CCNA Routing and Switching

ICND2 200-105

Official Cert Guide

WENDELL ODOM, CCIE No. 1624

with contributing author

SCOTT HOGG, CCIE No. 5133

Cisco Press

800 East 96th Street

Indianapolis, IN 46240

CCNA Routing and Switching ICND2 200-105 Official Cert Guide

Wendell Odom with contributing author Scott Hogg

Published by:
Cisco Press
800 East 96th Street
Indianapolis, IN 46240 USA

Printed in the United States of America

6   18

Library of Congress Control Number: 2016936746

ISBN-13: 978-1-58720-579-8

ISBN-10: 1-58720-579-3

Warning and Disclaimer

This book is designed to provide information about the Cisco ICND2 200-105 exam for CCNA Routing and Switching certification. Every effort has been made to make this book as complete and as accurate as possible, but no warranty or fitness is implied.

The information is provided on an "as is" basis. The authors, Cisco Press, and Cisco Systems, Inc. shall have neither liability nor responsibility to any person or entity with respect to any loss or damages arising from the information contained in this book or from the use of the discs or programs that may accompany it.

The opinions expressed in this book belong to the author and are not necessarily those of Cisco Systems, Inc.

Trademark Acknowledgments

All terms mentioned in this book that are known to be trademarks or service marks have been appropriately capitalized. Cisco Press or Cisco Systems, Inc., cannot attest to the accuracy of this information. Use of a term in this book should not be regarded as affecting the validity of any trademark or service mark.

Special Sales

For information about buying this title in bulk quantities, or for special sales opportunities (which may include electronic versions; custom cover designs; and content particular to your business, training goals, marketing focus, or branding interests), please contact our corporate sales department at corpsales@pearsoned.com or (800) 382-3419.

For government sales inquiries, please contact governmentsales@pearsoned.com.

For questions about sales outside the U.S., please contact intlcs@pearson.com.

Feedback Information

At Cisco Press, our goal is to create in-depth technical books of the highest quality and value. Each book is crafted with care and precision, undergoing rigorous development that involves the unique expertise of members from the professional technical community.

Readers' feedback is a natural continuation of this process. If you have any comments regarding how we could improve the quality of this book, or otherwise alter it to better suit your needs, you can contact us through email at feedback@ciscopress.com. Please make sure to include the book title and ISBN in your message.

We greatly appreciate your assistance.

Editor-in-Chief: Mark Taub

Product Line Manager: Brett Bartow

Business Operation Manager, Cisco Press: Jan Cornelssen

Managing Editor: Sandra Schroeder

Development Editor: Drew Cupp

Senior Project Editor: Tonya Simpson

Copy Editor: Bill McManus

Technical Editor(s): Aubrey Adams, Elan Beer

Editorial Assistant: Vanessa Evans

Cover Designer: Chuti Prasertsith

Composition: Bronkella Publishing

Indexer: Publishing Works, Inc.

Proofreader: Paula Lowell

CISCO

Americas Headquarters
Cisco Systems, Inc.
San Jose, CA

Asia Pacific Headquarters
Cisco Systems (USA) Pte. Ltd.
Singapore

Europe Headquarters
Cisco Systems International BV
Amsterdam, The Netherlands

Cisco has more than 200 offices worldwide. Addresses, phone numbers, and fax numbers are listed on the Cisco Website at www.cisco.com/go/offices.

CCDE, CCENT, Cisco Eos, Cisco HealthPresence, the Cisco logo, Cisco Lumin, Cisco Nexus, Cisco StadiumVision, Cisco TelePresence, Cisco WebEx, DCE, and Welcome to the Human Network are trademarks; Changing the Way We Work, Live, Play, and Learn and Cisco Store are service marks; and Access Registrar, Aironet, AsyncOS, Bringing the Meeting To You, Catalyst, CCDA, CCDP, CCIE, CCIP, CCNA, CCNP, CCSP, CCVP, Cisco, the Cisco Certified Internetwork Expert logo, Cisco IOS, Cisco Press, Cisco Systems, Cisco Systems Capital, the Cisco Systems logo, Cisco Unity, Collaboration Without Limitation, EtherFast, EtherSwitch, Event Center, Fast Step, Follow Me Browsing, FormShare, GigaDrive, HomeLink, Internet Quotient, IOS, iPhone, iQuick Study, IronPort, the IronPort logo, LightStream, Linksys, MediaTone, MeetingPlace, MeetingPlace Chime Sound, MGX, Networkers, Networking Academy, Network Registrar, PCNow, PIX, PowerPanels, ProConnect, ScriptShare, SenderBase, SMARTnet, Spectrum Expert, StackWise, The Fastest Way to Increase Your Internet Quotient, TransPath, WebEx, and the WebEx logo are registered trademarks of Cisco Systems, Inc. and/or its affiliates in the United States and certain other countries.

All other trademarks mentioned in this document or website are the property of their respective owners. The use of the word partner does not imply a partnership relationship between Cisco and any other company. (0812R)

About the Author

Wendell Odom, CCIE No. 1624 (Emeritus), has been in the networking industry since 1981. He has worked as a network engineer, consultant, systems engineer, instructor, and course developer; he currently works writing and creating certification study tools. This book is his 27th edition of some product for Pearson, and he is the author of all editions of the CCNA Routing and Switching and CCENT Cert Guides from Cisco Press. He has written books about topics from networking basics, and certification guides throughout the years for CCENT, CCNA R&S, CCNA DC, CCNP ROUTE, CCNP QoS, and CCIE R&S. He helped develop the popular Pearson Network Simulator. He maintains study tools, links to his blogs, and other resources at http://www.certskills.com.

About the Contributing Author

Scott Hogg, CCIE No. 5133, CISSP No. 4610, is the CTO for Global Technology Resources, Inc. (GTRI). Scott authored the Cisco Press book *IPv6 Security*. Scott is a Cisco Champion, founding member of the Rocky Mountain IPv6 Task Force (RMv6TF), and a member of the Infoblox IPv6 Center of Excellence (COE). Scott is a frequent presenter and writer on topics including IPv6, SDN, Cloud, and Security.

About the Technical Reviewers

Aubrey Adams is a Cisco Networking Academy instructor in Perth, Western Australia. With a background in telecommunications design, Aubrey has qualifications in electronic engineering and management; graduate diplomas in computing and education; and associated industry certifications. He has taught across a broad range of both related vocational and education training areas and university courses. Since 2007, Aubrey has technically reviewed a number of Pearson Education and Cisco Press publications, including video, simulation, and online products.

Elan Beer, CCIE No. 1837, is a senior consultant and Cisco instructor specializing in data center architecture and multiprotocol network design. For the past 27 years, Elan has designed networks and trained thousands of industry experts in data center architecture, routing, and switching. Elan has been instrumental in large-scale professional service efforts designing and troubleshooting internetworks, performing data center and network audits, and assisting clients with their short- and long-term design objectives. Elan has a global perspective of network architectures via his international clientele. Elan has used his expertise to design and troubleshoot data centers and internetworks in Malaysia, North America, Europe, Australia, Africa, China, and the Middle East. Most recently, Elan has been focused on data center design, configuration, and troubleshooting as well as service provider technologies. In 1993, Elan was among the first to obtain the Cisco Certified System Instructor (CCSI) certification, and in 1996, he was among the first to attain Cisco System's highest technical certification, the Cisco Certified Internetworking Expert. Since then, Elan has been involved in numerous large-scale data center and telecommunications networking projects worldwide.

Dedications

For Kris Odom, my wonderful wife: The best part of everything we do together in life. Love you, doll.

Acknowledgments

Brett Bartow again served as associate publisher and executive editor on the book. We've worked together on probably 20+ titles now. Besides the usual wisdom and good decision making to guide the project, he was the driving force behind adding all the new apps to the DVD/web. As always, Brett has been a pleasure to work with, and an important part of deciding what the entire Official Cert Guide series direction should be.

As part of writing these books, we work in concert with Cisco. A special thanks goes out to various people on the Cisco team who work with Pearson to create Cisco Press books. In particular, Greg Cote, Joe Stralo, and Phil Vancil were a great help while we worked on these titles.

Drew Cupp did his usual wonderful job with this book as development editor. He took over the job for this book during a pretty high-stress and high-load timeframe, and delivered with excellence. Thanks Drew for jumping in and getting into the minutia while keeping the big-picture features on track. And thanks for the work on the online/DVD elements as well!

Aubrey Adams and Elan Beer both did a great job as technical editors for this book, just as they did for the ICND1 100-105 Cert Guide. This book presented a little more of a challenge, from the breadth of some of the new topics, just keeping focus with such a long pair of books in a short time frame. Many thanks to Aubrey and Elan, for the timely input, for taking the time to read and think about every new part of the book, for finding those small technical areas, and for telling me where I need to do more. Truly, it's a much better book because of the two of you.

Hank Preston of Cisco Systems, IT as a Service Architect, and co-author of the Cisco Press *CCNA Cloud CLDADM 210-455 Cert Guide*, gave me some valuable assistance when researching before writing the cloud computing chapter (27). Hank helped me refine my understanding based on his great experience with helping Cisco customers implement cloud computing. Hank did not write the chapter, but his insights definitely made the chapter much better and more realistic.

Welcome and thanks to Lisa Matthews for her work on the DVD and online tools, like the Key Topics reviews. That work included many new math-related apps in the ICND1 book, but also many new features that sit on the DVD and on this book's website as review tools. Thanks for the hard work, Lisa!

I love the magic wand that is production. Presto, Word docs with gobs of queries and comments feed into the machine, and out pops these beautiful books. Thanks to Sandra Schroeder, Tonya Simpson, and all the production team for making the magic happen. From fixing all my grammar, crummy word choices, and passive-voice sentences to pulling the design and layout together, they do it all; thanks for putting it all together and making it look easy. And Tonya, once again getting the "opportunity" to manage two books with many elements at the same timeline. Once again, the juggling act continues, and once again, it is done well and beautifully. Thanks for managing the whole production process again.

The figures in the book continue to be an important part of the book, by design, with a great deal of attention paid to choosing how to use figures to communicate ideas. Mike Tanamachi, illustrator and mind reader, did his usual great job creating the finished figure files once again. Thanks for the usual fine work, Mike!

I could not have made the timeline for this book without Chris Burns of Certskills Professional. Chris owns the mind map process now, owns big parts of the lab development process for the associated labs added to my blogs, does various tasks related to specific chapters, and then catches anything I need to toss over my shoulder so I can focus on the books. Chris, you are the man!

Sean Wilkins played the largest role he's played so far with one of my books. A long-time co-collaborator with Pearson's CCNA Simulator, Sean did a lot of technology work behind the scenes. No way the books are out on time without Sean's efforts; thanks for the great job, Sean!

A special thanks to you readers who submit suggestions and point out possible errors, and especially to those of you who post online at the Cisco Learning Network. Without question, past comments I have received directly and "overheard" by participating at CLN have made this edition a better book.

Thanks to my wonderful wife, Kris, who helps make this sometimes challenging work lifestyle a breeze. I love walking this journey with you, doll. Thanks to my daughter Hannah. And thanks to Jesus Christ, Lord of everything in my life.

Contents at a Glance

Introduction   xxxv

Your Study Plan   2

Part I   Ethernet LANs   13

Chapter 1   Implementing Ethernet Virtual LANs   14

Chapter 2   Spanning Tree Protocol Concepts   42

Chapter 3   Spanning Tree Protocol Implementation   68

Chapter 4   LAN Troubleshooting   98

Chapter 5   VLAN Trunking Protocol   120

Chapter 6   Miscellaneous LAN Topics   142

Part I Review   164

Part II   IPv4 Routing Protocols   169

Chapter 7   Understanding OSPF Concepts   169

Chapter 8   Implementing OSPF for IPv4   194

Chapter 9   Understanding EIGRP Concepts   224

Chapter 10   Implementing EIGRP for IPv4   244

Chapter 11   Troubleshooting IPv4 Routing Protocols   272

Chapter 12   Implementing External BGP   300

Part II Review   324

Part III   Wide-Area Networks   327

Chapter 13   Implementing Point-to-Point WANs   328

Chapter 14   Private WANs with Ethernet and MPLS   362

Chapter 15   Private WANs with Internet VPN   386

Part III Review   434

Part IV   IPv4 Services: ACLs and QoS   437

Chapter 16   Basic IPv4 Access Control Lists   438

Chapter 17   Advanced IPv4 Access Control Lists   460

Chapter 18   Quality of Service (QoS)   488

Part IV Review   516

Part V   IPv4 Routing and Troubleshooting   519

Chapter 19   IPv4 Routing in the LAN   520

Chapter 20   Implementing HSRP for First-Hop Routing   544

Chapter 21   Troubleshooting IPv4 Routing   566

Part V Review   588

Part VI   IPv6   591

Chapter 22   IPv6 Routing Operation and Troubleshooting   592

Chapter 23   Implementing OSPF for IPv6   616

Chapter 24   Implementing EIGRP for IPv6   644

Chapter 25   IPv6 Access Control Lists   664

Part VI Review   688

Part VII   Miscellaneous   691

Chapter 26   Network Management   692

Chapter 27   Cloud Computing   730

Chapter 28   SDN and Network Programmability   760

Part VII Review   780

Part VIII   Final Prep   783

Chapter 29   Final Review   784

Part IX   Appendixes   801

Appendix A   Numeric Reference Tables   803

Appendix B   Technical Content   810

              Glossary   813

              Index   852

DVD Appendixes

Appendix C   Answers to the "Do I Know This Already?" Quizzes

Appendix D   Practice for Chapter 16: Basic IPv4 Access Control Lists

Appendix E   Mind Map Solutions

Appendix F   Study Planner

Appendix G   Learning IPv4 Routes with RIPv2

Appendix H   Understanding Frame Relay Concepts

Appendix I   Implementing Frame Relay

Appendix J   IPv4 Troubleshooting Tools

Appendix K   Topics from Previous Editions

Appendix L   Exam Topic Cross Reference

Contents

Introduction   xxxv

Your Study Plan   2

A Brief Perspective on Cisco Certification Exams   2

Five Study Plan Steps   3

Step 1: Think in Terms of Parts and Chapters   3

Step 2: Build Your Study Habits Around the Chapter   4

Step 3: Use Book Parts for Major Milestones   5

Step 4: Use the Final Review Chapter to Refine Skills and Uncover
Weaknesses   6

Step 5: Set Goals and Track Your Progress   7

Things to Do Before Starting the First Chapter   8

Find Review Activities on the Web and DVD   8

Should I Plan to Use the Two-Exam Path or One-Exam Path?   8

Study Options for Those Taking the 200-125 CCNA Exam   9

Other Small Tasks Before Getting Started   10

Getting Started: Now   11

Part I   Ethernet LANs   13

Chapter 1   Implementing Ethernet Virtual LANs   14

"Do I Know This Already?" Quiz   14

Foundation Topics   16

Virtual LAN Concepts   16

Creating Multiswitch VLANs Using Trunking   18

VLAN Tagging Concepts   18

The 802.1Q and ISL VLAN Trunking Protocols   20

Forwarding Data Between VLANs   21

Routing Packets Between VLANs with a Router   21

Routing Packets with a Layer 3 Switch   23

VLAN and VLAN Trunking Configuration and Verification   24

Creating VLANs and Assigning Access VLANs to an Interface   24

VLAN Configuration Example 1: Full VLAN Configuration   25

VLAN Configuration Example 2: Shorter VLAN Configuration   28

VLAN Trunking Protocol   29

VLAN Trunking Configuration   30

Implementing Interfaces Connected to Phones   34

Data and Voice VLAN Concepts   34

Data and Voice VLAN Configuration and Verification   36

Summary: IP Telephony Ports on Switches   38

Chapter Review   39

Chapter 2   Spanning Tree Protocol Concepts   42

"Do I Know This Already?" Quiz   43

Foundation Topics   44

Spanning Tree Protocol (IEEE 802.1D)   44

The Need for Spanning Tree   45

What IEEE 802.1D Spanning Tree Does   47

How Spanning Tree Works   48

The STP Bridge ID and Hello BPDU   49

Electing the Root Switch   50

Choosing Each Switch's Root Port   52

Choosing the Designated Port on Each LAN Segment   54

Influencing and Changing the STP Topology   54

Making Configuration Changes to Influence the STP Topology   55

Reacting to State Changes That Affect the STP Topology   55

How Switches React to Changes with STP   56

Changing Interface States with STP   57

Rapid STP (IEEE 802.1w) Concepts   58

Comparing STP and RSTP   59

RSTP and the Alternate (Root) Port Role   60

RSTP States and Processes   62

RSTP and the Backup (Designated) Port Role   62

RSTP Port Types   63

Optional STP Features   64

EtherChannel   64

PortFast   65

BPDU Guard   65

Chapter Review   66

Chapter 3   Spanning Tree Protocol Implementation   68

"Do I Know This Already?" Quiz   69

Foundation Topics   71

Implementing STP   71

Setting the STP Mode 72

Connecting STP Concepts to STP Configuration Options 72

Per-VLAN Configuration Settings 72

The Bridge ID and System ID Extension 73

Per-VLAN Port Costs 74

STP Configuration Option Summary 74

Verifying STP Operation 75

Configuring STP Port Costs 78

Configuring Priority to Influence the Root Election 80

Implementing Optional STP Features 81

Configuring PortFast and BPDU Guard 81

Configuring EtherChannel 84

Configuring a Manual EtherChannel 84

Configuring Dynamic EtherChannels 86

Implementing RSTP 88

Identifying the STP Mode on a Catalyst Switch 88

RSTP Port Roles 91

RSTP Port States 92

RSTP Port Types 92

Chapter Review 94

Chapter 4 LAN Troubleshooting 98

"Do I Know This Already?" Quiz 99

Foundation Topics 99

Troubleshooting STP 99

Determining the Root Switch 99

Determining the Root Port on Nonroot Switches 101

STP Tiebreakers When Choosing the Root Port 102

Suggestions for Attacking Root Port Problems on the Exam 103

Determining the Designated Port on Each LAN Segment 104

Suggestions for Attacking Designated Port Problems on the Exam 105

STP Convergence 105

Troubleshooting Layer 2 EtherChannel 106

Incorrect Options on the channel-group Command 106

Configuration Checks Before Adding Interfaces to EtherChannels 108

Analyzing the Switch Data Plane Forwarding   109

   Predicting STP Impact on MAC Tables   110

   Predicting EtherChannel Impact on MAC Tables   111

   Choosing the VLAN of Incoming Frames   112

Troubleshooting VLANs and VLAN Trunks   113

   Access VLAN Configuration Incorrect   113

   Access VLANs Undefined or Disabled   114

   Mismatched Trunking Operational States   116

   Mismatched Supported VLAN List on Trunks   117

   Mismatched Native VLAN on a Trunk   118

Chapter Review   119

Chapter 5   VLAN Trunking Protocol   120

"Do I Know This Already?" Quiz   120

Foundation Topics   122

VLAN Trunking Protocol (VTP) Concepts   122

   Basic VTP Operation   122

      Synchronizing the VTP Database   124

      Requirements for VTP to Work Between Two Switches   126

   VTP Version 1 Versus Version 2   127

   VTP Pruning   127

   Summary of VTP Features   128

VTP Configuration and Verification   129

   Using VTP: Configuring Servers and Clients   129

   Verifying Switches Synchronized Databases   131

   Storing the VTP and Related Configuration   134

   Avoiding Using VTP   135

VTP Troubleshooting   135

   Determining Why VTP Is Not Synchronizing   136

   Common Rejections When Configuring VTP   137

   Problems When Adding Switches to a Network   137

Chapter Review   139

Chapter 6   Miscellaneous LAN Topics   142

"Do I Know This Already?" Quiz   143

Foundation Topics   144

Securing Access with IEEE 802.1x   144

AAA Authentication   147

   AAA Login Process   147

   TACACS+ and RADIUS Protocols   147

   AAA Configuration Examples   148

DHCP Snooping   150

   DHCP Snooping Basics   151

   An Example DHCP-based Attack   152

   How DHCP Snooping Works   152

   Summarizing DHCP Snooping Features   154

Switch Stacking and Chassis Aggregation   155

   Traditional Access Switching Without Stacking   155

   Switch Stacking of Access Layer Switches   156

   Switch Stack Operation as a Single Logical Switch   157

   Cisco FlexStack and FlexStack-Plus   158

   Chassis Aggregation   159

     High Availability with a Distribution/Core Switch   159

     Improving Design and Availability with Chassis Aggregation   160

Chapter Review   162

Part I Review   164

Part II　　**IPv4 Routing Protocols   169**

Chapter 7　　**Understanding OSPF Concepts   170**

"Do I Know This Already?" Quiz   170

Foundation Topics   172

Comparing Dynamic Routing Protocol Features   172

   Routing Protocol Functions   172

   Interior and Exterior Routing Protocols   173

   Comparing IGPs   175

     IGP Routing Protocol Algorithms   175

     Metrics   175

     Other IGP Comparisons   176

   Administrative Distance   177

OSPF Concepts and Operation   178

   OSPF Overview   179

     Topology Information and LSAs   179

     Applying Dijkstra SPF Math to Find the Best Routes   180

Becoming OSPF Neighbors   180

    The Basics of OSPF Neighbors   181

    Meeting Neighbors and Learning Their Router ID   181

Exchanging the LSDB Between Neighbors   183

    Fully Exchanging LSAs with Neighbors   183

    Maintaining Neighbors and the LSDB   184

    Using Designated Routers on Ethernet Links   185

Calculating the Best Routes with SPF   186

OSPF Area Design   188

    OSPF Areas   189

    How Areas Reduce SPF Calculation Time   190

    OSPF Area Design Advantages   191

Chapter Review   191

Chapter 8   Implementing OSPF for IPv4   194

"Do I Know This Already?" Quiz   194

Foundation Topics   196

Implementing Single-Area OSPFv2   196

    OSPF Single-Area Configuration   197

    Matching with the OSPF network Command   198

    Verifying OSPFv2 Single Area   200

    Configuring the OSPF Router ID   203

    OSPF Passive Interfaces   204

Implementing Multiarea OSPFv2   206

    Single-Area Configurations   207

    Multiarea Configuration   209

    Verifying the Multiarea Configuration   210

        Verifying the Correct Areas on Each Interface on an ABR   210

        Verifying Which Router Is DR and BDR   211

        Verifying Interarea OSPF Routes   212

Additional OSPF Features   213

    OSPF Default Routes   213

    OSPF Metrics (Cost)   215

        Setting the Cost Based on Interface Bandwidth   216

        The Need for a Higher Reference Bandwidth   217

    OSPF Load Balancing   217

OSPFv2 Interface Configuration 218

OSPFv2 Interface Configuration Example 218

Verifying OSPFv2 Interface Configuration 219

Chapter Review 221

Chapter 9   Understanding EIGRP Concepts 224

"Do I Know This Already?" Quiz 224

Foundation Topics 226

EIGRP and Distance Vector Routing Protocols 226

Introduction to EIGRP 226

Basic Distance Vector Routing Protocol Features 227

The Concept of a Distance and a Vector 228

Full Update Messages and Split Horizon 229

Route Poisoning 231

EIGRP as an Advanced DV Protocol 232

EIGRP Sends Partial Update Messages, As Needed 232

EIGRP Maintains Neighbor Status Using Hello 233

Summary of Interior Routing Protocol Features 233

EIGRP Concepts and Operation 234

EIGRP Neighbors 234

Exchanging EIGRP Topology Information 235

Calculating the Best Routes for the Routing Table 236

The EIGRP Metric Calculation 236

An Example of Calculated EIGRP Metrics 237

Caveats with Bandwidth on Serial Links 238

EIGRP Convergence 239

Feasible Distance and Reported Distance 240

EIGRP Successors and Feasible Successors 241

The Query and Reply Process 242

Chapter Review 243

Chapter 10   Implementing EIGRP for IPv4 244

"Do I Know This Already?" Quiz 244

Foundation Topics 246

Core EIGRP Configuration and Verification 246

EIGRP Configuration 246

Configuring EIGRP Using a Wildcard Mask 248

Verifying EIGRP Core Features   249

Finding the Interfaces on Which EIGRP Is Enabled   250

Displaying EIGRP Neighbor Status   253

Displaying the IPv4 Routing Table   253

EIGRP Metrics, Successors, and Feasible Successors   255

Viewing the EIGRP Topology Table   255

Finding Successor Routes   257

Finding Feasible Successor Routes   258

Convergence Using the Feasible Successor Route   260

Examining the Metric Components   262

Other EIGRP Configuration Settings   262

Load Balancing Across Multiple EIGRP Routes   263

Tuning the EIGRP Metric Calculation   265

Autosummarization and Discontiguous Classful Networks   266

Automatic Summarization at the Boundary of a Classful Network   266

Discontiguous Classful Networks   267

Chapter Review   269

Chapter 11   Troubleshooting IPv4 Routing Protocols   272

"Do I Know This Already?" Quiz   272

Foundation Topics   273

Perspectives on Troubleshooting Routing Protocol Problems   273

Interfaces Enabled with a Routing Protocol   274

EIGRP Interface Troubleshooting   275

Examining Working EIGRP Interfaces   276

Examining the Problems with EIGRP Interfaces   278

OSPF Interface Troubleshooting   281

Neighbor Relationships   284

EIGRP Neighbor Verification Checks   285

EIGRP Neighbor Troubleshooting Example   286

OSPF Neighbor Troubleshooting   288

Finding Area Mismatches   290

Finding Duplicate OSPF Router IDs   291

Finding OSPF Hello and Dead Timer Mismatches   293

Other OSPF Issues   294

Shutting Down the OSPF Process   294

Mismatched MTU Settings   296

Chapter Review   296

Chapter 12   Implementing External BGP   300

"Do I Know This Already?" Quiz   300

Foundation Topics   302

BGP Concepts   302

Advertising Routes with BGP   303

Internal and External BGP   304

Choosing the Best Routes with BGP   305

eBGP and the Internet Edge   306

Internet Edge Designs and Terminology   306

Advertising the Enterprise Public Prefix into the Internet   307

Learning Default Routes from the ISP   309

eBGP Configuration and Verification   309

BGP Configuration Concepts   310

Configuring eBGP Neighbors Using Link Addresses   311

Verifying eBGP Neighbors   312

Administratively Disabling Neighbors   314

Injecting BGP Table Entries with the network Command   314

Injecting Routes for a Classful Network   315

Advertising Subnets to the ISP   318

Advertising a Single Prefix with a Static Discard Route   319

Learning a Default Route from the ISP   320

Chapter Review   321

Part II Review   324

Part III   Wide-Area Networks   327

Chapter 13   Implementing Point-to-Point WANs   328

"Do I Know This Already?" Quiz   328

Foundation Topics   330

Leased-Line WANs with HDLC   330

Layer 1 Leased Lines   331

The Physical Components of a Leased Line   332

The Role of the CSU/DSU   334

Building a WAN Link in a Lab   335

Layer 2 Leased Lines with HDLC   336

Configuring HDLC   337

Leased-Line WANs with PPP   340

PPP Concepts   340

PPP Framing   341

PPP Control Protocols   341

PPP Authentication   342

Implementing PPP   343

Implementing PPP CHAP   344

Implementing PPP PAP   346

Implementing Multilink PPP   347

Multilink PPP Concepts   348

Configuring MLPPP   349

Verifying MLPPP   351

Troubleshooting Serial Links   353

Troubleshooting Layer 1 Problems   354

Troubleshooting Layer 2 Problems   354

Keepalive Failure   355

PAP and CHAP Authentication Failure   356

Troubleshooting Layer 3 Problems   357

Chapter Review   358

Chapter 14   Private WANs with Ethernet and MPLS   362

"Do I Know This Already?" Quiz   363

Foundation Topics   364

Metro Ethernet   364

Metro Ethernet Physical Design and Topology   365

Ethernet WAN Services and Topologies   366

Ethernet Line Service (Point-to-Point)   367

Ethernet LAN Service (Full Mesh)   368

Ethernet Tree Service (Hub and Spoke)   369

Layer 3 Design Using Metro Ethernet   370

Layer 3 Design with E-Line Service   370

Layer 3 Design with E-LAN Service   371

Layer 3 Design with E-Tree Service   372

Ethernet Virtual Circuit Bandwidth Profiles   373

Charging for the Data (Bandwidth) Used   373

Controlling Overages with Policing and Shaping   374

Multiprotocol Label Switching (MPLS)   375

    MPLS VPN Physical Design and Topology   377

    MPLS and Quality of Service   378

    Layer 3 with MPLS VPN   379

        OSPF Area Design with MPLS VPN   381

        Routing Protocol Challenges with EIGRP   382

Chapter Review   383

Chapter 15   Private WANs with Internet VPN   386

"Do I Know This Already?" Quiz   386

Foundation Topics   389

Internet Access and Internet VPN Fundamentals   389

    Internet Access   389

        Digital Subscriber Line   390

        Cable Internet   391

        Wireless WAN (3G, 4G, LTE)   392

        Fiber Internet Access   393

    Internet VPN Fundamentals   393

        Site-to-Site VPNs with IPsec   395

        Client VPNs with SSL   396

GRE Tunnels and DMVPN   397

    GRE Tunnel Concepts   398

        Routing over GRE Tunnels   398

        GRE Tunnels over the Unsecured Network   400

    Configuring GRE Tunnels   402

    Verifying a GRE Tunnel   404

    Troubleshooting GRE Tunnels   406

        Tunnel Interfaces and Interface State   406

        Layer 3 Issues for Tunnel Interfaces   409

        Issues with ACLs and Security   409

    Multipoint Internet VPNs Using DMVPN   410

PPP over Ethernet   413

    PPPoE Concepts   414

    PPPoE Configuration   415

        PPPoE Configuration Breakdown: Dialers and Layer 1   416

        PPPoE Configuration Breakdown: PPP and Layer 2   417

        PPPoE Configuration Breakdown: Layer 3   417

PPPoE Configuration Summary 418

A Brief Aside About Lab Experimentation with PPPoE 419

PPPoE Verification 420

Verifying Dialer and Virtual-Access Interface Bindings 421

Verifying Virtual-Access Interface Configuration 422

Verifying PPPoE Session Status 424

Verifying Dialer Interface Layer 3 Status 425

PPPoE Troubleshooting 425

Step 0: Status Before Beginning the First Step 426

Step 1: Status After Layer 1 Configuration 427

Step 2: Status After Layer 2 (PPP) Configuration 428

Step 3: Status After Layer 3 (IP) Configuration 429

PPPoE Troubleshooting Summary 430

Chapter Review 430

Part III Review 434

Part IV   IPv4 Services: ACLs and QoS 437

Chapter 16   Basic IPv4 Access Control Lists 438

"Do I Know This Already?" Quiz 438

Foundation Topics 440

IPv4 Access Control List Basics 440

ACL Location and Direction 440

Matching Packets 441

Taking Action When a Match Occurs 442

Types of IP ACLs 442

Standard Numbered IPv4 ACLs 443

List Logic with IP ACLs 444

Matching Logic and Command Syntax 445

Matching the Exact IP Address 445

Matching a Subset of the Address with Wildcards 446

Binary Wildcard Masks 447

Finding the Right Wildcard Mask to Match a Subnet 448

Matching Any/All Addresses 448

Implementing Standard IP ACLs 448

Standard Numbered ACL Example 1 449

Standard Numbered ACL Example 2 450

Troubleshooting and Verification Tips 452

Practice Applying Standard IP ACLs 453

Practice Building access-list Commands 454

Reverse Engineering from ACL to Address Range 454

Chapter Review 456

Chapter 17   Advanced IPv4 Access Control Lists   460

"Do I Know This Already?" Quiz 461

Foundation Topics 462

Extended Numbered IP Access Control Lists 462

Matching the Protocol, Source IP, and Destination IP 463

Matching TCP and UDP Port Numbers 464

Extended IP ACL Configuration 467

Extended IP Access Lists: Example 1 468

Extended IP Access Lists: Example 2 469

Practice Building access-list Commands 470

Named ACLs and ACL Editing 471

Named IP Access Lists 471

Editing ACLs Using Sequence Numbers 473

Numbered ACL Configuration Versus Named ACL Configuration 475

ACL Implementation Considerations 476

Troubleshooting with IPv4 ACLs 477

Analyzing ACL Behavior in a Network 477

ACL Troubleshooting Commands 479

Example Issue: Reversed Source/Destination IP Addresses 480

Steps 3D and 3E: Common Syntax Mistakes 481

Example Issue: Inbound ACL Filters Routing Protocol Packets 481

ACL Interactions with Router-Generated Packets 483

Local ACLs and a Ping from a Router 483

Router Self-Ping of a Serial Interface IPv4 Address 483

Router Self-Ping of an Ethernet Interface IPv4 Address 484

Chapter Review 485

Chapter 18   Quality of Service (QoS)   488

"Do I Know This Already?" Quiz 488

Foundation Topics 490

Introduction to QoS 490

QoS: Managing Bandwidth, Delay, Jitter, and Loss 491

Types of Traffic 492

Data Applications 492

Voice and Video Applications 493

QoS as Mentioned in This Book   495

QoS on Switches and Routers   495

Classification and Marking   495

Classification Basics   495

Matching (Classification) Basics   496

Classification on Routers with ACLs and NBAR   497

Marking IP DSCP and Ethernet CoS   499

Marking the IP Header   499

Marking the Ethernet 802.1Q Header   500

Other Marking Fields   501

Defining Trust Boundaries   501

DiffServ Suggested Marking Values   502

Expedited Forwarding (EF)   502

Assured Forwarding (AF)   502

Class Selector (CS)   503

Congestion Management (Queuing)   504

Round Robin Scheduling (Prioritization)   505

Low Latency Queuing   505

A Prioritization Strategy for Data, Voice, and Video   507

Shaping and Policing   507

Policing   508

Where to Use Policing   509

Shaping   510

Setting a Good Shaping Time Interval for Voice and Video   511

Congestion Avoidance   512

TCP Windowing Basics   512

Congestion Avoidance Tools   513

Chapter Review   514

Part IV Review   516

Part V   IPv4 Routing and Troubleshooting   519

Chapter 19   IPv4 Routing in the LAN   520

"Do I Know This Already?" Quiz   521

Foundation Topics   522

VLAN Routing with Router 802.1Q Trunks   522

Configuring ROAS   524

Verifying ROAS   526

Troubleshooting ROAS   528

VLAN Routing with Layer 3 Switch SVIs   529

    Configuring Routing Using Switch SVIs   529

    Verifying Routing with SVIs   531

    Troubleshooting Routing with SVIs   532

VLAN Routing with Layer 3 Switch Routed Ports   534

    Implementing Routed Interfaces on Switches   535

    Implementing Layer 3 EtherChannels   537

    Troubleshooting Layer 3 EtherChannels   541

Chapter Review   541

Chapter 20   Implementing HSRP for First-Hop Routing   544

"Do I Know This Already?" Quiz   544

Foundation Topics   546

FHRP and HSRP Concepts   546

    The Need for Redundancy in Networks   547

    The Need for a First Hop Redundancy Protocol   549

    The Three Solutions for First-Hop Redundancy   550

    HSRP Concepts   551

        HSRP Failover   552

        HSRP Load Balancing   553

Implementing HSRP   554

    Configuring and Verifying Basic HSRP   554

    HSRP Active Role with Priority and Preemption   556

    HSRP Versions   559

Troubleshooting HSRP   560

    Checking HSRP Configuration   560

    Symptoms of HSRP Misconfiguration   561

Chapter Review   563

Chapter 21   Troubleshooting IPv4 Routing   566

"Do I Know This Already?" Quiz   567

Foundation Topics   567

Problems Between the Host and the Default Router   567

    Root Causes Based on a Host's IPv4 Settings   568

        Ensure IPv4 Settings Correctly Match   568

        Mismatched Masks Impact Route to Reach Subnet   569

        Typical Root Causes of DNS Problems   571

        Wrong Default Router IP Address Setting   572

Root Causes Based on the Default Router's Configuration   572

DHCP Issues   573

Router LAN Interface and LAN Issues   575

Problems with Routing Packets Between Routers   576

IP Forwarding by Matching the Most Specific Route   577

Using show ip route and Subnet Math to Find the Best Route   577

Using show ip route address to Find the Best Route   579

show ip route Reference   579

Routing Problems Caused by Incorrect Addressing Plans   581

Recognizing When VLSM Is Used or Not   581

Overlaps When Not Using VLSM   581

Overlaps When Using VLSM   583

Configuring Overlapping VLSM Subnets   584

Pointers to Related Troubleshooting Topics   585

Router WAN Interface Status   585

Filtering Packets with Access Lists   586

Chapter Review   586

Part V Review   588

Part VI   IPv6   591

Chapter 22   IPv6 Routing Operation and Troubleshooting   592

"Do I Know This Already?" Quiz   592

Foundation Topics   592

Normal IPv6 Operation   592

Unicast IPv6 Addresses and IPv6 Subnetting   593

Assigning Addresses to Hosts   595

Stateful DHCPv6   596

Stateless Address Autoconfiguration   597

Router Address and Static Route Configuration   598

Configuring IPv6 Routing and Addresses on Routers   598

IPv6 Static Routes on Routers   599

Verifying IPv6 Connectivity   600

Verifying Connectivity from IPv6 Hosts   600

Verifying IPv6 from Routers   601

Troubleshooting IPv6   604

Pings from the Host Work Only in Some Cases   605

Pings Fail from a Host to Its Default Router   606

Problems Using Any Function That Requires DNS   607

Host Is Missing IPv6 Settings: Stateful DHCP Issues   608

Host Is Missing IPv6 Settings: SLAAC Issues   609

Traceroute Shows Some Hops, But Fails   610

Routing Looks Good, But Traceroute Still Fails   612

Chapter Review   612

Chapter 23   Implementing OSPF for IPv6   616

"Do I Know This Already?" Quiz   616

Foundation Topics   618

OSPFv3 for IPv6 Concepts   618

IPv6 Routing Protocol Versions and Protocols   619

Two Options for Implementing Dual Stack with OSPF   619

OSPFv2 and OSPFv3 Internals   621

OSPFv3 Configuration   621

Basic OSPFv3 Configuration   621

Single-Area Configuration on the Three Internal Routers   623

Adding Multiarea Configuration on the Area Border Router   625

Other OSPFv3 Configuration Settings   626

Setting OSPFv3 Interface Cost to Influence Route Selection   626

OSPF Load Balancing   627

Injecting Default Routes   627

OSPFv3 Verification and Troubleshooting   628

OSPFv3 Interfaces   630

Verifying OSPFv3 Interfaces   630

Troubleshooting OSPFv3 Interfaces   631

OSPFv3 Neighbors   632

Verifying OSPFv3 Neighbors   632

Troubleshooting OSPFv3 Neighbors   633

OSPFv3 LSDB and LSAs   636

The Issue of IPv6 MTU   636

OSPFv3 Metrics and IPv6 Routes   638

Verifying OSPFv3 Interface Cost and Metrics   638

Troubleshooting IPv6 Routes Added by OSPFv3   640

Chapter Review   642

Chapter 24   Implementing EIGRP for IPv6   644

"Do I Know This Already?" Quiz   644

Foundation Topics   646

EIGRP for IPv6 Configuration   646

    EIGRP for IPv6 Configuration Basics   647

    EIGRP for IPv6 Configuration Example   648

    Other EIGRP for IPv6 Configuration Settings   650

        Setting Bandwidth and Delay to Influence EIGRP for IPv6 Route
Selection   650

        EIGRP Load Balancing   651

        EIGRP Timers   652

EIGRP for IPv6 Verification and Troubleshooting   653

    EIGRP for IPv6 Interfaces   654

    EIGRP for IPv6 Neighbors   656

    EIGRP for IPv6 Topology Database   657

    EIGRP for IPv6 Routes   659

Chapter Review   661

Chapter 25   IPv6 Access Control Lists   664

"Do I Know This Already?" Quiz   664

Foundation Topics   666

IPv6 Access Control List Basics   666

    Similarities and Differences Between IPv4 and IPv6 ACLs   666

    ACL Location and Direction   667

    IPv6 Filtering Policies   668

    ICMPv6 Filtering Caution   668

    Capabilities of IPv6 ACLs   669

    Limitations of IPv6 ACLs   669

        Matching Tunneled Traffic   670

        IPv4 Wildcard Mask and IPv6 Prefix Length   670

        ACL Logging Impact   670

        Router Originated Packets   670

Configuring Standard IPv6 ACLs   671

Configuring Extended IPv6 ACLs   674

    Examples of Extended IPv6 ACLs   676

    Practice Building ipv6 access-list Commands   678

Other IPv6 ACL Topics   679

   Implicit IPv6 ACL Rules   679

      An Example of Filtering ICMPv6 NDP and the Negative Effects   679

      How to Avoid Filtering ICMPv6 NDP Messages   683

      IPv6 ACL Implicit Filtering Summary   684

   IPv6 Management Control ACLs   685

Chapter Review   686

Part VI Review   688

Part VII   Miscellaneous   691

Chapter 26   Network Management   692

"Do I Know This Already?" Quiz   692

Foundation Topics   694

Simple Network Management Protocol   694

   SNMP Concepts   695

      SNMP Variable Reading and Writing: SNMP Get and Set   696

      SNMP Notifications: Traps and Informs   696

      The Management Information Base   697

      Securing SNMP   698

   Implementing SNMP Version 2c   699

      Configuring SNMPv2c Support for Get and Set   699

      Configuring SNMPv2c Support for Trap and Inform   701

      Verifying SNMPv2c Operation   702

   Implementing SNMP Version 3   704

      SNMPv3 Groups   705

      SNMPv3 Users, Passwords, and Encryption Keys   707

      Verifying SNMPv3   708

      Implementing SNMPv3 Notifications (Traps and Informs)   710

      Summarizing SNMPv3 Configuration   711

IP Service Level Agreement   712

   An Overview of IP SLA   713

   Basic IP SLA ICMP-Echo Configuration   714

   Troubleshooting Using IP SLA Counters   715

   Troubleshooting Using IP SLA History   716

SPAN   718

   SPAN Concepts   718

      The Need for SPAN When Using a Network Analyzer   719

      SPAN Session Concepts   720

Configuring Local SPAN   721

SPAN Session Parameters for Troubleshooting   724

Choosing to Limit SPAN Sources   725

Chapter Review   726

Chapter 27   Cloud Computing   730

"Do I Know This Already?" Quiz   730

Foundation Topics   732

Cloud Computing Concepts   732

Server Virtualization   732

Cisco Server Hardware   732

Server Virtualization Basics   733

Networking with Virtual Switches on a Virtualized Host   735

The Physical Data Center Network   736

Workflow with a Virtualized Data Center   737

Cloud Computing Services   739

Private Cloud   739

Public Cloud   741

Cloud and the "As a Service" Model   741

Infrastructure as a Service   742

Software as a Service   743

(Development) Platform as a Service   743

WAN Traffic Paths to Reach Cloud Services   744

Enterprise WAN Connections to Public Cloud   744

Accessing Public Cloud Services Using the Internet   745

Pros and Cons with Connecting to Public Cloud with Internet   745

Private WAN and Internet VPN Access to Public Cloud   746

Pros and Cons with Connecting to Cloud with Private WANs   747

Intercloud Exchanges   748

Summarizing the Pros and Cons of Public Cloud WAN Options   749

A Scenario: Branch Offices and the Public Cloud   749

Migrating Traffic Flows When Migrating to Email SaaS   750

Branch Offices with Internet and Private WAN   751

Virtual Network Functions and Services   752

Virtual Network Functions: Firewalls and Routers   752

DNS Services   754

Address Assignment Services and DHCP   756

NTP   757

Chapter Review   758

Chapter 28   SDN and Network Programmability   760

"Do I Know This Already?" Quiz   761

Foundation Topics   762

SDN and Network Programmability Basics   762

The Data, Control, and Management Planes   762

The Data Plane   762

The Control Plane   763

The Management Plane   764

Cisco Switch Data Plane Internals   765

Controllers and Network Architecture   766

Controllers and Centralized Control   766

The Southbound Interface   767

The Northbound Interface   768

SDN Architecture Summary   770

Examples of Network Programmability and SDN   770

Open SDN and OpenFlow   771

The OpenDaylight Controller   771

Cisco Open SDN Controller   772

The Cisco Application Centric Infrastructure   773

The Cisco APIC Enterprise Module   774

Comparing the Three Examples   776

Cisco APIC-EM Path Trace ACL Analysis Application   777

APIC-EM Path Trace App   777

APIC-EM Path Trace ACL Analysis Tool Timing and Exam Topic   778

Chapter Review   778

Part VII Review   780

Part VIII   Final Prep   783

Chapter 29   Final Review   784

Advice About the Exam Event   784

Learn the Question Types Using the Cisco Certification Exam Tutorial   784

Think About Your Time Budget Versus Number of Questions   785

A Suggested Time-Check Method   786

Miscellaneous Pre-Exam Suggestions   786

Exam-Day Advice   787

Reserve the Hour After the Exam in Case You Fail   788

Exam Review   788

    Take Practice Exams   789

        Practicing Taking the ICND2 or CCNA R&S Exam   790

        Advice on How to Answer Exam Questions   790

        Taking Other Practice Exams   792

    Find Knowledge Gaps Through Question Review   792

    Practice Hands-On CLI Skills   794

        Review Mind Maps from Part Review   795

        Do Labs   795

    Assess Whether You Are Ready to Pass (and the Fallacy of Exam Scores)   796

    Study Suggestions After Failing to Pass   797

    Other Study Tasks   798

    Final Thoughts   799

Part IX   **Appendixes   801**

Appendix A   **Numeric Reference Tables   803**

Appendix B   **CCNA ICND2 200-105 Exam Updates   810**

                Glossary   813

                Index   852

DVD Appendixes

Appendix C   **Answers to the "Do I Know This Already?" Quizzes**

Appendix D   **Practice for Chapter 16: Basic IPv4 Access Control Lists**

Appendix E   **Mind Map Solutions**

Appendix F   **Study Planner**

Appendix G   **Learning IPv4 Routes with RIPv2**

Appendix H   **Understanding Frame Relay Concepts**

Appendix I   **Implementing Frame Relay**

Appendix J   **IPv4 Troubleshooting Tools**

Appendix K   **Topics from Previous Editions**

Appendix L   **Exam Topic Cross Reference**

Reader Services

To access additional content for this book, simply register your product. To start the registration process, go to www.ciscopress.com/register and log in or create an account*. Enter the product ISBN 9781587205798 and click Submit. After the process is complete, you will find any available bonus content under Registered Products.

*Be sure to check the box that you would like to hear from us to receive exclusive discounts on future editions of this product.

Icons Used in This Book

Printer	PC	Laptop	Server	Phone
IP Phone	Router	Switch	Frame Relay Switch	Cable Modem
Access Point	ASA	DSLAM	WAN Switch	CSU/DSU
Hub	PIX Firewall	Bridge	Layer 3 Switch	Network Cloud
Ethernet Connection	Serial Line	Virtual Circuit	Ethernet WAN	Wireless

Command Syntax Conventions

The conventions used to present command syntax in this book are the same conventions used in the IOS Command Reference. The Command Reference describes these conventions as follows:

- **Boldface** indicates commands and keywords that are entered literally as shown. In actual configuration examples and output (not general command syntax), boldface indicates commands that are manually input by the user (such as a **show** command).
- *Italic* indicates arguments for which you supply actual values.
- Vertical bars (|) separate alternative, mutually exclusive elements.
- Square brackets ([ ]) indicate an optional element.
- Braces ({ }) indicate a required choice.
- Braces within brackets ([{ }]) indicate a required choice within an optional element.

Introduction

About the Exams

Congratulations! If you're reading far enough to look at this book's Introduction, you've probably already decided to go for your Cisco certification. If you want to succeed as a technical person in the networking industry at all, you need to know Cisco. Cisco has a ridiculously high market share in the router and switch marketplace, with more than 80 percent market share in some markets. In many geographies and markets around the world, networking equals Cisco. If you want to be taken seriously as a network engineer, Cisco certification makes perfect sense.

The Exams to Achieve CCENT and CCNA R&S

Cisco announced changes to the CCENT and CCNA Routing and Switching certifications, and the related 100-105 ICND1, 200-105 ICND2, and 200-125 CCNA exams, early in the year 2016. Most everyone new to Cisco certifications begins with either CCENT or CCNA Routing and Switching (CCNA R&S). However, the paths to certification are not quite obvious at first.

The CCENT certification requires a single step: pass the ICND1 exam. Simple enough.

Cisco gives you two options to achieve CCNA R&S certification, as shown in Figure I-1: pass both the ICND1 and ICND2 exams, or just pass the CCNA exam. Both paths cover the same exam topics, but the two-exam path does so spread over two exams rather than one. You also pick up the CCENT certification by going through the two-exam path, but you do not when working through the single-exam (200-125) option.

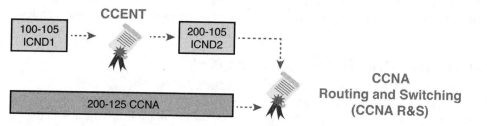

Figure I-1 *Cisco Entry-Level Certifications and Exams*

Note that Cisco has begun referencing some exams with a version number on some of their websites. If that form holds true, the exams in Figure I-1 will likely be called version 3 (or v3 for short). Historically, the 200-125 CCNA R&S exam is the seventh separate version of the exam (which warrants a different exam number), dating back to 1998. To make sure you reference the correct exam, when looking for information, using forums, and registering for the test, just make sure to use the correct exam number as shown in the figure.

Types of Questions on the Exams

The ICND1, ICND2, and CCNA R&S exams all follow the same general format. At the testing center, you sit in a quiet room with a PC. Before the exam timer begins, you have a chance to do a few other tasks on the PC; for instance, you can take a sample quiz just to get accustomed to the PC and the testing engine. Anyone who has user-level skills in getting around a PC should have no problems with the testing environment. The question types are

- Multiple-choice, single-answer
- Multiple-choice, multiple-answer
- Testlet (one scenario with several multiple-choice questions)
- Drag-and-drop
- Simulated lab (sim)
- Simlet

You should take the time to learn as much as possible by using the Cisco Certification Exam Tutorial, which you can find by going to Cisco.com and searching for "exam tutorial." This tool walks through each type of question Cisco may ask on the exam.

Although the first four types of questions in the list should be familiar to anyone who has taken standardized tests or similar tests in school, the last two types are more common to IT tests and Cisco exams in particular. Both use a network simulator to ask questions, so that you control and use simulated Cisco devices. In particular:

- **Sim questions:** You see a network topology, a lab scenario, and can access the devices. Your job is to fix a problem with the configuration.
- **Simlet questions:** This style combines sim and testlet question formats. Like a sim question, you see a network topology, a lab scenario, and can access the devices. However, like a testlet, you also see several multiple-choice questions. Instead of changing/fixing the configuration, you answer questions about the current state of the network.

Using these two question styles with the simulator enables Cisco to test your configuration skills with sim questions, and your verification and troubleshooting skills with simlet questions.

What's on the CCNA Exams...and in the Book?

Ever since I was in grade school, whenever the teacher announced that we were having a test soon, someone would always ask, "What's on the test?" Even in college, people would try to get more information about what would be on the exams. At heart, the goal is to know what to study hard, what to study a little, and what to not study at all.

You can find out more about what's on the exam from two primary sources: this book and the Cisco website.

The Cisco Published Exam Topics

First, Cisco tells the world the specific topics on each of their certification exams. For every Cisco certification exam, Cisco wants the public to know both the variety of topics and what kinds of knowledge and skills are required for each topic. Just go to http://www.cisco.com/go/certifications, look for the CCENT and CCNA Routing and Switching pages, and navigate until you see the exam topics.

Note that this book lists those same exam topics in Appendix L, "Exam Topic Cross Reference." This PDF appendix lists two cross references: one with a list of the exam topics in the order in which Cisco lists them on their website; and the other with a list of chapters in this book with the corresponding exam topics included in each chapter.

Cisco does more than just list the topic (for example, IPv4 addressing); they also list the depth to which you must master the topic. The primary exam topics each list one or more verbs that describe the skill level required. For example, consider the following exam topic, which describes one of the most important topics in both CCENT and CCNA R&S:

Configure, verify, and troubleshoot IPv4 addressing and subnetting

Note that this one exam topic has three verbs (configure, verify, and troubleshoot). So, you should be able to not only configure IPv4 addresses and subnets, but also understand them well enough to verify that the configuration works, and to troubleshoot problems when it is not working. And if to do that you need to understand concepts and need to have other knowledge, those details are implied. The exam questions will attempt to assess whether you can configure, verify, and troubleshoot.

The Cisco exam topics provide the definitive list of topics and skill levels required by Cisco for the exams. But the list of exam topics provides only a certain level of depth. For example, the ICND1 100-105 exam topics list has 41 primary exam topics (topics with verbs), plus additional subtopics that provide more details about that technology area. Although very useful, the list of exam topics would take about five pages of this book if laid out in a list.

You should take the time to not only read the exam topics, but read the short material above the exam topics as listed at the Cisco web page for each certification and exam. Look for notices about the use of unscored items, and how Cisco intends the exam topics to be a set of general guidelines for the exams.

This Book: About the Exam Topics

This book provides a complete study system for the Cisco published exam topics for the ICND2 200-105 exam. All the topics in this book either directly relate to some ICND2 exam topic or provide more basic background knowledge for some exam topic. The scope of the book is defined by the exam topics.

For those of you thinking more specifically about the CCNA R&S certification, and the CCNA 200-125 single-exam path to CCNA, this book covers about one-half of the CCNA exam topics. The *CCENT/CCNA ICND1 100-105 Official Cert Guide* (and ICND1 100-105 exam topics) covers about half of the topics listed for the CCNA 200-125 exam, and this book (and the ICND2 200-105 exam topics) covers the other half. In short, for content, CCNA = ICND1 + ICND2.

Book Features

This book (and the related *CCENT/CCNA ICND1 100-105 Official Cert Guide*) goes beyond what you would find in a simple technology book. It gives you a study system designed to help you not only learn facts but also to develop the skills you need to pass the exams. To do that, in the technology chapters of the book, about three-quarters of the chapter is about the technology, and about one-quarter is for the related study features.

The "Foundation Topics" section of each chapter contains rich content to explain the topics on the exam and to show many examples. This section makes extensive use of figures, with lists and tables for comparisons. It also highlights the most important topics in each chapter as key topics, so you know what to master first in your study.

Most of the book's features tie in some way to the need to study beyond simply reading the "Foundation Topics" section of each chapter. The rest of this section explains these book features. And because the book organizes your study by chapter, and then by part (a part contains multiple chapters), and then a final review at the end of the book, the next section of this Introduction discusses the book features introduced by chapter, part, and for final review.

Chapter Features and How to Use Each Chapter

Each chapter of this book is a self-contained short course about one topic area, organized for reading and study as follows:

- **"Do I Know This Already?" quiz:** Each chapter begins with a prechapter quiz.
- **Foundation Topics:** This is the heading for the core content section of the chapter.
- **Chapter Review:** This section includes a list of study tasks useful to help you remember concepts, connect ideas, and practice skills-based content in the chapter.

Figure I-2 shows how each chapter uses these three key elements. You start with the "Do I Know This Already?" (DIKTA) quiz. You can use the score to determine whether you already know a lot, or not so much, and determine how to approach reading the Foundation Topics (that is, the technology content in the chapter). When finished with the Foundation Topics, use the Chapter Review tasks to start working on mastering your memory of the facts and skills with configuration, verification, and troubleshooting.

DIKTA Quiz	Foundation Topics	Chapter Review
Take Quiz — High Score → (Skim) Foundation Topics / (Read) Foundation Topics ← Low Score	·····→	1) In-Chapter, or... 2) Companion Website 3) DVD

Figure I-2   *Three Primary Tasks for a First Pass Through Each Chapter*

In addition to these three main chapter features, each "Chapter Review" section presents a variety of other book features, including the following:

- **Review Key Topics:** In the "Foundation Topics" section, the Key Topic icon appears next to the most important items, for the purpose of later review and mastery. While all content matters, some is, of course, more important to learn, or needs more review to master, so these items are noted as key topics. The "Review Key Topics" section lists the key topics in a table; scan the chapter for these items to review them.

■ **Complete Tables from Memory:** Instead of just rereading an important table of information, some tables have been marked as memory tables. These tables exist in the Memory Table app that is available on the DVD and from the companion website. The app shows the table with some content removed, and then reveals the completed table, so you can work on memorizing the content.

■ **Key Terms You Should Know:** You do not need to be able to write a formal definition of all terms from scratch. However, you do need to understand each term well enough to understand exam questions and answers. This section lists the key terminology from the chapter. Make sure you have a good understanding of each term, and use the DVD Glossary to cross-check your own mental definitions.

■ **Labs:** Many exam topics use the verbs "configure," "verify," and "troubleshoot"; all these refer to skills you should practice at the command-line interface (CLI) of a router or switch. The Chapter Review refers you to these other tools. The Introduction's section titled "About Building Hands-On Skills" discusses your options.

■ **Command References:** Some book chapters cover a large number of router and switch commands. This section includes reference tables for the commands used in that chapter, along with an explanation. Use these tables for reference, but also use them for study— just cover one column of the table, and see how much you can remember and complete mentally.

■ **Review DIKTA Questions:** Re-answering the DIKTA questions from the chapter is a useful way to review facts. The Part Review element that comes at the end of each book Part suggests that you repeat the DIKTA questions. The Part Review also suggests using the Pearson IT Certification Practice Test (PCPT) exam software that comes with the book, for extra practice in answering multiple-choice questions on a computer.

Part Features and How to Use Part Review

The book organizes the chapters into seven parts. Each part contains a number of related chapters. Figure I-3 lists the titles of the parts and identifies the chapters in those parts by chapter numbers.

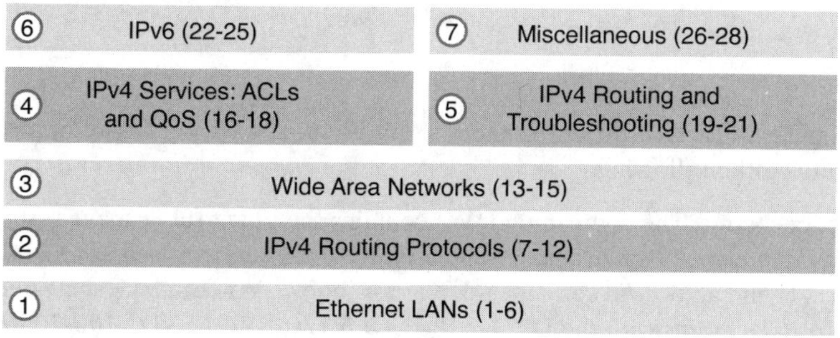

⑥ IPv6 (22-25)	⑦ Miscellaneous (26-28)
④ IPv4 Services: ACLs and QoS (16-18)	⑤ IPv4 Routing and Troubleshooting (19-21)
③ Wide Area Networks (13-15)	
② IPv4 Routing Protocols (7-12)	
① Ethernet LANs (1-6)	

Figure I-3 *The Book Parts and Corresponding Chapter Numbers*

Each book part ends with a "Part Review" section that contains a list of activities for study and review, much like the "Chapter Review" section at the end of each chapter. However, because the Part Review takes place after completing a number of chapters, the Part Review includes some tasks meant to help pull the ideas together from this larger body of work. The following list explains the types of tasks added to each Part Review beyond the types mentioned for the Chapter Review:

■ **Answer Part Review Questions:** The books come with exam software and databases of questions. One database holds questions written specifically for Part Reviews. These questions tend to connect multiple ideas together, to help you think about topics from multiple chapters, and to build the skills needed for the more challenging analysis questions on the exams.

■ **Mind Maps:** Mind maps are graphical organizing tools that many people find useful when learning and processing how concepts fit together. The process of creating mind maps helps you build mental connections. The Part Review elements make use of mind maps in several ways: to connect concepts and the related configuration commands, to connect **show** commands and the related networking concepts, and even to connect terminology. (For more information about mind maps, see the section "About Mind Maps" later in this Introduction.)

■ **Labs:** Each "Part Review" section will direct you to the kinds of lab exercises you should do with your chosen lab product, labs that would be more appropriate for this stage of study and review. (Check out the later section "About Building Hands-On Skills" for information about lab options.)

In addition to these tasks, many "Part Review" sections have you perform other tasks with book features mentioned in the "Chapter Review" section: repeating DIKTA quiz questions, reviewing key topics, and doing more lab exercises.

Final Review

Chapter 29, "Final Review," lists a series of preparation tasks that you can best use for your final preparation before taking the exam. Chapter 29 focuses on a three-part approach to helping you pass: practicing your skills, practicing answering exam questions, and uncovering your weak spots. To that end, Chapter 29 uses the same familiar book features discussed for the Chapter Review and Part Review elements, along with a much larger set of practice questions.

Other Features

In addition to the features in each of the core chapters, this book, as a whole, has additional study resources, including the following:

■ **DVD-based practice exams:** The companion DVD contains the powerful Pearson Test Prep practice test exam engine. You can take simulated ICND2 exams, as well as CCNA exams, with the DVD and activation code included in this book. (You can take simulated ICND1 and CCNA R&S exams with the DVD in the *CCENT/CCNA ICND1 100-105 Official Cert Guide*.)

- **CCNA ICND2 Simulator Lite:** This lite version of the best-selling CCNA Network Simulator from Pearson provides you with a means, right now, to experience the Cisco CLI. No need to go buy real gear or buy a full simulator to start learning the CLI. Just install it from the DVD in the back of this book.

- **eBook:** If you are interested in obtaining an eBook version of this title, we have included a special offer on a coupon card inserted in the DVD sleeve in the back of the book. This offer allows you to purchase the *CCNA Routing and Switching ICND2 200-105 Official Cert Guide Premium Edition eBook and Practice Test* at a 70 percent discount off the list price. In addition to three versions of the eBook, PDF (for reading on your computer), EPUB (for reading on your tablet, mobile device, or Nook or other eReader), and Mobi (the native Kindle version), you also receive additional practice test questions and enhanced practice test features.

- **Mentoring Videos:** The DVD included with this book includes four other instructional videos about the following topics: OSPF, EIGRP, EIGRP metrics, plus PPP and CHAP.

- **Companion website:** The website http://www.ciscopress.com/title/9781587205798 posts up-to-the-minute materials that further clarify complex exam topics. Check this site regularly for new and updated postings written by the author that provide further insight into the more troublesome topics on the exam.

- **PearsonITCertification.com:** The website http://www.pearsonitcertification.com is a great resource for all things IT-certification related. Check out the great CCNA articles, videos, blogs, and other certification preparation tools from the industry's best authors and trainers.

- **CCNA Simulator:** If you are looking for more hands-on practice, you might want to consider purchasing the CCNA Network Simulator. You can purchase a copy of this software from Pearson at http://pearsonitcertification.com/networksimulator or other retail outlets. To help you with your studies, I have created a mapping guide that maps each of the labs in the simulator to the specific sections in these CCNA cert guides. You can get this mapping guide for free on the Extras tab of the companion website.

- **Author's website and blogs:** I maintain a website that hosts tools and links that are useful when studying for CCENT and CCNA. The site lists information to help you build your own lab, study pages that correspond to each chapter of this book and the ICND1 book, and links to my CCENT Skills blog and CCNA Skills blog. Start at http://www.certskills.com; click the Blog tab for a page about the blogs in particular, with links to the pages with the labs related to this book.

A Big New Feature: Review Applications

One of the single biggest new features of this edition of the book is the addition of study apps for many of the Chapter Review activities. In the past, all Chapter Review activities used only the book chapter, or the chapter plus a DVD-only appendix. Readers tell us they find that content useful, but the content is static.

This book and the *CCENT/CCNA ICND1 100-105 Official Cert Guide* are the first Cisco Press Cert Guides with extensive interactive applications. Basically, most every activity that can be done in the "Chapter Review" sections can now be done with an application. The apps can be found both on the DVD that comes with the book and on the book's companion website. On the DVD you can find the apps under the "Chapter and Part Review" tab.

The advantages of using these apps are as follows:

- **Easier to use:** Instead of having to print out copies of the appendixes and do the work on paper, these new apps provide you with an easy-to-use, interactive experience that you can easily run over and over.

- **Convenient:** When you have a spare 5–10 minutes, go to the book's website, and review content from one of your recently finished chapters.

- **Untethered from book/DVD:** Because these apps are available on the book's companion website in addition to the DVD, you can access your review activities from anywhere— no need to have the book or DVD with you.

- **Good for tactile learners:** Sometimes looking at a static page after reading a chapter lets your mind wander. Tactile learners may do better by at least typing answers into an app, or clicking inside an app to navigate, to help keep you focused on the activity.

Our in-depth reader surveys show that readers who use the Chapter Review tools like them, but that not everyone uses them consistently. So, we want to increase the number of people using the review tools, and make them both more useful and more interesting. Table I-1 summarizes these new applications and the traditional book features that cover the same content.

Table I-1   Book Features with Both Traditional and App Options

Feature	Traditional	App
Key Topics	Table with list; flip pages to find	Key Topics Table app
Config Checklist	Just one of many types of key topics	Config Checklist app
Memory Table	Two static PDF appendixes (one with sparse tables for you to complete, one with completed tables)	Memory Table app
Key Terms	Listed in each "Chapter Review" section, with the Glossary in the back of the book	Glossary Flash Cards app
IPv4 ACL Practice	A static PDF appendix (D) with practice problems	An interactive app that asks the same problems as listed in the appendix

How to Get the Electronic Elements of This Book

Traditionally, all chapter review activities use the book chapter plus appendixes, with the appendixes often being located on the DVD. But most of that content is static—useful, but static.

If you buy the print book, and have a DVD drive, you have all the content on the DVD. Just spin the DVD and use the disk menu (which should automatically start) to explore all the content.

If you buy the print book but do not have a DVD drive, you can get the DVD files by registering your book on the Cisco Press website. To do so, simply go to http://www.ciscopress.com/register and enter the ISBN of the print book: 9781587205798. After you have registered your book, go to your account page and click the **Registered Products** tab. From there, click the **Access Bonus Content** link to get access to the book's companion website.

If you buy the *CCNA Routing and Switching ICND2 200-105 Official Cert Guide Premium Edition eBook and Practice Test* from Cisco Press, your book will automatically be registered on your account page. Simply go to your account page, click the **Registered Products** tab, and select **Access Bonus Content** to access the book's companion website.

If you buy the eBook from some other bookseller, the very last page of your eBook file will contain instructions for how to register the book and access the companion website. The steps are the same as noted earlier for those who buy the print book but do not have a DVD drive.

Book Organization, Chapters, and Appendixes

This book contains 28 core chapters, Chapters 1 through 28, with Chapter 29 as the "Final Review" chapter. Each core chapter covers a subset of the topics on the ICND2 exam. The core chapters are organized into sections. The core chapters cover the following topics:

Part I: Ethernet LANs

■ **Chapter 1, "Implementing Ethernet Virtual LANs,"** explains the concepts and configuration surrounding virtual LANs, including VLAN trunking.

■ **Chapter 2, "Spanning Tree Protocol Concepts,"** discusses the concepts behind IEEE Spanning Tree Protocol (STP) and how it makes some switch interfaces block frames to prevent frames from looping continuously around a redundant switched LAN.

■ **Chapter 3, "Spanning Tree Protocol Implementation,"** shows how to configure and verify STP on Cisco switches.

■ **Chapter 4, "LAN Troubleshooting,"** examines the most common LAN switching issues and how to discover those issues when troubleshooting a network. The chapter includes troubleshooting topics for STP/RSTP, Layer 2 EtherChannel, LAN switching, VLANs, and VLAN trunking.

■ **Chapter 5, "VLAN Trunking Protocol,"** shows how to configure, verify, and troubleshoot the use of VLAN Trunking Protocol (VTP) to define and advertise VLANs across multiple Cisco switches.

■ **Chapter 6, "Miscellaneous LAN Topics,"** as the last chapter in the book specifically about LANs, discusses a variety of small topics, including: 802.1x, AAA authentication, DHCP snooping, switch stacking, and chassis aggregation.

Part II: IPv4 Routing Protocols

■ **Chapter 7, "Understanding OSPF Concepts,"** introduces the fundamental operation of the Open Shortest Path First (OSPF) protocol, focusing on link state fundamentals, neighbor relationships, flooding link state data, and calculating routes based on the lowest cost metric.

- Chapter 8, "Implementing OSPF for IPv4," takes the concepts discussed in the previous chapter and shows how to configure and verify those same features.

- Chapter 9, "Understanding EIGRP Concepts," introduces the fundamental operation of the Enhanced Interior Gateway Routing Protocol (EIGRP) for IPv4 (EIGRPv4), focusing on EIGRP neighbor relationships, how EIGRP calculates metrics, and how it quickly converges to alternate feasible successor routes.

- Chapter 10, "Implementing EIGRP for IPv4," takes the concepts discussed in the previous chapter and shows how to configure and verify those same features.

- Chapter 11, "Troubleshooting IPv4 Routing Protocols," walks through the most common problems with IPv4 routing protocols, while alternating between OSPF examples and EIGRP examples.

- Chapter 12, "Implementing External BGP," examines the basics of the Border Gateway Protocol (BGP) and its use between an enterprise and an ISP, showing how to configure, verify, and troubleshoot BGP in limited designs.

Part III: Wide Area Networks

- Chapter 13, "Implementing Point-to-Point WANs," explains the core concepts of how to build a leased-line WAN and the basics of the two common data link protocols on these links: HDLC and PPP.

- Chapter 14, "Private WANs with Ethernet and MPLS," explores the concepts behind building a WAN service using Ethernet through different Metro Ethernet services, as well as using Multiprotocol Label Switching (MPLS) VPNs.

- Chapter 15, "Private WANs with Internet VPNs," works through a variety of conceptual material, plus some configuration and verification topics, for several technologies related to using the Internet to create a private WAN connection between different enterprise sites.

Part IV: IPv4 Services: ACLs and QoS

- Chapter 16, "Basic IPv4 Access Control Lists," examines how standard IP ACLs can filter packets based on the source IP address so that a router will not forward the packet.

- Chapter 17, "Advanced IPv4 Access Control Lists," examines both named and numbered ACLs, and both standard and extended IP ACLs.

- Chapter 18, "Quality of Service (QoS)," discusses a wide variety of concepts all related to the broad topic of QoS.

Part V: IPv4 Routing and Troubleshooting

- Chapter 19, "IPv4 Routing in the LAN," shows to a configuration and troubleshooting depth different methods to route between VLANs, including Router on a Stick (ROAS), Layer 3 switching with SVIs, Layer 3 switching with routed ports, and using Layer 3 EtherChannels.

- Chapter 20, "Implementing HSRP for First-Hop Routing," discusses the need for a First Hop Redundancy Protocol (FHRP), and specifically how to configure, verify, and troubleshoot Hot Standby Router Protocol (HSRP)

- **Chapter 21, "Troubleshooting IPv4 Routing,"** looks at the most common IPv4 problems and how to find the root causes of those problems when troubleshooting.

Part VI: IPv6

- **Chapter 22, "IPv6 Routing Operation and Troubleshooting,"** reviews IPv6 routing as discussed in the ICND1 book. It then shows some of the most common problems with IPv6 routing and discusses how to troubleshoot these problems to discover the root cause.

- **Chapter 23, "Implementing OSPF for IPv6,"** explores OSPFv3 and its use as an IPv6 routing protocol, showing traditional configuration, verification, and troubleshooting topics.

- **Chapter 24, "Implementing EIGRP for IPv6,"** takes the EIGRP concepts discussed for IPv4 in Chapter 9 and shows how those same concepts apply to EIGRP for IPv6. It then shows how to configure, verify, and troubleshoot EIGRP for IPv6.

- **Chapter 25, "IPv6 Access Control Lists,"** examines the similarities and differences between IPv4 ACLs and IPv6 ACLs, then shows how to configure, verify, and troubleshoot IPv6 ACLs.

Part VII: Miscellaneous

- **Chapter 26, "Network Management,"** discusses several network management topics that Cisco did not choose to put into ICND1, namely: SNMP, IP SLA, and SPAN.

- **Chapter 27, "Cloud Computing,"** is one of two chapters about topics that strays from traditional CCNA R&S topics as one of the Cisco emerging technology topics. This chapter explains the basic concepts and then generally discusses the impact that cloud computing has on a typical enterprise network.

- **Chapter 28, "SDN and Network Programmability,"** is the other chapter that moves away from traditional CCNA R&S topics to discuss many concepts and terms related to how Software Defined Networking (SDN) and network programmability are impacting typical enterprise networks.

Part VIII: Final Prep

- **Chapter 29, "Final Review,"** suggests a plan for final preparation once you have finished the core parts of the book, in particular explaining the many study options available in the book.

Part IX: Appendixes (In Print)

- **Appendix A, "Numeric Reference Tables,"** lists several tables of numeric information, including a binary-to-decimal conversion table and a list of powers of 2.

- **Appendix B, "CCNA ICND2 200-105 Exam Updates,"** is a place for the author to add book content mid-edition. Always check online for the latest PDF version of this appendix; the appendix lists download instructions.

- The **Glossary** contains definitions for all of the terms listed in the "Key Terms You Should Know" sections at the conclusion of Chapters 1 through 28.

Part X: DVD Appendixes

The following appendixes are available in digital format on the DVD that accompanies this book:

- **Appendix C, "Answers to the 'Do I Know This Already?' Quizzes,"** includes the explanations to all the questions from Chapters 1 through 28.

- **Appendix D, "Practice for Chapter 16: Basic IPv4 Access Control Lists,"** is a copy of the *CCENT/CCNA ICND1 100-105 Official Cert Guide*'s Appendix I.

- **Appendix E, "Mind Map Solutions,"** shows an image of sample answers for all the part-ending mind map exercises.

- **Appendix F, "Study Planner,"** is a spreadsheet with major study milestones, where you can track your progress through your study.

- **Appendix G, "Learning IPv4 Routes with RIPv2,"** explains how routers work together to find all the best routes to each subnet using a routing protocol. This chapter also shows how to configure the RIPv2 routing protocol for use with IPv4. (This appendix is a copy of ICND1's Chapter 19, and is included with the ICND2 book for convenience.)

- **Appendix H, "Understanding Frame Relay Concepts,"** explains how to build a Frame Relay WAN between routers, focusing on the protocols and concepts rather than the configuration. (This chapter is a chapter that covers old exam topics from the previous edition of the book, included here for those who might be interested.)

- **Appendix I, "Implementing Frame Relay,"** takes the concepts discussed in Appendix H and shows how to configure, verify, and troubleshoot those same features. (This chapter is a chapter that covers old exam topics from the previous edition of the book, included here for those who might be interested.)

- **Appendix J, "IPv4 Troubleshooting Tools,"** focuses on how to use two key troubleshooting tools to find routing problems: the **ping** and **traceroute** commands. (This appendix is a copy of ICND1's Chapter 23, and is included with the ICND2 book for convenience.)

- **Appendix K, "Topics from Previous Editions,"** is a collection of information about topics that have appeared on previous versions of the CCNA exams. While you most likely will not encounter exam questions on these topics, the concepts are still of interest to someone with the CCENT or CCNA certification.

- **Appendix L, "Exam Topic Cross Reference,"** provides some tables to help you find where each exam objective is covered in the book.

ICND1 Chapters in this Book

For this current edition of the ICND1 and ICND2 Cert Guides, I designed several chapters to be used in both books. These chapters include some topics that are listed in the exam topics of both exams:

- Chapter 1, "Implementing Ethernet Virtual LANs" (Chapter 11 in the ICND1 100-105 book).

- Chapter 16, "Basic IPv4 Access Control Lists" (Chapter 25 in the ICND1 100-105 book).

- Chapter 17, "Advanced IPv4 Access Control Lists" (Chapter 26 in the ICND1 100-105 book).

- Chapter 21, "Troubleshooting IPv4 Routing" (Chapter 24 in the ICND1 100-105 book).

I designed these four chapters for use in both books to be a help to those reading both books while avoiding any problems for those who might be reading only this ICND2 Cert Guide. Cisco has traditionally had some topics that overlap between the two exams that make up the two-exam path to CCNA R&S, and this current pair of exams is no exception. So, for those of you who have already read the ICND1 100-105 book, you can move more quickly through the above four chapters in this book. If you did not read the ICND1 100-105 book, then you have all the material you need right here in this book.

Extra Content Found in DVD Appendixes

Note that several appendixes on the DVD, namely G, H, I, J, and K, contain extra content outside the ICND2 200-105 exam topics. This short section explains why.

First, two appendixes are here to aid the transition when Cisco announced the exams. Appendixes G (about RIP) and J (about **ping** and **traceroute**) are copies of two chapters in the ICND1 100-105 book, and are part of the exam topics for the ICND1 100-105 exam. These two chapters might be particularly useful for anyone who was far along in their studies on the date when Cisco announced the ICND1 100-105 and ICND2 200-105 exams in 2016. I included Appendixes G and J to aid that transition for those who buy the ICND2 200-105 Cert Guide but not the ICND1 100-105 Cert Guide.

Three other appendixes are included for instructors who use these books for classes, as well as for the occasional reader who is mostly interested in the technology instead of the certification. Appendixes H, I, and K contain content that is no longer mentioned by the exam topics for the current exams. Appendixes H and I are copies of complete chapters about Frame Relay from the prior edition of this book, and Appendix K is a compilation of small topics I removed from the prior edition of this book when creating this current edition. This material might be helpful to some instructors during the transition time for their courses, or for those who want to read more broadly just for the sake of learning.

You do not need to use these extra appendixes (G through K) to prepare for the ICND2 200-105 exam or the CCNA R&S 200-125 exam, but feel free to use them if you are interested.

Reference Information

This short section contains a few topics available for reference elsewhere in the book. You may read these when you first use the book, but you may also skip these topics and refer back to them later. In particular, make sure to note the final page of this introduction, which lists several contact details, including how to get in touch with Cisco Press.

Install the Pearson Test Prep Practice Test Engine and Questions

This book, like many other Cisco Press books, includes the rights to use the Pearson Test Prep practice test (PTP) software, along with rights to use some exam questions related to this book. PTP has many options, including the option to answer questions in study mode, so you can see the answers and explanations for each question as you go along; the option to take a simulated exam that mimics real exam conditions; and the option to view questions in flash card mode, where all the answers are stripped out, challenging you to answer questions from memory.

You should install PTP so it is ready to use even for the earliest chapters. This book's Part Review sections ask you specifically to use PTP, and you can even take the DIKTA chapter quizzes using PTP.

You can also access the PTP software online by going to www.pearsontestprep.com. Unlike the Windows desktop application, the online version can be run on any OS with Internet connectivity and also works on smartphones and tablets.

> **NOTE**   The right to use the exams associated with this book is based on an activation code. For those with a paper book, the code is in the DVD sleeve at the back of the book. (Flip over the paper with the exam activation code to find a one-time-use coupon code for 70 percent off the purchase of the *CCNA Routing and Switching ICND2 200-105 Official Cert Guide, Premium Edition eBook and Practice Test*.) For those who purchase the Premium Edition eBook and Practice Test directly from the Cisco Press website, the activation code will be populated on your account page after purchase. For those who purchase a Kindle edition, the access code will be supplied directly from Amazon. Note that if you purchase an eBook version from any other source, the practice test is not included, as other vendors are not able to vend the required unique access code. *Do not lose the activation code.*

PTP Exam Databases with This Book

This book includes an activation code that allows you to load a set of practice questions. The questions come in different exams or exam databases. When you install the PTP software and type in the activation code, the PTP software downloads the latest version of all these exam databases. And with the ICND2 book alone, you get six different "exams," or six different sets of questions, as listed in Figure I-4.

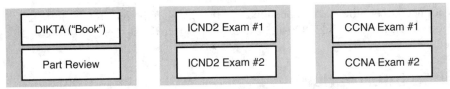

| DIKTA ("Book") | ICND2 Exam #1 | CCNA Exam #1 |
| Part Review | ICND2 Exam #2 | CCNA Exam #2 |

Figure I-4   *PTP Exams/Exam Databases and When to Use Them*

You can choose to use any of these exam databases at any time, both in study mode and practice exam mode. However, many people find it best to save some of the exams until exam review time, after you have finished reading the entire book. Figure I-4 begins to suggest a plan, spelled out here:

■ During Part Review, use PTP to review the DIKTA questions for that part, using study mode.

- During Part Review, use the questions built specifically for Part Review (the Part Review questions) for that part of the book, using study mode.
- Save the remaining exams to use with the "Final Review" chapter at the end of the book; if preparing for the ICND2 exam, use those practice exams, but if preparing for the CCNA exam, use those exams.

The two modes inside PTP give you better options for study versus practicing a timed exam event. In study mode, you can see the answers immediately, so you can study the topics more easily. Also, you can choose a subset of the questions in an exam database; for instance, you can view questions from only the chapters in one part of the book.

PTP practice mode lets you practice an exam event somewhat like the actual exam. It gives you a preset number of questions, from all chapters, with a timed event. Practice exam mode also gives you a score for that timed event.

How to View Only DIKTA Questions by Chapter or Part

Most chapters begin with a DIKTA quiz. You can take the quiz to start a chapter, take it again during Chapter Review for more practice, and, as suggested in the "Part Review" sections, repeat the questions for all chapters in the same part.

You can use the DIKTA quiz as printed in the book, or use the PTP software. The book lists the questions, with the letter answers on the page following the quiz. Appendix C, on the DVD, lists the answers along with an explanation; you might want to keep that PDF handy.

Using PTP for these questions has some advantages. It gives you a little more practice in how to read questions from testing software. Also, the explanations to the questions are conveniently located in the PTP software.

To view these DIKTA questions inside the PTP software, you need to select **Book Questions**, which is the way PTP references questions found inside the printed book. Then you have to deselect all chapters (with a single click), and then select one or more chapters, as follows:

Step 1.   Start the PTP software.

Step 2.   From the main (home) menu, select the item for this product, with a name like *CCNA Routing and Switching ICND2 200-105 Official Cert Guide*, and click **Open Exam**.

Step 3.   The top of the next window that appears should list some exams; check the **ICND2 Book Questions** box, and uncheck the other boxes. This selects the "book" questions (that is, the DIKTA questions from the beginning of each chapter).

Step 4.   On this same window, click at the bottom of the screen to deselect all objectives (chapters). Then select the box beside each chapter in the part of the book you are reviewing.

Step 5.   Select any other options on the right side of the window.

Step 6.   Click **Start** to start reviewing the questions.

How to View Part Review Questions

The exam databases you get with this book include a database of questions created solely for study during the Part Review process. DIKTA questions focus more on facts, to help you determine whether you know the facts contained within the chapter. The Part Review questions instead focus more on application of those facts to typical real scenarios, and look more like real exam questions.

To view these questions, follow the same process as you did with DIKTA/book questions, but select the Part Review database rather than the book database. PTP has a clear name for this database: Part Review Questions.

About Mind Maps

Mind maps are a type of visual organization tool that you can use for many purposes. For instance, you can use mind maps as an alternative way to take notes.

You can also use mind maps to improve how your brain organizes concepts. Mind maps improve your brain's connections and relationships between ideas. When you spend time thinking about an area of study, and organize your ideas into a mind map, you strengthen existing mental connections and create new connections, all into your own frame of reference.

In short, mind maps help you internalize what you learn.

Each mind map begins with a blank piece of paper or blank window in a mind mapping application. You then add a large central idea, with branches that move out in any direction. The branches contain smaller concepts, ideas, commands, pictures...whatever idea needs to be represented. Any concepts that can be grouped should be put near each other. As need be, you can create deeper and deeper branches, although for this book's purposes, most mind maps will not go beyond a couple of levels.

NOTE   Many books have been written about mind maps, but Tony Buzan often gets credit for formalizing and popularizing mind maps. You can learn more about mind maps at his website, http://www.tonybuzan.com.

For example, Figure I-5 shows a sample mind map that begins to output some of the IPv6 content from Part VIII of the ICND1 book. You might create this kind of mind map when reviewing IPv6 addressing concepts, starting with the big topic of "IPv6 addressing," and then writing down random terms and ideas. As you start to organize them mentally, you draw lines connecting the ideas, reorganize them, and eventually reach the point where you believe the organization of ideas makes sense to you.

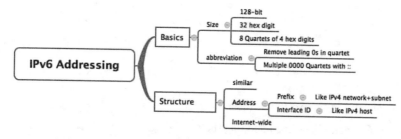

Figure I-5 *Sample Mind Map*

Mind maps may be the least popular but most effective study tool suggested in this book. I personally find a huge improvement in learning new areas of study when I mind map; I hope you will make the effort to try these tools and see if they work well for you too.

Finally, for mind mapping tools, you can just draw them on a blank piece of paper, or find and download a mind map application. I have used Mind Node Pro on a Mac, and we build the sample mind maps with XMIND, which has free versions for Windows, Linux, and OS X.

About Building Hands-On Skills

You need skills in using Cisco routers and switches, specifically the Cisco CLI. The Cisco CLI is a text-based command-and-response user interface; you type a command, and the device (a router or switch) displays messages in response. To answer sim and simlet questions on the exams, you need to know a lot of commands, and you need to be able to navigate to the right place in the CLI to use those commands.

This section walks through the options included in the book, with a brief description of lab options outside the book.

Config Lab Exercises

Some router and switch features require multiple configuration commands. Part of the skill you need to acquire is the ability to remember which configuration commands work together, which ones are required, and which ones are optional. So, the challenge level goes beyond just picking the right parameters on one command. You have to choose which commands to use, in which combination, typically on multiple devices. And getting good at that kind of task requires practice.

The Config Labs feature, introduced as a new feature in this edition of the book, helps provide that practice. Each lab presents a sample lab topology, with some requirements, and you have to decide what to configure on each device. The answer then shows a sample configuration. Your job is to create the configuration, and then check your answer versus the supplied answer.

Also for the first time, this edition places the content not only outside the book but also on the author's blog site. To reach my blog sites for ICND1 content or for ICND2 content (two different blogs) and access the Config Labs feature, you can start at my blog launch site (blog.certskills.com) and click from there.

Figure I-6 *Config Lab Logo in the Author's Blogs*

These Config Labs have several benefits, including the following:

- **Untethered and responsive:** Do them from anywhere, from any web browser, from your phone or tablet, untethered from the book or DVD.

- **Designed for idle moments:** Each lab is designed as a 5- to 10-minute exercise if all you are doing is typing in a text editor or writing your answer on paper.

- **Two outcomes, both good:** Practice getting better and faster with basic configuration, or if you get lost, you have discovered a topic that you can now go back and reread to complete your knowledge. Either way, you are a step closer to being ready for the exam!

- **Blog format:** Allows easy adds and changes by me, and easy comments by you.

- **Self-assessment:** As part of final review, you should be able to do all the Config Labs, without help, and with confidence.

Note that the blog organizes these Config Lab posts by book chapter, so you can easily use these at both Chapter Review and Part Review. See the "Your Study Plan" element that follows the Introduction for more details about those review sections.

A Quick Start with Pearson Network Simulator Lite

The decision of how to get hands-on skills can be a little scary at first. The good news is that you have a free and simple first step to experience the CLI: Install and use the Pearson NetSim Lite that comes with this book.

This book comes with a lite version of the best-selling CCNA Network Simulator from Pearson, which provides you with a means, right now, to experience the Cisco CLI. No need to go buy real gear or buy a full simulator to start learning the CLI. Just install NetSim Lite from the DVD in the back of this book.

The latest version of NetSim Lite includes labs associated with Part II of this book. Part I includes concepts only, with Part II being the first part with commands. So, make sure and use NetSim Lite to learn the basics of the CLI to get a good start.

Of course, one reason that NetSim Lite comes on the DVD is that the publisher hopes you will buy the full product. However, even if you do not use the full product, you can still learn from the labs that come with NetSim Lite while deciding about what options to pursue.

NOTE The ICND1 and ICND2 books each contain a different version of the Sim Lite product, each with labs that match the book content. If you bought both books, make sure you install both Sim Lite products.

The Pearson Network Simulator

The Config Labs and the Pearson Network Simulator Lite both fill specific needs, and they both come with the book. However, you need more than those two tools.

The single best option for lab work to do along with this book is the paid version of the Pearson Network Simulator. This simulator product simulates Cisco routers and switches so that you can learn for the CCENT and CCNA R&S certifications. But more importantly, it focuses on learning for the exam by providing a large number of useful lab exercises. Reader surveys tell us that those people who use the Simulator along with the book love the learning process, and rave about how the book and Simulator work well together.

Of course, you need to make a decision for yourself, and consider all the options. Thankfully, you can get a great idea of how the full Simulator product works by using the Pearson Network Simulator Lite product included with the book. Both have the same base code and same user interface, and the same types of labs. Try the Lite version, and check out the full product. There is a full product for CCENT only, and another for CCNA R&S (which includes all the labs in the CCENT product, plus others for the ICND2 parts of the content).

Note that the Simulator and the books work on a different release schedule. For a time in 2016, the version of the Simulator available for purchase will be the Simulator created for the previous versions of the exams (ICND1 100-101, ICND2 200-101, and CCNA 200-120). That product includes approximately 80 percent of the CLI topics in the ICND1 100-105 and ICND2 200-105 books. So during that time, the Simulator is still very useful.

On a practical note, when you want to do labs while reading a chapter or doing Part Review, the Simulator organizes the labs to match the book. Just look for the "Sort by Chapter" tab in the Simulator's user interface. However, during the months in 2016 for which the available Simulator is the older edition listing the older exams in the title, you will need to refer back to a PDF that lists those labs versus this book's organization; find that PDF at http://www.ciscopress.com/title/9781587205798.

More Lab Options

If you decide against using the full Pearson Network Simulator, you still need hands-on experience. You should plan to use some lab environment to practice as much CLI interaction as possible.

First, you can use real Cisco routers and switches. You can buy them, new or used, or borrow them at work. You can rent them for a fee. If you have the right mix of gear, you could even do the Config Lab exercises from my blog on that gear, or try and re-create examples from the book.

Cisco offers a virtualization product that lets you run router and switch operating system (OS) images in a virtual environment. This tool, the Virtual Internet Routing Lab (VIRL), lets you create a lab topology, start the topology, and connect to real router and switch OS images. Check out http://virl.cisco.com for more information.

You can even rent virtual Cisco router and switch lab pods from Cisco, in an offering called Cisco Learning Labs.

All these previously mentioned options cost some money, but the next two are generally free to the user, but with a different catch for each. First, GNS3 works somewhat like VIRL, creating a virtual environment running real Cisco IOS. However, GNS3 is not a Cisco product, and cannot provide you with the IOS images for legal reasons.

Cisco also makes a simulator that works very well as a learning tool: Cisco Packet Tracer. However, Cisco intends Packet Tracer for use by people currently enrolled in Cisco Networking Academy courses, and not for the general public. So, if you are part of a Cisco Academy, definitely use Packet Tracer.

This book does not tell you what option to use, but you should plan on getting some hands-on practice somehow. The important thing to know is that most people need to practice using the Cisco CLI to be ready to pass these exams.

For More Information

If you have any comments about the book, submit them via http://www.ciscopress.com. Just go to the website, select **Contact Us**, and type your message.

Cisco might make changes that affect the CCNA certification from time to time. You should always check http://www.cisco.com/go/ccna and http://www.cisco.com/go/ccent for the latest details.

The *CCNA ICND2 200-105 Official Cert Guide* helps you attain CCNA Routing and Switching certification. This is the CCNA and ICND2 certification book from the only Cisco-authorized publisher. We at Cisco Press believe that this book certainly can help you achieve CCNA certification, but the real work is up to you! I trust that your time will be well spent.

Your Study Plan

You just got this book. You have probably already read (or quickly skimmed) the Introduction. You are probably now wondering whether to start reading here or skip ahead to Chapter 1, "Implementing Ethernet Virtual LANs."

Stop for a moment to read this section about how to create your own study plan for the exam(s) you plan to take (ICND1 100-105, ICND2 200-105, and/or CCNA 200-125). Your study will go much better if you take time (maybe 15 minutes) to think about a few key points about how to study before starting on this journey. That is what this section will help you do.

A Brief Perspective on Cisco Certification Exams

Cisco sets the bar pretty high for passing the ICND1, ICND2, and CCNA R&S exams. Most anyone can study and pass these exams, but it takes more than just a quick read through the book and the cash to pay for the exam.

The challenge of these exams comes from many angles. Each of these exams covers a lot of concepts and many commands specific to Cisco devices. Beyond knowledge, these Cisco exams also require deep skills. You must be able to analyze and predict what really happens in a network. You must be able to configure Cisco devices to work correctly in those networks. And you must be ready to troubleshoot problems when the network does not work correctly.

The more challenging questions on these exams work a lot like a jigsaw puzzle, but with four out of every five puzzle pieces not even in the room. To solve the puzzle, you have to mentally re-create the missing pieces. To do that, you must know each networking concept and remember how the concepts work together.

For instance, the ICND2 exam includes many troubleshooting topics, like troubleshooting for Open Shortest Path Version 2 (OSPFv2). OSPFv2 might fail to form a neighbor relationship with another neighboring router. But a more exam-realistic question would make you think about why a router is missing a route, and that symptom might have a root cause related to OSPF neighbors. Then the question might supply some parts of what you would need to know, like some pieces of the jigsaw puzzle, as represented with the white pieces in Figure 1. You have to apply your knowledge of IP routing and OSPF theory to the facts to come up with some of the other pieces of the puzzle.

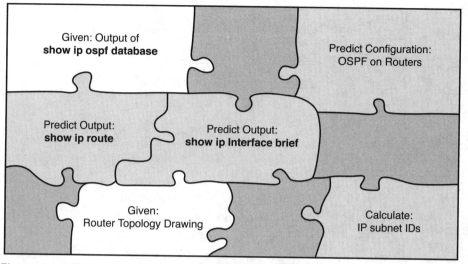

Figure 1 *Filling In Puzzle Pieces with Your Analysis Skills*

These skills require that you prepare by doing more than just reading and memorizing what you read. Of course, you need to read many pages in this book to learn many individual facts and how these facts relate to each other. But a big part of this book lists exercises beyond reading, exercises that help you build the skills to solve these networking puzzles.

Five Study Plan Steps

These exams are challenging, but many people pass them every day. So, what do you need to do to be ready to pass, beyond reading and remembering all the facts? You need to develop skills. You need to mentally link each idea with other related ideas. Doing that requires additional work. To help you along the way, the next few pages give you five key planning steps to take so that you can more effectively build those skills and make those connections, before you dive into this exciting but challenging world of learning networking on Cisco gear.

Step 1: Think in Terms of Parts and Chapters

The first step in your study plan is to get the right mindset about the size and nature of the task you have set out to accomplish. This is a large book. So you cannot think about the book as one huge task or you might get discouraged. And besides, you never sit down to read 900+ pages in one study session. So break the task down into smaller tasks.

The good news here is that the book is designed with obvious breakpoints and built-in extensive review activities. In short, the book is more of a study system than a book.

So the first step in your Study Plan is to visualize the book not as one large book, but as 7 parts. Then, within each part, visualize an average of 4 chapters. Your study plan has you work through the chapters in each part, and then review the material in that part before moving on, as shown in Figure 2.

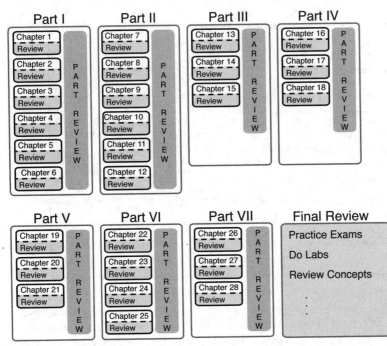

Figure 2   *7 Parts, with an Average of 4 Chapters Each, with Part Reviews*

Now your plan has the following:

1 large task: Read and master all content in the book.

7 medium tasks/book: Read and master a part.

4 small tasks/part: Read and master a chapter.

Step 2: Build Your Study Habits Around the Chapter

For your second step, possibly the most important step, approach each chapter with the same process: read it, and then study the chapter before moving on.

Each chapter follows the same design with three parts, as shown in Figure 3. The chapter pre-quiz (called a "Do I Know This Already?" quiz, or simply DIKTA quiz) helps you decide how much time to spend reading versus skimming the core of the chapter, called the Foundation Topics. The "Chapter Review" section then gives you instructions about how to study and review what you just read.

Figure 3   *Suggested Approach to Each Chapter*

The book has only a few long chapters, on purpose. They average 22 pages for the Foundation Topics. By keeping the size reasonable, you can complete all of a chapter in one or two short study sessions. Go into each study session that begins a new chapter thinking that you have a chance to complete the chapter, or at least make a great start on it. And if you do not have enough time, look for the major headings inside the chapter—each chapter has two to three major headings, and those make a great place to stop reading when you need to wait to complete the reading in the next study session.

The Chapter Review tasks are very important to your exam-day success. Doing these tasks, and doing them at the end of the chapter, really does help you get ready. Do not put off using these tasks until later! The chapter-ending Chapter Review tasks help you with the first phase of deepening your knowledge and skills of the key topics, remembering terms, and linking the concepts together in your brain so that you can remember how it all fits together. The following list describes most of the activities you will find in the "Chapter Review" sections:

- Review key topics
- Review key terms
- Answer DIKTA questions
- Do labs
- Review memory tables
- Review config checklists
- Review command tables

Check out the section titled "Find Review Activities on the Web and DVD" later in this planning section for more details.

Step 3: Use Book Parts for Major Milestones

Studies show that to master a concept and/or skill, you should plan to go through multiple study sessions to review the concept and to practice the skill. The "Chapter Review" section at the end of each chapter is the first such review, while "Part Review," at the end of each part, acts as that second review.

Plan time to do the Part Review task at the end of each part, using the Part Review elements found at the end of each part. You should expect to spend about as much time on one Part Review as you would on one entire chapter, or maybe a little more for some parts. So in terms of planning your time, think of the Part Review itself as another chapter.

Figure 4 lists the names of the parts in this book, with some color coding. Note that Parts II, IV, and V are the parts specific to IPv4. Parts I and III have to do with LANs and WANs, respectively. The top of the figure shows the final two parts of the book, with Part VI about IPv6, and Part VII about a few miscellaneous topics: network management, cloud, and network programmability. Each part ends with a "Part Review" section of 2 to 4 pages, with notes about what tools and activities to use.

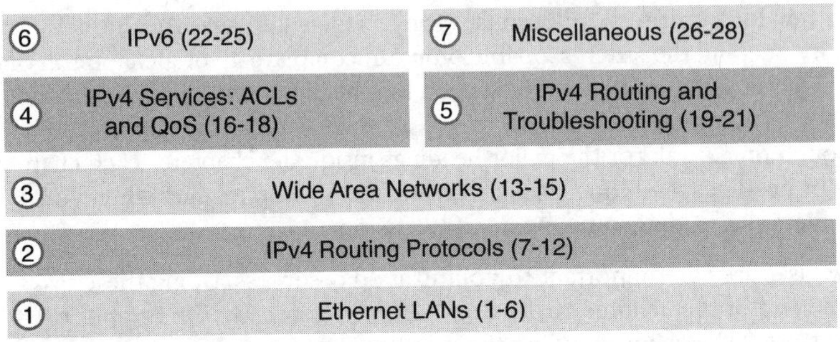

⑥	IPv6 (22-25)	⑦	Miscellaneous (26-28)
④	IPv4 Services: ACLs and QoS (16-18)	⑤	IPv4 Routing and Troubleshooting (19-21)
③	Wide Area Networks (13-15)		
②	IPv4 Routing Protocols (7-12)		
①	Ethernet LANs (1-6)		

Figure 4   *Parts as Major Milestones*

Chapter Review and Part Review differ in some ways. Chapter Review tasks tend to provide a lot of context, so you can focus on mentally adding a specific piece of knowledge, or practicing a specific skill. Part Review activities instead remove a lot of the context, more like real life and the real exams. Removing that context means that you have to exercise your own knowledge and skills. The result: You uncover your weaknesses. The better you become at uncovering weaknesses, and then learning what you are missing in that area, the better prepared you will be for the exam.

The "Part Review" sections use the following kinds of tools in additional to some of the same tools used for Chapter Review:

- Mind maps
- Part Review questions with PCPT
- Labs

Also, consider setting a goal date for finishing each part of the book (and a reward, as well). Plan a break, some family time, some time out exercising, eating some good food, whatever helps you get refreshed and motivated for the next part.

Step 4: Use the Final Review Chapter to Refine Skills and Uncover Weaknesses

Your fourth step has one overall task: Follow the details outlined in Chapter 29, "Final Review," at the end of this book for what to do between finishing the book and taking the exam.

The "Final Review" chapter has two major goals. First, it helps you further develop the analysis skills you need to answer the more complicated questions on the exam. Many questions require that you connect ideas about concepts, configuration, verification, and troubleshooting. The closer you get to taking the exam, the less reading you should do, and the more you should do other learning activities; this chapter's tasks give you activities to further develop these skills.

The tasks in the "Final Review" chapter also help you uncover your weak areas. This final element gives you repetition with high-challenge exam questions, uncovering any gaps in your knowledge. Many of the questions are purposefully designed to test your knowledge of the most common mistakes and misconceptions, helping you avoid some of the common pitfalls people experience with the actual exam.

Step 5: Set Goals and Track Your Progress

Your fifth study plan step spans across the entire timeline of your study effort. Before you start reading the book and doing the rest of these study tasks, take the time to make a plan, set some goals, and be ready to track your progress.

While making lists of tasks may or may not appeal to you, depending on your personality, goal setting can help everyone studying for these exams. And to do the goal setting, you need to know what tasks you plan to do.

NOTE   If you decide after reading this section that you want to try and do better with goal setting beyond your exam study, check out a blog series I wrote about planning your networking career here: http://blog.certskills.com/ccna/tag/development-plan/.

As for the list of tasks to do when studying, you do not have to use a detailed task list. (You could list every single task in every chapter-ending "Chapter Review" section, every task in the Part Reviews, and every task in the "Final Review" chapter.) However, listing the major tasks can be enough.

You should track at least two tasks for each typical chapter: reading the "Foundation Topics" section and doing the Chapter Review at the end of the chapter. And, of course, do not forget to list tasks for Part Reviews and Final Review. Table 1 shows a sample for Part I of this book.

Table 1   Sample Excerpt from a Planning Table

Element	Task	Goal Date	First Date Completed	Second Date Completed (Optional)
Chapter 1	Read Foundation Topics			
Chapter 1	Do Chapter Review tasks			
Chapter 2	Read Foundation Topics			
Chapter 2	Do Chapter Review tasks			
Chapter 3	Read Foundation Topics			
Chapter 3	Do Chapter Review tasks			
Chapter 4	Read Foundation Topics			
Chapter 4	Do Chapter Review tasks			
Chapter 5	Read Foundation Topics			
Chapter 5	Do Chapter Review tasks			
Chapter 6	Read Foundation Topics			
Chapter 6	Do Chapter Review tasks			
Part I Review	Do Part Review activities			

NOTE   Appendix F, "Study Planner," on the DVD that comes with this book, contains a complete planning checklist like Table 1 for the tasks in this book. This spreadsheet allows you to update and save the file to note your goal dates and the tasks you have completed.

Use your goal dates as a way to manage your study, and not as a way to get discouraged if you miss a date. Pick reasonable dates that you can meet. When setting your goals, think about how fast you read and the length of each chapter's "Foundation Topics" section, as listed in the table of contents. Then, when you finish a task sooner than planned, move up the next few goal dates.

If you miss a few dates, do *not* start skipping the tasks listed at the ends of the chapters! Instead, think about what is impacting your schedule—real life, commitment, and so on— and either adjust your goals or work a little harder on your study.

Things to Do Before Starting the First Chapter

Now that you understand the big ideas behind a good study plan for the book, take a few more minutes for a few overhead actions that will help. Before leaving this section, look at some other tasks you should do either now or around the time you are reading the first few chapters, to help make a good start in the book.

Find Review Activities on the Web and DVD

The earlier editions of the book have used review activities that relied on the chapter, plus PDF appendixes found on the DVD. Some activities also rely on the PCPT testing software.

This edition is the first Cisco Press certification guide to offer a large set of apps to use instead of the traditional study features. The Introduction's section titled "A Big New Feature: Review Applications" details some of the reasons.

I encourage you to go ahead and access the book's companion website to find the review apps and explore. Also, spin the DVD, and find the review apps there. Both methods organize the review activities by chapter and by part.

Note that this book includes the traditional methods of review as well, with instructions in the book, and matching PDF appendixes in some cases. For instance, all the Key Topics can be reviewed from the companion website and just by flipping pages in the book—you choose which works better for you.

Should I Plan to Use the Two-Exam Path or One-Exam Path?

To get a CCNA Routing and Switching certification, you choose either a one-exam or two-exam path. Which should you use? The following is my opinion, but it's based on chatter and opinions from readers from many years. You can consider the one-exam path if

- You already know about half the topics well, through prior experience or study.
- You have already proven that you are excellent at learning through self-study.

Otherwise, in my opinion, you would be better off taking the two-exam path. First, there are no cost savings for most people with the one-exam path. Check the exam prices in your country, for ICND1, ICND2, and CCNA, and then make some comparisons. Assume you pass the tests on the first try: traditionally, the cost is identical for both the ICND1 + ICND2 path and the CCNA path. Or, assume that you fail each exam once: again, the costs are identical.

Next, consider the number of topics. From a content perspective, CCNA = ICND1 + ICND2. So, both paths require learning the same content.

Next, which would you rather have done in school: take an exam over a single semester's material, or an exam covering the whole year? It is just harder to prepare for an exam that covers more material, so the two-exam path again has an advantage.

Finally, the most compelling reason for the two-exam path is that you probably have no experience with Cisco exams yet. I hope you have a chance to pass many Cisco exams during your career. The two-exam path gets you to that first exam attempt sooner, and the exam experience teaches you things about the exam and yourself that no study tool can teach you.

Study Options for Those Taking the 200-125 CCNA Exam

Studying for the two-exam path has an obvious approach: just use the ICND1 book for the ICND1 exam, and the ICND2 book for the ICND2 exam. Simple enough.

If you do plan to take the 200-125 CCNA R&S exam, you have a couple of study options. First, to be clear: The 200-125 CCNA exam covers the topics in the combined ICND1 and ICND2 books. So, using both the ICND1 and ICND2 books covers everything for the 200-125 CCNA R&S exam. The only question is when to read each part of the two books. You have two reasonable options when going with the one-exam option:

- Complete all the ICND1 book, then move on to the ICND2 book.
- Move back and forth between the ICND1 and ICND2 books, by part, based on topics, as shown in Figure 5.

The first option is pretty obvious, but the second one is less obvious. Figure 5 shows a study plan in which you complete the Ethernet Parts in the ICND1, then the Ethernet Part in ICND2. Similarly, you complete the IPv4 Parts in ICND1, then ICND2, and then the IPv6 Part in both books, and then the final part in both books.

Personally, I am a fan of completing the ICND1 book completely, and then moving on to the ICND2 book. However, for those of you with a large amount of experience already, this alternate reading plan may work well.

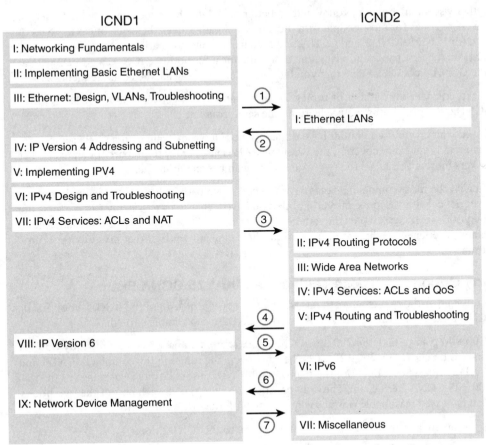

Figure 5 *Alternate Reading Plan for CCNA: Moving Between Books by Part*

Other Small Tasks Before Getting Started

You need to do a few overhead tasks to install software, find some PDFs, and so on. You can do these tasks now or do them in your spare moments when you need a study break during the first few chapters of the book. But do these early. That way, if you do stumble upon an installation problem, you have time to work through it before you need a particular tool.

Register (for free) at the Cisco Learning Network (CLN, http://learningnetwork.cisco.com) and join the CCENT/CCNA R&S study group. This group allows you to both lurk and participate in discussions about topics related to the ICND1 exam, ICND2 exam, and CCNA R&S exam. Register, join the groups, and set up an email filter to redirect the messages to a separate folder. Even if you do not spend time reading all the posts as they arrive, later, when you have time to read, you can browse through the posts to find interesting topics (or just search the posts from the CLN website).

Explore the electronic elements of this book, as detailed in the Introduction's section titled "How to Get the Electronic Elements of This Book." That includes the installation of the PCPT and Sim Lite software.

Also find my blog site as listed in the Introduction, and bookmark the pages that list the Config Labs, to have those handy for later study. (The URL is http://blog.certskills.com/ccna/category/hands-on/config-lab.)

Getting Started: Now

Now dive in to your first of many short, manageable tasks: reading Chapter 1, which happens to duplicate some of the topics also covered in the ICND1 book. Enjoy!

The ICND1 half of the CCNA R&S exam topics introduces the basics of Ethernet LANs and LAN switching. Part I of this ICND2 Cert Guide builds on that knowledge with six more chapters about LANs and LAN switching.

Part I discusses two major topics in depth, to a configuration, verification, and trouble-shooting level on each: Spanning Tree Protocol (STP) and VLAN Trunking Protocol (VTP). Chapters 2 and 3 get fairly deep on STP, a switch feature that requires basic configuration skills, but one that requires a lot of thought to master verification and troubleshooting. Chapter 5 discusses VTP and how it can be used to advertise VLAN configuration around a network of switches, again to a troubleshooting depth.

Besides the major focus on STP and VTP, Chapter 6 introduces a small set of new topics: 802.1x, AAA authentication, DHCP snooping, and switch stacking.

Beyond the four chapters that focus on completely new material (Chapters 2, 3, 5, and 6), Chapters 1 and 4 revisit some topics you will already be comfortable with if you remember most of what you learned for the ICND1 half of the CCNA R&S certification. Chapter 1 discusses VLANs and VLAN trunks, topics duplicated in ICND1 and ICND2 exam top-ics. So, this book includes the same chapter in both books. For those of you who read the *CCENT/CCNA ICND1 100-105 Official Cert Guide*, specifically Chapter 11 of that book, then use Chapter 1 of this book as a review. Make sure you recall the details, and move quickly through that chapter.

Part I

Ethernet LANs

Chapter 1: Implementing Ethernet Virtual LANs

Chapter 2: Spanning Tree Protocol Concepts

Chapter 3: Spanning Tree Protocol Implementation

Chapter 4: LAN Troubleshooting

Chapter 5: VLAN Trunking Protocol

Chapter 6: Miscellaneous LAN Topics

Part I Review

Implementing Ethernet Virtual LANs

This chapter covers the following exam topics:

1.0 LAN Switching Technologies

1.1 Configure, verify, and troubleshoot VLANs (normal/extended range) spanning multiple switches

    1.1.a Access ports (data and voice)

    1.1.b Default VLAN

1.2 Configure, verify, and troubleshoot interswitch connectivity

    1.2.a Add and remove VLANs on a trunk

    1.2.b DTP and VTP (v1&v2)

Virtual LANs (VLAN) have an impact on many parts of a switch's logic. Frame forwarding happens per VLAN. MAC learning adds MAC table entries, and those entries include the associated VLAN. Even Spanning Tree Protocol (STP), a big focus in Part I of this book, often happens per-VLAN.

This chapter examines how many switch core features work in the context of VLANs. The chapter breaks the topics into concepts in the first section of the chapter, with configuration and verification in the second half. The topics include VLANs, VLAN trunking, routing between VLANs, plus voice and data VLANs. (Chapter 4, "LAN Troubleshooting," revisits some of these topics from a troubleshooting perspective.)

For you ICND1 Cert Guide readers, note that this chapter is identical to the ICND1 100-105 Cert Guide's Chapter 11. Both the ICND1 and ICND2 exams include specific exam topics about most of the content in this chapter. By using the exact same chapter for duplicate exam topics between the two books, hopefully those of you who remember a lot about these topics can move quickly through this chapter. For those who do not remember as much, just treat it as a normal chapter.

"Do I Know This Already?" Quiz

Take the quiz (either here, or use the PCPT software) if you want to use the score to help you decide how much time to spend on this chapter. The answers are at the bottom of the page following the quiz, and the explanations are in DVD Appendix C and in the PCPT software.

Table 1-1 "Do I Know This Already?" Foundation Topics Section-to-Question Mapping

Foundation Topics Section	Questions
Virtual LAN Concepts	1–3
VLAN and VLAN Trunking Configuration and Verification	4–6

1. In a LAN, which of the following terms best equates to the term *VLAN*?

   a. Collision domain

   b. Broadcast domain

   c. Subnet

   d. Single switch

   e. Trunk

2. Imagine a switch with three configured VLANs. How many IP subnets are required, assuming that all hosts in all VLANs want to use TCP/IP?

   a. 0

   b. 1

   c. 2

   d. 3

   e. You cannot tell from the information provided.

3. Switch SW1 sends a frame to switch SW2 using 802.1Q trunking. Which of the answers describes how SW1 changes or adds to the Ethernet frame before forwarding the frame to SW2?

   a. Inserts a 4-byte header and does change the MAC addresses

   b. Inserts a 4-byte header and does not change the MAC addresses

   c. Encapsulates the original frame behind an entirely new Ethernet header

   d. None of the other answers are correct.

4. Imagine that you are told that switch 1 is configured with the **dynamic auto** parameter for trunking on its Fa0/5 interface, which is connected to switch 2. You have to configure switch 2. Which of the following settings for trunking could allow trunking to work? (Choose two answers.)

   a. trunk

   b. dynamic auto

   c. dynamic desirable

   d. access

5. A switch has just arrived from Cisco. The switch has never been configured with any VLANs, but VTP has been disabled. An engineer configures the **vlan 22** and **name Hannahs-VLAN** commands, and then exits configuration mode. Which of the following are true? (Choose two answers.)

    a. VLAN 22 is listed in the output of the **show vlan brief** command.

    b. VLAN 22 is listed in the output of the **show running-config** command.

    c. VLAN 22 is not created by this process.

    d. VLAN 22 does not exist in that switch until at least one interface is assigned to that VLAN.

6. Which of the following commands identify switch interfaces as being trunking interfaces: interfaces that currently operate as VLAN trunks? (Choose two answers.)

    a. show interfaces

    b. show interfaces switchport

    c. show interfaces trunk

    d. show trunks

Foundation Topics

Virtual LAN Concepts

Before understanding VLANs, you must first have a specific understanding of the definition of a LAN. For example, from one perspective, a LAN includes all the user devices, servers, switches, routers, cables, and wireless access points in one location. However, an alternative narrower definition of a LAN can help in understanding the concept of a virtual LAN:

    A LAN includes all devices in the same broadcast domain.

A broadcast domain includes the set of all LAN-connected devices, so that when any of the devices sends a broadcast frame, all the other devices get a copy of the frame. So, from one perspective, you can think of a LAN and a broadcast domain as being basically the same thing.

Without VLANs, a switch considers all its interfaces to be in the same broadcast domain. That is, for one switch, when a broadcast frame entered one switch port, the switch forwarded that broadcast frame out all other ports. With that logic, to create two different LAN broadcast domains, you had to buy two different Ethernet LAN switches, as shown in Figure 1-1.

Figure 1-1 *Creating Two Broadcast Domains with Two Physical Switches and No VLANs*

With support for VLANs, a single switch can accomplish the same goals of the design in Figure 1-1—to create two broadcast domains—with a single switch. With VLANs, a switch can configure some interfaces into one broadcast domain and some into another, creating multiple broadcast domains. These individual broadcast domains created by the switch are called virtual LANs (VLAN).

For example, in Figure 1-2, the single switch creates two VLANs, treating the ports in each VLAN as being completely separate. The switch would never forward a frame sent by Dino (in VLAN 1) over to either Wilma or Betty (in VLAN 2).

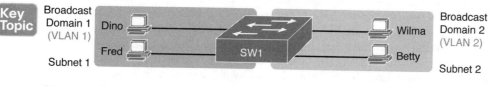

Figure 1-2 *Creating Two Broadcast Domains Using One Switch and VLANs*

Designing campus LANs to use more VLANs, each with a smaller number of devices, often helps improve the LAN in many ways. For example, a broadcast sent by one host in a VLAN will be received and processed by all the other hosts in the VLAN—but not by hosts in a different VLAN. Limiting the number of hosts that receive a single broadcast frame reduces the number of hosts that waste effort processing unneeded broadcasts. It also reduces security risks, because fewer hosts see frames sent by any one host. These are just a few reasons for separating hosts into different VLANs. The following list summarizes the most common reasons for choosing to create smaller broadcast domains (VLANs):

■ To reduce CPU overhead on each device by reducing the number of devices that receive each broadcast frame

■ To reduce security risks by reducing the number of hosts that receive copies of frames that the switches flood (broadcasts, multicasts, and unknown unicasts)

■ To improve security for hosts that send sensitive data by keeping those hosts on a separate VLAN

■ To create more flexible designs that group users by department, or by groups that work together, instead of by physical location

■ To solve problems more quickly, because the failure domain for many problems is the same set of devices as those in the same broadcast domain

■ To reduce the workload for the Spanning Tree Protocol (STP) by limiting a VLAN to a single access switch

This chapter does not examine all the reasons for VLANs in more depth. However, know that most enterprise networks use VLANs quite a bit. The rest of this chapter looks closely

Answers to the "Do I Know This Already?" quiz:
1 B **2** D **3** B **4** A, C **5** A, B **6** B, C

at the mechanics of how VLANs work across multiple Cisco switches, including the required configuration. To that end, the next section examines VLAN trunking, a feature required when installing a VLAN that exists on more than one LAN switch.

Creating Multiswitch VLANs Using Trunking

Configuring VLANs on a single switch requires only a little effort: You simply configure each port to tell it the VLAN number to which the port belongs. With multiple switches, you have to consider additional concepts about how to forward traffic between the switches.

When using VLANs in networks that have multiple interconnected switches, the switches need to use *VLAN trunking* on the links between the switches. VLAN trunking causes the switches to use a process called *VLAN tagging*, by which the sending switch adds another header to the frame before sending it over the trunk. This extra trunking header includes a *VLAN identifier* (VLAN ID) field so that the sending switch can associate the frame with a particular VLAN ID, and the receiving switch can then know in what VLAN each frame belongs.

Figure 1-3 shows an example that demonstrates VLANs that exist on multiple switches, but it does not use trunking. First, the design uses two VLANs: VLAN 10 and VLAN 20. Each switch has two ports assigned to each VLAN, so each VLAN exists in both switches. To forward traffic in VLAN 10 between the two switches, the design includes a link between switches, with that link fully inside VLAN 10. Likewise, to support VLAN 20 traffic between switches, the design uses a second link between switches, with that link inside VLAN 20.

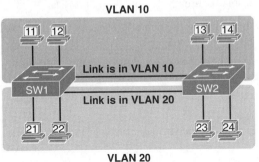

Figure 1-3 *Multiswitch VLAN Without VLAN Trunking*

The design in Figure 1-3 functions perfectly. For example, PC11 (in VLAN 10) can send a frame to PC14. The frame flows into SW1, over the top link (the one that is in VLAN 10) and over to SW2.

The design shown in Figure 1-3 works, but it simply does not scale very well. It requires one physical link between switches to support every VLAN. If a design needed 10 or 20 VLANs, you would need 10 or 20 links between switches, and you would use 10 or 20 switch ports (on each switch) for those links.

VLAN Tagging Concepts

VLAN trunking creates one link between switches that supports as many VLANs as you need. As a VLAN trunk, the switches treat the link as if it were a part of all the VLANs. At the same time, the trunk keeps the VLAN traffic separate, so frames in VLAN 10 would not go to devices in VLAN 20, and vice versa, because each frame is identified by VLAN number as it crosses the trunk. Figure 1-4 shows the idea, with a single physical link between the two switches.

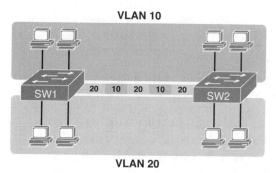

Figure 1-4 *Multiswitch VLAN with Trunking*

The use of trunking allows switches to pass frames from multiple VLANs over a single physical connection by adding a small header to the Ethernet frame. For example, Figure 1-5 shows PC11 sending a broadcast frame on interface Fa0/1 at Step 1. To flood the frame, switch SW1 needs to forward the broadcast frame to switch SW2. However, SW1 needs to let SW2 know that the frame is part of VLAN 10, so that after the frame is received, SW2 will flood the frame only into VLAN 10, and not into VLAN 20. So, as shown at Step 2, before sending the frame, SW1 adds a VLAN header to the original Ethernet frame, with the VLAN header listing a VLAN ID of 10 in this case.

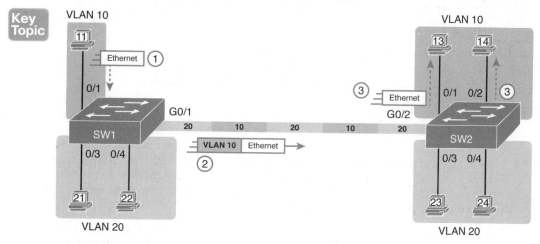

Figure 1-5 *VLAN Trunking Between Two Switches*

When SW2 receives the frame, it understands that the frame is in VLAN 10. SW2 then removes the VLAN header, forwarding the original frame out its interfaces in VLAN 10 (Step 3).

For another example, consider the case when PC21 (in VLAN 20) sends a broadcast. SW1 sends the broadcast out port Fa0/4 (because that port is in VLAN 20) and out Gi0/1 (because it is a trunk, meaning that it supports multiple different VLANs). SW1 adds a trunking header to the frame, listing a VLAN ID of 20. SW2 strips off the trunking header after determining that the frame is part of VLAN 20, so SW2 knows to forward the frame out only ports Fa0/3 and Fa0/4, because they are in VLAN 20, and not out ports Fa0/1 and Fa0/2, because they are in VLAN 10.

The 802.1Q and ISL VLAN Trunking Protocols

Cisco has supported two different trunking protocols over the years: Inter-Switch Link (ISL) and IEEE 802.1Q. Cisco created ISL long before 802.1Q, in part because the IEEE had not yet defined a VLAN trunking standard. Years later, the IEEE completed work on the 802.1Q standard, which defines a different way to do trunking. Today, 802.1Q has become the more popular trunking protocol, with Cisco not even supporting ISL in some of its newer models of LAN switches, including the 2960 switches used in the examples in this book.

While both ISL and 802.1Q tag each frame with the VLAN ID, the details differ. 802.1Q inserts an extra 4-byte 802.1Q VLAN header into the original frame's Ethernet header, as shown at the top of Figure 1-6. As for the fields in the 802.1Q header, only the 12-bit VLAN ID field inside the 802.1Q header matters for topics discussed in this book. This 12-bit field supports a theoretical maximum of 2^{12} (4096) VLANs, but in practice it supports a maximum of 4094. (Both 802.1Q and ISL use 12 bits to tag the VLAN ID, with two reserved values [0 and 4095].)

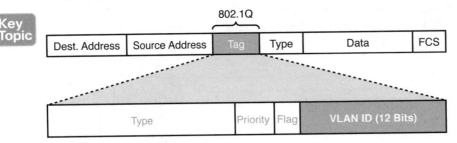

Figure 1-6 *802.1Q Trunking*

Cisco switches break the range of VLAN IDs (1–4094) into two ranges: the normal range and the extended range. All switches can use normal-range VLANs with values from 1 to 1005. Only some switches can use extended-range VLANs with VLAN IDs from 1006 to 4094. The rules for which switches can use extended-range VLANs depend on the configuration of the VLAN Trunking Protocol (VTP), which is discussed briefly in the section "VLAN Trunking Configuration," later in this chapter.

802.1Q also defines one special VLAN ID on each trunk as the *native VLAN* (defaulting to use VLAN 1). By definition, 802.1Q simply does not add an 802.1Q header to frames in the native VLAN. When the switch on the other side of the trunk receives a frame that does not have an 802.1Q header, the receiving switch knows that the frame is part of the native VLAN. Note that because of this behavior, both switches must agree on which VLAN is the native VLAN.

The 802.1Q native VLAN provides some interesting functions, mainly to support connections to devices that do not understand trunking. For example, a Cisco switch could be cabled to a switch that does not understand 802.1Q trunking. The Cisco switch could send frames in the native VLAN—meaning that the frame has no trunking header—so that the other switch would understand the frame. The native VLAN concept gives switches the capability of at least passing traffic in one VLAN (the native VLAN), which can allow some basic functions, like reachability to telnet into a switch.

Forwarding Data Between VLANs

If you create a campus LAN that contains many VLANs, you typically still need all devices to be able to send data to all other devices. This next topic discusses some concepts about how to route data between those VLANs.

First, it helps to know a few terms about some categories of LAN switches. All the Ethernet switch functions described in the ICND1 Cert Guide use the details and logic defined by OSI Layer 2 protocols. For example, many chapters of the ICND1 Cert Guide discussed how LAN switches receive Ethernet frames (a Layer 2 concept), look at the destination Ethernet MAC address (a Layer 2 address), and forward the Ethernet frame out some other interface. This chapter has already discussed the concept of VLANs as broadcast domains, which is yet another Layer 2 concept.

While some LAN switches work just as described in the ICND1 Cert Guide, some LAN switches have even more functions. LAN switches that forward data based on Layer 2 logic often go by the name *Layer 2 switch*. However, some other switches can do some functions like a router, using additional logic defined by Layer 3 protocols. These switches go by the name *multilayer switch*, or *Layer 3 switch*. This section first discusses how to forward data between VLANs when using Layer 2 switches and ends with a brief discussion of how to use Layer 3 switches.

Routing Packets Between VLANs with a Router

When including VLANs in a campus LAN design, the devices in a VLAN need to be in the same subnet. Following the same design logic, devices in different VLANs need to be in different subnets. For example, in Figure 1-7, the two PCs on the left sit in VLAN 10, in subnet 10. The two PCs on the right sit in a different VLAN (20), with a different subnet (20).

Figure 1-7 *Layer 2 Switch Does Not Route Between the VLANs*

> **NOTE** The figure refers to subnets somewhat generally, like "subnet 10," just so the subnet numbers do not distract. Also, note that the subnet numbers do not have to be the same number as the VLAN numbers.

Figure 1-7 shows the switch as if it were two switches broken in two to emphasize the point that Layer 2 switches will not forward data between two VLANs. When configured with some ports in VLAN 10 and others in VLAN 20, the switch acts like two separate switches in which it will forward traffic. In fact, one goal of VLANs is to separate traffic in one VLAN from another, preventing frames in one VLAN from leaking over to other VLANs.

For example, when Dino (in VLAN 10) sends any Ethernet frame, if SW1 is a Layer 2 switch, that switch will not forward the frame to the PCs on the right in VLAN 20.

The network as a whole needs to support traffic flowing into and out of each VLAN, even though the Layer 2 switch does not forward frames outside a VLAN. The job of forwarding data into and out of a VLAN falls to routers. Instead of switching Layer 2 Ethernet frames between the two VLANs, the network must route Layer 3 packets between the two subnets.

That previous paragraph has some very specific wording related to Layers 2 and 3, so take a moment to reread and reconsider it for a moment. The Layer 2 logic does not let the Layer 2 switch forward the Layer 2 protocol data unit (L2PDU), the Ethernet frame, between VLANs. However, routers can route Layer 3 PDUs (L3PDU), packets, between subnets as their normal job in life.

For example, Figure 1-8 shows a router that can route packets between subnets 10 and 20. The figure shows the same Layer 2 switch as shown in Figure 1-7, with the same perspective of the switch being split into parts with two different VLANs, and with the same PCs in the same VLANs and subnets. Now Router R1 has one LAN physical interface connected to the switch and assigned to VLAN 10, and a second physical interface connected to the switch and assigned to VLAN 20. With an interface connected to each subnet, the Layer 2 switch can keep doing its job—forwarding frames inside a VLAN, while the router can do its job—routing IP packets between the subnets.

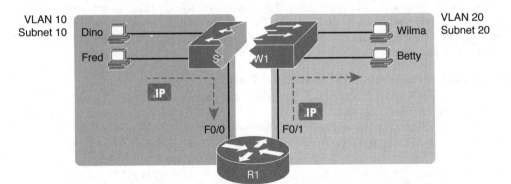

Figure 1-8   *Routing Between Two VLANs on Two Physical Interfaces*

The figure shows an IP packet being routed from Fred, which sits in one VLAN/subnet, to Betty, which sits in the other. The Layer 2 switch forwards two different Layer 2 Ethernet frames: one in VLAN 10, from Fred to R1's F0/0 interface, and the other in VLAN 20, from R1's F0/1 interface to Betty. From a Layer 3 perspective, Fred sends the IP packet to its default router (R1), and R1 routes the packet out another interface (F0/1) into another subnet where Betty resides.

While the design shown in Figure 1-8 works, it uses too many physical interfaces, one per VLAN. A much less expensive (and much preferred) option uses a VLAN trunk between the switch and router, requiring only one physical link between the router and switch, while supporting all VLANs. Trunking can work between any two devices that choose to support it: between two switches, between a router and a switch, or even between server hardware and a switch.

Figure 1-9 shows the same design idea as Figure 1-8, with the same packet being sent from Fred to Betty, except now R1 uses VLAN trunking instead of a separate link for each VLAN.

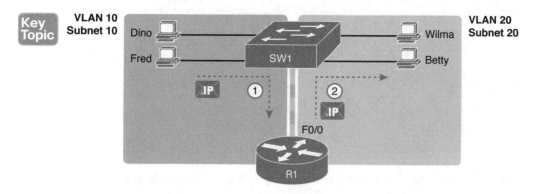

Figure 1-9   *Routing Between Two VLANs Using a Trunk on the Router*

> **NOTE**   Because the router has a single physical link connected to the LAN switch, this design is sometimes called a *router-on-a-stick*.

As a brief aside about terminology, many people describe the concept in Figures 1-8 and 1-9 as "routing packets between VLANs." You can use that phrase, and people know what you mean. However, note that this phrase is not literally true, because it refers to routing packets (a Layer 3 concept) and VLANs (a Layer 2 concept). It just takes fewer words to say something like "routing between VLANs" rather than the literally true but long "routing Layer 3 packets between Layer 3 subnets, with those subnets each mapping to a Layer 2 VLAN."

Routing Packets with a Layer 3 Switch

Routing packets using a physical router, even with the VLAN trunk in the router-on-a-stick model shown in Figure 1-9, still has one significant problem: performance. The physical link puts an upper limit on how many bits can be routed, and less expensive routers tend to be less powerful, and might not be able to route a large enough number of packets per second (pps) to keep up with the traffic volumes.

The ultimate solution moves the routing functions inside the LAN switch hardware. Vendors long ago started combining the hardware and software features of their Layer 2 LAN switches, plus their Layer 3 routers, creating products called *Layer 3 switches* (also known as *multilayer switches*). Layer 3 switches can be configured to act only as a Layer 2 switch, or they can be configured to do both Layer 2 switching as well as Layer 3 routing.

Today, many medium- to large-sized enterprise campus LANs use Layer 3 switches to route packets between subnets (VLANs) in a campus.

In concept, a Layer 3 switch works a lot like the original two devices on which the Layer 3 switch is based: a Layer 2 LAN switch and a Layer 3 router. In fact, if you take the concepts and packet flow shown in Figure 1-8, with a separate Layer 2 switch and Layer 3 router, and then imagine all those features happening inside one device, you have the general idea of what a Layer 3 switch does. Figure 1-10 shows that exact concept, repeating many details of Figure 1-8, but with an overlay that shows the one Layer 3 switch doing the Layer 2 switch functions and the separate Layer 3 routing function.

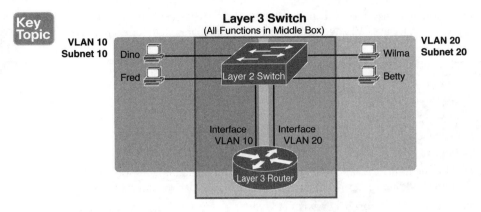

Figure 1-10 *Multilayer Switch: Layer 2 Switching with Layer 3 Routing in One Device*

This chapter introduces the core concepts of routing IP packets between VLANs (or more accurately, between the subnets on the VLANs). Chapter 19, "IPv4 Routing in the LAN," shows how to configure designs that use an external router with router-on-a-stick. This chapter now turns its attention to configuration and verification tasks for VLANs and VLAN trunks.

VLAN and VLAN Trunking Configuration and Verification

Cisco switches do not require any configuration to work. You can purchase Cisco switches, install devices with the correct cabling, turn on the switches, and they work. You would never need to configure the switch, and it would work fine, even if you interconnected switches, until you needed more than one VLAN. But if you want to use VLANs—and most enterprise networks do—you need to add some configuration.

This chapter separates the VLAN configuration details into two major sections. The first section looks at how to configure access interfaces, which are switch interfaces that do not use VLAN trunking. The second part shows how to configure interfaces that do use VLAN trunking.

Creating VLANs and Assigning Access VLANs to an Interface

This section shows how to create a VLAN, give the VLAN a name, and assign interfaces to a VLAN. To focus on these basic details, this section shows examples using a single switch, so VLAN trunking is not needed.

For a Cisco switch to forward frames in a particular VLAN, the switch must be configured to believe that the VLAN exists. In addition, the switch must have nontrunking interfaces (called *access interfaces*) assigned to the VLAN, and/or trunks that support the VLAN. The configuration steps for access interfaces are as follows, with the trunk configuration shown later in the section "VLAN Trunking Configuration":

Config Checklist

Step 1.   To configure a new VLAN, follow these steps:

A. From configuration mode, use the **vlan** *vlan-id* command in global configuration mode to create the VLAN and to move the user into VLAN configuration mode.

B. (Optional) Use the **name** *name* command in VLAN configuration mode to list a name for the VLAN. If not configured, the VLAN name is VLANZZZZ, where ZZZZ is the four-digit decimal VLAN ID.

Step 2.   For each access interface (each interface that does not trunk, but instead belongs to a single VLAN), follow these steps:

A. Use the **interface** *type number* command in global configuration mode to move into interface configuration mode for each desired interface.

B. Use the **switchport access vlan** *id-number* command in interface configuration mode to specify the VLAN number associated with that interface.

C. (Optional) Use the **switchport mode access** command in interface configuration mode to make this port always operate in access mode (that is, to not trunk).

While the list might look a little daunting, the process on a single switch is actually pretty simple. For example, if you want to put the switch's ports in three VLANs—11, 12, and 13—you just add three **vlan** commands: **vlan 11**, **vlan 12**, and **vlan 13**. Then, for each interface, add a **switchport access vlan 11** (or **12** or **13**) command to assign that interface to the proper VLAN.

> **NOTE** The term *default VLAN* (as shown in the exam topics) refers to the default setting on the **switchport access vlan** *vlan-id* command, and that default is VLAN ID 1. In other words, by default, each port is assigned to access VLAN 1.

VLAN Configuration Example 1: Full VLAN Configuration

Example 1-1 shows the configuration process of adding a new VLAN and assigning access interfaces to that VLAN. Figure 1-11 shows the network used in the example, with one LAN switch (SW1) and two hosts in each of three VLANs (1, 2, and 3). The example shows the details of the two-step process for VLAN 2 and the interfaces in VLAN 2, with the configuration of VLAN 3 deferred until the next example.

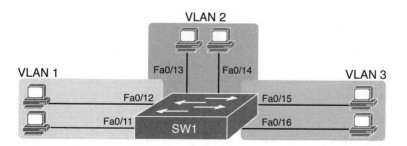

Figure 1-11   *Network with One Switch and Three VLANs*

Example 1-1 *Configuring VLANs and Assigning VLANs to Interfaces*

```
SW1# show vlan brief
VLAN Name                             Status    Ports
---- -------------------------------- --------- -------------------------------
1    default                          active    Fa0/1, Fa0/2, Fa0/3, Fa0/4
                                                Fa0/5, Fa0/6, Fa0/7, Fa0/8
                                                Fa0/9, Fa0/10, Fa0/11, Fa0/12
                                                Fa0/13, Fa0/14, Fa0/15, Fa0/16
                                                Fa0/17, Fa0/18, Fa0/19, Fa0/20
                                                Fa0/21, Fa0/22, Fa0/23, Fa0/24
                                                Gi0/1, Gi0/2
1002 fddi-default                     act/unsup
1003 token-ring-default               act/unsup
1004 fddinet-default                  act/unsup
1005 trnet-default                    act/unsup
! Above, VLANs 2 and 3 do not yet exist. Below, VLAN 2 is added, with name Freds-vlan,
! with two interfaces assigned to VLAN 2.

SW1# configure terminal
Enter configuration commands, one per line.  End with CNTL/Z.
SW1(config)# vlan 2
SW1(config-vlan)# name Freds-vlan
SW1(config-vlan)# exit
SW1(config)# interface range fastethernet 0/13 - 14
SW1(config-if-range)# switchport access vlan 2
SW1(config-if-range)# switchport mode access
SW1(config-if-range)# end

! Below, the show running-config command lists the interface subcommands on
! interfaces Fa0/13 and Fa0/14.
SW1# show running-config
! Many lines omitted for brevity
! Early in the output:
vlan 2
 name Freds-vlan
!
! more lines omitted for brevity
interface FastEthernet0/13
 switchport access vlan 2
 switchport mode access
!
interface FastEthernet0/14
 switchport access vlan 2
 switchport mode access
!
```

```
SW1# show vlan brief

VLAN Name                             Status    Ports
---- --------------------------------  --------  ------------------------------
1    default                          active    Fa0/1, Fa0/2, Fa0/3, Fa0/4
                                                Fa0/5, Fa0/6, Fa0/7, Fa0/8
                                                Fa0/9, Fa0/10, Fa0/11, Fa0/12
                                                Fa0/15, Fa0/16, Fa0/17, Fa0/18
                                                Fa0/19, Fa0/20, Fa0/21, Fa0/22
                                                Fa0/23, Fa0/24, Gi0/1, Gi0/2
2    Freds-vlan                       active    Fa0/13, Fa0/14
1002 fddi-default                     act/unsup
1003 token-ring-default               act/unsup
1004 fddinet-default                  act/unsup
1005 trnet-default                    act/unsup

SW1# show vlan id 2
VLAN Name                             Status    Ports
---- --------------------------------  --------  ------------------------------
2    Freds-vlan                       active    Fa0/13, Fa0/14

VLAN Type  SAID       MTU   Parent RingNo BridgeNo Stp  BrdgMode Trans1 Trans2
---- ----- ---------- ----- ------ ------ -------- ---- -------- ------ ------
2    enet  100010     1500  -      -      -        -    -        0      0

Remote SPAN VLAN
----------------
Disabled

Primary Secondary Type              Ports
------- --------- ----------------- ----------------------------------------
```

The example begins with the **show vlan brief** command, confirming the default settings of five nondeletable VLANs, with all interfaces assigned to VLAN 1. (VLAN 1 cannot be deleted, but can be used. VLANs 1002–1005 cannot be deleted and cannot be used as access VLANs today.) In particular, note that this 2960 switch has 24 Fast Ethernet ports (Fa0/1–Fa0/24) and two Gigabit Ethernet ports (Gi0/1 and Gi0/2), all of which are listed as being in VLAN 1 per that first command's output.

Next, the example shows the process of creating VLAN 2 and assigning interfaces Fa0/13 and Fa0/14 to VLAN 2. Note in particular that the example uses the **interface range** command, which causes the **switchport access vlan 2** interface subcommand to be applied to both interfaces in the range, as confirmed in the **show running-config** command output at the end of the example.

After the configuration has been added, to list the new VLAN, the example repeats the **show vlan brief** command. Note that this command lists VLAN 2, name Freds-vlan, and the interfaces assigned to that VLAN (Fa0/13 and Fa0/14). The **show vlan id 2** command that follows then confirms that ports Fa0/13 and Fa0/14 are assigned to VLAN 2.

The example surrounding Figure 1-11 uses six switch ports, all of which need to operate as access ports. That is, each port should not use trunking, but instead should be assigned to a single VLAN, as assigned by the **switchport access vlan** *vlan-id* command. However, as configured in Example 1-1, these interfaces could negotiate to later become trunk ports, because the switch defaults to allow the port to negotiate trunking and decide whether to act as an access interface or as a trunk interface.

For ports that should always act as access ports, add the optional interface subcommand **switchport mode access**. This command tells the switch to only allow the interface to be an access interface. The upcoming section "VLAN Trunking Configuration" discusses more details about the commands that allow a port to negotiate whether it should use trunking.

NOTE The book includes a video that works through a different VLAN configuration example as well. You can find the video on the DVD and on the companion website.

VLAN Configuration Example 2: Shorter VLAN Configuration

Example 1-1 shows several of the optional configuration commands, with a side effect of being a bit longer than is required. Example 1-2 shows a much briefer alternative configuration, picking up the story where Example 1-1 ended and showing the addition of VLAN 3 (as shown in Figure 1-11). Note that SW1 does not know about VLAN 3 at the beginning of this example.

Example 1-2 *Shorter VLAN Configuration Example (VLAN 3)*

```
SW1# configure terminal
Enter configuration commands, one per line.  End with CNTL/Z.
SW1(config)# interface range Fastethernet 0/15 - 16
SW1(config-if-range)# switchport access vlan 3
% Access VLAN does not exist. Creating vlan 3
SW1(config-if-range)# ^Z

SW1# show vlan brief

VLAN Name                             Status    Ports
---- -------------------------------- --------- -------------------------------
1    default                          active    Fa0/1, Fa0/2, Fa0/3, Fa0/4
                                                Fa0/5, Fa0/6, Fa0/7, Fa0/8
                                                Fa0/9, Fa0/10, Fa0/11, Fa0/12
                                                Fa0/17, Fa0/18, Fa0/19, Fa0/20
                                                Fa0/21, Fa0/22, Fa0/23, Fa0/24
                                                Gi0/1, Gi0/2

2    Freds-vlan                       active    Fa0/13, Fa0/14
3    VLAN0003                         active    Fa0/15, Fa0/16
1002 fddi-default                     act/unsup
1003 token-ring-default               act/unsup
1004 fddinet-default                  act/unsup
1005 trnet-default                    act/unsup
```

Example 1-2 shows how a switch can dynamically create a VLAN—the equivalent of the **vlan** *vlan-id* global config command—when the **switchport access vlan** interface sub-command refers to a currently unconfigured VLAN. This example begins with SW1 not knowing about VLAN 3. When the **switchport access vlan 3** interface subcommand was used, the switch realized that VLAN 3 did not exist, and as noted in the shaded message in the example, the switch created VLAN 3, using a default name (VLAN0003). No other steps are required to create the VLAN. At the end of the process, VLAN 3 exists in the switch, and interfaces Fa0/15 and Fa0/16 are in VLAN 3, as noted in the shaded part of the **show vlan brief** command output.

VLAN Trunking Protocol

Before showing more configuration examples, you also need to know something about a Cisco protocol and tool called the VLAN Trunking Protocol (VTP). VTP is a Cisco proprietary tool on Cisco switches that advertises each VLAN configured in one switch (with the **vlan** *number* command) so that all the other switches in the campus learn about that VLAN. However, for various reasons, many enterprises choose not to use VTP.

Each switch can use one of three VTP modes: server, client, or transparent. Switches use either VTP server or client mode when the switch wants to use VTP for its intended purpose of dynamically advertising VLAN configuration information. However, with many Cisco switches and IOS versions, VTP cannot be completely disabled on a Cisco switch; instead, the switch disables VTP by using VTP transparent mode.

Chapter 5, "VLAN Trunking Protocol," discusses how to make use of VTP. Chapters 1 through 4 mostly ignore VTP. To that end, all examples in this book use switches that have been set either to use VTP transparent mode (with the **vtp mode transparent** global command) or to disable it (with the **vtp mode off** global command). Both options allow the administrator to configure both standard- and extended-range VLANs, and the switch lists the **vlan** commands in the running-config file.

Finally, on a practical note, if you happen to do lab exercises with real switches or with simulators, and you see unusual results with VLANs, check the VTP status with the **show vtp status** command. If your switch uses VTP server or client mode, you will find:

- The server switches can configure VLANs in the standard range only (1–1005).
- The client switches cannot configure VLANs.
- Both servers and clients may be learning new VLANs from other switches, and seeing their VLANs deleted by other switches, because of VTP.
- The **show running-config** command does not list any **vlan** commands.

If possible in lab, switch to VTP transparent mode and ignore VTP for your switch configuration practice until you are ready to focus on how VTP works when studying for the ICND2 exam topics.

NOTE   Do not change VTP settings on any switch that also connects to the production network until you know how VTP works as explained in Chapter 5.

VLAN Trunking Configuration

Trunking configuration between two Cisco switches can be very simple if you just statically configure trunking. For example, if two Cisco 2960 switches connect to each other, they support only 802.1Q and not ISL. You could literally add one interface subcommand for the switch interface on each side of the link (**switchport mode trunk**), and you would create a VLAN trunk that supported all the VLANs known to each switch.

However, trunking configuration on Cisco switches includes many more options, including several options for dynamically negotiating various trunking settings. The configuration can either predefine different settings or tell the switch to negotiate the settings, as follows:

- **The type of trunking:** IEEE 802.1Q, ISL, or negotiate which one to use
- **The administrative mode:** Whether to always trunk, always not trunk, or negotiate

First, consider the type of trunking. Cisco switches that support ISL and 802.1Q can negotiate which type to use, using the Dynamic Trunking Protocol (DTP). If both switches support both protocols, they use ISL; otherwise, they use the protocol that both support. Today, many Cisco switches do not support the older ISL trunking protocol. Switches that support both types of trunking use the **switchport trunk encapsulation {dot1q | isl | negotiate}** interface subcommand to either configure the type or allow DTP to negotiate the type.

DTP can also negotiate whether the two devices on the link agree to trunk at all, as guided by the local switch port's administrative mode. The administrative mode refers to the configuration setting for whether trunking should be used. Each interface also has an *operational* mode, which refers to what is currently happening on the interface, and might have been chosen by DTP's negotiation with the other device. Cisco switches use the **switchport mode** interface subcommand to define the administrative trunking mode, as listed in Table 1-2.

Key Topic

Table 1-2   Trunking Administrative Mode Options with the **switchport mode** Command

Command Option	Description
access	Always act as an access (nontrunk) port
trunk	Always act as a trunk port
dynamic desirable	Initiates negotiation messages and responds to negotiation messages to dynamically choose whether to start using trunking
dynamic auto	Passively waits to receive trunk negotiation messages, at which point the switch will respond and negotiate whether to use trunking

For example, consider the two switches shown in Figure 1-12. This figure shows an expansion of the network shown in Figure 1-11, with a trunk to a new switch (SW2) and with parts of VLANs 1 and 3 on ports attached to SW2. The two switches use a Gigabit Ethernet link for the trunk. In this case, the trunk does not dynamically form by default, because both (2960) switches default to an administrative mode of *dynamic auto*, meaning that neither switch initiates the trunk negotiation process. By changing one switch to use *dynamic desirable* mode, which does initiate the negotiation, the switches negotiate to use trunking, specifically 802.1Q because the 2960s support only 802.1Q.

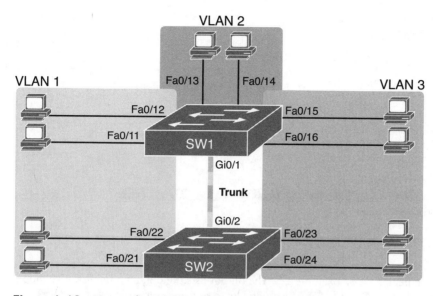

Figure 1-12 *Network with Two Switches and Three VLANs*

Example 1-3 begins by showing the two switches in Figure 1-12 with the default configuration so that the two switches do not trunk.

Example 1-3 *Initial (Default) State: Not Trunking Between SW1 and SW2*

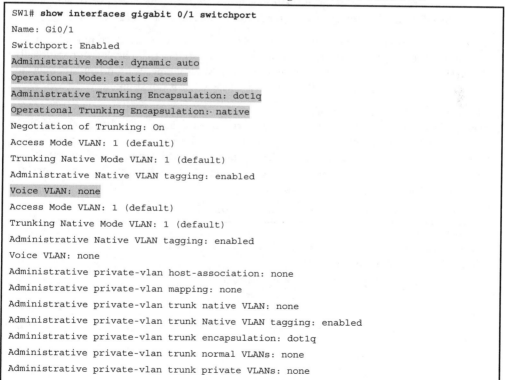

```
SW1# show interfaces gigabit 0/1 switchport
Name: Gi0/1
Switchport: Enabled
Administrative Mode: dynamic auto
Operational Mode: static access
Administrative Trunking Encapsulation: dot1q
Operational Trunking Encapsulation: native
Negotiation of Trunking: On
Access Mode VLAN: 1 (default)
Trunking Native Mode VLAN: 1 (default)
Administrative Native VLAN tagging: enabled
Voice VLAN: none
Access Mode VLAN: 1 (default)
Trunking Native Mode VLAN: 1 (default)
Administrative Native VLAN tagging: enabled
Voice VLAN: none
Administrative private-vlan host-association: none
Administrative private-vlan mapping: none
Administrative private-vlan trunk native VLAN: none
Administrative private-vlan trunk Native VLAN tagging: enabled
Administrative private-vlan trunk encapsulation: dot1q
Administrative private-vlan trunk normal VLANs: none
Administrative private-vlan trunk private VLANs: none
```

```
Operational private-vlan: none
Trunking VLANs Enabled: ALL
Pruning VLANs Enabled: 2-1001
Capture Mode Disabled
Capture VLANs Allowed: ALL


Protected: false
Unknown unicast blocked: disabled
Unknown multicast blocked: disabled
Appliance trust: none


! Note that the next command results in a single empty line of output.
SW1# show interfaces trunk
SW1#
```

First, focus on the highlighted items from the output of the **show interfaces switchport** command at the beginning of Example 1-3. The output lists the default administrative mode setting of dynamic auto. Because SW2 also defaults to dynamic auto, the command lists SW1's operational status as "access," meaning that it is not trunking. ("Dynamic auto" tells both switches to sit there and wait on the other switch to start the negotiations.) The third shaded line points out the only supported type of trunking (802.1Q) on this 2960 switch. (On a switch that supports both ISL and 802.1Q, this value would by default list "negotiate," to mean that the type of encapsulation is negotiated.) Finally, the operational trunking type is listed as "native," which is a reference to the 802.1Q native VLAN.

The end of the example shows the output of the **show interfaces trunk** command, but with no output. This command lists information about all interfaces that currently operationally trunk; that is, it lists interfaces that currently use VLAN trunking. With no interfaces listed, this command also confirms that the link between switches is not trunking.

Next, consider Example 1-4, which shows the new configuration that enables trunking. In this case, SW1 is configured with the **switchport mode dynamic desirable** command, which asks the switch to both negotiate as well as to begin the negotiation process, rather than waiting on the other device. As soon as the command is issued, log messages appear showing that the interface goes down and then back up again, which happens when the interface transitions from access mode to trunk mode.

Example 1-4   *SW1 Changes from Dynamic Auto to Dynamic Desirable*

```
SW1# configure terminal
Enter configuration commands, one per line.  End with CNTL/Z.
SW1(config)# interface gigabit 0/1
SW1(config-if)# switchport mode dynamic desirable
SW1(config-if)# ^Z
SW1#
%LINEPROTO-5-UPDOWN: Line protocol on Interface GigabitEthernet0/1, changed state to
  down
%LINEPROTO-5-UPDOWN: Line protocol on Interface GigabitEthernet0/1, changed state to
  up
```

```
SW1# show interfaces gigabit 0/1 switchport
Name: Gi0/1
Switchport: Enabled
Administrative Mode: dynamic desirable
Operational Mode: trunk
Administrative Trunking Encapsulation: dot1q
Operational Trunking Encapsulation: dot1q
Negotiation of Trunking: On
Access Mode VLAN: 1 (default)
Trunking Native Mode VLAN: 1 (default)
! lines omitted for brevity


! The next command formerly listed a single empty line of output; now it lists
! information about the 1 operational trunk.
SW1# show interfaces trunk

Port          Mode            Encapsulation  Status          Native vlan
Gi0/1         desirable       802.1q         trunking        1


Port          Vlans allowed on trunk
Gi0/1         1-4094


Port          Vlans allowed and active in management domain
Gi0/1         1-3


Port          Vlans in spanning tree forwarding state and not pruned
Gi0/1         1-3


SW1# show vlan id 2
VLAN Name                             Status    Ports
---- -------------------------------- --------- -------------------------------
2    Freds-vlan                       active    Fa0/13, Fa0/14, G0/1


VLAN Type  SAID       MTU   Parent RingNo BridgeNo Stp  BrdgMode Trans1 Trans2
---- ----- ---------- ----- ------ ------ -------- ---- -------- ------ ------
2    enet  100010     1500  -      -      -        -    -        0      0


Remote SPAN VLAN
----------------
Disabled


Primary Secondary Type              Ports
------- --------- ----------------- -------------------------------------------
```

To verify whether trunking is working now, the middle of Example 1-4 lists the **show interfaces switchport** command. Note that the command still lists the administrative settings, which denote the configured values along with the operational settings, which list what the switch is currently doing. In this case, SW1 now claims to be in an operational mode of *trunk*, with an operational trunking encapsulation of dot1Q.

The end of the example shows the output of the **show vlan id 2** command, which now lists G0/1, confirming that G0/1 is now operationally trunking. The next section discusses the meaning of the output of this command.

For the exams, you should be ready to interpret the output of the **show interfaces switchport** command, realize the administrative mode implied by the output, and know whether the link should operationally trunk based on those settings. Table 1-3 lists the combinations of the trunking administrative modes and the expected operational mode (trunk or access) resulting from the configured settings. The table lists the administrative mode used on one end of the link on the left, and the administrative mode on the switch on the other end of the link across the top of the table.

Key Topic

Table 1-3   Expected Trunking Operational Mode Based on the Configured Administrative Modes

Administrative Mode	Access	Dynamic Auto	Trunk	Dynamic Desirable
access	Access	Access	Do Not Use[1]	Access
dynamic auto	Access	Access	Trunk	Trunk
trunk	Do Not Use[1]	Trunk	Trunk	Trunk
dynamic desirable	Access	Trunk	Trunk	Trunk

[1] When two switches configure a mode of "access" on one end and "trunk" on the other, problems occur. Avoid this combination.

Finally, before leaving the discussion of configuring trunks, Cisco recommends disabling trunk negotiation on most ports for better security. The majority of switch ports on most switches will be used to connect to users. As a matter of habit, you can disable DTP negotiations altogether using the **switchport nonegotiate** interface subcommand.

Implementing Interfaces Connected to Phones

This next topic is a strange topic, at least in the context of access links and trunk links. In the world of IP telephony, telephones use Ethernet ports to connect to an Ethernet network so they can use IP to send and receive voice traffic sent via IP packets. To make that work, the switch's Ethernet port acts like an access port—but at the same time, the port acts like a trunk in some ways. This last topic of the chapter works through those main concepts.

Data and Voice VLAN Concepts

Before IP telephony, a PC could sit on the same desk as a phone. The phone happened to use UTP cabling, with that phone connected to some voice device (often called a *voice switch* or a *private branch exchange [PBX]*). The PC, of course, connected using an unshielded twisted-pair (UTP) cable to the usual LAN switch that sat in the wiring closet—sometimes in the same wiring closet as the voice switch. Figure 1-13 shows the idea.

User's Desk   Closet

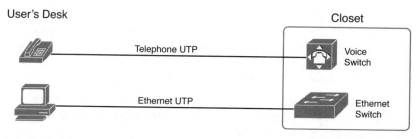

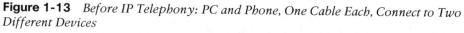

Figure 1-13 *Before IP Telephony: PC and Phone, One Cable Each, Connect to Two Different Devices*

The term *IP telephony* refers to the branch of networking in which the telephones use IP packets to send and receive voice as represented by the bits in the data portion of the IP packet. The phones connect to the network like most other end-user devices, using either Ethernet or Wi-Fi. These new IP phones did not connect via cable directly to a voice switch, instead connecting to the IP network using an Ethernet cable and an Ethernet port built in to the phone. The phones then communicated over the IP network with software that replaced the call setup and other functions of the PBX. (The current product from Cisco that perform this IP telephony control function is called *Cisco Unified Communications Manager*.)

The migration from using the already-installed telephone cabling, to these new IP phones that needed UTP cables that supported Ethernet, caused some problems in some offices. In particular:

- The older non-IP phones used a category of UTP cabling that often did not support 100-Mbps or 1000-Mbps Ethernet.

- Most offices had a single UTP cable running from the wiring closet to each desk, but now two devices (the PC and the new IP phone) both needed a cable from the desktop to the wiring closet.

- Installing a new cable to every desk would be expensive, plus you would need more switch ports.

To solve this problem, Cisco embedded small three-port switches into each phone.

IP telephones have included a small LAN switch, on the underside of the phone, since the earliest IP telephone products. Figure 1-14 shows the basic cabling, with the wiring closet cable connecting to one physical port on the embedded switch, the PC connecting with a short patch cable to the other physical port, and the phone's internal CPU connecting to an internal switch port.

User's Desk   Wiring Closet

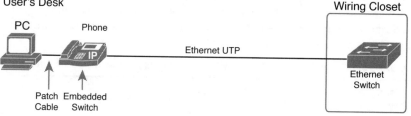

Figure 1-14 *Cabling with an IP Phone, a Single Cable, and an Integrated Switch*

Sites that use IP telephony, which includes most every company today, now have two devices off each access port. In addition, Cisco best practices for IP telephony design tell us to put the phones in one VLAN, and the PCs in a different VLAN. To make that happen, the switch port acts a little like an access link (for the PC's traffic), and a little like a trunk (for the phone's traffic). The configuration defines two VLANs on that port, as follows:

Data VLAN: Same idea and configuration as the access VLAN on an access port, but defined as the VLAN on that link for forwarding the traffic for the device connected to the phone on the desk (typically the user's PC).

Voice VLAN: The VLAN defined on the link for forwarding the phone's traffic. Traffic in this VLAN is typically tagged with an 802.1Q header.

Figure 1-15 illustrates this design with two VLANs on access ports that support IP telephones.

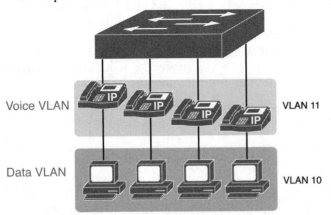

Figure 1-15 *A LAN Design, with Data in VLAN 10 and Phones in VLAN 11*

Data and Voice VLAN Configuration and Verification

Configuring a switch port to support IP phones, once you know the planned voice and data VLAN IDs, is easy. Making sense of the **show** commands once they are configured can be a challenge. The port acts like an access port in many ways. However, with most configuration options, the voice frames flow with an 802.1Q header, so that the link supports frames in both VLANs on the link. But that makes for some different **show** command output.

Example 1-5 shows an example. In this case, all four switch ports F0/1–F0/4 begin with default configuration. The configuration adds the new data and voice VLANs. The example then configures all four ports as access ports, and defines the access VLAN, which is also called the data VLAN when discussing IP telephony. Finally, the configuration includes the **switchport voice vlan 11** command, which defines the voice VLAN used on the port. The example matches Figure 1-15, using ports F0/1–F0/4.

Example 1-5 *Configuring the Voice and Data VLAN on Ports Connected to Phones*

```
SW1# configure terminal
Enter configuration commands, one per line.  End with CNTL/Z.
SW1(config)# vlan 10
SW1(config-vlan)# vlan 11
```

```
SW1(config-vlan)# interface range FastEthernet0/1 - 4
SW1(config-if)# switchport mode access
SW1(config-if)# switchport access vlan 10
SW1(config-if)# switchport voice vlan 11
SW1(config-if)#^Z
SW1#
```

NOTE   CDP, discussed in the ICND1 book's Chapter 33, "Device Management Protocols," must be enabled on an interface for a voice access port to work with Cisco IP Phones. CDP is enabled by default, so its configuration is not shown here.

The following list details the configuration steps for easier review and study:

Step 1.   Use the **vlan** *vlan-id* command in global configuration mode to create the data and voice VLANs if they do not already exist on the switch.

Step 2.   Configure the data VLAN like an access VLAN, as usual:

> **A.** Use the **interface** *type number* command in global configuration mode to move into interface configuration mode.
>
> **B.** Use the **switchport access vlan** *id-number* command in interface configuration mode to define the data VLAN.
>
> **C.** Use the **switchport mode access** command in interface configuration mode to make this port always operate in access mode (that is, to not trunk).

Step 3.   Use the **switchport voice vlan** *id-number* command in interface configuration mode to set the voice VLAN ID.

Verifying the status of a switch port configured like Example 1-5 shows some different output compared to the pure access port and pure trunk port configurations seen earlier in this chapter. For example, the **show interfaces switchport** command shows details about the operation of an interface, including many details about access ports. Example 1-6 shows those details for port F0/4 after the configuration in Example 1-5 was added.

Example 1-6   *Verifying the Data VLAN (Access VLAN) and Voice VLAN*

```
SW1# show interfaces FastEthernet 0/4 switchport
Name: Fa0/4
Switchport: Enabled
Administrative Mode: static access
Operational Mode: static access
Administrative Trunking Encapsulation: dot1q
Operational Trunking Encapsulation: native
Negotiation of Trunking: Off
Access Mode VLAN: 10 (VLAN0010)
Trunking Native Mode VLAN: 1 (default)
Administrative Native VLAN tagging: enabled
Voice VLAN: 11 (VLAN0011)
! The rest of the output is omitted for brevity
```

Working through the first three highlighted lines in the output, all those details should look familiar for any access port. The **switchport mode access** configuration command statically configures the administrative mode to be an access port, so the port of course operates as an access port. Also, as shown in the third highlighted line, the **switchport access vlan 10** configuration command defined the access mode VLAN as highlighted here.

The fourth highlighted line shows the one small new piece of information: the voice VLAN ID, as set with the **switchport voice vlan 11** command in this case. This small line of output is the only piece of information in the output that differs from the earlier access port examples in this chapter.

These ports act more like access ports than trunk ports. In fact, the **show interfaces** *type number* **switchport** command boldly proclaims, "Operational Mode: static access." However, one other **show** command reveals just a little more about the underlying operation with 802.1Q tagging for the voice frames.

As mentioned earlier, the **show interfaces trunk** command—that is, the command that does not include a specific interface in the middle of the command—lists the operational trunks on a switch. With IP telephony ports, the ports do not show up in the list of trunks either— providing evidence that these links are *not* treated as trunks. Example 1-7 shows just such an example.

However, the **show interfaces trunk** command with the interface listed in the middle of the command, as is also shown in Example 1-7, does list some additional information. Note that in this case, the **show interfaces F0/4 trunk** command lists the status as not-trunking, but with VLANs 10 and 11 allowed on the trunk. (Normally, on an access port, only the access VLAN is listed in the "VLANs allowed on the trunk" list in the output of this command.)

Example 1-7 *Allowed VLAN List and the List of Active VLANs*

```
SW1# show interfaces trunk
SW1# show interfaces F0/4 trunk


Port          Mode            Encapsulation  Status       Native vlan
Fa0/4         off             802.1q         not-trunking 1


Port          Vlans allowed on trunk
Fa0/4         10-11


Port          Vlans allowed and active in management domain
Fa0/4         10-11


Port          Vlans in spanning tree forwarding state and not pruned
Fa0/4         10-11
```

Summary: IP Telephony Ports on Switches

It might seem like this short topic about IP telephony and switch configuration includes a lot of small twists and turns and trivia, and it does. The most important items to remember are as follow:

■ Configure these ports like a normal access port to begin: Configure it as a static access port and assign it an access VLAN.

■ Add one more command to define the voice VLAN (**switchport voice vlan** *vlan-id*).

■ Look for the mention of the voice VLAN ID, but no other new facts, in the output of the **show interfaces** *type number* **switchport** command.

■ Look for both the voice and data (access) VLAN IDs in the output of the **show interfaces** *type number* **trunk** command.

■ Do not expect to see the port listed in the list of operational trunks as listed by the **show interfaces trunk** command.

Chapter Review

One key to doing well on the exams is to perform repetitive spaced review sessions. Review this chapter's material using either the tools in the book, DVD, or interactive tools for the same material found on the book's companion website. Refer to the "Your Study Plan" element for more details. Table 1-4 outlines the key review elements and where you can find them. To better track your study progress, record when you completed these activities in the second column.

Table 1-4   Chapter Review Tracking

Review Element	Review Date(s)	Resource Used
Review key topics		Book, DVD/website
Review key terms		Book, DVD/website
Answer DIKTA questions		Book, PCPT
Do labs		Blog
Review memory tables		DVD/website
Review config checklists		Book, DVD/website
Review command tables		Book

Review All the Key Topics

Table 1-5   Key Topics for Chapter 1

Key Topic Element	Description	Page Number
Figure 1-2	Basic VLAN concept	17
List	Reasons for using VLANs	17
Figure 1-5	Diagram of VLAN trunking	19
Figure 1-6	802.1Q header	20
Figure 1-9	Routing between VLANs with router-on-a-stick	23
Figure 1-10	Routing between VLANs with Layer 3 switch	24

Key Topic Element	Description	Page Number
Table 1-2	Options of the **switchport mode** command	30
Table 1-3	Expected trunking results based on the configuration of the **switchport mode** command	34
List	Definitions of data VLAN and voice VLAN	36
List	Summary of data and voice VLAN concepts, configuration, and verification	39

Key Terms You Should Know

802.1Q, trunk, trunking administrative mode, trunking operational mode, VLAN, VTP, VTP transparent mode, Layer 3 switch, access interface, trunk interface, data VLAN, voice VLAN

Command References

Tables 1-6 and 1-7 list configuration and verification commands used in this chapter, respectively. As an easy review exercise, cover the left column in a table, read the right column, and try to recall the command without looking. Then repeat the exercise, covering the right column, and try to recall what the command does.

Table 1-6   Chapter 1 Configuration Command Reference

Command	Description
vlan *vlan-id*	Global config command that both creates the VLAN and puts the CLI into VLAN configuration mode
name *vlan-name*	VLAN subcommand that names the VLAN
[no] shutdown	VLAN mode subcommand that enables (**no shutdown**) or disables (**shutdown**) the VLAN
[no] shutdown vlan *vlan-id*	Global config command that has the same effect as the **[no] shutdown** VLAN mode subcommands
vtp mode {**server** | **client** | **transparent** | **off**}	Global config command that defines the VTP mode
switchport mode {**access** | **dynamic** {**auto** | **desirable**} | **trunk**}	Interface subcommand that configures the trunking administrative mode on the interface
switchport access vlan *vlan-id*	Interface subcommand that statically configures the interface into that one VLAN
switchport trunk encapsulation {**dot1q** | **isl** | **negotiate**}	Interface subcommand that defines which type of trunking to use, assuming that trunking is configured or negotiated
switchport trunk native vlan *vlan-id*	Interface subcommand that defines the native VLAN for a trunk port
switchport nonegotiate	Interface subcommand that disables the negotiation of VLAN trunking

Command	Description
switchport voice vlan *vlan-id*	Interface subcommand that defines the voice VLAN on a port, meaning that the switch uses 802.1Q tagging for frames in this VLAN
**switchport trunk allowed vlan {add	all	except	remove}** *vlan-list*	Interface subcommand that defines the list of allowed VLANs

Table 1-7   Chapter 1 EXEC Command Reference

Command	Description
show interfaces *interface-id* **switchport**	Lists information about any interface regarding administrative settings and operational state
show interfaces *interface-id* **trunk**	Lists information about all operational trunks (but no other interfaces), including the list of VLANs that can be forwarded over the trunk
**show vlan [brief	id** *vlan-id* **| name** *vlan-name* **| summary]**	Lists information about the VLAN
show vlan [vlan**]**	Displays VLAN information
show vtp status	Lists VTP configuration and status information

CHAPTER 2

Spanning Tree Protocol Concepts

This chapter covers the following exam topics:

1.0 LAN Switching Technologies

1.3 Configure, verify, and troubleshoot STP protocols

    1.3.a STP mode (PVST+ and RPVST+)

    1.3.b STP root bridge selection

1.4 Configure, verify, and troubleshoot STP-related optional features

    1.4.a PortFast

    1.4.b BPDU guard

1.5 Configure, verify, and troubleshoot (Layer 2/Layer 3) EtherChannel

    1.5.a Static

    1.5.b PAGP

    1.5.c LACP

Spanning Tree Protocol (STP) allows Ethernet LANs to have the added benefits of installing redundant links in a LAN, while overcoming the known problems that occur when adding those extra links. Using redundant links in a LAN design allows the LAN to keep working even when some links fail or even when some entire switches fail. Proper LAN design should add enough redundancy so that no single point of failure crashes the LAN; STP allows the design to use redundancy without causing some other problems.

STP affects many aspects of how switch forwarding logic works. Because Cisco puts the STP exam topics into the ICND2 half of the CCNA Routing and Switching exam, all the detailed examples in the ICND1 Cert Guide avoid showing redundant links in the LANs. For this ICND2 book, most of the LAN examples include redundancy. Therefore, you need to be prepared to rethink what you learned about LANs from reading the ICND1 book while thinking about LANs that have redundant links, and how STP and related features make those LANs work.

This chapter organizes the material into three sections. The first section presents core STP concepts that apply to most types of STP. STP has been improved and changed over the years, with Rapid STP (RSTP) being one major improvement. The first section looks at STP concepts without the RSTP logic added, while the second major section details RSTP concepts. The final major section discusses a small number of features that optimize and secure STP: PortFast, BPDU Guard, and EtherChannels.

As for the exam topics for this chapter, note that they all use the same three verbs: configure, verify, and troubleshoot. This chapter does not get into that level of depth on any of the specific topics, but instead lays the foundation to understand these features so that you are prepared to delve into the configuration, verification, and troubleshooting details in Chapters 3 and 4.

"Do I Know This Already?" Quiz

Take the quiz (either here, or use the PCPT software) if you want to use the score to help you decide how much time to spend on this chapter. The answers are at the bottom of the page following the quiz, and the explanations are in DVD Appendix C and in the PCPT software.

Table 2-1 "Do I Know This Already?" Foundation Topics Section-to-Question Mapping

Foundation Topics Section	Questions
Spanning Tree Protocol (IEEE 802.1D)	1–4
Rapid STP (IEEE 802.1w) Concepts	5, 6
Optional STP Features	7

1. Which of the following IEEE 802.1D port states are stable states used when STP has completed convergence? (Choose two answers.)

   a. Blocking

   b. Forwarding

   c. Listening

   d. Learning

   e. Discarding

2. Which of the following are transitory IEEE 802.1D port states used only during the process of STP convergence? (Choose two answers.)

   a. Blocking

   b. Forwarding

   c. Listening

   d. Learning

   e. Discarding

3. Which of the following bridge IDs wins election as root, assuming that the switches with these bridge IDs are in the same network?

   a. 32769:0200.1111.1111

   b. 32769:0200.2222.2222

   c. 4097:0200.1111.1111

   d. 4097:0200.2222.2222

   e. 40961:0200.1111.1111

4. Which of the following facts determines how often a nonroot bridge or switch sends an 802.1D STP Hello BPDU message?

   a. The Hello timer as configured on that switch.

   b. The Hello timer as configured on the root switch.

   c. It is always every 2 seconds.

   d. The switch reacts to BPDUs received from the root switch by sending another BPDU 2 seconds after receiving the root BPDU.

5. Which of the following RSTP port states have the same name and purpose as a port state in traditional 802.1D STP? (Choose two answers.)

   a. Blocking

   b. Forwarding

   c. Listening

   d. Learning

   e. Discarding

6. RSTP adds some concepts to STP that enable ports to be used for a role if another port on the same switch fails. Which of the following statements correctly describe a port role that is waiting to take over for another port role? (Choose two answers.)

   a. An alternate port waits to become a root port.

   b. A backup port waits to become a root port.

   c. An alternate port waits to become a designated port.

   d. A backup port waits to become a designated port.

7. What STP feature causes an interface to be placed in the forwarding state as soon as the interface is physically active?

   a. STP

   b. EtherChannel

   c. Root Guard

   d. PortFast

Foundation Topics

Spanning Tree Protocol (IEEE 802.1D)

Without Spanning Tree Protocol (STP), a LAN with redundant links would cause Ethernet frames to loop for an indefinite period of time. With STP enabled, some switches block ports so that these ports do not forward frames. STP intelligently chooses which ports block, with two goals in mind:

■ All devices in a VLAN can send frames to all other devices. In other words, STP does not block too many ports, cutting off some parts of the LAN from other parts.

■ Frames have a short life and do not loop around the network indefinitely.

STP strikes a balance, allowing frames to be delivered to each device, without causing the problems that occur when frames loop through the network over and over again.

STP prevents looping frames by adding an additional check on each interface before a switch uses it to send or receive user traffic. That check: If the port is in STP forwarding state in that VLAN, use it as normal; if it is in STP blocking state, however, block all user traffic and do not send or receive user traffic on that interface in that VLAN.

Note that these STP states do not change the other information you already know about switch interfaces. The interface's state of connected/notconnect does not change. The interface's operational state as either an access or trunk port does not change. STP adds this additional STP state, with the blocking state basically disabling the interface.

In many ways, those last two paragraphs sum up what STP does. However, the details of how STP does its work can take a fair amount of study and practice. This first major section of the chapter begins by explaining the need for STP and the basic ideas of what STP does to solve the problem of looping frames. The majority of this section then looks at how STP goes about choosing which switch ports to block to accomplish STP's goals.

The Need for Spanning Tree

STP prevents three common problems in Ethernet LANs. All three problems occur as a side effect of one fact: without STP, some Ethernet frames would loop around the network for a long time (hours, days, literally forever if the LAN devices and links never failed). By default, Cisco switches run STP, but you can disable STP. Do not disable it unless you know exactly what you are doing!

Just one looping frame causes what is called a *broadcast storm*. Broadcast storms happen when any kind of Ethernet frames—broadcast frames, multicast frames, or unknown-destination unicast frames—loop around a LAN indefinitely. Broadcast storms can saturate all the links with copies of that one single frame, crowding out good frames, as well as significantly impacting end-user device performance by making the PCs process too many broadcast frames.

To help you understand how this occurs, Figure 2-1 shows a sample network in which Bob sends a broadcast frame. The dashed lines show how the switches forward the frame when STP does not exist.

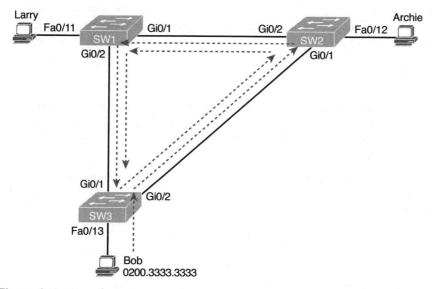

Figure 2-1   *Broadcast Storm*

NOTE   Bob's original broadcast would also be forwarded around the other direction as well, with SW3 sending a copy of the original frame out its Gi0/1 port. To reduce clutter, Figure 2-1 does not show that frame.

Remember that LAN switch? That logic tells switches to flood broadcasts out all interfaces in the same VLAN except the interface in which the frame arrived. In Figure 2-1, that means SW3 forwards Bob's frame to SW2, SW2 forwards the frame to SW1, SW1 forwards the frame back to SW3, and SW3 forwards it back to SW2 again.

When broadcast storms happen, frames like the one in Figure 2-1 keep looping until something changes—someone shuts down an interface, reloads a switch, or does something else to break the loop. Also note that the same event happens in the opposite direction. When Bob sends the original frame, SW3 also forwards a copy to SW1, SW1 forwards it to SW2, and so on.

The storm also causes a much more subtle problem called *MAC table instability*. MAC table instability means that the switches' MAC address tables keep changing, because frames with the same source MAC arrive on different ports. To see why, follow this example, in which SW3 begins Figure 2-1 with a MAC table entry for Bob, at the bottom of the figure, associated with port Fa0/13:

    0200.3333.3333   Fa0/13   VLAN 1

However, now think about the switch-learning process that occurs when the looping frame goes to SW2, then SW1, and then back into SW3's Gi0/1 interface. SW3 thinks, "Hmm... the source MAC address is 0200.3333.3333, and it came in my Gi0/1 interface. Update my MAC table!" This results in the following entry on SW3, with interface Gi0/1 instead of Fa0/13:

    0200.3333.3333   Gi0/1   VLAN 1

At this point, SW3 itself cannot correctly deliver frames to Bob's MAC address. At that instant, if a frame arrives at SW3 destined for Bob—a different frame than the looping frame that causes the problems—SW3 incorrectly forwards the frame out Gi0/1 to SW1, creating even more congestion.

The looping frames in a broadcast storm also cause a third problem: multiple copies of the frame arrive at the destination. Consider a case in which Bob sends a frame to Larry but none of the switches know Larry's MAC address. Switches flood frames sent to unknown destination unicast MAC addresses. When Bob sends the frame destined for Larry's MAC address, SW3 sends a copy to both SW1 and SW2. SW1 and SW2 also flood the frame, causing copies of the frame to loop. SW1 also sends a copy of each frame out Fa0/11 to Larry. As a result, Larry gets multiple copies of the frame, which may result in an application failure, if not more pervasive networking problems.

Table 2-2 summarizes the main three classes of problems that occur when STP is not used in a LAN that has redundancy.

Table 2-2   Three Classes of Problems Caused by Not Using STP in Redundant LANs

Problem	Description
Broadcast storms	The forwarding of a frame repeatedly on the same links, consuming significant parts of the links' capacities
MAC table instability	The continual updating of a switch's MAC address table with incorrect entries, in reaction to looping frames, resulting in frames being sent to the wrong locations
Multiple frame transmission	A side effect of looping frames in which multiple copies of one frame are delivered to the intended host, confusing the host

What IEEE 802.1D Spanning Tree Does

STP prevents loops by placing each switch port in either a forwarding state or a blocking state. Interfaces in the forwarding state act as normal, forwarding and receiving frames. However, interfaces in a blocking state do not process any frames except STP messages (and some other overhead messages). Interfaces that block do not forward user frames, do not learn MAC addresses of received frames, and do not process received user frames.

Figure 2-2 shows a simple STP tree that solves the problem shown in Figure 2-1 by placing one port on SW3 in the blocking state.

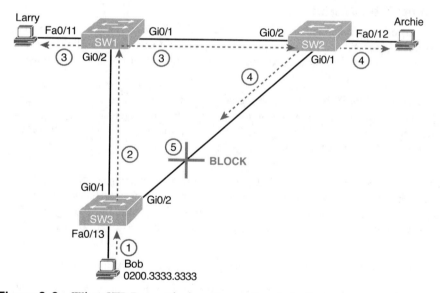

Figure 2-2   *What STP Does: Blocks a Port to Break the Loop*

Now when Bob sends a broadcast frame, the frame does not loop. As shown in the steps in the figure:

Step 1.   Bob sends the frame to SW3.

Step 2.   SW3 forwards the frame only to SW1, but not out Gi0/2 to SW2, because SW3's Gi0/2 interface is in a blocking state.

Step 3.   SW1 floods the frame out both Fa0/11 and Gi0/1.

Step 4.   SW2 floods the frame out Fa0/12 and Gi0/1.

Step 5.   SW3 physically receives the frame, but it ignores the frame received from SW2 because SW3's Gi0/2 interface is in a blocking state.

With the STP topology in Figure 2-2, the switches simply do not use the link between SW2 and SW3 for traffic in this VLAN, which is the minor negative side effect of STP. However, if either of the other two links fails, STP converges so that SW3 forwards instead of blocks on its Gi0/2 interface.

NOTE   The term *STP convergence* refers to the process by which the switches collectively realize that something has changed in the LAN topology and determine whether they need to change which ports block and which ports forward.

That completes the description of what STP does, placing each port into either a forwarding or blocking state. The more interesting question, and the one that takes a lot more work to understand, is the question of how and why STP makes its choices. How does STP manage to make switches block or forward on each interface? And how does it converge to change state from blocking to forwarding to take advantage of redundant links in response to network outages? The following sections answer these questions.

How Spanning Tree Works

The STP algorithm creates a spanning tree of interfaces that forward frames. The tree structure of forwarding interfaces creates a single path to and from each Ethernet link, just like you can trace a single path in a living, growing tree from the base of the tree to each leaf.

NOTE   STP was created before LAN switches even existed. In those days, Ethernet bridges used STP. Today, switches play the same role as bridges, implementing STP. However, many STP terms still refer to bridge. For the purposes of STP and this chapter, consider the terms *bridge* and *switch* synonymous.

The process used by STP, sometimes called the *spanning-tree algorithm* (STA), chooses the interfaces that should be placed into a forwarding state. For any interfaces not chosen to be in a forwarding state, STP places the interfaces in blocking state. In other words, STP simply picks which interfaces should forward, and any interfaces left over go to a blocking state.

STP uses three criteria to choose whether to put an interface in forwarding state:

- STP elects a root switch. STP puts all working interfaces on the root switch in forwarding state.

- Each nonroot switch considers one of its ports to have the least administrative cost between itself and the root switch. The cost is called that switch's *root cost*. STP places its port that is part of the least root cost path, called that switch's *root port* (RP), in forwarding state.

- Many switches can attach to the same Ethernet segment, but in modern networks, normally two switches connect to each link. The switch with the lowest root cost, as compared with the other switches attached to the same link, is placed in forwarding state.

That switch is the designated switch, and that switch's interface, attached to that segment, is called the *designated port* (DP).

> **NOTE** The real reason the root switches place all working interfaces in a forwarding state is that all its interfaces will become DPs, but it is easier to just remember that all the root switches' working interfaces will forward frames.

All other interfaces are placed in blocking state. Table 2-3 summarizes the reasons STP places a port in forwarding or blocking state.

Key Topic

Table 2-3 STP: Reasons for Forwarding or Blocking

Characterization of Port	STP State	Description
All the root switch's ports	Forwarding	The root switch is always the designated switch on all connected segments.
Each nonroot switch's root port	Forwarding	The port through which the switch has the least cost to reach the root switch (lowest root cost).
Each LAN's designated port	Forwarding	The switch forwarding the Hello on to the segment, with the lowest root cost, is the designated switch for that segment.
All other working ports	Blocking	The port is not used for forwarding user frames, nor are any frames received on these interfaces considered for forwarding.

> **NOTE** STP only considers working interfaces (those in a connected state). Failed interfaces (for example, interfaces with no cable installed) or administratively shutdown interfaces are instead placed into an STP disabled state. So, this section uses the term *working ports* to refer to interfaces that could forward frames if STP placed the interface into a forwarding state.

The STP Bridge ID and Hello BPDU

The STA begins with an election of one switch to be the root switch. To better understand this election process, you need to understand the STP messages sent between switches as well as the concept and format of the identifier used to uniquely identify each switch.

The STP *bridge ID* (BID) is an 8-byte value unique to each switch. The bridge ID consists of a 2-byte priority field and a 6-byte system ID, with the system ID being based on a universal (burned-in) MAC address in each switch. Using a burned-in MAC address ensures that each switch's bridge ID will be unique.

STP defines messages called *bridge protocol data units* (BPDU), which switches use to exchange information with each other. The most common BPDU, called a Hello BPDU, lists many details, including the sending switch's BID. By listing its own unique BID, switches can tell which switch sent which Hello BPDU. Table 2-4 lists some of the key information in the Hello BPDU.

Key Topic

Table 2-4   Fields in the STP Hello BPDU

Field	Description
Root bridge ID	The bridge ID of the switch the sender of this Hello currently believes to be the root switch
Sender's bridge ID	The bridge ID of the switch sending this Hello BPDU
Sender's root cost	The STP cost between this switch and the current root
Timer values on the root switch	Includes the Hello timer, MaxAge timer, and forward delay timer

For the time being, just keep the first three items from Table 2-4 in mind as the following sections work through the three steps in how STP chooses the interfaces to place into a forwarding state. Next, the text examines the three main steps in the STP process.

Electing the Root Switch

Switches elect a root switch based on the BIDs in the BPDUs. The root switch is the switch with the lowest numeric value for the BID. Because the two-part BID starts with the priority value, essentially the switch with the lowest priority becomes the root. For example, if one switch has priority 4096, and another switch has priority 8192, the switch with priority 4096 wins, regardless of what MAC address was used to create the BID for each switch.

If a tie occurs based on the priority portion of the BID, the switch with the lowest MAC address portion of the BID is the root. No other tiebreaker should be needed because switches use one of their own universal (burned-in) MAC addresses as the second part of their BIDs. So if the priorities tie, and one switch uses a MAC address of 0200.0000.0000 as part of the BID and the other uses 0911.1111.1111, the first switch (MAC 0200.0000.0000) becomes the root switch.

STP elects a root switch in a manner not unlike a political election. The process begins with all switches claiming to be the root by sending Hello BPDUs listing their own BID as the root BID. If a switch hears a Hello that lists a better (lower) BID, that switch stops advertising itself as root and starts forwarding the superior Hello. The Hello sent by the better switch lists the better switch's BID as the root. It works like a political race in which a less-popular candidate gives up and leaves the race, throwing his support behind the more popular candidate. Eventually, everyone agrees which switch has the best (lowest) BID, and everyone supports the elected switch—which is where the political race analogy falls apart.

NOTE   A better Hello, meaning that the listed root's BID is better (numerically lower), is called a *superior Hello*; a worse Hello, meaning that the listed root's BID is not as good (numerically higher), is called an *inferior Hello*.

Figure 2-3 shows the beginning of the root election process. In this case, SW1 has advertised itself as root, as have SW2 and SW3. However, SW2 now believes that SW1 is a better root, so SW2 is now forwarding the Hello originating at SW1. So, at this point, the figure shows SW1 is saying Hello, claiming to be root; SW2 agrees, and is forwarding SW1's Hello that lists SW1 as root; but, SW3 is still claiming to be best, sending its own Hello BPDUs, listing SW3's BID as the root.

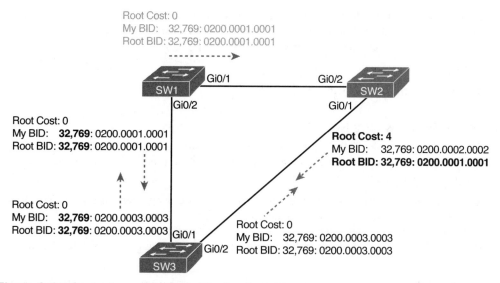

Figure 2-3 *Beginnings of the Root Election Process*

Two candidates still exist in Figure 2-3: SW1 and SW3. So who wins? Well, from the BID, the lower-priority switch wins; if a tie occurs, the lower MAC address wins. As shown in the figure, SW1 has a lower BID (32769:0200.0001.0001) than SW3 (32769:0200.0003.0003), so SW1 wins, and SW3 now also believes that SW1 is the better switch. Figure 2-4 shows the resulting Hello messages sent by the switches.

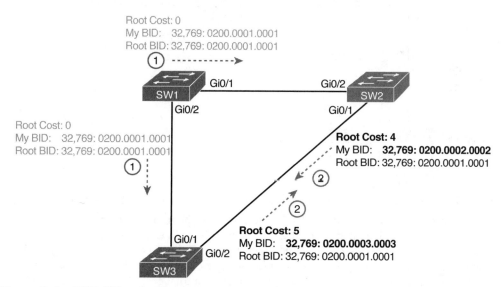

Figure 2-4 *SW1 Wins the Election*

After the election is complete, only the root switch continues to originate STP Hello BPDU messages. The other switches receive the Hellos, update the sender's BID field (and root cost field), and forward the Hellos out other interfaces. The figure reflects this fact, with SW1 sending Hellos at Step 1, and SW2 and SW3 independently forwarding the Hello out their other interfaces at Step 2.

Summarizing, the root election happens through each switch claiming to be root, with the best switch being elected based on the numerically lowest BID. Breaking down the BID into its components, the comparisons can be made as

- The lowest priority
- If that ties, the lowest switch MAC address

Choosing Each Switch's Root Port

The second part of the STP process occurs when each nonroot switch chooses its one and only *root port*. A switch's RP is its interface through which it has the least STP cost to reach the root switch (least root cost).

The idea of a switch's cost to reach the root switch can be easily seen for humans. Just look at a network diagram that shows the root switch, lists the STP cost associated with each switch port, and identifies the nonroot switch in question. Switches use a different process than looking at a network diagram, of course, but using a diagram can make it easier to learn the idea.

Figure 2-5 shows just such a figure, with the same three switches shown in the last several figures. SW1 has already won the election as root, and the figure considers the cost from SW3's perspective.

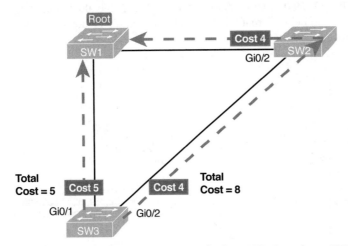

Figure 2-5 *How a Human Might Calculate STP Cost from SW3 to the Root (SW1)*

SW3 has two possible physical paths to send frames to the root switch: the direct path to the left, and the indirect path to the right through switch SW2. The cost is the sum of the costs of all the *switch ports the frame would exit* if it flowed over that path. (The calculation ignores the inbound ports.) As you can see, the cost over the direct path out SW3's G0/1 port has a total cost of 5, and the other path has a total cost of 8. SW3 picks its G0/1 port as root port because it is the port that is part of the least-cost path to send frames to the root switch.

Switches come to the same conclusion, but using a different process. Instead, they add their local interface STP cost to the root cost listed in each received Hello BPDU. The STP port cost is simply an integer value assigned to each interface, per VLAN, for the purpose of providing an objective measurement that allows STP to choose which interfaces to add to the STP topology. The switches also look at their neighbor's root cost, as announced in Hello BPDUs received from each neighbor.

Figure 2-6 shows an example of how switches calculate their best root cost and then choose their root port, using the same topology and STP costs as shown in Figure 2-5. STP on SW3 calculates its cost to reach the root over the two possible paths by adding the advertised cost (in Hello messages) to the interface costs listed in the figure.

Focus on the process for a moment. The root switch sends Hellos, with a listed root cost of 0. The idea is that the root's cost to reach itself is 0.

Next, look on the left of the figure. SW3 takes the received cost (0) from the Hello sent by SW1, and adds the interface cost (5) of the interface on which that Hello was received. SW3 calculates that the cost to reach the root switch, out that port (G0/1), is 5.

On the right side, SW2 has realized its best cost to reach the root is cost 4. So, when SW2 forwards the Hello toward SW3, SW2 lists a root cost 4. SW3's STP port cost on port G0/2 is 4, so SW3 determines a total cost to reach root out its G0/2 port of 8.

As a result of the process depicted in Figure 2-6, SW3 chooses Gi0/1 as its RP, because the cost to reach the root switch through that port (5) is lower than the other alternative (Gi0/2, cost 8). Similarly, SW2 chooses Gi0/2 as its RP, with a cost of 4 (SW1's advertised cost of 0 plus SW2's Gi0/2 interface cost of 4). Each switch places its root port into a forwarding state.

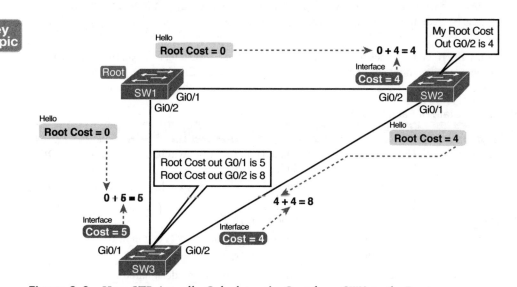

Figure 2-6 *How STP Actually Calculates the Cost from SW3 to the Root*

In more complex topologies, the choice of root port will not be so obvious. Chapter 4, "LAN Troubleshooting," discusses these more complex examples, including the tiebreakers to use if the root costs tie.

Choosing the Designated Port on Each LAN Segment

STP's final step to choose the STP topology is to choose the designated port on each LAN segment. The designated port (DP) on each LAN segment is the switch port that advertises the lowest-cost Hello onto a LAN segment. When a nonroot switch forwards a Hello, the nonroot switch sets the root cost field in the Hello to that switch's cost to reach the root. In effect, the switch with the lower cost to reach the root, among all switches connected to a segment, becomes the DP on that segment.

For example, earlier Figure 2-4 shows in bold text the parts of the Hello messages from both SW2 and SW3 that determine the choice of DP on that segment. Note that both SW2 and SW3 list their respective cost to reach the root switch (cost 4 on SW2 and cost 5 on SW3). SW2 lists the lower cost, so SW2's Gi0/1 port is the designated port on that LAN segment.

All DPs are placed into a forwarding state; so in this case, SW2's Gi0/1 interface will be in a forwarding state.

If the advertised costs tie, the switches break the tie by choosing the switch with the lower BID. In this case, SW2 would also have won, with a BID of 32769:0200.0002.0002 versus SW3's 32769:0200.0003.0003.

> **NOTE**   Two additional tiebreakers are needed in some cases, although these would be unlikely today. A single switch can connect two or more interfaces to the same collision domain by connecting to a hub. In that case, the one switch hears its own BPDUs. So, if a switch ties with itself, two additional tiebreakers are used: the lowest interface STP priority and, if that ties, the lowest internal interface number.

The only interface that does not have a reason to be in a forwarding state on the three switches in the examples shown in Figures 2-3 through 2-6 is SW3's Gi0/2 port. So, the STP process is now complete. Table 2-5 outlines the state of each port and shows why it is in that state.

Table 2-5   State of Each Interface

Switch Interface	State	Reason Why the Interface Is in Forwarding State
SW1, Gi0/1	Forwarding	The interface is on the root switch, so it becomes the DP on that link.
SW1, Gi0/2	Forwarding	The interface is on the root switch, so it becomes the DP on that link.
SW2, Gi0/2	Forwarding	The root port of SW2.
SW2, Gi0/1	Forwarding	The designated port on the LAN segment to SW3.
SW3, Gi0/1	Forwarding	The root port of SW3.
SW3, Gi0/2	Blocking	Not the root port and not the designated port.

Influencing and Changing the STP Topology

Switches do not just use STP once and never again. The switches continually watch for changes. Those changes can be because a link or switch fails or it can be a new link that can now be used. The configuration can change in a way that changes the STP topology. This section briefly discusses the kinds of things that change the STP topology, either through configuration or through changes in the status of devices and links in the LAN.

Making Configuration Changes to Influence the STP Topology

The network engineers can choose to change the STP settings to then change the choices STP makes in a given LAN. Two main tools available to the engineer are to configure the bridge ID and to change STP port costs.

Switches have a way to create a default BID, by taking a default priority value, and adding a universal MAC address that comes with the switch hardware. However, engineers typically want to choose which switch becomes the root. Chapter 3, "Spanning Tree Protocol Implementation," shows how to configure a Cisco switch to override its default BID setting to make a switch become root.

Port costs also have default values, per port, per VLAN. You can configure these port costs, or you can use the default values. Table 2-6 lists the default port costs suggested by IEEE. IOS on Cisco switches has long used the default settings as defined in the 1998 version of the 802.1D standard. The newer standard, useful when using links faster than 10 Gbps, can be used by adding a single configuration command to each switch (**spanning-tree pathcost method long**).

Table 2-6   Default Port Costs According to IEEE

Ethernet Speed	IEEE Cost: 1998 (and Before)	IEEE Cost: 2004 (and After)
10 Mbps	100	2,000,000
100 Mbps	19	200,000
1 Gbps	4	20,000
10 Gbps	2	2000
100 Gbps	N/A	200
1 Tbps	N/A	20

With STP enabled, all working switch interfaces will settle into an STP forwarding or blocking state, even access ports. For switch interfaces connected to hosts or routers, which do not use STP, the switch still forwards Hellos on to those interfaces. By virtue of being the only device sending a Hello onto that LAN segment, the switch is sending the least-cost Hello on to that LAN segment, making the switch become the designated port on that LAN segment. So, STP puts working access interfaces into a forwarding state as a result of the designated port part of the STP process.

Reacting to State Changes That Affect the STP Topology

Once the engineer has finished all STP configuration, the STP topology should settle into a stable state and not change, at least until the network topology changes. This section examines the ongoing operation of STP while the network is stable, and then it covers how STP converges to a new topology when something changes.

The root switch sends a new Hello BPDU every 2 seconds by default. Each nonroot switch forwards the Hello on all DPs, but only after changing items listed in the Hello. The switch sets the root cost to that local switch's calculated root cost. The switch also sets the "sender's bridge ID" field to its own bridge ID. (The root's bridge ID field is not changed.)

By forwarding the received (and changed) Hellos out all DPs, all switches continue to receive Hellos every 2 seconds. The following steps summarize the steady-state operation when nothing is currently changing in the STP topology:

Step 1. The root creates and sends a Hello BPDU, with a root cost of 0, out all its working interfaces (those in a forwarding state).

Step 2. The nonroot switches receive the Hello on their root ports. After changing the Hello to list their own BID as the sender's BID, and listing that switch's root cost, the switch forwards the Hello out all designated ports.

Step 3. Steps 1 and 2 repeat until something changes.

Each switch relies on these periodically received Hellos from the root as a way to know that its path to the root is still working. When a switch ceases to receive the Hellos, or receives a Hello that lists different details, something has failed, so the switch reacts and starts the process of changing the spanning-tree topology.

How Switches React to Changes with STP

For various reasons, the convergence process requires the use of three timers. Note that all switches use the timers as dictated by the root switch, which the root lists in its periodic Hello BPDU messages. Table 2-7 describes the timers.

Table 2-7   STP Timers

Timer	Default Value	Description
Hello	2 seconds	The time period between Hellos created by the root.
MaxAge	10 times Hello	How long any switch should wait, after ceasing to hear Hellos, before trying to change the STP topology.
Forward delay	15 seconds	Delay that affects the process that occurs when an interface changes from blocking state to forwarding state. A port stays in an interim listening state, and then an interim learning state, for the number of seconds defined by the forward delay timer.

If a switch does not get an expected Hello BPDU within the Hello time, the switch continues as normal. However, if the Hellos do not show up again within MaxAge time, the switch reacts by taking steps to change the STP topology. With default settings, MaxAge is 20 seconds (10 times the default Hello timer of 2 seconds). So, a switch would go 20 seconds without hearing a Hello before reacting.

After MaxAge expires, the switch essentially makes all its STP choices again, based on any Hellos it receives from other switches. It reevaluates which switch should be the root switch. If the local switch is not the root, it chooses its RP. And it determines whether it is DP on each of its other links. The best way to describe STP convergence is to show an example using the same familiar topology. Figure 2-7 shows the same familiar figure, with SW3's Gi0/2 in a blocking state, but SW1's Gi0/2 interface has just failed.

SW3 reacts to the change because SW3 fails to receive its expected Hellos on its Gi0/1 interface. However, SW2 does not need to react because SW2 continues to receive its periodic Hellos in its Gi0/2 interface. In this case, SW3 reacts either when MaxAge time passes without hearing the Hellos, or as soon as SW3 notices that interface Gi0/1 has failed. (If the interface fails, the switch can assume that the Hellos will not be arriving in that interface anymore.)

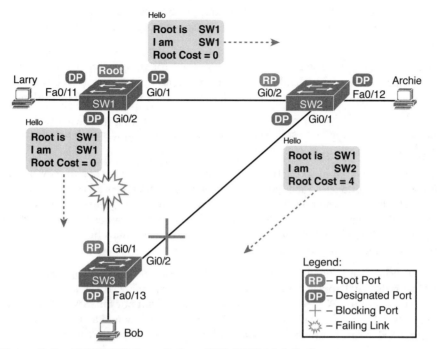

Figure 2-7 *Initial STP State Before SW1-SW3 Link Fails*

Now that SW3 can act, it begins by reevaluating the choice of root switch. SW3 still receives the Hellos from SW2, as forwarded from the root (SW1). SW1 still has a lower BID than SW3; otherwise, SW1 would not have already been the root. So, SW3 decides that SW1 is still the best switch and that SW3 is not the root.

Next, SW3 reevaluates its choice of RP. At this point, SW3 is receiving Hellos on only one interface: Gi0/2. Whatever the calculated root cost, Gi0/2 becomes SW3's new RP. (The cost would be 8, assuming the STP costs had no changes since Figures 2-5 and 2-6.)

SW3 then reevaluates its role as DP on any other interfaces. In this example, no real work needs to be done. SW3 was already DP on interface Fa0/13, and it continues to be the DP because no other switches connect to that port.

Changing Interface States with STP

STP uses the idea of roles and states. *Roles*, like root port and designated port, relate to how STP analyzes the LAN topology. *States*, like forwarding and blocking, tell a switch whether to send or receive frames. When STP converges, a switch chooses new port roles, and the port roles determine the state (forwarding or blocking).

Switches can simply move immediately from forwarding to blocking state, but they must take extra time to transition from blocking state to forwarding state. For instance, when a switch formerly used port G0/1 as its RP (a role), that port was in a forwarding state. After convergence, G0/1 might be neither an RP nor DP; the switch can immediately move that port to a blocking state.

When a port that formerly blocked needs to transition to forwarding, the switch first puts the port through two intermediate interface states. These temporary states help prevent temporary loops:

Key Topic

- **Listening:** Like the blocking state, the interface does not forward frames. The switch removes old stale (unused) MAC table entries for which no frames are received from each MAC address during this period. These stale MAC table entries could be the cause of the temporary loops.

- **Learning:** Interfaces in this state still do not forward frames, but the switch begins to learn the MAC addresses of frames received on the interface.

STP moves an interface from blocking to listening, then to learning, and then to forwarding state. STP leaves the interface in each interim state for a time equal to the forward delay timer, which defaults to 15 seconds. As a result, a convergence event that causes an interface to change from blocking to forwarding requires 30 seconds to transition from blocking to forwarding. In addition, a switch might have to wait MaxAge seconds before even choosing to move an interface from blocking to forwarding state.

For example, follow what happens with an initial STP topology as shown in Figures 2-3 through 2-6, with the SW1-to-SW3 link failing as shown in Figure 2-7. If SW1 simply quit sending Hello messages to SW3, but the link between the two did not fail, SW3 would wait MaxAge seconds before reacting (20 seconds is the default). SW3 would actually quickly choose its ports' STP roles, but then wait 15 seconds each in listening and learning states on interface Gi0/2, resulting in a 50-second convergence delay.

Table 2-8 summarizes spanning tree's various interface states for easier review.

Key Topic

Table 2-8 IEEE 802.1D Spanning-Tree States

State	Forwards Data Frames?	Learns MACs Based on Received Frames?	Transitory or Stable State?
Blocking	No	No	Stable
Listening	No	No	Transitory
Learning	No	Yes	Transitory
Forwarding	Yes	Yes	Stable
Disabled	No	No	Stable

Rapid STP (IEEE 802.1w) Concepts

The original STP worked well given the assumptions about networks and networking devices in that era. However, as with any computing or networking standard, as time passes, hardware and software capabilities improve, so new protocols emerge to take advantage of those new capabilities. For STP, one of the most significant improvements over time has been the introduction of Rapid Spanning Tree Protocol (RSTP), introduced as standard IEEE 802.1w.

Before getting into the details of RSTP, it helps to make sense of the standards numbers a bit. 802.1w was actually an amendment to the 802.1D standard. 802.1D was published anew in 1998 (and a few times before that). After the 1998 version of 802.1D, the IEEE published the 802.1w amendment in 2001. Later, when the IEEE 802.1 committee updated the 802.1D standard in 2004, the IEEE pulled the 802.1w amendment details into the 802.1D-2004 standard.

So, why do we care? Sometimes people use the term *STP* to refer to the original pre-RSTP rules for STP. Some use STP to mean anything in the 802.1D standard, which now includes RSTP. So for real life, make sure you know what people mean when they use STP: do they mean STP to include RSTP concepts, or not? For this book, throughout the book, if the distinction between STP and RSTP matters, the book will use STP for the original STP rules and RSTP for the new ones introduced by 802.1w.

> **NOTE**   The IEEE sells its standards, but through the "Get IEEE 802" program, you can get free PDFs of the current 802 standards. To read about RSTP 802.1w, you will need to download the 802.1D standard, and then look for the sections about RSTP.

Now on to the details about RSTP in this chapter. There are similarities between RSTP and STP, so this section next compares and contrasts the two. Following that, the rest of this section discusses the concepts unique to RSTP that are not found in STP: alternate root ports, different port states, backup ports, and the port roles used by RSTP.

Comparing STP and RSTP

RSTP (802.1w) works just like STP (the original 802.1D) in several ways:

- It elects the root switch using the same parameters and tiebreakers.
- It elects the root port on nonroot switches with the same rules.
- It elects designated ports on each LAN segment with the same rules.
- It places each port in either forwarding or blocking state, although RSTP calls the blocking state the discarding state.

In fact, RSTP works so much like STP that they can both be used in the same network. RSTP and STP switches can be deployed in the same network, with RSTP features working in switches that support it, and traditional 802.1D STP features working in the switches that support only STP.

With all these similarities, you might be wondering why the IEEE bothered to create RSTP in the first place. The overriding reason is convergence. STP takes a relatively long time to converge (50 seconds with the default settings when all the wait times must be followed). RSTP improves network convergence when topology changes occur, usually converging within a few seconds (or in slow conditions, in about 10 seconds).

IEEE 802.1w RSTP changes and adds to IEEE 802.1D STP in ways that avoid waiting on STP timers, resulting in quick transitions from forwarding to blocking state and vice versa. Specifically, RSTP, compared to STP, defines more cases in which the switch can avoid waiting for a timer to expire, such as the following:

- Adds a new mechanism to replace the root port, without any waiting to reach a forwarding state (in some conditions)
- Adds a new mechanism to replace a designated port, without any waiting to reach a forwarding state (in some conditions)
- Lowers waiting times for cases in which RSTP must wait

For instance, when a link remains up, but Hello BPDUs simply stop arriving regularly on a port, STP requires a switch to wait for MaxAge seconds. STP defines the MaxAge timers based on ten times the Hello timer, or 20 seconds, by default. RSTP shortens this timer, defining MaxAge as three times the Hello timer.

The best way to get a sense for these mechanisms is to see how the RSTP alternate port and the backup port both work. RSTP uses the term *alternate port* to refer to a switch's other ports that could be used as root port if the root port ever fails. The *backup port* concept provides a backup port on the local switch for a designated port, but only applies to some topologies that frankly do not happen often with a modern network design. However, both are instructive about how RSTP works. Table 2-9 lists these RSTP port roles.

Table 2-9   Port Roles in 802.1w RSTP

Function	Port Role
Nonroot switch's best path to the root	Root port
Replaces the root port when the root port fails	Alternate port
Switch port designated to forward onto a collision domain	Designated port
Replaces a designated port when a designated port fails	Backup port
Port that is administratively disabled	Disabled port

RSTP and the Alternate (Root) Port Role

With STP, each nonroot switch places one port in the STP root port (RP) role. RSTP follows that same convention, with the same exact rules for choosing the RP. RSTP then takes another step, naming other possible RPs, identifying them as *alternate ports*.

To be an alternate port, both the RP and the alternate port must receive Hellos that identify the same root switch. For instance, in Figure 2-8, SW1 is the root. SW3 will receive Hello BPDUs on two ports: G0/1 and G0/2. Both Hellos list SW1's bridge ID (BID) as the root switch, so whichever port is not the root port meets the criteria to be an alternate port. SW3 picks G0/1 as its root port in this case, and then makes G0/2 an alternate port.

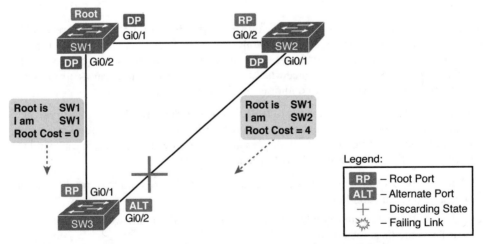

Figure 2-8   *Example of SW3 Making G0/2 Become an Alternate Port*

An alternate port basically works like the second-best option for root port. The alternate port can take over for the former root port, often very rapidly, without requiring a wait in other interim RSTP states. For instance, when the root port fails, or when Hellos stop arriving on the original root port, the switch changes the former root port's role and state: (a) the role from root port to a disabled port, and (b) the state from forwarding to discarding (the equivalent of STP's blocking state). Then, without waiting on any timers, the switch changes roles and state for the alternate port: its role changes to be the root port, with a forwarding state.

Notably, the new root port also does not need to spend time in other states, such as learning state, instead moving immediately to forwarding state.

Figure 2-9 shows an example of RSTP convergence. SW3's root port before the failure shown in this figure is SW3's G0/1, the link connected directly to SW1 (the root switch). Then SW3's link to SW1 fails as shown in Step 1 of the figure.

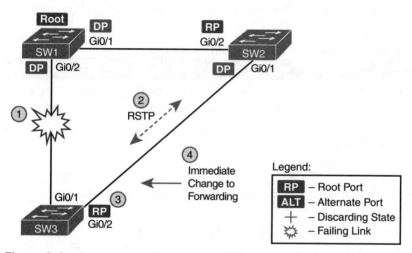

Figure 2-9   *Convergence Events with SW3 G0/1 Failure*

Following the steps in Figure 2-9:

Step 1.   The link between SW1 and SW3 fails, so that SW3's current root port (Gi0/1) fails.

Step 2.   SW3 and SW2 exchange RSTP messages to confirm that SW3 will now transition its former alternate port (Gi0/2) to be the root port. This action causes SW2 to flush the required MAC table entries.

Step 3.   SW3 transitions G0/1 to the disabled role and G0/2 to the root port role.

Step 4.   SW3 transitions G0/2 to a forwarding state immediately, without using learning state, because this is one case in which RSTP knows the transition will not create a loop.

As soon as SW3 realizes its G0/1 interface has failed, the process shown in the figure takes very little time. None of the processes rely on timers, so as soon as the work can be done, the convergence completes. (This particular convergence example takes about 1 second in a lab.)

RSTP States and Processes

The depth of the previous example does not point out all details of RSTP, of course; however, the example does show enough details to discuss RSTP states and internal processes.

Both STP and RSTP use *port states*, but with some differences. First, RSTP keeps both the learning and forwarding states as compared with STP, for the same purposes. However, RSTP does not even define a listening state, finding it unnecessary. Finally, RSTP renames the blocking state to the discarding state, and redefines its use slightly.

RSTP uses the discarding state for what 802.1D defines as two states: disabled state and blocking state. Blocking should be somewhat obvious by now: The interface can work physically, but STP/RSTP chooses to not forward traffic to avoid loops. STP's disabled state simply meant that the interface was administratively disabled. RSTP just combines those into a single discarding state. Table 2-10 shows the list of STP and RSTP states for comparison purposes.

Key Topic

Table 2-10   Port States Compared: 802.1D STP and 802.1w RSTP

Function	802.1D State	802.1w State
Port is administratively disabled	Disabled	Discarding
Stable state that ignores incoming data frames and is not used to forward data frames	Blocking	Discarding
Interim state without MAC learning and without forwarding	Listening	Not used
Interim state with MAC learning and without forwarding	Learning	Learning
Stable state that allows MAC learning and forwarding of data frames	Forwarding	Forwarding

RSTP also changes some processes and message content (compared to STP) to speed convergence. For example, STP waits for a time (forward delay) in both listening and learning states. The reason for this delay in STP is that, at the same time, the switches have all been told to time out their MAC table entries. When the topology changes, the existing MAC table entries may actually cause a loop. With STP, the switches all tell each other (with BPDU messages) that the topology has changed, and to time out any MAC table entries using the forward delay timer. This removes the entries, which is good, but it causes the need to wait in both listening and learning state for forward delay time (default 15 seconds each).

RSTP, to converge more quickly, avoids relying on timers. RSTP switches tell each other (using messages) that the topology has changed. Those messages also direct neighboring switches to flush the contents of their MAC tables in a way that removes all the potentially loop-causing entries, without a wait. As a result, RSTP creates more scenarios in which a formerly discarding port can immediately transition to a forwarding state, without waiting, and without using the learning state, as shown in the example in Figure 2-9.

RSTP and the Backup (Designated) Port Role

The RSTP backup port role acts as yet another new RSTP port role as compared to STP. As a reminder, the RSTP alternate port role creates a way for RSTP to quickly replace a switch's root port. Similarly, the RSTP backup port role creates a way for RSTP to quickly replace a switch's designated port on some LAN.

The need for a backup port can be a bit confusing at first, because the need for the backup port role only happens in designs that are a little unlikely today. The reason is that a design must use hubs, which then allows the possibility that one switch connects more than one port to the same collision domain.

Figure 2-10 shows an example. SW3 and SW4 both connect to the same hub. SW4's port F0/1 happens to win the election as designated port (DP). The other port on SW4 that connects to the same collision domain, F0/2, acts as a backup port.

With a backup port, if the current designated port fails, SW4 can start using the backup port with rapid convergence. For instance, if SW4's F0/1 interface were to fail, SW4 could transition F0/2 to the designated port role, without any delay in moving from discarding state to a forwarding state.

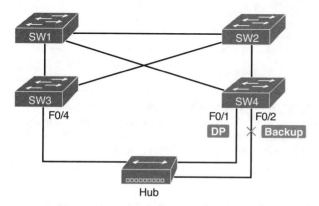

Figure 2-10   *RSTP Backup Port Example*

RSTP Port Types

The final RSTP concept included here relates to some terms RSTP uses to refer to different types of ports and the links that connect to those ports.

To begin, consider the basic figure of Figure 2-11. It shows several links between two switches. RSTP considers these links to be point-to-point links and the ports connected to them to be point-to-point ports, because the link connects exactly two devices (points).

RSTP further classifies point-to-point ports into two categories. Point-to-point ports that connect two switches are not at the edge of the network and are simply called *point-to-point ports*. Ports that instead connect to a single endpoint device at the edge of the network, like a PC or server, are called *point-to-point edge ports*, or simply *edge ports*. In Figure 2-11, SW3's switch port connected to a PC is an edge port.

Finally, RSTP defines the term *shared* to describe ports connected to a hub. The term *shared* comes from the fact that hubs create a shared Ethernet; hubs also force the attached switch port to use half-duplex logic. RSTP assumes that all half-duplex ports may be connected to hubs, treating ports that use half duplex as shared ports. RSTP converges more slowly on shared ports as compared to all point-to-point ports.

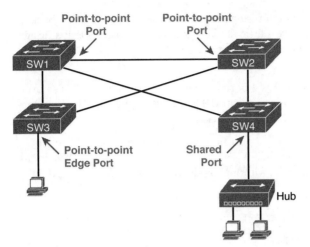

Figure 2-11 *RSTP Link Types*

Optional STP Features

At this point, you have learned plenty of details that will be useful to next configure and verify STP operations, as discussed in Chapter 3. However, before moving to that chapter, the final section of the chapter briefly introduces a few related topics that make STP work even better or be more secure: EtherChannel, PortFast, and BPDU Guard.

EtherChannel

One of the best ways to lower STP's convergence time is to avoid convergence altogether. EtherChannel provides a way to prevent STP convergence from being needed when only a single port or cable failure occurs.

EtherChannel combines multiple parallel segments of equal speed (up to eight) between the same pair of switches, bundled into an EtherChannel. The switches treat the EtherChannel as a single interface with regard to STP. As a result, if one of the links fails, but at least one of the links is up, STP convergence does not have to occur. For example, Figure 2-12 shows the familiar three-switch network, but now with two Gigabit Ethernet connections between each pair of switches.

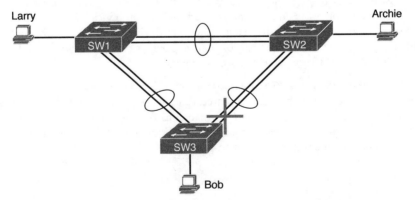

Figure 2-12 *Two-Segment EtherChannels Between Switches*

With each pair of Ethernet links configured as an EtherChannel, STP treats each EtherChannel as a single link. In other words, both links to the same switch must fail for a switch to need to cause STP convergence. Without EtherChannel, if you have multiple parallel links between two switches, STP blocks all the links except one. With EtherChannel, all the parallel links can be up and working at the same time, while reducing the number of times STP must converge, which in turn makes the network more available.

When a switch makes a forwarding decision to send a frame out an EtherChannel, the switch then has to take an extra step in logic: Out which physical interface does it send the frame? The switch has load-balancing logic that lets it pick an interface for each frame, with a goal of spreading the traffic load across all active links in the channel. As a result, a LAN design that uses EtherChannels makes much better use of the available bandwidth between switches, while also reducing the number of times that STP must converge.

Note that EtherChannels may be Layer 2 EtherChannels (as described here) or Layer 3 EtherChannels (as discussed in Chapter 19, "IPv4 Routing in the LAN"). Layer 2 EtherChannels combine links that switches use as switch ports, with the switches using Layer 2 switching logic to forward and receive Ethernet frames over the EtherChannels. Layer 3 EtherChannels also combine links, but the switches use Layer 3 routing logic to forward packets over the EtherChannels. All references to EtherChannel in Part I of this book refer to Layer 2 EtherChannels unless otherwise noted.

PortFast

PortFast allows a switch to immediately transition from blocking to forwarding, bypassing listening and learning states. However, the only ports on which you can safely enable PortFast are ports on which you know that no bridges, switches, or other STP-speaking devices are connected. Otherwise, using PortFast risks creating loops, the very thing that the listening and learning states are intended to avoid.

PortFast is most appropriate for connections to end-user devices. If you turn on PortFast on ports connected to end-user devices, when an end-user PC boots, the switch port can move to an STP forwarding state and forward traffic as soon as the PC NIC is active. Without PortFast, each port must wait while the switch confirms that the port is a DP, and then wait while the interface sits in the temporary listening and learning states before settling into the forwarding state.

PortFast is a popular feature for edge ports; in fact, RSTP incorporates PortFast concepts. You may recall the mention of RSTP port types, particularly point-to-point edge port types, around Figure 2-11. RSTP, by design of the protocol, converges quickly on these point-to-point edge type ports by bypassing the learning state, which is the same idea Cisco originally introduced with PortFast. In practice, Cisco switches enable RSTP point-to-point edge ports by enabling PortFast on the port.

BPDU Guard

STP opens up the LAN to several different types of possible security exposures. For example:

■ An attacker could connect a switch to one of these ports, one with a low STP priority value, and become the root switch. The new STP topology could have worse performance than the desired topology.

- The attacker could plug into multiple ports, into multiple switches, become root, and actually forward much of the traffic in the LAN. Without the networking staff realizing it, the attacker could use a LAN analyzer to copy large numbers of data frames sent through the LAN.

- Users could innocently harm the LAN when they buy and connect an inexpensive consumer LAN switch (one that does not use STP). Such a switch, without any STP function, would not choose to block any ports and could cause a loop.

The *Cisco BPDU Guard* feature helps defeat these kinds of problems by disabling a port if any BPDUs are received on the port. So, this feature is particularly useful on ports that should be used only as an access port and never connected to another switch.

In addition, the BPDU Guard feature helps prevent problems with PortFast. PortFast should be enabled only on access ports that connect to user devices, not to other LAN switches. Using BPDU Guard on these same ports makes sense because if another switch connects to such a port, the local switch can disable the port before a loop is created.

Chapter Review

One key to doing well on the exams is to perform repetitive spaced review sessions. Review this chapter's material using either the tools in the book, DVD, or interactive tools for the same material found on the book's companion website. Refer to the "Your Study Plan" element for more details. Table 2-11 outlines the key review elements and where you can find them. To better track your study progress, record when you completed these activities in the second column.

Table 2-11 Chapter Review Tracking

Review Element	Review Date(s)	Resource Used
Review key topics		Book, DVD/website
Review key terms		Book, DVD/website
Answer DIKTA questions		Book, PCPT
Review memory tables		Book, App

Review All the Key Topics

Key Topic

Table 2-12 Key Topics for Chapter 2

Key Topic Element	Description	Page Number
Table 2-2	Lists the three main problems that occur when not using STP in a LAN with redundant links	47
Table 2-3	Lists the reasons why a switch chooses to place an interface into forwarding or blocking state	49
Table 2-4	Lists the most important fields in Hello BPDU messages	50
List	Logic for the root switch election	52
Figure 2-6	Shows how switches calculate their root cost	53

Key Topic Element	Description	Page Number
Table 2-6	Lists the original and current default STP port costs for various interface speeds	55
Step list	A summary description of steady-state STP operations	56
Table 2-7	STP timers	56
List	Definitions of what occurs in the listening and learning states	58
Table 2-8	Summary of 802.1D states	58
List	Key similarities between 802.1D STP and 802.1w RSTP	59
Table 2-9	List of 802.1w port roles	60
Table 2-10	Comparisons of port states with 802.1D and 802.1w	62

Key Terms You Should Know

blocking state, BPDU Guard, bridge ID, bridge protocol data unit (BPDU), designated port, EtherChannel, forward delay, forwarding state, Hello BPDU, IEEE 802.1D, learning state, listening state, MaxAge, PortFast, root port, root switch, root cost, Spanning Tree Protocol (STP), rapid STP (RSTP), IEEE 802.1w, alternate port, backup port, disabled port, discarding state

CHAPTER 3

Spanning Tree Protocol Implementation

This chapter covers the following exam topics:

1.0 LAN Switching Technologies

1.3 Configure, verify, and troubleshoot STP protocols

  1.3.a STP mode (PVST+ and RPVST+)

  1.3.b STP root bridge selection

1.4 Configure, verify, and troubleshoot STP-related optional features

  1.4.a PortFast

  1.4.b BPDU guard

1.5 Configure, verify, and troubleshoot (Layer 2/Layer 3) EtherChannel

  1.5.a Static

  1.5.b PAGP

  1.5.c LACP

Cisco IOS–based LAN switches enable Spanning Tree Protocol (STP) by default on all interfaces in every VLAN. However, network engineers who work with medium-size to large-size Ethernet LANs usually want to configure at least some STP settings. First and foremost, Cisco IOS switches traditionally default to use STP rather than Rapid STP (RSTP), and the simple upgrade to RSTP improves convergence. For most LANs with more than a few switches, the network engineer will likely want to influence the choices made by STP, whether using traditional STP or RSTP—choices such as which switch becomes root, with predictability about which switch ports will block/discard when all ports are physically working. The configuration can also be set so that when links or switches fail, the engineer can predict the STP topology in those cases, as well.

This chapter discusses configuration and verification of STP. The first major section weaves a story of how to change different settings, per VLAN, with the **show** commands that reveal the current STP status affected by each configuration command. Those settings impact both STP and RSTP, but the examples use switches that use traditional 802.1D STP rather than RSTP. The second major section shows how to configure the same optional STP features mentioned in Chapter 2: PortFast, BPDU Guard, and EtherChannel (specifically Layer 2 EtherChannel). The final major section of this chapter looks at the simple (one command) configuration to enable RSTP, and the differences and similarities in **show** command output that occur when using RSTP versus STP.

"Do I Know This Already?" Quiz

Take the quiz (either here, or use the PCPT software) if you want to use the score to help you decide how much time to spend on this chapter. The answers are at the bottom of the page following the quiz, and the explanations are in DVD Appendix C and in the PCPT software.

Table 3-1 "Do I Know This Already?" Foundation Topics Section-to-Question Mapping

Foundation Topics Section	Questions
Implementing STP	1–3
Implementing Optional STP Features	4
Implementing RSTP	5, 6

1. On a 2960 switch, which of the following commands change the value of the bridge ID? (Choose two answers.)

   a. **spanning-tree bridge-id** *value*

   b. **spanning-tree vlan** *vlan-number* **root {primary | secondary}**

   c. **spanning-tree vlan** *vlan-number* **priority** *value*

   d. **set spanning-tree priority** *value*

2. Examine the following extract from the **show spanning-tree** command on a Cisco switch:

   ```
   Bridge ID  Priority    32771  (priority 32768 sys-id-ext 3)
              Address     0019.e86a.6f80
   ```

   Which of the following answers is true about the switch on which this command output was gathered?

   a. The information is about the STP instance for VLAN 1.

   b. The information is about the STP instance for VLAN 3.

   c. The command output confirms that this switch cannot possibly be the root switch.

   d. The command output confirms that this switch is currently the root switch.

3. A switch's G0/1 interface, a trunk that supports VLANs 1–10, has autonegotiated a speed of 100 Mbps. The switch currently has all default settings for STP. Which of the following actions results in the switch using an STP cost of 19 for that interface in VLAN 3? (Choose two answers.)

   a. **spanning-tree cost 19**

   b. **spanning-tree port-cost 19**

   c. **spanning-tree vlan 3 port-cost 19**

   d. Adding no configuration

4. An engineer configures a switch to put interfaces G0/1 and G0/2 into the same Layer 2 EtherChannel. Which of the following terms is used in the configuration commands?

    a. EtherChannel

    b. PortChannel

    c. Ethernet-Channel

    d. Channel-group

5. Examine the following first seven lines of output from the **show spanning-tree** command on a Cisco switch:

```
SW1# show spanning-tree vlan 5


VLAN0005
  Spanning tree enabled protocol rstp
  Root ID    Priority    32773
             Address     1833.9d7b.0e80
             Cost        15
             Port        25 (GigabitEthernet0/1)
             Hello Time   2 sec  Max Age 20 sec  Forward Delay 15 sec
```

Which of the following answers is true about the switch on which this command output was gathered?

    a. The root switch's MAC address is 1833.9d7b.0e80 and the local switch is the root.

    b. The local switch's MAC address is 1833.9d7b.0e80 and it is not the root.

    c. This switch uses STP and not RSTP.

    d. This switch uses RSTP.

6. The following output shows the last lines of output of a **show spanning-tree** command extracted from a Cisco switch running IOS:

```
SW1# show spanning-tree vlan 10
! lines omitted


Interface           Role Sts Cost      Prio.Nbr Type
------------------- ---- --- --------- -------- -----------------------

Fa0/1               Desg FWD 100       128.1    P2p Edge
Fa0/2               Desg FWD 19        128.2    Shr
Gi0/1               Desg FWD 4         128.25   P2p
Gi0/2               Root FWD 4         128.26   P2p
```

The answers all mention an interface and the state listed in the Type column of the output, along with a reason why that port should be listed as that type of STP port. Which answers list what could be a correct reason for the interface to be listed as that type of STP port? (Choose two answers.)

    a. Fa0/1 is P2p Edge because of the **spanning-tree rstp edge** interface subcommand.

    b. Fa0/2 is Shr because Fa0/2 uses half duplex.

    c. Gi0/1 is P2p because it is a VLAN trunk.

    d. Gi0/2 is P2p because the switch had no reason to make it Shr or P2p Edge.

Foundation Topics

Implementing STP

Cisco IOS switches usually use STP (IEEE 802.1D) by default rather than RSTP, and with effective default settings. You can buy some Cisco switches and connect them with Ethernet cables in a redundant topology, and STP will ensure that frames do not loop. And you never even have to think about changing any settings!

Although STP works without any configuration, most medium-size to large-size campus LANs benefit from some STP configuration. With all defaults, the switches choose the root based on the lowest burned-in MAC address on the switches because they all default to use the same STP priority. As a better option, configure the switches so that the root is predictable.

For instance, Figure 3-1 shows a typical LAN design model, with two distribution layer switches (D1 and D2). The design may have dozens of access layer switches that connect to end users; the figure shows just three access switches (A1, A2, and A3). For a variety of reasons, most network engineers make the distribution layer switches be the root. For instance, the configuration could make D1 be the root by having a lower priority, with D2 configured with the next lower priority, so it becomes root if D1 fails.

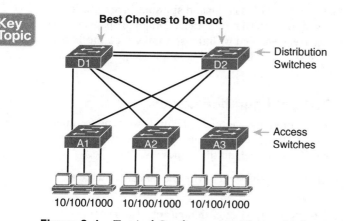

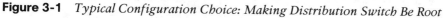

Figure 3-1 *Typical Configuration Choice: Making Distribution Switch Be Root*

This first section of the chapter examines a variety of topics that somehow relate to STP configuration. It begins with a look at STP configuration options, as a way to link the concepts of Chapter 2 to the configuration choices in this chapter. Following that, this section introduces some **show** commands for the purpose of verifying the default STP settings before changing any configuration.

___

Answers to the "Do I Know This Already?" quiz:
1 B, C **2** B **3** A, D **4** D **5** D **6** B, D

Setting the STP Mode

Chapter 2 described how 802.1D STP works in one VLAN. Now that this chapter turns our attention to STP configuration in Cisco switches, one of the first questions is this: Which kind of STP do you intend to use in a LAN? And to answer that question, you need to know a little more background.

The IEEE first standardized STP as the IEEE 802.1D standard, first published back in 1990. To put some perspective on that date, Cisco sold no LAN switches at the time, and virtual LANs did not exist yet. Instead of multiple VLANs in a LAN, there was just one broadcast domain, and one instance of STP. However, the addition of VLANs and the introduction of LAN switches into the market have created a need to add to and extend STP.

Today, Cisco IOS–based LAN switches allow you to use one of three STP configuration modes that reflect that history. The first two sections of this chapter use the mode called Per-VLAN Spanning Tree Plus (PVST+, or sometimes PVSTP), a Cisco-proprietary improvement of 802.1D STP. The *per-VLAN* part of the name gives away the main feature: PVST+ creates a different STP topology per VLAN, whereas 802.1D actually did not. PVST+ also introduced PortFast. Cisco switches often use PVST+ as the default STP mode per a default global command of **spanning-tree mode pvst**.

Over time, Cisco added RSTP support as well, with two STP modes that happen to use RSTP. One mode basically takes PVST+ and upgrades it to use RSTP logic as well, with a mode called *Rapid PVST+*, enabled with the global command **spanning-tree mode rapid-pvst**. Cisco IOS–based switches support a third mode, called Multiple Spanning Tree (MST) (or Multiple Instance of Spanning Tree), enabled with the **spanning-tree mode mst** command. (This book does not discuss MST beyond this brief mention; the CCNP Switch exam typically includes MST details.)

Connecting STP Concepts to STP Configuration Options

If you think back to the details of STP operation in Chapter 2, STP uses two types of numbers for most of its decisions: the BID and STP port costs. Focusing on those two types of numbers, consider this summary of what STP does behind the scenes:

- Uses the BID to elect the root switch, electing the switch with the numerically lowest BID

- Uses the total STP cost in each path to the root, when each nonroot switch chooses its own root port (RP)

- Uses each switch's root cost, which is in turn based on STP port costs, when switches decide which switch port becomes the designated port (DP) on each LAN segment

Unsurprisingly, Cisco switches let you configure part of a switch's BID and the STP port cost, which in turn influences the choices each switch makes with STP.

Per-VLAN Configuration Settings

Beyond supporting the configuration of the BID and STP port costs, Cisco switches support configuring both settings per VLAN. By default, Cisco switches use IEEE 802.1D, not RSTP (802.1w), with a Cisco-proprietary feature called Per-VLAN Spanning Tree Plus (PVST+). PVST+ (often abbreviated as simply PVST today) creates a different instance of STP for each VLAN. So, before looking at the tunable STP parameters, you need to have a basic understanding of PVST+, because the configuration settings can differ for each instance of STP.

PVST+ gives engineers a load-balancing tool with STP. By changing some STP configuration parameters differently for different VLANs, the engineer could cause switches to pick different RPs and DPs in different VLANs. As a result, some traffic in some VLANs can be forwarded over one trunk, and traffic for other VLANs can be forwarded over a different trunk.

Figure 3-2 shows the basic idea, with SW3 forwarding odd-numbered VLAN traffic over the left trunk (Gi0/1) and even-numbered VLANs over the right trunk (Gi0/2).

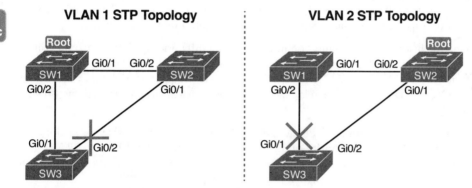

Figure 3-2 *Load Balancing with PVST+*

The next few pages look specifically at how to change the BID and STP port cost settings, per VLAN, when using the default PVST+ mode.

The Bridge ID and System ID Extension

Originally, a switch's BID was formed by combining the switch's 2-byte priority and its 6-byte MAC address. Later, the IEEE changed the rules, splitting the original priority field into two separate fields, as shown in Figure 3-3: a 4-bit priority field and a 12-bit subfield called the *system ID extension* (which represents the VLAN ID).

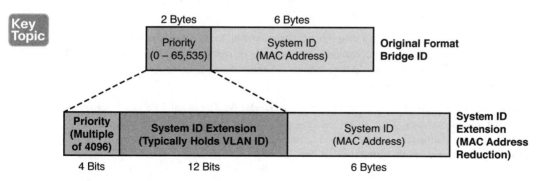

Figure 3-3 *STP System ID Extension*

Cisco switches let you configure the BID, but only the priority part. The switch fills in its universal (burned-in) MAC address as the system ID. It also plugs in the VLAN ID of a

VLAN in the 12-bit system ID extension field. The only part configurable by the network engineer is the 4-bit priority field.

Configuring the number to put in the priority field, however, is one of the strangest things to configure on a Cisco router or switch. As shown at the top of Figure 3-3, the priority field was originally a 16-bit number, which represented a decimal number from 0 to 65,535. Because of that history, the current configuration command (**spanning-tree vlan** *vlan-id* **priority** *x*) requires a decimal number between 0 and 65,535. But not just any number in that range will suffice—it must be a multiple of 4096: 0, 4096, 8192, 12288, and so on, up through 61,440.

The switch still sets the first 4 bits of the BID based on the configured value. As it turns out, of the 16 allowed multiples of 4096, from 0 through 61,440, each has a different binary value in their first 4 bits: 0000, 0001, 0010, and so on, up through 1111. The switch sets the true 4-bit priority based on the first 4 bits of the configured value.

Although the history and configuration might make the BID priority idea seem a bit convoluted, having an extra 12-bit field in the BID works well in practice because it can be used to identify the VLAN ID. VLAN IDs range from 1 to 4094, requiring 12 bits. Cisco switches place the VLAN ID into the system ID extension field, so each switch has a unique BID per VLAN.

For example, a switch configured with VLANs 1 through 4, with a default base priority of 32,768, has a default STP priority of 32,769 in VLAN 1, 32,770 in VLAN 2, 32,771 in VLAN 3, and so on. So, you can view the 16-bit priority as a base priority (as configured in the **spanning-tree vlan** *vlan-id* **priority** *x* command) plus the VLAN ID.

NOTE Cisco switches must use the system ID extension version of the bridge ID; it cannot be disabled.

Per-VLAN Port Costs

Each switch interface defaults its per-VLAN STP cost based on the IEEE recommendations listed in Table 2-6 in Chapter 2. On interfaces that support multiple speeds, Cisco switches base the cost on the current actual speed. So, if an interface negotiates to use a lower speed, the default STP cost reflects that lower speed. If the interface negotiates to use a different speed, the switch dynamically changes the STP port cost as well.

Alternatively, you can configure a switch's STP port cost with the **spanning-tree [vlan** *vlan-id*] **cost** *cost* interface subcommand. You see this command most often on trunks because setting the cost on trunks has an impact on the switch's root cost, whereas setting STP costs on access ports does not.

For the command itself, it can include the VLAN ID, or not. The command only needs a **vlan** parameter on trunk ports to set the cost per VLAN. On a trunk, if the command omits the VLAN parameter, it sets the STP cost for all VLANs whose cost is not set by a **spanning-tree vlan** *x* **cost** command for that VLAN.

STP Configuration Option Summary

Table 3-2 summarizes the default settings for both the BID and the port costs and lists the optional configuration commands covered in this chapter.

Table 3-2   STP Defaults and Configuration Options

Setting	Default	Command(s) to Change Default
BID priority	Base: 32,768	**spanning-tree vlan** *vlan-id* **root {primary	secondary}**
		spanning-tree vlan *vlan-id* **priority** *priority*
Interface cost	100 for 10 Mbps	**spanning-tree vlan** *vlan-id* **cost** *cost*
	19 for 100 Mbps	
	4 for 1 Gbps	
	2 for 10 Gbps	
PortFast	Not enabled	**spanning-tree portfast**
BPDU Guard	Not enabled	**spanning-tree bpduguard enable**

Next, the configuration section shows how to examine the operation of STP in a simple network, along with how to change these optional settings.

Verifying STP Operation

Before taking a look at how to change the configuration, first consider a few STP verification commands. Looking at these commands first will help reinforce the default STP settings. In particular, the examples in this section use the network shown in Figure 3-4.

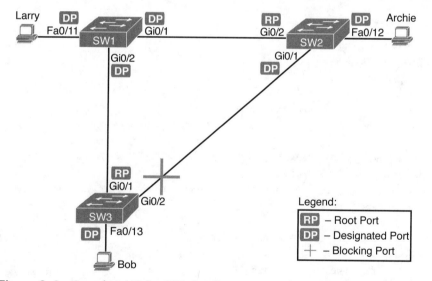

Figure 3-4   *Sample LAN for STP Configuration and Verification Examples*

Example 3-1 begins the discussion with a useful command for STP: the **show spanning-tree vlan 10** command. This command identifies the root switch and lists settings on the local switch. Example 3-1 lists the output of this command on both SW1 and SW2, as explained following the example.

Example 3-1   *STP Status with Default STP Parameters on SW1 and SW2*

```
SW1# show spanning-tree vlan 10


VLAN0010
  Spanning tree enabled protocol ieee
  Root ID     Priority     32778
              Address      1833.9d7b.0e80
              This bridge is the root
              Hello Time    2 sec  Max Age 20 sec  Forward Delay 15 sec


  Bridge ID   Priority     32778   (priority 32768 sys-id-ext 10)
              Address      1833.9d7b.0e80
              Hello Time    2 sec  Max Age 20 sec  Forward Delay 15 sec
              Aging Time   300 sec


Interface           Role Sts Cost      Prio.Nbr Type
------------------- ---- --- --------- -------- -------------------------------
Fa0/11              Desg FWD 19        128.11   P2p Edge
Gi0/1               Desg FWD 4         128.25   P2p
Gi0/2               Desg FWD 4         128.26   P2p
```

```
SW2# show spanning-tree vlan 10


VLAN0010
  Spanning tree enabled protocol ieee
  Root ID     Priority     32778
              Address      1833.9d7b.0e80
              Cost         4
              Port         26 (GigabitEthernet0/2)
              Hello Time    2 sec  Max Age 20 sec  Forward Delay 15 sec


  Bridge ID   Priority     32778   (priority 32768 sys-id-ext 10)
              Address      1833.9d7b.1380
              Hello Time    2 sec  Max Age 20 sec  Forward Delay 15 sec
              Aging Time   300 sec


Interface           Role Sts Cost      Prio.Nbr Type
------------------- ---- --- --------- -------- -------------------------------
Fa0/12              Desg FWD 19        128.12   P2p
Gi0/1               Desg FWD 4         128.25   P2p
Gi0/2               Root FWD 4         128.26   P2p
```

Example 3-1 begins with the output of the **show spanning-tree vlan 10** command on
SW1. This command first lists three major groups of messages: one group of messages
about the root switch, followed by another group about the local switch, and ending with
interface role and status information. In this case, SW1 lists its own BID as the root, with

even a specific statement that "This bridge is the root," confirming that SW1 is now the root of the VLAN 10 STP topology.

Next, compare the highlighted lines of the same command on SW2 in the lower half of the example. SW2 lists SW1's BID details as the root; in other words, SW2 agrees that SW1 has won the root election. SW2 does not list the phrase "This bridge is the root." SW2 then lists its own (different) BID details in the lines after the details about the root's BID.

The output also confirms a few default values. First, each switch lists the priority part of the BID as a separate number: 32778. This value comes from the default priority of 32768, plus VLAN 10, for a total of 32778. The output also shows the interface cost for some Fast Ethernet and Gigabit Ethernet interfaces, defaulting to 19 and 4, respectively.

Finally, the bottom of the output from the **show spanning-tree** command lists each interface in the VLAN, including trunks, with the STP port role and port state listed. For instance, on switch SW1, the output lists three interfaces, with a role of Desg for designated port (DP) and a state of FWD for forwarding. SW2 lists three interfaces, two DPs, and one root port, so all three are in an FWD or forwarding state.

Example 3-1 shows a lot of good STP information, but two other commands, shown in Example 3-2, work better for listing BID information in a shorter form. The first, **show spanning-tree root**, lists the root's BID for each VLAN. This command also lists other details, like the local switch's root cost and root port. The other command, **show spanning-tree vlan 10 bridge**, breaks out the BID into its component parts. In this example, it shows SW2's priority as the default of 32768, the VLAN ID of 10, and the MAC address.

Example 3-2 *Listing Root Switch and Local Switch BIDs on Switch SW2*

```
SW2# show spanning-tree root

                                     Root   Hello Max Fwd
Vlan                     Root ID     Cost   Time  Age Dly  Root Port
---------------- -------------------- --------- ----- --- ---  ------------
VLAN0001         32769 1833.9d5d.c900     23     2   20  15  Gi0/1
VLAN0010         32778 1833.9d7b.0e80      4     2   20  15  Gi0/2
VLAN0020         32788 1833.9d7b.0e80      4     2   20  15  Gi0/2
VLAN0030         32798 1833.9d7b.0e80      4     2   20  15  Gi0/2
VLAN0040         32808 1833.9d7b.0e80      4     2   20  15  Gi0/2


SW2# show spanning-tree vlan 10 bridge

                                             Hello  Max  Fwd
Vlan                     Bridge ID           Time   Age  Dly  Protocol
---------------- ---------------------------------- ----- --- ---  --------
VLAN0010         32778 (32768,  10) 1833.9d7b.1380    2    20   15  ieee
```

Note that both the commands in Example 3-2 have a VLAN option: **show spanning-tree [vlan x] root** and **show spanning-tree [vlan x] bridge**. Without the VLAN listed, each command lists one line per VLAN; with the VLAN, the output lists the same information, but just for that one VLAN.

Configuring STP Port Costs

Changing the STP port costs requires a simple interface subcommand: **spanning-tree [vlan x] cost x**. To show how it works, consider the following example, which changes what happens in the network shown in Figure 3-4.

Back in Figure 3-4, with default settings, SW1 became root, and SW3 blocked on its G0/2 interface. A brief scan of the figure, based on the default STP cost of 4 for Gigabit interfaces, shows that SW3 should have found a cost 4 path and a cost 8 path to reach the root, as shown in Figure 3-5.

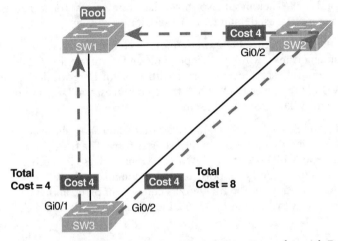

Figure 3-5 *Analysis of SW3's Current Root Cost of 4 with Defaults*

To show the effects of changing the port cost, the next example shows a change to SW3's configuration, setting its G0/1 port cost higher so that the better path to the root goes out SW3's G0/2 port instead. Example 3-3 also shows several other interesting effects.

Example 3-3 *Manipulating STP Port Cost and Watching the Transition to Forwarding State*

```
SW3# debug spanning-tree events
Spanning Tree event debugging is on
SW3# configure terminal
Enter configuration commands, one per line.  End with CNTL/Z.
SW3(config)# interface gigabitethernet0/1
SW3(config-if)# spanning-tree vlan 10 cost 30
SW3(config-if)# ^Z
SW3#
*Mar 11 06:28:00.860: STP: VLAN0010 new root port Gi0/2, cost 8
*Mar 11 06:28:00.860: STP: VLAN0010 Gi0/2 -> listening
*Mar 11 06:28:00.860: STP: VLAN0010 sent Topology Change Notice on Gi0/2
*Mar 11 06:28:00.860: STP[10]: Generating TC trap for port GigabitEthernet0/1
*Mar 11 06:28:00.860: STP: VLAN0010 Gi0/1 -> blocking
*Mar 11 06:28:15.867: STP: VLAN0010 Gi0/2 -> learning
*Mar 11 06:28:30.874: STP[10]: Generating TC trap for port GigabitEthernet0/2
*Mar 11 06:28:30.874: STP: VLAN0010 sent Topology Change Notice on Gi0/2
*Mar 11 06:28:30.874: STP: VLAN0010 Gi0/2 -> forwarding
```

This example starts with the **debug spanning-tree events** command on SW3. This command tells the switch to issue debug log messages whenever STP performs changes to an interface's role or state. These messages show up in the example as a result of the configuration.

Next, the example shows the configuration to change SW3's port cost, in VLAN 10, to 30, with the **spanning-tree vlan 10 cost 30** interface subcommand. Based on the figure, the root cost through SW3's G0/1 will now be 30 instead of 4. As a result, SW3's best cost to reach the root is cost 8, with SW3's G0/2 as its root port.

The debug messages tell us what STP on SW3 is thinking behind the scenes, with timestamps. Note that the first five debug messages, displayed immediately after the user exited configuration mode in this case, all happen at the same time (down to the same millisecond). Notably, G0/1, which had been forwarding, immediately moves to a blocking state. Interface G0/2, which had been blocking, does not go to a forwarding state, instead moving to a listening state (at least, according to this message).

Now look for the debug message that lists G0/2 transitioning to learning state, and then the next one that shows it finally reaching forwarding state. How long between the messages? In each case, the message's timestamps show that 15 seconds passed. In this experiment, the switches used a default setting of forward delay (15 seconds). So, these debug messages confirm the steps that STP takes to transition an interface from blocking to forwarding state.

If you did not happen to enable a debug when configuring the cost, using **show** commands later can confirm the same choice by SW3, to now use its G0/2 port as its RP. Example 3-4 shows the new STP port cost setting on SW3, along with the new root port and root cost, using the **show spanning-tree vlan 10** command. Note that G0/2 is now listed as the root port. The top of the output lists SW3's root cost as 8, matching the analysis shown in Figure 3-5.

Example 3-4 *New STP Status and Settings on SW3*

```
SW3# show spanning-tree vlan 10


VLAN0010
  Spanning tree enabled protocol ieee
  Root ID    Priority    32778
             Address     1833.9d7b.0e80
             Cost        8
             Port        26 (GigabitEthernet0/2)
             Hello Time   2 sec  Max Age 20 sec  Forward Delay 15 sec

  Bridge ID  Priority    32778  (priority 32768 sys-id-ext 10)
             Address     f47f.35cb.d780
             Hello Time   2 sec  Max Age 20 sec  Forward Delay 15 sec
             Aging Time  300 sec


Interface          Role Sts Cost      Prio.Nbr Type
------------------ ---- --- --------- -------- --------------------------------
Fa0/23             Desg FWD 19        128.23   P2p
Gi0/1              Altn BLK 30        128.25   P2p
Gi0/2              Root FWD 4         128.26   P2p
```

Configuring Priority to Influence the Root Election

The other big STP configuration option is to influence the root election by changing the priority of a switch. The priority can be set explicitly with the **spanning-tree vlan** *vlan-id* **priority** *value* global configuration command, which sets the base priority of the switch. (This is the command that requires a parameter of a multiple of 4096.)

However, Cisco gives us a better configuration option than configuring a specific priority value. In most designs, the network engineers pick two switches to be root: one to be root if all switches are up, and another to take over if the first switch fails. Switch IOS supports this idea with the **spanning-tree vlan** *vlan-id* **root primary** and **spanning-tree vlan** *vlan-id* **root secondary** commands.

The **spanning-tree vlan** *vlan-id* **root primary** command tells the switch to set its priority low enough to become root right now. The switch looks at the current root in that VLAN, and at the root's priority. Then the local switch chooses a priority value that causes the local switch to take over as root.

Remembering that Cisco switches use a default base priority of 32,768, this command chooses the base priority as follows:

- If the current root has a base priority higher than 24,576, the local switch uses a base priority of 24,576.

- If the current root's base priority is 24,576 or lower, the local switch sets its base priority to the highest multiple of 4096 that still results in the local switch becoming root.

For the switch intended to take over as the root if the first switch fails, use the **spanning-tree vlan** *vlan-id* **root secondary** command. This command is much like the **spanning-tree vlan** *vlan-id* **root primary** command, but with a priority value worse than the primary switch but better than all the other switches. This command sets the switch's base priority to 28,672 regardless of the current root's current priority value.

For example, in Figures 3-4 and 3-5, SW1 was the root switch, and as shown in various commands, all three switches defaulted to use a base priority of 32,768. Example 3-5 shows a configuration that makes SW2 the primary root, and SW1 the secondary, just to show the role move from one to the other. These commands result in SW2 having a base priority of 24,576, and SW1 having a base priority of 28,672.

Example 3-5 *Making SW2 Become Root Primary, and SW1 Root Secondary*

```
! First, on SW2:
SW2# configure terminal
Enter configuration commands, one per line.  End with CNTL/Z.
SW2(config)# spanning-tree vlan 10 root primary
SW2(config)# ^Z
! Next, SW1 is configured to back-up SW1
SW1# configure terminal
Enter configuration commands, one per line.  End with CNTL/Z.
SW1(config)# spanning-tree vlan 10 root secondary
SW1(config)# ^Z
SW1#
```

```
! The next command shows the local switch's BID (SW1)
SW1# show spanning-tree vlan 10 bridge


                                             Hello  Max  Fwd
Vlan                           Bridge ID     Time   Age  Dly  Protocol
----------------  ------------------------   -----  ---  ---  --------

VLAN0010           28682 (28672, 10) 1833.9d7b.0e80   2    20   15   ieee

! The next command shows the root's BID (SW2)
SW1# show spanning-tree vlan 10 root


                                   Root   Hello Max Fwd
Vlan                   Root ID     Cost   Time  Age Dly  Root Port
----------------  --------------------  ---------  ----- --- ---  ------------

VLAN0010           24586 1833.9d7b.1380      4    2    20  15   Gi0/1
```

The output of the two **show** commands clearly points out the resulting priority values on each switch. First, the **show spanning-tree bridge** command lists the local switch's BID information, while the **show spanning-tree root** command lists the root's BID, plus the local switch's root cost and root port (assuming it is not the root switch). So, SW1 lists its own BID, with priority 28,682 (base 28,672, with VLAN 10) with the **show spanning-tree bridge** command. Still on SW1, the output lists the root's priority as 24,586 in VLAN 10, implied as base 24,576 plus 10 for VLAN 10, with the **show spanning-tree root** command.

Note that alternatively you could have configured the priority settings specifically. SW1 could have used the **spanning-tree vlan 10 priority 28672** command, with SW2 using the **spanning-tree vlan 10 priority 24576** command. In this particular case, both options would result in the same STP operation.

Implementing Optional STP Features

This just-completed first major section of the chapter showed examples that used PVST+ only, assuming a default global command of **spanning-tree mode pvst**. At the same time, all the configuration commands shown in that first section, commands that influence STP operation, would influence both traditional STP and RSTP operation.

This section, the second of three major sections in this chapter, now moves on to discuss some useful but optional features that make both STP and RSTP work even better.

Configuring PortFast and BPDU Guard

You can easily configure the PortFast and BPDU Guard features on any interface, but with two different configuration options. One option works best when you want to enable these features only on a few ports, and the other works best when you want to enable these features on most every access port.

First, to enable the features on just one port at a time, use the **spanning-tree portfast** and the **spanning-tree bpduguard enable** interface subcommands. Example 3-6 shows an example of the process, with SW3's F0/4 interface enabling both features. (Also, note the long warning message IOS lists when enabling PortFast; using PortFast on a port connected to other switches can indeed cause serious problems.)

Example 3-6 *Enabling PortFast and BPDU Guard on One Interface*

```
SW3# configure terminal
Enter configuration commands, one per line.  End with CNTL/Z.
SW3(config)# interface fastEthernet 0/4
SW3(config-if)# spanning-tree portfast
%Warning: portfast should only be enabled on ports connected to a single
 host. Connecting hubs, concentrators, switches, bridges, etc... to this
 interface  when portfast is enabled, can cause temporary bridging loops.
 Use with CAUTION

%Portfast has been configured on FastEthernet0/4 but will only
 have effect when the interface is in a non-trunking mode.

SW3(config-if)# spanning-tree bpduguard ?
  disable  Disable BPDU guard for this interface
  enable   Enable BPDU guard for this interface

SW3(config-if)# spanning-tree bpduguard enable
SW3(config-if)# ^Z
SW3#
```

Example 3-7 shows some brief information about the interface configuration of both PortFast and BPDU Guard. Of course, the **show running-config** command (not shown) would confirm the configuration commands from Example 3-6. The **show spanning-tree interface fastethernet0/4 portfast** command in Example 3-7 lists the PortFast status of the interface; note that the status value of *enabled* is displayed only if PortFast is configured and the interface is up. The **show spanning-tree interface detail** command then shows a line near the end of the output that states that PortFast and BPDU Guard are enabled. Note that this command would not list those two highlighted lines of output if these two features were not enabled.

Example 3-7 *Verifying PortFast and BPDU Guard Configuration*

```
SW3# show spanning-tree interface fastethernet0/4 portfast
VLAN0104               enabled

SW11# show spanning-tree interface F0/4 detail
 Port 4 (FastEthernet0/4) of VLAN0001 is designated forwarding
   Port path cost 19, Port priority 128, Port Identifier 128.4.
   Designated root has priority 32769, address bcc4.938b.a180
   Designated bridge has priority 32769, address bcc4.938b.e500
   Designated port id is 128.4, designated path cost 19
   Timers: message age 0, forward delay 0, hold 0
   Number of transitions to forwarding state: 1
```

```
  The port is in the portfast mode
    Link type is point-to-point by default
  Bpdu guard is enabled
  BPDU: sent 1721, received 0
```

PortFast and BPDU Guard are disabled by default on all interfaces, and to use them, each interface requires interface subcommands like those in Example 3-6. Alternately, for both features, you can enable the feature globally. Then, for interfaces for which the feature should be disabled, you can use another interface subcommand to disable the feature.

The ability to change the global default for these features reduces the number of interface subcommands required. For instance, on an access layer switch with 48 access ports and two uplinks, you probably want to enable both PortFast and BPDU Guard on all 48 access ports. Rather than requiring the interface subcommands on all 48 of those ports, enable the features globally, and then disable them on the uplink ports.

Table 3-3 summarizes the commands to enable and disable both PortFast and BPDU Guard, both globally and per interface. For instance, the global command **spanning-tree portfast default** changes the default so that all interfaces use PortFast, unless a port also has the **spanning-tree portfast disable** interface subcommand configured.

Table 3-3   Enabling and Disabling PortFast and BPDU Guard, Globally and Per Interface

Action	Globally	One Interface
Disable PortFast	**no spanning-tree portfast default**	**spanning-tree portfast disable**
Enable PortFast	**spanning-tree portfast default**	**spanning-tree portfast**
Disable BPDU Guard	**no spanning-tree portfast bpduguard default**	**spanning-tree bpduguard disable**
Enable BPDU Guard	**spanning-tree portfast bpduguard default**	**spanning-tree bpduguard enable**

Example 3-8 shows another new command, **show spanning-tree summary**. This command shows the current global settings for several STP parameters, including the PortFast and BPDU Guard features. This output was gathered on a switch that had enabled both PortFast and BPDU Guard globally.

Example 3-8   *Displaying Status of Global Settings for PortFast and BPDU Guard*

```
SW1# show spanning-tree summary
Switch is in pvst mode
Root bridge for: none
EtherChannel misconfig guard is enabled
Extended system ID         is enabled
Portfast Default           is enabled
PortFast BPDU Guard Default is enabled
Portfast BPDU Filter Default is disabled
Loopguard Default          is disabled
UplinkFast                 is disabled
BackboneFast               is disabled
```

```
Configured Pathcost method used is short

Name                    Blocking Listening Learning Forwarding STP Active
---------------------   -------- --------- -------- ---------- ----------
VLAN0001                       3         0        0          2          5
---------------------   -------- --------- -------- ---------- ----------
1 vlan                         3         0        0          2          5
```

Configuring EtherChannel

As introduced back in Chapter 2, two neighboring switches can treat multiple parallel links between each other as a single logical link called an *EtherChannel*. STP operates on the EtherChannel, instead of the individual physical links, so that STP either forwards or blocks on the entire logical EtherChannel for a given VLAN. As a result, a switch in a forwarding state can then load balance traffic over all the physical links in the EtherChannel. Without EtherChannel, only one of the parallel links between two switches would be allowed to forward traffic, with the rest of the links blocked by STP.

> **NOTE**   All references to EtherChannel in this Chapter refer to Layer 2 EtherChannels, and not to Layer 3 EtherChannels (as discussed in Chapter 19, "IPv4 Routing in the LAN").

EtherChannel may be one of the most challenging switch features to make work. First, the configuration has several options, so you have to remember the details of which options work together. Second, the switches also require a variety of other interface settings to match among all the links in the channel, so you have to know those settings as well.

This section focuses on the correct EtherChannel configuration. Chapter 4's section "Troubleshooting Layer 2 EtherChannel" looks at many of the potential problems with EtherChannel, including all those other configuration settings that a switch checks before allowing the EtherChannel to work.

Configuring a Manual EtherChannel

The simplest way to configure an EtherChannel is to add the correct **channel-group** configuration command to each physical interface, on each switch, all with the **on** keyword. The **on** keyword tells the switches to place a physical interface into an EtherChannel.

Before getting into the configuration and verification, however, you need to start using three terms as synonyms: *EtherChannel*, *PortChannel*, and *Channel-group*. Oddly, IOS uses the **channel-group** configuration command, but then to display its status, IOS uses the **show etherchannel** command. Then, the output of this **show** command refers to neither an "EtherChannel" nor a "Channel-group," instead using the term "PortChannel." So, pay close attention to these three terms in the example.

To configure an EtherChannel manually, follow these steps:

Step 1.   Add the **channel-group** *number* **mode on** command in interface configuration mode under each physical interface that should be in the channel to add it to the channel.

Step 2. Use the same number for all commands on the same switch, but the channel-group number on the neighboring switch can differ.

Example 3-9 shows a simple example, with two links between switches SW1 and SW2, as shown in Figure 3-6. The configuration shows SW1's two interfaces placed into channel-group 1, with two **show** commands to follow.

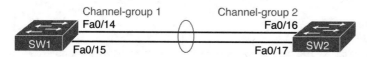

Figure 3-6 *Sample LAN Used in EtherChannel Example*

Example 3-9 *Configuring and Monitoring EtherChannel*

```
SW1# configure terminal
Enter configuration commands, one per line.  End with CNTL/Z.
SW1(config)# interface fa 0/14
SW1(config-if)# channel-group 1 mode on
SW1(config)# interface fa 0/15
SW1(config-if)# channel-group 1 mode on
SW1(config-if)# ^z


SW1# show spanning-tree vlan 3


VLAN0003
  Spanning tree enabled protocol ieee
  Root ID    Priority    28675
             Address     0019.e859.5380
             Cost        12
             Port        72 (Port-channel1)
             Hello Time   2 sec  Max Age 20 sec  Forward Delay 15 sec


  Bridge ID  Priority    28675  (priority 28672 sys-id-ext 3)
             Address     0019.e86a.6f80
             Hello Time   2 sec  Max Age 20 sec  Forward Delay 15 sec
             Aging Time 300


Interface         Role Sts Cost     Prio.Nbr Type
---------------- ---- --- --------- -------- -------------------------------
Po1               Root FWD 12       128.64   P2p Peer(STP)


SW1# show etherchannel 1 summary
Flags:  D - down         P - bundled in port-channel
        I - stand-alone s - suspended
        H - Hot-standby (LACP only)
        R - Layer3       S - Layer2
        U - in use       f - failed to allocate aggregator
```

```
          M - not in use, minimum links not met
          u - unsuitable for bundling
          w - waiting to be aggregated
          d - default port




Number of channel-groups in use: 1
Number of aggregators:           1


Group  Port-channel  Protocol    Ports
------+-------------+-----------+-----------------------------------------------
1       Po1(SU)          -        Fa0/14(P)    Fa0/15(P)
```

Take a few moments to look at the output in the two **show** commands in the example, as well. First, the **show spanning-tree** command lists Po1, short for PortChannel1, as an interface. This interface exists because of the **channel-group** commands using the **1** parameter. STP no longer operates on physical interfaces F0/14 and F0/15, instead operating on the PortChannel1 interface, so only that interface is listed in the output.

Next, note the output of the **show etherchannel 1 summary** command. It lists as a heading "Port-channel," with Po1 below it. It also lists both F0/14 and F0/15 in the list of ports, with a (P) beside each. Per the legend, the *P* means that the ports are bundled in the port channel, which is a code that means these ports have passed all the configuration checks and are valid to be included in the channel.

> **NOTE**   Cisco uses the term *EtherChannel* to refer to the concepts discussed in this section. To refer to the item configured in the switch, Cisco instead uses the term *port channel*, with the command keyword **port-channel**. For the purposes of understanding the technology, you may treat these terms as synonyms. However, it helps to pay close attention to the use of the terms *port channel* and *EtherChannel* as you work through the examples in this section, because IOS uses both.

Configuring Dynamic EtherChannels

Cisco switches support two different protocols that allow the switches to negotiate whether a particular link becomes part of an EtherChannel or not. Basically, the configuration enables the protocol for a particular channel-group number. At that point, the switch can use the protocol to send messages to/from the neighboring switch and discover whether their configuration settings pass all checks. If a given physical link passes, the link is added to the EtherChannel and used; if not, it is placed in a down state, and not used, until the configuration inconsistency can be resolved.

Cisco switches support the Cisco-proprietary Port Aggregation Protocol (PAgP) and the IEEE standard Link Aggregation Control Protocol (LACP), based on IEEE standard 802.3ad. Although differences exist between the two, to the depth discussed here, they both accomplish the same task: negotiate so that only links that pass the configuration checks are actually used in an EtherChannel.

To configure either protocol, a switch uses the **channel-group** configuration commands on each switch, but with a keyword that either means "use this protocol and begin negotiations" or "use this protocol and wait for the other switch to begin negotiations." As shown in Figure 3-7, the **desirable** and **auto** keywords enable PAgP, and the **active** and **passive** keywords enable LACP. With these options, at least one side has to begin the negotiations. In other words, with PAgP, at least one of the two sides must use **desirable**, and with LACP, at least one of the two sides must use **active**.

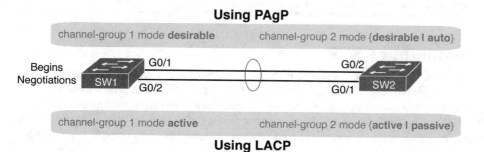

Using PAgP

channel-group 1 mode **desirable**   channel-group 2 mode {**desirable I auto**}

Begins Negotiations   SW1   G0/1
                              G0/2   G0/2   SW2
                                                      G0/1

channel-group 1 mode **active**   channel-group 2 mode {**active I passive**}

Using LACP

Figure 3-7 *Correct EtherChannel Configuration Combinations*

NOTE   Do not use the **on** parameter on one end, and either **auto** or **desirable** (or for LACP, **active** or **passive**) on the neighboring switch. The **on** option uses neither PAgP nor LACP, so a configuration that uses **on**, with PAgP or LACP options on the other end, would prevent the EtherChannel from working.

For example, in the design shown in Figure 3-7, imagine both physical interfaces on both switches were configured with the **channel-group 2 mode desirable** interface subcommand. As a result, the two switches would negotiate and create an EtherChannel. Example 3-10 shows the verification of that configuration, with the command **show etherchannel 2 port-channel**. This command confirms the protocol in use (PAgP, because the **desirable** keyword was configured), and the list of interfaces in the channel.

Example 3-10 *EtherChannel Verification: PAgP Desirable Mode*

```
SW1# show etherchannel 2 port-channel
                Port-channels in the group:
                ---------------------------


Port-channel: Po2
------------


Age of the Port-channel   = 0d:00h:04m:04s
Logical slot/port   = 16/1          Number of ports = 2
GC                  = 0x00020001      HotStandBy port = null
Port state          = Port-channel Ag-Inuse
Protocol            =     PAgP
Port security       = Disabled
```

```
Ports in the Port-channel:


Index  Load   Port    EC state         No of bits

------+------+------+------------------+------------

   0    00    Gi0/1   Desirable-S1        0

   0    00    Gi0/2   Desirable-S1        0


Time since last port bundled:     0d:00h:03m:57s    Gi0/2
```

Implementing RSTP

All you have to do to migrate from STP to RSTP is to configure the **spanning-tree mode rapid-pvst** global command on all the switches. However, for exam preparation, it helps to work through the various **show** commands, particularly to prepare for Simlet questions. Those questions can ask you to interpret **show** command output without allowing you to look at the configuration, and the output of **show** commands when using STP versus RSTP is very similar.

This third and final major section of this chapter focuses on pointing out the similarities and differences between STP and RSTP as seen in Catalyst switch configuration and verification commands. This section explains the configuration and verification of RSTP, with emphasis on how to identify RSTP features.

Identifying the STP Mode on a Catalyst Switch

Cisco Catalyst switches operate in some STP mode as defined by the **spanning-tree mode** global configuration command. Based on this command's setting, the switch is using either 802.1D STP or 802.1w RSTP, as noted in Table 3-4.

Table 3-4   Cisco Catalyst STP Configuration Modes

Parameter on spanning-tree mode Command	Uses STP or RSTP?	Protocol Listed in Command Output	Description
pvst	STP	ieee	Default; Per-VLAN Spanning Tree instance
rapid-pvst	RSTP	rstp	Like PVST, but uses RSTP rules instead of STP for each STP instance
mst	RSTP	mst	Creates multiple RSTP instances but does not require one instance per each VLAN

To determine whether a Cisco Catalyst switch uses RSTP, you can look for two types of information. First, you can look at the configuration, as noted in the left column of Table 3-4. Also, some **show** commands list the STP protocol as a reference to the configuration of the **spanning-tree mode** global configuration command. A protocol of **rstp** or **mst** refers to one of the modes that uses RSTP, and a protocol of **ieee** refers to the mode that happens to use STP.

Before looking at an example of the output, review the topology in Figure 3-8. The remaining RSTP examples in this chapter use this topology. In the RSTP examples in this chapter, SW1 will become root, and SW3 will block on one port (G0/2), as shown.

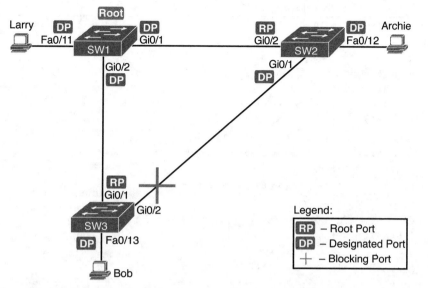

Figure 3-8 *Network Topology for STP and RSTP Examples*

The first example focuses on VLAN 10, with all switches using 802.1D STP and the default setting of **spanning-tree mode pvst**. This setting creates an instance of STP per VLAN (which is the per-VLAN part of the name) and uses 802.1D STP. Each switch places the port connected to the PC into VLAN 10 and enables both PortFast and BPDU Guard. Example 3-11 shows a sample configuration from switch SW3, with identical interface subcommands configured on SW1's F0/11 and SW2's F0/12 ports, respectively.

Example 3-11   *Sample Configuration from Switch SW3*

```
SW3# show running-config interface Fastethernet 0/13

Building configuration...

Current configuration : 117 bytes
!
interface FastEthernet0/13
 switchport access vlan 10
 spanning-tree portfast
 spanning-tree bpduguard enable
end
```

At this point, the three switches use 802.1D STP because all use the default PVST mode. Example 3-12 shows the evidence of STP's work, with only subtle and indirect clues that STP happens to be in use.

Example 3-12 *Output That Confirms the Use of 802.1D STP on Switch SW3*

```
SW3# show spanning-tree vlan 10


VLAN0010
 Spanning tree enabled protocol ieee
  Root ID    Priority    32778
             Address     1833.9d7b.0e80
             Cost        4
             Port        25 (GigabitEthernet0/1)
             Hello Time   2 sec  Max Age 20 sec  Forward Delay 15 sec

  Bridge ID  Priority    32778  (priority 32768 sys-id-ext 10)
             Address     f47f.35cb.d780
             Hello Time   2 sec  Max Age 20 sec  Forward Delay 15 sec
             Aging Time  300 sec


Interface          Role Sts Cost      Prio.Nbr Type
------------------ ---- --- --------- -------- --------------------------------
Fa0/13             Desg FWD 19        128.13   P2p Edge
Gi0/1              Root FWD 4         128.25   P2p
Gi0/2              Altn BLK 4         128.26   P2p



SW3# show spanning-tree vlan 10 bridge


                                       Hello  Max  Fwd
Vlan                     Bridge ID     Time   Age  Dly  Protocol
---------------- -------------------------------- ----- --- --- --------
VLAN0010         32778 (32768,  10) f47f.35cb.d780   2    20  15   ieee
```

The highlighted parts of the example note the references to the STP protocol as ieee, which implies that STP is in use. The term *ieee* is a reference to the original IEEE 802.1D STP standard.

To migrate this small network to use RSTP, configure the **spanning-tree mode rapid-pvst** command. This continues the use of per-VLAN spanning-tree instances, but it applies RSTP logic to each STP instance. Example 3-13 shows the output of the same two commands from Example 3-12 after configuring the **spanning-tree mode rapid-pvst** command on all three switches.

Example 3-13 *Output That Confirms the Use of 802.1w RSTP on Switch SW3*

```
SW3# show spanning-tree vlan 10


VLAN0010
  Spanning tree enabled protocol rstp
  Root ID    Priority    32778
             Address     1833.9d7b.0e80
```

```
               Cost        4
               Port       25  (GigabitEthernet0/1)
               Hello Time   2 sec  Max Age 20 sec  Forward Delay 15 sec

  Bridge ID  Priority   32778  (priority 32768 sys-id-ext 10)
             Address    f47f.35cb.d780
             Hello Time   2 sec  Max Age 20 sec  Forward Delay 15 sec
             Aging Time 300 sec


Interface        Role Sts Cost      Prio.Nbr Type
---------------- ---- --- --------- -------- --------------------------------

Fa0/13           Desg FWD 19        128.13   P2p Edge
Gi0/1            Root FWD 4         128.25   P2p
Gi0/2            Altn BLK 4         128.26   P2p



SW3# show spanning-tree vlan 10 bridge


                                            Hello  Max  Fwd
Vlan                     Bridge ID          Time   Age  Dly  Protocol
---------------- -------------------------- -----  ---  ---  --------
VLAN0010         32778 (32768,  10) f47f.35cb.d780  2    20   15   rstp
```

Pay close attention to the differences between the 802.1D STP output in Example 3-12 and the 802.1w RSTP output in Example 3-13. Literally, the only difference is rstp instead of ieee in one place in the output of each of the two commands listed. In this case, rstp refers to the configuration of the **spanning-tree mode rapid-pvst** global config command, which implied the use of RSTP.

RSTP Port Roles

RSTP adds two port roles to STP: the alternate port and the backup port. Example 3-14 repeats an excerpt from the **show spanning-tree vlan 10** command on switch SW3 to show an example of the alternate port role. SW3 (as shown earlier in Figure 3-8) is not the root switch, with G0/1 as its root port and G0/2 as an alternate port.

Example 3-14   *Output Confirming SW3's Root Port and Alternate Port Roles*

```
SW3# show spanning-tree vlan 10
! Lines omitted for brevity
Interface        Role Sts Cost      Prio.Nbr Type
---------------- ---- --- --------- -------- --------------------------------

Fa0/13           Desg FWD 19        128.13   P2p Edge
Gi0/1            Root FWD 4         128.25   P2p
Gi0/2            Altn BLK 4         128.26   P2p
```

The good news is that the output clearly lists which port is the root port (Gi0/1) and which port is the alternate root port (Gi0/2). The only trick is to know that Altn is a shortened version of the word *alternate*.

Pay close attention to this short description of an oddity about the STP and RSTP output on Catalyst switches! Cisco Catalyst switches often show the alternate and backup ports in output even when using STP and not RSTP. The alternate and backup port concepts are RSTP concepts. The switches only converge faster using these concepts when using RSTP. But **show** command output, when using STP and not RSTP, happens to identify what would be the alternate and backup ports if RSTP were used.

Why might you care about such trivia? Seeing output that lists an RSTP alternate port does not confirm that the switch is using RSTP. So, do not make that assumption on the exam. To confirm that a switch uses RSTP, you must look at the configuration of the **spanning-tree mode** command, or look for the protocol as summarized back in Table 3-4.

For instance, just compare the output of Example 3-12 and Example 3-14. Example 3-12 shows output for this same SW3, with the same parameters, except that all switches used PVST mode, meaning all the switches used STP. Example 3-12's output (based on STP) lists SW3's G0/2 as Altn, meaning alternate, even though the alternate port concept is not an STP concept, but an RSTP concept.

RSTP Port States

RSTP added one new port state compared to STP, discarding, using it as a replacement for the STP port states of disabled and blocking. You might think that after you configure a switch to use RSTP rather than STP, instead of seeing ports in a blocking state, you would now see the discarding state. However, the Cisco Catalyst switch output basically ignores the new term *discarding*, continuing to use the old term *blocking* instead.

For example, scan back to the most recent RSTP example (Example 3-14), to the line for SW3's port G0/2. Then look for the column with heading STS, which refers to the status or state. The output shows G0/2 is listed as BLK, or blocking. In theory, because SW3 uses RSTP, the port state ought to be discarding, but the switch IOS continues to use the older notation of BLK for blocking.

Just as one more bit of evidence, the command **show spanning-tree vlan 10 interface gigabitethernet0/2 state** lists the STP or RSTP port state with the state fully spelled out. Example 3-15 shows this command, taken from SW3, for interface G0/2. Note the fully spelled-out *blocking* term instead of the RSTP term *discarding*.

Example 3-15   *SW3, an RSTP Switch, Continues to Use the Old Blocking Term*

```
SW3# show spanning-tree vlan 10 interface gigabitEthernet 0/2 state
VLAN0010                blocking
```

RSTP Port Types

Cisco Catalyst switches determine the RSTP port type based on two port settings: the current duplex (full or half) and whether the PortFast feature is enabled. First, full duplex tells the switch to use port type point-to-point, with half duplex telling the switch to use port type shared. Enabling PortFast tells the switch to treat the port as an edge port. Table 3-5 summarizes the combinations.

Table 3-5 RSTP Port Types

Type	Current Duplex Status	Is Spanning-Tree PortFast Configured?
Point-to-point	Full	No
Point-to-point edge	Full	Yes
Shared	Half	No
Shared edge[1]	Half	Yes

[1] Cisco recommends against using this combination, to avoid causing loops.

You can easily find the RSTP port types in the output of several commands, including the same **show spanning-tree** command in Example 3-16. Example 3-16 lists output from switch SW2, with a hub added off SW2's F0/18 port (not shown in Figure 3-8). The hub was added so that the output in Example 3-16 lists a shared port (noted as Shr) to go along with the point-to-point ports (noted as P2p).

Example 3-16 *RSTP Port Types*

```
SW2# show spanning-tree vlan 10


VLAN0010
  Spanning tree enabled protocol rstp
  Root ID    Priority    32778
             Address     1833.9d7b.0e80
             Cost        4
             Port        26 (GigabitEthernet0/2)
             Hello Time   2 sec  Max Age 20 sec  Forward Delay 15 sec

  Bridge ID  Priority    32778   (priority 32768 sys-id-ext 10)
             Address     1833.9d7b.1380
             Hello Time   2 sec  Max Age 20 sec  Forward Delay 15 sec
             Aging Time  300 sec


Interface          Role Sts Cost      Prio.Nbr Type
------------------ ---- --- --------- -------- --------------------------------
Fa0/12             Desg FWD 19        128.12   P2p Edge
Fa0/18             Desg FWD 19        128.18   Shr
Gi0/1              Desg FWD 4         128.25   P2p
Gi0/2              Root FWD 4         128.26   P2p
```

For exam prep, again note an odd fact about the highlighted output in Example 3-16: The port type details appear in the output when using both STP and RSTP. For example, refer to Example 3-12 again, which shows output from SW3 when using STP (when configured for PVST mode). The Type column also identifies point-to-point and edge interfaces.

Chapter Review

One key to doing well on the exams is to perform repetitive spaced review sessions. Review this chapter's material using either the tools in the book, DVD, or interactive tools for the same material found on the book's companion website. Refer to the "Your Study Plan" element for more details. Table 3-6 outlines the key review elements and where you can find them. To better track your study progress, record when you completed these activities in the second column.

Table 3-6 Chapter Review Tracking

Review Element	Review Date(s)	Resource Used
Review key topics		Book, DVD/website
Review key terms		Book, DVD/website
Repeat DIKTA questions		Book, PCPT
Review memory tables		Book, DVD/website
Review command reference tables		Book (in Chapter Review)
Do labs		Blog

Review All the Key Topics

Table 3-7 Key Topics for Chapter 3

Key Topic Element	Description	Page Number
Figure 3-1	Typical design choice for which switches should be made to be root	71
Figure 3-2	Conceptual view of load-balancing benefits of PVST+	73
Figure 3-3	Shows the format of the system ID extension of the STP priority field	73
Table 3-2	Lists default settings for STP optional configuration settings and related configuration commands	75
List	Two branches of logic in how the **spanning-tree root primary** command picks a new base STP priority	80
List	Steps to manually configure an EtherChannel	84
Table 3-4	Commands to set a switch's STP mode	88
Paragraph	Key statement that seeing an alternate port in **show** command output does not imply that the switch uses RSTP	92

Key Terms You Should Know

Rapid PVST+, PVST+, system ID extension, PAgP, LACP, PortChannel, Channel-group

Command References

Tables 3-8 and 3-9 list configuration and verification commands used in this chapter. As an easy review exercise, cover the left column in a table, read the right column, and try to recall the command without looking. Then repeat the exercise, covering the right column, and try to recall what the command does.

Table 3-8   Chapter 3 Configuration Command Reference

Command	Description
spanning-tree mode {pvst | rapid-pvst | mst}	Global configuration command to set the STP mode.
spanning-tree [vlan *vlan-number*] root primary	Global configuration command that changes this switch to the root switch. The switch's priority is changed to the lower of either 24,576 or 4096 less than the priority of the current root bridge when the command was issued.
spanning-tree [vlan *vlan-number*] root secondary	Global configuration command that sets this switch's STP base priority to 28,672.
spanning-tree [vlan *vlan-id*] {priority *priority*}	Global configuration command that changes the bridge priority of this switch for the specified VLAN.
spanning-tree [vlan *vlan-number*] cost *cost*	Interface subcommand that changes the STP cost to the configured value.
spanning-tree [vlan *vlan-number*] port-priority *priority*	Interface subcommand that changes the STP port priority in that VLAN (0 to 240, in increments of 16).
channel-group *channel-group-number* mode {auto | desirable | active | passive | on}	Interface subcommand that enables EtherChannel on the interface.
spanning-tree portfast	Interface subcommand that enables PortFast on the interface.
spanning-tree bpduguard enable	Interface subcommand that enables BPDU Guard on an interface.
spanning-tree portfast default	Global command that changes the switch default for PortFast on access interfaces from disabled to enabled.
spanning-tree portfast bpduguard default	Global command that changes the switch default for BPDU Guard on access interfaces from disabled to enabled.
no spanning-tree portfast default	Global command that changes the global setting for PortFast to disabled.
no spanning-tree portfast bpduguard default	Global command that changes the global setting for BPDU Guard to disabled.
spanning-tree portfast disable	Interface subcommand that disables PortFast on the interface.
spanning-tree bpduguard disable	Interface subcommand that disables BPDU Guard on an interface.

3

Table 3-9 Chapter 3 EXEC Command Reference

Command	Description
show spanning-tree	Lists details about the state of STP on the switch, including the state of each port.
show spanning-tree interface *interface-id*	Lists STP information only for the specified port.
show spanning-tree vlan *vlan-id*	Lists STP information for the specified VLAN.
show spanning-tree [vlan *vlan-id*] root	Lists information about each VLAN's root or for just the specified VLAN.
show spanning-tree [vlan *vlan-id*] bridge	Lists STP information about the local switch for each VLAN or for just the specified VLAN.
show spanning-tree summary	Lists global STP settings for a switch, including the default PortFast and BPDU Guard settings, and the VLANs for which this switch is the root switch.
debug spanning-tree events	Causes the switch to provide informational messages about changes in the STP topology.
show spanning-tree interface *type number* portfast	Lists a one-line status message about PortFast on the listed interface.
show etherchannel [*channel-group-number*] {brief | detail | port | port-channel | summary}	Lists information about the state of EtherChannels on this switch.

CHAPTER 4

LAN Troubleshooting

This chapter covers the following exam topics:

1.0 LAN Switching Technologies

1.1 Configure, verify, and troubleshoot VLANs (normal/extended range) spanning multiple switches

   1.1.a Access ports (data and voice)

   1.1.b Default VLAN

1.2 Configure, verify, and troubleshoot interswitch connectivity

   1.2.a Add and remove VLANs on a trunk

   1.2.b DTP and VTP (v1&v2)

1.3 Configure, verify, and troubleshoot STP protocols

   1.3.a STP mode (PVST+ and RPVST+)

   1.3.b STP root bridge selection

1.5 Configure, verify, and troubleshoot (Layer 2/Layer 3) EtherChannel

   1.5.a Static

   1.5.b PAGP

   1.5.c LACP

1.7 Describe common access layer threat mitigation techniques

   1.7.c Non-default native VLAN

This chapter discusses the LAN topics discussed in depth in the first three chapters, plus a few prerequisite topics, from a troubleshooting perspective.

Troubleshooting for any networking topic requires a slightly different mindset as compared to thinking about configuration and verification. When thinking about configuration and verification, it helps to think about basic designs, learn how to configure the feature correctly, and learn how to verify the correct configuration is indeed working correctly. However, to learn how to troubleshoot, you need to think about symptoms when the design is incorrect, or if the configuration does not match the good design. What symptoms occur when you make one type of mistake or another? This chapter looks at the common types of mistakes, and works through how to look at the status with **show** commands to find those mistakes.

This chapter breaks the material into four major sections. The first section tackles the largest topic, STP troubleshooting. STP is not likely to fail as a protocol; instead, STP may not be operating as designed, so the task is to find how STP is currently working and discover how to then make the configuration implement the correct design. The second major section then moves on to Layer 2 EtherChannels, which have a variety of small potential problems that can prevent the dynamic formation of an EtherChannel.

The third major section of the chapter focuses on the data plane forwarding of Ethernet frames on LAN switches, in light of VLANs, trunks, STP, and EtherChannels. That same section reviews the Layer 2 forwarding logic of a switch in light of these features. The fourth and final major section then examines VLAN and trunking issues, and how those issues impact switch forwarding.

Note that a few of the subtopics listed within the exam topics at the beginning of this chapter are not discussed in this chapter. This chapter does not discuss VTP beyond its basic features (VTP is discussed in depth in Chapter 5) or Layer 3 EtherChannels (discussed in Chapter 19).

"Do I Know This Already?" Quiz

A few of the troubleshooting chapters in this book not only discuss troubleshooting of specific topics but also serve as a tool to summarize and review some important topics. This chapter is one of those chapters. As a result, it is useful to read these chapters regardless of your current knowledge level. Therefore, this chapter does not include a "Do I Know This Already?" quiz. However, if you feel particularly confident about troubleshooting LAN features covered in this book, feel free to move to the "Chapter Review" section near the end of this chapter to bypass the majority of the chapter.

Foundation Topics

Troubleshooting STP

STP questions tend to intimidate many test takers. STP uses many rules, with tiebreakers in case one rule ends with a tie. Without much experience with STP, people tend to distrust their own answers. Also, even those of us with networking jobs already probably do not troubleshoot STP very often, because STP works well. Often, troubleshooting STP is not about STP failing to do its job but rather about STP working differently than designed, with a different root switch, or different root ports (RP), and so on. Seldom does STP troubleshooting begin with a case in which STP has failed to prevent a loop.

This section reviews the rules for STP, while emphasizing some important troubleshooting points. In particular, this section takes a closer look at the tiebreakers that STP uses to make decisions. It also makes some practical suggestions about how to go about answering exam questions such as "which switch is the root switch?"

Determining the Root Switch

Determining the STP root switch is easy if you know all the switches' BIDs: Just pick the lowest value. If the question lists the priority and MAC address separately, as is common in some **show** command output, pick the switch with the lowest priority, or in the case of a tie, pick the lower MAC address value.

And just to be extra clear, STP does not have nor need a tiebreaker for electing the root switch. The BID uses a switch universal MAC address as the last 48 bits of the BID. These MAC addresses are unique in the universe, so there should never be identical BIDs or the need for a tiebreaker.

For the exam, a question that asks about the root switch might not be so simple as listing a bunch of BIDs and asking you which one is "best." A more likely question is a simulator (sim) question in which you have to do any **show** commands you like or a multiple choice question that lists the output from only one or two commands. Then you have to apply the STP algorithm to figure out the rest.

When faced with an exam question using a simulator, or just the output in an exhibit, use a simple strategy of ruling out switches, as follows:

Step 1. Begin with a list or diagram of switches, and consider all as possible root switches.

Step 2. Rule out any switches that have an RP (**show spanning-tree, show spanning-tree root**), because root switches do not have an RP.

Step 3. Always try **show spanning-tree**, because it identifies the local switch as root directly: "This switch is the root" on the fifth line of output.

Step 4. Always try **show spanning-tree root**, because it identifies the local switch as root indirectly: The RP column is empty if the local switch is the root.

Step 5. When using a sim, rather than try switches randomly, chase the RPs. For example, if starting with SW1, and SW1's G0/1 is an RP, next try the switch on the other end of SW1's G0/1 port.

Step 6. When using a sim, use **show spanning-tree vlan x** on a few switches and record the root switch, RP, and designated port (DP). This strategy can quickly show you most STP facts.

The one step in this list that most people ignore is the idea of ruling out switches that have an RP. Root switches do not have an RP, so any switch with an RP can be ruled out as not being the root switch for that VLAN. Example 4-1 shows two commands on switch SW2 in some LAN that confirms that SW2 has an RP and is therefore not the root switch.

Example 4-1 *Ruling Out Switches as Root Based on Having a Root Port*

```
SW2# show spanning-tree vlan 20 root

                                       Root Hello Max Fwd
Vlan                 Root ID           Cost Time Age Dly Root Port
---------------- -------------------- --------- ----- --- --- ------------
VLAN0020        32788 1833.9d7b.0e80      4    2   20  15  Gi0/2

SW2# show spanning-tree vlan 20

VLAN0020
  Spanning tree enabled protocol ieee
    Root ID    Priority    32788
```

```
            Address       1833.9d7b.0e80
            Cost          4
            Port          26 (GigabitEthernet0/2)
            Hello Time    2 sec   Max Age 20 sec   Forward Delay 15 sec

  Bridge ID Priority      32788  (priority 32768 sys-id-ext 20)
            Address       1833.9d7b.1380
            Hello Time    2 sec   Max Age 20 sec   Forward Delay 15 sec
            Aging Time  15  sec


Interface           Role Sts Cost        Prio.Nbr Type
------------------- ---- --- ---------   -------- --------------------------------
Gi0/1               Desg FWD 4           128.25   P2p
Gi0/2               Root FWD 4           128.26   P2p
```

Both commands identify SW2's G0/2 port as its RP, so if you follow the suggestions, the next switch to try in a sim question would be the switch on the other end of SW2's G0/2 interface.

Determining the Root Port on Nonroot Switches

Determining the RP of a switch when **show** command output is available is relatively easy. As shown recently in Example 4-1, both **show spanning-tree** and **show spanning-tree root** list the root port of the local switch, assuming it is not the root switch. The challenge comes more when an exam question makes you think through how the switches choose the RP based on the root cost of each path to the root switch, with some tiebreakers as necessary.

As a review, each nonroot switch has one, and only one, RP for a VLAN. To choose its RP, a switch listens for incoming Hello bridge protocol data units (BPDU). For each received Hello, the switch adds the cost listed in the hello BPDU to the cost of the incoming interface (the interface on which the Hello was received). That total is the root cost over that path. The lowest root cost wins, and the local switch uses its local port that is part of the least root cost path as its root port.

Although that description has a lot of twists and turns in the words, it is the same concept described for Chapter 2's Figure 2-8.

Most humans can analyze what STP chooses by using a network diagram and a slightly different algorithm. Instead of thinking about Hello messages and so on, approach the question as this: the sum of all outgoing port costs between the nonroot switch and the root. Repeating a familiar example, with a twist, Figure 4-1 shows the calculation of the root cost. Note that SW3's Gi0/1 port has yet again had its cost configured to a different value.

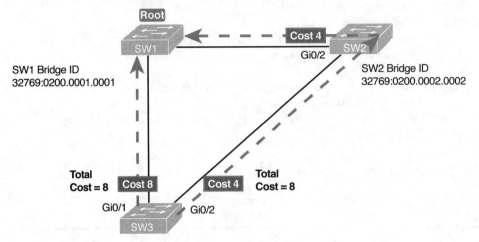

Figure 4-1 *SW3's Root Cost Calculation Ends in a Tie*

STP Tiebreakers When Choosing the Root Port

Figure 4-1 shows the easier process of adding the STP costs of the outgoing interfaces over each from SW3, a nonroot, to SW1, the root. It also shows a tie (on purpose), to talk about the tiebreakers.

When a switch chooses its root port, the first choice is to choose the local port that is part of the least root cost path. When those costs tie, the switch picks the port connected to the neighbor with the lowest BID. This tiebreaker usually breaks the tie, but not always. So, for completeness, the three tiebreakers are, in the order a switch uses them, as follows:

1. Choose based on the lowest neighbor bridge ID.
2. Choose based on the lowest neighbor port priority.
3. Choose based on the lowest neighbor internal port number.

(Note that the switch only considers the root paths that tie when thinking about these tie-breakers.)

For example, Figure 4-1 shows that SW3 is not root and that its two paths to reach the root tie with their root costs of 8. The first tiebreaker is the lowest neighbor's BID. SW1's BID value is lower than SW2's, so SW3 chooses its G0/1 interface as its RP in this case.

The last two RP tiebreakers come into play only when two switches connect to each other with multiple links, as shown in Figure 4-2. In that case, a switch receives Hellos on more than one port from the same neighboring switch, so the BIDs tie.

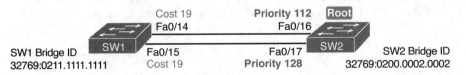

Figure 4-2 *Topology Required for the Last Two Tiebreakers for Root Port*

In this particular example, SW2 becomes root, and SW1 needs to choose its RP. SW1's port costs tie, at 19 each, so SW1's root cost over each path will tie at 19. SW2 sends Hellos over each link to SW1, so SW1 cannot break the tie based on SW1's neighbor BID because both list SW2's BID. So, SW1 has to turn to the other two tiebreakers.

> **NOTE** In real life, most engineers would put these two links into an EtherChannel.

The next tiebreaker is a configurable option: the neighboring switch's port priority on each neighboring switch interface. Cisco switch ports default to a setting of 128, with a range of values from 0 through 255, with lower being better (as usual). In this example, the network engineer has set SW2's F0/16 interface with the **spanning-tree vlan 10 port-priority 112** command. SW1 learns that the neighbor has a port priority of 112 on the top link and 128 on the bottom, so SW1 uses its top (F0/14) interface as the root port.

If the port priority ties, which it often does due to the default values, STP relies on an internal port numbering on the neighbor. Cisco switches assign an internal integer to identify each interface on the switch. The nonroot looks for the neighbor's lowest internal port number (as listed in the Hello messages) and chooses its RP based on the lower number.

Cisco switches use an obvious numbering, with Fa0/1 having the lowest number, then Fa0/2, then Fa0/3, and so on. So, in Figure 4-2, SW2's Fa0/16 would have a lower internal port number than Fa0/17; SW1 would learn those numbers in the Hello; and SW1 would use its Fa0/14 port as its RP.

Suggestions for Attacking Root Port Problems on the Exam

Exam questions that make you think about the RP can be easy if you know where to look and the output of a few key commands is available. However, the more conceptual the question, the more you have to calculate the root cost over each path, correlate that to different **show** commands, and put the ideas together. The following list makes a few suggestions about how to approach STP problems on the exam:

1. If available, look at the **show spanning-tree** and **show spanning-tree root** commands. Both commands list the root port and the root cost (see Example 4-1).

2. The **show spanning-tree** command lists cost in two places: the root cost at the top, in the section about the root switch; and the interface cost, at the bottom, in the per-interface section. Be careful, though; the cost at the bottom is the interface cost, not the root cost!

3. For problems where you have to calculate a switch's root cost:

   a. Memorize the default cost values: 100 for 10 Mbps, 19 for 100 Mbps, 4 for 1 Gbps, and 2 for 10 Gbps.

   b. Look for any evidence of the **spanning-tree cost** configuration command on an interface, because it overrides the default cost. Do not assume default costs are used.

   c. When you know a default cost is used, if you can, check the current actual speed as well. Cisco switches choose STP cost defaults based on the current speed, not the maximum speed.

Determining the Designated Port on Each LAN Segment

Each LAN segment has a single switch that acts as the designated port (DP) on that segment. On segments that connect a switch to a device that does not even use STP—for example, segments connecting a switch to a PC or a router—the switch always wins, because it is the only device sending a Hello onto the link. However, links with two switches require a little more work to discover which should be the DP. By definition:

Step 1.   For switches connected to the same LAN segment, the switch with the lowest cost to reach the root, as advertised in the Hello they send onto the link, becomes the DP on that link.

Step 2.   In case of a tie, among the switches that tied on cost, the switch with the lowest BID becomes the DP.

For example, consider Figure 4-3. This figure notes the root, RPs, and DPs and each switch's least cost to reach the root over its respective RP.

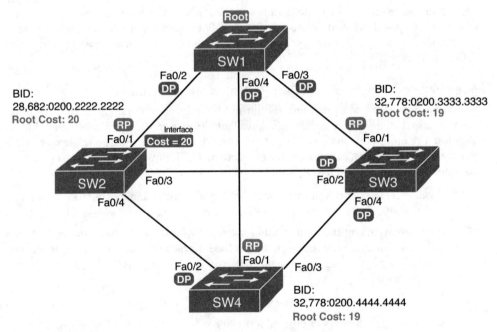

Figure 4-3   *Picking the DPs*

Focus on the segments that connect the nonroot switches for a moment:

> **SW2–SW4 segment:** SW4 wins because of its root cost of 19, compared to SW2's root cost of 20.

> **SW2–SW3 segment:** SW3 wins because of its root cost of 19, compared to SW2's root cost of 20.

> **SW3–SW4 segment:** SW3 and SW4 tie on root cost, both with root cost 19. SW3 wins due to its better (lower) BID value.

Interestingly, SW2 loses and does not become DP on the links to SW3 and SW4 even though SW2 has the better (lower) BID value. The DP tiebreaker does use the lowest BID, but the first DP criteria is the lowest root cost, and SW2's root cost happens to be higher than SW3's and SW4's.

> **NOTE**   A single switch can connect two or more interfaces to the same collision domain, and compete to become DP, if hubs are used. In such cases, two different switch ports on the same switch tie, the DP choice uses the same two final tiebreakers as used with the RP selection: the lowest interface STP priority, and if that ties, the lowest internal interface number.

Suggestions for Attacking Designated Port Problems on the Exam

As with exam questions asking about the RP, exam questions that make you think about the DP can be easy if you know where to look and the output of a few key commands is available. However, the more conceptual the question, the more you have to think about the criteria for choosing the DP: first the root cost of the competing switches, and then the better BID if they tie based on root cost.

The following list gives some tips to keep in mind when digging into a given DP issue. Some of this list repeats the suggestions for finding the RP, but to be complete, this list includes each idea as well.

1. If available, look at the **show spanning-tree** commands, at the list of interfaces at the end of the output. Then, look for the Role column, and look for Desg, to identify any DPs.

2. Identify the root cost of a switch directly by using the **show spanning-tree** command. But be careful! This command lists the cost in two places, and only the mention at the top, in the section about the root, lists the root cost.

3. For problems where you have to calculate a switch's root cost, do the following:

    a. Memorize the default cost values: 100 for 10 Mbps, 19 for 100 Mbps, 4 for 1 Gbps, and 2 for 10 Gbps.

    b. Look for any evidence of the **spanning-tree cost** configuration command on an interface, because it overrides the default cost. Do not assume default costs are used.

    c. When you know a default cost is used, if you can, check the current actual speed as well. Cisco switches choose STP cost defaults based on the current speed, not the maximum speed.

STP Convergence

STP puts each RP and DP into a forwarding state, and ports that are neither RP nor DP into a blocking state. Those states may remain as is for days, weeks, or months. But at some point, some switch or link will fail, a link may change speeds (changing the STP cost), or the STP configuration may change. Any of these events can cause switches to repeat their STP algorithm, which may in turn change their own RP and any ports that are DPs.

When STP converges based on some change, not all the ports have to change their state. For instance, a port that was forwarding, if it still needs to forward, just keeps on forwarding. Ports that were blocking that still need to block keep on blocking. But when a port needs to change state, something has to happen, based on the following rules:

- For interfaces that stay in the same STP state, nothing needs to change.
- For interfaces that need to move from a forwarding state to a blocking state, the switch immediately changes the state to blocking.
- For interfaces that need to move from a blocking state to a forwarding state, the switch first moves the interface to listening state, then learning state, each for the time specified by the forward delay timer (default 15 seconds). Only then is the interface placed into forwarding state.

Because the transition from blocking to forwarding does require some extra steps, you should be ready to respond to conceptual questions about the transition. To be ready, review the section "Reacting to State Changes That Affect the STP Topology" in Chapter 2.

Troubleshooting Layer 2 EtherChannel

EtherChannels can prove particularly challenging to troubleshoot for a couple of reasons. First, you have to be careful to match the correct configuration, and there are many more incorrect configuration combinations than there are correct combinations. Second, many interface settings must match on the physical links, both on the local switch and on the neighboring switch, before a switch will add the physical link to the channel. This second major section in the chapter works through both sets of issues.

Incorrect Options on the channel-group Command

In Chapter 3, the section titled "Configuring EtherChannel" listed the small set of working configuration options on the **channel-group** command. Those rules can be summarized as follows, for a single EtherChannel:

1. On the local switch, all the **channel-group** commands for all the physical interfaces must use the same channel-group number.
2. The channel-group number can be different on the neighboring switches.
3. If using the **on** keyword, you must use it on the corresponding interfaces of both switches.
4. If you use the **desirable** keyword on one switch, the switch uses PAgP; the other switch must use either **desirable** or **auto**.
5. If you use the **active** keyword on one switch, the switch uses LACP; the other switch must use either **active** or **passive**.

These rules summarize the correct configuration options, but the options actually leave many more incorrect choices. The following list shows some incorrect configurations that the switches allow, even though they would result in the EtherChannel not working. The list compares the configuration on one switch to another based on the physical interface configuration. Each lists the reasons why the configuration is incorrect.

- Configuring the **on** keyword on one switch, and **desirable**, **auto**, **active**, or **passive** on the other switch. The **on** keyword does not enable PAgP, and does not enable LACP, and the other options rely on PAgP or LACP.

■ Configuring the **auto** keyword on both switches. Both use PAgP, but both wait on the other switch to begin negotiations.

■ Configuring the **passive** keyword on both switches. Both use LACP, but both wait on the other switch to begin negotiations.

■ Configuring the **active** keyword on one switch and either **desirable** or **auto** on the other switch. The **active** keyword uses LACP, whereas the other keywords use PAgP.

■ Configuring the **desirable** keyword on one switch and either **active** or **passive** on the other switch. The **desirable** keyword uses PAgP, whereas the other keywords use LACP.

Example 4-2 shows an example that matches the last item in the list. In this case, SW1's two ports (F0/14 and F0/15) have been configured with the **desirable** keyword, and SW2's matching F0/16 and F0/17 have been configured with the **active** keyword. The example lists some telling status information about the failure, with notes following the example.

Example 4-2 *Incorrect Configuration Using Mismatched PortChannel Protocols*

```
SW1# show etherchannel summary
Flags:  D - down         P - bundled in port-channel
        I - stand-alone  s - suspended
        H - Hot-standby (LACP only)
        R - Layer3        S - Layer2
        U - in use        f - failed to allocate aggregator

        M - not in use, minimum links not met
        u - unsuitable for bundling
        w - waiting to be aggregated
        d - default port


Number of channel-groups in use: 1
Number of aggregators:           1


Group  Port-channel  Protocol    Ports
------+-------------+-----------+-----------------------------------------------
1       Po1(SD)         PAgP       Fa0/14(I)   Fa0/15(I)

SW1# show interfaces status | include Po|14|15
Port       Name              Status       Vlan      Duplex  Speed Type
Fa0/14                       connected    301       a-full  a-100 10/100BaseTX
Fa0/15                       connected    301       a-full  a-100 10/100BaseTX
Po1                          notconnect   unassigned auto    auto
```

Start at the top, in the legend of the **show etherchannel summary** command. The *D* code letter means that the channel itself is down, with *S* meaning that the channel is a Layer 2 EtherChannel. Code *I* means that the physical interface is working independently from the PortChannel (described as "stand-alone"). Then, the bottom of that command's output highlights PortChannel 1 (Po1) as Layer 2 EtherChannel in a down state (SD), with F0/14 and F0/15 as stand-alone interfaces (I).

Interestingly, because the problem is a configuration mistake, the two physical interfaces still operate independently, as if the PortChannel did not exist. The last command in the example shows that while the PortChannel 1 interface is down, the two physical interfaces are in a connected state.

> **NOTE**   As a suggestion for attacking EtherChannel problems on the exam, rather than memorizing all the incorrect configuration options, concentrate on the list of correct configuration options. Then look for any differences between a given question's configuration as compared to the known correct configurations and work from there.

Configuration Checks Before Adding Interfaces to EtherChannels

Even when the **channel-group** commands have all been configured correctly, other configuration settings can cause problems as well. This last topic examines those configuration settings and their impact.

First, a local switch checks each new physical interface that is configured to be part of an EtherChannel, comparing each new link to the existing links. That new physical interface's settings must be the same as the existing links' settings; otherwise, the switch does not add the new link to the list of approved and working interfaces in the channel. That is, the physical interface remains configured as part of the PortChannel, but it is not used as part of the channel, often being placed into some nonworking state.

The list of items the switch checks includes the following:

- Speed
- Duplex
- Operational access or trunking state (all must be access, or all must be trunks)
- If an access port, the access VLAN
- If a trunk port, the allowed VLAN list (per the **switchport trunk allowed** command)
- If a trunk port, the native VLAN
- STP interface settings

In addition, switches check the settings on the neighboring switch. To do so, the switches either use PAgP or LACP (if already in use), or use Cisco Discovery Protocol (CDP) if using manual configuration. The neighbor must match on all parameters in this list except the STP settings.

As an example, SW1 and SW2 again use two links in one EtherChannel. Before configuring the EtherChannel, SW1's F0/15 was given a different STP port cost than F0/14. Example 4-3 picks up the story just after configuring the correct **channel-group** commands, when the switch is deciding whether to use F0/14 and F0/15 in this EtherChannel.

Example 4-3   *Local Interfaces Fail in EtherChannel Because of Mismatched STP Cost*

```
*Mar  1 23:18:56.132: %PM-4-ERR_DISABLE: channel-misconfig (STP) error detected on
 Po1, putting Fa0/14 in err-disable state
*Mar  1 23:18:56.132: %PM-4-ERR_DISABLE: channel-misconfig (STP) error detected on
 Po1, putting Fa0/15 in err-disable state
```

```
*Mar  1 23:18:56.132: %PM-4-ERR_DISABLE: channel-misconfig (STP) error detected on
  Po1, putting Po1 in err-disable state
*Mar  1 23:18:58.120: %LINK-3-UPDOWN: Interface FastEthernet0/14, changed state to
  down
*Mar  1 23:18:58.137: %LINK-3-UPDOWN: Interface Port-channel1, changed state to down
*Mar  1 23:18:58.137: %LINK-3-UPDOWN: Interface FastEthernet0/15, changed state to
  down

SW1# show etherchannel summary
Flags:  D - down         P - bundled in port-channel
        I - stand-alone s - suspended
        H - Hot-standby (LACP only)
        R - Layer3       S - Layer2
        U - in use       f - failed to allocate aggregator

        M - not in use, minimum links not met
        u - unsuitable for bundling
        w - waiting to be aggregated
        d - default port


Number of channel-groups in use: 1
Number of aggregators:           1


Group  Port-channel  Protocol    Ports
------+-------------+-----------+----------------------------------------------
1      Po1(SD)          -        Fa0/14(D)   Fa0/15(D)
```

The messages at the top of the example specifically state what the switch does when determining whether the interface settings match. In this case, SW1 detects the different STP costs. SW1 does not use F0/14, does not use F0/15, and even places them into an err-disabled state. The switch also puts the PortChannel into err-disabled state. As a result, the PortChannel is not operational, and the physical interfaces are also not operational.

To solve this problem, you must reconfigure the physical interfaces to use the same STP settings. In addition, the PortChannel and physical interfaces must be **shutdown**, and then **no shutdown**, to recover from the err-disabled state. (Note that when a switch applies the **shutdown** and **no shutdown** commands to a PortChannel, it applies those same commands to the physical interfaces, as well; so, just do the **shutdown/no shutdown** on the PortChannel interface.)

Analyzing the Switch Data Plane Forwarding

STP and EtherChannel both have an impact on what a switch's forwarding logic can use. STP limits which interfaces the data plane even considers using by placing some ports in a blocking state (STP) or discarding state (RSTP), which in turn tells the data plane to simply not use that port. EtherChannel gives the data plane new ports to use in the switch's MAC address table—EtherChannels—while telling the data plane to not use the underlying physical interfaces in an EtherChannel in the MAC table.

This (short) third major section of the chapter explores the impact of STP and EtherChannel on data plane logic and a switch's MAC address table.

Predicting STP Impact on MAC Tables

Consider the small LAN shown in Figure 4-4. The LAN has only three switches, with redundancy, just big enough to make the point for this next example. The LAN supports two VLANs, 1 and 2, and the engineer has configured STP such that SW3 blocks on a different port in each of the two VLANs. As a result, VLAN 1 traffic would flow from SW3 to SW1 next, and in VLAN 2, traffic would flow from SW3 to SW2 next instead.

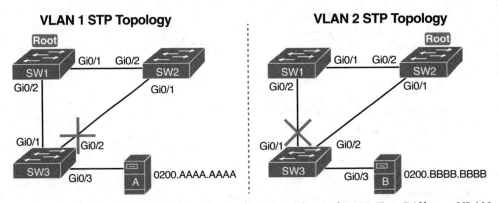

Figure 4-4 *Two Different STP Topologies for Same Physical LAN, Two Different VLANs*

Looking at diagrams like those in Figure 4-4 makes the forwarding path obvious. Although the figure shows the traffic path, that path is determined by switch MAC learning, which is then impacted by the ports on which STP has set a blocking or discarding state.

For example, consider VLAN 1's STP topology in Figure 4-4. Remember, STP blocks on a port on one switch, not on both ends of the link. So, in the case of VLAN 1, SW3's G0/2 port blocks, but SW2's G0/1 does not. Even so, by blocking on a port on one end of the link, that act effectively stops any MAC learning from happening by either device on the link. That is, SW3 learns no MAC addresses on its G0/2 port, and SW2 learns no MAC addresses on its G0/1 port, for these reasons:

- **SW2 learns no MAC addresses on G0/1:** On the blocking (SW3) end of the SW3–SW2 trunk, SW3 will not send frames out that link to SW2, so SW2 will never receive frames from which to learn MAC addresses on SW2's G0/1.

- **SW3 learns no MAC addresses on G0/2:** On the not blocking (SW2) end of the SW3–SW2 trunk, SW2 will flood frames out that port. SW3 receives those frames, but because SW3 blocks, SW3 ignores those received frames and does not learn their MAC addresses.

Given that discussion, can you predict the MAC table entries on each of the three switches for the MAC addresses of servers A and B in Figure 4-4? On switch SW2, the entry for server A, in VLAN 1, should refer to SW2's G0/2 port, pointing to SW1 next, matching the figure. But SW2's entry for server B, in VLAN 2, references SW2's G0/1 port, again matching the figure. Example 4-4 shows the MAC tables on SW1 and SW2 as a confirmation.

Example 4-4   *Examining SW1 and SW2 Dynamic MAC Address Table Entries*

```
SW1# show mac address-table dynamic
          Mac Address Table
-------------------------------------------


Vlan    Mac Address         Type        Ports
----    -----------         --------    -----
  1     0200.AAAA.AAAA      DYNAMIC     Gi0/2
  2     0200.BBBB.BBBB      DYNAMIC     Gi0/1
SW2# show mac address-table dynamic
          Mac Address Table
-------------------------------------------


Vlan    Mac Address         Type        Ports
----    -----------         --------    -----
  1     0200.AAAA.AAAA      DYNAMIC     Gi0/2
  2     0200.BBBB.BBBB      DYNAMIC     Gi0/1
```

Predicting EtherChannel Impact on MAC Tables

Most designs use multiple links between switches, with those links configured to be part of an EtherChannel. What does that do to the MAC forwarding logic? In short, the switch uses the PortChannel interfaces, and not the physical interfaces bundled into the EtherChannel, in the MAC address table. Specifically:

MAC learning: Frames received in a physical interface that is part of a PortChannel are considered to arrive on the PortChannel interface. So, MAC learning adds the PortChannel interface rather than the physical interface to the MAC address table.

MAC forwarding: The forwarding process will find a PortChannel port as an outgoing interface when matching the MAC address table. Then the switch must take the additional step to choose the outgoing physical interface, based on the load-balancing preferences configured for that PortChannel.

For example, consider Figure 4-5, which updates previous Figure 4-4 with two-link PortChannels between each pair of switches. With VLAN 1 blocking again on switch SW3, but this time on SW3's PortChannel3 interface, what MAC table entries would you expect to see in each switch? Similarly, what MAC table entries would you expect to see for VLAN 2, with SW3 blocking on its PortChannel2 interface?

The logic of which entries exist on which ports mirrors the logic with the earlier example surrounding Figure 4-4. In this case, the interfaces just happen to be PortChannel interfaces. Example 4-5 shows the same command from the same two switches as Example 4-4: **show mac address-table dynamic** from both SW1 and SW2. (Note that to save length, the MAC table output shows only the entries for the two servers in Figure 4-5.)

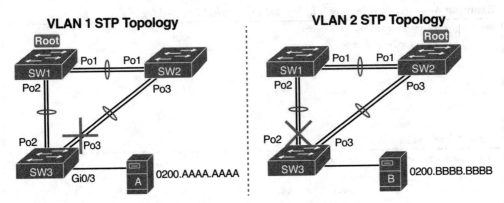

Figure 4-5 *VLAN Topology with PortChannels Between Switches*

Example 4-5 *SW1 and SW2 MAC Tables with PortChannel Ports Listed*

```
SW1# show mac address-table dynamic
          Mac Address Table
-------------------------------------------

Vlan    Mac Address     Type      Ports
----    -----------     --------  -----
 1      0200.AAAA.AAAA  DYNAMIC   Po2
 2      0200.BBBB.BBBB  DYNAMIC   Po1

SW2# show mac address-table dynamic
          Mac Address Table
-------------------------------------------

Vlan    Mac Address     Type      Ports
----    -----------     --------  -----
 1      0200.AAAA.AAAA  DYNAMIC   Po1
 2      0200.BBBB.BBBB  DYNAMIC   Po3
```

Switches use one of many load-balancing options to then choose the physical interface
to use after matching MAC table entries like those shown in Example 4-5. By default,
Cisco Layer 2 switches often default to use a balancing method based on the source MAC
address. In particular, the switch looks at the low-order bits of the source MAC address
(which are on the far right of the MAC address in written form). This approach increases
the chances that the balancing will be spread somewhat evenly based on the source MAC
addresses in use.

Choosing the VLAN of Incoming Frames

To wrap up the analysis of switch data plane forwarding, this section mostly reviews topics already discussed, but it serves to emphasize some important points. The topic is simply
this: How does a switch know which VLAN a frame is a part of as the frame enters a switch?
You have seen all the information needed to answer this question already, but take the time
to review.

First, some interfaces trunk, and in those cases, the frame arrives with a VLAN ID listed
in the incoming trunking header. In other cases, the frame does not arrive with a trunking

header, and the switch must look at local configuration. But because the switch will match both the destination MAC address and the frame VLAN ID when matching the MAC address table, knowing how the switch determines the VLAN ID is important.

The following list reviews and summarizes the key points of how a switch determines the VLAN ID to associate with an incoming frame:

Step 1. If the port is an access port, associate the frame with the configured access VLAN (**switchport access vlan** *vlan_id*).

Step 2. If the port is a voice port, or has both an IP Phone and PC (or other data device) connected to the phone:

    A. Associate the frames from the data device with the configured access VLAN (as configured with the **switchport access vlan** *vlan_id* command).

    B. Associate the frames from the phone with the VLAN ID in the 802.1Q header (as configured with the **switchport voice vlan** *vlan_id* command).

Step 3. If the port is a trunk, determine the frame's tagged VLAN, or if there is no tag, use that incoming interface's native VLAN ID (**switchport trunk native** *vlan_id*).

Troubleshooting VLANs and VLAN Trunks

A switch's data plane forwarding processes depend in part on VLANs and VLAN trunking. Before a switch can forward frames in a particular VLAN, the switch must know about a VLAN and the VLAN must be active. And before a switch can forward a frame over a VLAN trunk, the trunk must currently allow that VLAN to pass over the trunk.

This final major section in this chapter focuses on VLAN and VLAN trunking issues, specifically issues that impact the frame switching process. The issues are as follows:

Step 1. Identify all access interfaces and their assigned access VLANs and reassign into the correct VLANs if incorrect.

Step 2. Determine whether the VLANs both exist (either configured or learned with the VLAN Trunking Protocol [VTP]) and are active on each switch. If not, configure and activate the VLANs to resolve problems as needed.

Step 3. Check the allowed VLAN lists, on the switches on both ends of the trunk, and ensure that the lists of allowed VLANs are the same.

Step 4. Check for incorrect configuration settings that result in one switch operating as a trunk, with the neighboring switch not operating as a trunk.

Step 5. Check the allowed VLANs on each trunk, to make sure that the trunk has not administratively removed a VLAN from being supported on a trunk.

Access VLAN Configuration Incorrect

To ensure that each access interface has been assigned to the correct VLAN, engineers simply need to determine which switch interfaces are access interfaces instead of trunk interfaces, determine the assigned access VLANs on each interface, and compare the information to the documentation. The **show** commands listed in Table 4-1 can be particularly helpful in this process.

Key Topic

Table 4-1   Commands That Can Find Access Ports and VLANs

EXEC Command	Description
show vlan brief show vlan	Lists each VLAN and all interfaces assigned to that VLAN (but does not include operational trunks)
show vlan id *num*	Lists both access and trunk ports in the VLAN
show interfaces *type number* switchport	Identifies the interface's access VLAN and voice VLAN, plus the configured and operational mode (access or trunk)
show mac address-table	Lists MAC table entries, including the associated VLAN

If possible, start this step with the **show vlan** and **show vlan brief** commands, because they list all the known VLANs and the access interfaces assigned to each VLAN. Be aware, however, that these two commands do not list operational trunks. The output does list all other interfaces (those not currently trunking), no matter whether the interface is in a working or nonworking state.

If the **show vlan** and **show interface switchport** commands are not available in a particular exam question, the **show mac address-table** command can also help identify the access VLAN. This command lists the MAC address table, with each entry including a MAC address, interface, and VLAN ID. If the exam question implies that a switch interface connects to a single device, you should only see one MAC table entry that lists that particular access interface; the VLAN ID listed for that same entry identifies the access VLAN. (You cannot make such assumptions for trunking interfaces.)

After you determine the access interfaces and associated VLANs, if the interface is assigned to the wrong VLAN, use the **switchport access vlan** *vlan-id* interface subcommand to assign the correct VLAN ID.

Access VLANs Undefined or Disabled

Switches do not forward frames for VLANs that are (a) not known because the VLAN is not configured or has not been learned with VTP or (b) the VLAN is known, but it is disabled (shut down). This section summarizes the best ways to confirm that a switch knows that a particular VLAN exists, and if it exists, determines the shutdown state of the VLAN.

First, on the issue of whether a VLAN exists on a switch, a VLAN can be defined to a switch in two ways: using the **vlan** *number* global configuration command, or it can be learned from another switch using VTP. Chapter 5, "VLAN Trunking Protocol," discusses VTP and how VTP can be used by a switch to learn about VLANs. For this discussion, consider that the only way for a switch to know about a VLAN is to have a **vlan** command configured on the local switch.

Next, the **show vlan** command always lists all VLANs known to the switch, but the **show running-config** command does not. Switches configured as VTP servers and clients do not list the **vlan** commands in the running-config file nor the startup-config file; on these switches, you must use the **show vlan** command. Switches configured to use VTP transparent mode, or that disable VTP, list the **vlan** configuration commands in the configuration files. (Use the **show vtp status** command to learn the current VTP mode of a switch.)

After you determine that a VLAN does not exist on a switch, the problem might be that the VLAN simply needs to be configured. If so, follow the VLAN configuration process as covered in detail in Chapter 1.

Even for existing VLANs, you must also verify whether the VLAN is active. The **show vlan** command should list one of two VLAN state values, depending on the current state: either *active* or *act/lshut*. The second of these states means that the VLAN is shut down. Shutting down a VLAN disables the VLAN on that switch only, so that *the switch will not forward frames in that VLAN*.

Switch IOS gives you two similar configuration methods with which to disable (**shutdown**) and enable (**no shutdown**) a VLAN. Example 4-6 shows how, first by using the global command [no] **shutdown vlan** *number* and then using the VLAN mode subcommand [no] **shutdown**. The example shows the global commands enabling and disabling VLANs 10 and 20, respectively, and using VLAN subcommands to enable and disable VLANs 30 and 40 (respectively).

Example 4-6 *Enabling and Disabling VLANs on a Switch*

```
SW2# show vlan brief

VLAN Name                             Status    Ports
---- -------------------------------- --------- -------------------------------
1    default                          active    Fa0/1, Fa0/2, Fa0/3, Fa0/4
                                                Fa0/5, Fa0/6, Fa0/7, Fa0/8
                                                Fa0/9, Fa0/10, Fa0/11, Fa0/12
                                                Fa0/14, Fa0/15, Fa0/16, Fa0/17
                                                Fa0/18, Fa0/19, Fa0/20, Fa0/21
                                                Fa0/22, Fa0/23, Fa0/24, Gi0/1
10   VLAN0010                         act/lshut Fa0/13
20   VLAN0020                         active
30   VLAN0030                         act/lshut
40   VLAN0040                         active
SW2# configure terminal
Enter configuration commands, one per line.  End with CNTL/Z.
SW2(config)# no shutdown vlan 10
SW2(config)# shutdown vlan 20
SW2(config)# vlan 30
SW2(config-vlan)# no shutdown
SW2(config-vlan)# vlan 40
SW2(config-vlan)# shutdown
SW2(config-vlan)#
```

Mismatched Trunking Operational States

Trunking can be configured correctly so that both switches forward frames for the same set of VLANs. However, trunks can also be misconfigured, with a couple of different results. In some cases, both switches conclude that their interfaces do not trunk. In other cases, one switch believes that its interface is correctly trunking, while the other switch does not.

The most common incorrect configuration—which results in both switches not trunking—is a configuration that uses the **switchport mode dynamic auto** command on both switches on the link. The word "auto" just makes us all want to think that the link would trunk automatically, but this command is both automatic and passive. As a result, both switches passively wait on the other device on the link to begin negotiations.

With this particular incorrect configuration, the **show interfaces switchport** command on both switches confirms both the administrative state (auto) and the fact that both switches operate as "static access" ports. Example 4-7 highlights those parts of the output from this command.

Example 4-7   *Operational Trunking State*

```
SW2# show interfaces gigabit0/2 switchport
Name: Gi0/2
Switchport: Enabled
Administrative Mode: dynamic auto
Operational Mode: static access
Administrative Trunking Encapsulation: dot1q
Operational Trunking Encapsulation: native
! lines omitted for brevity
```

A different incorrect trunking configuration results in one switch with an operational state of "trunk," while the other switch has an operational state of "static access." When this combination of events happens, the interface works a little. The status on each end will be up/up or connected. Traffic in the native VLAN will actually cross the link successfully. However, traffic in all the rest of the VLANs will not cross the link.

Figure 4-6 shows the incorrect configuration along with which side trunks and which does not. The side that trunks (SW1 in this case) enables trunking always, using the command **switchport mode trunk**. However, this command does not disable Dynamic Trunking Protocol (DTP) negotiations. To cause this particular problem, SW1 also disables DTP negotiation using the **switchport nonegotiate** command. SW2's configuration also helps create the problem, by using a trunking option that relies on DTP. Because SW1 has disabled DTP, SW2's DTP negotiations fail, and SW2 does not trunk.

In this case, SW1 treats its G0/1 interface as a trunk, and SW2 treats its G0/2 interface as an access port (not a trunk). As shown in the figure at Step 1, SW1 could (for example) forward a frame in VLAN 10. However, SW2 would view any frame that arrives with an 802.1Q header as illegal, because SW2 treats its G0/2 port as an access port. So, SW2 discards any 802.1Q frames received on that port.

To deal with the possibility of this problem, always check the trunk's operational state on both sides of the trunk. The best commands to check trunking-related facts are **show interfaces trunk** and **show interfaces switchport**.

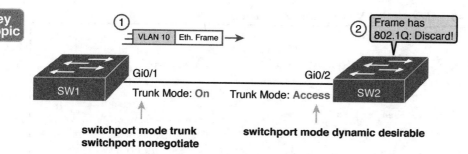

Figure 4-6 *Mismatched Trunking Operational States*

> **NOTE**   Frankly, in real life, just avoid this kind of configuration. However, the switches do not prevent you from making these types of mistakes, so you need to be ready. Note that Chapter 1's Table 1-3 summarizes the list of options on the **switchport trunk** command, which combinations work, and which ones to completely avoid (like the combination shown here in Figure 4-6.)

Mismatched Supported VLAN List on Trunks

VLAN trunks on Cisco switches can forward traffic for all defined and active VLANs. However, a particular trunk may not forward traffic for a defined and active VLAN for a variety of other reasons. You should know how to identify which VLANs a particular trunk port currently supports, and the reasons why the switch might not be forwarding frames for a VLAN on that trunk port.

The first category in this step can be easily done using the **show interfaces trunk** command, which only lists information about currently operational trunks. The best place to begin with this command is the last section of output, which lists the VLANs whose traffic will be forwarded over the trunk. Any VLANs that make it to this final list of VLANs in the command output meet the following criteria:

- The VLAN exists and is active on the local switch (as seen in the **show vlan** command).
- The VLAN has not been removed from the *allowed VLAN list* on the trunk (as configured with the **switchport trunk allowed vlan** interface subcommand).
- The VLAN has not been VTP-pruned from the trunk. (This is a VTP feature, discussed in Chapter 5, which this section will now otherwise ignore, deferring discussion until Chapter 5. It is only listed here because the **show** command output mentions it.)
- The trunk is in an STP forwarding state in that VLAN (as also seen in the **show spanning-tree vlan** *vlan-id* command).

Example 4-8 shows a sample of the command output from the **show interfaces trunk** command, with the final section of the command output shaded. In this case, the trunk only forwards traffic in VLANs 1 and 4.

Example 4-8   *Allowed VLAN List and List of Active VLANs*

```
SW1# show interfaces trunk

Port         Mode         Encapsulation  Status        Native vlan
Gi0/1        desirable    802.1q         trunking      1


Port         Vlans allowed on trunk
Gi0/1        1-2,4-4094


Port         Vlans allowed and active in management domain
Gi0/1        1,4


Port         Vlans in spanning tree forwarding state and not pruned
Gi0/1        1,4
```

The absence of a VLAN in this last part of the command's output does not necessarily mean that a problem has occurred. In fact, a VLAN might be legitimately excluded from a trunk for any of the reasons in the list just before Example 4-8. However, for a given exam question, it can be useful to know why traffic for a VLAN will not be forwarded over a trunk, and the details inside the output identify the specific reasons.

The output of the **show interfaces trunk** command creates three separate lists of VLANs, each under a separate heading. These three lists show a progression of reasons why a VLAN is not forwarded over a trunk. Table 4-2 summarizes the headings that precede each list and the reasons why a switch chooses to include or not include a VLAN in each list.

Key Topic

Table 4-2   VLAN Lists in the **show interfaces trunk** Command

List Position	Heading	Reasons
First	VLANs allowed	VLANs 1–4094, minus those removed by the **switchport trunk allowed** command
Second	VLANs allowed and active...	The first list, minus VLANs not defined to the local switch (that is, there is not a **vlan** global configuration command or the switch has not learned of the VLAN with VTP), and also minus those VLANs in shutdown mode
Third	VLANs in spanning tree...	The second list, minus VLANs in an STP blocking state for that interface, and minus VLANs VTP pruned from that trunk

Mismatched Native VLAN on a Trunk

Closing with a brief mention of one other trunking topic, you should also check a trunk's native VLAN configuration at this step. Unfortunately, it is possible to set the native VLAN ID to different VLANs on either end of the trunk, using the **switchport trunk native vlan** *vlan-id* command. If the native VLANs differ according to the two neighboring switches, the switches will accidentally cause frames to leave one VLAN and enter another.

For example, if switch SW1 sends a frame using native VLAN 1 on an 802.1Q trunk, SW1 does not add a VLAN header, as is normal for the native VLAN. When switch SW2 receives the frame, noticing that no 802.1Q header exists, SW2 assumes that the frame is part of

SW2's configured native VLAN. If SW2 has been configured to think VLAN 2 is the native VLAN on that trunk, SW2 will try to forward the received frame into VLAN 2.

Chapter Review

One key to doing well on the exams is to perform repetitive spaced review sessions. Review this chapter's material using either the tools in the book, DVD, or interactive tools for the same material found on the book's companion website. Refer to the "Your Study Plan" element for more details. Table 4-3 outlines the key review elements and where you can find them. To better track your study progress, record when you completed these activities in the second column.

Table 4-3   Chapter Review Tracking

Review Element	Review Date(s)	Resource Used
Review key topics		Book, DVD/website
Review memory tables		Book, DVD/website

Review All the Key Topics

Table 4-4   Key Topics for Chapter 4

Key Topic Element	Description	Page Number
List	Strategy for finding the root switch for exam questions	100
List	Strategy for finding the root port on nonroot switches for exam questions	103
List	Strategy for finding the designated port for exam questions	104
List	Suggestions when examining questions as a designated port	105
List	Summary of STP convergence actions	106
List	List of configuration combinations that cause a Layer 2 EtherChannel to fail	106
List	Interface settings that must match with other interfaces on the same switch for an interface to be included in an EtherChannel	108
List	Switch logic used to determine the VLAN used for an incoming frame	113
List	Potential issues to examine for VLANs and VLAN trunks	113
Table 4-1	Commands that identify access VLANs assigned to ports	114
Figure 4-6	How to poorly configure switches to reach a mismatched trunk operational state on the two ends of the trunk	117
Table 4-2	VLAN lists in the **show interfaces trunk** command	118

Command References

Although this chapter does show several examples, all the commands were introduced earlier in Chapters 1 and 3, so this section does not include any command reference tables. Refer to those chapters for command reference tables.

CHAPTER 5

VLAN Trunking Protocol

This chapter covers the following exam topics:

1.0 LAN Switching Technologies

1.2 Configure, verify, and troubleshoot interswitch connectivity

1.2.a DTP and VTP (v1&v2)

Engineers sometimes have a love/hate relationship with VLAN Trunking Protocol (VTP). VTP serves a useful purpose, distributing the configuration of the [no] vlan *vlan-id* command among switches. As a result, the engineer configures the **vlan** command on one switch, and all the rest of the switches are automatically configured with that same command.

Unfortunately, the automated update powers of VTP can also be dangerous. For example, an engineer could delete a VLAN on one switch, not realizing that the command actually deleted the VLAN on all switches. And deleting a VLAN impacts a switch's forwarding logic: Switches do not forward frames for VLANs that are not defined to the switch.

This chapter discusses VTP, from concept through troubleshooting. The first major section discusses VTP concepts, while the second section shows how to configure and verify VTP. The third section walks through troubleshooting, with some discussion of the risks that cause some engineers to just not use VTP. (In fact, the entirety of the ICND1 Cert Guide's discussion of VLAN configuration assumes VTP uses the VTP transparent mode, which effectively disables VTP from learning and advertising VLAN configuration.)

As for exam topics, note that the Cisco exam topics that mention VTP also mention DTP. Chapter 1, "Implementing Ethernet Virtual LANs," discussed how Dynamic Trunking Protocol (DTP) is used to negotiate VLAN trunking. This chapter does not discuss DTP, leaving that topic for Chapter 1.

"Do I Know This Already?" Quiz

Take the quiz (either here, or use the PCPT software) if you want to use the score to help you decide how much time to spend on this chapter. The answers are at the bottom of the page following the quiz, and the explanations are in DVD Appendix C and in the PCPT software.

Table 5-1 "Do I Know This Already?" Foundation Topics Section-to-Question Mapping

Foundation Topics Section	Questions
VLAN Trunking Protocol (VTP) Concepts	1, 2
VTP Configuration and Verification	3, 4
VTP Troubleshooting	5, 6

1. Which of the following VTP modes allow VLANs to be configured on a switch? (Choose two answers.)

   a. Client

   b. Server

   c. Transparent

   d. Dynamic

2. An engineer plans to connect three switches (SW1, SW2, and SW3) in a lab. Before connecting the switches, he starts by configuring all three switches as VTP servers, with matching VTP domain name and password. He then configures some VLANs on each switch so that switch SW3 has a revision number of 10, switch SW2 has a revision number of 6, and switch SW1 has a revision number of 8. Only then does the engineer connect the switches with trunks: first SW1 to SW2, then SW2 to SW3, and then SW3 to SW1. Switch SW1 is elected the STP root switch in VLAN 1. Which answer most accurately states which VLAN configuration database is used, and why?

   a. All use switch SW1's database because it has the highest revision number between the first two connected switches.

   b. All use switch SW1's database because VTP uses the same election logic as STP.

   c. All use SW3's database because SW3 has the highest revision number.

   d. All use SW2's database because SW2 has the lowest revision number.

3. An engineer compares the output of the **show vtp status** command on two neighboring switches. One switch, SW1, acts as VTP server, while the other, SW2, acts as a VTP client. What items in the command output confirm that synchronization has completed? (Choose two answers.)

   a. Both list the same "last updater" IP address and timestamp.

   b. Both list the neighbor's MAC address and the word "synchronized."

   c. SW2 (the client) lists the phrase "synchronized with server."

   d. Both list the same configuration revision number.

4. Switches SW1, SW2, SW3, and SW4 are configured as VTP server, client, transparent, and off, respectively, all using VTP version 1. A junior engineer has been told to try to configure the following two commands on each switch directly from the CLI: **vlan 200** and **vlan 2000**. Which answers correctly state which commands will be rejected, on which switch? (Choose two answers.)

   a. **vlan 2000** will be rejected on SW1 (VTP server).

   b. **vlan 200** will be rejected on SW2 (VTP client).

   c. **vlan 200** will be rejected on SW3 (VTP transparent).

   d. **vlan 200** will be rejected on SW1 (VTP server).

5. Two neighboring LAN switches are connected with an operational 802.1Q trunk. Switch SW1 has been configured with the **vtp mode client, vtp domain fred,** and **vtp version 2** commands. SW1 has no other VTP configuration commands configured. Which answer lists a possible reason why switch SW2, on the other end of the trunk, is not synchronizing its VLAN database with switch SW1? (Choose two answers.)

   a. SW2 has a **vtp version 1** command configured.

   b. SW2 has a **vtp password G0BeeZ** command configured.

   c. SW2 has a **vtp domain Fred** command configured.

   d. SW2 has a **vtp mode client** command configured.

6. Switches SW1 and SW2 connect through an operational trunk. The engineer wants to use VTP to communicate VLAN configuration changes. The engineer configures a new VLAN on SW1, VLAN 44, but SW2 does not learn about the new VLAN. Which of the following configuration settings on SW1 and SW2 would be a potential root cause why SW2 does not learn about VLAN 44? (Choose two answers.)

   a. VTP domain names of larry and LARRY, respectively

   b. VTP passwords of bob and BOB, respectively

   c. VTP pruning enabled and disabled, respectively

   d. VTP modes of server and client, respectively

Foundation Topics

VLAN Trunking Protocol (VTP) Concepts

The Cisco-proprietary *VLAN Trunking Protocol* (VTP) provides a means by which Cisco switches can exchange VLAN configuration information. In particular, VTP advertises about the existence of each VLAN based on its VLAN ID and the VLAN name.

This first major section of the chapter discusses the major features of VTP in concept, in preparation for the VTP implementation (second section) and VTP troubleshooting (third section).

Basic VTP Operation

Think for a moment about what has to happen in a small network of four switches when you need to add two new hosts, and to put those hosts in a new VLAN that did not exist before. Figure 5-1 shows some of the main configuration concepts.

First, remember that for a switch to be able to forward frames in a VLAN, that VLAN must be defined on that switch. In this case, Step 1 shows the independent configuration of VLAN 10 on the four switches: the two distribution switches and the two access layer switches. With the rules discussed in Chapter 1 (which assumed VTP transparent mode, by the way), all four switches need to be configured with the **vlan 10** command.

Step 2 shows the additional step to configure each access port to be in VLAN 10 as per the design. That is, in addition to creating the VLAN, the individual ports need to be added to the VLAN, as shown for servers A and B with the **switchport access vlan 10** command.

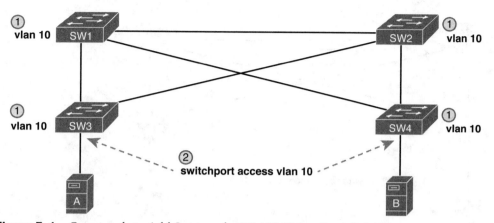

Figure 5-1 *Commands to Add Support for VLAN 10 in a Sample LAN*

VTP, when used for its intended purpose, would allow the engineer to create the VLAN (the **vlan 10** command) on one switch only, with VTP then automatically updating the configuration of the other switches.

VTP defines a Layer 2 messaging protocol that the switches can use to exchange VLAN configuration information. When a switch changes its VLAN configuration—including the **vlan** *vlan-id* command—VTP causes all the switches to synchronize their VLAN configuration to include the same VLAN IDs and VLAN names. The process is somewhat like a routing protocol, with each switch sending periodic VTP messages. However, routing protocols advertise information about the IP network, whereas VTP advertises VLAN configuration.

Figure 5-2 shows one example of how VTP works in the same scenario used for Figure 5-1. Figure 5-2 starts with the need for a new VLAN 10, and two servers to be added to that VLAN. At Step 1, the network engineer creates the VLAN with the **vlan 10** command on switch SW1. SW1 then uses VTP to advertise that new VLAN configuration to the other switches, as shown at Step 2; note that the other three switches do not need to be configured with the **vlan 10** command. At Step 3, the network engineer still must configure the access ports with the **switchport access vlan 10** command, because VTP does not advertise the interface and access VLAN configuration.

VTP advertises the **vlan** *vlan-id* command, the **name** *vlan-name* subcommand, and several VTP-specific commands. Of particular importance, note that VTP does not advertise the command that associates an access port with a particular VLAN (**switchport access vlan** *vlan-id*), so those still need to be configured on the individual switches.

Also, for historical reasons, VTP limits VTP servers and clients to use VLANs 1 through 1005. This range of VLAN IDs is known as standard range VLANs, and includes VLAN 1, which is the default access VLAN and the default native VLAN on each port. The standard range ends with four reserved VLANs, 1002–1005, which are reserved for historical reasons. VTP servers can then configure any of the other standard range VLAN IDs (2–1001) and advertise those.

Answers to the "Do I Know This Already?" quiz:

1 B, C **2** C **3** A, D **4** A, B **5** B, C **6** A, B

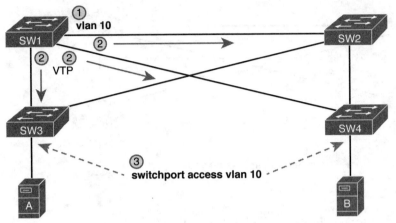

Figure 5-2 *Distributing the vlan 10 Command with VTP*

Note that switches in VTP transparent mode, or a switch that has disabled VTP, can configure and use extended range VLANs, which in IOS switches extends the VLAN ID range up to 4094.

Synchronizing the VTP Database

To use VTP to announce and/or learn VLAN configuration information, a switch must use either VTP *server mode* or *client mode*. The third VTP mode, *transparent mode*, tells a switch to not learn VLAN configuration and to not advertise VLAN configuration, effectively making a VTP transparent mode switch act as if it were not there, at least for the purposes of VTP. This next topic works through the mechanisms used by switches acting as either VTP server or client.

VTP servers allow the network engineer to create VLANs (and other related commands) from the CLI, whereas VTP clients do not allow the network engineer to create VLANs. You have seen many instances of the **vlan** *vlan-id* command at this point in your study, the command that creates a new VLAN in a switch. VTP servers are allowed to continue to use this command to create VLANs, but switches placed in VTP client mode reject the **vlan** *vlan-id* command, because VTP client switches cannot create VLANs.

With that main difference in mind, VTP servers allow the creation of VLANs (and related configuration) via the usual commands. The server then advertises that configuration information over VLAN trunks. The overall flow works something like this:

1. For each trunk, send VTP messages, and listen to receive them.

2. Check my local VTP parameters versus the VTP parameters announced in the VTP messages received on a trunk.

3. If the VTP parameters match, attempt to synchronize the VLAN configuration databases between the two switches.

NOTE The name *VLAN Trunking Protocol* is based on the fact that this protocol works specifically over VLAN trunks, as noted in item 1 in this list.

Done correctly, VTP causes all the switches in the same administrative *VTP domain*—the set of switches with the same domain name and password—to converge to have the exact same configuration of VLAN information. Over time, each time the VLAN configuration is changed on any VTP server, all other switches in the VTP automatically learn of those configuration changes.

VTP does not think of the VLAN configuration as lots of small pieces of information, but rather as one *VLAN configuration database*. The configuration database has a configuration revision number which is incremented by 1 each time a server changes the VLAN configuration. The VTP synchronization process hinges on the idea of making sure each switch uses the VLAN configuration database that has the best (highest) revision number.

Figure 5-3 begins an example that demonstrates how the VLAN configuration database revision numbers work. At the beginning of the example, all the switches have converged to use the VLAN database that uses revision number 3. The example then shows:

1. The network engineer defines a new VLAN with the **vlan 10** command on switch SW1.

2. SW1, a VTP server, changes the VTP revision number for its own VLAN configuration database from 3 to 4.

3. SW1 sends VTP messages over the VLAN trunk to SW2 to begin the process of telling SW2 about the new VTP revision number for the VLAN configuration database.

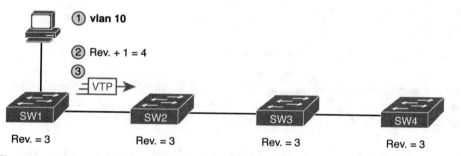
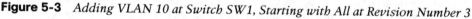

Figure 5-3 *Adding VLAN 10 at Switch SW1, Starting with All at Revision Number 3*

At this point, only switch SW1 has the best VLAN configuration database with the highest revision number (4). Figure 5-4 shows the next few steps, picking up the process where Figure 5-3 stopped. Upon receiving the VTP messages from SW1, as shown in Step 3 of Figure 5-3, at Step 4 in Figure 5-4, SW2 starts using that new LAN database. Step 5 emphasizes the fact that as a result, SW2 now knows about VLAN 10. SW2 then sends VTP messages over the trunk to the next switch, SW3 (Step 6).

With VTP working correctly on all four switches, all the switches will eventually use the exact same configuration, with VTP revision number 4, as advertised with VTP.

Figure 5-4 also shows a great example of one key similarity between VTP clients and servers: both will learn and update their VLAN database from VTP messages received from another switch. Note that the process shown in Figures 5-3 and 5-4 works the same whether switches SW2, SW3, and SW4 are VTP clients or servers, in any combination. In this scenario, the only switch that must be a VTP server is switch SW1, where the **vlan 10** command was configured; a VTP client would have rejected the command.

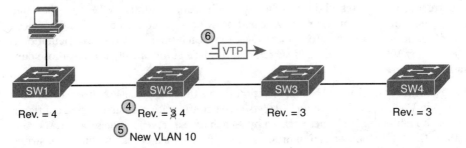

Figure 5-4 *Adding VLAN 10 at Switch SW1, Starting with All at Revision Number 3*

For instance, in Figure 5-5, imagine switches SW2 and SW4 were VTP clients, but switch SW3 was a VTP server. With the same scenario discussed in Figures 5-3 and 5-4, the new VLAN configuration database is propagated just as described in those earlier figures, with SW2 (client), SW3 (server), and SW4 (client) all learning of and using the new database with revision number 4.

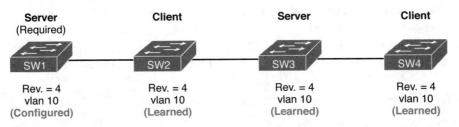

Figure 5-5 *Stable State, VTP Revision Number 4, All Switches Know VLAN 10*

NOTE The complete process by which a server changes the VLAN configuration and all VTP switches learn the new configuration, resulting in all switches knowing the same VLAN IDs and name, is called *VTP synchronization.*

After VTP synchronization is completed, VTP servers and clients also send periodic VTP messages every 5 minutes. If nothing changes, the messages keep listing the same VLAN database revision number, and no changes occur. Then when the configuration changes in one of the VTP servers, that switch increments its VTP revision number by 1, and its next VTP messages announce a new VTP revision number, so that the entire VTP domain (clients and servers) synchronize to use the new VLAN database.

Requirements for VTP to Work Between Two Switches

When a VTP client or server connects to another VTP client or server switch, Cisco IOS requires that the following three facts be true before the two switches will process VTP messages received from the neighboring switch:

- The link between the switches must be operating as a VLAN trunk (ISL or 802.1Q).
- The two switches' case-sensitive VTP domain name must match.
- If configured on at least one of the switches, both switches must have configured the same case-sensitive VTP password.

The VTP domain name provides a design tool by which engineers can create multiple groups of VTP switches, called *VTP domains*, whose VLAN configurations are autonomous. To do so, the engineer can configure one set of switches in one VTP domain and another set in another VTP domain. Switches in one domain will ignore VTP messages from switches in the other domain, and vice versa.

The VTP password mechanism provides a means by which a switch can prevent malicious attackers from forcing a switch to change its VLAN configuration. The password itself is never transmitted in clear text.

VTP Version 1 Versus Version 2

Cisco supports three VTP versions, aptly numbered versions 1, 2, and 3. Interestingly, the current ICND2/CCNA exam topics mention versions 1 and 2 specifically, but omit version 3. Version 3 adds more capabilities and features beyond versions 1 and 2, and as a result is a little more complex. Versions 1 and 2 are relatively similar, with version 2 updating version 1 to provide some specific feature updates. For example, version 2 added support for a type of LAN called Token Ring, but Token Ring is no longer even found in Cisco's product line.

For the purposes of configuring, verifying, and troubleshooting VTP today, versions 1 and 2 have no meaningful difference. For instance, two switches can be configured as VTP servers, one using VTP version 1 and one using VTP version 2, and they do exchange VTP messages and learn from each other.

The one difference between VTP versions 1 and 2 that might matter has to do with the behavior of a VTP transparent mode switch. By design, VTP transparent mode is meant to allow a switch to be configured to not synchronize with other switches, but to also pass the VTP messages to VTP servers and clients. That is, the transparent mode switch is transparent to the intended purpose of VTP: servers and clients synchronizing. One of the requirements for transparent mode switches to forward the VTP messages sent by servers and clients is that the VTP versions must match.

VTP Pruning

By default, Cisco IOS on LAN switches allows frames in all configured VLANs to be passed over a trunk. Switches flood broadcasts (and unknown destination unicasts) in each active VLAN out these trunks.

However, using VTP can cause too much flooded traffic to flow into parts of the network. VTP advertises any new VLAN configured in a VTP server to the other server and client switches in the VTP domain. However, when it comes to frame forwarding, there may not be any need to flood frames to all switches, because some switches may not connect to devices in a particular VLAN. For example, in a campus LAN with 100 switches, all the devices in VLAN 50 may exist on only 3 to 4 switches. However, if VTP advertises VLAN 50 to all the switches, a broadcast in VLAN 50 could be flooded to all 100 switches.

One solution to manage the flow of broadcasts is to manually configure the allowed VLAN lists on the various VLAN trunks. However, doing so requires a manual configuration process. A better option might be to allow VTP to dynamically determine which switches do not have access ports in each VLAN, and prune (remove) those VLANs from the appropriate trunks to limit flooding. *VTP pruning* simply means that the appropriate switch trunk interfaces do not flood frames in that VLAN.

> **NOTE**   The section "Mismatched Supported VLAN List on Trunks" in Chapter 4, "LAN Troubleshooting," discusses the various reasons why a switch trunk does not forward frames in a VLAN, including the allowed VLAN list. That section also briefly references VTP pruning.

Figure 5-6 shows an example of VTP pruning, showing a design that makes the VTP pruning feature more obvious. In this figure, two VLANs are used: 10 and 20. However, only switch SW1 has access ports in VLAN 10, and only switches SW2 and SW3 have access ports in VLAN 20. With this design, a frame in VLAN 20 does not need to be flooded to the left to switch SW1, and a frame in VLAN 10 does not need to be flooded to the right to switches SW2 and SW3.

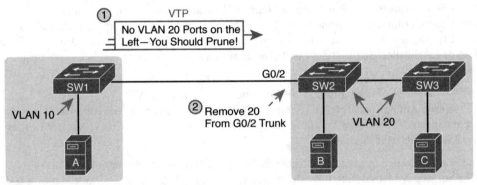

Figure 5-6   *VTP Pruning Example*

Figure 5-6 shows two steps that result in VTP pruning VLAN 10 from SW2's G0/2 trunk:

Step 1.   SW1 knows about VLAN 20 from VTP, but switch SW1 does not have access ports in VLAN 20. So SW1 announces to SW2 that SW1 would like to prune VLAN 20, so that SW1 no longer receives data frames in VLAN 20.

Step 2.   VTP on switch SW2 prunes VLAN 20 from its G0/2 trunk. As a result, SW2 will no longer flood VLAN 20 frames out trunk G0/2 to SW1.

VTP pruning increases the available bandwidth by restricting flooded traffic. VTP pruning is one of the two most compelling reasons to use VTP, with the other reason being to make VLAN configuration easier and more consistent.

Summary of VTP Features

Table 5-2 offers a comparative overview of the three VTP modes.

Table 5-2   VTP Features

Function	Server	Client	Transparent
Only sends VTP messages out ISL or 802.1Q trunks	Yes	Yes	Yes
Allows CLI configuration of VLANs	Yes	No	Yes
Can use normal range VLANs (1–1005)	Yes	Yes	Yes
Can use extended range VLANs (1006–4095)	No	No	Yes

Function	Server	Client	Transparent
Synchronizes its own config database when receiving VTP messages with a higher revision number	Yes	Yes	No
Creates and sends periodic VTP updates every 5 minutes	Yes	Yes	No
Does not process received VTP updates, but does forward received VTP updates out other trunks	No	No	Yes

VTP Configuration and Verification

VTP configuration requires only a few simple steps, but VTP has the power to cause significant problems, either by accidental poor configuration choices or by malicious attacks. This second major section of the chapter focuses on configuring VTP correctly and verifying its operation. The third major section then looks at troubleshooting VTP, which includes being careful to avoid harmful scenarios.

Using VTP: Configuring Servers and Clients

Before configuring VTP, the network engineer needs to make some choices. In particular, assuming that the engineer wants to make use of VTP's features, the engineer needs to decide which switches will be in the same VTP domain, meaning that these switches will learn VLAN configuration information from each other. The VTP domain name must be chosen, along with an optional but recommended VTP password. (Both the domain name and password are case sensitive.) The engineer must also choose which switches will be servers (usually at least two for redundancy) and which will be clients.

After the planning steps are completed, the following steps can be used to configure VTP:

Step 1. Use the **vtp mode** {**server** | **client**} command in global configuration mode to enable VTP on the switch as either a server or client.

Step 2. On both clients and servers, use the **vtp domain** *domain-name* command in global configuration mode to configure the case-sensitive VTP domain name.

Step 3. (Optional) On both clients and servers, use the **vtp password** *password-value* command in global configuration mode to configure the case-sensitive password.

Step 4. (Optional) On servers, use the **vtp pruning** global configuration command to make the domain-wide VTP pruning choice.

Step 5. (Optional) On both clients and servers, use the **vtp version** {**1** | **2**} command in global configuration mode to tell the local switch whether to use VTP version 1 or 2.

As a network to use in the upcoming configuration examples, Figure 5-7 shows a LAN with the current VTP settings on each switch. At the beginning of the example in this section, both switches have all default VTP configuration: VTP server mode with a null domain name and password. With these default settings, even if the link between two switches is a trunk, VTP would still not work.

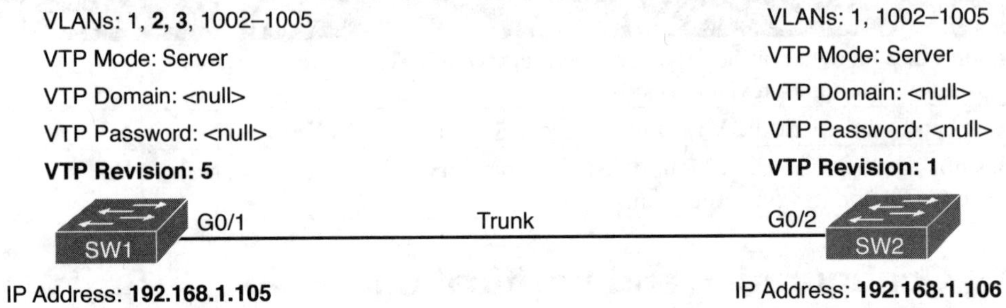

VLANs: 1, **2, 3**, 1002–1005
VTP Mode: Server
VTP Domain: <null>
VTP Password: <null>
VTP Revision: 5

VLANs: 1, 1002–1005
VTP Mode: Server
VTP Domain: <null>
VTP Password: <null>
VTP Revision: 1

G0/1   Trunk   G0/2

SW1   SW2

IP Address: **192.168.1.105**   IP Address: **192.168.1.106**

Figure 5-7   *Beginning Settings for VTP Example*

Per the figure, the switches do have some related configuration beyond the VTP configuration. SW1 has been configured to know about two additional VLANs (VLAN 2 and 3). Additionally, both switches have been configured with IP addresses—a fact that will be useful in upcoming **show** command output.

To move toward using VTP in these switches, and synchronizing their VLAN configuration databases, Figure 5-8 repeats Figure 5-7, but with some new configuration settings in bold text. Note that both switches now use the same VTP domain name and password. Switch SW1 remains at the default setting of being a VTP server, while switch SW2 is now configured to be a VTP client. Now, with matching VTP domain and password, and with a trunk between the two switches, the two switches will use VTP successfully.

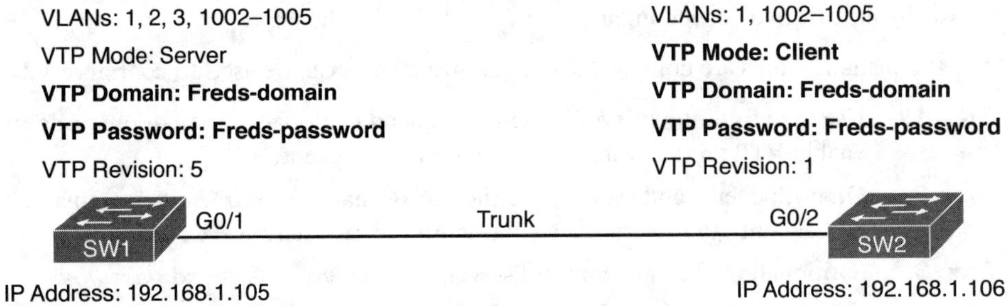

VLANs: 1, 2, 3, 1002–1005
VTP Mode: Server
VTP Domain: Freds-domain
VTP Password: Freds-password
VTP Revision: 5

VLANs: 1, 1002–1005
VTP Mode: Client
VTP Domain: Freds-domain
VTP Password: Freds-password
VTP Revision: 1

G0/1   Trunk   G0/2

SW1   SW2

IP Address: 192.168.1.105   IP Address: 192.168.1.106

Figure 5-8   *New VTP Configuration Settings Planned for Example 5-1*

Example 5-1 shows the configuration shown in Figure 5-8 as added to each switch.

Example 5-1   *Basic VTP Client and Server Configuration*

```
! IOS generates at least one informational message after each VTP command listed
! below. Those lines are not added as text by the author; they are generated by IOS.
SW1# configure terminal
Enter configuration commands, one per line.  End with CNTL/Z.
SW1(config)# vtp mode server
Setting device to VTP SERVER mode
SW1(config)# vtp domain Freds-domain
Changing VTP domain name from NULL to Freds-domain
SW1(config)# vtp password Freds-password
Setting device VLAN database password to Freds-password
```

```
SW1(config)# vtp pruning
Pruning switched on
SW1(config)# ^z
! Switching to SW2 now
SW2# configure terminal
Enter configuration commands, one per line.  End with CNTL/Z.
SW2(config)# vtp mode client
Setting device to VTP CLIENT mode.
SW2(config)# vtp domain Freds-domain
Domain name already set to Freds-domain.
SW2(config)# vtp password Freds-password
Setting device VLAN database password to Freds-password
SW2(config)# ^z
```

Make sure and take the time to work through the configuration commands on both switches. The domain name and password, case-sensitive, match. Also, SW2, as client, does not need the **vtp pruning** command, because the VTP server dictates to the domain whether or not pruning is used throughout the domain. (Note that all VTP servers should be configured with the same VTP pruning setting.)

Verifying Switches Synchronized Databases

Configuring VTP takes only a little work, as shown in Example 5-1. Most of the interesting activity with VTP happens in what it learns dynamically, and how VTP accomplishes that learning. For instance, Figure 5-7 showed the switch SW1 had revision number 5 for its VLAN configuration database, while SW2's was revision 1. Once configured as shown in Example 5-1, the following logic happened through an exchange of VTP messages between SW1 and SW2:

1. SW1 and SW2 exchanged VTP messages.

2. SW2 realized that its own revision number (1) was lower (worse) than SW1's revision number 5.

3. SW2 received a copy of SW1's VLAN database and updated SW2's own VLAN (and related) configuration.

4. SW2's revision number also updated to revision number 5.

To confirm that two neighboring switches synchronized their VLAN database, use the **show vtp status** command. Example 5-2 shows this command first on switch SW2, which had a lower revision number (1) at the start of the example, so it should have synchronized its VLAN configuration database with switch SW1. The example shows the output of the **show vtp status** command first on switch SW2, and then from switch SW1.

Example 5-2 *Demonstrating the Switch SW2's VLAN Database Updated to Revision 5*

```
! First, the output from SW2, the VTP Client, formerly revision 1, now revision 5
SW2# show vtp status
VTP Version capable             : 1 to 3
VTP version running             : 1
VTP Domain Name                 : Freds-domain
```

```
VTP Pruning Mode                  : Enabled
VTP Traps Generation              : Disabled
Device ID                         : bcc4.938b.a180
Configuration last modified by 192.168.1.105 at 2-21-16 11:45:33
Local updater ID is 192.168.1.105 on interface Vl1 (lowest numbered VLAN interface
   found)


Feature VLAN:
--------------
VTP Operating Mode                : Client
Maximum VLANs supported locally   : 1005
Number of existing VLANs          : 7
Configuration Revision            : 5
MD5 digest                        : 0xF3 0x07 0x44 0xA4 0xDE 0x82 0xCD 0xB0
                                    0x9E 0x8F 0x0B 0xD1 0xFD 0xE7 0xE7 0xB3
```

```
! Switching to SW1 now; all highlighted items match switch SW2
! Back on SW1, the output below confirms the same revision number as SW2, meaning
! that the two switches have synchronized their VLAN databases.
SW1# show vtp status
VTP Version capable               : 1 to 3
VTP version running               : 1
VTP Domain Name                   : Freds-domain
VTP Pruning Mode                  : Enabled
VTP Traps Generation              : Disabled
Device ID                         : bcc4.938b.e500
Configuration last modified by 192.168.1.105 at 2-21-16 11:45:33
Local updater ID is 192.168.1.105 on interface Vl1 (lowest numbered VLAN interface
   found)


Feature VLAN:
--------------
VTP Operating Mode                : Server
Maximum VLANs supported locally   : 1005
Number of existing VLANs          : 7
Configuration Revision            : 5
MD5 digest                        : 0xF3 0x07 0x44 0xA4 0xDE 0x82 0xCD 0xB0
                                    0x9E 0x8F 0x0B 0xD1 0xFD 0xE7 0xE7 0xB3
SW1# show vtp password
VTP Password: Freds-password
```

The example shows two facts that confirm that the two switches have synchronized to use the same VLAN configuration database due to VTP:

■ The highlighted line that states "Configuration last modified by…" lists the same IP address and timestamp. Both SW1 and SW2 list the exact same switch, with address 192.168.1.105. (Per Figure 5-8, 192.168.1.105 is switch SW1.) Also, note the text on SW1 lists "Local updater ID is 192.168.1.105…" which means that the local switch (SW1) is 192.168.1.105. The fact that both switches list the same IP address and timestamp confirm that they use the same database, in this case as supplied by 192.168.1.105, which is switch SW1.

■ The "Configuration Revision" of 5 listed by both switches also confirms that they both use the same VLAN database.

> **NOTE** Using NTP along with VTP can be useful so that the timestamps in the **show vtp status** command on neighboring switches have the same time listed.

Beyond those two key facts, the **show vtp status** command shows several key pieces of information that must match on two neighboring switches before they can succeed at exchanging their database. As highlighted only in switch SW1's output in Example 5-2:

■ Both use the same domain name (Freds-domain).

■ Both have the same MD5 digest.

Note that while it is a good practice to set the switches to all use either version 1 or version 2, mismatched versions do not prevent VTP servers and clients from exchanging VTP configuration databases.

The last item in the list, about the MD5 hash, needs a little further explanation. VTP on a switch takes the domain name and the VTP password and applies MD5 to create an MD5 digest, as displayed in the **show vtp status** command's output. If either the domain name or password does not match, the MD5 digests will not match, and the two switches will not exchange VLAN configuration with VTP. (Note that the end of Example 5-2 lists a sample **show vtp password** command, which lists the clear text VTP password.)

Any command that lists the VLANs known to a switch can also confirm that VTP worked. Once a VTP client or server learns a new VLAN configuration database from a neighbor, its list of VLANs should be identical to that of the neighbor.

For instance, with the configuration suggested in Figure 5-8, as shown in Example 5-1, VTP server SW1 began with VLANs 1, 2, 3 and default VLANs 1002–1005, while switch SW2 only knew about the default VLANs: 1 and 1002–1005. Example 5-3 lists the output of **show vlan brief** on switch SW2, confirming that it now also knows about VLANs 2 and 3. Note that switch SW2 also learned the names of the VLANs, not just the VLAN IDs.

Example 5-3 *Switch SW2 Now Knows About VLANs 2 and 3*

```
SW2# show vlan brief

VLAN Name                             Status    Ports
---- -------------------------------- --------- -------------------------------
1    default                          active    Fa0/1, Fa0/2, Fa0/3, Fa0/4
                                                Fa0/5, Fa0/6, Fa0/7, Fa0/8
                                                Fa0/9, Fa0/10, Fa0/11, Fa0/12
                                                Fa0/13, Fa0/14, Fa0/15, Fa0/16
                                                Fa0/17, Fa0/18, Fa0/19, Fa0/20
                                                Fa0/21, Fa0/22, Fa0/23, Fa0/24
                                                Gi0/1
```

2	Freds-vlan	active
3	VLAN0003	active
1002	fddi-default	act/unsup
1003	token-ring-default	act/unsup
1004	fddinet-default	act/unsup
1005	trnet-default	act/unsup

Storing the VTP and Related Configuration

Interestingly, even though VTP synchronizes VLAN and VTP configuration, you cannot just issue a **show running-config** command to discover if a switch has synchronized its VLAN configuration database. VTP does not place the configuration commands into the running-config or startup-config file of the VTP server or client. Instead, VTP server and client mode switches store the **vtp** configuration commands, and some VLAN configuration commands, in the vlan.dat file in flash. To verify these configuration commands and their settings, use the **show vtp status** and **show vlan** commands.

Figure 5-9 shows an example. It shows three key VTP commands (**vtp mode, vtp domain,** and **vtp password**), plus a **vlan 10** command that creates VLAN 10. It also shows the **switchport access vlan 10** interface subcommand for contrast. Of these, on a VTP server or client, only the **switchport access vlan 10** command would be part of the running-config or startup-config file.

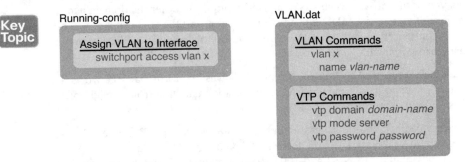

Figure 5-9 *Where VTP Stores Configuration: VTP Client and Server*

There is no equivalent of a **show running-config** command to display the contents of the vlan.dat file. Instead, you have to use various **show vtp** and **show vlan** commands to view information about VLANs and VTP. For reference, Table 5-3 lists the VLAN-related configuration commands, the location in which a VTP server or client stores the commands, and how to view the settings for the commands.

Table 5-3 Where VTP Clients and Servers Store VLAN-Related Configuration

Configuration Command	Where Stored	How to View
vtp domain	vlan.dat	show vtp status
vtp mode	vlan.dat	show vtp status
vtp password	vlan.dat	show vtp password
vtp pruning	vlan.dat	show vtp status

Configuration Command	Where Stored	How to View
vlan *vlan-id*	vlan.dat	**show vlan [brief]**
name *vlan-name*	vlan.dat	**show vlan [brief]**
[no] shutdown vlan *vlan-id*	running-config	**show vlan [brief]**
switchport access vlan *vlan-id*	running-config	**show running-config, show interfaces switchport**
switchport voice vlan *vlan-id*	running-config	**show running-config, show interfaces switchport**

Note that switches using VTP transparent mode (**vtp mode transparent**), or with VTP disabled (**vtp mode off**), store all the commands listed in Table 5-3 in the running-config and startup-config files.

An interesting side effect of how VTP stores configuration is that when you use a VTP client or server switch in a lab, and you want to remove all the configuration to start with a clean switch with all default VTP and VLAN configuration, you must issue more than the **erase startup-config** command. If you only erase the startup-config and reload the switch, the switch remembers all VLAN config and VTP configuration that is instead stored in the vlan.dat file in flash. To remove those configuration details before reloading a switch, you would have to delete the vlan.dat file in flash with a command such as **delete flash:vlan.dat**.

Avoiding Using VTP

For most of the history of VTP, one option existed for avoiding using VTP: using VTP transparent mode. That is, each switch technically had to use VTP in one of three modes (server, client, or transparent).

In transparent mode, a switch never updates its VLAN database based on a received VTP message, and never causes other switches to update their databases based on the transparent mode switch's VLAN database. The only VTP action performed by the switch is to forward VTP messages received on one trunk out all the other trunks, which allows other VTP clients and servers to work correctly.

Configuring VTP transparent mode is simple: Just issue the **vtp mode transparent** command in global configuration mode.

Cisco eventually added an option to disable VTP altogether, with the **vtp mode off** global command. Note that one key difference exists versus using transparent mode: switches using **vtp mode off** do not forward VTP messages. In short, if you want a switch to ignore VTP, but forward VTP message from other switches, use transparent mode. If you want a switch to ignore VTP, including not forwarding any VTP messages, disable VTP.

VTP Troubleshooting

Troubleshooting VTP can be both simple and tricky at the same time. To troubleshoot issues in which VTP fails to cause synchronization to happen, you just have to work a short checklist, find the configuration or status issue, and solve the problem. From the complete opposite direction, VTP can cause synchronization, but with bad results, using the wrong switch's VLAN database. This last section looks at the straightforward case of troubleshooting why VTP does not synchronize, as well as a few cases as to the dangers of VTP synchronizing with unfortunate results.

Determining Why VTP Is Not Synchronizing

VTP troubleshooting can be broken down to a pair of neighboring switches at a time. For any VTP domain, with a number of switches, find any two neighboring switches. Then troubleshoot to discover whether those two switches fail to meet the requirements to allow VTP to synchronize, and then fix the problem. Then work through every pair until VTP works throughout the VTP domain.

The troubleshooting process must begin with some basics. You need to learn about the LAN topology to then find and choose some neighboring switches to investigate. Then you need to determine whether the neighbors have synchronized or not, mainly by checking their list of VLANs, or by looking at information in the **show vtp status** command. For any pair of neighboring switches that have not synchronized, work through the list of configuration settings until the problem is fixed.

The following list details a good process to find VTP configuration problems, organized into a list for easier study and reference.

Step 1. Confirm the switch names, topology (including which interfaces connect which switches), and switch VTP modes.

Step 2. Identify sets of two neighboring switches that should be either VTP clients or servers whose VLAN databases differ with the **show vlan** command.

Step 3. On each pair of two neighboring switches whose databases differ, verify the following:

A. Because VTP messages only flow over trunks, at least one operational trunk should exist between the two switches (use the **show interfaces trunk**, **show interfaces switchport**, or **show cdp neighbors** command).

B. The switches must have the same (case-sensitive) VTP domain name (**show vtp status**).

C. If configured, the switches must have the same (case-sensitive) VTP password (**show vtp password**).

D. The MD5 digest should be the same, as evidence that both the domain name and any configured passwords are the same on both switches (**show vtp status**).

E. While VTP pruning should be enabled or disabled on all servers in the same domain, having two servers configured with opposite pruning settings does not prevent the synchronization process.

Step 4. For each pair of switches identified in Step 3, solve the problem by either troubleshooting the trunking problem or reconfiguring a switch to correctly match the domain name or password.

VTP also has a few related commands that you might think would prevent synchronization, but they do not. Remember these facts about VTP for items that do not cause a problem for VTP synchronization:

■ The VTP pruning setting does not have to match on neighboring switches (even though in a real VTP network you would likely use the same setting on all switches).

- The VTP version does not have to match between two switches that are any combination of VTP server and client for neighboring switches to synchronize.

- When deciding if VTP has synchronized, note that the administrative status of a VLAN (per the **shutdown vlan** *vlan-id* global configuration command and the **shutdown** command in VLAN configuration mode) is not communicated by VTP. So two neighboring switches can know about the same VLAN, with that VLAN shut down on one switch and active on the other.

Common Rejections When Configuring VTP

VTP clients cannot configure VLANs at all, to either add them, delete them, or name them. VTP servers (when using VTP versions 1 and 2) have the restriction of working with standard number VLANs only. This next short topic looks at the error messages shown when you attempt to add those VLANs in spite of what the chapter claims is allowed, just so you know what the error message looks like.

Example 5-4 shows some output on a switch (SW3) that is a VTP client. Focus first on the rejection of the **vlan 200** command. The result is clear and obvious: The user issued the **vlan 200** command, and IOS lists an error message about the switch being a VTP client.

Example 5-4   *Attempting* **vlan** *Commands on VTP Clients and Servers*

```
SW3# configure terminal
Enter configuration commands, one per line.  End with CNTL/Z.
SW3(config)# vlan 200
VTP VLAN configuration not allowed when device is in CLIENT mode.
SW3(config)# vlan 2000
SW3(config-vlan)# exit
% Failed to create VLANs 2000
Extended VLAN(s) not allowed in current VTP mode.
%Failed to commit extended VLAN(s) changes.
SW3(config)#
```

The second half of the example shows a couple of oddities. First, the **vlan 200** command is immediately rejected. Second, the **vlan 2000** command is also rejected, but not immediately. IOS, in an odd twist of logic, does not actually try and add the configuration of extended mode VLANs until the user exits VLAN configuration mode. Once the **exit** command was issued, IOS issued the three highlighted error messages—all messages that confirm in some way that the VLAN 2000 was not created.

Note that on a VTP server, the **vlan 200** command would have been accepted but the **vlan 2000** command would have been rejected, with the same process as shown in the example.

Problems When Adding Switches to a Network

VTP can be running just fine for months, and then one day, the help desk receives a rash of calls describing cases in which large groups of users can no longer use the network. After further examination, it appears that most every VLAN in the campus has been deleted. The switches still have many interfaces with **switchport access vlan** commands that refer to the now-deleted VLANs. None of the devices on those now-deleted VLANs work, because Cisco switches do not forward frames for nonexistent VLANs.

VTP can cause the kind of pervasive LAN problems described in that previous paragraph, so you have to be careful when using VTP. This kind of problem can occur when a new switch is connected to an existing network. Whether this problem happens by accident or as a denial of service (DoS) attack, the root cause is this:

> When two neighboring switches first connect with a trunk, and they also meet all the requirements to synchronize with VTP, the switch with the lower revision number accepts the VLAN database from the neighbor with the higher revision number.

Note in particular that the preceding statement says nothing about which switch is the server or client, or which switch is the older production switch versus the newly added switch. That is, no matter whether a server has the higher revision number or the client does, the two switches converge to both use the VLAN database with the higher revision number. There is no logic about which switch might be client or server, or which switch is the new switch in the network and which is the old established switch.

This VTP behavior of using the higher revision number when connecting new switches has some pretty powerful implications. For instance, consider the following scenario: Someone is studying for the CCNA R&S exam, using the equipment in the small lab room at work. The lab has a couple of LAN switches isolated from the production network—that is, the switches have no links even cabled to the production network. But because the engineer knows the VTP domain name and password used in production, when configuring in the lab, the engineer uses that same VTP domain name and password. That causes no problems (yet), because the lab switches do not even connect to the production network. (In real life, use a different VTP domain name and password in your lab gear!)

This same engineer continues CCNA studying and testing in the lab, making lots of changes to the VLAN configuration. Each change kicks the VLAN configuration database revision number up by 1. Eventually, the lab switches have a high VTP configuration revision number, so high that the number is higher than that of the production switches. But the lab is still isolated, so there is still no problem.

Do you see the danger? All that has to happen now is for someone to connect a link from a lab switch to a production switch and make it trunk. For instance, imagine now that some other engineer decides to do some testing in the lab and does not think to check the VTP status on the lab switches versus the production switches. That second engineer walks into the lab and connects the lab switches to the production network. The link negotiates trunking...VTP synchronizes between a lab switch and a production switch...and those two switches discover that the lab switch's configuration database has a higher revision number. At this point, VTP is now happily doing its job, synchronizing the VLAN configuration database, but unfortunately, VTP is distributing the lab's VLAN configuration, deleting production VLANs.

In real life, you have several ways to help reduce the chance of such problems when installing a new switch to an existing VTP domain. In particular, before connecting a new switch to an existing VTP domain, reset the new switch's VTP revision number to 0 by either of the following methods:

- Configure the new switch for VTP transparent mode and then back to VTP client or server mode.

- Erase the new switch's vlan.dat file in flash and reload the switch. (The vlan.dat file contains the switch's VLAN database, including the revision number.)

Besides the suggestion of resetting the VLAN database revision number before installing a new switch, a couple of other good VTP conventions, called best practices, can help avoid some of the pitfalls of VTP:

Key Topic

■ If you do not intend to use VTP, configure each switch to use transparent mode (**vtp mode transparent**) or off mode (**vtp mode off**).

■ If using VTP server or client mode, always use a VTP password. That way a switch that uses default settings (server mode, with no password set) will not accidentally overwrite the production VLAN database if connected to the production network with a trunk.

■ In a lab, if using VTP, always use a different domain name and password than you use in production.

■ Disable trunking with the **switchport mode access** and **switchport nonegotiate** commands on all interfaces except known trunks, preventing VTP attacks by preventing the dynamic establishment of trunks.

It is possible that an attacker might attempt a DoS attack using VTP. Preventing the negotiation of trunking on most ports can greatly reduce the attacker's opportunities to even try. Also, with a VTP password set on all switches, even if the attacker manages to get trunking working between the attacker's switch and a production switch, the attacker would then have to know the password to do any harm. And of course, either using transparent mode or disabling VTP completely removes the risk.

Chapter Review

One key to doing well on the exams is to perform repetitive spaced review sessions. Review this chapter's material using either the tools in the book, DVD, or interactive tools for the same material found on the book's companion website. Refer to the "Your Study Plan" element for more details. Table 5-4 outlines the key review elements and where you can find them. To better track your study progress, record when you completed these activities in the second column.

Table 5-4   Chapter Review Tracking

Review Element	Review Date(s)	Resource Used
Review key topics		Book, DVD/website
Review key terms		Book, DVD/website
Answer DIKTA questions		Book, PCPT
Do labs		Blog
Review memory tables		DVD/website
Review config checklists		Book, DVD/website
Review command tables		Book

Review All the Key Topics

Table 5-5   Key Topics for Chapter 5

Key Topic Element	Description	Page Number
List	Requirements for VTP to work between two switches	126
Table 5-2	VTP features summary	128
Figure 5-9	Description of where VTP client and server switches store configuration	134
Table 5-3	List of commands and where a VTP client and server store those commands	134
List	Troubleshooting checklist for VTP	136
List	VTP best practices	139

Key Terms You Should Know

VLAN configuration database, configuration revision number, vlan.dat, VTP, VTP client mode, VTP pruning, VTP server mode, VTP transparent mode, VTP synchronization

Command References

Tables 5-6 and 5-7 list configuration and verification commands used in this chapter, respectively. As an easy review exercise, cover the left column in a table, read the right column, and try to recall the command without looking. Then repeat the exercise, covering the right column, and try to recall what the command does.

Table 5-6   Chapter 5 Configuration Command Reference

Command	Description
vtp domain *domain-name*	Global config command that defines the VTP domain name
vtp password *password*	Global config command that defines the VTP password
vtp mode {server | client | transparent | off}	Global config command that defines the VTP mode
vtp version {1 | 2}	Global config command that sets the VTP version
[no] vtp pruning	Global config command that tells the VTP server to tell all switches to use VTP pruning
[no] shutdown vlan *vlan-id*	Global configuration command that administratively disables (or enables, if using the **no** option) the listed VLAN on the local switch only; not propagated by VTP

Table 5-7   Chapter 5 EXEC Command Reference

Command	Description
show vlan [**brief** | **id** *vlan-id* | **name** *vlan-name* | **summary**]	Lists information about the VLAN
show vlan [*vlan*]	Displays VLAN information
show vtp status	Lists VTP configuration and status information
show vtp password	Lists the current VTP password on the local switch

5

CHAPTER 6

Miscellaneous LAN Topics

This chapter covers the following exam topics:

1.0 LAN Switching Technologies

1.6 Describe the benefits of switch stacking and chassis aggregation

1.7 Describe common access layer threat mitigation techniques

1.7.a 802.1x

1.7.b DHCP snooping

5.0 Infrastructure Maintenance

5.4 Describe device management using AAA with TACACS+ and RADIUS

Between this book and the ICND1 100-105 Cert Guide, 14 chapters have been devoted to topics specific to LANs. This chapter is the last of those chapters. This chapter completes the LAN-specific discussion with a few small topics that just do not fit neatly in the other chapters.

The chapter begins with three security topics. The first section addresses IEEE 802.1x, which defines a mechanism to secure user access to a LAN by requiring the user to supply a username and password before a switch allows the device's sent frames into the LAN. This tool helps secure the network against attackers gaining access to the network. The second section, "AAA Authentication," discusses network device security, protecting router and switch CLI access by requiring username/password login with an external authentication server. The third section, "DHCP Snooping," explores how switches can prevent security attacks that take advantage of DHCP messages and functions. By watching DHCP messages, noticing when they are used in abnormal ways not normally done with DHCP, DHCP can prevent attacks by simply filtering certain DHCP messages.

The final of the four major sections in this chapter looks at two similar design tools that make multiple switches act like one switch: switch stacking and chassis aggregation. Switch stacking allows a set of similar switches that sit near to each other (in the same wiring closet, typically in the same part of the same rack) to be cabled together and then act like a single switch. Using a switch stack greatly reduces the amount of work to manage the switch, and it reduces the overhead of control and management protocols used in the network. Switch chassis aggregation has many of the same benefits, but is supported more often as a distribution or core switch feature, with switch stacking as a more typical access layer switch feature.

All four sections of this chapter have a matching exam topic that uses the verb "describe," so this chapter touches on the basic descriptions of a tool, rather than deep configuration. A few of the topics will show some configuration as a means to describe the topic, but the chapter is meant to help you come away with an understanding of the fundamentals, rather than an ability to configure the features.

"Do I Know This Already?" Quiz

Take the quiz (either here, or use the PCPT software) if you want to use the score to help you decide how much time to spend on this chapter. The answers are at the bottom of the page following the quiz, and the explanations are in DVD Appendix C and in the PCPT software.

Table 6-1 "Do I Know This Already?" Foundation Topics Section-to-Question Mapping

Foundation Topics Section	Questions
Securing Access with IEEE 802.1x	1
AAA Authentication	2
DHCP Snooping	3–4
Switch Stacking and Chassis Aggregation	5

1. With IEEE 802.1x, which role does a LAN switch typically play?

    a. Authentication server

    b. Supplicant

    c. Translator

    d. Authenticator

2. Which of the following answers is true of TACACS+ but not true of RADIUS?

    a. The protocol encrypts the password for transmission.

    b. Uses UDP as the transport protocol.

    c. Supports ability to authorize different users to use different subsets of CLI commands.

    d. Defined by an RFC.

3. An engineer hears about DHCP snooping and decides to implement it. The network includes devices that act primarily as Layer 2 switches, multilayer switches (that is, they perform both Layer 2 and Layer 3 switching), and routers. Which of the following are the devices on which DHCP snooping could be implemented? (Choose two answers.)

    a. Layer 2 switches

    b. Routers

    c. Multilayer switches

    d. A LAN hub

4. Layer 2 switch SW2 connects to several devices: a Layer 2 switch (SW1), a router, a DHCP server, and three PCs (PC1, PC2, and PC3). All PCs are expected to use DHCP to lease their IP addresses. A network engineer implements DHCP snooping on switch SW2. Unknown to the engineer, a malicious attacker is using PC3. Which of the following is the most likely DHCP snooping trust state configuration on SW2 for the ports connected to the listed devices? (Choose two answers.)

    a. The port connected to the router is untrusted.

    b. The port connected to switch SW1 is trusted.

    c. The port connected to PC1 is untrusted.

    d. The port connected to PC3 is trusted.

5. A network engineer takes four 2960-X switches and creates a switch stack using either FlexStack or FlexStack-Plus stacking from Cisco. Now consider data plane functions, such as frame forwarding; control plane functions, such as STP and VTP; and management plane functions, such as Telnet and SSH support. Once the stack is cabled and working, which of the following is true about how the stack of four switches works?

    a. The stack acts as one switch for data plane functions, and separate switches for control and management plane functions.

    b. The stack acts as one switch for data plane and control plane functions, and separate switches for management plane functions.

    c. The stack acts as one switch for data plane, control plane, and management plane functions.

    d. The stack does not act as one switch for data, control, or management plane functions, instead providing backup uplinks if all of one switch's uplinks fail.

Foundation Topics

Securing Access with IEEE 802.1x

In some enterprise LANs, the LAN is built with cables run to each desk, in every cubicle and every office. When you move to a new space, all you have to do is connect a short patch cable from your PC to the RJ-45 socket on the wall and you are connected to the network. Once booted, your PC can send packets anywhere in the network. Security? That happens mostly at the devices you try to access, for instance, when you log in to a server.

That previous paragraph is true of how many networks work. That attitude views the network as an open highway between the endpoints in the network, and the network is there to create connectivity, with high availability, and to make it easy to connect your device. Those goals are worthy goals. However, making the LAN accessible to anyone, so that anyone can attempt to connect to servers in the network, allows attackers to connect and then try and break in to the security that protects the server. That approach may be too insecure. For instance, any attacker who could gain physical access could plug in his laptop and start running tools to try to exploit all those servers attached to the internal network.

Today, many companies secure access to the network. Sure, they begin by creating basic connectivity: cabling the LAN and connecting cables to all the desks at all the cubicles and offices. All those ports physically work. But a user cannot just plug in her PC and start working; she must go through a security process before the LAN switch will allow the user to send any other messages in the network.

Switches can use IEEE standard 802.1x to secure access to LAN ports. To set up the feature, the LAN switches must be configured to enable 802.1x. Additionally, the IT staff must implement an authentication, authorization, and accounting (AAA) server. The AAA server (commonly pronounced "triple A" server) will keep the usernames and passwords, and when the user supplies that information, it is the AAA server that determines if what the user typed was correct or not.

Once implemented, the LAN switch acts as an 802.1x *authenticator*, as shown in Figure 6-1. As an 802.1x authenticator, a switch can be configured to enable some ports for 802.1x, most likely the access ports connected to end users. Enabling a port for 802.1x defines that when the port first comes up, the switch filters all incoming traffic (other than 802.1x traffic). 802.1x must first authenticate the user that uses that device.

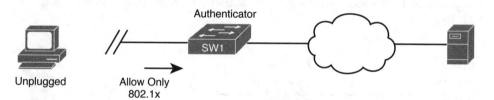

Figure 6-1   *Switch as 802.1x Authenticator, with AAA Server, and PC Not Yet Connected*

Note that the switch usually configures access ports that connect to end users with 802.1x, but does not enable 802.1x on ports connected to IT-controlled devices, such as trunk ports, or ports connected in parts of the network that are physically more secure.

The 802.1x authentication process works like the flow in Figure 6-2. Once the PC connects and the port comes up, the switch uses 802.1x messages to ask the PC to supply a username/password. The PC user must then supply that information. For that process to work, the end-user device must be using an 802.1x client called a *supplicant*; many OSs include an 802.1x supplicant, so it may just be seen as a part of the OS settings.

At Steps 3 and 4 in Figure 6-2, the switch authenticates the user, to find out if the username and password combination is legitimate. The switch, acting as 802.1x authenticator, asks the AAA server if the supplied username and password combo is correct, with the AAA server answering back. If the username and password were correct, then the switch authorizes the port. Once authorized, the switch no longer filters incoming messages on that port. If the username/password check shows that the username/password was incorrect, or the process fails for any reason, the port remains in an unauthorized state. The user can continue to retry the attempt.

Answers to the "Do I Know This Already?" quiz:

1 D **2** C **3** A, C **4** B, C **5** C

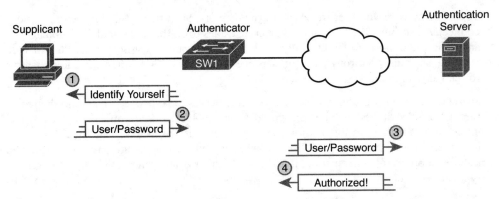

Figure 6-2 *Generic 802.1x Authentication Flows*

Figure 6-3 rounds out this topic by showing an example of one key protocol used by 802.1x: Extensible Authentication Protocol (EAP). The switch (the authenticator) uses RADIUS between itself and the AAA server, which itself uses IP and UDP. However, 802.1x, an Ethernet protocol, does not use IP or UDP. But 802.1x wants to exchange some authentication information all the way to the RADIUS AAA server. The solution is to use EAP, as shown in Figure 6-3.

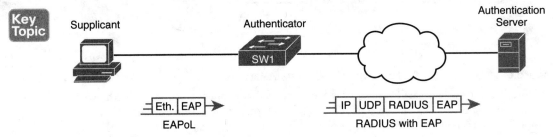

Figure 6-3 *EAP and Radius Protocol Flows with 802.1x*

As shown in the figure, the EAP message flows from the supplicant to the authentication server, just in different types of messages. The flow from the supplicant (the end-user device) to the switch transports the EAP message directly in an Ethernet frame with an encapsulation called *EAP over LAN* (EAPoL). The flow from the authenticator (switch) to the authentication server flows in an IP packet. In fact, it looks much like a normal message used by the RADIUS protocol (RFC 2865). The RADIUS protocol works as a UDP application, with an IP and UDP header, as shown in the figure.

Now that you have heard some of the details and terminology, this list summarizes the entire process:

■ A AAA server must be configured with usernames and passwords.

■ Each LAN switch must be enabled for 802.1x, to enable the switch as an authenticator, to configure the IP address of the AAA server, and to enable 802.1x on the required ports.

■ Users must know a username/password combination that exists on the AAA server, or they will not be able to access the network from any device.

AAA Authentication

The ICND1 100-105 Cert Guide discusses many details about device management, in particular how to secure network devices. However, all those device security methods shown in the ICND1 half of the CCNA R&S exam topics use locally configured information to secure the login to the networking device.

Using locally configured usernames and passwords configured on the switch causes some administrative headaches. For instance, every switch and router needs the configuration for all users who might need to log in to the devices. Good security practices tell us to change our passwords regularly, but logging in to hundreds of devices to change passwords is a large task, so often, the passwords remain unchanged for long periods.

A better option would be to use an external AAA server. The AAA server centralizes and secures all the username/password pairs. The switches and routers still need some local security configuration to refer to the AAA server, but the username/password exist centrally, greatly reducing the administrative effort, and increasing the chance that passwords are changed regularly and are more secure. It is also easier to track which users logged in to which devices and when, and to revoke access as people leave their current job.

This short section discusses the basics of how networking devices can use a AAA server.

AAA Login Process

First, to use AAA, the site would need to install and configure a AAA server, such as the Cisco Access Control Server (ACS). Cisco ACS is AAA software that you can install on your own server (physical or virtual).

The networking devices would each then need new configuration to tell the device to start using the AAA server. That configuration would point to the IP address of the AAA server, and define which AAA protocol to use: either TACACS+ or RADIUS. The configuration includes details about TCP (TACACS+) or UDP (RADIUS) ports to use.

When using a AAA server for authentication, the switch (or router) simply sends a message to the AAA server asking whether the username and password are allowed, and the AAA server replies. Figure 6-4 shows an example, with the user first supplying his username/password, the switch asking the AAA server, and the server replying to the switch stating that the username/password is valid.

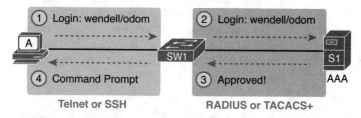

Figure 6-4 *Basic Authentication Process with an External AAA Server*

TACACS+ and RADIUS Protocols

While Figure 6-4 shows the general idea, note that the information flows with a couple of different protocols. On the left, the connection between the user and the switch or router uses Telnet or SSH. On the right, the switch and AAA server typically use either the RADIUS or TACACS+ protocol, both of which encrypt the passwords as they traverse the network.

The AAA server can also provide authorization and accounting features as well. For instance, for networking devices, IOS can be configured so that each user can be allowed to use only a specific subset of CLI commands. So, instead of having basically two levels of authority—user mode and privileged mode—each device can configure a custom set of command authority settings per user. Alternately, those details can be centrally configured at the AAA server, rather than configuring the details at each device. As a result, different users can be allowed to use different subsets of the commands, but as identified through requests to the AAA server, rather than repetitive laborious configuration on every device. (Note that TACACS+ supports this particular command authorization function, whereas RADIUS does not.)

Table 6-2 lists some basic comparison points between TACACS+ and RADIUS.

Key Topic

Table 6-2   Comparisons Between TACACS+ and RADIUS

Features	TACACS+	RADIUS
Most often used for	Network devices	Users
Transport protocol	TCP	UDP
Authentication port number(s)	49	1645, 1812
Protocol encrypts the password	Yes	Yes
Protocol encrypts entire packet	Yes	No
Supports function to authorize each user to a subset of CLI commands	Yes	No
Defined by	Cisco	RFC 2865

AAA Configuration Examples

Learning how to configure a router or switch to use a AAA server can be difficult. AAA requires that you learn several new commands. Besides all that, enabling AAA actually changes the rules used on a router for login authentication—for instance, you cannot just add a **login** command on the console line anymore after you have enabled AAA.

The exam topics use the phrase "describe" regarding AAA features, rather than configure, verify, or troubleshoot. However, to understand AAA on switches or routers, it helps to work through an example configuration. This next topic focuses on the big ideas behind a AAA configuration, instead of worrying about working through all the parameters, verifying the results, or memorizing a checklist of commands. The goal is to help you see how AAA on a switch or router changes login security.

NOTE   Throughout this book and the ICND1 Cert Guide, the login security details work the same on both routers and switches, with the exception that switches do not have an auxiliary port, whereas routers often do. But the configuration works the same on both routers and switches, so when this section mentions a switch for login security, the same concept applies to routers as well.

Everything you learned about switch login security for ICND1 in the ICND1 Cert Guide assumed an unstated default global command: **no aaa new-model**. That is, you had not yet added the **aaa new-model** global command to the configuration. Configuring AAA requires the **aaa new-model** command, and this single global command changes how that switch does login security.

The **aaa new-model** global command enables AAA services in the local switch (or router). It even enables new commands, commands that would not have been accepted before, and that would not have shown up when getting help with a question mark from the CLI. The **aaa new-model** command also changes some default login authentication settings. So, think of this command as the dividing line between using the original simple ways of login security versus a more advanced method.

After configuring the **aaa new-model** command on a switch, you need to define each AAA server, plus configure one or more groups of AAA servers aptly named a AAA group. For each AAA server, configure its IP address and a key, and optionally the TCP or UDP port number used, as seen in the middle part of Figure 6-5. Then you create a server group for each group of AAA servers to group one or more AAA servers, as seen in the bottom of Figure 6-5. (Other configuration settings will then refer to the AAA server group rather than the AAA server.)

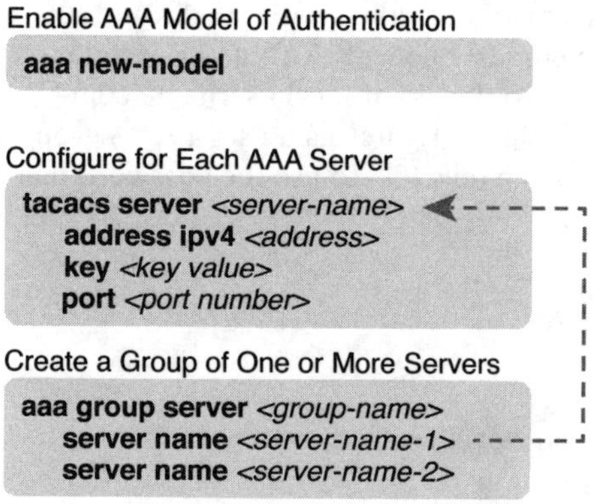

Enable AAA Model of Authentication

aaa new-model

Configure for Each AAA Server

tacacs server *<server-name>*
    address ipv4 *<address>*
    key *<key value>*
    port *<port number>*

Create a Group of One or More Servers

aaa group server *<group-name>*
    server name *<server-name-1>*
    server name *<server-name-2>*

Figure 6-5   *Enabling AAA and Defining AAA Servers and Groups*

The configuration concepts in Figure 6-5 still have not completed the task of configuring AAA authentication. IOS uses the following additional logic to connect the rest of the logic:

- IOS does login authentication for the console, vty, and aux port, by default, based on the setting of the **aaa authentication login default** global command.

- The **aaa authentication login default** *method1 method2...* global command lists different authentication methods, including referencing a AAA group to be used (as shown at the bottom of Figure 6-5).

- The methods include: a defined AAA group of AAA servers; **local**, meaning a locally configured list of usernames/passwords; or **line**, meaning to use the password defined by the **password** line subcommand.

Basically, when you want to use AAA for login authentication on the console or vty lines, the most straightforward option uses the **aaa authentication login default** command. As

Figure 6-6 shows with this command, it lists multiple authentication methods. The switch tries the first method, and if that method returns a definitive answer, the process is done. However, if that method is not available (for instance, none of the AAA servers is reachable over the IP network), IOS on the local device moves on to the next method.

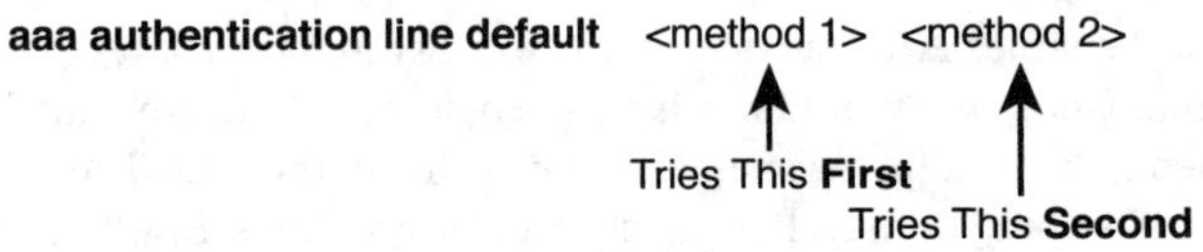

aaa authentication line default   <method 1>   <method 2>

Tries This **First**
Tries This **Second**

Figure 6-6   *Default Login Authentication Rules*

The idea of defining at least a couple of methods for login authentication makes good sense. For instance, the first method could be a AAA group so that each engineer logs in to each device with that engineer's unique username and password. However, you would not want the engineer to fail to log in just because the IP network is having problems and the AAA servers cannot send packets back to the switch. So, using a backup login method (a second method listed in the command) makes good sense.

Figure 6-7 shows three sample commands for perspective. All three commands reference the same AAA group (WO-AAA-Group). The command labeled with a 1 in the figure takes a shortsighted approach, using only one authentication method with the AAA group. Command 2 in the figure uses two authentication methods: one with AAA and a second method (**local**). (This command's **local** keyword refers to the list of local **username** commands as configured on the local switch.) Command 3 in the figure again uses a AAA group as the first method, followed by the keyword **line**, which tells IOS to use the **password** line subcommand.

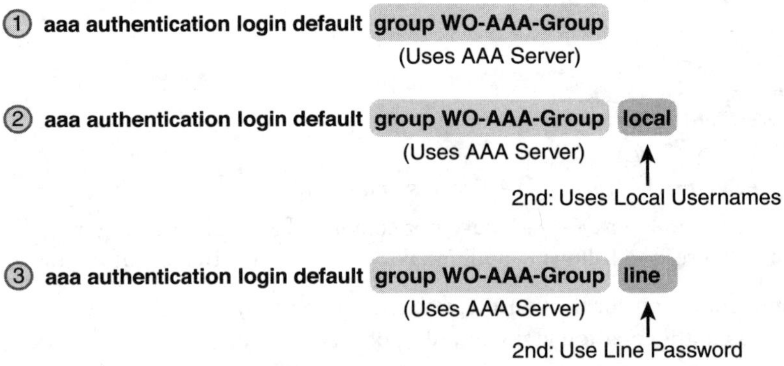

(1) **aaa authentication login default**   group WO-AAA-Group
                                           (Uses AAA Server)

(2) **aaa authentication login default**   group WO-AAA-Group   local
                                           (Uses AAA Server)
                                                               2nd: Uses Local Usernames

(3) **aaa authentication login default**   group WO-AAA-Group   line
                                           (Uses AAA Server)
                                                               2nd: Use Line Password

Figure 6-7   *Examples of AAA Login Authentication Method Combinations*

DHCP Snooping

To understand the kinds of risks that exist in modern networks, you have to first understand the rules. Then you have to think about how an attacker might take advantage of those rules in different ways. Some attacks might cause harm, and might be called a denial-of-service (DoS) attack. Or an attacker may gather more data to prepare for some other attack. Whatever the goal, for every protocol and function you learn in networking, there are possible methods to take advantage of those features to give an attacker an advantage.

Cisco chose to add one exam topic for this current CCNA R&S exam that focuses on mitigating attacks based on a specific protocol: DHCP. DHCP has become a very popular protocol, used in most every enterprise, home, and service provider. As a result, attackers have looked for methods to take advantage of DHCP. One way to help mitigate the risks of DHCP is to use a LAN switch feature called DHCP snooping.

This third of four major sections of the chapter works through the basics of DHCP snooping. It starts with the main idea, and then shows one example of how an attacker can misuse DHCP to gain an advantage. The last section explains the logic used by DHCP snooping.

DHCP Snooping Basics

DHCP snooping on a switch acts like a firewall or an ACL in many ways. It will watch for incoming messages on either all ports or some ports (depending on the configuration). It will look for DHCP messages, ignoring all non-DHCP messages and allowing those through. For any DHCP messages, the switch's DHCP snooping logic will make a choice: allow the message or discard the message.

To be clear, DHCP snooping is a Layer 2 switch feature, not a router feature. Specifically, any switch that performs Layer 2 switching, whether it does only Layer 2 switching or acts as a multilayer switch, typically supports DHCP snooping. DHCP snooping must be done on a device that sits between devices in the same VLAN, which is the role of a Layer 2 switch rather than a Layer 3 switch or router.

The first big idea with DHCP snooping is the idea of trusted ports and untrusted ports. To understand why, ponder for a moment all the devices that might be connected to one switch. The list includes routers, servers, and even other switches. It includes end-user devices, such as PCs. It includes wireless access points, which in turn connect to end-user devices. Figure 6-8 shows a representation.

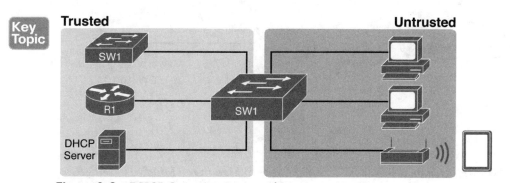

Figure 6-8 *DHCP Snooping Basics: Client Ports Are Untrusted*

DHCP snooping begins with the assumption that end-user devices are untrusted, while devices more within the control of the IT department are trusted. However, a device on an untrusted port can still use DHCP. Instead, making a port untrusted for DHCP snooping means this:

Watch for incoming DHCP messages, and discard any that are considered to be abnormal for an untrusted port and therefore likely to be part of some kind of attack.

An Example DHCP-based Attack

To give you perspective, Figure 6-9 shows a legitimate user's PC on the far right and the legitimate DHCP sever on the far left. However, an attacker has connected his laptop to the LAN and started his DHCP attack. Remember, PC1's first DHCP message will be a LAN broadcast, so the attacker's PC will receive those LAN broadcasts from any DHCP clients like PC1. (In this case, assume PC1 is attempting to lease an IP address while the attacker is making his attack.)

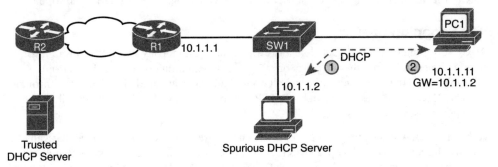

Figure 6-9   *DHCP Attack Supplies Good IP Address but Wrong Default Gateway*

In this example, the DHCP server created and used by the attacker actually leases a useful IP address to PC1, in the correct subnet, with the correct mask. Why? The attacker wants PC1 to function, but with one twist. Notice the default gateway assigned to PC1: 10.1.1.2, which is the attacker's PC address, rather than 10.1.1.1, which is R1's address. Now PC1 thinks it has all it needs to connect to the network, and it does—but now all the packets sent by PC1 flow first through the attacker's PC, creating a man-in-the-middle attack, as shown in Figure 6-10.

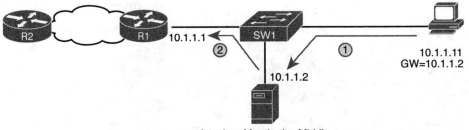

Figure 6-10   *Unfortunate Result: DHCP Attack Leads to Man-in-the-Middle*

The two steps in the figure show data flow once DHCP has completed. For any traffic destined to leave the subnet, PC1 sends its packets to its default gateway, 10.1.1.2, which happens to be the attacker. The attacker forwards the packets to R1. The PC1 user can connect to any and all applications just like normal, but now the attacker can keep a copy of anything sent by PC1.

How DHCP Snooping Works

The preceding example shows just one attack. Some attacks use an extra DHCP server (called a spurious DHCP server), and some attacks happen by using DHCP client functions in different ways. DHCP snooping considers how DHCP should work and filters out any messages that would not be part of a normal use of DHCP.

DHCP snooping needs a few configuration settings. First, the engineer enables DHCP snooping either globally on a switch or by VLAN (that is, enabled on some VLANs, and not on others). Once enabled, all ports are considered untrusted until configured as trusted.

Next, some switch ports need to be configured as trusted. Any switch ports connected to legitimate DHCP servers should be trusted. Additionally, ports connected to other switches, and ports connected to routers, should also be trusted. Why? Trusted ports are basically ports that could receive messages from legitimate DHCP servers in the network. The legitimate DHCP servers in a network are well known.

Just for a quick review, the ICND1 Cert Guide described the DHCP messages used in normal DHCP lease flows (DISCOVER, OFFER, REQUEST, ACK [DORA]). For these and other DHCP messages, a message is normally sent by either a DHCP client or a server, but not both. In the DORA messages, the client sends the DISCOVER and REQUEST, and the server sends the OFFER and ACK. Knowing that only DHCP servers should send DHCP OFFER and ACK messages, DHCP snooping allows incoming OFFER and ACK messages on trusted ports, but filters those messages if they arrive on untrusted ports.

So, the first rule of DHCP snooping is for the switch to trust any ports on which legitimate messages from trusted DHCP servers might arrive. Conversely, by leaving a port untrusted, the switch is choosing to discard any incoming DHCP server-only messages. Figure 6-11 summarizes these points, with the legitimate DHCP server on the left, on a port marked as trusted.

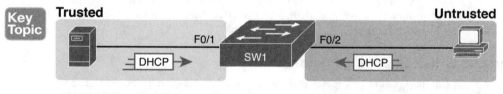

DHCP All Messages: **Approved!**   **DHCP Server** Messages: **Rejected!**
                                       DHCP Client Messages: **Check Binding Table**

Figure 6-11 *Summary of Rules for DHCP Snooping*

The logic for untrusted DHCP ports is a little more challenging. Basically, the untrusted ports are the real user population, all of which rely heavily on DHCP. Those ports also include those few people trying to attack the network with DHCP, and you cannot predict which of the untrusted ports have legitimate users and which are attacking the network. So the DHCP snooping function has to watch the DHCP messages over time, and even keep some state information in a DHCP Binding Table, so that it can decide when a DHCP message should be discarded.

The DHCP Binding Table is a list of key pieces of information about each successful lease of an IPv4 address. Each new DHCP message received on an untrusted port can then be compared to the DHCP Binding Table, and if the switch detects conflicts when comparing the DHCP message to the Binding Table, then the switch will discard the message.

To understand more specifically, first look at Figure 6-12, which shows a switch building one entry in its DHCP Binding Table. In this simple network, the DHCP client on the right leases IP address 10.1.1.11 from the DHCP server on the left. The switch's DHCP snooping feature combines the information from the DHCP messages, with information about the port (interface F0/2, assigned to VLAN 11 by the switch), and puts that in the DHCP Binding Table.

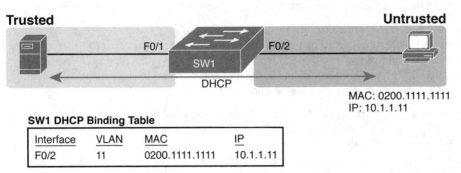

SW1 DHCP Binding Table

Interface	VLAN	MAC	IP
F0/2	11	0200.1111.1111	10.1.1.11

Figure 6-12 *Legitimate DHCP Client with DHCP Binding Entry Built by DHCP Snooping*

Because of this DHCP binding table entry, DHCP snooping would now prevent another client on another switch port from claiming to be using that same IP address (10.1.1.11) or the same MAC address (2000.1111.1111). (Many DHCP client attacks will use the same IP address or MAC address as a legitimate host.)

Note that beyond firewall-like rules of filtering based on logic, DHCP snooping can also be configured to rate limit the number of DHCP messages on an interface. For instance, by rate limiting incoming DHCP messages on untrusted interfaces, DHCP snooping can help prevent a DoS attack designed to overload the legitimate DHCP server, or to consume all the available DHCP IP address space.

Summarizing DHCP Snooping Features

DHCP snooping can help reduce risk, particularly because DHCP is such a vital part of most networks. The following list summarizes some of the key points about DHCP snooping for easier exam study:

Trusted ports: Trusted ports allow all incoming DHCP messages.

Untrusted ports, server messages: Untrusted ports discard all incoming messages that are considered server messages.

Untrusted ports, client messages: Untrusted ports apply more complex logic for messages considered client messages. They check whether each incoming DHCP message conflicts with existing DHCP binding table information and, if so, discard the DHCP message. If the message has no conflicts, the switch allows the message through, which typically results in the addition of new DHCP Binding Table entries.

Rate limiting: Optionally limits the number of received DHCP messages per second, per port.

Switch Stacking and Chassis Aggregation

Cisco offers several options that allow customers to configure their Cisco switches to act cooperatively to appear as one switch, rather than as multiple switches. This final major section of the chapter discusses two major branches of these technologies: switch stacking, which is more typical of access layer switches, and chassis aggregation, more commonly found on distribution and core switches.

Traditional Access Switching Without Stacking

Imagine for a moment that you are in charge of ordering all the gear for a new campus, with several multistory office buildings. You take a tour of the space, look at drawings of the space, and start thinking about where all the people and computers will be. At some point, you get to the point of thinking about how many Ethernet ports you need in each wiring closet.

Imagine for one wiring closet you need 150 ports today, and you want to build enough switch port capacity to 200 ports. What size switches do you buy? Do you get one switch for the wiring closet, with at least 200 ports in the switch? (The books do not discuss various switch models very much, but yes, you can buy LAN switches with hundreds of ports in one switch.) Or do you buy a pair of switches with at least 100 ports each? Or eight or nine switches with 24 access ports each?

There are pros and cons for using smaller numbers of large switches, and vice versa. To meet those needs, vendors such as Cisco offer switches with a wide range of port densities. However, a switch feature called *switch stacking* gives you some of the benefits of both worlds.

To appreciate the benefits of switch stacking, imagine a typical LAN design like the one shown in Figure 6-13. The figure shows the conceptual design, with two distribution switches and four access layer switches.

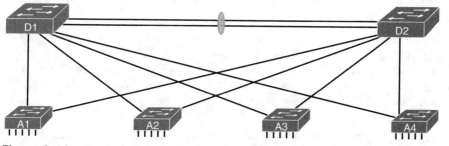
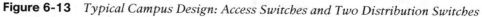

Figure 6-13 *Typical Campus Design: Access Switches and Two Distribution Switches*

For later comparison, let me emphasize a few points here. Access switches A1 through A4 all operate as separate devices. The network engineer must configure each. They each have an IP address for management. They each run CDP, STP, and maybe VTP. They each have a MAC address table, and they each forward Ethernet frames based on that MAC address table. Each switch probably has very similar configuration, but that configuration is separate, and all the functions are separate.

Now picture those same four access layer switches physically, not in Figure 6-13, but as you would imagine them in a wiring closet, even in the same rack. In this case, imagine all four access switches sit in the same rack in the same closet. All the wiring on that floor of the building runs back to the wiring closet, and each cable is patched into some port in one of these four switches. Each switch might be one rack unit (RU) tall (1.75 inches), and they all sit one on top of the other.

Switch Stacking of Access Layer Switches

The scenario described so far is literally a stack of switches one above the other. Switch stacking technology allows the network engineer to make that stack of physical switches act like one switch. For instance, if a switch stack was made from the four switches in Figure 6-13, the following would apply:

Key Topic

- The stack would have a single management IP address.
- The engineer would connect with Telnet or SSH to one switch (with that one management IP address), not multiple switches.
- One configuration file would include all interfaces in all four physical switches.
- STP, CDP, VTP would run on one switch, not multiple switches.
- The switch ports would appear as if all are on the same switch.
- There would be one MAC address table, and it would reference all ports on all physical switches.

The list could keep going much longer for all possible switch features, but the point is that switch stacking makes the switches act as if they are simply parts of a single larger switch.

To make that happen, the switches must be connected together with a special network. The network does not use standard Ethernet ports. Instead, the switches have special hardware ports called *stacking ports*. With the Cisco FlexStack and FlexStack-Plus stacking technology, a stacking module must be inserted into each switch, and then connected with a stacking cable.

NOTE Cisco has created a few switch stacking technologies over the years, so to avoid having to refer to them all, note that this section describes Cisco's FlexStack and FlexStack Plus options. These stacking technologies are supported to different degrees in the popular 2960-S, 2960-X, and 2960-XR switch families.

The stacking cables together make a ring between the switches as shown in Figure 6-14. That is, the switches connect in series, with the last switch connecting again to the first. Using full duplex on each link, the stacking modules and cables create two paths to forward data between the physical switches in the stack. The switches use these connections to communicate between the switches to forward frames and to perform other overhead functions.

Note that each stacking module has two ports with which to connect to another switch's stacking module. For instance, if the four switches were all 2960XR switches, each would need one stacking module, and four cables total to connect the four switches as shown. Figure 6-15 shows the same idea in Figure 6-14, but as a photo that shows the stacking cables on the left side of the figure.

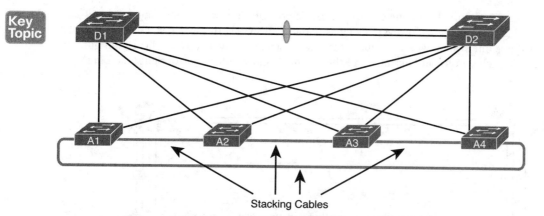

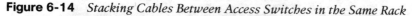

Stacking Cables

Figure 6-14 *Stacking Cables Between Access Switches in the Same Rack*

Figure 6-15 *Photo of Four 2960X Switches Cabled on the Left with Stacking Cables*

You should think of switch stacks as literally a stack of switches in the same rack. The stacking cables are short, with the expectation that the switches sit together in the same room and rack. For instance, Cisco offers stacking cables of .5, 1, and 3 meters long for the FlexStack and FlexStack-Plus stacking technology discussed in more depth at the end of this section.

Switch Stack Operation as a Single Logical Switch

With a switch stack, the switches together act as one *logical switch*. This term (logical switch) is meant to emphasize that there are obviously physical switches, but they act together as one switch.

To make it all work, one switch acts as a *stack master* to control the rest of the switches. The links created by the stacking cables allow the physical switches to communicate, but the stack master is in control of the work. For instance, if you number the physical switches as 1, 2, 3, and 4, a frame might arrive on switch 4 and need to exit a link on switch 3. If switch 1 were the stack master, switches 1, 3, and 4 would all need to communicate over the stack links to forward that frame. But switch 1, as stack master, would do the matching of the MAC address table to choose where to forward the frame.

Figure 6-16 focuses on the LAN design impact of how a switch stack acts like one logical switch. The figure shows the design with no changes to the cabling between the four access switches and the distribution switches. Formerly, each separate access switch had two links to the distribution layer: one connected to each distribution switch (see Figure 6-13). That cabling is unchanged. However, acting as one logical switch, the switch stack now operates as if it is one switch, with four uplinks to each distribution switch. Add a little configuration to put each set of four links into an EtherChannel, and you have the design shown in Figure 6-16.

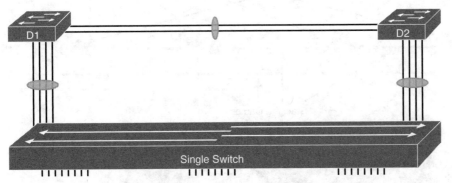

Figure 6-16   *Stack Acts Like One Switch*

The stack also simplifies operations. Imagine for instance the scope of an STP topology for a VLAN that has access ports in all four of the physical access switches in this example. That Spanning Tree would include all six switches. With the switch stack acting as one logical switch, that same VLAN now has only three switches in the STP topology, and is much easier to understand and predict.

Cisco FlexStack and FlexStack-Plus

Just to put a finishing touch on the idea of a switch stack, this closing topic examines a few particulars of Cisco's FlexStack and FlexStack-Plus stacking options.

Cisco's stacking technologies require that Cisco plan to include stacking as a feature in a product, given that it requires specific hardware. Cisco has a long history of building new model series of switches with model numbers that begin with 2960. Per Cisco's documentation, Cisco created one stacking technology, called FlexStack, as part of the introduction of the 2960-S model series. Cisco later enhanced FlexStack with FlexStack-Plus, adding support with products in the 2960-X and 2960-XR model series. For switch stacking to support future designs, the stacking hardware tends to increase over time as well, as seen in the comparisons between FlexStack and FlexStack-Plus in Table 6-3.

Table 6-3   Comparisons of Cisco's FlexStack and FlexStack-Plus Options

	FlexStack	FlexStack-Plus
Year introduced	2010	2013
Switch model series	2960-S, 2960-X	2960-X, 2960-XR
Speed of single stack link, in both directions (full duplex)	10 Gbps	20 Gbps
Maximum number of switches in one stack	4	8

Chassis Aggregation

The term *chassis aggregation* refers to another Cisco technology used to make multiple switches operate as a single switch. From a big picture perspective, switch stacking is more often used and offered by Cisco in switches meant for the access layer. Chassis aggregation is meant for more powerful switches that sit in the distribution and core layers. Summarizing some of the key differences, chassis aggregation

- Typically is used for higher-end switches used as distribution or core switches

- Does not require special hardware adapters, instead using Ethernet interfaces

- Aggregates two switches

- Arguably is more complex but also more functional

The big idea of chassis aggregation is the same as for a switch stack: make multiple switches act like one switch, which gives you some availability and design advantages. But much of the driving force behind chassis aggregation is about high-availability design for LANs. This section works through a few of those thoughts to give you the big ideas about the thinking behind high availability for the core and distribution layer.

NOTE   This section looks at the general ideas of chassis aggregation, but for further reading about a specific implementation, search at Cisco.com for Cisco's Virtual Switching System (VSS) that is supported on 6500 and 6800 series switches.

6

High Availability with a Distribution/Core Switch

Even without chassis aggregation, the distribution and core switches need to have high availability. The next few pages look at how the switches built for use as distribution and core switches can help improve availability, even without chassis aggregation.

If you were to look around a medium to large enterprise campus LAN, you would typically find many more access switches than distribution and core switches. For instance, you might have four access switches per floor, with ten floors in a building, for 40 access switches. That same building probably has only a pair of distribution switches.

And why two distribution switches instead of one? Because if the design used only one distribution switch, and it failed, none of the devices in the building could reach the rest of the network. So, if two distribution switches are good, why not four? Or eight? One reason is cost, another complexity. Done right, a pair of distribution switches for a building can provide the right balance of high availability and low cost/complexity.

The availability features of typical distribution and core switches allow network designers to create a great availability design with just two distribution or core switches. Cisco makes typical distribution/core switches with more redundancy. For instance, Figure 6-17 shows a representation of a typical chassis-based Cisco switch. It has slots that can be used for line cards—that is, cards with Ethernet ports. It has dual supervisor cards that do frame and packet forwarding. And it has two power supplies, each of which can be connected to power feeds from different electrical substations if desired.

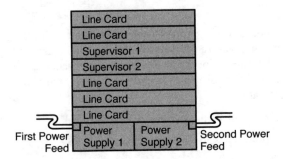

Figure 6-17 *Common Line-Card Arrangement in a Modular Cisco Distribution/Core Switch*

Now imagine two distribution switches sitting beside each other in a wiring closet as shown in Figure 6-18. A design would usually connect the two switches with an EtherChannel. For better availability, the EtherChannel could use ports from different line cards, so that if one line card failed due to some hardware problem, the EtherChannel would still work.

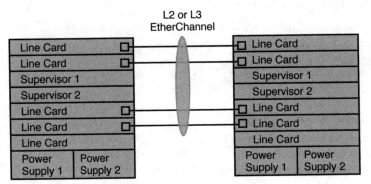

Figure 6-18 *Using EtherChannel and Different Line Cards*

Improving Design and Availability with Chassis Aggregation

Next, consider the effect of adding chassis aggregation to a pair of distribution switches. In terms of effect, the two switches act as one switch, much like switch stacking. The particulars of how chassis aggregation achieves that differs.

Figure 6-19 shows a comparison. On the left, the two distribution switches act independently, and on the right, the two distribution switches are aggregated. In both cases, each distribution switch connects with a single Layer 2 link to the access layer switches A1 and A2, which act independently—that is, they do not use switch stacking. So, the only difference between the left and right examples is that on the right the distribution switches use switch aggregation.

The right side of the figure shows the aggregated switch that appears as one switch to the access layer switches. In fact, even though the uplinks connect into two different switches, they can be configured as an EtherChannel through a feature called *Multichassis EtherChannel* (MEC).

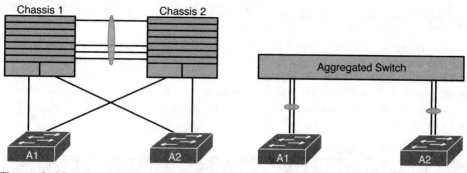

Figure 6-19 *One Design Advantage of Aggregated Distribution Switches*

The following list describes some of the advantages of using switch aggregation. Note that many of the benefits should sound familiar from the switch stacking discussion. The one difference in this list has to do with the active/active data plane.

Multichassis EtherChannel (MEC): Uses the EtherChannel between the two physical switches.

Active/Standby Control Plane: Simpler operation for control plane because the pair acts as one switch for control plane protocols: STP, VTP, EtherChannel, ARP, routing protocols.

Active/Active data plane: Takes advantage of forwarding power of supervisors on both switches, with active Layer 2 and Layer 3 forwarding the supervisors of both switches. The switches synchronize their MAC and routing tables to support that process.

Single switch management: Simpler operation of management protocols by running management protocols (Telnet, SSH, SNMP) on the active switch; configuration is synchronized automatically with the standby switch.

Finally, using chassis aggregation and switch stacking together in the same network has some great design advantages. Look back to Figure 6-13 at the beginning of this section. It showed two distribution switches and four access switches, all acting independently, with one uplink from each access switch to each distribution switch. If you enable switch stacking for the four access switches, and enable chassis aggregation for the two distribution switches, you end up with a topology as shown in Figure 6-20.

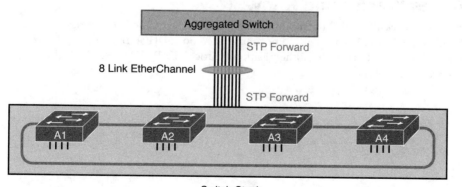

Switch Stack

Figure 6-20 *Making Six Switches Act like Two*

Chapter Review

One key to doing well on the exams is to perform repetitive spaced review sessions. Review this chapter's material using either the tools in the book, DVD, or interactive tools for the same material found on the book's companion website. Refer to the "Your Study Plan" element for more details. Table 6-4 outlines the key review elements and where you can find them. To better track your study progress, record when you completed these activities in the second column.

Table 6-4 Chapter Review Tracking

Review Element	Review Date(s)	Resource Used
Review key topics		Book, DVD/website
Review key terms		Book, DVD/website
Answer DIKTA questions		Book, PCPT
Review memory tables		Book, App

Review All the Key Topics

Table 6-5 Key Topics for Chapter 6

Key Topic Element	Description	Page Number
Figure 6-3	Protocols used by IEEE 802.1x	146
Table 6-2	Comparisons of TACACS+ and RADIUS	148
Figure 6-8	Concept: Trusted and untrusted ports for DHCP snooping	151
Figure 6-11	Summary of DHCP snooping filtering actions	153
List	Key points about DHCP snooping	154
List	Common Cisco switch stack features	156
Figure 6-14	Switch stacking cabling	157
Table 6-3	Comparisons of FlexStack and FlexStack-Plus	158
List	Key features of switch aggregation	161

Key Terms You Should Know

FlexStack, FlexStack-Plus, stacking module, stacking cable, switch stacking, chassis aggregation, Multichassis EtherChannel, trusted port, untrusted port, DHCP Binding Table, DHCP snooping, AAA server, Extensible Authentication Protocol (EAP), EAP over LAN (EAPoL), supplicant, authenticator

Part I Review

Keep track of your part review progress with the checklist shown in Table P1-1. Details about each task follow the table.

Table P1-1 Part I Part Review Checklist

Activity	1st Date Completed	2nd Date Completed
Repeat All DIKTA Questions		
Answer Part Review Questions		
Review Key Topics		
Create STP Concepts Mind Map		
Create Terminology Mind Map		
Create Command Mind Maps by Category		
Do Labs		

Repeat All DIKTA Questions

For this task, answer the "Do I Know This Already?" questions again for the chapters in this part of the book using the PCPT software. See the section "How to View Only DIKTA Questions by Chapter or Part" in the Introduction to this book to learn how to make the PCPT software show you DIKTA questions for this part only.

Answer Part Review Questions

For this task, answer the Part Review questions for this part of the book using the PCPT software. Refer to the Introduction to this book, in the section "How to View Part Review Questions," for more details.

Review Key Topics

Review all Key Topics in all chapters in this part, either by browsing the chapters or by using the Key Topics application on the DVD or companion website.

Create STP Concepts Mind Map

Spanning Tree Protocol (STP) defines a lot of ideas that you might find hard to mentally organize. Create a mind map to help your brain organize the various STP concepts. Some suggestions as to how to organize the concepts:

Rules: This section might include any of the rules a switch uses when making choices. For instance, the rules switches use for choosing a root switch.

Roles: STP defines both roles and states; an example of a role is the root port role.

States: For example, forwarding and blocking.

Within each of these sections, break down the details based on 802.1D STP and 802.1w RSTP.

Create Terminology Mind Map

The chapters in this part weave in and out of different topics. Without looking back at the chapters or your notes, create a mind map with all the terminology you can recall from Part I of the book. Your job is as follows:

- Think of every term that you can remember from Part I of the book.
- Organize the terms into these divisions: VLANs, VLAN trunks, STP, VTP, AAA, 802.1x, DHCP snooping, switch stacking/aggregation.
- After you have written every term you can remember into the mind map, review the Key Terms list at the end of Chapters 1 through 6. Add any terms you forgot to your mind map.

Create Command Mind Maps by Category

Part I of this book also introduced both configuration and EXEC commands. Create one mind map (or a section of a larger mind map) for each of the categories of commands in this list:

VLANs, 802.1Q trunking, STP/RSTP, EtherChannel, VTP

For each category, think of all configuration commands and all EXEC commands (mostly **show** commands). For each category, group the configuration commands separately from the EXEC commands. Figure P1-1 shows a sample for IPv4 commands on a switch.

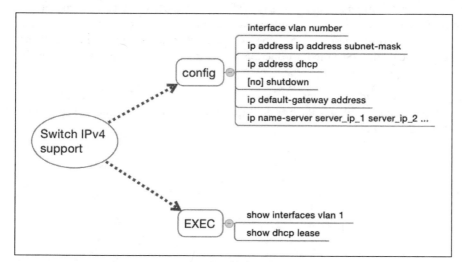

Figure P1-1 *Sample Command Mind Map*

NOTE For more information on mind mapping, refer to the Introduction, in the section "About Mind Maps."

Appendix E, "Mind Map Solutions," lists sample mind map answers. If you do choose to use mind map software, rather than paper, you might want to remember where you stored your mind map files. Table P1-2 lists the mind maps for this part review and a place to record those filenames.

Table P1-2   Configuration Mind Maps for Part I Review

Map	Description	Where You Saved It
1	STP Concepts Mind Map	
2	Terminology Mind Map	
3	Command Mind Maps	

Do Labs

If you have not done so, make your choices about what lab tools you intend to use and experiment with the commands in these chapters. Re-create examples in the chapters, and try all the **show** commands; the **show** commands are very important for answering simlet questions.

Sim Lite: You can use the Pearson Network Simulator Lite included with this book to do some labs and get used to the CLI. All the labs in the ICND2 Lite product are about topics in this part of the book, so make sure and work through those labs to start learning about the CLI.

Pearson Network Simulator: If you use the full Pearson CCNA simulator, focus more on the configuration scenario and troubleshooting scenario labs associated with the topics in this part of the book. These types of labs include a larger set of topics, and work well as Part Review activities. (See the Introduction for some details about how to find which labs are about topics in this part of the book.)

Config Labs: In your idle moments, review and repeat any of the Config Labs for this book part in the author's blog; launch from http://blog.certskills.com/ccna and navigate to **Hands-On > Config Lab.**

TCP/IP networks need IP routes. Part II collects six chapters focused on the IPv4 routing protocols discussed within the scope of ICND2.

The first four chapters in this part of the book deliver the details of OSPF Version 2 and then EIGRP. Chapter 7 begins with OSPFv2 concepts, followed by OSPFv2 implementation details (configuration and verification) in Chapter 8. Chapters 9 and 10 take the same approach to EIGRP, with one chapter of concepts (Chapter 9) and one chapter of implementation details (Chapter 10).

Chapter 11 pulls those four chapters about the OSPFv2 and EIGRP routing protocols together by discussing troubleshooting for both topics. Although they are different protocols, troubleshooting EIGRP and OSPFv2 requires the same kinds of logic and items to check. This chapter works through the details.

Finally, for the first time in the history of Cisco's CCNA R&S exam, Cisco has added more than a basic mention of BGP to the exam topics. Chapter 12 closes Part II with discussion of External BGP (eBGP), used between an enterprise and an ISP. That discussion includes basic concepts, configuration, and verification.

Part II

IPv4 Routing Protocols

Chapter 7: Understanding OSPF Concepts

Chapter 8: Implementing OSPF for IPv4

Chapter 9: Understanding EIGRP Concepts

Chapter 10: Implementing EIGRP for IPv4

Chapter 11: Troubleshooting IPv4 Routing Protocols

Chapter 12: Implementing External BGP

Part II Review

Understanding OSPF Concepts

This chapter covers the following exam topics:

2.0 Routing Technologies

2.2 Compare and contrast distance vector and link-state routing protocols

2.3 Compare and contrast interior and exterior routing protocols

2.4 Configure, verify, and troubleshoot single area and multiarea OSPFv2 for IPv4 (excluding authentication, filtering, manual summarization, redistribution, stub, virtual-link, and LSAs)

This chapter begins a series of four chapters with a similar flow. Open Shortest Path First (OSPF) and Enhanced Interior Gateway Protocol (EIGRP) are the two most popular IPv4 routing protocols used inside enterprises today. This chapter introduces OSPF concepts, followed by a chapter that gets into details about OSPF implementation. Chapters 9 and 10 do the same for EIGRP.

In particular, this chapter takes a long look at OSPF Version 2 (OSPFv2) concepts. OSPFv2 has been around over 20 years and is the most commonly used OSPF version for advertising IPv4 routes. It is the OSPF that has been part of CCNA R&S throughout most of the history of CCNA R&S.

This chapter has three major sections. The first section sets a bit of context about routing protocols in general, defining interior and exterior routing protocols and basic routing protocol features and terms. This information is duplicated somewhat in the ICND1 Cert Guide, but the exam topics of both the ICND1 and ICND2 Cert Guides include these topics, so the topics are covered here as well. The second major section presents the nuts and bolts of how OSPFv2 works, using OSPF neighbor relationships, database exchange, and then route calculation. The third section wraps up the discussion by looking at some OSPF design issues.

"Do I Know This Already?" Quiz

Take the quiz (either here, or use the PCPT software) if you want to use the score to help you decide how much time to spend on this chapter. The answers are at the bottom of the page following the quiz, and the explanations are in DVD Appendix C and in the PCPT software.

Table 7-1 "Do I Know This Already?" Foundation Topics Section-to-Question Mapping

Foundation Topics Section	Questions
Comparing Dynamic Routing Protocol Features	1–3
OSPF Concepts and Operation	4, 5
OSPF Area Design	6

1. Which of the following routing protocols is considered to use link-state logic?

   a. RIPv1

   b. RIPv2

   c. EIGRP

   d. OSPF

2. Which of the following routing protocols use a metric that is, by default, at least partially affected by link bandwidth? (Choose two answers.)

   a. RIPv1

   b. RIPv2

   c. EIGRP

   d. OSPF

3. Which of the following interior routing protocols support VLSM? (Choose three answers.)

   a. RIPv1

   b. RIPv2

   c. EIGRP

   d. OSPF

4. Two routers using OSPFv2 have become neighbors and exchanged all LSAs. As a result, Router R1 now lists some OSPF-learned routes in its routing table. Which of the following best describes how R1 uses those recently learned LSAs to choose which IP routes to add to its IP routing table?

   a. Each LSA lists a route to be copied to the routing table.

   b. Some LSAs list a route that can be copied to the routing table.

   c. Run some SPF math against the LSAs to calculate the routes.

   d. R1 does not use the LSAs at all when choosing what routes to add.

5. Which of the following OSPF neighbor states is expected when the exchange of topology information is complete between two OSPF neighbors?

   a. 2-way

   b. Full

   c. Up/up

   d. Final

6. A company has a small/medium-sized network with 15 routers and 40 subnets and uses OSPFv2. Which of the following is considered an advantage of using a single-area design as opposed to a multiarea design?

   a. Reduces the processing overhead on most routers.

   b. Status changes to one link may not require SPF to run on all other routers.

   c. Simpler planning and operations.

   d. Allows for route summarization, reducing the size of IP routing tables.

Foundation Topics

Comparing Dynamic Routing Protocol Features

Routers add IP routes to their routing tables using three methods: connected routes, static routes, and routes learned by using dynamic routing protocols. Before we get too far into the discussion, however, it is important to define a few related terms and clear up any misconceptions about the terms *routing protocol*, *routed protocol*, and *routable protocol*. The concepts behind these terms are not that difficult, but because the terms are so similar, and because many documents pay poor attention to when each of these terms is used, they can be a bit confusing. These terms are generally defined as follows:

- **Routing protocol:** A set of messages, rules, and algorithms used by routers for the overall purpose of learning routes. This process includes the exchange and analysis of routing information. Each router chooses the best route to each subnet (path selection) and finally places those best routes in its IP routing table. Examples include RIP, EIGRP, OSPF, and BGP.

- **Routed protocol and routable protocol:** Both terms refer to a protocol that defines a packet structure and logical addressing, allowing routers to forward or route the packets. Routers forward packets defined by routed and routable protocols. Examples include IP Version 4 (IPv4) and IP Version 6 (IPv6).

> **NOTE**   The term *path selection* sometimes refers to part of the job of a routing protocol, in which the routing protocol chooses the best route.

Even though routing protocols (such as OSPF) are different from routed protocols (such as IP), they do work together very closely. The routing process forwards IP packets, but if a router does not have any routes in its IP routing table that match a packet's destination address, the router discards the packet. Routers need routing protocols so that the routers can learn all the possible routes and add them to the routing table, so that the routing process can forward (route) routable protocols such as IP.

Routing Protocol Functions

Cisco IOS software supports several IP routing protocols, performing the same general functions:

1. Learn routing information about IP subnets from neighboring routers.

2. Advertise routing information about IP subnets to neighboring routers.

3. If more than one possible route exists to reach one subnet, pick the best route based on a metric.

4. If the network topology changes—for example, a link fails—react by advertising that some routes have failed and pick a new currently best route. (This process is called *convergence*.)

> **NOTE**   A neighboring router connects to the same link as another router, such as the same WAN link or the same Ethernet LAN.

Figure 7-1 shows an example of three of the four functions in the list. Both R1 and R3 learn about a route to subnet 172.16.3.0/24 from R2 (function 1). After R3 learns about the route to 172.16.3.0/24 from R2, R3 advertises that route to R1 (function 2). Then R1 must make a decision about the two routes it learned about for reaching subnet 172.16.3.0/24: one with metric 1 from R2 and one with metric 2 from R3. R1 chooses the lower metric route through R2 (function 3).

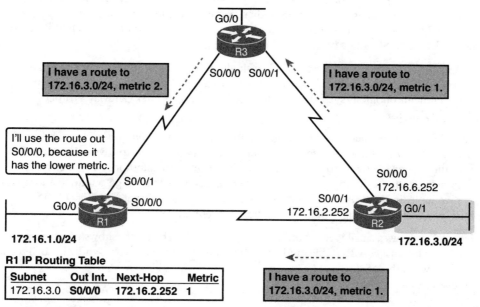

Figure 7-1 *Three of the Four Basic Functions of Routing Protocols*

Convergence is the fourth routing protocol function listed here. The term *convergence* refers to a process that occurs when the topology changes—that is, when either a router or link fails or comes back up again. When something changes, the best routes available in the network can change. Convergence simply refers to the process by which all the routers collectively realize something has changed, advertise the information about the changes to all the other routers, and all the routers then choose the currently best routes for each subnet. The ability to converge quickly, without causing loops, is one of the most important considerations when choosing which IP routing protocol to use.

In Figure 7-1, convergence might occur if the link between R1 and R2 failed. In that case, R1 should stop using its old route for subnet 172.16.3.0/24 (directly through R2) and begin sending packets to R3.

Interior and Exterior Routing Protocols

IP routing protocols fall into one of two major categories: *interior gateway protocols* (IGP) or *exterior gateway protocols* (EGP). The definitions of each are as follows:

- **IGP:** A routing protocol that was designed and intended for use inside a single autonomous system (AS)

- **EGP:** A routing protocol that was designed and intended for use between different autonomous systems

NOTE The terms *IGP* and *EGP* include the word "gateway" because routers used to be called gateways.

These definitions use another new term: *autonomous system* (AS). An AS is a network under the administrative control of a single organization. For example, a network created and paid for by a single company is probably a single AS, and a network created by a single school system is probably a single AS. Other examples include large divisions of a state or national government, where different government agencies might be able to build their own networks. Each ISP is also typically a single different AS.

Some routing protocols work best inside a single AS by design, so these routing protocols are called IGPs. Conversely, routing protocols designed to exchange routes between routers in different autonomous systems are called EGPs. Today, Border Gateway Protocol (BGP) is the only EGP used.

Each AS can be assigned a number called (unsurprisingly) an *AS number* (ASN). Like public IP addresses, the Internet Assigned Numbers Authority (IANA, http://www.iana.org) controls the worldwide rights to assigning ASNs. It delegates that authority to other organizations around the world, typically to the same organizations that assign public IP addresses. For example, in North America, the American Registry for Internet Numbers (ARIN, http://www.arin.net) assigns public IP address ranges and ASNs.

Figure 7-2 shows a small view of the worldwide Internet. The figure shows two enterprises and three ISPs using IGPs (OSPF and EIGRP) inside their own networks and with BGP being used between the ASNs.

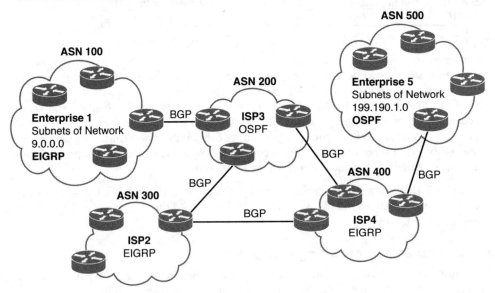

Figure 7-2 *Comparing Locations for Using IGPs and EGPs*

Comparing IGPs

Organizations have several options when choosing an IGP for their enterprise network, but most companies today use either OSPF or EIGRP. This book discusses both these routing protocols, with Chapters 7 and 8 covering OSPF and Chapters 9 and 10 covering EIGRP. Before getting into detail on these two protocols, the next section first discusses some of the main goals of every IGP, comparing OSPF, EIGRP, plus a few other IPv4 routing protocols.

IGP Routing Protocol Algorithms

A routing protocol's underlying algorithm determines how the routing protocol does its job. The term *routing protocol algorithm* simply refers to the logic and processes used by different routing protocols to solve the problem of learning all routes, choosing the best route to each subnet, and converging in reaction to changes in the internetwork. Three main branches of routing protocol algorithms exist for IGP routing protocols:

Key Topic

- Distance vector (sometimes called Bellman-Ford after its creators)
- Advanced distance vector (sometimes called "balanced hybrid")
- Link-state

Historically speaking, distance vector protocols were invented first, mainly in the early 1980s. Routing Information Protocol (RIP) was the first popularly used IP distance vector protocol, with the Cisco-proprietary Interior Gateway Routing Protocol (IGRP) being introduced a little later.

By the early 1990s, distance vector protocols' somewhat slow convergence and potential for routing loops drove the development of new alternative routing protocols that used new algorithms. Link-state protocols—in particular, Open Shortest Path First (OSPF) and Integrated Intermediate System to Intermediate System (IS-IS)—solved the main issues. They also came with a price: They required extra CPU and memory on routers, with more planning required from the network engineers.

Around the same time as the introduction of OSPF, Cisco created a proprietary routing protocol called Enhanced Interior Gateway Routing Protocol (EIGRP), which used some features of the earlier IGRP protocol. EIGRP solved the same problems as did link-state routing protocols, but less planning was required when implementing the network. As time went on, EIGRP was classified as a unique type of routing protocol. However, it used more distance vector features than link-state, so it is more commonly classified as an advanced distance vector protocol.

Metrics

Routing protocols choose the best route to reach a subnet by choosing the route with the lowest metric. For example, RIP uses a counter of the number of routers (hops) between a router and the destination subnet. OSPF totals the cost associated with each interface in the end-to-end route, with the cost based on link bandwidth. Table 7-2 lists the most important IP routing protocols for the CCNA exams and some details about the metric in each case.

7

Table 7-2 IP IGP Metrics

IGP	Metric	Description
RIPv2	Hop count	The number of routers (hops) between a router and the destination subnet
OSPF	Cost	The sum of all interface cost settings for all links in a route, with the cost defaulting to be based on interface bandwidth
EIGRP	Composite of bandwidth and delay	Calculated based on the route's slowest link and the cumulative delay associated with each interface in the route

A brief comparison of the metric used by the older RIP versus the metric used by EIGRP shows some insight into why OSPF and EIGRP surpassed RIP. Figure 7-3 shows an example in which Router B has two possible routes to subnet 10.1.1.0 on the left side of the net-work: a shorter route over a very slow 64-Kbps link, or a longer route over two higher-speed (T1) links.

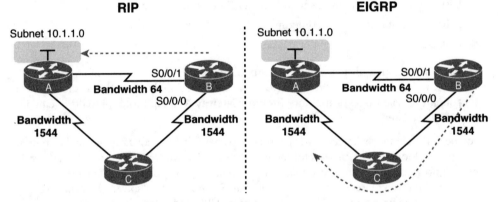

Figure 7-3 *RIP and EIGRP Metrics Compared*

The left side of the figure shows the results of RIP in this network. Using hop count, Router B learns of a one-hop route directly to Router A through B's S0/0/1 interface. B also learns of a two-hop route through Router C, through B's S0/0/0 interface. Router B chooses the lower hop count route, which happens to go over the slow-speed link.

The right side of the figure shows the arguably better choice made by EIGRP based on its better metric. To cause EIGRP to make the right choice, the engineer correctly configured the interface bandwidth to match the actual link speeds, thereby allowing EIGRP to choose the faster route. (The **bandwidth** interface subcommand does not change the actual physical speed of the interface. It just tells IOS what speed to assume the interface is using.)

Other IGP Comparisons

Some other IGP comparisons can be made. However, some topics require more fundamen-tal knowledge of specific routing protocols, or other features not yet covered in this book. For now, this section introduces a few more comparison points, and leaves the details until later in the book.

Routing protocols differ based on whether they are classless routing protocols or classful. Classless routing protocols support variable-length subnet masks (VLSM) as well as manual route summarization. *Classless routing protocols* support VLSM and manual route summarization by sending routing protocol messages that include the subnet masks in the message, whereas the generally older classful routing protocols do not send masks in the routing update messages. Table 7-3 summarizes the key IGP comparison points.

Key Topic

Table 7-3   Interior IP Routing Protocols Compared

Feature	RIPv1	RIPv2	EIGRP	OSPF	IS-IS
Classless/sends mask in updates/supports VLSM	No	Yes	Yes	Yes	Yes
Algorithm (DV, advanced DV, LS)	DV	DV	Advanced DV	LS	LS
Supports manual summarization	No	Yes	Yes	Yes	Yes
Cisco-proprietary	No	No	Yes[1]	No	No
Routing updates are sent to a multicast IP address	No	Yes	Yes	Yes	—
Convergence	Slow	Slow	Fast	Fast	Fast

[1] Although Cisco created EIGRP, and has kept it as a proprietary protocol for many years, Cisco chose to publish EIGRP as an informational RFC in 2013. This allows other vendors to implement EIGRP, while Cisco retains the rights to the protocol.

Administrative Distance

Many companies and organizations use a single routing protocol. However, in some cases, a company needs to use multiple routing protocols. For example, if two companies connect their networks so that they can exchange information, they need to exchange some routing information. If one company uses OSPF, and the other uses EIGRP, on at least one router, both OSPF and EIGRP must be used. Then, that router can take routes learned by OSPF and advertise them into EIGRP, and vice versa, through a process called *route redistribution*.

Depending on the network topology, the two routing protocols might learn routes to the same subnets. When a single routing protocol learns multiple routes to the same subnet, the metric tells it which route is best. However, when two different routing protocols learn routes to the same subnet, because each routing protocol's metric is based on different information, IOS cannot compare the metrics. For example, OSPF might learn a route to subnet 10.1.1.0 with metric 101, and EIGRP might learn a route to 10.1.1.0 with metric 2,195,416, but the EIGRP-learned route might be the better route—or it might not. There is simply no basis for comparison between the two metrics.

When IOS must choose between routes learned using different routing protocols, IOS uses a concept called *administrative distance*. Administrative distance is a number that denotes how believable an entire routing protocol is on a single router. The lower the number, the better, or more believable, the routing protocol. For example, RIP has a default administrative distance of 120, OSPF uses a default of 110, and EIGRP defaults to 90. When using OSPF and EIGRP, the router will believe the EIGRP route instead of the OSPF route (at least by default). The administrative distance values are configured on a single router and are not exchanged with other routers. Table 7-4 lists the various sources of routing information, along with the default administrative distances.

Table 7-4   Default Administrative Distances

Route Type	Administrative Distance
Connected	0
Static	1
BGP (external routes)	20
EIGRP (internal routes)	90
IGRP	100
OSPF	110
IS-IS	115
RIP	120
EIGRP (external routes)	170
BGP (internal routes)	200
DHCP default route	254
Unusable	255

NOTE   The **show ip route** command lists each route's administrative distance as the first of the two numbers inside the brackets. The second number in brackets is the metric.

The table shows the default administrative distance values, but IOS can be configured to change the administrative distance of a particular routing protocol, a particular route, or even a static route. For example, the command **ip route 10.1.3.0 255.255.255.0 10.1.130.253** defines a static route with a default administrative distance of 1, but the command **ip route 10.1.3.0 255.255.255.0 10.1.130.253 210** defines the same static route with an administrative distance of 210. So, you can actually create a static route that is only used when the routing protocol does not find a route, just by giving the static route a higher administrative distance.

OSPF Concepts and Operation

Routing protocols basically exchange information so routers can learn routes. The routers learn information about subnets, routes to those subnets, and metric information about how good each route is compared to others. The routing protocol can then choose the currently best route to each subnet, building the IP routing table.

Link-state protocols like OSPF take a little different approach to the particulars of what information they exchange and what the routers do with that information once learned. This next (second) major section narrows the focus to only link-state protocols, specifically OSPF.

This section begins with an overview of what OSPF does by exchanging data about the network in data structures called *link-state advertisements* (LSA). Then, the discussion backs up a bit to provide more details about each of three fundamental parts of how OSPF operates: how OSPF routers use neighbor relationships, how routers exchange LSAs with neighbors, and then how routers calculate the best routes once they learn all the LSAs.

OSPF Overview

Link-state protocols build IP routes with a couple of major steps. First, the routers together build a lot of information about the network: routers, links, IP addresses, status information, and so on. Then the routers flood the information, so all routers know the same information. At that point, each router can calculate routes to all subnets, but from each router's own perspective.

Topology Information and LSAs

Routers using link-state routing protocols need to collectively advertise practically every detail about the internetwork to all the other routers. At the end of the process of *flooding* the information to all routers, every router in the internetwork has the exact same information about the internetwork. Flooding a lot of detailed information to every router sounds like a lot of work, and relative to distance vector routing protocols, it is.

Open Shortest Path First (OSPF), the most popular link-state IP routing protocol, organizes topology information using LSAs and the link-state database (LSDB). Figure 7-4 represents the ideas. Each LSA is a data structure with some specific information about the network topology; the LSDB is simply the collection of all the LSAs known to a router. When sitting at the CLI of a router that uses OSPF, the **show ip ospf database** command lists information about the LSDB on that router by listing some of the information in each of the LSAs in the LSDB.

Link State Database (LSDB)

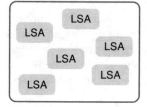

Figure 7-4 *LSA and LSDB Relationship*

Figure 7-5 shows the general idea of the flooding process, with R8 creating and flooding its router LSA. The router LSA for Router R8 describes the router itself, including the existence of subnet 172.16.3.0/24, as seen on the right side of the figure. (Note that Figure 7-5 actually shows only a subset of the information in R8's router LSA.)

Figure 7-5 shows the rather basic flooding process, with R8 sending the original LSA for itself, and the other routers flooding the LSA by forwarding it until every router has a copy. The flooding process has a way to prevent loops so that the LSAs do not get flooded around in circles. Basically, before sending an LSA to yet another neighbor, routers communicate, asking "Do you already have this LSA?," and then they avoid flooding the LSA to neighbors that already have it.

Once flooded, routers do occasionally reflood a particular LSA. Routers reflood an LSA when some information changes (for example, when a link goes up or comes down). They also reflood each LSA based on each LSA's separate aging timer (default 30 minutes).

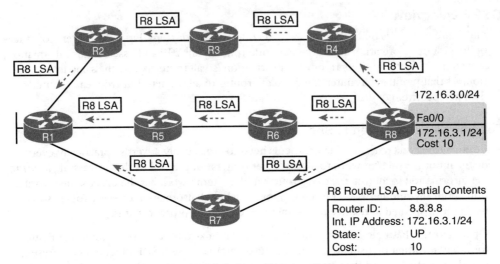

Figure 7-5 *Flooding LSAs Using a Link-State Routing Protocol*

Applying Dijkstra SPF Math to Find the Best Routes

The link-state flooding process results in every router having an identical copy of the LSDB in memory, but the flooding process alone does not cause a router to learn what routes to add to the IP routing table. Although incredibly detailed and useful, the information in the LSDB does not explicitly state each router's best route to reach a destination.

To build routes, link-state routers have to do some math. Thankfully, you and I do not have to know the math! However, all link-state protocols use a type of math algorithm, called the Dijkstra Shortest Path First (SPF) algorithm, to process the LSDB. That algorithm analyzes (with math) the LSDB, and builds the routes that the local router should add to the IP routing table—routes that list a subnet number and mask, an outgoing interface, and a next-hop router IP address.

Now that you have the big ideas down, the next several topics walk through the three main phases of how OSPF routers accomplish the work of exchanging LSAs and calculating routes. Those three phases are

Becoming neighbors: A relationship between two routers that connect to the same data link, created so that the neighboring routers have a means to exchange their LSDBs.

Exchanging databases: The process of sending LSAs to neighbors so that all routers learn the same LSAs.

Adding the best routes: The process of each router independently running SPF, on their local copy of the LSDB, calculating the best routes, and adding those to the IPv4 routing table.

Becoming OSPF Neighbors

Of everything you learn about OSPF in this chapter, OSPF neighbor concepts have the most to do with how you will configure and troubleshoot OSPF in Cisco routers. You configure OSPF in ways that make routers become neighbors, and much of the LSA exchange process and calculating the best routes happen in the background. This section discusses the fundamental concepts of OSPF neighbors.

The Basics of OSPF Neighbors

OSPF neighbors are routers that both use OSPF and both sit on the same data link. With the data link technology discussed so far in this book, that means two routers connected to the same VLAN become OSPF neighbors, or two routers on the ends of a serial link become OSPF neighbors.

Two routers need to do more than simply exist on the same link to become OSPF neighbors; they must send OSPF messages and agree to become neighbors. To do so, the routers send OSPF Hello messages, introducing themselves to the neighbor. Assuming the two neighbors have compatible OSPF parameters, the two form a neighbor relationship, and would be displayed in the output of the **show ip ospf neighbors** command.

The OSPF neighbor relationship also lets OSPF know when a neighbor might not be a good option for routing packets right now. Imagine R1 and R2 form a neighbor relationship, learn LSAs, and calculate routes that send packets through the other router. Months later, R1 notices that the neighbor relationship with R2 fails. That failed neighbor connection to R2 makes R1 react: R1 refloods LSAs that formerly relied on the link from R1 to R2, and R1 runs SPF to recalculate its own routes.

Finally, the OSPF neighbor model allows new routers to be dynamically discovered. That means new routers can be added to a network without requiring every router to be reconfigured. Instead, the configuration enables OSPF on a router's interfaces, and then the router reacts to any Hello messages from new neighbors, whenever those neighbors happen to be installed.

Meeting Neighbors and Learning Their Router ID

The OSPF Hello process, by which new neighbor relationships are formed, works somewhat like when you move to a new house and meet your various neighbors. When you see each other outside, you might walk over, say hello, and learn each other's name. After talking a bit, you form a first impression, particularly as to whether you think you'll enjoy chatting with this neighbor occasionally, or whether you can just wave and not take the time to talk the next time you see him outside.

Similarly, with OSPF, the process starts with messages called OSPF Hello messages. The Hellos in turn list each router's *router ID* (RID), which serves as each router's unique name or identifier for OSPF. Finally, OSPF does several checks of the information in the Hello messages to ensure that the two routers should become neighbors.

OSPF RIDs are 32-bit numbers. As a result, most command output lists these as dotted-decimal numbers (DDN). Additionally, by default, IOS chooses its OSPF RID based on an active interface IPv4 address, because those are some nearby convenient 32-bit numbers as well. However, the OSPF RID can be directly configured, as covered in the section "Configuring the OSPF Router ID" in Chapter 8, "Implementing OSPF for IPv4."

As soon as a router has chosen its OSPF RID and some interfaces come up, the router is ready to meet its OSPF neighbors. OSPF routers can become neighbors if they are connected to the same subnet (and in some other special cases not covered on the CCENT and

CCNA exams). To discover other OSPF-speaking routers, a router sends multicast OSPF Hello packets to each interface and hopes to receive OSPF Hello packets from other routers connected to those interfaces. Figure 7-6 outlines the basic concept.

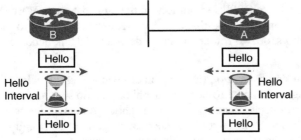

Figure 7-6 *OSPF Hello Packets*

Routers A and B both send Hello messages onto the LAN. They continue to send Hellos at a regular interval based on their Hello timer settings. The Hello messages themselves have the following features:

- The Hello message follows the IP packet header, with IP protocol type 89.
- Hello packets are sent to multicast IP address 224.0.0.5, a multicast IP address intended for all OSPF-speaking routers.
- OSPF routers listen for packets sent to IP multicast address 224.0.0.5, in part hoping to receive Hello packets and learn about new neighbors.

Taking a closer look, Figure 7-7 shows several of the neighbor states used by the early formation of an OSPF neighbor relationship. The figure shows the Hello messages in the center and the resulting neighbor states on the left and right edges of the figure. Each router keeps an OSPF state variable for how it views the neighbor.

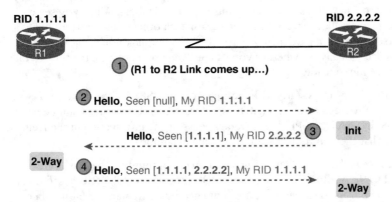

Figure 7-7 *Early Neighbor States*

Following the steps in the figure, the scenario begins with the link down, so the routers have no knowledge of each other as OSPF neighbors. As a result, they have no state (status) information about each other as neighbors, and they would not list each other in the output of the **show ip ospf neighbor** command. At Step 2, R1 sends the first Hello, so R2 learns of the existence of R1 as an OSPF router. At that point, R2 lists R1 as a neighbor, with an interim beginning state of init.

The process continues at Step 3, with R2 sending back a Hello. This message tells R1 that R2 exists, and it allows R1 to move through the init state and quickly to a 2-way state. At Step 4, R2 receives the next Hello from R1, and R2 can also move to a 2-way state.

The 2-way state is a particularly important OSPF state. At that point, the following major facts are true:

Key Topic

- The router received a Hello from the neighbor, with that router's own RID listed as being seen by the neighbor.

- The router has checked all the parameters in the Hello received from the neighbor, with no problems. The router is willing to become a neighbor.

- If both routers reach a 2-way state with each other, it means that both routers meet all OSPF configuration requirements to become neighbors. Effectively, at that point, they are neighbors, and ready to exchange their LSDB with each other.

Exchanging the LSDB Between Neighbors

One purpose of forming OSPF neighbor relationships is to allow the two neighbors to exchange their databases. This next topic works through some of the details of OSPF database exchange.

Fully Exchanging LSAs with Neighbors

7

The OSPF neighbor state 2-way means that the router is available to exchange its LSDB with the neighbor. In other words, it is ready to begin a 2-way exchange of the LSDB. So, once two routers on a point-to-point link reach the 2-way state, they can immediately move on to the process of database exchange.

The database exchange process can be quite involved, with several OSPF messages and several interim neighbor states. This chapter is more concerned with a few of the messages and the final state when database exchange has completed: the full state.

After two routers decide to exchange databases, they do not simply send the contents of the entire database. First, they tell each other a list of LSAs in their respective databases—not all the details of the LSAs, just a list. (Think of these lists as checklists.) Then, each router can check which LSAs it already has, and then ask the other router for only the LSAs that are not known yet.

For instance, R1 might send R2 a checklist that lists ten LSAs (using an OSPF Database Description, or DD, packet). R2 then checks its LSDB and finds six of those ten LSAs. So, R2 asks R1 (using a Link-State Request packet) to send the four additional LSAs.

Thankfully, most OSPFv2 work does not require detailed knowledge of these specific protocol steps. However, a few of the terms are used quite a bit and should be remembered. In particular, the OSPF messages that actually send the LSAs between neighbors are called Link-State Update (LSU) packets. That is, the LSU packet holds data structures called link-state advertisements (LSA). The LSAs are not packets, but rather data structures that sit inside the LSDB and describe the topology.

Figure 7-8 pulls some of these terms and processes together, with a general example. The story picks up the example shown in Figure 7-7, with Figure 7-8 showing an example of the database exchange process between Routers R1 and R2. The center shows the protocol messages, and the outer items show the neighbor states at different points in the process. Focus on two items in particular:

■ The routers exchange the LSAs inside LSU packets.

■ When finished, the routers reach a full state, meaning they have fully exchanged the contents of their LSDBs.

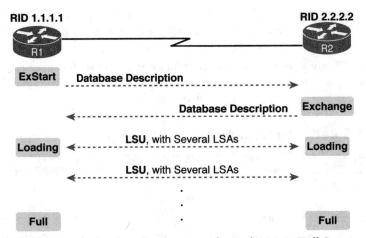

Figure 7-8 *Database Exchange Example, Ending in a Full State*

Maintaining Neighbors and the LSDB

Once two neighbors reach a full state, they have done all the initial work to exchange OSPF information between them. However, neighbors still have to do some small ongoing tasks to maintain the neighbor relationship.

First, routers monitor each neighbor relationship using Hello messages and two related timers: the Hello Interval and the Dead Interval. Routers send Hellos every Hello Interval to each neighbor. Each router expects to receive a Hello from each neighbor based on the Hello Interval, so if a neighbor is silent for the length of the Dead Interval (by default, four times as long as the Hello Interval), the loss of Hellos means that the neighbor has failed.

Next, routers must react when the topology changes as well, and neighbors play a key role in that process. When something changes, one or more routers change one or more LSAs. Then, the routers must flood the changed LSAs to each neighbor so that the neighbor can change its LSDB.

For example, imagine a LAN switch loses power, so a router's G0/0 interface fails from up/up to down/down. That router updates an LSA that shows the router's G0/0 as being down. That router then sends the LSA to its neighbors, and that neighbor in turn send it to its neighbors, until all routers again have an identical copy of the LSDB. Each router's LSDB now reflects the fact that the original router's G0/0 interface failed, so each router will then use SPF to recalculate any routes affected by the failed interface.

A third maintenance task done by neighbors is to reflood each LSA occasionally, even when the network is completely stable. By default, each router that creates an LSA also has the responsibility to reflood the LSA every 30 minutes (the default), even if no changes occur. (Note that each LSA has a separate timer, based on when the LSA was created, so there is no single big event where the network is overloaded with flooding LSAs.)

The following list summarizes these three maintenance tasks for easier review:

- Maintain neighbor state by sending Hello messages based on the Hello Interval, and listening for Hellos before the Dead Interval expires

- Flood any changed LSAs to each neighbor

- Reflood unchanged LSAs as their lifetime expires (default 30 minutes)

> **NOTE**   If you are curious to know a few more details about the LSAs themselves, Appendix K's section titled "(OSPFv2) Link-State Advertisements" provides a few more details.

Using Designated Routers on Ethernet Links

OSPF behaves differently on some types of interfaces, particularly comparing point-to-point and Ethernet links. In particular, on Ethernet links, OSPF elects one of the routers on the same subnet to act as the *designated router* (DR). The DR plays a key role in how the database exchange process works, with different rules than with point-to-point links. To see how, consider the example that begins with Figure 7-9. The figure shows five OSPFv2 routers on the same Ethernet VLAN. These five OSPF routers elect one router to act as the DR, and one router to be backup DR (BDR). The figure shows A and B as DR and BDR, for no other reason than the Ethernet must have one of each.

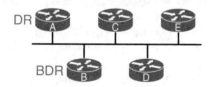

Figure 7-9   *Routers A and B Elected as DR and BDR*

The database exchange process on an Ethernet link does not happen between every pair of routers on the same VLAN/subnet. Instead, it happens between the DR and each of the other routers, with the DR making sure that all the other routers get a copy of each LSA. In other words, the database exchange happens over the flows shown in Figure 7-10.

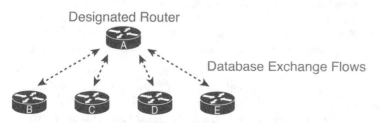

Figure 7-10   *Database Exchange to and from the DR on an Ethernet*

OSPF uses the BDR concept because the DR is so important to the database exchange process. The BDR watches the status of the DR and takes over for the DR if it fails. (When the DR fails, the BDR takes over, and then a new BDR is elected.)

At this point, you might be getting a little tired of some of the theory, but finally, the theory actually shows something that you may see in **show** commands on a router. Because the DR and BDR both do full database exchange with all the other OSPF routers in the LAN, they reach a full state with all neighbors. However, routers that are neither a DR nor a BDR—called *DROthers* by OSPF—never reach a full state because they do not do database exchange with each other. As a result, the **show ip ospf neighbor** command on these routers lists some neighbors, permanently, in a state of 2-way, and not in a full state.

For instance, with OSPF working normally on the Ethernet LAN in Figure 7-10, a **show ip ospf neighbor** command on router C (which is a DROther router) would show the following:

■ Two neighbors (A and B, the DR and BDR, respectively) with a full state (called *fully adjacent*)

■ Two neighbors (D and E) with a 2-way state (called *adjacent*)

This different behavior on OSPF neighbors on a LAN—where some neighbors reach full state and some do not—calls for the use of two more OSPF terms: *adjacent* and *fully adjacent*. Fully adjacent neighbors reach a full state after having exchanged their LSDBs directly. Adjacent neighbors are those DROther routers that (correctly) choose to stay in 2-way state but never reach a full state. Table 7-5 summarizes these key concepts and terms related to OSPF states.

Key Topic

Table 7-5   Stable OSPF Neighbor States and Their Meanings

Neighbor State	Adjacency Lingo	Meaning
2-way	Adjacent	The neighbor has sent a Hello that lists the local router's RID in the list of seen routers, also implying that neighbor verification checks all passed. If both neighbors are DROther routers, the neighbors should remain in this state.
Full	Fully adjacent	Both routers know the exact same LSDB details and are fully adjacent, meaning they have completed the exchange of LSDB contents.

Calculating the Best Routes with SPF

OSPF LSAs contain useful information, but they do not contain the specific information that a router needs to add to its IPv4 routing table. In other words, a router cannot just copy information from the LSDB into a route in the IPv4 routing table. The LSAs individually are more like pieces of a jigsaw puzzle. So, to know what routes to add to the routing table, each router must do some SPF math to choose the best routes from that router's perspective. The router then adds each route to its routing table: a route with a subnet number and mask, an outgoing interface, and a next-hop router IP address.

Although engineers do not need to know the details of how SPF does the math, they do need to know how to predict which routes SPF will choose as the best route. The SPF algorithm calculates all the routes for a subnet—that is, all possible routes from the router to the destination subnet. If more than one route exists, the router compares the metrics, picking the best (lowest) metric route to add to the routing table. Although the SPF math can be complex, engineers with a network diagram, router status information, and simple addition can calculate the metric for each route, predicting what SPF will choose.

Once SPF has identified a route, OSPF calculates the metric for a route as follows:

The sum of the OSPF interface costs for all outgoing interfaces in the route

Figure 7-11 shows an example with three possible routes from R1 to Subnet X (172.16.3.0/24) at the bottom of the figure.

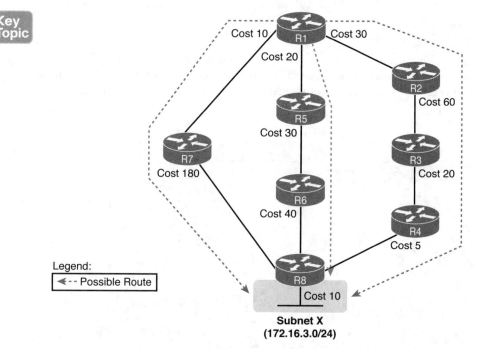

Figure 7-11   *SPF Tree to Find R1's Route to 172.16.3.0/24*

NOTE   OSPF considers the costs of the outgoing interfaces (only) in each route. It does not add the cost for incoming interfaces in the route.

Table 7-6 lists the three routes shown in Figure 7-11, with their cumulative costs, showing that R1's best route to 172.16.3.0/24 starts by going through R5.

Table 7-6   Comparing R1's Three Alternatives for the Route to 172.16.3.0/24

Route	Location in Figure 7-11	Cumulative Cost
R1–R7–R8	Left	10 + 180 + 10 = 200
R1–R5–R6–R8	Middle	20 + 30 + 40 + 10 = 100
R1–R2–R3–R4–R8	Right	30 + 60 + 20 + 5 + 10 = 125

As a result of the SPF algorithm's analysis of the LSDB, R1 adds a route to subnet 172.16.3.0/24 to its routing table, with the next-hop router of R5.

In real OSPF networks, an engineer can do the same process by knowing the OSPF cost for each interface. Armed with a network diagram, the engineer can examine all routes, add the costs, and predict the metric for each route.

> **NOTE**   OSPF calculates costs using different processes depending on the area design. The example surrounding Figure 7-11 best matches OSPF's logic when using a single-area design. OSPF areas are discussed in the next few pages.

OSPF Area Design

OSPF can be used in some networks with very little thought about design issues. You just turn on OSPF in all the routers, put all interfaces into the same area (usually area 0), and it works! Figure 7-12 shows one such network example, with 11 routers and all interfaces in area 0.

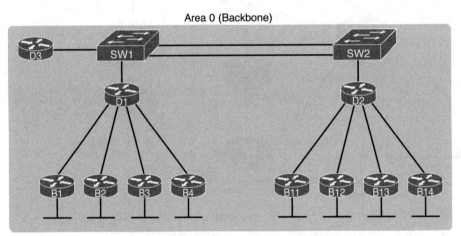

Figure 7-12   *Single-Area OSPF*

Larger OSPFv2 networks suffer with a single-area design. For instance, now imagine an enterprise network with 900 routers, rather than only 11, and several thousand subnets. As it turns out, the CPU time to run the SPF algorithm on all that topology data just takes time. As a result, OSPFv2 convergence time—the time required to react to changes in the network—can be slow. The routers may run low on RAM, as well. Additional problems include the following:

- A larger topology database requires more memory on each router.

- Processing the larger topology database with the SPF algorithm requires processing power that grows exponentially with the size of the topology database.

- A single interface status change, anywhere in the internetwork (up to down, or down to up), forces *every router* to run SPF again!

The solution is to take the one large LSDB and break it into several smaller LSDBs by using OSPF areas. With areas, each link is placed into one area. SPF does its complicated math on the topology inside the area, and that area's topology only. For instance, an internetwork with 1000 routers and 2000 subnets, broken in 100 areas, would average 10 routers and 20 subnets per area. The SPF calculation on a router would have to only process topology about 10 routers and 20 links, rather than 1000 routers and 2000 links.

So, how large does a network have to be before OSPF needs to use areas? Well, there is no set answer, because the behavior of the SPF process depends largely on CPU processing speed, the amount of RAM, the size of the LSDB, and so on. Generally, networks larger than a few dozen routers benefit from areas, and some documents over the years have listed 50 routers as the dividing line at which a network really should use areas.

The next few pages look at how OSPF area design works, with more reasons as to why areas help make larger OSPF networks work better.

OSPF Areas

OSPF area design follows a couple of basic rules. To apply the rules, start with a clean drawing of the internetwork, with routers, and all interfaces. Then, choose the area for each router interface, as follows:

Key Topic

- Put all interfaces connected to the same subnet inside the same area.
- An area should be contiguous.
- Some routers may be internal to an area, with all interfaces assigned to that single area.
- Some routers may be Area Border Routers (ABR), because some interfaces connect to the backbone area, and some connect to nonbackbone areas.
- All nonbackbone areas must connect to the backbone area (area 0) by having at least one ABR connected to both the backbone area and the nonbackbone area.

Figure 7-13 shows one example. Some engineer started with a network diagram that showed all 11 routers and their links. On the left, the engineer put four serial links, and the LANs connected to branch routers B1 through B4, into area 1. Similarly, he placed the links to branches B11 through B14, and their LANs, in area 2. Both areas need a connection to the backbone area, area 0, so he put the LAN interfaces of D1 and D2 into area 0, along with D3, creating the backbone area.

The figure also shows a few important OSPF area design terms. Table 7-7 summarizes the meaning of these terms, plus some other related terms, but pay closest attention to the terms from the figure.

7

Key Topic

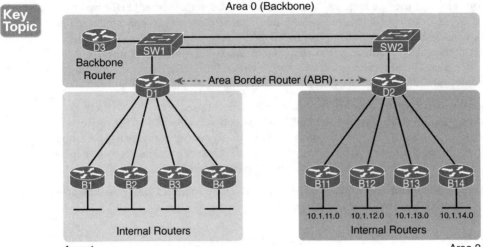

Figure 7-13 *Three-Area OSPF with D1 and D2 as ABRs*

Key Topic

Table 7-7   OSPF Design Terminology

Term	Description
Area Border Router (ABR)	An OSPF router with interfaces connected to the backbone area and to at least one other area
Backbone router	A router connected to the backbone area (includes ABRs)
Internal router	A router in one area (not the backbone area)
Area	A set of routers and links that shares the same detailed LSDB information, but not with routers in other areas, for better efficiency
Backbone area	A special OSPF area to which all other areas must connect—area 0
Intra-area route	A route to a subnet inside the same area as the router
Interarea route	A route to a subnet in an area of which the router is not a part

How Areas Reduce SPF Calculation Time

Figure 7-13 shows a sample area design and some terminology related to areas, but it does not show the power and benefit of the areas. To understand how areas reduce the work SPF has to do, you need to understand what changes about the LSDB inside an area, as a result of the area design.

SPF spends most of its processing time working through all the topology details, namely routers and the links that connect routers. Areas reduce SPF's workload because, for a given area, the LSDB lists only routers and links inside that area, as shown on the left side of Figure 7-14.

While the LSDB has less topology information, it still has to have information about all subnets in all areas, so that each router can create IPv4 routes for all subnets. So, with an area design, OSPFv2 uses very brief summary information about the subnets in other areas. These LSAs do not include topology information about the other areas, so they do not require much SPF processing at all. Instead, these subnets all appear like subnets connected to the ABR (in this case, ABR D1).

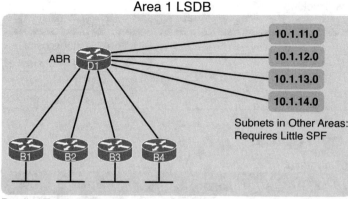

Area 1 LSDB

ABR D1

10.1.11.0
10.1.12.0
10.1.13.0
10.1.14.0

Subnets in Other Areas:
Requires Little SPF

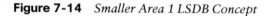

B1 B2 B3 B4

Detailed Topology Data (Routers and Links):
Requires Heavy SPF

Figure 7-14   *Smaller Area 1 LSDB Concept*

OSPF Area Design Advantages

In summary, using a single-area OSPF design works well for smaller OSPF networks. It avoids the added complexity, making the network slightly easier to operate. It also requires less planning effort because no one has to plan which parts of the network end up in which area.

Using multiple areas improves OSPF operations in many ways for larger networks. The following list summarizes some of the key points arguing for the use of multiple areas in larger OSPF networks:

- The smaller per-area LSDB requires less memory.

- Routers require fewer CPU cycles to process the smaller per-area LSDB with the SPF algorithm, reducing CPU overhead and improving convergence time.

- Changes in the network (for example, links failing and recovering) require SPF calculations only on routers connected to the area where the link changed state, reducing the number of routers that must rerun SPF.

- Less information must be advertised between areas, reducing the bandwidth required to send LSAs.

Chapter Review

One key to doing well on the exams is to perform repetitive spaced review sessions. Review this chapter's material using either the tools in the book, DVD, or interactive tools for the same material found on the book's companion website. Refer to the "Your Study Plan" element for more details. Table 7-8 outlines the key review elements and where you can find them. To better track your study progress, record when you completed these activities in the second column.

Table 7-8 Chapter Review Tracking

Review Element	Review Date(s)	Resource Used:
Review key topics		Book, DVD/website
Review key terms		Book, DVD/website
Answer DIKTA questions		Book, PCPT
Review memory tables		Book, DVD/website

Review All the Key Topics

Table 7-9 Key Topics for Chapter 7

Key Topic Element	Description	Page Number
List	Functions of IP routing protocols	172
List	Definitions of IGP and EGP	173
List	Types of IGP routing protocols	175
Table 7-2	IGP metrics	176
Table 7-3	Comparisons of IGP features	177
List	Key facts about the OSPF 2-way state	183
Table 7-5	Key OSPF neighbor states	186
Item	Definition of how OSPF calculates the cost for a route	187
Figure 7-11	Example of calculating the cost for multiple competing routes	187
List	OSPF area design rules	189
Figure 7-13	Sample OSPF multiarea design with terminology	190
Table 7-7	OSPF design terms and definitions	190

Key Terms You Should Know

convergence, shortest path first (SPF) algorithm, distance vector, interior gateway protocol (IGP), link-state, link-state advertisement (LSA), link-state database (LSDB), metric, 2-way state, full state, Area Border Router (ABR), designated router (DR), backup designated router (BDR), fully adjacent, Hello Interval, Dead Interval, link-state update, neighbor, router ID (RID), topology database, internal router, backbone area

CHAPTER 8

Implementing OSPF for IPv4

This chapter covers the following exam topics:

2.0 Routing Technologies

2.4 Configure, verify, and troubleshoot single area and multiarea OSPFv2 for IPv4 (excluding authentication, filtering, manual summarization, redistribution, stub, virtual-link, and LSAs)

Chapter 7, "Understanding OSPF Concepts," introduced you to the concepts, so this chapter moves on to the implementation details for Open Shortest Path First Version 2 (OSPFv2)—that is, OSPF as used for IPv4. This chapter looks at how to configure and verify a variety of OSPFv2 features.

This chapter touches on a wide variety of configuration options, so it breaks the content down into the three major sections. The first major section shows how to configure and verify basic OSPFv2 with a single-area design. With a single area, all interfaces sit in the same area, and that fact has an impact on the kinds of information lists in **show** command output. Also, the first section uses traditional OSPFv2 configuration using the OSPF **network** command. The second major section repeats the same kinds of configuration and verification as in the first major section, but now with multiarea OSPF designs.

The third major section of the chapter looks at a variety of common OSPFv2 features. These features include a completely different way to enable OSPFv2 on a Cisco router, using interface subcommands rather than the OSPF **network** command. It also includes the configuration of OSPF default routes, tuning OSPF metrics, and OSPF load balancing.

Finally, take a moment to reread the exam topics at the top of this page. Note that the exam topics specifically exclude some OSPF topics.

"Do I Know This Already?" Quiz

Take the quiz (either here, or use the PCPT software) if you want to use the score to help you decide how much time to spend on this chapter. The answers are at the bottom of the page following the quiz, and the explanations are in DVD Appendix C and in the PCPT software.

Table 8-1 "Do I Know This Already?" Foundation Topics Section-to-Question Mapping

Foundation Topics Section	Questions
Implementing Single-Area OSPFv2	1–3
Implementing Multiarea OSPFv2	4, 5
Additional OSPFv2 Features	6, 7

1. Which of the following **network** commands, following the command **router ospf 1**, tells this router to start using OSPF on interfaces whose IP addresses are 10.1.1.1, 10.1.100.1, and 10.1.120.1?

   a. network 10.0.0.0 255.0.0.0 area 0

   b. network 10.0.0.0 0.255.255.255 area 0

   c. network 10.0.0.1 0.0.0.255 area 0

   d. network 10.0.0.1 0.0.255.255 area 0

2. Which of the following **network** commands, following the command **router ospf 1**, tells this router to start using OSPF on interfaces whose IP addresses are 10.1.1.1, 10.1.100.1, and 10.1.120.1?

   a. network 10.1.0.0 0.0.255.255 area 0

   b. network 10.0.0.0 0.255.255.0 area 0

   c. network 10.1.1.0 0.x.1x.0 area 0

   d. network 10.1.1.0 255.0.0.0 area 0

   e. network 10.0.0.0 255.0.0.0 area 0

3. Which of the following commands list the OSPF neighbors off interface serial 0/0? (Choose two answers.)

   a. show ip ospf neighbor

   b. show ip ospf interface brief

   c. show ip neighbor

   d. show ip interface

   e. show ip ospf neighbor serial 0/0

4. Routers R1, R2, and R3 are internal routers in areas 1, 2, and 3, respectively. Router R4 is an ABR connected to the backbone area (0) and to areas 1, 2, and 3. Which of the following answers describes the configuration on Router R4, which is different from the other three routers, that makes it an ABR?

   a. The **abr enable** router subcommand.

   b. The **network** router subcommands refer to a single nonbackbone area.

   c. The **network** router subcommands refer to multiple areas, including the backbone.

   d. All the ABR's interfaces are assigned to OSPF area 0, while the other routers have their interfaces assigned to a different area, respectively.

5. An engineer connects to Router R1 and issues a **show ip ospf neighbor** command. The status of neighbor 2.2.2.2 lists FULL/BDR. What does the BDR mean?

   a. R1 is an Area Border Router.

   b. R1 is a backup designated router.

   c. Router 2.2.2.2 is an Area Border Router.

   d. Router 2.2.2.2 is a backup designated router.

6. An engineer migrates from a more traditional OSPFv2 configuration that uses **network** commands in OSPF configuration mode to instead use OSPFv2 interface configuration. Which of the following commands configures the area number assigned to an interface in this new configuration?

   a. The **area** command in interface configuration mode

   b. The **ip ospf** command in interface configuration mode

   c. The **router ospf** command in interface configuration mode

   d. The **network** command in interface configuration mode

7. Which of the following configuration settings on a router does not influence which IPv4 route a router chooses to add to its IPv4 routing table when using OSPFv2?

   a. auto-cost reference-bandwidth

   b. delay

   c. bandwidth

   d. ip ospf cost

Foundation Topics

Implementing Single-Area OSPFv2

OSPF configuration includes only a few required steps, but it has many optional steps. After an OSPF design has been chosen—a task that can be complex in larger IP internetworks—the configuration can be as simple as enabling OSPF on each router interface and placing that interface in the correct OSPF area.

This section shows several configuration examples, all with a single-area OSPF internetwork. Following those examples, the text goes on to cover several of the additional optional configuration settings. For reference, the following list outlines the configuration steps covered in this first major section of the chapter, as well as a brief reference to the required commands:

Config Checklist

Step 1. Use the **router ospf** *process-id* global command to enter OSPF configuration mode for a particular OSPF process.

Step 2. (Optional) Configure the OSPF router ID by doing the following:

   A. Use the **router-id** *id-value* router subcommand to define the router ID

   B. Use the **interface loopback** *number* global command, along with an **ip address** *address mask* command, to configure an IP address on a loopback interface (chooses the highest IP address of all working loopbacks)

   C. Rely on an interface IP address (chooses the highest IP address of all working nonloopbacks)

Step 3. Use one or more **network** *ip-address wildcard-mask* **area** *area-id* router subcommands to enable OSPFv2 on any interfaces matched by the configured address and mask, enabling OSPF on the interface for the listed area.

Step 4. (Optional) Use the **passive-interface** *type number* router subcommand to configure any OSPF interfaces as passive if no neighbors can or should be discovered on the interface.

For a more visual perspective on OSPFv2 configuration, Figure 8-1 shows the relationship between the key OSPF configuration commands. Note that the configuration creates a routing process in one part of the configuration, and then indirectly enables OSPF on each interface. The configuration does not name the interfaces on which OSPF is enabled, instead requiring IOS to apply some logic by comparing the OSPF **network** command to the interface **ip address** commands. The upcoming example discusses more about this logic.

Configuration

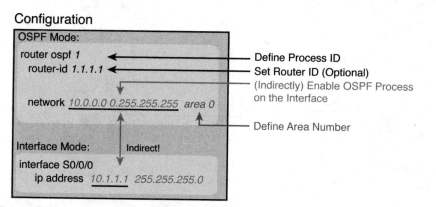

Figure 8-1   *Organization of OSPFv2 Configuration*

OSPF Single-Area Configuration

Figure 8-2 shows a sample network that will be used for the single-area OSPF configuration examples. All links sit in area 0. The design has four routers, each connected to one or two LANs. However, note that Routers R3 and R4, at the top of the figure, connect to the same two VLANs/subnets, so they will form neighbor relationships with each other over each of those VLANs as well. (The two switches at the top of the design are acting as Layer 2 switches.)

Example 8-1 shows the IPv4 addressing configuration on Router R3, before getting into the OSPF detail. The configuration enables 802.1Q trunking on R3's G0/0 interface, and assigns an IP address to each subinterface. (Not shown, switch S3 has configured trunking on the other side of that Ethernet link.)

Example 8-1   *IPv4 Address Configuration on R3 (Including VLAN Trunking)*

```
interface GigabitEthernet 0/0.341
 encapsulation dot1q 341
 ip address 10.1.3.1 255.255.255.128
!
interface GigabitEthernet 0/0.342
 encapsulation dot1q 342
 ip address 10.1.3.129 255.255.255.128
!
interface serial 0/0/0
 ip address 10.1.13.3 255.255.255.128
```

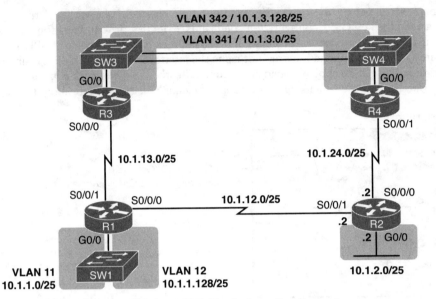

Figure 8-2   *Sample Network for OSPF Single-Area Configuration*

The beginning single-area configuration on R3, as shown in Example 8-2, enables OSPF on all the interfaces shown in Figure 8-2. First, the **router ospf 1** global command puts the user in OSPF configuration mode, and sets the OSPF *process-id*. This number just needs to be unique on the local router, allowing the router to support multiple OSPF processes in a single router by using different process IDs. (The **router** command uses the *process-id* to distinguish between the processes.) The *process-id* does not have to match on each router, and it can be any integer between 1 and 65,535.

Example 8-2   *OSPF Single-Area Configuration on R3 Using One* **network** *Command*

```
router ospf 1
 network 10.0.0.0 0.255.255.255 area 0
```

Speaking generally rather than about this example, the OSPF **network** command tells a router to find its local interfaces that match the first two parameters on the **network** command. Then, for each matched interface, the router enables OSPF on those interfaces, discovers neighbors, creates neighbor relationships, and assigns the interface to the area listed in the **network** command. (Note that the area can be configured as either an integer or a dotted-decimal number, but this book makes a habit of configuring the area number as an integer. The integer area numbers range from 0 through 4,294,967,295.)

For the specific command in Example 8-2, any matched interfaces are assigned to area 0. However, the first two parameters—the *ip_address* and *wildcard_mask* parameter values of 10.0.0.0 and 0.255.255.255—need some explaining. In this case, the command matches all three interfaces shown for Router R3; the next topic explains why.

Matching with the OSPF network Command

The key to understanding the traditional OSPFv2 configuration shown in this first example is to understand the OSPF **network** command. The OSPF **network** command compares the first parameter in the command to each interface IP address on the local router, trying to find a match. However, rather than comparing the entire number in the **network** command to the entire IPv4 address on the interface, the router can compare a subset of the octets, based on the wildcard mask, as follows:

Key Topic

Wildcard 0.0.0.0: Compare all 4 octets. In other words, the numbers must exactly match.

Wildcard 0.0.0.255: Compare the first 3 octets only. Ignore the last octet when comparing the numbers.

Wildcard 0.0.255.255: Compare the first 2 octets only. Ignore the last 2 octets when comparing the numbers.

Wildcard 0.255.255.255: Compare the first octet only. Ignore the last 3 octets when comparing the numbers.

Wildcard 255.255.255.255: Compare nothing—this wildcard mask means that all addresses will match the **network** command.

Basically, a wildcard mask value of 0 in an octet tells IOS to compare to see if the numbers match, and a value of 255 tells IOS to ignore that octet when comparing the numbers.

The **network** command provides many flexible options because of the wildcard mask. For example, in Router R3, many **network** commands could be used, with some matching all interfaces, and some matching a subset of interfaces. Table 8-2 shows a sampling of options, with notes.

Table 8-2 Example OSPF **network** Commands on R3, with Expected Results

Command	Logic in Command	Matched Interfaces
network 10.1.0.0 0.0.255.255	Match interface IP addresses that begin with 10.1	G0/0.341 G0/0.342 S0/0/0
network 10.0.0.0 0.255.255.255	Match interface IP addresses that begin with 10	G0/0.341 G0/0.342 S0/0/0
network 0.0.0.0 255.255.255.255	Match all interface IP addresses	G0/0.341 G0/0.342 S0/0/0
network 10.1.13.0 0.0.0.255	Match interface IP addresses that begin with 10.1.13	S0/0/0
network 10.1.3.1 0.0.0.0	Match one IP address: 10.1.3.1	G0/0.341

The wildcard mask gives the local router its rules for matching its own interfaces. For example, Example 8-2 shows R3 using the **network 10.0.0.0 0.255.255.255 area 0** command. However, the wildcard mask allows for many different valid OSPF configurations. For instance, in that same internetwork, Routers R1 and R2 could use the configuration shown in Example 8-3, with two other wildcard masks. In both routers, OSPF is enabled on all the interfaces shown in Figure 8-2.

Example 8-3 *OSPF Configuration on Routers R1 and R2*

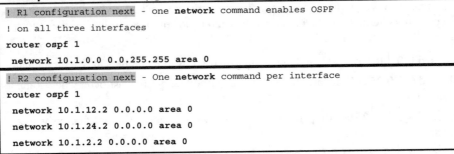

```
! R1 configuration next - one network command enables OSPF
! on all three interfaces
router ospf 1
 network 10.1.0.0 0.0.255.255 area 0

! R2 configuration next - One network command per interface
router ospf 1
 network 10.1.12.2 0.0.0.0 area 0
 network 10.1.24.2 0.0.0.0 area 0
 network 10.1.2.2 0.0.0.0 area 0
```

Finally, note that other wildcard mask values can be used as well, as long as the wildcard mask in binary is one unbroken string of 0s and another single string of binary 1s. Basically, that includes all wildcard masks that could be used to match all IP addresses in a subnet, as discussed in the "Finding the Right Wildcard Mask to Match a Subnet" section of Chapter 16, "Basic IPv4 Access Control Lists" (which is Chapter 25 of the ICND1 Cert Guide). For example, a mask of 0.255.255.0 would not be allowed.

NOTE The first two parameters of the **network** command are the address and the wildcard mask. By convention, if the wildcard mask octet is 255, the matching address octet should be configured as a 0. Interestingly, IOS will actually accept a **network** command that breaks this rule, but then IOS will change that octet of the address to a 0 before putting it into the running configuration file. For example, IOS will change a typed command that begins with **network 1.2.3.4 0.0.255.255** to **network 1.2.0.0 0.0.255.255**.

Verifying OSPFv2 Single Area

As mentioned in Chapter 7, OSPF routers use a three-step process to eventually add OSPF-learned routes to the IP routing table. First, they create neighbor relationships. Then they build and flood LSAs, so each router in the same area has a copy of the same LSDB. Finally, each router independently computes its own IP routes using the SPF algorithm and adds them to its routing table.

The **show ip ospf neighbor**, **show ip ospf database**, and **show ip route** commands display information for each of these three steps, respectively. To verify OSPF, you can use the same sequence. Or, you can just go look at the IP routing table, and if the routes look correct, OSPF probably worked.

For example, first, examine the list of neighbors known on Router R3 from the configuration in Examples 8-1, 8-2, and 8-3. R3 should have one neighbor relationship with R1, over the serial link. It also has two neighbor relationships with R4, over the two different VLANs to which both routers connect. Example 8-4 shows all three.

Key Topic

Example 8-4 *OSPF Neighbors on Router R3 from Figure 8-2*

```
R3# show ip ospf neighbor

Neighbor ID     Pri   State       Dead Time   Address        Interface
```

```
1.1.1.1            0    FULL/   -    00:00:33   10.1.13.1      Serial0/0/0
10.1.24.4          1    FULL/DR      00:00:35   10.1.3.130     GigabitEthernet0/0.342
10.1.24.4          1    FULL/DR      00:00:36   10.1.3.4       GigabitEthernet0/0.341
```

The detail in the output mentions several important facts, and for most people, working right to left works best in this case. For example, looking at the headings:

Interface: This is the local router's interface connected to the neighbor. For example, the first neighbor in the list is reachable through R3's S0/0/0 interface.

Address: This is the neighbor's IP address on that link. Again, for this first neighbor, the neighbor, which is R1, uses IP address 10.1.13.1.

State: While many possible states exist, for the details discussed in this chapter, FULL is the correct and fully working state in this case.

Neighbor ID: This is the router ID of the neighbor.

Next, Example 8-5 shows the contents of the LSDB on Router R3. Interestingly, when OSPF is working correctly in an internetwork with a single-area design, all the routers will have the same LSDB contents. So, the **show ip ospf database** command in Example 8-5 should list the same exact information, no matter on which of the four routers it is issued.

Example 8-5   *OSPF Database on Router R3 from Figure 8-2*

```
R3# show ip ospf database

            OSPF Router with ID (10.1.13.3) (Process ID 1)

                Router Link States (Area 0)

Link ID         ADV Router      Age         Seq#       Checksum Link count
1.1.1.1         1.1.1.1         498         0x80000006 0x002294 6
2.2.2.2         2.2.2.2         497         0x80000004 0x00E8C6 5
10.1.13.3       10.1.13.3       450         0x80000003 0x001043 4
10.1.24.4       10.1.24.4       451         0x80000003 0x009D7E 4

                Net Link States (Area 0)

Link ID         ADV Router      Age         Seq#       Checksum
10.1.3.4        10.1.24.4       451         0x80000001 0x0045F8
10.1.3.130      10.1.24.4       451         0x80000001 0x00546B
```

For the purposes of this book, do not be concerned about the specifics in the output of this command. However, for perspective, note that the LSDB should list one "Router Link State" (Type 1 Router LSA) for each of the routers in the same area. In this design, all four routers are in the same area, so there are four highlighted Type 1 LSAs listed.

Next, Example 8-6 shows R3's IPv4 routing table with the **show ip route** command. Note that it lists connected routes as well as OSPF routes. Take a moment to look back at Figure 8-2, and look for the subnets that are not locally connected to R3. Then look for those routes in the output in Example 8-5.

Example 8-6   *IPv4 Routes Added by OSPF on Router R3 from Figure 8-2*

```
R3# show ip route
Codes: L - local, C - connected, S - static, R - RIP, M - mobile, B - BGP
       D - EIGRP, EX - EIGRP external, O - OSPF, IA - OSPF inter area
       N1 - OSPF NSSA external type 1, N2 - OSPF NSSA external type 2
       E1 - OSPF external type 1, E2 - OSPF external type 2
! Legend lines omitted for brevity


      10.0.0.0/8 is variably subnetted, 11 subnets, 2 masks
O        10.1.1.0/25 [110/65] via 10.1.13.1, 00:13:28, Serial0/0/0
O        10.1.1.128/25 [110/65] via 10.1.13.1, 00:13:28, Serial0/0/0
O        10.1.2.0/25 [110/66] via 10.1.3.130, 00:12:41, GigabitEthernet0/0.342
                     [110/66] via 10.1.3.4, 00:12:41, GigabitEthernet0/0.341
C        10.1.3.0/25 is directly connected, GigabitEthernet0/0.341
L        10.1.3.1/32 is directly connected, GigabitEthernet0/0.341
C        10.1.3.128/25 is directly connected, GigabitEthernet0/0.342
L        10.1.3.129/32 is directly connected, GigabitEthernet0/0.342
O        10.1.12.0/25 [110/128] via 10.1.13.1, 00:13:28, Serial0/0/0
C        10.1.13.0/25 is directly connected, Serial0/0/0
L        10.1.13.3/32 is directly connected, Serial0/0/0
O        10.1.24.0/25
             [110/65] via 10.1.3.130, 00:12:41, GigabitEthernet0/0.342
             [110/65] via 10.1.3.4, 00:12:41, GigabitEthernet0/0.341
```

First, take a look at the bigger ideas confirmed by this output. The code of "O" on the left identifies a route as being learned by OSPF. The output lists five such IP routes. From Figure 8-2, five subnets exist that are not connected subnets off Router R3. Looking for a quick count of OSPF routes, versus nonconnected routes in the diagram, gives a quick check of whether OSPF learned all routes.

Next, take a look at the first route (to subnet 10.1.1.0/25). It lists the subnet ID and mask, identifying the subnet. It also lists two numbers in brackets. The first, 110, is the administrative distance of the route. All the OSPF routes in this example use the default of 110. The second number, 65, is the OSPF metric for this route.

Additionally, the **show ip protocols** command is also popular as a quick look at how any routing protocol works. This command lists a group of messages for each IPv4 routing protocol running on a router. Example 8-7 shows a sample, this time taken from Router R3.

Example 8-7   *The* **show ip protocols** *Command on R3*

```
R3# show ip protocols
*** IP Routing is NSF aware ***


Routing Protocol is "ospf 1"
  Outgoing update filter list for all interfaces is not set
  Incoming update filter list for all interfaces is not set
  Router ID 10.1.13.3
```

```
Number of areas in this router is 1. 1 normal 0 stub 0 nssa
Maximum path: 4
Routing for Networks:
   10.0.0.0 0.255.255.255 area 0
Routing Information Sources:
   Gateway          Distance      Last Update
   1.1.1.1               110      06:26:17
   2.2.2.2               110      06:25:30
   10.1.24.4             110      06:25:30
Distance: (default is 110)
```

The output shows several interesting facts. The first highlighted line repeats the parameters on the **router ospf 1** global configuration command. The second highlighted item points out R3's router ID, as discussed further in the next section. The third highlighted line repeats more configuration, listing the parameters of the **network 10.0.0.0 0.255.255.255 area 0** OSPF subcommand. Finally, the last highlighted item in the example acts as a heading before a list of known OSPF routers, by router ID.

Configuring the OSPF Router ID

While OSPF has many other optional features, most enterprise networks that use OSPF choose to configure each router's OSPF router ID. OSPF-speaking routers must have a router ID (RID) for proper operation. By default, routers will choose an interface IP address to use as the RID. However, many network engineers prefer to choose each router's router ID, so command output from commands like **show ip ospf neighbor** lists more recognizable router IDs.

To choose its RID, a Cisco router uses the following process when the router reloads and brings up the OSPF process. Note that when one of these steps identifies the RID, the process stops.

1. If the **router-id** *rid* OSPF subcommand is configured, this value is used as the RID.

2. If any loopback interfaces have an IP address configured, and the interface has an interface status of up, the router picks the highest numeric IP address among these loopback interfaces.

3. The router picks the highest numeric IP address from all other interfaces whose interface status code (first status code) is up. (In other words, an interface in up/down state will be included by OSPF when choosing its router ID.)

The first and third criteria should make some sense right away: the RID is either configured or is taken from a working interface's IP address. However, this book has not yet explained the concept of a *loopback interface*, as mentioned in Step 2.

A loopback interface is a virtual interface that can be configured with the **interface loopback** *interface-number* command, where *interface-number* is an integer. Loopback interfaces are always in an "up and up" state unless administratively placed in a shutdown state. For example, a simple configuration of the command **interface loopback 0**, followed by **ip address 2.2.2.2 255.255.255.0**, would create a loopback interface and assign it an IP address. Because loopback interfaces do not rely on any hardware, these interfaces can be up/up whenever IOS is running, making them good interfaces on which to base an OSPF RID.

Example 8-8 shows the configuration that existed in Routers R1 and R2 before the creation of the **show** command output in Examples 8-4, 8-5, and 8-6. R1 set its router ID using the direct method, while R2 used a loopback IP address.

Example 8-8 *OSPF Router ID Configuration Examples*

```
! R1 Configuration first
router ospf 1
router-id 1.1.1.1
 network 10.1.0.0 0.0.255.255 area 0


! R2 Configuration next
!
interface Loopback2
ip address 2.2.2.2 255.255.255.255
```

Each router chooses its OSPF RID when OSPF is initialized, which happens when the router boots or when a CLI user stops and restarts the OSPF process (with the **clear ip ospf process** command). So, if OSPF comes up, and later the configuration changes in a way that would impact the OSPF RID, OSPF does not change the RID immediately. Instead, IOS waits until the next time the OSPF process is restarted.

Example 8-9 shows the output of the **show ip ospf** command on R1, after the configuration of Example 8-8 was made, and after the router was reloaded, which made the OSPF router ID change.

Example 8-9 *Confirming the Current OSPF Router ID*

```
R1# show ip ospf
 Routing Process "ospf 1" with ID 1.1.1.1
! lines omitted for brevity
```

OSPF Passive Interfaces

Once OSPF has been enabled on an interface, the router tries to discover neighboring OSPF routers and form a neighbor relationship. To do so, the router sends OSPF Hello messages on a regular time interval (called the Hello Interval). The router also listens for incoming Hello messages from potential neighbors.

Sometimes, a router does not need to form neighbor relationships with neighbors on an interface. Often, no other routers exist on a particular link, so the router has no need to keep sending those repetitive OSPF Hello messages.

When a router does not need to discover neighbors off some interface, the engineer has a couple of configuration options. First, by doing nothing, the router keeps sending the messages, wasting some small bit of CPU cycles and effort. Alternately, the engineer can configure the interface as an OSPF passive interface, telling the router to do the following:

Key Topic

- Quit sending OSPF Hellos on the interface.
- Ignore received Hellos on the interface.
- Do not form neighbor relationships over the interface.

By making an interface passive, OSPF does not form neighbor relationships over the interface, but it does still advertise about the subnet connected to that interface. That is, the OSPF configuration enables OSPF on the interface (using the **network** router subcommand), and then makes the interface passive (using the **passive-interface** router subcommand).

To configure an interface as passive, two options exist. First, you can add the following command to the configuration of the OSPF process, in router configuration mode:

   passive-interface *type number*

Alternately, the configuration can change the default setting so that all interfaces are passive by default, and then add a **no passive-interface** command for all interfaces that need to not be passive:

   passive-interface default

   no passive-interface *type number*

For example, in the sample internetwork in Figure 8-2 (used in the single-area configuration examples), Router R1, at the bottom left of the figure, has a LAN interface configured for VLAN trunking. The only router connected to both VLANs is Router R1, so R1 will never discover an OSPF neighbor on these subnets. Example 8-10 shows two alternative configurations to make the two LAN subinterfaces passive to OSPF.

Example 8-10   *Configuring Passive Interfaces on R1 and R2 from Figure 8-2*

```
! First, make each subinterface passive directly
router ospf 1
 passive-interface GigabitEthernet0/0.11
 passive-interface GigabitEthernet0/0.12

! Or, change the default to passive, and make the other interfaces
! not be passive

router ospf 1
 passive-interface default
 no passive-interface serial0/0/0
 no passive-interface serial0/0/1
```

In real internetworks, the choice of configuration style reduces to which option requires the least number of commands. For example, a router with 20 interfaces, 18 of which are passive to OSPF, has far fewer configuration commands when using the **passive-interface default** command to change the default to passive. If only two of those 20 interfaces need to be passive, use the default setting, in which all interfaces are not passive, to keep the configuration shorter.

Interestingly, OSPF makes it a bit of a challenge to use **show** commands to find whether or not an interface is passive. The **show running-config** command lists the configuration directly, but if you cannot get into enable mode to use this command, note these two facts:

   The **show ip ospf interface brief** command lists all interfaces on which OSPF is enabled, *including passive interfaces.*

The **show ip ospf interface** command lists a single line that mentions that the interface is passive.

Example 8-11 shows these two commands on Router R1, with the configuration shown in the top of Example 8-10. Note that subinterfaces G0/0.11 and G0/0.12 both show up in the output of **show ip ospf interface brief**.

Example 8-11 *Displaying Passive Interfaces*

```
R1# show ip ospf interface brief

Interface    PID   Area        IP Address/Mask    Cost   State  Nbrs F/C
Gi0/0.12     1     0           10.1.1.129/25      1      DR     0/0
Gi0/0.11     1     0           10.1.1.1/25        1      DR     0/0
Se0/0/0      1     0           10.1.12.1/25       64     P2P    0/0
Se0/0/1      1     0           10.1.13.1/25       64     P2P    0/0


R1# show ip ospf interface g0/0.11
GigabitEthernet0/0.11 is up, line protocol is up
  Internet Address 10.1.1.1/25, Area 0, Attached via Network Statement
  Process ID 1, Router ID 10.1.1.129, Network Type BROADCAST, Cost: 1
  Topology-MTID    Cost    Disabled    Shutdown      Topology Name
       0            1        no          no           Base
  Transmit Delay is 1 sec, State DR, Priority 1
  Designated Router (ID) 10.1.1.129, Interface address 10.1.1.1
  No backup designated router on this network
  Timer intervals configured, Hello 10, Dead 40, Wait 40, Retransmit 5
    oob-resync timeout 40
    No Hellos (Passive interface)
! Lines omitted for brevity
```

Implementing Multiarea OSPFv2

Configuring the routers in a multiarea design is almost just like configuring OSPFv2 for a single area. The only difference is that the configuration places some interfaces on each ABR in different areas. The differences come in the verification and operation of OSPFv2.

This second major section of the chapter provides a second set of configurations to contrast multiarea configuration with single-area configuration. This new scenario shows the configuration for the routers in the multiarea OSPF design based on Figures 8-3 and 8-4. Figure 8-3 shows the internetwork topology and subnet IDs, and Figure 8-4 shows the area design. Note that Figure 8-3 lists the last octet of each router's IPv4 address near each interface, rather than the entire IPv4 address, to reduce clutter.

Take a moment to think about the area design shown in Figure 8-4, and look for the ABRs. Only R1 connects to the backbone area at all. The other three routers are internal routers in a single area. So, as it turns out, three of the four routers have single-area configurations, with all interfaces in the same area.

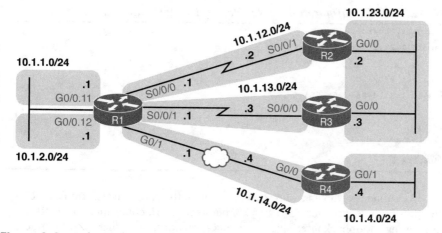

Figure 8-3 *Subnets for a Multiarea OSPF Configuration Example*

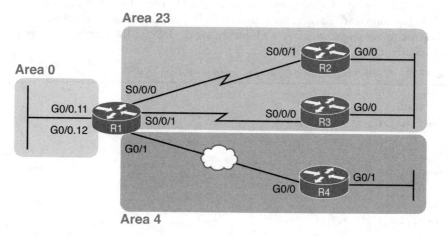

Figure 8-4 *Area Design for an Example Multiarea OSPF Configuration*

Note that the examples in this section use a variety of configuration options just so you can see those options. The options include different ways to set the OSPF RID, different wildcard masks on OSPF **network** commands, and the use of passive interfaces where no other OSPF routers should exist off an interface.

Single-Area Configurations

Example 8-12 begins the configuration example by showing the OSPF and IP address configuration on R2. Note that R2 acts as an internal router in area 23, meaning that the configuration will refer to only one area (23). The configuration sets R2's RID to 2.2.2.2 directly with the **router-id** command. And, because R2 should find neighbors on both its two interfaces, neither can reasonably be made passive, so R2's configuration lists no passive interfaces.

Example 8-12 *OSPF Configuration on R2, Placing Two Interfaces into Area 23*

```
interface GigabitEthernet0/0
 ip address 10.1.23.2 255.255.255.0
!
interface serial 0/0/1
 ip address 10.1.12.2 255.255.255.0
!
router ospf 1
 network 10.0.0.0 0.255.255.255 area 23
 router-id 2.2.2.2
```

Example 8-13 continues reviewing a few commands with the configuration for both R3 and R4. R3 puts both its interfaces into area 23, per its **network** command, sets its RID to 3.3.3.3 by using a loopback interface, and, like R2, cannot make either of its interfaces passive. The R4 configuration is somewhat different, with both interfaces placed into area 4, setting its RID based on a nonloopback interface (G0/0, for OSPF RID 10.1.14.4), and making R4's G0/1 interface passive, because no other OSPF routers sit on that link. (Note that the choice to use one method over another to set the OSPF RID is simply to show the variety of configuration options.)

Example 8-13 *OSPF Single-Area Configuration on R3 and R4*

```
! First, on R3
interface GigabitEthernet0/0
 ip address 10.1.23.3 255.255.255.0
!
interface serial 0/0/0
 ip address 10.1.13.3 255.255.255.0
!
interface loopback 0
 ip address 3.3.3.3 255.255.255.0
!
router ospf 1
 network 10.0.0.0 0.255.255.255 area 23
```
```
! Next, on R4
interface GigabitEthernet0/0
 description R4 will use this interface for its OSPF RID
 ip address 10.1.14.4 255.255.255.0
!
interface GigabitEthernet0/1
 ip address 10.1.4.4 255.255.255.0
!
router ospf 1
 network 10.0.0.0 0.255.255.255 area 4
 passive-interface GigabitEthernet0/1
```

Multiarea Configuration

The only router that has a multiarea config is an ABR, by virtue of the configuration referring to more than one area. In this design (as shown in Figure 8-4), only Router R1 acts as an ABR, with interfaces in three different areas. Example 8-14 shows R1's OSPF configuration. Note that the configuration does not state anything about R1 being an ABR; instead, it uses multiple **network** commands, some placing interfaces into area 0, some into area 23, and some into area 4.

Key Topic

Example 8-14   *OSPF Multiarea Configuration on Router R1*

```
interface GigabitEthernet0/0.11
 encapsulation dot1q 11
 ip address 10.1.1.1 255.255.255.0
!
interface GigabitEthernet0/0.12
 encapsulation dot1q 12
 ip address 10.1.2.1 255.255.255.0
!
interface GigabitEthernet0/1
 ip address 10.1.14.1 255.255.255.0
!
interface serial 0/0/0
 ip address 10.1.12.1 255.255.255.0
!
interface serial 0/0/1
 ip address 10.1.13.1 255.255.255.0
!
router ospf 1
 network 10.1.1.1 0.0.0.0 area 0
 network 10.1.2.1 0.0.0.0 area 0
 network 10.1.12.1 0.0.0.0 area 23
 network 10.1.13.1 0.0.0.0 area 23
 network 10.1.14.1 0.0.0.0 area 4
 router-id 1.1.1.1
 passive-interface GigabitEthernet0/0.11
 passive-interface GigabitEthernet0/0.12
```

Focus on the highlighted **network** commands in the example. All five commands happen to use a wildcard mask of 0.0.0.0, so that each command requires a specific match of the listed IP address. If you compare these **network** commands to the various interfaces on Router R1, you can see that the configuration enables OSPF, for area 0, on subinterfaces G0/0.11 and G0/0.12, area 23 for the two serial interfaces, and area 4 for R1's G0/1 interface.

NOTE   Many networks make a habit of using a 0.0.0.0 wildcard mask on OSPF **network** commands, requiring an exact match of each interface IP address, as shown in Example 8-14. This style of configuration makes it more obvious exactly which interfaces match which **network** command.

8

Finally, note that R1's configuration also sets its RID directly and makes its two LAN subinterfaces passive.

So, what's the big difference between single-area and multiarea OSPF configuration? Practically nothing. The only difference is that with multiarea, the ABR's **network** commands list different areas.

Verifying the Multiarea Configuration

The next few pages look at how to verify a few of the new OSPF features introduced in this chapter. Figure 8-5 summarizes the most important OSPF verification commands for reference.

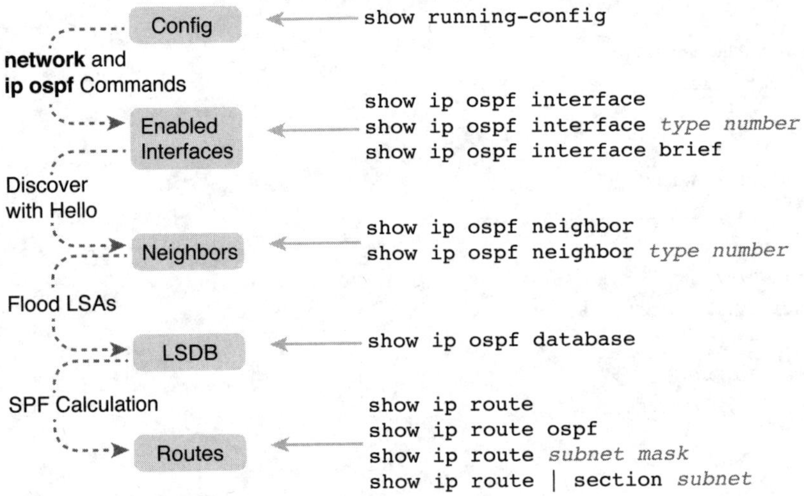

Figure 8-5 *OSPF Verification Commands*

This section looks at the following topics:

- Verifying the ABR interfaces are in the correct (multiple) areas
- Finding which router is DR and BDR on multiaccess links
- A brief look at the LSDB
- Displaying IPv4 routes

Verifying the Correct Areas on Each Interface on an ABR

The easiest place to make a configuration oversight with a multiarea configuration is to place an interface into the wrong OSPF area. Several commands mention the OSPF area. The **show ip protocols** command basically relists the OSPF **network** configuration commands, which indirectly identify the interfaces and areas. Also, the **show ip ospf interface** and **show ip ospf interface brief** commands directly show the area configured for an interface; Example 8-15 shows an example of the briefer version of these commands.

Key Topic

Example 8-15 *Listing the OSPF-Enabled Interfaces and the Matching OSPF Areas*

```
R1# show ip ospf interface brief
Interface     PID    Area        IP Address/Mask    Cost    State Nbrs F/C
Gi0/0.12      1      0           10.1.2.1/24        1       DR    0/0
Gi0/0.11      1      0           10.1.1.1/24        1       DR    0/0
Gi0/1         1      4           10.1.14.1/24       1       BDR   1/1
Se0/0/1       1      23          10.1.13.1/24       64      P2P   1/1
Se0/0/0       1      23          10.1.12.1/24       64      P2P   1/1
```

In the output, to correlate the areas, just look at the interface in the first column and the area in the third column. Also, for this example, double-check this information with Figures 8-3 and 8-4 to confirm that the configuration matches the design.

Verifying Which Router Is DR and BDR

Several **show** commands identify the DR and BDR in some way, as well. In fact, the **show ip ospf interface brief** command output, just listed in Example 8-15, lists the local router's state, showing that R1 is DR on two subinterfaces and BDR on its G0/1 interface.

Example 8-16 shows two other examples that identify the DR and BDR, but with a twist. The **show ip ospf interface** command lists detailed output about OSPF settings, per interface. Those details include the RID and interface address of the DR and BDR. At the same time, the **show ip ospf neighbor** command lists shorthand information about the neighbor's DR or BDR role as well; this command does not say anything about the local router's role.

Example 8-16 *Discovering the DR and BDR on the R1–R4 Ethernet (from R4)*

```
R4# show ip ospf interface gigabitEthernet 0/0
GigabitEthernet0/0 is up, line protocol is up
  Internet Address 10.1.14.4/24, Area 4, Attached via Network Statement
  Process ID 1, Router ID 10.1.14.4, Network Type BROADCAST, Cost: 1
  Topology-MTID    Cost    Disabled    Shutdown    Topology Name
        0           1         no          no          Base
  Transmit Delay is 1 sec, State DR, Priority 1
  Designated Router (ID) 10.1.14.4, Interface address 10.1.14.4
  Backup Designated router (ID) 1.1.1.1, Interface address 10.1.14.1
!
! Lines omitted for brevity
R4# show ip ospf neighbor

Neighbor ID      Pri    State        Dead Time    Address      Interface
1.1.1.1            1    FULL/BDR      00:00:33     10.1.14.1    GigabitEthernet0/0
```

First, focus on the highlighted lines from the **show ip ospf interface** command output. It lists the DR as RID 10.1.14.4, which is R4. It also lists the BDR as 1.1.1.1, which is R1.

The end of the example shows the **show ip ospf neighbor** command on R4, listing R4's single neighbor, with Neighbor RID 1.1.1.1 (R1). The command lists R4's concept of its neighbor state with neighbor 1.1.1.1 (R1), with the current state listed as FULL/BDR. The

8

FULL state means that R4 has fully exchanged its LSDB with R1. BDR means that the neighbor (R1) is acting as the BDR, implying that R4 (the only other router on this link) is acting as the DR.

Example 8-16 also shows the results of an DR/BDR election, with the router using the higher RID winning the election. The rules work like this:

■ When a link comes up, if two (or more) routers on the subnet send and hear each other's Hello messages, they elect a DR and BDR, with the higher OSPF RID becoming DR, and the second highest RID becoming the BDR.

■ Once the election has completed, new routers entering the subnet do not take over the DR or BDR role, even if they have better (higher) RID.

In this case, Routers R1 and R4, on the same Ethernet, heard each other's Hellos. R1, with RID 1.1.1.1, has a lower-value RID than R4's 10.1.14.1. As a result, R4 (10.1.14.1) won the DR election.

Verifying Interarea OSPF Routes

Finally, all this OSPF theory and all the **show** commands do not matter if the routers do not learn IPv4 routes. To verify the routes, Example 8-17 shows R4's IPv4 routing table.

Example 8-17   *Verifying OSPF Routes on Router R4*

```
R4# show ip route
Codes: L - local, C - connected, S - static, R - RIP, M - mobile, B - BGP
       D - EIGRP, EX - EIGRP external, O - OSPF, IA - OSPF inter area
       N1 - OSPF NSSA external type 1, N2 - OSPF NSSA external type 2
       E1 - OSPF external type 1, E2 - OSPF external type 2
       i - IS-IS, su - IS-IS summary, L1 - IS-IS level-1, L2 - IS-IS level-2
       ia - IS-IS inter area, * - candidate default, U - per-user static route
       o - ODR, P - periodic downloaded static route, H - NHRP, l - LISP
       + - replicated route, % - next hop override


      10.0.0.0/8 is variably subnetted, 9 subnets, 2 masks
O IA     10.1.1.0/24 [110/2] via 10.1.14.1, 11:04:43, GigabitEthernet0/0
O IA     10.1.2.0/24 [110/2] via 10.1.14.1, 11:04:43, GigabitEthernet0/0
C        10.1.4.0/24 is directly connected, GigabitEthernet0/1
L        10.1.4.4/32 is directly connected, GigabitEthernet0/1
O IA     10.1.12.0/24 [110/65] via 10.1.14.1, 11:04:43, GigabitEthernet0/0
O IA     10.1.13.0/24 [110/65] via 10.1.14.1, 11:04:43, GigabitEthernet0/0
C        10.1.14.0/24 is directly connected, GigabitEthernet0/0
L        10.1.14.4/32 is directly connected, GigabitEthernet0/0
O IA     10.1.23.0/24 [110/66] via 10.1.14.1, 11:04:43, GigabitEthernet0/0
```

This example shows a couple of new codes that are particularly interesting for OSPF. As usual, a single character on the left identifies the source of the route, with O meaning OSPF. In addition, IOS notes any interarea routes with an IA code as well. (The example does not list any intra-area OSPF routes, but these routes would simply omit the IA code; earlier

Example 8-6 lists some intra-area OSPF routes.) Also, note that R4 has routes to all seven subnets in the topology used in this example: two connected routes and five interarea OSPF routes.

Additional OSPF Features

So far this chapter has focused on the most common OSPF features using the traditional configuration using the OSPF **network** command. This final of three major sections discusses some very popular but optional OSPFv2 configuration features, as listed here in their order of appearance:

■ Default routes

■ Metrics

■ Load balancing

■ OSPF interface configuration

OSPF Default Routes

In some cases, routers benefit from using a default route. The ICND1 Cert Guide showed many of the details, with the configuration of static default routes in Chapter 18, learning default routes with DHCP in Chapter 20, and advertising default routes with RIP in Chapter 19. For those exact same reasons, networks that happen to use OSPFv2 can use OSPF to advertise default routes.

The most classic case for using a routing protocol to advertise a default route has to do with an enterprise's connection to the Internet. As a strategy, the enterprise engineer uses these design goals:

■ All routers learn specific routes for subnets inside the company; a default route is not needed when forwarding packets to these destinations.

■ One router connects to the Internet, and it has a default route that points toward the Internet.

■ All routers should dynamically learn a default route, used for all traffic going to the Internet, so that all packets destined to locations in the Internet go to the one router connected to the Internet.

Figure 8-6 shows the idea of how OSPF advertises the default route, with the specific OSPF configuration. In this case, a company connects to an ISP with its Router R1. That router has a static default route (destination 0.0.0.0, mask 0.0.0.0) with a next-hop address of the ISP router. Then, the use of the OSPF **default-information originate** command (Step 2) makes the router advertise a default route using OSPF to the remote routers (B1 and B2).

NOTE   The example in Figure 8-6 uses a static default route, but it could have used a default route as learned from the ISP with DHCP, as well as learning a default route with External BGP (eBGP), as discussed in Chapter 12, "Implementing External BGP."

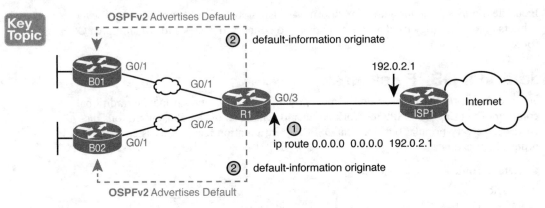

Figure 8-6 *Using OSPF to Create and Flood a Default Route*

Figure 8-7 shows the default routes that result from OSPF's advertisements in Figure 8-6. On the far left, the branch routers all have OSPF-learned default routes, pointing to R1. R1 itself also needs a default route, pointing to the ISP router, so that R1 can forward all Internet-bound traffic to the ISP.

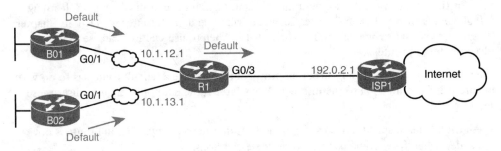

Figure 8-7 *Default Routes Resulting from the* **default-information originate** *Command*

Finally, this feature gives the engineer control over when the router originates this default route. First, R1 needs a default route, either defined as a static default route, learned from the ISP with DHCP, or learned from the ISP with a routing protocol like eBGP. The **default-information originate** command then tells R1 to advertise a default route when its own default route is working, and to advertise the default route as down when its own default route fails.

> **NOTE** Interestingly, the **default-information originate always** router subcommand tells the router to always advertise the default route, no matter whether the router's default route is working or not.

Example 8-18 shows details of the default route on both R1 and branch router B01. Beginning with Router R1, in this case, Router R1 used DHCP to learn its IP address on its G0/3 interface from the ISP. R1 then creates a static default route with the ISP router's IP address of 192.0.2.1 as the next-hop address, as highlighted in the output of the **show ip route static** command output.

Example 8-18 *Default Routes on Routers R1 and B01*

```
! The next command is from Router R1. Note the static code for the default route
R1# show ip route static
Codes: L - local, C - connected, S - static, R - RIP, M - mobile, B - BGP
! Rest of the legend omitted for brevity


Gateway of last resort is 192.0.2.1 to network 0.0.0.0


S*      0.0.0.0/0 [254/0] via 192.0.2.1
! The next command is from router B01; notice the External route code for the default
BO1# show ip route ospf
Codes: L - local, C - connected, S - static, R - RIP, M - mobile, B - BGP
        D - EIGRP, EX - EIGRP external, O - OSPF, IA - OSPF inter area
        N1 - OSPF NSSA external type 1, N2 - OSPF NSSA external type 2
        E1 - OSPF external type 1, E2 - OSPF external type 2
! Rest of the legend omitted for brevity


Gateway of last resort is 10.1.12.1 to network 0.0.0.0


O*E2    0.0.0.0/0 [110/1] via 10.1.12.1, 00:20:51, GigabitEthernet0/1
        10.0.0.0/8 is variably subnetted, 6 subnets, 2 masks
O          10.1.3.0/24 [110/3] via 10.1.12.1, 00:20:51, GigabitEthernet0/1
O          10.1.13.0/24 [110/2] via 10.1.12.1, 00:20:51, GigabitEthernet0/1
```

Keeping the focus on the command on Router R1, note that R1 indeed has a default route, that is, a route to 0.0.0.0/0. The "Gateway of last resort," which refers to the default route currently used by the router, points to next-hop IP address 192.0.2.1, which is the ISP router's IP address. (Refer back to Figure 8-7 for the particulars.)

Next look to the bottom half of the example, and router BO1's OSPF-learned default route. BO1 lists a route for 0.0.0.0/0 as well. The next-hop router in this case is 10.1.12.1, which is Router R1's IP address on the WAN link. The code on the far left is O*E2, meaning: an OSPF-learned route, which is a default route, and is specifically an external OSPF route. Finally, BO1's gateway of last resort setting uses that one OSPF-learned default route, with next-hop router 10.1.12.1.

OSPF Metrics (Cost)

Earlier, the Chapter 7 section "Calculating the Best Routes with SPF" discussed how SPF calculates the metric for each route, choosing the route with the best metric for each destination subnet. OSPF routers can influence that choice by changing the OSPF interface cost on any and all interfaces.

Cisco routers allow two different ways to change the OSPF interface cost. The one straightforward way is to set the cost directly, with an interface subcommand: **ip ospf cost** *x*. The other method is to let IOS choose default costs, based on a formula, but to change the inputs to the formula. This second method requires a little more thought and care and is the focus of this next topic.

Setting the Cost Based on Interface Bandwidth

The default OSPF cost values can actually cause a little confusion, for a couple of reasons. So, to get through some of the potential confusion, this section begins with some examples.

First, IOS uses the following formula to choose an interface's OSPF cost. IOS puts the interface's bandwidth in the denominator, and a settable OSPF value called the *reference bandwidth* in the numerator:

   Reference_bandwidth / Interface_bandwidth

With this formula, the following sequence of logic happens:

1.   A higher interface bandwidth—that is, a faster bandwidth—results in a lower number in the calculation.

2.   A lower number in the calculation gives the interface a lower cost.

3.   An interface with a lower cost is more likely to be used by OSPF when calculating the best routes.

Now for some examples. Assume a default reference bandwidth, set to 100 Mbps, which is the same as 100,000 Kbps. (The upcoming examples will use a unit of Kbps just to avoid math with fractions.) Assume defaults for interface bandwidth on serial, Ethernet, and Fast Ethernet interfaces, as shown in the output of the **show interfaces** command, respectively, of 1544 Kbps, 10,000 Kbps (meaning 10 Mbps), and 100,000 Kbps (meaning 100 Mbps). Table 8-3 shows the results of how IOS calculates the OSPF cost for some interface examples.

Table 8-3   OSPF Cost Calculation Examples with Default Bandwidth Settings

Interface	Interface Default Bandwidth (Kbps)	Formula (Kbps)	OSPF Cost
Serial	1544 Kbps	100,000/1544	64
Ethernet	10,000 Kbps	100,000/10,000	10
Fast Ethernet	100,000 Kbps	100,000/100,000	1

Example 8-19 shows the cost settings on R1's OSPF interfaces, all based on default OSPF (reference bandwidth) and default interface bandwidth settings.

Example 8-19   *Confirming OSPF Interface Costs*

```
R1# show ip ospf interface brief
Interface    PID    Area         IP Address/Mask    Cost   State Nbrs F/C
Gi0/0.12     1      0            10.1.2.1/24        1      DR    0/0
Gi0/0.11     1      0            10.1.1.1/24        1      DR    0/0
Gi0/1        1      4            10.1.14.1/24       1      BDR   1/1
Se0/0/1      1      23           10.1.13.1/24       64     P2P   1/1
Se0/0/0      1      23           10.1.12.1/24       64     P2P   1/1
```

To change the OSPF cost on these interfaces, the engineer simply needs to use the **bandwidth** *speed* interface subcommand to set the bandwidth on an interface. The interface bandwidth does not change the Layer 1 transmission speed at all; instead, it is used for other purposes, including routing protocol metric calculations. For instance, if you add the

bandwidth 10000 command to a serial interface, with a default reference bandwidth, the serial interface's OSPF cost could be calculated as 100,000 / 10,000 = 10.

Note that if the calculation of the default metric results in a fraction, OSPF rounds down to the nearest integer. For instance, the example shows the cost for interface S0/0/0 as 64. The calculation used the default serial interface bandwidth of 1.544 Mbps, with reference bandwidth 100 (Mbps), with the 100 / 1.544 calculation resulting in 64.7668394. OSPF rounds down to 64.

The Need for a Higher Reference Bandwidth

This default calculation works nicely as long as the fastest link in the network runs at 100 Mbps. The default reference bandwidth is set to 100, meaning 100 Mbps, the equivalent of 100,000 Kbps. As a result, with default settings, faster router interfaces end up with the same OSPF cost, as shown in Table 8-4, because the lowest allowed OSPF cost is 1.

Table 8-4   Faster Interfaces with Equal OSPF Costs

Interface	Interface Default Bandwidth (Kbps)	Formula (Kbps)	OSPF Cost
Fast Ethernet	100,000 Kbps	100,000/100,000	1
Gigabit Ethernet	1,000,000 Kbps	100,000/1,000,000	1
10 Gigabit Ethernet	10,000,000 Kbps	100,000/10,000,000	1
100 Gigabit Ethernet	100,000,000 Kbps	100,000/100,000,000	1

To avoid this issue, and change the default cost calculation, you can change the reference bandwidth with the **auto-cost reference-bandwidth** *speed* OSPF mode subcommand. This command sets a value in a unit of megabits per second (Mbps). To avoid the issue shown in Table 8-4, set the reference bandwidth value to match the fastest link speed in the network. For instance, **auto-cost reference-bandwidth 10000** accommodates links up to 10 Gbps in speed.

8

NOTE   Cisco recommends making the OSPF reference bandwidth setting the same on all OSPF routers in an enterprise network.

For convenient study, the following list summarizes the rules for how a router sets its OSPF interface costs:

Key Topic

1. Set the cost explicitly, using the **ip ospf cost** *x* interface subcommand, to a value between 1 and 65,535, inclusive.

2. Change the interface bandwidth with the **bandwidth** *speed* command, with *speed* being a number in kilobits per second (Kbps).

3. Change the reference bandwidth, using router OSPF subcommand **auto-cost reference-bandwidth** *ref-bw*, with a unit of megabits per second (Mbps).

OSPF Load Balancing

When a router uses SPF to calculate the metric for each of several routes to reach one subnet, one route may have the lowest metric, so OSPF puts that route in the routing table.

However, when the metrics tie for multiple routes to the same subnet, the router can put multiple equal-cost routes in the routing table (the default is four different routes) based on the setting of the **maximum-paths** *number* router subcommand. For example, if an internetwork has six possible paths between some parts of the network, and the engineer wants all routes to be used, the routers can be configured with the **maximum-paths 6** subcommand under **router ospf**.

The more challenging concept relates to how the routers use those multiple routes. A router could load balance the packets on a per-packet basis. For example, if the router has three equal-cost OSPF routes for the same subnet in the routing table, the router could send the one packet over the first route, the next packet over the second route, the next packet over the third route, and then start over with the first route for the next packet. Alternatively, the load balancing could be on a per-destination IP address basis.

Note that the default setting of **maximum-paths** varies by router platform.

OSPFv2 Interface Configuration

The newer interface-style OSPF configuration works mostly like the old style, for almost all features, with one important exception. The interface configuration enables OSPF directly on the interface with the **ip ospf** interface subcommand, while the traditional OSPFv2 configuration enables OSPFv2 on an interface, but indirectly, using the **network** command in OSPF configuration mode. The rest of the OSPF features discussed throughout this chapter are not changed by the use of OSPFv2 interface configuration.

Basically, instead of matching interfaces with indirect logic using **network** commands, you directly enable OSPFv2 on interfaces by configuring an interface subcommand on each interface.

OSPFv2 Interface Configuration Example

To show how OSPF interface configuration works, this example basically repeats the example shown earlier in the book using the traditional OSPFv2 configuration with **network** commands. So, before looking at the OSPFv2 interface configuration, take a moment to look back at Figures 8-3 and 8-4, along with Examples 8-12, 8-13, and 8-14. Once reviewed, for easier reference, Figure 8-8 repeats Figure 8-4 for reference in the upcoming interface configuration examples.

To convert from the old-style configuration in Examples 8-12, 8-13, and 8-14, simply do the following:

Config Checklist

Step 1. Use the **no network** *network-id* **area** *area-id* subcommands in OSPF configuration mode to remove the **network** commands.

Step 2. Add one **ip ospf** *process-id* **area** *area-id* command in interface configuration mode under each interface on which OSPF should operate, with the correct OSPF process (*process-id*) and the correct OSPF area number.

For example, Example 8-12 had a single **network** command that enabled OSPF on two interfaces on Router R2, putting both in area 23. Example 8-20 shows the replacement newer style of configuration.

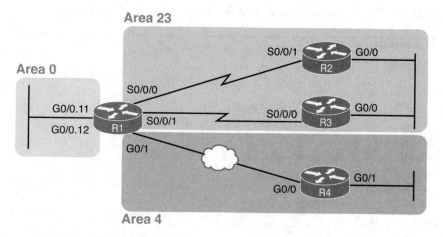

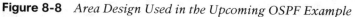

Figure 8-8   *Area Design Used in the Upcoming OSPF Example*

Example 8-20   *New-Style Configuration on Router R2*

```
interface GigabitEthernet0/0
 ip address 10.1.23.2 255.255.255.0
 ip ospf 1 area 23
!
interface serial 0/0/1
 ip address 10.1.12.2 255.255.255.0
 ip ospf 1 area 23

router ospf 1
 router-id 2.2.2.2
! Notice - no network commands here!
```

Verifying OSPFv2 Interface Configuration

OSPF operates the same way whether you use the new style or old style of configuration. The OSPF area design works the same, neighbor relationships form the same way, routers negotiate to become the DR and BDR the same way, and so on. However, you can see a few small differences in command output when using the newer OSPFv2 configuration if you look closely.

The **show ip protocols** command relists most of the routing protocol configuration, just in slightly different format, as shown in Example 8-21. With the newer-style configuration, the output lists the phrase "Interfaces Configured Explicitly," with the list of interfaces configured with the new **ip ospf** *process-id* **area** *area-id* commands, as highlighted in the example. With the old configuration, the output lists the contents of all the **network** commands, just leaving out the "network" word itself. Note that in the next two examples, R2 has been reconfigured to use OSPF interface configuration as shown in the previous example (Example 8-20), while Router R3 still uses the older-style **network** commands per earlier configuration Example 8-13.

Example 8-21 *Differences in* **show ip protocols** *Output: Old- and New-Style OSPFv2 Configuration*

```
R2# show ip protocols
*** IP Routing is NSF aware ***


Routing Protocol is "ospf 1"
  Outgoing update filter list for all interfaces is not set
  Incoming update filter list for all interfaces is not set
  Router ID 2.2.2.2
  Number of areas in this router is 1. 1 normal 0 stub 0 nssa
  Maximum path: 4
  Routing for Networks:
  Routing on Interfaces Configured Explicitly (Area 23):
    Serial0/0/1
    GigabitEthernet0/0
  Routing Information Sources:
    Gateway         Distance      Last Update
    3.3.3.3              110      00:04:59
    1.1.1.1              110      00:04:43
  Distance: (default is 110)

! Below, showing only the part that differs on R3:
R3# show ip protocols
! … beginning lines omitted for brevity
  Routing for Networks:
    10.0.0.0 0.255.255.255 area 23
! … ending line omitted for brevity
```

Basically, the **show ip protocols** command output differs depending on the style of configuration, either relisting the interfaces when using interface configuration or relisting the network commands if using **network** commands.

Next, the **show ip ospf interface** [*interface*] command lists details about OSPF settings for the interface(s) on which OSPF is enabled. The output also makes a subtle reference to whether that interface was enabled for OSPF with the old or new configuration style. As seen in Example 8-22, R2's new-style interface configuration results in the highlighted text, "Attached via Interface Enable," whereas R3's old-style configuration lists "Attached via Network Statement."

Key Topic

Example 8-22 *Differences in* **show ip ospf interface** *Output with OSPFv2 Interface Configuration*

```
R2# show ip ospf interface g0/0
GigabitEthernet0/0 is up, line protocol is up
  Internet Address 10.1.23.2/24, Area 23, Attached via Interface Enable
  Process ID 1, Router ID 22.2.2.2, Network Type BROADCAST, Cost: 1
  Topology-MTID    Cost    Disabled    Shutdown    Topology Name
       0            1         no          no         Base
  Enabled by interface config, including secondary ip addresses
```

```
    Transmit Delay is 1 sec, State DR, Priority 1
    Designated Router (ID) 2.2.2.2, Interface address 10.1.23.2
    Backup Designated router (ID) 3.3.3.3, Interface address 10.1.23.3
! Showing only the part that differs on R3:
R3# show ip ospf interface g0/0
GigabitEthernet0/0 is up, line protocol is up
   Internet Address 10.1.23.3/24, Area 23, Attached via Network Statement
! ... ending line omitted for brevity
```

Note that the briefer version of this command, the **show ip ospf interface brief** command, does not change whether the configuration uses traditional **network** commands or the alternative interface configuration with the **ip ospf** interface subcommand.

Chapter Review

One key to doing well on the exams is to perform repetitive spaced review sessions. Review this chapter's material using either the tools in the book, DVD, or interactive tools for the same material found on the book's companion website. Refer to the "Your Study Plan" element for more details. Table 8-5 outlines the key review elements and where you can find them. To better track your study progress, record when you completed these activities in the second column.

Table 8-5   Chapter Review Tracking

Review Element	Review Date(s)	Resource Used:
Review key topics		Book, DVD/website
Review key terms		Book, DVD/website
Answer DIKTA questions		Book, PCPT
Do labs		Blog
Review Config Checklists		Book, DVD/website
Review command tables		Book

Review All the Key Topics

Table 8-6   Key Topics for Chapter 8

Key Topic Element	Description	Page Number
List	Example OSPF wildcard masks and their meaning	199
Example 8-4	Example of the **show ip ospf neighbor** command	200
List	Rules for setting the router ID	203
List	Actions IOS takes when an OSPF interface is passive	204
Example 8-14	Example of a multiarea OSPFv2 configuration	209
Figure 8-5	Popular OSPF **show** commands and their general purposes	210

Key Topic Element	Description	Page Number
Example 8-15	Example of the **show ip ospf interface brief** showing interfaces in multiple areas	211
Figure 8-6	Actions taken by the OSPF **default-information originate** command	214
List	Rules for setting OSPF interface cost	217
Example 8-22	Differences in **show ip ospf interface** output with OSPF interface configuration	220

Key Terms You Should Know

reference bandwidth, interface bandwidth, maximum paths

Command References

Tables 8-7 and 8-8 list configuration and verification commands used in this chapter. As an easy review exercise, cover the left column in a table, read the right column, and try to recall the command without looking. Then repeat the exercise, covering the right column, and try to recall what the command does.

Table 8-7 Chapter 8 Configuration Command Reference

Command	Description
router ospf *process-id*	Enters OSPF configuration mode for the listed process.
network *ip-address wildcard-mask* **area** *area-id*	Router subcommand that enables OSPF on interfaces matching the address/wildcard combination and sets the OSPF area.
ip ospf *process-id* **area** *area-number*	Interface subcommand to enable OSPF on the interface and to assign the interface to a specific OSPF area.
ip ospf cost *interface-cost*	Interface subcommand that sets the OSPF cost associated with the interface.
bandwidth *bandwidth*	Interface subcommand that directly sets the interface bandwidth (Kbps).
auto-cost reference-bandwidth *number*	Router subcommand that tells OSPF the numerator in the Reference_bandwidth / Interface_bandwidth formula used to calculate the OSPF cost based on the interface bandwidth.
router-id *id*	OSPF command that statically sets the router ID.
interface loopback *number*	Global command to create a loopback interface and to navigate to interface configuration mode for that interface.
maximum-paths *number-of-paths*	Router subcommand that defines the maximum number of equal-cost routes that can be added to the routing table.
passive-interface *type number*	Router subcommand that makes the interface passive to OSPF, meaning that the OSPF process will not form neighbor relationships with neighbors reachable on that interface.
passive-interface *default*	OSPF subcommand that changes the OSPF default for interfaces to be passive instead of active (not passive).

Command	Description
no passive-interface *type number*	OSPF subcommand that tells OSPF to be active (not passive) on that interface or subinterface.
default-information originate [**always**]	OSPF subcommand to tell OSPF to create and advertise an OSPF default route, as long as the router has some default route (or to always advertise a default, if the **always** option is configured).

Table 8-8   Chapter 8 EXEC Command Reference

Command	Description
show ip ospf	Lists information about the OSPF process running on the router, including the OSPF router ID, areas to which the router connects, and the number of interfaces in each area.
show ip ospf interface brief	Lists the interfaces on which the OSPF protocol is enabled (based on the **network** commands), including passive interfaces.
show ip ospf interface [*type number*]	Lists a long section of settings, status, and counters for OSPF operation on all interfaces, or on the listed interface, including the Hello and Dead Timers.
show ip protocols	Shows routing protocol parameters and current timer values.
show ip ospf neighbor [*type number*]	Lists brief output about neighbors, identified by neighbor router ID, including current state, with one line per neighbor; optionally, limits the output to neighbors on the listed interface.
show ip ospf neighbor *neighbor-ID*	Lists the same output as the **show ip ospf neighbor** detail command, but only for the listed neighbor (by neighbor RID).
show ip ospf database	Lists a summary of the LSAs in the database, with one line of output per LSA. It is organized by LSA type (first type 1, then type 2, and so on).
show ip route	Lists all IPv4 routes.
show ip route ospf	Lists routes in the routing table learned by OSPF.
show ip route *ip-address mask*	Shows a detailed description of the route for the listed subnet/mask.
clear ip ospf process	Resets the OSPF process, resetting all neighbor relationships and also causing the process to make a choice of OSPF RID.

8

Understanding EIGRP Concepts

This chapter covers the following exam topics:

2.0 Routing Technologies

2.2 Compare and contrast distance vector and link-state routing protocols

2.3 Compare and contrast interior and exterior routing protocols

2.6 Configure, verify, and troubleshoot EIGRP for IPv4 (excluding authentication, filtering, manual summarization, redistribution, stub)

This chapter takes an in-depth look at a second option for an IPv4 routing protocol: the Enhanced Interior Gateway Routing Protocol, or EIGRP. This Cisco-proprietary routing protocol uses configuration commands much like Open Shortest Path First (OSPF), with the primary difference being that EIGRP configuration does not need to refer to an area. However, EIGRP does not use link-state (LS) logic, instead using some advanced distance vector (DV) logic. So, this chapter discusses quite a bit of detail about how routing protocols work and how EIGRP works before moving on to EIGRP configuration.

This chapter breaks the topics into two major sections. The first looks at some distance vector concepts, comparing some of the basic features of RIPv2 with the more advanced features of EIGRP. The second major section looks at the specifics of EIGRP operation, including EIGRP neighbors, exchanging routing information, and calculating the currently best routes to reach each possible subnet.

"Do I Know This Already?" Quiz

Take the quiz (either here, or use the PCPT software) if you want to use the score to help you decide how much time to spend on this chapter. The answers are at the bottom of the page following the quiz, and the explanations are in DVD Appendix C and in the PCPT software.

Table 9-1 "Do I Know This Already?" Foundation Topics Section-to-Question Mapping

Foundation Topics Section	Questions
EIGRP and Distance Vector Routing Protocols	1–3
EIGRP Concepts and Operation	4–6

1. Which of the following distance vector features prevents routing loops by causing the routing protocol to advertise only a subset of known routes, as opposed to the full routing table, under normal stable conditions?

   a. Route poisoning

   b. Poison reverse

   c. DUAL

   d. Split horizon

2. Which of the following distance vector features prevents routing loops by advertising an infinite metric route when a route fails?

a. Dijkstra SPF

b. DUAL

c. Split horizon

d. Route poisoning

3. Routers A and B use EIGRP. How does router A watch for the status of router B so that router A can react if router B fails?

a. By using EIGRP Hello messages, with A needing to receive periodic Hello messages to believe B is still working.

b. By using EIGRP update messages, with A needing to receive periodic update messages to believe B is still working.

c. Using a periodic ping of B's IP address based on the EIGRP neighbor timer.

d. None of the other answers are correct.

4. Which of the following affect the calculation of EIGRP metrics when all possible default values are used? (Choose two answers.)

a. Bandwidth

b. Delay

c. Load

d. Reliability

e. MTU

f. Hop count

5. Which of the following is true about the concept of EIGRP feasible distance?

a. A route's feasible distance is the calculated metric of a feasible successor route.

b. A route's feasible distance is the calculated metric of the successor route.

c. The feasible distance is the metric of a route from a neighboring router's perspective.

d. The feasible distance is the EIGRP metric associated with each possible route to reach a subnet.

6. Which of the following is true about the concept of EIGRP reported distance?

a. A route's reported distance is the calculated metric of a feasible successor route.

b. A route's reported distance is the calculated metric of the successor route.

c. A route's reported distance is the metric of a route from a neighboring router's perspective.

d. The reported distance is the EIGRP metric associated with each possible route to reach a subnet.

Foundation Topics

EIGRP and Distance Vector Routing Protocols

IPv4's long history has resulted in many competing interior gateway protocols (IGP). Each of those different IPv4 IGPs differs in some ways, including the underlying routing protocol algorithms like link state and distance vector. This first section of the chapter looks at how EIGRP acts like distance vector routing protocols to some degree, while at the same time, EIGRP does not fit easily into any category at all.

In particular, this first section positions EIGRP against the other common IPv4 routing protocols. Then this section looks at basic DV concepts as implemented with RIP. Using the simpler RIP to learn the basics helps the discussion focus on the DV concepts. This section ends then with a discussion of how EIGRP uses DV features but in a more efficient way than RIP uses them.

Introduction to EIGRP

Historically speaking, the first IPv4 routing protocols used DV logic. RIP Version 1 (RIPv1) was the first popularly used IP routing protocol, with the Cisco-proprietary Interior Gateway Routing Protocol (IGRP) being introduced a little later, as shown in Figure 9-1.

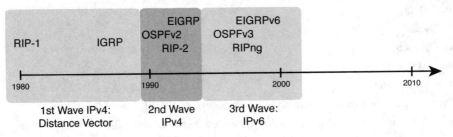

Figure 9-1 *Timeline for IP IGPs*

By the early 1990s, business and technical factors pushed the IPv4 world toward a second wave of better routing protocols. RIPv1 and IGRP had some technical limitations, even though they were great options for the technology levels of the 1980s. The world needed better routing protocols due to the widespread adoption and growth of TCP/IP in enterprise networks in the 1990s. Many enterprises migrated away from older vendor-proprietary networks to instead use networks built with routers, LANs, and TCP/IP. These businesses needed better performance from their routing protocols, including better metrics and better convergence. All these factors led to the introduction of a new wave of IPv4 interior routing protocols: RIP Version 2 (RIPv2), OSPF, and EIGRP.

Even today, EIGRP and OSPF remain the two primary competitors as the IPv4 routing protocol to use in a modern enterprise IPv4 internetwork. RIPv2 has fallen away as a serious competitor, in part due to its less robust hop-count metric, and in part due to its slower (worse) convergence time. Even today, you can walk in to most corporate networks and find either EIGRP or OSPF as the routing protocol used throughout the network.

Answers to the "Do I Know This Already?" quiz:

1 D **2** D **3** A **4** A, B **5** B **6** C

So, with so many IPv4 routing protocols, how does a network engineer choose which routing protocol to use? Well, consider two key points about EIGRP that drive engineers toward wanting to use it:

- EIGRP uses a robust metric based on both link bandwidth and link delay, so routers make good choices about the best route to use (see Figure 9-2).

- EIGRP converges quickly, meaning that when something changes in the internetwork, EIGRP quickly finds the currently best loop-free routes to use.

For example, RIP uses a basic metric of hop count, meaning the number of routers between the destination subnet and the local router. The hop count metric causes RIP to choose the least-hop route, even if those links are slow links, so RIP may choose an arguably poor route as the best route. EIGRP's metric calculation uses a math formula that avoids routes with slow links by giving those routes worse (higher) metrics. Figure 9-2 shows an example.

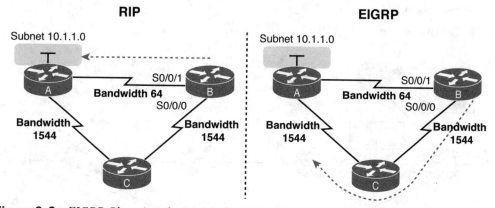

Figure 9-2   *EIGRP Choosing the Longer but Better Route to Subnet 10.1.1.0*

Traditionally, from the introduction of EIGRP in the 1990s until 2013, the one big negative about EIGRP was that Cisco kept the protocol as a Cisco-proprietary protocol. As a result, to run Cisco's EIGRP, you had to buy Cisco routers. In an interesting change, Cisco published EIGRP as an informational RFC, meaning that now other vendors can choose to implement EIGRP as well. In the past, many companies chose to use OSPF rather than EIGRP to give themselves options for what router vendor to use for future router hardware purchases. In the future, it might be that you can buy some routers from Cisco, some from other vendors, and still run EIGRP on all routers.

Today, EIGRP and OSPF remain the two best options for IPv4 interior routing protocols. Both converge quickly. Both use a good metric that considers link speeds when choosing the route. EIGRP can be much simpler to implement. Many reasonable network engineers have made these comparisons over the years, with some choosing OSPFv2 and others choosing EIGRP.

Basic Distance Vector Routing Protocol Features

EIGRP does not fit cleanly into the category of DV routing protocols or LS routing protocols. However, it most closely matches DV protocols. The next topic explains the basics of DV routing protocols as originally implemented with RIP, to give a frame of reference of how DV protocols work. In particular, the next examples show routes that use RIP's simple hop-count metric, which, although a poor option in real networks today, is a much simpler option for learning than EIGRP's more complex metric.

The Concept of a Distance and a Vector

The term *distance vector* describes what a router knows about each route. At the end of the process, when a router learns about a route to a subnet, all the router knows is some measurement of distance (the metric) and the next-hop router and outgoing interface to use for that route (a vector, or direction).

Figure 9-3 shows a view of both the vector and the distance as learned with RIP. The figure shows the flow of RIP messages that cause R1 to learn some IPv4 routes, specifically three routes to reach subnet X:

- The four-hop route through R2
- The three-hop route through R5
- The two-hop route through R7

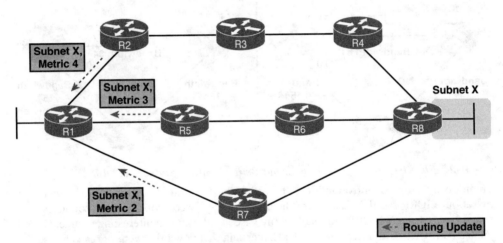

Figure 9-3 *Information Learned Using DV Protocols*

DV protocols learn two pieces of information about a possible route to reach a subnet: the distance (metric) and the vector (the next-hop router). In this case, R1 learns three routes to reach subnet X. When only one route for a single subnet exists, the router chooses that one route. However, with the three possible routes in this case, R1 picks the two-hop route through next-hop Router R7, because that route has the lowest RIP metric.

While Figure 9-3 shows how R1 learns the routes with RIP updates, Figure 9-4 gives a better view into R1's distance vector logic. R1 knows three routes, each with

Distance: The metric for a possible route

Vector: The direction, based on the next-hop router for a possible route

Note that R1 knows no other topology information about the internetwork. Unlike LS protocols, RIP's DV logic has no idea about the overall topology, instead just knowing about next-hop routers and metrics.

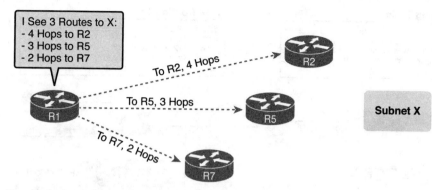

Figure 9-4 *Graphical Representation of the DV Concept*

Full Update Messages and Split Horizon

DV routing protocols have a couple of functions that require messages between neighboring routers.

First, routers need to send routing information inside some message, so that the sending router can advertise routing information to neighboring routers. For instance, in Figure 9-3, R1 received RIP messages to learn routes. As discussed in Chapter 7, OSPF calls those messages Link-State Updates (LSU). RIP and EIGRP both call their messages an *update* message.

In addition, routers need to monitor whether each neighboring router is still working or not; routers do so by sending and receiving regular messages with each neighbor. By quickly realizing when a neighboring router fails, routers can more quickly converge to use any still-available routes.

All routing protocols use some mechanism to monitor the state of neighboring routers. OSPF uses Hello messages, on a relatively short time interval (default 10 seconds on many interfaces). EIGRP uses a Hello message and process as well. However, old basic DV protocols such as RIP do not use a separate Hello type of message, instead using the same update message both to advertise routing information and be aware of whether the neighboring router is still alive. In other words, the function of advertising routing information, and the function of monitoring neighbor state, is done with the same update message.

These older basic DV routing protocols such as RIP send periodic full routing updates based on a relatively short time interval. *Full update* means that a router advertises all its routes, using one or more RIP update messages, no matter whether the route has changed or not. *Periodic* means that the router sends the message based on a short timed period (30 seconds with RIP).

Figure 9-5 illustrates this concept in an internetwork with two routers, three LAN subnets, and one WAN subnet. The figure shows both routers' full routing tables, plus listing the periodic full updates sent by each router.

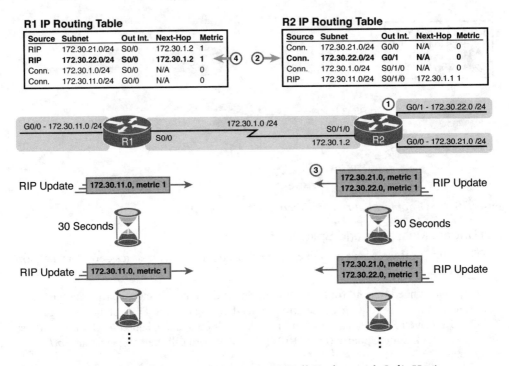

Figure 9-5 *Normal Steady-State RIP Operations: Full Update with Split Horizon*

This figure shows a lot of information, so take the time to work through the details. For example, consider what Router R1 learns for subnet 172.30.22.0/24, which is the subnet connected to R2's G0/1 interface:

1. R2 interface G0/1 has an IP address, and is in an up/up state.

2. R2 adds a connected route for 172.30.22.0/24, off interface G0/1, to R2's routing table.

3. R2 advertises its route for 172.30.22.0/24 to R1, with metric 1, meaning that R1's metric to reach this subnet will be metric 1 (hop count 1).

4. R1 adds a route for subnet 172.30.22.0/24, listing it as a RIP learned route with metric 1.

Also, take a moment to focus more on the route learned at Step 4: the bold route in R1's routing table. This route is for 172.30.22.0/24, as learned from R2. It lists R1's local S0/0 interface as the outgoing interface, because R1 receives the update on that interface. It also lists R2's serial IP address of 172.30.1.2 as next-hop router because that's the IP address from which R1 learned the route.

Next, look at the bottom of the figure, which shows the RIP update message being used to monitor neighbor state. The routers repeat the exact same update message based on 30-second timers. Note that in this internetwork, if nothing changed for a year, with RIP, every 30 seconds, the routers would repeat this same routing information to each other. Why? If a router fails to receive the update messages for a defined time period, the local router knows the silent neighbor has failed.

Finally, the figure shows an example of *split horizon*. Note that both routers list all four subnets in their IP routing tables, yet the RIP update messages do not list four subnets. The reason? Split horizon. Split horizon is a DV feature that tells the routing protocol to not advertise some routes in an update sent out an interface. Which routes? The routes that list that same interface as the outgoing interface. Those routes that are not advertised on an interface usually include the routes learned in routing updates received on that interface.

Split horizon is difficult to learn by reading words, and much easier to learn by seeing an example. Figure 9-6 continues the same example as 9-5, but focusing on R1's RIP update sent out R1's S0/0 interface to R2. This figure shows R1's routing table with three light-colored routes, all of which list S0/0 as the outgoing interface. When building the RIP update to send out S0/0, split-horizon rules tell R1 to ignore those light-colored routes, because all three routes list S0/0 as the outgoing interface. Only the bold route, which does not list S0/0 as an outgoing interface, can be included in the RIP update sent out S0/0.

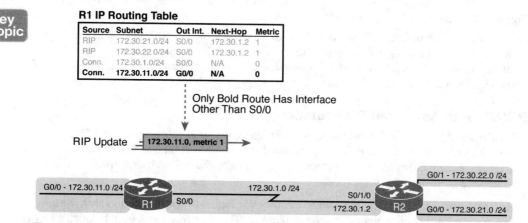

Figure 9-6   *R1 Does Not Advertise Three Routes Due to Split Horizon*

Route Poisoning

DV protocols help prevent routing loops by ensuring that every router learns that the route has failed, through every means possible, as quickly as possible. One of these features, *route poisoning*, helps all routers know for sure that a route has failed.

Route poisoning refers to the practice of advertising a failed route, but with a special metric value called *infinity*. Routers consider routes advertised with an infinite metric to have failed. Figure 9-7 shows an example of route poisoning with RIP, with R2's G0/1 interface failing, meaning that R2's route for 172.30.22.0/24 has failed. RIP defines infinity as 16.

Figure 9-7 shows the following process:

1. R2's G0/1 interface fails.

2. R2 removes its connected route for 172.30.22.0/24 from its routing table.

3. R2 advertises 172.30.22.0 with an infinite metric (which for RIP is 16).

4. Depending on other conditions, R1 either immediately removes the route to 172.30.22.0 from its routing table, or marks the route as unusable (with an infinite metric) for a few minutes before removing the route.

By the end of this process, Router R1 knows for sure that its old route for subnet 172.30.22.0/24 has failed, which helps R1 not introduce any looping IP routes.

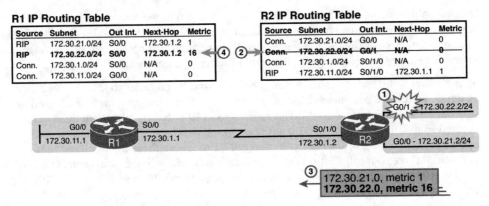

Figure 9-7 *Route Poisoning*

Each routing protocol has its own definition of an infinite metric. RIP uses 16, as shown in the figure, with 15 being a valid metric for a usable route. EIGRP has long used $2^{32} - 1$ as infinity (a little over 4 billion) with an option for a wider (larger) metric beyond the scope of this chapter. OSPFv2 uses $2^{24} - 1$ as infinity.

EIGRP as an Advanced DV Protocol

EIGRP acts a little like a DV protocol, and a little like no other routing protocol. Frankly, over the years, different Cisco documents and different books (mine included) have characterized EIGRP either as its own category, called a balanced hybrid routing protocol, or as some kind of advanced DV protocol.

Regardless of what label you put on EIGRP, the protocol uses several features that work like some other Distance Vector protocols like RIP. The next few pages walk through a few of the similarities and differences between RIP and EIGRP.

EIGRP Sends Partial Update Messages, As Needed

EIGRP does not use a short periodic update timer, sending a full update with all routes, like RIP does. EIGRP instead sends information about each route once, when the router learns the information. Then, the router sends only partial updates.

EIGRP *partial updates* are EIGRP update messages that list any new or changed information about a route. For instance, when a router interface fails, some routes will be affected. The router sends an immediate partial update message to any other neighboring EIGRP routers, listing new information. Or, when new routes become available, the router sends a partial update, about only the new routes. These update messages are not full updates, because they only contain changed or new information.

The idea works a little like OSPF's convention of flooding a link-state advertisement (LSA) once inside an area. However, the router that creates an OSPF LSA does reflood that LSA every 30 minutes. EIGRP does not even bother to reflood its routing information. For instance, if the routing information about an EIGRP route does not change for a year, EIGRP will literally remain silent about that route in its update messages for that whole year after it first advertises the route.

EIGRP Maintains Neighbor Status Using Hello

EIGRP does not send full or partial update messages based on a short periodic timer, so EIGRP cannot rely on update messages to monitor the state of EIGRP neighbors. So, using the same basic ideas as OSPF, EIGRP defines a Hello message. The EIGRP Hello message and protocol defines that each router should send a periodic Hello message on each interface, so that all EIGRP routers know that the router is still working. Figure 9-8 shows the idea.

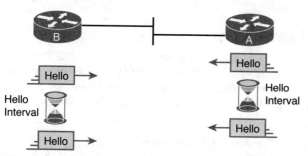

Figure 9-8   *EIGRP Hello Packets*

Normally, EIGRP neighbors use the same *Hello Interval*, which is the time period between each EIGRP Hello. Routers also must receive a Hello from a neighbor within a time called the *Hold Interval*, with a default setting of three times the Hello Interval.

For instance, imagine both R1 and R2 use default settings of 5 and 15 for their Hello and Hold Intervals. Under normal conditions, R1 receives Hellos from R2 every 5 seconds, well within R1's Hold Interval (15 seconds) before R1 would consider R2 to have failed. If R2 does fail, R2 no longer sends Hello messages. R1 notices that 15 seconds pass without receiving a Hello from R2, so then R1 can choose new routes that do not use R2 as a next-hop router.

Interestingly, EIGRP does not require two neighboring routers to use the same Hello and Hold intervals, but it makes good sense to use the same Hello and Hold intervals on all routers. Unfortunately, the flexibility to use different settings on neighboring routers makes it possible to prevent the neighbors from working properly, just by the poor choice of Hello and Hold intervals. For instance, if R2 changes its Hello/Hold Intervals to 30/60, respectively, but R1 keeps its Hello/Hold Intervals of 5/15 seconds, R1 will believe R2 has failed on a regular basis. R2 sends Hello messages only every 30 seconds, but R1 expects to receive them within its 15-second Hold Interval.

Summary of Interior Routing Protocol Features

Table 9-2 summarizes the features discussed in this chapter, for RIPv2, EIGRP, and OSPFv2. Following the table, the second major section of this chapter begins, which moves into depth about the specifics of how EIGRP works.

Key Topic

Table 9-2   Interior IP Routing Protocols Compared

Feature	RIPv2	EIGRP	OSPFv2
Metric is based on	Hop count	Bandwidth and delay	Cost
Sends periodic full updates	Yes	No	No
Sends periodic Hello messages	No	Yes	Yes

Feature	RIPv2	EIGRP	OSPFv2
Uses route poisoning for failed routes	Yes	Yes	Yes
Uses split horizon to limit updates about working routes	Yes	Yes	No
Address to which messages are sent	224.0.0.9	224.0.0.10	224.0.0.5, 224.0.0.6
Metric considered to be infinite	16	$2^{32} - 1$	$2^{24} - 1$

EIGRP Concepts and Operation

EIGRP differs from OSPF in some pretty obvious ways, but in some ways EIGRP acts a lot like OSPF. In fact, EIGRP uses a three-step model similar to OSPF when a router first joins a network. These steps each lead to a list or table: the neighbor table, the topology table, and the routing table. All these processes and tables lead toward building the IPv4 routes in the routing table, as follows:

1. **Neighbor discovery:** EIGRP routers send Hello messages to discover potential neighboring EIGRP routers and perform basic parameter checks to determine which routers should become neighbors. Neighbors that pass all parameter checks are added to the EIGRP neighbor table.

2. **Topology exchange:** Neighbors exchange full topology updates when the neighbor relationship comes up, and then only partial updates as needed based on changes to the network topology. The data learned in these updates is added to the router's EIGRP topology table.

3. **Choosing routes:** Each router analyzes its respective EIGRP topology tables, choosing the lowest-metric route to reach each subnet. EIGRP places the route with the best metric for each destination into the IPv4 routing table.

This second major section of this chapter discusses the particulars of how EIGRP goes about building its routing table, using these three steps. Although the overall three-step process looks similar to OSPF, the details differ greatly, especially those related to how OSPF uses LS logic to process topology data, whereas EIGRP does not. Also, in addition to these three steps, this section explains some unique logic EIGRP uses when converging and reacting to changes in an internetwork—logic that is not seen with the other types of routing protocols.

EIGRP Neighbors

From the perspective of one router, an EIGRP neighbor is another EIGRP-speaking router, connected to a common subnet, with which the first router is willing to exchange EIGRP topology information. EIGRP uses EIGRP Hello messages to dynamically discover potential neighbors, sending those updates to multicast address 224.0.0.10.

Once another EIGRP router is discovered using Hello messages, routers must perform some basic checking of each potential neighbor before that router becomes an EIGRP neighbor. (A potential neighbor is a router from which an EIGRP Hello has been received.) Then the router checks the following settings to determine whether the router should be allowed to be a neighbor:

- It must pass the authentication process if used.

- It must use the same configured autonomous system number (which is a configuration setting).

- The source IP address used by the neighbor's Hello must be in the same subnet as the local router's interface IP address/mask.

- The routers' EIGRP K-values must match. (However, Cisco recommends to not change these values.)

EIGRP uses relatively straightforward verification checks for neighbors. First, if authentication is configured, the two routers must be using the same type of authentication and the same authentication key (password). Second, EIGRP configuration includes a parameter called an *autonomous system number* (ASN), which must be the same on two neighboring routers. Finally, the IP addresses used to send the EIGRP Hello messages—the routers' respective interface IP addresses—must be in the range of addresses on the other routers' respective connected subnet.

Once two EIGRP routers become neighbors, the routers use the neighbor relationship in much simpler ways as compared to OSPF. Whereas OSPF neighbors have several interim states and a few stable states, EIGRP simply moves to a working state as soon as the neighbor passes the basic verification checks. At that point, the two routers can begin exchanging topology information using EIGRP update messages.

Exchanging EIGRP Topology Information

EIGRP uses EIGRP *update messages* to send topology information to neighbors. These update messages can be sent to multicast IP address 224.0.0.10 if the sending router needs to update multiple routers on the same subnet; otherwise, the updates are sent to the unicast IP address of the particular neighbor. (Hello messages are always sent to the 224.0.0.10 multicast address.) The use of multicast packets on LANs allows EIGRP to exchange routing information with all neighbors on the LAN efficiently.

EIGRP sends update messages without UDP or TCP, but it does use a protocol called *Reliable Transport Protocol* (RTP). RTP provides a mechanism to resend any EIGRP messages that are not received by a neighbor. By using RTP, EIGRP can better avoid loops because a router knows for sure that the neighboring router has received any updated routing information. (The use of RTP is just another example of a difference between basic DV protocols like RIP, which have no mechanism to know whether neighbors receive update messages, and the more advanced EIGRP.)

NOTE   The acronym *RTP* also refers to a different protocol, Real-time Transport Protocol (RTP), which is used to transmit voice and video IP packets.

EIGRP neighbors use both full routing updates and partial updates. A full update means that a router sends information about all known routes, whereas a partial update includes only information about recently changed routes. Full updates occur when neighbors first come up. After that, the neighbors send only partial updates in reaction to changes to a route.

Figure 9-9 summarizes many of the details discussed so far in this section, from top to bottom. It first shows neighbor discovery with Hellos, the sending of full updates, the maintenance of the neighbor relationship with ongoing Hellos, and partial updates.

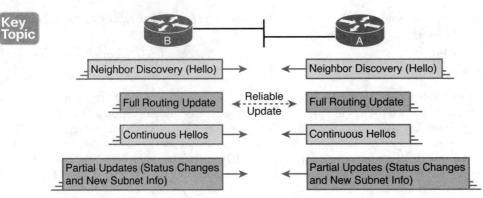

Figure 9-9 *Full and Partial EIGRP Updates*

Note that EIGRP refers to the information exchanged in the updates as topology informa-tion. The information is not nearly as detailed as OSPF LS topology data, and it does not attempt to describe every router and link in the network. However, it does describe more than just a distance (metric) and vector (next-hop router) for the local router—a local router also learns the metric as used by the next-hop router. This added information is used to help EIGRP converge quickly, without causing loops, as discussed in the upcoming section "EIGRP Convergence."

Calculating the Best Routes for the Routing Table

EIGRP calculates the metric for routes much differently than any other routing protocol. For instance, with OSPF, anyone with a network diagram and knowledge of the configured OSPF interface costs can calculate the exact OSPF metric (cost) for each route. EIGRP uses a math equation and a composite metric, making the exact metric value hard to predict.

The EIGRP Metric Calculation

The EIGRP composite metric means that EIGRP feeds multiple inputs (called metric com-ponents) into the math equation. By default, EIGRP feeds two metric components into the calculation: bandwidth and delay. The result of the calculation is an integer value and is the composite metric for that router.

Note that EIGRP includes other options for how it could calculate the metric, but those options are not normally used. EIGRP supports also using the interface load and interface reliability in the metric calculation. EIGRP also advertises the maximum transmission unit (MTU) associated with the route—that is, the longest IP packet allowed over the route—but does not support using the MTU when calculating the metric. For this book's purposes, EIGRP uses the default settings, calculating the composite metric based on the bandwidth and delay.

EIGRP's metric calculation formula actually helps describe some of the key points about the composite metric. (In real life, you seldom if ever need to sit down and calculate what a router will calculate with this formula.) The formula, assuming that the default settings that tell the router to use just bandwidth and delay, is as follows:

$$\text{Metric} = \left(\left(\frac{10^7}{\text{least-bandwidth}} \right) + \text{cumulative-delay} \right) * 256$$

In this formula, the term *least-bandwidth* represents the lowest-bandwidth link in the route, using a unit of kilobits per second. For instance, if the slowest link in a route is a 10-Mbps Ethernet link, the first part of the formula is $10^7 / 10^4$, which equals 1000. You use 10^4 in the formula because 10 Mbps is equal to 10,000 Kbps (10^4 Kbps).

The cumulative-delay value used in the formula is the sum of all the delay values for all outgoing interfaces in the route, with a unit of "tens of microseconds."

Using these two inputs helps EIGRP pick the best route with a little more balance than does OSPF. Using the least bandwidth lets EIGRP avoid routes with the slowest individual links, which are usually the links with the most congestion. At the same time, the delay part of the equation adds the delay for every link, so that routes with a large number of links will be relatively less desirable than a route with fewer links.

You can set both bandwidth and delay for each link, using the cleverly named **bandwidth** and **delay** interface subcommands.

> **NOTE**   Most **show** commands, including **show ip eigrp topology** and **show interfaces**, list delay settings as the number of microseconds of delay. Note that the EIGRP metric formula uses a unit of tens of microseconds.

An Example of Calculated EIGRP Metrics

Now that you have an idea of how the router's EIGRP math works, next consider an example that connects what a router learns in an EIGRP update message, local configuration settings, and the calculation of the metric for a single route.

To calculate the metric, a local router must consider the information received from the neighboring router as well as its local interface settings. First, EIGRP update messages list the subnet number and mask, along with all the metric components: the cumulative delay, minimum bandwidth, along with the other usually unused metric components. The local router then considers the bandwidth and delay settings on the interface on which the update was received, and calculates a new metric.

For example, Figure 9-10 shows Router R1 learning about subnet 10.1.3.0/24 from Router R2. The EIGRP update message from R2 lists a minimum bandwidth of 100,000 Kbps, and a cumulative delay of 100 microseconds. R1's S0/1 interface has an interface bandwidth set to 1544 Kbps—the default bandwidth on a serial link—and a delay of 20,000 microseconds.

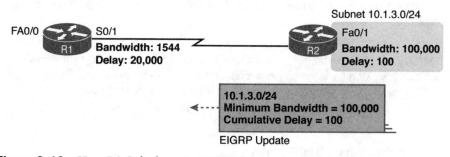

Figure 9-10   *How R1 Calculates Its EIGRP Metric for 10.1.3.0/24*

Next, consider how R1 thinks about the least-bandwidth part of the calculation. R1 discovers that its S0/1 interface bandwidth (1544 Kbps, or 1.544 Mbps) is less than the advertised minimum bandwidth of 100,000 Kbps, or 100 Mbps. R1 needs to use this new, slower bandwidth in the metric calculation. (If R1's S0/1 interface had a bandwidth of 100,000 Kbps or more in this case, R1 would instead use the minimum bandwidth listed in the EIGRP update from R2.)

As for interface delay, the router always adds its interface delay to the delay listed in the EIGRP update. However, the unit for delay can be a bit of a challenge. The units, and their use, are as follows:

Unit of microseconds: Listed in the output of **show** commands such as **show interfaces** and **show ip eigrp topology**, and in the EIGRP update messages

Unit of tens-of-microseconds: Used by the interface mode configuration command (**delay**), with which to set the delay, and in the EIGRP metric calculation

Because of this weird difference in units, when looking at the delay, make sure you keep the units straight. In this particular example:

- R1 received an update that lists delay of 100 (microseconds), which R1 converts to the equivalent 10 tens of microseconds before using it in the formula.

- R1 sees its S0/1 interface setting of 20,000 microseconds, which equals 2000 tens of microseconds

- For the purposes of the calculation, R1 adds 10 tens of microseconds from the update message to 2000 tens of microseconds for the interface for a total delay of 2010 tens of microseconds.

This example results in the following metric calculation:

$$\text{Metric} = \left(\left(\frac{10^7}{1544} \right) + (10 + 2000) \right) * 256 = 2{,}172{,}416$$

> **NOTE**   For those of you who repeat this math at home, IOS rounds down the division in this formula to the nearest integer before performing the rest of the formula. In this case, 10^7 / 1544 is rounded down to 6476, before adding the 2010 and then multiplying by 256.

If multiple possible routes to subnet 10.1.3.0/24 exist, Router R1 also calculates the metric for those routes and chooses the route with the best (lowest) metric to be added to the routing table.

> **NOTE**   The examples in this chapter show routers with Gigabit interfaces, which default their delay settings to 10 microseconds. However, IOS adjusts the delay based on the actual speed of a LAN interface. In the examples in this chapter and the next, all the LAN interfaces happen to be running at 100 Mbps, making the delay be 100 microseconds.

Caveats with Bandwidth on Serial Links

EIGRP's robust metric gives it the ability to choose routes that include more router hops but with faster links. However, to ensure that the right routes are chosen, engineers must take care to configure meaningful bandwidth and delay settings. In particular, serial links default to a bandwidth of 1544 and a delay of 20,000 microseconds, as used in the example shown in Figure 9-10. However, IOS cannot automatically change the bandwidth and delay settings based on the Layer 1 speed of a serial link. So, using default bandwidth and delay settings, particularly the bandwidth setting on serial links, can lead to problems.

Figure 9-11 shows the problem with using default bandwidth settings and how EIGRP uses the better (faster) route when the bandwidth is set correctly. The figure focuses on router B's route to subnet 10.1.1.0/24 in each case. In the left side of the figure, all serial interfaces use defaults, even though the top serial link actually runs at a slow 64 Kbps. The right side of the figure shows the results when the slow serial link's **bandwidth** command is changed to reflect the correct (slow) speed.

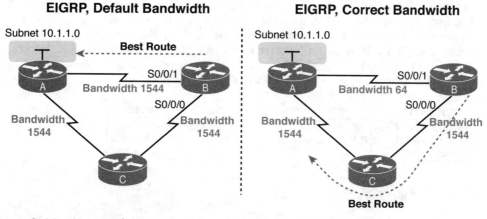

Figure 9-11 *Impact of the Bandwidth on EIGRP's Metric Calculation*

Generally, a good metric strategy for networks that use EIGRP is to set the WAN bandwidth to match the actual Layer 1 speed, use defaults for LAN interfaces, and EIGRP will usually choose the best routes.

EIGRP Convergence

Now that you have seen the details of how EIGRP forms neighbor relationships, exchanges routing information, and calculates the best route, the rest of this section looks at the most interesting part of EIGRP: EIGRP's work to converge to a new loop-free route.

Loop avoidance poses one of the most difficult problems with any dynamic routing protocol. DV protocols overcome this problem with a variety of tools, some of which create a large portion of the minutes-long convergence time after a link failure. LS protocols overcome this problem by having each router keep a full topology of the network, so by running a rather involved mathematical model (for example, OSPF's SPF algorithm), a router can avoid any loops.

EIGRP avoids loops by keeping some basic topological information, while keeping much less information as compared to LS protocols like OSPF. EIGRP keeps a record of each possible next-hop router for alternate routes, and some metric details related to those routes, but no information about the topology beyond the next-hop routers. This sparser topology information does not require the sophisticated Shortest Path First (SPF) algorithm, but it does allow quick convergence to loop-free routes.

Feasible Distance and Reported Distance

First, before getting into how EIGRP converges, you need to know a few additional EIGRP terms. With EIGRP, a local router needs to consider its own calculated metric for each route, but at the same time, the local router considers the next-hop router's calculated metric for that same destination subnet. And EIGRP has special terms for those metrics, as follows:

■ **Feasible distance (FD):** The local router's composite metric of the best route to reach a subnet, as calculated on the local router

■ **Reported distance (RD):** The next-hop router's best composite metric for that same subnet

As usual, the definition makes more sense with an example. Using the same advertisement as earlier in Figure 9-10, Figure 9-12 shows the two calculations done by R1. One calculation finds R1's own metric (FD) for its one route for subnet 10.1.3.0/24, as discussed around Figure 9-10. The other uses the metric components in the update received from R2, to calculate what R2 would have calculated for R2's metric to reach this same subnet. R1's second calculation based on R2's information—a slowest bandwidth of 100,000 Kbps and a cumulative delay of 100 microseconds—is R1's RD for this route.

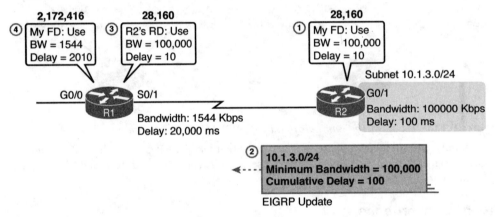

Figure 9-12 *How R1 Calculates RD and FD for 10.1.3.0/24*

Following the steps in the figure:

1. R2 calculates its own metric (its FD) for R2's route for 10.1.3.0/24, based on a bandwidth of 100,000 Kbps and a delay of 100 microseconds.

2. R2 sends the EIGRP update that lists 10.1.3.0/24, with these same metric components.

3. R1 calculates the RD for this route, using the same math R2 used at Step 1, using the information in the update message from Step 2.

4. R1 calculates its own metric, from R1's perspective, by considering the bandwidth and delay of R1's S0/1 interface, as discussed earlier around Figure 9-10.

In fact, based on the information in Figure 9-12, R2's FD to reach subnet 10.1.3.0/24, which is also R1's RD to reach 10.1.3.0/24, could be easily calculated:

$$\left(\left(\frac{10^7}{100,000}\right) + (10)\right) * 256 = 28,160$$

At this point, R1 knows its own calculated metric for the route, called the FD, and R1 knows next-hop Router R2's metric for R2's route to that same subnet. R1 calls that R2's RD.

Now that you have a general idea about the FD and RD concept, consider the EIGRP convergence process. EIGRP convergence has two branches in its logic, based on whether the failed route does or does not have a *feasible successor* route. The decision of whether a router has a feasible successor route depends on the FD and RD values of the competing routes to reach a given subnet. The next topic defines this concept of a feasible successor route and discusses what happens in that case.

EIGRP Successors and Feasible Successors

EIGRP calculates the metric for each route to reach each subnet. For a particular subnet, the route with the best metric is called the *successor*, with the router filling the IP routing table with this successor route. (This successor route's metric is called the feasible distance, as introduced earlier.)

Of the other routes to reach that same subnet—routes whose metrics were larger than the FD for the successor route—EIGRP needs to determine which alternate route can be used immediately if the currently best route fails, without causing a routing loop. EIGRP runs a simple algorithm to identify which routes could be used, keeping these loop-free backup routes in its topology table and using them if the currently best route fails. These alternative, immediately usable routes are called *feasible successor* routes because they can feasibly be used as the new successor route when the previous successor route fails.

A router determines whether a route is a feasible successor based on the feasibility condition:

  If a nonsuccessor route's RD is less than the FD, the route is a feasible successor route.

Although it is technically correct, this definition is much more understandable with an example. Figure 9-13 begins an example in which router E chooses its best route to subnet 1. Router E learns three routes to subnet 1, with next-hop routers B, C, and D. The figure shows the metrics as calculated on router E, as listed in router E's EIGRP topology table. Router E finds that the route through router D has the lowest metric, making that router E's successor route for subnet 1. Router E adds that route to its routing table, as shown. The FD is the metric calculated for this route, a value of 14,000 in this case.

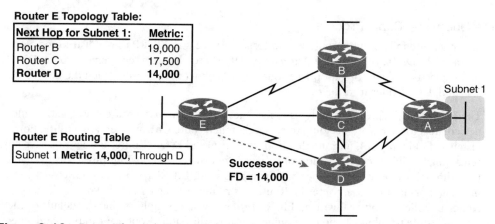

Figure 9-13 *Route Through Router D Is the Successor Route to Subnet 1*

At the same time, EIGRP on router E decides whether either of the other two routes to subnet 1 can be used immediately if the route through router D fails for whatever reason. Only a feasible successor route can be used. To meet the feasibility condition, the alternate route's RD must be less than the FD of the successor route.

Figure 9-14 demonstrates that one of the two other routes meets the feasibility condition and is therefore a feasible successor route. The figure shows an updated version of Figure 9-13. Router E uses the following logic to determine that the route through router B is not a feasible successor route, but the route through router C is, as follows:

- Router E compares the FD of 14,000 to the RD of the route through router B (15,000). Router B's RD is worse than router E's FD, so this route is not a feasible successor.

- Router E compares the FD of 14,000 to the RD of the route through router C (13,000). Router C's RD is better than router E's FD, making this route a feasible successor.

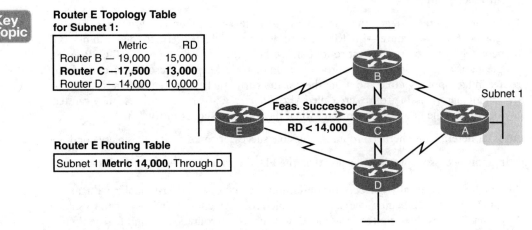

Figure 9-14 *Route Through Router C Is a Feasible Successor*

If the route to subnet 1 through router D fails, router E can immediately put the route through router C into the routing table without fear of creating a loop. Convergence occurs almost instantly in this case.

The Query and Reply Process

When a route fails, and the route has no feasible successor, EIGRP uses a distributed algorithm called *Diffusing Update Algorithm* (DUAL) to choose a replacement route. DUAL sends queries looking for a loop-free route to the subnet in question. When the new route is found, DUAL adds it to the routing table.

The EIGRP DUAL process simply uses messages to confirm that a route exists, and would not create a loop, before deciding to replace a failed route with an alternative route. For instance, in Figure 9-14, imagine that both routers C and D fail. Router E does not have any remaining feasible successor route for subnet 1, but there is an obvious physically available path through router B. To use the route, router E sends EIGRP *query* messages to its working neighbors (in this case, router B). Router B's route to subnet 1 is still working fine, so router B replies to router E with an EIGRP *reply* message, simply stating the details of the working route to subnet 1 and confirming that it is still viable. Router E can then add a new route to subnet 1 to its routing table, without fear of a loop.

Replacing a failed route with a feasible successor takes a very short amount of time, usually less than a second or two. When queries and replies are required, convergence can take slightly longer, but in most networks, convergence can still occur in less than 10 seconds.

Chapter Review

One key to doing well on the exams is to perform repetitive spaced review sessions. Review this chapter's material using either the tools in the book, DVD, or interactive tools for the same material found on the book's companion website. Refer to the "Your Study Plan" element for more details. Table 9-3 outlines the key review elements and where you can find them. To better track your study progress, record when you completed these activities in the second column.

Table 9-3 Chapter Review Tracking

Review Element	Review Date(s)	Resource Used:
Review key topics		Book, DVD/website
Review key terms		Book, DVD/website
Answer DIKTA questions		Book, PCPT
Review memory tables		Book, DVD/website

Review All the Key Topics

Key Topic

Table 9-4 Key Topics for Chapter 9

Key Topic Element	Description	Page Number
List	Key comparison points for EIGRP versus other routing protocols	227
List	Breakdown of the term *distance vector*	228
Figure 9-6	Example of split horizon	231
Table 9-2	More comparisons of IGPs	233
List	Reasons why EIGRP routers are prevented from becoming neighbors	234
Figure 9-9	Depicts the normal progression through neighbor discovery, full routing updates, ongoing Hellos, and partial updates	236
List	Definitions of feasible distance and reported distance	240
Definition	Feasibility condition	241
Figure 9-14	Example of how routers determine which routes are feasible successors	242

Key Terms You Should Know

convergence, distance vector, interior gateway protocol (IGP), partial update, poisoned route, split horizon, feasibility condition, feasible distance, feasible successor, full update, reported distance, successor

CHAPTER 10

Implementing EIGRP for IPv4

This chapter covers the following exam topics:

2.0 Routing Technologies

2.6 Configure, verify, and troubleshoot EIGRP for IPv4 (excluding authentication, filtering, manual summarization, redistribution, stub)

Whereas the preceding chapter looked solely at Enhanced Interior Gateway Routing Protocol (EIGRP) concepts, this chapter looks at the details of making it work in a Cisco router.

This chapter works through a variety of EIGRP configuration options, beginning with the most fundamental EIGRP configuration options. It then moves on to look at a few less-common configuration tasks, such as how to configure unequal-metric load balancing, as well as the autosummary feature, which might sound great, but which today is mostly a potential area for causing problems.

Throughout this chapter, the text moves back and forth between the configuration and the related commands to verify that the configured feature is working. In particular, this chapter takes a careful look at how to identify the feasible distance and reported distance, and find the successor and feasible successor routes.

"Do I Know This Already?" Quiz

Take the quiz (either here, or use the PCPT software) if you want to use the score to help you decide how much time to spend on this chapter. The answers are at the bottom of the page following the quiz, and the explanations are in DVD Appendix C and in the PCPT software.

Table 10-1 "Do I Know This Already?" Foundation Topics Section-to-Question Mapping

Foundation Topics Section	Questions
Core EIGRP Configuration and Verification	1–4
EIGRP Metrics, Successors, and Feasible Successors	5–6
Other EIGRP Configuration Settings	7

1. Which of the following **network** commands, following the command **router eigrp 1**, tells this router to start using EIGRP on interfaces whose IP addresses are 10.1.1.1, 10.1.100.1, and 10.1.120.1? (Choose two answers.)

   a. network 10.0.0.0

   b. network 10.1.1x.0

   c. network 10.0.0.0 0.255.255.255

   d. network 10.0.0.0 255.255.255.0

2. Routers R1 and R2 attach to the same VLAN with IP addresses 10.0.0.1 and 10.0.0.2, respectively. R1 is configured with the commands **router eigrp 99** and **network 10.0.0.0**. Which of the following commands might be part of a working EIGRP configuration on R2 that ensures that the two routers become neighbors and exchange routes? (Choose two answers.)

   a. **network 10**

   b. **network 10.0.0.1 0.0.0.0**

   c. **network 10.0.0.2 0.0.0.0**

   d. **network 10.0.0.0**

3. In the **show ip route** command, what code designation implies that a route was learned with EIGRP?

   a. E

   b. I

   c. G

   d. D

4. Examine the following excerpt from a **show** command on Router R1:

```
EIGRP-IPv4 Neighbors for AS(1)
H   Address         Interface       Hold Uptime    SRTT   RTO  Q  Seq
                                    (sec)          (ms)        Cnt Num
1   10.1.4.3        Se0/0/1         13 00:05:49    2      100  0  29
0   10.1.5.2        Se0/0/0         12 00:05:49    2      100  0  39
```

   Which of the following answers is true about this router based on this output?

   a. Address 10.1.4.3 identifies a working neighbor based on that neighbor's current EIGRP router ID.

   b. Address 10.1.5.2 identifies a router that may or may not become an EIGRP neighbor at some point after both routers check all neighbor requirements.

   c. Address 10.1.5.2 identifies a working neighbor based on that neighbor's interface IP address on the link between R1 and that neighbor.

   d. Address 10.1.4.3 identifies R1's own IP address on interface S0/0/1.

5. Examine the following excerpt from a router's CLI:

```
P 10.1.1.0/24, 1 successors, FD is 2172416
        via 10.1.6.3 (2172416/28160), Serial0/1
        via 10.1.4.2 (2684416/2284156), Serial0/0
        via 10.1.5.4 (2684416/2165432), Serial1/0
```

   Which of the following identifies a next-hop IP address on a feasible successor route?

   a. 10.1.6.3

   b. 10.1.4.2

   c. 10.1.5.4

   d. It cannot be determined from this command output.

6. Router R1's EIGRP process knows of three possible routes to subnet 1. One route is a successor, and one is a feasible successor. R1 is not using the **variance** command to allow for unequal-cost load balancing. Which of the following commands shows information about the feasible successor route, including its metric, whether as EIGRP topology information or as an IPv4 route?

   a. **show ip eigrp topology**

   b. **show ip eigrp database**

   c. **show ip route eigrp**

   d. **show ip eigrp interfaces**

7. Router R1 has four routes to subnet 2. The one successor route has a metric of 100, and the one feasible successor route has a metric of 350. The other routes have metrics of 450 and 550. R1's EIGRP configuration includes the **variance 5** command. Choose the answer that refers to the highest-metric route to subnet 2 that will be visible in the output of the **show ip route eigrp** command on R1.

   a. The successor route (metric 100)

   b. The feasible successor route (metric 350)

   c. The route with metric 450

   d. The route with metric 550

Foundation Topics

Core EIGRP Configuration and Verification

This first of three major sections of the chapter starts the discussion of EIGRP by showing the most commonly used parts of EIGRP configuration. As is usual with this book's implementation chapters, this section begins with configuration topics, followed by verification.

EIGRP Configuration

EIGRP configuration closely resembles OSPF configuration. The **router eigrp** command enables EIGRP and puts the user in EIGRP configuration mode, in which one or more **network** commands are configured. For each interface matched by a **network** command, EIGRP tries to discover neighbors on that interface, and EIGRP advertises the subnet connected to the interface.

The following configuration checklist outlines the main configuration tasks covered in this chapter:

Config Checklist

Step 1. Use the **router eigrp** *as-number* global command to enter EIGRP configuration mode and define the EIGRP autonomous system number (ASN).

Step 2. Configure one or more **network** *ip-address* [*wildcard-mask*] router subcommands. This enables EIGRP on any matched interface and causes EIGRP to advertise the connected subnet.

Step 3. (Optional) Use the **eigrp router-id** *value* router subcommand to set the EIGRP router ID (RID) explicitly.

Step 4. (Optional) Use the **ip hello-interval eigrp** *asn time* and **ip hold-time eigrp** *asn time* interface subcommands to change the interface Hello and hold timers.

Step 5. (Optional) Use the **bandwidth** *value* and **delay** *value* interface subcommands to impact metric calculations by tuning bandwidth and delay.

Step 6. (Optional) Use the **maximum-paths** *number* and **variance** *multiplier* router subcommands to configure support for multiple equal-cost routes.

Step 7. (Optional) Use the **auto-summary** router subcommand to enable automatic summarization of routes at the boundaries of classful IPv4 networks.

Example 10-1 begins the configuration discussion with the simplest possible EIGRP configuration. This configuration uses as many defaults as possible, but it does enable EIGRP on each router on all the interfaces shown in Figure 10-1. All three routers can use the exact same configuration, with only two commands required on each router.

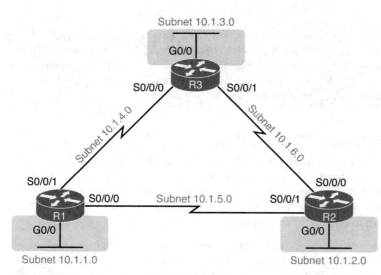

Figure 10-1 *Sample Internetwork Used in Most of the EIGRP Examples*

Example 10-1 *EIGRP Configuration on All Three Routers in Figure 10-1*

```
router eigrp 1
 network 10.0.0.0
```

This simple configuration only uses two parameters that the network engineer must choose: the autonomous system number and the classful network number in the **network** command.

The actual ASN does not matter, but all the routers must use the same ASN in the **router eigrp** command. For instance, they all use **router eigrp 1** in this example. (Routers that use different ASNs will not become EIGRP neighbors.) The range of valid ASNs is 1 through 65,535, which is the same range of valid process IDs with the **router ospf** command.

The EIGRP **network** command allows two syntax options: one with a wildcard mask at the end and one without, as shown with Example 10-1's **network 10.0.0.0** command. With no wildcard mask listed, this command must list a classful network (a Class A, B, or C network number). Once configured, this command tells the router to do the following:

■ Look for that router's own interfaces with addresses in that classful network

■ Enable EIGRP on those interfaces

Once enabled, EIGRP starts advertising about the subnet connected to an interface. It also starts sending Hello messages and listening for incoming Hello messages, trying to form neighbor relationships with other EIGRP routers.

> **NOTE** Interestingly, on real routers, you can type an EIGRP **network** *number* command and use a dotted-decimal number that is not a classful network number; in that case, IOS does not issue an error message. However, IOS changes the number you typed to be the classful network number in which that number resides. For example, IOS changes the **network 10.1.1.1** command to **network 10.0.0.0**.

Configuring EIGRP Using a Wildcard Mask

The EIGRP **network** command syntax without the wildcard mask, as shown in Example 10-1, may be exactly what an engineer wants to use, but it also might prove a bit clumsy. For instance, if an engineer wants to enable EIGRP on G0/0, and not on G0/1, and they both have IP addresses in Class A network 10.0.0.0, the **network 10.0.0.0** EIGRP subcommand would match both interfaces, instead of just G0/0.

IOS has a second option for the EIGRP **network** command that uses a wildcard mask so that the engineer can match exactly the correct interface IP addresses intended. In this case, the **network** command does not have to list a classful **network** number. Instead, IOS matches an interface IP address that would be matched if the address and wildcard mask in the **network** command were part of an access control list (ACL). The logic works just like an ACL address and wildcard mask, and just like the wildcard mask logic in the OSPF **network** commands discussed in Chapter 8, "Implementing OSPF for IPv4." (If you do not recall the details, look to Chapter 16, "Basic IPv4 Access Control Lists," for more details about ACL wildcard masks.)

For example, looking back at Figure 10-1, Router R3 has IP addresses in three subnets: 10.1.3.0/24, 10.1.4.0/24, and 10.1.6.0/24. Example 10-2 shows an alternate EIGRP configuration for Router R3 that uses a **network** command to match the range of addresses in each subnet for R3's three connected subnets. With a subnet mask of /24, each of the **network** commands uses a wildcard mask of 0.0.0.255, with an address parameter of the subnet ID off one of R3's interfaces.

Example 10-2 *Using Wildcard Masks with EIGRP Configuration*

```
R3(config)# router eigrp 1
R3(config-router)# network 10.1.3.0 0.0.0.255
R3(config-router)# network 10.1.4.0 0.0.0.255
R3(config-router)# network 10.1.6.0 0.0.0.255
```

Alternatively, R3 could have matched each interface with commands that use a wildcard mask of 0.0.0.0, listing the specific IP address of each interface. For instance, the **network 10.1.3.3 0.0.0.0** command would match R3's LAN interface address of 10.1.3.3, enabling EIGRP on that one interface.

> **NOTE** EIGRP for IPv4 supports two different configuration styles: *classic mode* (also called *autonomous system mode*) and *named mode*. In classic mode, which was the first of these two methods to be added to IOS, the **router eigrp** command uses an ASN. In named mode, the **router eigrp** command references a name instead of an ASN, hence the term EIGRP *named mode*. This chapter discusses classic mode only.

Verifying EIGRP Core Features

Like OSPF, EIGRP uses three tables to match its three major blocks of logic: a neighbor table, a topology table, and the IPv4 routing table. But before EIGRP even attempts to build these tables, IOS must connect the configuration logic to its local interfaces. Once enabled on an interface, a router can then start to build its three tables.

The next several pages walk through the verification steps to confirm a working internetwork that uses EIGRP. Figure 10-2 shows the progression of concepts from top to bottom on the left, with a reference for the various **show** commands on the right. The topics to follow use that same sequence.

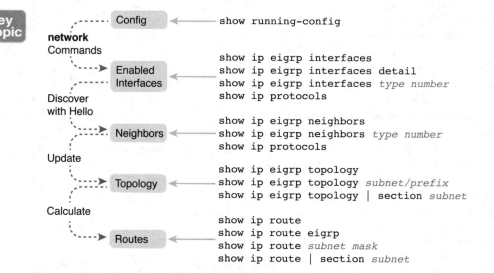

Figure 10-2 *Roadmap of Topics (Left) and Verification Commands (Right)*

> **NOTE**   All the upcoming verification examples list output taken from the routers in Figure 10-1. From that figure, Routers R1 and R2 use the EIGRP configuration Example 10-1, and Router R3 uses the configuration shown in Example 10-2. Also, note that all routers use Gigabit LAN interfaces that currently operate at 100 Mbps due to their connections to some 10/100 switch ports; this fact impacts the EIGRP metrics to a small degree.

Finding the Interfaces on Which EIGRP Is Enabled

Example 10-3 begins the verification process by connecting the configuration to the router interfaces on which EIGRP is enabled. IOS gives us three ways to find the list of interfaces:

- Use **show running-config** to look at the EIGRP and interface configuration, and apply the same logic as EIGRP to find the list of interfaces on which EIGRP should be enabled.

- Use **show ip protocols** to list a shorthand version of the EIGRP configuration, to again apply the same logic as EIGRP and predict the list of interfaces.

- Use **show ip eigrp interfaces** to list the interfaces on which the router has actually enabled EIGRP.

Of these three options, only the **show ip eigrp interfaces** command gives us the true list of interfaces as actually chosen by the router. The other two methods give us the configuration, and let us make an educated guess. (Both are important!)

The **show ip eigrp interfaces** command lists EIGRP-enabled interfaces directly, and briefly, with one line per interface. Alternatively, the **show ip eigrp interfaces detail** command lists much more detail per interface, including the Hello and Hold Intervals, as well as noting whether split horizon is enabled. Example 10-3 shows an example of both from Router R1.

Example 10-3   *Looking for Interfaces on Which EIGRP Has Been Enabled on R1*

```
R1# show ip eigrp interfaces
EIGRP-IPv4 Interfaces for AS(1)
                   Xmit Queue   PeerQ        Mean Pacing Time Multicast  Pending
Interface Peers  Un/Reliable Un/Reliable  SRTT Un/Reliable Flow Timer Routes
Gi0/0       0       0/0         0/0          0    0/0          0          0
Se0/0/0     1       0/0         0/0          2    0/16         50         0
Se0/0/1     1       0/0         0/0          1    0/15         50         0


R1# show ip eigrp interfaces detail S0/0/0
EIGRP-IPv4 Interfaces for AS(1)
                   Xmit Queue   PeerQ        Mean Pacing Time Multicast  Pending
Interface Peers  Un/Reliable Un/Reliable SRTT Un/Reliable Flow Timer Routes
Se0/0/0     1       0/0         0/0          2    0/16         50         0
   Hello-interval is 5, Hold-time is 15
   Split-horizon is enabled
! lines omitted for brevity
```

Note that the first command, **show ip eigrp interfaces**, lists all interfaces for which EIGRP is enabled and for which the router is currently sending Hello messages trying to find new

EIGRP neighbors. R1, with a single **network 10.0.0.0** EIGRP subcommand, enables EIGRP on all three of its interfaces (per Figure 10-1). The second command lists more detail per interface, including the local router's own Hello Interval and hold time and the split-horizon setting.

Note that neither command lists information about interfaces on which EIGRP is not enabled. For instance, had EIGRP not been enabled on S0/0/0, the **show ip eigrp interfaces detail S0/0/0** command would have simply listed no information under the heading lines. The shorter output of the **show ip eigrp interface** command omits interfaces on which EIGRP is not enabled.

Also, note that the **show ip eigrp interfaces...** command does not list information for passive interfaces. Like Open Shortest Path First (OSPF), EIGRP supports the **passive-interface** *type number* subcommand. On passive interfaces, EIGRP does not discover and form neighbor relationships. However, EIGRP still advertises about the subnet connected to the passive interface.

In summary, the **show ip eigrp interfaces** command lists information about interfaces enabled by EIGRP, but it does not list interfaces made passive for EIGRP.

The other two methods to find the EIGRP-enabled interfaces require an examination of the configuration and some thinking about the EIGRP rules. In real life, **show ip eigrp interfaces** is the place to start, but for the exam, you might have just the configuration, or you might not even have that. As an alternative, the **show ip protocols** command lists many details about EIGRP, including a shorthand repeat of the EIGRP **network** configuration commands. Example 10-4 lists these commands as gathered from Router R1.

Example 10-4   *Using* **show ip protocols** *to Derive the List of EIGRP-Enabled Interfaces on R1*

```
R1# show ip protocols
*** IP Routing is NSF aware ***

Routing Protocol is "eigrp 1"
  Outgoing update filter list for all interfaces is not set
  Incoming update filter list for all interfaces is not set
  Default networks flagged in outgoing updates
  Default networks accepted from incoming updates
  EIGRP-IPv4 Protocol for AS(1)
    Metric weight K1=1, K2=0, K3=1, K4=0, K5=0
    NSF-aware route hold timer is 240
    Router-ID: 10.1.5.1
    Topology: 0 (base)
      Active Timer: 3 min
      Distance: internal 90 external 170
      Maximum path: 4
      Maximum hopcount 100
      Maximum metric variance 1

Automatic Summarization: disabled
Maximum path: 4
```

10

```
Routing for Networks:
  10.0.0.0
Routing Information Sources:
  Gateway          Distance       Last Update
  10.1.4.3               90        00:22:32
  10.1.5.2               90        00:22:32
Distance: internal 90 external 170
```

To see the shorthand repeat of the EIGRP configuration, look toward the end of the example, under the heading Routing for Networks. In this case, the next line that lists 10.0.0.0 is a direct reference to the **network 10.0.0.0** configuration command shown in Example 10-1.

For configurations that use the wildcard mask option, the format of the **show ip protocols** command differs a little. Example 10-5 shows an excerpt of the **show ip protocols** command from R3. R3 uses the three **network** commands shown earlier in Example 10-2.

Example 10-5   *EIGRP Wildcard Masks Listed with* **show ip protocols** *on R3*

```
R3# show ip protocols
! Lines omitted for brevity


  Automatic Summarization: disabled
  Maximum path: 4
  Routing for Networks:
    10.1.3.0/24
    10.1.4.0/24
    10.1.6.0/24
! Lines omitted for brevity
```

To interpret the meaning of the highlighted portions of this **show ip protocols** command, you have to do a little math. The output lists a number in the format of /x (in this case, /24). It represents a wildcard mask with x binary 0s, or in this case, 0.0.0.255.

Before moving on from the **show ip protocols** command, take a moment to read some of the other details of this command's output from Example 10-4. For instance, it lists the EIGRP router ID (RID), which for R1 is 10.1.5.1. EIGRP allocates its RID just like OSPF, based on the following:

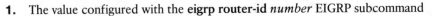

1. The value configured with the **eigrp router-id** *number* EIGRP subcommand

2. The numerically highest IP address of an up/up loopback interface at the time the EIGRP process comes up

3. The numerically highest IP address of a nonloopback interface at the time the EIGRP process comes up

The only difference compared to OSPF is that the EIGRP RID is configured with the **eigrp router-id** *value* router subcommand, whereas OSPF uses the **router-id** *value* subcommand.

Displaying EIGRP Neighbor Status

Once a router has enabled EIGRP on an interface, the router tries to discover neighboring routers by listening for EIGRP Hello messages. If two neighboring routers hear Hellos from each other and the required parameters match correctly, the routers become neighbors.

The best and most obvious command to list EIGRP neighbors is **show ip eigrp neighbors**. This command lists neighbors based on their interface IP address (and not based on their router ID, which is the convention with OSPF). The output also lists the local router's interface out which the neighbor is reachable.

For instance, Example 10-6 shows Router R1's neighbors, listing a neighbor with IP address 10.1.4.3 (R3). It is reachable from R1's S0/0/1 interface according to the first highlighted line in the example.

Example 10-6 *Displaying EIGRP Neighbors from Router R1*

```
R1# show ip eigrp neighbors
EIGRP-IPv4 Neighbors for AS(1)
H   Address                    Interface        Hold Uptime    SRTT   RTO  Q   Seq
                                                (sec)          (ms)        Cnt Num
1   10.1.4.3                   Se0/0/1            13 00:05:49     2   100   0   29
0   10.1.5.2                   Se0/0/0            12 00:05:49     2   100   0   39
```

The right side of the output also lists some interesting statistics. The four rightmost columns have to do with RTP, as discussed in Chapter 9, "Understanding EIGRP Concepts." The uptime lists the elapsed time since the neighbor relationship started. Finally, the hold time should be the current countdown from the Hold Interval (15 seconds in this case) down toward 0. In this case, with a Hello Interval of 5 and a Hold Interval of 15, this counter will vary from 15 down to 10 and then reset to 15 when the next Hello arrives.

Another less-obvious way to list EIGRP neighbors is the **show ip protocols** command. Look back again to Example 10-4, to the end of the **show ip protocols** command output from R1. That output under the heading Routing Information Sources lists the same two neighboring routers' IP addresses, as does the **show ip eigrp neighbors** command in Example 10-6.

Displaying the IPv4 Routing Table

Once EIGRP routers become neighbors, they exchange routing information, store it in their topology tables, and then calculate their best IPv4 routes. This section skips past the verification steps for the EIGRP topology table, saving that for the second major topic in the chapter, as an end to itself. However, you should find the IP routing table verification steps somewhat familiar at this point. Example 10-7 shows a couple of examples from R1 in Figure 10-1: the first showing the entire IPv4 routing table, and the second with the **show ip route eigrp** command listing only EIGRP-learned routes.

Example 10-7 *IP Routing Table on Router R1 from Figure 10-1*

```
R1# show ip route
Codes: L - local, C - connected, S - static, R - RIP, M - mobile, B - BGP
       D - EIGRP, EX - EIGRP external, O - OSPF, IA - OSPF inter area
       N1 - OSPF NSSA external type 1, N2 - OSPF NSSA external type 2
```

10

```
           E1 - OSPF external type 1, E2 - OSPF external type 2
           i - IS-IS, su - IS-IS summary, L1 - IS-IS level-1, L2 - IS-IS level-2
           ia - IS-IS inter area, * - candidate default, U - per-user static route
           o - ODR, P - periodic downloaded static route, H - NHRP, l - LISP
           + - replicated route, % - next hop override

Gateway of last resort is not set

      10.0.0.0/8 is variably subnetted, 9 subnets, 2 masks
C        10.1.1.0/24 is directly connected, GigabitEthernet0/0
L        10.1.1.1/32 is directly connected, GigabitEthernet0/0
D        10.1.2.0/24 [90/2172416] via 10.1.5.2, 00:06:39, Serial0/0/0
D        10.1.3.0/24 [90/2172416] via 10.1.4.3, 00:00:06, Serial0/0/1
C        10.1.4.0/24 is directly connected, Serial0/0/1
L        10.1.4.1/32 is directly connected, Serial0/0/1
C        10.1.5.0/24 is directly connected, Serial0/0/0
L        10.1.5.1/32 is directly connected, Serial0/0/0
D        10.1.6.0/24 [90/2681856] via 10.1.5.2, 00:12:20, Serial0/0/0
                     [90/2681856] via 10.1.4.3, 00:12:20, Serial0/0/1


R1# show ip route eigrp
! Legend omitted for brevity

      10.0.0.0/8 is variably subnetted, 9 subnets, 2 masks
D        10.1.2.0/24 [90/2172416] via 10.1.5.2, 00:06:43, Serial0/0/0
D        10.1.3.0/24 [90/2172416] via 10.1.4.3, 00:00:10, Serial0/0/1
D        10.1.6.0/24 [90/2681856] via 10.1.5.2, 00:12:24, Serial0/0/0
                     [90/2681856] via 10.1.4.3, 00:12:24, Serial0/0/1
```

The **show ip route** and **show ip route eigrp** commands both list the EIGRP-learned routes with a D beside them. Cisco chose to use D to represent EIGRP because when EIGRP was created, the letter E was already being used for a (now-extinct) Exterior Gateway Protocol (EGP) routing protocol. Cisco chose the next-closest unused letter, D, to denote EIGRP-learned routes.

Next, take a moment to think about the EIGRP routes learned by R1 versus R1's connected routes. Six subnets exist in the design in Figure 10-1: three on the LANs, and three on the WANs. The first command in the example lists three of these subnets as connected routes (10.1.1.0/24, 10.1.4.0/24, and 10.1.5.0/24). The other three subnets appear as EIGRP-learned routes.

Finally, note that the two numbers in brackets for each route list the administrative distance and the composite metric, respectively. IOS uses the administrative distance to choose the better route when IOS learns multiple routes for the same subnet but from two different sources of routing information. Refer back to the "Administrative Distance" section in Chapter 7, "Understanding OSPF Concepts," for a review.

EIGRP Metrics, Successors, and Feasible Successors

Both OSPF and EIGRP use similar big ideas: enabling the protocol on the router's interfaces, forming neighbor relationships, building topology tables, and adding IPv4 routes to the routing table. These two routing protocols differ most in the topology data they create and use. As a link-state protocol, OSPF creates and saves a lot of topology data, enough data to model the entire network topology in an area. EIGRP saves different kinds of data, in less detail, and uses a completely different algorithm to analyze the data.

This second major section in this chapter focuses on the details of the EIGRP topology database and specifically on the key ideas stored in the database. To review, as defined in Chapter 9, an EIGRP successor route is a router's best route to reach a subnet. Any of the other possible loop-free routes that can be used if the successor route fails are called feasible successor (FS) routes. And all the information used to determine which route is the successor, and which of the other routes meets the requirements to be an FS route, sits inside the EIGRP topology table.

This section demonstrates how to use **show** commands to identify successor routes and FS routes by looking at the EIGRP topology table. To make the discussion more interesting, the examples in this section use an expanded sample network that will result in multiple routes to reach each subnet, as shown in Figure 10-3.

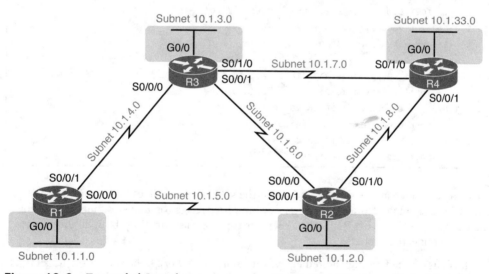

Figure 10-3 *Expanded Sample Internetwork with Multiple Routes to Each Subnet*

Viewing the EIGRP Topology Table

To begin, first consider the EIGRP topology table in Router R1, with this expanded network of Figure 10-3. The new network has five WAN and four LAN subnets, with multiple routes to reach each subnet. All the links use default bandwidth and delay settings. (Like the earlier examples, note that all router Gigabit interfaces happen to autonegotiate to use a speed of 100 Mbps, which changes the interface delay setting and therefore the EIGRP metric calculations.)

Example 10-8 begins the discussion with the output of the **show ip eigrp topology** command from R1. This command lists a few lines of information about each known subnet in R1's EIGRP topology table.

Example 10-8   *EIGRP Topology Table on Router R1*

```
R1# show ip eigrp topology
EIGRP-IPv4 Topology Table for AS(1)/ID(10.1.5.1)
Codes: P - Passive, A - Active, U - Update, Q - Query, R - Reply,
       r - reply Status, s - sia Status


P 10.1.5.0/24, 1 successors, FD is 2169856
        via Connected, Serial0/0/0
P 10.1.7.0/24, 1 successors, FD is 2681856
        via 10.1.4.3 (2681856/2169856), Serial0/0/1
P 10.1.3.0/24, 1 successors, FD is 2172416
        via 10.1.4.3 (2172416/28160), Serial0/0/1
P 10.1.2.0/24, 1 successors, FD is 2172416
        via 10.1.5.2 (2172416/28160), Serial0/0/0
P 10.1.6.0/24, 2 successors, FD is 2681856
        via 10.1.4.3 (2681856/2169856), Serial0/0/1
        via 10.1.5.2 (2681856/2169856), Serial0/0/0
P 10.1.4.0/24, 1 successors, FD is 2169856
        via Connected, Serial0/0/1
P 10.1.33.0/24, 2 successors, FD is 2684416
        via 10.1.4.3 (2684416/2172416), Serial0/0/1
        via 10.1.5.2 (2684416/2172416), Serial0/0/0
P 10.1.1.0/24, 1 successors, FD is 28160
        via Connected, GigabitEthernet0/0
P 10.1.8.0/24, 1 successors, FD is 2681856
        via 10.1.5.2 (2681856/2169856), Serial0/0/0
```

First, look through all the output, and count the subnets, in the lines that align with the left edge of the example. Note that R1 lists a group of messages for all nine subnets, including the connected subnets off R1. EIGRP keeps its topology information about all the subnets, even the connected subnets.

Next, focus on the first highlighted entry, for subnet 10.1.3.0/24, the subnet off R3's LAN interface. The first line for a given subnet lists the subnet ID and mask. It also lists the number of successor routes, and the feasible distance (FD). (As a reminder, the FD is the metric of the successor route, which is the best route to reach a particular subnet.)

To help make sure the items are clear, Figure 10-4 breaks down these items, using these same details about subnet 10.1.3.0/24 from R1's EIGRP topology table.

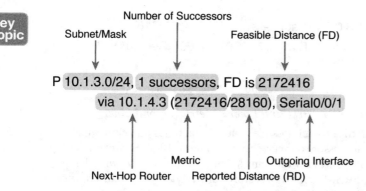

Figure 10-4 *Reference to Fields in the Output from* **show ip eigrp topology**

Continuing to focus on subnet 10.1.3.0/24 for a few more moments, the output lists one line per destination subnet and then one line per route below it, indented, beginning with the word *via*. In Figure 10-4, the main line (as usual) lists the subnet, prefix mask, the number of successor routes, and the FD. The second (indented) line lists information about the route, with the next-hop router (after the word *via*), and the outgoing interface. If the router puts this particular route into the IP routing table, the IP route would use this next-hop IP address and local outgoing interface in that route. Note that EIGRP can list multiple such lines that begin with *via* if EIGRP has multiple possible routes for that subnet.

Finally, note that the **show ip eigrp topology** command also lists two calculated EIGRP metrics in parentheses. The first is the metric as calculated by the local router for that route. The second is the reported distance (RD): the metric calculated from the perspective of the next-hop router. In the example shown in Figure 10-4, the RD of 28,160 is R1's RD for that route, which is the metric on next-hop router 10.1.4.3 (R3).

Finding Successor Routes

Unfortunately, the **show ip eigrp topology** command does not make it obvious which routes are successor (in other words, best) routes and which ones are feasible successor (in other words, quickly used loop-free replacement) routes. The next few pages walk through how to look at the data in the output of this command and identify the successor and FS routes.

First, for perspective, note that the output in Example 10-8 lists only successor routes, with no feasible successor routes. No routes happen to qualify as feasible successor routes in this network with all default bandwidth and delay settings. Upcoming Example 10-11 changes some settings, causing some routes to be feasible successors. For now, just note that all routes listed in Example 10-8 are successor routes.

The best way to recognize successor routes is that the successor route has the same metric value as the FD. The first line of topology output for a subnet lists the FD (that is, the best metric among all the routes to reach that destination subnet). The successor route, by definition, has the best metric, so the successor route's metric should equal the FD. As shown in Figure 10-5, just look for the FD on the first line and then for the individual routes that have the same metric in the first number inside parentheses.

10

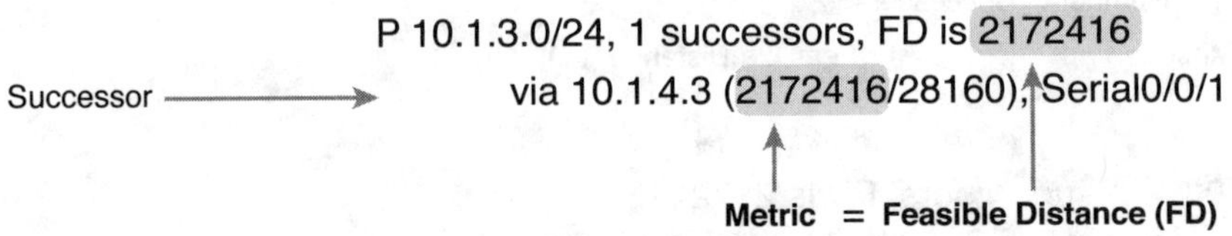

P 10.1.3.0/24, 1 successors, FD is 2172416

Successor ⟶ via 10.1.4.3 (2172416/28160), Serial0/0/1

Metric = Feasible Distance (FD)

Figure 10-5 *Identifying the Successor: FD (First Line) = Metric (Second Line)*

When EIGRP calculates the metrics for all possible routes, sometimes one clear winner exists, so EIGRP chooses one successor route (as shown in Figure 10-5). However, in other cases, the metrics for competing routes for the same subnet tie. In that case, with default EIGRP configuration settings, EIGRP supports a feature called *equal-cost load balancing*, which tells EIGRP to treat all the routes that tie as successor routes.

Example 10-9 shows two successor routes. The example shows an excerpt of the R1 EIGRP topology table for R1's route to subnet 10.1.33.0/24. That subnet exists off R4's LAN interface. In this case, R1 lists two routes, out two different interfaces to two different neighboring next-hop routers. Both routes list the same metric, which matches the FD (2,684,416), so both are successor routes.

Example 10-9 *Displaying Two Successor Routes on R1 for Subnet 10.1.33.0/24*

```
R1# show ip eigrp topology | section 10.1.33.0
P 10.1.33.0/24, 2 successors, FD is 2684416
        via 10.1.4.3 (2684416/2172416), Serial0/0/1
        via 10.1.5.2 (2684416/2172416), Serial0/0/0
```

In this case, with default settings, R1 would add both routes to its IP routing table. Later in this chapter, the section "EIGRP Maximum Paths and Variance" discusses some similar logic of how a router deals with somewhat equal-cost routes to the same subnet. That section also gives a little more insight into the equal-cost load-balancing option.

NOTE The command in Example 10-9 pipes the output of the **show ip eigrp topology** command to the **section** command. This process asks IOS to find a section or group of messages with the listed text (in this case, 10.1.33.0) and display only that group of messages. It is just a way to getting the desired subset of the output without listing the entire command.

Finding Feasible Successor Routes

The **show ip eigrp topology** command lists both successor and feasible successor routes when both exist. The examples so far in this chapter, which used all default bandwidth and delay settings, simply did not happen to result in any FS routes. The next topic changes the configuration, creating an FS route, and then shows how to recognize this route in the topology database.

First, consider Example 10-9's listing of R1's topology data for subnet 10.1.33.0/24, the LAN subnet off R4. From R1's perspective, with all default bandwidth and delay settings, two routes are as identical as they can be. The route from R1 through R3 uses two serial links with default settings for bandwidth of 1544 Kbps and delay of 20,000 microseconds on all the serial links. The route from R1 through R2 also uses two serial links, also with default bandwidth and delay. As a result, R1 has the two equal-cost routes for subnet 10.1.33.0/24, as shown on the left side of Figure 10-6.

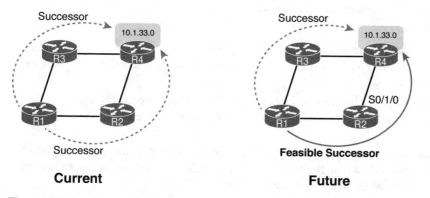

Figure 10-6   *Comparing Two Successor Routes to One Successor and One FS*

The next example makes the route through R2 worse than the route through R3, by simply lowering the bandwidth on R2's serial link connected to R4. Currently, the path R1-R2-R4 has, from R1's perspective, a slowest bandwidth of 1544 Kbps. By lowering the bandwidth to some other number lower than 1544 Kbps, the metrics of the two routes will no longer exactly tie. A slightly lower bandwidth will result in the upper R1-R3-R4 route being the only successor route, with the R1-R2-R4 route being an FS route.

First, to change the configuration to use a worse (slower) slowest bandwidth, Example 10-10 shows R2's S0/1/0 configuration being changed with the **bandwidth 1400** command.

Example 10-10   *Tuning EIGRP Routes by Changing Interface Bandwidth*

```
R2# configure terminal
Enter configuration commands, one per line.  End with CNTL/Z.
R2(config)# interface s0/1/0
R2(config-if)# bandwidth 1400
```

As soon as R2 changes its bandwidth, R2 sends a partial EIGRP update, as discussed back in Chapter 9. The other routers learn some new information, and they recalculate their own metrics, and the RD values, as appropriate. To see the differences, Example 10-11 repeats the **show ip eigrp topology | section 10.1.33.0** command on R1, as last seen in Example 10-9. In Example 10-9, that command showed R1 with two successor routes for this subnet. Now, in Example 10-11, R1 has only one successor route, but with the FS actually hidden there in the output, as explained after the example.

Example 10-11   *Viewing a Feasible Successor Route on R1 for 10.1.33.0/24*

```
R1# show ip eigrp topology | section 10.1.33.0
P 10.1.33.0/24, 1 successors, FD is 2684416
        via 10.1.4.3 (2684416/2172416), Serial0/0/1
        via 10.1.5.2 (2854912/2342912), Serial0/0/0
```

10

To see the feasible successor route, and why it is an FS, work through the various numbers in the output in Example 10-11. Or, work through that same output, repeated in Figure 10-7, with notes. In either case, the logic works like the notes in this list:

- Per the first line, one successor route exists.

- The FD is 2,684,416.

- Of the two lines that begin with via—the two possible routes listed—the first route's metric of 2,684,416 equals the FD. As a result, this first line lists the details of the one successor route.

- The other line that begins with via has a metric (first number in parentheses) of 2,854,912, which differs from the FD value of 2,684,416. As a result, this route is not a successor route.

- The second line that begins with via has a reported distance (RD, the second number) of 2,342,912, which is less than the FD of 2,684,416. This second route meets the feasibility condition, making it a feasible successor route.

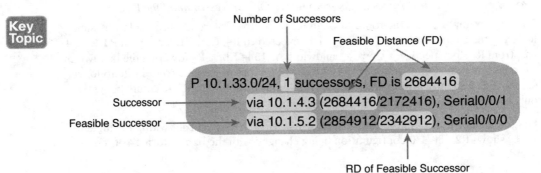

RD < FD: Meets Feasibility Condition!

Figure 10-7 *Identifying the Feasible Successor Route*

NOTE The **show ip eigrp topology** command lists only successor and FS routes. To see other routes, use the **show ip eigrp topology all-links** command, which lists all routes, even those that are neither successor nor feasible successor routes.

Convergence Using the Feasible Successor Route

One motivation for EIGRP to have an FS concept is to help EIGRP converge very quickly, using an FS route immediately when a successor route fails. The next example shows the convergence process, with R1 losing its current successor route to 10.1.33.0/24, through R3, and replacing it with the FS route through R2, as shown in Figure 10-8.

Example 10-12 shows not only the net results of the failover and convergence, but also the process by using some debug messages. Be warned, some of the debug messages might not make a lot of sense. However, the example removes some of the less-useful messages, and highlights the more understandable output, to demonstrate what happens with the failover.

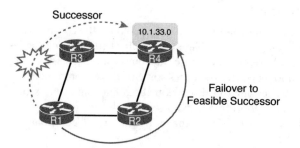

Figure 10-8 *Diagram of the Convergence Event Described in the Next Example*

For this example, the link between R3 and R4 is disabled (**shutdown**). The debug messages on R1 show the effects of EIGRP's logic in changing routes. Pay particular attention to the timestamps on the debug messages, which amazingly all occur within the same millisecond.

Example 10-12 *Debug Messages During Convergence to the FS Route for Subnet 10.1.33.0/24*

```
! Below, debug eigrp fsm is enabled, and then R3's S0/1/0 link to R4 is disabled,
! but not shown in the example text. SOME DEBUG MESSAGES are omitted to
! improve readability.
R1# debug eigrp fsm
EIGRP FSM Events/Actions debugging is on
R1#
*Nov 13 23:50:41.099: EIGRP-IPv4(1): Find FS for dest 10.1.33.0/24. FD is 2684416, RD
  is 2684416 on tid 0
*Nov 13 23:50:41.099: EIGRP-IPv4(1):     10.1.4.3 metric 72057594037927935/
  72057594037927936
*Nov 13 23:50:41.099: EIGRP-IPv4(1):     10.1.5.2 metric 2854912/2342912 found Dmin is
  2854912
*Nov 13 23:50:41.099: DUAL: AS(1) RT installed 10.1.33.0/24 via 10.1.5.2
!
! Next, R1 lists a new successor route, to 10.1.5.2: R2.
R1# show ip eigrp topology | section 10.1.33.0
P 10.1.33.0/24, 1 successors, FD is 2854912
        via 10.1.5.2 (2854912/2342912), Serial0/0/0
R1# show ip route | section 10.1.33.0
D       10.1.33.0/24 [90/2854912] via 10.1.5.2, 00:16:50, Serial0/0/0
```

Finally, make sure to note the ending state of the convergence, as shown at the end of the example. The example shows R1's updated topology database entries for subnet 10.1.33.0/24, with a new successor, new FD (2,854,912 versus the old 2,684,416 shown in Example 10-11), and a new next-hop router (R2, 10.1.5.2). The last command lists the new IPv4 route, with the new FD listed as the metric in brackets, and R2 (10.1.5.2) as the new next-hop router.

10

Examining the Metric Components

Most of the discussion about metrics in this chapter so far has centered on the composite EIGRP metric—that is, the rather large integer metric that is the result of the metric calculation on the local router. However, EIGRP does not advertise the composite metric. Instead, EIGRP advertises different metric components, and then uses some of those components to calculate the composite metric. Before leaving this discussion about choosing successor routes (with the best metric), and FS routes (loop-free backup routes), all based on their composite metrics, this short topic shows how to look at the individual metric components stored by EIGRP.

When using the defaults (which Cisco recommends), EIGRP bases its composite metric calculation on the minimum bandwidth link in a route and the total delay for all links in the route. However, the EIGRP routers still advertise all the metric components, which include the link reliability and load. Example 10-13 lists the output from the **show ip eigrp topology 10.1.3.0/24** command on Router R1, a command that lists the details of the EIGRP topology data for the routes for this subnet. The highlighted lines in the example list the composite metric as well as the individual components of the metric.

Example 10-13 *EIGRP Metric Components as Shown in the EIGRP Topology Database*

```
R1# show ip eigrp topology 10.1.3.0/24
EIGRP-IPv4 Topology Entry for AS(1)/ID(10.1.13.1) for 10.1.3.0/24
  State is Passive, Query origin flag is 1, 1 Successor(s), FD is 2172416
  Descriptor Blocks:
  10.1.4.3 (Serial0/0/1), from 10.1.4.3, Send flag is 0x0
       Composite metric is (2172416/28160), route is Internal
       Vector metric:
         Minimum bandwidth is 1544 Kbit
         Total delay is 20100 microseconds
         Reliability is 255/255
         Load is 1/255
         Minimum MTU is 1500
         Hop count is 1
         Originating router is 3.3.3.3
  10.1.5.2 (Serial0/0/0), from 10.1.5.2, Send flag is 0x0
       Composite metric is (2684416/2172416), route is Internal
       Vector metric:
         Minimum bandwidth is 1544 Kbit
         Total delay is 40100 microseconds
         Reliability is 255/255
         Load is 1/255
         Minimum MTU is 1500
         Hop count is 2
```

Other EIGRP Configuration Settings

So far, this chapter has focused on the core functions of EIGRP. The configuration details have been relatively sparse, just due to the nature of EIGRP. However, this chapter has spent a fair amount of time and effort to show the results of enabling EIGRP on the routers in a network, showing EIGRP working on interfaces, creating neighbor relationships, learning topology information, and ultimately adding routes to the IP routing table.

This third and final major section of this chapter turns away from these core features. The topics in this section are either completely optional or have default settings that the chapter has not discussed so far. This section now examines this small set of other EIGRP topics, including load balancing, EIGRP metric tuning, and autosummary.

Load Balancing Across Multiple EIGRP Routes

Like OSPF, EIGRP supports the ability to put multiple equal-metric routes in the IPv4 routing table. Like OSPF, EIGRP defaults to support four such routes for each subnet. That number of concurrent routes to each subnet can be configured with the **maximum-paths** *number* EIGRP subcommand. (Note that the maximum number of equal-cost paths depends on the IOS version and router platform.)

In fact, Example 10-9, earlier in this chapter, showed just such an example, with Router R1's route for subnet 10.1.33.0/24. Example 10-14 revisits that same scenario, this time with both the topology table and the IP routing table displayed. Due to the default EIGRP configuration setting of **maximum-paths 4**, R1 places both successor routes into R1's IP routing table.

Example 10-14   *R1's Routing Table with Multiple Equal-Cost EIGRP Routes*

```
R1# show ip eigrp topology | section 10.1.33.0
P 10.1.33.0/24, 2 successors, FD is 2684416
        via 10.1.4.3 (2684416/2172416), Serial0/0/1
        via 10.1.5.2 (2684416/2172416), Serial0/0/0

R1# show ip route | section 10.1.33.0
D       10.1.33.0/24 [90/2684416] via 10.1.5.2, 00:02:23, Serial0/0/0
                     [90/2684416] via 10.1.4.3, 00:02:23, Serial0/0/1
```

Although the ability to add multiple routes with exactly equal metrics may be useful, EIGRP often calculates similar metric values that are not exactly equal. EIGRP metrics often range into the millions, making it less likely that metrics would be exactly the same.

IOS also includes the concept of *unequal-cost load balancing* using an EIGRP setting called *variance*, to overcome this problem. Variance allows routes whose metrics are relatively close in value to be considered equal, allowing multiple unequal-metric routes to the same subnet to be added to the routing table.

The **variance** *multiplier* EIGRP router subcommand defines an integer between 1 and 128. The router then multiplies the variance times a route's FD—the best metric with which to reach that subnet. Any FS routes whose metric is less than the product of the variance times the FD are considered to be equal routes and may be placed in the routing table, depending on the setting of the **maximum-paths** command.

The previous paragraph does summarize the rules for variance and unequal-cost load balancing, but working through the idea with an example works much better. To keep the numbers more obvious, Table 10-2 lists an example with small metric values. The table lists the

10

metric for three routes to the same subnet, as calculated on Router R4. The table also lists the neighboring routers' RD and the decision to add routes to the routing table based on various variance settings.

Table 10-2   Example of Routes Chosen as Equal Because of Variance

Next Hop	Metric	RD	Added to Routing Table at Variance 1?	Added to Routing Table at Variance 2?	Added to Routing Table at Variance 3?
R1	50	30	Yes	Yes	Yes
R2	90	40	No	Yes	Yes
R3	120	60	No	No	No

Before considering the variance, note that in this case the route through R1 is the successor route because it has the lowest metric. This also means that the metric for the route through R1, 50, is the FD. The route through R2 is an FS route because its RD of 40 is less than the FD of 50. The route through R3 is not an FS route because its RD of 60 is more than the FD of 50.

At a default configuration of **variance 1**, the metrics must be exactly equal to be considered equal, so only the successor route is added to the routing table.

With the **variance 2** command configured, the FD (50) is multiplied by the variance (2) for a product of 100. The route through R2, with metric 90, is less than the calculated variance × FD = 100, so R4 adds the route through R2 to the routing table as well. The router can then load balance traffic across these two routes. The third route's metric, 120, is more than the calculated variance × FD = 100, so it is not added to the routing table.

With the **variance 3** command configured, the product of the FD (50) times 3 results in a product of 150, and all three routes' calculated metrics are less than 150. However, the route through R3 is not an FS route, so it cannot be added to the routing table for fear of causing a routing loop.

The following list summarizes the key points about variance:

- The variance is multiplied by the current FD (the metric of the best route to reach the subnet).

- Any FS routes whose calculated metric is less than or equal to the product of variance times the FD are added to the IP routing table, assuming that the **maximum-paths** setting allows more routes.

- Routes that are neither successor nor FS can never be added to the IP routing table, regardless of the variance setting, because doing so may cause packets to loop.

As soon as the routes have been added to the routing table, the router supports a variety of options for how to load balance traffic across the routes. The router can balance the traffic proportionally with the metrics, meaning that lower-metric routes send more packets. The router can send all traffic over the lowest-metric route, with the other routes just being in the routing table for faster convergence in case the best route fails. However, the details of the load-balancing process require a much deeper discussion of the internals of the forwarding process in IOS, and this topic is beyond the scope of this book.

Tuning the EIGRP Metric Calculation

By default, EIGRP calculates an integer composite metric based on interface bandwidth and delay. You can change the settings on any interface using the **bandwidth** *value* and the **delay** *value* interface subcommands, which in turn influences a router's choice of routes.

Cisco recommends setting each interface's bandwidth to an accurate value, rather than setting the bandwidth to some inaccurate value for the purpose of changing EIGRP's metric calculation. Router serial links should be configured with the **bandwidth** *speed* command, with a *speed* value in kilobits per second (Kbps), matching the interface's actual speed. Router Ethernet interfaces can use default settings; by default, IOS actually changes the router Ethernet interface bandwidth setting to match the actual physical transmission speed.

Because the delay interface setting impacts fewer other IOS features, Cisco recommends that if you want to tune the EIGRP metric, change the interface delay settings. To change an interface's delay setting, use the **delay** *value* command, where the *value* is a delay setting with an unusual unit: tens of microseconds. Interestingly, the EIGRP metric formula also uses the unit of tens of microseconds; however, **show** commands list the delay with a unit of microseconds, as shown in Example 10-15 with the following details:

1. The router's Fa0/0 has a default delay setting of 100 microseconds (usec), assuming the interface is actually running at a speed of 100 Mbps.

2. The **delay 123** command is configured on the interface, meaning 123 tens of microseconds.

3. The **show interfaces fa0/0** command now lists a delay of 1230 microseconds.

Example 10-15   *Configuring Interface Delay*

```
Yosemite# show interfaces fa0/0
FastEthernet0/0 is up, line protocol is up
  Hardware is Gt96k FE, address is 0013.197b.5026 (bia 0013.197b.5026)
  Internet address is 10.1.2.252/24
  MTU 1500 bytes, BW 100000 Kbit, DLY 100 usec,
! lines omitted for brevity


Yosemite# configure terminal
Enter configuration commands, one per line.  End with CNTL/Z.
Yosemite(config)# interface fa0/0
Yosemite(config-if)# delay 123
Yosemite(config-if)# ^Z


Yosemite# show interfaces fa0/0
FastEthernet0/0 is up, line protocol is up
  Hardware is Gt96k FE, address is 0013.197b.5026 (bia 0013.197b.5026)
  Internet address is 10.1.2.252/24
  MTU 1500 bytes, BW 100000 Kbit, DLY 1230 usec,
! lines omitted for brevity
```

10

Autosummarization and Discontiguous Classful Networks

Older routing protocols, namely RIPv1 and IGRP, were classified as *classful routing protocols*. This term comes from the fact that these classful routing protocols had to pay more attention to details about Class A, B, and C networks, in part because of the simplicity of the routing protocol.

These older classful routing protocols also had to use a more careful and cautious subnet design plan to avoid a problem called a discontiguous classful network. These simpler old routing protocols just got confused when a classful network became discontiguous, because of a required feature of classful routing protocols called autosummarization.

Today, most enterprises use OSPF or EIGRP, or in rare cases, RIPv2. All these protocols are classless routing protocols. As a result, these newer routing protocols can be configured so that the old problem with discontiguous classful networks is not a problem at all.

However, while the more recent IOS versions use good default settings so that this problem can be ignored, EIGRP allows the possibility of enabling the autosummary feature, which then requires the network engineer to be aware of this old discontiguous network problem. So, just in case, these next few pages first discuss the autosummary feature, followed by a discussion of the routing problems that can occur as a result.

NOTE In real networks, most people simply choose to avoid using autosummary today.

Automatic Summarization at the Boundary of a Classful Network

A routing protocol that uses autosummary automatically creates a summary route under certain conditions. In particular, when a router sits at the boundary between classful networks—that is, with some interfaces in one Class A, B, or C network and other interfaces in another Class A, B, or C network—the router summarizes routes. Routes from one classful network are summarized as one route to the entire Class A, B, or C network. More formally:

Routes related to subnets in network X, when advertised out an interface whose IP address is not in network X, are summarized and advertised as one route. That route is for the entire Class A, B, or C network X.

As usual, an example makes the concept much clearer. Consider Figure 10-9, which shows two networks in use: 10.0.0.0 and 172.16.0.0. R3 has four (connected) routes to subnets of network 10.0.0.0 on the right, and one interface on the left connected to a different classful network, Class B network 172.16.0.0. As a result, R3, with autosummary enabled, will summarize a route for all of Class A network 10.0.0.0.

Let's follow the steps in the figure:

1. R3 has autosummary enabled, with the EIGRP **auto-summary** router subcommand.

2. R3 advertises a route for all of Class A network 10.0.0.0, instead of advertising routes for each subnet inside network 10.0.0.0 because the link to R2 is a link in another network (172.16.0.0).

3. R2 learns one route in network 10.0.0.0: a route to 10.0.0.0/8, which represents all of network 10.0.0.0, with R3 as the next-hop router.

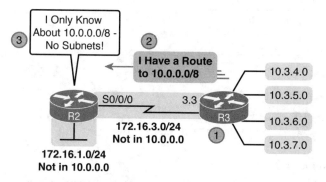

Figure 10-9   *Autosummarization*

Example 10-16 shows the output of the **show ip route** command on R2, confirming the effect of the **auto-summary** setting on R3.

Example 10-16   *R2 with a Single Route in Network 10.0.0.0 for the Entire Network*

```
R2# show ip route eigrp
! lines omitted for brevity


D     10.0.0.0/8 [90/2297856] via 172.16.3.3, 00:12:59, Serial0/0/0
```

Note that **auto-summary** by itself causes no problems. In the design shown in Figure 10-9, and in the command output in Example 10-16, no problems exist. R2 can forward packets to all subnets of network 10.0.0.0 using the one highlighted summary route, sending those packets to R3 next.

Discontiguous Classful Networks

Autosummarization does not cause any problems as long as the summarized network is contiguous rather than discontiguous. U.S. residents can appreciate the concept of a discontiguous network based on the common term *contiguous 48*, referring to the 48 U.S. states besides Alaska and Hawaii. To drive to Alaska from the contiguous 48, for example, you must drive through another country (Canada, for the geographically impaired), so Alaska is not contiguous with the 48 states. In other words, it is discontiguous.

To better understand what the terms *contiguous* and *discontiguous* mean in networking, refer to the following two formal definitions when reviewing the example of a discontiguous classful network that follows:

- **Contiguous network:** A classful network in which packets sent between every pair of subnets can pass only through subnets of that same classful network, without having to pass through subnets of any other classful network
- **Discontiguous network:** A classful network in which packets sent between at least one pair of subnets must pass through subnets of a different classful network

Figure 10-10 creates an expanded version of the internetwork shown in Figure 10-9 to create an example of a discontiguous network 10.0.0.0. In this design, some subnets of network 10.0.0.0 sit off R1 on the left, whereas others still connect to R3 on the right. Packets passing between subnets on the left to subnets on the right must pass through subnets of Class B network 172.16.0.0.

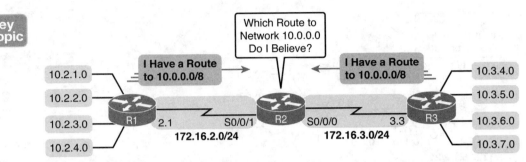

Figure 10-10   *Discontiguous Network 10.0.0.0*

Autosummarization causes problems in that routers like R2 that sit totally outside the discontiguous network become totally confused about how to route packets to the discontiguous network. Figure 10-10 shows the idea, with both R1 and R3 advertising a route for 10.0.0.0/8 to R2 in the middle of the network. Example 10-17 shows the resulting routes on Router R2.

Example 10-17   *R2 Routing Table: Autosummarization Causes Routing Problem with Discontiguous Network 10.0.0.0*

```
R2# show ip route | section 10.0.0.0
D     10.0.0.0/8 [90/2297856] via 172.16.3.3, 00:00:15, Serial0/0/0
                 [90/2297856] via 172.16.2.1, 00:00:15, Serial0/0/1
```

As shown in Example 10-17, R2 now has two routes to network 10.0.0.0/8: one pointing left toward R1 and one pointing right toward R3. R2 simply uses its usual load-balancing logic, because as far as R2 can tell, the two routes are simply equal-cost routes to the same destination: the entire network 10.0.0.0. Sometimes R2 happens to forward a packet toward the correct destination, and sometimes not.

This problem has two solutions. The old-fashioned solution is to create IP addressing plans that do not create discontiguous classful networks. The other: Just do not use autosummary, by using EIGRP defaults, or by disabling it with the **no auto-summary** EIGRP subcommand. Example 10-18 shows the resulting routing table in R2 for routes in network 10.0.0.0 with the **no auto-summary** command configured on Routers R1 and R3.

Example 10-18   *Classless Routing Protocol with No Autosummarization Allows Discontiguous Network*

```
R2# show ip route 10.0.0.0
Routing entry for 10.0.0.0/24, 8 known subnets
  Redistributing via eigrp 1
D     10.2.1.0 [90/2297856] via 172.16.2.1, 00:00:12, Serial0/0/1
D     10.2.2.0 [90/2297856] via 172.16.2.1, 00:00:12, Serial0/0/1
D     10.2.3.0 [90/2297856] via 172.16.2.1, 00:00:12, Serial0/0/1
D     10.2.4.0 [90/2297856] via 172.16.2.1, 00:00:12, Serial0/0/1
D     10.3.4.0 [90/2297856] via 172.16.3.3, 00:00:06, Serial0/0/0
D     10.3.5.0 [90/2297856] via 172.16.3.3, 00:00:06, Serial0/0/0
D     10.3.6.0 [90/2297856] via 172.16.3.3, 00:00:06, Serial0/0/0
D     10.3.7.0 [90/2297856] via 172.16.3.3, 00:00:06, Serial0/0/0
```

Chapter Review

One key to doing well on the exams is to perform repetitive spaced review sessions. Review this chapter's material using either the tools in the book, DVD, or interactive tools for the same material found on the book's companion website. Refer to the "Your Study Plan" element for more details. Table 10-3 outlines the key review elements and where you can find them. To better track your study progress, record when you completed these activities in the second column.

Table 10-3 Chapter Review Tracking

Review Element	Review Date(s)	Resource Used:
Review key topics		Book, DVD/website
Review key terms		Book, DVD/website
Answer DIKTA questions		Book, PCPT
Do Labs		Blog
Review config checklist		Book, DVD/website
Review command tables		Book

Review All the Key Topics

Key Topic

Table 10-4 Key Topics for Chapter 10

Key Topic Element	Description	Page Number
Figure 10-2	Roadmap of topics (left) and verification commands	249
Example 10-5	The **show ip protocols** command and how it reveals the configured **network** commands	252
List	Rules with which EIGRP chooses its router ID	252
Figure 10-4	Breakdown of the output of a successor route in the output of the **show ip eigrp topology** command	257
Figure 10-7	Breakdown of the output of an FS route in the output of the **show ip eigrp topology** command	260
List	Key points about EIGRP variance	264
Text	Definition of autosummary	266
List	Definitions of contiguous network and discontiguous network	267
Figure 10-10	An example of the problem caused by autosummary and the use of a discontiguous network	268

10

Key Terms You Should Know

feasibility condition, feasible distance, feasible successor, reported distance, successor, unequal-cost load balancing, variance, autosummary, discontiguous network

Command References

Tables 10-5 and 10-6 list configuration and verification commands used in this chapter. As an easy review exercise, cover the left column in a table, read the right column, and try to recall the command without looking. Then repeat the exercise, covering the right column, and try to recall what the command does.

Table 10-5   Chapter 10 Configuration Command Reference

Command	Description
router eigrp *autonomous-system*	Global command to move the user into EIGRP configuration mode for the listed ASN
network *network-number* [*wildcard-mask*]	EIGRP router subcommand that matches either all interfaces in a classful network or a subset of interfaces based on the ACL-style wildcard mask, enabling EIGRP on those interfaces
maximum-paths *number-paths*	Router subcommand that defines the maximum number of equal-cost routes that can be added to the routing table
variance *multiplier*	Router subcommand that defines an EIGRP multiplier used to determine whether an FS route's metric is close enough to the successor's metric to be considered equal
bandwidth *bandwidth*	Interface subcommand that directly sets the interface bandwidth (Kbps)
delay *delay-value*	Interface subcommand that sets the interface delay value with a unit of tens of microseconds
ip hello-interval eigrp *as-number timer-value*	Interface subcommand that sets the EIGRP Hello Interval for that EIGRP process
ip hold-time eigrp *as-number timer-value*	Interface subcommand that sets the EIGRP hold time for the interface
[no] **auto-summary**	Router subcommand that disables (with the **no** option) or enables the automatic summarization of routes at the boundary of a classful network
passive-interface *type number*	Router subcommand that makes the interface passive to EIGRP, meaning that the EIGRP process will not form neighbor relationships with neighbors reachable on that interface
passive-interface default	Router subcommand that changes the EIGRP default for interfaces to be passive instead of active (not passive)
no passive-interface *type number*	Router subcommand that tells EIGRP to be active (not passive) on that interface or subinterface

Table 10-6   Chapter 10 EXEC Command Reference

Command	Description
show ip eigrp interfaces	Lists one line per interface on which EIGRP has been enabled, but for which it is not made passive with the **passive-interface** configuration command
show ip eigrp interfaces *type number*	Lists statistics interfaces on which EIGRP has been enabled, but for which it is not made passive with the **passive-interface** configuration command
show ip eigrp interfaces detail [*type number*]	Lists detailed configuration and statistics, for all interfaces or for the listed interface, again for enabled interfaces that are not passive
show ip protocols	Shows routing protocol parameters and current timer values
show ip eigrp neighbors	Lists EIGRP neighbors and status
show ip eigrp neighbors *type number*	Lists EIGRP neighbors reachable off the listed interface
show ip eigrp topology	Lists the contents of the EIGRP topology table, including successors and FSs
show ip eigrp topology *subnet/prefix*	Lists detailed topology information about the listed subnet
show ip eigrp topology | section *subnet*	Lists a subset of the **show ip eigrp topology** command (just the section for the listed subnet ID)
show ip route	Lists all IPv4 routes
show ip route eigrp	Lists routes in the IPv4 routing table learned by EIGRP
show ip route *ip-address mask*	Shows a detailed description of the route for the listed subnet/mask
show ip route | section *subnet*	Lists a subset of the **show ip route** command: just the section for the listed subnet ID
debug eigrp fsm	Displays changes to the EIGRP successor and FS routes

10

CHAPTER 11

Troubleshooting IPv4 Routing Protocols

This chapter covers the following exam topics:

2.0 Routing Technologies

2.4 Configure, verify, and troubleshoot single area and multiarea OSPFv2 for IPv4 (excluding authentication, filtering, manual summarization, redistribution, stub, virtual-link, and LSAs)

2.6 Configure, verify, and troubleshoot EIGRP for IPv4 (excluding authentication, filtering, manual summarization, redistribution, stub)

To troubleshoot a possible IPv4 routing protocol problem, first focus on interfaces, and then on neighbors. The routing protocol configuration identifies the interfaces on which the router should use the routing protocol. After identifying those interfaces, a network engineer can look at the neighbors each router finds on each interface, searching for neighbors that should exist but do not.

This chapter focuses on issues related to these two main branches of logic: on which interfaces should a router enable the routing protocol, and which neighbor relationships should each router create. This chapter relies on the configuration discussed in Chapter 8 for OSPFv2 and in Chapter 10 for EIGRP. This chapter's troubleshooting discussions emphasize how to find incorrect configuration problems by using only **show** and **debug** commands.

This chapter first briefly introduces a few broad concepts related to troubleshooting problems with routing protocols. The next major section examines problems related to which interfaces on which a router enables the routing protocol, with the final major section focusing of routing protocol neighbor relationships. Note that the entire chapter moves back and forth between discussing both Enhanced Interior Gateway Routing Protocol (EIGRP) and Open Shortest Path First Version 2 (OSPFv2).

"Do I Know This Already?" Quiz

The troubleshooting chapters of this book pull in concepts from many other chapters, including some chapters in *CCENT/CCNA ICND1 100-105 Official Cert Guide*. They also show you how to approach some of the more challenging questions on the ICND2 and CCNA R&S exams. Therefore, it is useful to read these chapters regardless of your current knowledge level. For these reasons, the troubleshooting chapters do not include a "Do I Know This Already?" quiz. However, if you feel particularly confident about troubleshooting OSPFv2 and EIGRP, feel free to move to the "Chapter Review" section near the end of this chapter to bypass the majority of the chapter.

Perspectives on Troubleshooting Routing Protocol Problems

Because a routing protocol's job is to fill a router's routing table with the currently best routes, it makes sense that troubleshooting potential problems with routing protocols could begin with the IP routing table. Given basic information about an internetwork, including the routers, their IP addresses and masks, and the routing protocol, you could calculate the subnet numbers that should be in the router's routing table and list the likely next-hop routers for each route. For example, Figure 11-1 shows an internetwork with six subnets. Router R1's routing table should list all six subnets, with three connected routes, two routes learned from R2 (172.16.4.0/24 and 172.16.5.0/24), and one route learned from R3 (172.16.6.0/24).

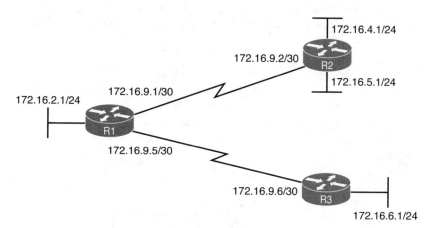

Figure 11-1 *Internetwork with Six Subnets*

So, one possible troubleshooting process is to analyze the internetwork, look at the routing table, and look for missing routes. If one or more expected routes are missing, the next step would be to determine whether that router has learned any routes from the expected next-hop (neighbor) router. The next steps to isolate the problem differ greatly if a router is having problems forming a neighbor relationship with another router, versus having a working neighbor relationship but not being able to learn all routes.

For example, suppose that R1 in Figure 11-1 has learned a route for subnet 172.16.4.0/24 in Figure 11-1 but not for subnet 172.16.5.0/24. In this case, it is clear that R1 has a working neighbor relationship with R2. In these cases, the root cause of this problem might still be related to the routing protocol, or it might not. For example, the problem may be that R2's lower LAN interface is down. However, if R1 did not have a route for both 172.16.4.0/24 and 172.16.5.0/24, R1's neighbor relationship with R2 could be the problem.

Troubleshooting routing protocol problems in real internetworks can be very complex—much more complex than even the most difficult CCNA R&S exam questions. Defining a generic troubleshooting process with which to attack both simple and complex routing protocol problems would require a lot of space and be counterproductive for preparing for the CCNA R&S exams. This chapter instead offers a straightforward process for attacking routing protocol problems—specifically, problems similar to the depth and complexity of the CCNA R&S exams.

If an exam question appears to be related to a problem with a routing protocol, you can quickly identify some common configuration errors with the following process—even if the question does not list the configuration. The process has three main tasks:

Step 1. Examine the internetwork design to determine on which interfaces the routing protocol should be enabled and which routers are expected to become neighbors.

Step 2. Verify whether the routing protocol is enabled on each interface (as per Step 1). If it isn't, determine the root cause and fix the problem.

Step 3. Verify that each router has formed all expected neighbor relationships. If it hasn't, find the root cause and fix the problem.

For instance, as noted with asterisks in Figure 11-2, each router should enable the routing protocol on each of the interfaces shown in the figure. Also, routing protocol neighbor relationships should form between R1 and R2, and R1 and R3, but not between R2 and R3.

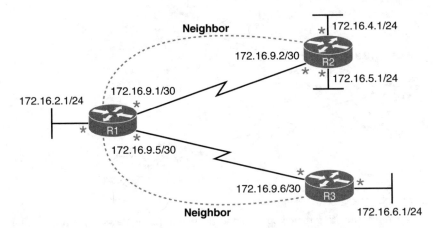

Figure 11-2 *Routing Protocol Interfaces and Neighbor Relationships*

While the concepts outlined in Figure 11-2 should be somewhat obvious by now, this chapter discusses how some of the most common configuration mistakes can impact the interfaces used by a routing protocol and whether a routing protocol creates neighbor relationships.

Interfaces Enabled with a Routing Protocol

This section examines the second major troubleshooting step outlined in the previous section of the chapter: how to verify the interfaces on which the routing protocol has been enabled. Both EIGRP and OSPF configuration enable the routing protocol on an interface by using the **network** router subcommand. For any interfaces matched by the **network** commands, the routing protocol tries the following two actions:

- Attempt to find potential neighbors on the subnet connected to the interface
- Advertise the subnet connected to that interface

At the same time, the **passive-interface** router subcommand can be configured so that the router does not attempt to find neighbors on the interface (the first action just listed), but still advertises the connected subnet (the second action).

Three **show** commands are all that is needed to know exactly which interfaces have been enabled with EIGRP and which interfaces are passive. In particular, the **show ip eigrp interfaces** command lists all EIGRP-enabled interfaces that are not passive interfaces. The **show ip protocols** command essentially lists the contents of the configured **network** commands for each routing protocol and a separate list of the passive interfaces. Comparing these two commands identifies all EIGRP-enabled interfaces and those that are passive.

For OSPF, the command works slightly differently, with the **show ip ospf interface brief** command listing all OSPF-enabled interfaces (including passive interfaces). Using this command, along with the list of passive interfaces listed by the **show ip protocols** command, again identifies all fully enabled OSPF interfaces as well as all passive interfaces.

Table 11-1 summarizes the commands that identify the interfaces on which OSPFv2 and EIGRP are enabled for easier reference.

Table 11-1   Key Commands to Find Routing Protocol-Enabled Interfaces

Command	Key Information	Lists Passive Interfaces?
show ip eigrp interfaces	Lists the interfaces on which EIGRP is enabled (based on the **network** commands), *excluding* passive interfaces.	No
show ip ospf interface brief	Lists the interfaces on which the OSPFv2 is enabled (based on the **network** router subcommands or **ip ospf** interface subcommands), *including* passive interfaces.	Yes
show ip protocols	Lists the contents of the **network** configuration commands for each routing process, and lists enabled but passive interfaces.	Yes

NOTE   All the commands in Table 11-1 list the interfaces regardless of interface status, in effect telling you the results of the **network** and **passive-interface** configuration commands.

So, for the major troubleshooting step covered in this section, the task is to use the commands in Table 11-1 and analyze the output. First, an EIGRP example will be shown, followed by an OSPF example.

EIGRP Interface Troubleshooting

This section shows a few examples of the commands in the context of Figure 11-3, which is used in all the examples in this chapter.

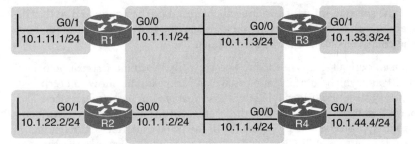

Figure 11-3 *Internetwork for EIGRP/OSPF Troubleshooting Examples*

This example includes four routers, with the following scenario in this case:

- R1 and R2 are configured correctly on both LAN interfaces.

- R3 is mistakenly not enabled with EIGRP on its G0/1 interface.

- R4 meant to use a **passive-interface G0/1** command because no other routers are off R4's G0/1 LAN. However, R4 has instead configured a **passive-interface G0/0** command.

This example begins by showing the working details between Routers R1 and R2, and then moves on to discuss the issues related to R3 and R4.

Examining Working EIGRP Interfaces

Examples 11-1 and 11-2 list configuration and **show** commands for R1 and R2, respectively. Each lists the related configuration, the **show ip eigrp interfaces** and **show ip protocols** command, and the EIGRP-learned routes on each router.

Example 11-1 *EIGRP Interfaces Problem: R1 Commands*

```
R1# show running-config
! only pertinent lines shown
router eigrp 99
 network 10.0.0.0
!
R1# show ip eigrp interfaces
EIGRP-IPv4 Interfaces for AS(99)
                  Xmit Queue    PeerQ        Mean   Pacing Time   Multicast    Pending
Interface  Peers  Un/Reliable   Un/Reliable  SRTT   Un/Reliable   Flow Timer   Routes
Gi0/0        2       0/0          0/0          2       0/0           50          0
Gi0/1        0       0/0          0/0          0       0/0            0          0


R1# show ip protocols
*** IP Routing is NSF aware ***

Routing Protocol is "eigrp 99"
  Outgoing update filter list for all interfaces is not set
  Incoming update filter list for all interfaces is not set
  Default networks flagged in outgoing updates
  Default networks accepted from incoming updates
```

```
    EIGRP-IPv4 Protocol for AS(99)
      Metric weight K1=1, K2=0, K3=1, K4=0, K5=0
      NSF-aware route hold timer is 240
      Router-ID: 1.1.1.1
      Topology : 0 (base)
        Active Timer: 3 min
        Distance: internal 90 external 170
        Maximum path: 4
        Maximum hopcount 100
        Maximum metric variance 1

   Automatic Summarization: disabled
   Maximum path: 4
   Routing for Networks:
     10.0.0.0
   Routing Information Sources:
     Gateway         Distance       Last Update
     10.1.1.2              90       09:55:51
     10.1.1.3              90       00:02:00
   Distance: internal 90 external 170

R1# show ip route eigrp
! Legend omitted for brevity


      10.0.0.0/8 is variably subnetted, 5 subnets, 2 masks
D         10.1.22.0/24 [90/30720] via 10.1.1.2, 00:00:40, GigabitEthernet0/0
```

Example 11-2   *EIGRP Interfaces Problem: R2 Commands*

```
R2# show running-config
! only pertinent lines shown
router eigrp 99
 network 10.1.0.0 0.0.255.255

R2# show ip eigrp interfaces
EIGRP-IPv4 Interfaces for AS(99)
                   Xmit Queue    PeerQ       Mean   Pacing Time   Multicast    Pending
Interface   Peers  Un/Reliable  Un/Reliable  SRTT   Un/Reliable   Flow Timer   Routes
Gi0/0          2      0/0          0/0          1      0/1            50          0
Gi0/1          0      0/0          0/0          0      0/0             0          0

R2# show ip protocols
*** IP Routing is NSF aware ***


Routing Protocol is "eigrp 99"
  Outgoing update filter list for all interfaces is not set
  Incoming update filter list for all interfaces is not set
```

11

```
Default networks flagged in outgoing updates
Default networks accepted from incoming updates
EIGRP-IPv4 Protocol for AS(99)
  Metric weight K1=1, K2=0, K3=1, K4=0, K5=0
  NSF-aware route hold timer is 240
  Router-ID: 2.2.2.2
  Topology : 0 (base)
    Active Timer: 3 min
    Distance: internal 90 external 170
    Maximum path: 4
    Maximum hopcount 100
    Maximum metric variance 1

Automatic Summarization: disabled
Maximum path: 4
Routing for Networks:
  10.1.0.0/16
Routing Information Sources:
  Gateway         Distance      Last Update
  10.1.1.3              90       00:02:30
  10.1.1.1              90       09:56:20
Distance: internal 90 external 170


R2# show ip route eigrp
! Legend omitted for brevity
     10.0.0.0/8 is variably subnetted, 5 subnets, 2 masks
D        10.1.11.0/24 [90/30720] via 10.1.1.1, 00:03:25, GigabitEthernet0/0
```

The **show ip eigrp interfaces** command output on both R1 and R2 shows how both R1 and R2 have configured EIGRP using process ID 99, and that EIGRP has been enabled on both G0/0 and G0/1 on both these routers. This command lists only interfaces on which EIGRP has been enabled, excluding passive interfaces.

The highlighted parts of the **show ip protocols** command output on each router are particularly interesting. These sections show the parameters of the configured **network** commands. The **show ip protocols** command lists a separate line under the header "Routing for Networks," one for each configured **network** command. Example 11-1's output suggests R1 has a **network 10.0.0.0** configuration command (as shown at the beginning of the example), and Example 11-2's "10.1.0.0/16" suggests R2 has a **network 10.1.0.0 0.0.255.255** command.

Examining the Problems with EIGRP Interfaces

The next few pages now look at the problems caused by the configuration on Routers R3 and R4.

First, Example 11-2 gives brief insight into the current problem caused by R3. The end of R2's **show ip protocols** command (Example 11-2) lists two routing information sources: 10.1.1.1 (R1) and 10.1.1.3 (R3). However, R2 has learned only one EIGRP route (10.1.11.0/24), as shown in the **show ip route eigrp** command output. When working properly, R2 should learn three EIGRP routes—one for each of the other LAN subnets shown in Figure 11-3.

Example 11-3 shows the root cause on R3. First, R3's **show ip eigrp interfaces** command lists G0/0, but not G0/1, so a problem might exist with how EIGRP has been configured on G0/1. The configuration at the top of the example lists the root cause: an incorrect **network** command, which does not enable EIGRP on R3's G0/1 interface.

Example 11-3   *EIGRP Problems on R3*

```
R3# show running-config
! lines omitted for brevity
router eigrp 99
 network 10.1.1.3 0.0.0.0
 network 10.1.13.3 0.0.0.0
 auto-summary


R3# show ip eigrp interfaces
EIGRP-IPv4 Interfaces for AS(99)
                    Xmit Queue    PeerQ        Mean   Pacing Time   Multicast    Pending
Interface   Peers   Un/Reliable   Un/Reliable  SRTT   Un/Reliable   Flow Timer   Routes
Gi0/0           2       0/0          0/0          1       0/1           50           0


R3# show ip protocols
*** IP Routing is NSF aware ***

Routing Protocol is "eigrp 99"
  Outgoing update filter list for all interfaces is not set
  Incoming update filter list for all interfaces is not set
  Default networks flagged in outgoing updates
  Default networks accepted from incoming updates
  EIGRP-IPv4 Protocol for AS(99)
    Metric weight K1=1, K2=0, K3=1, K4=0, K5=0
    NSF-aware route hold timer is 240
    Router-ID: 3.3.3.3
    Topology : 0 (base)
      Active Timer: 3 min
      Distance: internal 90 external 170
      Maximum path: 4
      Maximum hopcount 100
      Maximum metric variance 1

  Automatic Summarization: disabled
  Maximum path: 4
  Routing for Networks:
    10.1.1.3/32
    10.1.13.3/32
  Routing Information Sources:
    Gateway         Distance      Last Update
    10.1.1.2             90        00:05:14
    10.1.1.1             90        00:05:14
  Distance: internal 90 external 170
```

11

The root cause of R3's problem is that R3 has a **network 10.1.13.3 0.0.0.0** configuration command, which does not match R3's 10.1.33.3 G0/1 IP address. If the configuration was not available in the exam question, the **show ip protocols** command could be used to essentially see the same configuration details. In this case, the **show ip protocols** command on R3 lists the text "10.1.13.3/32" as a reference to the contents of the incorrect **network** command's parameters, with "/32" translating to a wildcard mask of 32 binary 0s, or decimal 0.0.0.0.

R3's incorrect configuration means that two actions do not happen on R3's G0/1 interface. First, R3 does not try to find neighbors on its G0/1 interface, which is not a big deal in this case. However, R3 also does not advertise subnet 10.1.33.0/24, the connected subnet off R3's G0/1 interface.

Moving on to R4's problem, Example 11-4 shows why R1 and R2 do not learn R4's 10.1.44.0/24 subnet. In this case, on R4, the engineer could have correctly used a **passive-interface gigabitethernet0/1** router subcommand because no other routers should exist off R4's G0/1 interface. However, the engineer mistakenly made R4's G0/0 interface passive.

Example 11-4   *EIGRP Problems on R4*

```
R4# show running-config
! lines omitted for brevity
router eigrp 99
 passive-interface GigabitEthernet0/0
 network 10.0.0.0
 auto-summary


R4# show ip eigrp interfaces
EIGRP-IPv4 Interfaces for AS(99)
                  Xmit Queue   PeerQ        Mean   Pacing Time  Multicast    Pending
Interface  Peers  Un/Reliable  Un/Reliable  SRTT   Un/Reliable  Flow Timer   Routes
Gi0/1        0      0/0          0/0          0       0/1          0            0


R4# show ip protocols | begin Routing for Networks
  Routing for Networks:
    10.0.0.0
  Passive Interface(s):
    GigabitEthernet0/0
  Routing Information Sources:
    Gateway         Distance      Last Update
  Distance: internal 90 external 170
```

NOTE   The last command on the example, **show ip protocols | begin Routing for Networks,** lists the command output, but starting with the line with the literal case-sensitive string **Routing for Networks.** You can use this feature with any output from a command when you prefer to view only later lines of the command's output.

To find this mistake without the configuration, Example 11-4 lists two useful commands. R4's **show ip eigrp interfaces** command omits the (G0/0) passive interface, which means that R4 will not attempt to find EIGRP neighbors off that interface. Also, the highlighted part of R4's **show ip protocols** command output lists G0/0 as a passive interface, which again means that R4 does not even attempt to become neighbors with others off its G0/0 interface.

OSPF Interface Troubleshooting

OSPF has the same basic requirements as EIGRP for interfaces, with a few exceptions. First, EIGRP routers need to use the same autonomous system number (ASN) as their neighboring routers, as configured in the **router eigrp** *asn* global configuration command. OSPF routers can use any process ID on the **router ospf** *process-id* command, with no need to match their neighbors. Second, OSPF requires that the interfaces connected to the same subnet be assigned to the same OSPF area, whereas EIGRP has no concept of areas.

Example 11-5 shows a mostly working OSPF internetwork, again based on Figure 11-3. The problem in this case relates to the area design, as shown in Figure 11-4, the revised version of Figure 11-3. All subnets should be placed into area 0. However, the engineer made a configuration mistake on R2, putting both its interfaces into area 1. As a result, R2's G0/0 interface breaks the OSPF design rule of being in the same subnet as R1, R3, and R4, but not being in the same OSPF area.

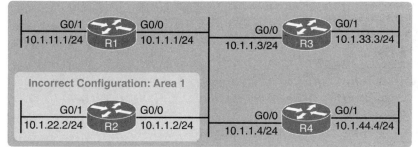

Figure 11-4 *Intended Area Design Using Only Area 0, with R2 Breaking the Design*

Example 11-5 begins to break down the problem by looking at the status of OSPF on the router interfaces of R1 and R2, using the **show ip ospf interface brief** command.

Example 11-5   show ip interface brief *on R1 and R2*

```
R1> show ip ospf interface brief

Interface    PID   Area        IP Address/Mask    Cost   State Nbrs F/C
Gi0/1         1     0          10.1.11.1/24       1      DR    0/0
Gi0/0         1     0          10.1.1.1/24        1      DROTH 2/2
! The following command is from R2
R2> show ip ospf interface brief

Interface    PID   Area        IP Address/Mask    Cost   State Nbrs F/C
Gi0/1         2     1          10.1.22.2/24       1      WAIT  0/0
Gi0/0         2     1          10.1.1.2/24        1      WAIT  0/0
```

11

From a general perspective, the **show ip ospf interface brief** command lists output similar to the **show ip eigrp interface** command, with one line for each enabled interface. The **show ip ospf interface** command, not shown in the example, lists detailed OSPF information for each interface.

Specific to this problem, the output in Example 11-5 shows that R1 and R2 both have OSPF enabled on both LAN interfaces. However, this command also lists the area number for each interface, with R2 having both LAN interfaces in area 1. Also, these commands repeat the IP address and mask of the interfaces, so together, you can see that R1's 10.1.1.1/24 address is in the same subnet as R2's 10.1.1.2/24 address, putting these two routers in the same subnet but in different OSPF areas.

Example 11-6 shows another way to look at the problem, with the **show ip protocols** commands on both R1 and R2. Because this command lists the OSPF **network** commands in shorthand form, it can point toward a possible configuration error, even if the configuration is not available.

Example 11-6 *Finding OSPF Configuration Errors with* **show ip protocols** *R1 and R2*

```
R1> show ip protocols
*** IP Routing is NSF aware ***

Routing Protocol is "ospf 1"
  Outgoing update filter list for all interfaces is not set
  Incoming update filter list for all interfaces is not set
  Router ID 1.1.1.1
  Number of areas in this router is 1. 1 normal 0 stub 0 nssa
  Maximum path: 4
  Routing for Networks:
    10.0.0.0 0.255.255.255 area 0
  Routing Information Sources:
    Gateway         Distance      Last Update
    2.2.2.2              110      00:14:32
    3.3.3.3              110      00:14:32
    10.1.44.4            110      00:14:42
  Distance: (default is 110)


R1> show ip route ospf
! Legend omitted for brevity


      10.0.0.0/8 is variably subnetted, 6 subnets, 2 masks
O        10.1.33.0/24 [110/2] via 10.1.1.3, 00:15:32, GigabitEthernet0/0
O        10.1.44.0/24 [110/2] via 10.1.1.4, 00:15:42, GigabitEthernet0/0
```

```
! Now moving to Router R2


R2> show ip protocols
*** IP Routing is NSF aware ***
```

```
Routing Protocol is "ospf 2"
  Outgoing update filter list for all interfaces is not set
  Incoming update filter list for all interfaces is not set
  Router ID 2.2.2.2
  Number of areas in this router is 1. 1 normal 0 stub 0 nssa
  Maximum path: 4
  Routing for Networks:
    10.0.0.0 0.255.255.255 area 1
  Routing Information Sources:
    Gateway         Distance      Last Update
  Distance: (default is 110)

R2>
Nov 15 12:16:39.377: %OSPF-4-ERRRCV: Received invalid packet: mismatched area
ID, from backbone area must be virtual-link but not found from 10.1.1.1,
GigabitEthernet0/0
```

Interestingly, a closer look at R2's **show ip protocols** command output, particularly the highlighted portion, points out the configuration error. As usual, the section with the heading "Routing for Networks:" points to a shorthand version of the configuration. In this case, the highlighted phrase "10.0.0.0 0.255.255.255 area 1" is actually the exact syntax of the one **network** command on Router R2, minus the word *network*, or **network 10.0.0.0 0.255.255.255 area 1**. Because Figure 11-4 shows the design should put all interfaces in area 0, reconfiguring this command to instead be **network 10.0.0.0 0.255.255.255 area 0** would solve this particular problem.

The end of the example also shows an unsolicited log message generated by Router R2, notifying the console user that this router has received a Hello from a router in a different area.

As you check the interfaces, you could also check several other details. It makes sense to go ahead and check the interface IP addresses, masks, and interface status values by using the **show interfaces** and **show ip interface brief** commands. In particular, it is helpful to note which interfaces are up/up, because a router will send no packets (including routing protocol packets) out interfaces that are not in an up/up state. These interface verification checks are part of the IPv4 troubleshooting topics in both the ICND1 and ICND2 exam topics, and are discussed in Chapter 21, "Troubleshooting IPv4 Routing," so they are not repeated here.

11

Neighbor Relationships

This final major section of the chapter examines the large number of facts that each router must check with each potential neighbor before the two routers become neighbors.

At a very basic level, routing protocols can easily create neighbor relationships using a Hello protocol. First, the routing protocol must be enabled on an interface. In addition, the interface may not be configured as a passive interface, because that stops the routing protocol from sending the Hello messages.

Beyond this basic process, the routing protocols actually check several other parameters to find out whether the routers should become neighbors. Both OSPF and EIGRP use Hello messages, and these messages each list information used to perform some basic verification checks. For example, as just shown in earlier Example 11-5, an OSPF router should not become neighbors with another router in another area because all routers on a common subnet should be in the same OSPF area by design.

After an EIGRP or OSPF router hears a Hello from a new neighbor, the routing protocol examines the information in the Hello, and compares that information with the local router's own settings. If the settings match, great. If not, the routers do not become neighbors. Because there is no formal term for all these items that a routing protocol considers, this book just calls them *neighbor requirements*.

Table 11-2 lists the neighbor requirements for both EIGRP and OSPF. Following the table, the next few pages examine some of these settings for both EIGRP and OSPF, again using examples based on Figure 11-3.

> **NOTE** Even though it is important to study and remember the items in this table, when reading this chapter the first time, just keep reading. When later reviewing the chapter or part, make sure you remember the details in the table.

Key Topic

Table 11-2 Neighbor Requirements for EIGRP and OSPF

Requirement	EIGRP	OSPF
Interfaces must be in an up/up state.	Yes	Yes
Interfaces must be in the same subnet.	Yes	Yes
Access control lists (ACL) must not filter routing protocol messages.	Yes	Yes
Must pass routing protocol neighbor authentication (if configured).	Yes	Yes
Must use the same ASN/PID on the **router** configuration command.	Yes	No
Hello and hold/dead timers must match.	No	Yes
Router IDs (RID) must be unique.	No[1]	Yes
K-values must match.	Yes	N/A
Must be in the same area.	N/A	Yes

[1] Having duplicate EIGRP RIDs does not prevent routers from becoming neighbors, but it can cause problems when external EIGRP routes are added to the routing table.

Unlike most of the neighbor requirements listed in Table 11-2, the first three requirements have very little to do with the routing protocols themselves. The two routers must be able to send packets to each other over the physical network to which they are both connected.

To do that, the router interfaces must be up/up, and they must be in the same subnet. In addition, the routers must not be using an ACL that filters the routing protocol traffic.

For instance, OSPF sends many messages to the well-known multicast IP addresses 224.0.0.5 and 224.0.0.6, whereas EIGRP uses 224.0.0.10. An ACL command like **access-list 101 deny ip any host 224.0.0.10**, in an inbound ACL on a router interface, would filter incoming EIGRP packets. Or, an ACL command like **access-list 102 deny ospf any any** could filter all OSPF traffic. Even more difficult to notice is an ACL that has lots of **permit** commands that match different TCP and UDP port numbers, but does not match the routing protocol explicitly, so the routing protocol packets match the implicit deny any at the end of the ACL. So, take extra care to watch for ACLs, especially when it seems like all the routing protocol configuration looks good.

In practice, before examining the rest of the details of why two routers do not become neighbors, confirm that the two routers can ping each other on the local subnet. If the ping fails, investigate all the Layer 1, 2, and 3 issues that could prevent the ping from working (such as an interface not being up/up). The details of troubleshooting IPv4 routing (that is, packet forwarding) can be found in several places, including Chapter 21, "Troubleshooting IPv4 Routing." Additionally, the ICND1 Cert Guide includes other related details, including a chapter about IPv4 troubleshooting tools such as ping and traceroute; that ICND1 chapter is made available to you in this ICND2 book as a DVD Appendix J, "IPv4 Troubleshooting Tools."

Now, on to the specific discussions about EIGRP and OSPF. Because the details differ slightly between the two routing protocols, this section first examines EIGRP, followed by OSPF.

> **NOTE** This section assumes that the routing protocol has actually been enabled on each required interface, as covered earlier in this chapter in the "Interfaces Enabled with a Routing Protocol" section.

EIGRP Neighbor Verification Checks

Any two EIGRP routers that connect to the same data link, and whose interfaces have been enabled for EIGRP and are not passive, will at least consider becoming neighbors. To quickly and definitively know which potential neighbors have passed all the neighbor requirements for EIGRP, just look at the output of the **show ip eigrp neighbors** command. This command lists only neighbors that have passed all the neighbor verification checks.

Example 11-7 shows an example of the **show ip eigrp neighbors** command, with the four routers from Figure 11-3 again. In this case, all the routers have been configured correctly, so each has a neighbor relationship with the other three routers on the same LAN subnet.

Example 11-7 *R1* show ip eigrp neighbors *Command with All Problems Fixed*

```
R1# show ip eigrp neighbors
EIGRP-IPv4 Neighbors for AS(99)
H   Address                 Interface        Hold Uptime    SRTT   RTO  Q  Seq
                                             (sec)          (ms)        Cnt Num
1   10.1.1.3                Gi0/0              13 00:00:20    1    100  0  31
2   10.1.1.4                Gi0/0              13 00:00:43   80    480  0  10
0   10.1.1.2                Gi0/0              13 00:13:52    1    100  0  20
```

11

If the **show ip eigrp neighbors** command does not list one or more expected neighbors, the first problem isolation step should be to find out if the two routers can ping each other's IP addresses on the same subnet. If that works, start looking at the list of neighbor verification checks, as relisted for EIGRP here in Table 11-3. Table 11-3 summarizes the EIGRP neighbor requirements, while noting the best commands with which to determine which requirement is the root cause of the problem.

Key Topic

Table 11-3   EIGRP Neighbor Requirements and the Best **show/debug** Commands

Requirement	Best Commands to Isolate the Problem
Must be in the same subnet.	show interfaces, show ip interface
Must use the same ASN on the **router** configuration command.	show ip eigrp interfaces, show ip protocols
Must pass EIGRP neighbor authentication.	debug eigrp packets
K-values must match.	show ip protocols

Of the four rows of requirements listed in Table 11-3, the first two have already been discussed in this chapter, and do not need further discussion.

For EIGRP authentication (the third item in the table), EIGRP supports the capability for routers to trust routers as EIGRP neighbors only if the routers share the same security key (password); if that check fails, the neighbor relationship fails. By default, routers do not attempt EIGRP authentication, which allows the routers to form EIGRP neighbor relationships. If one router uses authentication, and the other does not, they will not become neighbors. If both use authentication, they must use the same authentication key to become neighbors.

The last item in the table, EIGRP K-values, refers to the EIGRP metric components and the metric calculation. These K-values are variables that basically enable or disable the use of the different components in the EIGRP composite metric. Cisco recommends leaving these values at their default settings, using only bandwidth and delay in the metric calculation. The K-value settings must match before two routers will become neighbors; you can check the K-values on both routers with the **show ip protocols** command.

EIGRP Neighbor Troubleshooting Example

Example 11-8 shows three problems that can cause EIGRP routers to fail to become neighbors. This example uses the usual design for this chapter, as repeated in Figure 11-5. The figure shows the same routers, and same interfaces, but with the following problems:

- R2 has been configured with IP address 10.1.2.2/24 in a different subnet than R1, R3, and R4.

- R3 has been configured to use ASN 199 with the **router eigrp 199** command instead of ASN 99, as used on the other three routers.

- R4 has been configured to use message digest 5 (MD5) authentication, whereas the other routers use no authentication.

R1 can actually detect two of the problems using local commands and messages, as shown in Example 11-8. R1 generates an unsolicited log message for the mismatched subnet problem, and a **debug** command on R1 can reveal the authentication failure. The example shows some running commentary inside the example.

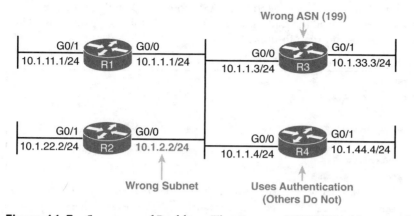

Figure 11-5 *Summary of Problems That Prevent EIGRP Neighbors on the Central LAN*

Example 11-8 *Common Problems Preventing the Formation of EIGRP Neighbors (R1)*

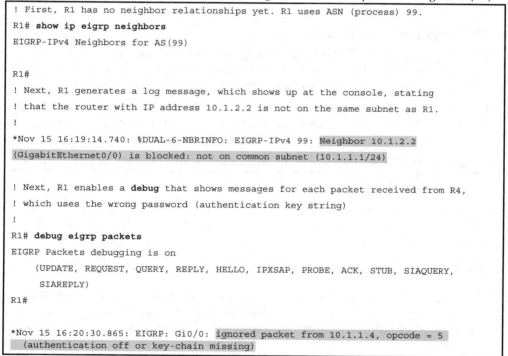

```
! First, R1 has no neighbor relationships yet. R1 uses ASN (process) 99.
R1# show ip eigrp neighbors
EIGRP-IPv4 Neighbors for AS(99)


R1#
! Next, R1 generates a log message, which shows up at the console, stating
! that the router with IP address 10.1.2.2 is not on the same subnet as R1.
!
*Nov 15 16:19:14.740: %DUAL-6-NBRINFO: EIGRP-IPv4 99: Neighbor 10.1.2.2
(GigabitEthernet0/0) is blocked: not on common subnet (10.1.1.1/24)


! Next, R1 enables a debug that shows messages for each packet received from R4,
! which uses the wrong password (authentication key string)
!
R1# debug eigrp packets
EIGRP Packets debugging is on
    (UPDATE, REQUEST, QUERY, REPLY, HELLO, IPXSAP, PROBE, ACK, STUB, SIAQUERY,
    SIAREPLY)
R1#

*Nov 15 16:20:30.865: EIGRP: Gi0/0: ignored packet from 10.1.1.4, opcode = 5
(authentication off or key-chain missing)
```

Example 11-8 shows some evidence of the mismatched subnet with R2, and the invalid authentication problem with R4. Note that the ICND2 200-105 and CCNA 200-125 exam topics specifically state that both OSPF and EIGRP authentication are excluded from the exam topics. However, even without knowing the details, it is easy to imagine that if one router's EIGRP process uses authentication with a defined password, and the other does not, that authentication will fail. The result? Neighbor relationships do not form.

Example 11-8 shows details about two of the problems, but not any details about the incorrect ASN configured on R3. Example 11-9 shows those details by listing excerpts from two

11

show commands on R3, both of which identify the ASN configured on that router. By using these same commands on all the routers, you could note that R1, R2, and R4 use ASN 99, whereas R3 uses 199, as shown in Example 11-9.

Example 11-9   *Displaying the Incorrect ASN (199) on R3*

```
R3# show ip protocols
Routing Protocol is "eigrp 199"
!
! The first line of output from show ip eigrp interfaces lists ASN 199
!
R3# show ip eigrp interfaces
EIGRP-IPv4 Interfaces for AS(199)
                        Xmit Queue   Mean   Pacing Time   Multicast    Pending
Interface      Peers    Un/Reliable  SRTT   Un/Reliable   Flow Timer   Routes
Gi0/0            0         0/0         0        0/1           0           0
Gi0/1            0         0/0         0        0/1           0           0
```

OSPF Neighbor Troubleshooting

Similar to EIGRP, a router's **show ip ospf neighbor** command lists all the neighboring routers that have met all the requirements to become an OSPF neighbor as listed in Table 11-2. So, the first step in troubleshooting OSPF neighbors is to look at the list of neighbors.

Example 11-10 lists the output of a **show ip ospf neighbor** command on Router R2, from Figure 11-4. All four routers sit on the same LAN subnet, in area 0, with correct configurations, so all four routers form a valid OSPF neighbor relationship.

Example 11-10   *Normal Working* **show ip ospf neighbors** *Command on Router R2*

```
R2# show ip ospf neighbor

Neighbor ID     Pri   State           Dead Time   Address     Interface
1.1.1.1           1   FULL/BDR        00:00:37    10.1.1.1    GigabitEthernet0/0
3.3.3.3           1   2WAY/DROTHER    00:00:37    10.1.1.3    GigabitEthernet0/0
4.4.4.4           1   FULL/DR         00:00:31    10.1.1.4    GigabitEthernet0/0
```

First, note that the neighbor IDs, listed in the first column, identify neighbors by their router ID (RID). For this example network, all four routers use an easily guessed RID. Further to the right, the Address column lists the interface IP address used by that neighbor on the common subnet.

A brief review of OSPF neighbor states (as explained in Chapter 7) can help you understand a few of the subtleties of the output in the example. A router's listed status for each of its OSPF neighbors—the neighbor's state—should settle into either a 2-way or full state under normal operation. For neighbors that do not need to directly exchange their databases, typically two non-designated router (DR) routers on a LAN, the routers should settle into a 2-way neighbor state. In most cases, two neighboring routers need to directly exchange their full link-state databases (LSDB) with each other. As soon as that process has been completed, the two routers settle into a full neighbor state.

In Example 11-10, Router R4 is the DR, and R1 is the backup DR (BDR), so R2 and R3 (as non-DRs) do not need to directly exchange routes. Therefore, R2's neighbor state for R3 (RID 3.3.3.3) in Example 11-10 is listed as 2-way.

> **NOTE** Notably, OSPF neighbors do not have to use the same process ID on the **router ospf** *process-id* command to become neighbors. In Example 11-10, all four routers use different PIDs.

If the **show ip ospf neighbor** command does not list one or more expected neighbors, you should confirm, even before moving on to look at OSPF neighbor requirements, that the two routers can ping each other on the local subnet. But if the two neighboring routers can ping each other, and the two routers still do not become OSPF neighbors, the next step is to examine each of the OSPF neighbor requirements. Table 11-4 summarizes the requirements, listing the most useful commands with which to find the answers.

Key Topic

Table 11-4   OSPF Neighbor Requirements and the Best **show/debug** Commands

Requirement	Best show Command	Best debug Command
Must be in the same subnet.	show interfaces	debug ip ospf hello
Hello and dead timers must match.	show ip ospf interface	debug ip ospf hello
Must be in the same area.	show ip ospf interface brief	debug ip ospf adj
RIDs must be unique.	show ip ospf	(N/A; log messages identify this problem)
Must pass any neighbor authentication.	show ip ospf interface	debug ip ospf adj

This topic looks at a couple of OSPF neighbor problems using the usual four-router network from Figure 11-4, with all interfaces in area 0. However, the following problems have been introduced into the design:

- R2 has been configured with both LAN interfaces in area 1, whereas the other three routers' G0/0 interfaces are assigned to area 0.
- R3 is using the same RID (1.1.1.1) as R1.
- R4 has been configured with a Hello/dead timer of 5/20 on its G0/0 interface, instead of the 10/40 used (by default) on R1, R2, and R3.

Figure 11-6 shows these same problems for reference.

11

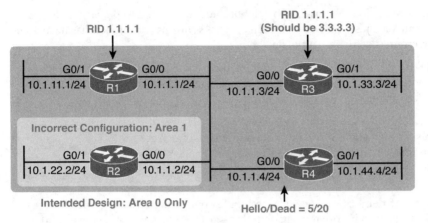

Figure 11-6   *Summary of Problems That Prevent OSPF Neighbors on the Central LAN*

Finding Area Mismatches

Earlier in this chapter, the "OSPF Interface Troubleshooting" section showed how to use the **show ip ospf interface** command to list the area numbers and find OSPF area mismatches. This next topic shows how to see that same issue using the **debug ip ospf adj** command, as shown in Example 11-11. This command lists messages related to OSPF neighbor adjacency events, and shows messages that identify the area mismatch (with R2).

Example 11-11   *Finding Mismatched Area Problem with R1 debug*

```
R1# debug ip ospf adj
OSPF adjacency events debugging is on
R1#
*Nov 15 13:42:02.288: OSPF-1 ADJ   Gi0/0: Rcv pkt from 10.1.1.2, area 0.0.0.0,
  mismatched area 0.0.0.1 in the header
R1#
R1# undebug all
All possible debugging has been turned off
```

As noted in Table 11-4, the **debug ip ospf adj** command helps troubleshoot mismatched OSPF area problems. The first part of the highlighted message in the example lists short-hand about a received packet ("Rcv pkt") from 10.1.1.2, which is R2's IP address. The rest of the message mentions R1's area (0.0.0.0), and the area claimed by the other router (0.0.0.1). (Note that the message lists the 32-bit area number as a dotted-decimal number.)

This particular example focuses on the symptom (that a neighbor relationship does not start), and the debug messages that identify the problem (mismatched areas). However, finding the configuration error may take some work, because the problem could be more complex than just having the wrong area number configured on a command.

One harder-to-notice configuration error happens when the configuration has multiple **network** commands, with different area numbers, that all happen to match one interface's IP address. IOS stores the OSPF **network** commands to the configuration in the same order they are configured (which is the same order listed in the output of **show running-config**). IOS processes the commands in sequence, so that the first **network** command that matches a particular interface is used to set the OSPF area number.

For instance, imagine a router with interface G0/1 configured with IP address 1.1.1.1. The OSPF configuration lists the following two **network** commands, in that order. Both would match the interface IP address of 1.1.1.1, so IOS uses the first command, which lists area 1. IOS would not use the second command, even though it uses a wildcard mask that is more specific.

- **network 1.0.0.0 0.255.255.255 area 1**

- **network 1.1.1.1 0.0.0.0 area 0**

Another tricky configuration error that can result in an area mismatch occurs when configuring both the **network** OSPF subcommand and the **ip ospf** interface subcommand on the same router. IOS supports using both on the same router at the same time. However, IOS does not prevent a case in which a **network** command attempts to enable OSPF in one area, and the **ip ospf** interface subcommand attempts to enable OSPF in a different area. When that happens, IOS uses the area number defined in the **ip ospf** interface subcommand.

For instance, with the two **network** commands just listed, if the **ip ospf 1 area 5** command was configured on that router's interface, that interface would be in area 5; IOS would prefer that setting over any OSPF **network** command.

> **NOTE** Using both **network** router subcommands and **ip ospf** interface subcommands allows an easier migration from the older to newer style OSPF configuration. However, most enterprises today would use either **network** commands or **ip ospf** commands in one router.

Finding Duplicate OSPF Router IDs

Next, Example 11-12 shows R1 and R3 both trying to use RID 1.1.1.1. Interestingly, both routers automatically generate a log message for the duplicate OSPF RID problem between R1 and R3; the end of Example 11-12 shows one such message. For the exams, just use the **show ip ospf** commands on both R3 and R1 to easily list the RID on each router, noting that they both use the same value.

Example 11-12 *Comparing OSPF Router IDs on R1 and R3*

```
! Next, on R3: R3 lists the RID of 1.1.1.1
!
R3# show ip ospf
Routing Process "ospf 3" with ID 1.1.1.1
 Start time: 00:00:37.136, Time elapsed: 02:20:37.200
! lines omitted for brevity
```

```
! Back to R1: R1 also uses RID 1.1.1.1

R1# show ip ospf
Routing Process "ospf 1" with ID 1.1.1.1
 Start time: 00:01:51.864, Time elapsed: 12:13:50.904
 Supports only single TOS(TOS0) routes
 Supports opaque LSA
```

11

```
Supports Link-local Signaling (LLS)
Supports area transit capability
Supports NSSA (compatible with RFC 3101)
Event-log enabled, Maximum number of events: 1000, Mode: cyclic
Router is not originating router-LSAs with maximum metric
Initial SPF schedule delay 5000 msecs
Minimum hold time between two consecutive SPFs 10000 msecs
Maximum wait time between two consecutive SPFs 10000 msecs
Incremental-SPF disabled
Minimum LSA interval 5 secs
Minimum LSA arrival 1000 msecs
LSA group pacing timer 240 secs
Interface flood pacing timer 33 msecs
Retransmission pacing timer 66 msecs
Number of external LSA 0. Checksum Sum 0x000000
Number of opaque AS LSA 0. Checksum Sum 0x000000
Number of DCbitless external and opaque AS LSA 0
Number of DoNotAge external and opaque AS LSA 0
Number of areas in this router is 1. 1 normal 0 stub 0 nssa
Number of areas transit capable is 0
External flood list length 0
IETF NSF helper support enabled
Cisco NSF helper support enabled
Reference bandwidth unit is 100 mbps
    Area BACKBONE(0) (Inactive)
        Number of interfaces in this area is 3
        Area has no authentication
        SPF algorithm last executed 00:52:42.956 ago
        SPF algorithm executed 9 times
        Area ranges are
        Number of LSA 1. Checksum Sum 0x00C728
        Number of opaque link LSA 0. Checksum Sum 0x000000
        Number of DCbitless LSA 0
        Number of indication LSA 0
        Number of DoNotAge LSA 0
        Flood list length 0

*May 29 00:01:25.679: %OSPF-4-DUP_RTRID_NBR: OSPF detected duplicate router-id
1.1.1.1 from 10.1.1.3 on interface GigabitEthernet0/0
```

First, focus on the problem: the duplicate RIDs. The first line of the **show ip ospf** command on the two routers quickly shows the duplicate use of 1.1.1.1. To solve the problem, assuming R1 should use 1.1.1.1 and R3 should use another RID (maybe 3.3.3.3), change the RID on R3, and restart the OSPF process. To do so, use the **router-id 3.3.3.3** OSPF subcommand and use the EXEC mode command **clear ip ospf process**.

Also, take a moment to read over the log message generated on each router when a duplicate RID exists.

Finally, note that the **show ip ospf** commands in Example 11-12 also show a common false positive for a root cause of OSPF neighbor problems. OSPF PIDs—the number of the **router ospf** command—do not have to match. Note that in Example 11-12 that same first line of output shows that R3 uses the **router ospf 3** command, per the phrase "Process ospf 3," whereas R1 uses the **router ospf 1** command, as noted with the phrase "Process ospf 1." These mismatched numbers are not a problem.

Finding OSPF Hello and Dead Timer Mismatches

Finally, consider the problem created on R4, with the configuration of a different Hello timer and dead timer as compared with the default settings on R1, R2, and R3. Whereas EIGRP allows neighbors to use a different Hello timer, OSPF does not, so this mismatch prevents R4 from becoming neighbors with any of the other three OSPF routers.

Example 11-13 shows the easiest way to find the mismatch, using the **show ip ospf interface** command on both R1 and R4. This command lists the Hello and dead timers for each interface, as highlighted in the example. Note that R1 uses 10 and 40 (Hello and dead), whereas R4 uses 5 and 20.

Example 11-13 *Finding Mismatched Hello/Dead Timers*

```
R1# show ip ospf interface G0/0
GigabitEthernet0/0 is up, line protocol is up
  Internet Address 10.1.1.1/24, Area 0, Attached via Network Statement
  Process ID 1, Router ID 1.1.1.1, Network Type BROADCAST, Cost: 1
  Topology-MTID    Cost    Disabled    Shutdown       Topology Name
       0            1         no          no            Base
  Transmit Delay is 1 sec, State DR, Priority 1
  Designated Router (ID) 1.1.1.1, Interface address 10.1.1.1
  No backup designated router on this network
  Timer intervals configured, Hello 10, Dead 40, Wait 40, Retransmit 5
! lines omitted for brevity
```

```
! Moving on to R4 next
!
R4# show ip ospf interface Gi0/0
GigabitEthernet0/0 is up, line protocol is up
  Internet Address 10.1.1.4/24, Area 0, Attached via Network Statement
  Process ID 4, Router ID 10.1.44.4, Network Type BROADCAST, Cost: 1
  Topology-MTID    Cost    Disabled    Shutdown       Topology Name
       0            1         no          no            Base
  Transmit Delay is 1 sec, State DR, Priority 1
  Designated Router (ID) 10.1.44.4, Interface address 10.1.1.4
  No backup designated router on this network
  Timer intervals configured, Hello 5, Dead 20, Wait 20, Retransmit 5
! lines omitted for brevity
```

11

The **debug ip ospf hello** command can also uncover this problem because it lists a message for each Hello that reveals the Hello/dead timer mismatch, as shown in Example 11-14.

Example 11-14 *Finding Mismatched Hello/Dead Timers with* **debug**

```
R1# debug ip ospf hello
OSPF hello events debugging is on
R1#
*Nov 15 14:05:10.616: OSPF-1 HELLO Gi0/0: Rcv hello from 10.1.44.4 area 0 10.1.1.4
*Nov 15 14:05:10.616: OSPF-1 HELLO Gi0/0: Mismatched hello parameters from 10.1.1.4
*Nov 15 14:05:10.616: OSPF-1 HELLO Gi0/0: Dead R 20 C 40, Hello R 5 C 10 Mask R
  255.255.255.0 C 255.255.255.0
```

Although debug messages can be a little difficult to understand, a few comments make the meaning of these messages much clearer. The highlighted message uses a *C* to mean "configured value"—in other words, the value on the local router, or R1 in this case. The *R* in the message means "received value," or the value listed in the received Hello. In this case

- "Dead R 20 C 40" means that R1 received a Hello with a dead timer set to 20, while R1's configured value is set to 40.

- "Hello R 5 C 10" means that R1 received a Hello with the Hello timer set to 5, while R1's configured value is set to 10.

Note that any IP subnet mismatch problems could also be found with this same debug, based on the received and configured subnet masks.

Other OSPF Issues

This last short discussion in this chapter looks at these two additional topics: shutting down the routing protocol process and the interface maximum transmission unit (MTU) size.

Shutting Down the OSPF Process

Cisco uses the IOS **shutdown** command in several contexts. You can use the **shutdown** command in interface configuration mode to disable the interface so that it no longer sends and receives packets. Cisco IOS switches allow the **shutdown** command in VLAN configuration mode, causing the switch to stop forwarding frames in that VLAN. In both cases, the **shutdown** command does not remove any configuration; it simply causes IOS to stop a particular function. Then, the **no shutdown** command in the same command mode re-enables that function.

IOS allows both the OSPFv2 and EIGRP routing protocol processes to be disabled and enabled with the **shutdown** and **no shutdown** commands, respectively, in routing protocol configuration mode. When a routing protocol process is shut down, IOS

- Brings down any existing neighbor relationships
- Does not form new neighbor relationships
- Quits sending Hello messages
- Does not remove routing protocol configuration

Basically, shutting down the routing protocol process gives the network engineer a way to stop using the routing protocol on that router, without having to remove all the configuration.

From a troubleshooting perspective, on the exam, what would you expect to see if a small design was configured perfectly, except that one router's OSPF process was shut down? First, the router with the shutdown routing protocol process would not have any OSPF neighbors, and other routers would not list that router as a neighbor. But because the OSPF **shutdown** subcommand does not remove any configuration, the **show ip ospf interfaces** command still shows evidence that OSPF is configured on the interfaces.

Example 11-15 shows an example on Router R5, as shown in Figure 11-7. R5 is a different router than the one used in earlier examples, but it begins the example with two OSPF neighbors, R2 and R3, with router IDs 2.2.2.2 and 3.3.3.3. The example shows the OSPF process being shut down, the neighbors failing, and those two key OSPF **show** commands: **show ip ospf neighbor** and **show ip ospf interface brief**.

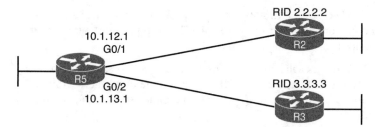

Figure 11-7   *Example Network to Demonstrate OSPF Process Shutdown*

Example 11-15   *Shutting Down an OSPF Process, and the Resulting Neighbor States*

```
R5# show ip ospf neighbor

Neighbor ID     Pri   State       Dead Time   Address       Interface
2.2.2.2          1    FULL/DR     00:00:35    10.1.12.2     GigabitEthernet0/1
3.3.3.3          1    FULL/DR     00:00:33    10.1.13.3     GigabitEthernet0/2
R5# configure terminal
Enter configuration commands, one per line.  End with CNTL/Z.
R5(config)# router ospf 1
R5(config-router)# shutdown
R5(config-router)# ^Z
R5#
*Mar 23 12:43:30.634: %OSPF-5-ADJCHG: Process 1, Nbr 2.2.2.2 on GigabitEthernet0/1
   from FULL to DOWN, Neighbor Down: Interface down or detached
*Mar 23 12:43:30.635: %OSPF-5-ADJCHG: Process 1, Nbr 3.3.3.3 on GigabitEthernet0/2
   from FULL to DOWN, Neighbor Down: Interface down or detached
R5#
R5# show ip ospf neighbor
R5#
R5# show ip ospf interface brief
Interface    PID   Area          IP Address/Mask      Cost   State  Nbrs F/C
Gi0/1         1     0            10.1.12.1/24          1      DOWN   0/0
Gi0/2         1     0            10.1.13.1/24          1      DOWN   0/0
```

11

The two **show** commands point out a couple of particularly important facts. First, before the **shutdown**, the **show ip ospf neighbor** command lists two neighbors. After the **shutdown**, the same command lists no neighbors at all. Second, the **show ip ospf interface brief** command does list the interfaces on which OSPF is enabled, on the local router's own IP addresses. However, it lists a state of DOWN, which is a reference to the neighbor's state.

Mismatched MTU Settings

The MTU size defines a per-interface setting used by the router for its Layer 3 forwarding logic, defining the largest network layer packet that the router will forward out each interface. For instance, the IPv4 MTU size of an interface defines the maximum size IPv4 packet that the router can forward out an interface.

Routers often use a default MTU size of 1500 bytes, with the ability to set the value as well. The **ip mtu** *size* interface subcommand defines the IPv4 MTU setting, and the **ipv6 mtu** *size* command sets the equivalent for IPv6 packets.

In an odd twist, two OSPFv2 routers can actually become OSPF neighbors, and reach 2-way state, even if they happen to use different IPv4 MTU settings on their interfaces. However, they fail to exchange their LSDBs. Eventually, after trying and failing to exchange their LSDBs, the neighbor relationship also fails.

The concepts behind what happens with an MTU mismatch work the same with both OSPFv2 and OSPFv3. In Chapter 23, "Implementing OSPF for IPv6," the "The Issue of IPv6 MTU" section shows an example of this particular problem with OSPFv3. Read that section for a little more detail about this issue.

Chapter Review

One key to doing well on the exams is to perform repetitive spaced review sessions. Review this chapter's material using either the tools in the book, DVD, or interactive tools for the same material found on the book's companion website. Refer to the "Your Study Plan" element for more details. Table 11-5 outlines the key review elements and where you can find them. To better track your study progress, record when you completed these activities in the second column.

Table 11-5   Chapter Review Tracking

Review Element	Review Date(s)	Resource Used:
Review key topics		Book, DVD/website
Review memory tables		DVD/website
Review command reference tables		Book

Review All the Key Topics

Table 11-6 Key Topics for Chapter 11

Key Topic Element	Description	Page Number
List	Two things that happen when EIGRP or OSPF is enabled on a router's interface	274
Table 11-1	Three commands that enable you to determine on which interfaces EIGRP or OSPF has been enabled	275
Table 11-2	Neighbor requirements for both EIGRP and OSPF	284
Table 11-3	EIGRP neighbor requirements and useful commands to isolate that requirement as the root cause of a neighbor problem	286
Table 11-4	The same information as Table 11-3, but for OSPF	289

Command References

Tables 11-7, 11-8, and 11-9 list configuration, verification, and debug commands used in this chapter. As an easy review exercise, cover the left column in a table, read the right column, and try to recall the command without looking. Then repeat the exercise, covering the right column, and try to recall what the command does.

Table 11-7 Chapter 11 Configuration Command Reference

Command	Description
ip hello-interval eigrp *as-number timer-value*	Interface subcommand that sets the EIGRP Hello interval for that EIGRP process
ip hold-time eigrp *as-number seconds*	Interface subcommand that sets the EIGRP hold time for the interface
ip ospf hello-interval *seconds*	Interface subcommand that sets the interval for periodic Hellos
ip ospf dead-interval *number*	Interface subcommand that sets the OSPF dead timer
passive-interface *type number*	Router subcommand, for both OSPF and EIGRP that tells the routing protocol to stop sending Hellos and stop trying to discover neighbors on that interface

Table 11-8 Chapter 11 **show** Command Reference

Command	Description
show ip protocols	Shows routing protocol parameters and current timer values, including an effective copy of the routing protocols' **network** commands and a list of passive interfaces
show ip eigrp interfaces	Lists the interfaces on which EIGRP has been enabled for each EIGRP process, except passive interfaces
show ip route eigrp	Lists only EIGRP-learned routes from the routing table
show ip eigrp neighbors	Lists EIGRP neighbors and status

11

Command	Description
show ip ospf interface brief	Lists the interfaces on which the OSPF protocol is enabled (based on the **network** commands), including passive interfaces
show ip ospf interface [*type number*]	Lists detailed OSPF settings for all interfaces, or the listed interface, including Hello and dead timers and OSPF area
show ip route ospf	Lists routes in the routing table learned by OSPF
show ip ospf neighbor	Lists neighbors and current status with neighbors, per interface
show ip ospf	Lists a group of messages about the OSPF process itself, listing the OSPF Router ID in the first line
show interfaces	Lists a long set of messages, per interface, that lists configuration, state, and counter information
show interfaces description	Lists one line of output per interface with brief status information

Table 11-9   Chapter 11 **debug** Command Reference

Command	Description
debug eigrp packets	Lists log messages for EIGRP packets that flow in and out of the router
debug ip ospf adj	Issues log messages for adjacency events, meaning events related to routers becoming neighbors
debug ip ospf events	Issues log messages for each action taken by OSPF, including the receipt of messages
debug ip ospf packet	Issues log messages describing the contents of all OSPF packets
debug ip ospf hello	Issues log messages describing Hellos and Hello failures
undebug all	EXEC command used to disable all current debugs

CHAPTER 12

Implementing External BGP

This chapter covers the following exam topics:

3.0 WAN Technologies

3.4 Describe WAN topology options

   3.4.d Single vs dual-homed

3.6 Configure and verify single-homed branch connectivity using eBGP IPv4 (limited to peering and route advertisement using Network command only)

For the first time in the long history of the Cisco CCNA Routing & Switching certification, Cisco has added Border Gateway Protocol (BGP) to the mix for this latest ICND2 and CCNA R&S exam. In the past, BGP might get a mention as the one current routing protocol used to exchange routes between companies (called autonomous systems for the purposes of BGP). Now for the first time in the history of the Cisco CCNA R&S the exam topics include BGP configuration and verification topics.

However, the lone BGP exam topic encompasses only one small slice of BGP, which limits the BGP discussion to this single chapter. BGP is a long-lived and flexible protocol, one that has many core features, with many features added to it over the years. This chapter introduces the small part that Cisco has chosen to inject into CCNA: the use of BGP for IPv4, between an enterprise and an ISP, with just a single Internet link.

"Do I Know This Already?" Quiz

Take the quiz (either here, or use the PCPT software) if you want to use the score to help you decide how much time to spend on this chapter. The answers are at the bottom of the page following the quiz, and the explanations are in DVD Appendix C and in the PCPT software.

Table 12-1 "Do I Know This Already?" Foundation Topics Section-to-Question Mapping

Foundation Topics Section	Questions
BGP Concepts	1–3
eBGP Configuration and Verification	4–6

1. Which of the following Internet edge designs include connections to two ISPs? (Choose two answers.)

   a. Single homed

   b. Single multihomed

   c. Dual homed

   d. Dual multihomed

2. Which of the following features is true of eBGP but not iBGP?

   a. Connects routers in the same ASN

   b. Uses TCP

   c. Exchanges routes between an ISP and an enterprise

   d. None of the other answers is correct

3. Consider the routes advertised over a typical single-homed Internet edge connection that uses eBGP. Which of the following answers describe a route typically advertised by eBGP in this case? (Choose two answers.)

   a. A default route advertised by the enterprise to the ISP

   b. A route for the enterprise's public IPv4 address block to the ISP

   c. A route for the enterprise's private IPv4 address block to the ISP

   d. A default route advertised by the ISP to the enterprise

4. Routers R1 and R2, in two different ASNs, connect directly to each other over a WAN link, with the two routers in the same subnet. If using the IP addresses on that common link to define the eBGP neighbors, how many different BGP **neighbor** commands would be required on Router R1 to make the eBGP peer work to Router R2?

   a. 1

   b. 2

   c. 3

   d. 4

5. An enterprise router (R1) has a working eBGP peer relationship with ISP router R2. Both routers use the default setting of **no auto-summary**. Examine the following output from R1. Based on that output, which of the following answers, when added to R1's BGP configuration, causes R1 to advertise a BGP route to Router R2?

```
R1# show ip route 200.1.1.0 255.255.255.0 longer-prefixes
      200.1.1.0/24 is variably subnetted, 3 subnets, 3 masks
C        200.1.1.0/27 is directly connected, Loopback1
L        200.1.1.1/32 is directly connected, Loopback1
O        200.1.1.32/28 [110/2] via 10.1.1.1, 03:11:00, GigabitEthernet0/2
```

   a. network 200.1.1.0 mask 255.255.255.0

   b. network 200.1.1.0

   c. network 200.1.1.0 mask 255.255.255.240

   d. None of the other answers causes R1 to advertise a route to R2.

6. Examine the output. Which of the following statements are true based on the output of this **show** command from Router R1? (Choose two answers.)

```
R1# show ip bgp summary
BGP router identifier 2.2.2.2, local AS number 101
BGP table version is 1, main routing table version 1

Neighbor        V    AS MsgRcvd MsgSent    TblVer  InQ OutQ Up/Down  State/PfxRcd
1.1.1.1         4   201       2       2         1    0    0 00:00:37            1
```

a. Neighbor 1.1.1.1 is an eBGP peer.

b. The TCP connection needed by BGP is not working at this point.

c. R1 has sent one prefix to neighbor 1.1.1.1.

d. R1 has a **neighbor 1.1.1.1 remote-as 201** command configured.

Foundation Topics

BGP Concepts

You have already learned a lot about what interior gateway protocols (IGP) such as Open Shortest Path First (OSPF) and Enhanced Interior Gateway Routing Protocol (EIGRP) do, and how they do it. To begin exploring BGP—the only option for an exterior gateway protocol (EGP) in use today—this section begins by making some basic comparisons between IGPs and EGPs.

So, ignoring the details of how the individual protocols work, instead focusing on what they do, what do IGPs like RIPv2, OSPF, and EIGRP accomplish? This list summarizes the main points:

Learn routes: Learn about subnets/masks, and calculate the local router's route for that subnet, with outgoing interface and next-hop router

Choose the best route: If one routing protocol learns of multiple routes existing for a single subnet, pick the best route, using some kind of metric

Converge: When network changes happen, *converge*—either remove routes, add new ones, or replace a failed route with a working route

RIPv2, OSPF, and EIGRP differ mostly in the mechanics of how they go about achieving the goals in this list. That is, each IGP needs to learn about new subnets and use metrics to choose the best route among competing routes for each subnet, and to converge as quickly as possible.

BGP has these same design goals, but with a much different emphasis compared to IGPs. First and foremost, BGP focuses on the first item in the list, called *reachability* in BGP terms. What prefixes (address blocks) are reachable? BGP, intended for use throughout the global Internet, must scale. And the first job—the most important job—is to make sure all routers learn about all public IP address prefixes reachable in the Internet.

Just to give you a sense of the scale of the IP routing tables used in the Internet core routers, check out the website http://bgp.potaroo.net, a site by Geoff Huston, who has been publishing statistics about the Internet for several decades. A check of this website while writing this chapter showed that the size of the BGP table in the Internet—which indicates the number of IPv4 routes expected to be in those routers—is at just over 600,000 entries. BGP has a big job to do.

Advertising Routes with BGP

BGP exchanges routing information by using the same general process used by IGPs, but with some differences of course. To begin the BGP process, one router must have knowledge of some IPv4 prefix. It then uses a BGP protocol message (a BGP *update* message) to exchange the routing information with another router, as shown in Figure 12-1. With BGP, the other router is called a *BGP neighbor* or *BGP peer*.

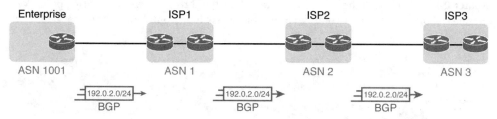

Figure 12-1   *Using BGP Between Autonomous Systems*

One big difference with BGP compared to IGPs is that BGP advertises the routes to other routers in other companies, shown in the figure as other ISPs. IGPs, by definition, advertise routes to other routers inside the same company.

> **NOTE**   While IGPs advertise blocks of addresses that we generally refer to as *subnets*, with BGP, we refer to the blocks of addresses as either *prefixes*, *address blocks*, or even the formal BGP name, *Network Layer Reachability Information* (NLRI). The reason for not using the word *subnet* is that, in practice, BGP seldom advertises address blocks as small as an individual subnet.

BGP differs from IGPs in its purpose, including the fact that, for an enterprise, BGP can be used to advertise the enterprise's public IPv4 prefix to its local ISP. In Figure 12-1, the enterprise sits on the far left, with a BGP peering relationship to the enterprise's ISP (ISP1 in this case). The enterprise then advertises its public prefix, Class C network 192.0.2.0/24, into ISP1. To create the global Internet, ISPs connect to each other, so ISP1 then advertises this prefix (192.0.2.0/24) to the other ISPs as shown, so that all parts of the Internet know how to forward packets to addresses in 192.0.2.0/24.

Answers to the "Do I Know This Already?" quiz:

1 B, D **2** C **3** B, D **4** A **5** D **6** A, D

The term *autonomous system number* (ASN) plays a key role in BGP, even more so than it does within EIGRP. With BGP, as with EIGRP, the term *autonomous system* (AS) refers to a network that operates separately from other networks (that is, autonomously). BGP uses the ASN—the number that identifies each AS—for many BGP features, including a part of the best path selection process (to choose the best BGP route). The ASN is also used as part of a routing loop prevention mechanism.

Internal and External BGP

The one BGP exam topic uses the acronym eBGP, rather than simply BGP. eBGP refers to *External BGP*, used in contrast to *Internal BGP* (iBGP). To see what those terms mean, you need to think in a little more detail about what happens with BGP update messages.

When an enterprise connects to an ISP, the physical connection is chosen to be as short as is reasonably possible, on purpose. For instance, in Figure 12-2, enterprise Router R1 and ISP1 Router ISP1-1 may sit in the same city; in fact, ISPs build their networks to place points of presence (PoP) near their customers, so that the WAN link from the customer to the ISP is short.

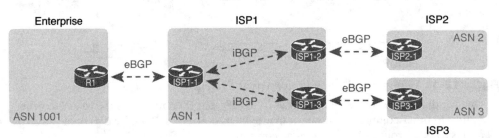

Figure 12-2 *eBGP Versus iBGP*

To create the global Internet, ISPs connect to each other. Some ISPs may be regional, or cover one country. Some cover major geographies of the world (for example, Europe), or a few may cover most of the globe. However, ISP1's sites may span the entire country, continent, or globe. ISP2 and ISP3 have different locations, in different geographies as well. To physically create the Internet, by connecting all ISPs to other ISPs in some way, the ISPs connect their routers someplace in the world. In fact, ISPs often co-locate routers in the same room, called an Internet exchange, for high-speed connections between ISPs.

Now think about BGP as used to exchange routes across enterprises, to their ISPs, and between all the ISPs, with the ISPs spread across major geographical regions. For BGP to work for the global Internet, BGP must first exchange prefix information between ASNs (External BGP). However, to then be able to advertise prefixes out other links in other parts of an ISP's network, the ISP must advertise those prefixes to other routers inside the same ASN (Internal BGP), as shown in the center of Figure 12-2.

Basically, eBGP refers to BGP's use in advertising routes between two different ASNs. iBGP refers to using BGP to advertise routes to other routers inside the same ASN. BGP uses slightly different rules and details of what it advertises and how it works based on whether a neighbor is an eBGP or iBGP peer. This chapter deals with eBGP only.

Choosing the Best Routes with BGP

The beginning of this chapter stated that all routing protocols learn prefixes, choose the best route if multiple routes exist, and converge when the network changes. BGP focuses on that first action—advertising reachability for a prefix. Additionally, like the IGPs, BGP has a concept like a metric, so that BGP can choose the best route among competing routes. However, BGP uses a much different approach to defining a metric and a different approach to the logic BGP uses to determine the best route.

First, BGP does not use a single idea of a metric. Instead, it uses *path attributes*. BGP advertises each prefix along with a list of different path attributes. The path attributes are different facts about the route (path) to reach that subnet. By using multiple concepts (multiple path attributes), BGP allows for a much wider variety of decisions about which route is best.

BGP then uses a process called the *best path selection* process to choose the best route between two competing routes. When receiving a BGP update that lists a prefix that already exists, the router has a simple choice to make: Is the old route better, or is this new one better? The best path selection process works through a series of comparisons (about ten) until a comparison shows one of the routes as being better. Understanding the process requires a detailed understanding of the path attributes by the network engineer (and is beyond the scope of this chapter). However, BGP on the routers requires very little work to make the comparisons, much less than, say, OSPF's SPF process, so the BGP best path selection process scales well.

While that general description of best path selection is accurate, a single example can help. BGP uses the AS_Path path attribute (PA) in one step of the best path selection process. AS_Path is a path attribute sent with routes in BGP, and this attribute lists the ASNs in the route. The best path selection process considers a shorter AS_Path as better; you can think of it a little like a hop count, but the hops are entire ASNs rather than single routers.

Figure 12-3 shows an example with two competing routes to reach prefix 192.0.2.0/24, one with a shorter AS_Path length. The enterprise advertises its public prefix 192.0.2.0/24 to ISP1, which then advertises it to other ISPs. ISP3 eventually learns two possible routes to that prefix, one that lists an AS_Path with three ASNs, and the shorter one with two ASNs (the best path, as noted with the >).

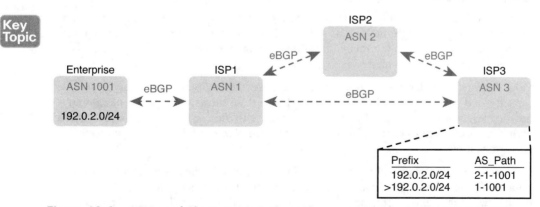

Figure 12-3 *ASNs and Shortest AS_Path as Chosen at ISP3 for Prefix 192.0.2.0/24*

If you continue down the routing and switching track in your Cisco studies, you will learn more and more about BGP and the best path algorithm. Both CCNP ROUTE and CCIE R&S include many details of BGP.

eBGP and the Internet Edge

The term *Internet edge* refers to the connection between an ISP customer and an ISP. The one BGP exam topic focuses the BGP discussion on the Internet edge, specifically the eBGP peering between an enterprise and an ISP, and what BGP can usefully do at the edge.

Internet Edge Designs and Terminology

The term *single homed* (used in the one BGP exam topic) refers to a particular Internet edge design with a single link to one ISP, as shown in Figure 12-4. A single-homed design has a single link between the enterprise and an ISP. You would typically find a single-homed Internet edge design used when connecting an enterprise branch office to the Internet, or for a simple connection from a core site at the enterprise.

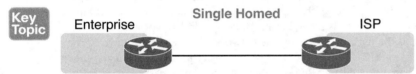

Figure 12-4 *Single-Homed Design: Single Link, One Home (ISP)*

A single-homed design allows any kind of WAN link. That is, it could be DSL, cable, fiber Ethernet, or even a wireless LTE connection. The more important points are that the enterprise site connects to a single ISP, and that only one link exists to that ISP. Figure 12-5 expands upon those concepts.

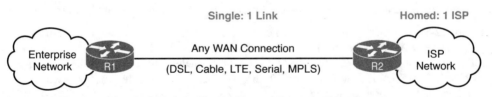

Figure 12-5 *Any Physical Link in Single-Homed Internet Edge*

A single-homed connection has some pros and cons. With only a single link, if the link fails, the ability to reach the Internet fails as well. A failure on either of the routers on the ends of the links also causes the Internet connection to fail. Of course, a single Internet connection, versus multiple, saves money.

Other Internet edge designs do exist, of course, mostly adding redundancy, increasing capacity, and raising the cost and complexity. Figure 12-6 shows three similar designs, in growing levels of complexity. Note that the designs with *dual* in the name refer to designs with two (or more) links to the same router, while *multihomed* refers to having connections to multiple ISPs.

You need basic BGP skills only to understand what happens in single-homed and dual-homed designs—in fact, this chapter focuses mostly on the needs of the single-homed designs, with some extra information useful to dual-homed designs. The added redundancy of the different multihomed designs requires a much deeper understanding of BGP concepts, path attributes, best path selection, and configuration.

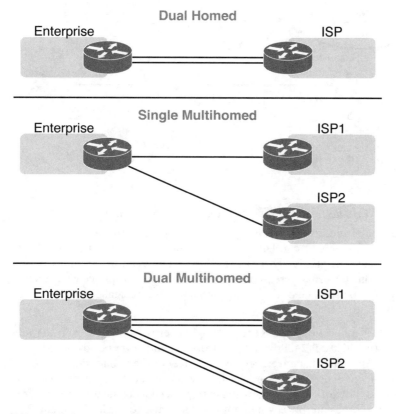

Figure 12-6 *Different Internet Edge Designs*

NOTE The one CCNA R&S exam topic limits BGP specifically to eBGP and to single-homed designs. Frankly, the enterprises that use a single-homed Internet connection often do not even bother to use eBGP, often using static routing instead. However, BGP has many rules and configuration options. Cisco's limits on the BGP exam topic gives CCNA candidates a chance to begin learning a little about BGP, but in a limited way that avoids most of BGP's complexity.

Advertising the Enterprise Public Prefix into the Internet

Next, consider what routes should be advertised between two eBGP peers at the Internet edge. Begin with routes advertised by the enterprise to the ISP, as with a typical enterprise site on the left side of Figure 12-7. In that particular design, the enterprise uses

Private 10.0.0.0/8: Like many companies, this enterprise uses private IP network 10.0.0.0 for most hosts in the enterprise.

Public 192.0.2.0/24: The public IPv4 network assigned to the company. As shown, it has been subnetted, one subnet for use with NAT, the other used for a DMZ with public-facing web servers.

12

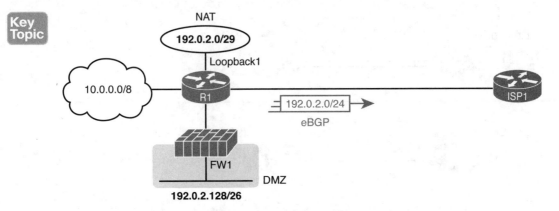

Figure 12-7   *Public and Private IPv4 Address Prefixes Advertised to an ISP*

Working through the public addressing in a little more detail, the enterprise uses public IP network 192.0.2.0/24. It uses a NAT configuration on the router, with subnet 192.0.2.0/29 configured on a loopback interface, ready for use by NAT. The design also includes a security demilitarized zone (DMZ), where public-facing servers, such as public web servers, can reside. These hosts also use some of the enterprise's public address range, from subnet 192.0.2.128/26 in this case.

Note that over the eBGP connection from R1 to ISP1, R1 advertises only one route: a route for public address prefix 192.0.2.0/24. Private IP networks should never be advertised into the Internet; the ISP would filter that advertisement anyway. For the public address range, the ISP wants to receive one route for each public address block, rather than hearing about each subnet, because the ISP does not care how the enterprise subnets the network. Figure 12-7 shows the one prefix the enterprise would normally advertise to the ISP in an eBGP update.

Why advertise the enterprise's public prefix to the ISP at all? So that the ISP can then advertise the prefix to other ISPs, and eventually all ISPs have a route to deliver packets to the enterprise's public IP address. Figure 12-8 shows the idea. At Step 1, R1, in the enterprise, uses eBGP to advertise its public IPv4 prefix to ISP1. At Step 2, ISP1 advertises that same prefix to two different ISPs.

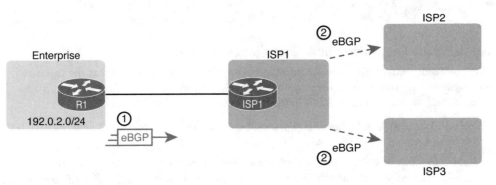

Figure 12-8   *Enterprise Advertises the Public Prefix; ISP Propagates*

Learning Default Routes from the ISP

Now turn the logic around, and think about what the ISP can and should advertise with eBGP to the enterprise. The Internet core routers have almost 600,000 IPv4 routes. An enterprise router at the Internet edge could learn all those routes from the ISP, and put those in its IPv4 routing table. Then, through a process called *redistribution*, that router could take all those BGP-learned routes and advertise them into the rest of the enterprise routers using the IGP.

However, what would all those new IP routes list as their next-hop addresses? All those new routes would send packets toward R1, and R1 would send them toward ISP1. Typically, the routers normally used by enterprises would not be designed to perform well with hundreds of thousands of routes in their routing tables.

Using a default route makes much more sense for a single-homed Internet edge design as compared with learning all those extra IP routes. The enterprise router that connects to the ISP needs one default route, so that for any unknown destinations, the packets are sent to the ISP. The idea is exactly what is discussed in regard to how OSPF advertises default routes back in Chapter 8.

When using a default routing strategy at the Internet edge, you can statically configure the default route, or learn it with eBGP. The OSPF chapter showed the static default route configuration, so of course, this chapter shows the effects of using eBGP.

Figure 12-9 shows the basic concept. At Step 1, the ISP advertises a default route with eBGP. At Step 2, router R1 takes the steps necessary with its IGP so that the IGP then reacts to the eBGP-learned default route, advertising a default route into the enterprise with the IGP.

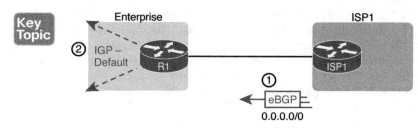
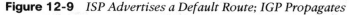

Figure 12-9 *ISP Advertises a Default Route; IGP Propagates*

That concludes the overview of BGP and eBGP in preparation for the configuration and verification topics. The rest of the chapter focuses on the eBGP peering between the enterprise and the ISP, particularly on the enterprise side of the configuration. That includes the details of configuring the peering relationship with the ISP router, advertising the public prefix (with the **network** BGP subcommand), and verifying the eBGP advertised and received routes.

eBGP Configuration and Verification

IGP configuration focuses on enabling the routing protocol on interfaces. The configuration may use the **network** router subcommand, which the router then compares to interface IPv4 addresses. Alternately, the IGP configuration may use an interface subcommand like

ip ospf *process-id* **area** *number*, which enables the IGP directly on the interface. Once enabled on an interface, the IGP

- Dynamically discovers neighbors that share the same data link off that interface
- Advertises known routes to those dynamically discovered neighbors
- Advertises about the subnet connected to the interface

BGP configuration, in contrast, does none of the actions in the preceding list. (BGP does use a **network** command, but for a different purpose.) BGP does form neighbor relationships, but BGP has no concept of being enabled on an interface, or of dynamically discovering neighbors. Instead, with BGP:

- Predefine neighbors with the **neighbor** *ip-address* **remote-as** *asn* BGP subcommand
- Advertise about prefixes that have been added to the BGP table using

  - The BGP **network** command
  - Route redistribution
  - By learning prefixes from a neighbor

In some ways, you have to unlearn some of what you know about IGP configuration to learn BGP configuration. This section walks you through the basics.

BGP Configuration Concepts

BGP uses TCP to transport its messages between two BGP peers, using well-known port 179. When you configure BGP, it opens port 179, waiting for incoming connection requests from other routers. Once a peer connects, the TCP connection is formed.

Once two routers form a TCP connection for use by BGP, the BGP process on each router must decide whether the two routers should become neighbors or not. The idea is much like the overall process with OSPF and EIGRP neighbors exchanging messages to decide if they should become neighbors. The two BGP routers send BGP messages that do some basic checks of parameters to make sure the two routers should become peers. If all checks are passed, the two routers become BGP peers (neighbors). At that point, the two routers can exchange routing information.

BGP uses the update message to exchange information. Once the BGP peer has been established, BGP peers send update messages which hold prefix/length (NLRI) information and the associated path attributes (PA). Those PAs include the AS_Path introduced earlier in the chapter. Figure 12-10 shows an example, the four steps of which are described as follows:

Step 1. Because of proper neighbor configuration in the two routers, the two routers create a TCP connection with each other and become BGP peers.

Step 2. Because of additional configuration, possibly the BGP **network** subcommand, Router R1 adds one or more NLRI and associated PAs to its local BGP table.

Step 3. eBGP on R1 advertises all the best routes in its BGP table—that is, the routes it considers as best for each NLRI—in a BGP update message sent to router ISP1. In this case, R1 advertises about NLRI 192.0.2.0/24.

Step 4. BGP on ISP1 processes that received update, adding a BGP table entry for 192.0.2.0/24.

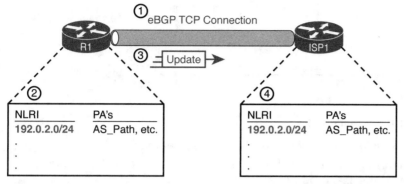

Figure 12-10 *Steps for Advertising a Public Prefix from the Enterprise to an ISP*

This process requires two key configuration steps: configuring neighbors, and configuration that adds entries to a router's BGP table. The next few pages explain both.

Configuring eBGP Neighbors Using Link Addresses

BGP configuration begins with a familiar type of command: the **router bgp** *asn* command, where *asn* is the AS number used by that enterprise or ISP. That command moves the CLI user into BGP configuration mode, much like the **router ospf**, **router eigrp**, and other similar commands.

In a single-homed eBGP design, one link exists between the two routers that need to be eBGP peers. As a result, the two routers can use their interface IP addresses. The **neighbor** *peer-ip-address* BGP subcommand defines the IP address of the neighbor, as shown in Figure 12-11.

Figure 12-11 *Using Link Addresses for BGP Peering in a Single-Homed Design*

However, the **neighbor 198.51.100.2** command shown in the figure for R1 (and the similar command on Router ISP1) is just a partial command. In IOS BGP configuration, you can define many different parameters for a single peer. To do so, IOS expects multiple **neighbor** commands for a single peer. Each command sets a different parameter. For instance, this chapter shows these options at various points in the chapter:

> **neighbor** *peer-ip-address* **remote-as** *asn*
>
> **neighbor** *peer-ip-address* **shutdown**

Of these, only the **neighbor** *peer-ip-address* **remote-as** command is required. The **router bgp** *asn* global command defines the local router's ASN, and each **neighbor** *peer-ip-address* **remote-as** *asn* command defines a neighbor's IP address and ASN, as shown in Figure 12-12.

12

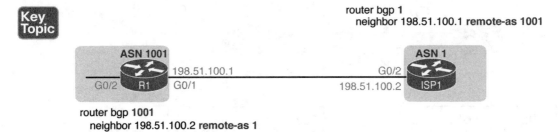

Figure 12-12 *Design for Sample eBGP Neighbor Configurations*

Example 12-1 shows the relevant eBGP configuration on Routers R1 and ISP1 for the design shown in Figures 12-11 and 12-12.

Example 12-1 *eBGP Neighbor Configuration*

```
! Configuration on R1
router bgp 1001
 neighbor 198.51.100.2 remote-as 1
! Configuration on ISP1
router bgp 1
 neighbor 198.51.100.1 remote-as 1001
```

NOTE This section shows examples that use the IPv4 addresses on the link between the two routers for the eBGP **neighbor** configuration. This chapter discusses only this case of using the common link's interface IP addresses in eBGP **neighbor** commands. eBGP allows the **neighbor** command to refer to any IPv4 address on the BGP neighbor, but other concepts must first be understood, and other BGP commands must be configured, for those alternate configurations to work.

Verifying eBGP Neighbors

The previous configuration gets BGP started, and causes an eBGP neighbor relationship to form, but it does not complete the initial configuration. Remember, from earlier Figure 12-10, that BGP must also add entries to its BGP table before it can then advertise that entry (NLRI and associated PAs). With the configuration so far, Routers R1 and ISP1 should be eBGP peers, but not yet have any BGP table entries to send to each other. Example 12-2 shows some sample output to confirm the neighbor relationship, and to confirm that BGP has an empty BGP table. The explanation follows the example.

Example 12-2 *eBGP Neighbor States and TCP Connection*

```
R1# show tcp brief
TCB        Local Address            Foreign Address          (state)
0D0D3F00   198.51.100.1.63680       198.51.100.2.179         ESTAB


R1# show ip bgp summary
BGP router identifier 192.0.2.1, local AS number 1001
BGP table version is 1, main routing table version 1
```

```
Neighbor        V       AS  MsgRcvd MsgSent   TblVer  InQ OutQ Up/Down  State/PfxRcd
198.51.100.2    4       1       2       2        1    0    0 00:00:49         0
R1#
R1# show ip bgp
R1#
```

First, the **show tcp brief** command shows all TCP connections that terminate at this router (R1), whether BGP or not. Each line lists the local router IP address and TCP port, and the foreign (other device) address and port. In this case, note that 198.51.100.2 uses BGP well-known port 179. With BGP, one router initiates the TCP connection and uses a dynamic port (R1 with port 63680 in this case), connecting to the well-known BGP TCP port 179 on the other peer.

The **show ip bgp summary** command lists one line per BGP peer. That one line identifies the neighbor IP address and the neighbor's ASN (both found in the **neighbor remote-as** command). However, that one line of output does not directly identify whether the peer is an eBGP or iBGP peer; instead, you have to compare the neighbor's AS (in the AS column of the output) with the local ASN in the first line of the output. In this case, with local ASN 1001 and neighbor ASN 1, this particular peer is an eBGP peer.

The **show ip bgp summary** command also lists the BGP process's BGP router ID. Like IGPs, BGP uses a router ID to identify itself in BGP messages. BGP also uses a familiar process to choose the router ID, with the same overall logic as OSPF and EIGRP:

1. Use the value in the **bgp router-id** *rid* BGP subcommand.

2. If unset per Step 1, choose the highest IPv4 address among all loopback interfaces in an interface up state.

3. If unset per Steps 1 and 2, use the same logic as Step 2, but for all nonloopback interfaces in an interface up state.

Continuing the tour of Example 12-2, make sure and look to the far right of the **show ip bgp summary** command, to the heading "State/PfxRcd." That column either lists the neighbor state or, if the neighbor is in a working ("established") state, lists the number of prefixes (BGP table entries) received from that neighbor. In the output of Example 12-2, the number of prefixes is listed as 0 because Router R1 has learned no prefixes as of yet from the ISP.

When the neighbor relationship is correct and complete, the final working state is the established state. When in that state, this column lists the number of prefixes learned from the neighbor. However, if the peer has not yet reached the established state, this column lists that interim state. Table 12-2 lists the various other BGP neighbor states.

Table 12-2   BGP Neighbor States

BGP Neighbor State	Typical Reasons
Idle	The neighbor has been administratively disabled (**neighbor shutdown**), or the router is waiting before the next retry.
Connect	The TCP connection is being attempted but has not completed.

12

BGP Neighbor State	Typical Reasons
Active	The TCP connection has been completed, but no BGP messages have been sent yet.
Opensent	The TCP connection exists, and this router has sent the first message to establish the BGP neighbor relationship (a BGP Open message).
Openconfirm	The TCP connection exists and the local router has received an Open message from the other router. The neighbor relationship may still be rejected.
Established	The routers are now neighbors/peers and can exchange update messages.

Administratively Disabling Neighbors

BGP attaches many configuration parameters to the **neighbor** commands that list a particular neighbor. So, to make it easy to bring down a neighbor, rather than requiring the complete removal of those multiple **neighbor** commands for that one neighbor, IOS supports the **neighbor shutdown** BGP subcommand. This command administratively disables that BGP neighbor. The **no neighbor shutdown** command then re-enables the neighbor connection. Example 12-3 shows an example, as well as the resulting BGP peer state (Idle).

Example 12-3 *Neighbor State with the Neighbor Shut Down*

```
R1# configure terminal
Enter configuration commands, one per line.  End with CNTL/Z.
R1(config)# router bgp 1001
R1(config-router)# neighbor 198.51.100.2 shutdown
*Nov 20 13:05:58.784: %BGP-5-NBR_RESET: Neighbor 198.51.100.2 reset (Admin. shutdown)
R1(config-router)# ^Z
R1#
R1# show ip bgp summary
BGP router identifier 192.0.2.1, local AS number 1001
BGP table version is 1, main routing table version 1

Neighbor        V          AS MsgRcvd MsgSent   TblVer  InQ OutQ Up/Down  State/PfxRcd
198.51.100.2    4           1       0       0        1    0    0 00:00:10 Idle (Admin)
```

Take the time to connect the State field value listed at the far right of the output of the **show ip bgp summary** command output at the end of Example 12-3. As mentioned in Table 12-2, the BGP neighbor Idle state simply refers to a neighbor that has been configured with the **neighbor shutdown** command.

Injecting BGP Table Entries with the network Command

At this point in the sample configurations, R1, the enterprise router, is not advertising any routes to the ISP with BGP. BGP has a couple of methods of injecting information into the BGP table so that BGP will then advertise those routes. The next few pages show how to make that happen with the BGP **network** command, which is the one method specifically mentioned in the exam topics.

The BGP **network** command works differently than the **network** command supported by the various IGPs. This section details several examples to show the differences, as follows:

- Advertising a route for an entire classful network or public address block
- Advertising routes for subnets of the public address block
- Advertising routes for larger address blocks when only subnets exist in the routing table

Injecting Routes for a Classful Network

To begin, consider this straightforward case of an eBGP connection. The enterprise uses a Class C public network (192.0.2.0/24), placing that entire Class C network in its DMZ, as shown in Figure 12-13.

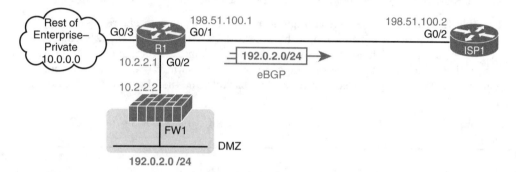

Figure 12-13   *All of Class C Network 192.0.2.0/24 Used as DMZ Subnet*

R1 needs to advertise its public prefix (192.0.2.0/24) to the ISP. R1 also needs to avoid advertising its private address space to the ISP (10.0.0.0/8). Why? Routers in the Internet need to know how to forward packets to the enterprise's public address range. However, many companies use the same private IPv4 networks, such as IPv4 network 10.0.0.0, and by definition, these networks are not advertised into the Internet.

To advertise its public prefix, the enterprise network engineer can configure a BGP **network** command on R1. This command lets the engineer easily control which prefixes R1 adds to its BGP table. Once in the BGP table, the router then advertises the prefixes to the ISP. The **network** command basically tells BGP this:

> Put this prefix/length into the BGP table, assuming that prefix/length is in the IP routing table.

Figure 12-14 details the logic of the BGP **network** *prefix* **mask** *DDN-mask* command. The **network** command lists a prefix and DDN-style mask (Step 1 in the figure). IOS then compares that prefix and mask to the prefix/mask for the routes in the IPv4 routing table. BGP looks for an exact match (Step 2), meaning that the BGP **network** command's prefix and mask both exactly match a prefix and mask in a route in the routing table. If a match is found (Step 3), BGP on that router creates a matching BGP table entry. BGP advertises the best valid routes from its BGP table to its BGP peers (Step 4).

12

Router Internals

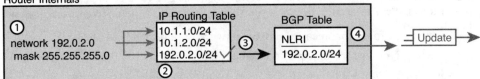

Figure 12-14 *Configuration Concept: the BGP **network** Command*

When the router using eBGP already has an IP route for the exact prefix it wants to advertise with BGP, configuring the BGP **network** command is easy. All you have to do is configure a BGP **network** command, listing that exact IPv4 prefix and mask. For example, in the design both shown in Figure 12-13 and represented logically in Figure 12-14, Router R1 will know a route for classful network 192.0.2.0/24, as learned via OSPF from the firewall.

Example 12-4 continues the same configuration example begun with Figure 12-12 and Example 12-1. It shows the addition of the **network 192.0.2.0 mask 255.255.255.0** BGP subcommand, which lists that exact prefix and exact mask (although in DDN format, not prefix format). The output at the end of the example confirms that R1 has that route, and the BGP table entry created on Router R1—basically the first three steps in Figure 12-14.

Example 12-4 *R1 BGP Configuration with **network** Command; Resulting BGP Table Entry*

```
R1# configure terminal
Enter configuration commands, one per line.  End with CNTL/Z.
R1(config)# router bgp 1001
R1(config-router)# network 192.0.2.0 mask 255.255.255.0
R1(config-router)# ^Z
R1# show ip route 192.0.2.0 255.255.255.0 longer-prefixes
! Legend omitted for brevity

O     192.0.2.0/24 [110/2] via 10.2.2.2, 00:01:13, GigabitEthernet0/2
R1#
R1# show ip bgp
BGP table version is 2, local router ID is 192.0.2.1
Status codes: s suppressed, d damped, h history, * valid, > best, i - internal,
              r RIB-failure, S Stale, m multipath, b backup-path, f RT-Filter,
              x best-external, a additional-path, c RIB-compressed,
Origin codes: i - IGP, e - EGP, ? - incomplete
RPKI validation codes: V valid, I invalid, N Not found

     Network          Next Hop            Metric LocPrf Weight Path
*>   192.0.2.0        10.2.2.2                 2           32768 i
R1#
```

> **NOTE**   In this case, because the **network 192.0.2.0 mask 255.255.255.0** command happens to list a Class C network ID and the default Class C mask, the mask 255.255.255.0 parameter could be omitted. If omitted, IOS assumes a default mask for the address class for the prefix.

Pay close attention to the two **show** commands in the output. The **show ip route 192.0.2.0 255.255.255.0 longer-prefixes** command lists all IPv4 routes in the range of 192.0.2.0 255.255.255.0, one route per line. Note that only one route exists in this range: a route for exactly 192.0.2.0/24, with next-hop address 10.2.2.2 (which is the firewall's IP address).

The **show ip bgp** command lists R1's BGP table, first with several lines of legend, followed by one line for each prefix in the table (only one entry in this case). First, look at the values in the network and next hop columns: it lists the same prefix and next-hop as taken from the IP routing table. Also, of particular importance, note the characters * and > on the far left, which per the legend mean that the route is valid and that this route is the best route to reach this prefix. In cases for which BGP has learned multiple routes to reach one prefix, BGP lists a > beside the best route per the BGP best path algorithm.

Now that R1 has a table entry for the enterprise's public prefix of 192.0.2.0/24, R1 advertises that prefix and associated PAs to its eBGP peer. Example 12-5 shows the BGP table and IPv4 routing table on Router ISP1.

Example 12-5   *ISP1's BGP and IP Routing Tables*

```
ISP1# show ip bgp
BGP table version is 2, local router ID is 2.2.2.2
Status codes: s suppressed, d damped, h history, * valid, > best, i - internal,
              r RIB-failure, S Stale, m multipath, b backup-path, f RT-Filter,
              x best-external, a additional-path, c RIB-compressed,
Origin codes: i - IGP, e - EGP, ? - incomplete
RPKI validation codes: V valid, I invalid, N Not found


     Network          Next Hop            Metric LocPrf Weight Path
 *>  192.0.2.0        198.51.100.1             2          0 1001 i
ISP1# show ip route 192.0.2.0 255.255.255.0 longer-prefixes
! Legend omitted


B     192.0.2.0/24 [20/2] via 198.51.100.1, 00:01:52
ISP1#
```

Even with this basic example, the output on ISP1 reveals some key facts about how BGP works. Note that the **show ip bgp** command's Path column now lists ASN 1001, whereas that column in R1's output listed no ASNs. (That column lists the AS_Path PA, which in this case lists the enterprise's ASN.) Also, note ISP1's next-hop address for this prefix, 198.51.100.1, which is R1's IP address on the link between R1 and ISP1. By default, when a router learns a prefix with eBGP, like the route ISP1 is shown to learn in Example 12-5, the router uses the IP address of the eBGP neighbor as the next-hop address.

12

ISP1's **show ip route** command lists one route, the route for 192.0.2.0/24. Of note, see that the administrative distance is 20 (the first number inside square brackets). eBGP has a default administrative distance of 20, while iBGP routes use 200. The code on the far left lists "B," for a BGP-learned route, and the same next-hop IP address of 198.51.100.1 as listed in the BGP table.

Advertising Subnets to the ISP

Often, an enterprise takes its one public address block and breaks it into subnets. As a result, the Internet edge router likely has routes for each of those subnets, rather than one route for the entire public address block.

One method to solve this problem is to advertise the subnets of the public address block to the ISP. The ISP probably does not want to use this solution, but for the sake of showing another example, this section includes one example, based on Figure 12-15. The enterprise has been assigned Class C network 192.0.2.0/24, and has created two subnets: 192.0.2.128/26, used for the DMZ on the other side of a firewall, and 192.0.2.0/29, used for NAT, and assigned to interface loopback 1 on Router R1.

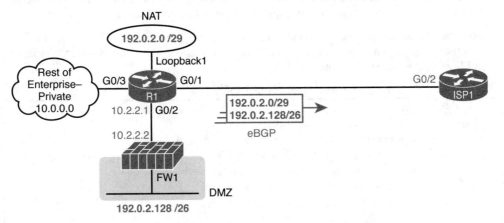

Figure 12-15 *Using Two Subnets of 192.0.2.0/24: DMZ and NAT*

Example 12-6 begins with all the IPv4 addressing configured per Figure 12-15, only needing the addition of the BGP configuration. For this solution, the engineer configured **network** commands that match the two specific subnets: 192.0.2.0/29 and 192.0.2.128/26.

Example 12-6 *R1 BGP Configuration with two **network** Commands*

```
R1# show ip route 192.0.2.0 255.255.255.0 longer-prefixes
      192.0.2.0/24 is variably subnetted, 3 subnets, 3 masks
C        192.0.2.0/29 is directly connected, Loopback1
L        192.0.2.1/32 is directly connected, Loopback1
O        192.0.2.128/26 [110/2] via 10.2.2.2, 03:45:00, GigabitEthernet0/2
R1#
R1# configure terminal
Enter configuration commands, one per line.  End with CNTL/Z.
R1(config)# router bgp 1001
R1(config-router)# network 192.0.2.0 mask 255.255.255.248
```

```
R1(config-router)# network 192.0.2.128 mask 255.255.255.192
R1(config-router)# ^Z
R1#
R1# show ip bgp
BGP table version is 5, local router ID is 198.51.100.1
Status codes: s suppressed, d damped, h history, * valid, > best, i - internal,
              r RIB-failure, S Stale, m multipath, b backup-path, f RT-Filter,
              x best-external, a additional-path, c RIB-compressed,
Origin codes: i - IGP, e - EGP, ? - incomplete
RPKI validation codes: V valid, I invalid, N Not found


     Network          Next Hop          Metric LocPrf Weight Path
 *>  192.0.2.0/29     0.0.0.0                0           32768 i
 *>  192.0.2.128/26   10.2.2.2               2           32768 i
```

Advertising a Single Prefix with a Static Discard Route

The end of the previous example shows the two subnets injected into R1's BGP table. R1 would then advertise both subnets to Router ISP1. However, in most cases, the ISP does not want to learn about the subnets of the enterprise's public address block: the ISP wants to learn one route for the whole public address block (in these examples, 192.0.2.0/24). The challenge with this latest example is that R1 does not have a route for 192.0.2.0/24, so the **network** command cannot trigger the process of adding a BGP table entry for 192.0.2.0/24.

One method to overcome that problem (and the only one shown in this chapter) uses a static IPv4 route called a *discard route*. In Example 12-6, the **network 192.0.2.0 mask 255.255.255.0** would not add a BGP table entry on R1 because R1 did not have a matching IPv4 route. The solution? Configure a static route for that exact prefix, causing a static route to be added to the IPv4 routing table. However, give the route an outgoing interface of **null0**. This route, the discard route, makes the router discard any packets that match the route. (If you are now confused, be patient and work through this next example. Using a discard route collects several concepts beyond BGP, so it takes a few moments to see how the pieces fit together.)

So, review Figure 12-15 again, to get your bearings. R1 has routes for 192.0.2.0/29 and 192.0.2.128/26. Then, instead of the BGP configuration shown in Example 12-6, use the configuration in Example 12-7, which includes the addition of the discard route.

Example 12-7   *R1 BGP Configuration with Discard Route for 192.0.2.0/24*

```
ip route 192.0.2.0 255.255.255.0 null0
!
router bgp 1001
 network 192.0.2.0 mask 255.255.255.0
```

Next, look just at the IPv4 routes in the range of 192.0.2.0/24, as shown in Example 12-8. It shows the 192.0.2.0/29 subnet used by NAT (and the 192.0.2.1/32 route for the interface IP address for that interface). It shows the route for prefix 192.0.2.128/26 used for the DMZ. And it shows an overlapping route, the discard route, for 192.0.2.0/24.

Example 12-8 *Evidence of Discard Route*

```
R1# show ip route 192.0.2.0 255.255.255.0 longer-prefixes
! Legend omitted for brevity
      192.0.2.0/24 is variably subnetted, 4 subnets, 4 masks
S        192.0.2.0/24 is directly connected, Null0
C        192.0.2.0/29 is directly connected, Loopback1
L        192.0.2.1/32 is directly connected, Loopback1
O        192.0.2.128/26 [110/2] via 10.2.2.2, 00:06:02, GigabitEthernet0/2
```

Remember, when IPv4 routes overlap, IOS matches the most specific route—that is, the route with the longer prefix length. As a result, with these overlapping routes:

1. Packets sent to the NAT subnet (192.0.2.0/29) would match both the 192.0.2.0/29 route and the route to 192.0.2.0/24, but IOS uses the more specific (longer prefix) route with the /29 prefix length.

2. Packets sent to the DMZ subnet (192.0.2.128/26) would match both the 192.0.2.128/26 route and the route to 192.0.2.0/24, but IOS uses the more specific (longer prefix) route with the /26 prefix length, and forwards packets to the firewall.

3. Other packets in the range of network 192.0.2.0/24 that do not also match 192.0.2.0/29 or 192.0.2.128/26 would match only the discard route (192.0.2.0/24) and are discarded.

Adding this static discard route has not harmed IPv4 routing at all, in that packets going to the used IP addresses in the 192.0.2.0/24 address range already have a more specific working route. However, adding that static discard route solves our BGP problem: the BGP **network** command now sees a route for 192.0.2.0/24 in the IP routing table, so BGP adds an entry to the BGP table per that route. Example 12-9 shows the resulting BGP table entry on Router R1.

Example 12-9 *Resulting /24 Route in BGP Table Due to Discard Route*

```
R1# show ip bgp
BGP table version is 8, local router ID is 198.51.100.1
Status codes: s suppressed, d damped, h history, * valid, > best, i - internal,
              r RIB-failure, S Stale, m multipath, b backup-path, f RT-Filter,
              x best-external, a additional-path, c RIB-compressed,
Origin codes: i - IGP, e - EGP, ? - incomplete
RPKI validation codes: V valid, I invalid, N Not found

     Network          Next Hop            Metric LocPrf Weight Path
 *>  192.0.2.0        0.0.0.0                  0         32768 i
```

Learning a Default Route from the ISP

Most of the configuration and verification steps in this chapter focus on configuring the enterprise router to advertise its public IPv4 prefix to the ISP. The ISP may also advertise a default route to the enterprise eBGP router as well. Example 12-10 shows the BGP table and IPv4 routing tables on Router R1, the same enterprise eBGP router used in the other examples in this chapter, after learning a default route from Router ISP1.

> **NOTE** This chapter focuses on the enterprise router's BGP configuration. However, if you want to try this in a lab, beyond the configuration shown in Example 12-1, add the following to Router ISP1: **ip route 0.0.0.0 0.0.0.0 null0**, **router bgp 1**, and **network 0.0.0.0**.

Example 12-10 *Receiving a Default Route from Router ISP1*

```
R1# show ip bgp
BGP table version is 3, local router ID is 192.0.2.1
Status codes: s suppressed, d damped, h history, * valid, > best, i - internal,
              r RIB-failure, S Stale, m multipath, b backup-path, f RT-Filter,
              x best-external, a additional-path, c RIB-compressed,
Origin codes: i - IGP, e - EGP, ? - incomplete
RPKI validation codes: V valid, I invalid, N Not found

     Network          Next Hop            Metric LocPrf Weight Path
*>  0.0.0.0          198.51.100.2             0             0 1 i
*>  192.0.2.0        0.0.0.0                  0         32768 i
R1# show ip route
! Legend omitted for brevity


Gateway of last resort is 198.51.100.2 to network 0.0.0.0


B*   0.0.0.0/0 [20/0] via 198.51.100.2, 00:00:18
! Lines omitted for brevity
```

First, look at the highlighted parts of the **show ip bgp** command output. The route to prefix 0.0.0.0 lists next-hop 198.51.100.2—Router ISP1's IP address on the link between R1 and ISP1. This route is another eBGP-learned route, so it lists the eBGP neighbor as the next-hop address by default. At the far right, the AS_Path lists one short ASN (ASN 1), ISP1's ASN. Both facts point to the idea that R1 learned this BGP prefix from Router ISP1.

The **show ip route** command (excerpt) confirms that R1 now has a default route, with Router ISP1 (198.51.100.2) as the next-hop router.

To make use of this route, R1 could advertise the default route into its IGP as described in Chapters 8 (for OSPF) and 10 (for EIGRP). For instance, with OSPF configured for this enterprise, Router R1 would simply need to add the **default-information originate** command in OSPF configuration mode.

Chapter Review

12

One key to doing well on the exams is to perform repetitive spaced review sessions. Review this chapter's material using either the tools in the book, DVD, or interactive tools for the same material found on the book's companion website. Refer to the "Your Study Plan" element for more details. Table 12-3 outlines the key review elements and where you can find them. To better track your study progress, record when you completed these activities in the second column.

Table 12-3 Chapter Review Tracking

Review Element	Review Date(s)	Resource Used
Review key topics		Book, DVD/website
Review key terms		Book, DVD/website
Answer DIKTA questions		Book, PCPT
Do labs		Blog
Review command tables		Book

Review All the Key Topics

Table 12-4 Key Topics for Chapter 12

Key Topic Element	Description	Page Number
Figure 12-3	Shortest AS_Path choice for BGP best path selection	305
Figure 12-4	Single-homed Internet edge design	306
Figure 12-7	Description of routes advertised by an enterprise to an ISP using eBGP	308
Figure 12-9	Description of routes advertised by an ISP to an enterprise using eBGP	309
List	eBGP configuration basics	310
Figure 12-12	eBGP configuration—matching the remote ASN	312
Example 12-2	BGP neighbor status and TCP connection status	312
Figure 12-14	Logic of how the BGP **network** command matches the IP routing table	316

Key Terms You Should Know

Border Gateway Protocol (BGP), autonomous system (AS), autonomous system number ASN, Internal BGP (iBGP), External BGP (eBGP), single homed, Internet edge, BGP table, BGP peer, discard route

Command References

Tables 12-5 and 12-6 list configuration and verification commands used in this chapter. As an easy review exercise, cover the left column in a table, read the right column, and try to recall the command without looking. Then repeat the exercise, covering the right column, and try to recall what the command does.

Table 12-5 Chapter 12 Configuration Commands

Command	Mode and Purpose
neighbor *ip-address* **remote-as** *asn*	Defines a BGP neighbor and the neighbor's AS number
[no] **neighbor** *ip-address* **shutdown**	Administratively disables or enables a BGP peer

Command	Mode and Purpose
network *prefix* [mask *mask*]	Directs the BGP process to add a BGP table entry for the prefix/mask if the prefix/mask exists in the IP routing table
ip route *prefix mask* null0	Defines a discard route, so that packets routed by the router that use this route will be discarded by the router

Table 12-6 Chapter 12 EXEC Command Reference

Command	Purpose
show ip bgp	Displays the BGP table
show ip bgp summary	Displays basic configuration for the local router, and one line of configuration and state information per BGP peer
show tcp brief	Lists a line of information about each TCP connection that terminates at the router
show ip route *prefix mask* longer-prefixes	Lists a subset of IP routes, listing one line per route that exists within the address range defined by the prefix and mask

12

Part II Review

Keep track of your part review progress with the checklist in Table P2-1. Details about each task follow the table.

Table P2-1   Part II Part Review Checklist

Activity	First Date Completed	Second Date Completed
Repeat All DIKTA Questions		
Answer Part Review Questions		
Review Key Topics		
Create Mind Maps		
Do Labs		

Repeat All DIKTA Questions

For this task, answer the "Do I Know This Already?" questions again for the chapters in this part of the book using the PCPT software. See the section "How to View Only DIKTA Questions by Chapter or Part" in the Introduction to this book to learn how to make the PCPT software show you DIKTA questions for this part only.

Answer Part Review Questions

For this task, answer the Part Review questions for this part of the book using the PCPT software. See the section "How to View Part Review Questions" in the Introduction to this book to learn how to make the PCPT software show you DIKTA questions for this part only.

Review Key Topics

Review all Key Topics in all chapters in this part, either by browsing the chapters or by using the Key Topics application on the DVD or companion website.

Create OSPF and EIGRP Root Causes Mind Map

Chapter 11, "Troubleshooting IPv4 Routing Protocols," focuses on how to troubleshoot problems with both Open Shortest Path First (OSPF) and Enhanced Interior Gateway Routing Protocol (EIGRP), specifically related to interfaces and to neighbor relationships. For this mind map, work through all the items you can think of that can fail and cause a problem that prevents a routing protocol from working in IPv4 internetworks, like those discussed in this part of the book. In other words, think about the root causes. Then organize those into a mind map.

To organize the mind map, start by just listing whatever comes to mind. Then, once you see several root causes that are related, group those root causes by whatever category comes to mind. There is no right or wrong organization to the root causes.

Create OSPF, EIGRP, and BGP Commands Mind Map

Part II also discussed OSPF, EIGRP, and BGP configuration and verification. Create a command mind map, like in many other part reviews. The first level of organization should be for OSPF, EIGRP, and BGP, then for configuration versus verification. Inside the verification area, further organize the commands similar to the organization in Chapter 10, "Implementing EIGRP for IPv4," with commands related to interfaces, neighbors, topology, and routes.

Appendix E, "Mind Map Solutions," lists sample mind map answers. If you do choose to use mind map software, rather than paper, you might want to remember where you stored your mind map files. Table P2-2 lists the mind maps for this part review and a place to record those filenames.

Table P2-2 Configuration Mind Maps for Part II Review

Map	Description	Where You Saved It
1	OSPF and EIGRP Root Causes Mind Map	
2	OSPF, EIGRP, and BGP Commands Mind Map	

Do Labs

Depending on your chosen lab tool, here are some suggestions for what to do in lab:

Pearson Network Simulator: If you use the full Pearson CCNA simulator, there are many labs for the routing protocol topics in particular. Note that labs on eBGP will require the Simulator for the CCNA 200-125 exam, while the Simulator for the earlier CCNA 200-200-120 exam has many labs on OSPF and EIGRP.

Config Labs: In your idle moments, review and repeat any of the Config Labs for this book part in the author's blog; launch from http://blog.certskills.com/ccna and navigate to **Hands-On > Config Lab.**

The world of networking offers a large variety of wide-area network (WAN) options. Part III of this book looks at one long-available option, in Chapter 13, breaking down the idea of a serial link and the protocols that control those links. Chapter 14 then moves on to the more common private WAN technologies seen today, namely Metro Ethernet and MPLS. Part III closes with Chapter 15, which examines how a company can use the Internet to create a private WAN using Virtual Private Network (VPN) technology. Chapter 15 goes into some implementation depth with two protocols that enable the VPNs in the Internet, specifically GRE and PPPoE.

Part III

Wide-Area Networks

Chapter 13: Implementing Point-to-Point WANs

Chapter 14: Private WANs with Ethernet and MPLS

Chapter 15: Private WANs with Internet VPNs

Part III Review

Implementing Point-to-Point WANs

This chapter covers the following exam topics:

3.0 WAN Technologies

3.1 Configure and verify PPP and MLPPP on WAN interfaces using local authentication

Leased-line WANs—also known as serial links—require much less thought than many other topics, at least to the depth required for the CCENT and CCNA R&S exams. That simplicity allows the Cisco exams to discuss leased lines briefly for the ICND1 exam, while using leased lines as part of larger discussions of IP routing.

This chapter finally takes the discussion of leased-line WANs deeper than has been discussed so far. This chapter briefly repeats the leased line concepts from the ICND1 book, to lay a foundation to discuss other concepts. More important, this chapter looks at the configuration, verification, and troubleshooting steps for leased lines that use the familiar High-level Data Link Control (HDLC) data-link protocol and the Point-to-Point Protocol (PPP).

This chapter breaks the material down into three major sections. The first looks at leased-line WANS that use HDLC, by reviewing and adding details about the physical links themselves, along with HDLC (and related) configuration. The second major section discusses PPP, an alternate data-link protocol that you can use instead of HDLC, with a focus on concepts and configuration. The final major section then discusses typical root causes of serial link problems and how to find those problems.

"Do I Know This Already?" Quiz

Take the quiz (either here, or use the PCPT software) if you want to use the score to help you decide how much time to spend on this chapter. The answers are at the bottom of the page following the quiz, and the explanations are in DVD Appendix C and in the PCPT software.

Table 13-1 "Do I Know This Already?" Foundation Topics Section-to-Question Mapping

Foundation Topics Section	Questions
Leased-Line WANs with HDLC	1–2
Leased-Line WANs with PPP	3–6
Troubleshooting Serial Links	7

1. In the cabling for a leased line, which of the following usually connects to a four-wire line provided by a telco?

   a. Router serial interface without internal CSU/DSU

   b. CSU/DSU

   c. Router serial interface with internal transceiver

   d. Switch serial interface

2. Two routers connect with a serial link, each using its S0/0/0 interface. The link is currently working using PPP. The network engineer wants to migrate to use the Cisco-proprietary HDLC that includes a protocol type field. Which of the following commands can be used to migrate to HDLC successfully? (Choose two answers.)

   a. encapsulation hdlc

   b. encapsulation cisco-hdlc

   c. no encapsulation ppp

   d. encapsulation-type auto

3. Which of the following PPP authentication protocols authenticates a device on the other end of a link without sending any password information in clear text?

   a. MD5

   b. PAP

   c. CHAP

   d. DES

4. Two routers have no initial configuration whatsoever. They are connected in a lab using a DTE cable connected to R1 and a DCE cable connected to R2, with the DTE and DCE cables then connected to each other. The engineer wants to create a working PPP link by configuring both routers. Which of the following commands are required in the R1 configuration for the link to reach a state in which R1 can ping R2's serial IP address, assuming that the physical back-to-back link physically works? (Choose two answers.)

   a. encapsulation ppp

   b. no encapsulation hdlc

   c. clock rate

   d. ip address

5. Consider the following excerpt from the output of a **show** command:

```
Serial0/0/1 is up, line protocol is up
   Hardware is GT96K Serial
   Internet address is 192.168.2.1/24
   MTU 1500 bytes, BW 1544 Kbit, DLY 20000 usec,
      reliability 255/255, txload 1/255, rxload 1/255
   Encapsulation PPP, LCP Open
   Open: CDPCP, IPCP, loopback not set
```

Which of the following are true about this router's S0/0/1 interface? (Choose two answers.)

   a. The interface is using HDLC.

   b. The interface is using PPP.

   c. The interface currently cannot pass IPv4 traffic.

   d. The link should be able to pass PPP frames at the present time.

6. Two routers, R1 and R2, connect to each other using three serial links. The network engineer configures these links to be part of the same multilink PPP group, along with configuring CHAP configuration, IPv4, and OSPFv2 using interface configuration. Which of the following answers list a configuration command along with the correct configuration mode for that command? (Choose two answers.)

    a. **encapsulation ppp** while in multilink interface configuration mode

    b. **ip address** address mask while in serial interface configuration mode

    c. **ppp authentication chap** while in multilink interface configuration mode

    d. **ip ospf 1 area 0** while in serial interface configuration mode

    e. **ppp multilink** while in serial interface configuration mode

7. Consider the following excerpt from the output of a **show interfaces** command on an interface configured to use PPP:

    ```
    Serial0/0/1 is up, line protocol is down
      Hardware is GT96K Serial
      Internet address is 192.168.2.1/24
    ```

    A ping of the IP address on the other end of the link fails. Which of the following are reasons for the failure, assuming that the problem listed in the answer is the only problem with the link? (Choose two answers.)

    a. The CSU/DSU connected to the other router is not powered on.

    b. The IP address on the router at the other end of the link is not in subnet 192.168.2.0/24.

    c. CHAP authentication failed.

    d. The router on the other end of the link has been configured to use HDLC.

    e. None of the above.

Foundation Topics

Leased-Line WANs with HDLC

A physical leased-line WAN works a lot like in an Ethernet crossover cable connecting two routers, but with no distance limitations. As shown in Figure 13-1, each router can send at any time (full duplex). The speed is also symmetric, meaning that both routers send bits at the same speed.

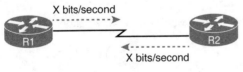

Figure 13-1 *Leased Line: Same Speed, Both Directions, Always On*

Although the leased line provides a physical layer bit transmission facility, routers also need to use a data link protocol on the WAN link to send bits over the link. The story should be familiar by now: routers receive frames in LAN interfaces, and then the router de-encapsulates the network layer packet. Before forwarding the packet, the router encapsulates the packet inside a WAN data link protocol like High-level Data Link Control (HDLC), as shown at Step 2 of Figure 13-2.

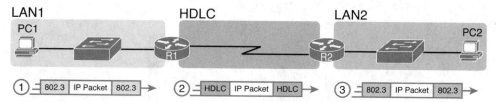

Figure 13-2   *Routers and Their Use of HDLC to Encapsulate Packets*

These first two figures review some of the Layer 1 and Layer 2 details, respectively, of leased-line WANs. This first major section of this chapter begins by discussing these links again, first with the Layer 1 details, followed by the Layer 2 details. This section ends with an explanation of HDLC configuration details.

Layer 1 Leased Lines

Leased lines have been around a long time, roughly 20 years longer than LANs. However, they still exist today as a WAN service.

As a result of their long history in the market, the networking world has used a large number of different terms. First, the term *leased line* refers to the fact that the company using the leased line does not own the line, but instead pays a monthly lease fee to use it. Often, you lease the service from a telephone company, or *telco*. However, many people today use the generic term *service provider* to refer to a company that provides any form of WAN connectivity, including Internet services. Table 13-2 lists some of those names so that you can understand the different terms you will encounter in a real networking job.

Table 13-2   Different Names for a Leased Line

Name	Meaning or Reference
Leased circuit, circuit	The words *line* and *circuit* are often used as synonyms in telco terminology; *circuit* makes reference to the electrical circuit between the two endpoints.
Serial link, serial line	The words *link* and *line* are also often used as synonyms. *Serial* in this case refers to the fact that the bits flow serially and that routers use serial interfaces.
Point-to-point link, point-to-point line	Refers to the fact that the topology stretches between two points, and two points only. (Some older leased lines allowed more than two devices.)
T1	A specific type of leased line that transmits data at 1.544 megabits per second (1.544 Mbps).
WAN link, link	Both these terms are very general, with no reference to any specific technology.

13

Answers to the "Do I Know This Already?" quiz:

1 B **2** A, C **3** C **4** A, D **5** B, D **6** A, E **7** C, D

The Physical Components of a Leased Line

To create a leased line, the telco must create some physical transmission path between the two routers on the ends of the link. The physical cabling must leave the buildings where each router sits. Then the telco must create the equivalent of a two-pair circuit from end to end, with one circuit to send data in each direction (full duplex). Figure 13-3 shows one such example, in which the telco uses a couple of traditional central office (CO) switches to create a short leased line between two routers.

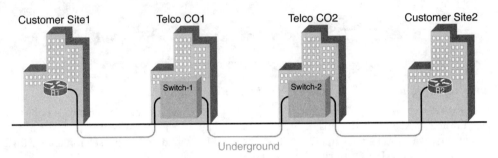

Figure 13-3   *Possible Cabling Inside a Telco for a Short Leased Line*

The details in the center of Figure 13-3 probably show more than you ever need to know about leased-line WANs, at least from the enterprise customer perspective. More commonly, most network engineers think more about a leased line from the perspective of Figure 13-4, which shows a few key components and terms for the equipment on the ends of a leased line, as follows:

Customer premises equipment (CPE): This telco term refers to the gear that sits at their customers' sites on the ends on the link.

Channel service unit/data service unit (CSU/DSU): This device provides a function called *clocking*, in which it physically controls the speed and timing at which the router serial interface sends and receives each bit over the serial cable.

Serial cable: This is a short cable that connects the CSU and the router serial interface.

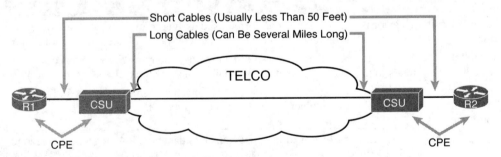
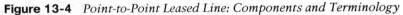

Figure 13-4   *Point-to-Point Leased Line: Components and Terminology*

The CPE includes several separately orderable parts. When using an external CSU/DSU, a serial cable must be used to connect the CSU to the router serial interface. These serial interfaces usually exist as part of a removable card on the router, called either WAN interface cards (WIC), High-speed WICs (HWIC), or Network Interface Modules (NIM). Most of the serial interfaces use one style (size/shape) of physical connector called a smart serial connector, whereas the CSU has one of several other types of connectors. So, when installing the leased line, the engineer must choose the correct cable type, with connectors to match the WIC on one end and the CSU/DSU on the other. Figure 13-5 shows a drawing of one type of serial cable, with the smart serial connector on the left, and the popular V.35 connector on the right. The figure shows a side view of the entire cable, plus direct views into the connector on the ends of the cable.

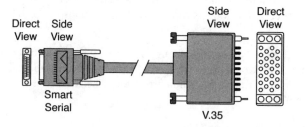

Figure 13-5   *Serial Cables Used Between a CSU and a Router*

Today, many leased lines make use of Cisco WICs with an integrated CSU/DSU. That is, the WIC hardware includes the same functions as a CSU/DSU, so an external CSU/DSU is not needed. Compared to Figure 13-4, the external CSU/DSU and serial cable on each end are not needed, with the cable from the telco connecting directly to the WIC.

Figure 13-6 shows a photo of a router with two NIM slots. Each slot currently shows a faceplate with no NIM cards installed. The foreground of the figure shows a NIM with two serial ports, with smart serial interfaces. The cable end on the left of the drawing in Figure 13-5 would attach to one of these smart serial ports on the NIM in Figure 13-6.

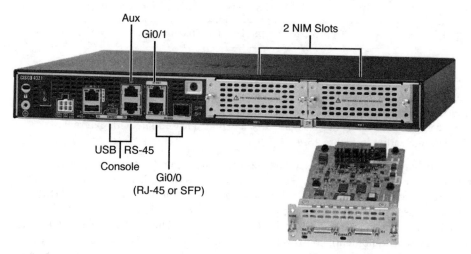

Figure 13-6   *Photo of Router with Serial NIM on the Right*

Telcos offer a wide variety of speeds for leased lines. However, a telco customer cannot pick just any speed. Instead, the speeds follow the standards of an age-old technology called the T-carrier system.

13

Back in the 1950s and 1960s, the U.S.-based Bell companies developed and deployed digital voice and the T-carrier system. As part of that work, they standardized different transmission speeds, including 64 Kbps, 1.544 Mbps, and 44.736 Mbps.

Those same Bell companies developed time-division multiplexing (TDM) technology that let them combine multiples of these base speeds onto a single line. For instance, one popular standard, a Digital Signal level 1 (DS1), or T1, combines 24 DS0s (at 64 Kbps) plus 8 Kbps of overhead into one physical line that runs at 1.544 Mbps. However, to allow flexibility of speeds offered to customers, the telco could install a T1 line to many sites, but run some at slower speeds and some at faster speeds—as long as those speeds were multiples of 64 Kbps.

Now back to the idea of the speed of a leased line. What can you actually buy? Basically, at slower speeds, you get any multiple of 64 Kbps, up to T1 speed. At faster speeds, you can get multiples of T1 speed, up to T3 speed. Table 13-3 summarizes the speeds typically seen in the United States, with a few from Europe.

Key Topic

Table 13-3   WAN Speed Summary

Names of Line	Bit Rate
DS0	64 Kbps
Fractional T1	Multiples of 64 Kbps, up to 24X
DS1 (T1)	1.544 Mbps (24 DS0s, for 1.536 Mbps, plus 8 Kbps overhead)
E1 (Europe)	2.048 Mbps (32 DS0s)
Fractional T3	Multiples of 1.536 Mbps, up to 28X
DS3 (T3)	44.736 Mbps (28 DS1s, plus management overhead)
E3 (Europe)	Approx. 34 Mbps (16 E1s, plus management overhead)

The Role of the CSU/DSU

For our last bit of discussion about WAN links in a working enterprise internetwork, next consider the role of the CSU/DSU (called CSU for short). For the sake of discussion, the next few paragraphs, leading up to Figure 13-7, assume a leased line with external CSU/DSUs, like earlier in Figure 13-4.

The CSU sits between the telco leased line and the router; it understands both worlds and their conventions at Layer 1. On the telco side, that means the CSU connects to the line from the telco, so it must understand all these details about the T-carrier system, TDM, and the speed used by the telco. On the router side of the equation, the CSU connects to the router, with roles called the DCE and DTE, respectively. The CSU, acting as DCE (data circuit-terminating equipment), controls the speed of the router serial interface. The router, acting as DTE (data terminal equipment), is controlled by the clocking signals from the CSU (DCE). That is, the CSU tells the router when to send and receive bits; the router attempts to send and receive bits only when the DCE creates the correct electrical impulses (called clocking) on the cable. Figure 13-7 shows a diagram of those main concepts of the role of the CSU/DSU.

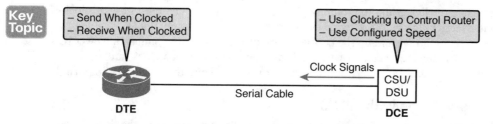

Figure 13-7 *DCE and DTE Roles for a CSU/DSU and a Router Serial Interface*

Building a WAN Link in a Lab

On a practical note, to prepare for the CCENT and CCNA R&S exams, you might choose to buy some used router and switch hardware for hands-on practice. If you do, you can create the equivalent of a leased line, without a real leased line from a telco, and without CSU/DSUs, just using a cabling trick. This short discussion tells you enough information to create a WAN link in your home lab.

First, when building a real WAN link with a real telco facility between sites, the serial cables normally used between a router and an external CSU/DSU are called *DTE cables*. That is, the serial cables in earlier Figure 13-4 are DTE cables.

You can create an equivalent WAN link just by connecting two routers' serial interfaces using one DTE cable and a slightly different DCE cable, with no CSUs and with no leased line from the telco. The DCE cable has a female connector, and the DTE cable has a male connector, which allows the two cables to be attached directly. That completes the physical connection, providing a path for the data. The DCE cable also does the equivalent of an Ethernet crossover cable by swapping the transmit and receive wire pairs, as shown in Figure 13-8.

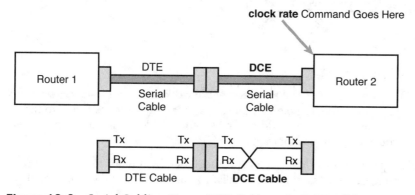

Figure 13-8 *Serial Cabling Uses a DTE Cable and a DCE Cable*

The figure shows the cable details at the top, with the wiring details at the bottom. In particular, at the bottom of the figure, note that the DTE serial cable acts as a straight-through cable and does not swap the transmit and receive pair, whereas the DCE cable does swap the pairs.

NOTE   Many vendors, for convenience, sell a single cable that combines the two cables shown in Figure 13-8 into a single cable. Search online for "Cisco serial crossover" to find examples.

13

Finally, to make the link work, the router with the DCE cable installed must provide clocking. A router serial interface can provide clocking, but it can do so only if a DCE cable is connected to the interface and by the configuration of the **clock rate** command. Newer IOS versions will sense the presence of a DCE cable and automatically set a clock rate, so that the link will work, but old IOS versions require that you configure the **clock rate** command.

Layer 2 Leased Lines with HDLC

A leased line provides a Layer 1 service. It promises to deliver bits between the devices connected to the leased line. However, the leased line itself does not define a data link layer protocol to be used on the leased line. HDLC provides one option for a data link protocol for a leased line.

HDLC has only a few big functions to perform with the simple point-to-point topology of a point-to-point leased line. First, the frame header lets the receiving router know that a new frame is coming. Plus, like all the other data link protocols, the HDLC trailer has a Frame Check Sequence (FCS) field that the receiving router can use to decide whether the frame had errors in transit, and if so, discard the frame.

Cisco adds another function to the ISO standard HDLC protocol by adding an extra field (a Type field) to the HDLC header, creating a Cisco-specific version of HDLC, as shown in Figure 13-9. The Type field allows Cisco routers to support multiple types of network layer packets to cross the HDLC link. For example, an HDLC link between two Cisco routers can forward both IPv4 and IPv6 packets because the Type field can identify which type of packet is encapsulated inside each HDLC frame.

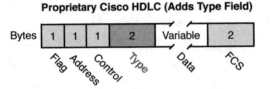

Figure 13-9   *Cisco HDLC Framing*

Today, the HDLC Address and Control fields have little work to do. For instance, with only two routers on a link, when a router sends a frame, it is clear that the frame is sent to the only other router on the link. Both the Address and Control fields had important purposes in years past, but today they are unimportant.

Routers use HDLC just like any other data link protocol used by routers: to move packets to the next router. Figure 13-10 shows three familiar routing steps, with the role of HDLC sitting at Step 2.

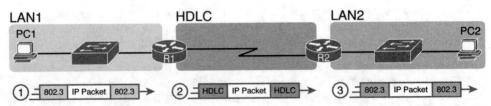

Figure 13-10   *General Concept of Routers De-encapsulating and Re-encapsulating IP Packets*

Here is a walkthrough of the steps in the figure:

1. To send the IP packet to router R1, PC1 encapsulates the IP packet in an Ethernet frame.

2. Router R1 de-encapsulates (removes) the IP packet, encapsulates the packet into an HDLC frame using an HDLC header and trailer, and forwards the HDLC frame to router R2.

3. Router R2 de-encapsulates (removes) the IP packet, encapsulates the packet into an Ethernet frame, and forwards the Ethernet frame to PC2.

In summary, a leased line with HDLC creates a WAN link between two routers so that they can forward packets for the devices on the attached LANs. The leased line itself provides the physical means to transmit the bits, in both directions. The HDLC frames provide the means to encapsulate the network layer packet correctly so it crosses the link between routers.

Configuring HDLC

Think back to router Ethernet interfaces for a moment. Router Ethernet interfaces require no configuration related to Layers 1 and 2 for the interface to be up and working, forwarding IP traffic. The Layer 1 details occur by default once the cabling has been installed correctly. Router Ethernet interfaces, of course, use Ethernet as the data link protocol by default. The router only needs to configure an IP address on the interface, and possibly enable the interface with the **no shutdown** command if the interface is in an "administratively down" state.

Similarly, serial interfaces on Cisco routers need no specific Layer 1 or 2 configuration commands. For Layer 1, the cabling needs to be completed, of course, but the router attempts to use the serial interface once the **no shutdown** command is configured. For Layer 2, IOS defaults to use HDLC on serial interfaces. As on Ethernet interfaces, router serial interfaces usually only need an **ip address** command, and possibly the **no shutdown** command, assuming both routers' interfaces otherwise have default settings.

Config Checklist

However, many optional commands exist for serial links. The following list outlines some configuration steps, listing the conditions for which some commands are needed, plus commands that are purely optional:

Step 1. Use the **ip address** *address mask* command in interface configuration mode to configure the interface IP address.

Step 2. The following tasks are required only when the specifically listed conditions are true:

    A. If an **encapsulation** *protocol* interface subcommand already exists, for a non-HDLC protocol, use the **encapsulation hdlc** command in interface configuration mode to enable HDLC. Alternatively, use the **no encapsulation** *protocol* command in interface configuration mode to use the default setting of HDLC as the data link protocol.

    B. If the interface line status is administratively down, use the **no shutdown** command in interface configuration mode to enable the interface.

13

C. If the serial link is a back-to-back serial link in a lab (or a simulator), use the **clock rate** *speed* command in interface configuration mode to configure the clocking rate. Use this command only on the one router with the DCE cable (per the **show controllers serial** *number* command).

Step 3. The following steps are always optional and have no impact on whether the link works and passes IP traffic:

A. Use the **bandwidth** *speed-in-kbps* command in interface configuration mode to configure the link's documented speed so that it matches the actual clock rate of the link.

B. For documentation purposes, use the **description** *text* command in interface configuration mode to configure a description of the purpose of the interface.

In practice, when you configure a Cisco router with no preexisting interface configuration and install a normal production serial link with CSU/DSUs, the **ip address** and **no shutdown** commands are likely the only configuration commands you would need.

Figure 13-11 shows a sample internetwork, and Example 13-1 shows the matching HDLC configuration. In this case, the serial link was created with a back-to-back serial link in a lab, requiring Steps 1 (**ip address**) and 2C (**clock rate**) from the preceding list. It also shows optional Step 3B (**description**).

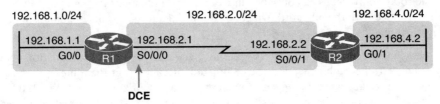

Figure 13-11 *Typical Serial Link Between Two Routers*

Example 13-1 *HDLC Configuration*

```
R1# show running-config
! Note - only the related lines are shown
interface GigabitEthernet0/0
 ip address 192.168.1.1 255.255.255.0
!
interface Serial0/0/0
 ip address 192.168.2.1 255.255.255.0
 description link to R2
 clock rate 2000000
!
router eigrp 1
 network 192.168.1.0
 network 192.168.2.0
```

The configuration on R1 is relatively simple. The matching configuration on R2's S0/0/1 interface simply needs an **ip address** command plus the default settings of **encapsulation hdlc** and **no shutdown**. The **clock rate** command would not be needed on R2 because R1 has the DCE cable, so R2 must be connected to a DTE cable.

Example 13-2 lists two commands that confirm the configuration on R1 and some other default settings. First, it lists the output from the **show controllers** command for S0/0/0, which confirms that R1 indeed has a DCE cable installed and that the clock rate has been set to 2000000 bps. The **show interfaces S0/0/0** command lists the various configuration settings near the top, including the default encapsulation value (HDLC) and default bandwidth setting on a serial interface (1544, meaning 1544 Kbps or 1.544 Mbps). It also lists the IP address, prefix-style mask (/24), and description, as configured in Example 13-1.

Example 13-2 *Verifying the Configuration Settings on R1*

```
R1# show controllers serial 0/0/0
Interface Serial0/0/0
Hardware is SCC
DCE V.35, clock rate 2000000
! lines omitted for brevity


R1# show interfaces s0/0/0
Serial0/0/0 is up, line protocol is up
  Hardware is WIC MBRD Serial
  Description: link to R2
  Internet address is 192.168.2.1/24
  MTU 1500 bytes, BW 1544 Kbit/sec, DLY 20000 usec,
     reliability 255/255, txload 1/255, rxload 1/255
  Encapsulation HDLC, loopback not set
  Keepalive set (10 sec)
  Last input 00:00:01, output 00:00:00, output hang never
  Last clearing of "show interface" counters never
  Input queue: 0/75/0/0 (size/max/drops/flushes); Total output drops: 0
  Queueing strategy: fifo
  Output queue: 0/40 (size/max)
  5 minute input rate 0 bits/sec, 0 packets/sec
  5 minute output rate 0 bits/sec, 0 packets/sec
     276 packets input, 19885 bytes, 0 no buffer
     Received 96 broadcasts (0 IP multicasts)
     0 runts, 0 giants, 0 throttles
     0 input errors, 0 CRC, 0 frame, 0 overrun, 0 ignored, 0 abort
     284 packets output, 19290 bytes, 0 underruns
     0 output errors, 0 collisions, 5 interface resets
     0 unknown protocol drops
     0 output buffer failures, 0 output buffers swapped out
     7 carrier transitions
     DCD=up  DSR=up  DTR=up  RTS=up  CTS=up
```

13

Finally, the router uses the serial interface only if it reaches an up/up interface status, as shown in the first line of the output of the **show interfaces S0/0/0** command in Example 13-2. Generally speaking, the first status word refers to Layer 1 status, and the second refers to Layer 2 status. For a quicker look at the interface status, instead use either the **show ip interface brief** or **show interfaces description** commands, as listed in Example 13-3.

Example 13-3 *Brief Lists of Interfaces and Interface Status*

```
R1# show ip interface brief
Interface              IP-Address      OK? Method Status                Protocol
GigabitEthernet0/0     192.168.1.1     YES manual up                    up
GigabitEthernet0/1     unassigned      YES manual administratively down down
Serial0/0/0            192.168.2.1     YES manual up                    up
Serial0/0/1            unassigned      YES NVRAM  administratively down down
Serial0/1/0            unassigned      YES NVRAM  administratively down down
Serial0/1/1            unassigned      YES NVRAM  administratively down down


R1# show interfaces description
Interface              Status      Protocol Description
Gi0/0                  up          up       LAN at Site 1
Gi0/1                  admin down  down
Se0/0/0                up          up       link to R2
Se0/0/1                admin down  down
Se0/1/0                admin down  down
Se0/1/1                admin down  down
```

Leased-Line WANs with PPP

Point-to-Point Protocol (PPP) plays the same role as HDLC: a data link protocol for use on serial links. However, HDLC was created for a world without routers. In contrast, PPP, defined in the 1990s, was designed with routers, TCP/IP, and other network layer protocols in mind, with many more advanced features.

This second major section of this chapter first discusses PPP concepts, including one example of a more advanced PPP feature (authentication). This section ends with some configuration examples using PPP.

PPP Concepts

PPP provides several basic but important functions that are useful on a leased line that connects two devices:

- Definition of a header and trailer that allows delivery of a data frame over the link
- Support for both synchronous and asynchronous links
- A protocol Type field in the header, allowing multiple Layer 3 protocols to pass over the same link
- Built-in authentication tools: Password Authentication Protocol (PAP) and Challenge Handshake Authentication Protocol (CHAP)

■ Control protocols for each higher-layer protocol that rides over PPP, allowing easier integration and support of those protocols

The next several pages take a closer look at the protocol field, authentication, and the control protocols.

PPP Framing

Unlike the standard version of HDLC, the PPP standard defines a protocol field. The protocol field identifies the type of packet inside the frame. When PPP was created, this field allowed packets from the many different Layer 3 protocols to pass over a single link. Today, the protocol Type field still provides the same function, usually supporting packets for the two different versions of IP (IPv4 and IPv6). Figure 13-12 shows the PPP framing, which happens to mirror the Cisco-proprietary HDLC framing that includes a protocol Type field (as shown earlier in Figure 13-9).

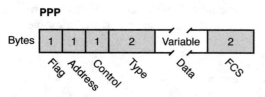

Figure 13-12   *PPP Framing*

PPP Control Protocols

In addition to HDLC-like framing, PPP defines a set of Layer 2 control protocols that perform various link control functions. The idea of these extra protocols works a little like how Ethernet includes additional protocols like Spanning Tree Protocol (STP). Ethernet has headers and trailers to deliver frames, plus it defines overhead protocols like STP to help make the frame forwarding process work better. Likewise, PPP defines the frame format in Figure 13-12, plus it defines other protocols to help manage and control the serial link.

PPP separates these control protocols into two main categories:

■ **Link Control Protocol (LCP):** This one protocol has several different individual functions, each focused on the data link itself, ignoring the Layer 3 protocol sent across the link.

■ **Network Control Protocols (NCP):** This is a category of protocols, one per network layer protocol. Each protocol performs functions specific to its related Layer 3 protocol.

The PPP LCP implements the control functions that work the same regardless of the Layer 3 protocol. For features related to any higher-layer protocols, usually Layer 3 protocols, PPP uses a series of PPP *control protocols* (CP), such as IP Control Protocol (IPCP). PPP uses one instance of LCP per link and one NCP for each Layer 3 protocol defined on the link. For example, on a PPP link using IPv4, IPv6, and Cisco Discovery Protocol (CDP), the link uses one instance of LCP plus IPCP (for IPv4), IPv6CP (for IPv6), and CDPCP (for CDP).

Table 13-4 summarizes the functions of LCP, gives the LCP feature names, and describes the features briefly. Following the table, the text explains one of the features, PPP authentication, in more detail. Later, the section "Implementing Multilink PPP" discusses the Multilink PPP (MLPPP) feature.

13

Table 13-4 PPP LCP Features

Function	LCP Feature	Description
Looped link detection	Magic number	Detects whether the link is looped, and disables the interface, allowing rerouting over a working route
Error detection	Link-quality monitoring (LQM)	Disables an interface that exceeds an error percentage threshold, allowing rerouting over better routes
Multilink support	Multilink PPP	Load balances traffic over multiple parallel links
Authentication	PAP and CHAP	Exchanges names and passwords so that each device can verify the identity of the device on the other end of the link

PPP Authentication

In networking, *authentication* gives one device a way to confirm that another device is truly the correct and approved device with which communications should occur. In other words, authentication confirms that the other party is the authentic other party, and not some imposter.

For instance, with PPP, if R1 and R2 are supposed to be communicating over a serial link, R1 might want R2 to somehow prove that the device claiming to be R2 really is R2. In that scenario, R1 wants to authenticate R2, with the authentication process providing a way for R2 to prove its identity.

WAN authentication is most often needed when dial lines are used. However, the configuration of the authentication features remains the same whether a leased line or dial line is used.

PPP defines two authentication protocols: PAP and CHAP. Both protocols require the exchange of messages between devices, but with different details. With PAP, the process works with the to-be-authenticated device starting the messages, claiming to be legitimate by listing a secret password in clear text, as shown in Figure 13-13.

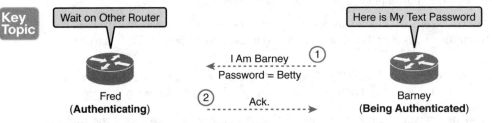

Figure 13-13 *PAP Authentication Process*

In the figure, when the link comes up, authentication takes two steps. At Step 1, Barney sends the shared password in clear text. Fred, who wants to authenticate Barney—that is, confirm that Barney is the real Barney—sees the password. Fred, configured with Barney's name and password, checks that configuration, confirming that it is the correct password, and sends back an acknowledgment that Barney has passed the authentication process.

CHAP, a much more secure option, uses different messages, and it hides the password. With CHAP, the device doing the authentication (Fred) begins with a message called a *challenge*, which asks the other device to reply. The big difference is that the second message in the flow (as shown in Figure 13-14) hides the authentication password by instead sending a hashed version of the password. Router Fred has been preconfigured with Barney's name and password in such a way that Fred can confirm that the hashed password sent by Barney is indeed the same password that Fred lists in his configuration for Barney. If the password is indeed the correct password, Fred sends back a third message to confirm the successful authentication of Barney.

Figure 13-14 *CHAP Authentication Process*

Both Figures 13-13 and 13-14 show authentication flows when authentication works. When it fails (for instance, if the passwords do not match), a different final message flows. Also, if the authentication fails, PPP leaves the interface in an up/down state, and the router cannot forward and receive frames on the interface.

PAP flows are much less secure than CHAP because PAP sends the hostname and password in clear text in the message. These can be read easily if someone places a tracing tool in the circuit. CHAP instead uses a one-way hash algorithm, called message digest 5 (MD5), with input to the algorithm being a password that never crosses the link plus a shared random number.

The CHAP process also uses a hash value only one time so that an attacker cannot just make a copy of the hashed value and send it at a later date. To make that work, the CHAP challenge (the first CHAP message) states a random number. The challenged router runs the hash algorithm using the just-learned random number and the secret password as input, and sends the results back to the router that sent the challenge. The router that sent the challenge runs the same algorithm using the random number (sent across the link) and the password (as stored locally); if the results match, the passwords must match. Later, the next time the authentication process work occurs, the authenticating router generates and uses a different random number.

PAP and CHAP are a few examples of the work done by PPP's LCP. The next topic looks at how to configure and verify PPP.

Implementing PPP

Configuring PPP, as compared to HDLC, requires only one change: using the **encapsulation ppp** command on both ends of the link. As with HDLC, other items can be optionally configured, such as the interface **bandwidth**, and a **description** of the interface. And of course, the interface must be enabled (**no shutdown**). But the configuration to migrate from HDLC to PPP just requires the **encapsulation ppp** command on both routers' serial interfaces.

Example 13-4 shows a simple configuration using the two routers shown in Figure 13-11, the same internetwork used for the HDLC example. The example includes the IP address configuration, but the IP addresses do not have to be configured for PPP to work.

13

Example 13-4 *Basic PPP Configuration*

```
! The example starts with router R1
interface Serial0/0/0
 ip address 192.168.2.1 255.255.255.0
 encapsulation ppp
 clock rate 2000000
! Next, the configuration on router R2
interface Serial0/0/1
 ip address 192.168.2.2 255.255.255.0
 encapsulation ppp
```

The one **show** command that lists PPP details is the **show interfaces** command, with an example from R1 listed in Example 13-5. The output looks just like it does for HDLC up until the first highlighted line in the example. The two highlighted lines confirm the configuration ("Encapsulation PPP"). These lines also confirm that LCP has completed its work successfully, as noted with the "LCP Open" phrase. Finally, the output lists the fact that two CPs, CDPCP and IPCP, have also successfully been enabled—all good indications that PPP is working properly.

Example 13-5 *Finding PPP, LCP, and NCP Status with* **show interfaces**

```
R1# show interfaces serial 0/0/0
Serial0/0/0 is up, line protocol is up
  Hardware is WIC MBRD Serial
  Description: link to R2
  Internet address is 192.168.2.1/24
  MTU 1500 bytes, BW 1544 Kbit/sec, DLY 20000 usec,
     reliability 255/255, txload 1/255, rxload 1/255
  Encapsulation PPP, LCP Open
  Open: IPCP, CDPCP, loopback not set
! Lines omitted for brevity
```

Implementing PPP CHAP

The simplest version of CHAP configuration requires only a few commands. The configuration uses a password configured on each router. (As an alternative, the password could be configured on an external authentication, authorization, and accounting [AAA] server outside the router.)

To configure PPP along with CHAP on an interface that has all default configuration on the serial interfaces of both routers, follow these steps:

Step 1. Use the **encapsulation ppp** command in interface configuration mode, on the serial interfaces on both routers, to enable PPP on the interfaces.

Step 2. Define the usernames and passwords used by the two routers:

A. Use the **hostname** *name* command in global configuration mode on each router, to set the local router's name to use when authenticating.

B. Use the **username** *name* **password** *password* command in global configuration mode on each router, to define the name (case-sensitive) used by the neighboring router, and the matching password (case-sensitive). (The name in the **username** command should match the name in the neighboring router's **hostname** command.)

Step 3. Use the **ppp authentication chap** command in interface configuration mode on each router to enable CHAP on each interface.

Figure 13-15 shows the configuration on both R1 and R2 to both enable PPP and add CHAP to the link. The figure shows how the name in the **hostname** command on one router must match the **username** command on the other router. It also shows that the password defined in each **username** command must be the same (mypass in this case).

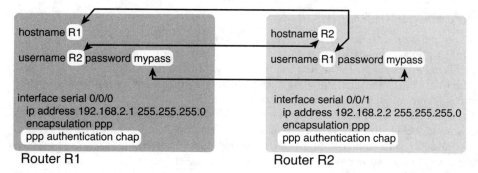

Figure 13-15 *CHAP Configuration*

You can confirm that CHAP authentication has succeeded in a couple of ways. First, if CHAP authentication is enabled but CHAP authentication fails, the protocol status of the interface falls to a down state. To check that status, use the usual **show interfaces** [*type number*] command or **show interfaces status** command. Additionally, if CHAP is enabled but CHAP authentication fails, the **show interfaces** command does not list "LCP Open" as shown in this example. Example 13-6 lists the output of the **show interfaces serial0/0/0** command from R1, with CHAP enabled per Figure 13-15, with CHAP working. However, note that this command does not tell us whether authentication has been configured or not.

Example 13-6 *Confirming CHAP Authentication with* **show interfaces**

```
R1# show interfaces serial 0/0/0
Serial0/0/0 is up, line protocol is up
  Hardware is WIC MBRD Serial
  Description: link to R2
  Internet address is 192.168.2.1/24
  MTU 1500 bytes, BW 1544 Kbit/sec, DLY 20000 usec,
     reliability 255/255, txload 1/255, rxload 1/255
  Encapsulation PPP, LCP Open
  Open: IPCP, CDPCP, loopback not set
  Keepalive set (10 sec)
! Lines omitted for brevity
```

13

```
R1# show ppp all
Interface/ID  OPEN+ Nego* Fail-       Stage    Peer Address    Peer Name
------------  --------------------- -------- --------------- --------------------
Se0/0/0       LCP+ CHAP+ IPCP+ CDP> LocalT   192.168.2.2     R2
```

The more obvious way to confirm that CHAP works is to use the **show ppp all** command, as shown at the end of Example 13-6. This command lists a single line per PPP connection in the router. The highlighted header in the example is the column where this command lists various PPP protocols and their status, with a plus sign (+) meaning that the listed protocol is OPEN, and a minus sign (−) meaning that the protocol has failed. The highlighted parts of this command in the example confirm that Serial0/0/0 uses PPP, with CHAP authentication, and that CHAP authentication worked (as proved by the OPEN status of the CHAP protocol).

Implementing PPP PAP

PAP configuration differs from CHAP configuration in a couple of ways. First, PAP uses the similar **ppp authentication pap** command instead of the **ppp authentication chap** command. Then, PAP configures the sent username/password pair much differently than CHAP. A router defines the username/password pair it will send using the **ppp pap sent-username** command, configured as an interface subcommand. Once sent, the other router receives that username/password pair, and compares those values with its various **username password** global commands. Figure 13-16 shows a completed configuration for two routers (R1 and R2), with emphasis on matching the **ppp pap sent-username** command on one router with the **username password** commands on the other router.

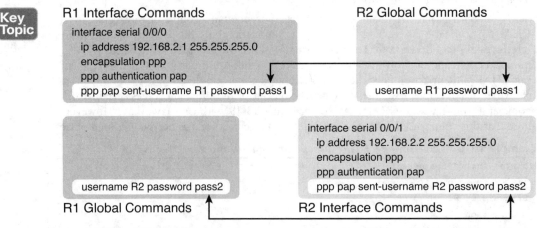

Figure 13-16 *PAP Configuration*

Example 13-7 now shows two commands used to verify PAP operation. In particular, note that the **show interfaces** command tells us nothing more and nothing less as compared to using CHAP authentication. The line protocol status being up confirms that authentication, if configured, worked. (However, nothing in the **show interfaces** command output tells us whether or not CHAP or PAP has been configured.) As with CHAP, the LCP status of Open also confirms that authentication worked, again assuming authentication is configured.

However, just as is the case when using CHAP, or when using no authentication at all, this command does not confirm whether authentication has been configured or, if it is configured, which authentication protocol is used. The better confirmation comes from the **show ppp all** command at the bottom of the example, which identifies PAP as configured on interface Serial0/0/0, and in this case the protocol is OPEN, meaning that authentication worked.

Example 13-7   *Configuring and Verifying PAP Authentication*

```
R1# show interfaces serial 0/0/0
Serial0/0/0 is up, line protocol is up
  Hardware is WIC MBRD Serial
  Description: link to R2
  Internet address is 192.168.2.1/24
  MTU 1500 bytes, BW 1544 Kbit/sec, DLY 20000 usec,
     reliability 255/255, txload 1/255, rxload 1/255
  Encapsulation PPP, LCP Open
  Open: IPCP, CDPCP, loopback not set
  Keepalive set (10 sec)
! Lines omitted for brevity
R1# show ppp all
Interface/ID OPEN+ Nego* Fail-    Stage    Peer Address    Peer Name
------------ --------------------- -------- --------------- --------------------
Se0/0/0      LCP+ PAP+ IPCP+ CDPC> LocalT   192.168.2.2     ciscouser2
```

Finally, note that you can configure the interface to try using the PAP process first, but if the other side does not support PAP, it then tries CHAP. You can configure to try PAP first or CHAP first. Just configure the commands to support both, and add the **ppp authentication pap chap** command to try PAP first, or the **ppp authentication chap pap** command to try CHAP first.

Implementing Multilink PPP

Network designers sometimes use multiple parallel serial links between two routers, rather than a single serial link. That motivation may be to improve availability, so if one link fails, at least the others are working. The motivation may be simple economics—it may be cheaper to install two or three parallel T1 lines (at about 1.5 Mbps each) rather than move up to the next faster type of line, a T3 line, using a fractional T3 service. Whatever the reasons, you end up with a design that looks like the design in Figure 13-17, with multiple serial links between two routers.

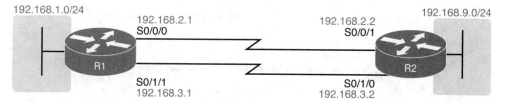

192.168.1.0/24   192.168.9.0/24

192.168.2.1   192.168.2.2
S0/0/0   S0/0/1

R1   R2

S0/1/1   S0/1/0
192.168.3.1   192.168.3.2

13

Figure 13-17   *Multiple Parallel Serial Links Between Routers*

If the network engineer configures the parallel serial links as discussed so far in this chapter, each link has IP addresses and can be used to forward IP packets. To make that happen, the interior routing protocol would run over each of the parallel links, with routing protocol neighbor relationships formed over each link. As a result, each router would learn multiple routes to every remote destination subnet—one such route for each parallel link.

Figure 13-18 shows the concept of having multiple equal-metric routes, one for each of the parallel serial links. It shows the same design as Figure 13-17, with two links. R1 has one route for network 192.168.9.0/24 over the top link, and one over the bottom link. If using EIGRP, R1 would have two EIGRP neighbor relationships with R2, one over each link.

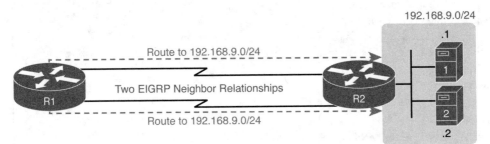

Figure 13-18 *Two IP Routes for One Network, One Per Parallel Serial Link*

The Layer 3 routing logic in Cisco IOS will then balance packets across the multiple links using the routes as shown in the figure. By default, IOS balances on a destination-by-destination address basis—for instance, in Figure 13-18, all packets to 192.168.9.1 might flow over the top link, with all packets going to destination address 192.168.9.2 being routed over the lower link. IOS can be configured to balance on a packet-by-packet basis.

Using the Layer 3 features discussed in the last page or so works, and works well in many cases. However, PPP offers a feature that simplifies the Layer 3 operations in topologies that use multiple parallel PPP links, with a feature called Multilink PPP (MLPPP).

Multilink PPP Concepts

Multilink PPP (MLPPP) is a PPP feature useful when using multiple parallel serial links between two devices. It provides two important features. First, it reduces the Layer 3 complexity by making the multiple serial interfaces on each router look like a single interface from a Layer 3 perspective. Instead of multiple subnets between routers, with multiple routing protocol neighbor relationships, and multiple equal-metric routes learned for each remote subnet, routers would have one subnet between routers, one routing protocol neighbor relationship, and one route per destination subnet. Figure 13-19 shows these main ideas for the same physical topology shown in Figure 13-18, which has multiple physical links.

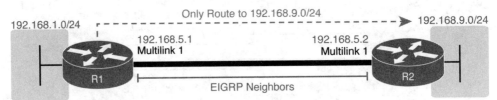

Figure 13-19 *Layer 3 Concept Created by Multilink Interface*

MLPPP makes the multiple physical links work like a single link by using a virtual interface called a multilink interface. The Layer 3 configuration (like IPv4 and IPv6 addresses and routing protocol interface subcommands) is added to the multilink interface. Then the configuration associates the physical serial interfaces with the multilink interface, connecting the Layer 2 logic that works with the multiple serial links with the Layer 3 logic that works on the single multilink interface.

In addition to simplifying Layer 3 details as just described, MLPPP balances the frames sent at Layer 2 over the multiple links. With MLPPP, a router's Layer 3 forwarding logic forwards each packet out the multilink interface. When IOS internally routes a packet out a multilink interface, MLPPP load-balancing logic takes over, encapsulating the packet into a new data link frame, and load balancing the frame.

Interestingly, MLPPP load balances the data link frame by fragmenting the frame into multiple smaller frames, one per active link, as shown with the process in Figure 13-20. Steps 1 and 2 show normal routing, with an encapsulated IP packet arriving at Step 1, and the router making the usual routing decision at Step 2. However, with the packet exiting a multilink interface, MLPPP fragments the packet into pieces (called fragments), with a PPP header/trailer around each, with a few extra header bytes to manage the fragmentation process. The receiving router reassembles the fragments back into the original packet (Step 4), with normal IP routing shown at Step 5.

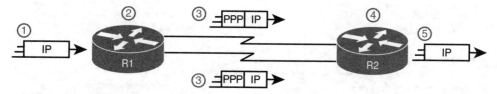
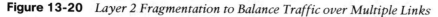

Figure 13-20   *Layer 2 Fragmentation to Balance Traffic over Multiple Links*

MLPPP's load-balancing process allows for some small variations in the sizes of the fragments, but for the most part, Cisco routers will balance the bytes sent equally across the active links in the multilink bundle. For instance, if three links are active, the router forwards about one-third of the byte volume of traffic.

Configuring MLPPP

Implementing MLPPP requires a longer configuration than most features discussed in this book. So first, to set the context a bit, think about these main three configuration requirements for MLPPP:

Key Topic

Step 1.   Configure matching multilink interfaces on the two routers, configuring the interface subcommands for all Layer 3 features (IPv4, IPv6, and routing protocol) under the multilink interfaces (and not on the serial interfaces).

Step 2.   Configure the serial interfaces with all Layer 1 and 2 commands, like **clock rate** (Layer 1) and **ppp authentication** (Layer 2).

Step 3.   Configure some PPP commands on both the multilink and serial interfaces, to both enable MLPPP and associate the multilink interface with the serial interfaces.

13

Figure 13-21 shows all the specific MLPPP commands in a working example. The example is based on the design in Figures 13-19 and 13-20. Note that for space, Figure 13-21 shows the configuration for only one of the two serial interfaces, but all serial interfaces would have the same subcommands when used for MLPPP.

First, focus on the six configuration commands noted with white highlight boxes in Figure 13-21 as pointed to with arrows. The **interface multilink 1** command on each router creates the multilink interface on that router. The network engineer chooses the interface number, but the number must be the same on both routers, or the link will not work. Additionally, the multilink interfaces and the physical serial interfaces must all have both a **ppp multilink group 1** command, and they must all again refer to that same number (1 in this example). Any number in range could be used, but the number must match with the commands highlighted in the figure.

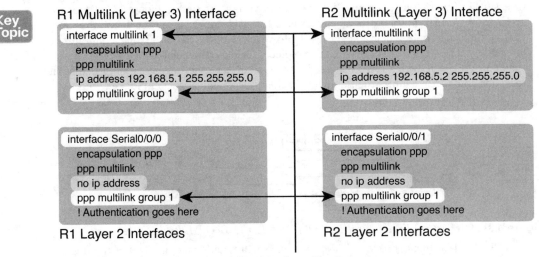

Figure 13-21 *MLPPP Configuration*

Now look at the **ip address** commands. Note that the configuration shows IPv4 addresses configured on the multilink interfaces, but no IPv4 address at all on the serial interface. In short, the multilink interface has the Layer 3 configuration, and the serial interfaces do not. As a result, the routing and routing protocol logic will work with the multilink interface.

Finally, note that both the multilink and serial interfaces have two additional commands: **encapsulation ppp** (which enables PPP), and **ppp multilink** (which adds multilink support).

NOTE Figure 13-21 shows only one serial interface, but each serial interface in the multilink group would need the same configuration.

Verifying MLPPP

To verify that an MLPPP interface is working, it helps to think about the Layer 3 features separately from Layer 1 and Layer 2 details. For Layer 3, all the usual IPv4, IPv6, and routing protocol commands will now list the multilink interface rather than the physical serial interfaces. You can also just ping the IP address on the other end of the multilink to test the link. Example 13-8 shows a few commands to confirm the current working state of the MLPPP link, taken from the working configuration in Figure 13-21.

Example 13-8 *Verifying Layer 3 Operations with an MLPPP Multilink Interface*

```
R1# show ip route
! Legend omitted for brevity


      192.168.1.0/24 is variably subnetted, 2 subnets, 2 masks
C        192.168.1.0/24 is directly connected, GigabitEthernet0/0
L        192.168.1.1/32 is directly connected, GigabitEthernet0/0
      192.168.5.0/24 is variably subnetted, 3 subnets, 2 masks
C        192.168.5.0/24 is directly connected, Multilink1
L        192.168.5.1/32 is directly connected, Multilink1
C        192.168.5.2/32 is directly connected, Multilink1
D      192.168.9.0/24 [90/1343488] via 192.168.5.2, 16:02:07, Multilink1


R1# show ip eigrp interfaces
EIGRP-IPv4 Interfaces for AS(1)

                   Xmit Queue    PeerQ        Mean  Pacing Time  Multicast    Pending
Interface   Peers  Un/Reliable   Un/Reliable  SRTT  Un/Reliable  Flow Timer   Routes
Mu1          1       0/0           0/0          1     0/8           50           0
Gi0/0        1       0/0           0/0          1     0/0           50           0


R1# show ip interface brief
Interface                    IP-Address    OK? Method Status                  Protocol
Embedded-Service-Engine0/0   unassigned    YES NVRAM  administratively down   down
GigabitEthernet0/0           192.168.1.1   YES manual up                      up
GigabitEthernet0/1           unassigned    YES manual up                      up
Serial0/0/0                  unassigned    YES manual up                      up
Serial0/0/1                  unassigned    YES manual administratively down   down
Serial0/1/0                  unassigned    YES NVRAM  administratively down   down
Serial0/1/1                  unassigned    YES NVRAM  up                      up
Multilink1                   192.168.5.1   YES manual up                      up
```

Working from the top of the example to the bottom, note that the IPv4 routing table lists interface multilink 1 as the outgoing interface in a variety of routes. However, the two serial interfaces are not listed at all, because they do not have IP addresses and the router's routing logic works with the multilink interface instead. Similarly, the **show ip eigrp interfaces**

13

command lists interfaces on which EIGRP is enabled, listing Mu1 (Multilink 1), and not listing either of the two serial interfaces in the MLPPP bundle. Finally, note that the **show ip interface brief** command does list both the serial interfaces and the multilink interface, but the output confirms that no IP address has been configured on the serial interfaces, as noted with the "unassigned" text under the IP-Address column.

Each multilink interface has a line and protocol status like any other interface, and if that status is up/up, IOS believes the multilink interface is working. By default, that working state implies that at least one of the physical links in the MLPPP group is also working—that is, some of the physical links can fail, and the multilink stays up. You can always directly verify the serial interfaces in the multilink group with the same commands discussed earlier in the chapter (**show controllers, show interfaces**). Additionally, the two commands in Example 13-9 give some insight into the specifics of MLPPP operation.

Example 13-9 *Verifying Operational Details of an MLPPP Group*

```
R1# show interfaces multilink 1
Multilink1 is up, line protocol is up
  Hardware is multilink group interface
  Internet address is 192.168.5.1/24
  MTU 1500 bytes, BW 3088 Kbit/sec, DLY 20000 usec,
     reliability 255/255, txload 1/255, rxload 1/255
  Encapsulation PPP, LCP Open, multilink Open
  Open: IPCP, CDPCP, loopback not set
  Keepalive set (10 sec)
! lines omitted for brevity


R1# show ppp multilink

Multilink1
  Bundle name: R2
  Remote Username: R2
  Remote Endpoint Discriminator: [1] R2
  Local Username: R1
  Local Endpoint Discriminator: [1] R1
  Bundle up for 16:50:33, total bandwidth 3088, load 1/255
  Receive buffer limit 24000 bytes, frag timeout 1000 ms
    0/0 fragments/bytes in reassembly list
    0 lost fragments, 96 reordered
    0/0 discarded fragments/bytes, 0 lost received
    0x654D7 received sequence, 0x654D5 sent sequence
  Member links: 2 active, 0 inactive (max 255, min not set)
    Se0/1/1, since 16:50:33
    Se0/0/0, since 16:23:16
No inactive multilink interfaces
```

First, notice that the **show interfaces multilink 1** command lists many familiar details and some mentions about multilink. In particular, the output shows the traditional line and protocol status, both in an up state, meaning that the interface is working. On the sixth line, the output mentioned a working multilink state of "Open" in the section about PPP control protocols, confirming that MLPPP is in effect.

Finally, the output of the **show ppp multilink** command identifies the links configured in each multilink bundle, as well as which ones are active. In this case, on R1, interfaces S0/0/0 and S0/1/1 are active, as highlighted at the bottom of the example. The timer to the side shows that both have been active a little over 16 hours. Seeing these two interfaces in the list confirms not only that the physical interfaces are working, but that the MLPPP configuration includes both of these links in multilink group 1.

Troubleshooting Serial Links

This final major section discusses how to isolate and find the root cause of problems related to topics covered earlier in this chapter. Also, this section does not attempt to repeat the IP troubleshooting coverage in Part II of this book, but it does point out some of the possible symptoms on a serial link when a Layer 3 subnet mismatch occurs on opposite ends of a serial link, which prevents the routers from routing packets over the serial link.

A simple **ping** command can determine whether a serial link can or cannot forward IP packets. A ping of the other router's serial IP address—for example, a working **ping 192.168.2.2** command on R1 in Figure 13-11, the figure used for both the HDLC and PPP configuration examples—proves that the link either works or does not.

If the **ping** does not work, the problem could be related to functions at Layer 1, 2, or 3. The best way to isolate which layer is the most likely cause is to examine the interface status codes described in Table 13-5.

Table 13-5   Interface Status Codes and Typical Meanings When a Ping Does Not Work

Line Status	Protocol Status	Likely General Reason/Layer
Administratively down	Down	Interface shutdown
Down	Down	Layer 1
Up	Down	Layer 2
Up	Up	Layer 3

The serial link verification and troubleshooting process should begin with a simple three-step process:

Step 1.   From one router, ping the other router's serial IP address.

Step 2.   If the ping fails, examine the interface status on both routers and investigate problems related to the likely problem areas listed in Table 13-5.

Step 3.   If the ping works, also verify that any routing protocols are exchanging routes over the link, as discussed in Chapter 11, "Troubleshooting IPv4 Routing Protocols."

13

NOTE   The interface status codes can be found using the **show interfaces, show ip interface brief,** and **show interfaces description** commands.

The rest of this section explores the specific items to be examined when the ping fails, based on the combinations of interface status codes listed in Table 13-5.

Troubleshooting Layer 1 Problems

The interface status codes, or interface state, play a key role in isolating the root cause of problems on serial links. In fact, the status on both ends of the link may differ, so it is important to examine the status on both ends of the link to help determine the problem.

For example, a serial link fails when just one of the two routers has administratively disabled its serial interface with the **shutdown** interface subcommand. When one router shuts down its serial interface, the other router sits in a down/down state (line status down, line protocol status down), assuming the second router's interface is not also shut down. The solution is to just configure a **no shutdown** interface configuration command on the interface.

A serial interface with a *down* line status on both ends of the serial link—that is, both ends in a down/down state—usually points to some Layer 1 problem. Figure 13-22 summarizes the most common causes of this state. In the figure, R2's serial interface has no problems at all; the center and left side of the figure show common root causes that then result in R2's serial interface being in a down/down state.

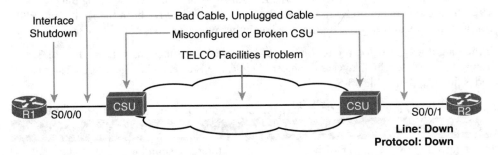

Figure 13-22 *Problems That Result in a Down/Down State on Router R2*

Troubleshooting Layer 2 Problems

Data link layer problems on serial links usually result in at least one of the routers having a serial interface status of up/down. In other words, the line status (the first status code) is up, while the second status (the line protocol status) is down. Table 13-6 lists some of these types of problems.

Table 13-6 Likely Reasons for Data Link Problems on Serial Links

Line Status	Protocol Status	Likely Reason
Up	Down on both ends[1]	Mismatched **encapsulation** commands
Up	Down on one end, up on the other	Keepalive disabled on the end in an up state when using HDLC
Up	Down on both ends	PAP/CHAP authentication failure

[1] In this case, the state may flap from up/up, to up/down, to up/up, and so on, while the router keeps trying to make the encapsulation work.

The first of these problems—a mismatch between the configured data link protocols—is easy to identify and fix. The **show interfaces** command lists the encapsulation type on about the seventh line of the output, so using this command on both routers can quickly identify the problem. Alternatively, a quick look at the configuration, plus remembering that HDLC is the default serial encapsulation, can confirm whether the encapsulations are mismatched. The solution is simple: Reconfigure one of the two routers to match the other router's **encapsulation** command.

The other two root causes require a little more discussion to understand the issue and determine if they are the real root cause. The next two sections take a closer look at each.

Keepalive Failure

The router *keepalive* feature helps a router notice when a link is no longer functioning. Once a router believes the link no longer works, the router can bring down the interface, allowing the routing protocol to converge to use other routes it they exist.

The keepalive function on an interface causes routers to send keepalive messages to each other every keepalive interval, defaulting to 10 seconds. For instance, on a serial link between R1 and R2, R1 sends a keepalive message every 10 seconds, and R2 expects to receive those keepalive messages every 10 seconds. If R2 fails to receive the keepalive messages for a set number of consecutive keepalive intervals (usually three or five intervals), R2 believes R1 has failed, and R2 changes the link to an up/down state. The keepalive process happens in both directions as well—R1 sends keepalives with R2 expecting to receive them, and R2 sends keepalives with R1 expecting to receive them.

A keepalive mismatch occurs when one router has keepalives enabled and one router does not. That combination is a mistake, and should not be used. Note that this keepalive mismatch mistake only breaks HDLC links; the PPP keepalive feature prevents the problem. Figure 13-23 shows one such example with HDLC and with R1 mistakenly disabling keepalives.

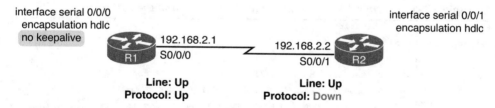

Figure 13-23 *Results when Using HDLC with a Keepalive Mismatch*

Note that the router interface that disables keepalives remains in an up/up state. In the scenario shown in Figure 13-23, R2's interface fails because

■ R1 does not send keepalive messages, because keepalives are disabled.

■ R2 still expects to receive keepalive messages, because keepalives are enabled.

You can verify the keepalive setting by looking at the configuration or by using the **show interfaces** command. The examples in this chapter list several examples of the **show interfaces** command that happen to list the text "Keepalive set (10 second)," meaning that keepalives are enabled with a 10-second interval. R1 would list the text "Keepalive not set" in this case.

13

PAP and CHAP Authentication Failure

As mentioned earlier, a failure in the PAP/CHAP authentication process results in both router interfaces failing to an up and down state. As shown in Examples 13-6 and 13-7, you can use the **show interfaces** and **show ppp all** commands to look further into the status of the PPP authentication process. By doing so, you can isolate and discover the root cause of why the interface is in an up/down state, ruling out or ruling in PPP authentication as the root cause.

Another deeper method to troubleshoot PPP authentication problems uses the **debug ppp authentication** command.

CHAP uses a three-message exchange, as shown back in Figure 13-14, with a set of messages flowing for authentication in each direction by default. If you enable the debug, shut down the link, and bring it back up, you will see debug messages that match that three-way exchange. If authentication fails, you see a failure message at the point at which the process fails, which may help you decide what specifically needs to be fixed.

Example 13-10 shows the three related debug messages when a link comes up. The network connects R1's S0/0/0 to router R2. The example extracts the three related debug messages from what would be a few dozen debug messages, so you would have to look for these. However, the output highlights the important parts of the process as seen back in Figure 13-14, as follows:

1. The "O" refers to output, meaning that this local router, R1, has output (sent) a Challenge message. Note the "from R1" at the end of the debug message, stating who the message is from.

2. The "I" refers to input, meaning that this local router, R1, has input (received) a Response message. Note the "from R2" at the end of the line.

3. The "O FAILURE" refers to R1 sending out a Failure message, telling R2 that the authentication process failed.

Example 13-10 *Debug Messages on Router R1 Confirming the Failure of CHAP*

```
R1# debug ppp authentication
PPP authentication debugging is on
! Lines omitted for brevity
*Nov 18 23:45:48.820: Se0/0/0 CHAP: O CHALLENGE id 1 len 23 from "R1"
*Nov 18 23:45:48.820: Se0/0/0 CHAP: I RESPONSE id 1 len 23 from "R2"
*Nov 18 23:45:48.820: Se0/0/0 CHAP: O FAILURE id 1 len 25 msg is "Authentication
  failed"
```

While using a **debug** command may tell us something about the problem, it does not always point to the specific command that is misconfigured. In this case, the fact that both routers send at least one CHAP message implies that both router interfaces can send frames, and that they have enabled CHAP. It looks more like R1 has rejected the hashed password supplied by R2. Note that this example was built by changing the **username** command to have an incorrect password, so that the CHAP process worked but the authentication was rejected.

Troubleshooting Layer 3 Problems

This chapter suggests that the best starting place to troubleshoot serial links is to ping the IP address of the router on the other end of the link—specifically, the IP address on the serial link. Interestingly, the serial link can be in an up and up state but the ping can still fail because of Layer 3 misconfiguration. In some cases, the ping may work but the routing protocols might not be able to exchange routes. This short section examines the symptoms, which differ slightly depending on whether HDLC or PPP is used and the root cause.

First, consider an HDLC link on which the physical and data link details are working fine. In this case, both routers' interfaces are in an up and up state. However, if the IP addresses configured on the serial interfaces on the two routers are in different subnets, a ping to the IP address on the other end of the link will fail because the routers do not have a matching route. For example, consider an example with a working HDLC link with the IP addresses shown earlier in Figure 13-23. Then, if R1's serial IP address remained 192.168.2.1, and R2's was changed to 192.168.3.2 (instead of 192.168.2.2), still with a mask of /24, the two routers would have connected routes to different subnets. They would not have a route matching the opposite router's serial IP address.

Finding and fixing a mismatched subnet problem with HDLC links is relatively simple. You can find the problem by doing the usual first step of pinging the IP address on the other end of the link and failing. If both interfaces have a status of up/up, the problem is likely this mismatched IP subnet.

For PPP links with the same IP address/mask misconfiguration, the ping to the other router's IP address actually works. However, the IP subnet mismatch still prevents EIGRP and OSPF neighbor relationships from forming, so it is still a good idea to follow the rules and put both serial interface IP addresses in the same subnet.

PPP makes the ping work with the mismatched subnet by adding a host route, with a /32 prefix length, for the IP address of the other router. Example 13-11 shows the working PPP link with addresses in different subnets.

> **NOTE** A route with a /32 prefix, representing a single host, is called a *host route*.

Example 13-11 *PPP Allowing a Ping over a Serial Link, Even with Mismatched Subnets*

```
R1# show ip route
! Legend omitted for brevity
      192.168.1.0/24 is variably subnetted, 2 subnets, 2 masks
C        192.168.1.0/24 is directly connected, GigabitEthernet0/0
L        192.168.1.1/32 is directly connected, GigabitEthernet0/0
      192.168.2.0/24 is variably subnetted, 2 subnets, 2 masks
C        192.168.2.0/24 is directly connected, Serial0/0/0
L        192.168.2.1/32 is directly connected, Serial0/0/0
      192.168.3.0/32 is subnetted, 1 subnets
C        192.168.3.2 is directly connected, Serial0/0/0

R1# ping 192.168.3.2
```

13

```
Type escape sequence to abort.
Sending 5, 100-byte ICMP Echos to 192.168.3.2, timeout is 2 seconds:
!!!!!
Success rate is 100 percent (5/5), round-trip min/avg/max = 1/2/4 ms
```

The first highlighted line in the example shows the normal connected route on the serial link, for network 192.168.2.0/24. R1 thinks this subnet is the subnet connected to S0/0/0 because of R1's configured IP address (192.168.2.1/24). The second highlighted line shows the host route created by PPP, specifically for R2's new serial IP address (192.168.3.2). (R2 will have a similar route for 192.168.2.1/32, R1's serial IP address.) So, both routers have a route to allow them to forward packets to the IP address on the other end of the link, even though the other router's address is in a different subnet. This extra host route allows the ping to the other side of the serial link to work in spite of the addresses on each end being in different subnets.

Table 13-7 summarizes the behavior on HDLC and PPP links when the IP addresses on each end do not reside in the same subnet but no other problems exist.

Table 13-7   Summary of Symptoms for Mismatched Subnets on Serial Links

Symptoms When IP Addresses on a Serial Link Are in Different Subnets	HDLC	PPP
Does a ping of the other router's serial IP address work?	No	Yes
Can routing protocols exchange routes over the link?	No	No

Chapter Review

One key to doing well on the exams is to perform repetitive spaced review sessions. Review this chapter's material using either the tools in the book, DVD, or interactive tools for the same material found on the book's companion website. Refer to the "Your Study Plan" element for more details. Table 13-8 outlines the key review elements and where you can find them. To better track your study progress, record when you completed these activities in the second column.

Table 13-8   Chapter Review Tracking

Review Element	Review Date(s)	Resource Used
Review key topics		Book, DVD/website
Review key terms		Book, DVD/website
Repeat DIKTA questions		Book, PCPT
Do labs		Blog
Review memory tables		Book, DVD/website
Review config checklists		Book, DVD/website
Review command tables		Book

Review All the Key Topics

Key Topic

Table 13-9   Key Topics for Chapter 13

Key Topic Element	Description	Page Number
Table 13-3	Speeds for WAN links per the T-carrier system	334
Figure 13-7	Role of the CSU/DSU and the router as DCE and DTE	335
List	PPP features	340
List	Comparison of PPP LCP and NCP	341
Figure 13-13	Example of messages sent by PAP	342
Figure 13-14	Example of messages sent by CHAP	343
Figure 13-16	Sample PAP configuration	346
List	MLPPP major configuration concepts	349
Figure 13-21	Sample MLPPP configuration	350

Key Terms You Should Know

leased line, telco, serial link, WAN link, T1, DS0, DS1, T3, customer premises equipment, CSU/DSU, serial cable, DCE, DTE, HDLC, PPP, CHAP, PAP, IP Control Protocol, keepalive, Link Control Protocol, Multilink PPP

Command References

Tables 13-10 and 13-11 list configuration and verification commands used in this chapter. As an easy review exercise, cover the left column in a table, read the right column, and try to recall the command without looking. Then repeat the exercise, covering the right column, and try to recall what the command does.

Table 13-10   Chapter 13 Configuration Command Reference

Command	Description
encapsulation {hdlc | ppp}	Interface subcommand that defines the serial data-link protocol
[no] shutdown	Administratively disables (**shutdown**) or enables (**no shutdown**) the interface in whose mode the command is issued
clock rate *speed*	Serial interface subcommand that, when used on an interface with a DCE cable, sets the clock speed in bps
bandwidth *speed-kbps*	Interface subcommand that sets the router's opinion of the link speed, in kilobits per second, but has no effect on the actual speed
description *text*	Interface subcommand that can set a text description of the interface
ppp authentication {pap | chap}	Interface subcommand that enables only PAP or only CHAP authentication
username *name* password *secret*	Global command that sets the password that this router expects to use when authenticating the router with the listed hostname
ppp pap sent-username *name* password *secret*	Interface subcommand that defines the username/password pair sent over this link when using PAP authentication

13

Command	Description
interface multilink *number*	Creates a multilink interface and moves the user to interface configuration mode on that interface
ppp multilink	Interface subcommand that enables MLPPP features
ppp multilink group *number*	Interface subcommand that associates the interface with a particular multilink interface and multilink group

Table 13-11   Chapter 13 EXEC Command Reference

Command	Description
show interfaces [*type number*]	Lists statistics and details of interface configuration, including the encapsulation type
show interfaces [*type number*] description	Lists a single line per interface (or if the interface is included, just one line of output total) that lists the interface status and description
show ip interface brief	Lists one line of output per interface, with IP address and interface status
show controllers serial *number*	Lists whether a cable is connected to the interface, and if so, whether it is a DTE or DCE cable
show ppp multilink	Lists detailed status information about each of the PPP multilink groups configured on the router
show ppp all	Lists one line of status information per PPP link on the router, including the status for each control protocol
debug ppp authentication	Generates messages for each step in the PAP or CHAP authentication process
debug ppp negotiation	Generates **debug** messages for the LCP and NCP negotiation messages sent between the devices

CHAPTER 14

Private WANs with Ethernet and MPLS

This chapter covers the following exam topics:

3.0 WAN Technologies

3.4 Describe WAN topology options

   3.4.a Point-to-point

   3.4.b Hub and spoke

   3.4.c Full mesh

3.5 Describe WAN access connectivity options

   3.5.a MPLS

   3.5.b MetroEthernet

This chapter details the concepts behind two types of private WAN service: Metro Ethernet (MetroE) and Multiprotocol Label Switching (MPLS). As usual for this book's discussion of WAN services, the service is viewed mostly from the perspective of the enterprise, as the customer of some WAN service provider (SP). That means the discussion focuses on what the enterprise receives from the service, rather than how the service provider implements the service inside its network. (Note that Cisco's Service Provider certification track explores the details of how an SP implements its network.)

This chapter reflects probably the biggest single change to what Cisco includes for WAN topics in the CCNA R&S certification for the entire history of the certification. Cisco introduced the CCNA certification back in 1998 (now called CCNA Routing and Switching). At that time, Frame Relay was the dominant WAN technology, and leased lines, an older technology, were still used. Cisco has included both leased lines and Frame Relay in CCNA R&S for the certification's entire history until the release of new exams in 2016, with the CCNA 200-125 exam (which is sometimes referenced by Cisco as CCNA v3.0). Frame Relay is not mentioned at all in the current exam topics, although serial links do still get a brief mention because of some related data link protocols.

Cisco replaces Frame Relay in the exam topics with two notable WAN technologies more commonly used today: Metro Ethernet and MPLS. For perspective, Figure 14-1 shows a timeline of approximately when some of the more common private WAN services entered the marketplace.

This chapter begins with Metro Ethernet in the first major section, followed by MPLS VPNs in the second, even though MPLS VPNs came first historically. Introducing Metro Ethernet first should be easier to learn, given the many similarities between using Ethernet in the LAN and using Ethernet in the WAN.

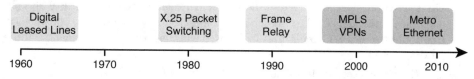

Figure 14-1 *General Timeline of Entering the Market for Some Private WAN Services*

> **NOTE** For those of you interested in reading about the old Frame Relay topics, the previous edition's two chapters about Frame Relay are included with this book, as Appendixes H and I.

"Do I Know This Already?" Quiz

Take the quiz (either here, or use the PCPT software) if you want to use the score to help you decide how much time to spend on this chapter. The answers are at the bottom of the page following the quiz, and the explanations are in DVD Appendix C and in the PCPT software.

Table 14-1 "Do I Know This Already?" Foundation Topics Section-to-Question Mapping

Foundation Topics Section	Questions
Metro Ethernet	1–3
Multiprotocol Label Switching (MPLS)	4–6

1. Which of the following topology terms most closely describe the topology created by a Metro Ethernet Tree (E-Tree) service? (Choose two answers.)

   a. Full mesh

   b. Partial mesh

   c. Hub and Spoke

   d. Point-to-point

2. Which of the following is the most likely technology used for an access link to a Metro Ethernet service?

   a. 100Base-LX10

   b. High-speed TDM (for example, T3, E3)

   c. MPLS

   d. 100Base-T

3. An enterprise uses a Metro Ethernet WAN with an Ethernet LAN (E-LAN) service, with the company headquarters plus ten remote sites connected to the service. The enterprise uses EIGRP at all sites, with one router connected to the service from each site. Which of the following are true about the Layer 3 details most likely used with this service and design? (Choose two answers.)

   a. The WAN uses one IP subnet.

   b. The WAN uses ten or more IP subnets.

   c. A remote site router would have one EIGRP neighbor.

   d. A remote site router would have ten EIGRP neighbors.

4. An enterprise uses an MPLS Layer 3 VPN with the company headquarters connected plus ten remote sites connected to the service. The enterprise uses EIGRP at all sites, with one router connected to the service from each site. Which of the following are true about the Layer 3 details most likely used with this service and design? (Choose two answers.)

    a. The WAN uses one IP subnet.

    b. The WAN uses ten or more IP subnets.

    c. A remote site router would have one EIGRP neighbor.

    d. A remote site router would have ten or more EIGRP neighbors.

5. Which of the following answers is most accurate about access link options for an MPLS network?

    a. Uses only TDM (T1, T3, E1, E3, etc.)

    b. Uses only Ethernet

    c. Uses only DSL and cable

    d. Uses a wide variety of Layer 1 and Layer 2 networking technologies

6. An enterprise connects 20 sites into an MPLS VPN WAN. The enterprise uses OSPF for IPv4 routes at all sites. Consider the OSPF area design options, and the PE-CE links. Which of the following answers is most accurate about OSPF areas and the PE-CE links?

    a. The PE-CE link may or may not be chosen to be in backbone area 0.

    b. The PE-CE link must not be in the backbone area 0.

    c. The PE-CE link must be in the backbone area 0.

    d. The PE-CE link will not be in any OSPF area.

Foundation Topics

Metro Ethernet

Metro Ethernet (MetroE) includes a variety of WAN services with some common features. Each MetroE service uses Ethernet physical links to connect the customer's device to the service provider's device. Second, the service is a Layer 2 service in that the WAN provider forwards Ethernet frames from one customer device to another.

To begin the conversation with a basic view, Metro Ethernet acts much as if the WAN service were created by one Ethernet switch, as shown in Figure 14-2. The figure shows four sites in the same company, each with a router. Each router is connected to the WAN service with an Ethernet link of some kind; those Ethernet links typically use one of the fiber Ethernet standards due to the distances involved. From the customer's perspective (that is, from the perspective of the enterprise that is the customer of the WAN SP), the WAN service acts like a LAN switch in that it forwards Ethernet frames.

NOTE Throughout this chapter, the word *customer* refers to the customer of the service provider; that is, the enterprise that is purchasing the WAN service.

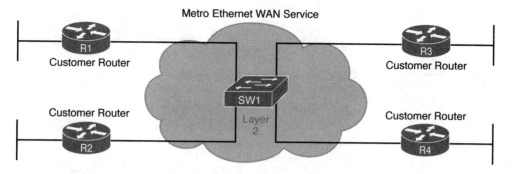

Figure 14-2 *Metro Ethernet Concept as a Large Ethernet Switch*

Although the main concept makes a Metro Ethernet service act like a big LAN switch, there are many options, and you should understand the basics of each. Additionally, many customers connect to a Metro Ethernet service with either routers or Layer 3 switches, which brings up some Layer 3 issues with IP addressing and routing protocols. This section closes with a discussion of the Layer 3 issues.

Metro Ethernet Physical Design and Topology

From an enterprise perspective, to use a Metro Ethernet service, each site needs to connect to the service with (at least) one Ethernet link. There is no need to connect each enterprise router to each other enterprise router directly with a physical link. For instance, in Figure 14-2 in the previous section, each of the four enterprise routers connects to the SP's MetroE service with one physical Ethernet link, rather than connecting directly to the other enterprise routers.

From the SP perspective, the SP needs to build a network to create the Metro Ethernet service. To keep costs lower the SP puts a device (typically an Ethernet switch) physically near to as many customer sites as possible, in an SP facility called a *point of presence* (PoP). Those SP switches need to be near enough to many customer locations so that some Ethernet standard supports the distance from the SP's PoP to each customer site. Figure 14-3 collects some of these terms and ideas together.

Working through the details in the figure, the physical link between the customer and the SP is called an *access link* or, when using Ethernet specifically, an *Ethernet access link*. Everything that happens on that link falls within the definition of the *user network interface*, or UNI. Breaking down the term UNI, the word *network* refers to the SP's network, while the SP's customer (the enterprise) is known as the *user* of the network.

Focusing on the center of Figure 14-3, the SP's network remains hidden to a great extent. The SP promises to deliver Ethernet frames across the WAN. To do that, the access links connect to an Ethernet switch. As you can imagine, the switch will look at the Ethernet header's MAC address fields and at 802.1Q trunking headers for VLAN tags, but the details inside the network remain hidden.

Answers to the "Do I Know This Already?" quiz:

1 B, C **2** A **3** A, D **4** B, C **5** D **6** A

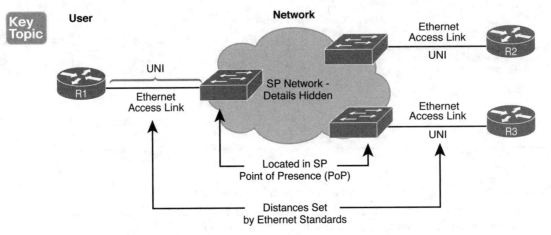

Figure 14-3 *Ethernet Access Links into a Metro Ethernet Service*

> **NOTE** The term *carrier Ethernet*, meaning Ethernet WAN service provider by a carrier (that is, service provider) is also used instead of Metro Ethernet. Metro Ethernet began as a technology used to create networks in metropolitan areas of cities (generically called metropolitan-area networks, or MANs), so the name Metro Ethernet made more sense. Carrier Ethernet is a better name today, because it is not limited to a single city.

The UNI references a variety of standards, including the fact that any IEEE Ethernet standard can be used for the access link. Table 14-2 lists some of the standards you might expect to see used as Ethernet access links, given their support of longer distances than the standards that use UTP cabling.

Table 14-2 IEEE Ethernet Standards Useful for Metro Ethernet Access

Name	Speed	Distance
100Base-LX10	100 Mbps	10 Km
1000Base-LX	1 Gbps	5 Km
1000Base-LX10	1 Gbps	10 Km
1000Base-ZX	1 Gbps	100 Km
10GBase-LR	10 Gbps	10 Km
10GBase-ER	10 Gbps	40 Km

Ethernet WAN Services and Topologies

Beyond adding a physical Ethernet connection from each site into the SP's Metro Ethernet WAN service, the enterprise must choose between several possible variations of MetroE services. Those variations use different topologies that meet different customer needs.

MEF (http://www.mef.net) defines the standards for Metro Ethernet, including the specifications for different kinds of MetroE services. Table 14-3 lists three service types described in this chapter, and their topologies. The next few pages after the table go into more depth about each.

Key Topic

Table 14-3   Three MEF Service Types and Their Topologies

MEF Service Name	MEF Short Name	Topology Terms	Description
Ethernet Line Service	E-Line	Point-to-point	Two customer premise equipment (CPE) devices can exchange Ethernet frames, similar in concept to a leased line.
Ethernet LAN Service	E-LAN	Full mesh	Acts like a LAN, in that all devices can send frames to all other devices.
Ethernet Tree Service	E-Tree	Hub-and-spoke; partial mesh; point-to-multipoint	A central site can communicate to a defined set of remote sites, but the remote sites cannot communicate directly.

NOTE   You may see the term *Virtual Private Wire Service* (VPWS) used for what MEF defines as E-Line service, and *Virtual Private LAN Service* (VPLS) used for what MEF defines as E-LAN service. You might also see the term *Ethernet over MPLS* (EoMPLS). All these terms refer to cases in which the SP uses MPLS internally to create what the customer sees as an Ethernet WAN service.

Ethernet Line Service (Point-to-Point)

The Ethernet Line Service, or E-Line, is the simplest of the Metro Ethernet services. The customer connects two sites with access links. Then the MetroE service allows the two customer devices to send Ethernet frames to each other. Figure 14-4 shows an example, with routers as the CPE devices.

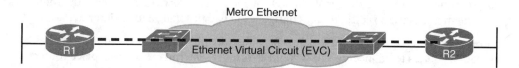

Figure 14-4   *Point-point Topology in Metro Ethernet E-Line Service Between Routers*

As with all MetroE services, the promise made by the service is to deliver Ethernet frames across the service, as if the two customer routers had a rather long crossover cable connected between them. In fact, the E-Line service is the same Ethernet WAN service you have already seen in many examples throughout the ICND1 Cert Guide and in this book. For instance, in this case:

- The routers would use physical Ethernet interfaces.
- The routers would configure IP addresses in the same subnet as each other.
- Their routing protocols would become neighbors and exchange routes.

The MetroE specifications define the concept of an *Ethernet Virtual Connection*, or EVC, to define which user (customer) devices can communicate with which. By definition, an E-Line service (as shown in Figure 14-4) creates a point-to-point EVC, meaning that the service allows two endpoints to communicate.

It may be that an enterprise wants to implement a network exactly as shown in Figure 14-4, with two sites and two routers, with MetroE WAN connectivity using an E-Line service. Other variations exist, even other variations using an E-Line.

For example, think of a common enterprise WAN topology with a central site and 100 remote sites. As shown so far, with an E-Line service, the central site router would need 100 Ethernet interfaces to connect to those 100 remote sites. That could be expensive. As an alternative, the enterprise could use the design partially shown in Figure 14-5 (just three remote sites shown). In this case:

- The central site router uses a single 10-Gbps access link.
- The central site connects to 100 E-Lines (only three shown).
- All the E-Lines send and receive frames over the same access link.

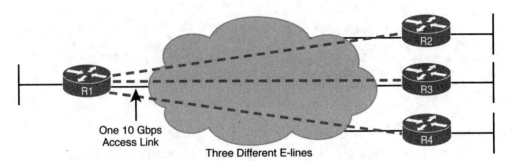

Figure 14-5 *Using Multiple E-Lines, One for Each Remote Site*

Note that this chapter does not get into the configuration details for WAN services. However, designs like Figure 14-5, with multiple E-Line services on a single access link, use 802.1Q trunking, with a different VLAN ID for each E-Line service. As a result, the router configuration can use a typical router configuration with trunking and subinterfaces.

Before moving on to the next MetroE service, note that the customer could use switches instead of routers to connect to the WAN. Historically, enterprise engineers place routers at the edge of a WAN, in part because that device connected to both the WAN and the LAN, and the LAN and WAN used different types of physical interfaces and different data link protocols. As a result of how routing works, routers served as the perfect device to sit at the edge between LAN and WAN (called the WAN edge). With MetroE, the LAN and WAN are both Ethernet, so an Ethernet switch becomes an option.

Ethernet LAN Service (Full Mesh)

Imagine an enterprise needs to connect several sites to a WAN, and the goal is to allow every site to send frames directly to every other site. You could do that with E-Lines, but you would need possibly lots of E-Lines. For instance, to connect three sites with E-Lines so that each site could send frames directly to each other, you only need three E-Lines. But with four, five, and six sites, you would need 6, 10, and 15 E-Lines, respectively. Get up to 20 sites for which all could send frames directly to each other, and you would need 190 E-Lines. (The formula is $N(N - 1) / 2$.)

The people who created MetroE anticipated the need for designs that allow a full mesh—that is, for each pair of nodes in the service to send frames to each other directly. In fact, allowing all devices to send directly to every other device sounds a lot like an Ethernet LAN, so the MetroE service is called an *Ethernet LAN service*, or E-LAN.

One E-LAN service allows all devices connected to that service to send Ethernet frames directly to every other device, just as if the Ethernet WAN service were one big Ethernet switch. Figure 14-6 shows a representation of a single E-LAN EVC. In this case, the one EVC connects to four customer sites, creating one E-LAN. Routers R1, R2, R3, and R4 can all send frames directly to each other. They would also all be in the same Layer 3 subnet on the WAN.

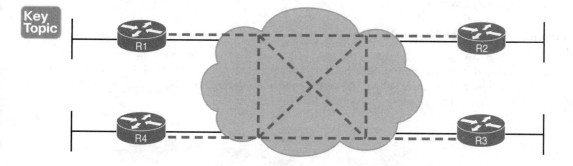

Figure 14-6 *MetroE Ethernet LAN Service—Any-to-Any Forwarding over the Service*

An E-LAN service connects the sites in a full mesh. The term *full mesh* refers to a design that, for a set of devices, creates a direct communication path for each pair. In contrast, a partial mesh refers to a design in which only some of the pairs can communicate directly. Ethernet Tree service (E-Trees), as discussed in the next topic, create a partial mesh design.

Ethernet Tree Service (Hub and Spoke)

The Ethernet Tree service (E-Tree) creates a WAN topology in which the central site device can send Ethernet frames directly to each remote (leaf) site, but the remote (leaf) sites can send only to the central site. Figure 14-7 shows the topology, again with a single EVC. In this case, Router R1 is the root site, and can send to all three remote sites. Routers R2, R3, and R4 can send only to R1.

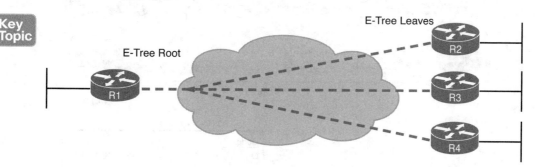

Figure 14-7 *E-Tree Service Creates a Hub-and-Spoke Topology*

With an E-Tree, the central site serves as the root of a tree, and each remote site as one of the leaves. The topology goes by many names: partial mesh, hub-and-spoke, and point-to-multipoint. Regardless of the term you use, an E-Tree service creates a service that works well for designs with a central site plus many remote sites.

Layer 3 Design Using Metro Ethernet

Now that you know the basics of the E-Line (point-to-point), E-LAN (full mesh), and E-Tree (point-to-multipoint, hub-and-spoke) services, this next topic reviews some Layer 3 design details when using each of these three services. That is, if the enterprise uses routers or Layer 3 switches as its WAN edge devices, how should the engineer plan for IP addresses and subnets? What is the impact on routing protocols? This section answers those questions.

Note that this section uses routers as the enterprise's devices, but the concepts apply to Layer 3 switches as well.

Layer 3 Design with E-Line Service

Every E-Line uses a point-to-point topology. As a result, the two routers on the ends of an E-Line need to be in the same subnet. Similarly, when an enterprise uses multiple E-Lines, each should be in a different subnet. As an example, consider Figure 14-8, which shows two E-Lines, both of which connect to Router R1 on the left.

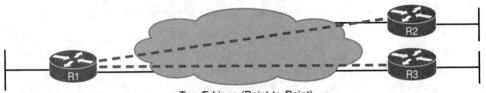

Two E-Lines (Point-to-Point)

Figure 14-8 *Routing Protocol Neighbor Relationships over Metro Ethernet E-Line*

Focusing on the E-Lines, and ignoring the access links for the most part, think of each E-Line as a subnet. Each router needs an IP address in each subnet, and the subnets need to be unique. All the addresses come from the enterprise's IP address space. Figure 14-9 shows an example of the addresses, subnets, and three OSPF-learned routes in the routing table of R3.

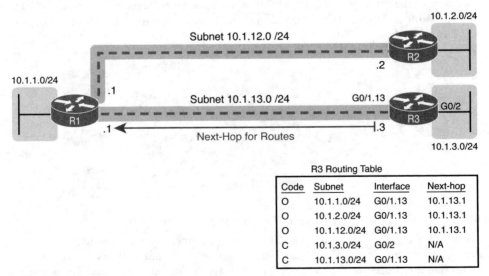

R3 Routing Table

Code	Subnet	Interface	Next-hop
O	10.1.1.0/24	G0/1.13	10.1.13.1
O	10.1.2.0/24	G0/1.13	10.1.13.1
O	10.1.12.0/24	G0/1.13	10.1.13.1
C	10.1.3.0/24	G0/2	N/A
C	10.1.13.0/24	G0/1.13	N/A

Figure 14-9 *Layer 3 Forwarding Between Remote Sites—Through Central Site*

Examine the IP routing table in the lower right of the figure, first focusing on the route to subnet 10.1.1.0/24, which is the LAN subnet off Router R1. R3's route points to a next-hop router IP address that is R1's IP address on the Ethernet WAN, specifically the address on the other side of the E-Line that connects R1 and R3. This route should not be a surprise: For R3 to send packets to a subnet connected to R1, R3 sends the packets to R1. Also, it happens to use a subinterface (G0/1.13), which means that the design is using 802.1Q trunking on the link.

Next, look at R3's route for subnet 10.1.2.0/24, which supports the fact that R3 cannot send packets directly to R2 with the current WAN design. R3 does not have an E-Line that allows R3 to send frames directly to R2. R3 will not become routing protocol neighbors with R2 either. So, R3 will learn its route for subnet 10.1.2.0/24 from R1, with R1's 10.1.13.1 address as the next-hop address. As a result, when forwarding packets, R3 will forward packets to R1, which will then forward them over the other E-Line to R2.

Layer 3 Design with E-LAN Service

If you connected four routers to one LAN switch, all in the same VLAN, what would you expect for the IP addresses on those routers? And if all four routers used the same routing protocol, which would become neighbors? Typically, with four routers connected to the same switch, on the same VLAN, using the same routing protocol, normally all four routers would have IP addresses in the same subnet, and all would become neighbors.

On an E-LAN service, the same IP addressing design is used, with the same kinds of routing protocol neighbor relationships. Figure 14-10 shows an example that includes subnets and addresses, plus one route as an example. Note that the four routers connected to the E-LAN service in the center all have addresses in subnet 10.1.99.0/24.

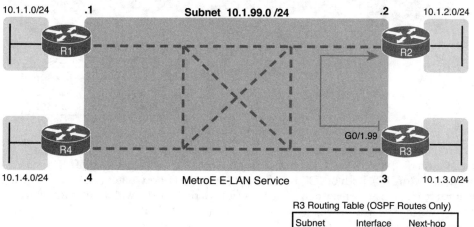

R3 Routing Table (OSPF Routes Only)		
Subnet	Interface	Next-hop
10.1.2.0/24	G0/1.99	**10.1.99.2**
10.1.1.0/24	G0/1.99	10.1.99.1
10.1.4.0/24	G0/1.99	10.1.99.4

Figure 14-10 *Layer 3 Forwarding Between Sites with E-LAN Service*

Look at R3's routing table in the figure, the route from R3 to R2's LAN subnet (10.1.2.0/24). In this case, R3's next-hop address is the WAN address on R2 (10.1.99.2), and R3 will send packets (encapsulated in Ethernet frames) directly to R2. Note also that the other two routes in the routing table list the next-hop addresses of R1 (10.1.99.1) and R4 (10.1.99.4).

Layer 3 Design with E-Tree Service

With an E-Tree service, the Layer 3 design again matches the EVC. That is, all the devices using the same single EVC have an address in the same subnet. However, an E-Tree can present some challenges for routing protocols, because of the three services discussed in this chapter, it is the only one in which some of the sites in the same EVC cannot send frames directly to each other.

For example, Figure 14-11 shows one E-Tree service with R1 as the root. Routers R2 and R3, as leaves, cannot send frames directly to each other, and therefore do not form routing protocol neighbor relationships. However, all three connect to the same E-Tree service. As a result:

■ All three routers have an IP address in the same subnet (10.1.123.0/24).

■ R1 will form a routing protocol neighbor relationship with both R2 and R3, but R2 will not form a routing protocol neighbor relationship with R3.

■ As a result, packets between the leaf sites will flow through the root site.

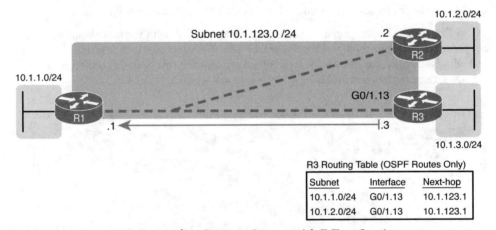

Figure 14-11 *Layer 3 Forwarding Between Leaves with E-Tree Service*

The routing (forwarding) process follows the path of the EVC, as shown in R3's routing table in the figure. The two routes are for remote subnets 10.1.1.0/24 (off R1) and 10.1.2.0/24 (off R2). Both of R3's routes list R1 as the next-hop router (10.1.123.1), because that is the only possible next-hop router available to the leaf site with Router R3 on the WAN. When R3 needs to send packets to subnet 10.1.2.0/24, R3 will route them to R1, which will then route them to R2.

This example may seem a lot like the example with E-Lines shown with Figure 14-9, but there are a couple of key differences. First, an E-Tree uses one subnet for all devices on the E-Tree service, while the example showing multiple E-Lines in Figure 14-9 shows one subnet for each (point-to-point) E-Line. Additionally, some routing protocols require additional configuration effort to work when using an E-Tree service, but those details are beyond the scope of this book.

Ethernet Virtual Circuit Bandwidth Profiles

Before leaving MetroE to move on to MPLS, it helps to consider some ideas about data usage over the WAN links and a whole topic area related to EVC Bandwidth Profiles (BWP).

First, ignoring MetroE for a moment, anyone who has shopped for mobile phone data plans in the 2010s has already thought about data usage with carrier networks. With mobile phones, many carriers offer some kind of tiered pricing: the more data you want to send and receive, the more money you spend per month. Why do they charge more based on usage? The SP spends a lot of capital and a lot of ongoing operational expense to build and operate its network. It seems fair to charge those who use less of the network a little less money, and those who use more a little more money. Simple enough.

Most private WAN services use the same kind of usage-based pricing, and this last MetroE topic discusses some of the terminology and concepts.

The first big idea is this: The access links transmit bits at a set predefined speed based on Ethernet standards. Each Ethernet access link on a MetroE WAN uses a specific Ethernet standard that runs at a specific speed. Those speeds are 10 Mbps, 100 Mbps, 1000 Mbps (that is, 1 Gbps), 10 Gbps, and so on. And while the IEEE has begun adding some new speeds for Ethernet standards, speeds that are not a multiple of 10 versus the next slower speed, the point is this: If a site's MetroE access link is using an Ethernet standard that is a 100-Mbps standard, then the bits are transmitted at 100 Mbps.

At the same time, the MetroE SP wants to be able to charge customers based on usage, and to be a little more flexible than pricing based on the speed of the access links. These final few pages of the MetroE topics in this chapter show how a MetroE SP can charge for speeds other than the access link speeds.

Charging for the Data (Bandwidth) Used

Think through this scenario. A potential customer looks at a MetroE provider's pricing. This customer wants an E-Line service between two sites only. They know that they need at least 100 Mbps of capacity (that is, bandwidth) between the sites. But because the service has the word "Ethernet" in it, the potential customer thinks the service is either 10 Mbps, 100 Mbps, 1 Gbps, and so on. So they look up pricing for an E-Line service at those prices, and think:

- **100 Mbps:** Reasonably good price, but we need more capacity
- **1000 Mbps:** More than we want to spend, it's enough capacity, but probably too much

As it turns out, what this customer really wants is 200 Mbps between the two sites. However, there is no Ethernet standard that runs at 200 Mbps, so there is no way to use access links that run at 200 Mbps. But there is a solution: an E-Line service, with a Bandwidth Profile that defines a 200-Mbps committed information rate (CIR) over the point-to-point EVC between the customer's two routers. Figure 14-12 shows the ideas and terms.

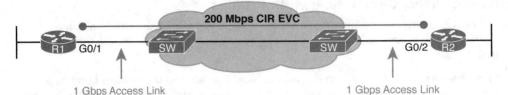

Figure 14-12   *Example: 200-Mbps CIR Supported by 1-Gbps Access Links*

The big ideas are simple, although the methods to control the data are new. The SP, per the contract with the customer, agrees to not only forward Ethernet frames between the two E-Line sites, but commits to a CIR of 200 Mbps. That is, the carrier commits to pass 200 Mbps worth of Ethernet frames over time.

When a customer asks for a new E-Line with a 200-Mbps CIR, they could send lots more data than 200 Mbps. Remember, the literal transmission rate would be 1 Gbps in this example, because the access links are 1-Gbps links. But over time, if all the customers that asked for a 200-Mbps CIR E-Line sent lots more than 200 Mbps worth of data, the SP's network could become too congested. The SP builds its network to support the traffic it has committed to send, plus some extra for expected overuse, and some extra for growth. But it is too expensive to build a network that allows customers that ask for and pay for 200 Mbps to send at 1 Gbps all the time.

Controlling Overages with Policing and Shaping

To make the idea of fast access links with a slower CIR on the EVCs work, and work well, both the SP and the customer have to cooperate. The tools are two Quality of Service (QoS) tools called policing and shaping.

Historically, in some similar WAN services (like Frame Relay), the SP would actually let you send more data than your CIR, but MetroE networks typically use policing to discard the excess. A policer can watch incoming frames and identify the frames associated with each EVC. It counts the bytes in each frame, and determines a bit rate over time. When the customer has sent more bits than the CIR, the SP discards enough of the currently arriving frames to keep the rate down to the CIR. Figure 14-13 shows the location of policing in the same example shown in Figure 14-12.

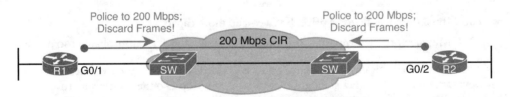

Figure 14-13   *SP Polices Incoming Traffic to Discard Excess Beyond CIR*

Recapping this scenario, the customer decides to ask the MetroE SP for an E-Line. The customer's routers use a 1-Gbps access link that allows the E-Line to support a 200-Mbps CIR. To protect the SP's network, the SP now uses ingress policing to monitor the bits/second received over each end of the E-Line's point-to-point EVC. And the SP discards some incoming frames when the rate gets too high.

Having the SP discard a few frames is actually not that harmful if QoS is implemented correctly, but with MetroE, if the SP is policing as shown in Figure 14-13, the customer needs to use the other QoS tool: shaping. Shaping, as implemented on the customer routers, lets the routers slow down. Shaping tells the routers, on the MetroE access link, to send some frames, and then wait; then send more, then wait; and to do that repeatedly. Shaping can be configured for that same rate as the CIR (200 Mbps in this case), so that the SP does not have to discard any traffic.

Summarizing some of these key points:

■ MetroE uses the concept of an Ethernet Virtual Connection (EVC), tying a committed number of bits/second called the committed information rate (CIR) to the EVC.

■ The access links need to be fast enough to handle the combined CIRs for all EVCs that cross the link.

■ For each EVC, the SP commits to forward the bits/second defined as the CIR for that EVC.

■ To protect its network from being overrun with too much traffic, the SP can use policing, monitoring the incoming traffic rate on each EVC and discarding traffic that goes beyond the CIR.

■ To prevent too much of its traffic from being discarded by the SP, the customer slows down its rate of sending over the EVC to match that same CIR, using shaping on the customer router.

Multiprotocol Label Switching (MPLS)

From your CCENT and CCNA R&S exam preparation, you have already learned a lot about how to build the basic components of an enterprise network. For each site, you buy some routers and switches. You connect the wired LAN devices to the switches, which in turn connect to a couple of routers. The routers connect to some WAN links that connect to other sites, where you installed more routers and switches.

You already understand a lot about the Layer 3 routing as well, as represented by the packet flowing left to right in Figure 14-14. Each router makes a separate forwarding decision to forward the packet, as shown as Steps 1, 2, and 3 in the figure. Each router makes a comparison between the packet's destination IP address and that router's IP routing table; the matching IP routing table entry tells the router where to forward the packet next. To learn those routes, the routers typically run some routing protocol.

An MPLS WAN service appears very much like that same model of how an IP network works with routers. This section discusses MPLS Layer 3 virtual private network (VPN) services, which create a Layer 3 WAN service. As a Layer 3 service, MPLS VPNs promise to forward IP packets across the WAN between the customer's routers.

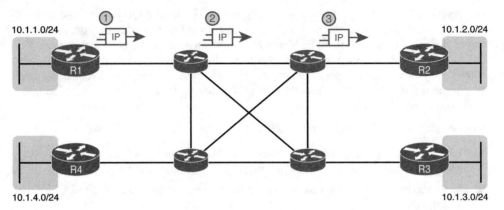

Figure 14-14 *Basic IP Routing of IP Packets*

An SP could just build an IP network and connect customers to it. However, MPLS allows the SP to connect to many customers and keep their IP traffic separated in some important ways. For instance, packets sent by one customer will not be forwarded to a second customer, and vice versa. So, rather than just build a generic IP network with routers, SPs use MPLS, which gives them many advantages when creating a Layer 3 service for their customers.

As with all the WAN services, how the SP creates the service is hidden from the customer for the most part. However, just to give you a little insight as to why MPLS is not just an IP network with routers, internally, the devices in an MPLS network use label switching, hence the name MPLS. The routers on the edge of the MPLS network add and remove an MPLS header as packets enter and exit the MPLS network. The devices inside the MPLS network then use the label field inside that MPLS header when forwarding data across the MPLS network.

NOTE While MPLS VPNs provide a Layer 3 service to customers, MPLS itself is sometimes called a Layer 2.5 protocol, because it adds the MPLS header between the data link header (Layer 2) and the IP header (Layer 3).

As usual, the discussion of WAN services in this book ignores as much of the SP's network as possible. For instance, you do not need to know how MPLS labels work. However, because MPLS VPNs create a Layer 3 service, the customer must be more aware of what the SP does, so you need to know a few facts about how an MPLS network approaches some Layer 3 functions. In particular, the SP's MPLS network:

- Needs to know about the customer's IP subnets
- Will run IP routing protocols to learn those routes
- Will use routes about the customer's IP address space to make forwarding decisions

MPLS Virtual Private Networks (MPLS VPNs) is one common offering from SPs, available since the early 2000s, and is one of the most commonly used private WAN services today. Note that MPLS standards can be used to create other services besides Layer 3 MPLS VPNs. However, for the purposes of this chapter, all references to MPLS are specifically about MPLS VPNs.

As an aside, note that an MPLS VPN service does not encrypt data to make the network private, as is done in some VPN services. Instead, MPLS VPNs make the data private by ensuring that data sent by one customer is not sent to a second customer, and vice versa, even though the packets for those two customers may pass through the same devices and links inside the MPLS network.

This second of two major sections of the chapter works through the basics of MPLS, specifically MPLS VPNs. This section first looks at the design, topology, and terminology related to building the customer-facing parts of an MPLS network. It then looks at the impact and issues created by the fact that the MPLS network provides a Layer 3 service.

MPLS VPN Physical Design and Topology

MetroE provides a Layer 2 service by forwarding Layer 2 Ethernet frames. To do that, the SP often uses Ethernet switches at the edge of its network. Those switches are configured to do more than what you learn about Ethernet LAN switches for CCNA, but a LAN switch's most fundamental job is to forward an Ethernet frame, so it makes sense for MetroE to use an Ethernet switch at the edge of the SP's MetroE network.

MPLS provides a Layer 3 service in that it promises to forward Layer 3 packets (IPv4 and IPv6). To support that service, MPLS SPs typically use routers at the edge of the MPLS networks, because routers provide the function of forwarding Layer 3 packets.

As usual, each WAN technology has its own set of terms and acronyms, so Figure 14-15 shows two important MPLS terms in context: customer edge (CE) and provider edge (PE). Because MPLS requires so much discussion about the devices on the edge of the customer and SP network, MPLS uses specific terms for each. The *customer edge* (CE) device is typically a router, and it sits at a customer site—that is, at a site in the company that is buying the MPLS service. The *provider edge* (PE) devices sit at the edge of the SP's network, on the other end of the access link.

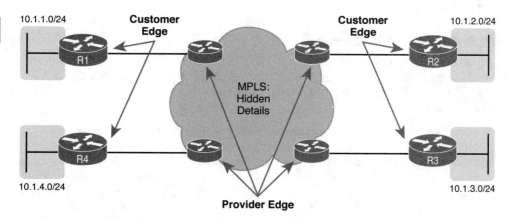

Figure 14-15 *MPLS Layer 3 Design, with PE and CE Routers*

Next, to appreciate what MPLS does, think back to how routers use their different kinds of physical interfaces and different kinds of data link protocols. When routing a packet, routers discard an incoming data link frame's data link header and trailer, and then build a new data link header/trailer. That action allows the incoming packet to arrive inside a frame of one data link protocol, and leave out an interface with another data link protocol.

With MPLS, the fact that the devices are routers, discarding and adding new data link headers, means that MPLS networks support a variety of access links. The fact that MPLS acts as a Layer 3 service, discarding incoming data link headers, means that any data link protocol could in theory be used on MPLS access links. In reality, MPLS does support many types of access links, as shown in Figure 14-16.

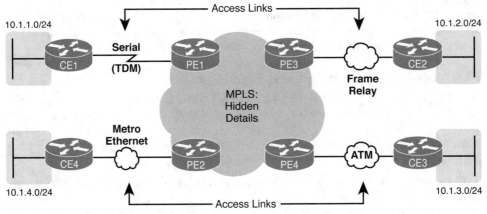

Figure 14-16 *Popular MPLS Access Link Technologies*

The variety of access links available for MPLS networks makes MPLS a great option for building large enterprise networks. For sites that are near MetroE services, especially for sites that need at least 10 Mbps of bandwidth, using MetroE as an access link makes great sense. Then, for sites that are more remote, the carrier may not offer MetroE services to that area, but many carriers can install a serial link to remote sites. Or, the enterprise may replace an existing Frame Relay or ATM network with MPLS, and in that case, the same physical links can be used, and the carrier can move those over to the MPLS network as MPLS access links.

MPLS and Quality of Service

MPLS was also the first WAN service for which the SP provided effective quality of service (QoS) features. And even though you have not yet gotten to Chapter 18, "Quality of Service (QoS)," you should be able to get a general idea of an MPLS QoS benefit with the following basic example.

IP networks can and often do forward voice traffic in IP packets, called Voice over IP (VoIP). If a WAN service does not provide QoS, that means that the WAN service does not treat one packet any differently than any other packet. With QoS, the SP's network can treat packets differently, giving some packets (like VoIP) better treatment. For a voice call to sound good, each voice packet must have low loss (that is, few packets are discarded); low one-way delay through the network; and low variation in delay (called jitter). Without QoS, a voice call over an IP network will not sound good.

With a QoS-capable WAN, the customer can mark VoIP packets so that the MPLS network can recognize VoIP packets and treat them better, resulting in better voice call quality. But to make it work correctly, the customer and MPLS provider need to cooperate.

For instance, for VoIP packets travelling left to right in Figure 14-17, Router CE1 could be configured with QoS marking tools. Marking tools could recognize VoIP packets, and place a specific value in the IP header of VoIP packets (a value called DSCP EF, per the figure). The MPLS WAN provider would then configure its QoS tools to react for packets that have that marking, typically sending that packet as soon as possible. The result: low delay, low jitter, low loss, and a better call quality.

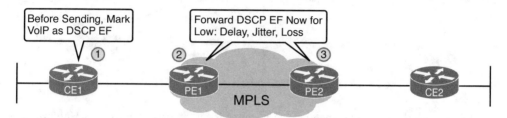

Figure 14-17 *MPLS VPN QoS Marking and Reaction in the MPLS WAN*

Note that Chapter 18 is devoted to these same mechanisms, and others like it.

Summarizing the ideas so far, MPLS supports a variety of access links. An enterprise would select the type and speed of access link for each site based on the capacity (bandwidth) required for each site. Beyond that basic connectivity, the enterprise will want to work with the SP to define other features of the service. The customer and SP will need to work through the details of some Layer 3 design choices (as discussed in more depth in the next section). The customer will also likely want to ask for QoS services from the MPLS provider, and define those details.

Layer 3 with MPLS VPN

Because MetroE provides a Layer 2 service, the SP has no need to understand anything about the customer's Layer 3 design. The SP knows nothing about the customer's IP addressing plan, and has no need to participate with routing protocols.

MPLS VPNs take the complete opposite approach. As a Layer 3 service, MPLS must be aware of the customer IP addressing. The SP will even use routing protocols and advertise those customer routes across the WAN. This section takes a closer look at what that means.

First, keep the primary goals in mind. The customer pays good money for a WAN service to deliver data between sites, with certain levels of availability and quality (for instance, low delay, jitter, and loss for VoIP). But to support that base function of allowing packet delivery from each WAN site to the other, the CE routers need to exchange routes with the PE routers in the MPLS network. Additionally, all the CE routers need to learn routes from the other CE routers—a process that relies on the PE routers.

To move into the specifics, first, the CE routers and the PE router on the ends of the same access link need to exchange routes, as shown in Figure 14-18. The figure shows the CE-PE routing protocol neighbor relationships (as lines with circles on the ends). In this case, the customer chose to use EIGRP. However, MPLS allows for many familiar routing protocols on the edge of the MPLS network: RIPv2, EIGRP, OSPF, and even eBGP.

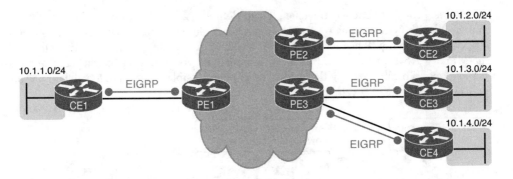

Figure 14-18 *Routing Protocol Neighbor Relationships with MPLS Customer Edge Routers*

Additionally, all the CE routers need to learn routes from the other CE routers. However, a CE router does not form routing protocol neighbor relationships directly with the other CE routers, as noted in Figure 14-18. Summarizing what does and does not happen:

- A CE router does become neighbors with the PE router on the other end of the access link.
- A CE router does not become neighbors with other CE routers.
- The MPLS network will advertise the customer's routes between the various PE routers, so that the CE routers can learn all customer routes through their PE-CE routing protocol neighbor relationship.

To advertise the customer routes between the PE routers, the PE routers use another routing protocol along with a process called *route redistribution*. Route redistribution happens inside one router, taking routes from one routing protocol process and injecting them into another. MPLS does route redistribution in the PE routers between the routing protocol used by the customer and a variation of BGP called Multiprotocol BGP (MPBGP). (Redistribution is needed when the PE-CE routing protocol is not BGP.) Figure 14-19 shows the idea.

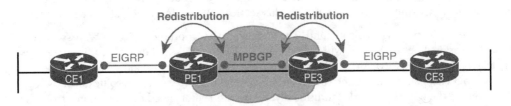

Figure 14-19 *MPLS VPN Using Redistribution with MPBGP at PE Router*

Just as a quick aside about MPBGP, MPLS VPNs use MPBGP (as opposed to other routing protocols) because MPBGP can advertise routes from multiple customers while keeping the routes logically separated. For instance, continuing the example in Figure 14-19, Router PE1 might sit in one PoP but connect to dozens of different customers. Likewise, Router PE3 might connect to many of those same customers. MPBGP can advertise routes for all those customers and mark which routes are from which customers, so that only the correct routes are advertised to each CE router for different customers.

OSPF Area Design with MPLS VPN

Now that you know the basics about what happens with routing protocols at the edge of an MPLS network, take a step back and ponder OSPF area design. For all the other WAN services discussed in the book, the WAN service is just one more data link, so the WAN sits inside one area. With MPLS, the MPLS service acts like a bunch of routers. If you use OSPF as the PE-CE routing protocol, some choices must be made about OSPF areas, and about which WAN links are in which area, and where the backbone area can and should be.

MPLS allows for a couple of variations on OSPF area design, but they all use an idea that was added to OSPF for MPLS VPNs, an idea that has come to be known informally as the OSPF *super backbone*. The idea is an elegant solution that meets OSPF needs and the requirement that the MPLS PEs, when using OSPF, must be in some OSPF area:

- The MPLS PEs form a backbone area by the name of a super backbone.
- Each PE-CE link can be any area—a non-backbone area or the backbone area.

Although the super backbone supports some functions and logic beyond the scope of this book, for the purposes of getting a basic understanding of OSPF's use with MPLS, you can think of the super backbone as simply the majority of an enterprise's OSPF backbone area, but with the option to make the backbone area larger. The CE routers at a customer site may not be part of the backbone area, or may be, at the choice of the customer network engineers.

For example, for a nice clean design, each of the four customer sites in Figure 14-20 uses a different area. The PE-CE links are part of those individual areas. The OSPF backbone area still exists, and each area connects to the backbone area, but the backbone exists in the MPLS PE routers only.

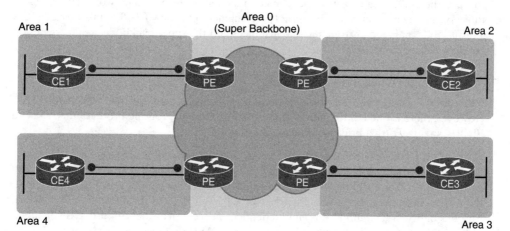

Figure 14-20 *MPLS Design with (Super Backbone) Area 0, Non-Backbone Area for Each Site*

The area design in Figure 14-20 provides a clean OSPF area design. However, if migrating from some other type of WAN service, with an existing OSPF design, the network engineers may prefer to keep parts of an existing OSPF design, which means some sites may still need to include the backbone area. In fact, multiple WAN sites can be configured to be in the backbone area, and still function correctly. Figure 14-21 shows one such example.

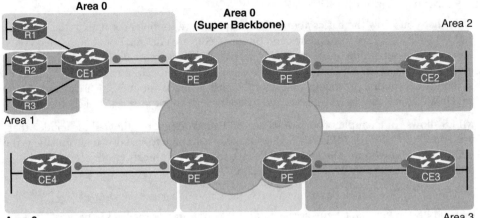

Figure 14-21 *Using Area 0 on CE-PE Link, or for Entire Site*

In effect, the super backbone combines with the two other parts of the network configured as area 0 for one contiguous backbone area. Notice on the left side of Figure 14-21 the two sites with area 0 noted. Normally, if both customer sites implement area 0, but there were links from some other area between them, the design would break OSPF design rules. However, the OSPF backbone (area 0) links on the left, plus the OSPF super backbone area 0 created by MPLS, act together in regard to OSPF design.

Next, focus on the site at the upper left. That site represents what might have existed before migrating to an MPLS design, with Router R1's links in area 0, and the links connected to Routers R2 and R3 in area 1. The enterprise network engineer may have decided to leave the OSPF area design alone when connecting to the MPLS network. To support those backbone area links off Router R1, the engineer put the CE1-PE1 link into area 0. As a result, the combined customer area 0 instances and the super backbone area 0 creates one contiguous backbone area.

Routing Protocol Challenges with EIGRP

Using EIGRP as the PE-CE routing protocol poses fewer challenges than when using OSPF. However, there is one configuration setting that impacts the routing protocol metrics with EIGRP, so it is worth a brief mention.

With an MPLS service, because of the effects of route redistribution to exchange routes, the PE-CE configuration at each site could use a different EIGRP AS number (ASN) in the configurations. For example, in Figure 14-22, thinking about route exchange from CE1 all the way to CE2, the process uses EIGRP from CE1 to PE1, and from PE2 to CE2. But what happens between PE1 and PE2 is an independent process that does not use EIGRP, but rather MPBGP, so the requirement to use the same ASN on both ends is removed.

Although a customer could use different EIGRP ASNs, EIGRP metrics are more realistic if you use the same EIGRP ASN at all sites. In fact, if the enterprise did use the same EIGRP ASN, the entire MPLS network's impact on EIGRP metrics would act as if everything between the PEs (in the middle of the MPLS network) did not exist. For instance, with the same ASN used at all sites in Figure 14-22, the EIGRP topology, from a metrics perspective, looks more like the design in Figure 14-23.

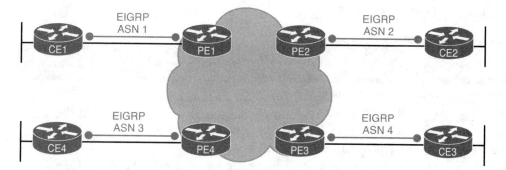

Figure 14-22 *Routing Protocol Neighbor Relationships with EIGRP*

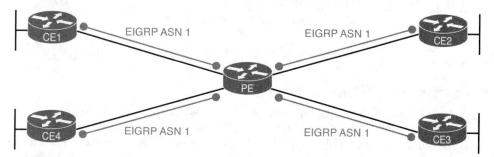

Figure 14-23 *EIGRP Metrics Unaffected by MPLS VPN Internals*

Chapter Review

One key to doing well on the exams is to perform repetitive spaced review sessions. Review this chapter's material using either the tools in the book, DVD, or interactive tools for the same material found on the book's companion website. Refer to the "Your Study Plan" element for more details. Table 14-4 outlines the key review elements and where you can find them. To better track your study progress, record when you completed these activities in the second column.

Table 14-4 Chapter Review Tracking

Review Element	Review Date(s)	Resource Used:
Review key topics		Book, DVD/website
Review key terms		Book, DVD/website
Answer DIKTA questions		Book, PCPT
Review memory tables		Book, DVD/website

Review All the Key Topics

Table 14-5 Key Topics for Chapter 14

Key Topic Element	Description	Page Number
Figure 14-3	Metro Ethernet terminology in context	366
Table 14-3	MetroE service types per MEF	367
Figure 14-6	MetroE Ethernet LAN (E-LAN) service concept	369
Figure 14-7	MetroE Ethernet Tree (E-Tree) service concept	369
List	Ideas about customer Layer 3 addressing and what an MPLS VPN provider needs to know	376
Figure 14-15	MPLS terminology in context	377
List	Ideas about routing protocol neighbor relationships with MPLS VPN	380
List	Two key facts about OSPF backbone area design with MPLS VPNs	381

Key Terms You Should Know

point-to-point, hub-and-spoke, partial mesh, full mesh, Multiprotocol Label Switching (MPLS), MPLS VPN, Ethernet WAN, Metro Ethernet, carrier Ethernet, service provider (SP), point of presence (PoP), access link, E-Line, E-LAN, E-Tree, Ethernet Virtual Connection (EVC), committed information rate (CIR), customer edge (CE), provider edge (PE), Multiprotocol BGP (MPBGP), OSPF super backbone

CHAPTER 15

Private WANs with Internet VPN

This chapter covers the following exam topics:

3.0 WAN Technologies

3.2 Configure, verify and troubleshoot PPPoE client-side interfaces using local authentication

3.3 Configure, verify and troubleshoot GRE tunnel connectivity

3.4 Describe WAN topology options

  3.4.a Point-to-point

3.5 Describe WAN access connectivity options

  3.5.c Broadband PPPoE

  3.5.d Internet VPN (DMVPN, site-to-site VPN, client VPN)

This lengthy chapter covers a wide variety of topics related to how companies can use the Internet as a private wide-area network (WAN) by using virtual private network (VPN) technologies. The stars of this chapter are generic routing encapsulation (GRE) tunnels and PPP over Ethernet (PPPoE). To support those topics, the chapter touches on a variety of related topics, including some Internet access technologies, security basics, and some important VPN protocols such as IP Security (IPsec) and Secure Sockets Layer (SSL).

This chapter breaks the material into three major sections. The first discusses Internet access options and the basics of VPN protocols used over the Internet. The second and third major sections are traditional concept, configure, verify, and troubleshoot sections, with the second section about GRE, and the third about PPPoE.

From a study planning perspective, this chapter is one of the longest chapters in the book. All the topics are related, so I decided to keep them in one larger chapter. However, you can easily treat each major section as a separate chapter from the sense of managing your time.

"Do I Know This Already?" Quiz

Take the quiz (either here, or use the PCPT software) if you want to use the score to help you decide how much time to spend on this chapter. The answers are at the bottom of the page following the quiz, and the explanations are in DVD Appendix C and in the PCPT software.

Table 15-1 "Do I Know This Already?" Foundation Topics Section-to-Question Mapping

Foundation Topics Section	Questions
Internet Access and Internet VPN Fundamentals	1
GRE Tunnels and DMVPN	2–4
PPP over Ethernet	5–7

1. A colleague mentions using a client VPN. Which of the following protocols or technologies would you expect your colleague to have used?

    a. SSL

    b. IPsec

    c. GRE

    d. DMVPN

2. An engineer configures a point-to-point GRE tunnel between two Cisco routers, called A and B. The routers use public IP addresses assigned by ISPs, and private addresses from network 10.0.0.0. Which of the following answers accurately describes where the addresses could be referenced in the GRE configuration?

    a. Router A's private address on an **ip address** command on Router A's tunnel interface

    b. Router A's private address on a **tunnel destination** command on Router B

    c. Router B's public address on a **tunnel source** command on Router A

    d. Router B's public address on an **ip address** command on Router B's tunnel interface

3. An enterprise uses a site-to-site GRE tunnel that runs over the Internet between two routers (R1 and R2). R1 uses tunnel interface 22. The tunnel has a source of 1.1.1.1 and a destination of 2.2.2.2. All the answers list facts that could be true, but which of the following must be true when Router R1's tunnel 22 is in an up/up state?

    a. 2.2.2.2 is pingable from Router R1.

    b. 1.1.1.1 is pingable from Router R2.

    c. R1 has a working (up/up) interface with address 1.1.1.1.

    d. R2 has a working (up/up) interface with address 2.2.2.2.

4. An enterprise has 1000 small retail locations and a central site. The enterprise uses Internet access links to each retail store and DMVPN to securely create a VPN back to the central site. Which of the following answers is true about the operation and configuration of DMVPN?

    a. The hub router needs at least 1000 tunnel interfaces.

    b. The hub router needs less than 10 tunnel interfaces.

    c. All packets between retail stores must route through the central hub site.

    d. Packets cannot be forwarded from one retail store to another.

5. An enterprise uses Cisco IOS routers and DSL connections to local ISPs for their retail locations. The ISPs require the use of PPPoE. The routers at each retail site use dynamically learned public IP addresses as learned from the ISPs. Each router uses its F0/0 interface to connect to an external DSL modem, which then connects to a phone line. Which of the following is the most likely choice for configuring the router to use the IP address as assigned by the ISP?

   a. Interface F0/0 has an **ip address dhcp** interface subcommand.

   b. Some dialer interface has an **ip address dhcp** interface subcommand.

   c. Some dialer interface has an **ip address negotiated** interface subcommand.

   d. Interface F0/0 has an **ip address negotiated** interface subcommand.

6. An enterprise uses Cisco IOS routers and DSL connections to local ISPs for their retail locations. The ISPs require the use of PPPoE. The following output listed comes from one such router (R1). Which of the following answers are true about the configuration on Router R1 and its current PPPoE state? (Choose two answers.)

   ```
   R1# show pppoe session
       1 client session

   Uniq ID  PPPoE  RemMAC          Port          VT  VA       State
            SID    LocMAC                             VA-st    Type
       N/A    1    0200.0000.3333  Gi0/0         Di1 Vi1      UP
                   0200.0000.3003                     UP
   ```

   a. The configuration includes PPPoE commands under interface virtual-access 1.

   b. Dialer interface 1 and virtual-access 1 are bound together.

   c. Interface G0/0 is using MAC address 0200.0000.3333.

   d. The PPPoE session is currently working.

7. An enterprise uses Cisco IOS routers and DSL connections to local ISPs for their retail locations. The ISPs require the use of PPPoE. A network engineer connects to the console of one router at a retail office, issues the **show pppoe session** command, and the router just returns a command prompt, with no lines of output. If you knew the problem was related to the configuration on the local router, which one of the four following areas would be the best area to recommend for your colleagues to investigate in their next troubleshooting step?

   a. Look at the commands on the physical Ethernet interface

   b. Look at the dialer interface commands specific to PPP

   c. Look at the commands specific to IPv4 address learning

   d. Look at the commands in the running-config file for the virtual-access interface

Foundation Topics

Internet Access and Internet VPN Fundamentals

To build the Internet, Internet service providers (ISP) need links to other ISPs as well as links to the ISPs' customers. The Internet core connects ISPs to each other using a variety of high-speed technologies. Additionally, Internet access links connect an ISP to each customer, again with a wide variety of technologies. The combination on ISP networks and customer networks that connect to the ISPs together create the worldwide Internet.

For these customer access links, the technologies need to be inexpensive so that a typical consumer can afford to pay for the service. But businesses can use many of these same technologies to connect to the Internet. Some WAN technologies happen to work particularly well as Internet access technologies. For example, several use the same telephone line installed into most homes by the phone company so that the ISPs do not have to install additional cabling. Others use the cable TV cabling, whereas others use wireless.

While consumers connect to the Internet to reach destinations on the Internet, businesses can also use the Internet as a WAN service. An enterprise can connect each business site to the Internet. Then, using virtual private network (VPN) technology, the enterprise can create an Internet VPN. An Internet VPN can keep the enterprise's packet private through encryption and other means, even while sending the data over the Internet.

This first of three major sections of the chapter reviews some of the basics of Internet access links. These details are needed as background for some of the exam topics discussed later in the chapter. This section then introduces the basics of how an enterprise can communicate securely over the internet, making the public Internet act like a private network, by creating an Internet VPN.

Internet Access

Private WAN technology may be used to access an ISP's network, including all the private WAN technologies discussed in Chapter 14, "Private WANs with Ethernet and MPLS." Businesses often use time-division multiplexing (TDM) serial links, Multiprotocol Label Switching (MPLS), or Metro Ethernet to access the Internet. Figure 15-1 shows a few of these, just as a visual reminder of these options.

The next few pages review some of the Internet access technologies not yet discussed elsewhere in the book. These topics exist to give you a little more context about the more detailed topics of building Internet VPNs.

Answers to the "Do I Know This Already?" quiz:
1 A **2** A **3** C **4** B **5** C **6** B, D **7** A

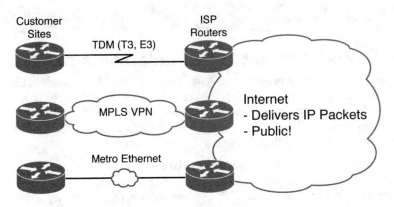

Figure 15-1 *Three Examples of Internet Access Links for Companies*

Digital Subscriber Line

In the consumer Internet access space, one big speed breakthrough happened with the introduction of the digital subscriber line (DSL). It represented a big technological breakthrough in terms of raw speed in comparison to some older technologies, such as analog modems. These faster speeds available through DSL also changed how people could use the Internet, because many of today's common applications would be unusable with the earlier Internet access technologies (analog modems and Integrated Services Digital Network, or ISDN).

> **NOTE** If you are interested in a few pages of information about the older Internet access technologies of analog modems and ISDN, look to this book's DVD Appendix K, "Topics from Previous Editions," for a section titled "Dial Access with Modems and ISDN."

Telephone companies (telcos) greatly influenced the creation of DSL. As a technology, DSL gave telcos a way to offer much faster Internet access speeds. As a business opportunity, DSL gave telcos a way to offer a valuable high-speed Internet service to many of their existing telephone customers, over the same physical phone line already installed, which created a great way for telcos to make money.

Figure 15-2 shows some of the details of how DSL works on a home phone line. The phone can do what it has always done: plug into a phone jack and send analog signals. For the data, a DSL modem connects to a spare phone outlet. The DSL modem sends and receives the data, as digital signals, at higher frequencies, over the same local loop, even at the same time as a telephone call. (Note that the physical installation often uses frequency filters that are not shown in the figure or discussed here.)

Because DSL sends analog (voice) and digital (data) signals on the same line, the telco has to somehow split those signals on the telco side of the connection. To do so, the local loop must be connected to a *DSL access multiplexer* (DSLAM) located in the nearby telco central office (CO). The DSLAM splits out the digital data over to the router on the lower right in Figure 15-2, which completes the connection to the Internet. The DSLAM also splits out the analog voice signals over to the voice switch on the upper right.

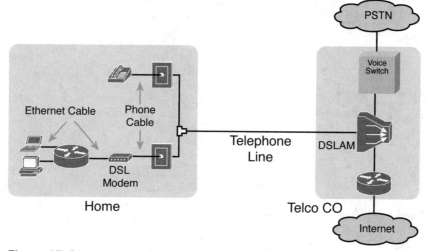

Figure 15-2 *Wiring and Devices for a Home DSL Link*

DSL has some advantages and disadvantages, of course. For instance, one variation of DSL, called asymmetric DSL (ADSL), offers a faster speed toward the customer (download speed), which better matches the traffic patterns of most consumer traffic. Many consumer ADSL offerings routinely support speeds in the 5-Mbps range, and up to 24 Mbps in ideal conditions. (DSL includes other options that have symmetric speeds as well.) However, DSL works only at certain distances from the CO to the customer site, and the speeds degrade at those longer cabling distances. So, the quality of the DSL service, or availability of the service at all, may be impacted simply by the distance between the home/business site and the CO.

Cable Internet

DSL uses the local link (telephone line) from the local telco. Cable Internet instead uses the cabling from what has become the primary competitor to the telco in most markets: the cable company.

Cable Internet creates an Internet access service which, when viewed generally rather than specifically, has many similarities to DSL. Like DSL, cable Internet takes full advantage of existing cabling, using the existing cable TV (CATV) cable to send data. Like DSL, cable Internet uses asymmetric speeds, sending data faster downstream than upstream, which works well for most consumer locations. And cable Internet still allows the normal service on the cable (cable TV), at the same time as the Internet access service is working.

Cable Internet also uses the same general idea for in-home cabling as DSL, just using CATV cabling instead of telephone cabling. The left side of Figure 15-3 shows a TV connected to the CATV cabling, just as it would normally connect. At another cable outlet, a cable modem connects to the same cable. The Internet service flows over one frequency, like yet another TV channel, just reserved for Internet service.

Similar to DSL, on the CATV company side of the connection (on the right side of the figure), the CATV company must split out the data and video traffic. Data flows to the lower right, through a router, to the Internet. The video comes in from video dishes for distribution out to the TVs in people's homes.

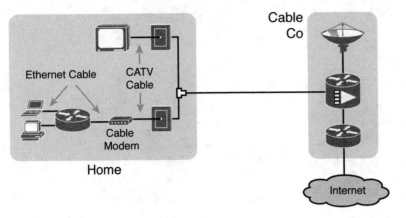

Figure 15-3 *Wiring and Devices for a Home Cable Internet Link*

Wireless WAN (3G, 4G, LTE)

Many of you reading this book have a mobile phone that has Internet access. That is, you can check your email, surf the Web, download apps, and watch videos. Many of us today rely on our mobile phones, and the Internet access built in to those phones, for most of our tweets and the like. This section touches on the big concepts behind the Internet access technology connecting those mobile phones.

Mobile phones use radio waves to communicate through a nearby mobile phone tower. The phone has a small radio antenna, and the provider has a much larger antenna sitting at the top of a tower somewhere within miles of you and your phone. Phones, tablet computers, laptops, and even routers (with the correct interface cards) can communicate through to the Internet using this technology, as represented in Figure 15-4.

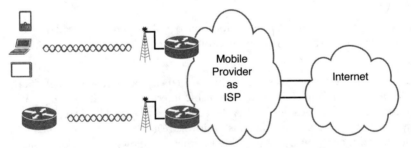

Figure 15-4 *Wireless Internet Access Using 3G/4G Technology*

The mobile phone radio towers also have cabling and equipment, including routers. The mobile provider builds its own IP network, much like an ISP builds out an IP network. The customer IP packets pass through the IP router at the tower into the mobile provider's IP network and then out to the Internet.

The market for mobile phones and wireless Internet access for other devices is both large and competitive. As a result, the mobile providers spend a lot of money advertising their services, with lots of names for one service or the other. Frankly, it can be difficult to tell what all the marketing jargon means, but a few terms tend to be used throughout the industry:

Wireless Internet: A general term for Internet services from a mobile phone or from any device that uses the same technology.

3G/4G Wireless: Short for third generation and fourth generation, these terms refer to the major changes over time to the mobile phone companies' wireless networks.

LTE: Long-Term Evolution, which is a newer and faster technology considered to be part of fourth generation (4G) technology.

The takeaway from all this jargon is this: When you hear about wireless Internet services with a mobile phone tower in the picture—whether the device is a phone, tablet, or PC—it is probably a 3G, 4G, or LTE wireless Internet connection.

Fiber Internet Access

The consumer-focused Internet access technologies discussed in this section use a couple of different physical media. DSL uses the copper wiring installed between the telco CO and the home. Cable uses the copper CATV cabling installed from the cable company to the home. And of course wireless WAN technologies do not use cables.

The cabling used by DSL and cable Internet uses copper wires, but, comparing different types of physical media, fiber-optic cabling generally supports faster speeds for longer distances. That is, just comparing physical layer technologies across the breadth of networking, fiber-optic cabling supports longer links, and those links often run at equivalent or faster speeds.

Some ISPs now offer Internet access that goes by the name of *fiber Internet*, or simply *fiber*. To make that work, some local company that owns the rights to install cabling underground in a local area (often a telephone company) installs new fiber-optic cabling. Once the cable plant is in place (a process that often takes years as well as a large budget), the fiber ISP then connects customers to the Internet using the fiber-optic cabling. Often, the fiber uses Ethernet protocols over the fiber. The end result: high-speed Internet to the home, often using Ethernet technology.

Internet VPN Fundamentals

Private WANs have some wonderful security features. In particular, the customers who send data through the WAN have good reason to believe that no attackers saw the data in transit, or even changed the data to cause some harm. The private WAN service provider promises to send one customer's data to other sites owned by that customer, but not to sites owned by other customers, and vice versa.

VPNs try to provide the same secure features as a private WAN while sending data over a network that is open to other parties (such as the Internet). Compared to a private WAN, the Internet does not provide for a secure environment that protects the privacy of an enterprise's data. Internet VPNs can provide important security features, like:

- **Confidentiality (privacy):** Preventing anyone in the middle of the Internet (man in the middle) from being able to read the data

- **Authentication:** Verifying that the sender of the VPN packet is a legitimate device and not a device used by an attacker

- **Data integrity:** Verifying that the packet was not changed as the packet transited the Internet

■ **Anti-replay:** Preventing a man in the middle from copying and later replaying the packets sent by a legitimate user, for the purpose of appearing to be a legitimate user

To accomplish these goals, two devices near the edge of the Internet create a VPN, sometimes called a *VPN tunnel*. These devices add headers to the original packet, with these headers including fields that allow the VPN devices to make the traffic secure. The VPN devices also encrypt the original IP packet, meaning that the original packet's contents are undecipherable to anyone who happens to see a copy of the packet as it traverses the Internet.

Figure 15-5 shows the general idea of what typically occurs with a VPN tunnel. The figure shows a VPN created between a branch office router and a Cisco Adaptive Security Appliance (ASA), which is one of Cisco's product names for a firewall. In this case, the VPN is called a *site-to-site VPN* because it connects two sites of a company.

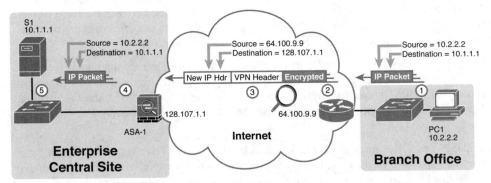

Figure 15-5 *VPN Tunnel Concepts for a Site-to-Site Intranet VPN*

The figure shows the following steps, which explain the overall flow:

1. Host PC1 (10.2.2.2) on the right sends a packet to the web server (10.1.1.1), just as it would without a VPN.

2. The router encrypts the packet, adds some VPN headers, adds another IP header (with public IP addresses), and forwards the packet.

3. An attacker in the Internet copies the packet (called a man-in-the-middle attack). However, the attacker cannot change the packet without being noticed and cannot read the contents of the original packet.

4. Device ASA-1 receives the packet, confirms the authenticity of the sender, confirms that the packet has not been changed, and then decrypts the original packet.

5. Server S1 receives the unencrypted packet.

The benefits of using an Internet-based VPN as shown in Figure 15-5 are many. The cost of a high-speed Internet connection as discussed in the early pages of this chapter is usually much less than that of many private WAN options. The Internet is seemingly everywhere, making this kind of solution available worldwide. And by using VPN technology and protocols, the communications are secure.

NOTE The term *tunnel* refers to any protocol's packet that is sent by encapsulating the packet inside another packet. The term *VPN tunnel* may or may not imply that the tunnel also uses encryption. Many of the VPN tunnels discussed in this chapter would normally include encryption when used in production.

Site-to-Site VPNs with IPsec

As just discussed regarding the example shown in Figure 15-5, a site-to-site VPN means that two enterprise sites create a VPN tunnel by encrypting and sending data between two devices. One set of rules for creating a site-to-site VPN is defined by IPsec.

IPsec is an architecture or framework for security services for IP networks. The name itself is not an acronym, but rather a name derived from the title of the RFC that defines it (RFC 4301, *Security Architecture for the Internet Protocol*), more generally called IP Security, or IPsec.

IPsec defines how two devices, both of which connect to the Internet, can achieve the main goals of a VPN as listed at the beginning of this chapter: confidentiality, authentication, data integrity, and anti-replay. IPsec does not define just one way to implement a VPN, instead allowing several different protocol options for each VPN feature. One of IPsec's strengths is that its role as an architecture allows it to be added to and changed over time as improvements to individual security functions are made.

This chapter does not go through the details of each part of IPsec, but to give you some general idea of some of IPsec's work, this section shows how two IPsec endpoints encrypt data and add IPsec VPN headers to the encrypted data.

The idea of IPsec encryption might sound intimidating, but if you ignore the math—and thankfully, you can—IPsec encryption is not too difficult to understand. IPsec encryption uses a pair of encryption algorithms, which are essentially math formulas, to meet a couple of requirements. First, the two math formulas are a matched set:

- One to hide (encrypt) the data
- Another to re-create (decrypt) the original data based on the encrypted data

Besides those somewhat obvious functions, the two math formulas were chosen so that if an attacker intercepted the encrypted text but did not have the secret password (called an *encryption key*), decrypting that one packet would be difficult. In addition, the formulas are also chosen so that if an attacker did happen to decrypt one packet, that information would not give the attacker any advantages in decrypting the other packets.

The process for encrypting data for an IPsec VPN works generally as shown in Figure 15-6. Note that the *encryption key* is also known as the *session key*, *shared key*, or *shared session key*.

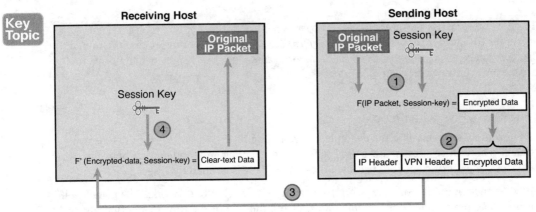

Figure 15-6 *Basic IPsec Encryption Process*

The four steps highlighted in the figure are as follows:

1. The sending VPN device (like the remote office router in Figure 15-5) feeds the original packet and the session key into the encryption formula, calculating the encrypted data.

2. The sending device encapsulates the encrypted data into a packet, which includes the new IP header and VPN header.

3. The sending device sends this new packet to the destination VPN device (ASA-1 back in Figure 15-5).

4. The receiving VPN device runs the corresponding decryption formula, using the encrypted data and session key—the same key value as was used on the sending VPN device—to decrypt the data.

Client VPNs with SSL

The Secure Sockets Layer (SSL) protocol serves as an alternative VPN technology to IPsec. In particular, today's web browsers support SSL as a way to dynamically create a secure connection from the web browser to a web server, supporting safe online access to financial transactions. This brief topic explains a few details about how you can use SSL to create client VPNs.

Web browsers use HTTP as the protocol with which to connect to web servers. However, when the communications with the web server need to be secure, the browser switches to use SSL. SSL uses well-known port 443, encrypting data sent between the browser and the server and authenticating the user. Then, the HTTP messages flow over the SSL VPN connection.

The built-in SSL functions of a web browser create one secure web browsing session, but this same SSL technology can be used to create a client VPN using a *Cisco VPN client*. The Cisco AnyConnect Secure Mobility Client (or AnyConnect Client for short) is software that sits on a user's PC and uses SSL to create one end of a VPN remote-access tunnel. As a result, all the packets sent to the other end of the tunnel are encrypted, not just those sent over a single HTTP connection in a web browser.

For example, the VPN tunnel shown for PC A in Figure 15-7 uses the AnyConnect Client to create a client VPN. The AnyConnect Client creates an SSL tunnel to the ASA firewall that has been installed to expect VPN clients to connect to it. The tunnel encrypts all traffic, so that PC A can use any application available at the enterprise network on the right.

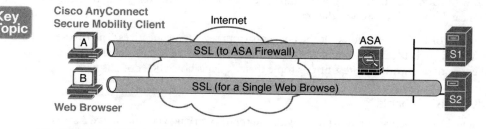

Figure 15-7 *Client VPN Options (SSL)*

Note that while the figure shows an ASA firewall used at the main enterprise site, many types of devices can be used on the server side of an SSL connection as well. The web server itself can be the endpoint of an SSL connection from a web browser, but often, to improve server performance, the SSL tunnel on the server side terminates on specialized devices like the Cisco ASA or a router.

The bottom of Figure 15-7 shows a client VPN that supports a web application for a single web browser tab. The experience is much like when you connect to any other secure website today: the session uses SSL, so all traffic sent to and from that web browser tab is encrypted with SSL. Note that PC B does not use the AnyConnect Client; the user simply opens a web browser to browse to server S2. However, by using SSL, that one session is encrypted with SSL, providing better security.

GRE Tunnels and DMVPN

The device on the endpoint of an Internet VPN takes a normal unencrypted packet and performs several functions before forwarding that packet. One of those functions is to encrypt the packet, and another is to encapsulate the packet in a new IP header. The new IP header uses addresses in the unsecured network (usually the Internet), allowing the routers between the two VPN tunnel endpoints to forward the VPN IP packet. The original IP packet, including the original IP header, is encrypted and unreadable.

This second major section of this chapter examines a subset of the work to create that kind of site-to-site VPN tunnel. In particular, this section looks at how to set up the tunnel, while ignoring the encryption function. Specifically, this section looks at the concepts and configuration of how routers create a tunnel, encapsulating the original IP packet inside another IP packet. The goal is to give you some general ideas about how tunneling works, while leaving the detailed security configuration to other certifications like CCNA Security.

This section concludes with a short discussion of Dynamic Multipoint VPN (DMVPN). DMVPN helps solve some shortcomings with deploying point-to-point GRE tunnels on a larger scale.

GRE Tunnel Concepts

This chapter looks at one type of IP tunnel: generic routing encapsulation (GRE). GRE, defined in RFC 2784, defines an additional header used by GRE to perform tunneling, along with the new IP header, that encapsulates the original packet. Two routers work together, with matching configuration settings, to create a GRE IP tunnel. Then, IPsec configuration can be added to encrypt the traffic.

The discussion of GRE tunnels looks at the concepts from several perspectives. The first section shows how packets can be routed over a GRE tunnel, much like using a serial link inside a secured enterprise network. The rest of this topic then explains how GRE does its work.

Routing over GRE Tunnels

A GRE tunnel exists between two routers, with the tunnel working very much like a serial link with regard to packet forwarding. So, before discussing GRE tunnels, this section first reviews some familiar facts about routers and serial links, using Figure 15-8 as an example.

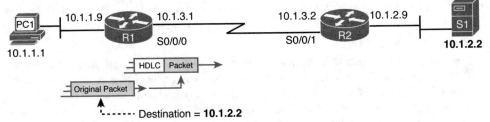

Figure 15-8 *Routing an IP Packet over a Serial Link*

The small network in Figure 15-8 looks like a part of many enterprise networks. It uses private IP addresses (network 10.0.0.0). It has an IP address on each router interface, including on each serial interface. The IP addresses on the serial interfaces (10.1.3.1 and 10.1.3.2, respectively) are in the same subnet. And when PC1 sends a packet to destination IP address 10.1.2.2, R1 will encapsulate the packet in the data link protocol used on the link, like the default High-level Data Link Control (HDLC) encapsulation shown in the figure.

Also, note that all the parts of this small enterprise network exist in secure spaces. This network has no need to encrypt data using a VPN.

GRE creates a concept that works just like the serial link in Figure 15-8, at least with regard to IP routing. Instead of a serial link with serial interfaces, the routers use virtual interfaces called *tunnel interfaces*. The two routers have IP addresses on their tunnel interfaces in the same subnet. Figure 15-9 shows an example where the serial link has been replaced with these virtual tunnel interfaces.

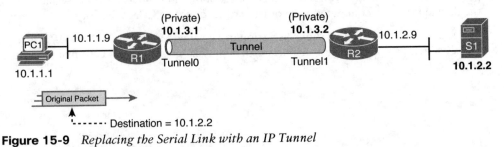

Figure 15-9 *Replacing the Serial Link with an IP Tunnel*

Sticking with the big ideas about IP routing for now, the tunnel looks like just another link in the secure part of the network. The tunnel IP addresses are from the secure enterprise network. The routers encapsulate the original packet inside a tunnel header, which takes the place of the serial link's HDLC header. And the routers will even have routes that list the tunnel interfaces (Tunnel0 and Tunnel1 in this case) as the outgoing interfaces.

To make use of the GRE tunnel, the routers treat it like any other link with a point-to-point topology. The routers have IPv4 addresses in the same subnet. The routers use a routing protocol to become neighbors and exchange routes over the tunnel. And the routes learned over the tunnel list the tunnel interface as the outgoing interface, with the neighboring router's tunnel interface IP address as the next-hop router. Figure 15-10 shows an example, with the routes learned by each router listed at the bottom.

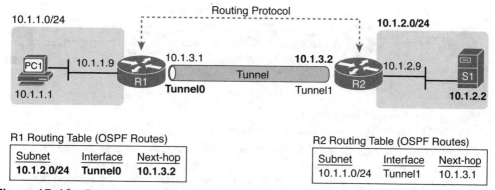

Figure 15-10   *Routes Learned with a Routing Protocol over the IP Tunnel*

Look closely at the route for subnet 10.1.2.0/24. The subnet exists on the right side of the figure, connected to R2. R1 has learned a route for the 10.1.2.0/24 subnet, as learned from R2. (R1's routing table is on the left side of the figure.) To create that route, first R2 will have a connected route to subnet 10.1.2.0/24. R1 and R2 will use some routing protocol (for instance, OSPF) to exchange routing information. R1 will add a new route for subnet 10.1.2.0/24.

Most importantly, note the use of the tunnel interface in the route as shown beneath Router R1 in the figure. That route will list R1's own tunnel interface, Tunnel0, as the outgoing interface. That route lists R2's tunnel interface IP address, 10.1.3.2, as the next-hop router, as shown in R1's IP routing table in the bottom-left part of the figure.

> **NOTE**   From a Layer 3 perspective, the tunnel interface shown in this example works like a point-to-point link. In fact, the tunnel shown in the examples so far is called a *point-to-point GRE tunnel*. DMVPN also uses GRE, but it uses multipoint GRE tunnels, which have more than two endpoints in the same tunnel.

All these concepts show how the GRE tunnel acts like just one more link in the secure part of an internetwork. The next few pages look at how GRE tunnels forward these packets over an unsecure network between the two routers.

GRE Tunnels over the Unsecured Network

The previous few figures have a tunnel between two routers, one that looks like a pipe, but those diagrams do not tell us much about the physical network behind the tunnel. The tunnel can exist over any IP network. The tunnel is created using an IP network to forward the original packets, so any IP network between Routers R1 and R2 would allow the tunnel to exist.

Often, site-to-site VPNs, like the one shown in Figure 15-10, use an unsecured network like the Internet as the IP network. The whole idea ties back to economics. The monthly cost of high-speed Internet access at each site is often less than paying for other private WAN services. But no matter what type of Internet connection exists, the routers on the tunnel can use the Internet as a way to forward the packets between the two tunnel routers, as shown in Figure 15-11.

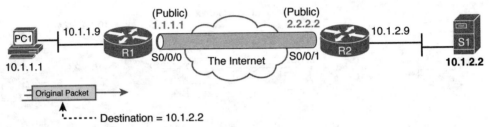

Figure 15-11 *Sending the Tunnel over the Internet*

The routers on the ends of the GRE tunnel create the tunnel by agreeing to send each other packets over the unsecure network between the two. Figure 15-11 shows many of the details that the engineer needs to know about the two routers before configuring the GRE tunnel on both ends. The figure shows the interfaces R1 and R2 each use to connect to the Internet. And it shows the IP addresses each router uses on its Internet connections, in this case 1.1.1.1 and 2.2.2.2 just to use more memorable numbers.

The router configuration uses virtual interfaces called *tunnel interfaces*. These interfaces do not exist until the engineer creates the tunnel with the **interface tunnel** command. For instance, the command **interface tunnel 0** creates a tunnel interface numbered as 0. To create a tunnel, both routers create a tunnel interface and use IP addresses as if the tunnel were a point-to-point link.

Figure 15-12 shows a conceptual diagram of a packet coming into Router R1 from PC1, one that needs to be forwarded over the GRE tunnel to Server S1 (10.1.2.2). When the router uses its IP routing logic from the secured part of the network, as shown in Figure 15-9, R1 wants to send the packet over the tunnel. Figure 15-12 shows the encapsulation done by R1.

NOTE If the two routers creating this tunnel also configured the IPsec encryption part of the tunnel, before encapsulating the original packet as shown in Figure 15-11, the sending router would first encrypt the original packet.

GRE specifies the use of two headers to create the tunnel. GRE defines its own header, used to manage the tunnel itself. GRE also defines the use of a complete 20-byte IP header, called the *delivery header*. This header will use IP addresses from the unsecure network. In this case, the delivery IP header will list R1's 1.1.1.1 Internet IP address as the source and R2's 2.2.2.2 Internet IP address as the destination.

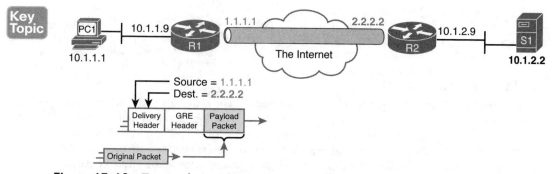

Figure 15-12 *Encapsulating the Original IP Packet in a GRE-Formatted Packet*

While this packet passes through the Internet, the routers in the Internet use this outer GRE delivery IP header to route the packet. The fact that this packet happens to hold another entire IP packet inside does not matter to the IP forwarding process in those routers; they just forward the IP packet based on the 2.2.2.2 destination IP address. Figure 15-13 shows the concept; note that this packet may be routed by many routers in the Internet before arriving at R2.

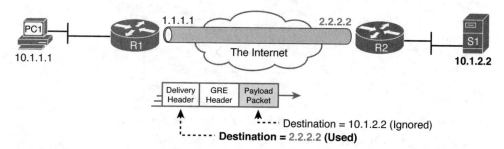

Figure 15-13 *Internet Routers Forwarding GRE IP Packet Based on Public IP Addresses*

When the GRE packet in Figure 15-13 finally arrives on the right side of the Internet, at R2, R2 needs to extract the original IP packet. With physical links, R2 would normally simply remove the old incoming data link header. With a GRE-encapsulated packet, the receiving router (R2) also needs to remove the delivery header and the GRE header, leaving the original packet, as shown in Figure 15-14.

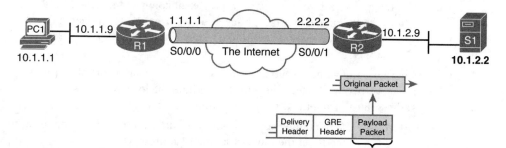

Figure 15-14 *Destination Tunnel Endpoint Decapsulates the Original Packet and Forwards It*

NOTE If the routers also configured the IPsec encryption part of the tunnel, just after the steps shown in Figure 15-14, the receiving router would then decrypt the original packet.

Configuring GRE Tunnels

Configuring GRE tunnels requires only a few commands. The challenge with GRE configuration comes in organizing the configuration parameters. The configuration requires a tunnel interface, with IP addresses from the secured part of the network configured with the **ip address** interface command. It also requires that the two routers declare both their own IP address (source) and the other router's IP address (destination), used in the unsecure part of the network. Figure 15-15 shows the organization of the various configuration parameters.

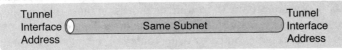

Addresses from Secured Network

Addresses from Unsecured Network (Usually Internet)

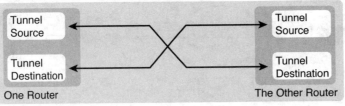

Figure 15-15 *GRE Tunnel Configuration: Relationship of Parameters*

The following list details the configuration steps on each router:

Step 1. Use the **interface tunnel** *number* global command to create a tunnel interface. The interface numbers have local meaning only and do not have to match between the two routers.

Step 2. (Optional) Use the **tunnel mode gre ip** interface subcommand in tunnel interface mode to tell IOS to use GRE encapsulation on the tunnel. (This is the default setting for a tunnel interface.)

Step 3. Use the **ip address** *address mask* interface subcommand to assign an IP address to the tunnel interface, using a subnet from the secure network's address range. The two routers on the tunnel should use addresses from the same subnet.

Step 4. Configure the tunnel's source IP address in the unsecured part of the network in one of two ways. Regardless of the method, the local router's source IP address must match the other router's tunnel destination.

  Step 4A. Use the **tunnel source** *ip-address* tunnel interface subcommand to directly set the tunnel's source IP address.

  Step 4B. Use the **tunnel source** *interface-id* tunnel interface subcommand to indirectly set the tunnel's source IP address by referencing an interface on the local router.

Step 5.   Use the **tunnel destination** {*ip-address* | *hostname*} command to configure the tunnel's destination IP address in the unsecured part of the network. (This value must match the IP address used by the other router as its tunnel source IP address.)

Step 6.   Add routes that use the tunnel by enabling a dynamic routing protocol on the tunnel or by configuring static IP routes.

As usual, an example can help quite a bit. The example, as you probably guessed, matches the example used throughout the last several pages, as shown in Figures 15-9 through 15-14. Figure 15-16 repeats all the interface numbers and IP addresses for reference. R1 and R2 form a tunnel using public addresses 1.1.1.1 and 2.2.2.2, respectively, in the unsecured network (the Internet). The tunnel uses private subnet 10.1.3.0/24, with R1 and R2 using IP addresses 10.1.3.1 and 10.1.3.2, respectively. Example 15-1 shows the configuration on R1, and Example 15-2 shows the configuration on R2.

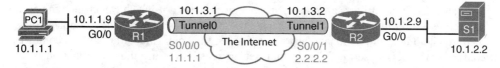

Figure 15-16   *Summary Diagram for Upcoming GRE Examples*

Example 15-1   *Tunnel Configuration on R1*

```
R1# show running-config
! Only the related configuration is listed
interface serial 0/0/0
 ip address 1.1.1.1 255.255.255.0
!
interface tunnel0
 ip address 10.1.3.1 255.255.255.0
 tunnel mode gre ip
 tunnel source serial0/0/0
 tunnel destination 2.2.2.2

! The OSPF configuration enables OSPF on the tunnel interface as well.
router ospf 1
 network 10.0.0.0 0.255.255.255 area 0
```

Example 15-2   *Tunnel Configuration on R2*

```
R2# show running-config
! Only the related configuration is listed
interface serial 0/0/1
 ip address 2.2.2.2 255.255.255.0
!
interface tunnel1
 ip address 10.1.3.2 255.255.255.0
```

```
tunnel mode gre ip
tunnel source serial0/0/1
tunnel destination 1.1.1.1

! The OSPF configuration enables OSPF on the tunnel interface as well.
router ospf 1
 network 10.0.0.0 0.255.255.255 area 0
```

Just to make sure the matching logic is clear, take a look at R2's configuration. R2's S0/0/1 interface has been configured with IP address 2.2.2.2. Then, under interface tunnel 1, the **tunnel source Serial0/0/1** command refers to that same interface, making R2's source IP address for the tunnel 2.2.2.2. Finally, referring back up to R1's configuration, its **tunnel destination 2.2.2.2** command clearly refers to the same IP address used by R2 as its source address. The same trail can be checked for R1's source address of 1.1.1.1 and R2's destination address 1.1.1.1.

Note also that IOS supports a variety of tunnel modes, each of which can change the encapsulation used on the tunnel as well as changing some other behaviors. The example shows the **tunnel mode gre ip** command just to let you see the command, although this command configures the default setting. That default setting tells IOS to use the encapsulation as shown in Figure 15-12: a delivery header that uses IP (that is, IPv4), with a GRE header to follow.

Although this chapter does not happen to include configurations that use other **tunnel mode** command options, it is easy to understand a few other options. For instance, a **tunnel mode gre ipv6** command would be used to create a point-to-point GRE tunnel that uses IPv6 to encapsulate the packets instead of IPv4. As another example, the command **tunnel mode gre multipoint** is used when configuring Dynamic Multipoint VPN (DMVPN), a topic discussed to a conceptual level later in this chapter.

Verifying a GRE Tunnel

The ultimate test of the tunnel is whether it can pass end-user traffic. However, some other **show** commands from the router tell us a lot about the status before trying a ping or traceroute from the user's device.

First, because the tunnel acts very much like a serial link, with interfaces on both routers, the usual commands that list interface status, IP addresses, and IP routes all show information about the GRE tunnel. For instance, Example 15-3 shows the familiar **show ip interface brief** command on R1, with R1's Tunnel0 interface highlighted.

Example 15-3 *Displaying the Interface State and IP Addresses, Including the Tunnel Interface*

```
R1# show ip interface brief
Interface              IP-Address     OK? Method Status                Protocol
GigabitEthernet0/0     10.1.1.9       YES manual up                    up
GigabitEthernet0/1     unassigned     YES manual administratively down down
Serial0/0/0            1.1.1.1        YES manual up                    up
Serial0/0/1            unassigned     YES manual administratively down down
Tunnel0                10.1.3.1       YES manual up                    up
```

The **show interfaces tunnel** *interface-number* command lists many counters plus the configuration settings, in addition to the interface status. Example 15-4 lists a sample, again for R1's Tunnel0 interface. Note that it lists the local router (R1) configuration of the source (1.1.1.1) and destination (2.2.2.2) IP addresses, and it confirms the use of GRE encapsulation over IP (IPv4), as highlighted in the example.

Example 15-4 *Tunnel Interface Details*

```
R1# show interfaces tunnel0
Tunnel0 is up, line protocol is up
  Hardware is Tunnel
  Internet address is 10.1.3.1/24
  MTU 17916 bytes, BW 100 Kbit/sec, DLY 50000 usec,
     reliability 255/255, txload 1/255, rxload 1/255
  Encapsulation TUNNEL, loopback not set
  Keepalive not set
  Tunnel source 1.1.1.1 (Serial0/0/0), destination 2.2.2.2
   Tunnel Subblocks:
      src-track:
         Tunnel0 source tracking subblock associated with Serial0/0/0
          Set of tunnels with source Serial0/0/0, 1 member (includes iterators), on
             interface <OK>
  Tunnel protocol/transport GRE/IP
! Lines omitted for brevity
```

Although a working tunnel interface is important, the routers will not use the tunnel interface unless routes try to forward packets over the tunnel interface. The configuration in this example shows that OSPF has been enabled on all interfaces in Class A network 10.0.0.0, the secure part of the internetwork. As a result, the routers should exchange OSPF routes and learn the same routes shown earlier in Figure 15-10. Example 15-5 shows proof, with R1 listing an OSPF-learned route to R2's LAN subnet of 10.1.2.0/24.

Example 15-5 *R1 Routes in Network 10.0.0.0*

```
R1# show ip route 10.0.0.0
Routing entry for 10.0.0.0/8, 5 known subnets
  Attached (4 connections)
  Variably subnetted with 2 masks
C        10.1.1.0/24 is directly connected, GigabitEthernet0/0
L        10.1.1.9/32 is directly connected, GigabitEthernet0/0
O        10.1.2.0/24 [110/1001] via 10.1.3.2, 00:07:55, Tunnel0
C        10.1.3.0/24 is directly connected, Tunnel0
L        10.1.3.1/32 is directly connected, Tunnel0
! Lines omitted for brevity
```

NOTE   The **show ip route 10.0.0.0** command lists the known routes inside network 10.0.0.0.

Finally, to prove the tunnel can forward traffic, the user can generate some traffic, or a handy extended ping or traceroute can serve as well. Example 15-6 shows an extended traceroute, sourced from R1's LAN IP address of 10.1.1.9, and sent to server 1's 10.1.2.2 IP address.

Example 15-6 *Extended Traceroute Shows the Tunnel Is Working*

```
R1# traceroute
Protocol [ip]:
Target IP address: 10.1.2.2
Source address: 10.1.1.9
Numeric display [n]:
Timeout in seconds [3]:
Probe count [3]:
Minimum Time to Live [1]:
Maximum Time to Live [30]:
Port Number [33434]:
Loose, Strict, Record, Timestamp, Verbose[none]:
Type escape sequence to abort.
Tracing the route to 10.1.2.2
VRF info: (vrf in name/id, vrf out name/id)
  1 10.1.3.2 0 msec 4 msec 0 msec
  2 10.1.2.2 4 msec 4 msec 0 msec
R1#
```

Example 15-6 shows that the traceroute completes, and it also lists R2's tunnel IP address (10.1.3.2) as the first router in the route. Note that the **traceroute** command does not list any routers in the unsecure part of the network, because the packets created by the **traceroute** command get encapsulated and sent from R1 to R2, just like any other packet.

Troubleshooting GRE Tunnels

In its most basic form, the configuration for a point-to-point GRE tunnel between two Cisco routers is simple. You refer to your own public IP address, either directly or by referencing an interface. You refer to the destination router, either by IP address or hostname. And you probably will configure some private IP addresses to make use of the tunnel. That is all you need to do to make a GRE tunnel work, assuming everything else works, such as the Internet connections on both ends.

From that summary, it may seem like there is little to discuss for troubleshooting GRE. This section takes a few pages to work through a couple of items that could prevent a GRE tunnel from working, going a bit beyond a configuration mistake in the relatively sparse GRE configuration.

Tunnel Interfaces and Interface State

The first and easiest configuration item to check is to make sure that the two routers refer to the correct IP addresses in the unsecure part of the network (typically the Internet). These are the addresses referenced by the **tunnel source** and **tunnel destination** commands. Earlier, Figure 15-15 showed the idea: The source address on one router should be the destination address on the other, and vice versa.

Of all the items that must be true before a point-to-point GRE tunnel works correctly, most, but not all, are tied to the tunnel interface state. For the tunnel to work, the tunnel interfaces on the endpoint routers must both reach an up/up state. To reach an up/up state, a tunnel interface must be configured with a **tunnel source** command and a **tunnel destination** command. Additionally, the following must be true of the tunnel source:

1. If configuring the **tunnel source** command by referencing a source interface, the interface must

   ■ Have an IP address assigned to it

   ■ Be in an up/up state

2. If configuring the **tunnel source** command by referencing a source IP address, the address must

   ■ Be an address assigned to an interface on the local router

   ■ Be in an up/up state for that interface on which the address is configured

In short, however it is referenced, the tunnel source must be an IP address on the local router on a currently working interface. If that is not true, the tunnel interface will remain in an up/down state. (Note that when a tunnel interface is created, it begins with an up/down state, because it has neither a **tunnel source** nor **tunnel destination** configured by default.)

A router's tunnel interface state is also impacted by the **tunnel destination** configuration, but those details can be a little trickier. Some settings cause IOS to accept the configuration, but cause the tunnel interface to not reach an up/up state. Other incorrect **tunnel destination** configuration settings cause IOS to reject the configuration. Those checks are

1. If configuring the **tunnel destination** command by referencing a destination IP address, the router

   ■ Must have a matching route to the destination address, or IOS will not move the tunnel interface to an up/up state

   ■ May use its default route as the matching route

2. If configuring the **tunnel destination** command by referencing a hostname, the router immediately attempts to resolve the name into an address per its name resolution settings. If:

   ■ The hostname does not resolve to an IP address, IOS rejects the **tunnel destination** command and does not store it in the configuration.

   ■ The hostname does resolve to an IP address, IOS stores that IP address in the **tunnel destination** command in the configuration, and does not store the hostname. Then the earlier rules about the tunnel destination IP address apply.

Basically, if you configure using a hostname, IOS immediately resolves the name, and if name resolution works, IOS stores the address, not the name. Then, for the tunnel interface to reach an up/up state, the router must have a route that matches the tunnel destination.

Example 15-7 shows a few samples to drive home the points about the tunnel destination. The example shows the configuration of two tunnel interfaces, both with the same source interface. The source interface meets all requirements. Focusing on the tunnel destination, the configuration uses two different hostnames with the following **tunnel destination** commands:

tunnel destination test1: Resolves to 10.1.6.1, which also has a matching route

tunnel destination test2: Name does not resolve

Example 15-7 *Examples of Using Hostnames with Tunnels*

```
R1# configure terminal
Enter configuration commands, one per line.  End with CNTL/Z.
R1(config)# interface tunnel 11
R1(config-if)# tunnel source G0/1
R1(config-if)# tunnel destination test1

R1(config)# interface tunnel 12
R1(config-if)# tunnel source G0/1
R1(config-if)# tunnel destination test2
Translating "test2"
                                              ^
% Invalid input detected at '^' marker.
R1(config-if)# ^Z
! Below, note that hostname test1 resolved to IP address 10.1.6.1 as stored in
! the tunnel destination command
R1# show running-config interface tunnel 11
interface Tunnel11
 no ip address
 tunnel source GigabitEthernet0/1
 tunnel destination 10.1.6.1
end
! Below, note the absence of the tunnel destination command because it was rejected
R1# show running-config interface tunnel 12
interface Tunnel12
 no ip address
 tunnel source GigabitEthernet0/1
end


R1# show ip interface brief | include Tunnel
Tunnel11                    unassigned      YES unset  up                      up
Tunnel12                    unassigned      YES unset  up                      down
```

Working through the example, first look at the portions related to tunnel 11. The configuration on interface tunnel 11 uses a hostname (test1). The **show running-config interface tunnel11** command reveals that the router resolved that name to address 10.1.6.1. Finally, the **show ip interface brief** command at the bottom of the example reveals that interface tunnel 11 reaches an up/up state. (Not shown: there is a route that matches 10.1.6.1.)

Now focus on interface tunnel 12. In the configuration section, note that the **tunnel destination test2** command was rejected by IOS. The message stating "Translating test2" means that it is doing name resolution, and that process fails. Because hostname test2 did not resolve to an IP address, the **tunnel destination test2** command was rejected; note that the **show running-config interface tunnel12** command does not list a **tunnel destination** command. Finally, the **show ip interface brief** command at the end of the example shows that interface tunnel 12 remains in an up/down state, because it does not yet have a tunnel destination configured.

15

Layer 3 Issues for Tunnel Interfaces

Getting both routers' tunnel interfaces to an up/up state is an important starting point. However, even once both routers have an up/up tunnel interface, other problems can exist. For instance, routers do not send packets to each other to test the tunnel to determine whether to put the tunnel in an up/up state.

Two tests give some great clues about whether the tunnel is really working:

- Ping the private IP address on the other end of the tunnel. For that to work, both routers' tunnel interfaces must be in an up/up state. Additionally, both routers must be able to place the packet into a GRE header, add a new IP header, forward over the tunnel, and remove the original packet.

- Enable a routing protocol on both ends of the tunnel. If a routing protocol neighbor relationship is formed, that also proves that packets can flow over the tunnel.

Issues with ACLs and Security

Almost every networking feature can then be broken by access control lists (ACL) and other security features like firewalls. In the case of Internet VPNs using GRE tunnels, those tunnels have endpoints at the edge of an enterprise network, but the tunnel itself runs through the Internet. So, not only can the enterprise's own devices filter traffic that makes the GRE tunnel fail, other devices not in direct control of the enterprise network engineer might also be filtering packets that impact the GRE tunnel.

For the part of the network in the control of the enterprise network engineer, you should be ready to notice issues with ACLs. In particular, the GRE protocol can be easily overlooked and discarded by an ACL, even an ACL on the router where the tunnel is configured.

First, as you will review later in Chapter 17, "Advanced IPv4 Access Control Lists," an outbound ACL on a router does not filter packets that the same router creates. That rule applies for the new packets created by a GRE tunnel. As a result, a router that is a GRE tunnel endpoint will not filter the packets it creates to send over the tunnel, at least with an outbound ACL on that same router.

However, routers do not bypass any ACL logic for inbound ACLs. Routers will look at all inbound packets, so a router might filter GRE packets entering the router, depending on the matching logic in the ACL.

So, the first item when thinking about GRE and possible ACL issues is to find inbound ACLs on one of the tunnel routers. The second is to make sure the GRE traffic is permitted by those ACLs and any others in the network, and GRE is a bit different compared to some other protocols.

GRE is not a TCP or UDP application. Instead, GRE acts like another transport protocol in that the GRE header follows the IPv4 header, like TCP and UDP. The IP header identifies the next protocol after the header with the IP header's protocol field, as noted in Figure 15-17.

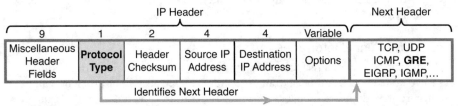

GRE = 47, TCP = 6, UDP = 17...

Figure 15-17   *GRE Shown as the Next Header After IP, as IP Protocol 47*

IP ACLs match the IP protocol field with a series of keywords, with the **ip** keyword matching all the protocols. That is the most common mistake. An ACL could have dozens of **permit** commands, with **permit tcp** this, and **permit udp** that, and none of those would match GRE. GRE is a different IP protocol, and is not a TCP or UDP application. To match GRE with a **permit** command, the ACL needs to

- Have a **permit ip …** command that matches the GRE tunnel's unsecured (public) addresses, or…

- Have a **permit gre …** command (which matches the GRE protocol specifically) that also matches the GRE tunnel's unsecured (public) IP addresses

Example 15-8 shows some pseudocode for an ACL added to Router R1 that explicitly permits GRE. First, it has a couple of pseudocode **permit** commands that use **permit tcp** and **permit udp**, to represent the kinds of matching you would do for other purposes. No matter what was configured in those commands, they could not match the GRE traffic. The **permit gre any any** command then matches all GRE packets from all sources and destinations, matching GRE (IP protocol 47).

Example 15-8   *ACL That Correctly Permits GRE*

```
R1# configure terminal
R1(config)# ip access-list extended inbound-from-Internet
R1(config-ext-nacl)# permit tcp (whatever you want)
R1(config-ext-nacl)# permit udp (whatever you want)
R1(config-ext-nacl)# permit gre any any
R1(config-ext-nacl)# interface S0/0/0
R1(config-if)# ip access-group inbound-from-Internet in
R1(config-if)# ^z
R1#
```

Multipoint Internet VPNs Using DMVPN

Site-to-site VPNs with GRE work well, but the point-to-point topology has some shortcomings. For instance, consider a company with a central site and hundreds of small retail sites. Those retail sites need Internet access as well as a private WAN to connect back to the central site. Given the relatively low pricing of Internet access options, the company decides to implement a plan with using the Internet as a WAN, using site-to-site VPN tunnels with GRE and IPsec. Figure 15-18 shows the general idea.

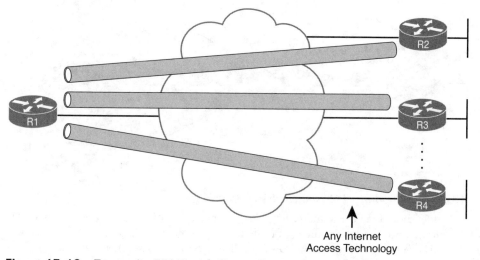

Figure 15-18   *Enterprise WAN with Site-to-Site Internet VPN*

Using GRE tunnels on a large scale has some drawbacks, mainly related to the static configuration, the fact that the central site device has a tunnel interface and configuration per tunnel, and the traffic flow. In particular:

- With static configuration on both ends of each GRE tunnel, adding a new remote site means that you also have to add configuration at the central site.

- The central site configuration can get large due to the per-tunnel configuration.

- The traffic flow works well for networks in which most traffic goes between the hub-and-spoke sites, but if the spoke (remote) sites want to send packets to each other, the network engineer must either

  - Allow routing to send spoke-to-spoke packets through the hub

  - Manually configure tunnels between spoke sites so that the spokes can send packets directly to each other (which adds even more configuration to manage).

The Cisco Dynamic Multipoint VPN (DMVPN) IOS feature solves these problems while still using GRE and IPsec. Focusing on the word *multipoint* for a moment, DMVPN uses a multipoint GRE tunnel. With a multipoint tunnel, a site can send and receive with any other site on the same multipoint tunnel. Figure 15-19 shows a drawing meant to represent a multipoint GRE tunnel.

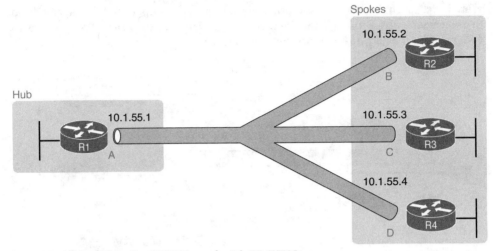

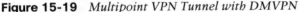

Figure 15-19   *Multipoint VPN Tunnel with DMVPN*

DMVPN does more than use a multipoint GRE tunnel instead of a point-to-point tunnel. To reduce configuration, and make the operation more dynamic, DMVPN adds some dynamic processes. Those processes rely on a protocol called *Next Hop Resolution Protocol* (NHRP), which works as follows:

1. One site on the tunnel acts as the hub site and as NHRP server.

2. The spoke sites initially can communicate only with the hub site.

3. The spoke sites (as NHRP clients) register their matching public and private IP addresses with the NHRP server (using NHRP protocol messages). (This is a key step in avoiding any configuration on the hub router for each new spoke site added to the network.)

Figure 15-20 shows an example of the process. Router R1, as the hub, has only a little configuration, including the configuration that sets aside an unsecure (public) IP address to use to send packets over the Internet, and the tunnel interface private IP address. However, the NHRP server (the hub router) learns the information and stores it in an NHRP mapping table, as shown in Figure 15-20 on the lower left. The figure shows an example of R3 registering its private IP address (10.1.55.3) and public IP address (C). (Note that the figure uses A, B, C, and D to represent the public IP addresses; the actual addresses would be assigned by the ISPs to which each site connects.)

So far in this DMVPN discussion, the hub router now has one tunnel interface to talk to many hub sites, rather than one tunnel interface per site. Also, the hub site does not need to configure any commands to support a new spoke site, because NHRP learns the relevant information. However, the discussion so far has not yet shown how DMVPN allows spokes to send packets directly to each other without any configuration about the other spoke.

Using the network in Figure 15-20 as an example, imagine that spoke Router R2 needs to send IP packets to subnets off spoke Router R3. R2 will use a routing protocol, and learn routes for those subnets. Router R2 learns about the subnets at R3's sites, but R2 does not know R3's public IP address. How can R2 learn R3's unsecure (public) IP address, and do so dynamically, without having to configure that setting? The solution is simple: The NHRP server already knows all that information, so just ask the NHRP server. Figure 15-21 shows the idea, the hub router R1 using NHRP messages to announce R3's public and private address pair to the other spoke sites.

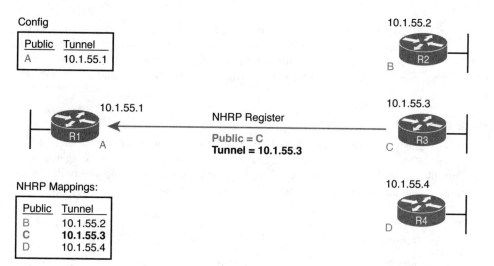

Figure 15-20 *Spoke Site Registers with NHRP Server to Enable Dynamic Mapping*

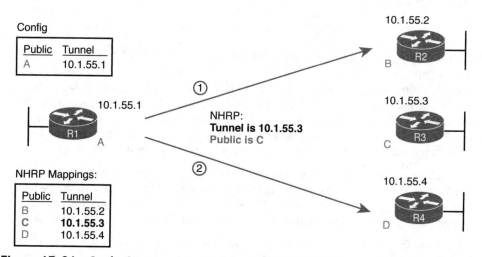

Figure 15-21 *Spoke Sites Learning Information with NHRP to Enable Spoke-to-Spoke Communication*

Once Router R2 knows Router R3's tunnel and public IP addresses, R2 has enough information to start sending packets directly to R3 over the multipoint GRE tunnel.

PPP over Ethernet

This third and final major section of the chapter revisits a familiar protocol: Point-to-Point Protocol, or PPP. While PPP is used on serial links, as shown in Chapter 13, "Implementing Point-to-Point WANs," it is also used over some types of Internet access links, like DSL links, by extending the PPP protocol using PPP over Ethernet (PPPoE). PPPoE keeps all the useful PPP features, like its different control protocols, as well as PPP authentication like CHAP. However, the PPP protocol is transported inside Ethernet frames out Ethernet interfaces.

The Cisco R&S and ICND2 200-105 exam topics list PPPoE Client functions as a topic to be covered for not only concepts, but also configuration, verification, and troubleshooting. This last major section of the chapter mirrors those verbs from the exam topics, with four subheadings, one each on PPPoE concepts, configuration, verification, and then troubleshooting.

PPPoE Concepts

PPP was originally used on serial links, which includes those links created with dial-up analog and ISDN modems. For instance, the link from a dial user to an ISP, using analog modems, likely uses PPP today, and has for a long time. Figure 15-22 shows a basic representation of that analog dial connection with a modem that uses PPP.

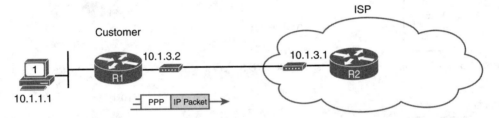

Figure 15-22   *PPP Frames Between Routers over a Dial Connection to an ISP*

ISPs used PPP as the data link protocol for a couple of reasons. First, PPP supports a way to assign IP addresses to the other end of the PPP link. ISPs can use PPP to assign each customer one public IPv4 address to use. But more important for this discussion is that PPP supports CHAP, and ISPs often want to use CHAP to authenticate customers. Then, when using CHAP to authenticate, ISPs could check accounting records to determine whether the customer's bill was paid before letting the customer connect to the Internet.

Now, think back a bit to the history of some of these Internet access technologies. ISPs in the 1990s had mostly dial customers using analog modems and PPP. Even into the 2000s, ISPs still had analog dial customers using PPP. However, by the early 2000s, DSL was becoming more common in the market, and DSL is a natural replacement for analog dial.

So, telcos and ISPs liked analog dial with PPP, but they wanted to move customers to the faster DSL...and they still wanted to use PPP! However, the DSL connect often connects a customer device (PC or router) with an Ethernet link to a DSL modem, which then connects to the phone line (see earlier Figure 15-2). That Ethernet interface on the customer PC or router only supported Ethernet data link protocols, and not PPP.

The solution was to create a new RFC that defined how to send PPP frames over Ethernet, encapsulated in an Ethernet frame, with the protocol called PPP over Ethernet. PPPoE basically creates a tunnel through the DSL connection for the purpose of sending PPP frames between the customer router and the ISP router, as shown in Figure 15-23.

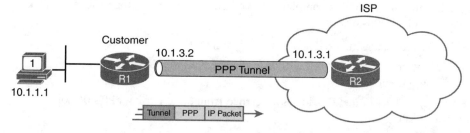

Figure 15-23 *Tunneling Concept to Create a PPP Link over Ethernet*

DSL does not create a single point-to-point physical link between the customer router and the ISP router, but it does create a logical equivalent called a PPPoE session. With PPPoE (and related protocols), the routers logically create such a tunnel. From one perspective, the routers create and send PPP frames, as if the link were a dial link between the routers. But before sending the frames over any physical link, the routers encapsulate the frames inside various headers, shown generically in the figure as a tunnel header.

> **NOTE**   For the purposes of this chapter, the specifics of the tunnel header shown in Figure 15-23 do not matter. However, the PPPoE tunnel header in this case has a typical Ethernet header, a short PPPoE header, and then the usual PPP frame (which includes the IP packet).

PPPoE Configuration

PPPoE configuration and verification can be a bit challenging compared to some other router features discussed in this book. You configure PPPoE in a couple of different configuration modes. Then, once configured, PPPoE dynamically adds some important components as well. So it is important to take your time through the PPPoE configuration and verification sections.

The rest of this section uses a physical topology as shown in Figure 15-24. It uses two routers with a crossover Ethernet cable between them. Note that while it does not use DSL, the PPPoE concepts and configuration still work the same on the customer side.

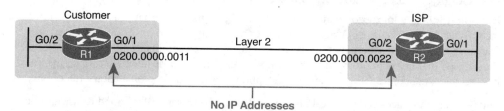

Figure 15-24 *Network Used for PPPoE Examples*

Note that IP is not enabled on the link between the routers. That is, neither router has an **ip address** subcommand on its Ethernet interface for that link in the middle. As a result, the routers treat the link as a Layer 2 link. But something else in the router has to make the router want to send the frames out those interfaces, and that is where the PPPoE configuration meets the physical interfaces.

To begin, Example 15-9 shows a completed PPPoE configuration on Router R1 that works. In this case, it follows this design:

- Use CHAP, with username Fred and password Barney.

- R1's G0/1 interface connects to the ISP and is a Layer 2 interface (that is, it has no IP address configured).

- Use a dynamically assigned IP address as learned from the ISP using PPP's IP Control Protocol (IPCP).

- Optionally, but to make the later verification commands more obvious, define a recognizable MAC address on the physical interface.

Example 15-9   *PPPoE Configuration on R1 (PPPoE Client)*

```
interface dialer 2
! Layer 3 details next
 ip address negotiated
 mtu 1492
! Layer 2 details next
 encapsulation ppp
 ppp chap hostname Fred
 ppp chap password Barney
! Layer 1 details next
 dialer pool 1
! Physical interface - the one connected towards the ISP
interface G0/1
 no ip address                        ! Physical link has no layer 3 address
 pppoe-client dial-pool-number 1
 pppoe enable                         ! auto-generated by previous command
 mac-address 0200.0000.0011          ! Not required; personal choice
 no shutdown
```

PPPoE Configuration Breakdown: Dialers and Layer 1

Example 15-9 has a lot of commands to work through. First, note that it uses a dialer interface. Dialer interfaces have been in IOS for a long time, and Cisco has found a variety of features that make use of a dialer interface. Originally, IOS used dialer interfaces when a router used dial-up technology to make a phone call to another device to set up a physical link, so the name comes from the ancient telephony term of dialing on a rotary telephone.

Today, dialer interfaces act as logical interfaces that can be dynamically bound to use another interface. These interfaces cooperate to perform a function. For instance, for PPPoE, the dialer interface holds configuration for IP and PPP, but it is not a physical Ethernet interface. So, to let the dialer interface use G0/1 as the physical interface in this scenario:

- The configuration puts interface G0/1 into a dial pool, specifically numbered dial pool 1, per the **pppoe-client dial-pool-number 1** command. This command means that G0/1 is available to be used by dialer interfaces wanting to do PPPoE.

- Dialer interface 2 references dial pool number 1 with the **dialer pool 1** command. Because the dial pool number matches, interface dialer 2 will use G0/1 for PPPoE.

Note that the dialer interface number (2 in this case) and dialer pool number (1 in this case) do not have to match. The customer network engineer can just choose an integer value to use; they do not have to match the ISP router. However, the dial pool number listed by the **dialer pool** command on the dialer interface, and the dial pool number listed by the **pppoe-client dial-pool-number** subcommand on the physical interface, must match.

The configuration of the dial pool gives the logical dialer interface a physical interface to use, so it is in some ways a physical layer (Layer 1) feature. In fact, you can break down all of Example 15-9's configuration into groupings by Layers 1, 2, and 3, a theme carried through the rest of this section. Figure 15-25 shows the commands versus the layers.

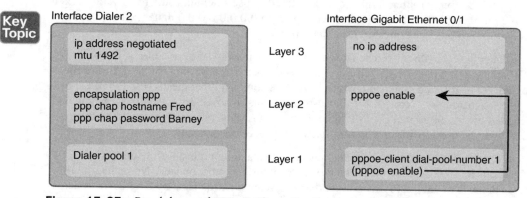

Figure 15-25 *Breakdown of PPPoE Client Configuration on Router R1*

PPPoE Configuration Breakdown: PPP and Layer 2

The dialer interface holds the PPP configuration used to create the PPPoE session. Focusing only on the configuration for now, start with the dialer interface. The dialer uses PPP directly, but not PPPoE. So, it needs the **encapsulation ppp** command to define the data link protocol. This is the same **encapsulation ppp** command you may remember from Chapter 13.

The dialer typically includes PPP CHAP authentication as well, mainly because the session happens between an ISP and its customer. The configuration here for PPPoE differs slightly from the CHAP configuration shown back in Chapter 13. Here, the authentication happens in one direction: the ISP authenticates the customer router, in this case R1. That small change in logic creates the small change in configuration. R1 simply needs to configure the username and password as shown.

Finally, the physical Ethernet interface (G0/1 in this example) does need one command to enable PPPoE on the interface: the **pppoe enable** subcommand. However, IOS adds this command to the interface automatically if you configure the **pppoe-client** interface subcommand. So, while Figure 15-25 shows the **pppoe enable** command in the Layer 1 section because it is automatically configured, it in effect enables PPPoE on the physical interface.

PPPoE Configuration Breakdown: Layer 3

The Layer 3 configuration, as noted at the top of Figure 15-25, has a couple of surprising ideas compared to earlier IP addressing commands.

First, the physical interface connected to the ISP (G0/1 in this example) has no IP address, will not learn an IP address, and does not need one for the duration of using PPPoE. Yes, IP traffic will be forwarded to and from the ISP in and out that physical interface, but not through enabling IP on the physical interface (G0/1 in this case). (Instead, the Layer 3 logic is applied to the dialer interface, which then uses the physical interface.) So the physical interface needs a **no ip address** command to make sure no address exists there.

Second, the dialer interface serves as the primary Layer 3 interface for PPPoE. The dialer interface will be listed in the output of the **show ip route** command as an outgoing interface, and the dialer interface can be referenced in commands that define static routes. In fact, if the customer router in this example wanted to use a default route to forward packets to the Internet, it might be configured with **ip route 0.0.0.0 0.0.0.0 dialer 2**. The command would not reference the physical Ethernet interface.

The dialer interface does need an IP address. To dynamically learn an address, PPPoE uses PPP's IPCP rather than DHCP. To cause that to happen, the customer router (R1) uses the **ip address negotiated** command, which is the IOS command that means "use PPP IPCP to negotiate an address." Note that if the customer wants to use a static IP address, maybe one assigned by the ISP so that the PPPoE configuration is stable, the address could be configured with the usual **ip address** *address mask* interface subcommand.

Finally, as an important housekeeping item, set the maximum transmission unit (MTU) for IP packets to 1492 as shown with the **mtu 1492** interface subcommand. Normally, the IP MTU defaults to 1500. PPPoE adds another 8-byte header, reducing by 8 bytes the space for the IP packet, so reducing the IP MTU to 1492 prevents the router from having to do unnecessary work to fragment packets.

PPPoE Configuration Summary

This section introduced the commands to configure PPPoE in the context of a single example. The following configuration checklist summarizes the configuration for easier review and study.

Config Checklist

Step 1. Configure Layer 1 details.

> **Step 1A.** Configure a dialer interface:
>
> > **I.** Use the **interface dialer** *number* command to create the dialer interface; choose a number not already used on the local router by some other dialer interface.
> >
> > **II.** Use the **dialer pool** *number* interface subcommand to refer to a pool of Ethernet-family interfaces that can be used for PPPoE.
>
> **Step 1B.** Configure the physical interface(s):
>
> > **I.** Use the **pppoe-client dial-pool-number** *number* interface subcommand to add the interface to the same pool number configured on the dialer interface.

Step 2. Configure Layer 2 details.

> **Step 2A.** Configure PPP on the dialer interface:
>
> > **I.** Use the **encapsulation ppp** interface subcommand to enable PPP on the dialer interface.

> **II.** Use the **ppp chap hostname** *name* interface subcommand to define the username with which to authenticate to the ISP.
>
> **III.** Use the **ppp chap password** *password* interface subcommand to define the password with which to authenticate to the ISP.

Step 2B. Configure PPPoE on the Ethernet interface(s):

> **I.** Use the **pppoe enable** interface subcommand to enable PPPoE. (IOS adds this command automatically when the **pppoe-client** interface subcommand is configured.)

Step 3.   Configure Layer 3 details.

Step 3A. Configure IP on the dialer interface:

> **I.** Use the **ip address negotiated** interface subcommand to tell the dialer interface to use PPP's IPCP to learn the IP address to use.
>
> **II.** Use the **mtu 1492** interface subcommand to change from the default of 1500 to allow for the 8 extra header bytes used by PPPoE.

Step 3B. Disable IP on the Ethernet interface(s):

> **I.** Use the **no ip address** interface subcommand to disable IP routing on the physical interface and remove the IPv4 address from the interface.

A Brief Aside About Lab Experimentation with PPPoE

For most configuration topics in this book, you learn enough information to go into a lab and configure a couple of routers and switches to make the feature work and then experiment with **show** commands. However, this chapter does not explain the details of the ISP's PPPoE configuration, because the PPPoE exam topic states that it is about the client side only. And the configuration is not the same on both the customer and ISP routers.

However, for those of you who want to try to re-create the examples shown in this section of the book, please do. To give you a start, use a configuration like Example 15-10 for the ISP; it is a copy of the relevant configuration from the router labeled R2 that was used when creating the upcoming examples. Then use a lab with a crossover Ethernet cable between two routers, with a topology like Figure 15-24.

Example 15-10 *ISP Router Configuration Sample*

```
ip local pool WOPool 10.1.3.2 10.1.3.254
bba-group pppoe WOGroup
 virtual-template 1
!
username Fred password Barney
!
interface virtual-template 1
  ip address 10.1.3.1 255.255.255.0
  peer default ip address pool WOPool
  ppp authentication chap callin
!
```

```
interface GigabitEthernet0/2
  no ip address
  pppoe enable group WOGroup
  no shutdown
  mac-address 0200.0000.0022
```

NOTE   Check out the Config Lab section of my CCNA blog (http://blog.certskills.com/ccna) for a couple of Config Labs about PPPoE.

PPPoE Verification

While PPPoE configuration has enough detail to be a challenge, PPPoE verification has a few more challenges because of how PPPoE works internally in IOS. Before reviewing a bunch of command output, it helps to get an idea about those internals. So, consider the ideas in Figure 15-26. The figure shows the two familiar interfaces from the configuration section, namely, a dialer interface and Ethernet interface. It adds two boxes for discussion:

PPPoE Session: A reference to the IOS internal process that performs the PPPoE work and keeps status variables for the PPPoE control protocols

Virtual-Access Interface: Another logical interface, dynamically created by IOS once the PPPoE session is up and working, and bound to the dialer interface

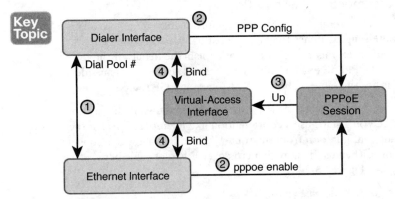

Figure 15-26   *PPPoE Verification Concepts and Interfaces*

The figure represents some big ideas with what IOS displays in PPPoE **show** commands. Working through the concepts represented in the figure can help you make more sense of the upcoming command output. Following the numbered steps in the figure:

Step 1.   The dial interface and Ethernet interface are associated by referencing the same dial pool number in the configuration.

Step 2.   Some part of IOS must act to implement PPP and the PPPoE specifics. Call this part of IOS the *PPPoE session*, as represented on the far right of the figure. That box represents the IOS PPPoE session logic, status variables for the PPP Control Protocols (CP), and sends and receives the PPPoE messages to/from the ISP.

Step 3. IOS creates a virtual-access interface if the PPPoE session reaches the desired up state. This dynamically created interface acts as a PPPoE interface. The virtual-access interface holds much of the Layer 2 PPPoE operational settings and counters.

Step 4. The three interfaces in the figure are separate, but they work closely together, and are considered to be bound together for the purposes of PPPoE. Various **show** commands identify these bindings.

Summarizing the ideas about the interfaces, the physical interface sends Ethernet frames; the virtual-access interface (as the PPPoE interface) sends PPPoE frames by making use of the physical interface; and the dialer interface (as the Layer 3 interface) sends packets, relying on the PPPoE interface to encapsulate the packet and then send it out the physical interface.

With those big ideas in mind, now take a look at some of the related **show** commands. The rest of this section assumes the topology shown in Figure 15-24 and the configuration shown in Example 15-9. Note also that Figure 15-25 repeats the configuration in Example 15-9 but organizes the commands based on TCP/IP layers. The upcoming examples list **show** command output taken when PPPoE was working correctly.

Verifying Dialer and Virtual-Access Interface Bindings

With PPPoE, the output of the **show interfaces dialer** *number* command has a lot of interesting information. In particular:

■ When a PPPoE session exists, the dialer interface is bound to a dynamically created virtual-access interface. As a result, the **show interfaces dialer** command lists output for not just one interface, but two: one group of about 20 output lines for the dialer interface, and another set for the virtual-access interface to which it is bound.

■ Both sections of output list some information about binding to the other interface (dialer bound to virtual-access, and vice versa).

■ The dialer interface output confirms the Layer 3 focus of the dialer interface (listing the IP address), but with PPP's Link Control Protocol (LCP) closed.

■ The virtual-access interface output confirms the Layer 2 focus of the interface, with PPP's LCP open, but with no IP address.

Example 15-11 shows the output from the **show interfaces dialer 2** command taken from customer router R1. The highlighted lines are discussed following the example.

Example 15-11 *Displaying the Dialer and Virtual-Access Interfaces*

```
R1# show interfaces dialer 2
Dialer2 is up, line protocol is up (spoofing)
  Hardware is Unknown
  Internet address is 10.1.3.2/32
  MTU 1492 bytes, BW 56 Kbit/sec, DLY 20000 usec,
     reliability 255/255, txload 1/255, rxload 1/255
  Encapsulation PPP, LCP Closed, loopback not set
  Keepalive set (10 sec)
```

```
    DTR is pulsed for 1 seconds on reset
    Interface is bound to Vi2
 ! Interface counter lines removed for brevity
Bound to:
Virtual-Access2 is up, line protocol is up
   Hardware is Virtual Access interface
   MTU 1492 bytes, BW 56 Kbit/sec, DLY 20000 usec,
       reliability 255/255, txload 1/255, rxload 1/255
   Encapsulation PPP, LCP Open
   Stopped: CDPCP
   Open: IPCP
PPPoE vaccess, cloned from Dialer2
   Vaccess status 0x44, loopback not set
   Keepalive set (10 sec)
   Interface is bound to Di2 (Encapsulation PPP)
    ! Counter lines removed for brevity
```

First off, PPPoE is working in this example. It shows the dialer interface with a line status of up, and a line protocol status of "up (spoofing)," which is the normal working state. (The word *spoofing* is a reference to the fact that the data link logic sits elsewhere, in this case on the virtual-access interface.) If you look about halfway down the output, you can find the second half of the output, about interface virtual-access 2. This interface has a line and protocol status of up and up, again which is the normal state when PPPoE is working.

Also, it is important to note that Example 15-11 shows the output from one command only; it just happens to list information about both the dialer interface and the bound virtual-access interface.

Focusing on the top half of the output, for the dialer interface, the output lists the configured IP MTU of 1492, and the learned IP address of 10.1.3.2. It shows the fact that it uses PPP encapsulation, but LCP is closed—the dialer interface (the Layer 3 interface) does not do the PPP work, so the output lists LCP as closed for this interface. Finally, the dialer interface output lines state that the dialer interface is bound to Vi2, which is shorthand for Virtual-access 2.

The second half of the output, for interface Vi2, lists similar info. While it shows PPP in use, it also shows LCP as open, because this interface does the PPP/PPPoE functions, and LCP is part of PPP. However, the virtual-access interface has no Layer 3 function, so look for an IP address; there is none. The IP address sits on the dialer interface. Finally, the bottom of the output confirms that this interface is bound to Di2, which is shorthand for Dialer2.

Note that while the **show interfaces dialer 2** command lists information about the bound virtual-access interface (when PPPoE is working), you can also list the virtual-access interface details with a command like **show interfaces virtual-access 2**.

Verifying Virtual-Access Interface Configuration

That one command in Example 15-11, **show interfaces dialer 2**, reveals many details about a working PPPoE session, including details about the dynamically created virtual-access interface. This next short topic looks at how IOS builds the configuration for that virtual-access interface.

Interestingly, IOS uses the dialer interface as a configuration template to build the virtual-access interface's configuration. To see what IOS does, use the **show interfaces virtual-access 2 configuration** command (or **show int vi2 conf** for short). This command shows the configuration for the dynamically created virtual-access interface, which copies some of the dialer interface configuration, as shown in Example 15-12. Working through the three commands in the example:

1. The first command is a reminder of the configuration of interface dialer 2, as seen earlier in Example 15-9.

2. The second command, **show interfaces virtual-access 2 configuration**, shows the IOS-generated configuration. Note the highlighted lines from the first command are the ones that IOS copies to the configuration of the virtual-access interface. (Additionally, the first highlighted line is a great description of what the interface does: it is the PPPoE interface.)

3. The third (last) command shows the running-config section for interface virtual-access 2. Note that the configuration file holds fewer commands, and does not include the PPP configuration that IOS dynamically pulls from the dialer interface.

Example 15-12 *Displaying Layer 2 PPP Orientation of Virtual-Access Interface*

```
R1# show running-config interface dialer 2
Building configuration…

Current configuration: 159 bytes
!
interface Dialer 2
 mtu 1492
 ip address negotiated
 encapsulation ppp
 dialer pool 1
 ppp chap hostname Fred
 ppp chap password 0 Barney
 no cdp enable

! The next command shows the configuration generated by IOS for the virtual-access
! interface
R1# show interfaces virtual-access 2 configuration
Virtual-Access2 is a PPP over Ethernet link (sub)interface
Derived configuration : 109 bytes
!
interface Virtual-Access2
 mtu 1492
 ppp chap hostname Fred
 ppp chap password 0 Barney
 pulse-time 0
end
```

```
R1# show running-config interface virtual-access2
Building configuration...

Current configuration : 58 bytes
!
interface Virtual-Access2
 mtu 1492
 no ip address
end
```

Verifying PPPoE Session Status

As discussed back in Chapter 13, PPP uses a variety of control protocols, including LCP for core PPP functions. When PPPoE starts on the customer router, it sends and receives PPPoE messages, including those for LCP, to decide whether the PPP session can work or not. Each router then keeps track of the status of the PPPoE state, which can be displayed with the **show pppoe session** command.

Figure 15-27 shows a representation of the data found about the PPPoE session with the **show pppoe session interface g0/1** command. In particular, it shows all three interfaces involved in making PPPoE work, along with the MAC address used by both devices. The figure organizes the information to act as a comparison to upcoming Example 15-13, which lists the same information.

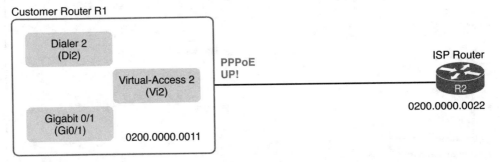

Figure 15-27 *Details Found in Example 15-13 Output*

Example 15-13 *Connecting the Physical, Virtual-Access, Dialer, and PPPoE State*

```
R1# show pppoe session interface gigabitEthernet 0/1
    1 client session

Uniq ID  PPPoE  RemMAC          Port          VT   VA         State
         SID    LocMAC                              VA-st      Type
   N/A     1    0200.0000.0022  Gi0/1         Di2  Vi2        UP
                0200.0000.0011                     UP
```

Note that the **show pppoe session** command lists the same kind of information shown in Example 15-13, but for all PPPoE sessions on the router. The **show pppoe session interface gigabitethernet0/1** command in the example limits the output to a message group for all PPPoE sessions off the listed interface (G0/1).

Verifying Dialer Interface Layer 3 Status

The dialer interface acts as a Layer 3 interface for the router in addition to being a configuration template for creating the virtual-access interface. So, the dialer interface should have an IP address. If learned dynamically, the address is typically learned with PPPoE, specifically by IPCP. Additionally, all routes in the IP routing table will reference the dialer interface instead of the virtual-access or Ethernet interface used by PPPoE.

In the continuing example in this section, two commands on customer router R1 confirm that the dialer has an IP address and that routes use the dialer interface. The **show ip route** command lists a connected route for both R1's learned interface address of 10.1.3.2 and the neighboring ISP's address of 10.1.3.1. PPP IPCP announces the address on the other end of the PPP link, so R1 learns R2's IP address (10.1.3.1) and adds a connected route as shown, as shown in Example 15-14.

Example 15-14   *Displaying Layer 3 Orientation of Dialer Interface*

```
R1# show ip route
! Legend omitted for brevity

      10.0.0.0/8 is variably subnetted, 4 subnets, 2 masks
C        10.1.1.0/24 is directly connected, GigabitEthernet0/2
L        10.1.1.9/32 is directly connected, GigabitEthernet0/2
C        10.1.3.1/32 is directly connected, Dialer2
C        10.1.3.2/32 is directly connected, Dialer2
R1# show ip interface brief dialer 2
Interface              IP-Address      OK? Method Status          Protocol
Dialer2                10.1.3.2        YES IPCP   up              up
```

The second command in the example lists the one line in the **show ip interface brief** command output for the dialer interface. Note that it lists the address, but more importantly, it lists the method as "IPCP." This is a confirmation that R1 learned the address through PPPoE, specifically PPP's IPCP.

PPPoE Troubleshooting

Like many networking features, the Layer 3 features simply do not work if the Layer 2 function they rely upon has a problem. Similarly, a Layer 2 problem often cannot be noticed if the underlying Layer 1 also has problems. In most cases, if you have problems with the network, data link, and physical layers, you have to work from the lower layers up the stack to find the issues.

This troubleshooting section takes a similar approach. Trying to cover every combination of missing or incorrect PPPoE configuration, with the resulting differences in **show** command output, would be pretty laborious. Instead, this section takes a structured approach to rebuild the configuration shown throughout the earlier PPPoE topics, specifically as listed in Example 15-9 and repeated in Figure 15-25. By configuring a few related commands and then stopping to show and discuss the current status, you can learn about what status to expect if a configuration omits some configuration or uses the wrong parameters on some configuration.

15

This section builds the configuration on the dialer interface, plus on the physical interface, in three different steps, as listed here. Note that the figure organizes the configuration based on TCP/IP Layers 1, 2, and 3, as outlined earlier in Figure 15-25 (repeated here as Figure 15-28 for convenience).

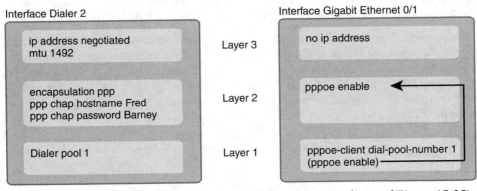

Figure 15-28   *PPPoE Client Configuration on Router R1 (Duplicate of Figure 15-25)*

The next few topics in this chapter work through an analysis of the status of PPPoE at various stages of configuration, until the configuration is completed, based on these steps. At each step, the text makes some comments to point out the key facts about the current state.

Step 1.   Add the Layer 1 configuration per Figure 15-28.

Step 2.   Add the Layer 2 configuration per Figure 15-28.

Step 3.   Add the Layer 3 configuration per Figure 15-28.

Step 0: Status Before Beginning the First Step

This troubleshooting scenario begins with R1 having all default configuration in relation to PPPoE, except that the configuration does begin with a few statements already on Router R1 (the customer router), as shown in Example 15-15. Note that the MAC address is set on the interface, for the sole purpose of making it easier to find in **show** command output. For the same reason, ISP Router R2 has been set to use MAC address 0200.0000.0022.

Example 15-15   *Relevant Configuration on Customer Router (R1) at Beginning of Troubleshooting*

```
R1# show running-config interface gigabitethernet0/1
Building configuration...

Current configuration : 202 bytes
!
interface GigabitEthernet0/1
 mac-address 0200.0000.0011
 no ip address
end
R1# show running-config interface Dialer2
Building configuration...
```

```
Current configuration : 55 bytes
!
interface Dialer2
 no ip address
```

15

Additionally, the dialer 2 interface has been created with the **interface dialer 2** command, but with no further interface configuration commands added. The reason for configuring the dialer interface first, without other configuration, is to emphasize some details about the dialer interface's status.

The interface status of a dialer interface, before adding any configuration at all, is different than the status of most any interface on a router or switch. You could configure the dialer interface with a **shutdown** command, and it would have an administratively disabled line status like any other router interface. However, the dialer interface is in a **no shutdown** state by default.

When a dialer interface is not fully working, which is true when there are no subcommands configured on the dialer interface, both the interface and protocol status will be "up (spoofing)," as shown in Example 15-16. The **show ip interface brief** command will list the two status codes (the interface status and the protocol status) both as up. However, the **show interfaces** command lists a longer status value of up (spoofing). (Note that the **show interfaces dialer 2 | include line** command filters the output to list only the line with "line" in it.)

Example 15-16 *Step 0: Status of Dialer 2 After Creation but with No Other Configuration*

```
R1# show interfaces dialer 2 | include line
Dialer2 is up (spoofing), line protocol is up (spoofing)
R1# show ip interface brief dialer 2
Interface              IP-Address      OK? Method Status         Protocol
Dialer2                unassigned      YES unset  up             up
R1# show pppoe session
R1#
```

At the bottom of the output, the **show pppoe session** command implies that PPPoE is not working yet, because it returns no lines of output. With PPPoE working, this command lists a small group of output lines for every PPPoE session on the router.

Step 1: Status After Layer 1 Configuration

The bottom of Figure 15-28 shows commands labeled as Layer 1. This next section begins by adding those commands to the router. Specifically:

1. The **dialer pool 1** command is added under the dialer interface.

2. The **pppoe-client dial-pool-number 1** command is added under interface G0/1.

3. IOS automatically adds the **pppoe enable** command under interface G0/1.

At this point, the dialer interface has referenced a pool, and an Ethernet interface is in the pool (G0/1 in this case), so the dialer interface has a physical interface to use. Example 15-17 confirms that the dialer and physical interfaces can now work together (Layer 1), but that PPPoE (Layer 2) does not yet work. Of particular note in this case:

- The dialer interface state is still up (spoofing). The interface state will remain in this state until PPPoE is functional.

- R1 is at least trying to create a PPPoE session because of the automatic configuration of the **pppoe enable** command on G0/1. Now the **show pppoe session** command lists some evidence of that attempt. However, if you compare the highlighted items to the working output in Example 15-13, you will see

  - The state is not up (it is PADISNT).

  - It does not list a VA (virtual-access) interface, listing instead N/A for "not applicable."

  - It lists placeholders for the MAC addresses (all 0s) at this point, which are not the addresses used by the routers.

Example 15-17 *Status After Step 1: Layer 1 Configuration (Per Figure 15-28)*

```
R1# show interfaces dialer 2 | include line
Dialer2 is up (spoofing), line protocol is up (spoofing)
R1# show pppoe session
  1 client session

Uniq ID  PPPoE  RemMAC          Port                  VT  VA        State
         SID    LocMAC                                    VA-st     Type
   N/A     0    0000.0000.0000  Gi0/1                 Di2 N/A       PADISNT
                0000.0000.0000
```

Also, the example does not bother to look at the Layer 3 information, like the dialer interface IP address and connected routes. Because PPPoE still does not work (Layer 2), the Layer 3 address discovery could not yet have worked either.

Step 2: Status After Layer 2 (PPP) Configuration

Per the Figure 15-28 comments about Layer 2, at this step, R1 next adds three PPP commands to the dialer interface: **encapsulation ppp**, **ppp chap hostname Fred**, and **ppp chap password Barney**. This new configuration completes all PPP and PPPoE configuration for R1, so the PPPoE session should work The output in Example 15-18 confirms many facts about a working PPPoE design, including:

- The dialer 2 interface state is up instead of up (spoofing). (The protocol state remains up (spoofing) even when all is working.)

- The **show pppoe session** command lists a state of UP.

- The **show pppoe session** command lists all three key interfaces: dialer 2 (Di2), virtual-access 1 (Vi1), and GigabitEthernet0/1 (Gi0/1).

- The **show pppoe session** command lists the MAC addresses of the local and ISP router.

Example 15-18 *Status After Step 3: Layer 2 Configuration (Per Figure 15-28)*

```
R1# show interfaces dialer 2 | include line
Dialer2 is up, line protocol is up (spoofing)
R1# show pppoe session interface g0/1
  1 client session


Uniq ID  PPPoE  RemMAC          Port              VT  VA       State
         SID    LocMAC                                VA-st    Type
   N/A    35    0200.0000.0022  Gi0/1             Di2 Vi1      UP
                0200.0000.0011                                 UP
```

Although not shown here, now that PPPoE is up, the **show interfaces dialer 2** command would list two groups of messages: the first set for the dialer interface, and the second set for interface Vi1. Before the PPPoE session comes up and binds the Vi1 interface to Di2, the **show interfaces dialer 2** command would list messages for dialer 2 only. (See Example 15-11 for an example of this output.)

Problems still exist. At this point, the configuration for Layers 1 and 2 has been added and the functions have been verified, but the Layer 3 configuration has not yet been added. To confirm those issues before adding the configuration, Example 15-19 shows the status of the dialer interface's IPv4 address and the lack of associated IP routes that result. Note that the dialer interface has no IP address assigned, and there are no routes listing dialer 2 as an outgoing interface; only G0/2, an interface ignored for this lab, is listed as an outgoing interface.

Example 15-19 *Layer 3 Status After Step 2, with No IP Configuration for the Dialer Interface*

```
R1# show ip interface brief dialer 2
Interface               IP-Address      OK? Method Status          Protocol
Dialer2                 unassigned      YES unset  up              up
R1# show ip route
! Legend omitted for brevity
      10.0.0.0/8 is variably subnetted, 2 subnets, 2 masks
C        10.1.1.0/24 is directly connected, GigabitEthernet0/2
L        10.1.1.9/32 is directly connected, GigabitEthernet0/2
```

Step 3: Status After Layer 3 (IP) Configuration

Figure 15-28 lists three configuration commands in the Layer 3 area, with two on the dialer interface. This step adds two commands to interface dialer 2, namely the **ip address negotiated** and **mtu 1492** commands. (The third command for Layer 3 in Figure 15-28, the **no ip address** command for interface G0/1, was preconfigured as noted earlier in Example 15-15.)

At this point, all should be working properly. The configuration for this troubleshooting scenario should exactly match Example 15-9 and Figure 15-28, which is the same configuration used to gather all the verification commands shown in Examples 15-11 through 15-14. Rather than repeat all those commands again, feel free to refer to those examples to review the status shown when all is working well. For the Layer 3 status, make sure and review Example 15-14, which shows the Layer 3 status on the dialer interface.

PPPoE Troubleshooting Summary

The sections about PPPoE verification and troubleshooting show a lot of command examples. This section summarizes a few suggestions for what to look for to help with review and exam preparation.

Layer 1: If the **show pppoe session [interface** *type number*] command does not list output, or does not list both the physical and dialer interfaces, check for the existence of the Layer 1 commands as noted in Figure 15-28. Check for errors in those commands as well; for instance, the dial pool numbers must match. Also check to make sure both the dialer and physical interfaces are not shut down. (See Example 15-16.)

Layer 2: If the **show pppoe session [interface** *type number*] command does list output, and lists the physical and dialer interfaces, but no Vi interface, check the Layer 2 configuration as noted in Figure 15-28. Those could be missing, or there could be mistakes. For instance, something as simple as a mistyped CHAP password ends with this result. (See Example 15-17.)

Layer 2: If the **show interfaces dialer** *number* command lists an interface status (the first status value) of up (spoofing), that is another confirmation that PPPoE is not yet working. If so, check the PPP configuration on the dialer interface, and confirm the username/password matches with what the ISP requires. (See Example 15-18.)

Layer 2: To be confident PPPoE is working, look for three items, all seen in Example 15-18's **show pppoe session** command output:

- A status of UP
- Three interfaces listed in shorthand: the Ethernet interface (Gi0/1 in the example), the dialer interface (Di2), and the virtual-access interface (Vi1)
- The MAC addresses of the two routers; check the local MAC address with a **show interfaces** command on the local router

Layer 3: If the **show interfaces** or **show ip interface brief** command does not list an IP address for the dialer interface, then look for missing or incorrect Layer 3 commands per Figure 15-28.

Here are a couple of possible false positives to avoid as well:

Dialer interface status: If the **show interfaces dialer** *number* command lists a protocol status (the second status value) of up (spoofing), do not be concerned. It will always list that status, both when working and not working. (See Example 15-18.)

Physical interface IP address: The physical Ethernet interface will not have an IP address. It is used to send Ethernet frames only. So, it is appropriate with PPPoE to configure the physical Ethernet interface with the **no ip address** command.

Chapter Review

One key to doing well on the exams is to perform repetitive spaced review sessions. Review this chapter's material using either the tools in the book, DVD, or interactive tools for the same material found on the book's companion website. Refer to the "Your Study Plan" element for more details. Table 15-2 outlines the key review elements and where you can find them. To better track your study progress, record when you completed these activities in the second column.

Table 15-2   Chapter Review Tracking

Review Element	Review Date(s)	Resource Used:
Review key topics		Book, DVD/website
Review key terms		Book, DVD/website
Answer DIKTA questions		Book, PCPT
Do labs		Blog
Review command tables		Book

Review All the Key Topics

Key Topic

Table 15-3   Key Topics for Chapter 15

Key Topic Element	Description	Page Number
Figure 15-6	IPsec encryption process	396
Figure 15-7	Client VPN options with SSL	397
Figure 15-10	Site-to-site tunnel with IP routes learned	399
Figure 15-12	Addresses in GRE tunnel packet	401
Figure 15-15	GRE tunnel address concepts: secured and unsecured networks	402
List	Rules for the GRE **tunnel source** command before the tunnel interface will reach an up/up state	407
List	Rules for the GRE **tunnel destination** command before the tunnel interface will reach an up/up state	407
List	Dial pool logic	416
Figure 15-25	Breakdown of PPPoE configuration by OSI layers	417
Figure 15-26	PPPoE verification concepts and interfaces	420
List	List of possible issues with PPPoE	430
List	List of possible false positive indicators of PPPoE problems	430

Key Terms You Should Know

IPsec, shared key, SSL, VPN, VPN client, client VPN, generic routing encapsulation (GRE), GRE tunnel, encrypt/encryption, decrypt/decryption, site-to-site VPN, encryption key, Secure Sockets Layer (SSL), Cisco VPN Client, Cisco AnyConnect Secure Mobility Client, tunnel interface, Dynamic Multipoint VPN (DMVPN), Next Hop Resolution Protocol (NHRP), NHRP server, NHRP client, PPPoE session, dialer interface, virtual-access interface, dial pool, digital subscriber line (DSL), DSL modem, cable Internet, 3G/4G Internet, fiber Internet, PPP over Ethernet (PPPoE)

Command References

Tables 15-4 and 15-5 list configuration and verification commands used in this chapter. As an easy review exercise, cover the left column in a table, read the right column, and try to recall the command without looking. Then repeat the exercise, covering the right column, and try to recall what the command does.

Table 15-4   Chapter 15 Configuration Command Reference

Command	Description
tunnel source *interface-type interface-number*	Tunnel interface subcommand that defines the source IP address of the tunnel on the local router, but indirectly; the router uses the IP address configured on the listed interface.
tunnel source *ip-address*	Tunnel interface subcommand that directly defines the source IP address of the tunnel on the local router.
tunnel destination *ip-address*	Tunnel interface subcommand that defines the destination IP address of the tunnel, which exists on the other end of the tunnel.
tunnel mode gre ip	Tunnel interface subcommand that defines the mode of the tunnel, which must match on both ends of the tunnel. The default is **gre ip**.
interface tunnel *number*	Global command that creates a tunnel interface based on the integer interface number and moves the user to tunnel configuration mode.
permit gre *source-ip source-mask destination-ip destination-mask*	Extended named ACL mode command that matches GRE messages per IP protocol 47.
interface dialer *number*	Global command that creates a dialer interface based on the integer interface number and moves the user to dialer configuration mode.
ip address negotiated	Interface subcommand that causes the interface to use PPP IPCP to discover its IP address.
mtu *size*	Interface subcommand to define the maximum size IP packet allowed to be sent out an interface without fragmenting.
encapsulation ppp	Interface subcommand for serial and dialer interfaces that sets the data link protocol to PPP.
ppp chap hostname *name*	Interface subcommand that tells the interface, when using CHAP, to use this name instead of its hostname.
ppp chap password *value*	Interface subcommand that tells the interface, when using CHAP, to use this password.
dialer pool *number*	Interface subcommand used on dialer interfaces to reference a dialer pool.
pppoe-client dial-pool-number *number*	Interface subcommand used on Ethernet interfaces to add the interface to a pool available to dialer interfaces.
pppoe enable	Interface subcommand used on Ethernet interfaces to enable the PPPoE feature.
mac-address *address*	Interface subcommand used on Ethernet interfaces to assign the MAC address for use by the interface.

Table 15-5 Chapter 15 EXEC Command Reference

Command	Description
show interfaces tunnel *number*	Displays the status of a tunnel interface.
show interfaces dialer *number*	Displays the status of a dialer interface.
show interfaces virtual-access *number*	Displays the status of a virtual-access interface.
show interfaces virtual-access *number* configuration	Displays the configuration that IOS builds for a virtual-access interface based on a dialer interface.
show pppoe session [interface *type number*]	Displays a few lines of status output about each PPPoE session (or if listed, only those sessions on a particular interface).

15

Part III Review

Keep track of your part review progress with the checklist shown in Table P3-1. Details about each task follow the table.

Table P3-1 Part III Part Review Checklist

Activity	1st Date Completed	2nd Date Completed
Repeat All DIKTA Questions		
Answer Part Review Questions		
Review Key Topics		
Create Mind Maps		
Do Labs		

Repeat All DIKTA Questions

For this task, answer the "Do I Know This Already?" questions again for the chapters in this part of the book using the PCPT software.

Answer Part Review Questions

For this task, answer the Part Review questions for this part of the book using the PCPT software. Refer to the Introduction to this book, in the section "How to View Part Review Questions," for more details.

Review Key Topics

Review all key topics in all chapters in this part, either by browsing the chapters or by using the Key Topics application on the DVD or companion website.

Create Terminology Mind Map

The chapters in this part weave in and out of different topics. Without looking back at the chapters or your notes, create a mind map with all the terminology you can recall from Part III of the book. Your job is as follows:

- Think of every term that you can remember from Part III of the book.

- Organize the terms into these divisions: serial links, PPP/MLPPP, Metro Ethernet, MPLS, Internet access, VPN concepts, GRE, DMVPN, and PPPoE.

- After you have written every term you can remember into the mind map, review the Key Terms list at the end of Chapters 13 through 15. Add any terms you forgot to your mind map.

Create Command Mind Maps by Category

Part III of this book also introduced both configuration and EXEC commands. Create one mind map (or a section of a larger mind map) for each of the categories of commands in this list:

PPP, MLPPP, GRE, PPPoE

For each category, think of all configuration commands and all EXEC commands (mostly **show** commands). For each category, group the configuration commands separately from the EXEC commands.

Appendix E, "Mind Map Solutions," lists sample mind map answers. If you do choose to use mind map software, rather than paper, you might want to remember where you stored your mind map files. Table P3-2 lists the mind maps for this part review and a place to record those filenames.

Table P3-2 Configuration Mind Maps for Part I Review

Map	Description	Where You Saved It
1	Terminology Mind Map	
2	Command Mind Maps	

Do Labs

Depending on your chosen lab tool, here are some suggestions for what to do in lab.

Pearson Network Simulator: Once the Pearson network simulator has been updated for the 100-105, 200-105, and 200-125 exams, you will see labs for all these topics that are easily found in the "Sort by Chapter" tab of the Sim. Do those labs. (The version of the Sim that existed when this book was released also included labs on GRE and PPP.)

Config Labs: In your idle moments, review and repeat any of the Config Labs for this book part in the author's blog; launch from http://blog.certskills.com/ccna and navigate to **Hands-On > Config Lab**.

Other: If using other lab tools, everything in this section can be tested with a couple of routers. The PPP labs require serial interfaces, while the PPPoE labs require Ethernet interfaces.

Part IV continues this book's extensive coverage of IPv4 topics, with two main topics: IPv4 access control lists (ACL) and Quality of Service (QoS). Both topics are interesting both from a technology perspective and from what Cisco has done with these topics on the exams.

First, for IPv4 ACLs, Chapters 16 and 17 discuss the basics and more advanced features of IPv4 ACLs. ACLs are IPv4 packet filters that can be programmed to look at IPv4 packet headers, make choices, and either allow a packet through or discard the packet.

From an exam perspective, Cisco has included overlapping exam topics about IPv4 ACLs in both the ICND1 100-105 and ICND2 200-105 exams. To meet that need, both the ICND1 and ICND2 Official Cert Guides include the same chapters: The contents in this book's Chapters 16 and 17 are identical (other than the chapter numbers) to the ICND1 book's Chapters 25 and 26. By using the same book content for these overlapping exam topics, those of you who read the ICND1 100-105 Cert Guide can simply review this book's Chapters 16 and 17, remind yourself of the details, and pick up some speed in your study time.

Chapter 18, the last chapter in this part, discusses QoS. QoS tools allow the network engineer to direct the routers and switches to change their internal processing details for each packet, resulting in a change to the bandwidth, delay, jitter, and loss characteristics experienced by certain types of packets. QoS is about improving those behaviors for some packets, and managing the unfortunate price paid to worsening those behaviors for other packets.

QoS is also an interesting topic from an exam perspective for the current exams. In past CCNA R&S exam blueprints, QoS at most has gotten a minor mention. The current exams' mentions of QoS represent a big new addition to the content as listed in the CCNA R&S exam topics.

Part IV

IPv4 Services: ACLs and QoS

Chapter 16: Basic IPv4 Access Control Lists

Chapter 17: Advanced IPv4 Access Control Lists

Chapter 18: Quality of Service (QoS)

Part IV Review

Basic IPv4 Access Control Lists

This chapter covers the following exam topics:

4.0 Infrastructure Services

4.4 Configure, verify, and troubleshoot IPv4 and IPv6 access list for traffic filtering

4.4.a Standard

IPv4 access control lists (ACL) give network engineers the ability to program a filter into a router. Each router, on each interface, for both the inbound and outbound direction, can enable a different ACL with different rules. Each ACL's rules tell the router which packets to discard, and which to allow through.

This chapter discusses the basics of IPv4 ACLs, and in particular, one type of IP ACL: standard numbered IP ACLs. The next chapter, titled, "Advanced IPv4 Access Control Lists," completes the discussion by describing other types of IP ACLs.

Those of you who have already read the ICND1 100-105 Cert Guide will probably begin to recognize a lot of similar figures and examples. In fact, this chapter's content is identical to the ICND1 book's Chapter 25. Likewise, this book's Chapter 17 is identical to the ICND1 book's Chapter 26. I kept the IPv4 ACL content identical in both books in an attempt to make you a little more efficient in your use of time. Here's why:

■ Cisco's ICND1 and ICND2 ACL exam topics overlap quite a bit, so both books need to cover those topics.

■ If this book had some ACL content that was not identical to the ICND1 book, you would probably want to read it all, in case there was something new.

■ With these two chapters, the version in the ICND1 and ICND2 books have the exact same content, so you can make better use of your time here with ICND2. If you have read these chapters in the ICND1 book, refer to your notes, skim this chapter as appropriate, and use the chapter review tools to make sure you have mastered the content.

I believe this plan will work better for those of you using both books, and will be of no difference to those of you using only the ICND1 book or only the ICND2 book. Regardless, jump in and read/review about IPv4 ACLs.

"Do I Know This Already?" Quiz

Take the quiz (either here, or use the PCPT software) if you want to use the score to help you decide how much time to spend on this chapter. The answers are at the bottom of the page following the quiz, and the explanations are in DVD Appendix C and in the PCPT software.

Table 16-1 "Do I Know This Already?" Foundation Topics Section-to-Question Mapping

Foundation Topics Section	Questions
IP Access Control List Basics	1
Standard Numbered IPv4 ACLs	2–5
Practice Applying Standard IP ACLs	6

1. Barney is a host with IP address 10.1.1.1 in subnet 10.1.1.0/24. Which of the following are things that a standard IP ACL could be configured to do? (Choose two answers.)

   a. Match the exact source IP address.

   b. Match IP addresses 10.1.1.1 through 10.1.1.4 with one **access-list** command without matching other IP addresses.

   c. Match all IP addresses in Barney's subnet with one **access-list** command without matching other IP addresses.

   d. Match only the packet's destination IP address.

2. Which of the following answers list a valid number that can be used with standard numbered IP ACLs? (Choose two answers.)

   a. 1987

   b. 2187

   c. 187

   d. 87

3. Which of the following wildcard masks is most useful for matching all IP packets in subnet 10.1.128.0, mask 255.255.255.0?

   a. 0.0.0.0

   b. 0.0.0.31

   c. 0.0.0.240

   d. 0.0.0.255

   e. 0.0.15.0

   f. 0.0.248.255

4. Which of the following wildcard masks is most useful for matching all IP packets in subnet 10.1.128.0, mask 255.255.240.0?

   a. 0.0.0.0

   b. 0.0.0.31

   c. 0.0.0.240

   d. 0.0.0.255

   e. 0.0.15.255

   f. 0.0.248.255

5. ACL 1 has three statements, in the following order, with address and wildcard mask values as follows: 1.0.0.0 0.255.255.255, 1.1.0.0 0.0.255.255, and 1.1.1.0 0.0.0.255. If a router tried to match a packet sourced from IP address 1.1.1.1 using this ACL, which ACL statement does a router consider the packet to have matched?

   a. First

   b. Second

   c. Third

   d. Implied deny at the end of the ACL

6. Which of the following **access-list** commands matches all packets sent from hosts in subnet 172.16.4.0/23?

   a. access-list 1 permit 172.16.0.5 0.0.255.0

   b. access-list 1 permit 172.16.4.0 0.0.1.255

   c. access-list 1 permit 172.16.5.0

   d. access-list 1 permit 172.16.5.0 0.0.0.127

Foundation Topics

IPv4 Access Control List Basics

IPv4 access control lists (IP ACL) give network engineers a way to identify different types of packets. To do so, the ACL configuration lists values that the router can see in the IP, TCP, UDP, and other headers. For example, an ACL can match packets whose source IP address is 1.1.1.1, or packets whose destination IP address is some address in subnet 10.1.1.0/24, or packets with a destination port of TCP port 23 (Telnet).

IPv4 ACLs perform many functions in Cisco routers, with the most common use as a packet filter. Engineers can enable ACLs on a router so that the ACL sits in the forwarding path of packets as they pass through the router. After it is enabled, the router considers whether each IP packet will either be discarded or allowed to continue as if the ACL did not exist.

However, ACLs can be used for many other IOS features as well. As an example, ACLs can be used to match packets for applying Quality of Service (QoS) features. QoS allows a router to give some packets better service, and other packets worse service. For example, packets that hold digitized voice need to have very low delay, so ACLs can match voice packets, with QoS logic in turn forwarding voice packets more quickly than data packets.

This first section introduces IP ACLs as used for packet filtering, focusing on these aspects of ACLs: the locations and direction in which to enable ACLs, matching packets by examining headers, and taking action after a packet has been matched.

ACL Location and Direction

Cisco routers can apply ACL logic to packets at the point at which the IP packets enter an interface, or the point at which they exit an interface. In other words, the ACL becomes associated with an interface and for a direction of packet flow (either in or out). That is, the ACL can be applied inbound to the router, before the router makes its forwarding (routing) decision, or outbound, after the router makes its forwarding decision and has determined the exit interface to use.

The arrows in Figure 16-1 show the locations at which you could filter packets flowing left to right in the topology. For example, imagine that you wanted to allow packets sent by host A to server S1, but to discard packets sent by host B to server S1. Each arrowed line represents a location and direction at which a router could apply an ACL, filtering the packets sent by host B.

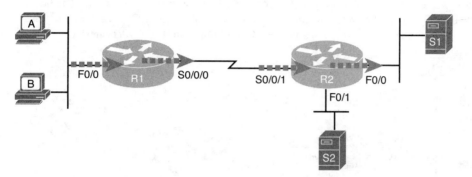

Figure 16-1   *Locations to Filter Packets from Hosts A and B Going Toward Server S1*

The four arrowed lines in the figure point out the location and direction for the router interfaces used to forward the packet from host B to server S1. In this particular example, those interfaces and direction are inbound on R1's F0/0 interface, outbound on R1's S0/0/0 interface, inbound on R2's S0/0/1 interface, and outbound on R2's F0/0 interface. If, for example, you enabled an ACL on R2's F0/1 interface, in either direction, that ACL could not possibly filter the packet sent from host B to server S1, because R2's F0/1 interface is not part of the route from B to S1.

In short, to filter a packet, you must enable an ACL on an interface that processes the packet, in the same direction the packet flows through that interface.

When enabled, the router then processes every inbound or outbound IP packet using that ACL. For example, if enabled on R1 for packets inbound on interface F0/0, R1 would compare every inbound IP packet on F0/0 to the ACL to decide that packet's fate: to continue unchanged, or to be discarded.

Matching Packets

When you think about the location and direction for an ACL, you must already be thinking about what packets you plan to filter (discard), and which ones you want to allow through. To tell the router those same ideas, you must configure the router with an IP ACL that matches packets. *Matching packets* refers to how to configure the ACL commands to look at each packet, listing how to identify which packets should be discarded, and which should be allowed through.

Answers to the "Do I Know This Already?" quiz:

1 A, C **2** A, D **3** D **4** E **5** A **6** B

Each IP ACL consists of one or more configuration commands, with each command listing details about values to look for inside a packet's headers. Generally, an ACL command uses logic like "look for these values in the packet header, and if found, discard the packet." (The action could instead be to allow the packet, rather than discard.) Specifically, the ACL looks for header fields you should already know well, including the source and destination IP addresses, plus TCP and UDP port numbers.

For example, consider an example with Figure 16-2, in which you want to allow packets from host A to server S1, but to discard packets from host B going to that same server. The hosts all now have IP addresses, and the figure shows pseudocode for an ACL on R2. Figure 16-2 also shows the chosen location to enable the ACL: inbound on R2's S0/0/1 interface.

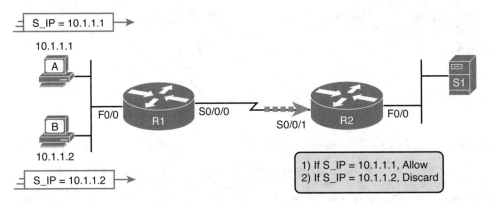

Figure 16-2   *Pseudocode to Demonstrate ACL Command-Matching Logic*

Figure 16-2 shows a two-line ACL in a rectangle at the bottom, with simple matching logic: both statements just look to match the source IP address in the packet. When enabled, R2 looks at every inbound IP packet on that interface and compares each packet to those two ACL commands. Packets sent by host A (source IP address 10.1.1.1) are allowed through, and those sourced by host B (source IP address 10.1.1.2) are discarded.

Taking Action When a Match Occurs

When using IP ACLs to filter packets, only one of two actions can be chosen. The configuration commands use the keywords **deny** and **permit**, and they mean (respectively) to discard the packet or to allow it to keep going as if the ACL did not exist.

This book focuses on using ACLs to filter packets, but IOS uses ACLs for many more features. Those features typically use the same matching logic. However, in other cases, the **deny** or **permit** keywords imply some other action.

Types of IP ACLs

Cisco IOS has supported IP ACLs since the early days of Cisco routers. Beginning with the original standard numbered IP ACLs in the early days of IOS, which could enable the logic shown earlier around Figure 16-2, Cisco has added many ACL features, including the following:

- Standard numbered ACLs (1–99)
- Extended numbered ACLs (100–199)
- Additional ACL numbers (1300–1999 standard, 2000–2699 extended)
- Named ACLs
- Improved editing with sequence numbers

This chapter focuses solely on standard numbered IP ACLs, while the next chapter discusses the other three primary categories of IP ACLs. Briefly, IP ACLs will be either numbered or named in that the configuration identifies the ACL either using a number or a name. ACLs will also be either standard or extended, with extended ACLs having much more robust abilities in matching packets. Figure 16-3 summarizes the big ideas related to categories of IP ACLs.

Key Topic

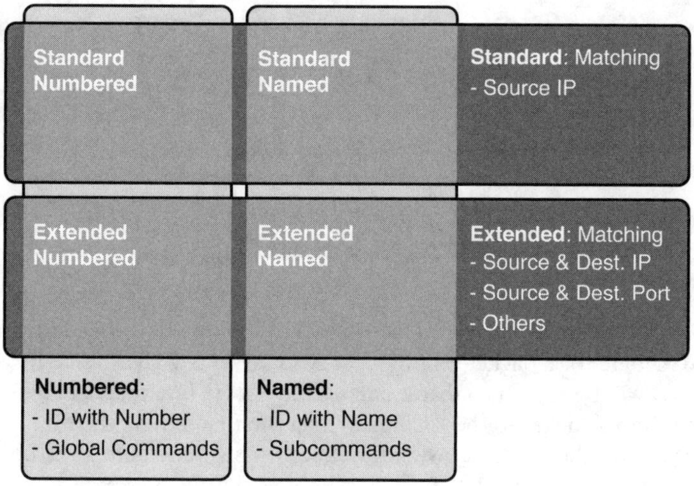

Standard Numbered	Standard Named	**Standard**: Matching - Source IP
Extended Numbered	Extended Named	**Extended**: Matching - Source & Dest. IP - Source & Dest. Port - Others
Numbered: - ID with Number - Global Commands	**Named**: - ID with Name - Subcommands	

Figure 16-3 *Comparisons of IP ACL Types*

Standard Numbered IPv4 ACLs

The title of this section serves as a great introduction, if you can decode what Cisco means by each specific word. This section is about a type of Cisco filter (*ACL*) that matches only the source IP address of the packet (*standard*), is configured to identify the ACL using numbers rather than names (*numbered*), and looks at IPv4 packets.

This section examines the particulars of standard numbered IP ACLs. First, it examines the idea that one ACL is a list, and what logic that list uses. Following that, the text closely looks at how to match the source IP address field in the packet header, including the syntax of the commands. This section ends with a complete look at the configuration and verification commands to implement standard ACLs.

List Logic with IP ACLs

A single ACL is both a single entity and, at the same time, a list of one or more configuration commands. As a single entity, the configuration enables the entire ACL on an interface, in a specific direction, as shown earlier in Figure 16-1. As a list of commands, each command has different matching logic that the router must apply to each packet when filtering using that ACL.

When doing ACL processing, the router processes the packet, compared to the ACL, as follows:

ACLs use first-match logic. Once a packet matches one line in the ACL, the router takes the action listed in that line of the ACL, and stops looking further in the ACL.

To see exactly what that means, consider the example built around Figure 16-4. The figure shows an example ACL 1 with three lines of pseudocode. This example applies ACL 1 on R2's S0/0/1 interface, inbound (the same location as in earlier Figure 16-2).

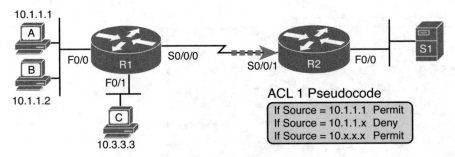

Figure 16-4 *Backdrop for Discussion of List Process with IP ACLs*

Consider the first-match ACL logic for a packet sent by host A to server S1. The source IP address will be 10.1.1.1, and it will be routed so that it enters R2's S0/0/1 interface, driving R2's ACL 1 logic. R2 compares this packet to the ACL, matching the first item in the list with a permit action. So this packet should be allowed through, as shown in Figure 16-5, on the left.

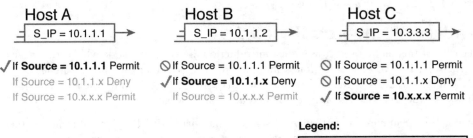

Figure 16-5 *ACL Items Compared for Packets from Hosts A, B, and C in Figure 16-4*

Next, consider a packet sent by host B, source IP address 10.1.1.2. When the packet enters R2's S0/0/1 interface, R2 compares the packet to ACL 1's first statement, and does not make a match (10.1.1.1 is not equal to 10.1.1.2). R2 then moves to the second statement, which requires some clarification. The ACL pseudocode, back in Figure 16-4, shows 10.1.1.x, which is meant to be shorthand that any value can exist in the last octet. Comparing only the first three octets, R2 decides that this latest packet does have a source IP address that begins with the first three octets 10.1.1, so R2 considers that to be a match on the second statement. R2 takes the listed action (deny), discarding the packet. R2 also stops ACL processing on the packet, ignoring the third line in the ACL.

Finally, consider a packet sent by host C, again to server S1. The packet has source IP address 10.3.3.3, so when it enters R2's S0/0/1 interface, and drives ACL processing on R2, R2 looks at the first command in ACL 1. R2 does not match the first ACL command (10.1.1.1 in the command is not equal to the packet's 10.3.3.3). R2 looks at the second command, compares the first three octets (10.1.1) to the packet source IP address (10.3.3), and still finds no match. R2 then looks at the third command. In this case, the wildcard means ignore the last three octets, and just compare the first octet (10), so the packet matches. R2 then takes the listed action (permit), allowing the packet to keep going.

This sequence of processing an ACL as a list happens for any type of IOS ACL: IP, other protocols, standard or extended, named or numbered.

Finally, if a packet does not match any of the items in the ACL, the packet is discarded. The reason is that every IP ACL has a *deny all* statement implied at the end of the ACL. It does not exist in the configuration, but if a router keeps searching the list, and no match is made by the end of the list, IOS considers the packet to have matched an entry that has a **deny** action.

Matching Logic and Command Syntax

Standard numbered IP ACLs use the following global command:

```
access-list {1-99 | 1300-1999} {permit | deny} matching-parameters
```

Each standard numbered ACL has one or more **access-list** commands with the same number, any number from the ranges shown in the preceding line of syntax. (One number is no better than the other.)

Besides the ACL number, each **access-list** command also lists the action (**permit** or **deny**), plus the matching logic. The rest of this section examines how to configure the matching parameters, which for standard ACLs, means that you can only match the source IP address, or portions of the source IP address using something called an ACL wildcard mask.

Matching the Exact IP Address

To match a specific source IP address, the entire IP address, all you have to do is type that IP address at the end of the command. For example, the previous example uses pseudocode for "permit if source = 10.1.1.1." The following command configures that logic with correct syntax using ACL number 1:

```
access-list 1 permit 10.1.1.1
```

Matching the exact full IP address is that simple.

In earlier IOS versions, the syntax included a **host** keyword. Instead of simply typing the full IP address, you first typed the **host** keyword, and then the IP address. Note that in later

IOS versions, if you use the **host** keyword, IOS accepts the command, but then removes the keyword.

```
access-list 1 permit host 10.1.1.1
```

Matching a Subset of the Address with Wildcards

Often, the business goals you want to implement with an ACL do not match a single particular IP address, but rather a range of IP addresses. Maybe you want to match all IP addresses in a subnet. Maybe you want to match all IP addresses in a range of subnets. Regardless, you want to check for more than one IP address in a range of addresses.

IOS allows standard ACLs to match a range of addresses using a tool called a *wildcard mask*. Note that this is not a subnet mask. The wildcard mask (which this book abbreviates as *WC mask*) gives the engineer a way to tell IOS to ignore parts of the address when making comparisons, essentially treating those parts as wildcards, as if they already matched.

You can think about WC masks in decimal and in binary, and both have their uses. To begin, think about WC masks in decimal, using these rules:

Decimal 0: The router must compare this octet as normal.

Decimal 255: The router ignores this octet, considering it to already match.

Keeping these two rules in mind, consider Figure 16-6, which demonstrates this logic using three different but popular WC masks: one that tells the router to ignore the last octet, one that tells the router to ignore the last two octets, and one that tells the router to ignore the last three octets.

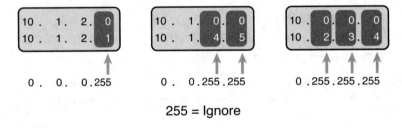

255 = Ignore

Figure 16-6 *Logic for WC Masks 0.0.0.255, 0.0.255.255, and 0.255.255.255*

All three examples in the boxes of Figure 16-6 show two numbers that are clearly different. The WC mask causes IOS to compare only some of the octets, while ignoring other octets. All three examples result in a match, because each wildcard mask tells IOS to ignore some octets. The example on the left shows WC mask 0.0.0.255, which tells the router to treat the last octet as a wildcard, essentially ignoring that octet for the comparison. Similarly, the middle example shows WC mask 0.0.255.255, which tells the router to ignore the two octets on the right. The rightmost case shows WC mask 0.255.255.255, telling the router to ignore the last three octets when comparing values.

To see the WC mask in action, think back to the earlier example related to Figure 16-4 and Figure 16-5. The pseudocode ACL in those two figures used logic that can be created using a WC mask. As a reminder, the logic in the pseudocode ACL in those two figures included the following:

Line 1: Match and permit all packets with a source address of exactly 10.1.1.1.

Line 2: Match and deny all packets with source addresses with first three octets 10.1.1.

Line 3: Match and permit all addresses with first single octet 10.

Figure 16-7 shows the updated version of Figure 16-4, but with the completed, correct syntax, including the WC masks. In particular, note the use of WC mask 0.0.0.255 in the second command, telling R2 to ignore the last octet of the number 10.1.1.0, and the WC mask 0.255.255.255 in the third command, telling R2 to ignore the last three octets in the value 10.0.0.0.

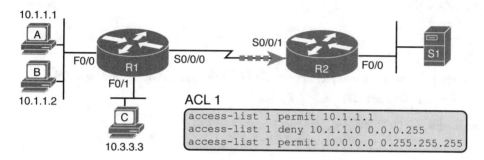

Figure 16-7 *Syntactically Correct ACL Replaces Pseudocode from Figure 16-4*

Finally, note that when using a WC mask, the **access-list** command's loosely defined *source* parameter should be a 0 in any octets where the WC mask is a 255. IOS will specify a source address to be 0 for the parts that will be ignored, even if nonzero values were configured.

Binary Wildcard Masks

Wildcard masks, as dotted-decimal number (DDN) values, actually represent a 32-bit binary number. As a 32-bit number, the WC mask actually directs the router's logic bit by bit. In short, a WC mask bit of 0 means the comparison should be done as normal, but a binary 1 means that the bit is a wildcard, and can be ignored when comparing the numbers.

Thankfully, for the purposes of CCENT and CCNA R&S study, and for most real-world applications, you can ignore the binary WC mask. Why? Well, we generally want to match a range of addresses that can be easily identified by a subnet number and mask, whether it be a real subnet, or a summary route that groups subnets together. If you can describe the range of addresses with a subnet number and mask, you can find the numbers to use in your ACL with some simple decimal math, as discussed next.

NOTE If you really want to know the binary mask logic, take the two DDN numbers the ACL will compare (one from the **access-list** command, and the other from the packet header) and convert both to binary. Then, also convert the WC mask to binary. Compare the first two binary numbers bit by bit, but also ignore any bits for which the WC mask happens to list a binary 1, because that tells you to ignore the bit. If all the bits you checked are equal, it's a match!

Finding the Right Wildcard Mask to Match a Subnet

In many cases, an ACL needs to match all hosts in a particular subnet. To match a subnet with an ACL, you can use the following shortcut:

- Use the subnet number as the source value in the **access-list** command.
- Use a wildcard mask found by subtracting the subnet mask from 255.255.255.255.

For example, for subnet 172.16.8.0 255.255.252.0, use the subnet number (172.16.8.0) as the address parameter, and then do the following math to find the wildcard mask:

$$
\begin{array}{r}
255.255.255.255 \\
-255.255.252.0 \\
\hline
0.\ \ 0.\ \ 3.255
\end{array}
$$

Continuing this example, a completed command for this same subnet would be as follows:

```
access-list 1 permit 172.16.8.0 0.0.3.255
```

The upcoming section, "Practice Applying Standard IP ACLs," gives you a chance to practice matching subnets when configuring ACLs.

Matching Any/All Addresses

In some cases, you will want one ACL command to match any and all packets that reach that point in the ACL. First, you have to know the (simple) way to match all packets using the **any** keyword. More importantly, you need to think about when to match any and all packets.

First, to match any and all packets with an ACL command, just use the **any** keyword for the address. For example, to permit all packets:

```
access-list 1 permit any
```

So, when and where should you use such a command? Remember, all Cisco IP ACLs end with an implicit deny any concept at the end of each ACL. That is, if a router compares a packet to the ACL, and the packet matches none of the configured statements, the router discards the packet. Want to override that default behavior? Configure a **permit any** at the end of the ACL.

You might also want to explicitly configure a command to deny all traffic (for example, **access-list 1 deny any**) at the end of an ACL. Why, when the same logic already sits at the end of the ACL anyway? Well, the ACL **show** commands list counters for the number of packets matched by each command in the ACL, but there is no counter for that implicit deny any concept at the end of the ACL. So, if you want to see counters for how many packets are matched by the deny any logic at the end of the ACL, configure an explicit **deny any**.

Implementing Standard IP ACLs

This chapter has already introduced all the configuration steps in bits and pieces. This section summarizes those pieces as a configuration process. The process also refers to the **access-list** command, whose generic syntax is repeated here for reference:

```
access-list access-list-number {deny | permit} source [source-wildcard]
```

Key Topic

Step 1.   Plan the location (router and interface) and direction (in or out) on that interface:

   A. Standard ACLs should be placed near to the destination of the packets so that they do not unintentionally discard packets that should not be discarded.

   B. Because standard ACLs can only match a packet's source IP address, identify the source IP addresses of packets as they go in the direction that the ACL is examining.

Step 2.   Configure one or more **access-list** global configuration commands to create the ACL, keeping the following in mind:

   A. The list is searched sequentially, using first-match logic.

   B. The default action, if a packet does not match any of the **access-list** commands, is to **deny** (discard) the packet.

Step 3.   Enable the ACL on the chosen router interface, in the correct direction, using the **ip access-group** *number* {**in** | **out**} interface subcommand.

The rest of this section shows a couple of examples.

Standard Numbered ACL Example 1

The first example shows the configuration for the same requirements demonstrated with Figure 16-4 and Figure 16-5. Restated, the requirements for this ACL are as follows:

1. Enable the ACL inbound on R2's S0/0/1 interface.

2. Permit packets coming from host A.

3. Deny packets coming from other hosts in host A's subnet.

4. Permit packets coming from any other address in Class A network 10.0.0.0.

5. The original example made no comment about what to do by default, so simply deny all other traffic.

Example 16-1 shows a completed correct configuration, starting with the configuration process, followed by output from the **show running-config** command.

Example 16-1   *Standard Numbered ACL Example 1 Configuration*

```
R2# configure terminal
Enter configuration commands, one per line.  End with CNTL/Z.
R2(config)# access-list 1 permit 10.1.1.1
R2(config)# access-list 1 deny 10.1.1.0 0.0.0.255
R2(config)# access-list 1 permit 10.0.0.0 0.255.255.255
R2(config)# interface S0/0/1
R2(config-if)# ip access-group 1 in
R2(config-if)# ^z
R2# show running-config
! Lines omitted for brevity

access-list 1 permit 10.1.1.1
access-list 1 deny 10.1.1.0 0.0.0.255
access-list 1 permit 10.0.0.0 0.255.255.255
```

16

First, pay close attention to the configuration process at the top of the example. Note that the **access-list** command does not change the command prompt from the global configuration mode prompt, because the **access-list** command is a global configuration command. Then, compare that to the output of the **show running-config** command: the details are identical compared to the commands that were added in configuration mode. Finally, make sure to note the **ip access-group 1 in** command, under R2's S0/0/1 interface, which enables the ACL logic (both location and direction).

Example 16-2 lists some output from Router R2 that shows information about this ACL. The **show ip access-lists** command lists details about IPv4 ACLs only, while the **show access-lists** command lists details about IPv4 ACLs plus any other types of ACLs that are currently configured, for example, IPv6 ACLs.

Example 16-2   *ACL show Commands on R2*

```
R2# show ip access-lists
Standard IP access list 1
    10 permit 10.1.1.1 (107 matches)
    20 deny    10.1.1.0, wildcard bits 0.0.0.255 (4 matches)
    30 permit 10.0.0.0, wildcard bits 0.255.255.255 (10 matches)
R2# show access-lists
Standard IP access list 1
    10 permit 10.1.1.1 (107 matches)
    20 deny    10.1.1.0, wildcard bits 0.0.0.255 (4 matches)
    30 permit 10.0.0.0, wildcard bits 0.255.255.255 (10 matches)
R2# show ip interface s0/0/1
Serial0/0/1 is up, line protocol is up
  Internet address is 10.1.2.2/24
  Broadcast address is 255.255.255.255
  Address determined by setup command
  MTU is 1500 bytes
  Helper address is not set
  Directed broadcast forwarding is disabled
  Multicast reserved groups joined: 224.0.0.9
  Outgoing access list is not set
  Inbound  access list is 1
! Lines omitted for brevity
```

The output of these commands shows two items of note. The first line of output in this case notes the type (standard), and the number. If more than one ACL existed, you would see multiple stanzas of output, one per ACL, each with a heading line like this one. Next, these commands list packet counts for the number of packets that the router has matched with each command. For example, 107 packets so far have matched the first line in the ACL.

Finally, the end of the example lists the **show ip interface** command output. This command lists, among many other items, the number or name of any IP ACL enabled on the interface per the **ip access-group** interface subcommand.

Standard Numbered ACL Example 2

For the second example, use Figure 16-8, and imagine your boss gave you some requirements hurriedly in the hall. At first, he tells you he wants to filter packets going from the servers on the right toward the clients on the left. Then, he says he wants you to allow access for hosts A, B, and other hosts in their same subnet to server S1, but deny access to that server to the hosts in host C's subnet. Then, he tells you that, additionally, hosts in host A's subnet should be denied access to server S2, but hosts in host C's subnet should be allowed access to server S2—all by filtering packets going right to left only. He then tells you to put the ACL inbound on R2's F0/0 interface.

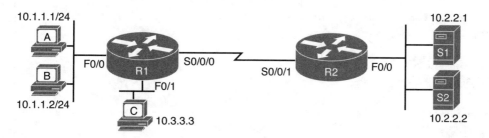

Figure 16-8 *Standard Numbered ACL Example 2*

If you cull through all the boss's comments, the requirements might reduce to the following:

1. Enable the ACL inbound on R2's F0/0 interface.
2. Permit packets from server S1 going to hosts in A's subnet.
3. Deny packets from server S1 going to hosts in C's subnet.
4. Permit packets from server S2 going to hosts in C's subnet.
5. Deny packets from server S2 going to hosts in A's subnet.
6. (There was no comment about what to do by default; use the implied **deny all** default.)

As it turns out, you cannot do everything your boss asked with a standard ACL. For example, consider the obvious command for requirement number 2: **access-list 2 permit 10.2.2.1**. That permits all traffic whose source IP is 10.2.2.1 (server S1). The very next requirement asks you to filter (deny) packets sourced from that same IP address! Even if you added another command that checked for source IP address 10.2.2.1, the router would never get to it, because routers use first-match logic when searching the ACL. You cannot check both the destination and source IP address, because standard ACLs cannot check the destination IP address.

To solve this problem, you should get a new boss! No, seriously, you have to rethink the problem and change the rules. In real life, you would probably use an extended ACL instead, which lets you check both the source and destination IP address.

For the sake of practicing another standard ACL, imagine your boss lets you change the requirements. First, you will use two outbound ACLs, both on Router R1. Each ACL will permit traffic from a single server to be forwarded onto that connected LAN, with the following modified requirements:

1. Using an outbound ACL on R1's F0/0 interface, permit packets from server S1, and deny all other packets.
2. Using an outbound ACL on R1's F0/1 interface, permit packets from server S2, and deny all other packets.

Example 16-3 shows the configuration that completes these requirements.

Example 16-3   *Alternative Configuration in Router R1*

```
access-list 2 remark This ACL permits server S1 traffic to host A's subnet
access-list 2 permit 10.2.2.1
!
access-list 3 remark This ACL permits server S2 traffic to host C's subnet
access-list 3 permit 10.2.2.2
!
interface F0/0
 ip access-group 2 out
!
interface F0/1
 ip access-group 3 out
```

As highlighted in the example, the solution with ACL number 2 permits all traffic from server S1, with that logic enabled for packets exiting R1's F0/0 interface. All other traffic will be discarded because of the implied deny all at the end of the ACL. In addition, ACL 3 permits traffic from server S2, which is then permitted to exit R1's F0/1 interface. Also, note that the solution shows the use of the **access-list remark** parameter, which allows you to leave text documentation that stays with the ACL.

NOTE   When routers apply an ACL to filter packets in the outbound direction, as shown in Example 16-3, the router checks packets that it routes against the ACL. However, a router does not filter packets that the router itself creates with an outbound ACL. Examples of those packets include routing protocol messages, and packets sent by the **ping** and **traceroute** commands on that router.

Troubleshooting and Verification Tips

Troubleshooting IPv4 ACLs requires some attention to detail. In particular, you have to be ready to look at the address and wildcard mask and confidently predict the addresses matched by those two combined parameters. The upcoming practice problems a little later in this chapter can help prepare you for that part of the work. But a few other tips can help you verify and troubleshoot ACL problems on the exams as well.

First, you can tell if the router is matching packets or not with a couple of tools. Example 16-2 already showed that IOS keeps statistics about the packets matched by each line of an ACL. In addition, if you add the **log** keyword to the end of an **access-list** command, IOS then issues log messages with occasional statistics about matches of that particular line of the ACL. Both the statistics and the log messages can be helpful in deciding which line in the ACL is being matched by a packet.

For example, Example 16-4 shows an updated version of ACL 2 from Example 16-3, this time with the **log** keyword added. The bottom of the example then shows a typical log message, this one showing the resulting match based on a packet with source IP address 10.2.2.1 (as matched with the ACL), to destination address 10.1.1.1.

Example 16-4 *Creating Log Messages for ACL Statistics*

```
R1# show running-config
! lines removed for brevity
access-list 2 remark This ACL permits server S1 traffic to host A's subnet
access-list 2 permit 10.2.2.1 log
!
interface F0/0
 ip access-group 2 out

R1#
Feb  4 18:30:24.082: %SEC-6-IPACCESSLOGNP: list 2 permitted 0 10.2.2.1 -> 10.1.1.1, 1
  packet
```

Anytime you troubleshoot an ACL for the first time, before getting into the details of the matching logic, take the time to think about both the interface on which the ACL is enabled, and the direction of packet flow. Sometimes, the matching logic is perfect—but the ACL has been enabled on the wrong interface, or for the wrong direction, to match the packets as configured for the ACL.

For example, Figure 16-9 repeats the same ACL shown earlier in Figure 16-7. The first line of that ACL matches the specific host address 10.1.1.1. If that ACL exists on Router R2, placing that ACL as an inbound ACL on R2's S0/0/1 interface can work, because packets sent by host 10.1.1.1—on the left side of the figure—can enter R2's S0/0/1 interface. However, if R2 enables ACL 1 on its F0/0 interface, for inbound packets, the ACL will never match a packet with source IP address 10.1.1.1, because packets sent by host 10.1.1.1 will never enter that interface. Packets sent by 10.1.1.1 will exit R2's F0/0 interface, but never enter it, just because of the network topology.

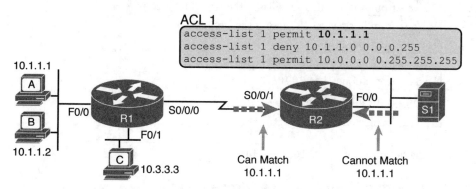

Figure 16-9 *Example of Checking the Interface and Direction for an ACL*

Practice Applying Standard IP ACLs

Some CCENT and CCNA R&S topics, like ACLs, simply require more drills and practice than others. ACLs require you to think of parameters to match ranges of numbers, and that of course requires some use of math, and some use of processes.

This section provides some practice problems and tips, from two perspectives. First, this section asks you to build one-line standard ACLs to match some packets. Second, this section asks you to interpret existing ACL commands to describe what packets the ACL will match. Both skills are useful for the exams.

Practice Building access-list Commands

In this section, practice getting comfortable with the syntax of the **access-list** command, particularly with choosing the correct matching logic. These skills will be helpful when reading about extended and named ACLs in the next chapter.

First, the following list summarizes some important tips to consider when choosing matching parameters to any **access-list** command:

Key Topic

- To match a specific address, just list the address.
- To match any and all addresses, use the **any** keyword.
- To match based only on the first one, two, or three octets of an address, use the 0.255.255.255, 0.0.255.255, and 0.0.0.255 WC masks, respectively. Also, make the source (address) parameter have 0s in the wildcard octets (those octets with 255 in the wildcard mask).
- To match a subnet, use the subnet ID as the source, and find the WC mask by subtracting the DDN subnet mask from 255.255.255.255.

Table 16-2 lists the criteria for several practice problems. Your job: Create a one-line standard ACL that matches the packets. The answers are listed in the section "Answers to Earlier Practice Problems," later in this chapter.

Table 16-2   Building One-Line Standard ACLs: Practice

Problem	Criteria
1	Packets from 172.16.5.4
2	Packets from hosts with 192.168.6 as the first three octets
3	Packets from hosts with 192.168 as the first two octets
4	Packets from any host
5	Packets from subnet 10.1.200.0/21
6	Packets from subnet 10.1.200.0/27
7	Packets from subnet 172.20.112.0/23
8	Packets from subnet 172.20.112.0/26
9	Packets from subnet 192.168.9.64/28
10	Packets from subnet 192.168.9.64/30

Reverse Engineering from ACL to Address Range

In some cases, you may not be creating your own ACL. Instead, you may need to interpret some existing **access-list** commands. To answer these types of questions on the exams, you need to determine the range of IP addresses matched by a particular address/wildcard mask combination in each ACL statement.

Under certain assumptions that are reasonable for CCENT and CCNA R&S certifications, calculating the range of addresses matched by an ACL can be relatively simple. Basically, the range of addresses begins with the address configured in the ACL command. The range of addresses ends with the sum of the address field and the wildcard mask. That's it.

For example, with the command **access-list 1 permit 172.16.200.0 0.0.7.255**, the low end of the range is simply 172.16.200.0, taken directly from the command itself. Then, to find the high end of the range, just add this number to the WC mask, as follows:

172.16.200.0

+ 0. 0.   7.255

172.16.207.255

For this last bit of practice, look at the existing **access-list** commands in Table 16-3. In each case, make a notation about the exact IP address, or range of IP addresses, matched by the command.

Table 16-3 Finding IP Addresses/Ranges Matching by Existing ACLs

Problem	Commands for Which to Predict the Source Address Range
1	access-list 1 permit 10.7.6.5
2	access-list 2 permit 192.168.4.0 0.0.0.127
3	access-list 3 permit 192.168.6.0 0.0.0.31
4	access-list 4 permit 172.30.96.0 0.0.3.255
5	access-list 5 permit 172.30.96.0 0.0.0.63
6	access-list 6 permit 10.1.192.0 0.0.0.31
7	access-list 7 permit 10.1.192.0 0.0.1.255
8	access-list 8 permit 10.1.192.0 0.0.63.255

Interestingly, IOS lets the CLI user type an **access-list** command in configuration mode, and IOS will potentially change the address parameter before placing the command into the running-config file. This process of just finding the range of addresses matched by the **access-list** command expects that the **access-list** command came from the router, so that any such changes were complete.

The change IOS can make with an **access-list** command is to convert to 0 any octet of an address for which the wildcard mask's octet is 255. For example, with a wildcard mask of 0.0.255.255, IOS ignores the last two octets. IOS expects the address field to end with two 0s. If not, IOS still accepts the **access-list** command, but IOS changes the last two octets of the address to 0s. Example 16-5 shows an example, where the configuration shows address 10.1.1.1, but wildcard mask 0.0.255.255.

Example 16-5 *IOS Changing the Address Field in an* **access-list** *Command*

```
R2# configure terminal
Enter configuration commands, one per line.  End with CNTL/Z.
R2(config)# access-list 21 permit 10.1.1.1 0.0.255.255
R2(config)# ^Z
R2#
R2# show ip access-lists
Standard IP access list 21
    10 permit 10.1.0.0, wildcard bits 0.0.255.255
```

The math to find the range of addresses relies on the fact that either the command is fully correct, or that IOS has already set these address octets to 0, as shown in the example.

> **NOTE**   The most useful WC masks, in binary, do not interleave 0s and 1s. This book assumes the use of only these types of WC masks. However, Cisco IOS allows WC masks that interleave 0s and 1s, but using these WC masks breaks the simple method of calculating the range of addresses. As you progress through to CCIE studies, be ready to dig deeper to learn how to determine what an ACL matches.

Chapter Review

One key to doing well on the exams is to perform repetitive spaced review sessions. Review this chapter's material using either the tools in the book, DVD, or interactive tools for the same material found on the book's companion website. Refer to the "Your Study Plan" element for more details. Table 16-4 outlines the key review elements and where you can find them. To better track your study progress, record when you completed these activities in the second column.

Table 16-4   Chapter Review Tracking

Review Element	Review Date(s)	Resource Used
Review key topics		Book, DVD/website
Review key terms		Book, DVD/website
Repeat DIKTA questions		Book, PCPT
Review command tables		Book

Review All the Key Topics

Table 16-5   Key Topics for Chapter 16

Key Topic Element	Description	Page Number
Paragraph	Summary of the general rule of the location and direction for an ACL	441
Figure 16-3	Summary of four main categories of IPv4 ACLs in Cisco IOS	443
Paragraph	Summary of first-match logic used by all ACLs	444
List	Wildcard mask logic for decimal 0 and 255	446
List	Wildcard mask logic to match a subnet	448
List	Steps to plan and implement a standard IP ACL	449
List	Tips for creating matching logic for the source address field in the **access-list** command	454

Key Terms You Should Know

standard access list, wildcard mask

Additional Practice for This Chapter's Processes

For additional practice with analyzing subnets, you may do the same set of practice problems using your choice of tools:

Application: Use the Basic IPv4 Access Control Lists application on the DVD or companion website.

PDF: Alternatively, practice the same problems found in these apps using DVD Appendix D, "Practice for Chapter 16: Basic IPv4 Access Control Lists."

Command References

Tables 16-6 and 16-7 list configuration and verification commands used in this chapter. As an easy review exercise, cover the left column in a table, read the right column, and try to recall the command without looking. Then repeat the exercise, covering the right column, and try to recall what the command does.

Table 16-6   Chapter 16 Configuration Command Reference

Command	Description
access-list *access-list-number* {**deny** | **permit**} *source* [*source-wildcard*] [**log**]	Global command for standard numbered access lists. Use a number between 1 and 99 or 1300 and 1999, inclusive.
access-list *access-list-number* **remark** *text*	Defines a remark that helps you remember what the ACL is supposed to do
ip access-group *number* {**in** | **out**}	Interface subcommand to enable access lists

Table 16-7   Chapter 16 EXEC Command Reference

Command	Description
show ip interface [*type number*]	Includes a reference to the access lists enabled on the interface
show access-lists [*access-list-number* | *access-list-name*]	Shows details of configured access lists for all protocols
show ip access-lists [*access-list-number* | *access-list-name*]	Shows IP access lists

Answers to Earlier Practice Problems

Table 16-8 lists the answers to the problems listed earlier in Table 16-2.

Table 16-8   Building One-Line Standard ACLs: Answers

Problem	Answers
1	access-list 1 permit 172.16.5.4
2	access-list 2 permit 192.168.6.0 0.0.0.255
3	access-list 3 permit 192.168.0.0 0.0.255.255
4	access-list 4 permit any
5	access-list 5 permit 10.1.200.0 0.0.7.255
6	access-list 6 permit 10.1.200.0 0.0.0.31
7	access-list 7 permit 172.20.112.0 0.0.1.255
8	access-list 8 permit 172.20.112.0 0.0.0.63
9	access-list 9 permit 192.168.9.64 0.0.0.15
10	access-list 10 permit 192.168.9.64 0.0.0.3

Table 16-9 lists the answers to the problems listed earlier in Table 16-3.

Table 16-9   Address Ranges for Problems in Table 16-3: Answers

Problem	Address Range
1	One address: 10.7.6.5
2	192.168.4.0 – 192.168.4.127
3	192.168.6.0 – 192.168.6.31
4	172.30.96.0 – 172.30.99.255
5	172.30.96.0 – 172.30.96.63
6	10.1.192.0 – 10.1.192.31
7	10.1.192.0 – 10.1.193.255
8	10.1.192.0 – 10.1.255.255

Advanced IPv4 Access Control Lists

This chapter covers the following exam topics:

4.0 Infrastructure Services

4.4 Configure, verify, and troubleshoot IPv4 and IPv6 access list for traffic filtering

4.4.a Standard

4.4.b Extended

4.4.c Named

IPv4 ACLs are either standard or extended ACLs, with standard ACLs matching only the source IP address, and extended matching a variety of packet header fields. At the same time, IP ACLs are either numbered or named. Figure 17-1 shows the categories, and the main features of each, as introduced in the previous chapter.

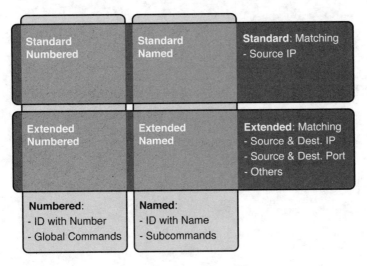

Figure 17-1 *Comparisons of IP ACL Types*

This chapter discusses the other three categories of ACLs beyond standard numbered IP ACLs, and ends with a few miscellaneous features to secure Cisco routers and switches. Note that this chapter's technical content is identical to the ICND1 100-105 Cert Guide's Chapter 26; use that fact to speed your reading now if you have already read that chapter.

"Do I Know This Already?" Quiz

Take the quiz (either here, or use the PCPT software) if you want to use the score to help you decide how much time to spend on this chapter. The answers are at the bottom of the page following the quiz, and the explanations are in DVD Appendix C and in the PCPT software.

Table 17-1 "Do I Know This Already?" Foundation Topics Section-to-Question Mapping

Foundation Topics Section	Questions
Extended IP Access Control Lists	1–3
Named ACLs and ACL Editing	4
Troubleshooting with IPv4 ACLs	5–6

1. Which of the following fields cannot be compared based on an extended IP ACL? (Choose two answers.)

   a. Protocol

   b. Source IP address

   c. Destination IP address

   d. TOS byte

   e. URL

   f. Filename for FTP transfers

2. Which of the following **access-list** commands permit packets going from host 10.1.1.1 to all web servers whose IP addresses begin with 172.16.5? (Choose two answers.)

   a. access-list 101 permit tcp host 10.1.1.1 172.16.5.0 0.0.0.255 eq www

   b. access-list 1951 permit ip host 10.1.1.1 172.16.5.0 0.0.0.255 eq www

   c. access-list 2523 permit ip host 10.1.1.1 eq www 172.16.5.0 0.0.0.255

   d. access-list 2523 permit tcp host 10.1.1.1 eq www 172.16.5.0 0.0.0.255

   e. access-list 2523 permit tcp host 10.1.1.1 172.16.5.0 0.0.0.255 eq www

3. Which of the following **access-list** commands permits packets going to any web client from all web servers whose IP addresses begin with 172.16.5?

   a. access-list 101 permit tcp host 10.1.1.1 172.16.5.0 0.0.0.255 eq www

   b. access-list 1951 permit ip host 10.1.1.1 172.16.5.0 0.0.0.255 eq www

   c. access-list 2523 permit tcp any eq www 172.16.5.0 0.0.0.255

   d. access-list 2523 permit tcp 172.16.5.0 0.0.0.255 eq www 172.16.5.0 0.0.0.255

   e. access-list 2523 permit tcp 172.16.5.0 0.0.0.255 eq www any

4. In a router running a recent IOS version (at least version 15.0), an engineer needs to delete the second line in ACL 101, which currently has four commands configured. Which of the following options could be used? (Choose two answers.)

   a. Delete the entire ACL and reconfigure the three ACL statements that should remain in the ACL.

   b. Delete one line from the ACL using the **no access-list...** global command.

   c. Delete one line from the ACL by entering ACL configuration mode for the ACL and then deleting only the second line based on its sequence number.

   d. Delete the last three lines from the ACL from global configuration mode, and then add the last two statements back into the ACL.

5. An engineer is considering configuring an ACL on Router R1. The engineer could use ACL A, which would be enabled with the **ip access-group A out** command on interface G0/1, or ACL B, which would be enabled with the **ip access-group B in** command on that same interface. R1's G0/1 interface uses IPv4 address 1.1.1.1. Which of the answers are true when comparing these options? (Choose two answers.)

   a. ACL A creates more risk of filtering important overhead traffic than ACL B.

   b. ACL B creates more risk of filtering important overhead traffic than ACL A.

   c. A **ping 1.1.1.1** command on R1 would bypass ACL A even if enabled.

   d. A **ping 1.1.1.1** command on R1 would bypass ACL B even if enabled.

6. An engineer configures an ACL but forgets to save the configuration. At that point, which of the following commands display the configuration of an IPv4 ACL, including line numbers? (Choose two answers.)

   a. show running-config

   b. show startup-config

   c. show ip access-lists

   d. show access-lists

Foundation Topics

Extended Numbered IP Access Control Lists

Extended IP access lists have many similarities compared to the standard numbered IP ACLs discussed in the previous chapter. Just like standard IP ACLs, you enable extended access lists on interfaces for packets either entering or exiting the interface. IOS searches the list sequentially. Extended ACLs also use first-match logic, because the router stops the search through the list as soon as the first statement is matched, taking the action defined in the first-matched statement. All these features are also true of standard numbered access lists (and named ACLs).

Extended ACLs differ from standard ACLs mostly because of the larger variety of packet header fields that can be used to match a packet. One extended ACL statement can examine multiple parts of the packet headers, requiring that all the parameters be matched correctly to match that one ACL statement. That powerful matching logic makes extended access lists both more useful and more complex than standard IP ACLs.

Matching the Protocol, Source IP, and Destination IP

Like standard numbered IP ACLs, extended numbered IP ACLs also use the **access-list** global command. The syntax is identical, at least up through the **permit** or **deny** keyword. At that point, the command lists matching parameters, and those differ, of course. In particular, the extended ACL **access-list** command requires three matching parameters: the IP protocol type, the source IP address, and the destination IP address.

The IP header's Protocol field identifies the header that follows the IP header. Figure 17-2 shows the location of the IP Protocol field, the concept of it pointing to the type of header that follows, along with some details of the IP header for reference.

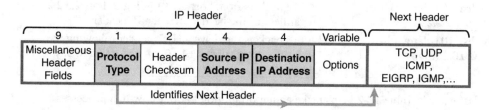

Figure 17-2   *IP Header, with Focus on Required Fields in Extended IP ACLs*

IOS requires that you configure parameters for the three highlighted parts of Figure 17-2. For the protocol type, you simply use a keyword, such as **tcp**, **udp**, or **icmp**, matching IP packets that happen to have a TCP, UDP, or ICMP header, respectively, following the IP header. Or you can use the keyword **ip**, which means "all IPv4 packets." You also must configure some values for the source and destination IP address fields that follow; these fields use the same syntax and options for matching the IP addresses as discussed in Chapter 16, "Basic IPv4 Access Control Lists." Figure 17-3 shows the syntax.

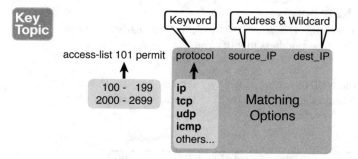

Figure 17-3   *Extended ACL Syntax, with Required Fields*

NOTE   When matching IP addresses in the source and destination fields, there is one difference with standard ACLs: When matching a specific IP address, the extended ACL requires the use of the **host** keyword. You cannot simply list the IP address alone.

Answers to the "Do I Know This Already?" quiz:

1 E, F **2** A, E **3** E **4** A, C **5** B, C **6** C, D

Table 17-2 lists several sample **access-list** commands that use only the required matching parameters. Feel free to cover the right side and use the table for an exercise, or just review the explanations to get an idea for the logic in some sample commands.

Table 17-2 Extended **access-list** Commands and Logic Explanations

access-list Statement	What It Matches
access-list 101 deny tcp any any	Any IP packet that has a TCP header
access-list 101 deny udp any any	Any IP packet that has a UDP header
access-list 101 deny icmp any any	Any IP packet that has an ICMP header
access-list 101 deny ip host 1.1.1.1 host 2.2.2.2	All IP packets from host 1.1.1.1 going to host 2.2.2.2, regardless of the header after the IP header
access-list 101 deny udp 1.1.1.0 0.0.0.255 any	All IP packets that have a UDP header following the IP header, from subnet 1.1.1.0/24, and going to any destination

The last entry in Table 17-2 helps make an important point about how IOS processes extended ACLs:

In an extended ACL **access-list** command, all the matching parameters must match the packet for the packet to match the command.

For example, in that last example from Table 17-2, the command checks for UDP, a source IP address from subnet 1.1.1.0/24, and any destination IP address. If a packet with source IP address 1.1.1.1 were examined, it would match the source IP address check, but if it had a TCP header instead of UDP, it would not match this **access-list** command. All parameters must match.

Matching TCP and UDP Port Numbers

Extended ACLs can also examine parts of the TCP and UDP headers, particularly the source and destination port number fields. The port numbers identify the application that sends or receives the data.

The most useful ports to check are the well-known ports used by servers. For example, web servers use well-known port 80 by default. Figure 17-4 shows the location of the port numbers in the TCP header, following the IP header.

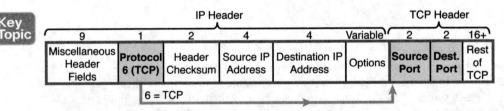

Figure 17-4 *IP Header, Followed by a TCP Header and Port Number Fields*

When an extended ACL command includes either the **tcp** or **udp** keyword, that command can optionally reference the source and/or destination port. To make these comparisons, the syntax uses keywords for equal, not equal, less than, greater than, and for a range of port numbers. In addition, the command can use either the literal decimal port numbers, or more convenient keywords for some well-known application ports. Figure 17-5 shows the positions of the source and destination port fields in the **access-list** command and these port number keywords.

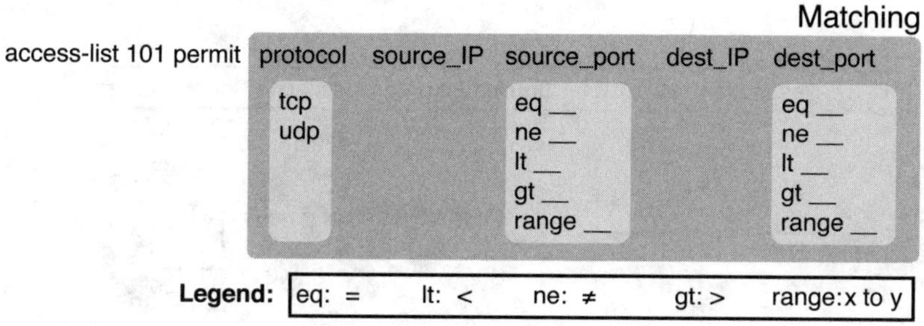

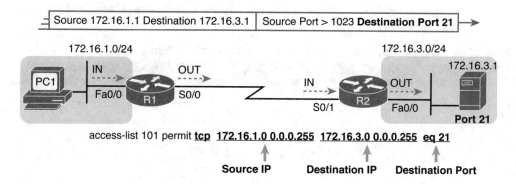

Figure 17-5 *Extended ACL Syntax with TCP and UDP Port Numbers Enabled*

For example, consider the simple network shown in Figure 17-6. The FTP server sits on the right, with the client on the left. The figure shows the syntax of an ACL that matches the following:

- Packets that include a TCP header
- Packets sent from the client subnet
- Packets sent to the server subnet
- Packets with TCP destination port 21 (FTP server control port)

Figure 17-6 *Filtering Packets Based on Destination Port*

To fully appreciate the matching of the destination port with the **eq 21** parameters, consider packets moving from left to right, from PC1 to the server. Assuming the server uses well-known port 21 (FTP control port), the packet's TCP header has a destination port value of 21. The ACL syntax includes the **eq 21** parameters after the destination IP address. The position after the destination address parameters is important: That position identifies the fact that the **eq 21** parameters should be compared to the packet's destination port. As a result, the ACL statement shown in Figure 17-6 would match this packet, and the destination port of 21, if used in any of the four locations implied by the four dashed arrowed lines in the figure.

Conversely, Figure 17-7 shows the reverse flow, with a packet sent by the server back toward PC1. In this case, the packet's TCP header has a source port of 21, so the ACL must check the source port value of 21, and the ACL must be located on different interfaces. In this case, the **eq 21** parameters follow the source address field, but come before the destination address field.

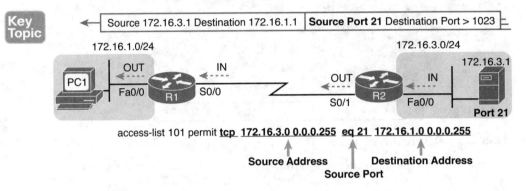

Figure 17-7 *Filtering Packets Based on Source Port*

When examining ACLs that match port numbers, first consider the location and direction in which the ACL will be applied. That direction determines whether the packet is being sent to the server, or from the server. At that point, you can decide whether you need to check the source or destination port in the packet. For reference, Table 17-3 lists many of the popular port numbers and their transport layer protocols and applications. Note that the syntax of the **access-list** commands accepts both the port numbers and a shorthand version of the application name.

Table 17-3 Popular Applications and Their Well-Known Port Numbers

Port Number(s)	Protocol	Application	access-list Command Keyword
20	TCP	FTP data	**ftp-data**
21	TCP	FTP control	**ftp**
22	TCP	SSH	—
23	TCP	Telnet	**telnet**
25	TCP	SMTP	**smtp**
53	UDP, TCP	DNS	**domain**
67	UDP	DHCP Server	**bootps**
68	UDP	DHCP Client	**bootpc**
69	UDP	TFTP	**tftp**
80	TCP	HTTP (WWW)	**www**
110	TCP	POP3	**pop3**
161	UDP	SNMP	**snmp**
443	TCP	SSL	—
514	UDP	Syslog	—
16,384 – 32,767	UDP	RTP (voice, video)	—

Table 17-4 lists several example **access-list** commands that match based on port numbers. Cover the right side of the table, and try to characterize the packets matched by each command. Then, check the right side of the table to see if you agree with the assessment.

Table 17-4 Extended **access-list** Command Examples and Logic Explanations

access-list Statement	What It Matches
access-list 101 deny tcp any gt 1023 host 10.1.1.1 eq 23	Packets with a TCP header, any source IP address, with a source port greater than (gt) 1023, a destination IP address of exactly 10.1.1.1, and a destination port equal to (eq) 23.
access-list 101 deny tcp any host 10.1.1.1 eq 23	The same as the preceding example, but any source port matches, because that parameter is omitted in this case.
access-list 101 deny tcp any host 10.1.1.1 eq telnet	The same as the preceding example. The **telnet** keyword is used instead of port 23.
access-list 101 deny udp 1.0.0.0 0.255.255.255 lt 1023 any	A packet with a source in network 1.0.0.0/8, using UDP with a source port less than (lt) 1023, with any destination IP address.

Extended IP ACL Configuration

Because extended ACLs can match so many different fields in the various headers in an IP packet, the command syntax cannot be easily summarized in a single generic command. However, the two commands in Table 17-5 summarize the syntax options as covered in this book.

Table 17-5 Extended IP Access List Configuration Commands

Command	Configuration Mode and Description
access-list *access-list-number* {deny | permit} *protocol source source-wildcard destination destination-wildcard* [log | log-input]	Global command for extended numbered **access lists**. Use a number between 100 and 199 or 2000 and 2699, inclusive.
access-list *access-list-number* {deny | permit} {tcp | udp} *source source-wildcard* [*operator* [*port*]] *destination destination-wildcard* [*operator* [*port*]] [established] [log]	A version of the **access-list** command with parameters specific to TCP and/or UDP.

The configuration process for extended ACLs mostly matches the same process used for standard ACLs. You must choose the location and direction in which to enable the ACL, particularly the direction, so that you can characterize whether certain addresses and ports will be either the source or destination. Configure the ACL using **access-list** commands, and when complete, then enable the ACL using the same **ip access-group** command used with standard ACLs. All these steps mirror what you do with standard ACLs; however, when configuring, keep the following differences in mind:

- Place extended ACLs as close as possible to the source of the packets that will be filtered. Filtering close to the source of the packets saves some bandwidth.

- Remember that all fields in one **access-list** command must match a packet for the packet to be considered to match that **access-list** statement.
- Use numbers of 100–199 and 2000–2699 on the **access-list** commands; no one number is inherently better than another.

Extended IP Access Lists: Example 1

This example focuses on understanding basic syntax. In this case, the ACL denies Bob access to all FTP servers on R1's Ethernet, and it denies Larry access to server1's web server. Figure 17-8 shows the network topology; Example 17-1 shows the configuration on R1.

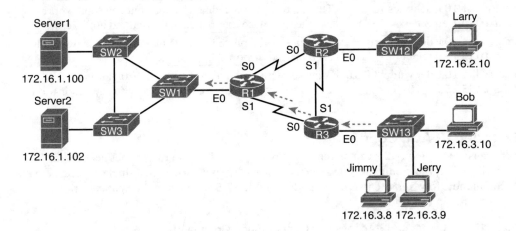

Figure 17-8 *Network Diagram for Extended Access List Example 1*

Example 17-1 *R1's Extended Access List: Example 1*

```
interface Serial0
 ip address 172.16.12.1 255.255.255.0
 ip access-group 101 in
!
interface Serial1
 ip address 172.16.13.1 255.255.255.0
 ip access-group 101 in
!
access-list 101 remark Stop Bob to FTP servers, and Larry to Server1 web
access-list 101 deny tcp host 172.16.3.10 172.16.1.0 0.0.0.255 eq ftp
access-list 101 deny tcp host 172.16.2.10 host 172.16.1.100 eq www
access-list 101 permit ip any any
```

The first ACL statement prevents Bob's access to FTP servers in subnet 172.16.1.0. The second statement prevents Larry's access to web services on Server1. The final statement permits all other traffic.

Focusing on the syntax for a moment, there are several new items to review. First, the access-list number for extended access lists falls in the range of 100 to 199 or 2000 to 2699. Following the **permit** or **deny** action, the *protocol* parameter defines whether you want to check for all IP packets or specific headers, such as TCP or UDP headers. When you check for TCP or UDP port numbers, you must specify the TCP or UDP protocol. Both FTP and the web use TCP.

This example uses the **eq** parameter, meaning "equals," to check the destination port numbers for FTP control (keyword **ftp**) and HTTP traffic (keyword **www**). You can use the numeric values—or, for the more popular options, a more obvious text version is valid. (If you were to type **eq 80**, the config would show **eq www**.)

This example enables the ACL in two places on R1: inbound on each serial interface. These locations achieve the goal of the ACL. However, that initial placement was made to make the point that Cisco suggests that you locate them as close as possible to the source of the packet. Therefore, Example 17-2 achieves the same goal as Example 17-1 of stopping Bob's access to FTP servers at the main site, and it does so with an ACL on R3.

Example 17-2   *R3's Extended Access List Stopping Bob from Reaching FTP Servers Near R1*

```
interface Ethernet0
 ip address 172.16.3.1 255.255.255.0
 ip access-group 103 in


access-list 103 remark deny Bob to FTP servers in subnet 172.16.1.0/24
access-list 103 deny tcp host 172.16.3.10 172.16.1.0 0.0.0.255 eq ftp
access-list 103 permit ip any any
```

The new configuration on R3 meets the goals to filter Bob's traffic, while also meeting the overarching design goal of keeping the ACL close to the source of the packets. ACL 103 on R3 looks a lot like ACL 101 on R1 from Example 17-1, but this time, the ACL does not bother to check for the criteria to match Larry's traffic, because Larry's traffic will never enter R3's Ethernet 0 interface. ACL 103 filters Bob's FTP traffic to destinations in subnet 172.16.1.0/24, with all other traffic entering R3's E0 interface making it into the network.

Extended IP Access Lists: Example 2

Example 17-3, based on the network shown in Figure 17-9, shows another example of how to use extended IP access lists. This example uses the following criteria:

■ Sam is not allowed access to the subnet of Bugs or Daffy.

■ Hosts on the Seville Ethernet are not allowed access to hosts on the Yosemite Ethernet.

■ All other combinations are allowed.

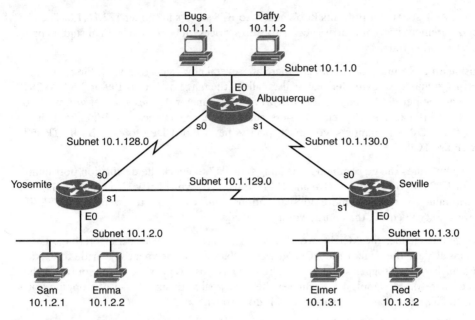

Figure 17-9 *Network Diagram for Extended Access List Example 2*

Example 17-3 *Yosemite Configuration for Extended Access List Example*

```
interface ethernet 0
 ip access-group 110 in
!
access-list 110 deny ip host 10.1.2.1 10.1.1.0 0.0.0.255
access-list 110 deny ip 10.1.2.0 0.0.0.255 10.1.3.0 0.0.0.255
access-list 110 permit ip any any
```

This configuration solves the problem with few statements while keeping to the Cisco design guideline of placing extended ACLs as close as possible to the source of the traffic. The ACL filters packets that enter Yosemite's E0 interface, which is the first router interface that packets sent by Sam enter. If the route between Yosemite and the other subnets changes over time, the ACL still applies. Also, the filtering mandated by the second requirement (to disallow Seville's LAN hosts from accessing Yosemite's) is met by the second **access-list** statement. Stopping packet flow from Yosemite's LAN subnet to Seville's LAN subnet stops effective communication between the two subnets. Alternatively, the opposite logic could have been configured at Seville.

Practice Building access-list Commands

Table 17-6 supplies a practice exercise to help you get comfortable with the syntax of the extended **access-list** command, particularly with choosing the correct matching logic. Your job: create a one-line extended ACL that matches the packets. The answers are in the section "Answers to Earlier Practice Problems," later in this chapter. Note that if the criteria mentions a particular application protocol, for example, "web client," that means to specifically match for that application protocol.

Table 17-6 Building One-Line Extended ACLs: Practice

Problem	Criteria
1	From web client 10.1.1.1, sent to a web server in subnet 10.1.2.0/24.
2	From Telnet client 172.16.4.3/25, sent to a Telnet server in subnet 172.16.3.0/25. Match all hosts in the client's subnet as well.
3	ICMP messages from the subnet in which 192.168.7.200/26 resides to all hosts in the subnet where 192.168.7.14/29 resides.
4	From web server 10.2.3.4/23's subnet to clients in the same subnet as host 10.4.5.6/22.
5	From Telnet server 172.20.1.0/24's subnet, sent to any host in the same subnet as host 172.20.44.1/23.
6	From web client 192.168.99.99/28, sent to a web server in subnet 192.168.176.0/28. Match all hosts in the client's subnet as well.
7	ICMP messages from the subnet in which 10.55.66.77/25 resides to all hosts in the subnet where 10.66.55.44/26 resides.
8	Any and every IPv4 packet.

Named ACLs and ACL Editing

Now that you have a good understanding of the core concepts in IOS IP ACLs, this section examines a few enhancements to IOS support for ACLs: named ACLs and ACL editing with sequence numbers. Although both features are useful and important, neither adds any function as to what a router can and cannot filter. Instead, named ACLs and ACL sequence numbers make it easier to remember ACL names and edit existing ACLs when an ACL needs to change.

Named IP Access Lists

Named IP ACLs have many similarities with numbered IP ACLs. They can be used for filtering packets, plus for many other purposes. They can match the same fields as well: Standard numbered ACLs can match the same fields as a standard named ACL, and extended numbered ACLs can match the same fields as an extended named ACL.

Of course, there are differences between named and numbered ACLs. Named ACLs originally had three big differences compared to numbered ACLs:

- Using names instead of numbers to identify the ACL, making it easier to remember the reason for the ACL
- Using ACL subcommands, not global commands, to define the action and matching parameters
- Using ACL editing features that allow the CLI user to delete individual lines from the ACL and insert new lines

You can easily learn named ACL configuration by just converting numbered ACLs to use the equivalent named ACL configuration. Figure 17-10 shows just such a conversion, using a simple three-line standard ACL number 1. To create the three **permit** subcommands for the named ACL, you literally copy parts of the three numbered ACL commands, beginning with the **permit** keyword.

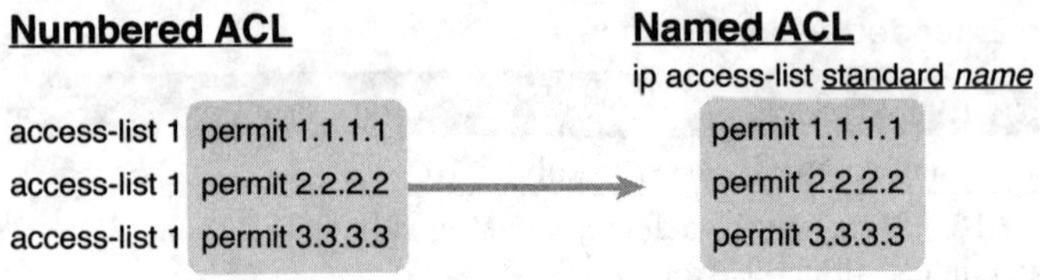

Numbered ACL

access-list 1 | permit 1.1.1.1
access-list 1 | permit 2.2.2.2
access-list 1 | permit 3.3.3.3

Named ACL

ip access-list <u>standard</u> <u>*name*</u>

permit 1.1.1.1
permit 2.2.2.2
permit 3.3.3.3

Figure 17-10 *Named ACL Versus Numbered ACL Configuration*

The only truly new part of the named ACL configuration is the **ip access-list** global configuration command. This command defines whether an ACL is a standard or extended ACL, and defines the name. It also moves the user to ACL configuration mode, as shown in upcoming Example 17-4. Once in ACL configuration mode, you configure **permit**, **deny**, and **remark** commands that mirror the syntax of numbered ACL **access-list** commands. If you're configuring a standard named ACL, these commands match the syntax of standard numbered ACLs; if you're configuring extended named ACLs, they match the syntax of extended numbered ACLs.

Example 17-4 shows the configuration of a named extended ACL. Pay particular attention to the configuration mode prompts, which show ACL configuration mode.

Example 17-4 *Named Access List Configuration*

```
Router# configure terminal
Enter configuration commands, one per line.  End with Ctrl-Z.
Router(config)# ip access-list extended barney
Router(config-ext-nacl)# permit tcp host 10.1.1.2 eq www any
Router(config-ext-nacl)# deny udp host 10.1.1.1 10.1.2.0 0.0.0.255
Router(config-ext-nacl)# deny ip 10.1.3.0 0.0.0.255 10.1.2.0 0.0.0.255
Router(config-ext-nacl)# deny ip 10.1.2.0 0.0.0.255 10.2.3.0 0.0.0.255
Router(config-ext-nacl)# permit ip any any
Router(config-ext-nacl)# interface serial1
Router(config-if)# ip access-group barney out
Router(config-if)# ^Z
Router# show running-config
Building configuration...


Current configuration:

! lines omitted for brevity


interface serial 1
 ip access-group barney out
!
ip access-list extended barney
 permit tcp host 10.1.1.2 eq www any
 deny   udp host 10.1.1.1 10.1.2.0 0.0.0.255
 deny   ip 10.1.3.0 0.0.0.255 10.1.2.0 0.0.0.255
 deny   ip 10.1.2.0 0.0.0.255 10.2.3.0 0.0.0.255
 permit ip any any
```

Example 17-4 begins with the creation of an ACL named barney. The **ip access-list extended barney** command creates the ACL, naming it barney and placing the user in ACL configuration mode. This command also tells the IOS that barney is an extended ACL. Next, five different **permit** and **deny** statements define the matching logic and action to be taken upon a match. The **show running-config** command output lists the named ACL configuration before the single entry is deleted.

Named ACLs allow the user to delete and add new lines to the ACL from within ACL configuration mode. Example 17-5 shows how, with the **no deny ip . . .** command deleting a single entry from the ACL. Notice that the output of the **show access-list** command at the end of the example still lists the ACL, with four **permit** and **deny** commands instead of five.

Example 17-5 *Removing One Command from a Named ACL*

```
Router# configure terminal
Enter configuration commands, one per line.  End with Ctrl-Z.
Router(config)# ip access-list extended barney
Router(config-ext-nacl)# no deny ip 10.1.2.0 0.0.0.255 10.2.3.0 0.0.0.255
Router(config-ext-nacl)# ^Z
Router# show access-list

Extended IP access list barney
    10 permit tcp host 10.1.1.2 eq www any
    20 deny    udp host 10.1.1.1 10.1.2.0 0.0.0.255
    30 deny    ip 10.1.3.0 0.0.0.255 10.1.2.0 0.0.0.255
    50 permit ip any any
```

Editing ACLs Using Sequence Numbers

Numbered ACLs have existed in IOS since the early days of Cisco routers and IOS; however, for many years, through many IOS versions, the ability to edit a numbered IP ACL was poor. For example, to simply delete a line from the ACL, the user had to delete the entire ACL and then reconfigure it.

The ACL editing feature uses an ACL sequence number that is added to each ACL **permit** or **deny** statement, with the numbers representing the sequence of statements in the ACL. ACL sequence numbers provide the following features for both numbered and named ACLs:

New configuration style for numbered: Numbered ACLs use a configuration style like named ACLs, as well as the traditional style, for the same ACL; the new style is required to perform advanced ACL editing.

Deleting single lines: An individual ACL **permit** or **deny** statement can be deleted with a **no** *sequence-number* subcommand.

Inserting new lines: Newly added **permit** and **deny** commands can be configured with a sequence number before the **deny** or **permit** command, dictating the location of the statement within the ACL.

Automatic sequence numbering: IOS adds sequence numbers to commands as you configure them, even if you do not include the sequence numbers.

To take advantage of the ability to delete and insert lines in an ACL, both numbered and named ACLs must use the same overall configuration style and commands used for named ACLs. The only difference in syntax is whether a name or number is used. Example 17-6 shows the configuration of a standard numbered IP ACL, using this alternative configuration style. The example shows the power of the ACL sequence number for editing. In this example, the following occurs:

Step 1. Numbered ACL 24 is configured using this new-style configuration, with three **permit** commands.

Step 2. The **show ip access-lists** command shows the three **permit** commands with sequence numbers 10, 20, and 30.

Step 3. The engineer deletes only the second **permit** command using the **no 20** ACL subcommand, which simply refers to sequence number 20.

Step 4. The **show ip access-lists** command confirms that the ACL now has only two lines (sequence numbers 10 and 30).

Step 5. The engineer adds a new **deny** command to the beginning of the ACL, using the **5 deny 10.1.1.1** ACL subcommand.

Step 6. The **show ip access-lists** command again confirms the changes, this time listing three commands, sequence numbers 5, 10, and 30.

NOTE For this example, note that the user does not leave configuration mode, instead using the **do** command to tell IOS to issue the **show ip access-lists** EXEC command from configuration mode.

Example 17-6 *Editing ACLs Using Sequence Numbers*

```
! Step 1: The 3-line Standard Numbered IP ACL is configured.
R1# configure terminal
Enter configuration commands, one per line.  End with Ctrl-Z.
R1(config)# ip access-list standard 24
R1(config-std-nacl)# permit 10.1.1.0 0.0.0.255
R1(config-std-nacl)# permit 10.1.2.0 0.0.0.255
R1(config-std-nacl)# permit 10.1.3.0 0.0.0.255


! Step 2: Displaying the ACL's contents, without leaving configuration mode.
R1(config-std-nacl)# do show ip access-lists 24
Standard IP access list 24
    10 permit 10.1.1.0, wildcard bits 0.0.0.255
    20 permit 10.1.2.0, wildcard bits 0.0.0.255
    30 permit 10.1.3.0, wildcard bits 0.0.0.255


! Step 3: Still in ACL 24 configuration mode, the line with sequence number 20 is
  deleted.
R1(config-std-nacl)# no 20


! Step 4: Displaying the ACL's contents again, without leaving configuration mode.
```

```
! Note that line number 20 is no longer listed.
R1(config-std-nacl)#do show ip access-lists 24
Standard IP access list 24
    10 permit 10.1.1.0, wildcard bits 0.0.0.255
    30 permit 10.1.3.0, wildcard bits 0.0.0.255


! Step 5: Inserting a new first line in the ACL.
R1(config-std-nacl)# 5 deny 10.1.1.1


! Step 6: Displaying the ACL's contents one last time, with the new statement
!(sequence number 5) listed first.
R1(config-std-nacl)# do show ip access-lists 24
Standard IP access list 24
    5 deny    10.1.1.1
    10 permit 10.1.1.0, wildcard bits 0.0.0.255
    30 permit 10.1.3.0, wildcard bits 0.0.0.255
```

Note that although Example 17-6 uses a numbered ACL, named ACLs use the same process to edit (add and remove) entries.

Numbered ACL Configuration Versus Named ACL Configuration

As a brief aside about numbered ACLs, note that IOS actually allows two ways to configure numbered ACLs in the more recent versions of IOS. First, IOS supports the traditional method, using the **access-list** global commands shown earlier in Examples 17-1, 17-2, and 17-3. IOS also supports the numbered ACL configuration with commands just like named ACLs, as shown in Example 17-6.

Oddly, IOS always stores numbered ACLs with the original style of configuration, as global **access-list** commands, no matter which method is used to configure the ACL. Example 17-7 demonstrates these facts, picking up where Example 17-6 ended, with the following additional steps:

Step 7.   The engineer lists the configuration (**show running-config**), which lists the old-style configuration commands—even though the ACL was created with the new-style commands.

Step 8.   The engineer adds a new statement to the end of the ACL using the old-style **access-list 24 permit 10.1.4.0 0.0.0.255** global configuration command.

Step 9.   The **show ip access-lists** command confirms that the old-style **access-list** command from the previous step followed the rule of being added only to the end of the ACL.

Step 10.   The engineer displays the configuration to confirm that the parts of ACL 24 configured with both new-style commands and old-style commands are all listed in the same old-style ACL (**show running-config**).

Example 17-7   *Adding to and Displaying a Numbered ACL Configuration*

```
! Step 7: A configuration snippet for ACL 24.
R1# show running-config
```

```
! The only lines shown are the lines from ACL 24
access-list 24 deny   10.1.1.1
access-list 24 permit 10.1.1.0 0.0.0.255
access-list 24 permit 10.1.3.0 0.0.0.255


! Step 8: Adding a new access-list 24 global command
R1# configure terminal
Enter configuration commands, one per line.  End with CNTL/Z.
R1(config)# access-list 24 permit 10.1.4.0 0.0.0.255
R1(config)# ^Z


! Step 9: Displaying the ACL's contents again, with sequence numbers. Note that even
! the new statement has been automatically assigned a sequence number.
R1# show ip access-lists 24
Standard IP access list 24
    5 deny   10.1.1.1
    10 permit 10.1.1.0, wildcard bits 0.0.0.255
    30 permit 10.1.3.0, wildcard bits 0.0.0.255
    40 permit 10.1.4.0, wildcard bits 0.0.0.255


! Step 10: The numbered ACL configuration remains in old-style configuration commands.
R1# show running-config
! The only lines shown are the lines from ACL 24
access-list 24 deny   10.1.1.1
access-list 24 permit 10.1.1.0 0.0.0.255
access-list 24 permit 10.1.3.0 0.0.0.255
access-list 24 permit 10.1.4.0 0.0.0.255
```

ACL Implementation Considerations

ACLs can be a great tool to enhance the security of a network, but engineers should think about some broader issues before simply configuring an ACL to fix a problem. To help, Cisco makes the following general recommendations in the courses on which the CCNA R&S exams are based:

■ Place extended ACLs as close as possible to the source of the packet. This strategy allows ACLs to discard the packets early.

■ Place standard ACLs as close as possible to the destination of the packet. This strategy avoids the mistake with standard ACLs (which match the source IPv4 address only) of unintentionally discarding packets that did not need to be discarded.

■ Place more specific statements early in the ACL.

■ Disable an ACL from its interface (using the **no ip access-group** interface subcommand) before making changes to the ACL.

The first point deals with the concept of where to locate your ACLs. If you intend to filter a packet, filtering closer to the packet's source means that the packet takes up less bandwidth in the network, which seems to be more efficient—and it is. Therefore, Cisco suggests locating extended ACLs as close to the source as possible.

However, the second point seems to contradict the first point, at least for standard ACLs, to locate them close to the destination. Why? Well, because standard ACLs look only at the source IP address, they tend to filter more than you want filtered when placed close to the source. For example, imagine that Fred and Barney are separated by four routers. If you filter Barney's traffic sent to Fred on the first router, Barney can't reach any hosts near the other three routers. So, the Cisco courses make a blanket recommendation to locate standard ACLs closer to the destination to avoid filtering traffic you do not mean to filter.

For the third item in the list, by placing more specific matching parameters early in each list, you are less likely to make mistakes in the ACL. For example, imagine that the ACL first listed a command that permitted traffic going to 10.1.1.0/24, and the second command denied traffic going to host 10.1.1.1. Packets sent to host 10.1.1.1 would match the first command, and never match the more specific second command. Note that later IOS versions prevent this mistake during configuration in some cases, as shown later in this chapter in Example 17-11.

Finally, Cisco recommends that you disable the ACLs on the interfaces before you change the statements in the list. By doing so, you avoid issues with the ACL during an interim state. First, if you delete an entire ACL, and leave the IP ACL enabled on an interface with the **ip access-group** command, IOS does not filter any packets (that was not always the case in far earlier IOS versions)! As soon as you add one ACL command to that enabled ACL, however, IOS starts filtering packets based on that ACL. Those interim ACL configurations could cause problems.

For example, suppose you have ACL 101 enabled on S0/0/0 for output packets. You delete list 101 so that all packets are allowed through. Then, you enter a single **access-list 101** command. As soon as you press Enter, the list exists, and the router filters all packets exiting S0/0/0 based on the one-line list. If you want to enter a long ACL, you might temporarily filter packets you don't want to filter! Therefore, the better way is to disable the list from the interface, make the changes to the list, and then reenable it on the interface.

Troubleshooting with IPv4 ACLs

The use of IPv4 ACLs makes troubleshooting IPv4 routing more difficult. Any data plane troubleshooting process can include a catchall phrase to include checking for ACLs. A network can have all hosts working, DHCP settings correct, all LANs working, all router interfaces working, and all routers having learned all routes to all subnets—and ACLs can still filter packets. Although ACLs provide that important service of filtering some packets, ACLs can make the troubleshooting process that much more difficult.

This third of the three major sections of this chapter focuses on troubleshooting in the presence of IPv4 ACLs. It breaks the discussion into two parts. The first part gives advice about common problems you might see on the exam, and how to find those with **show** commands and some analysis. The second part then looks at how ACLs impact the **ping** command.

Analyzing ACL Behavior in a Network

ACLs cause some of the biggest challenges when troubleshooting problems in real networking jobs. The packets created by commands like **ping** and **traceroute** do not exactly match the fields in packets created by end users. The ACLs sometimes filter the **ping** and **traceroute** traffic, making the network engineer think some other kind of problems exists when no problems exist at all. Or, the problem with the end-user traffic really is caused by the ACL, but the ping and traceroute traffic works fine, because the ACL matches the end-user traffic with a **deny** action but matches the ping and traceroute traffic with a **permit** action.

As a result, much of ACL troubleshooting requires thinking about ACL configuration versus the packets that flow in a network, rather than using a couple of IOS commands that identify the root cause of the problem. The **show** commands that help are those that give you the configuration of the ACL, and on what interfaces the ACL is enabled. You can also see statistics about which ACL statements have been matched. And using pings and traceroutes can help—as long as you remember that ACLs may apply different actions to those packets versus the end-user traffic.

The following phrases the ACL troubleshooting steps into a list for easier study. The list also expands on the idea of analyzing each ACL in Step 3. None of the ideas in the list are new compared to this chapter and the previous chapter, but it acts more as a summary of the common issues:

Step 1. Determine on which interfaces ACLs are enabled, and in which direction (**show running-config, show ip interfaces**).

Step 2. Find the configuration of each ACL (**show access-lists, show ip access-lists, show running-config**).

Step 3. Analyze the ACLs to predict which packets should match the ACL, focusing on the following points:

    A. **Misordered ACLs:** Look for misordered ACL statements. IOS uses first-match logic when searching an ACL.

    B. **Reversed source/destination addresses:** Analyze the router interface, the direction in which the ACL is enabled, compared to the location of the IP address ranges matched by the ACL statements. Make sure the source IP address field could match packets with that source IP address, rather than the destination, and vice versa for the destination IP address field.

    C. **Reversed source/destination ports:** For extended ACLs that reference UDP or TCP port numbers, continue to analyze the location and direction of the ACL versus the hosts, focusing on which host acts as the server using a well-known port. Ensure that the ACL statement matches the correct source or destination port depending on whether the server sent or will receive the packet.

    D. **Syntax:** Remember that extended ACL commands must use the **tcp** and **udp** keywords if the command needs to check the port numbers.

    E. **Syntax:** Note that ICMP packets do not use UDP or TCP; ICMP is considered to be another protocol matchable with the **icmp** keyword (instead of **tcp** or **udp**).

    F. **Explicit deny any:** Instead of using the implicit **deny any** at the end of each ACL, use an explicit configuration command to deny all traffic at the end of the ACL so that the **show** command counters increment when that action is taken.

    G. **Dangerous inbound ACLs:** Watch for inbound ACLs, especially those with deny all logic at the end of the ACL. These ACLs may discard incoming overhead protocols, like routing protocol messages.

> **H. Standard ACL location:** Standard ACLs enabled close to the source of matched addresses can discard the packets as intended, but also discard packets that should be allowed through. Always pay close attention to the requirements of the ACL in these cases.

This chapter (and the previous) have already discussed the details of Step 3. The first two steps are important for Simlet questions in case you are not allowed to look at the configuration; you can use other **show** commands to determine all the relevant ACL configuration. The next few pages show some of the related commands and how they can uncover some of the issues described in the just-completed ACL troubleshooting checklist.

ACL Troubleshooting Commands

If you suspect ACLs are causing a problem, the first problem-isolation step is to find the location and direction of the ACLs. The fastest way to do this is to look at the output of the **show running-config** command and to look for **ip access-group** commands under each interface. However, in some cases, enable mode access may not be allowed, and **show** commands are required. Instead, use the **show ip interfaces** command to find which ACLs are enabled on which interfaces, as shown in Example 17-8.

Example 17-8   *Sample* show ip interface *Command*

```
R1> show ip interface s0/0/1
Serial0/0/1 is up, line protocol is up
  Internet address is 10.1.2.1/24
  Broadcast address is 255.255.255.255
  Address determined by setup command
  MTU is 1500 bytes
  Helper address is not set
  Directed broadcast forwarding is disabled
  Multicast reserved groups joined: 224.0.0.9
  Outgoing access list is not set
  Inbound  access list is 102
! roughly 26 more lines omitted for brevity
```

Note that the command output lists whether an ACL is enabled, in both directions, and which ACL it is. The example shows an abbreviated version of the **show ip interface S0/0/1** command, which lists messages for just this one interface. The **show ip interface** command would list the same messages for every interface in the router.

Step 2 of the ACL troubleshooting checklist then says that the contents of the ACL must be found. Again, the quickest way to look at the ACL is to use the **show running-config** command. If it's not available, the **show access-lists** and **show ip access-lists** commands list the same details shown in the configuration. These commands also list a useful counter that lists the number of packets that have matched each line in the ACL. Example 17-9 shows an example.

Example 17-9   show ip access-lists *Command Example*

```
R1# show ip access-lists
Extended IP access list 102
    10 permit ip 10.1.2.0 0.0.0.255 10.1.4.0 0.0.1.255 (15 matches)
```

The counter can be very useful for troubleshooting. If you can generate traffic that you think should match a particular line in an ACL, then you should see the matches increment on that counter. If you keep generating traffic that should match, but that line's counter never goes up, then those packets do not match that line in that ACL. Those packets could be matching an earlier line in the same ACL, or might not even be reaching that router (for any reason).

After the locations, directions, and configuration details of the various ACLs have been discovered in Steps 1 and 2, the hard part begins—analyzing what the ACL really does. For example, one of the most common tasks you will do is to look at the address fields and decide the range of addresses matched by that field. Remember, for an ACL that sits in a router configuration, you can easily find the address range. The low end of the range is the address (the first number), and the high end of the range is the sum of the address and wildcard mask. For instance, with ACL 102 in Example 17-9, which is obviously configured in some router, the ranges are as follows:

> **Source 10.1.2.0, wildcard 0.0.0.255:** Matches from 10.1.2.0 through 10.1.2.255
>
> **Destination 10.1.4.0, wildcard 0.0.1.255:** Matches from 10.1.4.0 through 10.1.5.255

The next few pages work through some analysis of a few of the items from Step 3 in the troubleshooting checklist.

Example Issue: Reversed Source/Destination IP Addresses

IOS cannot recognize a case in which you attempt to match the wrong addresses in the source or destination address field. So, be ready to analyze the enabled ACLs and their direction versus the location of different subnets in the network. Then ask yourself about the packets that drive that ACL: what could the source and destination addresses of those packets be? And does the ACL match the correct address ranges, or not?

For example, consider Figure 17-11, a figure that will be used in several troubleshooting examples in this chapter. The requirements for the next ACL follow the figure.

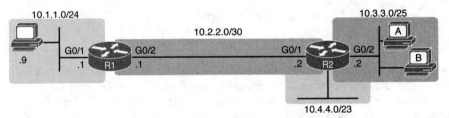

Figure 17-11 *Example Network Used in IPv4 ACL Troubleshooting Examples*

For this next ACL, the requirements ask that you allow and prevent various flows, as follows:

■ Allow hosts in subnet 10.3.3.0/25 and subnet 10.1.1.0/24 to communicate

■ Prevent hosts in subnet 10.4.4.0/23 and subnet 10.1.1.0/24 from communicating

■ Allow all other communications between hosts in network 10.0.0.0

■ Prevent all other communications

Example 17-10 shows the ACL used in this case on R2. At first glance, it meets all those requirements straight down the list.

Example 17-10 *Troubleshooting Example 2 per Step 3B: Source and Destination Mismatch*

```
R2# show ip access-lists
Standard IP access list Step3B
 10 permit 10.3.3.0 0.0.0.127
 20 deny 10.4.4.0 0.0.1.255
 30 permit 10.0.0.0 0.255.255.255 (12 matches)
R2#
R2# show ip interface G0/1 | include Inbound
  Inbound access list is Step3B
```

The problem in this case is that the ACL has been enabled on R2's G0/1 interface, inbound. Per the figure, packets coming from a source address in subnets 10.3.3.0/25 and 10.4.4.0/23 should be forwarded out R2's G0/1 interface, rather than coming in that interface. So, do not let the matching logic in the ACL that perfectly mirrors the requirements fool you; make sure and check the location of the ACL, direction, and the location of the IP addresses.

Note that Step 3C suggests a similar issue regarding matching well-known ports with TCP and UDP. The earlier section in this chapter titled "Matching TCP and UDP Port Numbers" has already discussed those ideas in plenty of detail. Just make sure to check where the server sits versus the location and direction of the ACL.

Steps 3D and 3E: Common Syntax Mistakes

Steps 3D and 3E describe a couple of common syntax mistakes. First, to match a TCP port in an ACL statement, you must use a **tcp** protocol keyword instead of **ip** or any other value. Otherwise, IOS rejects the command as having incorrect syntax. Same issue with trying to match UDP ports: a **udp** protocol keyword is required.

To match ICMP, IOS includes an **icmp** protocol keyword to use instead of **tcp** or **udp**. In fact, the main conceptual mistake is to think of ICMP as an application protocol that uses either UDP or TCP; it uses neither. To match all ICMP messages, for instance, use the **permit icmp any any** command in an extended named ACL.

Example Issue: Inbound ACL Filters Routing Protocol Packets

A router bypasses outbound ACL logic for packets the router itself generates. That might sound like common sense, but it is important to stop and think about that fact in context. A router can have an outgoing ACL, and that ACL can and will discard packets that the router receives in one interface and then tries to forward out some other interface. But if the router creates the packet, for instance, for a routing protocol message, the router bypasses the outbound ACL logic for that packet.

However, a router does not bypass inbound ACL logic. If an ACL has an inbound ACL enabled, and a packet arrives in that interface, the router checks the ACL. Any and all IPv4 packets are considered by the ACL—including important overhead packets like routing protocol updates.

For example, consider a seemingly good ACL on a router, like the Step3G ACL in Example 17-11. That ACL lists a couple of **permit** commands, and has an implicit deny any at the end of the list. At first, it looks like any other reasonable ACL.

Example 17-11 *Troubleshooting Example 2 per Step 3G: Filtering RIP by Accident*

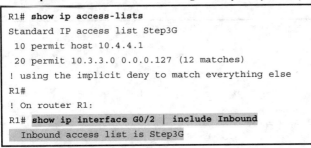

```
R1# show ip access-lists
Standard IP access list Step3G
 10 permit host 10.4.4.1
 20 permit 10.3.3.0 0.0.0.127 (12 matches)
! using the implicit deny to match everything else
R1#
! On router R1:
R1# show ip interface G0/2 | include Inbound
  Inbound access list is Step3G
```

Now look at the location and direction (inbound on R1, on R1's G0/2) and consider that location versus the topology Figure 17-11 for a moment. None of those **permit** statements match the RIP updates sent by R2, sent out R2's G0/1 interface toward R1. RIP messages use UDP (well-known port 520), and R2's G0/1 interface is 10.2.2.2 per the figure. R1 would match incoming RIP messages with the implicit deny all at the end of the list. The symptoms in this case, assuming only that one ACL exists, would be that R1 would not learn routes from R2, but R2 could still learn RIP routes from R1.

Of the three routing protocols discussed in the ICND1 and ICND2 books, RIPv2 uses UDP as a transport, while OSPF and EIGRP do not even use a transport protocol. As a result, to match RIPv2 packets with an ACL, you need the **udp** keyword and you need to match well-known port 520. OSPF and EIGRP can be matched with special keywords as noted in Table 17-7. The table also list the addresses used by each protocol.

Table 17-7 Key Fields for Matching Routing Protocol Messages

Protocol	Source IP Address	Destination IP Addresses	ACL Protocol Keyword
RIPv2	Source interface	224.0.0.9	**udp** (port 520)
OSPF	Source interface	224.0.0.5, 224.0.0.6	**ospf**
EIGRP	Source interface	224.0.0.10	**eigrp**

Example 17-12 shows a sample ACL with three lines, one to match each routing protocol, just to show the syntax. Note that in this case, the ACL matches the address fields with the **any** keyword. You could include lines like these in any inbound ACL to ensure that routing protocol packets would be permitted.

Example 17-12 *Example ACL that Matches all RIPv2, OSPF, and EIGRP with a Permit*

```
R1# show ip access-lists
ip access-list extended RoutingProtocolExample
 10 permit udp any any eq 520
 20 permit ospf any any
 30 permit eigrp any any
 remark a complete ACL would also need more statements here
R1#
```

ACL Interactions with Router-Generated Packets

Routers bypass outbound ACL logic for packets generated by that same router. This logic helps avoid cases in which a router discards its own overhead traffic. This logic applies to packets that a router creates for overhead processes like routing protocols, as well as for commands, like **ping** and **traceroute**. This section adds a few perspectives about how ACLs impact troubleshooting, and how this exception to outbound ACL logic applies, particularly commands used from the router CLI.

Local ACLs and a Ping from a Router

For the first scenario, think about a **ping** command issued by a router. The command generates packets, and the router sends those packets (holding the ICMP echo request messages) out one of the router interfaces, and typically some ICMP echo reply messages are received back. As it turns out, not all ACLs will attempt to filter those packets.

As a backdrop to discuss what happens, Figure 17-12 illustrates a simple network topology with two routers connected to a serial link. Note that in this figure four IP ACLs exist, named A, B, C, and D, as noted by the thick arrows in the drawing. That is, ACL A is an outbound ACL on R1's S0/0/0, ACL B is an inbound ACL on R2's S0/0/1, and so on.

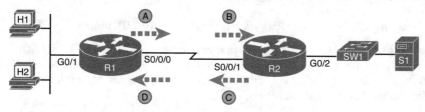

Figure 17-12 *Sample Network with IP ACLs in Four Locations*

As an example, consider a **ping** command issued from R1's CLI (after a user connects to R1's CLI using SSH). The **ping** command pings server S1's IP address. The IPv4 packets with the ICMP messages flow from R1 to S1 and back again. Which of those four ACLs could possibly filter the ICMP Echo Request toward S1, and the ICMP Echo Reply back toward R1?

Routers bypass their own outbound ACLs for packets generated by the router, as shown in Figure 17-13. Even though ACL A exists as an outgoing ACL on Router R1, R1 bypasses its own outgoing ACL logic of ACL A for the ICMP Echo Requests generated by R1.

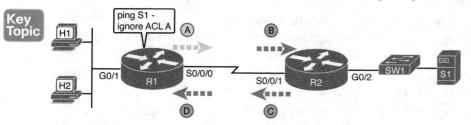

Figure 17-13 *R1 Ignores Outgoing ACL for Packets Created by Its Own* **ping** *Command*

Router Self-Ping of a Serial Interface IPv4 Address

The previous example uses a router's **ping** command when pinging a host. However, network engineers often need to ping router IP addresses, including using a self-ping. The term *self-ping* refers to a ping of a device's own IPv4 address. And for point-to-point serial links, a self-ping actually sends packets over the serial link, which causes some interesting effects with ACLs.

When a user issues a self-ping for that local router's serial IP address, the router actually sends the ICMP echo request out the link to the other router. The neighboring router then receives the packet and routes the packet with the ICMP echo request back to the original router. Figure 17-14 shows an example of a self-ping (**ping 172.16.4.1**) of Router R1's own IP address on a point-to-point serial link, with the ICMP echo request out the link to Router R2. At Step 2, R2 treats it like any other packet not destined for one of R2's own IPv4 addresses: R2 routes the packet. Where? Right back to Router R1, as shown in the figure.

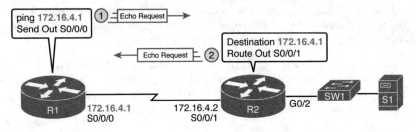

Figure 17-14 *The First Steps in a Self-Ping on R1, for R1's S0/0/0 IP Address*

Now think about those four ACLs in the earlier figures compared to Figure 17-14. R1 generates the ICMP echo request, so R1 bypasses outbound ACL A. ACLs B, C, and D could filter the packet. Note that the packet sent by R2 back to R1 is not generated by R2 in this case; R2 is just routing R1's original packet back to R1.

A self-ping of a serial interface actually tests many parts of a point-to-point serial link, as follows:

■ The link must work at Layers 1, 2, and 3. Specifically, both routers must have a working (up/up) serial interface, with correct IPv4 addresses configured.

■ ACLs B, C, and D must permit the ICMP echo request and reply packets.

So, when troubleshooting, if you choose to use self-pings and they fail, but the serial interfaces are in an up/up state, do not forget to check to see whether the ACLs have filtered the Internet Control Management Protocol (ICMP) traffic.

Router Self-Ping of an Ethernet Interface IPv4 Address

A self-ping of a router's own Ethernet interface IP address works a little like a self-ping of a router's serial IP address, but with a couple of twists:

■ Like with serial interface, the local router interface must be working (in an up/up state); otherwise, the ping fails.

■ Unlike serial interfaces, the router does not forward the ICMP messages physically out the interface, so security features on neighboring switches (like port security) or routers (like ACLs) cannot possibly filter the messages used by the **ping** command.

■ Like serial interfaces, an incoming IP ACL on the local router does process the router self-ping of an Ethernet-based IP address.

Figure 17-15 walks through an example. In this case, R2 issues a **ping 172.16.2.2** command to ping its own G0/2 IP address. Just like with a self-ping on serial links, R2 creates the

ICMP echo request. However, R2 basically processes the ping down its own TCP/IP stack and back up again, with the ICMP echo never leaving the router's Ethernet interface. R2 does check the Ethernet interface status, showing a failure if the interface is not up/up. R2 does not apply outbound ACL logic to the packet, because R2 created the packet, but R2 will apply inbound ACL logic to the packet, as if the packet had been physically received on the interface.

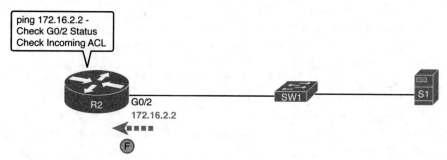

Figure 17-15   *Self-Ping of a Router's Ethernet Address*

Chapter Review

One key to doing well on the exams is to perform repetitive spaced review sessions. Review this chapter's material using either the tools in the book, DVD, or interactive tools for the same material found on the book's companion website. Refer to the "Your Study Plan" element for more details. Table 17-8 outlines the key review elements and where you can find them. To better track your study progress, record when you completed these activities in the second column.

Table 17-8   Chapter Review Tracking

Review Element	Review Date(s)	Resource Used
Review key topics		Book, DVD/website
Review key terms		Book, DVD/website
Repeat DIKTA questions		Book, PCPT
Review memory tables		Book, DVD/website
Review command tables		Book

Review All the Key Topics

Table 17-9   Key Topics for Chapter 17

Key Topic Element	Description	Page Number
Figure 17-3	Syntax and notes about the three required matching fields in the extended ACL **access-list** command	463
Paragraph	Summary of extended ACL logic that all parameters must match in a single **access-list** statement for a match to occur	464

Key Topic Element	Description	Page Number
Figure 17-4	Drawing of the IP header followed by a TCP header	464
Figure 17-5	Syntax and notes about matching TCP and UDP ports with extended ACL **access-list** commands	465
Figure 17-7	Logic and syntax to match TCP source ports	466
List	Guidelines for using extended numbered IP ACLs	467
List	Differences between named and numbered ACLs when named ACLs introduced	471
List	Features enabled by IOS 12.3 ACL sequence numbers	473
List	ACL implementation recommendations	476
Checklist	ACL troubleshooting checklist	478
Figure 17-13	Example of a router bypassing its outbound ACL logic for packets the router generates	483

Key Terms You Should Know

extended access list, named access list

Command References

Tables 17-10 and 17-11 list configuration and verification commands used in this chapter. As an easy review exercise, cover the left column in a table, read the right column, and try to recall the command without looking. Then repeat the exercise, covering the right column, and try to recall what the command does.

Table 17-10   Chapter 17 ACL Configuration Command Reference

Command	Description
access-list *access-list-number* {**deny** | **permit**} *protocol source source-wildcard destination destination-wildcard* [**log**]	Global command for extended numbered **access lists.** Use a number between 100 and 199 or 2000 and 2699, inclusive.
access-list *access-list-number* {**deny** | **permit**} **tcp** *source source-wildcard* [*operator* [*port*]] *destination destination-wildcard* [*operator* [*port*]] [**log**]	A version of the **access-list** command with TCP-specific parameters.
access-list *access-list-number* **remark** *text*	Defines a remark that helps you remember what the ACL is supposed to do.
ip access-group {*number* | *name* [**in** | **out**]}	Interface subcommand to enable access lists.
access-class *number* | *name* [**in** | **out**]	Line subcommand to enable either standard or extended access lists on vty lines.
ip access-list {**standard** | **extended**} *name*	Global command to configure a named standard or extended ACL and enter ACL configuration mode.
{**deny** | **permit**} *source* [*source wildcard*] [**log**]	ACL mode subcommand to configure the matching details and action for a standard named ACL.

Command	Description
{deny | permit} *protocol source source-wildcard destination destination-wildcard* [log]	ACL mode subcommand to configure the matching details and action for an extended named ACL.
{deny | permit} tcp *source source-wildcard* [*operator* [*port*]] *destination destination-wildcard* [*operator* [*port*]] [log]	ACL mode subcommand to configure the matching details and action for a named ACL that matches TCP segments.
remark *text*	ACL mode subcommand to configure a description of a named ACL.

Table 17-11   Chapter 17 EXEC Command Reference

Command	Description
show ip *interface* [*type number*]	Includes a reference to the access lists enabled on the interface
show access-lists [*access-list-number* | *access-list-name*]	Shows details of configured access lists for all protocols
show ip access-lists [*access-list-number* | *access-list-name*]	Shows IP access lists

Answers to Earlier Practice Problems

Table 17-12 lists the answers to the practice problems listed in Table 17-6. Note that for any question that references a client, you might have chosen to match port numbers greater than 1023. The answers in this table mostly ignore that option, but just to show one sample, the answer to the first problem lists one with a reference to client ports greater than 1023 and one without. The remaining answers simply omit this part of the logic.

Table 17-12   Building One-Line Extended ACLs: Answers

	Criteria
1	access-list 101 permit tcp host 10.1.1.1 10.1.2.0 0.0.0.255 eq www or access-list 101 permit tcp host 10.1.1.1 gt 1023 10.1.2.0 0.0.0.255 eq www
2	access-list 102 permit tcp 172.16.4.0 0.0.0.127 172.16.3.0 0.0.0.127 eq telnet
3	access-list 103 permit icmp 192.168.7.192 0.0.0.63 192.168.7.8 0.0.0.7
4	access-list 104 permit tcp 10.2.2.0 0.0.1.255 eq www 10.4.4.0 0.0.3.255
5	access-list 105 permit tcp 172.20.1.0 0.0.0.255 eq 23 172.20.44.0 0.0.1.255
6	access-list 106 permit tcp 192.168.99.96 0.0.0.15 192.168.176.0 0.0.0.15 eq www
7	access-list 107 permit icmp 10.55.66.0 0.0.0.127 10.66.55.0 0.0.0.63
8	access-list 108 permit ip any any

CHAPTER 18

Quality of Service (QoS)

This chapter covers the following exam topics:

4.0 Infrastructure Services

4.3 Describe Basic QoS concepts

    4.3.a Marking

    4.3.b Device trust

    4.3.c Prioritization

        4.3.c.(i) Voice

        4.3.c.(ii) Video

        4.3.c.(iii) Data

    4.3.d Shaping

    4.3.e Policing

    4.3.f Congestion Management

Quality of Service (QoS) refers to tools that network devices can use to manage several related characteristics of what happens to a packet while it flows through a network. Specifically, these tools manage the bandwidth made available to that type of packet, the delay the packet experiences, the jitter (variation in delay) between successive packets in the same flow, and the percentage of packet loss for packets of each class. These tools balance the tradeoffs of which types of traffic receive network resources, and when, giving more preference to some traffic, and less preference to others.

In the entire history of CCNA R&S, the exam topics have not focused on QoS beyond the barest small mention—until this latest version of the ICND2 (200-105) and CCNA (200-125) exams. Cisco adds one major topic, "Describe Basic QoS concepts," with a list of subitems that list specific QoS tools. As listed in the exam topics, this new QoS material is concepts only—not configuration and verification—and basic.

This chapter works through the QoS tools listed in the exam topics, with an emphasis on the problems they solve and how each tool manages bandwidth, delay, jitter, and loss.

"Do I Know This Already?" Quiz

Take the quiz (either here, or use the PCPT software) if you want to use the score to help you decide how much time to spend on this chapter. The answers are at the bottom of the page following the quiz, and the explanations are in DVD Appendix C and in the PCPT software.

Table 18-1 "Do I Know This Already?" Foundation Topics Section-to-Question Mapping

Foundation Topics Section	Questions
Introduction to QoS	1
Classification and Marking	2, 3
Congestion Management (Queuing)	4
Shaping and Policing	5
Congestion Avoidance	6

1. Which of the following attributes do QoS tools manage? (Choose three answers.)

    a. Bandwidth

    b. Delay

    c. Load

    d. MTU

    e. Loss

2. Which of the following QoS marking fields could remain with a packet while being sent through four different routers, over different LAN and WAN links? (Choose two answers.)

    a. CoS

    b. IPP

    c. DSCP

    d. MPLS EXP

3. Which of the following are available methods of classifying packets in DiffServ on Cisco routers? (Choose three answers.)

    a. Matching the IP DSCP field

    b. Matching the 802.1p CoS field

    c. Matching fields with an extended IP ACL

    d. Matching the SNMP Location variable

4. Which of the following behaviors is applied to a low latency queue in a Cisco router or switch?

    a. Congestion management

    b. Shaping

    c. Policing

    d. Priority scheduling

    e. Round robin scheduling

5. Think about a policing function that is currently working, and also think about a shaping function that is also currently working. That is, the current bit rate of traffic exceeds the respective policing and shaping rates. Which statements are true about these features? (Choose two answers.)

    a. The policer may or may not be discarding packets.

    b. The policer is definitely discarding packets.

    c. The shaper may or may not be queuing packets to slow down the sending rate.

    d. The shaper is definitely queuing packets to slow down the sending rate.

6. A queuing system has three queues serviced with round robin scheduling and one low latency queue that holds all voice traffic. Round robin queue 1 holds predominantly UDP traffic, while round robin queues 2 and 3 hold predominantly TCP traffic. The packets in each queue happen to have a variety of DSCP markings per the QoS design. In which queues would it make sense to use a congestion avoidance (drop management) tool? (Choose two answers.)

    a. The LLQ

    b. Queue 1

    c. Queue 2

    d. Queue 3

Foundation Topics

Introduction to QoS

Routers typically sit at the WAN edge, with both WAN interfaces and LAN interfaces. Those LAN interfaces typically run at much faster speeds, while the WAN interfaces run at slower speeds. While that slower WAN interface is busy sending the packets waiting in the router, hundreds or even thousands more IP packets could arrive in the LAN interfaces, all needing to be forwarded out that same WAN interface. What should the router do? Send them all, in the same order in which they arrived? Prioritize the packets, to send some earlier than others, preferring one type of traffic over another? Discard some of the packets when the number of packets waiting to exit the router gets too large?

That first paragraph described some of the many classic Quality of Service (QoS) questions in networking. QoS refers to the tools that networking devices use to apply some different treatment to packets in the network as they pass through the device. For instance, the WAN edge router would queue packets waiting for the WAN interface to be available. The router could also use a queue scheduling algorithm to determine which packets should be sent next, using some other order than the arrival order—giving some packets better service, and some worse service.

QoS: Managing Bandwidth, Delay, Jitter, and Loss

Cisco offers a wide range of QoS tools on both routers and switches. All these tools give you the means to manage four characteristics of network traffic:

Key Topic

- Bandwidth
- Delay
- Jitter
- Loss

Bandwidth refers to the speed of a link, in bits per second (bps). But while we think of bandwidth as speed, it helps to also think of bandwidth as the capacity of the link, in terms of how many bits can be sent over the link per second. The networking device's QoS tools determine what packet is sent over the link next, so the networking device is in control of which messages get access to the bandwidth next, and how much of that bandwidth (capacity) each type of traffic gets over time.

For example, consider that typical WAN edge router that has hundreds of packets waiting to exit the WAN link. An engineer might configure a queuing tool to reserve 10 percent of the bandwidth for voice traffic, 50 percent for mission-critical data applications, and leave the rest of the bandwidth for all other types of traffic. The queuing tool could then use those settings to make the choice about which packets to send next.

Delay can be described as one-way delay or round-trip delay. *One-way delay* refers to the time between sending one packet and that same packet arriving at the destination host. *Round-trip delay* counts the one-way delay plus the time for the receiver of the first packet to send back a packet—in other words, the time it takes to send one packet between two hosts, and receive one back. Many different individual actions impact delay; this chapter will discuss a few of those, including queuing and shaping delay.

Jitter refers to the variation in one-way delay between consecutive packets sent by the same application. For instance, imagine an application sends a few hundred packets to one particular host. The first packet's one-way delay is 300 milliseconds (300 ms, or .3 seconds). The next packet's one-way delay is 300 ms; so is the third's; and so on. In that case, there is no jitter. However, if instead the first packet has a one-way delay of 300 ms, the next has a one-way delay of 310 ms, and the next has 325 ms, then there is some variation in the delay, 10 ms between packets 1 and 2, and another 15 ms between packets 2 and 3. That difference is called jitter.

Finally, *loss* refers to the amount of lost messages, usually as a percentage of packets sent. The comparison is simple: If the sender for some application sends 100 packets, and only 98 arrive at the destination, that particular application flow experienced 2 percent loss. Loss can be caused by many factors, but often, people think of loss as something caused by faulty cabling or poor WAN services. That is one cause. However, more loss happens because of the normal operation of the networking devices, in which the devices' queues get too full, so the device has nowhere to put new packets, and discards the packet. Several QoS tools manage queuing systems to help control and avoid loss.

Answers to the "Do I Know This Already?" quiz:

1 A, B, E **2** B, C **3** A, B, C **4** D **5** A, D **6** C, D

Types of Traffic

With QoS, a network engineer sets about to prefer one type of traffic over another in regard to bandwidth, delay, jitter, and loss. Sometimes, that choice relates to the specific business. For example, if all the mission-critical applications sit on servers in three known subnets, then the QoS plan could be set up to match packets going to/from that subnet, and give that traffic better treatment compared to other traffic. However, in other cases, the choice of how to apply QoS tools relates to the nature of different kinds of applications. Some applications have different QoS needs than others. This next topic compares the basic differences in QoS needs based on the type of traffic.

Data Applications

First, consider a basic web application, with a user at a PC or tablet. The user types in a URI to request a web page. That request may require a single packet going to the web server, but it may result in hundreds or thousands of packets coming back to the web client, as shown in Figure 18-1.

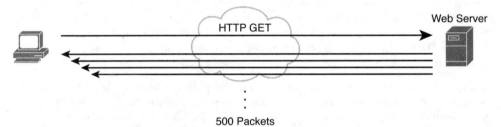

500 Packets

Figure 18-1 *Interactive Data Application*

> **NOTE** If you wonder how one web page might require thousands of packets, consider this math: with a 1500-byte IP maximum transmission unit (MTU), the data part of a TCP segment could be at most 1460 bytes (1500 bytes, minus 20 bytes each for the IP and TCP header). 1000 such packets total to 1,460,000 bytes, or about 1.5 MB. It is easy to imagine a web page with just a few graphics that totals more than 1.5 MB in size.

So, what is the impact of bandwidth, delay, jitter, and loss on an interactive web-based application? First, the packets require a certain amount of bandwidth capacity. As for delay, each of those packets from the server to the client takes some amount of one-way delay, with some jitter as well. Of the 500 packets shown in Figure 18-1, if some are lost (transmission errors, discarded by devices, or other reasons), then the server's TCP logic will retransmit—but parts of the web page may not show up right away.

While QoS tools focus on managing bandwidth, delay, jitter, and loss, the user mainly cares about the quality of the overall experience. For instance, with a web application, how long after clicking do you see something useful in your web browser? So, as a user, you care about the *Quality of Experience* (QoE), which is a term referring to users' perception of their use of the application on the network. QoS tools directly impact bandwidth, delay, jitter, and loss, which then should have some overall good effect to influence the users' QoE. And you can use QoS tools to create a better QoE for more important traffic—for instance, you might give certain business-critical applications better QoS treatment, which improves QoE for users of those apps.

In contrast, a noninteractive data application (historically called *batch* traffic)—for instance, data backup or file transfers—has different QoS requirements than interactive data applications. Batch applications typically send more data than interactive applications, but because no one is sitting there waiting to see something pop on the screen, the delay and jitter does not matter much. Much more important for these applications is meeting the need to complete the larger task (transferring files) within a larger time window. QoS tools can be used to provide enough bandwidth to meet the capacity needs of these applications, and manage loss to reduce the number of retransmissions.

Voice and Video Applications

Voice and video applications each have a similar breakdown of interactive and noninteractive flows. To make the main points about both voice and video, this section looks more deeply at voice traffic.

Before looking at voice, though, first think about the use of the term *flow* in networking. A flow is all the data moving from one application to another over the network, with one flow for each direction. For example, if you open a website and connect to a web server, the web page content that moves from the server to the client is one flow. Listen to some music with a music app on your phone, and that creates a flow from your app to the music app's server, and a flow from the server back to your phone. From a voice perspective, a phone call between two IP phones would create a flow for each direction. For video, it could be the traffic from one video surveillance camera collected by security software.

Now on to voice, specifically Voice over IP (VoIP). VoIP defines the means to take the sound made at one telephone and send it inside IP packets over an IP network, playing the sound back on the other telephone. Figure 18-2 shows the general idea. The steps in the figure include

Step 1.   The phone user makes a phone call and begins speaking.

Step 2.   A chip called a *codec* processes (digitizes) the sound to create a binary code (160 bytes with the G.711 codec, for example) for a certain time period (usually 20 ms).

Step 3.   The phone places the data into an IP packet.

Step 4.   The phone sends the packet to the destination IP phone.

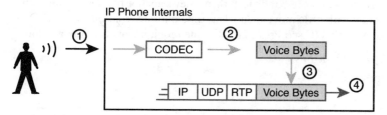

Figure 18-2   *Creating VoIP Packets with an IP Phone and a G.711 Codec*

If you work through the math a bit, this single call, with the G.711 Codec, requires about 80 Kbps of bandwidth (ignoring the data link header and trailer overhead). Counting the headers and VoIP payload as shown in the figure, each of the IP packets has 200 bytes. Each holds 20 ms of digitized voice, so the phone sends 50 packets per second. 50 packets at 200 bytes each is 10,000 bytes per second, or 80,000 bits per second, which is 80 Kbps. Other voice codecs require even less bandwidth, with the commonly used G.729 taking about 24 Kbps (again ignoring data link overhead).

At first, it may look like VoIP calls require little in regard to QoS. For bandwidth, a single voice call or flow requires only a little bandwidth in comparison to many data applications. However, interactive voice does require a much better level of quality for delay, jitter, and loss.

For instance, think about making a phone call with high one-way delay. You finish speaking, and pause for the other person to respond. And they do not, so you speak again—and hear the other person's voice overlaid on your own. The problem: too much delay. Or, consider calls for which the sound breaks up. The problem? It could have been packet loss, or it could have been jitter.

You can achieve good-quality voice traffic over an IP network, but you must implement QoS to do so. QoS tools set about to give different types of traffic the QoS behavior they need. Cisco's *Enterprise QoS Solution Reference Network Design Guide*, which itself quotes other sources in addition to relying on Cisco's long experience in implementing QoS, suggests the following guidelines for interactive voice:

Key Topic

- **Delay (one-way):** 150 ms or less
- **Jitter:** 30 ms or less
- **Loss:** 1% or less

In comparison, interactive voice requires more attention than interactive data applications for QoS features. Data applications generally tolerate more delay, jitter, and loss than voice (and video). A single voice call does generally take less bandwidth than a typical data application, but that bandwidth requirement is consistent. Data applications tend to be bursty, with data bursts in reaction to the user doing something with the application.

Video has a much more varied set of QoS requirements. Generally, think of video like voice, but with a much higher bandwidth requirement than voice (per flow), and similar requirements for low delay, jitter, and loss. As for bandwidth, video can use a variety of codecs that impact the amount of data sent, but many other technical features impact the amount of bandwidth required for a single video flow. (For instance, a sporting event with lots of movement on screen takes more bandwidth than a news anchor reading the news in front of a solid background with little movement.) This time quoting from *End-to-End QoS Network Design*, Second Edition (Cisco Press, 2013), some requirements for video include

Key Topic

- **Bandwidth:** 384 Kbps to 20+ Mbps
- **Delay (one-way):** 200–400 ms
- **Jitter:** 30–50 ms
- **Loss:** 0.1%–1%

NOTE *End-to-End QoS Network Design* is written by some of the same people who created the Cisco *Enterprise QoS Solutions Reference Network Design Guide* (available at Cisco.com). If you are looking for a book to dig into more depth on QoS, this book is an excellent modern reference for Cisco QoS.

QoS as Mentioned in This Book

QoS tools change the QoS characteristics of certain flows in the network. The rest of the chapter focuses on the specific tools mentioned in the sub-bullets under the lone CCNA R&S exam topic about QoS, presented in the following major sections:

- "Classification and Marking," about the marking of packets and the definition of trust boundaries.

- "Congestion Management (Queuing)" describes the scheduling of packets to give one type of packet priority over another.

- "Shaping and Policing" explains these two tools together because they are often used on opposite ends of a link.

- "Congestion Avoidance" addresses how to manage the packet loss that occurs when network devices get too busy.

QoS on Switches and Routers

Before moving on to several sections of the chapter about specific QoS tools, let me make a point about the terms *packet* and *frame* as used in this chapter.

The QoS tools discussed in this chapter can be used on both switches and routers. There are some differences in the features, and differences in implementation, due to the differences of internal architecture between routers and switches. However, to the depth discussed here, the descriptions apply equally to both LAN switches and IP routers.

This chapter uses the word *packet* in a general way, to refer to any message being processed by a networking device, just for convenience. Normally, throughout this book and the ICND1 Cert Guide, the term *packet* refers to the IP header and encapsulated headers and data, but without the data link header and trailer. The term *frame* refers to the data link header/trailer with its encapsulated headers and data. For this chapter, those differences do not matter to the discussion, but at the same time, the discussion often shows a message that sometimes is literally a packet (without the data link header/trailer) and sometimes a frame.

Throughout the chapter, the text uses *packet* for all messages, because the fact of whether or not the message happens to have a data link header/trailer at that point is immaterial to the basic discussion of features.

Additionally, note that all the examples in the chapter refer to routers, just to be consistent.

Classification and Marking

The first QoS tool discussed in this chapter, classification and marking, or simply marking, refers to a type of QoS tool that classifies packets based on their header contents, and then marks the message by changing some bits in specific header fields. This section looks first at the role of classification across all QoS tools, and then it examines the marking feature.

Classification Basics

QoS tools sit in the path that packets take when being forwarded through a router or switch, much like the positioning of ACLs. Like ACLs, QoS tools are enabled on an interface. Also like ACLs, QoS tools are enabled for a direction: packets entering the interface (before the forwarding decision) or for messages exiting the interface (after the forwarding decision).

The term *classification* refers to the process of matching the fields in a message to make a choice to take some QoS action. So, again comparing QoS tools to ACLs, ACLs perform classification and filtering; that is, ACLs match (classify) packet headers. ACLs can have the purpose (action) of choosing which packets to discard. QoS tools perform classification (matching of header fields) to decide which packets to take certain QoS actions against. Those actions include the other types of QoS tools discussed in this chapter, such as queuing, shaping, policing, and so on.

For example, consider the internal processing done by a router as shown in Figure 18-3. In this case, an output queuing tool has been enabled on an interface. Routers use queuing tools to place some packets in one output queue, other packets in another, and so on, when the outgoing interface happens to be busy. Then, when the outgoing interface becomes available to send another message, the queuing tool's scheduler algorithm can pick the next message from any one of the queues, prioritizing traffic based on the rules configured by the network engineer.

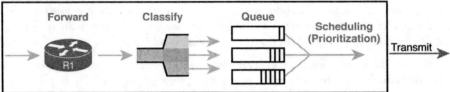

Figure 18-3 *Big Idea: Classification for Queuing in a Router*

The figure shows the internals of a router, and what happens to the packet during part of that internal processing, moving left to right inside the router, as follows:

Step 1. The router makes a forwarding (routing) decision.

Step 2. The output queuing tool uses classification logic to determine which packets go into which output queue.

Step 3. The router holds the packets in the output queue waiting for the outgoing interface to be available to send the next message.

Step 4. The queuing tool's scheduling logic chooses the next packet, effectively prioritizing one packet over another.

While the example shows a queuing tool, note that the queuing tool requires the ability to classify messages by comparing the messages to the configuration, much like ACLs.

Matching (Classification) Basics

Now think about classification from an enterprise-wide perspective, which helps us appreciate the need for marking. Every QoS tool can examine various headers to make comparisons to classify packets. However, you might apply QoS tools on most every device in the network, sometimes at both ingress and egress on most of the interfaces. Using complex matching of many header fields in every device and on most interfaces requires lots of configuration. The work to match packets can even degrade device performance of some devices. So, while you could have every device use complex packet matching, doing so is a poor strategy.

A better strategy, one recommended both by Cisco and by RFCs, suggests doing complex matching early in the life of a packet, and then marking the packet. *Marking* means that the QoS tool changes one or more header fields, setting a value in the header. Several header fields have been designed for the purpose of marking the packets for QoS processing. Then, devices that process the packet later in its life can use much simpler classification logic.

Figure 18-4 shows an example, with a PC on the left sending an IP packet to some host off of the right side of the figure (not shown). Switch SW1, the first networking device to forward the packet, does some complex comparisons and marks the packet's Differentiated Services Code Point (DSCP) field, a 6-bit field in the IP header meant for QoS marking. The next three devices that process this message—SW2, R1, and R2—then use simpler matching to classify the packet by comparing the packet's DSCP value, placing packets with one DSCP value in class 1, and packets with another DSCP value in class 2.

More Complex Matching
Less Complex Matching
DSCP=X? CLASS 1.
DSCP=Y? CLASS 2.
Mark DSCP at Ingress
*
SW1
SW2
R1
WAN
R2
...

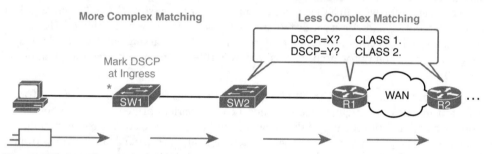

Figure 18-4 *Systematic Classification and Marking for the Enterprise*

Classification on Routers with ACLs and NBAR

Now that you know the basics of what classification and marking do together, this section takes the discussion a little deeper with a closer look at classification on routers, which is followed by a closer look at the marking function.

First, QoS classification sounds a lot like what ACLs do, and it should. In fact, many QoS tools support the ability to simply refer to an IP ACL, with this kind of logic:

> For any packet matched by the ACL with a permit action, consider that packet a match for QoS, so do a particular QoS action.

As a reminder, Figure 18-5 shows the IP and TCP header. All these fields are matchable for QoS classification.

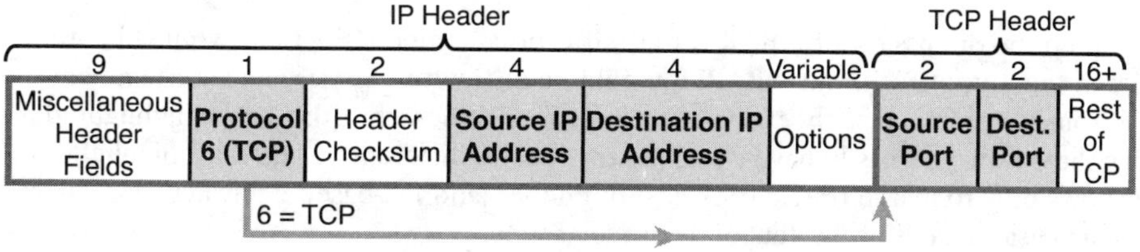

IP Header
TCP Header
9
1
2
4
4
Variable
2
2
16+
Miscellaneous Header Fields
Protocol 6 (TCP)
Header Checksum
Source IP Address
Destination IP Address
Options
Source Port
Dest. Port
Rest of TCP
6 = TCP

Figure 18-5 *Classification with Five Fields Used by Extended ACLs*

Now think about the enterprise's QoS plan for a moment. That plan should list details like which types of traffic should be classified as being in the same class for queuing purpose, for shaping, and for any other QoS tool. That plan should detail the fields in the header that can be matched. For instance, if all the IP phones sit in subnets within the range of addresses 10.3.0.0/16, then the QoS plan should state that. Then the network engineer could configure an extended ACL to match all packets to/from IP addresses inside 10.3.0.0/16 and apply appropriate QoS actions to that voice traffic.

However, not every classification can be easily made by matching with an ACL. In more challenging cases, Cisco Network Based Application Recognition (NBAR) can be used. NBAR is basically in its second major version, called NBAR2, or next-generation NBAR. In short, NBAR2 matches packets for classification in a large variety of ways that are very useful for QoS.

NBAR2 looks far beyond what an ACL can examine in a message. Many applications cannot be identified based on well-known port alone. NBAR solves those problems.

Cisco also organizes what NBAR can match in ways that make it easy to separate the traffic into different classes. For instance, the Cisco WebEx application provides audio and video conferencing on the web. In a QoS plan, you might want to classify WebEx differently than other video traffic, and classify it differently than voice calls between IP phones. That is, you might classify WebEx traffic and give it a unique DSCP marking. NBAR provides easy built-in matching ability for WebEx, plus well over 1000 different subcategories of applications.

Just to drive the point home with NBAR, Example 18-1 lists four lines of help output for one of many NBAR configuration commands. I chose a variety of items that might be more memorable. With the use of the keywords on the left in the correct configuration command, you could match the following: entertainment video from Amazon, video from Cisco's video surveillance camera products, voice from Cisco IP Phones, and video from sports channel ESPN. (NBAR refers to this idea of defining the characteristics of different applications as *application signatures*.)

Example 18-1   *Example of the Many NBAR2 Matchable Applications*

```
R1#(config)# class-map matchingexample
R1(config-cmap)# match protocol attribute category voice-and-video ?
! output heavily edited for length
    amazon-instant-video      VOD service by Amazon
    cisco-ip-camera           Cisco video surveillance camera
    cisco-phone               Cisco IP Phones and PC-based Unified Communicators
    espn-video                ESPN related websites and mobile applications video
    facetime                  Facetime video calling software
! Output snipped.
```

To wrap up the discussion of NBAR for classification, compare the first two highlighted entries in the output. Without NBAR, it would be difficult to classify an entertainment video from Amazon versus the video from a security camera, but those two highlighted entries show how you easily have classified that traffic differently. The third highlighted item shows how to match traffic for Cisco IP Phones (and PC-based equivalents), again making for an easier match of packets of a particular type.

Marking IP DSCP and Ethernet CoS

The QoS plan for an enterprise centers on creating classes of traffic that should receive certain types of QoS treatment. That plan would note how to classify packets into each classification, and the values that should be marked on the packets, basically labeling each packet with a number to associate it with that class. For example, that plan might state the following:

- Classify all voice payload traffic that is used for business purposes as IP DSCP EF and CoS 5.
- Classify all video conferencing and other interactive video for business purposes as IP DSCP AF41 and CoS 4.
- Classify all business-critical data application traffic as IP DSCP AF21 and CoS 2.

This next topic takes a closer look at the specific fields that can be marked, defining the DSCP and CoS marking fields.

Marking the IP Header

Marking a QoS field in the IP header works well with QoS because the IP header exists for the entire trip from the source host to the destination host. When a host sends data, the host sends a data link frame that encapsulates an IP packet. Each router that forwards the IP packet discards the old data link header, and adds a new header. By marking the IP header, the marking can stay with the data from the first place it is marked until it reaches the destination host.

IPv4 defines a Type of Service (ToS) byte in the IPv4 header, as shown in Figure 18-6. The original RFC defined a 3-bit IP Precedence (IPP) field for QoS marking. That field gave us eight separate values—binary 000, 001, 010, and so on, through 111—which when converted to decimal are decimal 0 through 7.

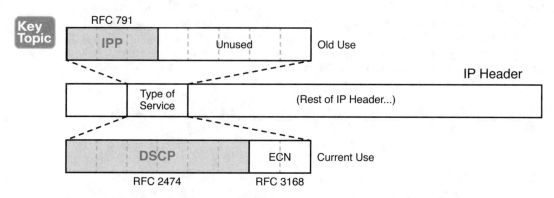

Figure 18-6 *IP Precedence and Differentiated Services Code Point Fields*

> **NOTE**   Those last 5 bits of the ToS byte per RFC 791 were mostly defined for some purpose, but were not used in practice to any significant extent.

While a great idea, IPP gave us only eight different values to mark, so later RFCs redefined the ToS byte with the DSCP field. DSCP increased the number of marking bits to 6 bits, allowing for 64 unique values that can be marked. The DiffServ RFCs, which became RFCs back in the late 1990s, have become accepted as the most common method to use when doing QoS, and using the DSCP field for marking has become quite common.

IPv6 has a similar field to mark as well. The 6-bit field also goes by the name DSCP, with the byte in the IPv6 header being called the IPv6 *Traffic Class* byte. Otherwise, think of IPv4 and IPv6 being equivalent in terms of marking.

IPP and DSCP fields can be referenced by their decimal values as well as some convenient text names as well. The section titled "DiffServ Suggested Marking Values" later in this section details some of the names.

Marking the Ethernet 802.1Q Header

Another useful marking field exists in the 802.1Q header, in a field originally defined by the IEEE 802.1p standard. This field sits in the third byte of the 4-byte 802.1Q header, as a 3-bit field, supplying eight possible values to mark (see Figure 18-7). It goes by two different names: *Class of Service*, or CoS, and *Priority Code Point*, or PCP.

Key Topic

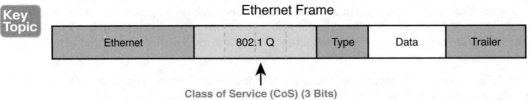

Figure 18-7   *Class of Service Field in 802.1Q/p Header*

The figure uses two slightly different shades of gray (in print) for the Ethernet header and trailer fields versus the 802.1Q header, as a reminder: The 802.1Q header is not included in all Ethernet frames. The 802.1Q header only exists when 802.1Q trunking is used on a link. As a result, QoS tools can only make use of the CoS field for QoS features enabled on interfaces that use trunking, as shown in Figure 18-8.

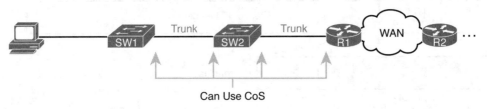

Figure 18-8   *Useful Life of CoS Marking*

For instance, if the PC on the left were to send data to a server somewhere off the figure to the right, the DSCP field would exist for that entire trip. However, the CoS field would exist over the two trunks only, and would be useful mainly on the four interfaces noted with the arrow lines.

Other Marking Fields

Other marking fields exist in other headers as well. Table 18-2 lists those fields for reference.

Table 18-2   Marking Fields

Field Name	Header(s)	Length (bits)	Where Used
DSCP	IPv4, IPv6	6	End-to-end packet
IPP	IPv4, IPv6	3	End-to-end packet
CoS	802.1Q	3	Over VLAN trunk
TID	802.11	3	Over Wi-Fi
EXP	MPLS Label	3	Over MPLS WAN

Defining Trust Boundaries

The end-user device can mark the DSCP field, and even the CoS field if trunking is used on the link. Would you, as the network engineer, trust those settings, and let your networking devices trust and react to those markings for their various QoS actions?

Most of us would not, because anything the end user controls might be used inappropriately at times. For instance, a PC user could know enough about DiffServ and DSCPs to know that most voice traffic is marked with a DSCP called Expedited Forwarding (EF), which has a decimal value of 46. Voice traffic gets great QoS treatment, so PC users could mark all their traffic as DSCP 46, hoping to get great QoS treatment.

The people creating a QoS plan for an enterprise have to choose where to place the trust boundary for the network. The *trust boundary* refers to the point in the path of a packet flowing through the network at which the networking devices can trust the current QoS markings. That boundary typically sits in a device under the control of the IT staff.

For instance, a typical trust boundary could be set in the middle of the first ingress switch in the network, as shown in Figure 18-9. The markings on the message as sent by the PC cannot be trusted. However, because SW1 performed classification and marking as the packets entered the switch, the markings can be trusted at that point.

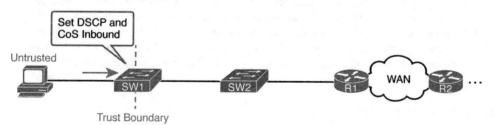

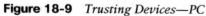

Figure 18-9   *Trusting Devices—PC*

Interestingly, when the access layer includes an IP Phone, the phone is typically the trust boundary, instead of the access layer switch. IP Phones can set the CoS and DSCP fields of the messages created by the phone, as well as those forwarded from the PC through the phone. The specific marking values are actually configured on the attached access switch. Figure 18-10 shows the typical trust boundary in this case, with notation of what the phone's marking logic usually is: mark all of the PC's traffic with a particular DSCP and/or CoS, and the phone's traffic with different values.

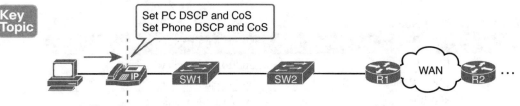

Figure 18-10   *Trusting Devices—IP Phone*

DiffServ Suggested Marking Values

Everything in this chapter follows the DiffServ architecture as defined originally by RFC 2475, plus many other DiffServ RFCs. In particular, DiffServ goes beyond theory in several areas, including making suggestions about the specific DSCP values to use when marking IP packets. By suggesting specific markings for specific types of traffic, DiffServ hoped to create a consistent use of DSCP values in all networks. By doing so, product vendors could provide good default settings for their QoS features, QoS could work better between an enterprise and service provider, and many other benefits could be realized.

The next two topics outline three sets of DSCP values as used in DiffServ.

Expedited Forwarding (EF)

DiffServ defines the *Expedited Forwarding* (EF) DSCP value—a single value—as suggested for use for packets that need low latency (delay), low jitter, and low loss. The Expedited Forwarding RFC (RFC 3246) defines the specific DSCP value (decimal 46) and an equivalent text name (Expedited Forwarding). QoS configuration commands allow the use of the decimal value or text name, but one purpose of having a text acronym to use is to make the value more memorable, so many QoS configurations refer to the text names.

Most often QoS plans use EF to mark voice payload packets. With voice calls, some packets carry voice payload, and other packets carry call signaling messages. Call signaling messages set up (create) the voice call between two devices, and they do not require low delay, jitter, and loss. Voice payload packets carry the digitized voice, as shown back in Figure 18-2, and these packets do need better QoS. By default, Cisco IP Phones mark voice payload with EF, and mark voice signaling packets sent by the phone with another value called CS3.

Assured Forwarding (AF)

The Assured Forwarding (AF) DiffServ RFC (2597) defines a set of 12 DSCP values meant to be used in concert with each other. First, it defines the concept of four separate queues in a queuing system. Additionally, it defines three levels of drop priority within each queue for use with congestion avoidance tools. With four queues, and three drop priority classes per queue, you need 12 different DSCP markings, one for each combination of queue and drop priority. (Queuing and congestion avoidance mechanisms are discussed later in this chapter.)

Assured Forwarding defines the specific AF DSCP text names and equivalent decimal values as listed in Figure 18-11. The text names follow a format of AFXY, with X referring to the queue (1 through 4), and Y referring to the drop priority (1 through 3).

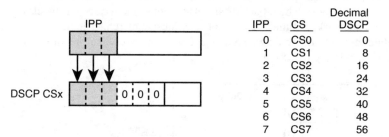

Best Drop ◄────── Worst Drop

Best Queue	AF41 (34)	AF42 (36)	AF43 (38)
	AF31 (26)	AF32 (28)	AF33 (30)
	AF21 (18)	AF22 (20)	AF23 (22)
Worst Queue	AF11 (10)	AF12 (12)	AF13 (14)

Figure 18-11 *Differentiated Services Assured Forwarding Values and Meaning*

For example, if you marked packets with all 12 values, those with AF11, AF12, and AF13 would all go into one queue; those with AF21, AF22, and AF23 would go into another queue; and so on. Inside the queue with all the AF2y traffic, you would treat the AF21, AF22, and AF23 each differently in regard to drop actions (congestion avoidance), with AF21 getting the preferred treatment and AF23 the worst treatment.

Class Selector (CS)

Originally, the ToS byte was defined with a 3-bit IP Precedence (IPP) field. When DiffServ redefined the ToS byte, it made sense to create eight DSCP values for backward compatibility with IPP values. The Class Selector (CS) DSCP values are those settings.

Figure 18-12 shows the main idea along with the eight CS values, both in name and in decimal value. Basically, the DSCP values have the same first 3 bits as the IPP field, and with binary 0s for the last 3 bits, as shown on the left side of the figure. CSx represents the text names, where x is the matching IPP value (0 through 7).

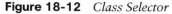

IPP	CS	Decimal DSCP
0	CS0	0
1	CS1	8
2	CS2	16
3	CS3	24
4	CS4	32
5	CS5	40
6	CS6	48
7	CS7	56

Figure 18-12 *Class Selector*

This section on classification and marking has given you a solid foundation for understanding the tools explored in the next three major sections of this chapter: queuing, shaping, policing, and congestion avoidance.

Congestion Management (Queuing)

All networking devices use queues. Network devices receive messages, make a forwarding decision, and then send the message—but sometimes the outgoing interface is busy. So, the device keeps the outgoing message in a queue, waiting for the outgoing interface to be available—simple enough.

The term *congestion management* (found in the QoS exam topics) refers to the QoS toolset for managing the queues that hold packets while they wait their turn to exit an interface (and in other cases in which a router holds packets waiting for some resource). But congestion management refers to more than one idea, so you have to look inside devices to think about how they work. For instance, consider Figure 18-13, which shows the internals of a router. The router of course makes a forwarding decision, and it needs to be ready to queue packets for transmission once the outgoing interface is available. At the same time, the router may take a variety of other actions as well—ingress ACL, ingress NAT (on the inside interface), egress ACLs after the forwarding decision is made, and so on.

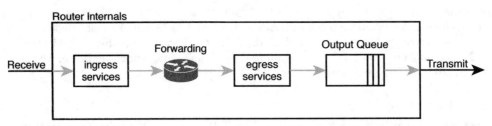

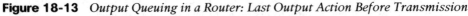

Figure 18-13 *Output Queuing in a Router: Last Output Action Before Transmission*

The figure shows *output queuing*, one aspect of congestion management, in which the device holds messages until the output interface is available. The queuing system may use a single output queue, with a first-in, first-out (FIFO) scheduler. (In other words, it's like ordering lunch at the sandwich shop that has a single ordering line.)

Next, think a little more deeply about the queuing system. Most networking devices can have a queuing system with multiple queues. To use multiple queues, the queuing system needs a classifier function to choose which packets are placed into which queue. (The classifier can react to previously marked values, or do a more extensive match.) The queuing system needs a scheduler as well, to decide which message to take next when the interface becomes available, as shown in Figure 18-14.

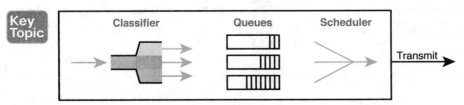

Figure 18-14 *Congestion Management (Queuing) Components*

Of all these components of the queuing system, the scheduler can be the most interesting part, because it can perform prioritization. *Prioritization* (yet another term from the exam topics) refers to the concept of giving priority to one queue over another in some way.

Round Robin Scheduling (Prioritization)

One scheduling algorithm used by Cisco routers and switches uses round robin logic. In its most basic form, round robin cycles through the queues in order, taking turns with each queue. In each cycle, the scheduler either takes one message or takes a number of bytes from each queue by taking enough messages to total that number of bytes. Take some messages from queue 1, move on and take some from queue 2, then take some from queue 3, and so on, starting back at queue 1 after finishing a complete pass through the queues.

Round robin scheduling also includes the concept of *weighting* (generally called *weighted round robin*). Basically, the scheduler takes a different number of packets (or bytes) from each queue, giving more preference to one queue over another.

For example, routers use a popular tool called *Class-Based Weighted Fair Queuing* (CBWFQ) to guarantee a minimum amount of bandwidth to each class. That is, each class receives at least the amount of bandwidth configured during times of congestion, but maybe more. Internally, CBWFQ uses a weighted round robin scheduling algorithm, while letting the network engineer define the weightings as a percentage of link bandwidth. Figure 18-15 shows an example in which the three queues in the system have been given 20, 30, and 50 percent of the bandwidth each, respectively.

18

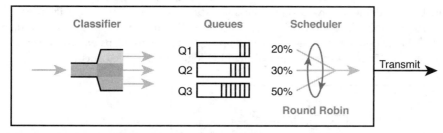

Figure 18-15   *CBWFQ Round Robin Scheduling*

With the queuing system shown in the figure, if the outgoing link is congested, the scheduler guarantees the percentage bandwidth shown in the figure to each queue. That is, queue 1 gets 20 percent of the link even during busy times.

Low Latency Queuing

Earlier in the chapter, the section titled "Voice and Video Applications" discussed the reasons why voice and video, particularly interactive voice and video like phone calls and videoconferencing, need low latency (low delay), low jitter, and low loss. Unfortunately, a round robin scheduler does not provide low enough delay, jitter, or loss. The solution: add Low Latency Queuing (LLQ) to the scheduler.

First, for a quick review, Table 18-3 lists the QoS requirements for a voice call. The numbers come from the *Enterprise QoS Solution Reference Network Design Guide*, referenced earlier in the chapter. The amount of bandwidth required per call varies based on the codec used by the call. However, the delay, jitter, and loss requirements remain the same for all voice calls. (Interactive video has similar requirements for delay, jitter, and loss.)

Table 18-3   QoS Requirements for a VoIP Call Per Cisco Voice Design Guide

Bandwidth/call	One-way Delay (max)	Jitter (max)	Loss (max)
30–320 Kbps	150 ms	30 ms	<1%

A round robin queuing system adds too much delay for these voice and video packets. To see why, imagine a voice packet arrives and is routed to be sent out some interface with the queuing system shown in Figure 18-16. However, that next voice packet arrives just as the round robin scheduler moves on to service the queue labeled "data 1." Even though the voice queue has been given 50 percent of the link bandwidth, the scheduler does not send that voice message until it sends some messages from the other three queues—adding delay and jitter.

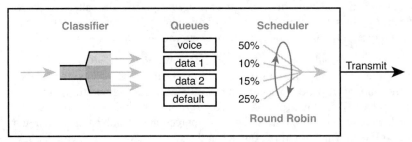

Figure 18-16   *Round Robin Not Good for Voice Delay (Latency) and Jitter*

The solution, LLQ, tells the scheduler to treat one or more queues as special *priority queues*. The LLQ scheduler always takes the next message from one of these special priority queues. Problem solved: very little delay for packets in that queue, resulting in very little jitter as well. Plus the queue never has time to fill up, so there are no drops due to the queue filling up. Figure 18-17 shows the addition of the LLQ logic for the voice queue.

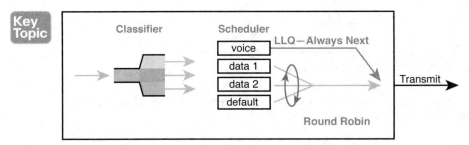

Figure 18-17   *LLQ Always Schedules Voice Packet Next*

Using LLQ, or a priority queue, provides the needed low delay, jitter, and loss for the traffic in that queue. However, think about those other queues. Do you see the problem? What happens if the speed of the interface is X bits/second, but more than X bits/second come into the voice queue? The scheduler never services the other queues (called *queue starvation*).

As you might guess, there is a solution: limit the amount of traffic placed into the priority queue, using a feature called policing. The next section talks about policers in more detail, but for now, think of it as a cap on the bandwidth used by the priority queue. For instance, you could reserve 20 percent of the link's bandwidth for the voice queue, and make it a priority queue. However, in this case, instead of 20 percent being the minimum bandwidth, it is the maximum for that queue. If more than 20 percent of the link's worth of bits shows up in that queue, the router will discard the excess.

Limiting the amount of bandwidth in the priority queue protects the other queues, but it causes yet another problem. Voice and video need low loss, and with LLQ, we put the voice and video into a priority queue that will discard the excess messages beyond the bandwidth limit. The solution? Find a way to limit the amount of voice and video that the network routes out this link, so that the policer never discards any of the traffic. There are QoS tools to help you do just that, called Call Admission Control (CAC) tools. However, CAC tools did not get a mention in the exam topics, so this chapter leaves those tools at a brief mention.

A Prioritization Strategy for Data, Voice, and Video

This section about queuing introduces several connected ideas, so before leaving the discussion of queuing, think about this strategy for how most enterprises approach queuing in their QoS plans:

Key Topic

1. Use a round robin queuing method like CBWFQ for data classes and for noninteractive voice and video.

2. If faced with too little bandwidth compared to the typical amount of traffic, give data classes that support business-critical applications much more guaranteed bandwidth than is given to less important data classes.

3. Use a priority queue with LLQ scheduling for interactive voice and video, to achieve low delay, jitter, and loss.

4. Put voice in a separate queue from video, so that the policing function applies separately to each.

5. Define enough bandwidth for each priority queue so that the built-in policer should not discard any messages from the priority queues.

6. Use Call Admission Control (CAC) tools to avoid adding too much voice or video to the network, which would trigger the policer function.

Shaping and Policing

This section introduces two related QoS tools, shaping and policing. These tools have a more specialized use, and are not found in as many locations in a typical enterprise. These tools are most often used at the WAN edge in an enterprise network design.

Both policing and shaping monitor the bit rate of the combined messages that flow through a device. Once enabled, the policer or shaper notes each packet that passes, and measures the number of bits per second over time. Both attempt to keep the bit rate at or below the configured speed, but by using two different actions: policers discard packets and shapers hold packets in queues to delay the packets.

Shapers and policers monitor the traffic rate (the bits/second that move through the shaper or policer) versus a configured shaping rate or policing rate, respectively. The basic question that both ask is listed below, with the actions based on the answers:

Key Topic

1. Does this next packet push the measured rate past the configured shaping rate or policing rate?

2. If no:

   a. Let the packet keep moving through the normal path and do nothing extra to the packet.

3. If yes:

   a. If shaping, delay the message by queuing it.

   b. If policing, either discard the message or mark it differently.

This section first explains policing, which discards or re-marks messages that exceed the policing rate, followed by shaping, which slows down messages that exceed the shaping rate.

Policing

Focus on the traffic rate versus the configured policing rate for a moment, and the policing action of discarding messages. Those concepts sit at the core of what the policing function does.

Traffic arrives at networking devices at a varying rate, with valleys and spikes. That is, if you graph the bit rate of the collective bits that enter or exit any interface, the graph would look something like the one on the left side of Figure 18-18. The policer would measure that rate, and make a similar measurement. Still on the left side of the figure, the horizontal dashed line represents the policing rate, which is the rate configured for the policer. So, the policer has some awareness of the measured bit rate over time, which can be compared to the configured rate.

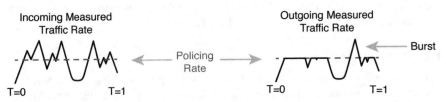

Figure 18-18 *Effect of a Policer and Shaper on an Offered Traffic Load*

The right side of the figure shows a graph of what happens to the traffic when a policer discards any messages that would have otherwise pushed the rate over the configured policing rate. In effect, the policer chops off the top of the graph at the policing rate.

The graph on the right also shows one example of a policer allowing a burst of traffic. Policers allow for a burst beyond the policing rate for a short time, after a period of low activity. So, that one peak that exceeds the policing rate on the graph on the right side allows for the nature of bursty data applications.

Where to Use Policing

Now that you understand the basics of policing, take a moment to ponder. Policers monitor messages, measure a rate, and discard some messages. How does that help a network in regard to QoS? At first glance, it seems to hurt the network, discarding messages, many of which the transport or application layer will have to resend. How does that improve bandwidth, delay, jitter, or loss?

Policing makes sense only in certain cases, and as a general tool, it can be best used at the edge between two networks. For instance, consider a typical point-to-point metro Ethernet WAN connection between two enterprise routers, R1 and R2. Usually, the enterprise network engineers just view the WAN as a cloud, with Ethernet interfaces on the routers, as shown at the top of Figure 18-19.

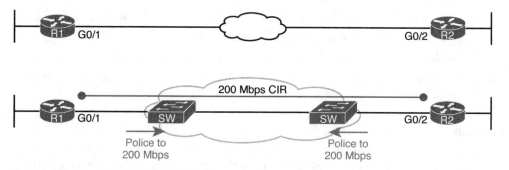

Figure 18-19 *Ethernet WAN: Link Speed Versus CIR*

Now think about the contract for this MetroE connection, as shown at the bottom of Figure 18-19. In this case, this connection uses Gigabit Ethernet for the access links, and a 200-Mbps *committed information rate* (CIR). That is, the SP providing the WAN service agrees to allow the enterprise to send 200 Mbps of traffic in each direction. However, as discussed back in Chapter 14, remember that the enterprise routers transmit the data at the speed of the access link, or 1 Gbps in this case.

Think like the SP for a moment, and think about supporting tens of thousands of Gigabit Ethernet links into your WAN service, all with 200-Mbps CIRs. What would happen if you just let all those customers send data that, over time, averaged close to 1000 Mbps (1 Gbps)? That is, if all customers kept sending data far beyond their contracted CIR, that much traffic could cause congestion in the WAN service. Also, those customers might choose to pay for a lower CIR, knowing that the SP would send the data anyway. And customers that were well behaved, and did not send more data than their CIR, might suffer from the congestion just as much as the customers that send far too much data.

Figure 18-19 also notes the solution to the problem: The SP can police incoming packets, setting the policing rate to match the CIR that the customer chooses for that link. By doing so, the SP protects all customers from the negative effects of the customers that send too much traffic. Customers receive what they paid for. And the SP can provide reports of actual traffic rates, so the enterprise knows when to buy a faster CIR for each link.

Policers can discard excess traffic, but they can also re-mark packets as well. Think again about what an SP does with an ingress policer as shown in Figure 18-19: they are discarding their customer's messages. So, the SP might want to make a compromise that works better for its customers, while still protecting the SP's network. The SP could mark the messages with a new marking value, with this strategy:

1. Re-mark packets that exceed the policing rate, but let them into the SP's network.

2. If other SP network devices are experiencing congestion when they process the packet, the different marking means that device can discard the packet. However...

3. ...if no other SP network devices are experiencing congestion when forwarding that re-marked packet, it gets through the SP network anyway.

With this strategy, the SP can treat their customers a little better by discarding less traffic, while still protecting the SP's network during times of stress.

Summarizing the key features of policing:

- It measures the traffic rate over time for comparison to the configured policing rate.

- It allows for a burst of data after a period of inactivity.

- It is enabled on an interface, in either direction, but typically at ingress.

- It can discard excess messages, but can also re-mark the message so that it is a candidate for more aggressive discard later in its journey.

Shaping

You have a 1-Gbps link from a router into an SP, but a 200-Mbps CIR for traffic to another site, as seen in Figure 18-19. The SP has told you that they always discard incoming traffic that exceeds the CIR. The solution? Use a shaper to slow the traffic down, in this case to a 200-Mbps shaping rate.

That scenario—shaping before sending data to an SP that is policing—is one of the typical uses of a shaper. Shapers can be useful in other cases as well, but generally speaking, shapers make sense when a device can send at a certain speed, but there is a benefit to slowing down the rate.

The shaper slows messages down by queuing the messages. The shaper then services the shaping queues, but not based on when the physical interface is available. Instead, the shaper schedules messages from the shaping queues based on the shaping rate, as shown in Figure 18-20. Following the left-to-right flow in the figure, for a router, the packet is routed out an interface; the shaper queues packets so that the sending rate through the shaper does not exceed the shaping rate; and then output queuing works as normal, if needed.

Note that in some cases, the output queuing function has little to do. For instance, in the earlier example shown in Figure 18-19, the SP is policing incoming messages at 200 Mbps. If the router (R1 for instance) were to shape all traffic exiting toward the SP to 200 Mbps as well, with that 1-Gbps interface, the output queue would seldom if ever be congested.

Because shapers create queues where messages wait, you should apply a congestion management tool to those queues. It is perfectly normal to apply the round robin and priority queuing features of CBWFQ and LLQ, respectively, to the shaping queues, as noted in the figure.

Router Internals

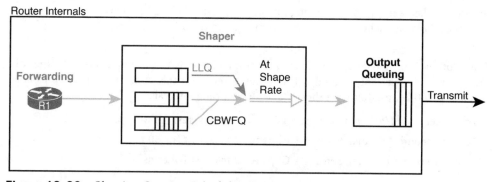

Figure 18-20 *Shaping Queues: Scheduling with LLQ and CBWFQ*

Setting a Good Shaping Time Interval for Voice and Video

Once again, a QoS tool has attempted to solve one QoS problem, but introduces another. The unfortunate side effect of a shaper is that is slows down packets, which then creates more delay, and probably more jitter. The delay occurs in part because of the message simply waiting in a queue, but partly because of the mechanisms used by a shaper. Thankfully, you can (and should) configure a shaper's setting that changes the internal operation of the shaper, which then reduces the delay and jitter caused to voice and video traffic.

A shaper's *time interval* refers to its internal logic and how a shaper averages, over time, sending at a particular rate. A shaper basically sends as fast as it can, and then waits; sends and waits; sends and waits. For instance, the policing and shaping example in this section suggests shaping at 200 Mbps on a router that has a 1000-Mbps (1-Gbps) outgoing interface. In that case, the shaper would result in the interface sending data 20 percent of the time, and being silent 80 percent of the time.

Figure 18-21 shows a graph of the shaping time interval concept, assuming a time interval of 1 second. To average 200 million bits/second, the shaper would allow 200 million bits to exit its shaping queues and exit the interface each second. Because the interface transmits bits at 1 Gbps, it takes just .2 seconds, or 200 ms, to send all 200 million bits. Then the shaper must wait for the rest of the time interval, another 800 ms, before beginning the next time interval.

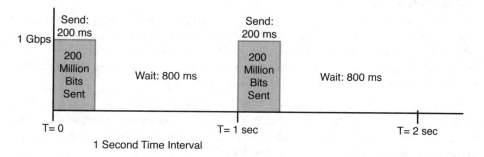

Figure 18-21 *1 Second (1000 ms) Shaping Time Interval, Shaping at 20% of Line Rate*

Now think about a voice or video packet that needs very low delay and jitter—and unfortunately, it arrives just as the shaper finishes sending data for a time interval. Even if that voice or video packet is in a priority shaping queue, the packet will wait 800 ms before the shaper schedules the next packet—far too long compared to the 150-ms one-way delay goal for voice.

The solution to this problem: configure a short time interval. For example, consider the following time intervals (abbreviated Tc), and their effects, for this same example (1-Gbps link, shaping to 200 Mbps), but with shorter and shorter time intervals:

Tc = 1 second (1000 ms): Send at 1 Gbps for 200 ms, rest for 800 ms

Tc = .1 second (100 ms): Send at 1 Gbps for 20 ms, rest for 80 ms

Tc = .01 second (10 ms): Send at 1 Gbps for 2 ms, rest for 8 ms

When shaping, use a short time interval. By recommendation, use a 10-ms time interval to support voice and video. With that setting, a voice or video packet should wait no more than 10 ms while waiting for the next shaping time interval, at which point the priority queue scheduling should take all the voice and video messages next.

Summarizing the key features of shapers:

- Shapers measure the traffic rate over time for comparison to the configured shaping rate.
- Shapers allow for bursting after a period of inactivity.
- Shapers are enabled on an interface for egress (outgoing packets).
- Shapers slow down packets by queuing them, and over time releasing them from the queue at the shaping rate.
- Shapers use queuing tools to create and schedule the shaping queues, which is very important for the same reasons discussed for output queuing.

Congestion Avoidance

The QoS feature called congestion avoidance attempts to reduce overall packet loss by preemptively discarding some packets used in TCP connections. To see how it works, you first need to look at how TCP works in regard to windowing, and then look at how congestion avoidance features work.

TCP Windowing Basics

TCP uses a flow control mechanism called *windowing*. Each TCP receiver grants a window to the sender. The window, which is a number, defines the number of bytes the sender can send over the TCP connection before receiving a TCP acknowledgement for at least some of those bytes. More exactly, the window size is the number of unacknowledged bytes that the sender can send before the sender must simply stop and wait.

The TCP window mechanism gives the receiver control of the sender's rate of sending data. Each new segment sent by the receiver back to the sender grants a new window, which can be smaller or larger than the previous window. By raising and lowering the window, the receiver can make the sender wait more or wait less.

NOTE Each TCP connection has two senders and two receivers; that is, each host sends and receives data. For this discussion, focus on one direction, with one host as the sender and the other as the receiver. If calling one host the "sender" and one the "receiver," note that the receiver then acknowledges data in TCP segments sent back to the sender by the receiver.

By choice, when all is well, the receiver keeps increasing the granted window, doubling it every time the receiver acknowledges data. Eventually, the window grows to the point that the sender never has to stop sending: the sender keeps receiving TCP acknowledgements before sending all the data in the previous window. Each new acknowledgement (as listed in a TCP segment and TCP header) grants a new window to the sender.

Also by choice, when a TCP receiver senses the loss of a TCP segment, he shrinks the window with the next window size listed in the next TCP segment the receiver sends back to the sender. For each TCP segment lost, the window can shrink by one-half, with multiple segment losses causing the window to shrink by half multiple times, slowing down the sender's rate significantly.

Now think about router queues for a moment. Without a congestion avoidance tool, an event called a *tail drop* causes the most drops in a network. Figure 18-22 shows the idea, showing the same queuing system, but in three separate conditions: little congestion, medium congestion, and much congestion. On the left, with little congestion, the output queues on an interface have not yet filled. In the middle, the queues have started to fill, with one queue being totally full. Any new packets that arrive for that queue right now will be dropped because there is no room at the tail of the queue (tail drop).

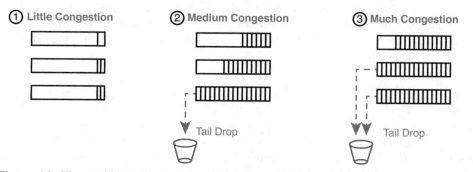

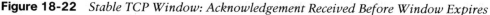

Figure 18-22 *Stable TCP Window: Acknowledgement Received Before Window Expires*

The worse the congestion in the queues, the more likely tail drop will occur, as shown with the most congested case on the right side of the figure. The more congestion, the bigger the negative impact on traffic—both in terms of loss and in terms of increasing delay in TCP connections.

Congestion Avoidance Tools

Congestion avoidance tools attempt to avoid the congestion, primarily through using TCP's own windowing mechanisms. These tools discard some TCP segments before the queues fill, hoping that enough TCP connections will slow down, reducing congestion, and avoiding a much worse problem: the effects of many more packets being dropped due to tail drop. The strategy is simple: discard some now in hopes that the device discards far fewer in the long term.

Congestion avoidance tools monitor the average queue depth over time, triggering more severe actions the deeper the queue, as shown in Figure 18-23. The height of the box represents the queue depth, or the number of packets in the queue. When the queue depth is low, below the minimum threshold values, the congestion avoidance tool does nothing. When the queue depth is between the minimum and maximum thresholds, the congestion avoidance tool discards a percentage of the packets—usually a small percentage, like 5, 10, or 20 percent. If the queue depth passes the maximum threshold, the tool drops all packets, in an action called *full drop*.

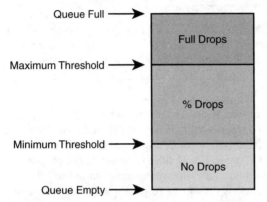

Figure 18-23 *Mechanisms of Congestion Avoidance*

Of course, like all the QoS tools mentioned in this chapter, congestion avoidance tools can classify messages to treat some packets better than others. In the same queue, packets with one marking might be dropped more aggressively, and those with better DSCP markings dropped less aggressively.

Chapter Review

One key to doing well on the exams is to perform repetitive spaced review sessions. Review this chapter's material using either the tools in the book, DVD, or interactive tools for the same material found on the book's companion website. Refer to the "Your Study Plan" element for more details. Table 18-4 outlines the key review elements and where you can find them. To better track your study progress, record when you completed these activities in the second column.

Table 18-4 Chapter Review Tracking

Review Element	Review Date(s)	Resource Used
Review key topics		Book, DVD/website
Review key terms		Book, DVD/website
Answer DIKTA questions		Book, PCPT
Review memory tables		Book, DVD/website

Review All the Key Topics

Table 18-5   Key Topics for Chapter 18

Key Topic Element	Description	Page Number
List	Four QoS characteristics	491
List	Voice call QoS requirements	494
List	Video QoS requirements	494
Figure 18-6	IP Precedence and IP DSCP marking fields	499
Figure 18-7	802.1Q CoS marking field	500
Figure 18-10	Trust boundary with IP Phones	502
Figure 18-14	Queuing components	504
Figure 18-17	LLQ scheduling logic with a priority queue	506
List	A strategy for using queuing (congestion management) to prioritize traffic	507
List	Logic steps for shapers and policers	508
List	Key features of policers	510
List	Key features of shapers	512

18

Key Terms You Should Know

marking, classification, quality of service (QoS), IP Precedence (IPP), Differentiated Services Code Point (DSCP), Class of Service (CoS), bandwidth, delay, jitter, loss, queuing, priority queue, round robin, policing, shaping, Differentiated Services (DiffServ), policing rate, shaping rate

Part IV Review

Keep track of your part review progress with the checklist in Table P4-1. Details about each task follow the table.

Table P4-1 Part IV Part Review Checklist

Activity	1st Date Completed	2nd Date Completed
Repeat All DIKTA Questions		
Answer Part Review Questions		
Review Key Topics		
Create Mind Maps		
Do Labs		

Repeat All DIKTA Questions

For this task, use the PCPT software to answer the "Do I Know This Already?" questions again for the chapters in this part of the book.

Answer Part Review Questions

For this task, use PCPT to answer the Part Review questions for this part of the book.

Review Key Topics

Review all key topics in all chapters in this part, either by browsing the chapters or by using the Key Topics application on the DVD or companion website.

Create Command Mind Map by Category

Create a command mind map to help you remember the ACL commands in Chapters 16 and 17. This exercise does not focus on every single parameter of every command, or even their meaning. The goal is to help you organize the commands internally so that you know which commands to consider when faced with a real-life problem or an exam question. Create a mind map with the following categories of commands from this part of the book:

numbered standard IPv4 ACLs, numbered extended IPv4 ACLs, named IPv4 ACLs

Create QoS Terminology Mind Map

Chapter 18, "Quality of Service (QoS)," introduces a large amount of terminology. Without looking back at the chapter or your notes, create a mind map with all the terminology you can recall from Chapter 18. Your job is as follows:

- Think of every term that you can remember from Chapter 18 of the book.
- Organize the terms into these divisions: general, classification and marking, queuing, shaping and policing, and congestion avoidance.

- After you have written every term you can remember into the mind map, review your notes for other terms, or add any terms from this list that you did not happen to add to your mind map:

  application signature, Assured Forwarding (AF), AutoQoS, bandwidth, Class of Service (CoS), Class Selector (CS), classification, delay, Differentiated Services (DiffServ), Differentiated Services Code Point (DSCP), Expedited Forwarding (EF), Integrated Services (IntServ), IP Precedence (IPP), jitter, loss, low latency queue, marking, MPLS Experimental Bits, Network Based Application Recognition (NBAR), one-way delay, policing, policing rate, Priority Code Point (PCP), priority queue, quality of experience (QoE), Quality of Service (QoS), queuing, Real-time Transport Protocol (RTP), round robin, round-trip delay, shaping, shaping rate, tail drop, TCP synchronization, TCP window, time interval (shaper), traffic class, trust boundary, Type of Service (ToS)

Appendix E, "Mind Map Solutions," lists sample mind map answers. If you do choose to use mind map software, rather than paper, you might want to remember where you stored your mind map files. Table P4-2 lists the mind maps for this part review and a place to record those filenames.

Table P4-2 Configuration Mind Maps for Part IV Review

Map	Description	Where You Saved It
1	Command Mind Map	
2	QoS Terminology Mind Map	

Do Labs

Depending on your chosen lab tool, here are some suggestions for what to do in lab:

Pearson Network Simulator: If you use the full Pearson CCNA simulator, focus more on the configuration scenario and troubleshooting scenario labs associated with the topics in this part of the book. These types of labs include a larger set of topics, and work well as Part Review activities. (See the Introduction for some details about how to find which labs are about topics in this part of the book.)

Config Labs: In your idle moments, review and repeat any of the Config Labs for this book part in the author's blog; launch from http://blog.certskills.com/ccna and navigate to **Hands-On > Config Lab**.

Other: If using other lab tools, here are a few suggestions: When building ACL labs, you can test with Telnet (port 23), SSH (port 22), ping (ICMP), and traceroute (UDP) traffic as generated from an extra router. So, do not just configure the ACL; make an ACL that can match these types of traffic, denying some and permitting others, and then test.

Part V completes this book's many chapters focused on IPv4 routing and related topics. Part II shows how to learn routes with various IPv4 routing protocols. Part III discusses WAN options and how to route IP packets over those WANs. Part IV discusses services over IPv4 networks, both to secure the network with ACLs and to improve the quality of user experience with QoS. Part V wraps up the parts focused on IPv4 routing with a couple of specific topics centered on the edge of the LAN, topping it off with an IPv4 troubleshooting discussion.

This part begins by drilling down into the device and configuration options for routing between LAN-based subnets. Those options include routers and Layer 3 switches, with a variety of configuration variations. This chapter works through all those variations, through to the point of troubleshooting each.

This part's second chapter (20) looks at a related topic: how to make the default gateway (router) function have redundancy for better availability. So, while Chapter 19 shows the various ways to configure routers to have an address connected to a LAN subnet, Chapter 20 then shows how multiple routers connected to the same subnet can cooperate to provide redundancy and better availability through a protocol: Hot Standby Router Protocol (HSRP).

Every topic related to IPv4 routing in this book has some troubleshooting aspect to learn per the current exam topics. To that end, this part's final chapter (21) caps this book's IPv4 routing discussions with a chapter devoted to IPv4 troubleshooting. Many of the earlier chapters in this book already discussed troubleshooting of the content in that same chapter or part. Chapter 21 reviews some of the basics that you may not have thought about since your ICND1 studies, and serves as a great review before moving on to Part VI, which is about IPv6.

Part V

IPv4 Routing and Troubleshooting

Chapter 19: IPv4 Routing in the LAN

Chapter 20: Implementing HSRP for First-Hop Routing

Chapter 21: Troubleshooting IPv4 Routing

Part V Review

CHAPTER 19

IPv4 Routing in the LAN

This chapter covers the following exam topics:

1.0 LAN Switching Technologies

1.5 Configure, verify, and troubleshoot (Layer 2/Layer 3) EtherChannel

    1.5.a Static

    1.5.b PaGP

    1.5.b LACP

2.0 Routing Technologies

2.1 Configure, verify, and troubleshoot Inter-VLAN routing

    2.1.a Router on a stick

    2.1.b SVI

5.0 Infrastructure Maintenance

5.6 Troubleshoot basic Layer 3 end-to-end connectivity issues

The CCNA Routing and Switching certification features two technology topics: routing and switching. This chapter focuses on routing, and one specific part of the routing space: routing between LAN subnets. This chapter focuses on configuration options on routers and Layer 3 switches that enable them to route packets between subnets that exist on VLANs.

This chapter breaks the discussion down into three major sections. The first section focuses on using routers to route between VLANs, with a feature many of you will remember from the ICND1 Cert Guide: routing over a VLAN trunk, also known as router-on-a-stick (ROAS). This option gives a router the means to connect to a switch with one Ethernet link, use trunking, and route packets that come in that trunk on one VLAN and go right back out that same trunk but tagged with another VLAN.

The second and third sections focuses on implementing Layer 3 switching, but with two major configuration options. The second section discusses using switched virtual interfaces (SVI) on switches, which are VLAN interfaces. (This is another topic with overlap in the ICND1 book and the ICND1 100-105 exam.) The third major section of the chapter discusses an alternative to SVIs called routed ports, in which the physical switch ports are made to act like interfaces on a router. This third section also introduces the concept of an EtherChannel as used as a routed port in a feature called Layer 3 EtherChannel.

"Do I Know This Already?" Quiz

Take the quiz (either here, or use the PCPT software) if you want to use the score to help you decide how much time to spend on this chapter. The answers are at the bottom of the page following the quiz, and the explanations are in DVD Appendix C and in the PCPT software.

Table 19-1 "Do I Know This Already?" Foundation Topics Section-to-Question Mapping

Foundation Topics Section	Questions
VLAN Routing with Router 802.1Q Trunks	1, 2
VLAN Routing with Layer 3 Switch SVIs	3, 4
VLAN Routing with Layer 3 Switch Routed Ports	5, 6

1. Router 1 has a Fast Ethernet interface 0/0 with IP address 10.1.1.1. The interface is connected to a switch. This connection is then migrated to use 802.1Q trunking. Which of the following commands could be part of a valid configuration for Router 1's Fa0/0 interface? (Choose two answers.)

    a.   interface fastethernet 0/0.4

    b.   dot1q enable

    c.   dot1q enable 4

    d.   trunking enable

    e.   trunking enable 4

    f.   encapsulation dot1q 4

2. Router R1 has a router-on-a-stick (ROAS) configuration with two subinterfaces of interface G0/1: G0/1.1 and G0/1.2. Physical interface G0/1 is currently in a down/down state. The network engineer then configures a **shutdown** command when in interface configuration mode for G0/1.1, and a **no shutdown** command when in interface configuration mode for G0/1.2. Which answers are correct about the interface state for the subinterfaces? (Choose two answers.)

    a.   G0/1.1 will be in a down/down state.

    b.   G0/1.2 will be in a down/down state.

    c.   G0/1.1 will be in an administratively down state.

    d.   G0/1.2 will be in an up/up state.

3. A Layer 3 switch has been configured to route IP packets between VLANs 1, 2, and 3 using SVIs, which connect to subnets 172.20.1.0/25, 172.20.2.0/25, and 172.20.3.0/25, respectively. The engineer issues a **show ip route connected** command on the Layer 3 switch, listing the connected routes. Which of the following answers lists a piece of information that should be in at least one of the routes?

    a.   Interface Gigabit Ethernet 0/0.3

    b.   Next-hop router 172.20.2.1

    c.   Interface VLAN 2

    d.   Mask 255.255.255.0

4. An engineer has successfully configured a Layer 3 switch with SVIs for VLANs 2 and 3. Hosts in the subnets using VLANs 2 and 3 can ping each other with the Layer 3 switch routing the packets. Next week, the network engineer receives a call that those same users can no longer ping each other. If the problem is with the Layer 3 switching function, which of the following could have caused the problem? (Choose two answers.)

   a. Six (or more) out of ten working VLAN 2 access ports failing due to physical problems

   b. A **shutdown** command issued from interface VLAN 4 configuration mode

   c. VTP on the switch removing VLAN 3 from the switch's VLAN list

   d. A **shutdown** command issued from VLAN 2 configuration mode

5. A LAN design uses a Layer 3 EtherChannel between two switches SW1 and SW2, with Port-Channel interface 1 used on both switches. SW1 uses ports G0/1, G0/2, and G0/3 in the channel. Which of the following are true about SW1's configuration to make the channel be able to route IPv4 packets correctly? (Choose two answers.)

   a. The **ip address** command must be on the port-channel 1 interface.

   b. The **ip address** command must be on interface G0/1 (lowest numbered port).

   c. The port-channel 1 interface must be configured with the **no switchport** command.

   d. Interface G0/1 must be configured with the **routedport** command.

6. A LAN design uses a Layer 3 EtherChannel between two switches SW1 and SW2, with port-channel interface 1 used on both switches. SW1 uses ports G0/1 and G0/2 in the channel. However, only interface G0/1 is bundled into the channel and working. Think about the configuration settings on port G0/2 that could have existed before adding G0/2 to the EtherChannel. Which answers identify a setting that could prevent IOS from adding G0/2 to the Layer 3 EtherChannel? (Choose two answers.)

   a. A different STP cost (**spanning-tree cost** *value*)

   b. A different speed (**speed** value)

   c. A default setting for switchport (**switchport**)

   d. A different access VLAN (**switchport access vlan** *vlan-id*)

Foundation Topics

VLAN Routing with Router 802.1Q Trunks

Almost all enterprise networks use VLANs. To route IP packets in and out of those VLANs, some devices (either routers or Layer 3 switches) need to have an IP address in each subnet and have a connected route to each of those subnets. Then the IP addresses on those routers or Layer 3 switches can serve as the default gateways in those subnets.

This chapter breaks down the LAN routing options into four categories:

- Use a router, with one router LAN interface and cable connected to the switch for each and every VLAN (typically not used)
- Use a router, with a VLAN trunk connecting to a LAN switch (known as router-on-a-stick, or ROAS)
- Use a Layer 3 switch with switched virtual interfaces (SVI)
- Use a Layer 3 switch with routed interfaces (which may or may not be Layer 3 EtherChannels)

Of the items in the list, the first option works, but to be practical it requires far too many interfaces. It is mentioned here only to make the list complete.

As for the other three options, this chapter discusses each in turn as the main focus of one of the three major sections in this chapter. Each feature is used in real networks today, with the choice to use one or the other driven by the design and needs for a particular part of the network. Figure 19-1 shows cases in which these options could be used.

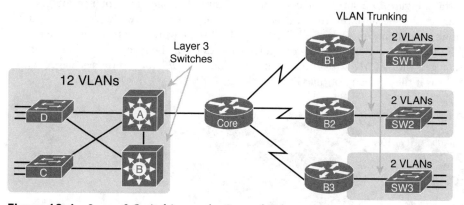

Figure 19-1 *Layer 3 Switching at the Central Site*

Figure 19-1 shows a classic case for using a router with a VLAN trunk at the branches on the right, and either of the two options in Layer 3 switches at the central site on the left. The figure shows a central site campus LAN on the left, with 12 VLANs. At the central site, two of the switches act as Layer 3 switches, combining the functions of a router and a switch, routing between all 12 subnets/VLANs. Those Layer 3 switches could configure routing using SVIs, routed interfaces, or both. Additionally, sites that have a WAN router and a switch, like the remote branch sites on the right side of the figure, might use ROAS to take advantage of the router's ability to route over an 802.1Q trunk.

Note that Figure 19-1 just shows an example. The engineer could use Layer 3 switching at each site, or routers with VLAN trunking at each site.

Answers to the "Do I Know This Already?" quiz:

1 A, F **2** B, C **3** C **4** C, D **5** A, C **6** B, C

Configuring ROAS

This next topic discusses how routers route packets to subnets associated with VLANs connected to a router 802.1Q trunk. That long description can be a bit of a chore to repeat each time someone wants to discuss this feature, so over time, the networking world has instead settled on a shorter and more interesting name for this feature: router-on-a-stick (ROAS).

ROAS uses router VLAN trunking configuration to give the router a logical router interface connected to each VLAN, and therefore each subnet that sits on a separate VLAN. That trunking configuration revolves around subinterfaces. The router needs to have an IP address/mask associated with each VLAN on the trunk. However, the router has only one physical interface on which to configure the **ip address** command. Cisco solves this problem by creating multiple virtual router interfaces, one associated with each VLAN on that trunk (at least for each VLAN that you want the trunk to support). Cisco calls these virtual interfaces *subinterfaces*.

The ROAS configuration creates a subinterface for each VLAN on the trunk, and the router then treats all frames tagged with that associated VLAN ID as if they came in or out of that subinterface. Figure 19-2 shows the concept with Router B1, one of the branch routers from Figure 19-1. Because this router needs to route between only two VLANs, the figure also shows two subinterfaces, named G0/0.10 and G0/0.20, which create a new place in the configuration where the per-VLAN configuration settings can be made. The router treats frames tagged with VLAN 10 as if they came in or out of G0/0.10, and frames tagged with VLAN 20 as if they came in or out G0/0.20.

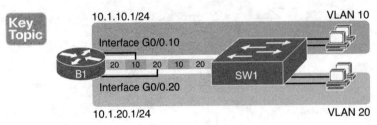

Figure 19-2 *Subinterfaces on Router B1*

In addition, note that most Cisco routers do not attempt to negotiate trunking, so both the router and switch need to manually configure trunking. This chapter discusses the router side of that trunking configuration; the matching switch interface would need to be configured with the **switchport mode trunk** command.

Example 19-1 shows a full example of the 802.1Q trunking configuration required on Router B1 in Figure 19-2. More generally, these steps detail how to configure 802.1Q trunking on a router:

Step 1. Use the **interface** *type number.subint* command in global configuration mode to create a unique subinterface for each VLAN that needs to be routed.

Step 2. Use the **encapsulation dot1q** *vlan_id* command in subinterface configuration mode to enable 802.1Q and associate one specific VLAN with the subinterface.

Step 3. Use the **ip address** *address mask* command in subinterface configuration mode to configure IP settings (address and mask).

Example 19-1   *Router Configuration for the 802.1Q Encapsulation Shown in Figure 19-2*

```
B1# show running-config
! Only pertinent lines shown
interface gigabitethernet 0/0
! No IP address up here! No encapsulation up here!
!
interface gigabitethernet 0/0.10
 encapsulation dot1q 10
 ip address 10.1.10.1 255.255.255.0
!
interface gigabitethernet 0/0.20
 encapsulation dot1q 20
 ip address 10.1.20.1 255.255.255.0
```

First, look at the subinterface numbers. The subinterface number begins with the period, like .10 and .20 in this case. These numbers can be any number from 1 up through a very large number (over 4 billion). The number just needs to be unique among all subinterfaces associated with this one physical interface. In fact, the subinterface number does not even have to match the associated VLAN ID. (The **encapsulation** command, and not the subinterface number, defines the VLAN ID associated with the subinterface.)

NOTE   Although not required, most sites do choose to make the subinterface number match the VLAN ID, as shown in Example 19-1, just to avoid confusion.

Each subinterface configuration lists two subcommands. One command (**encapsulation**) enables trunking and defines the VLAN whose frames are considered to be coming in and out of the subinterface. The **ip address** command works the same way it does on any other interface. Note that if the physical Ethernet interface reaches an up/up state, the subinterface should as well, which would then let the router add the connected routes shown at the bottom of the example.

Now that the router has a working interface, with IPv4 addresses configured, the router can route IPv4 packets on these subinterfaces. That is, the router treats these subinterfaces like any physical interface in terms of adding connected routes, matching those routes, and forwarding packets to/from those connected subnets.

NOTE   As a brief aside, while Example 19-1 shows 802.1Q configuration, the Inter-Switch Link (ISL) configuration on the same router would be practically identical. Just substitute the keyword **isl** instead of **dot1q** in each case.

The configuration and use of the native VLAN on the trunk requires a little extra thought. The native VLAN can be configured on a subinterface, or on the physical interface, or ignored as in Example 19-1. Each 802.1Q trunk has one native VLAN, and if the router needs to route packets for a subnet that exists in the native VLAN, then the router needs some configuration to support that subnet. The two options to define a router interface for the native VLAN are

- Configure the **ip address** command on the physical interface, but without an **encapsulation** command; the router considers this physical interface to be using the native VLAN.

- Configure the **ip address** command on a subinterface, and use the **encapsulation dot1q** *vlan-id* **native** subcommand to tell the router both the VLAN ID and the fact that it is the native VLAN.

Example 19-2 shows both native VLAN configuration options with a small change to the same configuration in Example 19-1. In this case, VLAN 10 becomes the native VLAN. The top part of the example shows the option to configure the router physical interface to use native VLAN 10. The second half of the example shows how to configure that same native VLAN on a subinterface. In both cases, the switch configuration also needs to be changed to make VLAN 10 the native VLAN.

Example 19-2 *Router Configuration Using Native VLAN 10 on Router B1*

```
! First option: put the native VLAN IP address on the physical interface
interface gigabitethernet 0/0
 ip address 10.1.10.1 255.255.255.0
!
interface gigabitethernet 0/0.20
 encapsulation dot1q 20
 ip address 10.1.20.1 255.255.255.0
! Second option: like Example 19-1, but add the native keyword
interface gigabitethernet 0/0.10
 encapsulation dot1q 10 native
 ip address 10.1.10.1 255.255.255.0
!
interface gigabitethernet 0/0.20
 encapsulation dot1q 20
 ip address 10.1.20.1 255.255.255.0
```

Verifying ROAS

Beyond using the **show running-config** command, ROAS configuration on a router can be best verified with two commands: **show ip route [connected]** and **show vlans**. As with any router interface, as long as the interface is in an up/up state, and has an IPv4 address configured, IOS will put a connected (and local) route in the IPv4 routing table. So, a first and obvious check would be to see if all the expected connected routes exist. Example 19-3 lists the connected routes per the configuration shown in Example 19-1.

Example 19-3 *Connected Routes Based on Example 19-1 Configuration*

```
B1# show ip route connected
Codes: L - local, C - connected, S - static, R - RIP, M - mobile, B - BGP
! Legend omitted for brevity

     10.0.0.0/8 is variably subnetted, 4 subnets, 2 masks
```

```
C        10.1.10.0/24 is directly connected, GigabitEthernet0/0.10
L        10.1.10.1/32 is directly connected, GigabitEthernet0/0.10
C        10.1.20.0/24 is directly connected, GigabitEthernet0/0.20
L        10.1.20.1/32 is directly connected, GigabitEthernet0/0.20
```

As for interface and subinterface state, note that the ROAS subinterface state does depend to some degree on the physical interface state. In particular, the subinterface state cannot be better than the state of the matching physical interface. For instance, on Router B1 in the examples so far, physical interface G0/0 is in an up/up state, and the subinterfaces are in an up/up state. But if you unplugged the cable from that port, the physical port would fail to a down/down state, and the subinterfaces would also fail to a down/down state. Example 19-4 shows another example, with the physical interface being shut down, with the subinterfaces then automatically changed to an administratively down state as a result.

Example 19-4   *Subinterface State Tied to Physical Interface State*

```
B1# configure terminal
Enter configuration commands, one per line.  End with CNTL/Z.
B1(config)# interface g0/0
B1(config-if)# shutdown
B1(config-if)# ^Z
B1# show ip interface brief | include 0/0
GigabitEthernet0/0       unassigned      YES manual administratively down down
GigabitEthernet0/0.10    10.1.10.1       YES manual administratively down down
GigabitEthernet0/0.20    10.1.20.1       YES manual administratively down down
```

Additionally, the subinterface state can also be enabled and disabled independently from the physical interface, using the **no shutdown** and **shutdown** commands in subinterface configuration mode.

Another useful ROAS verification command, **show vlans**, spells out which router trunk interfaces use which VLANs, which VLAN is the native VLAN, plus some packet statistics. The fact that the packet counters are increasing can be useful when verifying whether traffic is happening or not. Example 19-5 shows a sample, based on the Router B1 configuration in Example 19-2 (bottom half), in which native VLAN 10 is configured on subinterface G0/0.10. Note that the output identifies VLAN 1 associated with the physical interface, VLAN 10 as the native VLAN associated with G0/0.10, and VLAN 20 associated with G0/0.20. It also lists the IP addresses assigned to each interface/subinterface.

Example 19-5   *Sample* **show vlans** *Command to Match Sample Router Trunking Configuration*

```
R1# show vlans
Virtual LAN ID:  1 (IEEE 802.1Q Encapsulation)

   vLAN Trunk Interface:    GigabitEthernet0/0

   Protocols Configured:   Address:          Received:        Transmitted:
      Other                                         0                 83
```

```
         69 packets, 20914 bytes input
        147 packets, 11841 bytes output


Virtual LAN ID:  10 (IEEE 802.1Q Encapsulation)


    vLAN Trunk Interface:   GigabitEthernet0/0.10


 This is configured as native Vlan for the following interface(s) :
GigabitEthernet0/0         Native-vlan Tx-type: Untagged


    Protocols Configured:   Address:          Received:       Transmitted:
         IP             10.1.10.1              2                 3
        Other                                 0                 1


    3 packets, 722 bytes input
    4 packets, 264 bytes output


Virtual LAN ID:  20 (IEEE 802.1Q Encapsulation)


    vLAN Trunk Interface:   GigabitEthernet0/0.20


    Protocols Configured:   Address:        Received:       Transmitted:
         IP             10.1.20.1            0                 134
        Other                               0                 1


    0 packets, 0 bytes input
    135 packets, 10498 bytes output
```

Troubleshooting ROAS

The biggest challenge when troubleshooting ROAS has to do with the fact that if you mis-configure only the router, or misconfigure only the switch, the other device on the trunk has no way to know that the other side is misconfigured. That is, if you check the **show ip route** and **show vlans** commands on a router, and the output looks like it matches the intended configuration, and the connected routes for the correct subinterfaces show up, routing may still fail because of problems on the attached switch. So troubleshooting ROAS often begins with checking the configuration on both the router and switch, because there is no status output on either device that tells you where the problem might be.

First, to check ROAS on the router, you need to start with the intended configuration, and ask questions about the configuration:

1. Is each non-native VLAN configured on the router with an **encapsulation dot1q** *vlan-id* command on a subinterface?

2. Do those same VLANs exist on the trunk on the neighboring switch (**show interfaces trunk**), and are they in the allowed list, not VTP pruned, and not STP blocked?

3. Does each router ROAS subinterface have an IP address/mask configured per the planned configuration?

4. If using the native VLAN, is it configured correctly on the router either on a subinterface (with an **encapsulation dot1q** *vlan-id* **native** command) or implied on the physical interface?

5. Is the same native VLAN configured on the neighboring switch's trunk?

6. Are the router physical or ROAS subinterfaces configured with a **shutdown** command?

For some of these steps, you need to be ready to repeat all the VLAN and VLAN trunk troubleshooting as discussed back in the "Troubleshooting VLANs and VLAN Trunks" section of Chapter 4, "LAN Troubleshooting." The reason is that on many Cisco routers, router interfaces do not negotiate trunking. As a result, if the switch has any problems with VLANs or the VLAN trunking configuration on its side of the trunk, the router has no way to realize that the problem exists.

For example, imagine you configured ROAS on a router just like in Example 19-1 or Example 19-2. However, the switch on the other end of the link had no matching configuration. For instance, maybe the switch did not even define VLANs 10 and 20. Maybe the switch did not configure trunking on the port connected to the router. Even with blatant misconfiguration or missing configuration on the switch, the router still shows up/up ROAS interfaces and subinterfaces, IP routes in the output of **show ip route**, and meaningful configuration information in the output of the **show vlans** command.

VLAN Routing with Layer 3 Switch SVIs

Using a router with ROAS to route packets makes sense in some cases, particularly at small remote sites. In sites with a larger LAN, network designers choose to use Layer 3 switches for most inter-VLAN routing.

A Layer 3 switch (also called a multilayer switch) is one device, but it executes logic at two layers: Layer 2 LAN switching and Layer 3 IP routing. The Layer 2 switch function forwards frames inside each VLAN, but it will not forward frames between VLANs. The Layer 3 forwarding (routing) logic forwards IP packets between VLANs.

Layer 3 switches typically support two configuration options to enable IPv4 routing inside the switch, specifically to enable IPv4 on switch interfaces. This section explains one option, an option that uses switched virtual interfaces (SVI). The final major section of the chapter deals with the other option for configuring IPv4 addresses on Layer 3 switches: routed interfaces.

Configuring Routing Using Switch SVIs

The configuration of a Layer 3 switch mostly looks like the Layer 2 switching configuration shown back in Part I of this book, with a small bit of configuration added for the Layer 3 functions. The Layer 3 switching function needs a virtual interface connected to each VLAN internal to the switch. These *VLAN interfaces* act like router interfaces, with an IP address and mask. The Layer 3 switch has an IP routing table, with connected routes off each of these VLAN interfaces. (These interfaces are also referred to as switched virtual interfaces [SVI].)

To show the concept of Layer 3 switching with SVIs, Figure 19-3 shows the design changes and configuration concept for the same branch office used in Figures 19-1 and 19-2. The figure shows the Layer 3 switch function with a router icon inside the switch, to emphasize that the switch routes the packets. The branch still has two user VLANs, so the Layer 3 switch needs one VLAN interface for each VLAN. In addition, the traffic still needs to get to the router to access the WAN, so the switch uses a third VLAN (VLAN 30 in this case) for the link to Router B1. This link would not be a trunk, but would be an access link.

Key Topic

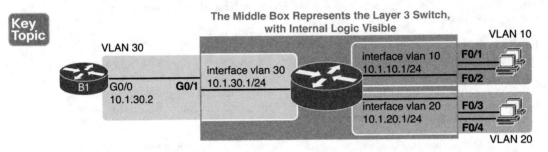

Figure 19-3 *Routing on VLAN Interfaces in a Layer 3 Switch*

Config Checklist

The following steps show how to configure Layer 3 switching using SVIs. Note that on some switches, like the 2960 and 2960-XR switches used for the examples in this book, the ability to route IPv4 packets must be enabled first, with a **reload** of the switch required to enable the feature. The rest of the steps after Step 1 would apply to all models of Cisco switches that are capable of doing Layer 3 switching.

Step 1. Enable IP routing on the switch, as needed:

  A. Use the **sdm prefer lanbase-routing** command (or similar) in global configuration mode to change the switch forwarding ASIC settings to make space for IPv4 routes at the next reload of the switch.

  B. Use the **reload** EXEC command in enable mode to reload (reboot) the switch to pick up the new **sdm prefer** command setting.

  C. Once reloaded, use the **ip routing** command in global configuration mode to enable the IPv4 routing function in IOS software and to enable key commands like **show ip route**.

Step 2. Configure each SVI interface, one per VLAN for which routing should be done by this Layer 3 switch:

  A. Use the **interface vlan** *vlan_id* command in global configuration mode to create a VLAN interface, and to give the switch's routing logic a Layer 3 interface connected into the VLAN of the same number.

  B. Use the **ip address** *address mask* command in VLAN interface configuration mode to configure an IP address and mask on the VLAN interface, enabling IPv4 routing on that VLAN interface.

  C. (As needed) Use the **no shutdown** command in interface configuration mode to enable the VLAN interface (if it is currently in a shutdown state).

Example 19-6 shows the configuration to match Figure 19-3. In this case, switch SW1, a 2960, has already used the **sdm prefer lanbase-routing** global command and has been reloaded. The example shows the related configuration on all three VLAN interfaces.

Example 19-6 *VLAN Interface Configuration for Layer 3 Switching*

```
ip routing
!
interface vlan 10
 ip address 10.1.10.1 255.255.255.0
!
interface vlan 20
 ip address 10.1.20.1 255.255.255.0
!
interface vlan 30
 ip address 10.1.30.1 255.255.255.0
```

Verifying Routing with SVIs

With the VLAN configuration shown in the previous section, the switch is ready to route packets between the VLANs as shown in Figure 19-3. To support the routing of packets, the switch adds connected IP routes, as shown in Example 19-7; note that each route is listed as being connected to a different VLAN interface.

Example 19-7 *Connected Routes on a Layer 3 Switch*

```
SW1# show ip route
! legend omitted for brevity

      10.0.0.0/8 is variably subnetted, 6 subnets, 2 masks
C        10.1.10.0/24 is directly connected, Vlan10
L        10.1.10.1/32 is directly connected, Vlan10
C        10.1.20.0/24 is directly connected, Vlan20
L        10.1.20.1/32 is directly connected, Vlan20
C        10.1.30.0/24 is directly connected, Vlan30
L        10.1.30.1/32 is directly connected, Vlan30
```

The switch would also need additional routes to the rest of the network (not shown in the figures in this chapter). The Layer 3 switch could use static routes or a routing protocol, depending on the capabilities of the switch. For instance, if you then enabled EIGRP on the Layer 3 switch, the configuration and verification would work the same as it does on a router, as discussed in Chapter 9, "Understanding EIGRP Concepts," and Chapter 10, "Implementing EIGRP for IPv4." The routes that IOS adds to the Layer 3 switch's IP routing table would list the VLAN interfaces as outgoing interfaces.

NOTE Some models of Cisco enterprise switches, based on model, IOS version, and IOS feature set, support different capabilities for IP routing and routing protocols, so for real networks, check the capabilities of the switch model by browsing at Cisco.com. In particular, check the Cisco Feature Navigator (CFN) tool at http://www.cisco.com/go/cfn.

19

Troubleshooting Routing with SVIs

There are two big topics to investigate when troubleshooting routing over LANs with SVIs. First, you have to make sure the switch has been enabled to support IP routing. Second, the VLAN associated with each VLAN interface must be known and active on the local switch, otherwise the VLAN interfaces do not come up.

First, about enabling IP routing, note that some models of Cisco switches default to enable Layer 3 switching, and some do not. So, to make sure your switch supports Layer 3 routing, look to those first few configuration commands listed in the configuration checklist found in the earlier section "Configuring Routing Using Switch SVIs." Those commands are **sdm prefer** (followed by a **reload**) and then **ip routing** (after the **reload**).

The **sdm prefer** command changes how the switch forwarding chips allocate memory for different forwarding tables, and changes to those tables requires a reload of the switch. By default, many access switches that support Layer 3 switching still have an SDM default that does not allocate space for an IP routing table. Once changed and reloaded, the **ip routing** command then enables IPv4 routing in IOS software. Both are necessary before some Cisco switches will act as a Layer 3 switch.

Example 19-8 shows some symptoms on a router for which Layer 3 switching had not yet been enabled by the **sdm prefer** command. As you can see, both the **show ip route** EXEC command and the **ip routing** config command are rejected because they do not exist to IOS until the **sdm prefer** command has been used (followed by a **reload** of the switch).

Example 19-8 *Evidence That a Switch Has Not Yet Enabled IPv4 Routing*

```
SW1# show ip route
              ^
% Invalid input detected at '^' marker.


SW3# configure terminal
Enter configuration commands, one per line.  End with CNTL/Z.
SW3(config)# ip routing
                ^
% Invalid input detected at '^' marker.
```

The second big area to investigate when troubleshooting SVIs relates to the SVI state, a state that ties to the state of the associated VLANs. Each VLAN interface has a matching VLAN of the same number, and the VLAN interface's state is tied to the state of the VLAN in certain ways. In particular, for a VLAN interface to be in an up/up state:

Step 1.   The VLAN must be defined on the local switch (either explicitly, or learned with VTP).

Step 2.   The switch must have at least one up/up interface using the VLAN, either/both:

A.   An up/up access interface assigned to that VLAN

B.   A trunk interface for which the VLAN is in the allowed list, is STP forwarding, and is not VTP pruned

Step 3.   The VLAN (not the VLAN interface) must be administratively enabled (that is, not **shutdown**).

Step 4.   The VLAN interface (not the VLAN) must be administratively enabled (that is, not **shutdown**).

When working through the steps in the list, keep in mind that the VLAN and the VLAN interface are related but separate ideas, and the configuration items are separate in the CLI. The VLAN interface is a switch's Layer 3 interface connected to the VLAN. If you want to route packets for the subnets on VLANs 11, 12, and 13, the matching VLAN interfaces must be numbered 11, 12, and 13. And both the VLANs and the VLAN interfaces can be disabled and enabled with the **shutdown** and **no shutdown** commands (as mentioned in Steps 3 and 4 in the previous list), so you have to check for both.

Example 19-9 shows three scenarios, each of which leads to one of the VLAN interfaces in the previous configuration example (Figure 19-3, Example 19-6) to fail. At the beginning of the example, all three VLAN interfaces are up/up. VLANs 10, 20, and 30 each have at least one access interface up and working. The example works through three scenarios:

- **Scenario 1:** The last access interface in VLAN 10 is shut down (F0/1), so IOS shuts down the VLAN 10 interface.

- **Scenario 2:** VLAN 20 (not VLAN interface 20, but VLAN 20) is deleted, which results in IOS then bringing down (not shutting down) the VLAN 20 interface.

- **Scenario 3:** VLAN 30 (not VLAN interface 30, but VLAN 30) is shut down, which results in IOS then bringing down (not shutting down) the VLAN 30 interface.

Example 19-9   *Three Examples That Cause VLAN Interfaces to Fail*

```
SW1# show interfaces status
! Only ports related to the example are shown
Port      Name            Status        Vlan    Duplex  Speed Type
Fa0/1                     connected     10      a-full  a-100 10/100BaseTX
Fa0/2                     notconnect    10       auto    auto 10/100BaseTX
Fa0/3                     connected     20      a-full  a-100 10/100BaseTX
Fa0/4                     connected     20      a-full  a-100 10/100BaseTX
Gi0/1                     connected     30      a-full a-1000 10/100/1000BaseTX


SW1# configure terminal
Enter configuration commands, one per line.  End with CNTL/Z.

! Case 1: Interface F0/1, the last up/up access interface in VLAN 10, is shutdown
SW1(config)# interface fastEthernet 0/1
SW1(config-if)# shutdown
SW1(config-if)#
*Apr  2 19:54:08.784: %LINEPROTO-5-UPDOWN: Line protocol on Interface Vlan10, changed
  state to down
SW1(config-if)#
*Apr  2 19:54:10.772: %LINK-5-CHANGED: Interface FastEthernet0/1, changed state to
  administratively down
```

```
*Apr  2 19:54:11.779: %LINEPROTO-5-UPDOWN: Line protocol on Interface FastEthernet0/1,
  changed state to down


! Case 2: VLAN 20 is deleted
SW1(config)# no vlan 20
SW1(config)#
*Apr  2 19:54:39.688: %LINEPROTO-5-UPDOWN: Line protocol on Interface Vlan20, changed
  state to down


! Case 3: VLAN 30, the VLAN from the switch to the router, is shutdown
SW1(config)# vlan 30
SW1(config-vlan)# shutdown
SW1(config-vlan)# exit
SW1(config)#
*Apr  2 19:55:25.204: %LINEPROTO-5-UPDOWN: Line protocol on Interface Vlan30, changed
  state to down


! Final status of all three VLAN interfaces are below
SW1# show ip interface brief | include Vlan
Vlan1                   unassigned      YES manual administratively down down
Vlan10                  10.1.10.1       YES manual up                    down
Vlan20                  10.1.20.1       YES manual up                    down
Vlan30                  10.1.30.1       YES manual up                    down
```

Note that the example ends with the three VLAN interfaces in an up/down state per the **show ip interface brief** command.

VLAN Routing with Layer 3 Switch Routed Ports

When configuring Layer 3 switching using SVIs, the physical interfaces on the switches act like they always have: as Layer 2 interfaces. That is, the physical interfaces receive Ethernet frames. The switch learns the source MAC address of the frame, and the switch forwards the frame based on the destination MAC address. The SVIs are then used when a frame happens to be destined to the SVI interface's MAC address, as if the SVI were attached to a router sitting within the center of the Layer 3 switch.

Alternately, the Layer 3 switch configuration can make a physical port act like a router interface instead of a switch interface. To do so, the switch configuration makes that port a *routed* port. On a *routed* port, when a frame is received on the physical interface, the switch does not perform Layer 2 switching logic on that frame. Instead, the switch performs routing actions, including

1. Stripping off the incoming frame's Ethernet data link header/trailer

2. Making a Layer 3 forwarding decision by comparing the destination IP address to the IP routing table

3. Adding a new Ethernet data link header/trailer to the packet

4. Forwarding the packet, encapsulated in a new frame

This third major section of the chapter examines routed interfaces as configured on Cisco Layer 3 switches, but with a particular goal in mind: to also discuss Layer 3 EtherChannels. The exam topics do not mention routed interfaces specifically, but the exam topics do mention L3 EtherChannels, meaning Layer 3 EtherChannels. Layer 3 EtherChannels are EtherChannels (as discussed in Chapters 2 and 3) that are also routed ports instead of switched ports. So this section first looks at routed ports on Cisco Layer 3 switches, and then discusses Layer 3 EtherChannels.

Implementing Routed Interfaces on Switches

When a Layer 3 switch needs a Layer 3 interface connected to a subnet, and only one physical interface connects to that subnet, the network engineer can choose to use a routed port instead of an SVI. Conversely, when the Layer 3 switch needs a Layer 3 interface connected to a subnet, and many physical interfaces on the switch connect to that subnet, an SVI needs to be used. (SVIs can forward traffic that the Layer 2 logic then sends out any of the ports in the VLAN, and routed ports cannot.)

To see why, consider the design in Figure 19-4, which repeats the same design from Figure 19-3 (used in the SVI examples). In that familiar design, at least two access ports sit in both VLAN 10 and VLAN 20. However, that figure shows a single link from the switch to Router B1. As a result, the switch could configure that link as a routed port.

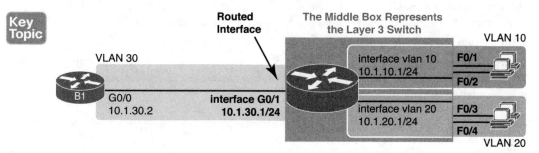

Figure 19-4 *Routing on a Routed Interface on a Switch*

Enabling a switch interface to be a routed interface instead of a switched interface is simple: just use the **no switchport** subcommand on the physical interface. Cisco switches capable of being a Layer 3 switch use a default of the **switchport** command to each switch physical interface. Think about the word *switchport* for a moment. With that term, Cisco tells the switch to treat the port like it is a port on a switch—that is, a Layer 2 port on a switch. To make the port stop acting like a switch port, and instead act like a router port, use the **no switchport** command on the interface.

Once the port is acting as a routed port, think of it like a router interface. That is, configure the IP address on the physical port, as implied in Figure 19-4. Example 19-10 shows a completed configuration for the interfaces configured on the switch in Figure 19-4. Note that the design uses the exact same IP subnets as the example that showed SVI configuration in Example 19-6, but now, the port connected to subnet 10.1.30.0 has been converted to a routed port. All you have to do is add the **no switchport** command to the physical interface, and configure the IP address on the physical interface.

Example 19-10 *Configuring Interface G0/1 on Switch SW1 as a Routed Port*

```
ip routing
!
interface vlan 10
 ip address 10.1.10.1 255.255.255.0
!
interface vlan 20
 ip address 10.1.20.1 255.255.255.0
!
interface gigabitethernet 0/1
 no switchport
 ip address 10.1.30.1 255.255.255.0
```

Once configured, the routed interface will show up differently in command output in the switch. In particular, for an interface configured as a routed port with an IP address, like interface GigabitEthernet0/1 in the previous example:

show interfaces: Similar to the same command on a router, the output will display the IP address of the interface. (For switch ports, this command does not list an IP address.)

show interfaces status: Under the "VLAN" heading, instead of listing the access VLAN or the word "trunk," the output lists the word "routed," meaning that it is a routed port.

show ip route: Lists the routed port as an outgoing interface in routes.

show interfaces *type number* **switchport:** If a routed port, the output is short and confirms that the port is not a switch port. (If the port is a Layer 2 port, this command lists many configuration and status details.)

Example 19-11 shows samples of all four of these commands as taken from the switch as configured in Example 19-10.

Example 19-11 *Verification Commands for Routed Ports on Switches*

```
SW11# show interfaces g0/1
GigabitEthernet0/1 is up, line protocol is up (connected)
  Hardware is Gigabit Ethernet, address is bcc4.938b.e541 (bia bcc4.938b.e541)
  Internet address is 10.1.30.1/24
! lines omitted for brevity


SW1# show interfaces status
! Only ports related to the example are shown; the command lists physical only
Port      Name          Status       Vlan       Duplex  Speed Type
Fa0/1                   connected    10          a-full  a-100 10/100BaseTX
Fa0/2                   notconnect   10           auto    auto 10/100BaseTX
Fa0/3                   connected    20          a-full  a-100 10/100BaseTX
Fa0/4                   connected    20          a-full  a-100 10/100BaseTX
Gi0/1                   connected    routed      a-full a-1000 10/100/1000BaseTX


SW1# show ip route
```

```
! legend omitted for brevity

      10.0.0.0/8 is variably subnetted, 6 subnets, 2 masks
C        10.1.10.0/24 is directly connected, Vlan10
L        10.1.10.1/32 is directly connected, Vlan10
C        10.1.20.0/24 is directly connected, Vlan20
L        10.1.20.1/32 is directly connected, Vlan20
C        10.1.30.0/24 is directly connected, GigabitEthernet0/1
L        10.1.30.1/32 is directly connected, GigabitEthernet0/1

SW1# show interfaces g0/1 switchport
Name: Gi0/1
Switchport: Disabled
```

So, with two options—SVI and routed ports—where should you use each? For any topologies with a point-to-point link between two devices that do routing, a routed interface works well. Figure 19-5 shows a typical core/distribution/access design with the core and distribution layers acting as Layer 3 switches. All the ports that are links directly between the Layer 3 switches can be routed interfaces. For VLANs for which many interfaces (access and trunk) connect to the VLAN, SVIs make sense, because the SVIs can send and receive traffic out multiple ports on the same switch.

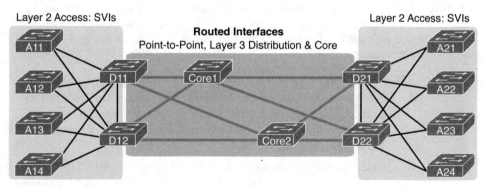

Figure 19-5 *Using Routed Interfaces for Core and Distribution Layer 3 Links*

Implementing Layer 3 EtherChannels

So far, this section has stated that routed interfaces can be used with a single point-to-point link between pairs of Layer 3 switches, or between a Layer 3 switch and a router. However, in most designs, the network engineers use at least two links between each pair of distribution and core switches, as shown in Figure 19-6.

While each individual port in the distribution and core could be treated as a separate routed port, it is better to combine each pair of parallel links into a Layer 3 EtherChannel. Without using EtherChannel, you can still make each port on each switch in the center of the figure be a routed port. It works. However, once you enable a routing protocol, each Layer 3 switch will now learn two IP routes with the same neighboring switch as the next hop—one route over one link, another route over the other link.

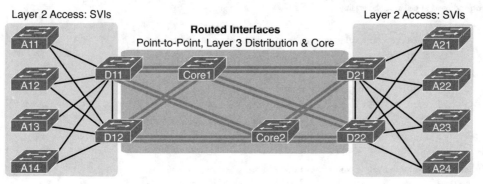

Figure 19-6 *Two Links Between Each Distribution and Core Switch*

Using a Layer 3 EtherChannel makes more sense with multiple parallel links between two switches. By doing so, each pair of links acts as one Layer 3 link. So, each pair of switches has one routing protocol neighbor relationship with the neighbor, and not two. Each switch learns one route per destination per pair of links, and not two. IOS then balances the traffic, often with better balancing than Layer 3 balancing. Overall, the Layer 3 EtherChannel approach works much better than leaving each link as a separate routed port and using Layer 3 balancing.

Compared to what you have already learned, configuring a Layer 3 EtherChannel takes only a little more work. Chapter 3, "Spanning Tree Protocol Implementation," already showed you how to configure an EtherChannel. This chapter has already shown how to make a port a Layer 3 routed port. So, to configure a Layer 3 EtherChannel, do both the EtherChannel and routed port configuration. The follow checklist shows the steps, assuming a static definition for the EtherChannel.

Config Checklist

Step 1.   Configure the physical interfaces as follows, in interface configuration mode:

A.   Add the **channel-group** *number* **mode on** command to add it to the channel. Use the same number for all physical interfaces on the same switch, but the number used (the channel-group number) can differ on the two neighboring switches.

B.   Add the **no switchport** command to make each physical port a routed port.

Step 2.   Configure the PortChannel interface:

A.   Use the **interface port-channel** *number* command to move to port-channel configuration mode for the same channel number configured on the physical interfaces.

B.   Add the **no switchport** command to make sure that the port-channel interface acts as a routed port. (IOS may have already added this command.)

C.   Use the **ip address** *address mask* command to configure the address and mask.

> **NOTE** Cisco uses the term *EtherChannel* in concepts discussed in this section, and then uses the term *PortChannel*, with command keyword **port-channel**, when verifying and configuring EtherChannels. For the purposes of understanding the technology, you may treat these terms as synonyms. However, it helps to pay close attention to the use of the terms PortChannel and EtherChannel as you work through the examples in this section, because IOS uses both.

Example 19-12 shows an example of the configuration for a Layer 3 EtherChannel for switch SW1 in Figure 19-7. The EtherChannel defines a port-channel interface 12, and uses subnet 10.1.12.0/24.

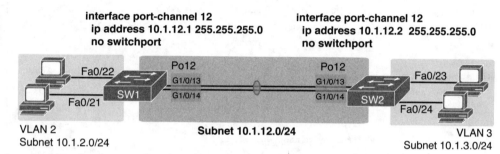

Figure 19-7 *Design Used in EtherChannel Configuration Examples*

Example 19-12 *Layer 3 EtherChannel Configuration on Switch SW1*

```
interface GigabitEthernet1/0/13
 no switchport
 no ip address
 channel-group 12 mode on
!
interface GigabitEthernet1/0/14
 no switchport
 no ip address
 channel-group 12 mode on
!
interface Port-channel12
 no switchport
 ip address 10.1.12.1 255.255.255.0
```

Of particular importance, note that although the physical interfaces and PortChannel interface are all routed ports, the IP address should be placed on the PortChannel interface only. In fact, when the **no switchport** command is configured on an interface, IOS adds the **no ip address** command to the interface. Then configure the IP address on the PortChannel interface only.

Once configured, the PortChannel interface appears in several commands, as shown in Example 19-13. The commands that list IP addresses and routes refer to the PortChannel interface. Also, note that the **show interfaces status** command lists the fact that the physical ports and the port-channel 12 interface are all routed ports.

Example 19-13 *Verification Commands Listing Interface Port-Channel12 from Switch SW1*

```
SW1# show interfaces port-channel 12
Port-channel12 is up, line protocol is up (connected)
  Hardware is EtherChannel, address is bcc4.938b.e543 (bia bcc4.938b.e543)
  Internet address is 10.1.12.1/24
! lines omitted for brevity


SW1# show interfaces status
! Only ports related to the example are shown.
Port       Name              Status       Vlan       Duplex  Speed Type
Gi1/0/13                     connected    routed     a-full a-1000 10/100/1000BaseTX
Gi1/0/14                     connected    routed     a-full a-1000 10/100/1000BaseTX
Po12                         connected    routed     a-full a-1000


SW1# show ip route
! legend omitted for brevity
      10.0.0.0/8 is variably subnetted, 4 subnets, 2 masks
C        10.1.2.0/24 is directly connected, Vlan2
L        10.1.2.1/32 is directly connected, Vlan2
C        10.1.12.0/24 is directly connected, Port-channel12
L        10.1.12.1/32 is directly connected, Port-channel12
```

For a final bit of verification, you can examine the EtherChannel directly with the **show etherchannel summary** command as listed in Example 19-14. (Although it has been a while, as a reminder, Chapters 3 and 4 showed examples of this command when used for Layer 2 EtherChannels.) Note in particular that it lists a flag legend for characters that identify key operational states, like whether a port is bundled (included) in the PortChannel (P), and whether it is acting as a routed (R) or switched (S) port.

Example 19-14 *Verifying the EtherChannel*

```
SW1# show etherchannel 12 summary
Flags:  D - down        P - bundled in port-channel
        I - stand-alone s - suspended
        H - Hot-standby (LACP only)
        R - Layer3       S - Layer2
        U - in use       f - failed to allocate aggregator

        M - not in use, minimum links not met
        u - unsuitable for bundling
        w - waiting to be aggregated
        d - default port


Number of channel-groups in use: 1
Number of aggregators:           1
```

```
Group   Port-channel   Protocol     Ports
------+-------------+-----------+-------------------------------------------------
12      Po12(RU)         -        Gi1/0/13(P)  Gi1/0/14(P)
```

Troubleshooting Layer 3 EtherChannels

When troubleshooting a Layer 3 EtherChannel, there are two main areas to consider. First, you need to look at the configuration of the **channel-group** command, which enables an interface for an EtherChannel. Second, you should check a list of settings that must match on the interfaces for a Layer 3 EtherChannel to work correctly.

As for the **channel-group** interface subcommand, this command can enable EtherChannel statically or dynamically. If dynamic, this command's keywords imply either Port Aggregation Protocol (PaGP) or Link Aggregation Control Protocol (LACP) as the protocol to negotiate between the neighboring switches whether they put the link into the EtherChannel.

If all this sounds vaguely familiar, it is the exact same configuration covered way back in the Chapter 3 section "Configuring Dynamic EtherChannels." The configuration of the **channel-group** subcommand is exactly the same, with the same requirements, whether configuring Layer 2 or Layer 3 EtherChannels. So, it might be a good time to review those EtherChannel configuration details from Chapter 3. However, regardless of when you review and master those commands, note that the configuration of the EtherChannel (with the **channel-group** subcommand) is the same, whether Layer 2 or Layer 3.

Additionally, you must do more than just configure the **channel-group** command correctly for all the physical ports to be bundled into the EtherChannel. Layer 2 EtherChannels have a longer list of requirements, but Layer 3 EtherChannels do require a few consistency checks between the ports before they can be added to the EtherChannel. The following is the list of requirements for Layer 3 EtherChannels:

Key Topic

no switchport: The PortChannel interface must be configured with the **no switchport** command, and so must the physical interfaces. If a physical interface is not also configured with the **no switchport** command, it will not become operational in the EtherChannel.

Speed: The physical ports in the channel must use the same speed.

duplex: The physical ports in the channel must use the same duplex.

Chapter Review

One key to doing well on the exams is to perform repetitive spaced review sessions. Review this chapter's material using either the tools in the book, DVD, or interactive tools for the same material found on the book's companion website. Refer to the "Your Study Plan" element for more details. Table 19-2 outlines the key review elements and where you can find them. To better track your study progress, record when you completed these activities in the second column.

Table 19-2   Chapter Review Tracking

Review Element	Review Date(s)	Resource Used
Review key topics		Book, DVD/website
Review key terms		Book, DVD/website
Repeat DIKTA questions		Book, PCPT
Do labs		Blog
Review config checklists		Book, DVD/website
Review command tables		Book

Review All the Key Topics

Table 19-3   Key Topics for Chapter 19

Key Topic Element	Description	Page Number
Figure 19-2	Concept of VLAN subinterfaces on a router	524
List	Two alternative methods to configure the native VLAN in a ROAS configuration	526
List	Troubleshooting suggestions for ROAS configuration	528
Figure 19-3	Layer 3 switching with SVIs concept and configuration	530
List	Troubleshooting suggestions for correct operation of a Layer 3 switch that uses SVIs	532
Figure 19-4	Layer 3 switching with routed ports concept and configuration	535
List	**show** commands that list Layer 3 routed ports in their output	536
Figure 19-7	Layer 3 EtherChannel concept and configuration	539
List	List of configuration settings that must be consistent before IOS will bundle a link with an existing Layer 3 EtherChannel	541

Key Terms You Should Know

router-on-a-stick (ROAS), switched virtual interface (SVI), VLAN interface, Layer 3 EtherChannel (L3 EtherChannel), routed port, Layer 3 switch, multilayer switch, subinterfaces

Command References

Tables 19-4 and 19-5 list configuration and verification commands used in this chapter. As an easy review exercise, cover the left column in a table, read the right column, and try to recall the command without looking. Then repeat the exercise, covering the right column, and try to recall what the command does.

Table 19-4   Chapter 19 Configuration Command Reference

Command	Description
interface *type number.subint*	Router global command to create a subinterface and to enter configuration mode for that subinterface
encapsulation dot1q *vlan-id* [native]	Router subinterface subcommand that tells the router to use 802.1Q trunking, for a particular VLAN, and with the **native** keyword, to not encapsulate in a trunking header
[no] ip routing	Global command that enables (**ip routing**) or disables (**no ip routing**) the routing of IPv4 packets on a router or Layer 3 switch
interface vlan *vlan-id*	A switch global command on a Layer 3 switch to create a VLAN interface and to enter configuration mode for that VLAN interface
sdm prefer lanbase-routing	Command on some Cisco switches that reallocates forwarding chip memory to allow for an IPv4 routing table
[no] switchport	Layer 3 switch subcommand that makes the port act as a Layer 2 port (**switchport**) or Layer 3 routed port (**no switchport**)
interface port-channel *channel-number*	A switch command to enter PortChannel configuration mode, and also to create the PortChannel if not already created
channel-group *channel-number* mode {auto | desirable | active | passive | on}	Interface subcommand that enables EtherChannel on the interface

Table 19-5   Chapter 19 EXEC Command Reference

Command	Description
show ip route	Lists the router's entire routing table
show ip route [connected]	Lists a subset of the IP routing table
show vlans	Lists VLAN configuration and statistics for VLAN trunks configured on routers
show interfaces [interface *type number*]	Lists detailed status and statistical information, including IP address and mask, about all interfaces (or the listed interface only)
show interfaces [interface *type number*] status	Among other facts, for switch ports, lists the access VLAN or the fact that the interface is a trunk; or, for routed ports, lists "routed"
show interfaces *interface-id* switchport	For switch ports, lists information about any interface regarding administrative settings and operational state; for routed ports, the output simply confirms the port is a routed (not switched) port
show interfaces vlan *number*	Lists the interface status, the switch's IPv4 address and mask, and much more
show etherchannel [*channel-group-number*] summary	Lists information about the state of EtherChannels on this switch, including whether the channel is a Layer 2 or Layer 3 EtherChannel

19

CHAPTER 20

Implementing HSRP for First-Hop Routing

This chapter covers the following exam topics:

4.0 Infrastructure Services

4.1 Configure, verify, and troubleshoot basic HSRP

  4.1.a Priority

  4.1.b Preemption

  4.1.c Version

5.0 Infrastructure Maintenance

5.6 Troubleshoot basic Layer 3 end-to-end connectivity issues

Businesses rely on their networks to get their work done. Some businesses rely more on the network than others, with a direct connection between network outages and lost revenue. For instance, when the network is down, some companies lose customers, or lose sales, or they cannot ship their goods to market, affecting sales volume in the future. Companies can design their networks to use redundancy—extra devices and extra links—so that when a device fails, or a link fails, the network still works. The extra devices may cost more money, but the cost may be justified, given the cost of an outage.

Networks that have redundant devices and links sometimes require additional protocols to deal with changes to how the network functions with the added redundancy. This chapter introduces the concepts behind one such class of protocols, called First Hop Redundancy Protocol (FHRP). Then the majority of the chapter gets into the details of how to configure, verify, and troubleshoot one particular FHRP: Cisco's Hot Standby Router Protocol (HSRP).

This chapter breaks the content into three major sections. The first looks at FHRP concepts, and introduces the three FHRP options: HSRP, Virtual Router Redundancy Protocol (VRRP), and Gateway Load Balancing Protocol (GLBP). The second section shows how to configure and verify HSRP, while the third section discusses how to troubleshoot HSRP.

"Do I Know This Already?" Quiz

Take the quiz (either here, or use the PCPT software) if you want to use the score to help you decide how much time to spend on this chapter. The answers are at the bottom of the page following the quiz, and the explanations are in DVD Appendix C and in the PCPT software.

Table 20-1 "Do I Know This Already?" Foundation Topics Section-to-Question Mapping

Foundation Topics Section	Questions
FHRP and HSRP Concepts	1–2
Implementing HSRP	3–5
Troubleshooting HSRP	6

1. R1 and R2 attach to the same Ethernet VLAN, with subnet 10.1.19.0/25, with addresses 10.1.19.1 and 10.1.19.2, respectively, configured with the **ip address** interface subcommand. Host A refers to 10.1.19.1 as its default router, and host B refers to 10.1.19.2 as its default router. The routers do not use an FHRP. Which of the following is a problem for this LAN?

   a. The design breaks IPv4 addressing rules, because two routers cannot connect to the same LAN subnet.

   b. If one router fails, neither host can send packets off-subnet.

   c. If one router fails, both hosts will use the one remaining router as a default router.

   d. If one router fails, the host that uses that router as a default router cannot send packets off-subnet.

2. R1 and R2 attach to the same Ethernet VLAN, with subnet 10.1.19.0/25, with addresses 10.1.19.1 and 10.1.19.2, respectively, configured with the **ip address** interface subcommand. The routers use an FHRP. Host A and host B attach to the same LAN and have correct default router settings per the FHRP configuration. Which of the following statements is true for this LAN?

   a. The design breaks IPv4 addressing rules, because two routers cannot connect to the same LAN subnet.

   b. If one router fails, neither host can send packets off-subnet.

   c. If one router fails, both hosts will use the one remaining router as a default router.

   d. If one router fails, only one of the two hosts will still be able to send packets off-subnet.

3. R1 and R2 attach to the same Ethernet VLAN, with subnet 10.1.19.0/25, with addresses 10.1.19.1 and 10.1.19.2, respectively, configured with the **ip address** interface subcommand. The routers use HSRP. The network engineer prefers to have R1 be the default router when both R1 and R2 are up. Which of the following is the likely default router setting for hosts in this subnet?

   a. 10.1.19.1

   b. 10.1.19.2

   c. Another IP address in subnet 10.1.19.0/25 other than 10.1.19.1 and 10.1.19.2

   d. A hostname that the FHRP mini-DNS will initially point to 10.1.19.1

4. The following text lists output taken from Router R3, which is using HSRP. Subnet 10.1.12.0 uses mask 255.255.255.0. Based on the output of this command, which of the following answers is true?

```
R3# show standby brief
Interface   Grp  Pri P State   Active   Standby      Virtual IP
Gi0/0        1   105   Active  local    10.1.12.1    10.1.12.2
```

   a. Hosts with a default router setting of 10.1.12.1 are sending their packets to Router R3.

   b. Hosts with a default router setting of 10.1.12.2 are sending their packets to Router R3.

   c. Router R3 has an **ip address 10.1.12.2 255.255.255.0** command configured on its G0/0 interface.

   d. Router R3 has an **ip address 10.1.12.1 255.255.255.0** command configured on its G0/0 interface.

5. Two routers, R1 and R2, are configured to be part of an HSRP group. R1's configuration includes the **standby 1 priority 1** command, and R2's configuration includes the **standby 1 priority 2** command. R1 powers up. An hour later, R2 powers up. Which of the following answers is true about which router is now the HSRP active router?

   a. R2 is active regardless of other configuration settings.

   b. R1 is active regardless of other configuration settings.

   c. R2 is active only if R2 is also configured with **standby 1 preempt**.

   d. R1 is active only if R1 is also configured with **no standby 1 preempt**.

6. Another engineer has configured HSRP on two routers that connect to the same LAN. You connect to the console of one of the routers, and see this log message:

```
*Mar  12 17:18:19.123: %IP-4-DUPADDR: Duplicate address 10.2.2.2 on
GigabitEthernet0/0, sourced by 0000.0c9f.f002
```

Which of the answers list an HSRP configuration mistake that would cause the router to list this message? (Choose two answers.)

   a. The two HSRP routers are configured with different HSRP group numbers.

   b. The local router is filtering all incoming HSRP messages.

   c. The two HSRP routers are configured with different HSRP version numbers.

   d. The two HSRP routers have configured different virtual IP addresses.

Foundation Topics

FHRP and HSRP Concepts

When networks use a design that includes redundant routers, switches, LAN links, and WAN links, in some cases other protocols are required to both take advantage of that redundancy and to prevent problems caused by it.

For instance, imagine a WAN with many remote branch offices. If each remote branch has two WAN links connecting it to the rest of the network, those routers can use an IP routing protocol to pick the best routes. The routing protocol learns routes over both WAN links, adding the best route into the routing table. When the better WAN link fails, the routing protocol adds the alternate route to the IP routing table, taking advantage of the redundant link.

As another example, consider a LAN with redundant links and switches, as discussed in Chapters 2, "Spanning Tree Protocol Concepts," and Chapter 3, "Spanning Tree Protocol Implementation," of this book. Those LANs have problems unless the switches use Spanning Tree Protocol (STP). STP prevents the problems created by frames that loop through those extra redundant paths in the LAN.

This chapter examines yet another type of protocol that helps when a network uses some redundancy, this time with redundant default routers. When two or more routers connect to the same LAN subnet, all those routers could be used as the default router for the hosts in the subnet. However, to make the best use of the redundant default routers, another protocol is needed. The term *First Hop Redundancy Protocol* (FHRP) refers to the category of protocols that can be used so that the hosts take advantage of redundant routers in a subnet.

This first major section of the chapter discusses the major concepts behind how different FHRPs work. This section begins by discussing a network's need for redundancy in general and the need for redundant default routers. It then shows how the three available FHRP options can each solve the problems that occur when using redundant default routers.

The Need for Redundancy in Networks

Networks need redundant links to improve the availability of the network. Eventually, something in the network will fail. A router power supply might fail, or a cable might break, or a switch might lose power. And those WAN links, drawn as simple lines in most drawings in this book, are actually the most complicated physical parts of the network, with many individual parts that can fail as well.

Depending on the design of the network, the failure of a single component might mean an outage that affects at least some part of the user population. Network engineers refer to any one component that, if it fails, brings down that part of the network as a *single point of failure*. For instance, in Figure 20-1, the LANs appear to have some redundancy, whereas the WAN does not. If most of the traffic flows between sites, many single points of failure exist, as shown in the figure.

The figure notes several components as a single point of failure. If any one of the noted parts of the network fails, packets cannot flow from the left side of the network to the right.

20

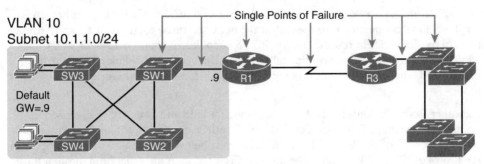

Figure 20-1 *R1 and the One WAN Link as Single Points of Failure*

Generally speaking, to improve availability the network engineer first looks at a design and finds the single points of failure. Then, the engineer chooses where to add to the network, so that one (or more) single points of failure now have redundant options, increasing availability. In particular, the engineer:

■ Adds redundant devices and links

■ Implements any necessary functions that take advantage of the redundant device or link

For instance, of all the single points of failure in Figure 20-1, the most expensive over the long term would likely be the WAN link, because of the ongoing monthly charge. However, statistically, the WAN links are the most likely component to fail. So, a reasonable upgrade from the network in Figure 20-1 would be to add a WAN link and possibly even connect to another router on the right side of the network, as shown in Figure 20-2.

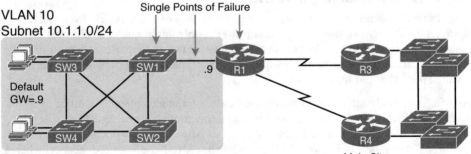
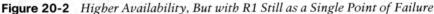

Figure 20-2 *Higher Availability, But with R1 Still as a Single Point of Failure*

Many real enterprise networks follow designs like Figure 20-2, with one router at each remote site, two WAN links connecting back to the main site, and redundant routers at the main site (on the right side of the figure). Compared to Figure 20-1, the design in Figure 20-2 has fewer single points of failure. Of the remaining single points of failure, a risk remains, but it is a calculated risk. For many outages, a reload of the router solves the problem, and the outage is short. But the risk still exists that the switch or router hardware fails completely and requires time to deliver a replacement device on-site before that site can work again.

For enterprises that can justify more expense, the next step in higher availability for that remote site is to protect against those catastrophic router and switch failures. In this particular design, adding one router on the left side of the network in Figure 20-2 removes all the single points of failure that had been noted earlier. Figure 20-3 shows the design with a second router, which connects to a different LAN switch so that SW1 is also no longer a single point of failure.

VLAN 10
Subnet 10.1.1.0/24

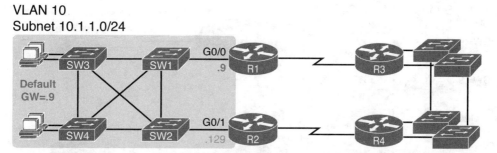

Figure 20-3 *Removing All Single Points of Failure from the Network Design*

> **NOTE** Medium to large enterprise networks work hard at striking a balance of high-availability features versus the available budget dollars. Cisco.com has many design documents that discuss trade-offs in high-availability design. If interested in learning more, search Cisco.com for "high availability campus network design."

The Need for a First Hop Redundancy Protocol

Now back to the topic of this chapter. Of the designs shown so far in this chapter, only Figure 20-3's design has two routers to support the LAN of the left side of the figure, specifically the same VLAN and subnet. While having the redundant routers on the same subnet helps, the network needs to use an FHRP when these redundant routers exist.

To see the need and benefit of using an FHRP, first think about how these redundant routers could be used as default routers by the hosts in VLAN 10/subnet 10.1.1.0/24, as shown in Figure 20-4. The host logic will remain unchanged, so each host has a single default router setting. So, some design options for default router settings include the following:

- All hosts in the subnet use R1 (10.1.1.9) as their default router, and they statically reconfigure their default router setting to R2's 10.1.1.129 if R1 fails.

- All hosts in the subnet use R2 (10.1.1.129) as their default router, and they statically reconfigure their default router setting to R1's 10.1.1.9 if R2 fails.

- Half the hosts use R1, and half use R2, as their default router, and if either router fails, that half of the users statically reconfigure their default router setting.

To make sure the concept is clear, Figure 20-4 shows this third option, with half the hosts using R1 and the other half using R2. The figure removes all the LAN switches just to unclutter the figure. Hosts A and B use R1 as their default router, and hosts C and D use R2 as their default router.

All of these options have a problem: The users have to take action. They have to know an outage occurred. They have to know how to reconfigure their default router setting. And they have to know when to change it back to the original setting.

FHRPs make this design work better. The two routers appear to be a single default router. The users never have to do anything: Their default router setting remains the same, and their ARP table even remains the same.

20

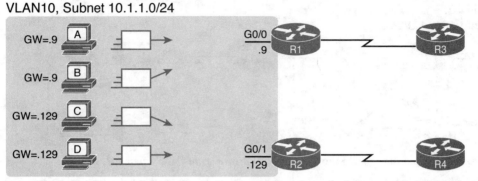

Figure 20-4   *Balancing Traffic by Assigning Different Default Routers to Different Clients*

To allow the hosts to remain unchanged, the routers have to do some more work, as defined by one of the FHRP protocols. Generically, each FHRP makes the following happen:

1.   All hosts act like they always have, with one default router setting that never has to change.

2.   The default routers share a virtual IP address in the subnet, defined by the FHRP.

3.   Hosts use the FHRP virtual IP address as their default router address.

4.   The routers exchange FHRP protocol messages, so that both agree as to which router does what work at any point in time.

5.   When a router fails, or has some other problem, the routers use the FHRP to choose which router takes over responsibilities from the failed router.

The Three Solutions for First-Hop Redundancy

The term *First Hop Redundancy Protocol* does not name any one protocol. Instead, it names a family of protocols that fill the same role. For a given network, like the left side of Figure 20-4, the engineer would pick one of the protocols from the FHRP family.

> **NOTE**   *First Hop* is a reference to the default router being the first router, or first router hop, through which a packet must pass.

Table 20-2 lists the three FHRP protocols in chronological order, based on when these were first used. Cisco first introduced the proprietary Hot Standby Router Protocol (HSRP), and it worked well for many of its customers. Later, the IETF developed an RFC for a very similar protocol, Virtual Router Redundancy Protocol (VRRP). Finally, Cisco developed a more robust option, Gateway Load Balancing Protocol (GLBP).

Table 20-2   Three FHRP Options

Acronym	Full Name	Origin	Redundancy Approach	Load Balancing
HSRP	Hot Standby Router Protocol	Cisco	Active/standby	Per subnet
VRRP	Virtual Router Redundancy Protocol	RFC 5798	Active/standby	Per subnet
GLBP	Gateway Load Balancing Protocol	Cisco	Active/active	Per host

This chapter focuses on HSRP and does not discuss VRRP and GLBP other than this brief mention. HSRP, the first of the three FHRP protocols to enter the market, remains a popular option in many networks. The next few pages walk through the concepts of how HSRP works. (Note that Appendix K contains a topic with more depth about GLBP, copied from an earlier edition of the book, if you are interested in reading more.)

HSRP Concepts

HSRP operates with an active/standby model (also more generally called *active/passive*). HSRP allows two (or more) routers to cooperate, all being willing to act as the default router. However, at any one time, only one router actively supports the end-user traffic. The packets sent by hosts to their default router flow to that one active router. Then, the other routers, with an HSRP standby state, sit there patiently waiting to take over should the active HSRP router have a problem.

The HSRP active router implements a virtual IP address and matching virtual MAC address. This virtual IP address exists as part of the HSRP configuration, which is an additional configuration item compared to the usual **ip address** interface subcommand. This virtual IP address is in the same subnet as the interface IP address, but it is a different IP address. The router then automatically creates the virtual MAC address. All the cooperating HSRP routers know these virtual addresses, but only the HSRP active router uses these addresses at any one point in time.

Hosts refer to the virtual IP address as their default router address, instead of any one router's interface IP address. For instance, in Figure 20-5, R1 and R2 use HSRP. The HSRP virtual IP address is 10.1.1.1, with the virtual MAC address referenced as VMAC1 for simplicity's sake.

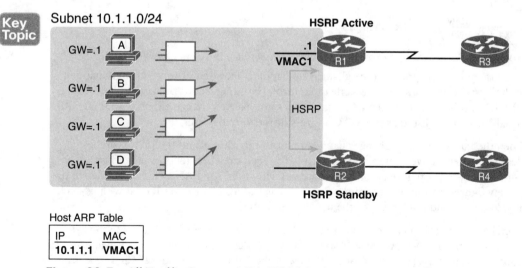

Figure 20-5 *All Traffic Goes to .1 (R1, Which Is Active); R2 Is Standby*

HSRP Failover

HSRP on each router has some work to do to make the network function as shown in Figure 20-5. The two routers need HSRP configuration, including the virtual IP address. The two routers send HSRP messages to each other to negotiate and decide which router should currently be active, and which should be standby. Then, the two routers continue to send messages to each other so that the standby router knows when the active router fails so that it can take over as the new active router.

Figure 20-6 shows the result when R1, the HSRP active router in Figure 20-5, fails. R1 quits using the virtual IP and MAC address, while R2, the new active router, starts using these addresses. The hosts do not need to change their default router settings at all, with traffic now flowing to R2 instead of R1.

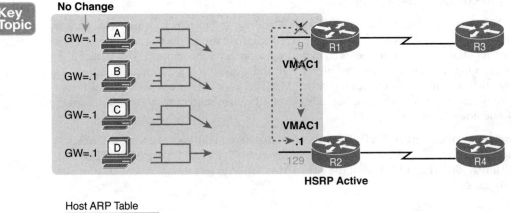

Figure 20-6 *Packets Sent Through R2 (New Active) Once It Takes Over for Failed R1*

When the failover happens, some changes do happen, but none of those changes happen on the hosts. The host keeps the same default router setting, set to the virtual IP address (10.1.1.1 in this case). The host's ARP table does not have to change either, with the HSRP virtual MAC being listed as the MAC address of the virtual router.

When the failover occurs, changes happen on both the routers and the LAN switches. Clearly, the new active router has to be ready to receive packets (encapsulated inside frames) using the virtual IP and MAC addresses. However, the LAN switches, hidden in the last few figures, formerly sent frames destined for VMAC1 to Router R1. Now the switches must know to send the frames to the new active router, R2.

To make the switches change their MAC address table entries for VMAC1, R2 sends an Ethernet frame with VMAC1 as the source MAC address. The switches, as normal, learn the source MAC address (VMAC1), but with new ports that point toward R2. The frame is also a LAN broadcast, so all the switches learn a MAC table entry for VMAC1 that leads toward R2. (By the way, this Ethernet frame holds an ARP Reply message, called a gratuitous ARP, because the router sends it without first receiving an ARP Request.)

HSRP Load Balancing

The active/standby model of HSRP means that in one subnet all hosts send their off-subnet packets through only one router. In other words, the routers do not share the workload, with one router handling all the packets. For instance, back in Figure 20-5, R1 was the active router, so all hosts in the subnet sent their packets through R1, and none of the hosts in the subnet sent their packets through R2.

HSRP does support load balancing by preferring different routers to be the active router in different subnets. Most sites that require a second router for redundancy are also big enough to use several VLANs and subnets at the site. The two routers will likely connect to all the VLANs, acting as the default router in each VLAN. HSRP then can be configured to prefer one router as active in one VLAN, and another router as active in another VLAN, balancing the traffic. Or you can configure multiple instances of HSRP in the same subnet (called multiple HSRP groups), preferring one router to be active in one group, and the other router to be preferred as active in another.

For instance, Figure 20-7 shows a redesigned LAN, now with two hosts in VLAN 1 and two hosts in VLAN 2. Both R1 and R2 connect to the LAN, and both use a VLAN trunking and router-on-a-stick (ROAS) configuration. Both routers use HSRP in each of the two subnets, supporting each other. However, on purpose, R1 has been configured so that it wins the negotiation to become HSRP active in VLAN 1, and R2 has been configured to win in VLAN 2.

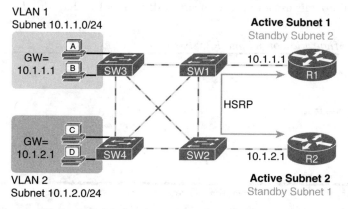

Figure 20-7 *Load Balancing with HSRP by Using Different Active Routers per Subnet*

Note that by having each router act as the HSRP active router in some subnets, the design makes use of both routers and both WAN links.

FHRPs are needed on any device that acts as a default router, which of course includes both traditional routers and Layer 3 switches. HSRP can be configured on routers and Layer 3 switches on interfaces that have IP addresses configured. However, in most cases, HSRP is used on interfaces to subnets that have hosts that need to use a default router. Those interfaces include router physical interfaces, router trunk subinterfaces, and Layer 3 switched Virtual interfaces (SVI).

> **NOTE**   This chapter refers to routers using HSRP, and shows examples on physical inter-faces, just to avoid having to repeatedly mention both routers and Layer 3 switches and the various interfaces. All concepts in this chapter about FHRPs and HSRP specifically apply to router physical interfaces, trunk subinterfaces, and SVIs.

Implementing HSRP

This second major section of this chapter shows the configuration for basic functions of HSRP, with the matching **show** commands. The goal of this section is to show enough of the operation of each tool to reinforce the concepts discussed in the first section.

Configuring and Verifying Basic HSRP

HSRP configuration requires only one command on the two (or more) routers that want to share default router responsibilities with HSRP: the **standby** *group* **ip** *virtual-ip* interface subcommand. The first value defines the HSRP group number, which must match on both routers. The group number lets one router support multiple HSRP groups at a time on the same interface, and it allows the routers to identify each other based on the group. The command also configures the virtual IP address shared by the routers in the same group; the virtual IP address is the address the hosts in the VLAN use as their default gateway.

Example 20-1 shows a configuration example, matching the HSRP examples related to Figures 20-5 and 20-6. Both routers use group 1, with virtual IP address 10.1.1.1, with the **standby 1 ip 10.1.1.1** interface subcommand.

Example 20-1   *HSRP Configuration on R1 and R2, Sharing IP Address 10.1.1.1*

```
R1# show running-config
! Lines omitted for brevity
interface GigabitEthernet0/0
 ip address 10.1.1.9 255.255.255.0
 standby version 2
 standby 1 ip 10.1.1.1
 standby 1 priority 110
 standby 1 name HSRP-group-for-book
! The following configuration, on R2, is identical except for the HSRP priority and
! the interface IP address
R2# show running-config
! Lines omitted for brevity
interface GigabitEthernet0/0
 ip address 10.1.1.129 255.255.255.0
 standby version 2
 standby 1 ip 10.1.1.1
 standby 1 name HSRP-group-for-book
```

The configuration shows other optional parameters, as well. For instance, R1 has a priority of 110 in this group, and R2 defaults to 100. With HSRP, if the two routers are brought up at the same time, the router with the higher priority wins the election to become the active router. The configuration also shows a name that can be assigned to the group (when using **show** commands) and a choice to use HSRP Version 2. (This chapter provides more details on these settings in the coming pages.)

Once configured, the two routers negotiate the HSRP settings and choose which router will currently be active and which will be standby. With the configuration as shown, R1 will win the election and become active because of its higher (better) priority. Both routers reach the same conclusion, as confirmed with the output of the **show standby brief** command on both R1 and R2 in Example 20-2.

Example 20-2 *HSRP Status on R1 and R2 with* **show standby brief**

```
! First, the group status as seen from R1
R1# show standby brief
                     P indicates configured to preempt.
                     |
Interface   Grp  Pri P State    Active        Standby      Virtual IP
Gi0/0        1   110   Active   local         10.1.1.129   10.1.1.1
! The output here on R2 shows that R2 agrees with R1.
R2# show standby brief
                     P indicates configured to preempt.
                     |
Interface   Grp  Pri P State    Active        Standby      Virtual IP
Gi0/0        1   100   Standby  10.1.1.9      local        10.1.1.1
```

The **show standby brief** command packs a lot of detail in the output, so take your time and work through the highlighted fields. First, look at the Grp column for each command. This lists the HSRP group number, so when looking at output from multiple routers, you need to look at the lines with the same group number to make sure the data relates to that one HSRP group. In this case, both routers have only one group number (1), so it is easy to find the information.

Each line of output lists the local router's view of the HSRP status for that group. In particular, based on the headings, the **show standby brief** command identifies the following:

Key Topic

Interface: The local router's interface on which the HSRP group is configured

Grp: The HSRP group number

Pri: The local router's HSRP priority

State: The local router's current HSRP state

Active: The interface IP address of the currently active HSRP router (or "local" if the local router is HSRP active)

Standby: The interface IP address of the currently standby HSRP router (or "local" if the local router is HSRP standby)

Virtual IP: The virtual IP address defined by this router for this group

For instance, following the highlighted text in Example 20-2, R2 believes that its own current state is standby, that the router with interface address 10.1.1.9 is active (which happens

20

to be Router R1), with a confirmation that the "local" router (R2, on which this command was issued) is the standby router.

In comparison, the **show standby** command (without the **brief** keyword) lists a more detailed description of the current state, while repeating many of the facts from the **show standby brief** command. Example 20-3 shows an example of the new information with the **show standby** command, listing several counters and timers about the HSRP protocol itself, plus the virtual MAC address 0000.0c9f.f001.

Example 20-3 *HSRP Status on R1 and R2 with* **show standby**

```
R1# show standby
GigabitEthernet0/0 - Group 1 (version 2)
  State is Active
    6 state changes, last state change 00:12:53
  Virtual IP address is 10.1.1.1
  Active virtual MAC address is 0000.0c9f.f001
    Local virtual MAC address is 0000.0c9f.f001 (v2 default)
  Hello time 3 sec, hold time 10 sec
    Next hello sent in 1.696 secs
  Preemption disabled
  Active router is local
  Standby router is 10.1.1.129, priority 100 (expires in 8.096 sec)
  Priority 110 (configured 110)
  Group name is "HSRP-group-for-book" (cfgd)
! The output here on R2 shows that R2 agrees with R1.
R2# show standby
GigabitEthernet0/0 - Group 1 (version 2)
  State is Standby
    4 state changes, last state change 00:12:05
  Virtual IP address is 10.1.1.1
  Active virtual MAC address is 0000.0c9f.f001
    Local virtual MAC address is 0000.0c9f.f001 (v2 default)
  Hello time 3 sec, hold time 10 sec
    Next hello sent in 0.352 secs
  Preemption disabled
  Active router is 10.1.1.9, priority 110 (expires in 9.136 sec)
    MAC address is 0200.0101.0101
  Standby router is local
  Priority 100 (default 100)
  Group name is "HSRP-group-for-book" (cfgd)
```

HSRP Active Role with Priority and Preemption

HSRP defines some rules to determine which router acts as the active HSRP router and which acts as standby. Those rules also define details about when a standby router should take over as active. The following list summarizes the rules; following the list, this section takes a closer look at those rules and the related configuration settings.

First, the HSRP rules. When a router (call it the local router) has an HSRP-enabled interface, and that interface comes up, the router sends HSRP messages to negotiate whether it should be active or standby. When it sends those messages, if it...

Step 1. ...discovers no other HSRP routers in the subnet, the local router becomes the active router.

Step 2. ...discovers an existing HSRP router, and both are currently negotiating to decide which should become the HSRP active router, the routers negotiate, with the router with the highest HSRP priority becoming the HSRP active router.

Step 3. ...discovers an existing HSRP router in the subnet, and that router is already acting as the active router:

A. If configured with no preemption (the default; **no standby preempt**), the local router becomes a standby router, even if it has a better (higher) priority.

B. If configured with preemption (**standby preempt**), the local router checks its priority versus the active router; if the local router priority is better (higher), the local router takes over (preempts) the existing active router to become the new active HSRP router.

Steps 1 and 2 in the list are pretty obvious, but Steps 3A and 3B could use a little closer look. For instance, the examples so far in this chapter show R1's G0/0 with a priority of 110 versus R2's G0/0 with priority 100. The **show** commands in Example 20-3 show that R1 is currently the HSRP active router. That same example also lists a line for both R1 and R2 that confirms "preemption disabled," which is the default.

To show a test of Step 3A logic, Example 20-4 shows a process by which R1's G0/0 interface is disabled and then enabled again, but after giving Router R2 long enough to take over and become active. That is, R1 comes up but R2 is already HSRP active for group 1. The bottom of the example lists output from the **show standby brief** command from R2, confirming that R2 becomes HSRP active and R1 becomes standby (10.1.1.9), proving that R1 does not preempt R2 in this case.

Example 20-4 *Showing How No Preemption Keeps R1 as Standby After R1 Recovers*

```
! First, R1's G0/0 is disabled and enabled; the ending log message shows a standby
! state.
R1# configure terminal
Enter configuration commands, one per line.  End with CNTL/Z.
R1(config)# interface gigabitEthernet 0/0
R1(config-if)# shutdown
*Mar  8 18:10:29.242: %HSRP-5-STATECHANGE: GigabitEthernet0/0 Grp 1 state Active ->
  Init
*Mar  8 18:10:31.205: %LINK-5-CHANGED: Interface GigabitEthernet0/0, changed state to
administratively down
*Mar  8 18:10:32.205: %LINEPROTO-5-UPDOWN: Line protocol on Interface GigabitEther
  net0/0, changed state to down
R1(config-if)#
R1(config-if)# no shutdown
```

```
R1(config-if)# ^Z
R1#
*Mar  8 18:11:08.355: %HSRP-5-STATECHANGE: GigabitEthernet0/0 Grp 1 state Speak ->
  Standby
```

```
! Now from R2, note R2 is active, and 10.1.1.9 (R1) is standby
R2# show standby brief
                      P indicates configured to preempt.
                      |
Interface   Grp  Pri P State   Active        Standby        Virtual IP
Gi0/1       1    100   Active  local         10.1.1.9       10.1.1.1
```

If R1 had been configured with preemption for that previous scenario, R1 would have taken over from R2 when R1's interface came back up. Example 20-5 shows exactly that. Before the output in Example 20-5 was gathered, the network had been put back to the same beginning state as at the beginning of Example 20-4, with R1 active and R2 as standby. Within Example 20-5, R1's interface is shut down, then configured with preemption using the **standby 1 preempt** command, enabling preemption. Then, after enabling the interface again, R1 takes over as HSRP active, as shown at the bottom of the example's **show standby brief** command from R2. That output now shows the local router's state as Standby, and the active as 10.1.1.9 (R1).

Example 20-5 *Showing How Preemption Causes R1 to Take over As Active upon Recovery*

```
! First, R1's G0/0 is disabled and enabled; the ending log message shows a standby
! state.
R1# configure terminal
Enter configuration commands, one per line.  End with CNTL/Z.
R1(config)# interface gigabitEthernet 0/0
R1(config-if)# shutdown
*Mar  8 18:10:29.242: %HSRP-5-STATECHANGE: GigabitEthernet0/0 Grp 1 state Active ->
  Init
*Mar  8 18:10:31.205: %LINK-5-CHANGED: Interface GigabitEthernet0/0, changed state to
administratively down
*Mar  8 18:10:32.205: %LINEPROTO-5-UPDOWN: Line protocol on Interface GigabitEther
  net0/0, changed state to down
R1(config-if)# standby 1 preempt
R1(config-if)# no shutdown
R1(config-if)# ^Z
R1#
*Mar  8 18:19:14.355: %HSRP-5-STATECHANGE: GigabitEthernet0/0 Grp 1 state Listen ->
  Active
```

```
! Now from R2, note it is active, and 10.1.1.9 (R1) is standby

*Mar  8 18:18:55.948: %HSRP-5-STATECHANGE: GigabitEthernet0/0 Grp 1 state Standby ->
  Active
*Mar  8 18:19:14.528: %HSRP-5-STATECHANGE: GigabitEthernet0/0 Grp 1 state Active ->
  Speak
*Mar  8 18:19:26.298: %HSRP-5-STATECHANGE: GigabitEthernet0/0 Grp 1 state Speak ->
  Standby
```

```
R2# show standby brief
                  P indicates configured to preempt.
                  |
Interface   Grp  Pri P State    Active        Standby      Virtual IP
Gi0/0       1    100   Standby 10.1.1.9       local        10.1.1.1
```

Note that it is the preemption setting on the router that is taking over (preempting) that determines if preemption happens. For instance, in this case, R1 came up when R2 was active; R1 was set to preempt; so R1 preempted R2.

HSRP Versions

Cisco IOS on routers and Layer 3 switches supports two versions of HSRP: versions 1 and 2. The versions have enough differences, like multicast IP addresses used and message formats, so that routers in the same HSRP group must use the same version. If two routers configured to be in the same HSRP group mistakenly configure to use different versions, they will not understand each other and ignore each other for the purposes of HSRP.

To configure the version, each interface/subinterface uses the **standby version** {1 | 2} interface subcommand. Note that the HSRP group number is not included in the command, because it sets the version for all HSRP messages sent out that interface/subinterface.

There are some good reasons to want to use the more recent HSRP version 2 (HSRPv2). For example, HSRPv1 existed before IPv6 became popular. Cisco enhanced HSRP to version 2 in part to make IPv6 support possible. Today, to use HSRP with IPv6 requires HSRPv2.

As another example of a benefit of HSRPv2, HSRP uses a Hello message, similar in concept to routing protocols, so that HSRP group members can realize when the active router is no longer reachable. HSRPv2 allows for shorter Hello timer configuration (as low as a small number of milliseconds), while HSRPv1 typically had a minimum of 1 second. So, HSRPv2 can be configured to react more quickly to failures with a lower Hello timer.

Beyond IPv6 support and shorter Hello timer options, other differences for version 2 versus version 1 include a different virtual MAC address base value and a different multicast IP address used as the destination for all messages. Table 20-3 lists the differences between HSRPv1 and HSRPv2.

Key Topic

Table 20-3   HSRPv1 Versus HSRPv2

Feature	Version 1	Version 2
IPv6 support	No	Yes
Smallest unit for Hello timer	Second	Millisecond
Range of group numbers	0..255	0..4095
MAC address used (xx or xxx is the hex group number)	0000.0C07.ACxx	0000.0C9F.Fxxx
IPv4 multicast address used	224.0.0.2	224.0.0.102
Does protocol use a unique identifier for each router?	No	Yes

20

Of the details in the table, make sure to look at the MAC addresses for both versions 1 and 2. Cisco reserves the prefixes of 0000.0C07.AC for HSRPv1 and 0000.0C9F.F for HSRPv2. HSRPv1, with 256 possible HSRP groups per interface, then uses the last two hex digits to identify the HSRP group. For example, an HSRP group 1 using version 1 would use a virtual MAC address that ends in hex 01. Similarly, because HSRPv2 supports 4096 groups per interface, the MAC address reserves three hex digits to identify the group. An HSRP group 1 using version 2 would use a virtual MAC address that ends in hex 001.

Troubleshooting HSRP

Troubleshooting HSRP follows some familiar themes in this book as far as the types of activities you should prepare to do. First, you need to master the configuration details so you can know when the configuration is correct or incorrect. As part of that, you need to be ready to figure out the configuration based on **show** commands other than the **show running-config** command; you need to be able to reverse engineer the configuration based on other **show** commands as much as possible.

Additionally, you should have a good idea of which HSRP configuration settings need to match on the routers in the same HSRP group. And it always helps to know what the **show** command output would look like when some common configuration mistakes are made.

Checking HSRP Configuration

First, for the issue of determining the configuration, take another moment to think about the output of the **show standby** command, but now with the goal of re-creating the configuration in mind. To that end, Example 20-6 repeats the configuration of Router R1 from the running example used throughout this chapter. It also repeats the same **show standby** command output from Example 20-3. In this new example, highlighted comments in the **show** command output list the matching configuration command on which the output is based.

Example 20-6 *Finding HSRP Configuration in the* **show standby** *Command Output*

```
! First, the configuration of the HSRP group:
interface GigabitEthernet0/0
 ip address 10.1.1.9 255.255.255.0
 standby version 2
 standby 1 ip 10.1.1.1
 standby 1 priority 110
 standby 1 name HSRP-group-for-book

! Next, the show standby command output
R1# show standby
GigabitEthernet0/0 - Group 1 (version 2)            ! standby version 2
  State is Active
    6 state changes, last state change 00:12:53
  Virtual IP address is 10.1.1.1                     ! standby 1 ip 10.1.1.1
  Active virtual MAC address is 0000.0c9f.f001
    Local virtual MAC address is 0000.0c9f.f001 (v2 default)
  Hello time 3 sec, hold time 10 sec
    Next hello sent in 1.696 secs
```

```
Preemption disabled                                    ! no standby 1 preempt
 (default)
Active router is local
Standby router is 10.1.1.129, priority 100 (expires in 8.096 sec)
Priority 110 (configured 110)                          ! standby 1 priority 110
Group name is "HSRP-group-for-book" (cfgd)             ! standby 1 name HSRP-group-for-book
```

If you work through the comments on the far right of the **show** command output (comments that begin with a !), you can mentally connect the concepts on that same line of **show** command output with the four **standby** configuration commands at the top of the example.

Next, for HSRP to work correctly, some of the HSRP parameters must match. For instance, if two routers were intended to be in the same HSRP group, but were configured with two different HSRP versions, they would not understand each other's messages, and would ignore each other, and would act independently from each other. The following list details some important items to check to make sure the configurations should work:

- Routers must be configured with the same HSRP version (**standby version** {1 | 2})
- Routers must be configured with the same HSRP group number (**standby** *number* ...).
- Routers must configure the same virtual IP address (**standby** *number* **ip** *address*).
- Virtual IP address must be (a) in the same subnet as the interface IP address and (b) not used by any other device in the subnet (including the other HSRP routers) (**standby** *number* **ip** *address*).
- In the attached Layer 2 network, the interfaces on the routers or Layer 3 switches must be in the same VLAN.
- No ACLs should filter HSRP messages between the two routers. (HSRP uses UDP, port 1985; version 1 sends to multicast address 224.0.0.2, while version 2 sends to 224.0.0.102.)

Symptoms of HSRP Misconfiguration

IOS cannot detect several configuration mistakes that vary from the good configuration suggestions in the previous list. So, think about what a good configuration would look like, and then imagine purposefully misconfiguring a single item. What would the symptoms be? Table 20-4 lists four such purposeful configuration mistakes. Each assumes that only one mistake is made. Following the table, the chapter takes a closer look at each.

Table 20-4   HSRP Misconfiguration Scenarios and Expected Results

Reference Number	Scenario	Routers Both Become Active?	Duplicate Address Detected?	VIP Changes Depending on Active Router?
1	HSRP version mismatch	Yes	Yes	N/A
2	HSRP group number mismatch	Yes	Yes	N/A
3	ACL blocks HSRP packets	Yes	No	N/A
4	Routers configure different VIPs	No	N/A	Yes

For example, consider item 1 in the table, with an HSRP version mismatch. Example 20-7 shows what happens, using the same design and configuration shown throughout this chapter, starting with the configuration in Example 20-1. As shown in Example 20-7, R1's HSRP version is changed to version 1, while R2's remains as version 2.

Example 20-7 *Misconfiguration Scenario: HSRP Routers Use Different HSRP Version*

```
! R1's HSRP version formerly matched R2's version 2. Below, R1 begins to use V1.
R1# configure terminal
Enter configuration commands, one per line.  End with CNTL/Z.
R1(config)# interface gigabitEthernet 0/0
R1(config-if)# standby version 1
R1(config-if)# ^Z
R1#
*Mar  9 17:53:43.275: %HSRP-5-STATECHANGE: GigabitEthernet0/0 Grp 1 state Active ->
  Init
*Mar  9 17:54:06.348: %HSRP-5-STATECHANGE: GigabitEthernet0/0 Grp 1 state Standby ->
  Active
*Mar  9 17:54:06.377: %IP-4-DUPADDR: Duplicate address 10.1.1.1 on GigabitEthernet0/0,
  sourced by 0000.0c9f.f001
*Mar  9 17:54:36.425: %IP-4-DUPADDR: Duplicate address 10.1.1.1 on GigabitEthernet0/0,
  sourced by 0000.0c9f.f001


R1# show standby brief
                   P indicates configured to preempt.
                   |
Interface   Grp  Pri P State  Active    Standby      Virtual IP
Gi0/0       1    100   Active  local     unknown      10.1.1.1
! next lines are from R2; R2 remains as HSRP version 2; R2 also acts as active
*Mar  9 17:53:38.618: %HSRP-5-STATECHANGE: GigabitEthernet0/0 Grp 1 state Standby ->
  Active
*Mar  9 17:54:01.724: %IP-4-DUPADDR: Duplicate address 10.1.1.1 on GigabitEthernet0/0,
  sourced by 0000.0c07.ac01


R2# show standby brief
                   P indicates configured to preempt.
                   |
Interface   Grp  Pri P State  Active    Standby      Virtual IP
Gi0/0       1    100   Active  local     unknown      10.1.1.1
```

Working through Example 20-7, as soon as the version changes to version 1 on R1, R1 starts sending HSRPv1 messages, stops sending HSRPv2 messages, and ignores incoming HSRPv2 messages from R2. Both R1 and R2 begin to act independently. As you can see from the log messages and the **show standby brief** command output from both routers, both become active, and neither knows of another router that acts as standby. Basically, they ignore each other.

Continuing in Example 20-7, because both routers are active, both attempt to make use of the same virtual IP address 10.1.1.1. However, because both use a different HSRP version, they use different MAC addresses. Each router notices the duplicate use of the same virtual IP address, and begins to issue log messages like the highlighted message in the example.

Working through the items in Table 20-4, number 2, the configuration of mismatched HSRP group numbers results in much the same results as shown in Example 20-7. The two routers do not attempt to work together. Both become active in their respective HSRP group, both try to use the same virtual IP address, and both notice the duplicate use of the virtual IP address, issuing log messages to that effect.

As for item 3, an inbound ACL on either router can filter HSRP traffic. HSRP messages use the local interface IP address as the source IP address. The destination address is either 224.0.0.2 (for version 1) or 224.0.0.102 (for version 2). Also, HSRP uses UDP port 1985. So, any ACL that happens to deny HSRP inbound would make the two routers again act independently. Often that also means that the routers do not notice use of duplicate IP addresses either.

Finally, for item 4, with the two routers configuring two different IP addresses to use as the virtual IP address, much different results occur. That is, if that is the only configuration mistake, both routers send and receive HSRP messages and choose the active and standby routers correctly. The active router uses the virtual IP address defined on the active router. But if that router fails, and the other router becomes active, that second router uses its different virtual IP address. Basically, the virtual IP address changes based on which router is active. As a result, devices that refer to one of the VIPs will only work when the matching router is active.

Chapter Review

One key to doing well on the exams is to perform repetitive spaced review sessions. Review this chapter's material using either the tools in the book, DVD, or interactive tools for the same material found on the book's companion website. Refer to the "Your Study Plan" element for more details. Table 20-5 outlines the key review elements and where you can find them. To better track your study progress, record when you completed these activities in the second column.

Table 20-5   Chapter Review Tracking

Review Element	Review Date(s)	Resource Used
Review key topics		Book, DVD/website
Review key terms		Book, DVD/website
Answer DIKTA questions		Book, PCPT
Do labs		Blog
Review memory tables		Book, DVD/website
Review command tables		Book

Review All the Key Topics

Key Topic

Table 20-6 Key Topics for Chapter 20

Key Topic Element	Description	Page Number
List	Common characteristics of all FHRPs	550
Figure 20-5	HSRP concepts	551
Figure 20-6	HSRP failover results	552
List	Interpretation of the output from the **show standby brief** command	555
List	HSRP preemption rules	557
Table 20-3	HSRP version differences	559
List	HSRP configuration setting that should match between routers in the same HSRP group	561
Table 20-4	HSRP misconfiguration scenarios and symptoms	561

Key Terms You Should Know

single point of failure, First Hop Redundancy Protocol (FHRP), Hot Standby Router Protocol (HSRP), Virtual Router Redundancy Protocol (VRRP), Gateway Load Balancing Protocol (GLBP), virtual IP address, virtual MAC address, HSRP active, HSRP standby

Command References

Tables 20-7 and 20-8 list configuration and verification commands used in this chapter. As an easy review exercise, cover the left column in a table, read the right column, and try to recall the command without looking. Then repeat the exercise, covering the right column, and try to recall what the command does.

Table 20-7 Chapter 20 Configuration Command Reference

Command	Description
standby *group-number* **ip** *virtual-ip*	Interface subcommand that enables HSRP, defines a virtual IP address, and associates it with a particular HSRP group.
standby *group-number* **priority** *0...255*	Interface subcommand that configures a priority, influencing which router becomes the active HSRP router. The higher number wins, with a default of 100. This command associates the setting with a particular HSRP group.
[no] **standby** *group-number* **preempt**	Interface subcommand that enables preemption (or disables if using the **no** version of the command).
standby *group-number* **name** *descriptive-name*	Interface subcommand that defines a name and associates it with a particular HSRP group.
**standby version 1	2**	Interface subcommand that sets the HSRP version used for all groups on the interface.

Table 20-8   Chapter 20 EXEC Command Reference

Command	Description
show standby	Lists details about HSRP status, including the virtual IP address, currently active and standby routers, virtual MAC addresses, and counters.
show standby brief	Lists a single line of status information for each HSRP group, with the currently active and standby routers and virtual IP address.

20

CHAPTER 21

Troubleshooting IPv4 Routing

This chapter covers the following exam topics:

5.0 Infrastructure Maintenance

5.6 Troubleshoot basic Layer 3 end-to-end connectivity issues

This chapter examines how to troubleshoot the IPv4 data plane. These topics form the foundation of how IP works: a host's logic and how that logic is impacted by its IPv4 settings, how those settings must match with the default router, how routers forward packets, and how the IP addressing plan can cause problems.

Note that the ICND1 book discusses these topics in depth—in fact, this very chapter exists in the ICND1 book as Chapter 24, "Troubleshooting IPv4 Routing." This chapter in the ICND2 book is identical in that all the words, figures, examples, and tables are the same; the items may appear in slightly different places on the page due to how the publishing process lays out the items on the pages.

The topics in this chapter exist in both the ICND1 and ICND2 book for a couple of reasons. First, the ICND2 exam topics list one specific exam topic that focuses on IPv4 data plane troubleshooting, and this chapter discusses most of those issues (with other issues like ACL troubleshooting discussed in other chapters). Beyond that, all IPv4 troubleshooting in both the ICND1 and ICND2 books rely on the kind of fundamental IPv4 data plane troubleshooting skills shown in this chapter.

So, if you have both books, there is no need to read and understand both ICND1 Chapter 24 and this chapter; they are indeed the same. But even if you read this chapter a while back when you read the ICND1 book, please take the time to review at least the key topics throughout the chapter, as noted with the Key Topic icons in the margins. Or, use the Key Topic review application on the book's DVD or website.

"Do I Know This Already?" Quiz

A few of the troubleshooting chapters in this book serve both to discuss troubleshooting of the topics, and to serve as a tool to summarize and review some important topics. This chapter is one of those chapters. As a result, it is useful to read these chapters regardless of your current knowledge level; so this chapter does not include a "Do I Know This Already?" quiz. However, if you feel particularly confident about troubleshooting IPv4 routing features covered in this book, feel free to move to the "Chapter Review" section near the end of this chapter to bypass the majority of the chapter.

Foundation Topics

Problems Between the Host and the Default Router

Imagine that you work as a customer support representative (CSR) fielding calls from users about problems. A user left a message stating that he couldn't connect to a server. You could not reach him when you called back, so you did a series of pings from that host's default router. At the end of those pings, you think the problem exists somewhere between the user's device and the default router—for instance, between Router R1 and host A, as shown in Figure 21-1.

Figure 21-1 *Focus of the Discussions in This Section of the Chapter*

This first major section of the chapter focuses on problems that can occur on hosts, their default routers, and between the two. To begin, this section looks at the host itself, and its four IPv4 settings, as listed in the figure. Following that, the discussion moves to the default router, with focus on the LAN interface, and the settings that must work for the router to serve as a host's default router.

Root Causes Based on a Host's IPv4 Settings

A typical IPv4 host gets its four key IPv4 settings in one of two ways: either through static configuration or by using Dynamic Host Configuration Protocol (DHCP). In both cases, the settings can actually be incorrect. Clearly, any static settings can be set to a wrong number just through human error when typing the values. More surprising is the fact that the DHCP can set the wrong values: The DHCP process can work, but with incorrect values configured at the DHCP server, the host can actually learn some incorrect IPv4 settings.

This section first reviews the settings on the host, and what they should match, followed by a discussion of typical issues.

Ensure IPv4 Settings Correctly Match

Once an engineer thinks that a problem exists somewhere between a host and its default router, the engineer should review the host's IPv4 settings versus the intended settings. That process begins by guiding the user through the graphical user interface (GUI) of the host operating system or by using command-line commands native to host operating systems, such as **ipconfig** and **ifconfig**. This process should uncover obvious issues, like completely missing parameters, or if using DHCP, the complete failure of DHCP to learn any of the IPv4 settings.

If the host has all its settings, the next step is to check the values to match them with the rest of the internetwork. The Domain Name System (DNS) server IP address—usually a list of at least two addresses—should match the DNS server addresses actually used in the internetwork. The rest of the settings should be compared to the correct LAN interface on the router that is used as this host's default router. Figure 21-2 collects all the pieces that should match, with some explanation to follow.

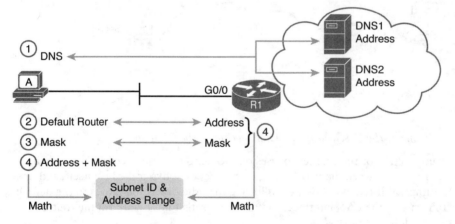

Figure 21-2 *Host IPv4 Settings Compared to What the Settings Should Match*

As numbered in the figure, these steps should be followed to check the host's IPv4 settings:

Step 1. Check the host's list of DNS server addresses against the actual addresses used by those servers.

Step 2. Check the host's default router settings against the router's LAN interface configuration, for the **ip address** command.

Step 3.   Check the subnet mask used by the router and the host; if they use a different mask, the subnets will not exactly match, which will cause problems for some host addresses.

Step 4.   The host and router should attach to the exact same subnet—same subnet ID and same range of IP addresses. So, use both the router's and host's IP address and mask, calculate the subnet ID and range of addresses, and confirm they are in the same subnet as the subnet implied by the address/mask of the router's **ip address** command.

If an IPv4 host configuration setting is missing, or simply wrong, checking these settings can quickly uncover the root cause. For instance, if you can log in to the router and do a **show interfaces G0/0** command, and then ask the user to issue an **ipconfig /all** (or similar) command and read the output to you, you can compare all the settings in Figure 21-2.

However, although checking the host settings is indeed very useful, some problems related to hosts are not so easy to spot. The next few topics walk through some example problems to show some symptoms that occur when some of these less obvious problems occur.

Mismatched Masks Impact Route to Reach Subnet

A host and its default router should agree about the range of addresses in the subnet. Sometimes, people are tempted to skip over this check, ignoring the mask either on the host or the router and assuming that the mask used on one device must be the same mask as on the other device. However, if the host and router have different subnet mask values, and therefore each calculates a different range of addresses in the subnet, problems happen.

To see one such example, consider the network in Figure 21-3. Host A has IP address/mask 10.1.1.9/24, with default router 10.1.1.150. Some quick math puts 10.1.1.150—the default router address—inside host A's subnet, right? Indeed it does, and it should. Host A's math for this subnet reveals subnet ID 10.1.1.0, with a range of addresses from 10.1.1.1 through 10.1.1.254, and subnet broadcast address 10.1.1.255.

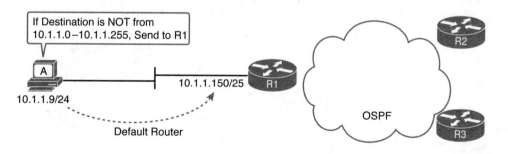

Figure 21-3   *Mismatched Subnet Calculations Appear to Work*

In this case, the host routing of packets, to destinations outside the subnet, works well. However, the reverse direction, from the rest of the network back toward the host, does not. A quick check of Router R1's configuration reveals the IP address/mask as shown in Figure 21-3, which results in the connected route for subnet 10.1.1.128/25, as shown in Example 21-1.

Example 21-1 *R1's IP Address, Mask, Plus the Connected Subnet That Omits Host A's Address*

```
R1# show running-config interface g0/0
Building configuration...

Current configuration: 185 bytes
!
interface GigabitEthernet0/0
 description LAN at Site 1
 mac-address 0200.0101.0101
 ip address 10.1.1.150 255.255.255.128
 ip helper-address 10.1.2.130
 duplex auto
 speed auto
end

R1# show ip route connected
! Legend omitted for brevity

      10.0.0.0/8 is variably subnetted, 9 subnets, 4 masks
C        10.1.1.128/25 is directly connected, GigabitEthernet0/0
L        10.1.1.150/32 is directly connected, GigabitEthernet0/0
! Other routes omitted for brevity
```

Because of this particular mismatch, R1's view of the subnet puts host A (10.1.1.9) outside R1's view of the subnet (10.1.1.128/25, range 10.1.1.129 to 10.1.1.254). R1 adds a connected route for subnet 10.1.1.128/25 into R1's routing table, and even advertises this route (with Open Shortest Path First [OSPF] in this case) to the other routers in the network, as shown in Figure 21-4. All the routers know how to route packets to subnet 10.1.1.128/25, but unfortunately that route does not include host A's 10.1.1.9 IP address.

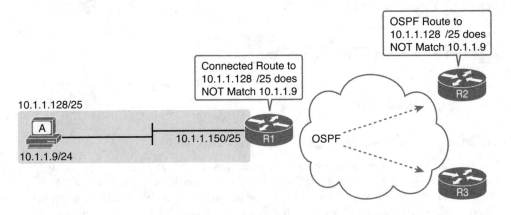

Figure 21-4 *Routers Have No Route That Matches Host A's 10.1.1.9 Address*

Hosts should use the same subnet mask as the default router, and the two devices should agree as to what subnet exists on their common LAN. Otherwise, problems may exist immediately, as in this example, or they might not exist until other hosts are added later.

Typical Root Causes of DNS Problems

When a host lists the wrong IP addresses for the DNS servers, the symptoms are somewhat obvious: Any user actions that require name resolution fail. Assuming that the only problem is the incorrect DNS setting, any network testing with commands like **ping** and **traceroute** fails when using names, but it works when using IP addresses instead of names.

When a ping of another host's hostname fails, but a ping of that same host's IP address works, some problem exists with DNS. For example, imagine a user calls the help desk complaining that he cannot connect to Server1. The CSR issues a **ping server1** command from the CSR's own PC, which both works and identifies the IP address of Server1 as 1.1.1.1. Then the CSR asks the user to try two commands from the user's PC: both a **ping Server1** command (which fails), and a **ping 1.1.1.1** command (which works). Clearly, the DNS name resolution process on the user's PC is having some sort of problem.

This book does not go into much detail about how DNS truly works behind the scenes, but even with a basic analysis, two major types of potential DNS issues are obvious:

- A user host (DNS client) that has an incorrect setting for the DNS server IP address(es)
- An IP connectivity problem between the user's host and the correct DNS server

Although the first problem may be more obvious, note that it can happen both with static settings on the host and with DHCP. If a host lists the wrong DNS server IP address, and the setting is static, just change the setting. If the wrong DNS server address is learned with DHCP, you need to examine the DHCP server configuration. (If using the IOS DHCP server feature, you make this setting with the **dns-server** *server-address* command in DHCP pool mode.)

The second bullet point brings up an important issue for troubleshooting any real-world networking problem. Most every real user application uses names, not addresses, and most hosts use DNS to resolve names. So, every connection to a new application involves two sets of packets: packets that flow between the host and the DNS server, and packets that flow between the host and the real server, as shown in Figure 21-5.

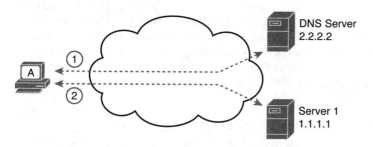
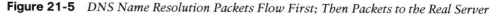

Figure 21-5 *DNS Name Resolution Packets Flow First; Then Packets to the Real Server*

Finally, before leaving the topic of name resolution, note that the router can be configured with the IP addresses of the DNS servers, so that router commands will attempt to resolve names. For instance, a user of the router command-line interface (CLI) could issue a command **ping server1** and rely on a DNS request to resolve server1 into its matching IP address. To configure a router to use a DNS for name resolution, the router needs the **ip name-server** *dns1-address dns2-address...* global command. It also needs the **ip domain-lookup** global command, which is enabled by default.

For troubleshooting, it can be helpful to set a router or switch DNS settings to match that of the local hosts. However, note that these settings have no impact on the user DNS requests.

> **NOTE**   On a practical note, IOS defaults with the **ip domain-lookup** command, but with no DNS IP address known. Most network engineers either add the configuration to point to the DNS servers or disable DNS using the **no ip domain-lookup** command.

Wrong Default Router IP Address Setting

Clearly, having a host that lists the wrong IP address as its default router causes problems. Hosts rely on the default router when sending packets to other subnets, and if a host lists the wrong default router setting, the host may not be able to send packets to a different subnet.

Figure 21-6 shows just such an example. In this case, hosts A and B both misconfigure 10.1.3.4 as the default router due to the same piece of bad documentation. Router R3 uses IP address 10.1.3.3. (For the sake of discussion, assume that no other host or router in this subnet currently uses address 10.1.3.4.)

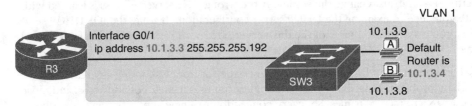

Figure 21-6   *Incorrect Default Router Setting on Hosts A and B*

In this case, several functions do work. For instance, hosts A and B can send packets to other hosts on the same LAN. The CSR at the router CLI can issue a **ping 10.1.3.9** and **ping 10.1.3.8** command, and both work. As a result of those two working pings, R3 would list the MAC address of the two PCs in the output of the **show arp** command. Similarly, the hosts would list R3's 10.1.3.3 IP address (and matching MAC address) in their ARP caches (usually displayed with the **arp –a** command). The one big problem in this case happens when the hosts try to send packets off-subnet. In that case, try to send the packets to IP address 10.1.3.4 next, which fails.

Root Causes Based on the Default Router's Configuration

Hosts must have correct IPv4 settings to work properly, but having correct settings does not guarantee that a LAN-based host can successfully send a packet to the default router. The LAN between the host and the router must work. In addition, the router itself must be working correctly, based on the design of the internetwork.

This next topic looks at problems between hosts and their default router, focusing on two problem areas. First, the text examines typical DHCP issues, followed by a discussion of router interfaces and what causes that interface to fail.

DHCP Issues

Hosts that use DHCP to lease an IP address, and learn other settings, rely on the network to pass the DHCP messages. In particular, if the internetwork uses a centralized DHCP server, with many remote LAN subnets using the centralized DHCP server, the routers have to enable a feature called *DHCP Relay* to make DHCP work. Without DHCP Relay, DHCP requests from hosts never leave the local LAN subnet.

Figure 21-7 shows some of the big ideas behind how DHCP Relay works. In this example, a DHCP client (Host A) sits on the left, with the DHCP server (172.16.2.11) on the right. The client begins the DHCP lease process by sending a DHCP Discover message, one that would flow only across the local LAN without DHCP Relay configured on Router R1. To be ready to forward the Discover message, R1 enables DHCP Relay with the **ip helper-address 172.16.2.11** command configured under its G0/0 interface.

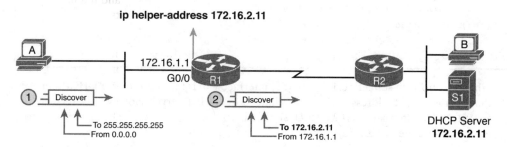

Figure 21-7 *IP Helper Address Effect*

The steps in the figure point out the need for DHCP Relay. At Step 1, host A sends a message, with destination IP and L2 broadcast address of 255.255.255.255 and ff:ff:ff:ff:ff:ff, respectively. Packets sent to this IP address, the "local subnet broadcast address," should never be forwarded past the router. All devices on the subnet receive and process the frame. In addition, because of the **ip helper-address** command configured on R1, Router R1 will continue to de-encapsulate the frame and packet to identify that it is a DHCP request and take action. Step 2 shows the results of DHCP Relay, where R1 changes both the source and destination IP address, with R1 routing the packet to the address listed in the command: 172.16.2.11.

The following troubleshooting checklist gives us a place to start when troubleshooting DHCP-related issues:

Key Topic

Step 1.   If using a centralized DHCP server, at least one router on each remote subnet that has DHCP clients must act as DHCP relay agent, and have a correctly configured **ip helper-address** *address* subcommand on the interface connected to that subnet.

Step 2.   Troubleshoot for any IP connectivity issues between the DHCP relay agent and the DHCP server, using the relay agent interface IP address and the server IP address as the source and destination of the packets.

Step 3. Whether using a local DHCP server or centralized server, troubleshoot for any LAN issues between the DHCP client and the DHCP relay agent.

Step 4. Troubleshoot incorrect server configuration.

Also, if the configuration includes the **ip helper-address** command but lists the wrong DHCP server IP address, again DHCP fails completely.

For instance, Example 21-2 shows an updated configuration for ROAS on Router R3, based on the same scenario as in Figure 21-7. The router configuration works fine for supporting IPv4 and making the router reachable. However, only one subinterface happens to list an **ip helper-address** command.

Example 21-2 *Forgetting to Support DHCP Relay on a ROAS Subinterface*

```
interface GigabitEthernet0/1
 ip address 10.1.3.3 255.255.255.192
 ip helper-address 10.1.2.130
!
interface GigabitEthernet0/1.2
 encapsulation dot1q 2
 ip address 10.1.3.65 255.255.255.192
! There is no ip helper-address command on this subinterface!
```

In this case, hosts in subnet 10.1.3.0/26 (off interface G0/1) that want to use DHCP can, assuming the host at address 10.1.2.130 is indeed the DHCP server. However, hosts in subnet 10.1.3.64/26 (off subinterface G0/1.2) will fail to learn settings with DHCP because of the lack of an **ip helper-address** command.

The second step in the checklist begs for the use of an extended **ping** or extended **traceroute** command. Remember, the DHCP relay agent changes the source and destination IP address of the original DHCP request, using the relay agent interface IP address as the source. Figure 21-8 shows an example, with the DHCP relay agent interface as 172.16.1.1 and the server at 172.16.2.11. From the relay agent router's CLI (Router R1), an extended ping of 172.16.2.11, using R1's G0/1 IP address of 172.16.1.1 as the source addresses, would use those exact same IP addresses.

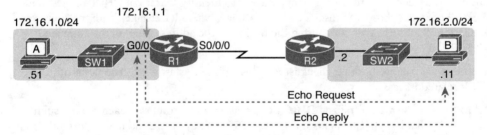

Figure 21-8 *IP Helper Address Effect*

As for Steps 3 and 4 in the list of DHCP relay agent troubleshooting tips, the next topic looks at the issues related to Step 3, focusing on interfaces on the local LAN. As for Step 4, which focuses on DHCP server misconfiguration, the ICND1 book's Chapter 20, "DHCP and IP Networking on Hosts," discusses server configuration issues in depth.

Router LAN Interface and LAN Issues

At some point, the problem isolation process may show that a host cannot ping its default router and vice versa. That is, neither device can send an IP packet to the other device on the same subnet. This basic test tells the engineer that the router, host, and LAN between them, for whatever reasons, cannot pass the packet encapsulated in an Ethernet frame between the two devices.

The root causes for this basic LAN connectivity issue fall into two categories:

■ Problems that cause the router LAN interface to fail
■ Problems with the LAN itself

A router's LAN interface must be in a working state before the router will attempt to send packets out that interface (or receive packets in that interface). Specifically, the router LAN interface must be in an up/up state; if in any other state, the router will not use the interface for packet forwarding. So, if a ping from the router to a LAN host fails (or vice versa), check the interface status, and if it's not up, find the root cause for the router interface to not be up.

Alternatively, the router interface can be in an up/up state, but problems can exist in the LAN itself. In this case, every topic related to Ethernet LANs may be a root cause. In particular, LAN details such as Ethernet cable pinouts, port security, and even Spanning Tree Protocol, may be root causes of LAN issues.

For instance, in Figure 21-9, Router R3 connects to a LAN with four switches. R3's LAN interface (G0/1) can reach an up/up state if the link from R3 to SW1 works. However, many other problems could prevent R3 from successfully sending an IP packet, encapsulated in an Ethernet frame, to the hosts attached to switches SW3 and SW4.

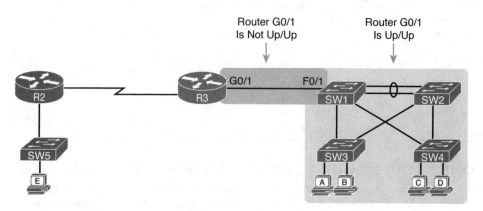

Figure 21-9 *Where to Look for Problems Based on Router LAN Interface Status*

> **NOTE** This book leaves the discussion of LAN issues, as shown on the right side of Figure 21-9, to the various LAN-focused chapters of the ICND1 and ICND2 books.

Router LAN interfaces can fail to reach a working up/up state for several reasons, including the common reasons listed in Table 21-1.

Key Topic

Table 21-1   Common Reasons Why Router LAN Interfaces Are Not Up/Up

Reason	Description	Router Interface State
Speed mismatch	The router and switch can both use the **speed** interface subcommand to set the speed, but to different speeds.	Down/down
Shutdown at router	The router interface has been configured with the **shutdown** interface subcommand.	Admin down/down
Shutdown at switch	The neighboring switch interface has been configured with the **shutdown** interface subcommand, while the router interface is **no shutdown**.	Down/down
Err-disabled switch	The neighboring switch port uses port security, which has put the port in an err-disabled state.	Down/down
No cable/bad cable	The router has no cable installed, or the cable pinouts are incorrect.*	Down/down

* Cisco switches use a feature called auto-mdix, which automatically detects some incorrect cabling pinouts and internally changes the pin logic to allow the cable to be used. As a result, not all incorrect cable pinouts result in an interface failing.

Using the speed mismatch root cause as an example, you could configure Figure 21-9's R3's G0/1 with the **speed 1000** command and SW1's F0/1 interface with the **speed 100** command. The link simply cannot work at these different speeds, so the router and switch interfaces both fall to a down/down state. Example 21-3 shows the resulting state, this time with the **show interfaces description** command, which lists one line of output per interface.

Example 21-3   show interfaces description *Command with Speed Mismatch*

```
R3# show interfaces description
Interface                Status         Protocol Description
Gi0/0                    up             up
Gi0/1                    down           down       link to campus LAN
Se0/0/0                  admin down     down
Se0/0/1                  up             up
Se0/1/0                  up             up
Se0/1/1                  admin down     down
```

Problems with Routing Packets Between Routers

The first half of this chapter focused on the first hop that an IPv4 packet takes when passing over a network. This second major section now looks at issues related to how routers forward the packet from the default router to the final host.

In particular, this section begins by looking at the IP routing logic inside a single router. These topics review how to understand what a router currently does. Following that, the discussion expands to look at some common root causes of routing problems, causes that come from incorrect IP addressing, particularly when the addressing design uses variable-length subnet masks (VLSM).

The end of this section turns away from the core IP forwarding logic, looking at other issues that impact packet forwarding, including issues related to router interface status (which needs to be up/up) and how IPv4 access control lists (ACL) can filter IPv4 traffic.

IP Forwarding by Matching the Most Specific Route

Any router's IP routing process requires that the router compare the destination IP address of each packet with the existing contents of that router's IP routing table. Often, only one route matches a particular destination address. However, in some cases, a particular destination address matches more than one of the router's routes.

The following router features can create overlapping subnets:

- Autosummarization
- Manual route summarization
- Static routes
- Incorrectly designed subnetting plans that cause subnets to overlap their address ranges

In some cases, overlapping routes cause a problem; in other cases, the overlapping routes are just a normal result of using some feature. This section focuses on how a router chooses which of the overlapping routes to use, for now ignoring whether the overlapping routes are a problem. The section "Routing Problems Caused by Incorrect Addressing Plans," later in this chapter, discusses some of the problem cases.

Now on to how a router matches the routing table, even with overlapping routes in its routing table. If only one route matches a given packet, the router uses that one route. However, when more than one route matches a packet's destination address, the router uses the "best" route, defined as follows:

When a particular destination IP address matches more than one route in a router's IPv4 routing table, the router uses the most specific route—in other words, the route with the longest prefix length mask.

Using show ip route and Subnet Math to Find the Best Route

We humans have a couple of ways to figure out what choice a router makes for choosing the best route. One way uses the **show ip route** command, plus some subnetting math, to decide the route the router will choose. To let you see how to use this option, Example 21-4 shows a series of overlapping routes.

Example 21-4   show ip route *Command with Overlapping Routes*

```
R1# show ip route ospf
Codes: L - local, C - connected, S - static, R - RIP, M - mobile, B - BGP
       D - EIGRP, EX - EIGRP external, O - OSPF, IA - OSPF inter area
       N1 - OSPF NSSA external type 1, N2 - OSPF NSSA external type 2
       E1 - OSPF external type 1, E2 - OSPF external type 2
       i - IS-IS, su - IS-IS summary, L1 - IS-IS level-1, L2 - IS-IS level-2
       ia - IS-IS inter area, * - candidate default, U - per-user static route
       o - ODR, P - periodic downloaded static route, H - NHRP, l - LISP
       + - replicated route, % - next hop override
```

```
Gateway of last resort is 172.16.25.129 to network 0.0.0.0

    172.16.0.0/16 is variably subnetted, 9 subnets, 5 masks
O      172.16.1.1/32 [110/50] via 172.16.25.2, 00:00:04, Serial0/1/1
O      172.16.1.0/24 [110/100] via 172.16.25.129, 00:00:09, Serial0/1/0
O      172.16.0.0/22 [110/65] via 172.16.25.2, 00:00:04, Serial0/1/1
O      172.16.0.0/16 [110/65] via 172.16.25.129, 00:00:09, Serial0/1/0
O      0.0.0.0/0 [110/129] via 172.16.25.129, 00:00:09, Serial0/1/0
!
```

NOTE As an aside, the **show ip route ospf** command lists only OSPF-learned routes, but the statistics for numbers of subnets and masks (9 and 5 in the example, respectively) are for all routes, not just OSPF-learned routes.

To predict which of its routes a router will match, two pieces of information are required: the destination IP address of the packet and the contents of the router's routing table. The subnet ID and mask listed for a route define the range of addresses matched by that route. With a little subnetting math, a network engineer can find the range of addresses matched by each route. For instance, Table 21-2 lists the five subnets listed in Example 21-4 and the address ranges implied by each.

Table 21-2 Analysis of Address Ranges for the Subnets in Example 21-4

Subnet/Prefix	Address Range
172.16.1.1/32	172.16.1.1 (just this one address)
172.16.1.0/24	172.16.1.0–172.16.1.255
172.16.0.0/22	172.16.0.0–172.16.3.255
172.16.0.0/16	172.16.0.0–172.16.255.255
0.0.0.0/0	0.0.0.0–255.255.255.255 (all addresses)

NOTE The route listed as 0.0.0.0/0 is the default route.

As you can see from these ranges, several of the routes' address ranges overlap. When matching more than one route, the route with the longer prefix length is used. That is, a route with /16 is better than a route with /10; a route with a /25 prefix is better than a route with a /20 prefix; and so on.

For example, a packet sent to 172.16.1.1 actually matches all five routes listed in the routing table in Example 21-4. The various prefix lengths range from /0 to /32. The longest prefix (largest /P value, meaning the best and most specific route) is /32. So, a packet sent to 172.16.1.1 uses the route to 172.16.1.1/32, and not the other routes.

The following list gives some examples of destination IP addresses. For each address, the list describes the routes from Table 21-2 that the router would match, and which specific route the router would use.

172.16.1.1: Matches all five routes; the longest prefix is /32, the route to 172.16.1.1/32.

172.16.1.2: Matches last four routes; the longest prefix is /24, the route to 172.16.1.0/24.

172.16.2.3: Matches last three routes; the longest prefix is /22, the route to 172.16.0.0/22.

172.16.4.3: Matches the last two routes; the longest prefix is /16, the route to 172.16.0.0/16.

Using show ip route *address* to Find the Best Route

A second way to identify the route a router will use, one that does not require any subnetting math, is the **show ip route** *address* command. The last parameter on this command is the IP address of an assumed IP packet. The router replies by listing the route it would use to route a packet sent to that address.

For example, Example 21-5 lists the output of the **show ip route 172.16.4.3** command on the same router used in Example 21-4. The first line of (highlighted) output lists the matched route: the route to 172.16.0.0/16. The rest of the output lists the details of that particular route, like the outgoing interface of S0/1/0 and the next-hop router of 172.16.25.129.

Example 21-5   show ip route *Command with Overlapping Routes*

```
R1# show ip route 172.16.4.3
Routing entry for 172.16.0.0/16
  Known via "ospf 1", distance 110, metric 65, type intra area
  Last update from 10.2.2.5 on Serial0/1/0, 14:22:06 ago
  Routing Descriptor Blocks:
  * 172.16.25.129, from 172.16.25.129, 14:22:05 ago, via Serial0/1/0
      Route metric is 65, traffic share count is 1
```

Certainly, if you have an option, just using a command to check what the router actually chooses is a much quicker option than doing the subnetting math.

show ip route Reference

The **show ip route** command plays a huge role in troubleshooting IP routing and IP routing protocol problems. Many chapters in both the ICND1 and ICND2 books mention various facts about this command. This section pulls the concepts together in one place for easier reference and study.

Figure 21-10 shows the output of a sample **show ip route** command. The figure numbers various parts of the command output for easier reference, with Table 21-3 describing the output noted by each number.

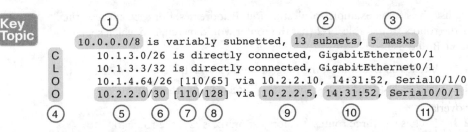

Figure 21-10 show ip route *Command Output Reference*

Table 21-3 Descriptions of the **show ip route** Command Output

Item	Idea	Value in the Figure	Description
1	Classful network	10.0.0.0/8	The routing table is organized by classful network. This line is the heading line for classful network 10.0.0.0; it lists the default mask for Class A networks (/8).
2	Number of subnets	13 subnets	Lists the number of routes for subnets of the classful network known to this router, from all sources, including local routes—the /32 routes that match each router interface IP address.
3	Number of masks	5 masks	The number of different masks used in all routes known to this router inside this classful network.
4	Legend code	C, L, O	A short code that identifies the source of the routing information. *O* is for OSPF, *D* for EIGRP, *C* for Connected, *S* for static, and *L* for local. (See Example 21-4 for a sample of the legend.)
5	Subnet ID	10.2.2.0	The subnet number of this particular route.
6	Prefix length	/30	The prefix mask used with this subnet.
7	Administrative distance	110	If a router learns routes for the listed subnet from more than one source of routing information, the router uses the source with the lowest administrative distance (AD).
8	Metric	128	The metric for this route.
9	Next-hop router	10.2.2.5	For packets matching this route, the IP address of the next router to which the packet should be forwarded.
10	Timer	14:31:52	For OSPF and EIGRP routes, this is the time since the route was first learned.
11	Outgoing interface	Serial0/0/1	For packets matching this route, the interface out which the packet should be forwarded.

Routing Problems Caused by Incorrect Addressing Plans

The existence of overlapping routes in a router's routing table does not necessarily mean a problem exists. Both automatic and manual route summarization result in overlapping routes on some routers, with those overlaps not causing problems. However, some overlaps, particularly those related to addressing mistakes, can cause problems for user traffic. So, when troubleshooting, if overlapping routes exist, the engineer should also look for the specific reasons for overlaps that actually cause a problem.

Simple mistakes in either the IP addressing plan or the implementation of that plan can cause overlaps that also cause problems. In these cases, one router claims to be connected to a subnet with one address range, while another router claims to be connected to another subnet with an overlapping range, breaking IP addressing rules. The symptoms are that the routers sometimes forward the packets to the right host, but sometimes not.

This problem can occur whether or not VLSM is used. However, the problem is much harder to find when VLSM is used. This section reviews VLSM, shows examples of the problem both with and without VLSM, and discusses the configuration and verification commands related to these problems.

Recognizing When VLSM Is Used or Not

An internetwork is considered to be using VLSM when multiple subnet masks are used for different subnets of *a single classful network*. For example, if in one internetwork all subnets come from network 10.0.0.0, and masks /24, /26, and /30 are used, the internetwork uses VLSM.

Sometimes people fall into the trap of thinking that any internetwork that uses more than one mask must be using VLSM, but that is not always the case. For instance, if an internetwork uses subnets of network 10.0.0.0, all of which use mask 255.255.240.0, and subnets of network 172.16.0.0, all of which use a 255.255.255.0 mask, the design does not use VLSM. Two different masks are used, but only one mask is used in any single classful network. The design must use more than one mask for subnets of a single classful network to be using VLSM.

Only classless routing protocols can support VLSM. The three IPv4 IGP routing protocols included in the current CCNA Routing and Switching certification (RIPv2, OSPF, and EIGRP) are all classless routing protocols.

Overlaps When Not Using VLSM

Even when you are not using VLSM, addressing mistakes that create overlapping subnets can occur. For instance, Figure 21-11 shows a sample network with router LAN IP address/mask information. An overlap exists, but it might not be obvious at first glance.

21

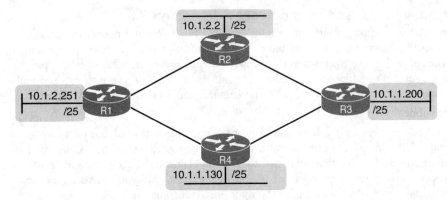

Figure 21-11 *IP Addresses on LAN Interfaces, with One Mask (/25) in Network 10.0.0.0*

If an overlap exists when all subnets use the same mask, the overlapping subnets have the exact same subnet ID, and the exact same range of IP addresses in the subnet. To find the overlap, all you have to do is calculate the subnet ID of each subnet and compare the numbers. For instance, Figure 21-12 shows an updated version of Figure 21-11, with subnet IDs shown and with identical subnet IDs for the LANs off R3 and R4.

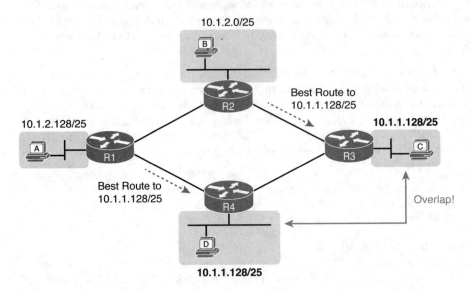

Figure 21-12 *Subnet IDs Calculated from Figure 21-11*

Using the same subnet in two different places (as is done in Figure 21-12) breaks the rules of IPv4 addressing because the routers get confused about where to send packets. In this case, for packets sent to subnet 10.1.1.128/25, some routers send packets so they arrive at R3, whereas others think the best route points toward R4. Assuming all routers use a routing protocol, such as OSPF, both R3 and R4 advertise a route for 10.1.1.128/25.

In this case, R1 and R2 will likely send packets to two different instances of subnet 10.1.1.128/25. With these routes, hosts near R1 will be able to communicate with 10.1.1.128/25 hosts off R4's LAN, but not those off R3's LAN, and vice versa.

Finally, although the symptoms point to some kind of routing issues, the root cause is an invalid IP addressing plan. No IP addressing plan should use the same subnet on two different LANs, as was done in this case. The solution: Change R3 or R4 to use a different, non-overlapping subnet on its LAN interface.

Overlaps When Using VLSM

When using VLSM, the same kinds of addressing mistakes can lead to overlapping subnets; they just may be more difficult to notice.

First, overlaps between subnets that have different masks will cause only a partial overlap. That is, two overlapping subnets will have different sizes and possibly different subnet IDs. The overlap occurs between all the addresses of the smaller subnet, but with only part of the larger subnet. Second, the problems between hosts only occur for some destinations (specifically the subset of addresses in the overlapped ranges), making it even tougher to characterize the problem.

For instance, Figure 21-13 shows an example with a VLSM overlap. The figure shows only the IP address/mask pairs of router and host interfaces. First, look at the example and try to find the overlap by looking at the IP addresses.

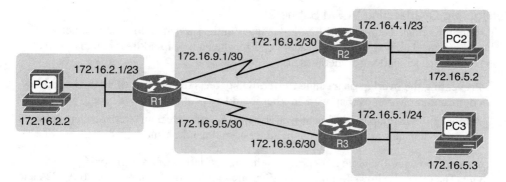

Figure 21-13 *VLSM IP Addressing Plan in Network 172.16.0.0*

To find the overlap, the person troubleshooting the problem needs to analyze each subnet, finding not only the subnet ID but also the subnet broadcast address and the range of addresses in the subnet. If the analysis stops with just looking at the subnet ID, the overlap may not be noticed (as is the case in this example).

Figure 21-14 shows the beginning analysis of each subnet, with only the subnet ID listed. Note that the two overlapping subnets have different subnet IDs, but the lower-right subnet (172.16.5.0/24) completely overlaps with part of the upper-right subnet (172.16.4.0/23). (Subnet 172.16.4.0/23 has a subnet broadcast address of 172.16.5.255, and subnet 172.16.5.0/24 has a subnet broadcast address of 172.16.5.255.)

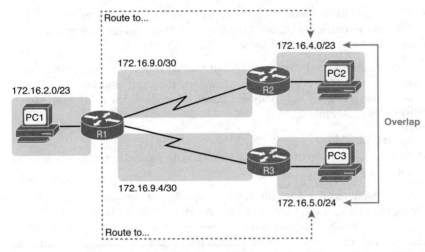

Figure 21-14 *A VLSM Overlap Example, but with Different Subnet IDs*

To be clear, the design with actual subnets whose address ranges overlap is incorrect and should be changed. However, once implemented, the symptoms show up as routing problems, like the similar case without VLSM. **ping** commands fail, and **traceroute** commands do complete for only certain hosts (but not all).

Configuring Overlapping VLSM Subnets

IP subnetting rules require that the address ranges in the subnets used in an internetwork should not overlap. IOS sometimes can recognize when a new **ip address** command creates an overlapping subnet, but sometimes not, as follows:

Preventing the overlap on a single router: IOS detects the overlap when the **ip address** command implies an overlap with another **ip address** command *on the same router*.

Allowing the overlap on different routers: IOS cannot detect an overlap when an **ip address** command overlaps with an **ip address** command on another router.

The router shown in Example 21-6 prevents the configuration of an overlapping VLSM subnet. The example shows Router R3 configuring Fa0/0 with IP address 172.16.5.1/24 and attempting to configure Fa0/1 with 172.16.5.193/26. The ranges of addresses in each subnet are as follows:

Subnet 172.16.5.0/24:   172.16.5.1–172.16.5.254

Subnet 172.16.5.192/26: 172.16.5.193–172.16.5.254

Example 21-6 *Single Router Rejects Overlapped Subnets*

```
R3# configure terminal
R3(config)# interface Fa0/0
R3(config-if)# ip address 172.16.5.1 255.255.255.0
R3(config-if)# interface Fa0/1
R3(config-if)# ip address 172.16.5.193 255.255.255.192
% 172.16.5.192 overlaps with FastEthernet0/0
R3(config-if)#
```

IOS knows that it is illegal to overlap the ranges of addresses implied by a subnet. In this case, because both subnets would be connected subnets, this single router knows that these two subnets should not coexist because that would break subnetting rules, so IOS rejects the second command.

As an aside of how IOS handles these errors, IOS only performs the subnet overlap check for interfaces that are not in a shutdown state. When configuring an interface in shutdown state, IOS actually accepts the **ip address** command that would cause the overlap. Later, when the **no shutdown** command is issued, IOS checks for the subnet overlap and issues the same error message shown in Example 21-6. IOS leaves the interface in the shutdown state until the overlap condition has been resolved.

IOS cannot detect the configuration of overlapping subnets on different routers, as shown in Example 21-7. The example shows the configuration of the two overlapping subnets on R2 and R3 from Figure 21-13.

Example 21-7 *Two Routers Accept Overlapped Subnets*

```
! First, on router R2
R2# configure terminal
R2(config)# interface G0/0
R2(config-if)# ip address 172.16.4.1 255.255.254.0
! Next, on router R3
R3# configure terminal
R3(config)# interface G0/0
R3(config-if)# ip address 172.16.5.1 255.255.255.0
```

Pointers to Related Troubleshooting Topics

A router's data plane may fail due to features beyond those mentioned in this chapter or in this book. However, other chapters of the ICND1 and ICND2 books explain troubleshooting of a couple of other features that directly impact a router's forwarding logic. This short section references those other topics for completeness, even though the details sit in other chapters.

Router WAN Interface Status

One of the steps in the IP routing troubleshooting process described earlier, in the "Router LAN Interface and LAN Issues" section, says to check the interface status, ensuring that the required interface is working. For a router interface to be working, the two interface status codes must both be listed as up, with engineers usually saying the interface is "up and up."

To fully troubleshoot the IPv4 data plane over WAN links, you should look closely at the troubleshooting topics in Chapter 13, "Implementing Point-to-point WANs," of this book. Anything that prevents a serial link from being in an up/up state would of course prevent the routers on that link from sending packets to each other.

In addition, note that a link can be in an up/up state on both ends but still have IPv4 forwarding issues. A serial link with both interfaces up/up means that Layers 1 and 2 work well, but Layer 3 might still have an issue. In particular, the classic case is the misconfiguration of IPv4 addresses on the two ends of the link, such that the addresses are in different subnets.

Make sure to review all these details about troubleshooting WAN links in Chapter 13.

Filtering Packets with Access Lists

Practically every networking device used today has some ability to filter traffic at the data plane. That is, the device can monitor packets during the forwarding process, compare those packets to a list of rules, and discard (filter) some packets based on those rules. Cisco IOS calls this feature *access control lists* (ACL).

Part IV of this book spent a fair amount of time on ACLs, with Chapter 17, "Advanced IPv4 Access Control Lists," specifically discussing troubleshooting IPv4 ACLs from the command line. This chapter does not repeat those same ideas, but make sure to keep those thoughts in mind when troubleshooting the IPv4 data plane. Note that Chapter 17 includes some details about how ACLs filter packets, as well as how ACLs impact the **ping** command.

Chapter Review

One key to doing well on the exams is to perform repetitive spaced review sessions. Review this chapter's material using either the tools in the book, DVD, or interactive tools for the same material found on the book's companion website. Refer to the "Your Study Plan" element for more details. Table 21-4 outlines the key review elements and where you can find them. To better track your study progress, record when you completed these activities in the second column.

Table 21-4   Chapter Review Tracking

Review Element	Review Date(s)	Resource Used
Review key topics		Book, DVD/website
Review memory tables		Book, DVD/website

Review All the Key Topics

Table 21-5   Key Topics for Chapter 21

Key Topic Element	Description	Page Number
Figure 21-2, checklist	A checklist of how to troubleshoot issues between the IPv4 settings on a host and its default router	568
List	Two root causes of DNS problems	571
List	Conditions that must be true for DHCP messages to be able to flow from a client to a DHCP server	573
Table 21-1	Common reasons why router LAN interfaces are not up/up	576
Definition	When more than one route matches a packet's destination address, the router uses the "best" (most specific) route	577
Figure 21-10, Table 21-3	**show ip route** field reference and explanations	580
List	Types of overlapping IP address configuration issues that IOS can and cannot recognize	584

Part V Review

Keep track of your part review progress with the checklist in Table P5-1. Details about each task follow the table.

Table P5-1 Part V Part Review Checklist

Activity	First Date Completed	Second Date Completed
Repeat All DIKTA Questions		
Answer Part Review Questions		
Review Key Topics		
Create Mind Maps		
Do Labs		

Repeat All DIKTA Questions

For this task, answer the "Do I Know This Already?" questions again for the chapters in this part of the book using the PCPT software. See the section "How to View Only DIKTA Questions by Chapter or Part" in the Introduction to this book to learn how to make the PCPT software show you DIKTA questions for this part only.

Answer Part Review Questions

For this task, answer the Part Review questions for this part of the book using the PCPT software.

Review Key Topics

Review all Key Topics in all chapters in this part, either by browsing the chapters or by using the Key Topics application on the DVD or companion website.

Create Troubleshooting Root Causes Mind Map

All three chapters in this section discuss troubleshooting for different topics. For this first Part Review mind map, work through these topics, all of which were discussed to a troubleshooting level of depth in the chapters. Think about root causes, or any configuration checks you would do. Then organize those thoughts into a mind map.

If you can, create one mind map for all topics. If not, break it into one map for the topics in Chapters 19 and 20, as listed next, and another map for the wide variety of topics in Chapter 21. The topics from Chapters 19 and 20 include:

ROAS, L3 switching with SVI, L3 switching with routed ports and L3 EtherChannels, HSRP

And the topics from Chapter 21:

host IP settings, default router issues, routing issues

You will find yourself going beyond what I might have put in the chapters, particularly for Chapter 21. That is great! That is part of what the mind map does, helping you own what you learned here and combining it with other things you know. So do not worry if you add something I did not happen to include in the sample mind map.

To organize the mind map, once you see several root causes that are related, group those root causes by whatever category comes to mind. These might be the same kinds of symptoms you would see when doing problem isolation. For instance, you might note root causes about Dynamic Host Configuration Protocol (DHCP), like a router missing its DHCP Relay configuration (**ip helper-address**), and another cause that no IP connectivity exists to the DHCP server. So, group these DHCP root causes together in one category, something like Host DHCP. Figure P5-1 shows an example.

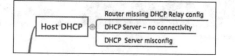

Figure P5-1 *Subset Example of the IPv4 Root Cause Mind Map*

> **NOTE** For more information about mind mapping, see the section "About Mind Maps" in the Introduction to this book.

Create Commands Mind Map

Part V also introduced the configuration and verification details for ROAS, L3 switching with SVIs, and L3 switching with routed interfaces and L3 EtherChannels. It also discussed HSRP. Create a mind map that organizes the commands by each of these topics, and inside each topic organize the commands as either configuration or verification commands.

Appendix E, "Mind Map Solutions," lists sample mind map answers. If you do choose to use mind map software, rather than paper, you might want to remember where you stored your mind map files. Table P5-2 lists the mind maps for this part review and a place to record those filenames.

Table P5-2 Configuration Mind Maps for Part II Review

Map	Description	Where You Saved It
1	Troubleshooting Root Causes Mind Map	
2	Commands Mind Map	

Do Labs

Depending on your chosen lab tool, here are some suggestions for what to do in lab:

Pearson Network Simulator: The full Pearson CCNA simulator, both the Sim that was available when this book published and the newer version expected within a year of the release of the current exam, have several labs on the topics in this part of the book.

Config Labs: In your idle moments, review and repeat any of the Config Labs for this book part in the author's blog; launch from http://blog.certskills.com/ccna and navigate to **Hands-On > Config Lab.**

As with IPv4, Cisco has organized the IP Version 6 (IPv6) topics for the exams by spreading the topics between the ICND1 and ICND2 exams. For ICND1, Cisco included the basics: addressing, subnetting, routing, router addresses, and static route configuration. ICND2 includes routing protocol topics, specifically with OSPF and EIGRP, as well as IPv6 ACLs.

Only three ICND2 exam topics mention IPv6 specifically: one that lists EIGRP for IPv6, one that lists OSPF for IPv6, and one that mentions IPv6 ACLs. All three exam topics include the verbs configure, verify, and troubleshoot. To meet those needs, Chapter 23 works through the OSPF for IPv6 details for configuration, verification, and troubleshooting, while Chapter 24 does the same for EIGRP for IPv6. Chapter 25 completes this part with the details of IPv6 ACLs.

This part begins with Chapter 22, a chapter that meets two purposes. First, to perform tasks for ICND2's IPv6 exam topics, you need solid skills with ICND1's IPv6 topics. Chapter 22 reviews those topics. Additionally, to be ready to troubleshoot OSPF for IPv6, EIGRP for IPv6, and IPv6 ACLs, you need to have IPv6 data plane troubleshooting concepts fresh in mind. Chapter 22 does just that by reviewing ICND1's IPv6 topics, and giving you some mental exercises while thinking through a variety of IPv6 troubleshooting issues.

Part VI

IPv6

Chapter 22: IPv6 Routing Operation and Troubleshooting

Chapter 23: Implementing OSPF for IPv6

Chapter 24: Implementing EIGRP for IPv6

Chapter 25: IPv6 Access Control Lists

Part VI Review

IPv6 Routing Operation and Troubleshooting

This chapter covers the following exam topics:

2.0 Routing Technologies

2.5 Configure, verify, and troubleshoot single area and multiarea OSPFv3 for IPv6 (excluding authentication, filtering, manual summarization, redistribution, stub, virtual-link, and LSAs)

2.7 Configure, verify, and troubleshoot EIGRP for IPv6 (excluding authentication, filtering, manual summarization, redistribution, stub)

The first step in troubleshooting any networking technology is to understand what should happen under normal conditions. Then, the troubleshooting process can compare the current network behavior with what should be happening, looking for differences, until the root cause of those differences can be found.

This chapter begins with a review of the ICND1 book's discussion about how IPv6 works normally. Thankfully, IPv6 has many similarities to IPv4, other than the obvious differences in addressing. This section builds on those similarities and summarizes the core features of IPv6 to set the stage for a discussion of troubleshooting IPv6.

The second major section of the chapter examines a variety of problems that can occur in an IPv6 network.

"Do I Know This Already?" Quiz

A few of the troubleshooting chapters in this book not only discuss troubleshooting of specific topics but also serve as a tool to summarize and review some important topics. This chapter is one of those chapters. As a result, it is useful to read these chapters regardless of your current knowledge level. Therefore, this chapter does not include a "Do I Know This Already?" quiz. However, if you feel particularly confident about IPv6 features covered in this book and in the *CCENT/CCNA ICND1 100-105 Official Cert Guide*, feel free to move to the "Chapter Review" section near the end of this chapter to bypass the majority of the chapter.

Foundation Topics

Normal IPv6 Operation

To be ready to troubleshoot an IPv6 problem, you have to remember many facts about how IPv6 works. Thankfully, many IPv6 concepts work much like IPv4, but there are enough differences to make it worth the time to review IPv6 as an end to itself. This first section of the chapter reviews the details of IPv6, condensing many of the concepts from the five IPv6 chapters of the ICND1 book into one concise review section.

This first section, from this page up to the heading "Troubleshooting IPv6," repeats concepts discussed in the ICND1 book. If you are using both books, you might need to go back and review, or you might be ready to skip this section, as suggested here:

Skip to "Troubleshooting IPv6": If you know IPv6 well, right now, skip ahead. For instance, maybe you are following a reading plan under which you just finished reading the ICND1 book's IPv6 chapters and the material is fresh in your mind. Just know that this first section introduces no new concepts as compared to the ICND1 book's IPv6 chapters.

Read this section: If you remember some of your IPv6 knowledge, but not all, this section is built for you. Keep reading!

Go back and review the ICND1 book: If you have not thought about IPv6 for quite a while, and you really do not remember much at all about it, you might be better off reviewing the IPv6 chapters in the ICND1 book first.

So, what is in this section? It hits the highlights of IPv6. Of course, it reviews IPv6 unicast addressing and subnetting. This section also discusses host IPv6 configuration, including stateless address autoconfiguration (SLAAC) and stateful Dynamic Host Configuration Protocol (DHCP). It reviews basic protocols, like Neighbor Discovery Protocol (NDP), and commands, like **ping** and **traceroute**. This section also reviews router configuration for addressing and static routes.

Unicast IPv6 Addresses and IPv6 Subnetting

IPv6 defines two major types of unicast IPv6 addresses. *Global unicast* addresses work like public IPv4 addresses in that the enterprise obtains a unique prefix with all addresses inside the enterprise beginning with that prefix. With all companies using unique prefixes, all addresses in the IPv6 Internet should be unique.

Unique local unicast addresses work more like private addresses. A company can randomly create a prefix and assign addresses that begin with that prefix. Unique local addresses let companies avoid having to register a prefix while still having a good statistical chance of not using the same address range as other companies.

To create subnets with global unicast addresses, a company starts with the global routing prefix—the prefix assigned to the enterprise—and then breaks the address structure into three parts. In almost all cases, including most cases in this book and the ICND1 book, the combined global routing prefix and subnet part of the address makes up the first half (64 bits) of the address structure. The subnet part gives the enterprise network engineer a place to number each subnet with a different value, uniquely identifying each subnet. Then, the remainder of the structure leaves room for a 64-bit interface ID (or host field). Figure 22-1 summarizes these rules.

For example, a company might receive a global routing prefix of 2001:DB8:1111::/48. That is, all addresses must begin with those 12 hex digits. The subnet part of the addresses exists in the entire fourth quartet. Those subnet numbers can be (hex) 0000, 0001, 0002, and so on, up through FFFF, for 65,536 possible subnets in this example. As a result, the company might end up with a subnet design as shown in Figure 22-2.

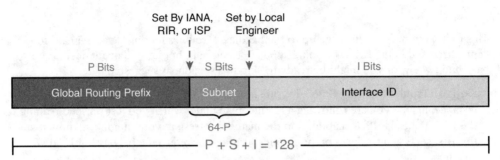

Figure 22-1   *Structure of Subnetted IPv6 Global Unicast Addresses*

NOTE   IPv6 formally uses the term *prefix* rather than *subnet*, but many people use either term when discussing IPv6 addressing.

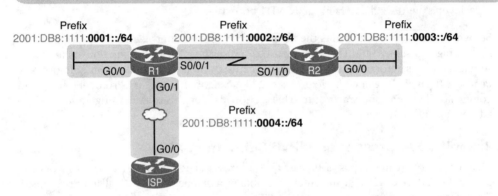

Figure 22-2   *Subnet Design with Global Routing Prefix of 2001:0DB8:1111*

Although Figure 22-2 is helpful for subnet planning, it does not list the specific IPv6 addresses. Like IPv4, IPv6 follows the same general rules. For example, hosts and routers connected to the same Ethernet VLAN need to be in the same IPv6 subnet. Figure 22-3 shows an example with the IPv6 addresses in the appropriate subnets to match Figure 22-2.

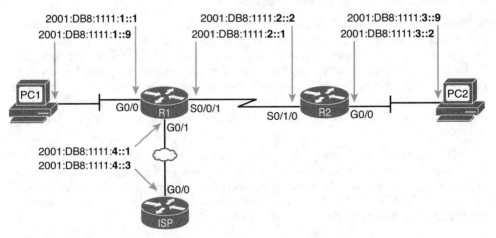

Figure 22-3   *Example Static IPv6 Addresses Based on the Subnet Design of Figure 22-2*

Hosts can use global unicast and unique local unicast addresses to send and receive IPv6 packets with other hosts, but IPv6 defines a special type of unicast address used for packets that stay on a single link: the *link-local* address. Many protocols need to send IPv6 packets that flow only in the local subnet, with no need for routers to forward the packets to any other subnets. IPv6 uses link-local addresses for these protocols. Note that hosts can create their own link-local address even before the host has a valid global unicast or unique local address.

IPv6 hosts and routers create their own link-local address for each interface using some basic rules. First, all link-local addresses start with the same 16-digit prefix (FE80:0000:0000:0000), as shown on the left side of Figure 22-4. The router or host then forms the final 16 hex digits using EUI-64 rules, as discussed in the upcoming section "Stateless Address Autoconfiguration."

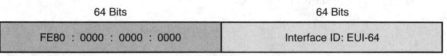

Figure 22-4 *Link-local Address Format*

Table 22-1 summarizes a few bits of reference information about global unicast and unique local unicasts for reference.

Table 22-1   Summary of IPv6 Unicast Address Types

Type	First Digits	Similar to IPv4 Public or Private?
Global unicast	2 or 3[1]	Public
Unique local unicast	FD	Private
Link-local	FE80	N/A

[1] IANA actually defines the global unicast address range as any address not otherwise reserved for some other purpose. However, actual address assignments normally happen from 2000::/3 because that was the original range used for these addresses. Many IPv6 references simply quote 2000::/3 as the prefix, which means the first hex digit is either a 2 or 3.

Assigning Addresses to Hosts

Once all the addressing details have been discussed, registered, and documented, the addresses must be configured on the various hosts and routers. This next topic examines how to add IPv6 configuration (including addressing) to IPv6 hosts.

From a learning perspective, IPv6 host configuration is a little more complex than IPv4. IPv6 adds another protocol to the mix—Neighbor Discovery Protocol (NDP)—and has two options through which hosts can learn their IPv6 settings. Learning how IPv6 hosts dynamically learn their IPv6 settings just takes a little more effort than with IPv4.

IPv6 hosts have three basic options to set their IPv6 options: static configuration, stateful DHCP, and SLAAC. With static configuration, someone just types the options into the right part of the user interface, so this section does not discuss the static configuration option further. The next two topics look at the two dynamic options.

22

Stateful DHCPv6

Stateful DHCPv6 follows the same general process as DHCP for IPv4 (DHCPv4):

1. A DHCP server or servers exist somewhere in the internetwork.

2. User hosts use DHCP messages to ask for a lease of an IP address and information about other settings.

3. The server replies, assigning an address to the host and informing the host of the other settings.

The one noticeable difference between DHCPv4 and stateful DHCPv6 is that the stateful DHCPv6 server does not supply the default router information. Instead, a built-in protocol, NDP, lets the host ask the local routers to identify themselves. Otherwise, hosts use the same general process as with DHCPv4. Figure 22-5 shows a comparison of what is learned by a host using DHCPv4 and stateful DHCPv6.

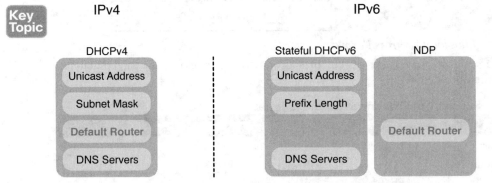

Figure 22-5 *Sources of Specific IPv6 Settings When Using Stateful DHCP*

If the stateful DHCPv6 server sits on a different subnet than the host, DHCPv6 relies on the DHCPv6 *relay agent* function, as shown in Figure 22-6. For instance, on the left, host A begins its attempt to learn an address to use by sending a DHCPv6 Solicit message. This message goes to an IPv6 multicast destination address of FF02::1:2, and routers, like R1, would not normally forward a packet sent to this local-scope multicast address. However, with the DHCPv6 relay agent configuration added to R1's G0/0 interface, as shown in the figure, R1 forwards host A's DHCPv6 message to the DHCP server.

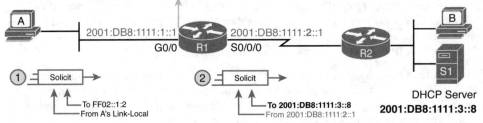

Figure 22-6 *DHCPv6 Relay Agent and DHCP IPv6 Addresses*

Stateless Address Autoconfiguration

IPv6's stateless address autoconfiguration (SLAAC) provides an alternative method for dynamic IPv6 address assignment—without needing a stateful server. In other words, SLAAC does not require a server to lease the IPv6 address and record (keep state information) about which host has which IPv6 address, as is the case with the stateful DHCPv6 service.

SLAAC defines an overall process that also uses NDP and DHCPv6 with a stateless service; the server keeps no state information. First, the process takes advantage of NDP, through which the host can learn the following from any router on the link: the IPv6 prefix (subnet ID), the prefix length (mask equivalent), and the default router IPv6 address. The host uses SLAAC rules to build the rest of its address. Finally, the host uses stateless DHCPv6 to learn the DNS server IPv6 addresses. Figure 22-7 summarizes these details for easy study and reference.

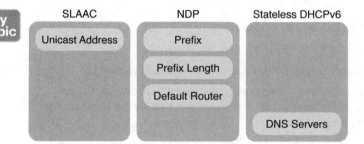

Figure 22-7 *Sources of Specific IPv6 Settings When Using SLAAC*

With SLAAC, a host learns values for three settings (prefix length, router address, and DNS servers), but the host builds the value to use as its address. To build the address, a host uses these steps:

1. Learn the IPv6 prefix used on the link, from any router, using NDP Router Solicitation (RS) and Router Advertisement (RA) messages.

2. Choose an interface ID value to follow the just-learned IPv6 prefix, either by randomly choosing a number, or by using the host's MAC address and using EUI-64 rules.

If the host uses the EUI-64 option, the address built by the host can be predicted. The prefix part of the address is the prefix as defined on the local IPv6 router. Then, the host's MAC address feeds into a few EUI-64 (also called modified EUI-64) rules to change the 48-bit MAC address into a 64-bit interface ID, as follows:

1. Split the 6-byte (12 hex digits) MAC address in two halves (6 hex digits each).

2. Insert FFFE in between the two, making the interface ID now have a total of 16 hex digits (64 bits).

3. Invert the seventh bit of the first byte.

Figure 22-8 shows the major pieces of how the address is formed.

22

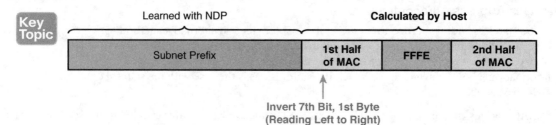

Figure 22-8   *IPv6 Address Format with Interface ID and EUI-64*

Router Address and Static Route Configuration

At this point in this section, you have reviewed IPv6 addresses, IPv6 subnetting, and how to assign addresses to hosts. This next topic looks at how to assign addresses to routers, enable IPv6 routing, and configure static IPv6 routes.

Configuring IPv6 Routing and Addresses on Routers

To enable IPv6 on a router, you have two basic tasks:

Step 1.   Use the **ipv6 unicast-routing** global command to enable IPv6 routing.

Step 2.   Use the **ipv6 address** *address/length* subcommand in interface configuration mode to enable IPv6 on each desired interface, and set the interface IPv6 address and prefix length.

In many cases inside enterprises, the IPv6 implementation plan uses a *dual-stack* strategy, at least on the routers and possibly on hosts. That is, the routers still route IPv4 packets and still have IPv4 addresses on their interfaces. The configuration then adds IPv6 routing as a second Layer 3 protocol routed by the routers, leading to the name "dual stack."

Example 22-1 shows a configuration example for adding IPv6 configuration to Router R1, based on what you saw in Figure 22-3. In that figure, R1 uses three interfaces, with the entire address shown in each case. As a result, Example 22-1 statically configures the entire address. Note also that the prefix length, /64 in this case, sits immediately after the address, without a space. (The IPv4 configuration, not shown, usually already exists with a dual-stack approach.)

Example 22-1   *IPv6 Addressing Configuration on Router R1 from Figure 22-3*

```
ipv6 unicast-routing
!
interface serial0/0/1
  ipv6 address 2001:db8:1111:2::1/64
!
interface gigabitethernet0/0
  ipv6 address 2001:db8:1111:1::1/64
!
interface gigabitethernet0/1
  ipv6 address 2001:db8:1111:4::1/64
```

Alternatively, routers can also use addresses formed using EUI-64 rules. To configure a router for this option, the **ipv6 address** command has two changes. First, the command lists only the prefix, and not the entire address, because the router creates the interface ID part of the address. The command also lists an **eui-64** keyword at the end. For instance, to instead use EUI-64 on R1's G0/0 interface, you use the command **ipv6 address 2001:db8:1111:1::/64 eui-64**.

IPv6 Static Routes on Routers

As for IPv6 routes, most enterprises use a dynamic IPv6 routing protocol, such as Open Shortest Path First Version 3 (OSPFv3; Chapter 23, "Implementing OSPF for IPv6") or Enhanced Interior Gateway Routing Protocol (EIGRP) for IPv6 (see Chapter 24, "Implementing EIGRP for IPv6"). However, routers also support static routes, of course.

Routers support three basic options for IPv6 static routes about how to tell a router where to send packets next. Figure 22-9 shows all three options, as follows:

1. Direct the packets out an interface on the local router.

2. Direct the packets to the unicast address of a neighboring router.

3. Direct the packets to the link-local address of a neighboring router (requires the outgoing interface, as well).

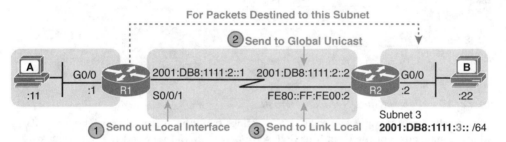

Figure 22-9 *Three Options for IPv6 Static Route Configuration*

Example 22-2 shows a static route to match the figure in each of the three styles. A single router would not use three static routes for the same destination IPv6 prefix; the example just shows all three as a review of the syntax of each command.

Example 22-2 *Static IPv6 Routes: Three Options*

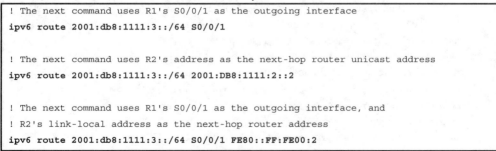

```
! The next command uses R1's S0/0/1 as the outgoing interface
ipv6 route 2001:db8:1111:3::/64 S0/0/1


! The next command uses R2's address as the next-hop router unicast address
ipv6 route 2001:db8:1111:3::/64 2001:DB8:1111:2::2


! The next command uses R1's S0/0/1 as the outgoing interface, and
! R2's link-local address as the next-hop router address
ipv6 route 2001:db8:1111:3::/64 S0/0/1 FE80::FF:FE00:2
```

Verifying IPv6 Connectivity

Most troubleshooting tasks, both on the job and for the exam, begin with a partially work-ing network. To find the existing problems, the engineer needs to try various commands to test the network to verify what works properly and what does not. This next topic reviews a few commands useful for verifying IPv6 connectivity both on hosts and on routers.

Verifying Connectivity from IPv6 Hosts

The first item to check with on any IPv6 host should be the four key IPv6 settings on a host, as shown on the left side of Figure 22-10. This verification step should not only look at the host itself but also compare the host's settings to the other devices in the network. For instance, the host's default router (default gateway) setting should match the address config-ured on a local router.

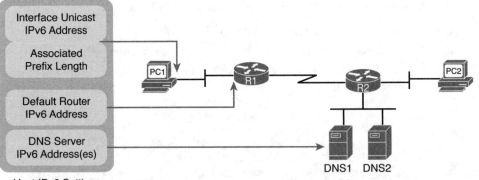

Host IPv6 Settings

Figure 22-10 *IPv6 Settings Needed on Hosts*

Hosts usually support some way to see IPv6 settings from the graphical user interface (GUI) and use commands. For the main four IPv6 settings, the **ipconfig** (Windows operating sys-tems) and **ifconfig** (Linux and Mac OS X) usually show some of the settings. Example 22-3 shows an **ifconfig** command from a Linux host with the address and prefix length highlight-ed for the global unicast and link-local addresses.

Example 22-3   ifconfig *Command Using Linux*

```
WOair$ ifconfig en0
eth0: Link encap:Ethernet  Hwaddr 02:00:11:11:11:11
        inet addr:10.1.1.99  Bcast:10.1.1.255  Mask:255.255.255.0
      inet6 addr: fe80::11ff:fe11:1111/64 Scope:Link
      inet6 2001:db8:1111:1::11/64 Scope:Global
     UP BROADCAST RUNNING MULTICAST  MTU:1500  Metric:1
     RX packets: 45 errors:0 dropped:0 overruns:0 frame:0
     TX packets: 804 errors:0 dropped:0 overruns:0 carrier:0
     collisions:0 txqueuelen:1000
     RX bytes:5110 (5.1 KB)  TX bytes:140120 (140.1 KB)
```

Of course, the best two commands for testing connectivity are the **ping** and **traceroute** commands. Some hosts use the same exact **ping** and **traceroute** commands for both IPv4 and IPv6, whereas others (notably Mac OS X and Linux) use a different command for IPv6 (for instance, the **ping6** and **traceroute6** commands).

When using **ping6** for troubleshooting, pinging the nearest IPv6 address and then pinging router addresses further and further away until one of the pings fails can help you isolate the problem. For instance, in Figure 22-11, from PC1 the user could first ping the nearer interface on R1, then the serial interface IPv6 address on R1, then R2's IPv6 address on S0/1/0, and so on.

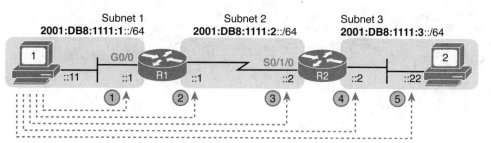

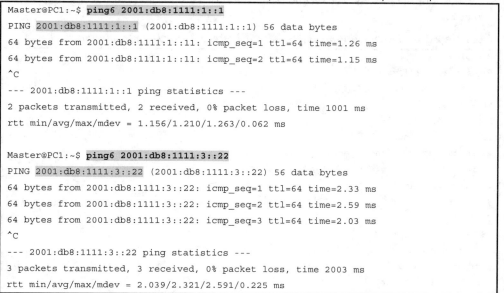

Figure 22-11   *Ping Sequence to Isolate an IPv6 Routing Problem*

Example 22-4 shows the pings from Steps 1 and 5 from Figure 22-11.

Example 22-4   *The* **ping6** *Command from PC, for R1's Nearer Interface and for PC2*

```
Master@PC1:~$ ping6 2001:db8:1111:1::1
PING 2001:db8:1111:1::1 (2001:db8:1111:1::1) 56 data bytes
64 bytes from 2001:db8:1111:1::11: icmp_seq=1 ttl=64 time=1.26 ms
64 bytes from 2001:db8:1111:1::11: icmp_seq=2 ttl=64 time=1.15 ms
^C
--- 2001:db8:1111:1::1 ping statistics ---
2 packets transmitted, 2 received, 0% packet loss, time 1001 ms
rtt min/avg/max/mdev = 1.156/1.210/1.263/0.062 ms


Master@PC1:~$ ping6 2001:db8:1111:3::22
PING 2001:db8:1111:3::22 (2001:db8:1111:3::22) 56 data bytes
64 bytes from 2001:db8:1111:3::22: icmp_seq=1 ttl=64 time=2.33 ms
64 bytes from 2001:db8:1111:3::22: icmp_seq=2 ttl=64 time=2.59 ms
64 bytes from 2001:db8:1111:3::22: icmp_seq=3 ttl=64 time=2.03 ms
^C
--- 2001:db8:1111:3::22 ping statistics ---
3 packets transmitted, 3 received, 0% packet loss, time 2003 ms
rtt min/avg/max/mdev = 2.039/2.321/2.591/0.225 ms
```

Verifying IPv6 from Routers

Cisco routers support IPv6 with the **ping** and **traceroute** commands. Both commands accept either an IPv4 or an IPv6 address or hostname, and both work either as a standard or an extended command.

The extended **ping** and **traceroute** commands give you a lot of power to sit at a router CLI and test the reverse route used by the hosts on the connected LANs. For a brief review here, the extended IPv6 options on the router **ping** and **traceroute** commands let you test routes back to the correct source subnet. For instance, in Figure 22-12, an extended ping from R1 to PC2's IPv6 address tests the forward route to PC2. However, if the extended ping uses R1's G0/0 interface as the source, this command also tests the reverse route back to PC1's IPv6 subnet.

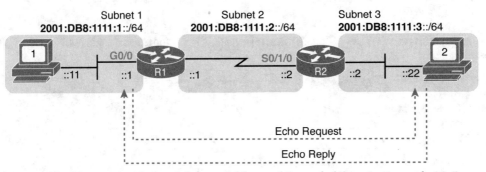

Figure 22-12 *Destination and Source Address of Extended Ping in Example 22-5*

Example 22-5 shows the extended IPv6 ping from R1 to PC2 using R1's G0/0 interface as the source of the packets. The second command shows a standard IPv6 **traceroute** from R1 to PC2.

Example 22-5 *Extended Ping and Standard Traceroute for IPv6 from Router R1*

```
R1# ping
Protocol [ip]: ipv6
Target IPv6 address: 2001:db8:1111:3::22
Repeat count [5]:
Datagram size [100]:
Timeout in seconds [2]:
Extended commands? [no]: yes
Source address or interface: GigabitEthernet0/0
UDP protocol? [no]:
Verbose? [no]:
Precedence [0]:
DSCP [0]:
Include hop by hop option? [no]:
Include destination option? [no]:
Sweep range of sizes? [no]:
Type escape sequence to abort.
Sending 5, 100-byte ICMP Echos to 2001:DB8:1111:3::22, timeout is 2 seconds:
Packet sent with a source address of 2001:DB8:1111:1::1
!!!!!
Success rate is 100 percent (5/5), round-trip min/avg/max = 0/1/4 ms

R1# traceroute 2001:db8:1111:3::22
Type escape sequence to abort.
```

```
Tracing the route to 2001:DB8:1111:3::22


  1 2001:DB8:1111:2::2  4 msec 0 msec 0 msec
  2 2001:DB8:1111:3::22  0 msec 4 msec 0 msec
```

When an IPv6 **ping** or **traceroute** points to some kind of routing problem, several more steps can help isolate the problem to find the root cause. However, this chapter leaves the IPv6 routing protocol troubleshooting discussions until Chapters 23 and 24. Both chapters discuss specific reasons why OSPFv3 and EIGRP might fail to put a route into the IPv6 routing table. For now, keep the following two examples in mind when troubleshooting IPv6 problems.

To display the specific IPv6 route a router would use to send packets to a specific destination address, just use the **show ipv6 route** *address* command. The command lists several lines that detail the route the router will use. If the router has no matching route, the router lists a message of "Route not found." Example 22-6 shows an example in which the matched route is a static route that forwards packets out interface S0/0/1. It also shows an example where no route was found.

Example 22-6   *Displaying the Router R1 Uses to Forward to 2001:DB8:1111:3::22*

```
R1# show ipv6 route 2001:db8:1111:3::22
Routing entry for 2001:DB8:1111:3::/64
  Known via "static", distance 1, metric 0
  Route count is 1/1, share count 0
  Routing paths:
    directly connected via Serial0/0/1
      Last updated 00:01:29 ago

R1# show ipv6 route 2001:1:1:1::1
% Route not found
```

In addition, the **show ipv6 neighbors** command lists the IPv6 replacement for the IPv4 Address Resolution Protocol (ARP) table. If a ping fails, and an expected entry is missing from this table, that fact might point to an issue that is preventing NDP from discovering the neighbor's MAC address. Example 22-7 shows this command on Router R2 from Figure 22-12, listing PC2's IPv6 and matching MAC address.

Example 22-7   *The* **show ipv6 neighbors** *Command on Router R2*

```
R2# show ipv6 neighbors
IPv6 Address                       Age Link-layer Addr State Interface
FE80::11FF:FE11:1111                  0 0200.1111.1111  STALE Gi0/0
FE80::22FF:FE22:2222                  1 0200.2222.2222  STALE Gi0/0
2001:DB8:1111:3::22                   0 0200.2222.2222  REACH Gi0/0
FE80::D68C:B5FF:FE7D:8200             1 d48c.b57d.8200  DELAY Gi0/0
2001:DB8:1111:3::33                   0 0200.1111.1111  REACH Gi0/0
2001:DB8:1111:3::3                    0 d48c.b57d.8200  REACH Gi0/0
```

Troubleshooting IPv6

Imagine that you work with a medium-sized enterprise network that uses IPv6. It works well, you go home on time every day, and life is good. Then one day you go to work and get a text about a problem with the network. So, what do you do? You try some commands, try to isolate the problem, and eventually, find the root cause of the problem. For example, maybe a user had a problem and a co-worker "helped" and configured that user's PC with static IPv6 settings and made a typo in the default router IPv6 address.

The rest of this chapter presents seven different IPv6 troubleshooting scenarios, as if an engineer had just started working a problem. Each problem assumes that the engineer has determined that the problem exists in a particular part of the network or for a particular set of reasons.

Each scenario then gives us a place to talk about potential root causes that happen to show up with a particular set of symptoms and to review the whys and wherefores behind those symptoms.

Before getting into the specific scenarios, the following three lists break down some important facts that should be true about a working IPv6 network. Many of the root causes of problems in this section of the chapter happen because one of these rules was broken.

Host-Focused Issues

1. Hosts should be in the same IPv6 subnet as their default router.
2. Hosts should use the same prefix length as their default router.
3. Hosts should have a default router setting that points to a real router's address.
4. Hosts should have correct Domain Name Service (DNS) server addresses.

Router-Focused Issues

1. Router interfaces in use should be in an up/up state.
2. Two routers that connect to the same data link should have addresses in the same IPv6 subnet.
3. Routers should have IPv6 routes to all IPv6 subnets as per the IPv6 subnet design.

Filtering Issues

1. Watch for MAC address filtering on the LAN switches.
2. Watch for missing VLANs in switches.
3. Watch for IPv6 access control lists (ACL) in routers.

Before diving into the scenarios, if you stop and think about these lists, all the items apply in concept to both IPv4 and IPv6. So, the IPv6 troubleshooting process and concepts should mirror IPv4 to some degree. Of course, the specifics do differ, and these scenarios bring out those differences as well.

Now on to a variety of IPv6 problem symptoms!

Pings from the Host Work Only in Some Cases

Our network engineer has responded to a new problem request by calling the user. The engineer asks the user to do some IPv6 **ping** commands from the user's PC. Some pings actually work, but some do not. What should he try next?

Frankly, at this point, if you ask that same question to ten experienced network engineers, you would probably get five or six different suggested next steps. But one highly productive next step when a host gets some pings to work and some do not work is to check the host's IPv6 settings.

The static IPv6 settings on a host can be one of the most common places to find a mistake, and some of those mistakes result in the "some pings work, some do not" symptom. First, the numbers are long and easy to mistype. Second, you have to make sure that you understand what has to match on the router and DNS server, as well. Finally, for exams, the people writing the exam questions have a lot of small settings to change to make new questions, so it is easy to create a new question by just editing a drawing and changing one number. So, just as with IPv4, you need to be ready to check IPv6 host settings.

Figure 22-13 collects all the pieces that should match. The concepts mirror the same concepts in IPv4.

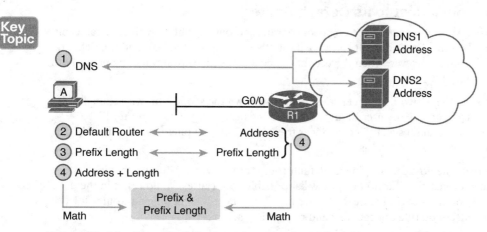

Figure 22-13 *Host IPv6 Settings Compared to What the Settings Should Match*

Next, think about the symptoms of the ping tests, assuming one, but only one, of these settings is wrong. (If more than one setting is wrong, it makes the symptoms harder to describe here.) Here is a walkthrough of the settings numbered in the figure:

1. With the DNS setting as the one incorrect setting, pings that refer to a hostname will fail, but pings to an IPv6 address should work (again assuming no other problems exist).

2. With the default router setting as the only incorrect setting, pings based on an IPv6 address in the local LAN should work. However, pings to addresses outside the subnet (that therefore use the default router) fail. Also, because name resolution would fail, all pings that use names would also fail.

3. If the prefix lengths do not match, the host and router disagree about the subnet on the LAN (see the next step).

4. If the host and router disagree about what IPv6 subnet exists on the VLAN, the routers might not be able to route packets back to the host. As a result, the same ping symptoms as Step 2 occur.

From an exam-taking perspective, you want to work through these symptoms as fast as possible. So, if the question gives you the host settings, check them against the router interface address and prefix length and the DNS server address info, because doing so should take only a little time.

From the perspective of troubleshooting for your job, these symptoms reduce to basically two sets of symptoms:

■ Pings that use names happen to fail

■ Pings that require off-subnet packets happen to fail

For these two sets of symptoms, the first case points to some DNS problem, and the second points to either a default router issue or a mismatched subnet issue.

Pings Fail from a Host to Its Default Router

Now, on to a second scenario. The engineer has checked out a problem with commands on the host and on that host's default router. All the IPv6 settings on the host and the default router look good. However, when the user at the host pings faraway servers, the pings, both by name and by IPv6 address, fail.

As a next step, the network engineer tries to narrow down the scope a bit with some local pings. The engineer asks the user to just ping from the host to the default router IPv6 address. This ping fails, as well. The engineer tries the reverse—a ping from the default router to the host—and it fails as well.

To summarize, the host cannot ping its default router or vice versa. With these initial problem symptoms, the question is this: What possible root causes would result in these symptoms? For instance, in Figure 22-14, what prevents host B from pinging Router R3, particularly after you rule out the host and router IPv6 settings?

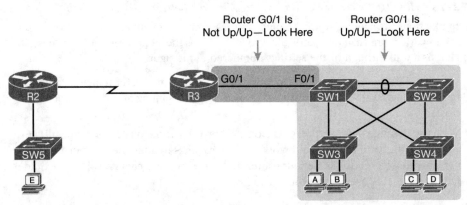

Figure 22-14 *Where to Look for Problems Based on Router LAN Interface Status*

To find the problem, the engineer needs to start thinking outside the IPv6 world and start thinking about the LAN between the host and the router. In particular, the probable root causes can be broken down into these categories:

1. The router or host LAN interface is administratively disabled.

2. The LAN has some problem that prevents the flow of Ethernet frames.

3. The LAN has filtering (for example, port security) that filters the Ethernet frames.

First, the router and host can be disabled. Routers, of course, use the **shutdown** interface subcommand; if R3's G0/1 were shut down at this point, the engineer would have seen the **ping** results described for this scenario. Hosts also have ways to disable and enable their interfaces, which again would result in this same set of ping symptoms. The solution? Use a **no shutdown** command on the router or enable the interface on the host.

As for the second problem in the list, Part I of this book has already discussed LAN problems at length. However, as a troubleshooting tip, note that if R3's G0/1 interface is in a down/down state, a LAN problem would likely exist on the Ethernet link directly connected to R3's G0/1 interface. However, if R3's G0/1 is in an up/up state, any LAN problem probably exists elsewhere in the LAN itself. If the ping still does not work, review the information covered in Chapter 4, "LAN Troubleshooting."

As for the third problem in the list, it could be that some filtering mechanism, like port security, is purposefully filtering the frames sent by the host (B) or the router (R3 G0/1). Also, Router R3 could have an inbound IPv6 ACL on its G0/1 interface, one that unfortunately filtered inbound ICMPv6 packets, which would discard the incoming packets generated by the **ping** commands. (Note that upcoming Chapter 25, "IPv6 Access Control Lists," discusses IPv6 ACLs.)

Problems Using Any Function That Requires DNS

Moving on to the third unique troubleshooting scenario, our engineer is troubleshooting a problem for host C. A ping from host C to a Server1 by hostname fails, but a ping to Server1's IPv6 address succeeds. The engineer tries another similar test, pinging another server (Server2), with the same results: The ping to the hostname fails, and the ping to the IPv6 address works.

These symptoms pretty clearly point to "some kind of name resolution problem." However, that does not define the specific root cause that the engineer can go fix to get the user working again. In this case, the root causes could fall into these categories:

1. An incorrect host DNS server setting, as statically defined on the host

2. An incorrect host DNS server setting, as learned with (stateless or stateful) DHCPv6

3. An IPv6 connectivity problem between the user's host and the DNS server

As for the first root cause listed here, if the host's DNS server setting is wrong, the host sends the DNS requests to the wrong destination address. As a result, the host gets no DNS response and does not learn the IPv6 address of the destination host. The root cause? Someone typed the wrong information into the host IPv6 configuration settings.

The second root cause in the list is similar to the first, but different enough to be worth having a second category. The user's computer has an incorrect DNS server setting, but that setting was learned using DHCPv6. Basically, you have the same problem symptoms but a different root cause. As a reminder, both with stateful DHCPv6 and with SLAAC, the host learns the DNS addresses using DHCPv6.

The third root cause requires a little more discussion and an example. The example shows host C in Figure 22-15, with the two-step process that happens the first time the host tests Server1 with a **ping Server1** command. First, IPv6 packets must flow from host C to the DNS server and back for the purpose of name resolution. At Step 2 in the figure, IPv6 packets can flow to Server1's IPv6 address.

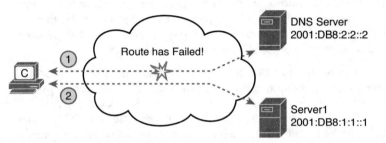

Figure 22-15   *DNS Name Resolution Before Forwarding the Packet to the Server*

Depending on the topology in the cloud, a connectivity problem may exist between host C and the DNS server, whereas no such problem exists between host C and Server1. So, when the problem symptoms point to a "name resolution is not working" set of symptoms, but the host appears to point to the right DNS server addresses, start looking at basic IPv6 connectivity from the host to the DNS server.

Host Is Missing IPv6 Settings: Stateful DHCP Issues

Turning the page to yet another new scenario, our network engineer is now working a problem for a user of a host D. The engineer has called and asked the user to issue a few commands, and the engineer has determined that the host is trying to dynamically learn its IPv6 settings and that the host does not have an IPv6 unicast address yet.

For the sake of discussion, assume that this network uses a strategy of assigning IPv6 addresses using DHCPv6. The engineer knows this strategy, so the engineer is already wondering why the process failed. This scenario walks through some potential root causes of straightforward mistakes.

> **NOTE**   This book leaves out some details of what happens in the process of how a host is told whether to use SLAAC or stateful DHCPv6. To keep the discussion clean and in scope of the topics in this book, assume that for this discussion only stateful DHCP is in use.

Stateful IPv6 DHCP troubleshooting follows the same basic logic as for IPv4 DHCP, as discussed in Chapter 21, "Troubleshooting IPv4 Routing," in the "DHCP Issues" section. So, reiterating a few concepts from that chapter, the following must be true for an IPv6 host to successfully use either stateful or stateless DHCPv6 to learn information from a DHCPv6 server:

1.   The server must be in the same subnet as the client.

   Or

2. The server may be in a different subnet, with

   a. The router that sits on the same subnet as the client host correctly implementing DHCP relay

   b. IPv6 connectivity working between that local router (the router near the client host) and the DHCPv6 server

The two most likely root causes of a host failing to dynamically learn its IPv6 settings with stateful DHCPv6 are root causes 2A and 2B. For 2A, the solution requires a configuration command on the correct interface on each LAN that is remote from the DHCPv6 server. For instance, in Figure 22-16, host D sits on a LAN subnet on the left, with R1's G0/0 interface connected to the same subnet. R1 should have the command listed at the bottom of the figure to enable the IPv6 DHCP relay function pointing to the DHCPv6 server on the right.

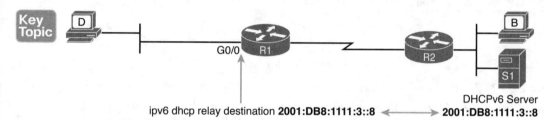

Figure 22-16 *IPv6 DHCP Relay*

If R1 is missing the **ipv6 dhcp relay** command or points to the wrong IPv6 address, host D's attempt to use DHCPv6 will fail.

The item listed as 2B is not actually a root cause. Instead, it is just another problem symptom that needs further investigation. Connectivity must exist between R1 and the DHCPv6 server, and back to the address R1 uses to source the DHCPv6 message. (R1 sources the DHCPv6 request from the outgoing interface of the sent message, not necessarily the same interface where the **ipv6 dhcp relay** command is configured; in this case, R1 would use its serial interface IPv6 address.) A good test of this problem is to ping the DHCPv6 server's IPv6 address from R1.

Host Is Missing IPv6 Settings: SLAAC Issues

For the fifth troubleshooting scenario, take the previous scenario but assume the enterprise uses SLAAC rather than stateful DHCPv6 for IPv6 address assignment. To review, the engineer has discovered that host D has not learned its IPv6 address. So, what could cause SLAAC to fail? This next topic explores the potential root causes.

To understand some of the root causes for such a problem, first review the three steps a host takes when using SLAAC to learn and build its IPv6 settings:

1. Use NDP to learn the prefix, prefix length, and default router address from a router on the same subnet.

2. Use SLAAC rules, locally on the host (no network messages required), to build the host's own IPv6 address.

3. Use stateless DHCPv6 to learn the addresses of the DNS servers from a DHCPv6 server.

The first of these steps uses the NDP Router Solicitation (RS) message, with the router sending back an NDP Router Advertisement (RA) message, as shown in Figure 22-17. The RS message, sent to the all IPv6 routers multicast address FF02::2, should go to all IPv6 routers on the same VLAN as host D in the figure. In this case, R1 replies, listing R1's IPv6 address (to be used as D's default router) and the prefix/length host D should use.

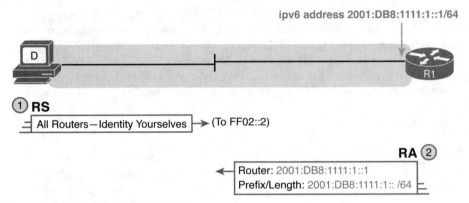

Figure 22-17 *NDP RS and RA Process*

Hosts that use SLAAC rely on the information in the RA message. So, when a host fails to learn and build these three settings when using SLAAC, including the IPv6 address, the next question really should be this: What could cause the NDP RS/RA process to fail? The following list details these potential root causes:

1. No LAN connectivity between the host and any router in the subnet.

2. The router is missing an **ipv6 address** interface subcommand.

3. The router is missing an **ipv6 unicast-routing** global configuration command.

Of these reasons, the first is somewhat obvious. If the LAN cannot forward Ethernet frames from the host to the router, or vice versa, the NDP RS and RA messages cannot be delivered.

As for the second reason, to respond to an RS message, a router must have an **ipv6 address** command. This command enables IPv6 on the interface, but it also defines the information that the router will list in the RA message. For instance, in Figure 22-17, R1 has been configured with the **ipv6 address 2001:db8:1111:1::1/64** command. This command directly lists two of the pieces of information R1 supplies in the RA message, and R1 uses the address and prefix length to calculate the IPv6 prefix as well.

The third root cause in the list may be the most surprising: The router must enable IPv6 routing with the **ipv6 unicast-routing** global command. Why? Without this command, Cisco routers do not try to route IPv6 packets. If omitted, the router does not consider itself an IPv6 router and does not reply to the NDP RS message with an RA.

Traceroute Shows Some Hops, But Fails

This chapter's sixth different troubleshooting scenario now moves away from the host and toward the routers, leading toward IPv6 routing issues.

In this case, the engineer hears that a host cannot connect to a server. Clearly, a ping from the host to the server fails, so the engineer does several of the steps discussed already in this chapter and finds the following:

■ The host IPv6 settings look good.

■ The host IPv6 settings match the default router and DNS server as they should.

■ The host can ping its default router.

To continue troubleshooting, the engineer next calls the user and asks him to try a **traceroute** command with a destination of the server's IPv6 address. The **traceroute** shows a couple of routers in the output, but then the command never completes until interrupted by the user. What could the root causes be? Usually, but not always, these symptoms point to some kind of an IPv6 routing problem. For the next page or two, this discussion examines some potential root causes for these routing problems.

Routing problems happen for many reasons. Some routing problems happen because routes are missing from a router (perhaps because of many specific root causes). Some routing problems happen because a router has an incorrect route. The following list gives just some of the reasons why a router might be missing a needed route or might have an incorrect route:

■ Links between routers are down.

■ Routing protocol neighbor problems exist.

■ Routing protocol route filtering prevents the route from being added to the IPv6 routing table.

■ Incorrect static routes send packets to the wrong next router.

■ Poor subnet design duplicates subnets in different locations in the network, falsely advertising a subnet.

For example, take a look at Figure 22-18. Host A fails when attempting to ping host C, which sits in subnet 33 (2001:DB8:1:33::/64). A traceroute of host C from host A lists R1's and R2's IPv6 addresses, but then it never finishes.

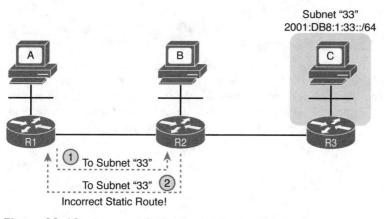

Figure 22-18 *Incorrect Static Route Creates Routing Loop*

As you can see from the notes in the figure, the routing problem exists because of an incorrect static route on R2. Host A can forward IPv6 packets to R1, its default router. R1 can correctly forward packets sent to host C to router R2. However, R2 has an incorrect static route for subnet 33 pointing back to R1.

As for other root causes of routing problems, take the list and look for those issues as well. Check the interfaces on routers that should be up to make sure the interfaces still work. Do troubleshooting for your routing protocol. (Chapters 23 and 24 discuss how to troubleshoot OSPFv3 and EIGRP, respectively.) And even look for the possibility that someone misconfigured a router interface, so that the routing protocols advertise about the same subnet number as existing in two places, which breaks design rules on paper and confuses the routing of packets to hosts in that IPv6 subnet.

Routing Looks Good, But Traceroute Still Fails

To finish this set of scenarios, this last scenario focuses on one particular root cause: IPv6 access control lists (ACL).

You have already learned how **ping** and **traceroute** commands can imply that a routing problem may exist. When **ping** and **traceroute** show that the host can forward a packet at least as far as the default router but not all the way to the destination, the problem probably sits in one of these two categories:

■ A routing problem exists.

■ Routing works, but some filter, like an IPv6 ACL, is discarding the packets.

IPv6 ACLs use some of the same general concepts as IPv4 ACLs, but of course, they filter IPv6 packets rather than IPv4 packets. IPv6 ACL configuration defines a list of statements, with each statement matching source and destination IPv6 address ranges, port numbers, and so on. You can enable the ACL to filter IPv6 packets as they flow in or out of an interface.

Chapter 25 shows the details for how to configure and verify IPv6 ACLs. As always, when troubleshooting a packet-forwarding issue, always check for ACLs that could be filtering the packets.

Chapter Review

One key to doing well on the exams is to perform repetitive spaced review sessions. Review this chapter's material using either the tools in the book, DVD, or interactive tools for the same material found on the book's companion website. Refer to the "Your Study Plan" element for more details. Table 22-2 outlines the key review elements and where you can find them. To better track your study progress, record when you completed these activities in the second column.

Table 22-2   Chapter Review Tracking

Review Element	Review Date(s)	Resource Used
Review key topics		Book, DVD/website
Review key terms		Book, DVD/website
Review memory tables		DVD/website
Review config checklist		Book, DVD/website
Review command reference tables		Book

Review All the Key Topics

Table 22-3   Key Topics for Chapter 22

Key Topic Element	Description	Page Number
Table 22-1	IPv6 address types	595
Figure 22-5	Comparisons of IPv4 DHCP versus IPv6 stateful DHCP	596
Figure 22-7	Details of source of host IPv6 settings when using SLAAC	597
List	Steps to build an address using SLAAC and EUI-64	597
Figure 22-8	Concepts behind using SLAAC and EUI-64	598
List	Working with hosts in IPv6 networks	604
List	Working with routers in IPv6 networks	604
List	Working with filtering in IPv6 networks	604
Figure 22-13	Specific host settings to compare to other devices when troubleshooting	605
List	Categories of issues that prevent an IPv6 host from pinging its default router	607
List	Categories of issues that prevent IPv6 hosts from using DNS server functions	607
List	Requirements for DHCPv6 to work correctly	608
Figure 22-16	DHCPv6 relay agent configuration in a router	609
List	Reasons why the NDP RS/RA process would fail between a host and router	610
List	Possible reasons for IPv6 routing problems	611

Key Terms You Should Know

Neighbor Discovery Protocol (NDP), Router Solicitation (RS), Router Advertisement (RA), stateless address autoconfiguration (SLAAC), stateful DHCPv6, stateless DHCPv6, global unicast address, unique local unicast address, link-local address, EUI-64, dual stack

Command References

Tables 22-4, 22-5, and 22-6 list configuration, verification, and debug commands used in this chapter. As an easy review exercise, cover the left column in a table, read the right column, and try to recall the command without looking. Then repeat the exercise, covering the right column, and try to recall what the command does.

Table 22-4   Chapter 22 Configuration Command Reference

Command	Description
ipv6 unicast-routing	Global command that enables IPv6 routing on the router
ipv6 address {*ipv6-address/ prefix-length*	*prefix-name sub-bits/prefix-length*} [**eui-64**]	Interface subcommand that manually configures either the entire interface IP address, or a /64 prefix with the router building the EUI-64 format interface ID automatically
ipv6 dhcp relay destination *server-address*	Interface subcommand that enables the IPv6 DHCP relay agent

Table 22-5   Chapter 22 EXEC Command Reference

Command	Description
show ipv6 interface [*type number*]	Lists IPv6 settings on an interface, including link-local and other unicast IP addresses
show ipv6 protocols	Lists briefer information than the IPv4 **show ip protocols** command, primarily listing all means through which a router can learn or build IPv6 routes and interfaces on which a routing protocol is enabled
ping {*host-name*	*ipv6-address*}	Tests IPv6 routes by sending an ICMP packet to the destination host
traceroute {*host-name*	*ipv6-address*}	Tests IPv6 routes by discovering the IP addresses of the routes between a router and the listed destination
show ipv6 route [**ospf**	**connected**	**static**]	Lists routes in the routing table, optionally limiting the output based on the routing source
show ipv6 neighbors	Lists the router's IPv6 neighbor table
show ipv6 routers	Lists any neighboring routers that advertised themselves through an NDP RA message

Table 22-6   Chapter 22 Host Command Reference

Command (Microsoft, Apple, Linux)	Description
ipconfig, ifconfig, ifconfig	Lists interface settings, including IPv4 and IPv6 addresses
ping, ping6, ping6	Tests IP routes by sending an ICMPv6 packet to the destination host
tracert, traceroute6, traceroute6	Tests IP routes by discovering the IPv6 addresses of the routes between a router and the listed destination
netsh interface ipv6 show neighbors, ndp -an, ip -6 neighbor show	Lists a host's IPv6 neighbor table

CHAPTER 23

Implementing OSPF for IPv6

This chapter covers the following exam topics:

2.0 Routing Technologies

2.5 Configure, verify, and troubleshoot single area and multiarea OSPFv3 for IPv6 (excluding authentication, filtering, manual summarization, redistribution, stub, virtual-link, and LSAs)

When IPv6 was defined back in the 1990s, Open Shortest Path First Version 2 (OSPFv2) was a popular routing protocol for IPv4 networks. IPv6 needed routing protocols. One solution was to create a new version of OSPF: OSPF Version 3 (OSPFv3). The original OSPFv3 RFC defined a routing protocol to advertise IPv6 routes, using many similar concepts as compared to OSPFv2, but with of course some differences.

Because OSPFv2 (for IPv4) and OSPFv3 (for IPv6) have many similarities, you already know a lot about OSPFv3 from earlier Chapters 7, 8, and 11 of this book. This chapter takes advantage of those similarities to help you learn OSPFv3 more quickly.

This chapter uses three major sections. The first major section of the chapter, which is rather short, works through a few details about terminology and the history of OSPFv2 and OSPFv3. Then the chapter moves on to the section about OSPFv3 configuration, with many details similar to OSPFv2 interface configuration. For the most part, this second section will look very similar to the OSPFv2 configuration you saw in Chapter 8, "Implementing OSPF for IPv4," except that OSPFv3 does not use a **network** command in OSPF configuration mode; it uses interface configuration instead.

The last major section of the chapter pulls many OSPFv3 concepts together with troubleshooting concepts and by showing verification commands. Many of these commands will look familiar from the earlier OSPFv2 chapters. The section points out the differences in command output compared to OSPFv2. At the same time, the discussion includes a list of common root causes of OSPFv3 problems and explains how to recognize those problems.

"Do I Know This Already?" Quiz

Take the quiz (either here, or use the PCPT software) if you want to use the score to help you decide how much time to spend on this chapter. The answers are at the bottom of the page following the quiz, and the explanations are in DVD Appendix C and in the PCPT software.

Table 23-1 "Do I Know This Already?" Foundation Topics Section-to-Question Mapping

Foundation Topics Section	Questions
OSPFv3 for IPv6 Concepts	1
OSPFv3 Configuration	2–4
OSPFv3 Verification and Troubleshooting	5–7

1. Which of the following are differences between OSPFv2 and OSPFv3? (Choose two answers.)

   a. OSPFv2 uses neighbor relationships, while OSPFv3 does not.

   b. OSPFv2 uses an SPF algorithm, while OSPFv3 uses the DUAL algorithm.

   c. OSPFv2 uses LSAs, while OSPFv3 uses LSAs but with differences.

   d. OSPFv2 is a link-state protocol, while OSPFv3 is an advanced distance vector protocol.

   e. OSPFv2 can advertise IPv4 routes, while OSPFv3 can advertise both IPv4 and IPv6 routes.

2. An engineer wants to set the OSPFv3 router ID for Router R1. Which of the following answers could affect R1's choice of OSPFv3 router ID?

   a. The **ipv6 address** command on interface Gigabit0/0

   b. The **ip address** command on interface Serial0/0/1

   c. The **ospf router-id** command in OSPFv3 configuration mode

   d. The **ipv6 address** command on interface loopback2

3. Router R1 has a Serial0/0/0 interface with address 2001:1:1:1::1/64, and a G0/0 interface with address 2001:2:2:2::1/64. The OSPFv3 process uses process ID 1. Which of the following OSPFv3 configuration commands enables OSPFv3 on R1's G0/0 interface and places it into area 0?

   a. A **network 2001:1:1:1::/64 1 area 0** command in router configuration mode

   b. An **ipv6 ospf 1 area 0** command in G0/0 interface configuration mode

   c. A **network 2001:1:1:1::/64 1 area 0** command in router configuration mode

   d. An **ospf 1 area 0** command in G0/0 interface configuration mode

4. An enterprise uses a dual-stack model of deployment for IPv4 and IPv6, using OSPF as the routing protocol for both. Router R1 has IPv4 and IPv6 addresses on its G0/0 and S0/0/0 interfaces only, with OSPFv2 and OSPFv3 enabled on both interfaces for area 0 and the router ID explicitly set for both protocols. Comparing the OSPFv2 and OSPFv3 configuration, which of the following statements is true?

   a. The OSPFv3 configuration, but not OSPFv2, uses the **router-id** *router-id* router subcommand.

   b. Both protocols use the **router-id** *router-id* router subcommand.

   c. Both protocols use the **network** *network-number wildcard* **area** *area-id* router subcommand.

   d. Both protocols use the **ipv6 ospf** *process-id* **area** *area-id* interface subcommand.

5. R1 and R2 are routers that connect to the same VLAN. Which of the answers list an item that can prevent the two routers from becoming OSPFv3 neighbors? (Choose three answers.)

   a. Mismatched Hello timers

   b. Mismatched process IDs

   c. IPv6 addresses in different subnets

   d. Equal router IDs

   e. One passive router interface (used on this link)

6. The example shows an excerpt from the **show ipv6 route ospf** command on a router (R1). Which of the answers are correct about the interpretation of the meaning of the output of this command? (Choose two answers.)

   ```
   R1# show ipv6 route ospf
   OI  2001:DB8:1:4::/64 [110/129]
        via FE80::FF:FE00:1, Serial0/0/1
   ```

   a. 110 is the metric for the route.

   b. S0/0/1 is an interface on R1.

   c. FE80::FF:FE00:1 is a link-local address on R1.

   d. OI means that the route is an interarea OSPF route.

7. Router R1 has been configured as a dual-stack IPv4/IPv6 router, using interfaces S0/0/0, S0/0/1, and GigabitEthernet0/1. As a new engineer hired at the company, you do not know whether any of the interfaces are passive. Which of the following commands lets you find whether G0/1 is passive, either by the command listing that fact or by that command leaving passive interfaces out of its list of interfaces?

   a. show ipv6 ospf interface brief

   b. show ipv6 protocols

   c. show ipv6 ospf interface G0/1

   d. show ipv6 ospf interface passive

Foundation Topics

OSPFv3 for IPv6 Concepts

As you might expect, OSPFv3—the version of OSPF that supports IPv6—happens to work a lot like OSPFv2. So, rather than repeat every detail, this first major section of the chapter begins by describing OSPFv3 expecting that you already know quite a bit about OSPFv2. These next few pages begin with some background information about routing protocols used for IPv6, and OSPFv3 in particular. This section ends with a long list of similarities between OSPFv2 and OSPFv3, which gives you a great start for learning OSPFv3.

IPv6 Routing Protocol Versions and Protocols

First, when most engineers refer to "OSPF," they are likely referring to OSPF as used with IPv4, and specifically, OSPF Version 2 (OSPFv2). To appreciate why, consider a few branches of the history of OSPF.

Once, there was an OSPF version 1 (OSPFv1), but OSPFv2 followed soon afterward (with the original OSPFv2 RFC dated 1991). When OSPF became widely used as an IPv4 routing protocol, back in the early to mid-1990s, OSPFv2 was already defined, and the router vendors used OSPFv2 and not OSPFv1. So, even in the early days of OSPF, there was no need for people to talk about whether they used OSPFv1 or OSPFv2; everyone used OSPFv2, and they just called it OSPF.

Next, consider the timeline for the development of the original IPv6 protocols, also back in early to mid-1990s. The introduction of IPv6 meant that many other protocols needed to be updated to make IPv6 work: ICMP, TCP, UDP, and so on, including OSPF. When a working group updated OSPF to support IPv6, what did they call it? OSPF version 3, of course. Figure 23-1 shows those events on the left and center of the timeline, with OSPFv3 first reaching RFC status in 1999.

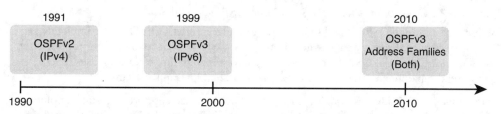

Figure 23-1 *Timeline of OSPF Standards*

For a little over 10 years, the OSPF version story could be told easily in one sentence. You used OSPFv2 to advertise IPv4 routes, and OSPFv3 to advertise IPv6 routes. In fact, OSPFv2 could advertise only IPv4 routes, with OSPFv3 supporting only IPv6 routes.

This particular story continued to change. Again based on RFC dates, in 2010, OSPFv3 added support for IPv4 through a feature called *address families*. Basically, if you want to run dual stack (that is, both IPv4 and IPv6 on your routers), then you can run OSPFv3 with address families. You treat IPv4 as one address family, IPv6 as another, but each router has one OSPFv3 routing protocol process. With these new features, now OSPFv3 supports the advertisement of both IPv4 and IPv6 routes.

Two Options for Implementing Dual Stack with OSPF

As previously indicated, *dual stack* means that routers support both IPv4 and IPv6. To implement dual stack, each router needs to learn both IPv4 and IPv6 routes. For many years, the OSPF solution for dual stack was clear: Run both OSPFv2 and OSPFv3 on all routers, as shown in Figure 23-2.

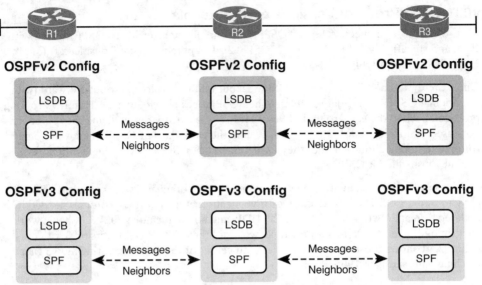

Figure 23-2   *Conceptual View of OSPFv2 and OSPFv3 Dual Stack*

Note that although OSPFv2 and OSPFv3 have similar internals, they act as completely separate processes with separate messages. That is, the OSPFv2 process on Router R1 does not communicate with the OSPFv3 process. They have separate link-state databases (LSDB). They send separate messages, as noted with the dashed lines in the figure.

Now that OSPFv3 address families exist in IOS, you can also support dual-stack implementations by running OSPFv3 only, and configuring it to support the IPv4 address family in addition to the IPv6 address family. However, as seen in Figure 23-3, the router would still have a separate LSDB for IPv4 and IPv6 routes, separate SPF calculations, with separate neighbor relationships and separate OSPF messages between the routers.

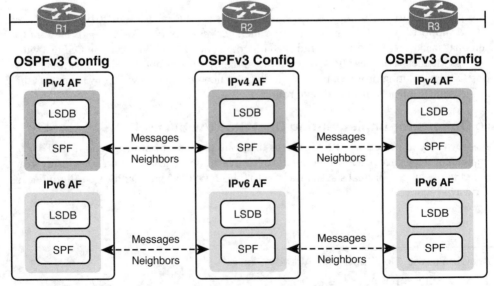

Figure 23-3   *Conceptual View of OSPFv3 Address Families Dual Stack*

OSPFv2 and OSPFv3 Internals

To the depth that this book discusses OSPF theory and concepts, OSPFv3 acts very much like OSPFv2. For example, both use link-state logic. Both use the same metric. And the list keeps getting longer, because the protocols do have many similarities. The following list notes many of the similarities for the features discussed both in this chapter and in Chapter 7, "Understanding OSPF Concepts":

Key Topic

- Both are link-state protocols.

- Both use the same area design concepts and design terms.

- Both require that the routing protocol be enabled on an interface.

- Once enabled on an interface, both then attempt to discover neighbors connected to the data link connected to an interface.

- Both perform a check of certain settings before a router will become neighbors with another router (the list of checks is slightly different between OSPFv2 and OSPFv3).

- After two routers become neighbors, both OSPFv2 and OSPFv3 proceed by exchanging the contents of their LSDB—the link-state advertisements (LSA) that describe the network topology—between the two neighbors.

- After all the LSAs have been exchanged, both OSPFv2 and OSPFv3 use the shortest path first (SPF) algorithm to calculate the best route to each subnet.

- Both use the same metric concept, based on the interface cost of each interface, with the same default cost values.

- Both use LSAs to describe the topology, with some differences in how LSAs work.

The biggest differences between OSPFv3 and the older OSPFv2 pertain to their internals. OSPFv3 changes the structure of some OSPF LSAs, and adds some new LSA types. However, these differences sit outside the scope of this book.

Now that you have a general idea about the similarities and differences between OSPFv3 and OSPFv2, the rest of this section shows examples of how to configure and verify OSPFv3. Note that for the rest of the chapter, all references to classic OSPFv3 refers to using OSPFv3 without using the address family configuration feature.

OSPFv3 Configuration

Remember how to configure OSPFv2 using interface configuration? OSPFv3 configuration follows that same interface configuration model. In fact, most of the commands have either similar syntax, replacing **ip** with **ipv6**, or the exact same syntax.

This second of three major sections focuses on OSPFv3 configuration. It begins with the basics, and then folds in many of the optional configuration topics, like setting OSPF costs, load balancing, and injecting default routes.

Basic OSPFv3 Configuration

As a first step, review the following OSPFv3 configuration checklist. It details the required configuration steps, plus a few optional steps. If you read it too quickly, you might not even notice the small differences for OSPFv3 versus OSPFv2—the configuration is that similar.

23

Config Checklist

Step 1. Use the **ipv6 router ospf** *process-id* global command to create an OSPFv3 process number and enter OSPF configuration mode for that process.

Step 2. Ensure that the router has an OSPF router ID, through either

    A. Configuring the **router-id** *id-value* router subcommand in OSPFv3 configuration mode

    B. Configuring an IPv4 address on a loopback interface (chooses the highest IPv4 address of all working loopbacks)

    C. Relying on an interface IPv4 address (chooses the highest IPv4 address of all working nonloopbacks)

Step 3. Configure the **ipv6 ospf** *process-id* **area** *area-number* interface subcommand on each interface on which OSPFv3 should be enabled, to both enable OSPFv3 on the interface and set the area number for the interface.

Step 4. (Optional) Use the **passive-interface** *type number* router subcommand to configure any OSPFv3 interfaces as passive if no neighbors can or should be discovered on the interface.

To get a better understanding of these basic commands, and to contrast them with their OSPFv2 cousins, this configuration section uses a multiarea configuration example with the exact same internetwork topology as the multiarea example shown in Chapter 8.

Figure 23-4 begins to describe the design, before getting into the configuration, showing the IPv6 subnets. The figure does not show the individual router IPv6 addresses, to reduce clutter, but to make the addresses easier to recognize, the addresses all end with the same number as the router. For example, all five of Router R1's interface addresses end with 1.

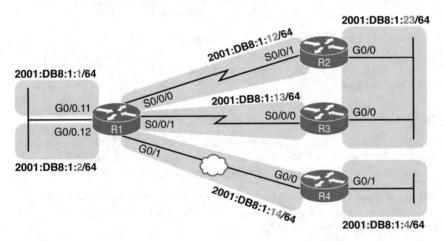

Figure 23-4 *Internetwork for an Example Multiarea OSPFv3 Configuration*

Figure 23-5 next shows the OSPFv3 area design. For those of you with an excellent memory, the design is identical to Chapter 8's Figure 8-8, which defined the area design for that chapter's multiarea design example. The design makes R2 and R3 internal routers inside area 23, R4 an internal router inside area 4, and R1 an Area Border Router (ABR) connected to all three areas.

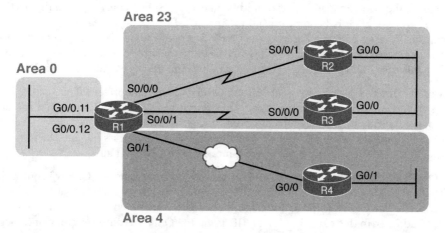

Figure 23-5 *Area Design for the Multiarea OSPFv3 Example*

Single-Area Configuration on the Three Internal Routers

The configurations on the three internal routers in this example review ICND1-level single-area OSPF configuration. In a multiarea OSPF design, the configuration on any internal routers—routers for which all interfaces connect to a single area—looks like a single-area configuration because all the interfaces are placed into one area.

Example 23-1 begins the example with R2's complete IPv6 configuration, including OSPFv3. In other words, all the commands needed on R2 to add IPv6 support are in the example. Note that for OSPFv3 in particular, the example shows the following actions, as highlighted in the example:

1. Creates an OSPFv3 process with process ID 2
2. Defines the OSPFv3 RID explicitly as 2.2.2.2
3. Enables OSPFv3 process 2 on two interfaces, putting both in area 23

Example 23-1 *IPv6 and OSPFv3 Configuration on Internal Router R2*

```
ipv6 unicast-routing
!
interface GigabitEthernet0/0
 mac-address 0200.0000.0002
 ipv6 address 2001:db8:1:23::2/64
 ipv6 ospf 2 area 23
!
interface serial 0/0/1
 ipv6 address 2001:db8:1:12::2/64
 ipv6 ospf 2 area 23
!
ipv6 router ospf 2
 router-id 2.2.2.2
```

23

First, focus on the two commands that should be in every OSPFv3 configuration: the **ipv6 router ospf** *process-id* global command and the **ipv6 ospf** *process-id* **area** *area-id* interface subcommand. The first command creates the OSPFv3 process by number. The second command, one per interface, enables that OSPFv3 process on the interface and assigns the area number. In this case, R2 has a process ID of 2, with both interfaces assigned to area 23.

Next, consider one completely optional feature: OSPFv3 passive interfaces. This feature uses the same concepts and literally the exact same command syntax as OSPFv2. If a router should not form neighbor relationships on an interface, that interface may be made passive. In this case, R2 should find at least one OSPFv3 neighbor on each of its two interfaces, so the configuration does not include the **passive-interface** command at all.

Finally, OSPFv3 follows the *exact* same rules as OSPFv2 when setting the OSPFv3 router ID (RID). The OSPFv3 RID is a 32-bit number, often written in dotted decimal, so it looks like an IPv4 address. The OSPFv3 RID is not a 128-bit number that is then represented to look like an IPv6 address. In this case, R2 sets its RID using the OSPFv3 **router-id** command, but you should be ready to configure all three ways.

Now on to the configuration on R3, which should have a very similar OSPFv3 configuration compared to R2. Both are internal routers in area 23, and both have at least one neighbor off their two interfaces, respectively, so neither can make either of their interfaces passive. Also, just to make the point that OSPFv3 neighbors may use different PID values, R3 uses OSPFv3 PID 3, while R2 uses PID 2. Example 23-2 shows the resulting configuration.

Example 23-2   *IPv6 and OSPFv3 Configuration on R3*

```
ipv6 unicast-routing
!
interface GigabitEthernet0/0
 mac-address 0200.0000.0003
 ipv6 address 2001:db8:1:23::3/64
 ipv6 ospf 3 area 23
!
interface serial 0/0/0
 ipv6 address 2001:db8:1:13::3/64
 ipv6 ospf 3 area 23
!
ipv6 router ospf 3
 router-id 3.3.3.3
```

Moving on to R4, in Example 23-3, the configuration differs slightly from that of the previous two routers. First, R4 can make its G0/1 interface passive because R4 expects to create no OSPFv3 neighbor relationships off that LAN interface. R4 also uses a different OSPFv3 PID.

NOTE   Although these examples use different OSPFv3 PIDs, to show that such a choice causes no problems, most enterprises would use the same PID value on all routers for consistency.

Example 23-3 *IPv6 and OSPFv3 Configuration on R4*

```
ipv6 unicast-routing
!
interface GigabitEthernet0/0
 mac-address 0200.0000.0004
 ipv6 address 2001:db8:1:14::4/64
 ipv6 ospf 4 area 4
!
interface GigabitEthernet0/1
 ipv6 address 2001:db8:1:4::4/64
 ipv6 ospf 4 area 4
!
ipv6 router ospf 4
 router-id 4.4.4.4
 passive-interface gigabitethernet0/1
```

Adding Multiarea Configuration on the Area Border Router

The configuration for multiarea OSPF is just as anticlimactic for OSPFv3 as it was for OSPFv2. Multiarea OSPF may lead to some interesting design discussions when deciding which links to put in which areas. Once decided, the configuration is just a matter of reading the documentation correctly and typing the correct area number into the **ipv6 ospf** *process-id* **area** *area-id* interface subcommand.

In this example, ABR R1 has an OSPFv3 process (PID 1), with OSPFv3 enabled on five interfaces, as follows, to match earlier Figure 23-5:

Area 0: G0/0.11 and G0/0.12

Area 23: S0/0/0 and S0/0/1

Area 4: G0/1

To be clear, nothing in R1's configuration mentions multiarea or ABR—R1 simply acts as an ABR because its configuration puts some interfaces in area 0 and others in other nonbackbone areas. Example 23-4 shows the configuration.

Example 23-4 *IPv6 and OSPFv3 Configuration on ABR R1*

```
ipv6 unicast-routing
!
interface GigabitEthernet0/0
 mac-address 0200.0000.0001
!
interface GigabitEthernet0/0.11
 encapsulation dot1q 11
 ipv6 address 2001:db8:1:1::1/64
 ipv6 ospf 1 area 0
!
interface GigabitEthernet0/0.12
```

23

```
 encapsulation dot1q 12
 ipv6 address 2001:db8:1:2::1/64
 ipv6 ospf 1 area 0
!
interface GigabitEthernet0/1
 ipv6 address 2001:db8:1:14::1/64
 ipv6 ospf 1 area 4
!
interface serial 0/0/0
 ipv6 address 2001:db8:1:12::1/64
 ipv6 ospf 1 area 23
!
interface serial 0/0/1
 ipv6 address 2001:db8:1:13::1/64
 ipv6 ospf 1 area 23
!
ipv6 router ospf 1
 router-id 1.1.1.1
```

Other OSPFv3 Configuration Settings

The next few short configuration topics take some other OSPFv2 features discussed back in Chapter 8 and show how to configure those for OSPFv3. And as usual, the details are nearly identical.

Setting OSPFv3 Interface Cost to Influence Route Selection

OSPFv3 works much like OSPFv2 in how it calculates the metric for a route, with some slight differences with the concepts, configuration commands, and verification commands.

To review the concepts, as discussed back in Chapters 7 and 8, SPF on a router finds all possible routes for a subnet. Then, it adds the OSPF interface cost for all outgoing interfaces in a route to calculate the metric for each route. It then chooses the route with the lowest metric as the best route, which is then added to the IP routing table.

For instance, Figure 23-6 repeats a figure from Chapter 7 (Figure 7-11), changed slightly to now show an IPv6 subnet. The figure shows a single-area design in which R1 finds three possible routes to reach subnet 33 (2001:DB8:1:33::/64), the middle route having the lowest cost.

To influence the metric for the route, OSPFv3 gives us a few ways to change an interface's OSPFv3 cost, with the same basic rules as OSPFv2, as summarized in this list:

Key Topic

1. Set the cost explicitly using the **ipv6 ospf cost** *x* interface subcommand to a value between 1 and 65,535, inclusive.

2. Change the interface bandwidth with the **bandwidth** *speed* command, with speed being a number in kilobits per second (Kbps), and let the router calculate the value based on the OSPFv3 **reference-bandwidth / interface-bandwidth**.

3. Change the reference bandwidth with router OSPFv3 subcommand **auto-cost reference-bandwidth** *ref-bw*, with a unit of megabits per second (Mbps).

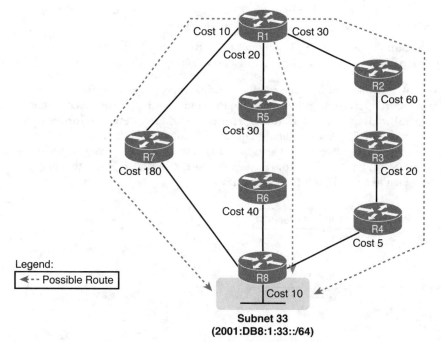

Figure 23-6   *SPF Tree to Find R1's Route to 2001:DB8:1:33::/64*

OSPF Load Balancing

OSPFv3 and OSPFv2 follow the same concept, with the exact same configuration command, to effect equal-cost load balancing.

When OSPFv3 on a router calculates multiple equal-metric routes to reach one subnet, the router can put multiple equal-cost routes in the routing table. The OSPFv3 **maximum-paths** *number* router subcommand defines just how many such routes OSPFv3 will add to the IPv6 routing table. For example, if an internetwork has six possible routes for some subnet, and all have the exact same metric, and the engineer wants all routes to be used, he could configure the router with the **maximum-paths 6** subcommand under the **ipv6 router ospf** command.

Injecting Default Routes

Finally, with yet another OSPFv3 feature that works very much like OSPFv2, OSPFv3 supports a router's capability to advertise a default route with OSPFv3. This function allows one router to have a default route and then basically tell all other routers, "Hey, if you need a default route, send packets to me, and I'll send them with my good default route."

One classic case for using a routing protocol to advertise a default route has to do with an enterprise's connection to the Internet. If a company has one IPv6-enabled Internet connection, that one router can use a default IPv6 route to route all IPv6 Internet traffic out that one link. But the rest of the enterprise's routers need to send their Internet traffic to this one router, so the enterprise engineer uses these design goals:

- All routers learn specific routes for subnets inside the company, so a default route is not needed for destinations inside the company.

- The one router that connects to the Internet has a static default IPv6 route that points all IPv6 traffic (that does not match any other IPv6 route) into the Internet.

- All routers learn (by using OSPFv3) a default route from the Internet-facing router so that all IPv6 packets going to the Internet first go to this one router.

Figure 23-7 shows the ideas of how the routing information is propagated from the Internet-facing router (R1) to the other routers in the company. In this case, a company connects to an ISP with its Router R1. Router R1 uses the OSPFv3 **default-information originate** command in OSPFv3 configuration mode; this command is literally the same command used for OSPFv2 (Step 1). As a result, R1 advertises a default route to the other OSPFv3 routers (Step 2). (The prefix for the default route with IPv6 is ::/0, with a prefix length 0, somewhat like the 0.0.0.0/0 used with IPv4.)

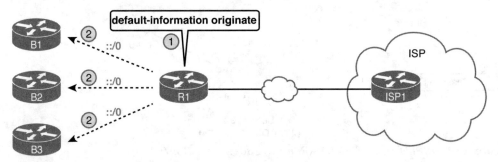

Figure 23-7   *Using OSPFv3 to Advertise a Default Route*

Once the process in Figure 23-7 completes, the three routers on the left each have a default route. Their default routes point to R1 as the next-hop router so that all traffic destined for the Internet first goes to R1 and then out to the ISP.

That completes the discussion of new configuration for OSPFv3. The next section discusses OSPFv3 verification and troubleshooting.

OSPFv3 Verification and Troubleshooting

To the depth discussed for CCNA Routing and Switching, OSPFv3 and OSPFv2 behave very much like each other. Just like the configuration of OSPFv2, using interface config is similar to OSPFv3 configuration, the OSPFv3 verification commands are also similar. Also, the types of issues that you need to troubleshoot for OSPFv3 are similar to the potential problems with OSPFv2. So, this last major section of the chapter just needs to show where OSPFv3 uses the same concepts as OSPFv2, and show where in those rare cases OSPFv3 differs from OSPFv2.

To the depth discussed in these books, OSPFv3 works much like OSPFv2 with regard to

- Area design and the related terms

- The configuration idea of enabling the routing process, per interface, for an area

- The neighbor discovery process with Hello messages

- Transitioning through neighbor states and the topology exchange process

- The use of full and 2-way as the normal stable state for working neighbor relationships, with other states being either temporary or pointing to some problem with the neighbor

- SPF and how it uses interface cost to calculate metrics

- Messages being sent to reserved multicast addresses (FF02::5 for all OSPF routers, FF02::6 for all DR and BDR routers), similar to OSPFv2's use of 224.0.0.5 and 224.0.0.6

So, what is different between OSPFv3 and OSPFv2? The next list mentions a few differences. However, note that many of the differences happen to be outside the scope of the coverage of topics in this book.

Key Topic

- OSPFv3 neighbors do not have to have IPv6 addresses in the same IPv6 subnet, whereas OSPFv2 neighbors must be in the same IPv4 subnet.

- They use different names for their Type 3 LSAs (called inter-area prefix LSAs in OSPFv3 and summary LSAs in OSPFv2).

- OSPFv3 introduces new LSA types not used by OSPFv2 (beyond scope of this book).

- The details defined inside LSA Types 1, 2, and 3 differ (beyond scope of this book).

As you can see, the list of differences is relatively short.

Because of the many similarities between OSPFv3 and OSPFv2, Cisco keeps the verification commands similar, too. Figure 23-8 summarizes the OSPFv3 verification commands relative to the kinds of information they show. Note that all the commands that list **ipv6** can be changed to **ip** to create the exact syntax of the matching OSPFv2 **show** command.

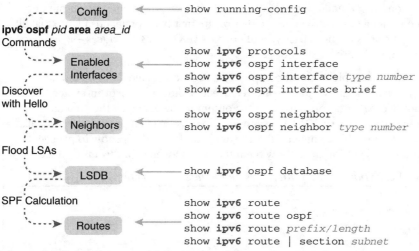

Figure 23-8 *Reference of OSPFv3 Verification Commands*

When a router first brings up the OSPFv3 process, IOS reads the OSPFv3 configuration and enables OSPFv3 on interfaces. So, this section begins by discussing OSPFv3 interface verification and troubleshooting. Following that, the discussion moves on to OSPFv3 neighbors, then to the OSPFv3 topology database, and finally to OSPFv3 routes added to the IPv6 routing table.

NOTE All the troubleshooting examples in the rest of this chapter use Routers R1, R2, R3, and R4 from the multiarea configuration example earlier in this chapter. Look back to Figures 23-4 and 23-5 for a reference to the topology and area diagrams for this network.

OSPFv3 Interfaces

The style of OSPFv3 configuration clearly identifies on which interfaces the OSPFv3 process should be working. The **ipv6 ospf** *process-id* **area** *area-id* interface subcommand basically means "run OSPFv3 on this interface." A quick scan of the interface in the output of the **show running-config** command can identify the interfaces and the area number for each.

The next few pages first take a look at a few other methods of verifying OSPFv3 interfaces, and then the discussion turns to some OSPFv3 interface troubleshooting tips.

Verifying OSPFv3 Interfaces

Suppose that, from studying, you have both seen and practiced OSPFv3 configuration and you feel confident about the configuration. Then, on the exam, you happen to get a simlet question on OSPFv3. Unfortunately, like many simlet questions, the question does not let you into enable mode, so you cannot see the configuration! A **show running-config** command plus your good configuration skills would let you answer any question, but you cannot see the config. How can you find out, for example, on which interfaces the OSPFv3 process has been enabled?

Three commands tell you something about interfaces enabled for OSPFv3: **show ipv6 protocols**, **show ipv6 ospf interface brief**, and **show ipv6 ospf interface**. All three commands list the interfaces on which OSPFv3 has been enabled. The first two commands list the information briefly, and the third command lists many, many lines of output per interface. (If you want a quick answer, use either of the first two commands.) Note that all three of these commands list both passive and nonpassive OSPFv3 interfaces—a handy fact to know when troubleshooting neighbor issues.

Example 23-5 shows a sample of the **show ipv6 protocols** command; later, Example 23-6 shows samples of the **show ipv6 ospf interface** and **show ipv6 ospf interface brief** commands. Note that before gathering the output in the example, the command **passive-interface gigabitethernet0/0.11** was added to R1's OSPFv3 process. In particular, notice that the output of this command differs quite a bit from IPv4's **show ip protocols** command, but the IPv6 version does show the interfaces on which OSPFv3 is enabled.

Example 23-5 *Verifying OSPFv3 Interfaces and Related Parameters*

```
R1# show ipv6 protocols
IPv6 Routing Protocol is "connected"
IPv6 Routing Protocol is "ND"
IPv6 Routing Protocol is "ospf 1"
  Interfaces (Area 0):
    GigabitEthernet0/0.12
    GigabitEthernet0/0.11
  Interfaces (Area 4):
    GigabitEthernet0/1
  Interfaces (Area 23):
    Serial0/0/1
    Serial0/0/0
  Redistribution:
    None
```

As you can see in the example, the output of the **show ipv6 protocols** command lists all five OSPFv3 interfaces on Router R1, including passive interface G0/0.11.

Troubleshooting OSPFv3 Interfaces

Most troubleshooting discussions with OSPFv3 revolve around the problems that can occur between two OSPFv3 neighbors. However, mistakes with interface subcommands can actually cause many of these OSPF neighbor problems. To get the discussions started, just consider the problems that can occur with the interface subcommands mentioned so far in this chapter:

■ Configuring the wrong area with the **ipv6 ospf** *process-id* **area** *area-id* interface subcommand prevents neighbor relationships off that interface.

■ Making an interface passive to the OSPFv3 process prevents the local router from forming neighbor relationships off that interface.

For the first item in the list, note that all OSPFv3 routers on the same data link need to be assigned to the same area. On the exam, you need to check any information about the intended area design. To find out which interfaces have been assigned to which area, use the **show ipv6 ospf interface** and **show ipv6 ospf interface brief** commands.

As for the issue in making an interface passive to OSPFv3, when a neighbor relationship needs to be made out that interface, the router should not make that interface passive to OSPFv3. Note that only the **show ipv6 ospf interface** command mentions which OSPFv3 interfaces happen to be passive.

Example 23-6 lists two commands that can be helpful for finding both of these problems. Both list area information, but only the second makes mention of an interface being passive.

Example 23-6   *Finding OSPFv3 Passive Interfaces on R1*

```
R1# show ipv6 ospf interface brief
Interface    PID   Area          Intf ID    Cost   State Nbrs F/C
Gi0/0.12     1     0             16         1      DR    0/0
Gi0/0.11     1     0             17         1      DR    0/0
Gi0/1        1     4             4          1      DR    1/1
Se0/0/1      1     23            7          64     P2P   1/1
Se0/0/0      1     23            6          64     P2P   1/1

R1# show ipv6 ospf interface G0/0.11
GigabitEthernet0/0.11 is up, line protocol is up
  Link Local Address FE80::FF:FE00:1, Interface ID 17
  Area 0, Process ID 1, Instance ID 0, Router ID 1.1.1.1
  Network Type BROADCAST, Cost: 1
  Transmit Delay is 1 sec, State DR, Priority 1
  Designated Router (ID) 1.1.1.1, local address FE80::FF:FE00:1
  No backup designated router on this network
  Timer intervals configured, Hello 10, Dead 40, Wait 40, Retransmit 5
    No Hellos (Passive interface)
! remaining lines omitted for brevity
```

23

Finally, to see an example of one of the problems, take another look at the configuration for Router R4. For the correct configuration in Example 23-3, the engineer made LAN interface G0/1 passive because no other routers existed on that LAN. However, note that R4 uses one Ethernet interface as its WAN interface (G0/0) and one as its LAN interface (G0/1). Suppose that the engineer made the simple mistake of making R4's G0/0 passive instead of G0/1. To show what happens, Example 23-7 changes R4's G0/0 interface to be passive to OSPFv3; note that R4's neighbor relationship to R1 fails almost immediately after the **passive-interface** command is issued.

Example 23-7 *Failure of R4's Neighbor Relationship with R1 Due to Passivity*

```
R4# configure terminal
Enter configuration commands, one per line.  End with CNTL/Z.
R4(config)# ipv6 router ospf 4
R4(config-rtr)# passive-interface gigabitEthernet 0/0
R4(config-rtr)# ^Z
R4#
Jan 17 23:49:56.379: %OSPFv3-5-ADJCHG: Process 4, Nbr 1.1.1.1 on GigabitEthernet0/0
  from FULL to DOWN, Neighbor Down: Interface down or detached
```

OSPFv3 Neighbors

As usual, OSPFv3 follows OSPFv2's conventions for how neighbors do their work as well. OSPFv3 uses many of the same protocol message names, neighbor states, and concepts from the processes to form neighbor relationships and exchange the LSDB. This next topic looks both at some samples of the process and, more important, at the number one place to look for OSPF problems: issues that prevent routers from becoming neighbors.

Verifying OSPFv3 Neighbors

Next, Example 23-8 shows some similarities between OSPFv3 and OSPFv2 message names and neighbor states. When reading through the debug output in the example, do not worry about all the detail; instead, focus on the highlighted portions. The highlights list some familiar neighbor states from OSPFv2, like 2-way, exstart, exchange, loading, and full, which is the final desired state in this case.

The example first shows the output from the **debug ipv6 ospf adj** command, which lists messages for OSPFv3 "adjacency" events—that is, what happens when neighbors work through their neighbor states. The end of the example shows R2's **show ipv6 ospf neighbor** command output, which confirms that R2's neighbor state with R3 is the final full state, as mentioned in the debug message. (Note that some debug messages were deleted for the sake of readability.)

Example 23-8 *From R2, Watching Changes to Its Neighbor State for R3*

```
R2# debug ipv6 ospf adj
R2#
Jan 15 14:50:58.098: OSPFv3-2-IPv6 ADJ   Gi0/0: Added 3.3.3.3 to nbr list
Jan 15 14:50:58.098: OSPFv3-2-IPv6 ADJ   Gi0/0: 2 Way Communication to 3.3.3.3, state
  2WAY
Jan 15 14:50:58.098: OSPFv3-2-IPv6 ADJ   Gi0/0: DR: 3.3.3.3 (Id)   BDR: 2.2.2.2 (Id)
```

```
Jan 15 14:50:58.098: OSPFv3-2-IPv6 ADJ   Gi0/0: Nbr 3.3.3.3: Prepare dbase exchange
Jan 15 14:50:58.098: OSPFv3-2-IPv6 ADJ   Gi0/0: Send DBD to 3.3.3.3 seq 0x2AC5B307 opt
  0x0013 flag 0x7 len 28
Jan 15 14:50:58.102: OSPFv3-2-IPv6 ADJ   Gi0/0: Rcv DBD from 3.3.3.3 seq 0xBD091ED opt
  0x0013 flag 0x7 len 28   mtu 1500 state EXSTART
Jan 15 14:50:58.102: OSPFv3-2-IPv6 ADJ   Gi0/0: NBR Negotiation Done. We are the SLAVE
Jan 15 14:50:58.102: OSPFv3-2-IPv6 ADJ   Gi0/0: Nbr 3.3.3.3: Summary list built, size
  14
Jan 15 14:50:58.106: OSPFv3-2-IPv6 ADJ   Gi0/0: Rcv DBD from 3.3.3.3 seq 0xBD091EE opt
  0x0013 flag 0x1 len 308  mtu 1500 state EXCHANGE
Jan 15 14:50:58.106: OSPFv3-2-IPv6 ADJ   Gi0/0: Exchange Done with 3.3.3.3
Jan 15 14:50:58.106: OSPFv3-2-IPv6 ADJ   Gi0/0: Synchronized with 3.3.3.3, state FULL
Jan 15 14:50:58.106: %OSPFv3-5-ADJCHG: Process 2, Nbr 3.3.3.3 on GigabitEthernet0/0
  from LOADING to FULL, Loading Done


R2# show ipv6 ospf neighbor


Neighbor ID     Pri   State           Dead Time   Interface ID    Interface
1.1.1.1           0   FULL/ -         00:00:38    6               Serial0/0/1
3.3.3.3           1   FULL/DR         00:00:37    3               GigabitEthernet0/0
```

Just like with OSPFv2, working OSPFv3 neighbors will stabilize either in a full state or a 2-way state. Most neighbors reach a full state, meaning that they fully exchanged their LSDBs directly to/from each other. However, for any OSPF network type that uses a designated router (DR), only the neighbor relationships with the DR and backup DR (BDR) reach a full state. Neighbor relationships between routers that are neither DR nor BDR—DROther routers—will stabilize to a 2-way state.

Troubleshooting OSPFv3 Neighbors

Any time it appears that OSPFv3 fails to learn routes that it should be learning, look at the expected OSPFv3 neighbor relationships. Then, if you find a relationship that does not exist, or exists but does not reach the expected state (full or 2-way), you can focus on the various reasons why a neighbor relationship would not work.

> **NOTE** As with OSPFv2, a neighbor in a full state is said to be *fully adjacent*, whereas two DROther neighbors that stabilize to a 2-way state are said to simply be *adjacent*.

Troubleshooting OSPF neighbor relationships requires that you remember many details about items that could prevent two routers from becoming neighbors at all. Thankfully, OSPFv3 uses the same list as OSPFv2, with one noticeable difference: OSPFv3 does not require the neighbors to be in the same subnet. Table 23-2 lists the items to consider when troubleshooting OSPF neighbor relationships.

23

Key Topic

Table 23-2   Neighbor Requirements for OSPFv2 and OSPFv3

Requirement	OSPFv2	OSPFv3
Interfaces must be in an up/up state.	Yes	Yes
Interfaces must be in the same subnet.	Yes	No
ACLs must not filter routing protocol messages.	Yes	Yes
Must pass routing protocol neighbor authentication (if configured).	Yes	Yes
Hello and dead timers must match.	Yes	Yes
Router IDs must be unique.	Yes	Yes
Must use the same process ID on the **router** configuration command.	No	No

When troubleshooting a problem, use the commands listed in Table 23-3 to quickly find the right piece of information to determine if that particular setting is preventing two routers from becoming neighbors.

Key Topic

Table 23-3   OSPF Neighbor Requirements and the Best **show** Commands

Requirement	Best Commands to Isolate the Problem
Must pass any neighbor authentication.	show ipv6 ospf interface
Hello and dead timers must match.	show ipv6 ospf interface
Must be in the same area.	show ipv6 ospf interface brief, show ipv6 protocols
Router IDs must be unique.	show ipv6 ospf
Interfaces must not be passive.	show ipv6 ospf interface

This section shows a couple of examples of problems that can exist between OSPFv3 neighbors. First, Example 23-9 shows a configuration in which a router (R4) purposefully sets its RID to the same number as a neighbor (R1, RID 1.1.1.1). Reading down in the example's highlighted portions, the following happens:

1. R4 changes its RID to 1.1.1.1.

2. R4 clears its OSPFv3 process, so that it starts using the new 1.1.1.1 RID.

3. R4 lists a syslog message stating the neighbor relationship went down (due to the clear command).

4. R4 lists a syslog message stating why R4 will not now become neighbors with R1 (1.1.1.1).

Example 23-9   *Results from R4 Changing Its RID to the Same 1.1.1.1 Value as R1*

```
R4# configure terminal
Enter configuration commands, one per line.  End with CNTL/Z.
R4(config)# ipv6 router ospf 4
R4(config-rtr)# router-id 1.1.1.1
% OSPFv3: Reload or use "clear ipv6 ospf process" command, for this to take effect
R4(config-rtr)# ^Z

R4# clear ipv6 ospf process
Reset ALL OSPF processes? [no]: yes
R4#
```

```
Jan 17 23:22:03.211: %OSPFv3-5-ADJCHG: Process 4, Nbr 1.1.1.1 on GigabitEthernet0/0
  from FULL to DOWN, Neighbor Down: Interface down or detached
R4#
Jan 17 23:22:05.635: %OSPFv3-4-DUP_RTRID_NBR: OSPF detected duplicate router-id
  1.1.1.1 from FE80::604:5FF:FE05:707 on interface GigabitEthernet0/0
R4#
R4# show ipv6 ospf neighbor
R4#
```

At the end of the example, the **show ipv6 ospf neighbor** command confirms that R4 now has no OSPFv3 neighbors. (Note that these examples still use the same network design shown in Figures 23-4 and 23-5, with the router normally having one neighbor, namely R1.) The duplicate RID now prevents R4 and R1 from becoming neighbors, so R4's **show ipv6 ospf neighbor** command lists no lines of output at all.

The next example (Example 23-10) mimics the OSPFv2 Hello and Dead timer mismatch issue shown back in Chapter 11, "Troubleshooting IPv4 Routing Protocols," in the section "Finding OSPF Hello and Dead Timer Mismatches." Again based on Figures 23-4 and 23-5, R3's Hello and Dead timers are 10 and 40, respectively, which are the default values on Ethernet interfaces. Before gathering this output, R2's configuration of the **ipv6 ospf hello-interval 5** interface subcommand on R2's G0/0 interface changed R2's Hello and Dead timers to 5 and 20, respectively. (This command sets the Hello timer, and IOS then sets the Dead timer to four times the Hello timer.)

Example 23-10 *R3 Missing from R2's OSPFv3 Neighbor Table*

```
R2# show ipv6 ospf neighbor

Neighbor ID     Pri   State         Dead Time    Interface ID    Interface
1.1.1.1           0   FULL/  -      00:00:35     6               Serial0/0/1

R2# show ipv6 ospf interface g0/0
GigabitEthernet0/0 is up, line protocol is up
  Link Local Address FE80::FF:FE00:2, Interface ID 3
  Area 23, Process ID 2, Instance ID 0, Router ID 2.2.2.2
  Network Type BROADCAST, Cost: 1
  Transmit Delay is 1 sec, State DR, Priority 1
  Designated Router (ID) 2.2.2.2, local address FE80::FF:FE00:2
  No backup designated router on this network
  Timer intervals configured, Hello 5, Dead 20, Wait 20, Retransmit 5
```

The two commands listed in Example 23-10 confirm that R2 and R3 are no longer neighbors over the LAN. However, just as with the similar OSPFv2 example back in Chapter 11, the router does not issue a syslog message telling us the root cause of the problem. With **show** commands, the only way to find this particular mismatch is to look at both routers with the **show ipv6 ospf interface** command; Example 23-10 shows an example from R2, listing its new values of 5 and 20 for the Hello and Dead timers.

23

Finally, note that as with OSPFv2, IOS allows the OSPFv3 routing process itself to be disabled with the **shutdown** command in routing protocol configuration mode. The process and results work just like they do for OSPFv2. When shut down, the router will not have any OSPFv3 neighbors, but the configuration will not be removed. Refer to the Chapter 11 section "Shutting Down the OSPF Process" for more details.

OSPFv3 LSDB and LSAs

Once OSPFv3 routers become neighbors, they proceed to exchange their LSDBs over that subnet. As with OSPFv2, in point-to-point topologies, the two routers exchange their LSDBs directly, and when finished, each router lists its neighbor as having reached a full state. In broadcast topologies like Ethernet, the routers elect a DR and BDR, and exchange their databases through the DR, with all routers reaching a full state with the DR and BDR. Once in a full state, the routers should have the same LSAs for that area. In short, the process works like OSPFv2.

Although the current ICND2 and CCNA R&S exam topics list LSAs as one of the excluded items (see the first page of the chapter), a quick look at LSAs can put some perspective on area design. For instance, Example 23-11 shows the output from the **show ipv6 ospf database** command on Router R4 from the configuration example used throughout the middle section of this chapter. As a brief review of that example:

- The design shows an area 4 (as well as area 0 and area 23).
- Router R4 is an internal router in area 4.
- Router R1 is an ABR between areas 4 and 0.

As a result, as seen in Example 23-11, Router R4 knows of two Type 1 LSAs. As with OSPFv2, with OSPFv3 each router creates a Type 1 router LSA for itself and floods that LSA throughout the area. As a result, R4 should see a Type 1 LSA for itself and Router R1, but not for the other routers in the network. (Note that the example uses obvious OSPF RIDs to make the LSAs easier to identify, with 1.1.1.1 being R1's RID, and 4.4.4.4 being R4's.)

Example 23-11   *LSDB Content in Area 4, as Viewed from R4*

```
R4# show ipv6 ospf database

            OSPFv3 Router with ID (4.4.4.4) (Process ID 4)


              Router Link States (Area 4)


ADV Router       Age        Seq#        Fragment ID  Link count  Bits
1.1.1.1          258        0x80000072  0            1           B
4.4.4.4          257        0x80000003  0            1           None
! Lines omitted for brevity
```

The Issue of IPv6 MTU

OSPFv3 can have problems in which neighbors come up, but fail to exchange their OSPF databases, due to an IPv6 MTU mismatch. This is the same problem that OSPFv2 can have, as discussed back in the Chapter 11 section "Mismatched MTU Settings."

Database exchange normally works correctly if two routers indeed become neighbors. That is, most of the problems for both OSPFv2 and OSPFv3 show up before the topology database exchange process happens. By way of review, two routers must first pass all the neighbor compatibility checks and reach 2-way state before attempting to exchange the topology databases. So, the configuration problems that prevent routers from becoming neighbors have been passed before the database exchange is attempted.

One misconfiguration problem actually allows two routers to become neighbors, attempt to do database exchange, and then fail after trying for a few minutes. The problem: mismatched IPv4 or IPv6 maximum transmission unit (MTU) sizes.

First, consider the idea of the MTU size, ignoring OSPF for a moment. The MTU size is a setting for a Layer 3 protocol, both IPv4 and IPv6. For now, consider only IPv6. The IPv6 MTU size of an interface defines the maximum size IPv6 packet that the router can forward out an interface. The same idea works for IPv4, with the IPv4 MTU.

NOTE In IPv4, routers can fragment IPv4 packets into smaller packets if a packet exceeds an interface MTU. In IPv6, hosts can detect the smallest MTU over an entire end-to-end route and avoid sending packets that exceed any MTU.

Most router interfaces default to an IPv4 and IPv6 MTU of 1500 bytes. You can change these values with the **ip mtu** *size* and **ipv6 mtu** *size* interface subcommands for IPv4 and IPv6, respectively.

Now think back to OSPFv3 and the fact that two routers can become neighbors and then fail to exchange their LSDBs because of unequal MTU settings. Specifically, the neighbors learn of each other with Hellos, reach a 2-way state, and reach exstart state at the beginning of the database exchange process. However, database exchange fails because of the MTU mismatch, and the neighbor relationship fails to a down state.

Example 23-12 shows an example of that specific failure on R4. The example first changes R4's G0/0 IPv6 MTU to 1400, and then resets the OSPFv3 process.

Example 23-12 *Failure to Exchange the LSDB Because of a Mismatched IPv6 MTU*

```
R4# configure terminal
Enter configuration commands, one per line.  End with CNTL/Z.
R4(config)# interface gigabitethernet0/0
R4(config-if)# ipv6 mtu 1400
R4(config-if)# ^Z
R4#
R4# clear ipv6 ospf 4 process
Reset OSPF process? [no]: yes
R4#
Jan 17 23:53:24.439: %OSPFv3-5-ADJCHG: Process 4, Nbr 1.1.1.1 on GigabitEthernet0/0
  from FULL to DOWN, Neighbor Down: Interface down or detached

R4# show ipv6 ospf neighbor
```

```
Neighbor ID      Pri    State           Dead Time    Interface ID    Interface
1.1.1.1            1    EXSTART/DR      00:00:37     4               GigabitEthernet0/0


Jan 17 23:55:29.063: %OSPFv3-5-ADJCHG: Process 4, Nbr 1.1.1.1 on GigabitEthernet0/0
  from EXSTART to DOWN, Neighbor Down: Too many retransmits
R4# show ipv6 ospf neighbor


Neighbor ID      Pri    State           Dead Time    Interface ID    Interface
1.1.1.1            1    DOWN/DROTHER    -            4               GigabitEthernet0/0
```

The last command in the example may be the key to noticing this particular problem on the exam. The two routers (R1 and R4) know of each other because the OSPF Hello messages have no problems at all. So, the **show ipv6 ospf neighbor** command on each router still lists the other router, as shown in R4's output that mentions neighbor R1 (1.1.1.1). However, after a while, the neighbor relationship fails to a down state. So, when you see a neighbor in what looks like a permanent down state, check the IPv6 MTU on both sides (with the **show ipv6 interface** command).

OSPFv3 Metrics and IPv6 Routes

At the end of all this noise about LSAs, database exchange, matching parameters for neighbors, and so on, the routers need to choose the best IPv6 routes to use. This final topic of the chapter reviews a few verification steps for how OSPFv3 calculates the metrics, and then looks at some more troubleshooting tips—this time about what to do with missing or suboptimal IPv6 routes.

Verifying OSPFv3 Interface Cost and Metrics

The SPF algorithm looks for all possible routes, or paths, from the local router to each and every subnet. When redundant paths exist between the local router and some remote subnet, the SPF algorithm has to pick the better route, based on the lower metric of the end-to-end route, as in the example shown earlier in Figure 23-6.

When OSPFv3 adds a route to the IPv6 routing table, the metric for the route is the second of the two numbers in brackets for the route. (The first number in brackets is the administrative distance [AD]; the IPv6 routing protocols use the same default AD values as their IPv4 counterparts.)

For example, first focus on the two metric 65 routes R1 learns for subnet 2001:DB8:1:23::/64, as shown in Figure 23-9. For the route through R2, R1 adds its S0/0/0 cost of 64 to R2's G0/0 cost of 1, for a total cost of 65. R1 calculates a metric 65 route through R3, as well. With a default setting of **maximum-paths 4**, R1 placed both routes into the routing table. (One route uses R2 as the next hop, and one uses R3.)

Example 23-13 shows these two routes for subnet 2001:DB8:1:23::/64, as highlighted in the output of the **show ipv6 route ospf** command on router R1. As usual, the OSPF-learned routes list a next-hop link-local address. To see which route refers to R2, and which refers to R3, check the outgoing interfaces and compare them to Figure 23-9.

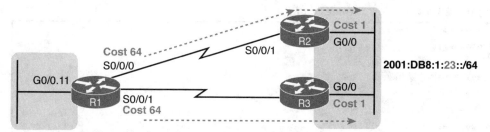

Figure 23-9 *Two Equal-Metric Routes from R1 to 2001:DB8:1:23::/64*

Example 23-13 *OSPFv3 Routes on R1*

```
R1# show ipv6 route ospf
! Legend omitted for brevity


O    2001:DB8:1:4::/64 [110/1]
     via GigabitEthernet0/1, directly connected
O    2001:DB8:1:23::/64 [110/65]
     via FE80::FF:FE00:3, Serial0/0/1
     via FE80::FF:FE00:2, Serial0/0/0
```

To see an example of what happens when a router has multiple routes but chooses one route because it has a better metric, next look at R2's OSPF-learned IPv6 routes in Example 23-14, focusing on the router to the subnet to the left side of Router R1 (subnet 2001:DB8:1:1::/64):

■ R2 has two possible routes (per the topology diagram in Figure 23-4) to reach subnet 2001:DB8:1:1::/64: one through R1, out R2's S0/0/1 interface; and one through R3, out R2's G0/0 interface.

■ R2 only placed one of these two routes into the IPv6 routing table: a route with metric 65, out R2's S0/0/1 interface. This cost is based on R2's default S0/0/1 cost of 64, plus R1's G0/0.11 cost of 1.

■ R2 decided the route through R3 was worse because the cost was the sum of R2's G0/0 cost (1), R3's S0/0/0 cost (64), and R1's G0/0.11 cost (1), for a total of 66.

Figure 23-10 shows the interface costs for these two competing routes. Note that the drawing omits parts of the network as shown earlier in Figure 23-4.

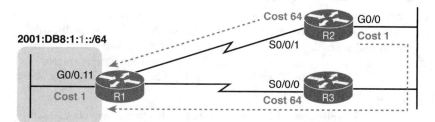

Figure 23-10 *R2's Competing Routes to Reach Subnet 1*

Example 23-14   *OSPFv3 Routes on R2*

```
R2# show ipv6 route ospf
! Legend omitted for brevity
OI  2001:DB8:1:1::/64 [110/65]
      via FE80::FF:FE00:1, Serial0/0/1
OI  2001:DB8:1:2::/64 [110/65]
      via FE80::FF:FE00:1, Serial0/0/1
OI  2001:DB8:1:4::/64 [110/65]
      via FE80::FF:FE00:1, Serial0/0/1
O   2001:DB8:1:13::/64 [110/65]
      via FE80::FF:FE00:3, GigabitEthernet0/0
OI  2001:DB8:1:14::/64 [110/65]
      via FE80::FF:FE00:1, Serial0/0/1
```

Also, note that the code letters on the left of most of these routes on R2 are *OI*. The *O* identifies the route as being learned by OSPF, and the *I* identifies the route as an interarea route. For instance, the highlighted entry lists prefix/subnet 1 (2001:DB8:1:1::/64), which sits in area 0, and R2 is in area 23. So, R2's route to this subnet is an interarea route. (Earlier, Example 23-13 showed several intra-area OSPF routes, each with code letter *O* instead of *OI*.)

OSPFv3 displays the settings for OSPFv3 interface cost with commands similar to those used in OSPFv2. For the default calculations, the **show ipv6 ospf** command lists the reference bandwidth, and the **show interfaces** command lists the interface bandwidth. Example 23-15 shows the current OSPFv3 interface costs on R1 with the **show ipv6 ospf interface brief** command.

Example 23-15   *Finding a Router's OSPFv3 Interface Costs*

```
R1# show ipv6 ospf interface brief
Interface   PID   Area        Intf ID   Cost   State  Nbrs F/C
Gi0/0.12    1     0           16        1      DR     0/0
Gi0/0.11    1     0           17        1      DR     0/0
Gi0/1       1     4           4         1      BDR    1/1
Se0/0/0     1     23          6         64     P2P    1/1
Se0/0/1     1     23          7         64     P2P    1/1
```

Troubleshooting IPv6 Routes Added by OSPFv3

If a problem appears to be related to IPv6 routing, the problems can be put into two broad categories. First, a router may be missing a route for some prefix, so the router discards the packet, and pings fail. Second, a router may have a working route, but it appears to take a suboptimal route to the destination. (Chapter 22, "IPv6 Routing Operation and Troubleshooting," in the "Traceroute Shows Some Hops, But Fails" section, discusses yet a third category in which a routing loop occurs.)

For example, in Figure 23-11, Router R1 has two possible routes to reach subnet 33, an IPv6 subnet off Router R3. The top route appears to be the better route, at least in terms of the number of routers between R1 and subnet 33. If R1 has no routes at all to subnet 33, you might look for one type of root cause; but if R1 uses the lower route through five routers, you might look for a different root cause.

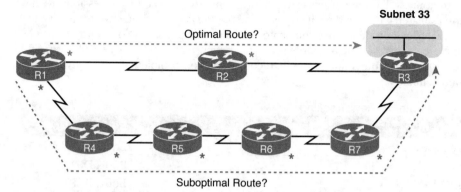

Figure 23-11   *Competing Long and Short Routes from R1 to Subnet 33*

When a router simply has no route to a given subnet—for instance, if R1 has no route at all for subnet 33—do the following:

Step 1.   Check the routers with interfaces directly connected to that IPv6 prefix. A router must have OSPFv3 enabled on that interface before OSPFv3 will advertise about the subnet.

Step 2.   Check OSPFv3 neighbor relationships for all routers between the local router and the routers with an interface connected to IPv6 prefix X.

For instance, in Figure 23-11, if Router R3 did not have an **ipv6 ospf** *process-id* **area** *area-id* command on its LAN interface, all seven routers could have working neighbor relationships, but R3 still would not advertise about subnet 33.

If a router has a route, but it appears to be the wrong (suboptimal) route, take these steps:

Step 1.   Check for broken neighbor relationships over what should be the optimal path from the local router and prefix Y.

Step 2.   Check the OSPFv3 cost settings on the interfaces in the optimal path.

For instance, in Figure 23-11, suppose that R1 indeed has one route for subnet 33, pointing over the lower route, with R4 as the next-hop router. The root cause of that choice could be the following:

■ The R2-R3 neighbor relationship is not working.

■ The sum of the costs for the top route is larger (worse) than the sum of the costs for the lower route. (Note that the figure shows an asterisk beside each interface whose cost is part of the calculation.)

Chapter Review

One key to doing well on the exams is to perform repetitive spaced review sessions. Review this chapter's material using either the tools in the book, DVD, or interactive tools for the same material found on the book's companion website. Refer to the "Your Study Plan" element for more details. Table 23-4 outlines the key review elements and where you can find them. To better track your study progress, record when you completed these activities in the second column.

Table 23-4   Chapter Review Tracking

Review Element	Review Date(s)	Resource Used
Review key topics		Book, DVD/website
Review key terms		Book, DVD/website
Answer DIKTA questions		Book, PCPT
Do labs		Blog
Review memory tables		Book, DVD/website
Review config checklists		Book, DVD/website
Review command reference tables		Book

Review All the Key Topics

Table 23-5   Key Topics for Chapter 23

Key Topic Element	Description	Page Number
List	Comparisons of OSPFv2 and OSPFv3	621
Example 23-4	Multiarea OSPFv3 configuration	625
List	Ways to impact the calculation of the metric for an OSPFv3 route	626
List	Similarities between OSPFv3 and OSPFv2	628
List	Differences between OSPFv3 and OSPFv2	629
List	Common OSPFv3 issues on interfaces	631
Table 23-2	Reasons why OSPF routers fail to become neighbors	634
Table 23-3	Commands to verify OSPFv3 neighbor requirements	634
List	Common OSPFv3 issues for missing IPv6 routes	641
List	Common OSPFv3 issues for having a suboptimal OSPFv3 route	641

Key Terms You Should Know

multiarea, Area Border Router (ABR), internal router, backbone area, router ID, full state, 2-way state, router LSA, MTU

Command References

Tables 23-6 and 23-7 list configuration and verification commands used in this chapter. As an easy review exercise, cover the left column in a table, read the right column, and try to recall the command without looking. Then repeat the exercise, covering the right column, and try to recall what the command does.

Table 23-6   Chapter 23 Configuration Command Reference

Command	Description
ipv6 router ospf *process-id*	Enters OSPF configuration mode for the listed process
ipv6 ospf *process-id* area *area-number*	Interface subcommand that enables OSPFv3 on the interface, for a particular process, and defines the OSPFv3 area
ipv6 ospf cost *interface-cost*	Interface subcommand that sets the OSPF cost associated with the interface
bandwidth *bandwidth*	Interface subcommand that directly sets the interface bandwidth (Kbps)
auto-cost reference-bandwidth *number*	Router subcommand that tells OSPF the numerator in the *Ref-BW/Int-BW* formula used to calculate the OSPF cost based on the interface bandwidth
router-id *id*	OSPF command that statically sets the router ID
maximum-paths *number-of-paths*	Router subcommand that defines the maximum number of equal-cost routes that can be added to the routing table

Table 23-7   Chapter 23 **show** Command Reference

Command	Description
show ipv6 ospf	Lists information about the OSPF process running on the router, including the OSPF router ID, areas to which the router connects, and the number of interfaces in each area
show ipv6 ospf interface brief	Lists the interfaces on which the OSPF protocol is enabled (based on the **network** commands), including passive interfaces
show ipv6 ospf interface *type number*	Lists a long section of settings, status, and counters for OSPF operation on all interfaces, or on the listed interface, including the Hello and Dead timers
show ipv6 protocols	Lists all means through which a router can learn or build IPv6 routes, including the interfaces on which each routing protocol is enabled
show ipv6 ospf neighbor [*type number*]	Lists brief output about neighbors, identified by neighbor router ID, including current state, with one line per neighbor; optionally, limit the output to neighbors on the listed interface
show ipv6 ospf neighbor *neighbor-ID*	Lists the same output as the **show ip ospf neighbor detail** command, but only for the listed neighbor (by neighbor router ID)
show ipv6 ospf database	Lists a summary of the LSAs in the database, with one line of output per LSA; organized by LSA type (first Type 1, then Type 2, and so on)
show ipv6 route	Lists all IPv6 routes
show ipv6 route ospf	Lists routes in the routing table learned by OSPF
show ipv6 route *prefix/length*	Shows a detailed description of the route for the listed subnet/mask

23

CHAPTER 24

Implementing EIGRP for IPv6

This chapter covers the following exam topics:

2.0 Routing Technologies

2.7 Configure, verify, and troubleshoot EIGRP for IPv6 (excluding authentication, filtering, manual summarization, redistribution, stub)

When creating Enhanced Interior Gateway Routing Protocol (EIGRP) for IPv6, Cisco made the new EIGRP for IPv6 as much like EIGRP for IPv4 as possible. How close are they? Incredibly close, even closer than the IPv4 and IPv6 versions of the Open Shortest Path First (OSPF) protocol. With EIGRP, the only noticeable difference is the configuration, which enables EIGRP for IPv6 directly on the interfaces and, of course, the use of IPv6 addresses and prefixes. However, the old and new EIGRP protocols are practically twins when it comes to the concepts, **show** commands, and troubleshooting steps.

This chapter has two major sections. The first major section shows the EIGRP for IPv6 configuration options for EIGRP for IPv6 classic mode, comparing those steps with the classic mode configuration of EIGRP for IPv4. The second major section shows how to verify EIGRP for IPv6 while giving some troubleshooting tips.

"Do I Know This Already?" Quiz

Take the quiz (either here, or use the PCPT software) if you want to use the score to help you decide how much time to spend on this chapter. The answers are at the bottom of the page following the quiz, and the explanations are in DVD Appendix C and in the PCPT software.

Table 24-1 "Do I Know This Already?" Foundation Topics Section-to-Question Mapping

Foundation Topics Section	Questions
EIGRP for IPv6 Configuration	1–3
EIGRP for IPv6 Verification and Troubleshooting	4–6

1. An enterprise uses a dual-stack model of deployment for IPv4 and IPv6, using EIGRP as the routing protocol for both. Router R1 has IPv4 and IPv6 addresses on its G0/0 and S0/0/0 interfaces only, with EIGRP for IPv4 and EIGRP for IPv6 enabled on both interfaces. Which of the following answers is a valid way to configure R1 so that it enables EIGRP for IPv6 on the exact same interfaces as EIGRP for IPv4 in this case?

   a. Adding the **dual-stack all-interfaces** router subcommand for EIGRP for IPv6

   b. Adding the **dual-stack** interface subcommand to interfaces G0/0 and S0/0/0

   c. Adding the **ipv6 eigrp** *asn* interface subcommand to interfaces G0/0 and S0/0/0

   d. Adding the **dual-stack all-interfaces** router subcommand for EIGRP for IPv4

2. Which of the following configuration settings does not have a separate IPv4/EIGRP for IPv4 and IPv6/EIGRP for IPv6 setting, instead using one setting that both EIGRP for IPv4 and EIGRP for IPv6 use?

   a. Interface bandwidth

   b. Hello timer

   c. Variance

   d. Maximum paths

3. An enterprise uses a dual-stack model of deployment for IPv4 and IPv6, using EIGRP as the routing protocol for both. Router R1 has IPv4 and IPv6 addresses on its G0/0 and S0/0/0 interfaces only, with EIGRP for IPv4 and EIGRP for IPv6 enabled on both interfaces and the router ID explicitly set for both protocols. Comparing the EIGRP for IPv4 and EIGRP for IPv6 configuration, which of the following statements is true?

   a. The EIGRP for IPv6 configuration uses the **router eigrp** *asn* global command.

   b. Both protocols use the **router-id** *router-id* router subcommand.

   c. Both protocols use the **network** *network-number* router subcommand.

   d. The EIGRP for IPv6 configuration uses the **ipv6 eigrp** *asn* interface subcommand.

4. Three redundant IPv6 routes exist on R1 to reach IPv6 subnet 9 (2009:9:9:9::/64), a subnet connected to Router R9's G0/0 interface. R1's current successor route uses R2 as the next hop, with feasible successor routes through Routers R3 and R4. Then, another engineer makes changes to the configuration in the network, resulting in R1 having no routes to reach subnet 9. Which of the answers lists one configuration that would result in R1 having no routes at all to subnet 9?

   a. Make R9's G0/0 interface passive.

   b. Change R2's EIGRP ASN to some other number, but otherwise keep the same configuration.

   c. Change the Hello timers on all of R1's interfaces from 5 to 4.

   d. Change R1's EIGRP ASN to some other number, but otherwise keep the same configuration.

5. R1 and R2 are routers that connect to the same VLAN. Which of the answers list an item that can prevent the two routers from becoming EIGRP for IPv6 neighbors? (Choose two answers.)

   a. Mismatched Hello timers

   b. Mismatched ASNs

   c. IPv6 addresses in different subnets

   d. Using the same router ID

   e. One passive router interface (used on this link)

6. The output of the **show ipv6 eigrp neighbors** command from R2 lists one neighbor. Which of the following answers is correct about the meaning of the output of the command in this example?

```
R2# show ipv6 eigrp neighbors
EIGRP-IPv6 Neighbors for AS(1)
H   Address             Interface     Hold Uptime     SRTT   RTO   Q   Seq
                                      (sec)           (ms)         Cnt Num
0   Link-local address: Gi0/0         11 06:46:11      1     100   0   30
    FE80::FF:FE22.2222
```

a. The neighbor's link-local address on its common link must be FE80::FF:FE22:2222.

b. The neighbor's EIGRP for IPv6 router ID must be FE80::FF:FE22:2222.

c. R2's link-local address on its common link must be FE80::FF:FE22:2222.

d. R2's EIGRP for IPv6 router ID must be FE80::FF:FE22:2222.

Foundation Topics

EIGRP for IPv6 Configuration

Internally, EIGRP for IPv6 behaves much like its IPv4 counterpart, EIGRP. Once enabled on all routers in an internetwork, the routers exchange EIGRP messages. Those messages allow the routers to discover neighbors, form neighbor relationships, advertise subnets along with their metric components, and calculate metrics for competing routes using the same old calculation. EIGRP for IPv6 also uses the same successor and feasible successor (FS) logic, and Diffusing Update Algorithm (DUAL) processing when no FS exists.

Differences do exist, of course, with the most obvious being that EIGRP for IPv6 advertises IPv6 prefixes, not IPv4 subnets. The messages flow in IPv6 packets, many going to IPv6 multicast address FF02::A. But most of the big ideas mirror EIGRP for IPv4.

As for configuration, EIGRP for IPv6 configuration looks much like the OSPFv3 configuration just discussed in Chapter 23. The EIGRP for IPv6 routing protocol process must be created, and then must be enabled on various interfaces using an interface subcommand. The rest of the EIGRP for IPv6 configuration is optional, to change some default setting, with changes to what happens between neighbors, what metric is calculated, and so on.

> **NOTE** This chapter shows one of two styles of EIGRP for IPv6 configuration called classic mode (also called autonomous system mode). EIGRP classic mode has existed since EIGRP for IPv6 first became available. The more involved EIGRP named mode, which uses address families, can be used as well but is not included in this book.

This first section first works through the most common EIGRP for IPv6 configuration commands, followed by a look at the various other commands used to change some small feature.

EIGRP for IPv6 Configuration Basics

EIGRP for IPv6 configuration works much like OSPFv3. That is, the commands create the EIGRP for IPv6 process in one part of the configuration, with interface subcommands enabling the routing protocol on the interface. Figure 24-1 shows the fundamentals of this core configuration for IPv6.

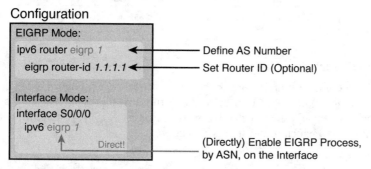

Figure 24-1 *Fundamentals of EIGRP for IPv6 Configuration*

If you remember EIGRP for IPv4 configuration, you will quickly see one key difference between the configuration in Figure 24-1 and what you know about EIGRP for IPv4. The example in the figure does not use any EIGRP **network** commands at all because EIGRP for IPv6 does not even support the **network** command. Instead, it uses the **ipv6 eigrp** *asn* interface subcommand. This process works like the OSPFv3 configuration from the preceding chapter, just with a slightly different command for EIGRP for IPv6.

The rest of the EIGRP for IPv6 configuration commands work either exactly like the EIGRP for IPv4 commands or very similarly to them. To show the similarities, Table 24-2 lists the EIGRP for IPv4 configuration options introduced in Chapter 10, "Implementing EIGRP for IPv4," making comparisons to the similar configuration options in EIGRP for IPv6.

Key Topic

Table 24-2 Comparison of EIGRP for IPv4 and EIGRP for IPv6 Configuration Commands

Function	EIGRP for IPv4	EIGRP for IPv6
Create process, define ASN	**router eigrp** *as-number*	**ipv6 router eigrp** *as-number*
Define router ID explicitly (router mode)	**eigrp router-id** *number*	Identical
Change number of concurrent routes (router mode)	**maximum-paths** *number*	Identical
Set the variance multiplier (router mode)	**variance** *multiplier*	Identical
Influence metric calculation (interface mode)	**bandwidth** *value* **delay** *value*	Identical

24

Answers to the "Do I Know This Already?" quiz:

1 C **2** A **3** D **4** D **5** B, E **6** A

Function	EIGRP for IPv4	EIGRP for IPv6
Change Hello and hold timers (interface mode)	**ip hello-interval eigrp** *asn time* **ip hold-time eigrp** *asn time*	Change **ip** to **ipv6**
Enable EIGRP on an interface	**network** *ip-address* [*wildcard-mask*]	**ipv6 eigrp** *as-number* (interface subcommand)
Disable and enable automatic summarization (router mode)	[**no**] **auto-summary**	Not needed for EIGRP for IPv6

EIGRP for IPv6 Configuration Example

To show EIGRP for IPv6 configuration in context, the next several pages show an example using the internetwork from Figure 24-2. The figure shows the IPv6 subnets. It also shows the last quartet of each router's interface IPv6 address as ::X, where X is the router number, to make it more obvious as to which router uses which address.

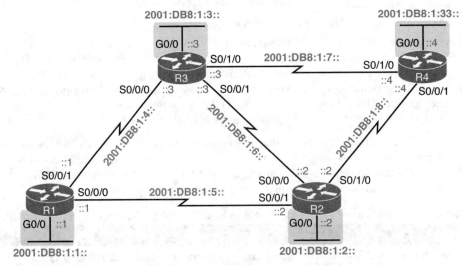

Figure 24-2 *Internetwork for an Example Multiarea EIGRP for IPv6 Configuration*

Note that Figure 24-2 mimics Figure 10-3, a figure used in several EIGRP for IPv4 examples in Chapter 10. Figure 24-2 uses the exact same interface types and numbers and router names. In fact, it uses a similar subnet numbering pattern. For instance, think of the four LAN-based IPv6 subnets as subnets 1, 2, 3, and 33, based on the last quartet values. Those same subnets in the examples in Chapter 10, based on the third octet of the IPv4 subnet numbers, are also 1, 2, 3, and 33, respectively.

Why does it matter that the internetwork used for this chapter mirrors the one used in Chapter 10? Not only are the EIGRP configuration commands similar but also the **show** command output. The **show** commands in this chapter, by using the exact same network topology, list almost the exact same output for EIGRP for IPv6 as they did for EIGRP for IPv4.

For this specific example, Example 24-1 begins by listing the additional IPv6 configuration required on R1 to make it a dual-stack router, including EIGRP for IPv6 configuration. The highlighted lines are the EIGRP for IPv6–specific configuration commands, while the rest of the configuration adds IPv6 routing and addressing.

Example 24-1 *IPv6 and EIGRP for IPv6 Configuration on Router R1*

```
ipv6 unicast-routing
!
ipv6 router eigrp 1
 eigrp router-id 1.1.1.1
!
interface GigabitEthernet0/0
 ipv6 address 2001:db8:1:1::1/64
 ipv6 eigrp 1
!
interface serial 0/0/0
 description link to R2
 ipv6 address 2001:db8:1:5::1/64
 ipv6 eigrp 1
!
interface serial 0/0/1
 description link to R3
 ipv6 address 2001:db8:1:4::1/64
 ipv6 eigrp 1
```

With this first example, take a few moments to review the configuration thoroughly. All the routers need to use the same EIGRP for IPv6 autonomous system number (ASN), as configured on the **ipv6 router eigrp** *asn* global command. Just after this command, R1 explicitly sets its EIGRP router ID (RID) using the **eigrp router-id** command. Note that EIGRP for IPv6 also uses a 32-bit RID, as does OSPFv3, with the same exact rules for how a router picks the value.

The rest of the configuration simply enables EIGRP for IPv6 on each interface by referring to the correct EIGRP for IPv6 process, by ASN, using the **ipv6 eigrp** *asn* interface subcommand.

Example 24-2 shows the configuration on a second router (R2). Note that it also uses ASN 1 because it must match the ASN used by Router R1. Otherwise, these two routers will not become neighbors. Also, note that R2 sets its RID to 2.2.2.2.

Example 24-2 *EIGRP for IPv6 Configuration on R2*

```
ipv6 unicast-routing
!
ipv6 router eigrp 1
 eigrp router-id 2.2.2.2
!
interface GigabitEthernet0/0
 ipv6 address 2001:db8:1:2::2/64
```

24

```
 ipv6 eigrp 1
!
interface serial 0/0/0
 description link to R3
 ipv6 address 2001:db8:1:6::2/64
 ipv6 eigrp 1
!
interface serial 0/0/1
 description link to R1
 ipv6 address 2001:db8:1:5::2/64
 ipv6 eigrp 1
!
interface serial 0/1/0
 description link to R4
 ipv6 address 2001:db8:1:8::2/64
 ipv6 eigrp 1
```

NOTE   IOS allows the EIGRP for IPv6 routing process to be disabled, and then reenabled, using the **shutdown** and **no shutdown** commands in EIGRP configuration mode. While enabled by default at later IOS versions, note that earlier IOS versions defaulted to a disabled state, requiring the configuration of a **no shutdown** command in EIGRP configuration mode before EIGRP for IPv6 would work.

Other EIGRP for IPv6 Configuration Settings

Examples 24-1 and 24-2 showed the basics for EIGRP for IPv6 configuration. The next few pages discuss a few configuration options in comparison to EIGRP for IPv4.

Setting Bandwidth and Delay to Influence EIGRP for IPv6 Route Selection

By default, EIGRP for IPv6 uses the exact same settings as EIGRP for IPv4 when calculating the metrics for each route. And to be extra clear, the settings are not similar or simply using the same command syntax. EIGRP for IPv6 uses the exact same settings as EIGRP for IPv4, specifically the interface bandwidth and delay settings, as configured with the **bandwidth** and **delay** interface subcommands. A change to these values impacts both EIGRP for IPv4's calculation of metrics and EIGRP for IPv6's calculation.

EIGRP for IPv6 also uses the exact same formula as EIGRP for IPv4 to calculate the metric for a route. As a result, in some conditions, the EIGRP for IPv4 metric for a route to an IPv4 subnet will be the same metric as the EIGRP for IPv6 route from the same router to IPv6 subnet in the same location.

For instance, in Figure 24-3, all the routers are dual-stack routers, with EIGRP for IPv4 and EIGRP for IPv6 enabled on all the interfaces in the design. Subnet 10.1.33.0/24 has been noted in the upper right, in the same location as IPv6 subnet 33 (2001:DB8:1:33::/64). R1's EIGRP for IPv4 and EIGRP for IPv6 processes will calculate the same exact metric for these routes based on the same collection of interface bandwidth and delay settings.

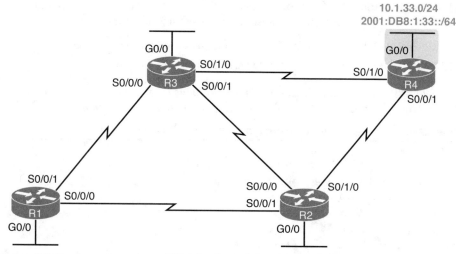

Figure 24-3 *Same Location off R4 for IPv4 Subnet 33 and IPv6 Subnet 33*

Example 24-3 shows the IPv4 and IPv6 routes on R1 for the subnets shown in Figure 24-3. Note the highlighted metrics in all cases are 2,684,416.

Example 24-3 *Identical Metrics for IPv4 and IPv6 Routes with EIGRP for IPv4 and EIGRP for IPv6*

```
R1# show ip route | section 10.1.33.0
D        10.1.33.0/24 [90/2684416] via 10.1.5.2, 00:02:23, Serial0/0/0
                      [90/2684416] via 10.1.4.3, 00:02:23, Serial0/0/1


R1# show ipv6 route | section 2001:DB8:1:33::/64
D   2001:DB8:1:33::/64 [90/2684416]
    via FE80::FF:FE00:3, Serial0/0/1
    via FE80::FF:FE00:2, Serial0/0/0
```

Note that both commands list two equal-cost routes on R1, for subnet 33, but the format of the output differs a little. The format of the **show ip route** command puts the destination subnet on the same first line as the first route's forwarding instructions. The **show ipv6 route** command lists the destination prefix on the first line, with each route's forwarding instructions on the second and third lines, respectively.

EIGRP Load Balancing

EIGRP for IPv6 and EIGRP for IPv4 use the exact same concepts, with the exact same configuration command syntax, for equal-cost and unequal-cost load balancing. However, EIGRP for IPv6 has its own configuration settings, made with the **maximum-paths** and **variance** commands inside EIGRP for IPv6 configuration mode. EIGRP for IPv4 has separate settings, using these same two commands, in EIGRP for IPv4 configuration mode.

For example, imagine that in a dual-stack network, the routers use EIGRP for IPv4 and EIGRP for IPv6. The network engineer would probably choose the same **variance** and

24

maximum-paths settings for both routing protocols. However, for the sake of pointing out the differences, imagine the engineer chose different settings, like these:

- **EIGRP for IPv4:** At most 2 routes, with variance 3 for unequal cost routes
- **EIGRP for IPv6:** At most 5 routes, with variance 4 for unequal cost routes

Example 24-4 shows how to make these different settings for these two different routing processes. However, note that the commands happen to use the exact same syntax.

Example 24-4 *Setting Load-Balancing Parameters per Routing Process*

```
R1# configure terminal
Enter configuration commands, one per line.  End with CNTL/Z.
! First, configure the settings for IPv4
R1(config)# router eigrp 10
R1(config-router)# maximum-paths 2
R1(config-router)# variance 3
! Next, configure the similar settings for IPv6
R1(config-router)# ipv6 router eigrp 11
R1(config-rtr)# maximum-paths 5
R1(config-rtr)# variance 4
R1(config-rtr)# ^Z
R1#
```

EIGRP Timers

EIGRP for IPv6 and EIGRP for IPv4 use the exact same concepts for the Hello and hold timers as does EIGRP for IPv4. To allow these values to be set differently for each routing process, IOS gives us slightly different syntax on the EIGRP for IPv6 and EIGRP for IPv4 commands, with the EIGRP for IPv6 commands using the keyword **ipv6** rather than **ip**. Otherwise, the EIGRP for IPv6 syntax mirrors the EIGRP for IPv4 version of the commands.

Example 24-5 shows a sample that changes both the EIGRP for IPv4 and EIGRP for IPv6 Hello timer, just to show the different commands side by side. For EIGRP for IPv4, the Hello timer is set to 6 seconds, and for EIGRP for IPv6, it is set to 7 seconds.

Example 24-5 *Setting the EIGRP for IPv4 and EIGRP for IPv6 Hello Timers*

```
R1# configure terminal
Enter configuration commands, one per line.  End with CNTL/Z.
R1(config)# interface gigabitethernet0/1
R1(config-if)# ip hello-interval eigrp 10 6
R1(config-if)# ipv6 hello-interval eigrp 11 7
R1(config-rtr)# ^Z
R1#
```

The choices for the timer values are arbitrary, just to make it clear which command is for each routing protocol. In real networks, these settings will likely have the same values for both EIGRP for IPv4 and EIGRP for IPv6.

EIGRP for IPv6 Verification and Troubleshooting

To the depth discussed in this book, EIGRP for IPv4 and EIGRP for IPv6 behave almost identically. Earlier, Table 24-2 listed the configuration commands, side by side, to show the similarities. This second major section of the chapter now looks at EIGRP for IPv6 verification and troubleshooting, with even more similarities between EIGRP for IPv6 and its older cousin EIGRP for IPv4.

So many similarities exist between EIGRP for IPv6 and EIGRP for IPv4 that you should just assume that they work the same, except for a few differences, as noted in the following list:

- EIGRP for IPv6 advertises IPv6 prefixes, whereas EIGRP for IPv4 advertises IPv4 subnets.

- EIGRP for IPv6 **show** commands use a keyword of **ipv6,** in the same position where EIGRP **show** commands use a keyword of **ip.**

- EIGRP for IPv6 uses the same checklist for choosing whether to become neighbors, except EIGRP for IPv6 routers may become neighbors if they have IPv6 addresses in different subnets. (EIGRP for IPv4 neighbors must be in the same IPv4 subnet.)

- EIGRP for IPv6 does not have an autosummary concept (while EIGRP for IPv4 does).

As you can see, the list of differences mentioned here is short. The similarities will become clearer through the many examples of **show** command output in the remainder of this chapter. To begin, Figure 24-4 reviews the EIGRP for IPv6 **show** commands discussed in this chapter. Note that all the commands in the figure use the same syntax as the EIGRP for IPv4 equivalent but with **ip** changed to **ipv6.**

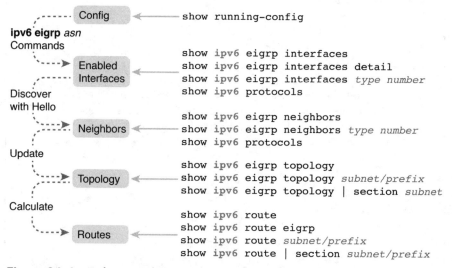

Figure 24-4 *Reference of EIGRP for IPv6 Verification Commands*

Similar to the preceding chapter's flow, this chapter's second major section breaks the discussion down in the same general sequence as EIGRP for IPv6 does when bringing up the EIGRP for IPv6 process. This section first examines EIGRP for IPv6 interfaces, then neighbors, topology, and finally, IPv6 routes.

NOTE   All the troubleshooting examples in the rest of this chapter use the example configuration from Routers R1, R2, R3, and R4, as shown in Figure 24-2.

EIGRP for IPv6 Interfaces

By enabling EIGRP for IPv6 on an interface, the router attempts to do two things:

1. Discover EIGRP for IPv6 neighbors off that interface

2. Advertise about the prefix connected to that interface

To make sure that EIGRP for IPv6 works correctly, an engineer should verify that EIGRP for IPv6 is enabled on the right interfaces. Or, from a troubleshooting perspective, one of the most common problems with EIGRP for IPv6 may be that a router did not enable EIGRP for IPv6 on an interface.

As was the case for EIGRP for IPv4, with EIGRP for IPv6, some commands list all interfaces on which EIGRP is enabled (including passive), some list all EIGRP interfaces but note which are passive, and some simply do not list the passive interfaces. Example 24-6 shows a sample that points out these differences, by first making R1's G0/0 interface passive. It then lists output from the **show ipv6 eigrp interfaces** command, which omits G0/0, and then the **show ipv6 protocols** command, which includes G0/0, but noted as a passive interface.

Example 24-6   *Verifying OSPFv3 Interfaces and Related Parameters*

```
R1# configure terminal
Enter configuration commands, one per line.  End with CNTL/Z.
R1(config)# ipv6 router eigrp 1
R1(config-rtr)# passive-interface g0/0
R1(config-rtr)# ^Z
R1#
R1# show ipv6 eigrp interfaces
EIGRP-IPv6 Interfaces for AS(1)
                        Xmit Queue   Mean   Pacing Time   Multicast    Pending
Interface      Peers   Un/Reliable  SRTT   Un/Reliable   Flow Timer   Routes
Se0/0/0          1        0/0         1        0/15          50          0
Se0/0/1          1        0/0         1        0/15          50          0

R1# show ipv6 protocols
IPv6 Routing Protocol is "connected"
IPv6 Routing Protocol is "eigrp 1"
EIGRP-IPv6 Protocol for AS(1)
  Metric weight K1=1, K2=0, K3=1, K4=0, K5=0
  NSF-aware route hold timer is 240
  Router-ID: 1.1.1.1
  Topology: 0 (base)
    Active Timer: 3 min
    Distance: internal 90 external 170
    Maximum path: 16
```

```
     Maximum hopcount 100
     Maximum metric variance 1


  Interfaces:
     Serial0/0/0
     Serial0/0/1
     GigabitEthernet0/0 (passive)
  Redistribution:
     None
IPv6 Routing Protocol is "ND"
```

Note that the **show ipv6 eigrp interfaces detail** command lists many lines of output per interface. Also, like the **show ipv6 eigrp interfaces** command, it lists all EIGRP-enabled interfaces, except passive interfaces.

Next, focus for a moment on troubleshooting related to EIGRP for IPv6 interfaces. As with OSPF, most troubleshooting revolves around the neighbor relationships. However, this short list describes two problems that can happen related to the interfaces:

- The omission of an **ipv6 eigrp** *asn* interface subcommand on an interface that has no possible neighbors may go overlooked. This omission does not impact EIGRP for IPv6 neighbors. However, this omission means that EIGRP for IPv6 is not enabled on that interface, and therefore the router will not advertise about that connected subnet. This problem shows up as a missing route.

- Making an interface passive to the EIGRP for IPv6 process, when a potential EIGRP for IPv6 neighbor is connected to that link, prevents the two routers from becoming neighbors. Note that the neighbor relationship fails with just one of the two routers having a passive interface.

For example, consider Router R4 in this chapter's sample network. Its G0/0 interface connects to a LAN, with no other routers. Currently, R4's configuration includes the **ipv6 eigrp 1** interface subcommand on R4's G0/0 interface. If instead that command were mistakenly missing (or if it were just removed as an experiment in lab), R4 would not advertise a route for the connected subnet (subnet 33, or 2001:DB8:1:33::/64).

Example 24-7 shows that specific example. To re-create the problem, though, before gathering the output in Example 24-7 on R4, the **no ipv6 eigrp 1** command was issued on R4's G0/0 interface, disabling EIGRP from that interface. Example 24-7 then shows R1 does not have a route to subnet 33 or EIGRP topology data.

Example 24-7 *Missing Route to Subnet 33 on R1*

```
R1# show ipv6 route 2001:DB8:1:33::
% Route not found

R1# show ipv6 eigrp topology | include 2001:DB8:1:33
R1#
```

EIGRP for IPv6 Neighbors

From one perspective, EIGRP neighbor relationships are simple. When two EIGRP for IPv6 routers sit on the same data link, they discover each other with EIGRP for IPv6 Hello messages. Those Hello messages list some parameters, and the neighbors check the Hello to determine whether the routers should become neighbors:

- If the parameters match, each router adds the other router to their EIGRP for IPv6 neighbor table, as listed with the **show ipv6 eigrp neighbors** command.

- If the parameters do not match, the routers do not become neighbors, do not add each other to their neighbor tables, and do not list each other in the output of the **show ipv6 eigrp neighbors** command.

From another perspective, troubleshooting EIGRP neighbor relationships means that you have to remember a lot of small details. The neighbors check lists of parameters that must match. At the same time, other problems can prevent the routers from becoming neighbors as well. Thankfully, EIGRP for IPv6 uses the same list as EIGRP for IPv4, with one noticeable difference: EIGRP for IPv6 does not require the neighbors to be in the same subnet.

Table 24-3 lists the items to consider when troubleshooting EIGRP neighbor relationships.

Key Topic

Table 24-3   Neighbor Requirements for EIGRP for IPv4 and EIGRP for IPv6

Requirement	EIGRP for IPv4	EIGRP for IPv6
Interfaces must be in an up/up state.	Yes	Yes
Interfaces must be in the same subnet.	Yes	No
Access control lists (ACL) must not filter routing protocol messages.	Yes	Yes
Must pass routing protocol neighbor authentication (if configured).	Yes	Yes
Must use the same ASN on the **router** configuration command.	Yes	Yes
K values must match.	Yes[1]	Yes[1]
Hello and hold timers must match.	No	No
Router IDs must be unique.	No[2]	No[2]

[1] K values define the EIGRP metric calculation algorithm. Cisco recommends that the settings be left as is; the **metric weights** command in router mode reconfigures the settings.

[2] Having duplicate EIGRP RIDs does not prevent routers from becoming neighbors, but it can cause problems when external EIGRP routes are added to the routing table.

For instance, in the configuration example in this chapter, all four routers use EIGRP for IPv6 ASN 1. However, suppose that Router R2's configuration had mistakenly used ASN 2, while the other three routers correctly used ASN 1. What would happen? R2 would have failed to form a neighbor relationship with any of the other routers.

Many EIGRP for IPv6 **show** commands mention the EIGRP for IPv6 ASN, but the **show ipv6 protocols** command shows the value in a couple of obvious places. Example 24-6, earlier, shows this.

As a troubleshooting strategy for the exam, note that every pair of EIGRP for IPv6 routers on the same link should become neighbors. So, when an exam question appears to point to some IPv6 routing problem, check the routers, count the EIGRP neighbor relationships, and make sure all the neighbor relationships exist. If any are missing, start troubleshooting EIGRP for IPv6 neighbor relationships based on Table 24-3.

To examine the neighbors, use the **show ipv6 eigrp neighbors** command. Because of the length of IPv6 addresses, this command lists two lines per neighbor rather than one line (as is the case with the EIGRP for IPv4 version of this command). The output in Example 24-8 shows this command's output from Router R2, with highlights in two lines for a single neighbor (R3).

Example 24-8 *R2's EIGRP for IPv6 Neighbors*

```
R2# show ipv6 eigrp neighbors
EIGRP-IPv6 Neighbors for AS(1)
H   Address                 Interface        Hold Uptime    SRTT   RTO  Q   Seq
                                             (sec)          (ms)        Cnt Num
2   Link-local address:     Se0/1/0           10 06:37:34   104    624  0   13
    FE80::D68C:B5FF:FE6B:DB48
1   Link-local address:     Se0/0/0           11 06:37:54   1      100  0   38
    FE80::FF:FE00:3
0   Link-local address:     Se0/0/1           11 06:46:11   1      100  0   30
    FE80::FF:FE00:1
```

Take a moment to focus on the IPv6 address and interface listed in the highlighted two lines. The output, taken from Router R2, lists R3's link-local address that sits on the other end of R2's S0/0/0 interface. The listed S0/0/0 interface is R2's interface. In summary, the details list the local router's interface and the neighbor's link-local address. So, to identify the EIGRP for IPv6 neighbor, you have to use that neighbor's link-local address (and not their EIGRP for IPv6 RID).

EIGRP for IPv6 Topology Database

If you keep the discussions to topics within the scope of this book, once EIGRP for IPv6 routers become neighbors, they should exchange all appropriate topology data. Outside the scope of this book, other router features can filter the topology data sent between routers. But for now, if the neighbor comes up, you can assume they exchange the topology data.

However, you should be ready to interpret the meaning of some of the topology data described by EIGRP for IPv6. Thankfully, the EIGRP for IPv6 topology data works just like it does for EIGRP for IPv4, other than one obvious difference: It lists IPv6 prefixes. The following list points out the concepts that remain identical between the two:

- The metric components (bandwidth, delay, reliability, load)
- The metric calculation
- The idea of a successor route (the best route)
- The idea of FS routes
- The feasibility condition, in which the reported distance (the composite metric reported by the neighbor) is lower (better) than the local router's metric

24

For example, Figure 24-5 shows an excerpt from the output of the **show ipv6 eigrp topology** command. This output shows R1's topology data for subnet 3 (2001:DB8:1:3::/64), the subnet off R3's G0/0 LAN interface. The left side shows the two details particular to IPv6: the IPv6 prefix/length and the next-hop router's link-local address.

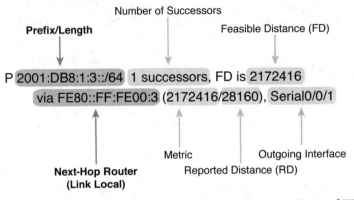

Figure 24-5   *Comparing IPv6 Details Versus Common Parts of EIGRP Topology Data*

Note that while the left side shows the IPv6 prefix and IPv6 next-hop router address, the right side shows the exact same ideas as used with EIGRP for IPv4. In fact, this example mirrors an example back in Chapter 10, shown there as Figure 10-4. That chapter also showed topology data from R1's database for the subnet off R3's G0/0 LAN interface. However, that example was for EIGRP for IPv4 and for subnet 10.1.3.0/24. If you take the time to flip back to Figure 10-4, you will see the exact same information for all the data on the right based on the EIGRP for IPv4 topology database, but IPv4 information about the subnet, mask, and next-hop address on the left.

In short, study the Chapter 10 details about the metric components, the metric computed as a formula, the successor and FS, and so on. If you master those details for EIGRP for IPv4, you have mastered the equivalent for EIGRP for IPv6.

Example 24-9 shows the EIGRP topology table for one last insight into the internals of EIGRP for IPv6. The output shows R1's detailed topology data for subnet 3 (2001:DB8:1:3::/64). Note that the first highlighted line lists the next-hop address and outgoing interface. It lists the composite metric—that is, the metric as calculated from the input of the various metric components—on the second highlighted line. The next two highlighted lines show the two metric components that impact the calculation (by default): bandwidth and delay. Finally, note that it mentions that EIGRP uses the minimum bandwidth (1544 Kbps) and the total delay (20,100).

Example 24-9   *R2's EIGRP for IPv6 Neighbors*

```
R1# show ipv6 eigrp topology 2001:DB8:1:3::/64
EIGRP-IPv6 Topology Entry for AS(1)/ID(1.1.1.1) for 2001:DB8:1:3::/64
  State is Passive, Query origin flag is 1, 1 Successor(s), FD is 2172416
  Descriptor Blocks:
  FE80::FF:FE00:3 (Serial0/0/1), from FE80::FF:FE00:3, Send flag is 0x0
      Composite metric is (2172416/28160), route is Internal
      Vector metric:
```

```
        Minimum bandwidth is 1544 Kbit
        Total delay is 20100 microseconds
        Reliability is 255/255
        Load is 1/255
        Minimum MTU is 1500
        Hop count is 1
        Originating router is 3.3.3.3
  FE80::FF:FE00:2 (Serial0/0/0), from FE80::FF:FE00:2, Send flag is 0x0
     Composite metric is (2684416/2172416), route is Internal
     Vector metric:
        Minimum bandwidth is 1544 Kbit
        Total delay is 40100 microseconds
        Reliability is 255/255
        Load is 1/255
        Minimum MTU is 1500
        Hop count is 2
```

EIGRP for IPv6 Routes

Verifying EIGRP for IPv6–learned routes is relatively easy as long as you realize that the code for EIGRP is D and not E. Example 24-10 shows R1's entire IPv6 routing table, with six EIGRP-learned IPv6 routes.

Example 24-10 *EIGRP for IPv6 Routes on R1*

```
R1# show ipv6 route
IPv6 Routing Table - default - 13 entries
Codes: C - Connected, L - Local, S - Static, U - Per-user Static route
       B - BGP, R - RIP, I1 - ISIS L1, I2 - ISIS L2
       IA - ISIS interarea, IS - ISIS summary, D - EIGRP, EX - EIGRP external
       ND - Neighbor Discovery, l - LISP
       O - OSPF Intra, OI - OSPF Inter, OE1 - OSPF ext 1, OE2 - OSPF ext 2
       ON1 - OSPF NSSA ext 1, ON2 - OSPF NSSA ext 2
C   2001:DB8:1:1::/64 [0/0]
     via GigabitEthernet0/0, directly connected
L   2001:DB8:1:1::1/128 [0/0]
     via GigabitEthernet0/0, receive
D   2001:DB8:1:2::/64 [90/2172416]
     via FE80::FF:FE00:2, Serial0/0/0
D   2001:DB8:1:3::/64 [90/2172416]
     via FE80::FF:FE00:3, Serial0/0/1
C   2001:DB8:1:4::/64 [0/0]
     via Serial0/0/1, directly connected
L   2001:DB8:1:4::1/128 [0/0]
     via Serial0/0/1, receive
C   2001:DB8:1:5::/64 [0/0]
     via Serial0/0/0, directly connected
```

24

```
L     2001:DB8:1:5::1/128 [0/0]
         via Serial0/0/0, receive
D     2001:DB8:1:6::/64 [90/2681856]
         via FE80::FF:FE00:3, Serial0/0/1
         via FE80::FF:FE00:2, Serial0/0/0
D     2001:DB8:1:7::/64 [90/2681856]
         via FE80::FF:FE00:3, Serial0/0/1
D     2001:DB8:1:8::/64 [90/2681856]
         via FE80::FF:FE00:2, Serial0/0/0
D     2001:DB8:1:33::/64 [90/2684416]
         via FE80::FF:FE00:3, Serial0/0/1
         via FE80::FF:FE00:2, Serial0/0/0
L     FF00::/8 [0/0]
         via Null0, receive
```

The pair of highlighted lines about halfway through the example describes the one route to IPv6 subnet 3 (2001:DB8:1:3::/64). Each route lists at least two lines, with the first line listing the prefix/length and, in brackets, the administrative distance and the metric (feasible distance). The second line lists the forwarding instructions for a route.

When a router has multiple routes to reach one IPv6 prefix, the output shows one line with the prefix and then one line for each route. The line for each route lists the forwarding instructions (neighbor's link-local address and local router's outgoing interface). The highlighted lines at the end of the example, for subnet 33, show one such example, with two routes, each with a different next-hop address and different outgoing interface.

As for troubleshooting IPv6 routes, again, most of the troubleshooting for routes begins with questions about neighbors. Thinking through a potential EIGRP for IPv6 problem actually follows the same logic as working through an OSPFv3 problem. Repeating some of the logic from the preceding chapter, when a router simply has no route to a given subnet—for instance, if R1 had no route at all for subnet 33—then do the following:

Step 1. Check the routers with interfaces directly connected to that IPv6 prefix. A router must have EIGRP for IPv6 enabled on that interface before EIGRP for IPv6 will advertise about the subnet.

Step 2. Check EIGRP for IPv6 neighbor relationships for all routers between the local router and the routers with an interface connected to IPv6 prefix X.

For instance, in Figure 24-2, if Router R4 did not have an **ipv6 eigrp 1** command under its G0/0 interface, all the routers would have their correct EIGRP for IPv6 neighbor relationships, but R4 would not advertise about subnet 33.

If a router has a route but it appears to be the wrong (suboptimal) route, take these steps:

Step 1. Check for broken neighbor relationships over what should be the optimal path from the local router and prefix Y.

Step 2. Check the interface bandwidth and delay settings. Pay particular attention to the lowest bandwidth in the end-to-end route, because EIGRP ignores the faster bandwidths, using only the lowest (slowest) bandwidth in its metric calculation.

Chapter Review

One key to doing well on the exams is to perform repetitive spaced review sessions. Review this chapter's material using either the tools in the book, DVD, or interactive tools for the same material found on the book's companion website. Refer to the "Your Study Plan" element for more details. Table 24-4 outlines the key review elements and where you can find them. To better track your study progress, record when you completed these activities in the second column.

Table 24-4   Chapter Review Tracking

Review Element	Review Date(s)	Resource Used
Review key topics		Book, DVD/website
Review key terms		Book, DVD/website
Answer DIKTA questions		Book, PCPT
Do labs		Blog
Review memory table		DVD/website
Review command tables		Book

Review All the Key Topics

Key Topic

Table 24-5   Key Topics for Chapter 24

Key Topic Element	Description	Page Number
Table 24-2	Comparison of EIGRP for IPv4 and EIGRP for IPv6 configuration commands	647
List	Differences in EIGRP for IPv4 and EIGRP for IPv6 concepts	653
List	Possible issues with EIGRP for IPv6 related to interfaces	655
Table 24-3	Items that may prevent EIGRP for IPv4 and EIGRP for IPv6 routers from becoming neighbors	656
List	Items to consider when using EIGRP for IPv6 and a route is missing	660
List	Items to consider when using EIGRP for IPv6 and a suboptimal route is used	660

Key Terms You Should Know

autonomous system number (ASN), EIGRP for IPv6, successor, feasible successor

Command References

Tables 24-6 and 24-7 list configuration and verification commands used in this chapter. As an easy review exercise, cover the left column in a table, read the right column, and try to recall the command without looking. Then repeat the exercise, covering the right column, and try to recall what the command does.

24

Table 24-6　Chapter 24 Configuration Command Reference

Command	Description
ipv6 router eigrp *autonomous-system*	Global command to move the user into EIGRP configuration mode for the listed ASN
ipv6 eigrp *asn*	Interface subcommand to enable EIGRP for IPv6 on the interface
maximum-paths *number-paths*	Router subcommand that defines the maximum number of equal-cost routes that can be added to the routing table
variance *multiplier*	Router subcommand that defines an EIGRP multiplier used to determine whether a FS route's metric is close enough to the successor's metric to be considered equal
bandwidth *bandwidth*	Interface subcommand that directly sets the interface bandwidth (Kbps)
delay *delay-value*	Interface subcommand to set the interface delay value with a unit of tens of microseconds
ipv6 hello-interval eigrp *as-number timer-value*	Interface subcommand that sets the EIGRP Hello Interval for that EIGRP process
ipv6 hold-time eigrp *as-number timer-value*	Interface subcommand that sets the EIGRP hold time for the interface
eigrp router-id *router-id*	Router subcommand to define the EIGRP for IPv6 router ID
[no] shutdown	Router subcommand to disable (**shutdown**) or enable (**no shutdown**) the EIGRP for IPv6 process
passive-interface *type number*	Router subcommand that makes the interface passive to EIGRP, meaning the EIGRP process will not form neighbor relationships with neighbors reachable on that interface
passive-interface default	Router subcommand that changes the EIGRP default for interfaces to be passive instead of active (not passive)
no passive-interface *type number*	Router subcommand that tells EIGRP to be active (not passive) on that interface or subinterface

Table 24-7　Chapter 24 **show** Command Reference

Command	Description
show ipv6 eigrp interfaces	Lists one line per interface on which EIGRP has been enabled, but for which it is not made passive with the **passive-interface** configuration command
show ipv6 eigrp interfaces *type number*	Lists interfaces on which EIGRP has been enabled, but for which it is not made passive with the **passive-interface** configuration command
show ipv6 eigrp interfaces detail [*type number*]	Lists detailed configuration and statistics, for all interfaces, or for the listed interface, again for enabled interfaces that are not passive
show ipv6 protocols	Shows brief information about each source of routing information, including listing interfaces enabled for EIGRP for IPv6 and noting which interfaces are passive

Command	Description
show ipv6 eigrp neighbors	Lists EIGRP neighbors and status
show ipv6 eigrp neighbors *type number*	Lists EIGRP neighbors reachable off the listed interface
show ipv6 eigrp topology	Lists the contents of the EIGRP topology table, including successors and feasible successors
show ipv6 eigrp topology *prefix/ length*	Lists detailed topology information about the listed prefix
show ipv6 eigrp topology | section *prefix/length*	Lists a subset of the **show ipv6 eigrp topology** command: just the section for the listed prefix/length
show ipv6 route	Lists all IPv6 routes
show ipv6 route eigrp	Lists routes in the IPv6 routing table learned by EIGRP for IPv6
show ipv6 route *prefix/length*	Shows a detailed description of the route for the listed prefix/length
show ipv6 route | section *prefix*	Lists a subset of the **show ip route** command (just the section for the listed prefix)

24

CHAPTER 25

IPv6 Access Control Lists

This chapter covers the following exam topics:

4.0 Infrastructure Services

4.4 Configure, verify, and troubleshoot IPv4 and IPv6 access list for traffic filtering

4.4.a Standard

4.4.b Extended

4.4.c Named

IP version 6 (IPv6) access control lists (ACL) provide a way for the network and security administrator to control the flow of IPv6 connections traversing the network. IPv6 ACLs provide a way to secure inbound and outbound connections as a part to the overall corporate security strategy and policy. Thus, IPv6 ACLs are a component of a layered security model that provides diversity of defensive techniques and defense in depth of complementary security approaches.

IPv6 ACLs share many of the same characteristics as IPv4 ACL, so your knowledge of IPv4 ACLs is directly transferable to IPv6 ACLs. As you have already learned, IPv6 is similar to IPv4, but it has some subtle differences in the way it works. Your knowledge of IPv4 is essential to learning IPv6, and at this point, your knowledge of IPv6 is solidifying. The same is true for the subtle differences between IPv4 and IPv6 ACLs. Both IP version ACLs can filter on IP addresses of packets and upper-layer information. IPv6 ACLs provide the ability to filter on IPv6-specific header values and other IPv6 packet attributes.

IPv6 ACLs can be used for a variety of reasons and purposes. IPv6 ACLs can filter traffic traversing the network, but IPv6 ACLs can also filter management access traffic. IPv6 ACLs can also be used to create Quality of Service (QoS) policies and to filter routing advertisements. However, the focus of this chapter will be on the ways in which IPv6 ACLs can be used to filter IPv6 packets arriving and departing router interfaces.

This chapter builds upon the IPv6 information in the ICND1 book and the IPv6 chapters earlier in this book. This chapter covers the fundamental concepts of IPv6 ACLs. The focus is on standard and extended IPv6 ACLs.

"Do I Know This Already?" Quiz

Take the quiz (either here, or use the PCPT software) if you want to use the score to help you decide how much time to spend on this chapter. The answers are at the bottom of the page following the quiz, and the explanations are in DVD Appendix C and in the PCPT software.

Table 25-1 "Do I Know This Already?" Foundation Topics Section-to-Question Mapping

Foundation Topics Section	Questions
IPv6 Access Control List Basics	1–2
Configuring Standard IPv6 ACLs	3
Configuring Extended IPv6 ACLs	4
Other IPv6 ACL Topics	5

1. IPv6 access control lists are configured in which of the following ways?

   a. Using ACL numbers 2300–2499

   b. Using ACL numbers 3000–3999

   c. Using ACL names to uniquely identify each ACL

   d. Using subinterfaces on the physical router's interface descriptor block

2. Which of the following statements is true about IPv6 ACLs?

   a. Cisco router interfaces can only have one IPv4 or one IPv6 ACLs applied in only one direction.

   b. Cisco router interfaces can have either an IPv4 or IPv6 ACL applied, but in both directions.

   c. Cisco router interfaces can have both IPv4 and IPv6 ACLs applied inbound and outbound on a single interface.

   d. Cisco router interfaces can have either an IPv4 or an IPv6 ACL applied, but only in one direction.

3. Which of the following IPv6 ACL entries would match and permit IPv6 packets coming from the Internet destined for the 2001:0db8:1111:0001:0000:0000:0000:0000 prefix with a 64-bit prefix length?

   a. **permit ipv6 any 2001:db8:1111:1::1**

   b. **permit ipv6 2001:db8:1111:1::/64 any**

   c. **permit ipv6 any 2001:db8:1111:1::1/128**

   d. **permit ipv6 any 2001:db8:1111:1::/64**

4. Which of the following packet header fields can be filtered using IPv6 extended access control lists?

   a. TCP source and destination port number

   b. ICMPv6 type and code values

   c. IPv6 extension header numbers

   d. IPv6 flow label values

   e. All of the other answers are correct.

5. The implicit rules at the bottom of IPv6 ACLs are there to permit which of the following packets?

    a. Router Solicitation (RS) and Router Advertisement (RA) messages

    b. Neighbor Solicitation (NS) and Neighbor Advertisement (NA) messages

    c. All ICMPv6 messages on a LAN interface

    d. All IPv6 multicast packets on a LAN interface

Foundation Topics

IPv6 Access Control List Basics

IPv6 ACLs provide the network engineer with a method to filter IPv6 packets. IPv6 packets can match the configuration of the ACL and then be permitted or denied from entering or exiting the router's interface. IPv6 ACLs can match on the various fields of the IPv6 header, including the source and destination addresses. IPv6 ACLs can also match on the other upper-layer header parameters and extension headers and Internet Control Message Protocol Version 6 (ICMPv6) packets.

There are several types of and uses for ACLs. ACLs can be used to filter control-plane activity, either to filter routing updates or to secure the router's own internal control plane. ACLs are used when matching and classifying types of data traffic when configuring QoS. ACLs can also be used to filter management plane packets to help secure configuration activities by allowing only management protocol access from approved network administrator systems.

The traditional use of ACLs, and the focus of this chapter, involves their ability to permit or deny packets traversing the router's data-plane interfaces. ACLs can filter many different types of packets, but this chapter narrows the focus to how ACLs can be used to filter IPv6 packets that are traversing the network. IPv6 ACLs can permit or deny specific types of IPv6 packets that are flowing from a source node to a destination node.

This first section of this chapter covers IPv6 ACLs and how they are used for filtering IPv6 packets in the data plane on router interfaces.

Similarities and Differences Between IPv4 and IPv6 ACLs

At this point you should be familiar with IPv4 ACLs but just starting to learn about IPv6 ACLs. As you learn about IPv6, you will notice subtle differences about IPv6 that have direct functional relationships with IPv4 protocol operations. Similarly, there are subtle similarities and differences between the way that IPv4 ACLs and IPv6 ACLs operate. Following are the ways that IPv4 and IPv6 are similar:

- Both match on the source address or the destination address in the protocol header.
- Both match individual host addresses or subnets/prefixes.
- Both can be applied directionally (inbound and outbound) to a router's interface.
- Both can match on transport layer protocol information such as TCP or UDP source or destination port numbers.

- Both can match on specific ICMP message types and codes.

- Both have an implicit deny statement at the end of the ACL that matches all remaining packets.

- Both support time ranges for time-based ACLs.

Of course, there are key differences between IPv4 and IPv6 ACLs as well. IPv4 ACLs match IPv4 packets only (and not IPv6), and match special fields found only in IPv4 headers. Likewise, IPv6 ACLs match against IPv6 address fields as well as other fields unique to an IPv6 header. The following is a summary of the key differences:

Key Topic

- IPv4 ACLs can only match IPv4 packets and IPv6 ACLs can only match IPv6 packets.

- IPv4 ACLs can be identified by number or name, while IPv6 ACLs use names only.

- IPv4 ACLs identify that an ACL is either standard or extended based on the ACL number range or by using the **standard** or **extended** keyword. IPv6 ACLs have a similar standard and extended ACL concept, but do not differentiate the styles with a different configuration keyword.

- IPv4 ACLs can match on specific values unique to an IPv4 header (e.g., option, precedence, ToS TTL, fragments).

- IPv6 ACLs can match on specific values unique to an IPv6 header (e.g., flow label, DSCP) as well as extension and option header values.

- IPv6 ACLs have some implicit **permit** statements at the end of each ACL, just before the implicit deny all at the end of the ACL, while IPv4 ACLs do not have implicit **permit** statements.

ACL Location and Direction

IPv6 ACLs, just like IPv4 ACLs, can be applied to any interface using that specific IP version protocol and can be applied to that interface in the inbound and the outbound direction. Furthermore, a router's interface that is operating in dual-protocol mode with both IPv4 and IPv6 can have an inbound and outbound IPv4 ACL and an inbound and outbound IPv6 ACL on the interface. The IPv4 ACLs will have no filtering function on the IPv6 packets and, vice versa, the IPv6 ACLs will not affect any IPv4 packets on the interface.

When ACLs are used to perform security filtering at the edge of a network, the more secure configuration method is to use inbound ACLs applied to the router interface that faces the untrusted network. This puts the router into a position to block incoming packets before they enter any part of the network. The less secure method is to use outbound ACLs applied to the perimeter router's internal interface. In this case, the router first computes the forwarding path, and then the ACL can block the packet before it begins to leave the interface. Furthermore, to filter packets leaving the trusted network, the best practice is to apply the ACL in the outbound direction on the interface that connects to the untrusted network. These best practices for ACLs also apply to IPv6 ACLs.

25

Answers to the "Do I Know This Already?" quiz:

1 C **2** C **3** D **4** E **5** B

IPv6 Filtering Policies

Choosing what packets to permit and deny—called the *filtering policy*—is the hard part of building IPv6 ACLs. Configuring those filtering policies once they are chosen is the easy part.

Most security practitioners agree on the concept of having a "fail-safe stance" whereby filters should only permit what is allowed and block all else. In other words, "that which is not permitted is blocked." This is the default method of configuration for Cisco IOS ACLs and is no different when it comes to IPv6 ACLs. Each IPv6 ACL has an implied **deny ipv6 any any** rule at the bottom, so that any packet that falls through the if-then-else rule base will be blocked by default.

When starting to create an IPv6 filter, you don't just take your IPv4 policy and then change the addresses to IPv6 addresses and paste in the new policy. Because IPv4 and IPv6 operate in completely separate data planes, you cannot simply replace an IPv4 address with an IPv6 address in the policy and make it work. For starters, in most cases your IPv4 network is fully established and your IPv6 environment is just beginning to develop. It is more realistic to start a new IPv6 policy and allow only those services that you want to permit for IPv6. Your IPv6 filters will grow in size over time as your IPv6 deployment develops and you require more permit statements in the ACLs.

The next step in creating an IPv6 ACL and filtering policy is to determine the types of IPv6 packets that should be allowed. This depends on the location of the router performing the filtering and the nature of the interface that the ACL is being applied to. For example, an ACL applied to the inbound direction of an Internet-connected router's external interface is much different than an ACL applied to the inbound direction of an internal data center router connecting to a LAN containing servers.

ICMPv6 Filtering Caution

For the sake of the exams, this chapter focuses mostly on how to configure and verify IPv6 ACLs. However, it helps to think about some more practical tips that will be of good use in production networks.

Taking an approach of explicitly filtering the traffic that should be allowed, and filtering all other traffic, actually requires that the network engineer fully understand the protocols that flow through the router. As it turns out, with IPv6, some types of ICMPv6 messages need to be permitted by IPv6 ACLs, otherwise the ACL can prevent IPv6 packet forwarding from working correctly.

First, with ICMP for IPv4, many network engineers filter most ICMP messages as a matter of habit. Many different attacks make use of ICMP for IPv4, and one way to deal with those attacks is to filter the messages. The temptation is to then do likewise and filter ICMPv6 messages.

Some ICMPv6 messages must be permitted by IPv6 ACLs. For instance, Neighbor Discovery Protocol (NDP) is part of ICMPv6. Additionally, endpoint hosts use a feature called Path MTU Discovery (PMTUD), which requires ICMP messages to flow through the network. (The PMTUD feature discovers the maximum-length IPv6 packet that can flow between the source and destination host; if the host sends larger packets, IPv6 routers discard those packets.) So, building IPv6 ACLs that filter the ICMPv6 messages used by PMTUD can prevent hosts from communicating over the IPv6 network.

Therefore, when building production IPv6 networks, allowing specific ICMPv6 message types to traverse a router interface is an essential practice for facilitating end-to-end connectivity. Understanding the ICMPv6 types and codes and their functions is useful when creating IPv6 ACLs. For future reference, the Internet Assigned Numbers Authority (IANA) maintains the list of ICMPv6 parameters:

http://www.iana.org/assignments/icmpv6-parameters/icmpv6-parameters.xhtml

For guidance on the types of IPv6 and ICMPv6 packets that should be permitted at these different locations, consult IETF RFC 4890, "Recommendations for Filtering ICMPv6 Messages in Firewalls," and NIST Special Publication (SP) 800-119, "Guidelines for the Secure Deployment of IPv6." These reference documents, found at the following URIs, provide real-world deployment guidance on the IPv6 packet types that should and must be dropped or allowed on WAN or LAN interfaces:

https://www.ietf.org/rfc/rfc4890.txt

http://csrc.nist.gov/publications/nistpubs/800-119/sp800-119.pdf

Capabilities of IPv6 ACLs

Even though IPv6 shares many commonalities with IPv4, there are subtle protocol differences that must be understood prior to configuring an IPv6 ACL. The way that IPv4 and IPv6 operate on a LAN is different. IPv4 utilizes LAN broadcast packets with Address Resolution Protocol (ARP). IPv6 uses multicast ICMPv6 messages with NDP. The IPv6 header includes fields such as the flow label and IPv6 uses extension headers for optional packet header functionality. This is different than IPv4's header structure.

Because ACLs are configured to match various elements of a packet header, IPv6 ACLs have their own capabilities that should be understood. The following mentions some values that IPv6 ACLs on IOS routers can match in an IPv6 packet:

- Traffic class (e.g., DSCP, 0 to 63)
- Flow label (0 to 1048575)
- IPv6 Next Header field indicating extension header type/number
- Source and destination 128-bit IPv6 addresses
- Upper-layer header details: TCP or UDP port numbers, TCP flags SYN, ACK, FIN, PUSH, URG, RST
- ICMPv6 type and code
- IPv6 extension header value and type (hop-by-hop headers, routing headers, fragmentation headers, IPsec, destination options, among others)

Limitations of IPv6 ACLs

There are several limitations of ACLs that you should take into consideration when planning and designing the router configurations. As mentioned previously, there are subtle nuances to how IPv6 is different than IPv4 that may affect how IPv6-enabled routers are configured. Following are the key limitations of IPv6 ACLs that you should be aware of and take into consideration when creating your filtering policy.

25

Matching Tunneled Traffic

IPv6 networks have a tendency to have more tunnels in use than in IPv4 networks. There are situations where IPv6 packets are being transported over IPv4 networks. For instance, these packets are carried within generic routing encapsulation (GRE). However, today, native IPv6 connectivity is more ubiquitous, so tunnels are not needed to join islands of IPv6 over an ocean of IPv4. Regardless, IPv6 ACLs are unable to filter based on the details of the IPv6 packets tunneled in IPv4 packets. The limitations of filtering based on the encapsulated traffic within any type of encapsulated or tunneled traffic has always been a limitation of ACLs.

IPv4 Wildcard Mask and IPv6 Prefix Length

IPv4 ACLs use a mask for the wildcard for the IPv4 subnet that is matched. Typically an IPv4 access list might look like the following entry that matches packets destined to the 10.1.1.0/24 subnet:

```
access-list 10 permit 10.1.1.0 0.0.0.255
```

However, those IPv4 wildcard mask bits do not have to be contiguous. It is possible, although not common, to have an IPv4 ACL that matches the IPv4 source or destination address using a noncontiguous wildcard mask.

With IPv6, you create an IPv6 ACL with a prefix length number value that indicates the number of contiguous prefix mask bits. In an IPv6 ACL, the prefix length number represents the number of contiguous bits that will be matched for that IPv6 address prefix. The syntax uses "slash" notation where the number after the slash indicates the number of bits of the prefix length. Therefore, you are only able to match on IPv6 address prefix and not use discontiguous masks with IPv6 ACLs. Furthermore, it is very common to have prefix lengths that are evenly divisible by 4 (e.g., /48, /52, /56, /60, /64) and nonstandard to have a prefix length that does not fall on a hex digit boundary.

ACL Logging Impact

It is important to remember that excessive logging can negatively impact router performance. The router's CPU is involved when a log entry is created. Therefore, any ACL entry that uses the **log** parameter and matches many packets per second could consume CPU resources on the router.

In this chapter there are IPv6 ACL examples that use the **log** keyword. This is for demonstration purposes only, to validate that IPv6 packets match specific IPv6 ACL entries. Although this may be a useful practice as the ACL is being created and tested, it may not be desirable to have a production ACL logging continuously.

With IPv6 ACLs, the log messages are generated for the first packet that matches that ACL entry. Subsequent ACL entry matches that are logged are generated on a 5-minute interval. This helps reduce the CPU impact, but is something to be aware of nonetheless.

Router Originated Packets

IPv6 ACLs, like IPv4 ACLs, have the ability to match and permit or deny packets traversing a router's interface in the data plane. However, there are limitations to ACLs matching router-originated traffic. IPv6 and IPv4 ACLs applied to interfaces in the inbound direction will block packets entering the router. However, outbound ACLs will not match packets that the router is originating.

NOTE   The idea of routers bypassing outbound ACLs for router-generated packets is the same concept discussed in some depth in Chapter 17, "Advanced IPv4 Access Control Lists," in the section "ACL Interactions with Router-Generated Packets."

Configuring Standard IPv6 ACLs

This section will show how to begin creating and testing simple examples of IPv6 ACLs. Demonstrations of this configuration process will use a network topology with two routers configured for IPv6 and two hosts connected to each of the router's LAN segments. Figure 25-1 will be used for the subsequent configuration examples in this chapter, so you may find yourself referring back to this topology frequently while reading examples.

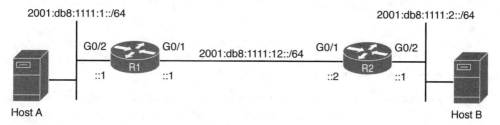

Figure 25-1   *IPv6 ACL Example Network Topology*

The first thing you will notice when you first learn the syntax differences between IPv4 ACLs and IPv6 ACLs is that IPv6 does not use any numbered ACLs. All IPv6 ACLs are named. As always, named ACLs allow you to use descriptive names that help you remember the ACL's intended purpose. To begin creating an IPv6 ACL, we need to enter the first command to name the ACL. After entering the first command and the ACL name, we then proceed with creating the access control entries, sometimes referred to as ACEs. Example 25-1 shows the syntax to create an ACL.

Example 25-1   *Configuring a Simple ACL*

```
R1# configure terminal
R1(config)# ipv6 access-list ?
  WORD        User selected string identifying this access list
  log-update  Control access list log updates


R1(config)# ipv6 access-list V6_ACL_IN
R1(config-ipv6-acl)# ?
IPv6 Access List configuration commands:
  default   Set a command to its defaults
  deny      Specify packets to reject
  evaluate  Evaluate an access list
  exit      Exit from access-list configuration mode
  no        Negate a command or set its defaults
  permit    Specify packets to forward
  remark    Access list entry comment
  sequence  Sequence number for this entry
```

25

Example 25-1 shows the creation of an IPv6 ACL with the name V6_ACL_IN. When the **?** is entered at the ACL configuration prompt, the router shows all the possible commands within an ACL. The **permit** and **deny** commands are the most common, but you could also use **remark** statements to help document the ACLs. The **sequence** command allows you to create or modify an ACL entry with a specific number whereby the ACL filtering is performed in order from the lowest sequence number to the highest sequence number. The **no** command can be used to remove a specific ACL entry.

Following is the syntax for standard IPv6 ACL **permit** and **deny** statements. IPv6 supports both standard and extended ACLs, although the configuration does not identify an ACL as one or the other. IPv6 standard ACLs can match the source and destination IPv6 address fields, but no other parts of an IPv6 packet.

```
[permit | deny] ipv6 {source-ipv6-prefix/prefix-length | any | host source-ipv6-
address} {destination-ipv6-prefix/prefix-length | any | host destination-ipv6-
address} [log]
```

The **permit** and **deny** commands in an IPv6 ACL have many similar concepts compared to a named IPv4 ACL's **permit** or **deny** commands, just with some slight variations. From this generic IPv6 **permit** command, you can see

- The **ipv6** parameter is one example of the protocol keyword, and means that the ACL will match all IPv6 packets. Other options match a subset of IPv6 packets and include **tcp**, **udp**, and **icmp**. These keywords mirror the **ip**, **tcp**, **udp**, and **icmp** keywords used in IPv4 ACLs.

- The source and destination IP address fields, followed by a prefix length, define the IPv6 prefix, much like an IPv4 ACL's combined subnet and wildcard mask field defines an IPv4 address range.

- The **host** *address* values (both source and destination) match a specific single IPv6 address, much like the **host** *address* option used in IPv4 ACLs.

Example 25-2 continues Example 25-1, in which the IPv6 ACL with the name V6_ACL_IN was created, proceeding to create the ACL entries. This ACL is going to have a single **permit** statement that allows any IPv6 node to send IPv6 packets to R2's LAN that contains host B (2001:db8:1111:2::/64). All other IPv6 packets will be implicitly dropped by this ACL. Once the ACL is created, then this ACL is applied to an IPv6-enabled interface in the specific direction.

Example 25-2 *Simple ACL*

```
R1(config-ipv6-acl)# permit ipv6 any 2001:db8:1111:2::/64
R1(config-ipv6-acl)# interface GigabitEthernet 0/2
R1(config-if)# ipv6 traffic-filter V6_ACL_IN in
```

IPv6 ACLs use the **ipv6 traffic-filter** command to apply the ACL to a router interface in a specific direction. This is a different syntax than the familiar IPv4 ACL **ip access-group** command that is used to apply an IPv4 ACL to a router interface.

Now it is a good idea to verify that the IPv6 ACL was created in the configuration and properly applied to the interface. Example 25-3 demonstrates the **show** commands that will be used to inspect the configuration steps performed.

Example 25-3   *Validating Simple ACL Configuration*

```
R1# show running-config
Building configuration...
! lines omitted for brevity
hostname R1
! lines omitted for brevity
interface GigabitEthernet0/2
 ipv6 address 2001:DB8:1111:1::1/64
 ipv6 traffic-filter V6_ACL_IN in
! lines omitted for brevity
ipv6 access-list V6_ACL_IN
 permit ipv6 any 2001:DB8:1111:2::/64
! lines omitted for brevity


R1# show ipv6 interface GigabitEthernet 0/2
GigabitEthernet0/2 is up, line protocol is up
  IPv6 is enabled, link-local address is FE80::F816:3EFF:FEC0:21D
  No Virtual link-local address(es):
  Global unicast address(es):
    2001:DB8:1111:1::1, subnet is 2001:DB8:1111:1::/64
! lines omitted for brevity
  Input features: Access List
  Inbound access list V6_ACL_IN
! lines omitted for brevity


R1# show ipv6 interface | include line|list
GigabitEthernet0/1 is up, line protocol is up
GigabitEthernet0/2 is up, line protocol is up
  Inbound access list V6_ACL_IN


R1# show ipv6 access-list
IPv6 access list V6_ACL_IN
    permit ipv6 any 2001:DB8:1111:2::/64 sequence 10
```

The Example 25-3 command output shows that the commands are now within the global configuration and the IPv6 ACL is applied to GigabitEthernet 0/2 in the inbound interface. The router's interfaces are up and operational and the ACL has its one **permit** statement.

25

The next step in the process is to test sending IPv6 traffic through the ACL. Using a simple **ping6** command from host A to host B will validate that the packets are being allowed. Example 25-4 shows the output from host A successfully executing the **ping6** command.

Example 25-4 *Validating* ping *Command's Packets Are Permitted by the ACL*

```
cisco@HostA:~$ ping6 2001:db8:1111:2:f816:3eff:fe9a:c89f
PING 2001:db8:1111:2:f816:3eff:fe9a:c89f(2001:db8:1111:2:f816:3eff:fe9a:c89f) 56 data
 bytes
64 bytes from 2001:db8:1111:2:f816:3eff:fe9a:c89f: icmp_seq=1 ttl=62 time=8.63 ms
64 bytes from 2001:db8:1111:2:f816:3eff:fe9a:c89f: icmp_seq=2 ttl=62 time=8.71 ms
64 bytes from 2001:db8:1111:2:f816:3eff:fe9a:c89f: icmp_seq=3 ttl=62 time=6.25 ms
^C
--- 2001:db8:1111:2:f816:3eff:fe9a:c89f ping statistics ---
3 packets transmitted, 3 received, 0% packet loss, time 2003ms
rtt min/avg/max/mdev = 6.257/7.869/8.712/1.142 ms
cisco@HostA:~$
```

Three ICMPv6 Echo Request messages were sent and it appears that they were successfully received and three ICMPv6 Echo Reply messages were returned. The next step is to check the IPv6 ACL on R1 and see how many packets have matched its single permit ACL entry. Example 25-5 shows the IPv6 ACL and shows that three packets have matched this ACL entry.

Example 25-5 *Finding Counters of Packets That Matched the ACL*

```
R1# show ipv6 access-list
IPv6 access list V6_ACL_IN
    permit ipv6 any 2001:DB8:1111:2::/64 (3 matches) sequence 10
R1#
```

To clear the IPv6 ACL traffic counters, use the following command:

```
clear access-list counters V6_ACL_IN
```

Configuring Extended IPv6 ACLs

The previous section covered a simplified syntax for a standard IPv6 ACL. This section will review the additional types of packets that extended IPv6 ACLs can match and the syntax for ACL configuration. Extended IPv6 ACLs can match on many more IPv6 header fields as well as ICMPv6 messages, TCP and UDP port numbers, and other IPv6 header items like IPv6 extension headers. Following is the complete syntax of an IPv6 ACL entry.

```
[permit | deny] protocol {source-ipv6-prefix/prefix-length | any | host source-ipv6-
address} [operator [port-number]] {destination-ipv6-prefix/prefix-length | any | host
destination-ipv6-address} [operator [port-number]] [dest-option-type [doh-number |
doh-type]] [dscp value] [flow-label value] [fragments] [log] [log-input] [mobility]
[mobility-type [mh-number | mh-type]] [reflect name [timeout value]] [routing]
[routing-type routing-number] [sequence value] [time-range name]
```

NOTE   The next few pages show many details of IPv6 ACL syntax so that you can see the large number of options. The upcoming Figure 25-2 reduces the complexity down to a few key values, similar to those used with IPv4 ACLs, more useful for preparing for the exam.

The generic **permit** and **deny** command shows the syntax for an extended IPv6 ACL. With IPv6, the difference between standard and extended ACLs is subtle. There is no keyword that distinguishes an IPv6 ACL as either standard or extended. Instead, an extended IPv6 ACL simply uses more than the source and destination IPv6 address fields when matching.

IPv6 extended ACLs can match on many of the values within the IPv6 header. IPv6 ACLs can match on the DSCP value for QoS marking, the flow label, and the source and destination IPv6 address. IPv6 extended ACLs have the ability to match not only on the source and destination IP addresses, but also on upper-layer protocol information. The next-header value in the IPv6 header indicates the number of the type of header that immediately follows the IPv6 header. In many cases, this would be either a TCP or UDP header where the protocol value would be **tcp** or **udp**, respectively. However, it could also be an ICMPv6 packet or it could be an extension header that has been added between the IPv6 header and the upper-layer header. IPv6 extended ACLs can match on destination option headers, fragmentation headers, routing headers, and Mobile IPv6 (MIPv6) headers. (To extend your learning about additional IPv6 extension header types, search for and read a copy of IETF RFC 2460.)

Besides matching IPv6 packets, IPv6 ACLs can also match ICMPv6 packets. ICMPv6 packets are IPv6 packets that also include an ICMPv6 header. By specifying **icmp** as the protocol keyword in the IPv6 ACL entry, the command matches the subset of IPv6 packets that also have an ICMPv6 header. Using the **icmp** keyword also enables many filtering options for ICMPv6 packets. For IPv6 ACL entries that match on ICMPv6 message headers, the following syntax defines how these ACL entries are configured:

```
[permit | deny] icmp { source-ipv6-prefix/prefix-length | any | host source-ipv6-
address | auth } [ operator [port-number] ] { destination-ipv6-prefix/prefix-length
| any | host destination-ipv6-address | auth } [ operator [port-number] ] [ icmp-
type [icmp-code] | icmp-message ] [ dest-option-type [ doh-number | doh-type ] ] [
dscp value ] [ flow-label value ] [fragments] [hbh] [log] [log-input] [mobility] [
mobility-type [ mh-number | mh-type ] ] [routing] [ routing-type routing-number ] [
sequence value ] [ time-range name ]
```

ICMPv6 ACLs can match on the source and destination IPv6 addresses, but also the ICMPv6 type and code values. ICMPv6 ACLs can also match on many other IPv6 extension headers like IPv6 extended ACLs.

It is possible to create an IPv6 ACL that matches TCP header values including source and destination port numbers. It is possible, although uncommon, for an ACL to match on TCP flags such as ACK, FIN, PSH, RST, SYN, and URG. TCP IPv6 ACLs can also match the other IPv6 extension header values. Following is the syntax for an IPv6 ACL that uses the **tcp** value for the protocol allowing this ACL to permit or deny a TCP packet:

```
[permit | deny] tcp { source-ipv6-prefix/prefix-length | any | host source-ipv6-
address | auth } [ operator [port-number] ] { destination-ipv6-prefix/prefix-length
| any | host destination-ipv6-address | auth } [ operator [port-number] ] [ack] [
dest-option-type [ doh-number | doh-type ] ] [ dscp value ] [established] [fin] [
flow-label value ] [fragments] [hbh] [log] [log-input] [mobility] [ mobility-type [
mh-number | mh-type ] ] [ neq { port | protocol } ] [psh] [ range { port | protocol }
] [ reflect name [ timeout value ] ] [routing] [ routing-type routing-number ] [rst]
[ sequence value ] [syn] [ time-range name ] [urg]
```

IPv6 ACLs also have the ability to match UDP packets. UDP packets do not have any of the flow-control flags used in TCP packets, and as a result, the ACL syntax is simpler. However, UDP IPv6 ACLs can still match on IPv6 extension header values. When the **udp** protocol value is used in an IPv6 ACL, the following syntax applies when creating an IPv6 ACL that can permit or deny a UDP packet:

```
[permit | deny] udp { source-ipv6-prefix/prefix-length | any | host source-ipv6-
address | auth } [ operator [port-number] ] { destination-ipv6-prefix/prefix-
length | any | host destination-ipv6-address | auth } [ operator [port-number] ]
[ dest-option-type [ doh-number | doh-type ] ] [ dscp value ] [ flow-label value ]
[fragments] [hbh] [log] [log-input] [mobility] [ mobility-type [ mh-number | mh-type
] ] [ neq { port | protocol } ] [ range { port | protocol } ] [ reflect name [
timeout value ] ] [routing] [ routing-type routing-number ] [ sequence value ] [
time-range name ]
```

When creating an IPv6 ACL that permits or denies TCP or UDP packets based on port numbers, IPv6 packets use the same port numbers as IPv4 packets. Therefore, an IPv6 ACL that blocks Telnet services using TCP destination port 23 would use the same port number as the functionally equivalent IPv4 ACL. Look to Table 17-3 in Chapter 17 for a list of most of the more common TCP and UDP port numbers.

Figure 25-2 points out some of the more common matching options specific to IPv6 extended ACL **permit** and **deny** commands when using the **tcp**, **udp**, and **icmp** keywords. When using any protocol keyword other than **ipv6**, the **permit** or **deny** command then matches a subset of IPv6 packets. For instance, using the **tcp** keyword as the protocol matches all IPv6 packets with a TCP header. Additionally, as with IPv4 ACLs, to match TCP port numbers, you must use the **tcp** keyword in the **permit** or **deny** command. Likewise, the command must use the **udp** keyword to match UDP port numbers, and the **icmp** keyword to then match ICMP message types.

Key Topic

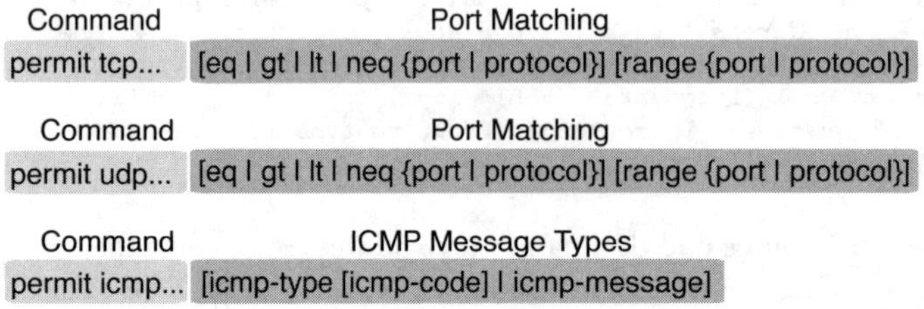

Command	Port Matching
permit tcp...	[eq l gt l lt l neq {port l protocol}] [range {port l protocol}]

Command	Port Matching
permit udp...	[eq l gt l lt l neq {port l protocol}] [range {port l protocol}]

Command	ICMP Message Types
permit icmp...	[icmp-type [icmp-code] l icmp-message]

Figure 25-2 *ICMP, TCP, and UDP Matching Fields in Extended IPv6 ACLs*

Examples of Extended IPv6 ACLs

Configuring an extended IPv6 ACL is similar to configuring a standard IPv6 ACL, but the ACL syntax is more complex, allowing matching of more types of packets.

This example will use the same network topology as in the previous standard IPv6 ACL example, repeated here as Figure 25-3. Example 25-6 will demonstrate the creation of an IPv6 ACL that filters packets entering R2's G0/1 interface. Example 25-6 shows an IPv6 extended ACL that

- Permits a custom application running on TCP port 51234
- Permits SSH running on TCP port 22
- Permits ICMv6 Echo Request packets

Figure 25-3 *IPv6 ACL Example Network Topology*

Example 25-6 *Configuring Extended ACL*

```
R2# configure terminal
Enter configuration commands, one per line.  End with CNTL/Z.
R2(config)# ipv6 access-list V6_APPS_ACL
R2(config-ipv6-acl)# permit tcp 2001:db8:1111:1::/64 2001:db8:1111:2::/64 eq 51234 log
R2(config-ipv6-acl)# permit tcp 2001:db8:1111:1::/64 2001:db8:1111:2::/64 eq 22 log
R2(config-ipv6-acl)# permit icmp 2001:db8:1111:1::/64 2001:db8:1111:2::/64
  echo-request log
R2(config-ipv6-acl)# interface GigabitEthernet0/1
R2(config-if)# ipv6 traffic-filter V6_APPS_ACL in
R2(config-if)# end
R2# show ipv6 access-list
IPv6 access list V6_APPS_ACL
    permit tcp 2001:DB8:1111:1::/64 2001:DB8:1111:2::/64 eq 51234 log sequence 10
    permit tcp 2001:DB8:1111:1::/64 2001:DB8:1111:2::/64 eq 22 log sequence 20
    permit icmp 2001:DB8:1111:1::/64 2001:DB8:1111:2::/64 echo-request log sequence 30
R2# show ipv6 interface | include line|list
GigabitEthernet0/1 is up, line protocol is up
  Inbound access list V6_APPS_ACL
GigabitEthernet0/2 is up, line protocol is up
R2#
```

Configuring this IPv6 ACL named V6_APPS_ACL starts with the creation of the ACL and its name, followed by the two **permit** statements for the two TCP applications and the ICMP Echo Request **permit** statement. Then the ACL is applied inbound to the specific R2 router interface. It is visible that the ACL is applied to the GigabitEthernet 0/1 interface in the inbound direction.

The next step is to test the IPv6 ACL by creating connections from host A to host B using these two specific TCP applications. The next step will be to test performing an IPv6 ping from host A to host B, which should succeed because ICMPv6 Echo Request messages are permitted by this ACL and should be replied to with ICMPv6 Echo Reply messages. The two TCP connections were completed successfully as well. After generating these connections on the hosts, the output in Example 25-7 was observed on R2, first with log messages, then with the **show ipv6 access-lists** command.

25

Example 25-7 *Check Counters on Extended ACL*

```
*Mar  6 21:59:12.230: %IPV6_ACL-6-ACCESSLOGP: list V6_APPS_ACL/10 permitted tcp
   2001:DB8:1111:1:F816:3EFF:FEF6:7296(52239) -> 2001:DB8:1111:2:F816:3EFF:FEE1:
   5CF5(51234), 1 packet
*Mar  6 21:59:16.069: %IPV6_ACL-6-ACCESSLOGP: list V6_APPS_ACL/10 permitted tcp
   2001:DB8:1111:1:F816:3EFF:FEF6:7296(52240) -> 2001:DB8:1111:2:F816:3EFF:FEE1:
   5CF5(51234), 1 packet
*Mar  6 21:59:17.798: %IPV6_ACL-6-ACCESSLOGP: list V6_APPS_ACL/10 permitted tcp
   2001:DB8:1111:1:F816:3EFF:FEF6:7296(52241) -> 2001:DB8:1111:2:F816:3EFF:FEE1:
   5CF5(51234), 1 packet
*Mar  6 21:59:49.769: %IPV6_ACL-6-ACCESSLOGP: list V6_APPS_ACL/20 permitted tcp
   2001:DB8:1111:1:F816:3EFF:FEF6:7296(57199) -> 2001:DB8:1111:2:F816:3EFF:FEE1:
   5CF5(22), 1 packet
*Mar  6 22:13:07.326: %IPV6_ACL-6-ACCESSLOGDP: list V6_APPS_ACL/40 permitted icmpv6
   2001:DB8:1111:1:F816:3EFF:FEF6:7296 -> 2001:DB8:1111:2:F816:3EFF:FEE1:5CF5 (128/0),
   1 packet
R2# show ipv6 access-list
IPv6 access list V6_APPS_ACL
    permit tcp 2001:DB8:1111:1::/64 2001:DB8:1111:2::/64 eq 51234 log (15 matches)
       sequence 10
    permit tcp 2001:DB8:1111:1::/64 2001:DB8:1111:2::/64 eq 22 log (34 matches)
       sequence 20
    permit icmp 2001:DB8:1111:1::/64 2001:DB8:1111:2::/64 echo-request log (3 matches)
       sequence 30
R2#
```

Because both entries of the IPv6 extended ACL are using the **log** keyword, R2 observes via console-level logging that connections were made on both TCP port 51234 and port 22 and that the ping worked. When the IPv6 ACL is checked on R2, the log messages and **show** command counters show that there are matches on all three ACL entries. Therefore, this extended IPv6 ACL is behaving as expected and as desired.

Practice Building ipv6 access-list Commands

In this section, practice getting comfortable with the syntax of the **ipv6 access-list permit** or **deny** ACL entry, particularly with choosing the correct matching logic. First, the following list summarizes some important tips to consider when choosing matching parameters to any **ipv6 access-list permit** or **deny** ACL entries:

Key Topic

■ To match a specific address, just list the address after the **host** keyword.

■ To match any and all addresses, use the **any** keyword.

■ To match based only on the IPv6 prefix, use the "slash" notation to designate the number of bits in the prefix length. For example, a /64 prefix length matches the first 64 bits of the 128-bit IPv6 address, and any Interface Identifier (IID) within the least-significant 64 bits of that address falls within that prefix range.

Table 25-2 lists the criteria for several practice problems. Your job: Create a one-line standard ACL that matches the packets. The answers are listed in the final section of this chapter, "Answers to Earlier Practice Problems."

Table 25-2 Building Permit and Deny Extended IPv6 ACLs: Practice

Problem	Criteria
1	Permit IPv6 packets from any address to the 2001:db8:45::/48 prefix
2	Permit and log IPv6 packets from the host 2001:db8:1:1::234 to the IPv6 network 2001:db8:1111:1111::/64
3	Permit any HTTP packets from anywhere to the web server with the IPv6 address 2001:db8:12:34::100
4	Permit and log HTTPS packets from host 2001:db8:11:22::1 to host 2001:db8:33:44::1
5	Permit Secure Shell (SSH) to the router with the IPv6 address 2001:db8:12:34::1
6	Permit ICMPv6 Echo Request packets from anywhere to the IPv6 network prefix 2001:db8:1111::/48
7	Permit IPv6 multicast packets sourced from any address

Other IPv6 ACL Topics

This last major section of the chapter discusses two topics that apply to both standard and extended IPv6 ACLs. First, IPv6 ACLs apply several implicit rules at the end of each ACL. The first topic in this section discusses the protocols matched by those rules and then shows what those implicit rules are. The second topic examines how to use IPv6 ACLs to control access to a router using IPv6 Telnet and SSH.

Implicit IPv6 ACL Rules

Every ACL has the default fail-safe stance whereby any packet that is not permitted is implicitly dropped. At the end of each IPv6 ACL is an implicit **deny ipv6 any any** statement that catches any packet that falls through the list unmatched, much like the implicit **deny ip any any** found at the end of IPv4 ACLs.

IPv6 requires the use of ICMPv6 to properly function, and multicast is a necessary forwarding method on each IPv6-enabled LAN. Unfortunately, that implicit deny all at the end of IPv6 ACLs would otherwise filter those ICMPv6 and multicast packets.

By way of review, the Neighbor Discovery Protocol (NDP) is a part of ICMPv6. As introduced in the ICND1 100-105 Cert Guide, Chapter 31, NDP includes neighbor discovery with the NDP Neighbor Solicitation (NS) and Neighbor Advertisement (NA) messages, as well as the Router Solicitation (RS) and Router Advertisement (RA) messages. Therefore, network engineers are unable to be overly aggressive with IPv6 ACLs to block ICMPv6 and multicast connections. However, in previous IPv6 ACL examples, the configuration did not explicitly allow IPv6 NDP messages to flow through the IPv6 ACLs configured earlier in this chapter. This section works through understanding what IOS does to make sure those ICMP messages flow correctly.

An Example of Filtering ICMPv6 NDP and the Negative Effects

To get a better understanding, let's try a little experiment to test this. Instead of relying on the implicit statements at the end of an IPv6 ACL, what would happen if an IPv6 ACL explicitly blocked all ICMPv6 and blocked all IPv6 multicast? The next three examples answer that question. Examples 25-8 and 25-9 show the background, with no ACLs used

25

at all, showing the information learned by ICMPv6's NDP protocols. Example 25-10 then shows an ACL that blocks all ICMPv6 and all IPv6 multicast packets, to see how that filtering affects a network.

This series of examples uses the network topology shown in Figure 25-4, which is the same topology shown previously in this chapter in Figures 25-1 and 25-3. Example 25-8 validates that Router R1 has a properly discovered IPv6 NDP neighbor cache. It also shows that R1's GigabitEthernet 0/1 interface is functioning properly with multicast and it is receiving RA messages from Router R2.

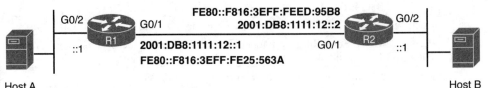

Figure 25-4   *Network Used to Examine How ACLs Filter ICMP NDP*

Example 25-8   *Check IPv6 NDP on R1*

```
R1# show ipv6 interface GigabitEthernet 0/1
GigabitEthernet0/1 is up, line protocol is up
  IPv6 is enabled, link-local address is FE80::F816:3EFF:FE25:563A
  No Virtual link-local address(es):
  Global unicast address(es):
    2001:DB8:1111:12::1, subnet is 2001:DB8:1111:12::/64
  Joined group address(es):
    FF02::1
    FF02::2
    FF02::1:FF00:1
    FF02::1:FF25:563A
! lines omitted for brevity
R1# show ipv6 neighbors GigabitEthernet0/1
IPv6 Address                          Age Link-layer Addr State Interface
2001:DB8:1111:12::2                    11 fa16.3eed.95b8  STALE Gi0/1
FE80::F816:3EFF:FEED:95B8              11 fa16.3eed.95b8  STALE Gi0/1

R1# show ipv6 routers
Router FE80::F816:3EFF:FEED:95B8 on GigabitEthernet0/1, last update 2 min
  Hops 64, Lifetime 1800 sec, AddrFlag=0, OtherFlag=0, MTU=1500
  HomeAgentFlag=0, Preference=Medium
  Reachable time 0 (unspecified), Retransmit time 0 (unspecified)
  Prefix 2001:DB8:1111:12::/64 onlink autoconfig
    Valid lifetime 2592000, preferred lifetime 604800
```

Example 25-8 reveals that R1 knows two IPv6 neighbor addresses in its neighbor cache, both of which are Router R2. One address is the global unicast address of R2's GigabitEthernet 0/1 interface and one is the link local address of that same interface. The **show ipv6 routers**

routers command output confirms that R1 has learned of one other IPv6 router (also R2). This command lists information learned by NDP, in this case confirming that R1 is receiving the RA messages that R2 is sending out from its GigabitEthernet 0/1 interface. Therefore, R2 can reach R1 perfectly.

In Example 25-9, the same checks are performed on Router R2.

Example 25-9 *Check IPv6 NDP on R2*

```
R2# show ipv6 interface GigabitEthernet 0/1
GigabitEthernet0/1 is up, line protocol is up
  IPv6 is enabled, link-local address is FE80::F816:3EFF:FEED:95B8
  No Virtual link-local address(es):
  Global unicast address(es):
    2001:DB8:1111:12::2, subnet is 2001:DB8:1111:12::/64
  Joined group address(es):
    FF02::1
    FF02::2
    FF02::1:FF00:2
    FF02::1:FFED:95B8
! lines omitted for brevity
R2# show ipv6 neighbors GigabitEthernet0/1
IPv6 Address                       Age Link-layer Addr State Interface
2001:DB8:1111:12::1                  11 fa16.3e25.563a  STALE Gi0/1
FE80::F816:3EFF:FE25:563A            11 fa16.3e25.563a  STALE Gi0/1

R2# show ipv6 routers
Router FE80::F816:3EFF:FE25:563A on GigabitEthernet0/1, last update 1 min
  Hops 64, Lifetime 1800 sec, AddrFlag=0, OtherFlag=0, MTU=1500
  HomeAgentFlag=0, Preference=Medium
  Reachable time 0 (unspecified), Retransmit time 0 (unspecified)
  Prefix 2001:DB8:1111:12::/64 onlink autoconfig
    Valid lifetime 2592000, preferred lifetime 604800
```

Example 25-9 reveals that R2 learns R1's two addresses (global unicast and link local), as well as learning about R1 as a router. The **show ipv6 neighbors** command lists R1's global unicast and link-local addresses, both of which Router R2 would have learned by receiving ICMPv6 NDP NA messages. The **show ipv6 routers** command output confirms that R2 has learned about R1, with R2 learning this information by receiving an ICMPv6 NDP RA message.

Example 25-10 shows the addition of an IPv6 ACL that prevents the two routers from learning from each other using ICMPv6 NDP. The example shows the configuration of an IPv6 ACL will block ICMPv6 packets and block all multicast traffic, but allow all other IPv6 packets. This extended IPv6 ACL will be applied inbound on R1's GigabitEthernet 0/1 interface and inbound on R2's GigabitEthernet 0/1 interface. After the ACLs are configured, the ACL will be checked that they are in the running configuration and operational. Following is the configuration on R1. R2's configuration is identical to R1's.

25

Example 25-10   *Configuring IPv6 Blocking ACL on R1*

```
R1# configure terminal
Enter configuration commands, one per line.  End with CNTL/Z.
R1(config)# ipv6 access-list BLOCKV6
R1(config-ipv6-acl)# deny icmp any any
R1(config-ipv6-acl)# deny ipv6 ff00::/8 any
R1(config-ipv6-acl)# deny ipv6 any ff00::/8
R1(config-ipv6-acl)# permit ipv6 any any
R1(config-ipv6-acl)# interface GigabitEthernet0/1
R1(config-if)# ipv6 traffic-filter BLOCKV6 in
R1(config-if)# end
R1#
R1# show ipv6 access-list
IPv6 access list BLOCKV6
    deny icmp any any sequence 10
    deny ipv6 FF00::/8 any sequence 20
    deny ipv6 any FF00::/8 sequence 30
    permit ipv6 any any sequence 40

R1# show ipv6 interface | include line|list
GigabitEthernet0/1 is up, line protocol is up
  Inbound access list BLOCKV6
```

The IPv6 ACL shown in Example 25-10 will filter Router Advertisement (RA) ICMPv6 messages for a couple of reasons. NDP RA and RS messages are part of ICMPv6, so those messages match the first line of the ACL. Even if they had not, NDP RA messages are sent to the all-nodes multicast group address (FF02::1). Routers periodically send RA messages, typically every 200 seconds, to inform nodes on the network about the local network characteristics and about the method for IPv6 address allocation. Router Solicitation (RS) ICMPv6 messages are sent to the all-routers multicast group address (FF02::2). When a node boots up or joins the network, it immediately sends an RS message to the local router to find out about the network and to determine the method it should use to acquire its IPv6 address. The **deny** commands that list address FF00::/8 would match all multicast addresses.

Note that blocking all multicast IPv6 packets, as is done with the ACL in Example 25-10, can have a big negative impact on router operation. If the BLOCKV6 ACL is blocking multicast packets, then it will inadvertently block other link-local multicasts such as: OSPFv3 (FF02::5, FF02::6), RIPng (FF02::9), EIGRP for IPv6 (FF02::A), and DHCPv6 (FF02::1:2, FF05::1:3). To further explore other well-known registered IPv6 multicast addresses, you can extend your learning and refer to the IANA IPv6 Multicast Address Space Registry at the following URI. (Or refer to the ICND1 Cert Guide's Chapter 30, section "Local Scope Multicast Addresses.")

http://www.iana.org/assignments/ipv6-multicast-addresses/ipv6-multicast-addresses.xhtml

The sample BLOCKV6 ACL will also prevent the two routers from learning each other's IPv6 addresses, which actually prevents the two routers from successfully forwarding packets to each other. The first line in the ACL will prevent all ICMPv6 messages, including all

NDP NS and NA messages. Even without the **deny icmp any any** command, the ACL would filter NS and NA based on the addresses used. NS ICMPv6 messages are sent to the solicited node multicast address (FF02:0:0:0:0:1:FF00::/104) of the destination node on the LAN. (NA ICMPv6 messages are sent back, typically to the unicast address of the node that sent the original NS packet.)

Now that this ACL is applied, it will block all ICMPv6 and multicast packets on this interface. After waiting for over 5 minutes, the neighbor cache and the router cache on the two routers can be inspected, as shown in Example 25-11. The observation shows that the neighbor cache entries on the interface have timed out and the RA cache is very old. In fact, now host A and host B are unable to ping each other because the connectivity between R1 and R2 has been disrupted by these two IPv6 ACLs.

Example 25-11 *Checking IPv6 Blocking ACL on R1*

```
R1# show ipv6 neighbors GigabitEthernet 0/1
R1# show ipv6 routers
Router FE80::F816:3EFF:FEED:95B8 on GigabitEthernet0/1, last update 17 min
  Hops 64, Lifetime 1800 sec, AddrFlag=0, OtherFlag=0, MTU=1500
  HomeAgentFlag=0, Preference=Medium
  Reachable time 0 (unspecified), Retransmit time 0 (unspecified)
  Prefix 2001:DB8:1111:12::/64 onlink autoconfig
    Valid lifetime 2592000, preferred lifetime 604800
```

Example 25-12 shows the output from R2 validating the contents of the neighbor cache and the router cache.

Example 25-12 *Checking IPv6 Blocking ACL on R2*

```
R2# show ipv6 neighbors GigabitEthernet 0/1
R2# show ipv6 routers
Router FE80::F816:3EFF:FE25:563A on GigabitEthernet0/1, last update 15 min
  Hops 64, Lifetime 1800 sec, AddrFlag=0, OtherFlag=0, MTU=1500
  HomeAgentFlag=0, Preference=Medium
  Reachable time 0 (unspecified), Retransmit time 0 (unspecified)
  Prefix 2001:DB8:1111:12::/64 onlink autoconfig
    Valid lifetime 2592000, preferred lifetime 604800
```

How to Avoid Filtering ICMPv6 NDP Messages

Network administrators must be careful when creating IPv6 ACLs that are filtering ICMPv6 messages and multicast packets so that the ACLs are not inadvertently stopping NDP from functioning properly. This is why it is important, on any interface, to permit NDP to operate. In other words, you should not filter ICMPv6 and multicast on a wholesale level.

For this very reason, Cisco IOS IPv6 ACLs have three implicit rules at the bottom of each ACL. These are invisible, but they are included at the end of each IPv6 ACL so as to implicitly permit NA and NS messages. The final implicit IPv6 ACL statement is the default deny that is commonly expected. The three implicit IPv6 ACL rules at the bottom of every ACL are shown in Example 25-13.

25

Key Topic

Example 25-13 *Implicit IPv6 ACL Entries*

```
permit icmp any any nd-na
permit icmp any any nd-ns
deny ipv6 any any
```

Note that these defaults do permit NDP NS and NA messages, but do not include an implicit permit of NDP RS and RA messages. If you wanted to add explicit statements to an ACL to match RS and RA messages, you could use commands like **permit icmp any any router-advertisement** and **permit icmp any any router-solicitation.**

> **NOTE** Even though CCNA R&S does not get into Cisco's IOS XE and NX-OS operating systems, on a practical note, they do use slightly different defaults. IOS-XE has no default permit of NS/NA packets, so you would need to add explicit **permit** commands at the end of each IPv6 ACL so as to not inadvertently affect NDP functionality. NX-OS has five implicit IPv6 ACL statements: one for NA messages, one for NS messages, one for RA messages, one for RS messages, and the final implicit default deny rule.

Because of these implicit IPv6 ACL rules allowing NA/NS messages, it is important to remember to change our ACLs if required to use a deny-log at the end of the policy. Therefore, if the desire is to create an ACL that logs all denied IPv6 packets, the IPv6 ACL would need to be configured like Example 25-14.

Example 25-14 *Explicitly Allowing NDP in IPv6 ACL*

```
R1(config)# ipv6 access-list MY_IPV6_ACL
R1(config-ipv6-acl)# permit ipv6 any 2001:db8:1111:1::/64
R1(config-ipv6-acl)# permit ipv6 any 2001:db8:1111:2::/64
R1(config-ipv6-acl)# permit icmp any any nd-na
R1(config-ipv6-acl)# permit icmp any any nd-ns
R1(config-ipv6-acl)# deny ipv6 any any log
```

In Example 25-14, this IPv6 ACL has explicit entries to permit NA and NS messages. Even though it does not explicitly permit RA messages, this ACL, if applied in the outbound direction, will not block the sending of RA messages because they are originated by the router. Similar to IPv4 ACLs, packets originating from the router will not be affected by an outbound interface IPv6 ACL. However, if this ACL is applied in the inbound direction, it will block RA messages from being received on this router's interface.

IPv6 ACL Implicit Filtering Summary

There are many ways that IPv6 packets can be used. Basic IPv6 ACLs can be used simply to filter communications between specific IPv6 hosts or IPv6 address prefixes. Extended IPv6 ACLs have the ability to match ICMPv6, TCP, UDP, or other IPv6 header fields and extension headers.

It is important to remember that IPv6 operations are different from IPv4 operations across a WAN or the Internet and that ACLs should not be overly aggressive at filtering ICMPv6 messages. It is also important to remember that ICMPv6 is critical to LAN connectivity and that ACLs should not block NDP messages to access nodes or between directly connected routers. There are implicit rules in IPv6 ACLs that can help us remember to permit these important IPv6 packet types.

IPv6 Management Control ACLs

IPv6 ACLs can be used for security purposes other than filtering data-plane traffic that passes through the router. ACLs can also be used to help harden the router from a security perspective and control the management-plane communications to the router.

Seldom do routers have fully out-of-band management network access, and frequently routers are configured in-band. To limit the exposure and restrict the management and configuration interaction with a router, ACLs can be used to filter these connections.

IPv6 ACLs can be applied to many other management functions of a router. IPv6 ACLs can be used to restrict SNMP communications, RADIUS, TACACS+, HTTP/HTTPS access, NTP, and Telnet/SSH CLI access. An example of how an IPv6 ACL can be used to restrict management access is when it is used with an IPv6 access class. This is when an ACL is used to filter IPv6 Telnet and/or SSH login connections.

In Example 25-15, the IPv6 ACL is created to restrict the IPv6 addresses of the authorized management workstations on R1's LAN. This ACL will be applied to the VTY ports on R1 and R2 using the **ipv6 access-class** command. This is similar to the familiar IPv4 command **ip access-class**. Example 25-15 shows the configuration that is applied to R2, but R1's configuration is identical.

Example 25-15 *Configuring IPv6 Access ACL on R2*

```
R2# configure terminal
Enter configuration commands, one per line.  End with CNTL/Z.
R2(config)# ipv6 access-list V6ACCESS
R2(config-ipv6-acl)# permit tcp 2001:db8:1111:1::/64 any eq 23
R2(config-ipv6-acl)# permit tcp 2001:db8:1111:1::/64 any eq 22
R2(config-ipv6-acl)# deny ipv6 any any log
R2(config-ipv6-acl)# line vty 0 4
R2(config-line)# login
R2(config-line)# password cisco
R2(config-line)# transport input telnet ssh
R2(config-line)# ipv6 access-class V6ACCESS in
R2(config-line)# end
```

In Example 25-15, the IPv6 ACL is configured and applied to the VTY ports. At this point, it is time to test this ACL. It is now possible to telnet from host A to both R1 and R2, but host B is disallowed from connecting to either router with Telnet.

Example 25-16 shows the attempt of host B to Telnet to R1, which failed as shown in the log message. The example also shows that the IPv6 ACL had matches for the connections from host A.

25

Example 25-16   *Checking IPv6 Access ACL on R1*

```
*Mar  6 23:31:19.926: %IPV6_ACL-6-ACCESSLOGP: list V6ACCESS/30 denied tcp 2001:DB8:111
1:2:F816:3EFF:FEE1:5CF5(34474) -> 2001:DB8:1111:1::1(23), 1 packet
R1# show ipv6 access-list
IPv6 access list V6ACCESS
    permit tcp 2001:DB8:1111:1::/64 any eq telnet (2 matches) sequence 10
    permit tcp 2001:DB8:1111:1::/64 any eq 22 sequence 20
    deny ipv6 any any log (1 match) sequence 30
```

Chapter Review

One key to doing well on the exams is to perform repetitive spaced review sessions. Review this chapter's material using either the tools in the book, DVD, or interactive tools for the same material found on the book's companion website. Refer to the "Your Study Plan" element for more details. Table 25-3 outlines the key review elements and where you can find them. To better track your study progress, record when you completed these activities in the second column.

Table 25-3   Chapter Review Tracking

Review Element	Review Date(s)	Resource Used
Review key topics		Book, DVD/website
Review key terms		Book, DVD/website
Repeat DIKTA questions		Book, PCPT
Review command tables		Book

Review All the Key Topics

Table 25-4   Key Topics for Chapter 25

Key Topic Element	Description	Page Number
List	Similarities between IPv4 and IPv6 ACLs	666
List	Differences between IPv4 and IPv6 ACLs	667
Paragraph	Format of a standard IPv6 ACL **permit** and **deny** command	672
Figure 25-2	Common fields in IPv6 extended ALs	676
List	Explanation of how to match IPv6 addresses with IPv6 ACLs	678
Example 25-13	Implicit statements at the end of each IPv6 ACL	684

Key Terms You Should Know

standard access list, extended access list, IPv6 prefix length, ICMPv6, Neighbor Discovery Protocol (NDP)

Command References

Tables 25-5 and 25-6 list configuration and verification commands used in this chapter. As an easy review exercise, cover the left column in a table, read the right column, and try to recall the command without looking. Then repeat the exercise, covering the right column, and try to recall what the command does.

Table 25-5   Chapter 25 Configuration Command Reference

Command	Description
ipv6 access-list *access-list-name* [log-update]	Global command to create a standard or extended named IPv6 ACL
permit ipv6 { *source-ipv6-prefix/prefix-length* | any | host *source-ipv6-address* | auth } [operator [*port-number*]] { *destination-ipv6-prefix/prefix-length* | any | host *destination-ipv6-address* | auth } [log] [log-input]	Syntax for a standard named IPv6 ACL entry
ipv6 traffic-filter *access-list-name* {in | out}	Interface subcommand to enable access lists in the specified direction

Table 25-6   Chapter 25 EXEC Command Reference

Command	Description
show ipv6 interface [*type number*]	Includes a reference to the IPv6 access lists enabled on the interface
show access-lists	Shows details of configured access lists for all protocols (IPv4 and IPv6)
show ipv6 access-list [*access-list-name*]	Shows IPv6 access lists

Answers to Earlier Practice Problems

Table 25-7 lists the answers to the problems listed earlier in Table 25-2.

Table 25-7   Building Permit and Deny Extended IPv6 ACLs: Answers

Problem	Answers
1	permit ipv6 any 2001:db8:45::/48
2	permit ipv6 host 2001:db8:1:1::234 2001:db8:1111:1111::/64 log
3	permit tcp any host 2001:db8:12:34::100 eq 80
4	permit tcp host 2001:db8:11:22::1 host 2001:db8:33:44::1 eq 443 log
5	permit tcp any host 2001:db8:12:34::1 eq 22
6	permit icmp any 2001:db8:1111::/48 echo-request
7	permit ipv6 any ff00::/8

25

Part VI Review

Keep track of your part review progress with the checklist in Table P6-1. Details about each task follow the table.

Table P6-1 Part VI Part Review Checklist

Activity	First Date Completed	Second Date Completed
Repeat All DIKTA Questions		
Answer Part Review Questions		
Review Key Topics		
Create Mind Maps		
Do Labs		

Repeat All DIKTA Questions

For this task, answer the "Do I Know This Already?" questions again for the chapters in this part of the book using the PCPT software. See the section "How to View Only DIKTA Questions by Chapter or Part" in the Introduction to this book to learn how to make the PCPT software show you DIKTA questions for this part only.

Answer Part Review Questions

For this task, answer the Part Review questions for this part of the book using the PCPT software.

Review Key Topics

Review all Key Topics in all chapters in this part, either by browsing the chapters or by using the Key Topics application on the DVD or companion website.

Create Troubleshooting Root Causes Mind Map

The chapters in this part of the book touch on different root causes for different kinds of problems. Chapter 22 focuses on how to troubleshoot IPv6 routing (forwarding) problems, while Chapters 23 and 24 focus on the root causes that prevent OSPFv3 and EIGRP, respectively, from exchanging routing information. Chapter 25 also discusses troubleshooting, but more from the perspective that IPv6 ACLs can be the root cause of IPv6 routing and routing protocol issues.

For this first mind map, try to collect all root causes of problems in an IPv6 network and organize those into a mind map. As usual, use short reminders, rather than long descriptions, with just enough information for you to remember the meaning. Also, organize the concepts in a way that makes sense to you. And avoid looking at the chapters when first building these; as usual, the point is to help you organize the ideas in your own head, rather than to read lists from the book again.

Create Commands Mind Map

This part also discussed OSPF for IPv6, EIGRP for IPv6, and IPv6 ACL configuration and verification. It also reviewed a wide variety of IPv6 configuration commands in Chapter 22. Create a command mind map, like in many other part reviews. The first level of organization should be for OSPF for IPv6, EIGRP for IPv6, and IPv6 ACLs. For the rest of the IPv6 commands (from Chapter 22), organize them to your own liking. Inside each of those categories, break the organization into configuration versus verification commands.

DVD Appendix E, "Mind Map Solutions," lists sample mind map answers. If you do choose to use mind map software, rather than paper, you might want to remember where you stored your mind map files. Table P6-2 lists the mind maps for this part review and a place to record those filenames.

Table P6-2 Configuration Mind Maps for Part VI Review

Map	Description	Where You Saved It
1	Troubleshooting Root Causes Mind Map	
2	Commands Mind Map	

Do Labs

Depending on your chosen lab tool, here are some suggestions for what to do in lab:

Pearson Network Simulator: If you use the full Pearson CCNA simulator, there are many labs for the routing protocol topics in particular. Work through the basic skill builder labs to the point where doing the labs is automatic, and then move on to the configuration scenario and troubleshooting scenario labs. (See the Introduction for some details about how to find which labs are about topics in this part of the book.)

Config Labs: In your idle moments, review and repeat any of the Config Labs for this book part in the author's blog; launch from http://blog.certskills.com/ccna and navigate to **Hands-On > Config Lab**.

Other: If using other lab tools, here are a few suggestions: When building ACL labs, you can test with Telnet (port 23), SSH (port 22), ping (ICMP), and traceroute (UDP) traffic as generated from an extra router. So, do not just configure the ACL; make an ACL that can match these types of traffic, denying some and permitting others, and then test.

Part VII is the final part of the book that introduces new content, so congratulations on working through most of the book!

This part collects topics that do not fit neatly into any of the other parts of the book. The first chapter, Chapter 26, discusses the implementation details of three different topics related to operating networks: SNMP, IP SLA, and SPAN. This chapter gets into specifics about concepts, configuration, verification, and some troubleshooting.

As much as Chapter 26 gets into small implementation details, the other two chapters instead focus on big ideas. Chapter 27 discusses many big ideas about a cloud computing approach to offering IT services. Cloud computing goes far beyond any one tool, or any one feature in a device. It is a chapter that requires you to slow down a bit and ponder while you read.

Chapter 28 is like Chapter 27 in that it requires a little more pondering rather than memorizing small details. Chapter 28 explains the fundamentals of network programmability and Software Defined Networking (SDN), with just enough detail so you can begin to learn more about this exciting new area of networking.

Part VII

Miscellaneous

Chapter 26: Network Management

Chapter 27: Cloud Computing

Chapter 28: SDN and Network Programmability

Part VII Review

CHAPTER 26

Network Management

This chapter covers the following exam topics:

5.0 Infrastructure Maintenance

5.1 Configure and verify device-monitoring protocols

    5.1.a SNMPv2

    5.1.b SNMPv3

5.2 Troubleshoot network connectivity issues using ICMP echo-based IP SLA

5.3 Use local SPAN to troubleshoot and resolve problems

This chapter discusses three major topics that are related by their theme. However, they have no direct impact on each other. From a study perspective, you can treat each of the major headings as a separate study task. In fact, because this chapter is rather long compared to other chapters, I would suggest breaking down the topics in this chapter by major heading, just so the new terminology does not get in the way.

This chapter begins with a detailed discussion of Simple Network Management Protocol (SNMP). The discussion begins with the core concepts, and moves on to configuration for two versions: SNMPv2c and SNMPv3. These versions differ significantly with their security features, so much of the configuration discussion revolves around sorting out those details.

The second section moves to a router-specific feature called IP Service Level Agreement (IP SLA). This tool lets network engineers configure routers so that the routers generate artificial probe traffic to send into the network. By sending the messages and receiving responses, the routers can measure availability and performance.

The final section then discusses a switch-specific feature: Switched Port Analyzer, or SPAN. This tool allows the network engineer to make the switch copy frames to a destination port. This feature is useful to direct frames to different kinds of networking tools, like network analyzer software.

"Do I Know This Already?" Quiz

Take the quiz (either here, or use the PCPT software) if you want to use the score to help you decide how much time to spend on this chapter. The answers are at the bottom of the page following the quiz, and the explanations are in DVD Appendix C and in the PCPT software.

Table 26-1 "Do I Know This Already?" Foundation Topics Section-to-Question Mapping

Foundation Topics Section	Questions
Simple Network Management Protocol	1–4
IP Service Level Agreement	5–6
SPAN	7–8

1. A Network Management Station (NMS) is using SNMP to manage some Cisco routers and switches with SNMPv2c. Which of the following answers most accurately describes how the SNMP agent on a router authenticates any SNMP Get requests received from the NMS?

   a. Using a username and hashed version of a password

   b. Using either the read-write or read-only community string

   c. Using only the read-write community string

   d. Using only the read-only community string

2. A router has been configured with the global command **snmp-server community** *textvalue1* **RO** *textvalue2*. Which of the following statements are true about the meaning of this command? (Choose two answers.)

   a. The router's read-only community is textvalue1.

   b. The router's read-only community is textvalue2.

   c. The router filters incoming SNMP messages using IPv4 ACL textvalue2.

   d. The router filters outgoing SNMP messages using IPv4 ACL textvalue2.

3. A router has been configured with the following command: **snmp-server group one v3 auth write v1default**. Which of the following answers lists a command that would correctly define a user to associate with this SNMPv3 group to correctly define security parameters to work with an SNMP manager?

   a. **snmp-server user fred1 one v3 auth md5 pass1 priv des keyvalue1**

   b. **snmp-server user fred2 v3**

   c. **snmp-server user fred3 one v3 auth 3des pass1**

   d. **snmp-server user fred4 one v3 auth sha pass1**

4. Which of the following commands primarily lists counters and status information, instead of configuration settings?

   a. **show snmp**

   b. **show snmp community**

   c. **show snmp group**

   d. **show snmp user**

5. Which of the following statements is true about ICMP Echo-based IP SLA?

   a. It sends messages to mimic Voice over IP (VoIP) traffic to measure jitter.

   b. It requires the use of one router as the source and another as the responder.

   c. It can collect and aggregate historical statistics.

   d. It sends ICMP Echo messages to measure jitter.

6. Examine the output taken from a router using IP SLA. Which of the following answers list a fact that can be confirmed based on this output? (Choose two answers.)

```
R3# show ip sla summary

IPSLAs Latest Operation Summary

Codes: * active, ^ inactive, ~ pending

ID          Type        Destination      Stats        Return      Last
                                         (ms)         Code        Run
------------------------------------------------------------------------
*1          icmp-echo   10.1.1.1         RTT=384      OK          54 seconds ago
```

   a. The probe sends ICMP Echos to address 10.1.1.1.

   b. The output confirms that an Echo Reply was received back as well.

   c. The one-way delay through the network for the latest test was 384 ms.

   d. The "1" means that this output is the first historical record for this probe.

7. Host1 and Host2 connect to ports F0/1 and F0/2 on a LAN switch, respectively, so that frames sent by Host1 to Host2 will enter switch port F0/1 and exit switch port F0/2. All FastEthernet ports on the switch are access ports in VLAN 5. A network analyzer connects to port F0/9. A network engineer wants to use SPAN to direct traffic to the network analyzer. Which one answer is the best answer for what traffic to direct to the analyzer with SPAN, if the goal is to gather all traffic sent between Host1 and Host2, but to avoid gathering multiple copies of the same frames?

   a. Use a SPAN source VLAN of VLAN 5 for both directions of traffic.

   b. Use a SPAN source port of F0/1 for the transmit direction of traffic.

   c. Use a SPAN source port of F0/2 for both directions of traffic.

   d. Use a SPAN source port of both F0/1 and F0/2 for both directions of traffic.

8. Which of the following are allowed when configuring Local SPAN sessions? (Choose two answers.)

   a. Using more than one SPAN source port in one SPAN session

   b. Using a SPAN source port and SPAN source VLAN in one SPAN session

   c. Using an EtherChannel port as a SPAN source port

   d. Using one SPAN destination port in two different SPAN sessions

Foundation Topics

Simple Network Management Protocol

The year was 1988 and RFC 1065 was published: *Structure and Identification of Management Information for TCP/IP-based Internets*. The superb idea behind this document was the fact that information about devices on a TCP/IP-based network—configuration settings, status information, counters, and so on—could be broken down into a database of variables. Those variables could then be collected by management software to monitor and manage the IP-based network. After all, the elements of any IP-based machines would have commonalities. For example, a PC, a network printer, and a router would all have commonalities such as interfaces, IP addresses, and buffers. Why not create a standardized database of these variables and a simple system for monitoring and managing them? This idea was brilliant, caught on, and became what we know today as *Simple Network Management Protocol* (SNMP).

This first major section of the chapter begins by explaining the concepts and terminology surrounding SNMP, along with how to configure the two most commonly used versions: SNMPv2c and SNMPv3.

SNMP Concepts

Simple Network Management Protocol (SNMP) is an application layer protocol that provides a message format for communication between what are termed *managers* and *agents*. An SNMP manager is a network management application running on a PC or server, with that host typically being called a Network Management Station (NMS). Many SNMP agents exist in the network, one per device that is managed. The SNMP agent is software running inside each device (router, switch, and so on), with knowledge of all the variables on that device that describe the device's configuration, status, and counters. The SNMP manager uses SNMP protocols to communicate with each SNMP agent.

Each agent keeps a database of variables that make up the parameters, status, and counters for the operations of the device. This database, called the Management Information Base (MIB), has some core elements in common across most networking devices. It also has a large number of variables unique to that type of device—for instance, router MIBs will include variables not needed on switch MIBs, and vice versa. (For perspective, I did a quick check on a router when writing this section, and found a little over 7000 MIB variables on a router running a 15.4M version of IOS.)

Figure 26-1 connects a few of these ideas and terms together. First, many companies sell SNMP management products. The Cisco Prime series of management products (http://www.cisco.com/go/prime) uses SNMP (and other protocols) to manage networks. IOS on routers and switches include an SNMP agent, with built-in MIB, that can be enabled with the configuration shown later in this chapter.

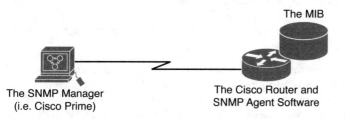

Figure 26-1   *Elements of Simple Network Management Protocol*

26

SNMP Variable Reading and Writing: SNMP Get and Set

The NMS typically polls the SNMP agent on each device. The NMS can notify the human user in front of the PC, or send emails, texts, and so on to notify the network operations staff of any issues identified by the data found by polling the devices. You can even reconfigure the device through these SNMP variables in the MIB if you permit this level of control.

Specifically, the NMS uses the SNMP Get, GetNext, and GetBulk messages (together referenced simply as Get messages) to ask for information from an agent. The NMS sends an SNMP Set message to write variables on the SNMP agent as a means to change the configuration of the device. These messages come in pairs, with, for instance, a Get Request asking the agent for the contents of a variable, and the Get Response supplying that information. Figure 26-2 shows an example of a typical flow, with the NMS using an SNMP Get to ask for the MIB variable that describes the status of a particular router interface.

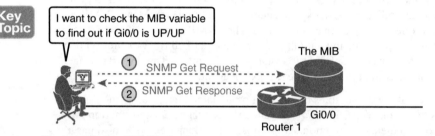

Figure 26-2 *SNMP Get Request and Get Response Message Flow*

SNMP permits much flexibility in how you monitor variables in the MIB. Most commonly, a network administrator gathers and stores statistics over time using the NMS. The NMS, with the stored data, can then analyze various statistical facts such as averages, minimums, and maximums. To be proactive, administrators can set thresholds for certain key variables, telling the NMS to send a notification (email, text, and so on) when a threshold is passed.

SNMP Notifications: Traps and Informs

In addition to asking for information with Get commands, and setting variables on agents with the Set command, SNMP agents can initiate communications to the NMS. These messages, generally called notifications, use two specific SNMP messages: Trap and Inform. SNMP agents send a Trap or Inform SNMP message to the NMS to list the state of certain MIB variables when those variables reach a certain state.

As an example of a Trap, suppose that Router 1's G0/0 interface fails, as shown at Step 1 of Figure 26-3. With Traps configured, the router would send an SNMP Trap message to the NMS, with that Trap message noting the down state of the G0/0 interface. Then, the NMS software can send a text message to the network support staff, pop up a window on the NMS screen, change to red the color of the correct router icon on the graphical interface, and so on.

SNMP Traps and Inform messages have the exact same purpose, but differ in the protocol mechanisms. SNMP Traps, available since the first version of SNMP from the late 1980s (SNMP Version 1, or SNMPv1), use a fire-and-forget process. The SNMP agent sends the Trap to the IP address of the NMS, with UDP as the transport protocol as with all SNMP messages, and with no application layer error recovery. If the Trap arrives, great; if it is lost in transit, it is lost.

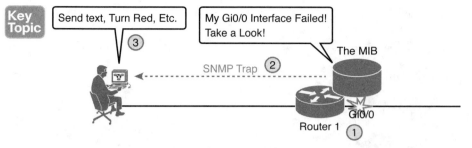

Figure 26-3 *SNMP Trap Notification Process*

Inform messages are like Trap messages but with reliability added. Added to the protocol with SNMP Version 2 (SNMPv2), Informs still use UDP, but add application layer reliability. The NMS must acknowledge receipt of the Inform or the SNMP agent will time out and resend the Inform.

Note that Traps and Informs both have a useful role today, and Traps are still frequently used. Both inform the NMS. Traps use less overhead on the agent, while Informs improve reliability of the messages but require a little more overhead effort.

The Management Information Base

Every SNMP agent has its own Management Information Base. The MIB defines variables whose values are set and updated by the agent. The MIB variables on the devices in the network enable the management software to monitor/control the network device.

More formally, the MIB defines each variable as an *object ID* (OID). On most devices, the MIB then organizes the OIDs based in part on RFC standards, and in part with vendor-proprietary variables. The MIB organizes all the variables into a hierarchy of OIDs, usually shown as a tree. Each node in the tree can be described based on the tree structure sequence, either by name or by number. Figure 26-4 shows a small part of the tree structure of a MIB that happens to be part of the Cisco-proprietary part of the MIB.

Working directly with a MIB, with long variable names and numbers, can be a bit of a challenge, so NMS software typically hides the complexity of the MIB variable numbering and names. However, to get a sense for the variable names, Figure 26-4 shows the tree structure for two variables, with the variable names being the long string of numbers shown at the bottom of the figure. Working with those numbers and the tree structure can be difficult at best. As a result, most people manage their networks using an NMS such as Cisco Prime. For perspective, you could use an SNMP manager and type a MIB variable 1.3.6.1.4.1.9.2.1.58.0 and click a button to get that variable, to see the current CPU usage percentage from a Cisco router. However, most users of an NMS would much prefer to ignore those details, and have a simple graphical interface to ask for the same information, never having to know that 1.3.6.1.4.9.2.1.58.0 represents the router CPU utilization MIB variable.

26

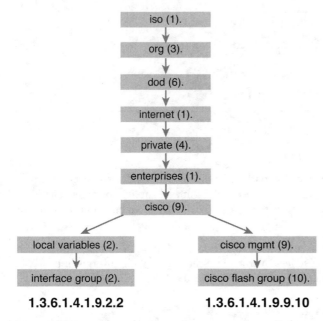

Figure 26-4   *Management Information Base (MIB)*

Securing SNMP

SNMP supports a few security mechanisms, depending in part on the particular version. This section works through the options.

First, one strong method to secure SNMP is to use ACLs to limit SNMP messages to those from known servers only. SNMP agents on Cisco routers and switches support SNMP messages that flow in both IPv4 and IPv6 packets. The SNMP agent can configure an IPv4 ACL to filter incoming SNMP messages that arrive in IPv4 packets, and an IPv6 ACL to filter SNMP messages that arrive in IPv6 packets.

Using an IPv4 and IPv6 ACL to secure an agent makes good sense. The only hosts that should be sending SNMP messages to the SNMP agent in a router or switch are the NMS hosts. Those NMS hosts seldom change and their IP addresses should be well known to the networking staff. It makes good sense to configure an ACL that permits packets sourced from the IP addresses of all NMS hosts, but no others.

As for the SNMP protocol messages, all versions of SNMP support a basic clear-text password mechanism, although none of those versions refer to the mechanism as using a password. SNMP Version 3 (SNMPv3) adds more modern security as well.

SNMPv1 defined clear-text passwords called SNMP *communities*. Basically, both the SNMP agent and the SNMP manager need prior knowledge of the same SNMP community value (called a *community string*). The SNMP Get messages and the Set message include the appropriate community string value, in clear text. If the NMS sends a Get or Set with the correct community string, as configured on the SNMP agent, the agent processes the message.

SNMPv1 defines both a read-only community and a read-write community. The *read-only (RO) community* allows Get messages, and the *read-write (RW) community* allows both reads and writes (Gets and Sets). Figure 26-5 shows the concepts. At Steps 1 and 2, the agent is configured with particular RO and RW community strings and the NMS configures the matching values. At Step 3, the SNMP Get can flow with either community, but at Step 4, the Set Request must use the RW community.

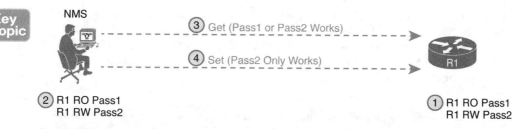

Figure 26-5 *RO and RW Communities with the Get and Set Commands*

SNMPv2, and the related Community-based SNMP Version 2 (SNMPv2c), added a wrinkle in naming, but basically kept the same community security feature as SNMPv1 once the standards process completed. The original specifications for SNMPv2 did not include communities. However, the marketplace still wanted communities, so an additional RFC added the communities mechanism back to SNMPv2. This updated RFC, Community-based SNMPv2, came to be known simply as SNMPv2c. Vendors (including Cisco) implemented SNMPv2c.

SNMPv3 arrived with much celebration among network administrators. Finally, security had arrived with the powerful network management protocol. SNMPv3 does away with communities, and replaces them with the following features:

- **Message integrity:** This mechanism, applied to all SNMPv3 messages, confirms whether or not each message has been changed during transit.

- **Authentication:** An optional feature that adds authentication with both a username and password, with the password never sent as clear text. Instead, it uses a hashing method like many other modern authentication processes.

- **Encryption (privacy):** An optional feature that encrypts the contents of SNMPv3 messages, so that attackers who intercept the messages cannot read their contents.

Implementing SNMP Version 2c

The exam topics mention SNMPv2c and SNMPv3 by name. As it turns out, SNMPv1 and SNMPv2c configuration is very similar, because both use communities. SNMPv3 varies quite a bit, mainly to implement the better SNMPv3 security features. This next section shows how to configure and verify SNMPv2c.

Configuring SNMPv2c Support for Get and Set

SNMP configuration in Cisco IOS routers and switches works a little differently than many other IOS features. First, the SNMP configuration exists in a series of global commands; there is no SNMP agent configuration mode in which to collect subcommands. Secondly, no single command enables the SNMP agent. Instead, IOS typically defaults for the SNMP agent to be disabled. Then, the first time an **snmp-server** global command is configured, IOS enables the SNMP agent.

> **NOTE**   To disable the SNMP agent, you must remove all the **snmp-server** commands. You can do this with a single **no snmp-server** command (with no parameters).

With that backdrop, a typical SNMPv2c configuration requires only one or two settings. To be useful, the agent needs at least a read-only (RO) community string. The agent will not reply to SNMPv2c Get messages without at least the RO community string configured. The network engineer may also want the agent to have a read-write (RW) community string, to support Set messages.

> **NOTE**   When configuring an RW community, use some caution: configuring an RW community means that you have defined a clear-text password that can be used to configure many settings on the router or switch.

The following checklist details the commands used to configure SNMPv2c on a Cisco router or switch. This list shows the method to configure the RO and RW communities, plus a few optional but common settings (location and contact information).

Config Checklist

Step 1.   Use the **snmp-server community** *communitystring* **RO** [**ipv6** *acl-name*] [*acl-name*] command in global configuration mode to enable the SNMP agent (if not already started), set the read-only community string, and restrict incoming SNMP messages based on the optional referenced IPv4 or IPv6 ACL.

Step 2.   (Optional) Use the **snmp-server community** *communitystring* **RW** [**ipv6** *acl-name*] [*acl-name*] command in global configuration mode to enable the SNMP agent (if not already started), set the read-write community string, and restrict incoming SNMP messages based on the optional referenced IPv4 or IPv6 ACL.

Step 3.   (Optional) If referenced by an **snmp-server community** command, configure an IPv4 or IPv6 ACL, with the same name or number referenced by the **snmp-server community** command, with the ACL permitting by matching the source IPv4 or IPv6 address of the allowed SNMP management hosts.

Step 4.   (Optional) Use the **snmp-server location** *text-describing-location* command in global configuration mode to document the location of the device.

Step 5.   (Optional) Use the **snmp-server contact** *contact-name* command in global configuration mode to document the person to contact if problems occur.

> **NOTE**   In the SNMP model, the SNMP agent acts as a server, with the NMS (SNMP Manager) acting as an SNMP client by requesting information with Get messages. The IOS **snmp-server** command happens to emphasize the idea that the SNMP agent on a router or switch acts as the SNMP server.

Example 26-1 shows a sample configuration based on Figure 26-6. The examples in this section come from Router R1, although the exact same SNMP configuration syntax could be used in the LAN switches or in R2. (The configuration of the location information would likely differ for each device, however.) Note that the configuration creates an IPv4 ACL that permits traffic with source IP address 10.1.3.3, which is the address of the NMS shown in the figure. It then defines read-only and read-write communities, along with the location and contact name for the router.

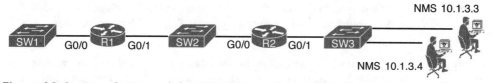

Figure 26-6   *Sample Network for SNMP Examples, with NMS at 10.1.3.3*

Example 26-1   *Configuring SNMP Version 2c on Router R1 to Support Get and Set*

```
ip access-list standard ACL_PROTECTSNMP
 permit host 10.1.3.3
!
snmp-server community secretROpw RO ACL_PROTECTSNMP
snmp-server community secretRWpw RW ACL_PROTECTSNMP
snmp-server location Atlanta
snmp-server contact Tyler B
```

To begin managing Router R1 (or any of the other devices that use the same community strings), the SNMP manager at address 10.1.3.3 now needs to configure the community strings listed in Example 26-1.

Configuring SNMPv2c Support for Trap and Inform

For an SNMPv2c agent in a router or switch to be able to send unsolicited notifications to an SNMP manager (that is, to send Trap and Inform messages), the device needs to be configured with the **snmp-server host** command. This command references the NMS to which the Traps or Informs should be sent, along with the SNMP version.

Beyond telling the SNMP agent the hostname or address of the NMS, the agent typically needs to know the *notification community* string used by the NMS. Think of the RO and RW community strings as protecting the SNMP agent from the messages originated by an NMS (Get or Set Requests), so the agent requires the NMS to supply the correct RO or RW community string. For Traps and Informs, the NMS can protect itself from the Trap and Inform messages originated by SNMP agents by requiring those agents to include the notification community with those messages. The agent can configure this value on the **snmp-server host** command as well.

26

The following list details the command to enable the sending of SNMPv2c Trap or Inform messages to an NMS:

Config Checklist

Step 1.   Use the **snmp-server host** {*hostname* | *ip-address*} [**informs**] **version 2c** *notification-community* command in global configuration mode to configure the SNMP agent to send either SNMPv2c Traps (default) or Informs to the listed host. Use this command once for each host to which this device should send Traps.

Step 2.   Use the **snmp-server enable traps** command in global configuration mode to enable the sending of all supported types of Trap and Inform messages.

Example 26-2 shows a sample configuration. In most cases, you would send either Traps or Informs to a particular NMS, but not both. So, for this example, the configuration shows how to configure to send Traps to one host (10.1.3.3), and Informs to another host (10.1.3.4). Note that this configuration is added to Router R1 from Figure 26-6, but it could have been added to Router R2 or to any of the LAN switches as well.

Example 26-2   *Configuring SNMP Version 2c on Router R1 to Support Sending Traps*

```
snmp-server host 10.1.3.3 version 2c secretTRAPpw
snmp-server host 10.1.3.4 informs version 2c secretTRAPpw
snmp-server enable traps
```

Verifying SNMPv2c Operation

Example 26-3 displays some of the status information based on the configuration seen in the previous two examples. The variations on the **show snmp** command highlight several configuration settings. For example, the **show snmp community** command repeats the community string values, with reference to any attached IPv4 or IPv6 ACLs. The **show snmp host** command lists the IP address or hostname of the NMS referenced by each **snmp-server host** configuration command.

Example 26-3   *Confirming SNMPv2c Configuration Settings on Router R1*

```
R1# show snmp community


Community name: secretROpw
Community Index: secretROpw
Community SecurityName: secretROpw
storage-type: nonvolatile          active access-list: ACL_PROTECTSNMP


Community name: secretRWpw
Community Index: secretRWpw
Community SecurityName: secretRWpw
storage-type: nonvolatile          active access-list: ACL_PROTECTSNMP


Community name: secretTRAPpw
Community Index: secretTRAPpw
```

```
Community SecurityName: secretTRAPpw
storage-type: nonvolatile          active


R1# show snmp location
Atlanta


R1# show snmp contact
Tyler B


R1# show snmp host
Notification host: 10.1.3.4     udp-port: 162    type: inform
user: secretTRAPpw        security model: v2c


Notification host: 10.1.3.3      udp-port: 162     type: trap
user: secretTRAPpw        security model: v2c
```

The **show snmp** command takes the opposite approach from the commands in Example 26-3, focusing almost completely on status and counter information, rather than repeating configuration settings. This command lists dozens of lines of detailed information, so the sample in Example 26-4 shows just enough of the output to give you a sense of the kinds of information found there, with comments following the example.

Example 26-4   *Finding SNMPv2c Message Load on Router R1*

```
R1# show snmp
Chassis: FTX162883H0
Contact: Tyler B
Location: Atlanta
7735 SNMP packets input
    0 Bad SNMP version errors
    9 Unknown community name
    0 Illegal operation for community name supplied
    2 Encoding errors
    51949 Number of requested variables
    2 Number of altered variables
    3740 Get-request PDUs
    3954 Get-next PDUs
    7 Set-request PDUs
    0 Input queue packet drops (Maximum queue size 1000)
7850 SNMP packets output
    0 Too big errors (Maximum packet size 1500)
    0 No such name errors
    0 Bad values errors
    0 General errors
    7263 Response PDUs
    126 Trap PDUs
! Lines omitted for brevity
```

26

The output in Example 26-4 was taken from Router R1 as shown in the earlier examples, after doing some testing from the NMS at address 10.1.3.3. The highlighted items point out the number of SNMP packets received (input) and sent (output), as well as the number of requested MIB variables—that is, the number of variables requested in different SNMP Get requests. (Note that SNMP also supports the GetNext and GetBulk commands, so a single NMS user click can cause the NMS to Get many variables from an agent; thus, it is not unusual for the requested variables counter to get very large.) The output also shows that seven Set requests were received, resulting in two changes to variables. The fact that two Set requests changed variables is a good fact to know if you are wondering if someone has reconfigured something on the device using SNMP.

Implementing SNMP Version 3

SNMPv3 configuration on Cisco routers and switches has some commands in common with SNMPv2c configuration, and some completely different commands. The configuration to support sending Traps and Informs, using the **snmp-server host** and **snmp-server enable traps** commands, works almost identically, with a few small differences. However, SNMPv3 replaces all references to communities, and as a result does not use the **snmp-server community** command at all. Instead, it uses the **snmp-server group** and **snmp-server user** commands to configure the security features available to SNMPv3.

SNMPv3 has many more configuration options, and it is easy to get confused by the details. So, to get started, first look at a short SNMPv3 configuration example, as shown in Example 26-5. The example highlights the values you would have to choose, but the values are either text fields (names and passwords) or the IP address of the NMS. This configuration could be used to replace the SNMPv2c configuration and use username/password authentication. The requirements met in the example are

- Use SNMPv3 authentication (basically replacing SNMPv2 communities).

- Use username Youdda and authentication password madeuppassword (in your network, you would choose your own values).

- Do not use SNMPv3 privacy (that is, message encryption).

- Allow both read (Get) and write (Set) access.

- Send Traps to an NMS (10.1.3.3), authenticating with the same username.

Example 26-5 *Configuring SNMPv3 on R1—Authentication Only*

```
R1(config)# snmp-server group BookGroup v3 auth write v1default
R1(config)# snmp-server user Youdda BookGroup v3 auth md5 madeuppassword
R1(config)# snmp-server host 10.1.3.3 version 3 auth Youdda
```

Given the list of requirements, you could probably just read the configuration in Example 26-5, compare that to the list of requirements preceding the example, and correctly guess what most of the command parameters mean. However, we need to get into more detail to work through these commands and their options so that you understand the entire configuration, which is exactly what the next few pages do.

SNMPv3 Groups

SNMPv3 authentication uses a username/password combination. When Cisco created its SNMPv3 implementation in IOS, it realized that it might be useful to have groups of users that use some of the same security settings. So, rather than have each **snmp-server user** command (the command that defines a user) define every single security parameter, Cisco put some of the security configuration settings into the **snmp-server group** command. This command holds SNMPv3 security settings that are often the same between a group of SNMPv3 users; each **snmp-server user** command then refers to one SNMP group. This next topic explores those security parameters defined on the **snmp-server group** command.

Figure 26-7 shows the entire **snmp-server group** command. The required parameters on the left include a name that the network engineer can make up; it only needs to match other commands on the local router. For SNMPv3 configuration, the **v3** keyword would always be used. The text following this figure then details the rest of the parameters in the figure.

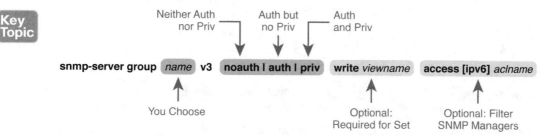

Figure 26-7   *SNMPv3 Groups—Configuration Command Parameters*

The next parameter in the command configures this group of users to use one of three SNMPv3 *security levels*. As you can see from the summary in Table 26-2, all three security levels provide message integrity for their messages, which confirms that the message has not been changed in transit. The **auth** option adds authentication to message integrity, using a username and password, with IOS storing the password with a hash and never sending the password as clear text. The last increase in security level, configured by using the **priv** security level, causes the SNMP manager and agent to encrypt the entire SNMP packet for all SNMP messages sent, in addition to performing message integrity and authentication.

Table 26-2   SNMPv3 Security Levels Keywords and Their Meanings

Command Keyword	Keyword in Messages	Checks Message Integrity?	Performs Authentication?	Encrypts Messages?
noauth	noAuthNoPriv	Yes	No	No
auth	authNoPriv	Yes	Yes	No
priv	priv	Yes	Yes	Yes

Continuing to look at the **snmp-server group** command in Figure 26-7, notice that it ends with an optional ACL to filter packets. This same idea is used in SNMPv2c to reference an IPv4 or IPv6 ACL to filter incoming messages coming from the SNMP manager.

So far, the discussion has ignored one part of the **snmp-server group** command: the idea of SNMPv3 MIB views. MIB views define a subset of the MIB. IOS supplies a series of MIB views for us, and you can define your own MIB views if you like. However, this book

26

discusses only one predefined MIB view that goes by the name *v1default*, which is a MIB view that includes all the useful parts of the MIB. Instead of focusing on the depths of how you might create different views of a router or switch MIB that has literally thousands of variables, focus on how the **snmp-server group** command uses that one MIB view that includes the majority of the MIB.

By default, each SNMPv3 group, as defined with the **snmp-server group** command, has a read MIB view of v1default, and no write view. As a result, the SNMP agent will process received SNMPv3 Get requests, but not process received SNMPv3 Set requests. That complete lack of a write MIB view basically results in read-only behavior for the SNMP agent, as shown at the top of Figure 26-8.

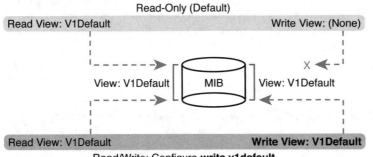

Figure 26-8   *SNMPv3 Views Creating Read-Only and Read-Write Effect*

The bottom of the figure shows the concept behind configuring an SNMP group with the **write v1default** parameters, causing the group to use the same write view of the MIB that is used for reading the MIB. By including **write v1default** in the **snmp-server group** command, you migrate from a default operation of allowing only Gets to now also allowing Sets.

To pull these ideas together, Example 26-6 shows four similar SNMPv3 groups, which could later be referenced by **snmp-server user** commands. Two commands use the parameters **write v1default**, and two do not, so two groups create read-write (Get and Set) support, and two groups create read-only (Get only) support. Also, note that two groups refer to an IPv4 ACL by name (SNMPACL), and two do not. The ends of the lines in the example list comments about each command.

Example 26-6   *SNMPv3 Groups—Comparisons with Write Views and ACL Security*

```
ip access-list standard SNMPACL
 permit host 10.1.3.3
!
snmp-server group Group1 v3 noauth                              ! No writes, no ACL
snmp-server group Group2 v3 noauth write v1default             ! Allows writes, no ACL
snmp-server group Group3 v3 noauth access SNMPACL             ! No writes, uses ACL
snmp-server group Group4 v3 noauth write v1default access SNMPACL  ! Allows writes,
                                                                    uses ACL
```

Note that while all four examples use an authentication type of **noauth**, groups could be defined that use the **auth** and **priv** types as well. Configuring groups with any one of the security levels does not change the meaning and use of the **write** and **access** keywords and their parameters. The security level simply needs to match the security level configured on the **snmp-server user** commands that refer to the group by name, as seen in the next section.

SNMPv3 Users, Passwords, and Encryption Keys

The **snmp-server user** command configures other security parameters for the SNMP agent. In particular, it configures

- The username
- The authentication password and the authentication hash algorithm (MD5 or SHA)
- The encryption key and the encryption algorithm (DES, 3DES, AES)
- A reference to an **snmp-server group** command by name, which holds more security configuration

The **snmp-server user** command still has plenty of moving parts, even with some of the security configuration sitting in the **snmp-server group** command. Figure 26-9 connects these configuration concepts together, showing both commands in one place. Some explanation follows the figure.

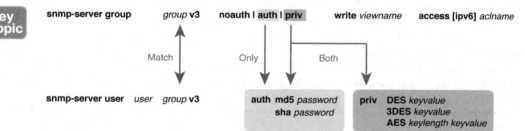

Figure 26-9 *SNMPv3 Users and Groups: Configured*

The **snmp-server user** command creates the username itself. The network engineer can make up a name. The next two parameters must match the chosen **snmp-server group** command associated with this user, by matching the group name and the **v3** keyword (meaning SNMPv3). Any mistakes here will result in this SNMP user not being associated with the SNMP group.

You must pay particular attention to the security type in the associated **snmp-server group** command, because it dictates what parameters must be configured toward the end of the **snmp-server user** command. As noted in Figure 26-9 with the arrowed lines, the use of the **auth** keyword in the **snmp-server group** command requires that you configure authentication parameters for the user in the **snmp-server user** command: the password and the choice of authentication hash algorithms. If using the **priv** keyword in the **snmp-server group** command, the **snmp-server user** command must define both authentication and privacy parameters as shown in the figure.

26

NOTE IOS allows you to misconfigure the **snmp-server user** command so that it omits the **auth** or **priv** keyword, even when the referenced **snmp-server group** command uses the **auth** or priv parameter. However, that misconfiguration causes the SNMP agent to not be able to communicate with the SNMP manager. For instance, if the **snmp-server user** command omits the **auth** keyword and associated parameters, but the **snmp-server group** command uses the **auth** keyword, IOS accepts the configuration commands, but authentication fails when the agent and NMS try to communicate.

Example 26-7 shows a series of **snmp-server group** and matching **snmp-server user** commands, one after the other, so you can more easily see the parameters. Note that the **snmp-server group** commands do not include the optional parameters to enable writes (**write v1default**) or to use an ACL, just to reduce clutter.

Example 26-7 *SNMPv3 Configuration Samples: Groups and Users*

```
! The group uses noauth, so the user Youdda1 has no auth nor priv keyword
snmp-server group BookGroup1 v3 noauth
snmp-server user Youdda1 BookGroup1 v3

! The next group uses auth, so the next two users use the auth keyword, but not priv
snmp-server group BookGroup2 v3 auth
snmp-server user Youdda2 BookGroup2 v3 auth md5 AuthPass2
snmp-server user Youdda3 BookGroup2 v3 auth sha AuthPass3

! The next group uses priv, so the next users use both the auth and priv keywords.
snmp-server group BookGroup3 v3 priv
snmp-server user Youdda4 BookGroup3 v3 auth md5 AuthPass3 priv des PrivPass4
snmp-server user Youdda5 BookGroup3 v3 auth md5 AuthPass3 priv 3des PrivPass5
snmp-server user Youdda6 BookGroup3 v3 auth sha AuthPass4 priv aes 128 PrivPass6
```

Note that the example also shows samples of several authentication and encryption options, as listed in Figure 26-9.

Verifying SNMPv3

Verifying SNMPv3 operation begins with confirming the details of the SNMPv3 configuration. You can of course find these with the **show running-config** command, but two commands in particular repeat the configuration settings. Example 26-8 shows the output from one of those commands, **show snmp user**, taken from Router R1 after adding the configuration listed in Example 26-7.

Example 26-8 *Verifying SNMPv3 Configuration Settings*

```
R3# show snmp user
User name: Youdda1
Engine ID: 800000090300D48CB57D8200
storage-type: nonvolatile        active
Authentication Protocol: None
Privacy Protocol: None
```

```
Group-name: BookGroup1


User name: Youdda2
Engine ID: 800000090300D48CB57D8200
storage-type: nonvolatile        active
Authentication Protocol: MD5
Privacy Protocol: None
Group-name: BookGroup2


! Skipping Youdda3, Youdda4, and Youdda5 for brevity


User name: Youdda6
Engine ID: 800000090300D48CB57D8200
storage-type: nonvolatile        active
Authentication Protocol: SHA
Privacy Protocol: AES128
Group-name: BookGroup3
```

In particular, work through the highlighted output for users Youdda1, Youdda2, and Youdda6, as compared to the configuration in Example 26-7. All the highlighted entries basically repeat the settings from the configuration.

Example 26-9 lists output from the **show snmp group** command, which also confirms configuration settings from Example 26-7. The most challenging thing to find in this output is what is missing, rather than what is there. Note that this command does not list the SNMP usernames that happen to refer to this group. Also, for groups that do not use an ACL, there is no obvious text that states that no ACL is used. Make sure to compare the output for BookGroup1, which uses an ACL, and the output for BookGroup2, which does not use an ACL.

Example 26-9 *Verifying SNMPv3 Using* **show snmp group**

```
R3# show snmp group
groupname: BookGroup1                    security model:v3 noauth
contextname: <no context specified>      storage-type: nonvolatile
readview : v1default                     <no writeview specified>
notifyview: <no notifyview specified>
row status: active       access-list: ACL_PROTECTSNMP


groupname: BookGroup2                    security model:v3 auth
contextname: <no context specified>      storage-type: nonvolatile
readview : v1default                     writeview: <no writeview specified>
notifyview: <no notifyview specified>
row status: active
! Lines omitted for brevity
```

Implementing SNMPv3 Notifications (Traps and Informs)

SNMP agents can use SNMPv3 to send unsolicited notifications—Trap and Inform messages—to SNMP managers. SNMPv2c uses communities, in this case using the SNMPv2c notification community concept. SNMPv3 uses the same security levels just discussed, but as applied to SNMPv3 notifications.

To configure an SNMPv3 agent to send notifications, you add the security level and the username to the **snmp-server host** command. That configuration links to the same kinds of **snmp-server user** commands discussed earlier in this section, which in turn link to an **snmp-server group** command. Figure 26-10 shows how the commands connect to each other.

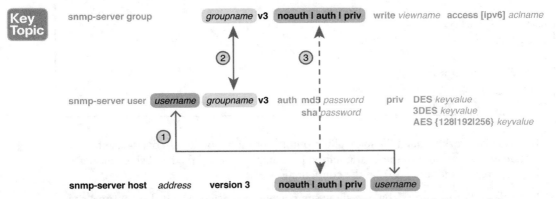

Figure 26-10 *Connecting SNMPv3 Notification Configuration with User and Group*

> **NOTE** IOS allows you to configure commands that refer to the correct username and group name, but with different security levels, with no error messages. However, communication with the NMS then fails.

Example 26-10 shows a few samples of configuration notifications that use SNMPv3. The samples rely on the SNMPv3 usernames and groups as defined in Example 26-7. Feel free to refer back to that example, and check to make sure that each **snmp-server host** command in Example 26-10 refers to the correct SNMP security level used by each linked **snmp-server group** command.

Example 26-10 *Verifying SNMPv3 Configuration Settings*

```
! The group uses noauth, so the user Youdda1 has no auth nor priv keyword
snmp-server enable traps
snmp-server host 10.1.3.3 version 3 noauth Youdda1          ! Traps w/ noauth
snmp-server host 10.1.3.4 informs version 3 auth Youdda2 ! Informs w/ auth
snmp-server host 10.1.3.5 version 3 priv Youdda4            ! Traps w/ priv
```

As always, the **show snmp** command lists the counters that show how many messages flow, including the number of Trap and Inform messages sent by the SNMP agent. To verify the configuration of SNMPv3 notification to NMS hosts, use the **show snmp host** command. Example 26-11 shows the results after configuring Example 26-10; note that almost all the fields in Example 26-11 repeat the configuration parameters from Example 26-10.

Example 26-11 *Verifying SNMPv3 Configuration Settings*

```
R3# show snmp host
Notification host: 10.1.3.4     udp-port: 162    type: inform
user: Youdda2    security model: v3 auth


Notification host: 10.1.3.3     udp-port: 162    type: trap
user: Youdda1    security model: v3 noauth


Notification host: 10.1.3.5     udp-port: 162    type: trap
user: Youdda4    security model: v3 priv
```

Summarizing SNMPv3 Configuration

SNMPv3 configuration has many parameters to choose from in several commands. As a result, putting the commands into a configuration checklist earlier in this section did not work as well for learning, so the text instead spelled out the pieces little by little. Now that you have seen how to configure the individual pieces, this configuration checklist summarizes all the different SNMPv3 configuration options discussed in this chapter, for easier review.

Config Checklist

Step 1. Use the **snmp-server group** *groupname* **v3** {**noauth** | **auth** | **priv**} [**write v1default**] [**access** [**ipv6**] *acl-name*] command in global configuration mode to enable the SNMP agent (if not already started), create a named SNMPv3 group of security settings, set the security level, optionally override the default write view with the same view as defaulted for use as the read MIB view (v1default), and optionally restrict incoming SNMP messages based on the optional referenced IPv4 or IPv6 ACL.

Step 2. To configure users whose referenced SNMPv3 group has a security level of **noauth**, use the **snmp-server user** *username groupname* **v3** command in global configuration mode, making sure to reference an SNMPv3 group with security level of **noauth** configured.

Step 3. To configure users whose referenced SNMPv3 group use the security level of **auth:**

    A. Use the **snmp-server user** *username groupname* **v3 auth md5** *password* command in global configuration mode to configure the user and authentication password, and to choose to use MD5 as the authentication hash algorithm.

    B. Alternatively, use the **snmp-server user** *username groupname* **v3 auth sha** *password* command in global configuration mode to configure the user and authentication password, and to choose to use SHA as the authentication hash algorithm.

26

Step 4. To configure users that use the security level of **priv**, you will add parameters to the end of the **snmp-server user** command syntax as configured in Step 3, as follows:

   A. Add the **priv des** *encryption-key* parameters in global configuration mode to the end of the **snmp-server user** command, to enable the use of DES as the encryption algorithm and to set the encryption key.

   B. Add the **priv 3des** *encryption-key* parameters in global configuration mode to the end of the **snmp-server user** command, to enable the use of triple DES (3DES) as the encryption algorithm and to set the encryption key.

   C. Add the **priv aes** {**128** | **192** | **256**} *encryption-key* parameters in global configuration mode to the end of the **snmp-server user** command, to enable the use of AES as the encryption algorithm, to set the length of the encryption key in bits, and to set the seed for the encryption key.

Step 5. Enable the SNMP agent to send notification messages (Traps and/or Informs) to an NMS as follows:

   A. Use the **snmp-server host** {*hostname* | *ip-address*} [**informs** | **traps**] **version 3** {**noauth** | **auth** | **priv**} *username* command in global configuration mode to configure the SNMP agent to send SNMPv3 Traps to the listed host, using the listed username. Use this command once for each host to which this device should send Traps. Include the **informs** keyword to send Informs; the **traps** keyword is the default setting. Use the same security level setting as the link SNMPv3 group.

   B. Use the **snmp-server enable traps** command in global configuration mode to enable the sending of all supported notifications to all hosts defined in **snmp-server host** commands.

Note that if you review this checklist and get lost, make sure to review and study this section again. SNMPv3 configuration uses a lot of different parameters on three different commands, so it is easy to get lost. The checklist is best used for review once you have a good understanding of the commands.

IP Service Level Agreement

A *service level agreement* (SLA) is a contract or agreement between two parties, with one supplying some service to the second party. The document defines the level of service; with IT, the definition could be for a percentage of the time a service is available, or the round-trip response time of an application, and so on. For instance, a service provider might agree to an SLA that defines the availability numbers for a WAN service to each enterprise site. The enterprise IT department then might agree to an SLA with its internal customers in different business units for application availability and performance.

The IP Service Level Agreement (IP SLA) feature of Cisco routers provides a means to measure and display several key performance and availability indicators. These IP SLA statistics can be used as measurements to determine if an SLA has been met over some period of time. Additionally, IP SLA features can be used for many other purposes as well, like better network monitoring and troubleshooting.

This next section takes a short look at IP SLA, but from a little different perspective than many other topics in this book. While this section does show some IP SLA configuration, the goal here is to show how to use IP SLA for troubleshooting, rather than to work through all the details of configuration. Think of it as if you need to operate the network, and another more experienced engineer may have set up some IP SLA configurations in different places in the network. Your job: use the information available from IP SLA to troubleshoot a network.

An Overview of IP SLA

Network engineers could measure network performance and availability for SLAs by measuring actual end-user traffic. However, measuring end-user traffic could require placing some kind of software on the user devices themselves, with those hidden applications then measuring key facts such as application response time, QoS metrics like jitter and loss, or simple availability information, like whether the host can ping a particular other host.

IP SLA gives network engineers a much different option that does not bother end-user devices. IP SLA runs on a router and generates traffic that mimics user traffic, but without placing any software on the end-user devices. IP SLA—a router-specific feature not found on Cisco switches—can be configured to perform over a dozen different types of IP SLA operations. These operations can be as simple as the equivalent of issuing a **ping** command (to send an ICMP Echo message), to sending messages whose headers mimic voice traffic so that VoIP delay, jitter, and loss can be measured with packets that receive the same QoS treatment as end-user voice traffic.

IP SLA *operations* generate this traffic, receive responses, measure the results, and then make that information available.

To see how IP SLA works at least in some cases, Figure 26-11 shows a simple design with a couple of routers. The two routers sit at different sites. The senior network engineer wants to track voice delay and jitter over the WAN in preparation for an upcoming revision to an end-user SLA. The engineer could use one of several IP SLA operations—for instance, the RTP-based VoIP operation, called a UDP Jitter probe, which generates IP packets that include a UDP and RTP header like normal VoIP traffic.

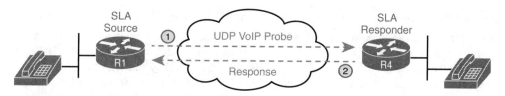

Figure 26-11 *Using ICMP UDP Jitter Probes*

Many of the IP SLA probes rely on one router to generate the packets (the *IP SLA source*), with another router replying back (the *IP SLA responder*), as shown in Figure 26-11. However, some IP SLA operations do not require an IP SLA responder, like the ICMP Echo probe. This operation generates an ICMP Echo Request message, so any host that will respond to a normal ICMP Echo Request (a normal ping) will reply back with an ICMP Echo Reply. Using the IP SLA ICMP Echo probe means that you can monitor the state of and performance sending packets to any IP address in the network, including servers and user hosts, as shown in Figure 26-12. Steps 1 and 2 show Router R1 as an IP SLA source,

26

with R4 replying to the normal ICMP packet. Steps 3 and 4 show the same idea, again with Router R1 as the IP SLA source, with the server replying to the ICMP Echo message.

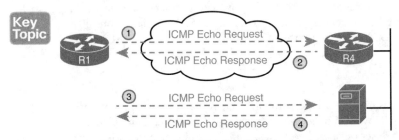

Figure 26-12 *Using IP SLA ICMP Echo Probes to Routers and Normal Hosts*

NOTE The term IP SLA *probe* is commonly used instead of the more formal term IP SLA *operation*.

Basic IP SLA ICMP-Echo Configuration

This section shows a couple of IP SLA ICMP-Echo operations configured on a router, just to give you a sense for what can be configured. In this scenario, the senior engineer decided to configure R1, the central site router in a network, as the IP SLA source. He configured an ICMP Echo probe, with the branch office router's LAN IP address (10.1.3.2) as the destination. He also used the central site router's LAN IP address (10.1.1.1) as the source. By using these addresses, the probe not only tests WAN connectivity, but tests the two routers' IP routing tables for the LAN subnet destinations.

Figure 26-13 shows a small subset of the network, with central site R1 on the left, and a sample branch office R2 on the right.

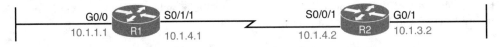

Figure 26-13 *Sample Network with IP SLA ICMP Echo Probes*

Example 26-12 shows an example IP SLA operation that the senior engineer is considering using. It refers to R2's LAN subnet address of 10.1.3.2 as the destination of the ICMP Echo, and uses R1's LAN IP address of 10.1.1.1 as the source IP address. In fact, of all the commands shown in the example, only the highlighted commands would be required to create the operations; the rest of the commands set related parameters.

Example 26-12 *IP SLA Configuration Used in This Section*

```
ip sla 1
  icmp-echo 10.1.3.2 source-ip 10.1.1.1   ! Echo from 10.1.1.1 to 10.1.3.2
  frequency 60                            ! Send it every 60 seconds; default
  threshold 300                           ! Round Trip Time of 300 milliseconds
  history filter all                      ! This means KEEP all data in history
  history buckets-kept 6                  ! Limits historical data to 6 groups (buckets)
```

```
    history lives-kept 1                    !
  !
  ip sla schedule 1 life forever start-time now
```

Also notice the **ip sla schedule** command at the end of Example 26-12 as well. IP SLA uses a concept of configuring the IP SLA operation with a number, with many subcommands defining the probe, as seen in the majority of the example. Separately, as shown at the bottom of the example, the **ip sla schedule** global configuration command tells IOS when to run the operation: when to start, and when to stop. An operation can be started at a certain date and time, or in so much time from when the command is issued, or to just start now (as is shown in the example with the **start-time now** parameters). This command can also limit how long the probe runs; in this case, the probe runs forever, which means until the engineer issues a command like **no ip sla schedule 1** to remove the command from the configuration.

Troubleshooting Using IP SLA Counters

The IP SLA ICMP-Echo operation does the equivalent of a single ping to another address, on a timed basis. So how does that help you troubleshoot problems, particularly in comparison to just using the **ping** command from the CLI? This section shows how, by taking a closer look at the data made available by IP SLA.

To begin, take a look at the most basic IP SLA **show** command, the **show ip sla summary** command, as listed in Example 26-13. The command lists a single line of output per SLA operation. It lists some configuration information, namely the address to which the ICMP Echo is being sent. It also lists the two key pieces of information you have seen many times in the output of **ping** commands: an indication of whether the Echo Request received a response, and the Round Trip Time (RTT), which measures the delay from sending the ICMP Echo Request until receiving the matching ICMP Echo Reply. With this command, the success or failure is shown in the Return Code column, with OK meaning that an Echo Reply was received.

Example 26-13 *Displaying the Return Code State and RTT with Basic IP SLA Commands*

```
R1# show ip sla summary
IPSLAs Latest Operation Summary
Codes: * active, ^ inactive, ~ pending

ID            Type          Destination     Stats       Return     Last
                                            (ms)        Code       Run

---------------------------------------------------------------------

*1            icmp-echo     10.1.3.2        RTT=124     OK         15 seconds ago

*2            icmp-echo     10.1.3.2        RTT=184     OK         11 seconds ago
R1# ping 10.1.3.2
Type escape sequence to abort.
Sending 5, 100-byte ICMP Echos to 10.1.3.2, timeout is 2 seconds:
!!!!!
Success rate is 100 percent (5/5), round-trip min/avg/max = 1/1/4 ms
R1#
```

26

Note that Example 26-13 shows the output of a **ping** command for comparison. That command lists the same basic information—success (or not) for the (default) five Echo Requests, and some stats about the RTT for those Echo Request/Response pairs.

An IP SLA ICMP-Echo operation can measure two facts: success/failure of the Echo, and the RTT. To use that information for better troubleshooting, beyond just issuing a **ping** command, you need to go beyond the status of the most recent IP SLA operation, and look at statistics about the history of previous IP SLA operations.

The **show ip sla statistics 1** command provides some basic history through a counter of successes and failures, as shown in Example 26-14. In addition to the return code and RTT of the most recent operation, you get a counter of successes and failures of past operations. So, you can get a sense of whether the pings have been failing or not.

Key Topic

Example 26-14   *Historical Success/Failure Counters with IP SLA*

```
R1# show ip sla statistics 1
IPSLAs Latest Operation Statistics


IPSLA operation id: 1
        Latest RTT: 16 milliseconds
Latest operation start time: 12:40:39 EST Tue Jan 5 2016
Latest operation return code: OK
Number of successes: 7
Number of failures: 0
Operation time to live: Forever
```

Think about a couple of troubleshooting scenarios with these stats. Imagine the stats show 22 successes, but 15 failures. You ping the address (with the same source address as well, using extended ping), and it works correctly now. But the statistics show that almost half of the most recent operations failed. Without that history, you might use the ping, see it work, and think that no problems existed at all. Conversely, if you see counters with only a few failures, and the ping fails right now, that could tell you that some problem exists, and it just happened, so that might give you some direction as well.

Seeing the counters with the numbers of successes and failures brings up a key question: How often does IP SLA perform an operation? As you probably would guess, that setting is configurable. The samples in Example 26-12 both set the operation **frequency** to 60 (seconds), which is the default for ICMP-Echo operations.

You may also want to reset those statistics when troubleshooting. For instance, imagine that you show up to do some troubleshooting on a router that acts as an IP SLA source. If the counters show 80 successes and 5 failures, with a 60-second frequency, you may find that information helpful, but maybe not. Those five failures could be spread across those 85 minutes, could have all happened over an hour ago, and so on. So, you might just want to reset the counters, and then check again a little later in the troubleshooting process. To do so, issue the **ip sla restart** *op-number* command in global configuration mode.

Troubleshooting Using IP SLA History

IP SLA has two other methods to keep historical data and even perform analysis on that data. IOS first had IP SLA history. Later, Cisco added new history features, referring to those as *enhanced history*. Both take the RTT concept, save the information, and in the case of enhanced history, aggregate the information to conserve memory, while keeping more details. This next topic shows an example using traditional IP SLA history.

Traditional IP SLA history data can be enabled and then displayed with the **show ip sla history** command, as shown in Example 26-15. (IP SLA operation 1 from Example 26-12 uses history; note that operation 2, with the **history enhanced** IP SLA subcommand, also enables enhanced history.)

With traditional IP SLA history, SLA takes the RTT and return code information and stores it in a history bucket. The **show ip sla history** command then displays one line per bucket. You can think of it as the same information in the **show ip sla summary** command seen back in Example 26-13, but going backward in time for the number of history buckets defined. Earlier Example 26-12 shows IP SLA operation 1 uses six buckets, so the output in Example 26-15 shows the results of the most recent six IP SLA operations for operation number 1.

Key Topic

Example 26-15 *Displaying the Traditional Historical State of an IP SLA ICMP Echo Probe*

```
R1# show ip sla history 1
         Point by point History
Entry    = Entry number
LifeI    = Life index
BucketI  = Bucket index
SampleI  = Sample index
SampleT  = Sample start time (milliseconds)
CompT    = RTT (milliseconds)
Sense    = Response return code


Entry LifeI    BucketI    SampleI    SampleT    CompT    Sense    TargetAddr
1     1        11         1          59438868   108      1        10.1.3.2
1     1        12         1          59498868   188      1        10.1.3.2
1     1        13         1          59558868   280      1        10.1.3.2
1     1        14         1          59618868   88       1        10.1.3.2
1     1        15         1          59678868   160      1        10.1.3.2
1     1        16         1          59738868   252      1        10.1.3.2
```

First, look at the legend information in the top half of Example 26-15, and the two highlighted lines in particular. Those show an odd quirk, with the two most useful fields for troubleshooting using different headings than the earlier commands: CompT and Sense. *Sense* refers to the same idea as return code in the commands in Examples 26-13 and 26-14, with a numeric 1 meaning that the probe succeeded. A return code of timeout and a sense of 4 means that the ICMP Echo probe did not receive a response to the ICMP Echo Request.

You can troubleshoot a little more easily with this historical data by looking for a few key trends. First, imagine that the probe configured 30 buckets and the frequency was 60 seconds, so that the operation keeps 30 minutes of historical data. You can look for spikes in the RTT (in the CompT column). You can also look to see if the return code (in the Sense column) had been working consistently, or if the Echo Requests had been failing off and on for a while. Those answers might lead you more toward issues of network performance or QoS, or more toward specific connectivity issues.

26

SPAN

This next major section of the chapter moves from the router-specific tool of IP SLA to a switch-specific tool: Switched Port Analyzer, or SPAN. SPAN enables switches to make copies of some of the Ethernet frames flowing through the switch, sending them out a specific port. Many networking tools can make use of the copies of these frames, from intrusion prevention systems (IPS), to offloading some workloads away from servers, and sending the frames to network analysis tools to help troubleshoot a problem.

This section introduces the concepts behind SPAN, along with how to configure Local SPAN on a Cisco switch. The discussion revolves around how to use SPAN to mirror traffic to a network analyzer, for the purpose of then troubleshooting problems.

SPAN Concepts

Network analyzers capture and analyze the contents of frames that enter and exit a network interface card (NIC) on the host where the analyzer is running. The analyzer may be a purpose-built hardware appliance, capturing the frames entering and exiting the appliance. Often, the analyzer is a software application installed on a PC or server, or as a virtual machine (VM) in a data center.

For example, a network engineer can install a network analyzer on a PC and start using it, capturing all Ethernet frames sent in and out the Ethernet NIC, or all 802.11 frames sent in/out the wireless NIC. (In fact, if you have never done so, take a few minutes to do a lab: download the free Wireshark network analyzer from https://www.wireshark.org, start it, and capture all the frames entering and exiting your own PC.) The network analyzer can then display the contents of each frame in hex and binary, but more importantly, it will separate out each message, each header in each message, and make it much easier to sift through the data to troubleshoot a problem. Figure 26-14 shows a copy of a screen from the Wireshark analyzer, taken when building an upcoming example in which a host pinged another host, with the output listing the details of one of the packets carrying the ICMP Echo Request.

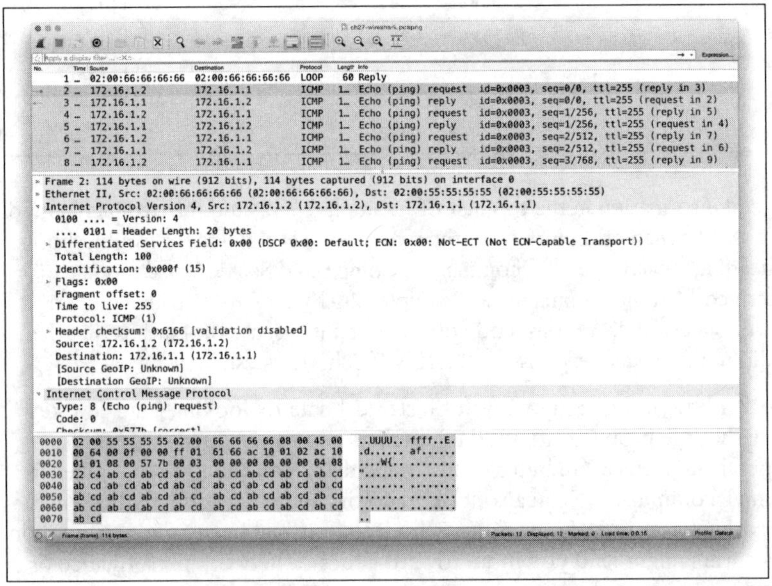

Figure 26-14 *Screenshot of Wireshark Network Analyzer User Interface*

The Need for SPAN When Using a Network Analyzer

Although you can install network analyzer software on your own PC, to be ready to troubleshoot problems in a network, network engineers place network analyzers around the network, connecting to one of the LAN switches in the network. However, the network analyzer needs to receive copies of the frames into its NIC so that the analyzer can capture and then analyze the frames. Because of the normal operation of a LAN switch, the network analyzer will not receive copies of frames unless the switch is configured to send copies of frames out another port, which is exactly what SPAN does.

To see an example of both the problem and the solution, Figures 26-15 and 26-16 show a before-and-after flow, before SPAN and after SPAN. In this case, the arrow line represents Ethernet frames being sent between a PC and a server. Without SPAN, after the first frame is sent by each device, the LAN switch will have learned the MAC addresses used by each device. Any frames sent from the PC to the server, and back, will be forwarded as unicast frames out ports G1/0/11 or G1/0/12. None of the frames addressed to the PC or server will be forwarded to the network analyzer.

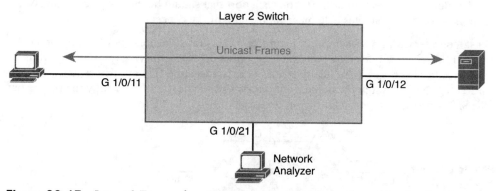

Figure 26-15   *Layer 2 Forwarding Logic: Network Analyzer Does Not Receive Frames*

NOTE   The examples in this section were taken from a Cisco 2960-XR switch, which uses a three-digit interface ID.

SPAN solves this problem by copying those frames from certain ports (*SPAN source ports*) to the port where the network analyzer sits (the *SPAN destination port*). Figure 26-16 shows the concept. In this case, the switch has two SPAN source ports, G1/0/11 and G1/0/12. Frames received on both ports are copied out to the SPAN destination port G1/0/21.

26

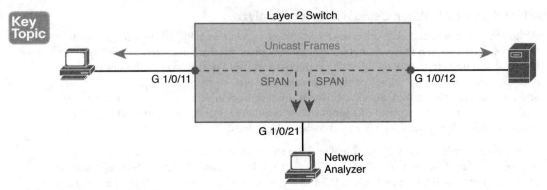

Figure 26-16 *SPAN Copies (Mirrors) Frames to the Network Analyzer*

SPAN Session Concepts

A collection of SPAN rules, called a SPAN *session*, can define one or more source ports, as well as define the direction of traffic on each port that should be then copied to the destination port. Some examples help make more sense of the concepts.

First, consider the SPAN example in Figure 26-17. It shows the concept of using port G1/0/11 as a source port. However, the logic goes beyond identifying the source port; it also specifies for the switch to copy frames being transmitted (Tx) out that switch port. The SPAN logic would watch for frames sent out that switch port, and then copy the frames out the SPAN destination port (G1/0/21 in this case).

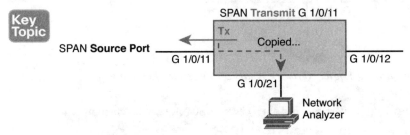

Figure 26-17 *SPAN Construct: Source Port G1/0/11, for Frames in the Transmit Direction*

Figure 26-18 shows the contrasting concepts behind using the receive direction. The example shown in Figure 26-18 is just like that shown in Figure 26-17, except the SPAN function monitors traffic received (Rx) on that same interface. In this case, frames received on the switch interface would be sent out to the SPAN destination port.

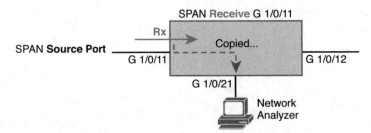

Figure 26-18 *SPAN Construct: Source Port G1/0/11, for Frames in the Receive Direction*

One SPAN session can be configured to monitor one or more ports and, on each port, to monitor for frames transmitted out the switch port, monitor for frames received in the switch port, or monitor in both directions.

SPAN also supports monitoring VLANs. However, the idea of monitoring the receive, transmit, and both directions for a VLAN does not apply to the VLAN as a whole. Instead, using SPAN on a VLAN means using SPAN on all ports in the VLAN (including trunks). For instance, if a switch has eight access ports in VLAN 3, a SPAN session that monitors VLAN 3 for received traffic monitors all eight ports in that VLAN for each port's received traffic. Later, if ports are added or removed from VLAN 3, the SPAN logic will adjust without requiring reconfiguration.

Finally, all the example topologies so far happen to show Local SPAN: instances in which the SPAN source ports and the SPAN destination port are attached to the same switch. In some cases, you might need to send the SPAN traffic to a device attached to another switch.

Cisco switches supply two solutions to use SPAN with remote destinations, each useful depending on the network topology between the switches. Remote SPAN (RSPAN), as seen at the top of Figure 26-19, forwards the SPAN traffic over a VLAN at Layer 2. Encapsulated RSPAN (ERSPAN) expects Layer 3 switches and a Layer 3 forwarding path between the switches, so it encapsulates the SPAN traffic in a GRE tunnel to forward the traffic to another switch.

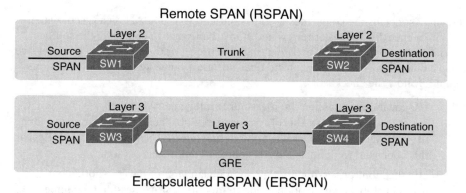

Figure 26-19 *RSPAN and ERSPAN Defined*

Configuring Local SPAN

Local SPAN enables network engineers to troubleshoot problems by using tools like network analyzers. The goal of the configuration then is to define the correct sources of information (ports and/or VLANs, and transmit/receive directions), and identify the correct destination port where the analyzer sits.

IOS uses a series of **monitor session** global commands to configure SPAN. SPAN allows the definition of multiple monitor sessions. Each monitor session defines one or more SPAN sources of the same type (either port or VLAN, but not a mix), plus a single SPAN destination port.

26

SPAN configuration actually has quite a few dependencies, with the following list mentioning some of the most important dependencies:

- A SPAN destination port can be used with only one SPAN session at a time.
- A SPAN destination port cannot also be a SPAN source port.
- When configured as a SPAN destination port, the switch no longer treats the port as a normal port. That is, the switch does not learn MAC addresses for received frames, or send frames based on matching the MAC table, for that port.
- A SPAN destination port can be unconfigured from one monitor session (**no monitor session** *number* **destination interface** *type number*) and then added to another monitor session.
- Multiple SPAN sources can be used in a single SPAN session.
- One SPAN session cannot mix interfaces and VLAN sources; that is, the sources must all be interfaces or all be VLANs.
- One SPAN session can use any combination of directions (transmit, receive, and both) as applied to different SPAN sources.
- EtherChannel interfaces can be used as source ports. Frames for all ports in the EtherChannel will be considered by SPAN.
- Trunks can be used as source ports. When used, by default, SPAN includes frames from all VLANs on that trunk, but SPAN VLAN filtering can limit the VLANs included.

The following list details the commands used to configure Local SPAN on a Cisco switch, collected into a checklist for easier review and study. Note that to configure the source port (interface), the command can refer to a single interface, or to the first and last interface numbers in a range. However, the command does not use a **range** keyword. (Explanations and examples follow the checklist.)

Step 1.   Use the **monitor session** *number* **source interface** *type number* [- *last-in-range*] [**rx** | **tx** | **both**] command in global configuration mode to identify a SPAN session by number, and define one SPAN source interface. Repeat this command to define all SPAN source ports for this session.

Step 2.   Use the **monitor session** *number* **source vlan** *vlan-id* [**rx** | **tx** | **both**] command in global configuration mode to identify a SPAN session by number, and define one SPAN source VLAN. Repeat this command to define all SPAN source VLANs for this session.

Step 3.   Use the **monitor session** *number* **destination interface** *type number* global command to define the one SPAN destination port for the monitor session.

For example, Figure 26-20 shows the ideas behind the configuration of two monitor sessions in Example 26-16, numbered 1 and 2. SPAN session 1 uses two source ports, monitoring frames received on those ports. (Session 1 matches the earlier example shown in Figure 26-16.) SPAN session 2 shows the ideas of monitoring VLAN 11, for frames going in both directions on each port in VLAN 11, and sending copies of those frames out destination port G1/0/22. Example 26-16 shows the configuration that matches the figure.

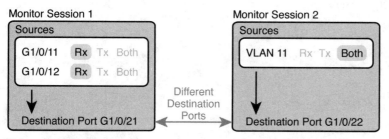

Figure 26-20 *SPAN Monitor Sessions—Some Dependencies*

Example 26-16 *Configuring SPAN Monitor Sessions 1 and 2*

```
! Monitor Session 1
monitor session 1 source interface Gi1/0/11 - 12 rx
monitor session 1 destination interface Gi1/0/21
!
! Monitor Session 2 - the default direction is both, so both does not appear in the
! command.
monitor session 2 source vlan 11
monitor session 2 destination interface Gi1/0/22
```

Once configured, all the network engineer would need to do is start using the network analyzer software on the hosts connected to port G1/0/21 (for SPAN session 1) or port G1/0/22 (for SPAN session 2). The details of how to use the output of the analyzer go beyond the scope of this book. However, when using the analyzer, if the capture does not appear to be working in that no frames are being captured, you can check the SPAN sessions with the **show monitor session all** command, as listed in Example 26-17. This command lists the configuration of each monitor session, including any default settings not listed in the configuration commands.

Example 26-17 *Configuring a SPAN Monitor Session 1 Per Figure 26-18*

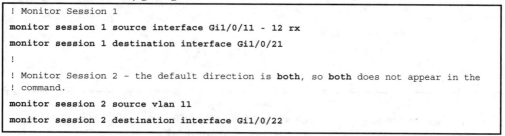

```
        Encapsulation       : Native
              Ingress       : Disabled


SW11# show monitor detail
Session 1
---------
Type                        : Local Session
Description          : -
Source Ports                :
    RX Only             : Gi1/0/11-12
    TX Only             : None
    Both                : None
Source VLANs                :
    RX Only             : None
    TX Only             : None
    Both                : None
! Lines omitted for brevity
```

Pay particular attention to the details around the SPAN sources in the **show monitor session** command, as compared with the **show monitor detail** command at the end of the example. The **show monitor session** output lists the source port or VLAN, but breaks down the information based on ports/VLANs configured for receive frames, transmit frames, or both, listing no lines for directions that do not happen to be configured for that SPAN session. The **show monitor detail** command (shown here for session 1 only) lists all three directions, for both ports and VLANs, so you can clearly see each port/VLAN and associated direction.

SPAN Session Parameters for Troubleshooting

To close this section and chapter, stop and think for a moment about what SPAN does. Think about interface speeds, and the work that must be done on the network analyzer connected to the SPAN destination port. And think about this question: How much SPAN is too much?

For example, consider a SPAN session that collects traffic in the receive direction for ten FastEthernet ports. If the destination port is also a FastEthernet port, it is easy to imagine that more than 100 Mbps of traffic needs to be sent out to the destination port, because at full speeds, those ten ports at 100 Mbps could generate 1000 Mbps (1 Gbps) of traffic.

Now think about that same case, but with the simple change to monitor for both directions of packets. That just doubled the potential amount of traffic sent out to the destination port.

Finally, think about the host where the network analyzer runs. It might be a purpose-built network analyzer appliance so that it can handle the load. Sometimes, it's the 7-year-old laptop that no one uses any more, except to connect to a switch to capture packets. That laptop might not handle the amount of traffic sent by SPAN.

All these scenarios result in the same kinds of problems. The network analyzer does not capture what you need to capture, you cannot troubleshoot the problem, and you have to waste time repeating the effort to get a good capture of what is happening in the network.

Choosing to Limit SPAN Sources

Good engineers do not just decide to use SPAN on the entire VLAN in both directions without giving any thought to what they really need to capture. Instead, engineers think about what needs to be captured, how to get SPAN to capture that traffic, and *capture as little other traffic as possible*.

For example, if the goal of a capture is to see traffic sent by the switch to all hosts in a VLAN, then create a SPAN session with that VLAN as the source, for the transmit direction. However, if you only really care about 3 of the 12 access ports in that VLAN, take the time to configure the SPAN session just for those ports.

It is also easy to make poor choices regarding the traffic direction—choices that work, but that overload the SPAN destination port. For instance, Figure 26-21 represents the SPAN logic applied to the four ports in the same VLAN (11), with a command like **monitor session 1 source VLAN 11 both**. Each Tx and Rx bubble represents a location where SPAN is monitoring either transmit or receive traffic. The figure then focuses on one Ethernet frame, sent by PC1 to PC3.

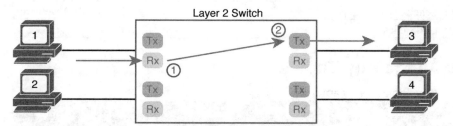

Figure 26-21 *Frame from PC1 to PC3—SPAN Copies Twice*

Enabling SPAN in this VLAN, for both directions, means that SPAN monitors both transmit and receive traffic on each port in that VLAN. The single frame shown in the figure would be seen by SPAN monitoring twice (on the receive function of the port on the left, and the transmit function of the port on the right), so SPAN would send two copies of this single frame to the destination port. Overall, this SPAN session would send twice as many frames as necessary out the SPAN destination port.

A much more efficient choice would be to use either the receive or transmit direction for the SPAN session. Figure 26-22 shows the logic, but now with the Tx bubbles removed, implying that SPAN has been enabled in the receive direction only. As a result, that one example frame sent by PC1 to PC3 is seen only once by SPAN's monitoring logic, and only one copy of the frame is sent to the destination port.

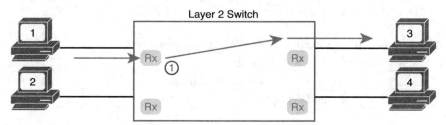

Figure 26-22 *Frame from PC1 to PC3—SPAN Copies Once*

26

Chapter Review

One key to doing well on the exams is to perform repetitive spaced review sessions. Review this chapter's material using either the tools in the book, DVD, or interactive tools for the same material found on the book's companion website. Refer to the "Your Study Plan" element for more details. Table 26-3 outlines the key review elements and where you can find them. To better track your study progress, record when you completed these activities in the second column.

Table 26-3 Chapter Review Tracking

Review Element	Review Date(s)	Resource Used
Review key topics		Book, DVD/website
Review key terms		Book, DVD/website
Answer DIKTA questions		Book, PCPT
Do labs		Blog
Review memory tables		Book, DVD/website
Review config checklists		Book, DVD/website
Review command tables		Book

Review All the Key Topics

Table 26-4 Key Topics for Chapter 26

Key Topic Element	Description	Page Number
Figure 26-2	The SNMP Get Request and Get Response message flow	696
Figure 26-3	SNMP notification with SNMP Trap messages	697
Figure 26-5	The use of SNMP RO and RW communities with SNMP Get and Set	699
List	SNMPv3 security features	699
Figure 26-7	SNMPv3 **snmp-server group** command syntax and meaning	705
Table 26-2	SNMPv3 security levels and the actions taken for each	705
Figure 26-9	Linkage and requirements between the **snmp-server group** and **snmp-server user** commands	707
Figure 26-10	Linkage between SNMPv3 Trap host definition, user, and group	710
Figure 26-12	IP SLA ICMP-Echo operation concepts	714
Example 26-14	Output that shows counters of success/failure of IP SLA operations	716
Example 26-15	Output of IP SLA history for an ICMP-Echo operation	717
Figure 26-16	SPAN copying frames to a destination port	720
Figure 26-17	SPAN monitoring in Transmit direction, concepts	720
List	SPAN exceptions and dependencies	722

Key Terms You Should Know

Simple Network Management Protocol, SNMP community, read-only community, read-write community, notification community, SNMP Get, SNMP Set, SNMP Trap, SNMP Inform, Management Information Base (MIB), SNMPv2c, SNMPv3, Network Management System (NMS), SNMP manager, SNMP agent, MIB view, service level agreement (SLA), IP Service Level Agreement (IP SLA), IP SLA operation, ICMP-Echo operation, IP SLA source, IP SLA responder, Round Trip Time (RTT), Switched Port Analyzer (SPAN), SPAN source port, SPAN source VLAN, SPAN destination port, network analyzer, Local SPAN, SPAN monitor session (SPAN session)

Command References

Tables 26-5 and 26-6 list configuration and verification commands used in this chapter. As an easy review exercise, cover the left column in a table, read the right column, and try to recall the command without looking. Then repeat the exercise, covering the right column, and try to recall what the command does.

Table 26-5   Chapter 26 Configuration Command Reference

Command	Description
SNMP Configuration Commands	
snmp-server community *communitystring* **RO** [**ipv6** *acl-name*] [*acl-name*]	Configures an SNMPv1 or SNMPv2c community string that allows reads (Get and related messages), and also enables the SNMP agent if not yet enabled by another **snmp-server** command. Optionally enables ACL filtering of the incoming SNMP messages that use this community string.
snmp-server community *communitystring* **RW** [**ipv6** *acl-name*] [*acl-name*]	Configures an SNMPv1 or SNMPv2c community string that allows both write and read (Get and Set messages), and also enables the SNMP agent if not yet enabled by another **snmp-server** command. Optionally enables ACL filtering of the incoming SNMP messages that use this community string.
snmp-server location *text-describing-location*	Defines the text setting of an SNMP variable meant to identify the location of the device.
snmp-server contact *contact-name*	Defines the text setting of an SNMP variable meant to identify the person to contact for questions about the device.
snmp-server host *hostname*	*ip-address* **version 2c** *community-string*	Identifies one SNMP manager (NMS) to which to send SNMPv2 Trap messages, using the listed notification community.
snmp-server host *hostname*	*ip-address* **informs version 2c** *community-string*	Identifies one SNMP manager (NMS) to which to send SNMPv2 Inform messages, using the listed notification community.
snmp-server enable traps	Enables the SNMP agent to send all supported Traps/Inform messages to any NMS hosts defined with the **snmp-server host** command.

26

Command	Description
IP SLA Configuration Commands	
ip sla *operation-number*	From global config mode, defines an IP SLA operation (probe) by number, and moves the user into SLA configuration mode for that operation.
icmp-echo *address* [**source-ip** *address*]	From IP SLA mode, defines this operation as an ICMP-Echo operation, always defines the destination of the ICMP Echo, and optionally defines the IP address on the local router to use as the source of the ICMP Echo.
frequency *seconds*	From IP SLA mode, defines how often an IP SLA operation is performed.
history filter all	From IP SLA mode, tells IOS to keep all historical data for the configured probe.
history buckets-kept 6	From IP SLA mode, for traditional IP SLA history, sets the number of historical buckets of data to keep.
history enhanced interval *seconds* **buckets** *number*	From IP SLA mode, enables the use of enhanced history for this operation, and defines the aggregation interval (the time for which probe stats are collected and aggregated), as well as the number of buckets of aggregated statistics to keep.
history lives-kept 1	From IP SLA mode, enables the keeping of historical data for the operation (a setting of 0 disables the tracking of history.)
ip sla restart *op-number*	Global configuration command that resets statistics for the listed operation.
SPAN Configuration Commands	
monitor session *number* **source interface** *type number [- last-in-range]* [**rx**	**tx**	**both**]	Global configuration command to enable SPAN on an interface, or range of consecutive interfaces, for the listed direction of frames.
monitor session *number* **source vlan** *vlan-id* [**rx**	**tx**	**both**]	Global configuration command to enable SPAN on all interfaces in a VLAN, for the listed direction of frames.
monitor session *number* **destination interface** *type number*	Global configuration command to define the one destination port for the SPAN session.

Table 26-6   Chapter 26 EXEC Command Reference

Command	Description
SNMP Verification Commands	
show snmp community	Displays a few lines of output about the configuration of each community configured with **snmp-server community**.
show snmp contact	Displays the contact information set with the command **snmp-server contact** *text*.
show snmp location	Displays the location information set with the command **snmp-server location** *text*.

Command	Description
show snmp host	Displays a few lines of configuration information based on each configured **snmp-server host** command.
show snmp	Displays a few dozen lines of output, mostly status and counter variables, which describe the operation of the SNMP agent, plus the numbers of and types of messages processed.
show snmp user	Displays a few lines of output per defined SNMPv3 user, listing configured and default settings.
show snmp group	Displays a few lines of output per defined SNMPv3 user group, listing configured and default settings.
IP SLA Verification Commands	
show ip sla summary	Lists one line of combined configuration and status information for each IP SLA operation configured on the IP SLA source router.
show ip sla statistics [*op-number*]	Lists several lines of information about each IP SLA operation (or just the listed operation number), including the return code for the most recent attempt, plus success and failure counters.
show ip sla history [*op-number*]	Displays any traditional IP SLA history information if configured, which includes one operation result per history bucket.
show ip sla enhanced-history distribution-statistics [*op-number*]	Displays any enhanced IP SLA history information if configured, which includes aggregated statistics based on multiple operations calculated and stored into each history bucket.
SPAN Verification Commands	
show monitor session [*number* | **all**]	Lists a few lines of output for each SPAN session, repeating each non-default configuration detail.
show monitor detail	Lists a few dozen lines of output per SPAN session, including the configured settings as well as for any values left as defaults.

26

CHAPTER 27

Cloud Computing

This chapter covers the following exam topics:

4.0 Infrastructure Services

4.2 Describe the effects of cloud resources on enterprise network architecture

4.2.a Traffic path to internal and external cloud services

4.2.b Virtual services

4.2.c Basic virtual network infrastructure

Cloud computing is an approach to offering IT services to customers. However, cloud computing is not a product, or a set of products, a protocol, or any single thing. So, while there are accepted descriptions and definitions of cloud computing today, it takes a broad knowledge of IT beyond networking to know whether a particular IT service is or is not worthy of being called a cloud computing service.

Cloud computing, or cloud, is an approach as to how to offer services to customers. For an IT service to be considered to be cloud computing, it should have these characteristics: It can be requested on-demand; it can dynamically scale (that is, it is elastic); it uses a pool of resources; it has a variety of network access options; and it can be measured and billed back to the user based on the amount used.

From an exam perspective, the cloud topic for this chapter (and the SDN/programmability topic in Chapter 28) departs from the typical CCNA R&S types of topics. Around the mid-2010s, Cisco began adding some coverage of emerging technologies to some of its exams, even technologies that might be unrelated to the core of the exam. While cloud was a popular IT practice by 2016 (the publication year of this book), cloud topics stray pretty far from the core routing and switching topics that comprise most of the ICND2 and CCNA R&S exams. So the cloud computing material poses a unique challenge.

This chapter attempts to give you a general idea of the cloud issues as described by several cloud exam topics. To do that, this chapter begins with one major section that defines cloud computing, with some background in server virtualization to start. Following that, the second major section discusses one of the key cloud exam topics, discussing the traffic patterns that occur with and without the use of cloud services. The third and final major section of this chapter then introduces the idea of a virtualized network function and how public cloud providers provide some services while customers provide others.

"Do I Know This Already?" Quiz

Take the quiz (either here, or use the PCPT software) if you want to use the score to help you decide how much time to spend on this chapter. The answers are at the bottom of the page following the quiz, and the explanations are in DVD Appendix C and in the PCPT software.

Table 27-1 "Do I Know This Already?" Foundation Topics Section-to-Question Mapping

Foundation Topics Section	Questions
Cloud Computing Concepts	1, 2
WAN Traffic Paths to Reach Cloud Services	3, 4
Virtual Network Functions and Services	5

1. Which of the following cloud services is most likely to be used for software development?

   a. IaaS

   b. PaaS

   c. SaaS

   d. SLBaaS

2. Which of the following cloud services is most likely to be purchased and then used to later install your own software applications?

   a. IaaS

   b. PaaS

   c. SaaS

   d. SLBaaS

3. An enterprise plans to start using a public cloud service, and is considering different WAN options. The answers list four options under consideration. Which one option has the most issues if the company chooses one cloud provider but then later wants to change to use a different cloud provider instead?

   a. Using private WAN connections directly to the cloud provider

   b. Using an Internet connection without VPN

   c. Using an intercloud exchange

   d. Using an Internet connection with VPN

4. An enterprise plans to start using a public cloud service, and is considering different WAN options. The answers list four options under consideration. Which options provide good security by keeping the data private while also providing good QoS services? (Choose two answers.)

   a. Using private WAN connections directly to the cloud provider

   b. Using an Internet connection without VPN

   c. Using an intercloud exchange

   d. Using an Internet connection with VPN

5. Which of the following best describes a virtual network function in a public cloud service?

    a. A subset of a physical networking device, configured by the cloud provider and allocated for use by that customer only

    b. A networking function implemented by the cloud provider for the customer, but with no direct customer access to the server that provides the service

    c. A networking function implemented by the cloud provider for the customer as a VM that is directly accessible and configurable by the customer

    d. Any networking feature implemented on a VM in a cloud service

Foundation Topics

Cloud Computing Concepts

From one perspective, the IT function in any business provides services: the service of supplying applications to the internal customers inside the company. We might think about IT as servers, and databases, and networks, and security, and all the related hardware and software. But from the other direction, the goal is to run the business operations of the enterprise, using different applications, and IT's business is to deliver those applications to the rest of the company.

Cloud computing refers to one approach to providing some kinds of IT services. That approach focuses on the service more than the technology. But before you can begin to appreciate cloud computing, this section needs to introduce some concepts and terminology from the world of virtualized data centers. Following that, this first section defines and explains cloud computing.

Server Virtualization

When you think of a server, what comes to mind? Is it a desktop computer with a fast CPU? A desktop computer with lots of RAM? Is it hardware that would not sit upright on the floor, but could be easily bolted into a rack in a data center? When you think of a server, do you not even think of hardware, but of the server operating system (OS), running somewhere as a virtual machine (VM)?

All those answers are accurate from one perspective or another, but in most every other discussion within the scope of the CCNA R&S certification, we ignore those details. From the perspective of most CCNA R&S discussions, a server is a place to run applications, with users connecting to those applications over the network. The book then represents the server with an icon that looks like a desktop computer (that is the standard Cisco icon for a server). This next topic breaks down some different perspectives on what it means to be a server, and prepares us to then discuss cloud computing.

Cisco Server Hardware

Think about the form factor of servers for a moment—that is, the shape and size of the physical server. If you were to build a server of your own, what would it look like? How big, how wide, how tall, and so on? Even if you have never seen a device characterized as a server, consider these key facts:

No KVM: For most servers, there is no permanent user that sits near the server; all the users and administrators connect to the server over the network. As a result, there is no need for a permanent keyboard, video display, or mouse (collectively referred to as KVM).

Racks of servers in a data center: In the early years of servers, a server was any computer with relatively fast CPU, large amounts of RAM, and so on. Today, companies put many servers into one room—a data center—and one goal is to not waste space. So, making servers with a form factor that fits in a standard rack makes for more efficient use of the available space—especially when you do not expect people to be sitting in front of each server.

As an example, Figure 27-1 shows a photo of server hardware from Cisco. While you might think of Cisco as a networking company, around 2010, Cisco expanded its product line into the server market, with the Cisco Unified Computing System (UCS) product line. The photo shows a product from the UCS B-Series (Blade series) that uses a rack-mountable chassis, with slots for server blades. The product shown in the figure can be mounted in a rack—note the holes on the sides—with eight server blades (four on each side) mounted horizontally. It also has four power supplies at the bottom of the chassis.

Figure 27-1 *Cisco UCS Servers: B-Series (Blade)*

No matter the form factor, server hardware today supplies some capacity of CPU chips, RAM, storage, and network interface cards (NIC). But you also have to think differently about the OS that runs on the server because of a tool called *server virtualization*.

Server Virtualization Basics

Think of a server—the hardware—as one computer. It can be one of the blades in Figure 27-1, a powerful computer you can buy at the local computer store...whatever. Traditionally, when you think of one server, that one server runs one OS. Inside, the hardware includes a CPU, some RAM, some kind of permanent storage (like disk drives), and

---

Answers to the "Do I Know This Already?" quiz:

1 B **2** A **3** A **4** A, C **5** C

one or more NICs. And that one OS can use all the hardware inside the server, and then run one or more applications. Figure 27-2 shows those main ideas.

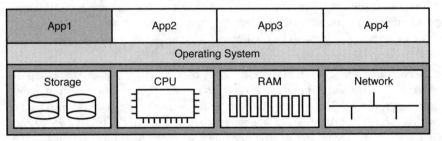

Figure 27-2 *Physical Server Model: Physical Hardware, One OS, and Applications*

With the physical server model shown in Figure 27-2, each physical server runs one OS, and that OS uses all the hardware in that one server. That was true of servers in the days before server virtualization.

Today, most companies instead create a virtualized data center. That means the company purchases server hardware, installs it in racks, and then treats all the CPU, RAM, and so on as capacity in the data center. Then, each OS instance is decoupled from the hardware, and is therefore virtual (in contrast to physical). Each piece of hardware that we would formerly have thought of as a server runs multiple instances of an OS at the same time, with each virtual OS instance called a *virtual machine*, or VM.

A single physical host (server) often has more processing power than you need for one OS. Thinking about processors for a moment, modern server CPUs have multiple cores (processors) in a single CPU chip. Each core may also be able to run multiple threads with a feature called *multithreading*. So, when you read about a particular Intel processor with 8 cores and multithreading (typically two threads per core), that one CPU chip can execute 16 different programs concurrently. The hypervisor (introduced shortly) can then treat each available thread as a virtual CPU (vCPU), and give each VM a number of vCPUs, with 16 available in this example.

A VM—that is, an OS instance that is decoupled from the server hardware—still must execute on hardware. Each VM has configuration as to the minimum number of vCPUs it needs, minimum RAM, and so on. The virtualization system then starts each VM on some physical server so that enough physical server hardware capacity exists to support all the VMs running on that host. So, at any one point in time, each VM is running on a physical server, using a subset of the CPU, RAM, storage, and NICs on that server. Figure 27-3 shows a graphic of that concept, with four separate VMs running on one physical server.

To make server virtualization work, each physical server (called a *host* in the server virtualization world) uses a *hypervisor*. The hypervisor manages and allocates the host hardware (CPU, RAM, etc.) to each VM based on the settings for the VM. Each VM runs as if it is running on a self-contained physical server, with a specific number of virtual CPUs and NICs and a set amount of RAM and storage. For instance, if one VM happens to be configured to use four CPUs, with 8 GB of RAM, the hypervisor allocates the specific parts of the CPU and RAM that the VM actually uses.

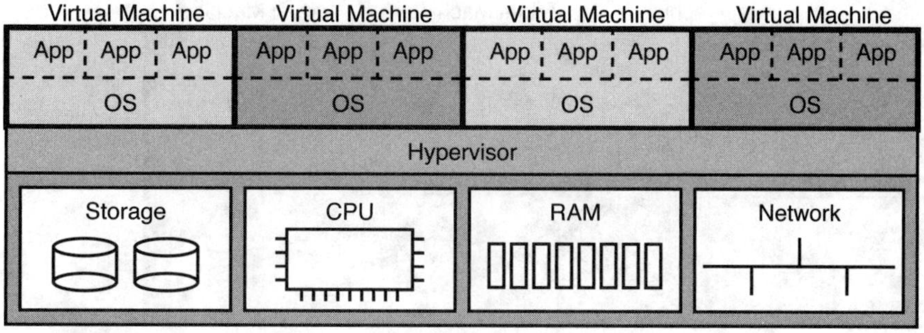

Figure 27-3 *Four VMs Running on One Host; Hypervisor Manages the Hardware*

To connect the marketplace to the big ideas discussed thus far, the following list includes a few of the vendors and product family names associated with virtualized data centers:

- VMware vCenter
- Microsoft HyperV
- Citrix XenServer
- Red Hat KVM

Beyond the hypervisor, companies like those in the list (and others) sell complete virtualization systems. These systems allow virtualization engineers to dynamically create VMs, start them, move them (manually and automatically) to different servers, and stop them. For instance, when hardware maintenance needs to be performed, the virtualization engineer can move the VMs to another host (often while running) so that the maintenance can be done.

Networking with Virtual Switches on a Virtualized Host

Server virtualization tools provide a wide variety of options for how to connect VMs to networks. This book does not attempt to discuss them all, but it can help to get some of the basics down before thinking more about cloud computing.

First, what does a physical server include for networking functions? Typically it has one or more NICs, maybe as slow as 1 Gbps, often 10 Gbps today, and maybe as fast as 40 Gbps.

Next, think about the VMs. Normally, an OS has one NIC, maybe more. To make the OS work as normal, each VM has (at least) one NIC, but for a VM, it is a virtual NIC. (For instance, in VMware's virtualization systems, the VM's virtual NIC goes by the name vNIC.)

Finally, the server must combine the ideas of the physical NICs with the vNICs used by the VMs into some kind of a network. Most often, each server uses some kind of an internal Ethernet switch concept, often called (you guessed it) a virtual switch, or vSwitch. Figure 27-4 shows an example, with four VMs, each with one vNIC. The physical server has two physical NICs. The vNICs and physical NICs connect internally to a virtual switch.

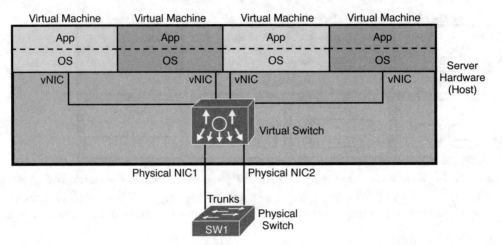

Figure 27-4   *Basic Networking in a Virtualized Host with a Virtual Switch*

Interestingly, the vSwitch can be supplied by the hypervisor vendor or by Cisco. For instance, Cisco's data center switch product line, Cisco Nexus switches, includes the Nexus 1000v (v for virtual). At your option, you can use the vSwitch included by the hypervisor, or install the Cisco Nexus 1000v (or similar products). The Nexus 1000v then supports some features unique to the Cisco Nexus series of switches. (Note that the Cisco data center switches, and the NX-OS operating system that runs on the Nexus models of switches, are covered in the CCNA, CCNP, and CCIE Data Center certifications.)

The networking details shown in Figure 27-4 show just the basics, but two important points remain for this chapter's buildup to cloud. First, networking in the data center has many options. Each VM can be in its own VLAN, or share the same VLAN, or even use VLAN trunking to the VM itself. Second, that configuration can be easily done from within the same virtualization software that controls the VMs. That programmability allows the virtualization software to move VMs between hosts (servers), and reprogram the vSwitches so that the VM has the same networking capabilities no matter where the VM is running.

The Physical Data Center Network

To pull these ideas together, next consider what happens with the physical network in a virtualized data center. Each host—that is, the physical host—needs a physical connection to the network. Looking again at Figure 27-4, that host, with two physical NICs, needs to connect those two physical NICs to a LAN in the data center.

Figure 27-5 shows the traditional cabling for a data center LAN. Each taller rectangle represents one rack inside a data center, with the tiny squares representing NIC ports, and the lines representing cables.

Often, each host is cabled to two different switches in the top of the rack—called Top of Rack (ToR) switches—to provide redundant paths into the LAN. Each ToR switch acts as an access layer switch from a design perspective. Each ToR switch is then cabled to an End of Row (EoR) switch, which acts as a distribution switch, and also connects to the rest of the network.

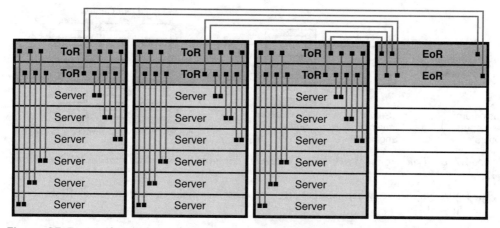

Figure 27-5 *Traditional Data Center Top-of-Rack and End-of-Row Physical Switch Topology*

Workflow with a Virtualized Data Center

So far, the first part of this chapter has described background information important to the upcoming discussions of cloud computing. Server virtualization has been a great improvement to the operations of many data centers, but virtualization alone does not create a cloud computing environment. Continuing the discussion of these fundamental technologies before discussing cloud computing, consider this example of a workflow through a virtualized (not cloud based) data center.

Some of the IT staff, call them server or virtualization engineers or administrators, order and install new hosts (servers). They gather requirements, plan for the required capacity, shop for hardware, order it, and install the hardware. They play the role of long-time server administrators and engineers, but now they work with the virtualization tools as well.

For the virtualization parts of the effort, the virtualization engineers also install and customize the virtualization tools. Beyond the hypervisor on each host, many other useful tools help manage and control a virtualized data center. For instance, one tool might give the engineers a view of the data center as a whole, with all VMs running there, with the idea that one data center is just a lot of capacity to run VMs. Over time, the server/virtualization engineers add new physical servers to the data center, and configure the virtualization systems to make use of the new physical servers, and make sure it all works.

So far in this scenario, the work has been in preparation for providing services to some internal customer—a development team member, the operations staff, and so on. Now, a customer is requesting a "server." In truth, the customer wants a VM (or many), with certain requirements: a specific number of vCPUs, a specific amount of RAM, and so on. The customer makes a request to the virtualization/server engineer to set up the VMs, as shown in Figure 27-6.

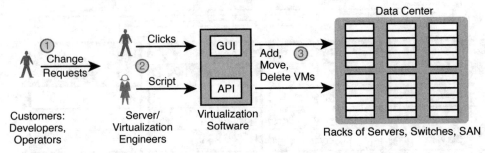

Figure 27-6 *Traditional Workflow: Customer (Human) Asks Virtualization (Human) for Service*

The figure emphasizes what happens after the customer makes a request, which flows something like this:

Step 1. The customer of the IT group, such as a developer or a member of the operations staff, wants some service, like a set of new VMs.

Step 2. The virtualization/server engineer reacts to the request from the customer. The server/virtualization engineer clicks away at the user interface, or if the number of VMs is large, they often run a program called a script to more efficiently create the VMs.

Step 3. Regardless of whether the virtualization engineer clicked or used scripts, the virtualization software could then create a number of new VMs and start those on some hosts inside the data center.

The process shown in Figure 27-6 works great. However, that approach to providing services breaks some of the basic criteria of a cloud service. For instance, cloud computing requires self-service. For the workflow to be considered to be a cloud service, the process as Step 2 should not require a human to service that request, but instead the request should be filled automatically. Want some new VMs in a cloud world? Click a user interface to ask for some new VMs, go get a cup of coffee, and your VMs will have been set up and started, to your specification, in minutes.

Summarizing some of the key points about a virtualized data center made so far, which enable cloud computing:

- The OS is decoupled from the hardware on which it runs, so that the OS, as a VM, can run on any server in a data center that has enough resources to run the VM.

- The virtualization software can automatically start and move the VM between servers in the data center.

- Data center networking includes virtual switches and virtual NICs within each host (server).

- Data center networking can be programmed by the virtualization software, allowing new VMs to be configured, started, moved as needed, and stopped, with the networking details configured automatically.

Cloud Computing Services

Cloud computing is an approach to offering IT services. Cloud computing makes use of products such as the virtualization products, but also uses products built specifically to enable cloud features. However, cloud computing is not just a set of products to be implemented; instead, it is a way of offering IT services. So, understanding what cloud computing is and is not takes a little work; this next topic introduces the basics.

From the just-completed discussions about virtualization, you already know one characteristic of a cloud service: it must allow self-service provisioning by the consumer of the service. That is, the consumer or customer of the service must be able to request the service and receive that service without the delay of waiting for a human to have time to work on it, consider the request, do the work, and so on.

To get a broader sense of what it means for a service to be a cloud service, examine this list of five criteria for a cloud computing service. The list is derived from the definition of cloud computing as put forth by the U.S. National Institute of Standards and Technology (NIST):

Key Topic

- **On-demand self-service:** The IT consumer chooses when to start and stop using the service, without any direct interaction with the provider of the service.

- **Broad network access:** The service must be available from many types of devices and over many types of networks (including the Internet).

- **Resource pooling:** The provider creates a pool of resources (rather than dedicating specific servers for use only by certain consumers), and dynamically allocates resources from that pool for each new request from a consumer.

- **Rapid elasticity:** To the consumer, the resource pool appears to be unlimited (that is, it expands quickly, so it is called *elastic*), and the requests for new service are filled quickly.

- **Measured service:** The provider can measure the usage and report that usage to the consumer, both for transparency and for billing.

Keep this list of five criteria in mind while you work through the rest of the chapter. Later parts of the chapter will refer back to the list.

To further develop this definition, the next few pages look at two branches of the cloud universe—private cloud and public cloud—also with the goal of further explaining some of the points from the NIST definition.

Private Cloud

Look back to the workflow example in Figure 27-6 with a virtualized data center. Now think about the five NIST criteria for cloud computing. If you break down the list versus the example around Figure 27-6, it seems like the workflow may meet at least some of these five NIST cloud criteria, and it does. In particular, as described so far in this chapter, a virtualized data center pools resources so they can be dynamically allocated. You could argue that a virtualized data center is elastic, in that the resource pool expands. However, the process may not be rapid, because the workflow requires human checks, balances, and time before provisioning new services.

Private cloud creates a service, inside a company, to internal customers, that meets the five criteria from the NIST list. To create a private cloud, an enterprise often expands its IT tools (like virtualization tools), changes internal workflow processes, adds additional tools, and so on.

As some examples, consider what happens when an application developer at a company needs VMs to use when developing an application. With private cloud, the developer can request those VMs and those VMs automatically start and are available within minutes, with most of the time lag being the time to boot the VMs. If the developer wants many more VMs, he can assume that the private cloud will have enough capacity, and new requests are still serviced rapidly. And all parties should know that the IT group can measure the usage of the services for internal billing.

Focus on the self-service aspect of cloud for a moment. To make that happen, many cloud computing services use a *cloud services catalog*. That catalog exists for the user as a web application that lists anything that can be requested via the company's cloud infrastructure. Before using a private cloud, developers and operators who needed new services (like new VMs) sent a change request asking the virtualization team to add VMs (see Figure 27-6). With private cloud, the (internal) consumers of IT services—developers, operators, and the like—can click to choose from the cloud services catalog. And if the request is for a new set of VMs, the VMs appear and are ready for use in minutes, without human interaction for that step, as seen at Step 2 of Figure 27-7.

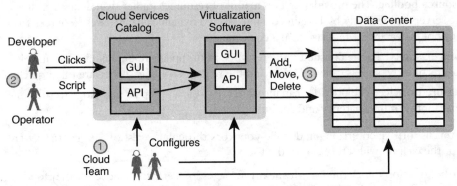

Figure 27-7 *Basic Private Cloud Workflow to Create One VM*

To make this process work, the cloud team has to add some tools and processes to its virtualized data center. For instance, it installs software to create the cloud services catalog, both with a user interface and with code that interfaces to the APIs of the virtualization systems. That services catalog software can react to consumer requests, using APIs into the virtualization software, to add, move, and create VMs, for instance. Also, the cloud team—composed of server, virtualization, network, and storage engineers—focuses on building the resource pool, testing and adding new services to the catalog, handling exceptions, and watching the reports (per the measured service requirement) to know when to add capacity to keep the resource pool ready to handle all requests.

Notably, with the cloud model, the cloud team no longer spends time handling individual requests for adding 10 VMs here, 50 there, with change requests from different groups.

Summarizing, with private cloud, you change your methods and tools to offer some of the same services. Private cloud is "private" in that one company owns the tools that create the cloud and employs the people who use the services. Even inside one company, using a cloud computing approach can improve the operational speed of deploying IT services.

Public Cloud

With a private cloud, the cloud provider and the cloud consumer are part of the same company. With public cloud, the reverse is true: a public cloud provider offers services, selling those services to consumers in other companies. In fact, if you think of Internet service providers and WAN service providers selling Internet and WAN services to many enterprises, the same general idea works here with public cloud providers selling their services to many enterprises.

The workflow in public cloud happens somewhat like private cloud when you start from the point of a consumer asking for some service (like a new VM). As shown on the right of Figure 27-8, at Step 1, the consumer asks for the new service from the service catalog web page. At Step 2, the virtualization tools react to the request to create the service. Once started, the services are available, but running in a data center that resides somewhere else in the world, and certainly not at the enterprise's data center (Step 3).

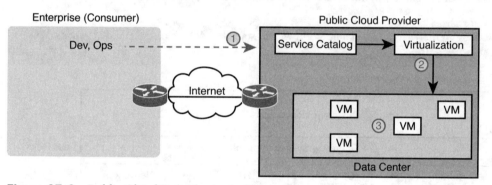

Figure 27-8 *Public Cloud Provider in the Internet*

Of course, the consumer is in a different network than the cloud provider with cloud computing, which brings up the issue of how to connect to a cloud provider. Cloud providers support multiple network options. They each connect to the Internet, so that apps and users inside the consumer's network can communicate with the apps that the consumer runs in the cloud provider's network. However, one of the five NIST criteria for cloud computing is broad network access, so cloud providers offer different networking options as well, including virtual private network (VPN) and private wide-area network (WAN) connections between consumers and the cloud.

Cloud and the "As a Service" Model

So what do you get with cloud computing? So far, this chapter has just shown a VM as a service. With cloud computing, there are a variety of services, and three stand out as the most common seen in the market today.

First, a quick word about some upcoming terminology. The cloud computing world works on a services model. Instead of buying (consuming) hardware, buying or licensing software, installing it yourself, and so on, the consumer receives some service from the provider. But that idea, receiving a service, is more abstract than the idea of buying a server and installing a particular software package. So with cloud computing, instead of keeping the discussion so generic, the industry uses a variety of terms that end in "as a Service." And each "-aaS" term has a different meaning.

This next topic explains those three most common cloud services: Infrastructure as a Service, Software as a Service, and Platform as a Service.

Infrastructure as a Service

Infrastructure as a Service (IaaS) may be the easiest of the cloud computing services to understand for most people. For perspective, think about any time you have shopped for a computer. You thought about the OS to run (the latest Microsoft OS, or Linux, or OS X if shopping for a Mac). You compared prices based on the CPU and its speed, how much RAM the computer had, the size of the disk drive, and so on.

IaaS offers a similar idea, but the consumer receives the use of a VM. You specify the amount of hardware performance/capacity to allocate to the VM (number of virtual CPUs, amount of RAM, and so on) as shown in Figure 27-9. You can even pick an OS to use. Once selected, the cloud provider starts the VM, which boots the chosen OS.

> **NOTE**   In the virtualization and cloud world, starting a VM is often called *spinning up a VM* or *instantiating a VM*.

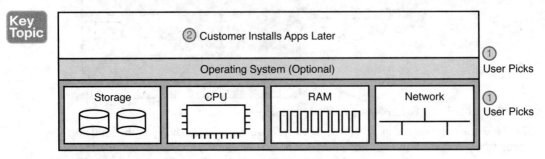

Figure 27-9   *IaaS Concept*

The provider also gives the consumer details about the VM so the consumer can connect to the OS's user interface, install more software, and customize settings. For example, imagine that the consumer wants to run a particular application on the server. If that customer wanted to use Microsoft Exchange as an email server, she would then need connect to the VM and install Exchange.

Figure 27-10 shows a web page from Amazon Web Services (AWS), a public cloud provider, from which you could create a VM as part of its IaaS service. The screenshot shows that the user selected a small VM called "micro." If you look closely at the text, you may be able to read the heading and numbers to see that this particular VM has one vCPU and 1 GB of RAM. (Note that this particular VM happens to be available as a free trial from AWS.)

27

Family	Type	vCPUs (i)	Memory (GiB)	Instance Storage (GB) (i)	EBS-Optimized Available (i)	Network Performance (i)
General purpose	t2.nano	1	0.5	EBS only	-	Low to Moderate
General purpose	t2.micro Free tier eligible	1	1	EBS only	-	Low to Moderate
General purpose	t2.small	1	2	EBS only	-	Low to Moderate
General purpose	t2.medium	2	4	EBS only	-	Low to Moderate
General purpose	t2.large	2	8	EBS only	-	Low to Moderate

Step 2: Choose an Instance Type
Filter by: All instance types ∨   Current generation ∨   Show/Hide Columns

Currently selected: t2.micro (Variable ECUs, 1 vCPUs, 2.5 GHz, Intel Xeon Family, 1 GiB memory, EBS only)

Cancel   Previous   Review and Launch   Next: Configure Instance Details

Figure 27-10 *AWS Screenshot—Set Up VM with Different CPU/RAM/OS*

Software as a Service

With Software as a Service (SaaS), the consumer receives a service with working software. The cloud provider may use VMs, possibly many VMs, to create the service, but those are hidden from the consumer. The cloud provider licenses, installs, and supports whatever software is required. The cloud provider then monitors performance of the application. However, the consumer chooses to use the application, signs up for the service, and starts using the application—no further installation work required. Figure 27-11 shows these main concepts.

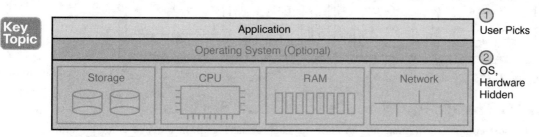

Figure 27-11 *SaaS Concept*

Many of you have probably used or at least heard of many public SaaS offerings. File storage services like Apple iCloud, Google Drive, Dropbox, and Box are all SaaS offerings. Most online email offerings can be considered SaaS services today. As another example, Microsoft offers its Exchange email server software as a service, so you can have private email services but offered as a service, along with all the other features included with Exchange—but without having to license, install, and maintain the Exchange software on some VMs.

(Development) Platform as a Service

Platform as a Service (PaaS) is a development platform, prebuilt as a service. A PaaS service is like IaaS in some ways. Both supply the consumer with one (or more) VMs, with a configurable amount of CPU, RAM, and other resources.

The key difference between PaaS and IaaS is that PaaS includes many more software tools beyond the basic OS. Those tools are useful to a software developer during the software development process. Once the development process is complete, and the application has been rolled out in production, those tools are not needed on the servers running the application. So the development tools are particular to the work done when developing.

A PaaS offering includes a set of development tools, and each PaaS offering has a different combination of tools. PaaS VMs often include an integrated development environment (IDE), which is a set of related tools that enables the developer to write and test code easily. PaaS VMs include continuous integration tools that allow the developer to update code and have that code automatically tested and integrated into a larger software project. Examples include Google's App Engine PaaS offering (https://cloud.google.com/appengine), the Eclipse integrated development environment (see http://www.eclipse.org), and the Jenkins continuous integration and automation tool (see https://jenkins.io).

The primary reasons to choose one PaaS service over another, or to choose a PaaS solution instead of IaaS, is the mix of development tools. Without experience as a developer, it can be difficult to tell whether one PaaS service might be better. You can still make some choices about sizing the PaaS VMs, similar to IaaS tools when setting up some PaaS services, as shown in Figure 27-12, but the developer tools included are the key to a PaaS service.

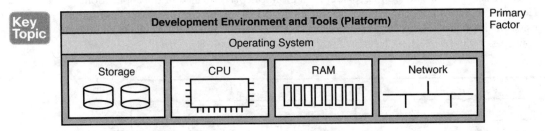

Figure 27-12 *PaaS Concept*

WAN Traffic Paths to Reach Cloud Services

The just-completed first major section of this chapter has set up the story of cloud computing enough to now discuss the cloud-related exam topics in the ICND2 and CCNA R&S exams. The first section has defined a few details about cloud computing, just enough to discuss the exam topics. This second section explains some networking issues about how to access those services.

This second major section of the chapter focuses on WAN options for public cloud, and the pros and cons of each. This section ignores private cloud for the most part, because using a private cloud—which is internal to an enterprise—has much less of an impact on an enterprise WAN compared to public cloud. With public cloud, the cloud services exist on the other side of some WAN connection as compared to the consumer of the services, so network engineers must think about how to best build a WAN when using public cloud services.

Enterprise WAN Connections to Public Cloud

Using the Internet to communicate between the enterprise and a public cloud provider is easy and convenient. However, it also has some negatives. This first section describes the basics, and points out the issues, which then leads to some of the reasons why using other WAN connections may be preferred.

Accessing Public Cloud Services Using the Internet

Imagine an enterprise that operates its network without cloud. All the applications it uses to run its business run on servers in a data center inside the enterprise. The OS instances where those applications run can be hosted directly on physical servers, or on VMs in a virtualized data center, but all the servers exist somewhere inside the enterprise.

Now imagine that the IT staff starts moving some of those applications out to a public cloud service. How do the users of the application (inside the enterprise) get to the user interface of the application (which runs at the public cloud provider's data center)? The Internet, of course. Both the enterprise and the cloud provider connect to the Internet, so using the Internet is the easy and convenient choice.

Now consider a common workflow to move an internal application to now run on the public cloud, for the purpose of making a couple of important points. First, Figure 27-13 shows the example. The cloud provider's services catalog can be reached by enterprise personnel, over the Internet, as shown at Step 1. After choosing the desired services—for instance, some VMs for an IaaS service—the cloud provider (Step 2) instantiates the VMs. Then, not shown as a step in the figure, the VMs are customized to now run the app that was formerly running inside the enterprise's data center.

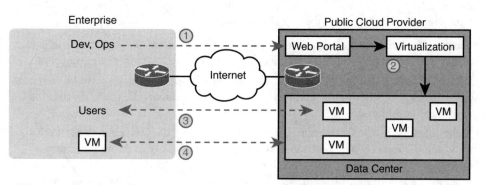

Figure 27-13 *Accessing a Public Cloud Service Using the Internet*

At this point, the new app is running in the cloud, and those services will require network bandwidth. In particular, Step 3 shows users communicating with the applications, just as would happen with any other application. Additionally, most apps send much more data than just the data between the application and the end user. For instance, you might move an app to the public cloud, but you might keep authentication services on an internal server, because those are used by a large number of applications—some internal and some hosted in the public cloud. So at Step 4, any application communication between VMs hosted in the cloud to/from VMs hosted inside the enterprise also needs to take place.

Pros and Cons with Connecting to Public Cloud with Internet

Using the Internet to connect from the enterprise to the public cloud has several advantages. The most obvious advantage is that all companies and cloud providers already have Internet connections, so getting started using public cloud services is easy. Using the Internet works particularly well with SaaS services and a distributed work force. For instance, maybe your sales division uses a SaaS customer contact app. Often, salespeople do not sit inside the enterprise network most of the work day. They likely connect to the Internet, and use a VPN to connect to the enterprise. For apps hosted on the public cloud, with this user base, it makes perfect sense to use the Internet.

While that was just one example, the following list summarizes some good reasons to use the Internet as the WAN connection to a public cloud service:

Agility: An enterprise can get started using public cloud without having to wait to order a private WAN connection to the cloud provider because cloud providers support Internet connectivity.

Migration: An enterprise can switch its workload from one cloud provider to another more easily because cloud providers all connect to the Internet.

Distributed users: The enterprise's users are distributed and connect to the Internet with their devices (as in the sales SaaS app example).

Using the Internet as the WAN connectivity to a public cloud is both a blessing and a curse in some ways. Using the Internet can help you get started with public cloud, and to get working quickly, but it also means that you do not have to do any planning before deploying a public cloud service. With a little planning, a network engineer can see some of the negatives of using the Internet—the same negatives when using the Internet for other purposes—which then might make you want to use alternative WAN connections. Those negatives for using the Internet for public cloud access are

Security: The Internet is less secure than private WAN connections in that a "man in the middle" can attempt to read the contents of data that passes to/from the public cloud.

Capacity: Moving an internal application to the public cloud increases network traffic, so the question of whether the enterprise's Internet links can handle the additional load needs to be considered.

Quality of Service (QoS): The Internet does not provide QoS, whereas private WANs can. Using the Internet may result in a worse user experience than desired, because of higher delay (latency), jitter, and packet loss.

No WAN SLA: ISPs typically will not provide a service level agreement (SLA) for WAN performance and availability to all destinations of a network. WAN service providers are much more likely to offer performance and availability SLAs.

This list of concerns does not mean that an enterprise cannot use the Internet to access its public cloud services. It does mean that it should consider the pros and cons of each WAN option.

Private WAN and Internet VPN Access to Public Cloud

The NIST definition for cloud computing lists "broad network access" as one of the five main criteria. In the case of public cloud, that often means supporting a variety of WAN connections, including the most common enterprise WAN technologies. Basically, an enterprise can connect to a public cloud provider with WAN technologies discussed in this book. For the sake of discussion, Figure 27-14 breaks it down into two broad categories.

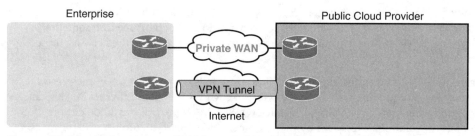

Figure 27-14 *Using Private WAN to a Public Cloud: Security, QoS, Capacity, Reporting*

To create a VPN tunnel between the enterprise and the cloud provider, you can use the same VPN features discussed earlier in Chapter 15, "Private WANs with Internet VPN." The cloud provider can offer a VPN service—that is, the cloud side of the VPN tunnel is implemented by the cloud provider—and the enterprise configures the matching VPN service on one of its own routers. Or the enterprise can use its own router inside the cloud provider's network—a virtual router, running as a VM—and configure VPN services on that router. In fact, Cisco makes the *Cloud Services Router* (CSR) to do exactly that: to be a router, but a router that runs as a VM in a cloud service, controlled by the cloud consumer, to do various functions that routers do, including terminating VPNs. (Also, by running a virtual router as a VM and managing the configuration internally, the enterprise might save some of the cost of using a similar service offered by the cloud provider.)

To make a private Multiprotocol Label Switching (MPLS) VPN or Ethernet WAN connection, the enterprise needs to work with the cloud provider and the WAN provider. Because cloud providers connect to many customers with private WAN connections, they often have published set instructions to follow. In the most basic form, with MPLS, the enterprise and the cloud provider connect to the same MPLS provider, with the MPLS provider connecting the enterprise and cloud sites. The same basic process happens with Ethernet WAN services, with one or more EVCs created between the public WAN and the enterprise.

NOTE Often, the server/virtualization engineers will dictate whether the WAN connection needs to support Layer 2 or Layer 3 connectivity, depending on other factors.

Private WAN connections also require some physical planning. Each of the larger public cloud providers has a number of large data centers spread around the planet, and with pre-built connection points into the major WAN services to aid the creation of private WAN connections to customers. An enterprise might then look at the cloud provider's documentation and work with that provider to choose the best place to install the private WAN connection. (Those larger public cloud companies include Amazon Web Services, Google Compute Cloud, Microsoft Azure, and Rackspace, if you would like to look at their websites for information about their locations.)

Pros and Cons with Connecting to Cloud with Private WANs

Private WANs overcome some of the issues of using the Internet without VPN, so working through those issues, consider some of the different WAN options.

First, considering the issue of security, all the private options, including adding a VPN to the existing Internet connection, improve security significantly. An Internet VPN would encrypt the data to keep it private. Private WAN connections with MPLS and Ethernet have traditionally been considered secure without encryption, but companies are sometimes encrypting data sent over private WAN connections as well to make the network more secure.

Regarding QoS, using an Internet VPN solution still fails to provide QoS because the Internet does not provide QoS. WAN services like MPLS VPN and Ethernet WANs can. As discussed in Chapter 18, "Quality of Service (QoS)," WAN providers will look at the QoS markings for frames/packets sent by the customer, and apply QoS tools to the traffic as it passes through the service provider's network.

Finally, as for the capacity issue, the concern of planning network capacity exists no matter what type of WAN is used. Any plan to migrate an app away from an internal data center to instead be hosted as a public cloud provider requires extra thought and planning.

Several negatives exist for using a private WAN, as you might expect. Installing the new private WAN connections takes time, delaying when a company gets started in cloud computing. Private WANs typically cost more than using the Internet. If using a WAN connection to one cloud provider (instead of using the Internet), then migrating to a new cloud provider can require another round of private WAN installation, again delaying work projects. Using the Internet (with or without VPN) would have made that migration much easier, but as shown in the next section, a strong compromise solution exists as well.

Intercloud Exchanges

Public cloud computing also introduces a whole new level of competition, because a cloud consumer can move their workload from one cloud provider to another. Moving the workload takes some effort, for a variety of reasons beyond the scope of this book. (Suffice it to say that most cloud providers differ in the detail of how they implement services.) But enterprises can and do migrate their workload from one cloud provider to another, choosing a new company for a variety of reasons, including looking for a less expensive cloud provider.

Now focus on the networking connections again. The main negative with using a private WAN for the cloud is that it adds another barrier to migrating to a new public cloud provider. One solution adds easier migration to the use of a private WAN through a cloud service called an intercloud exchange (or simply an intercloud).

Generically, the term *intercloud exchange* has come to be known as a company that creates a private network as a service. First, an intercloud exchange connects to multiple cloud providers on one side. On the other side, the intercloud connects to cloud consumers. Figure 27-15 shows the idea.

Once connected, the cloud consumer can be configured to communicate with one public cloud provider today, to specific cloud provider sites. Later, if the consumer wants to migrate to use another cloud provider, the consumer keeps the same private WAN links to the intercloud exchange, and asks the provider to reconfigure to set up new private WAN connections to the new cloud provider.

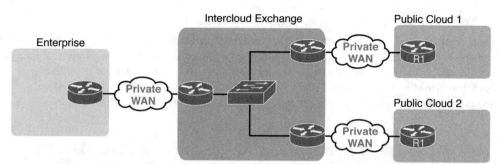

Figure 27-15 *Permanent Private WAN Connection to an Intercloud Exchange*

As for pros and cons, with an intercloud exchange, you get the same benefits as when connecting with a private WAN connection to a public cloud, but with the additional pro of easier migration to a new cloud provider. The main con is that using an intercloud exchange introduces another company into the mix.

Note that Cisco has a related set of products (called Cisco Intercloud Fabric) that helps solve many of the other migration challenges with moving workloads from one cloud provider to the next. These software tools from Cisco do not provide an intercloud exchange WAN service, but they do solve many of the challenges that exist when managing cloud workloads across both private and public cloud across a variety of WAN connection options. Look to http://www.cisco.com/go/intercloud for more details.

Summarizing the Pros and Cons of Public Cloud WAN Options

Table 27-2 summarizes some of these key pros and cons for the public WAN options for cloud computing, for study and reference.

Key Topic

Table 27-2 Comparison of Key Pros and Cons

	Internet	Internet VPN	MPLS VPN	Ethernet WAN	Intercloud Exchange
Secure	No	Yes	Yes	Yes	Yes
QoS	No	No	Yes	Yes	Yes
Requires capacity planning	Yes	Yes	Yes	Yes	Yes
Easier migration to new provider	Yes	Yes	No	No	Yes
Can begin using public cloud quickly	Yes	Yes	No	No	No

A Scenario: Branch Offices and the Public Cloud

So far in this major section about WAN design with public cloud, the enterprise has been shown as one entity, but most enterprise WANs have many sites. Those distributed enterprise sites impact some parts of WAN design for public cloud. The next discussion of WAN design issues with public cloud works through a scenario that shows an enterprise with a typical central site and branch office.

The example used in this section is a common one: the movement away from internal email servers, supported directly by the IT staff, to email delivered as a SaaS offering. Focus on the impact of the enterprise's remote sites like branch offices.

Migrating Traffic Flows When Migrating to Email SaaS

First, think of the traffic flow inside an enterprise before SaaS, when the company buys servers, licenses email server software, installs the hardware and software in an internal data center, and so on. The company may have hundreds or thousands of remote sites, like the branch office shown in Figure 27-16. To check email, an employee at the branch office sends packets back and forth with the email server at the central site, as shown.

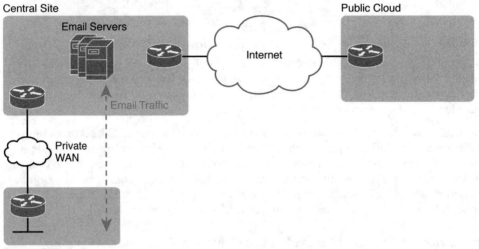

Figure 27-16 *Traffic Flow: Private WAN, Enterprise Implements Email Services*

The company then looks at the many different costs for email in this old model versus the new SaaS model. For instance, Microsoft Exchange is a very popular software package to build those enterprise email servers. Microsoft, who as a company is a major player in the public cloud space with their Microsoft Azure service, offers Exchange as a SaaS service. (During the writing of this book, this particular service could be found as part of Office 365 or as "Exchange Online.") So the enterprise considers the options and chooses to migrate an email SaaS offering.

Once migrated, the email servers run in the cloud, but as a SaaS service. The enterprise IT staff, who are the customers of the SaaS service, do not have to manage the servers. Just to circle back to some big ideas, as a SaaS service, the consumer does not worry about installing VMs, sizing them, installing Exchange or some other email server software, and so on. The consumer receives email service in this case. The company does have to do some migration work to move existing email, contacts, and so on, but once migrated, all users now communicate with email servers that run in the cloud as a SaaS service.

Now think about that enterprise branch office user, and the traffic flows shown in Figure 27-17, when a branch user sends or receives an email. For instance, think of an email with a large attachment, just to make the impact more dramatic. If the enterprise design connects branches to the central sites only, this is the net effect on WAN traffic:

■ No reduction in private WAN traffic at all occurs, because all the branch office email traffic flows to/from the central site.

■ 100 percent of the email traffic—even internal emails—that flows to/from branches now also flows over the Internet connection, consuming the bandwidth of the enterprise's Internet links.

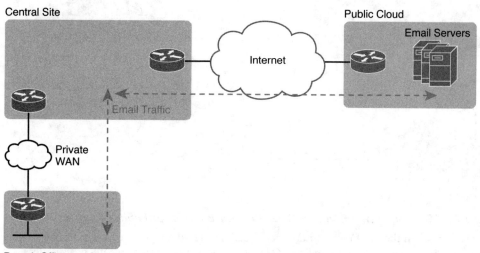

Figure 27-17   *Traffic Flow: Private WAN, Enterprise Implements Email Services*

Just to make the point, imagine two users at the same branch office. They can see each other across the room. One wants to share a file with the other, but the most convenient way they know to share a file is to email the file as an attachment. So one of them sends an email to the other, attaching the 20-MB file to the email. Before using SaaS, with an email server at the central site, that email and file would flow over the private WAN, to the email server, and then back to the second user's email client. With this new design, that email with the 20-MB attachment would flow over the private WAN, then over the Internet to the email server, and then back again over the Internet and over the private WAN when the second user downloads her email.

Branch Offices with Internet and Private WAN

For enterprises that place their Internet connections primarily at the central sites, this public cloud model can cause problems like the one just described. One way to deal with this particular challenge is to plan the right capacity for the Internet links; another is to plan capacity for some private WAN connections to the public cloud. Another option exists as well: redesign the enterprise WAN to a small degree, and consider placing direct Internet connections at the branch offices. Then all Internet traffic, including the email traffic to the new SaaS service, could be sent directly, and not consume the private WAN bandwidth or the central site Internet link bandwidth, as shown in Figure 27-18.

The design in Figure 27-18 has several advantages. The traffic flows much more directly. It does not waste the WAN bandwidth for the central site. And broadband Internet connections are relatively inexpensive today compared to private WAN connections.

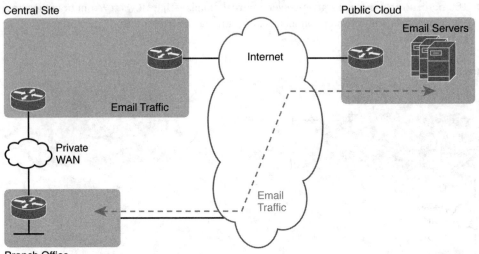

Figure 27-18 *Connecting Branches Directly to the Internet for Public Cloud Traffic*

However, when the per-branch Internet connections are added for the first time, the new Internet links create security concerns. One of the reasons an enterprise might use only a few Internet links, located at a central site, is to focus the security efforts at those links. Using an Internet connection at each branch changes that approach. But many enterprises not only use the Internet at each site, but rely on it as their only WAN connection, as shown with Internet VPNs back in Chapter 15.

Virtual Network Functions and Services

This third and final major section of the chapter now looks more closely at what happens with networking functions inside the public cloud environment. In particular, this section introduces the concept of a virtual network function (VNF), by showing how a public cloud installation could implement routers and firewalls as VMs. The remainder of this section looks at options for changing how DNS, DHCP, and NTP could work when migrating an application from inside an enterprise to being hosted in a public cloud service.

Virtual Network Functions: Firewalls and Routers

When you start to peel back the layers of what you get in a public cloud service, you can begin to see familiar functions and features. Public cloud providers may not use all the same old terminology for traditional approaches to IT, but to anyone who has worked in IT, many of the ideas should look familiar.

As an example, take the following basic scenario in which an enterprise orders an IaaS service from a public cloud provider:

■ The consumer wants a number of IaaS servers.

■ All VMs will run the same app; the consumer wants multiple VMs to deal with server load.

- Because they run the same app, the consumer does not care which particular server any one client uses, so the consumer wants the cloud provider to perform server load balancing (SLB).

- The consumer will use the Internet for all user traffic to the VMs.

Figure 27-19 shows the kind of information the consumer would receive back from the cloud provider, along with the functions provided. It includes a public IP address (198.51.100.1). Each IaaS server gets its own private IP address, from the cloud provider's private IPv4 address space. The provider performs SLB as a service (SLBaaS). (And not shown in the figure for now, the provider also supplies some security and DNS services.)

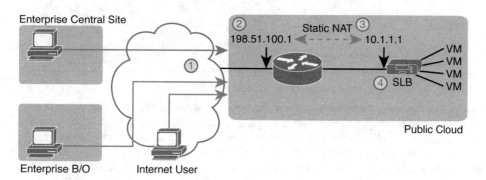

Figure 27-19 *Common Baseline Public Cloud Features Running Just One Instance*

Once the cloud provider instantiates the VMs, the consumer adds the applications to the VMs, and the users can connect to the public IP address as shown on the left of the figure. The users connect through the Internet (Step 1), to public IP address 198.51.100.1 (Step 2). The static NAT function at the cloud provider (Step 3) translates to the assigned private IPv4 address. Finally, at Step 4, the SLB function load balances each user to one of the VMs.

As shown, all the services provided by the cloud provider are services. The consumer can ask for particular types of service, like having a public address, and doing server load balancing. However, as shown here, the consumer does not get access to the cloud router that performs NAT, or the device that performs SLB. The consumer needed a service, the cloud provider offered it, the consumer asked for it. And it works.

In other cases, the consumer may feel the need to be in direct control over some networking function. For instance, many IT personnel might look at the design in Figure 27-19 and ask: Where is the firewall? Or maybe you want to use VPN services, maybe even DMVPN, terminated at a router. As the consumer, you might want to have a router in your part of the public cloud—not a router service, but a router of your very own, one that you control and configure. In that case, the cloud consumer can use a virtual network function.

A *virtual network function* (VNF) is a virtual instance of a traditional networking device that the consumer can choose to use in a cloud. For example, cloud providers offer different security services, but in addition, they offer to let consumers run their own firewall in the cloud. Similarly, the cloud provider routes packets and does other typical router functions, but if a consumer wants total control of a router, the cloud consumer can run a virtual router as a VM. Any such virtual networking device is a VNF.

Figure 27-20 shows a common public WAN design for one tenant (consumer) in which the consumer has chosen to add two VNFs: a virtual firewall and a virtual router. The virtual firewall could be a Cisco ASAv (that is, the virtual version of Cisco's ASA firewall), running as a VM. Similarly, the router could be a Cisco router, specifically a Cisco Cloud Services Router (CSR), which is a Cisco router with the IOS XE operating system running as a VM. Those devices would be available for the consumer to configure and use just like they would use a physical version of the same device.

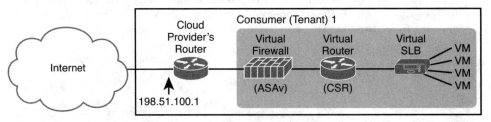

Figure 27-20 *Common Virtual Appliances Added by IT Staff*

The more you read about emerging network technology in the press, the more you will see a variety of terms related to the concept of virtual functions in a network, so it helps to be aware of some of the related terms. For instance, the exam topics refer to the term *virtual network infrastructure*, which is a broad term that refers to the fact traditional networking functions like routing, switching, and so on occur in software—that is, it is virtual instead of physical. The term *network functions virtualization* (NFV) is a term used primarily in the service provider space for how SPs virtualize network functions inside their network. (The terms are defined by ETSI, a European Telco standards body; see http://www.etsi.org.) With NFV, each networking function, like the CSR router in Figure 27-20, would then be called a VNF.

DNS Services

Many options exist for DNS services related to a public cloud. This next topic works through a couple of the common options.

First, because this book spends only a little time with DNS discussions, review some DNS basics without cloud, as shown in Figure 27-21. The figure shows what happens with DNS when a user goes to a web page and clicks a link for an app, App1, as shown at the bottom of the page. In this scenario, App1 runs inside the enterprise; that is, it is a traditional app, not running in a private or public cloud.

The action in the figure follows these numbered steps:

Step 1.   The user clicks the link for App1; the link includes domain name app1.example.com.

Step 2.   The user's device sends a DNS request for app1.example.com to the enterprise DNS server.

Step 3.   The DNS server returns the IP address associated with app1.example.com (10.1.1.1).

Step 4.   The user connects to App1 at the server that uses address 10.1.1.1.

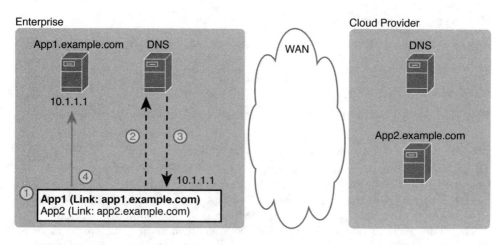

Figure 27-21   *DNS Request for Internal Application (App1)*

Now imagine that the enterprise IT staff migrates a different app, App2, to the public cloud. The public cloud provider wants all its customers to have a good experience, and for the service to work well. So when asking for the new IaaS VMs, the consumer chooses some configuration settings. As a result of those choices, the cloud provider allocates a public IP address (198.51.100.1) for the VMs, dynamically creates a matching name, and adds an address record for the name and address to the cloud provider's DNS server. The cloud provider also makes all this same information available to the consumer (hostname, IP address, and so on).

Given those steps, the enterprise can choose to do something simple: just update its own DNS to refer to the public IP address used by its application as running at the public cloud provider. Figure 27-22 shows the user flow after making changes to the enterprise DNS.

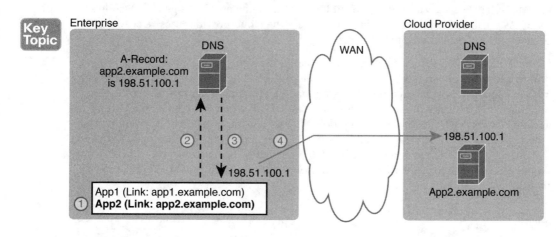

Figure 27-22   *Enterprise DNS Is Updated with Addresses of Public Cloud Apps*

Following the steps in the figure:

Step 1. The user clicks the link for App2; the link includes domain name app2.example.com.

Step 2. The user's device sends a DNS request for app2.example.com to the enterprise DNS server.

Step 3. The DNS returns the IP address associated with app2.example.com (198.51.100.1).

Step 4. The user connects to the app at the server that uses address 198.51.100.1.

As yet another option, the consumer can rely on the DNS service of the cloud provider. The cloud provider automatically creates a DNS record for each VM. In this scenario, the enterprise DNS still requires a change for name app2.example.com, but instead of an A-record that identifies the IP address, it points to the DNS server of the cloud provider. And user DNS resolution requests flow to the enterprise DNS, and then to the cloud provider's DNS, and then back again. However, the end result is that the user learns the same IP address (198.51.100.1 in this case) that is used for the IaaS service.

Address Assignment Services and DHCP

Cloud providers make a big effort to supply IP addresses to the hosts in the service, and to do that automatically and as simply as possible. They know that any VM defined by a cloud service, public or private, needs an IP address. So rather than make each customer take the time and effort to set up a VNF to run as a DHCP server, and then configure it, the cloud provider lets the consumer specify some criteria for the addresses. For instance, the consumer can let the cloud provider choose addresses, or the consumer can specify all the IP addresses to use. Then the cloud provider sets up the addressing automatically.

First, consider the case in which the consumer wants the application to be reachable directly over the Internet. The cloud provider can allocate a public IP address. Then, the cloud provider can give each VM a private IP address based on the provider's private IP address space. As usual, and as seen earlier in Figure 27-19, the cloud provider uses NAT to translate between the public and private addresses.

Figure 27-23 shows just such an example. The cloud provider uses network 10.0.0.0 for its private addresses, and in this case it allocates addresses from subnet 10.2.2.0/24 to the new VMs for a particular tenant (consumer). Note that the cloud provider may (and probably does) use DHCP behind the scenes, but there is no DHCP server required by the customer as a VNF, and no DHCP configuration required by the customer. The public IP address used for this service uses public IP address 198.51.100.1, which the cloud provider NATs to the correct private address in network 10.0.0.0 on behalf of the customer. As for configuration, the customer chooses options from the cloud services catalog, and the provider makes the addresses match.

Figure 27-23 *Public Cloud Addressing: Cloud Private Addresses for IaaS VMs*

Other cloud consumers may want a different network design in the cloud, requiring different IP addresses. For instance, when connecting a private WAN connection, the consumer may want only internal enterprise users to be able to reach the applications running in the cloud. In that case, it would make sense to use private addresses only, and use addresses from the consumer's IP address space. Those subnets would then be advertised into the rest of the enterprise, just like any other enterprise subnets.

Figure 27-24 shows just such an example. In this case, the enterprise creates a VPN connection to the cloud, terminating in a Cisco CSR (running as a VNF). That VPN tunnel's private addressing uses subnet 172.16.1.0/24 from the consumer's private IP address space. The VMs created by the cloud provider come from subnet 172.16.2.0/24. The enterprise can then advertise routes for 172.16.2.0/24 throughout the enterprise, so that all users can reach the cloud-based apps.

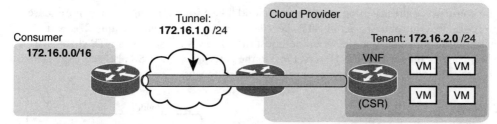

Figure 27-24 *Public Cloud Addressing: Consumer Private Addresses for IaaS VMs*

In the scenarios described with the last two figures, note that the cloud consumer does not run their own DHCP service as a VNF. Even in this second case, with Figure 27-24, the cloud provider performs the service of assigning the addresses, even with the addresses coming from the consumer's address space. The consumer just needs to make the correct choices at the cloud services catalog (that is, at the web page or APIs for the cloud provider).

NOTE If you find this discussion of IP addressing in public clouds interesting, do a search on the net for "Amazon EC2 Instance IP Addressing." You should find a link that summarizes a lot of the discussion about how Amazon Web Services (AWS) handles public and private addressing along with DNS.

NTP

To wrap up the discussion of virtual network functions and services, think back to the topic of Network Time Protocol (NTP), covered in the ICND1 half of the CCNA R&S exam. NTP uses the concept of servers that supply time-of-day clock information. NTP clients then receive that information in NTP messages and adjust (synchronize) their clocks to match the server's time. Over time, the client's clock should synchronize to have close to the same time as the server.

The VNFs and VMs in a cloud service, whether private or public, often need to synchronize their time with the rest of the devices and servers in the enterprise. To do that, the VMs and VNFs can be configured as NTP clients, referencing NTP servers inside the enterprise, as shown in Figure 27-25.

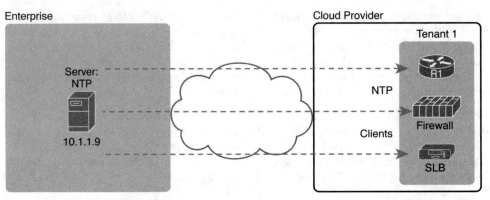

Figure 27-25 *Using the NTP Servers Inside the Enterprise*

If a consumer is already using a VNF in the cloud, like a router, it might make more sense to configure that router to act in NTP client/server mode, as shown in Figure 27-26. In this example, a CSR running in the cloud does just that. The CSR first acts as NTP client, synchronizing its time with the NTP server inside the enterprise. The CSR also acts as a server to the VMs and other VNFs used for that consumer (tenant).

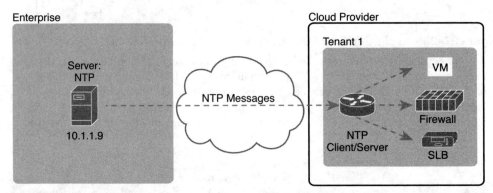

Figure 27-26 *Using a Tenant CSR Router as NTP Client/Server*

Chapter Review

One key to doing well on the exams is to perform repetitive spaced review sessions. Review this chapter's material using either the tools in the book, DVD, or interactive tools for the same material found on the book's companion website. Refer to the "Your Study Plan" element for more details. Table 27-3 outlines the key review elements and where you can find them. To better track your study progress, record when you completed these activities in the second column.

Table 27-3   Chapter Review Tracking

Review Element	Review Date(s)	Resource Used
Review key topics		Book, DVD/website
Review key terms		Book, DVD/website
Answer DIKTA questions		Book, PCPT
Review memory tables		Book, App

Review All the Key Topics

Table 27-4   Key Topics for Chapter 27

Key Topic Element	Description	Page Number
Figure 27-3	Organization of applications, on a VM, on an OS, with a hypervisor allocating and managing the host hardware	735
List	Definition of cloud computing (paraphrased) based on the NIST standard	739
Figure 27-9	Organization and concepts for an IaaS service	742
Figure 27-11	Organization and concepts for an SaaS service	743
Figure 27-12	Organization and concepts for a PaaS service	744
List	Cons for using the Internet to access public WAN services	746
Table 27-2	Summary of pros and cons with different public cloud WAN access options	749
Figure 27-22	Example of using DNS with a public cloud service	755

Key Terms You Should Know

Unified Computing System (UCS), virtual machine, virtual CPU (vCPU), hypervisor, Host (context: DC), virtual NIC (vNIC), virtual switch (vSwitch), on-demand self-service, resource pooling, rapid elasticity, cloud services catalog, public cloud, private cloud, Infrastructure as a Service (IaaS), Platform as a Service (PaaS), Software as a Service (SaaS), Cloud Services Router (CSR), ASAv, virtual network function (VNF), intercloud exchange

CHAPTER 28

SDN and Network Programmability

This chapter covers the following exam topics:

4.0 Infrastructure Services

4.5 Verify ACLs using the APIC-EM Path Trace ACL analysis tool

5.0 Infrastructure Maintenance

5.5 Describe network programmability in enterprise network architecture

    5.5.a Function of a controller

    5.5.b Separation of control plane and data plane

    5.5.c Northbound and southbound APIs

Welcome to the final technology-focused chapter of the book!

The broad topic area called network programmability by some, or Software Defined Networking by others, creates a new way to build networks.

The CCNA R&S certification teaches the traditional model for operating and controlling networks, a model that has existed for decades. You understand protocols that the devices use, understand the commands that can customize how those protocols operate, and add distributed configuration to the devices, device by device, to implement the network.

Network programmability changes the operational model for networks, requiring new methods of controlling the devices to enable the new operational models. The term *network programmability* itself refers to more focus on software control of the network, so that the network can be changed more easily to adapt to the ever-changing environment as virtual machines (VM) move in a data center, and traffic patterns change, and so forth. The similar term *Software Defined Networking* (SDN), used frequently in the trade press, also emphasizes the concept of software (programmatic) control of the network, rather than the more static configuration-controlled networking.

As with the previous chapter covering cloud computing, this chapter can only begin to introduce the concepts of network programmability and SDN, because the topic is simply too large. Thankfully, the related exam topics focus on the most fundamental ideas of SDN. The first major section of this chapter introduces the basic concepts mentioned in the exam topics, specifically the data and control planes, along with controllers and the related architecture. The second section then shows three separate product examples of network programmability, all of which use different methods to implement networking features. The last section focuses on one additional feature of the APIC-EM product.

"Do I Know This Already?" Quiz

Take the quiz (either here, or use the PCPT software) if you want to use the score to help you decide how much time to spend on this chapter. The answers are at the bottom of the page following the quiz, and the explanations are in DVD Appendix C and in the PCPT software.

Table 28-1   "Do I Know This Already?" Foundation Topics Section-to-Question Mapping

Foundation Topics Section	Questions
SDN and Network Programmability Basics	1–3
Examples of Network Programmability and SDN	4
Cisco APIC-EM ACL Analysis Application	5

1. A Layer 2 switch examines a frame's destination MAC address and chooses to forward that frame out port G0/1 only. That action is an action that occurs as part of which plane of the switch?

   a. Data plane

   b. Management plane

   c. Control plane

   d. Table plane

2. A router uses EIGRP to learn routes and adds those to the IPv4 routing table. That action is an action that occurs as part of which plane of the router?

   a. Data plane

   b. Management plane

   c. Control plane

   d. Table plane

3. A network uses an SDN architecture with switches and a centralized controller. Which of the following terms describes a function or functions expected to be found on the switches but not on the controller?

   a. A Northbound Interface

   b. A Southbound Interface

   c. Data plane functions

   d. Control plane functions

4. Which of the following controllers (if any) from Cisco uses a mostly centralized control plane model?

   a. Cisco Open SDN Controller

   b. Cisco Application Policy Infrastructure Controller (APIC)

   c. Cisco APIC Enterprise Module (APIC-EM)

   d. None of these controllers uses a mostly centralized control plane.

5. Host A and Host B sit in two different subnets. The path between the subnets of these two hosts runs through three different Layer 3 forwarding devices (routers and Layer 3 switches). A network engineer uses the APIC-EM Path Trace ACL Analysis tool to analyze the path used for Host A to send packets to Host B. Which part of the function is done specifically by the ACL Analysis or ACL Trace part of the tool?

    a. Discovery of the topology that exists between the two hosts

    b. Analysis of the Layer 3 forwarding decisions in the path from Host A to B

    c. Analysis of the Layer 2 forwarding decisions in the path from Host A to B

    d. Analysis of the impact of ACLs on the packets that would flow from Host A to B

Foundation Topics

SDN and Network Programmability Basics

Networking devices forward data in the form of messages, typically data link frames like Ethernet frames. You have learned about how switches and routers do that forwarding for the entire length of preparing for the CCNA R&S exam.

Network programmability and SDN takes those ideas, analyzes the pieces, finds ways to improve them for today's needs, and reassembles those ideas into a new way of making networks work. At the end of that rearrangement, the devices in the network still forward messages, but the how and why has changed.

This first major section explains the most central concepts of SDN and network programmability. It starts by breaking down some of the components of what exists in traditional networking devices. Then this section explains how some centralized controller software, called a controller, creates an architecture for easier programmatic control of a network.

The Data, Control, and Management Planes

Stop and think about what networking devices do. What does a router do? What does a switch do?

Many ideas should come to mind. For instance, they physically connect to each other with cables, and with wireless, to create networks. They forward messages: switches forward Ethernet frames, and routers forward packets. They use many different protocols to learn useful information, like routing protocols for learning network layer routes.

Everything that networking devices do can be categorized as being in a particular plane. This section takes those familiar facts about how networking devices work, and describes the three planes most often used to describe how network programmability works: the data plane, the control plane, and the management plane.

The Data Plane

The term *data plane* refers to the tasks that a networking device does to forward a message. In other words, anything to do with receiving data, processing it, and forwarding that same data—whether you call the data a frame, packet, or, more generically, a message—is part of the data plane.

For example, think about how routers forward IP packets, as shown in Figure 28-1. If you focus on the Layer 3 logic for a moment, the host sends the packet (Step 1) to its default router, R1. R1 does some processing on the received packet, makes a forwarding (routing) decision, and forwards the packet (Step 2). Routers R3 and R4 also receive, process, and forward the packet (Steps 3 and 4).

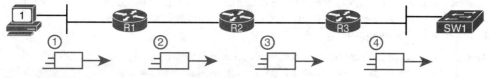

Figure 28-1   *Data Plane Processing on Routers: Basics*

Now broaden your thinking for a moment, and try to think of everything a router or switch might do when receiving, processing, and forwarding a message. Of course, the forwarding decision is part of the logic; in fact, the data plane is often called the *forwarding plane*. But think beyond matching the destination address to a table. For perspective, the following list details some of the more common actions that a networking device does that fit into the data plane:

Key Topic

- De-encapsulating and re-encapsulating a packet in a data link frame (routers, Layer 3 switches)

- Adding or removing an 802.1Q trunking header (routers and switches)

- Matching the destination MAC address to the MAC address table (Layer 2 switches)

- Matching the destination IP address to the IP routing table (routers, Layer 3 switches)

- Encrypting the data and adding a new IP header (for VPN processing)

- Changing the source or destination IP address (for NAT processing)

- Discarding a message due to a filter (ACLs, port security)

All the items in the list make up the data plane, because the data plane includes all actions done per message.

The Control Plane

Next, take a moment to ponder the kinds of information that the data plane needs to know beforehand so that it can work properly. For instance, routers need IP routes in a routing table before the data plane can forward packets. Layer 2 switches need entries in a MAC address table before they can forward Ethernet frames out the one best port to reach the destination. Switches must use Spanning Tree Protocol (STP) to limit which interfaces can be used for forwarding so that the data plane works well and does not loop frames forever.

From one perspective, the information supplied to the data plane controls what the data plane does. For instance, a router with no routes in the routing table cannot forward packets. The data plane is there, but when a router's data plane tries to match the routing table, and finds no matching route, the router discards the packet. However, once the router has

---

Answers to the "Do I Know This Already?" quiz:

1 A **2** C **3** C **4** A **5** D

some routes, the router's data plane processes can forward packets. And what controls the contents of the routing table? Various control plane processes.

The term *control plane* refers to any action that controls the data plane. Most of these actions have to do with creating the tables used by the data plane, tables like the IP routing table, an IP ARP table, a switch MAC address table, and so on. By adding, removing, and changing entries to the tables used by the data plane, the control plane processes control what the data plane does. You already know many control plane protocols, of course, including all IP routing protocols.

Traditional networking protocols and devices separate the control and data planes and distribute those functions into each individual device, as shown in the example in Figure 28-2. In this case, OSPF, the control plane protocol, runs on each router (that is, it is distributed among all the routers). OSPF on each router then adds to, removes from, and changes the IP routing table on each router. Once populated with useful routes, the data plane of the routers, also distributed to each router, can forward incoming packets, as shown from left to right across the bottom of the figure.

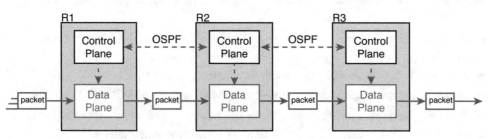

Figure 28-2 *Control and Data Planes of Routers—Conceptual*

The following list includes many of the more common control plane protocols:

- Routing protocols (OSPF, EIGRP, RIP, BGP)
- IPv4 ARP
- IPv6 NDP
- Switch MAC learning
- STP

Without the protocols and activities of the control plane, the data plane of traditional networking devices would not function well. Routers would be mostly useless without routes learned by a routing protocol. Without learning MAC table entries, a switch could still forward unicasts by flooding them, but doing that for all frames would create much more load on the LAN compared to normal switch operations. So the data plane must rely on the control plane to provide useful information.

The Management Plane

The control plane does overhead tasks that directly impact the behavior of the data plane. The *management plane* does overhead work as well, but that work does not directly impact the data plane. Instead, the management plane includes protocols that allow network engineers to manage the devices.

Telnet and SSH are two of the most obvious management plane protocols. To emphasize the difference with control plane protocols, think about two routers: one configured to allow Telnet and SSH into the router, and one that does not. Both could still be running a routing protocol and routing packets, whether or not they support Telnet and SSH.

Figure 28-3 lists some of the more common management plane protocols from the CCNA R&S exam.

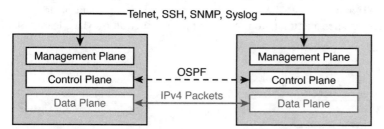

Figure 28-3 *Management Plane for Configuration of Control and Data Plane*

Cisco Switch Data Plane Internals

To better understand SDN and network programmability, it helps to think about the internals of switches. This next topic does just that.

From the very first days of devices called LAN switches, switches had to use specialized hardware to forward frames, because of the large number of frames per second (fps) required. To get a sense for the volume of frames a switch must be able to forward, consider the minimum frame size of an Ethernet frame, the number of ports on a switch, and the speeds of the ports; even low-end switches need to be able to forward millions of frames per second. For example, if a switch manufacturer wanted to figure out how fast their data plane needed to be in a new access layer switch with 24 ports, they might work through this bit of math:

- The switch has 24 ports.

- Each port runs at 100 Mbps each.

- For this analysis, assume frames 125 bytes in length (to make the math easier, because each frame is 1000 bits long).

- Use full duplex on all ports, so the switch can expect to receive on all 24 ports at the same time.

- Result: Each port would be receiving 100,000 fps, for 2.4 million fps total, so the switch data plane would need to be ready to process 2.4 million fps.

While 2.4 million fps may seem like a lot, the goal here is not to put an absolute number on how fast the data plane of a switch needs to be for any given era of switching technology. Instead, from their first introduction into the marketplace in the mid-1990s, LAN switches needed a faster data plane than a generalized CPU could process in software. As a result, hardware switches have always had specialized hardware to perform data plane processing.

First, the switching logic occurs not in the CPU with software, but in an *application-specific integrated circuit* (ASIC). An ASIC is a chip built for specific purposes, such as for message processing in a networking device.

Second, the ASIC needs to perform table lookup in the MAC address table, so for fast table lookup, the switch uses a specialized type of memory to store the equivalent of the MAC address table: *ternary content-addressable memory* (TCAM). TCAM memory does not require the ASIC to search the table. Instead, the ASIC can feed the fields to be matched, like a MAC address value, into the TCAM, and the TCAM returns the matching table entry, without a need to run a search algorithm.

Note that a switch still has a general-purpose CPU and RAM as well, as shown in Figure 28-4. IOS runs in the CPU and uses RAM. Most of the control and management plane functions run in IOS. The data plane function (and the control plane function of MAC learning) happens in the ASIC.

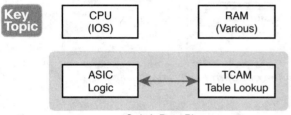

Switch Data Plane

Figure 28-4 *Key Internal Processing Points in a Typical Switch*

Note that some routers also use hardware for data plane functions, for the same kinds of reasons that switches use hardware. (For instance, check out the Cisco Quantum Flow Processor for interesting reading about hardware data plane forwarding in Cisco routers.) The ideas of a hardware data plane in routers are similar to those in switches: use a purpose-built ASIC for the forwarding logic, and TCAM to store the required tables for fast table lookup.

Controllers and Network Architecture

New approaches to networking have emerged in the 2010s, approaches that change where some of the control plane functions occur. Many of those approaches move parts of the control plane work into software that runs as a centralized application called a *controller*. This next topic looks at controller concepts, and the interfaces to the devices that sit below the controller and to any programs that use the controller.

Controllers and Centralized Control

Most traditional control plane processes use a distributed architecture. That is, the control plane is distributed, running on many devices. For example, each router runs its own OSPF routing protocol process. To do their work, those distributed control plane processes use messages to communicate with each other, like OSPF protocol messages between routers. As a result, traditional networks are said to use a *distributed control plane*.

The people who created today's control plane concepts, like STP, OSPF, EIGRP, and so on, could have chosen to use a centralized control plane. That is, they could have put the logic in one place, running on one device, or on a server. Then the centralized software could have used protocol messages to learn information from the devices, but with all the processing of the information at a centralized location. But they instead chose a distributed architecture.

There are pros and cons to using distributed and centralized architectures to do any function in a network. Many control plane functions have a long history of working well with a distributed architecture. However, a centralized application can be easier to write than a distributed application, because the centralized application has all the data gathered into one place. And this emerging world of network programmability and SDN often uses a centralized architecture, with a centralized control plane, with its foundations in a service called a controller.

A *controller*, or *SDN controller*, centralizes the control of the networking devices. The degree to which control is centralized can vary, from the controller performing all control plane functions, to the other end of the spectrum, in which the controller is simply aware of the ongoing work of the distributed control plane.

To better understand the idea of a controller, consider the case shown in Figure 28-5, in which one SDN controller centralizes all important control plane functions. First, the controller sits anywhere in the network that has IP reachability to the devices in the network. Each of the network devices still has a data plane. However, note that none of the devices has a control plane. In the variation of SDN as shown in Figure 28-5, the controller (or a program making use of the controller) directly programs the data plane entries into each device's tables. The networking devices do not populate their forwarding tables with traditional distributed control plane processes.

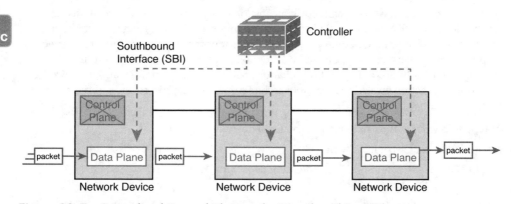

Figure 28-5 *Centralized Control Plane and a Distributed Data Plane*

Figure 28-5 shows one model for network programmability and SDN, but not all. The figure does give us a great backdrop to discuss a few more important basic concepts, in particular, the idea of a Southbound Interface (SBI) and Northbound Interface (NBI).

The Southbound Interface

In a controller-based network architecture, the controller needs to communicate to the networking devices. In most network drawings and architecture drawings, those network devices typically sit below the controller, as shown in Figure 28-5. There is an interface between the controller and those devices, and given its location in drawings, the interface came to be known as the *Southbound Interface*, or SBI, as labeled in Figure 28-5.

NOTE   The word "interface" is used throughout this book to refer to physical connectors on routers and switches. However, in the context of this chapter's discussion of SDN, the word "interface" (including in the names of SBI, NBI, and API) refers to software interfaces unless otherwise noted.

Several different options exist for the SBI. The overall goal is network programmability, so the interface moves away from being only a protocol. An SBI often includes a protocol, so that the controller and devices can communicate, but they often include an *application programming interface*, or API.

An API is a method for one application (program) to exchange data with another application. Rearranging the words to describe the idea, an API is an interface to an application program. Programs process data, so an API lets two programs exchange data. While a protocol exists as a document, often from a standards body, an API often exists as usable code— functions, variables, and data structures—that can be used by one program to communicate and copy structured data between the programs across a network.

So, back to the term *SBI*: It is an interface between a program (the controller) and a program (on the networking device) that lets the two programs communicate, with one goal being to allow the controller to program the data plane forwarding tables of the networking device.

Unsurprisingly, in a network architecture meant to enable network programmability, the capabilities of the SBIs and their APIs tell us a lot about what that particular architecture can and cannot do. For instance, some controllers may support one or a few SBIs, for a specific purpose, while others may support many more SBIs, allowing choice of SBIs to use. The comparisons of SBIs go far beyond this chapter, but it does help to think about a few; the second major section gives three example architectures that happen to show three separate SBIs, specifically:

- OpenFlow (from the ONF; https://www.opennetworking.org)
- OpFlex (from Cisco; used with ACI)
- CLI (Telnet/SSH) and SNMP (from Cisco; used with APIC-EM)

The Northbound Interface

Think about the programming required at the controller related to the example in Figure 28-5. The figure focuses on the fact that the controller can add entries to the networking device's forwarding tables. However, how does the controller know what to add? How does it choose? What kind of information would your program need to gather before it could attempt to add something like MAC table entries or IP routes to a network? You might think of these:

- A list of all the devices in the network
- The capabilities of each devices
- The interfaces/ports on each device
- The current state of each port
- The topology: which devices connect to which, over which interfaces
- Device configuration: IP addresses, VLANs, and so on as configured on the devices

A controller does much of the work needed for the control plane in a centralized control model. It gathers all sorts of useful information about the network, like the items in the previous list. The controller itself can create a centralized repository of all this useful information about the network.

A controller's Northbound Interface (NBI) opens the controller so its data and functions can be used by other programs, enabling network programmability, with much quicker development. Programs can pull information from the controller, using the controller's APIs. The NBIs also enable programs to use the controller's abilities to program flows into the devices using the controller's SBIs.

To see where the NBI resides, first think about the controller itself. The controller is software, running on some server, which can be a VM or a physical server. An application can run on the same server as the controller, and use an NBI, which is an API, so that two programs can communicate.

Figure 28-6 shows just such an example. The big box in the figure represents the system where the controller software resides. This particular controller happens to be written in Java, and has a Java-based native API. Anyone—the same vendor as the controller vendor, another company, or even you—can write an app that runs on this same operating system that uses the controller's Java API. By using that API to exchange data with the controller, the application can learn information about the network. The application can also program flows in the network—that is, ask the controller to add the specific match/action logic (flows) into the forwarding tables of the networking devices.

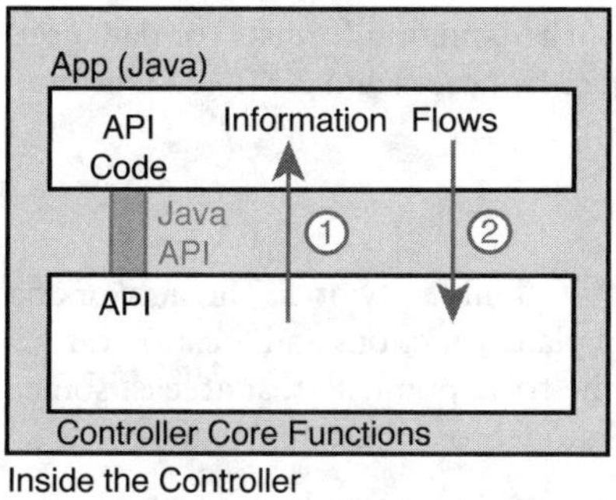

App (Java)

API Code   Information   Flows

Java API   ①   ②

API

Controller Core Functions

Inside the Controller

Figure 28-6 *Java API: Java Applications Communicates with Controller*

> **NOTE** The Northbound Interface (NBI) gets its name from its normal location as shown above the controller; that is, in what would be north on a map.

Before leaving the topic of NBIs, let me close with a brief explanation of a REST API as used for a controller. REST (*Representational State Transfer*) describes a type of API that allows applications to sit on different hosts, using HTTP messages to transfer data over the API. When you see SDN figures like Figure 28-6, with the application running on the same system as the controller, the API does not need to send messages over a network, because both programs run on the same system. But when the application runs on a different system somewhere else in the network other than running on the controller, the API needs a way to send the data back and forth over an IP network, and RESTful APIs meet that need.

Figure 28-7 shows the big ideas with a REST API. The application runs on a host at the top of the figure. In this case, at Step 1, it sends an HTTP GET request to a particular URI. The HTTP GET is like any other HTTP GET, even like those used to retrieve web pages. However, the URI is not for a web page, but rather identifies an object on the controller, typically a data structure that the application needs to learn and then process. For example, the URI might identify an object that is the list of physical interfaces on a specific device along with the status of each.

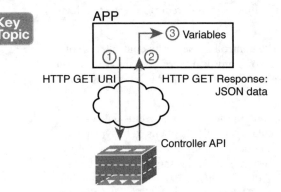

Figure 28-7   *Process Example of a GET Using a REST API*

At Step 2, the controller sends back an HTTP GET response message with the object. Most REST APIs will ask for and receive structured data. That is, instead of receiving data that is a web page, like a web browser would receive, the response holds variable names and their values, in a format that can be easily used by a program. The common formats for data used for network programmability are JSON (JavaScript Object Notation) and XML (eXtensible Markup Language), shown as Step 3.

SDN Architecture Summary

SDN and network programmability introduce a new way to build networks. The networking devices still exist, and still forward data, but the control plane functions and location can change dramatically. The centralized controller acts as the focal point, so that at least some of the control plane functions move from a distributed model to a centralized model.

However, the world of network programmability and SDN includes a wide array of options and solutions. Some options pull most control plane functions into the controller, while others pull only some of those functions into the controller. The next section takes a look at three different options, each of which takes a different approach to network programmability and the degree of centralized control.

Examples of Network Programmability and SDN

This second of three major sections of the chapter introduces three different SDN and network programmability solutions available from Cisco. Others exist as well. These three were chosen because they give a wide range of comparison points:

■ Open SDN Controller and OpenFlow

■ Cisco Application Centric Infrastructure (ACI) and OpFlex

■ Cisco APIC Enterprise Module (APIC-EM)

Open SDN and OpenFlow

One common form of SDN comes from the Open Networking Foundation, and is billed as Open SDN. The ONF (https://www.opennetworking.org) acts as a consortium of users and vendors to help establish SDN in the marketplace. Part of that work defines protocols, SBIs, NBIs, and anything that helps people implement their vision of SDN.

The ONF model of SDN features OpenFlow as the SBI. Part of OpenFlow defines an IP-based protocol used between the controller and the network devices. Just as important, OpenFlow defines a standard idea of what a switch's capabilities are, based on the ASICs and TCAMs commonly used in switches today. (That standardized idea of what a switch does is called a *switch abstraction*.) An OpenFlow switch can act as a Layer 2 switch, a Layer 3 switch, or in different ways and with great flexibility beyond the traditional model of a Layer 2/3 switch.

The Open SDN model centralizes most control plane functions, with control of the network done by the controller plus any applications that use the controller's NBIs. In fact, earlier Figure 28-5, which showed the network devices without a control plane, was meant to represent this mostly centralized ONF model of SDN. The applications may use any APIs (NBIs) supported on the controller platform. However, it calls for OpenFlow as the SBI protocol. Additionally, the networking devices need to be switches that support OpenFlow.

Because the ONF's Open SDN model has this common thread of a controller with an OpenFlow SBI, the controller plays a big role in the network. The next few pages provide a brief background about two such controllers.

The OpenDaylight Controller

First, if you were to look back at the history of OpenFlow, a wide variety of SDN controllers have been written. Some were more research oriented, while SDN was being developed and was more of an experimental idea. As time passed, more and more vendors began building their own controllers. And those controllers often had many similar features, because they were trying to accomplish many of the same goals.

Some companies got together to attempt to create an open source SDN controller, with many of the same principles of how Linux has been developed over the years. Part of the idea was that if enough vendors worked together on a common open source controller, then all would benefit. All those vendors could then use the open source controller as the basis for their own products, with each vendor focusing on the product differentiation part of the effort, rather than the fundamental features. The result was that back in the mid-2010s, the *OpenDaylight SDN controller* (https://www.opendaylight.org) was born.

The OpenDaylight (ODL) project exists as a project of the Linux Foundation. If that fact was not enough to convince you it is legit, OpenDaylight has backing from many vendors, including Cisco. Many of the corporate participants contribute significant money and people annually.

Figure 28-8 shows a generalized version of the ODL architecture. In particular, note the variety of SBIs listed in the lower part of the controller box: OpenFlow, NetConf, PCEP, BGP-LS, and OVSDB; many more exist. The ODL project has enough participants so that it includes a large variety of options, including multiple SBIs, not just OpenFlow.

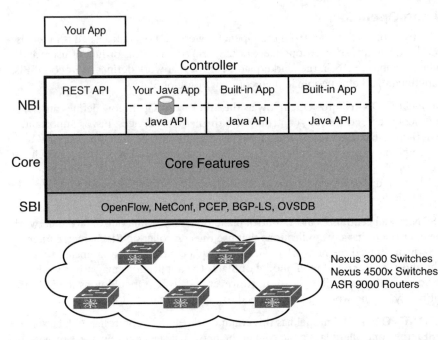

Figure 28-8 *Architecture of NBI, Controller Internals, and SBI to Network Devices*

ODL has many features, with many SBIs, and many core features. A vendor can then take ODL, use the parts that make sense for that vendor, add to it, and create a commercial ODL controller. Just a brief look around the OpenDaylight.org website when writing this chapter in early 2016 showed a listing of 15 commercial SDN controllers based on ODL, including the Cisco Open SDN Controller, described next.

Cisco Open SDN Controller

Cisco has a wide product line, with a large number of products, many of which support network programmability and SDN. One such product, the Cisco *Open SDN Controller* (OSC), acts as an SDN controller, and is Cisco's commercial version of ODL. Cisco follows the intended model for the ODL project: Cisco and others contribute labor and money to the ODL open source project; once a new release is completed, Cisco takes that release and builds new versions of their product. ODL licensing allows any vendor to take the open source code and package it with additional code and support.

The idea of having a free open source product, and a similar commercial product, is not a new concept in the open source world. In fact, the Linux OS follows that same model: You can download Linux for free to run on your own computer, but companies that use Linux in production may (and often do) want to run a supported and stable commercial version with support available.

Comparing the two controllers—that is, ODL and OSC—ODL has a longer list of features, but that is the normal progression of how a vendor would create its own offering. ODL includes many features based on the interests and goals of many participating companies. Each vendor picks the subset it wants to use, test, and support for its own commercial products.

Note that Cisco does support the OpenFlow and ONF model of OpenFlow through OSC and a small part of the Cisco router and switch product line. Cisco customers today (at least at publication) can purchase OSC, and some models of Cisco Nexus switches, plus some Cisco ASR series routers, with the routers and switches supporting OpenFlow. However, Cisco does not appear to be setting about to migrate its entire product line to support OpenFlow, instead taking a different approach to implementing SDN for different parts of a network and for different goals. The next two topics show two such offerings.

The Cisco Application Centric Infrastructure

The ONF Open SDN model with OpenFlow gives the centralized software great power and flexibility by enabling direct programming of the data plane forwarding tables on the devices. However, the end goal of that architecture is about enabling software control of the network and how it operates, so that software can automate and change the network based on current conditions in the network. The SDN movement that became OpenFlow meets those goals in particular ways. But SDN with OpenFlow is just one way to enable network programmability and automation.

Cisco looked at the same set of problems and goals for a modern IT infrastructure, the same issues that drove the development of OpenFlow, and reached some different conclusions about how to go about providing network programmability. One of those solutions focused on the data center, where applications run. So, instead of thinking about the network first, the solution began with applications, and what they need, and then built networking concepts around application architectures. Cisco made the network infrastructure become application centric, hence the name of the Cisco data center SDN solution: *Application Centric Infrastructure*, or ACI.

For example, Cisco looked at the data center world and saw lots of automation and control. As discussed in Chapter 27, virtualization software routinely starts, moves, and stops VMs, and cloud software enables self-service highly elastic services. From a networking perspective, some of those VMs need to communicate, but some do not. And those VMs can move based on the needs of the virtualization and cloud systems, so the idea of having a lot of per-physical-interface configuration on switches and routers was just a poor model.

The model that Cisco defines for ACI uses a concept of endpoints and policies. The *endpoints* are the VMs (or even traditional servers with the OS running directly on the hardware). Because several endpoints have the same needs, you group them together into aptly named *endpoint groups*. Then *policies* can be defined about which endpoint groups can communicate with whom—for instance, a group of web servers may need to communicate with a group of application servers. The policy also defines other key parameters, like which endpoint groups can access each other (or not), as well as QoS parameters and other services.

Note that at no point did the previous paragraph talk about which physical switch interfaces should be assigned to which VLAN, or which ports are in an EtherChannel—the discussion moves to an application-centric view of what happens in the network. Once all the endpoints, policies, and related details are defined, the controller can then direct the network as to what needs to be in the forwarding tables to make it all happen—and to more easily react when the VMs start, stop, or move.

To make it all work, ACI uses a centralized controller called the *Application Policy Infrastructure Controller* (APIC), as shown in Figure 28-9. The name defines the function in this case: It is the controller that creates application policies for the data center infrastructure. The APIC, of course, has a convenient GUI, but the power comes in software control—that is, network programmability. The same virtualization software, or cloud or automation software, even scripts written by the network engineer, can define the endpoint groups, policies, and so on to the APIC. But all these players access the ACI system by interfacing to the APIC; the network engineer no longer needs to connect to each individual switch and configure CLI commands.

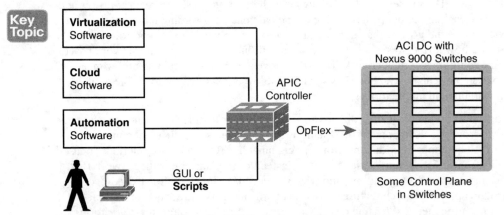

Figure 28-9   *Controlling the ACI Data Center Network Using the APIC*

ACI uses a partially centralized control plane, RESTful and native APIs, and OpFlex as an SBI. The NBIs allow software control from outside the controller. The controller communicates with the switches connected to the endpoints, and asks those switches to then create the correct flows to be added to the switches. Interestingly, ACI uses a partially distributed control plane, with the controller informing the switches about the desired policies to apply to each endpoint. The switches still have some control plane software that interprets those policies to then add the correct flows to the switch's own forwarding table.

For more information on Cisco ACI, go to http://www.cisco.com/go/aci.

The Cisco APIC Enterprise Module

The first two solutions discussed in this section move significant parts of the control plane functions into the controller, and require switches that support that model. The ONF's Open SDN model centralizes most of the control plane, with switches that support OpenFlow. The Cisco ACI solution centralizes much but not all of the control plane, leaving some of the control plane in the switches. However, those switches were newer models of switches with software that supports ACI. Neither the Open SDN model nor the Cisco ACI model uses switches and routers that act like the traditional switch and router discussed throughout this book and the ICND1 book.

The third example of a Cisco SDN solution in this section, called *APIC Enterprise Module* (APIC-EM), keeps the same traditional switches and routers as discussed throughout this book and the ICND1 Cert Guide. Cisco rejected the idea that its enterprise-wide SDN (network programmability) solution could begin with the assumption of replacing all hardware.

Instead, Cisco looked for ways to add the benefits of network programmability while keeping the same traditional switches and routers in place. That approach could certainly change over time, but with its initial introduction into the market in late 2015, the Cisco APIC-EM does just that: offer enterprise SDN using the same switches and routers already installed in networks.

> **NOTE**   Even though APIC-EM uses the same APIC acronym used for the controller with the Cisco ACI offering, the details of how it works differ significantly.

Per the Cisco product pages, APIC-EM is the Cisco SDN offering for the enterprise. To help with network programmability, the solution uses a centralized controller. At the same time, it attempts to support much of the more recent generations of Cisco enterprise routers and switches by using SBIs that should sound familiar. Summarizing some of the key points:

- The solution uses the APIC-EM controller.

- Cisco supplies a variety of applications that reside on the controller, some of which use information gathered by the controller, and some of which control the operation of the network devices.

- The controller has a RESTful Northbound API that can make available that collected information about the entire network over an easy-to-use API.

- The control and data planes of the network devices remain unchanged, as part of the effort to support existing devices.

- The SBI uses familiar protocols: Telnet, SSH, and SNMP.

Figure 28-10 shows a general view of the APIC-EM controller architecture, with a few of the APIC-EM apps, the REST API, and a list of the SBIs.

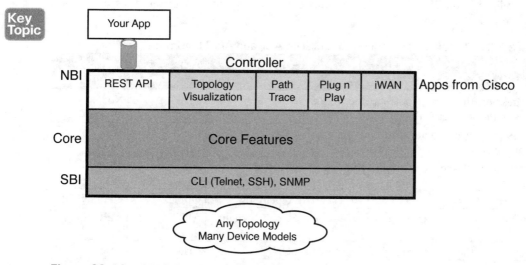

Figure 28-10   *APIC-EM Controller Model*

The fact that the data plane and control plane do not change needs more explanation. First, APIC-EM will likely change over time; the Cisco product pages even tell us that support for more SBIs will happen. But as it existed in early 2016 (when this chapter was finalized), when using APIC-EM, all the routers and switches still use their data and control planes in the same way, with no changes. The APIC-EM controller does not program flows into tables, nor ask the control plane in the devices to change how it operates. The switches and routers do not need to be ready to change how they operate internally. So, you might wonder, what does the APIC-EM controller do?

First, APIC-EM enables easier network automation for customers. To do that, APIC-EM gathers information about the network over the SBI. That information includes topology, devices, interfaces, operational status, and configuration. Next, APIC-EM makes that information available through extensive NBI APIs. Additionally, APIC-EM makes the data about devices consistent to a great extent, even if the devices use different operating systems.

Second, APIC-EM can still change how the devices operate by changing the configuration of the devices. The SBIs listed in Figure 28-10 include CLI, meaning that APIC-EM can use Telnet and SSH to log in to a device, use the CLI, and issue commands—including to reconfigure the device. With SNMP as the SBI, APIC-EM can also configure the network device with SNMP Set commands.

So in its first version, APIC-EM enables programmability with a centralized controller model, without changing the data and control plane concepts and configuration described throughout this book.

Comparing the Three Examples

The three example SDN branches in this section of the book were chosen to provide a wide variety for the sake of learning. For instance, with Cisco OSC (using OpenFlow) and with Cisco ACI, the network engineer now works with the controller rather than individual devices. However, they differ to some degree in how much of the control plane work is centralized. Table 28-2 lists those and other comparison points taken from this section, for easy review and study.

Table 28-2   Points of Comparison: Open SDN, ACI, and APIC Enterprise

Criteria	Open SDN	ACI	APIC Enterprise
Changes how the device control plane works versus traditional networking	Yes	Yes	No
Creates centralized point from which humans and automation control the network	Yes	Yes	Yes
Degree to which the architecture centralizes the control plane	Mostly	Partially	N/A[1]
SBIs used	OpenFlow	OpFlex	CLI, SNMP
Controllers mentioned in this chapter	OpenDaylight, Cisco OSC	APIC	APIC-EM
Organization that is the primary definer/owner	ONF	Cisco	Cisco

[1] The control plane remains the same in the networking devices, so in that sense, the control plane is not centralized at all.

Also, before leaving these topics, let me offer a few words about learning more about SDN. Cisco DevNet (https://developer.cisco.com), a site for anyone interested in network programming, has information about all the Cisco SDN solutions in this section. It also has free labs as well. You should definitely set up a free login at Cisco DevNet and check out the content there. Also, I blog about SDN from time to time at one of my blog sites (http://www.sdnskills.com); look there for posts with recommendations about what to study to learn about SDN.

Cisco APIC-EM Path Trace ACL Analysis Application

This final section of the chapter was designed to discuss a single exam topic, and only that exam topic, due to some timing challenges. This short section introduces the topic, with a promise of more information to be posted as a PDF on this book's companion website. Now that I have made you curious, this section first introduces the Path Trace app, then explains more about the ACL Analysis app and the reason why the details are in a free PDF on the website.

APIC-EM Path Trace App

Think of the APIC-EM controller as a set of base features plus a series of applications or apps. The list of supported applications will grow over time. The apps run natively on the controller; that is, they do not run elsewhere in the network but are installed as part of the controller. From a user interface perspective, they appear as just another feature in the user interface, but architecturally, the apps are separate from the base controller, and may even be developed by different groups within Cisco.

APIC-EM supports a variety of apps, and that list will almost certainly expand over time. Currently, when you download the APIC-EM software, the software includes all the apps built in. All the apps can run. As for licensing, some apps, called basic apps, do not require a license—they are free to use (just like APIC-EM itself). Other apps, called solution apps, require the purchase of a license for legal use of the app.

The APIC-EM Path Trace app has been available since version 1.0 of APIC-EM. The idea is simple, but it is a very powerful and useful tool. This tool predicts what happens in the data plane of the various devices in the network. The process works something like this:

1. Before using Path Trace, another APIC-EM app called Discovery discovers the network topology.

2. From the Path Trace part of the GUI, the user can type in a source and destination address of a packet.

3. The Path Trace app examines information pulled by APIC-EM from the devices in the network—the MAC tables, IP routing tables, and other forwarding details in the devices—to analyze where this imaginary packet would flow if sent in the network right now.

4. The Path Trace GUI displays the path, with notes, overlaid on a map of the network.

You and I could do the same work, but it would be laborious. APIC-EM's Path Trace app does the work with just a few clicks at the user interface.

APIC-EM Path Trace ACL Analysis Tool Timing and Exam Topic

The one exam topic that mentions an APIC-EM app uses a longish phrase: "APIC-EM Path Trace ACL Analysis tool." This phrase refers to a newer app (not available in version 1.0 or 1.1 of APIC-EM) that takes the work done by Path Trace a step further.

The ACL Analysis tool app depends on the Path Trace app, but it then extends the function of the Path Trace app. Path Trace by itself does not consider ACLs in its analysis of the forwarding path. That is, Path Trace shows where the packet would be forwarded based on MAC address tables and IP routing tables, while ignoring whether an ACL might discard the packet. The ACL Analysis app then examines the chosen path as determined by the Path Trace tool (hence the dependency), but it looks for any enabled ACLs. The ACL Analysis tool analyzes and then characterizes (with notes overlaid on the screen) what packets sent from source to destination would be filtered as it travelled along that path.

Unfortunately for our publishing process, the APIC-EM ACL Path Trace ACL Analysis tool creates a small challenge. The app was not available before we needed to send the book out for its first printing. However, the exam topic refers to that specific feature. The timing for the Cisco release of that feature into the APIC-EM product feature happened to be just a little too late for us to use the final version of the released software when writing this section.

While the timing of the release of the software feature impacted our book schedule, it should not impact your study schedule. We plan to deliver to you more detail about this one exam topic, as follows:

■ The book has an Appendix B, "Exam Updates," that is designed as a tool to add new content to the book over time without creating a new edition. (Basically, we create a new version of Appendix B, post it on the web page, and even email all those who register their books at ciscopress.com.)

■ Once the new APIC-EM version is out with the Path Trace ACL Analysis feature included, I will finish the material, including screen images, so you can see how it works.

■ You should learn this app by using it on DevNet as well. The updated Appendix B material will include a link to any specific Cisco DevNet labs about this new feature, but you can always browse for labs at developer.cisco.com and look for labs that have APIC-EM 1.2 installed. (That would be the best way to learn the features of a GUI-based tool anyway.)

■ If the code is available when we expect it, our new Appendix B will be sitting there on the website by the time you read this. Go look now; look at this book's current Appendix B for details about how to download (for free, of course).

Chapter Review

One key to doing well on the exams is to perform repetitive spaced review sessions. Review this chapter's material using either the tools in the book, DVD, or interactive tools for the same material found on the book's companion website. Refer to the "Your Study Plan" element for more details. Table 28-3 outlines the key review elements and where you can find them. To better track your study progress, record when you completed these activities in the second column.

Table 28-3   Chapter Review Tracking

Review Element	Review Date(s)	Resource Used
Review key topics		Book, DVD/website
Review key terms		Book, DVD/website
Answer DIKTA questions		Book, PCPT
Review memory tables		Book, App

Review All the Key Topics

Table 28-4   Key Topics for Chapter 28

Key Topic Element	Description	Page Number
List	Example actions of the networking device data plane	763
List	Example actions of the networking device control plane	764
Figure 28-4	Switch internals with ASIC and TCAM	766
Figure 28-5	Basic SDN architecture, with the centralized controller programming device data planes directly	767
Paragraph	Description of the role and purpose of the NBI	769
Figure 28-7	REST API basic concepts	770
Figure 28-9	Controlling the ACI data center network using APIC	774
Figure 28-10	APIC-EM: architecture, SBIs, and example apps	775
Table 28-2	Comparisons of Open SDN, Cisco ACI, and Cisco APIC Enterprise options	776

Key Terms You Should Know

application programming interface (API), Application Policy Infrastructure Controller (APIC), APIC Enterprise Module (APIC-EM), Application Centric Infrastructure (ACI), Northbound API, Southbound API, control plane, data plane, management plane, application-specific integrated circuit (ASIC), ternary content-addressable memory (TCAM), OpenFlow, Software Defined Networking (SDN), distributed control plane, centralized control plane, Representational State Transfer (REST), RESTful API, Northbound Interface (NBI), Southbound Interface (SBI), OpenDaylight (ODL), Cisco Open SDN Controller (OSC), Open Networking Foundation (ONF)

Part VII Review

Keep track of your part review progress with the checklist in Table P7-1. Details about each task follow the table.

Table P7-1 Part VII Part Review Checklist

Activity	1st Date Completed	2nd Date Completed
Repeat All DIKTA Questions		
Answer Part Review Questions		
Review Key Topics		
Create Mind Maps		
Do Labs		

Repeat All DIKTA Questions

For this task, answer the "Do I Know This Already?" questions again for the chapters in this part of the book using the PCPT software.

Answer Part Review Questions

For this task, use PCPT to answer the Part Review questions for this part of the book.

Review Key Topics

Review all key topics in all chapters in this part, either by browsing the chapters, or using the Key Topics application on the DVD or companion website.

Create Command Mind Map by Category

Part VII of this book has three chapters. Only Chapter 26 includes any new CLI commands, and those have an obvious organization: SNMP, SPAN, and IPS SLA. So, make a command mind map for those three topics, and within each, break down the commands based on which are configuration commands versus EXEC commands.

Create Terminology Mind Maps

All three chapters in this part of the book introduce a large number of new terms and concepts. The exercise of trying to remember all the terms you remember from those chapters would be useful by itself. Do just that, creating one mind map for each chapter, as listed in Table P7-2. Within each mind map, you may choose any organization you see fit.

Appendix E, "Mind Map Solutions," lists sample mind map answers. If you do choose to use mind map software, rather than paper, you might want to remember where you stored your mind map files. Table P7-2 lists the mind maps for this part review and a place to record those filenames.

Table P7-2 Configuration Mind Maps for Part IX Review

Map	Description	Where You Saved It
1	Command Mind Map	
2	Network Management Terminology Mind Map	
3	Cloud Computing Terminology Mind Map	
4	Network Programmability Terminology Mind Map	

Do Labs

Depending on your chosen lab tool, here are some suggestions for what to do in lab:

Pearson Network Simulator: Once the Pearson network simulator has been updated for the 100-105, 200-105, and 200-125 exams, you will see labs for all these topics that are easily found in the "Sort by Chapter" tab of the Sim. Do those labs.

Config Labs: In your idle moments, review and repeat any of the Config Labs for this book part in the author's blog; launch from http://blog.certskills.com/ccna/ and navigate to **Hands-On > Config Lab.**

Other: If using other lab tools, here are a few suggestions: The configurations in Chapter 26 can be tested in lab. You can find free SNMP management software with Internet searches. To test SPAN, if you have a LAN switch in your lab, just download the free Wireshark network analyzer (https://www.wireshark.org) and use it to capture the SPAN traffic.

Part VIII

Final Prep

Chapter 29: Final Review

Final Review

Congratulations! You made it through the book, and now it's time to finish getting ready for the exam. This chapter helps you get ready to take and pass the exam in two ways.

This chapter begins by talking about the exam itself. You know the content and topics. Now you need to think about what happens during the exam, and what you need to do in these last few weeks before taking the exam. At this point, everything you do should be focused on getting you ready to pass so that you can finish up this hefty task.

The second section of this chapter gives you some exam review tasks as your final preparation for your ICND1, ICND2, or CCNA exam.

Advice About the Exam Event

Now that you have finished the bulk of this book, you could just register for your Cisco ICND1, ICND2, or CCNA R&S exam; show up; and take the exam. However, if you spend a little time thinking about the exam event itself, learning more about the user interface of the real Cisco exams, and the environment at the Pearson VUE testing centers, you will be better prepared, particularly if this is your first Cisco exam. This first of two major sections in this chapter gives some advice about the Cisco exams and the exam event itself.

Learn the Question Types Using the Cisco Certification Exam Tutorial

In the weeks leading up to your exam, you should think more about the different types of exam questions and have a plan for how to approach those questions. One of the best ways to learn about the exam questions is to use the Cisco Certification Exam Tutorial.

To find the Cisco Certification Exam Tutorial, go to Cisco.com and search for "exam tutorial." The tutorial sits inside a web page with a Flash presentation of the exam user interface. The tutorial even lets you take control as if you were taking the exam. When using the tutorial, make sure that you take control and try the following:

- Try to click **Next** on the multiple-choice, single-answer question without clicking an answer, and see that the testing software tells you that you have too few answers.

- On the multiple-choice, multiple-answer question, select too few answers and click **Next** to again see how the user interface responds.

- In the drag-and-drop question, drag the answers to the obvious answer locations, but then drag them back to the original location. (You can do this on the real exam if you change your mind when answering a question.)

- On the simulation question, first just make sure that you can get to the command-line interface (CLI) on one of the routers. To do so, you have to click the PC icon for a PC connected to the router console; the console cable appears as a dashed line, whereas network cables are solid lines.

- Still on the sim question, make sure that you look at the scroll areas at the top, at the side, and in the terminal emulator window. These scrollbars let you view the entire question and scenario.

- Still on the sim question, make sure that you can toggle between the topology window and the terminal emulator window by clicking **Show topology** and **Hide topology**. Hang out here and click around until you are completely comfortable navigating—and do it again tomorrow and the next day.

- On the testlet question, answer one multiple-choice question, move to the second and answer it, and then move back to the first question, confirming that inside a testlet you can move around between questions.

- Again on the testlet question, click **Next** to see the pop-up window that Cisco uses as a prompt to ask whether you want to move on. (Testlets might actually allow you to give too few answers and still move on, so make extra sure that you answer with the correct number of answers in each testlet question.) After you click **Next** to move past the testlet, you cannot go back to change your answer for any of these questions.

Think About Your Time Budget Versus Number of Questions

On exam day, you need to keep an eye on your speed. Going too slowly hurts you because you might not have time to answer all the questions. Going too fast can be hurtful if you are rushing because you are fearful about running out of time. So, you need to be able to somehow know whether you are moving quickly enough to answer all the questions, while not rushing.

The exam user interface shows some useful information, namely a countdown timer and a question counter. The question counter shows a question number for the question you are answering, and it shows the total number of questions on your exam.

Unfortunately, some questions require lots more time than others, and for this and other reasons, time estimating can be a challenge.

First, before you show up to take the exam, you only know a range of the number of questions for the exam; for example, the Cisco website might list the CCNA R&S exam as having from 50 to 60 questions. But you do not know how many questions are on your exam until the exam begins, when you go through the screens that lead up to the point where you click Start Exam, which starts your timed exam.

Next, some questions (call them *time burners*) clearly take a lot more time to answer:

Normal-time questions: Multiple-choice and drag-and-drop, approximately 1 minute each

Time burners: Sims, simlets, and testlets, approximately 6–8 minutes each

Finally, in the count of 50 to 60 questions on a single exam, even though testlet and simlet questions contain several multiple-choice questions, the exam software counts each testlet and simlet question as one question in the question counter. For example, if a testlet question has four embedded multiple-choice questions, in the exam software's question counter, that counts as one question. So when you start the exam, you might see that you will have 50 questions, but you don't know how many of those are time burners.

> **NOTE**   Cisco does not tell us why one person taking the exam might get 50 questions while someone else taking the same exam might get 60 questions, but it seems reasonable to think that the person with 50 questions might have a few more of the time burners, making the two exams equivalent.

You need a plan for how you will check your time, a plan that does not distract you from the exam. You can ponder the facts listed here and come up with your own plan. If you want a little more guidance, the next topic shows one way to check your time that uses some simple math so it does not take much time away from the test.

A Suggested Time-Check Method

You can use the following math to do your time check in a way that weights the time based on those time-burner questions. You do not have to use this method. But this math uses only addition of whole numbers, to keep it simple. It gives you a pretty close time estimate, in my opinion.

The concept is simple. Just do a simple calculation that estimates the time you should have used so far. Here's the math:

Number of questions answered so far + 7 per time burner answered so far

Then you check the timer to figure out how much time you have spent:

- You have used exactly that much time, or a little more time: your timing is perfect.
- You have used less time: you are ahead of schedule.
- You have used noticeably more time: you are behind schedule.

For example, if you have already finished 17 questions, 2 of which were time burners, your time estimate is 17 + 7 + 7 = 31 minutes. If your actual time is also 31 minutes, or maybe 32 or 33 minutes, you are right on schedule. If you have spent less than 31 minutes, you are ahead of schedule.

So, the math is pretty easy: Questions answered, plus 7 per time burner, is the guesstimate of how long you should have taken so far if you are right on time.

> **NOTE**   This math is an estimate; I make no guarantees that the math will be an accurate predictor on every exam.

Miscellaneous Pre-Exam Suggestions

Here are just a few more suggestions for things to think about before exam day arrives:

- Get some earplugs. Testing centers often have some, but if you do not want to chance it, come prepared with your own. (They will not let you bring your own noise-canceling headphones into the room if they follow the rules disallowing any user electronic devices in the room, so think low-tech disposable earplugs, or even bring a cotton ball.) The testing center is typically one room within a building of a company that does something else as well, often a training center, and almost certainly you will share the room with other test takers coming and going. So, there are people talking in nearby rooms and other office noises. Earplugs can help.

- Some people like to spend the first minute of the exam writing down some notes for reference, before actually starting the exam. For example, maybe you want to write down the table of magic numbers for finding IPv4 subnet IDs. If you plan to do that, practice making those notes. Before each practice exam, transcribe those lists, just like you expect to do at the real exam.

- Plan your travel to the testing center with enough time so that you will not be rushing to make it just in time.

- If you tend to be nervous before exams, practice your favorite relaxation techniques for a few minutes before each practice exam, just to be ready to use them.

Exam-Day Advice

I hope the exam goes well for you. Certainly, the better prepared you are, the better chances you have on the exam. But these small tips can help you do your best on exam day:

- Rest the night before the exam rather than stay up late to study. Clarity of thought is more important than one extra fact, especially because the exam requires so much analysis and thinking rather than just remembering facts.

- If you did not bring earplugs, ask the testing center for some, even if you cannot imagine using them. You never know whether using them might help.

- You may bring personal effects into the building and testing company's space, but not into the actual room in which you take the exam. So, save a little stress and bring as little extra stuff with you as possible. If you have a safe place to leave briefcases, purses, electronics, and so on, leave them there. However, the testing center should have a place to store your things as well. Simply put, the less you bring, the less you have to worry about storing. (For example, I have been asked to remove even my analog wristwatch on more than one occasion.)

- The exam center will give you a laminated sheet and pen, as a place to take notes. (Test center personnel typically do not let you bring paper and pen into the room, even if supplied by the testing center.) I always ask for a second pen as well.

- If they're available, grab a few tissues from the box in the room, for two reasons. One, to avoid having to get up in the middle of the exam. Two, if you need to erase your laminated sheet, doing that with a tissue paper rather than your hand helps prevent the oil from your hand making the pen stop working well.

- Leave for the testing center with extra time so that you do not have to rush.

- Find a restroom to use before going into the testing center. If you cannot find one, you can use one in the testing center, and test personnel will direct you and give you time before your exam starts.

- Do not drink a 64-ounce caffeinated drink on the trip to the testing center. After the exam starts, the exam timer will not stop while you go to the restroom.

- On exam day, use any relaxation techniques that you have practiced to help get your mind focused while you wait for the exam.

Reserve the Hour After the Exam in Case You Fail

Some people pass these exams on the first attempt, and some do not. The exams are not easy. If you fail to pass the exam that day, you will likely be disappointed. And that is understandable. But it is not a reason to give up. In fact, I added this short topic to give you a big advantage in case you do fail.

The most important study hour for your next exam attempt is the hour just after your failed attempt.

Prepare to fail before you take the exam. That is, prepare your schedule to give yourself an hour, or at least a half an hour, immediately after the exam attempt, in case you fail. Then follow these suggestions:

- Bring pen and paper, preferably a notebook you can write in if you have to write standing up or sitting somewhere inconvenient.

- Make sure you know where pen and paper are so that you can take notes immediately after the exam. Keep these items in your backpack if using the train or bus, or on the car seat in the car.

- Install an audio recording app on your phone, and be prepared to start talking into your app when you leave the testing center.

- Before the exam, scout the testing center, and plan the place where you will sit and take your notes, preferably somewhere quiet.

- Write down anything in particular that you can recall from any question.

- Write down details of questions you know you got right as well, because doing so may help trigger a memory of another question.

- Draw the figures that you can remember.

- Most importantly, write down any tidbit that might have confused you: terms, configuration commands, **show** commands, scenarios, topology drawings, anything.

- Take at least three passes at remembering. That is, you will hit a wall where you do not remember more. So, start on your way back to the next place, and then find a place to pause and take more notes. And do it again.

- When you have sucked your memory dry, take one more pass while thinking of the major topics in the book, to see if that triggers any other memory of a question.

Once collected, *you cannot share the information with anyone*, because doing so would break the Cisco nondisclosure agreement (NDA). Cisco considers cheating a serious offense and strongly forbids sharing this kind of information publicly. But you can use your information to study for your next attempt. Remember, anything that uncovers what you do not know is valuable when studying for your next attempt. See the section "Study Suggestions After a Failed Attempt" in this chapter for the rest of the story.

Exam Review

This Exam Review completes the Study Plan materials as suggested by this book. At this point, you have read the other chapters of the book, and you have done the Chapter Review and Part Review tasks. Now you need to do the final study and review activities before taking the exam, as detailed in this section.

This section suggests some new activities and repeats some activities that have been previously mentioned. However, whether the activities are new or old to you, they all focus on filling in your knowledge gaps, finishing off your skills, and completing the study process. While repeating some tasks you did at Chapter Review and Part Review can help, you need to be ready to take an exam, so the Exam Review asks you to spend a lot of time answering exam questions.

The Exam Review walks you through suggestions for several types of tasks and gives you some tracking tables for each activity. The main categories are

- Taking practice exams
- Finding what you do not know well yet (knowledge gaps)
- Configuring and verifying functions from the CLI
- Repeating the Chapter Review and Part Review tasks

Take Practice Exams

One day soon, you need to pass a real Cisco exam at a Pearson VUE testing center. So, it's time to practice the real event as much as possible.

A practice exam using the Pearson IT Certification Practice Test (PCPT) exam software lets you experience many of the same issues as when taking a real Cisco exam. The software gives you a number of questions, with a countdown timer shown in the window. After you answer a question, you cannot go back to it (yes, that's true on Cisco exams). If you run out of time, the questions you did not answer count as incorrect.

The process of taking the timed practice exams helps you prepare in three key ways:

- To practice the exam event itself, including time pressure, the need to read carefully, and the need to concentrate for long periods
- To build your analysis and critical thinking skills when examining the network scenario built in to many questions
- To discover the gaps in your networking knowledge so that you can study those topics before the real exam

As much as possible, treat the practice exam events as if you were taking the real Cisco exam at a VUE testing center. The following list gives some advice on how to make your practice exam more meaningful, rather than just one more thing to do before exam day rolls around:

- Set aside 2 hours for taking the 90-minute timed practice exam.
- Make a list of what you expect to do for the 10 minutes before the real exam event. Then visualize yourself doing those things. Before taking each practice exam, practice those final 10 minutes before your exam timer starts. (The earlier section "Exam-Day Advice" lists some suggestions about what to do in those last 10 minutes.)
- You cannot bring anything with you into the VUE exam room, so remove all notes and help materials from your work area before taking a practice exam. You can use blank paper, a pen, and your brain only. Do not use calculators, notes, web browsers, or any other app on your computer.

- Real life can get in the way, but if at all possible, ask anyone around you to leave you alone for the time you will practice. If you must do your practice exam in a distracting environment, wear headphones or earplugs to reduce distractions.

- Do not guess, hoping to improve your score. Answer only when you have confidence in the answer. Then, if you get the question wrong, you can go back and think more about the question in a later study session.

Practicing Taking the ICND2 or CCNA R&S Exam

This book comes with both ICND2 and CCNA R&S practice exams. Depending on which exam you plan to take, you should select a different set of exam databases to use when you want to take a practice exam using the PCPT software. To take an ICND2 practice exam, you need to select one or both of the ICND2 exam databases from PCPT. If you plan to take the CCNA R&S 200-125 exam, select the NA exam databases instead.

If you followed the advice in the "Your Study Plan" guide provided early in this book, you will not have seen any of the questions in these exam databases before now. After you select the ICND2 or CCNA exam databases, you simply need to choose the **Practice Exam** option in the upper right and start the exam.

You should plan to take between one and three practice exam with these two exam databases. Even people who are already well prepared should do at least one practice exam, just to experience the time pressure and the need for prolonged concentration.

Table 29-1 gives you a checklist to record your different practice exam events. Note that recording both the date and the score is helpful for some other work you will do, so note both. Also, in the Time Notes section, if you finish on time, note how much extra time you had; if you run out of time, note how many questions you did not have time to answer.

Table 29-1   ICND2 Practice Exam Checklist

Exam	Date	Score	Time Notes
ICND2/ CCNA			
ICND2/ CCNA			
ICND2/ CCNA			

Advice on How to Answer Exam Questions

Open a web browser. Yes, take a break and open a web browser on any device. Do a quick search on a fun topic. Then, before you click a link, get ready to think where your eyes go for the first 5 to 10 seconds after you click the link. Now, click a link and look at the page. Where did your eyes go?

Interestingly, web browsers and the content in web pages have trained us all to scan. Web page designers actually design content expecting certain scan patterns from viewers. Regardless of the pattern, when reading a web page, almost no one reads sequentially, and no one reads entire sentences. People scan for the interesting graphics and the big words, and then scan the space around those noticeable items.

Other parts of our electronic culture have also changed how the average person reads. For example, many of you grew up using texting and social media, sifting through hundreds or thousands of messages—but each message barely fills an entire sentence. (In fact, that previous sentence would not fit in a tweet, being longer than 140 characters.)

Those everyday habits have changed how we all read and think in front of a screen. Unfortunately, those same habits often hurt our scores when taking computer-based exams.

If you scan exam questions like you read web pages, texts, and tweets, you will probably make some mistakes because you missed a key fact in the question, answer, or exhibits. It helps to start at the beginning and read all the words—a process that is amazingly unnatural for many people today.

29

> **NOTE**   I have talked to many college professors, in multiple disciplines, and Cisco Networking Academy instructors, and they consistently tell me that the number-one test-taking issue today is that people do not read the question well enough to understand the details.

When you are taking the practice exams and answering individual questions, consider these two strategies. First, before the practice exam, think about your own personal strategy for how you will read a question. Make your approach to multiple-choice questions in particular be a conscious decision on your part. Second, if you want some suggestions on how to read an exam question, use the following strategy:

Step 1.   Read the question itself, thoroughly, from start to finish.

Step 2.   Scan any exhibit (usually command output) or figure.

Step 3.   Scan the answers to look for the types of information. (Numeric? Terms? Single words? Phrases?)

Step 4.   Reread the question thoroughly, from start to finish, to make sure that you understand it.

Step 5.   Read each answer thoroughly, while referring to the figure/exhibit as needed. After reading each answer, before reading the next answer:

    A.   If correct, select as correct.

    B.   If for sure incorrect, mentally rule it out.

    C.   If unsure, mentally note it as a possible correct answer.

> **NOTE**   Cisco exams will tell you the number of correct answers. The exam software also helps you finish the question with the right number of answers noted. For example, the software prevents you from selecting too many answers. Also, if you try to move on to the next question but have too few answers noted, the exam software asks if you truly want to move on. And you should guess the answer when unsure on the actual exam—there is no penalty for guessing.

Use the practice exams as a place to practice your approach to reading. Every time you click to the next question, try to read the question following your approach. If you are feeling time pressure, that is the perfect time to keep practicing your approach, to reduce and eliminate questions you miss because of scanning the question instead of reading thoroughly.

Taking Other Practice Exams

Many people add other practice exams and questions other than those that come with this book. Frankly, using other practice exams in addition to the questions that come with this book can be a good idea, for many reasons. The other exam questions can use different terms in different ways, emphasize different topics, and show different scenarios that make you rethink some topics.

Note that Cisco Press does sell products that include additional test questions. The *CCNA ICND2 200-105 Official Cert Guide Premium Edition eBook and Practice Test* product is basically the publisher's eBook version of this book. It includes a soft copy of the book, in formats you can read on your computer and on the most common book readers and tablets. The product includes all the content you would normally get with the DVD that comes with the print book, including all the question databases mentioned in this chapter. Additionally, this product includes two more ICND2 exam databases and two more CCNA R&S exam databases.

NOTE   In addition to getting the extra questions, the Premium Editions have links to every test question, including those in the print book, to the specific section of the book for further reference. This is a great learning tool if you need more detail than what you find in the question explanations. You can purchase the eBooks and additional practice exams at 70 percent off the list price using the coupon on the back of the activation code card in the DVD sleeve, making the Premium Editions the best and most cost-efficient way to get more practice questions.

Find Knowledge Gaps Through Question Review

You just took a number of practice exams. You probably learned a lot, gained some exam-taking skills, and improved your networking knowledge and skills. But if you go back and look at all the questions you missed, you might be able to find a few small gaps in your knowledge.

One of the hardest things to find when doing your final exam preparation is to discover gaps in your knowledge and skills. In other words, what topics and skills do you need to know that you do not know? Or what topics do you think you know, but you misunderstand about some important fact? Finding gaps in your knowledge at this late stage requires more than just your gut feel about your strengths and weaknesses.

This next task uses a feature of PCPT to help you find those gaps. The PCPT software tracks each practice exam you take, remembering your answer for every question, and whether you got it wrong. You can view the results and move back and forth between seeing the question and seeing the results page. To find gaps in your knowledge, follow these steps:

Step 1.   Pick and review one of your practice exams.

Step 2.   Review each incorrect question until you are satisfied that you understand the question.

Step 3.   When finished with your review for a question, mark the question.

Step 4.   Review all incorrect questions from your exam until all are marked.

Step 5.   Move on to the next practice exam.

Figure 29-1 shows a sample Question Review page, in which all the questions were answered incorrectly. The results list a Correct column, with no check mark, meaning that the answer was incorrect.

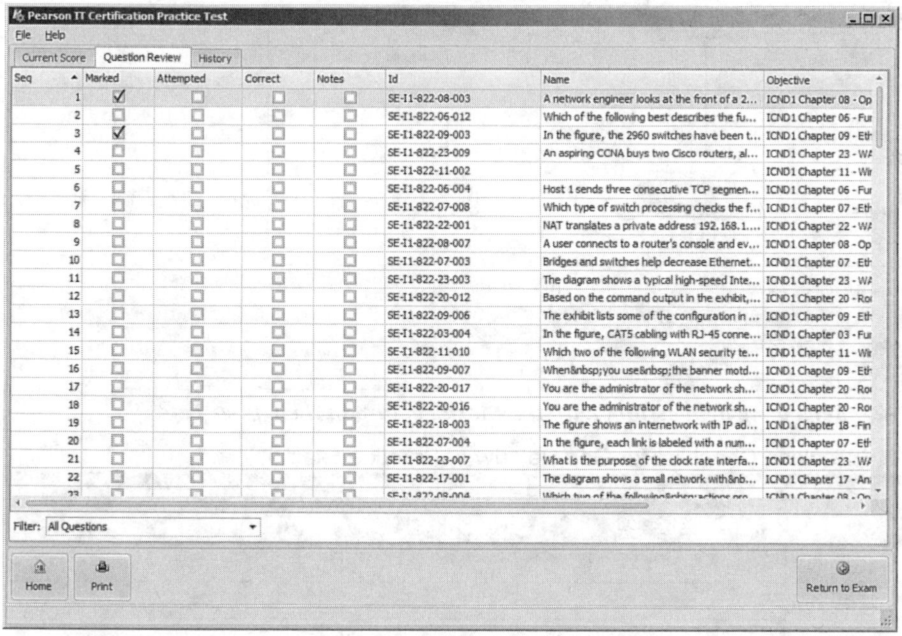

Figure 29-1   *PCPT Grading Results Page*

To perform the process of reviewing questions and marking them as complete, you can move between this Question Review page and the individual questions. Just double-click a question to move back to that question. From the question, you can click **Grade Exam** to move back to the grading results and to the Question Review page shown in Figure 29-1. The question window also shows the place to mark the question, in the upper left, as shown in Figure 29-2.

If you want to come back later to look through the questions you missed from an earlier exam, start at the PCPT home screen. From there, instead of clicking the Start button to start a new exam, click the **View Grade History** button to see your earlier exam attempts and work through any missed questions.

Track your progress through your gap review in Table 29-2. PCPT lists your previous practice exams by date and score, so it helps to note those values in the table for comparison to the PCPT menu.

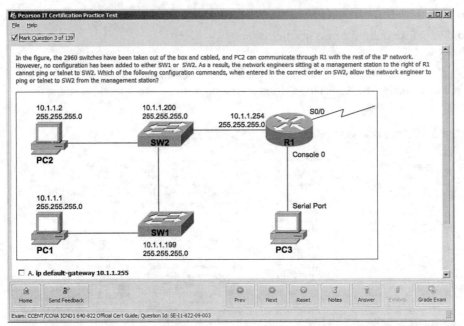

Figure 29-2 *Reviewing a Question, with the Mark Feature in the Upper Left*

Table 29-2 Tracking Checklist for Gap Review of Practice Exams

Exam (ICND1, ICND2, or CCNA)	Original Practice Exam Date	Original Exam Score	Date Gap Review Was Completed

Practice Hands-On CLI Skills

To do well on sim and simlet questions, you need to be comfortable with many Cisco router and switch commands, and how to use them from a Cisco CLI. As described in the introduction to this book, sim questions require you to decide what configuration command(s) need to be configured to fix a problem or to complete a working configuration. Simlet questions require you to answer multiple-choice questions by first using the CLI to issue **show** commands to look at the status of routers and switches in a small network.

To be ready for the exam, you need to know the following kinds of information:

CLI navigation: Basic CLI mechanics of moving into and out of user, enable, and configuration modes

Individual configuration: The meaning of the parameters of each configuration command

Feature configuration: The set of configuration commands, both required and optional, for each feature

Verification of configuration: The **show** commands that directly identify the configuration settings

Verification of status: The **show** commands that list current status values, and the ability to decide incorrect configuration or other problem causes of less-than-optimal status values

To help remember and review all this knowledge and skill, you can do the tasks listed in the next several pages.

Review Mind Maps from Part Review

During Part Review, you created different mind maps with both configuration and verification commands. To remember the specific mind maps, flip back to each part's Part Review section.

Do Labs

Whatever method you chose for building hands-on CLI skills, take some time to review and do some labs to practice the commands. At this point, you should have thought about configuration quite a bit, whether in a simulator, on real gear, or even just as paper exercises. While it might be impractical to repeat every lab, make it a point to practice any commands and features for which you feel a little unsure about the topics from your review of the mind maps.

First, make it a point to review labs for the major configuration topics in the chapter as listed in Table 29-3.

Table 29-3   Lab Topic Checklist

Topic	Chapter	Date You Finished Lab Review
VLANs	1	
VLAN trunking	1	
STP and RSTP	3	
Layer 2 EtherChannel, PortFast, and BPDU Guard	3	
VTP	5	
OSPFv2	8	
EIGRP	10	
eBGP	12	
PPP	13	
Multilink PPP	13	
PPPoE	15	
GRE Tunnels	15	
Standard ACLs	16	
Extended ACLs	17	

Topic	Chapter	Date You Finished Lab Review
Router on a Stick	19	
Layer 3 switching with SVIs	19	
Layer 3 switching with routed interfaces and L3 EtherChannels	19	
HSRP	20	
OSPF for IPv6	23	
EIGRP for IPv6	24	
IPv6 ACLs	25	
SNMPv2c and SNMPv3	26	
IP SLA Echo	26	
SPAN	26	

One great way to practice is to use the Pearson Network Simulator (the Sim) at http://www.pearsonitcertification.com/networksimulator.

Second, use the Config Checklist app available from the book DVD or companion website. Make sure you remember all the required and optional configuration commands. Third, you should be able to repeat any or all of the Config Labs found on my blog site. When you are truly prepared for the exam, you should be able to do these labs without much reference to your notes. The launch site for all CCNA (ICND2) Config Labs is http://blog.certskills.com/ccna. From there, navigate to the **Hands On > Config Lab** category from the site menus.

Assess Whether You Are Ready to Pass (and the Fallacy of Exam Scores)

When you take a practice exam with PCPT, PCPT gives you a score, on a scale from 300 to 1000. Why? Cisco gives a score of between 300 and 1000 as well. But the similarities end there.

With PCPT, the score is a basic percentage but expressed as a number from 0 to 1000. For example, answer 80 percent correct, and the score is 800; get 90 percent correct, and the score is 900. If you start a practice exam and click through it without answering a single question, you get a 0.

However, Cisco does not score exams in the same way. The following is what we do know about Cisco exam scoring:

■ Cisco uses a scoring scale from 300 to 1000.

■ Cisco tells us that it gives partial credit but provides no further details.

So, what does an 800 or a 900 mean on the actual Cisco exams? Many people think those scores mean 80 percent or 90 percent, but we don't know. Cisco doesn't reveal the details of scoring to us. It doesn't reveal the details of partial credit. It seems reasonable to expect a sim question to be worth more points than a multiple-choice, single-answer question, but we do not know.

The reason I mention all these facts to you is this:

> Do not rely too much on your PCPT practice exam scores to assess whether you are ready to pass. Those scores are a general indicator, in that if you make a 700 one time and a 900 a week later, you are probably now better prepared. But that 900 on your PCPT practice exam does not mean you will likely make a 900 on the actual exam—because we do not know how Cisco scores the exam.

So, what can you use as a way to assess whether you are ready to pass? Unfortunately, the answer requires some extra effort, and the answer will not be some nice, convenient number that looks like an exam score. But you can self-assess your skills as follows:

1. When you do take an exam with PCPT, you should understand the terms used in the questions and answers.

2. You should be able to look at the list of key topics from each chapter and explain a sentence or two about each topic to a friend.

3. You should be able to do subnetting math confidently with 100 percent accuracy at this point.

4. You should be able to do all the Config Labs, or labs of similar challenge level, and get them right consistently.

5. For chapters with **show** commands, you should understand the fields highlighted in gray in the examples spread about the book, and when looking at those examples, you should know which values show configuration settings and which show status information.

6. For the key topics that list various troubleshooting root causes, when you review those lists, you should remember and understand the concept behind each item in the list without needing to look further at the chapter.

Study Suggestions After Failing to Pass

None of us wants to take and fail any exam, but some of you will. And even if you pass the ICND2 200-105 or CCNA R&S 200-125 exam on your first try, if you keep going with Cisco certifications, you will probably fail some exams along the way. I mention failing an exam not to focus on the negative, but to help prepare you for how to pass the next attempt after failing an earlier attempt. This section collects some of the advice I have given to readers over the years who have contacted me after a failed attempt, asking for help about what to do next.

The single most important bit of advice is to change your mindset about Cisco exams. Cisco exams are not like high school or college exams where your failing grade matters. Instead, a Cisco exam is more like an event on the road to completing an impressive major accomplishment, one that most people have to try a few times to achieve.

For instance, achieving a Cisco certification is more like training to run a marathon in under 4 hours. The first time running a marathon, you may not even finish, or you may finish at 4:15 rather than under 4:00. But finishing a marathon in 4:15 means that you have prepared and are getting pretty close to your goal. Or maybe it is more like training to complete an obstacle course (for any *American Ninja Warrior* fans out there). Maybe you got past the first three obstacles today, but you couldn't climb over the 14-foot high warped wall. That just means you need to practice on that wall a little more.

So change your mindset. You're a marathon runner looking to improve your time or a Ninja Warrior looking to complete the obstacle course. And you are getting better skills every time you study, which helps you compete in the market.

With that attitude and analogy in mind, the rest of this section lists specific study steps that can help.

First, study the notes you took about your failed attempt. (See the earlier section "Reserve the Hour After the Exam in Case You Fail.") Do not share that information with others, but use it to study. Before you take the exam again, you should be able to answer every actual exam question you can remember from the last attempt. Even if you never see the exact same question again, you will still get a good return for your effort.

Second, spend more time on activities that uncover your weaknesses. When doing that, you have to slow down and be more self-aware. For instance, answer practice questions in study mode, and *do not guess*. Do not click on to the next question, but pause and ask yourself if you are really sure about both the wrong and correct answers. If unsure, fantastic! You just discovered a topic for which to go back and dig in to learn it more deeply. Or when you do a lab, you may refer to your notes without thinking, so now think about it when you turn to your notes because that tells you where you are unsure. That might be a reminder that you have not mastered those commands yet.

Third, think about your time spent on the exam. Did you run out of time? Go too fast? Too slow? If too slow, were you slow on subnetting, or sims, or something else? Then make a written plan as to how you will approach time on the next attempt and how you will track time use. And if you ran out of time, practice for the things that slowed you down.

Fourth, if you failed the CCNA R&S 200-125 exam, reconsider your choice for the one-exam path rather than the two-exam path. Think about the ICND1 topics on the CCNA exam. Did you know those pretty well? If so, you may be ready to pass ICND1 now. That's another step closer, and then you can focus on the ICND2 exam. (For perspective, the original *CCNA Official Cert Guide* was 500 pages long. The combined ICND1 and ICND2 books have grown to over 1,600 pages of technology chapters, for three times as much content as the original CCNA exam. It's just a lot of content.)

Other Study Tasks

If you got to this point and still feel the need to prepare some more, this last topic gives you three suggestions.

First, the Chapter Review and Part Review sections give you some useful study tasks.

Second, use more exam questions from other sources. You can always get more questions in the Cisco Press Premium Edition eBook and Practice Test products, which include an eBook copy of this book plus additional questions in additional PCPT exam banks. However, you can search the Internet for questions from many sources and review those questions as well.

NOTE   Some vendors claim to sell practice exams that contain the literal exam questions from the official exam. These exams, called "brain dumps," are against the Cisco testing policies. Cisco strongly discourages using any such tools for study.

Finally, join in the discussions on the Cisco Learning Network. Try to answer questions asked by other learners; the process of answering makes you think much harder about the topic. When someone posts an answer with which you disagree, think about why and talk about it online. This is a great way to both learn more and build confidence.

Final Thoughts

You have studied quite a bit, worked hard, and sacrificed time and money to be ready for the exam. I hope your exam goes well, that you pass, and that you pass because you really know your stuff and will do well in your IT and networking career.

I encourage you to celebrate when you pass and ask advice when you do not. The Cisco Learning Network is a great place to make posts to celebrate and to ask advice for the next time around. I personally would love to hear about your progress through Twitter (@wendellodom) or my Facebook page (https://www.facebook.com/wendellodom). I wish you well, and congratulations for working through the entire book!

29

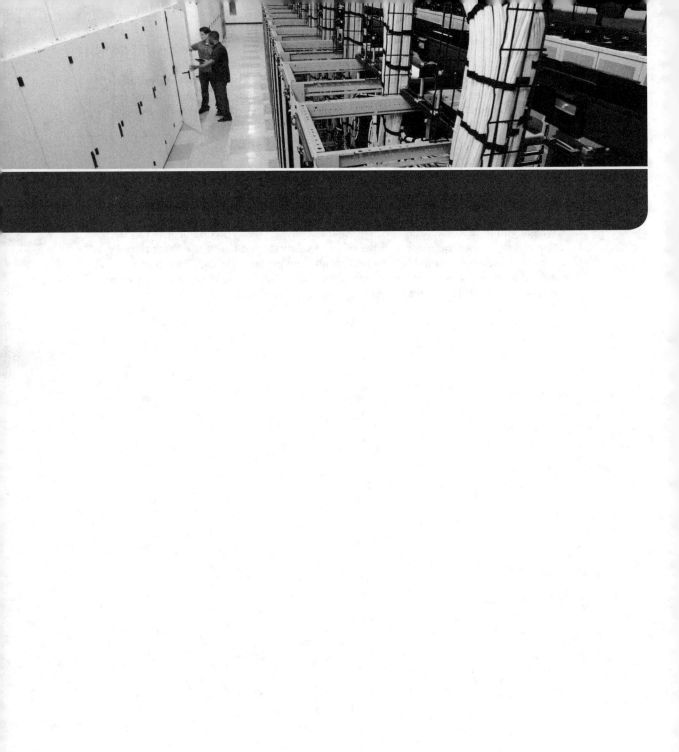

Part IX

Appendixes

Appendix A: Numeric Reference Tables

Appendix B: CCNA ICND2 200-105 Exam Updates

Glossary

Numeric Reference Tables

This appendix provides several useful reference tables that list numbers used throughout this book. Specifically:

Table A-1: A decimal-binary cross reference, useful when converting from decimal to binary and vice versa.

Table A-1   Decimal-Binary Cross Reference, Decimal Values 0–255

Decimal Value	Binary Value	Decimal Value	Binary Value	Decimal Value	Binary Value	Decimal Value	Binary Value
0	00000000	32	00100000	64	01000000	96	01100000
1	00000001	33	00100001	65	01000001	97	01100001
2	00000010	34	00100010	66	01000010	98	01100010
3	00000011	35	00100011	67	01000011	99	01100011
4	00000100	36	00100100	68	01000100	100	01100100
5	00000101	37	00100101	69	01000101	101	01100101
6	00000110	38	00100110	70	01000110	102	01100110
7	00000111	39	00100111	71	01000111	103	01100111
8	00001000	40	00101000	72	01001000	104	01101000
9	00001001	41	00101001	73	01001001	105	01101001
10	00001010	42	00101010	74	01001010	106	01101010
11	00001011	43	00101011	75	01001011	107	01101011
12	00001100	44	00101100	76	01001100	108	01101100
13	00001101	45	00101101	77	01001101	109	01101101
14	00001110	46	00101110	78	01001110	110	01101110
15	00001111	47	00101111	79	01001111	111	01101111
16	00010000	48	00110000	80	01010000	112	01110000
17	00010001	49	00110001	81	01010001	113	01110001
18	00010010	50	00110010	82	01010010	114	01110010
19	00010011	51	00110011	83	01010011	115	01110011
20	00010100	52	00110100	84	01010100	116	01110100
21	00010101	53	00110101	85	01010101	117	01110101
22	00010110	54	00110110	86	01010110	118	01110110
23	00010111	55	00110111	87	01010111	119	01110111
24	00011000	56	00111000	88	01011000	120	01111000
25	00011001	57	00111001	89	01011001	121	01111001
26	00011010	58	00111010	90	01011010	122	01111010
27	00011011	59	00111011	91	01011011	123	01111011
28	00011100	60	00111100	92	01011100	124	01111100
29	00011101	61	00111101	93	01011101	125	01111101
30	00011110	62	00111110	94	01011110	126	01111110
31	00011111	63	00111111	95	01011111	127	01111111

Decimal Value	Binary Value	Decimal Value	Binary Value	Decimal Value	Binary Value	Decimal Value	Binary Value
128	10000000	160	10100000	192	11000000	224	11100000
129	10000001	161	10100001	193	11000001	225	11100001
130	10000010	162	10100010	194	11000010	226	11100010
131	10000011	163	10100011	195	11000011	227	11100011
132	10000100	164	10100100	196	11000100	228	11100100
133	10000101	165	10100101	197	11000101	229	11100101
134	10000110	166	10100110	198	11000110	230	11100110
135	10000111	167	10100111	199	11000111	231	11100111
136	10001000	168	10101000	200	11001000	232	11101000
137	10001001	169	10101001	201	11001001	233	11101001
138	10001010	170	10101010	202	11001010	234	11101010
139	10001011	171	10101011	203	11001011	235	11101011
140	10001100	172	10101100	204	11001100	236	11101100
141	10001101	173	10101101	205	11001101	237	11101101
142	10001110	174	10101110	206	11001110	238	11101110
143	10001111	175	10101111	207	11001111	239	11101111
144	10010000	176	10110000	208	11010000	240	11110000
145	10010001	177	10110001	209	11010001	241	11110001
146	10010010	178	10110010	210	11010010	242	11110010
147	10010011	179	10110011	211	11010011	243	11110011
148	10010100	180	10110100	212	11010100	244	11110100
149	10010101	181	10110101	213	11010101	245	11110101
150	10010110	182	10110110	214	11010110	246	11110110
151	10010111	183	10110111	215	11010111	247	11110111
152	10011000	184	10111000	216	11011000	248	11111000
153	10011001	185	10111001	217	11011001	249	11111001
154	10011010	186	10111010	218	11011010	250	11111010
155	10011011	187	10111011	219	11011011	251	11111011
156	10011100	188	10111100	220	11011100	252	11111100
157	10011101	189	10111101	221	11011101	253	11111101
158	10011110	190	10111110	222	11011110	254	11111110
159	10011111	191	10111111	223	11011111	255	11111111

A

Table A-2: A hexadecimal-binary cross reference, useful when converting from hex to binary and vice versa.

Table A-2   Hex-Binary Cross Reference

Hex	4-Bit Binary
0	0000
1	0001
2	0010
3	0011
4	0100
5	0101
6	0110
7	0111
8	1000
9	1001
A	1010
B	1011
C	1100
D	1101
E	1110
F	1111

Table A-3: Powers of 2, from 2^1 through 2^{32}.

Table A-3   Powers of 2

X	2^X	X	2^X
1	2	17	131,072
2	4	18	262,144
3	8	19	524,288
4	16	20	1,048,576
5	32	21	2,097,152
6	64	22	4,194,304
7	128	23	8,388,608
8	256	24	16,777,216
9	512	25	33,554,432
10	1024	26	67,108,864
11	2048	27	134,217,728
12	4096	28	268,435,456
13	8192	29	536,870,912
14	16,384	30	1,073,741,824
15	32,768	31	2,147,483,648
16	65,536	32	4,294,967,296

A

Table A-4: Table of all 33 possible subnet masks, in all three formats.

Table A-4 All Subnet Masks

Decimal	Prefix	Binary			
0.0.0.0	/0	00000000	00000000	00000000	00000000
128.0.0.0	/1	10000000	00000000	00000000	00000000
192.0.0.0	/2	11000000	00000000	00000000	00000000
224.0.0.0	/3	11100000	00000000	00000000	00000000
240.0.0.0	/4	11110000	00000000	00000000	00000000
248.0.0.0	/5	11111000	00000000	00000000	00000000
252.0.0.0	/6	11111100	00000000	00000000	00000000
254.0.0.0	/7	11111110	00000000	00000000	00000000
255.0.0.0	/8	11111111	00000000	00000000	00000000
255.128.0.0	/9	11111111	10000000	00000000	00000000
255.192.0.0	/10	11111111	11000000	00000000	00000000
255.224.0.0	/11	11111111	11100000	00000000	00000000
255.240.0.0	/12	11111111	11110000	00000000	00000000
255.248.0.0	/13	11111111	11111000	00000000	00000000
255.252.0.0	/14	11111111	11111100	00000000	00000000
255.254.0.0	/15	11111111	11111110	00000000	00000000
255.255.0.0	/16	11111111	11111111	00000000	00000000
255.255.128.0	/17	11111111	11111111	10000000	00000000
255.255.192.0	/18	11111111	11111111	11000000	00000000
255.255.224.0	/19	11111111	11111111	11100000	00000000
255.255.240.0	/20	11111111	11111111	11110000	00000000
255.255.248.0	/21	11111111	11111111	11111000	00000000
255.255.252.0	/22	11111111	11111111	11111100	00000000
255.255.254.0	/23	11111111	11111111	11111110	00000000
255.255.255.0	/24	11111111	11111111	11111111	00000000
255.255.255.128	/25	11111111	11111111	11111111	10000000
255.255.255.192	/26	11111111	11111111	11111111	11000000
255.255.255.224	/27	11111111	11111111	11111111	11100000
255.255.255.240	/28	11111111	11111111	11111111	11110000
255.255.255.248	/29	11111111	11111111	11111111	11111000
255.255.255.252	/30	11111111	11111111	11111111	11111100
255.255.255.254	/31	11111111	11111111	11111111	11111110
255.255.255.255	/32	11111111	11111111	11111111	11111111

CCNA ICND2 200-105 Exam Updates

Over time, reader feedback allows Pearson to gauge which topics give our readers the most problems when taking the exams. To assist readers with those topics, the authors create new materials clarifying and expanding on those troublesome exam topics. As mentioned in the Introduction, the additional content about the exam is contained in a PDF on this book's companion website, at http://www.ciscopress.com/title/9781587205798.

This appendix is intended to provide you with updated information if Cisco makes minor modifications to the exam upon which this book is based. When Cisco releases an entirely new exam, the changes are usually too extensive to provide in a simple update appendix. In those cases, you might need to consult the new edition of the book for the updated content.

This appendix attempts to fill the void that occurs with any print book. In particular, this appendix does the following:

- Mentions technical items that might not have been mentioned elsewhere in the book
- Covers new topics if Cisco adds new content to the exam over time
- Provides a way to get up-to-the-minute current information about content for the exam

Always Get the Latest at the Book's Product Page

You are reading the version of this appendix that was available when your book was printed. However, given that the main purpose of this appendix is to be a living, changing document, it is important that you look for the latest version online at the book's companion website. To do so, follow these steps:

Step 1. Browse to www.ciscopress.com/title/9781587205798.

Step 2. Click the **Updates** tab.

Step 3. If there is a new Appendix B document on the page, download the latest Appendix B document.

NOTE   The downloaded document has a version number. Comparing the version of the print Appendix B (Version 1.0) with the latest online version of this appendix, you should do the following:

- **Same version:** Ignore the PDF that you downloaded from the companion website.

- **Website has a later version:** Ignore this Appendix B in your book and read only the latest version that you downloaded from the companion website.

Technical Content

The current Version 1.0 of this appendix does not contain additional technical coverage.

B

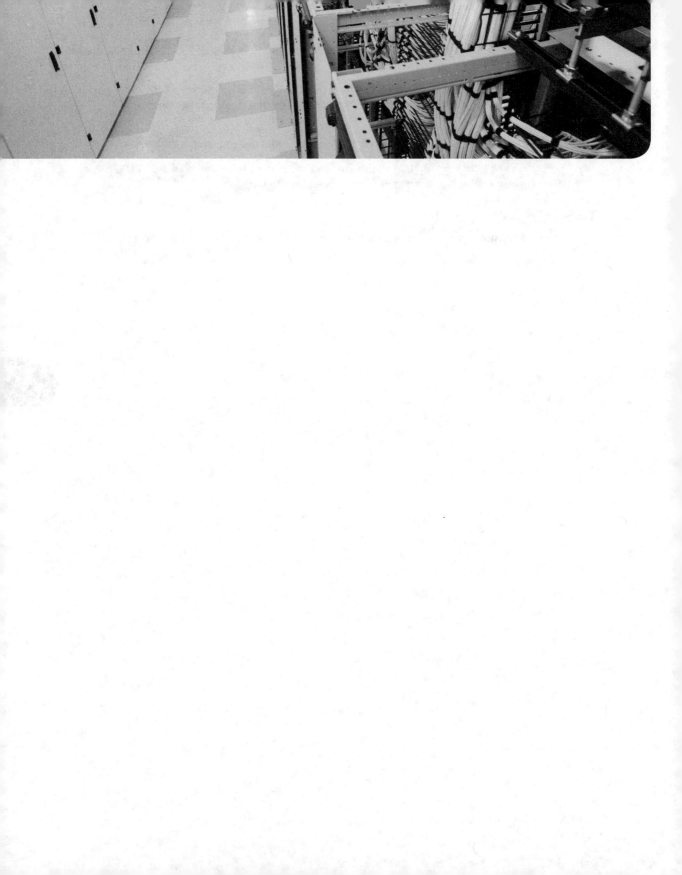

GLOSSARY

2-way state In OSPF, a neighbor state that implies that the router has exchanged Hellos with the neighbor and that all required parameters match.

3G/4G Internet An Internet access technology that uses wireless radio signals to communicate through mobile phone towers, most often used by mobile phones, tablets, and some other mobile devices.

802.1Q The IEEE standardized protocol for VLAN trunking.

A

AAA server *See* authentication, authorization, and accounting (AAA) server.

ABR Area Border Router. A router using OSPF in which the router has interfaces in multiple OSPF areas.

access interface A LAN network design term that refers to a switch interface connected to end-user devices, configured so that it does not use VLAN trunking.

access link (WAN) A physical link between a service provider and its customer that provides access to the SP's network from that customer site.

access rate The speed at which bits are sent over an access link.

ACI *See* Application Centric Infrastructure.

ACL Access control list. A list configured on a router to control packet flow through the router, such as to prevent packets with a certain IP address from leaving a particular interface on the router.

adjacency table In Cisco IOS CEF, a table that keeps a copy of the outgoing data link headers that a router will then add to a packet before forwarding the packet, for the purpose of reducing the per-packet processing done by the router.

administrative distance In Cisco routers, a means for one router to choose between multiple routes to reach the same subnet when those routes are learned by different routing protocols. The lower the administrative distance, the more preferred the source of the routing information.

administrative mode *See* trunking administrative mode.

ADSL Asymmetric digital subscriber line. One of many DSL technologies, ADSL is designed to deliver more bandwidth downstream (from the central office to the customer site) than upstream.

alternate port With 802.1w RSTP, a port role in which the port acts as an alternative to a switch's root port, so that when the switch's root port fails, the alternate port can immediately take over as the root port.

analog modem *See* modem.

anti-replay   Preventing a man in the middle from copying and later replying the packets sent by a legitimate user, for the purpose of appearing to be a legitimate user.

APIC   *See* Application Policy Infrastructure Controller.

APIC-EM   *See* Application Policy Infrastructure Controller – Enterprise Module.

Application Centric Infrastructure (ACI)   Cisco's data center SDN solution, the concepts of defining policies that the APIC controller then pushes to the switches in the network using the OpFlex protocol, with the partially distributed control plane in each switch building the forwarding table entries to support the policies learned from the controller. It also supports a GUI, a CLI, and APIs.

Application Policy Infrastructure Controller (APIC)   The software that plays the role of controller, controlling the flows that the switches create to define where frames are forwarded, in a Cisco data center that uses the Application Centric Infrastructure (ACI) approach, switches, and software.

Application Policy Infrastructure Controller – Enterprise Module (APIC-EM)   The software that plays the role of controller in an enterprise network of Cisco devices, in its first version as of the publication of this book, which leaves the distributed routing and switching control plane as is, instead acting as a management and automation platform. It provides robust APIs for network automation, and uses CLI (Telnet and SSH) plus SNMP southbound to control the existing routers and switches in an enterprise network.

application programming interface (API)   A software mechanism that enables software components to communicate with each other.

application signature   With Network Based Application Recognition (NBAR), the definition of a combination of matchable fields that Cisco has identified as being characteristic of a specific application, so that NBAR can be configured by the customer to match an application, while IOS then defines the particulars of that matching.

application-specific integrated circuit (ASIC)   An integrated circuit (computer chip) designed for a specific purpose or application, often used to implement the functions of a networking device rather than running a software process as part of the device's OS that runs on a general-purpose processor.

AR   *See* access rate.

Area Border Router   *See* ABR.

ARP   Address Resolution Protocol. An Internet protocol used to map an IP address to a MAC address. Defined in RFC 826.

AS_Path   A BGP path attribute that lists the ASNs in the path (other than the ASN of the router on which the AS_Path is examined).

ASAv   A Cisco ASA firewall software image that runs as a virtual machine rather than on Cisco hardware, intended to be used as a consumer-controlled firewall in a cloud service or in other virtualized environments.

ASBR   Autonomous System Border Router. A router using OSPF in which the router learns routes via another source, usually another routing protocol, exchanging routes that are external to OSPF with the OSPF domain.

ASIC   *See* application-specific integrated circuit.

Assured Forwarding (AF)   The name of a grid of 12 DSCP values, and a matching grid of per-hop behavior as defined by DiffServ. AF defines four queuing classes, and three packet drop priorities within each queuing class. The text names of the 12 DSCP values follow a format of AFXY, where X is the queuing class, and Y is the drop priority.

authentication   The ability to verify the identity of a user or a computer system on a computer network.

authentication, authorization, and accounting (AAA) server   A server that holds security information and provides services related to user login, particularly authentication (is the user who they say they are), authorization (once authenticated, what do we allow the user to do), and accounting (tracking the user).

authenticator   With IEEE 802.1x, the LAN switch that uses EAPoL to ask for the identification from the supplicant (the end-user device), and then passes the EAP messages to a AAA server to authenticate the user.

autonomous system (AS)   An internetwork that is managed by one organization.

Autonomous System Border Router   *See* ASBR.

autonomous system number (ASN)   A number used by BGP to identify a routing domain, often a single enterprise or organization. As used with EIGRP, a number that identifies the routing processes on routers that are willing to exchange EIGRP routing information with each other.

AutoQoS   In Cisco switches and routers, an IOS feature that configures a variety of QoS features with useful settings as defined by the Cisco reference design guide documents.

autosummarization   A routing protocol feature in which a router that connects to more than one classful network advertises summarized routes for each entire classful network when sending updates out interfaces connected to other classful networks.

autosummary   *See* autosummarization.

B

backbone area   In OSPFv2 and OSPFv3, the special area in a multiarea design, with all non-backbone areas needing to connect to the backbone area, area 0.

backup designated router   An OSPF router connected to a multiaccess network that monitors the work of the designated router (DR) and takes over the work of the DR if the DR fails.

backup port   With 802.1w RSTP, a port role in which the port acts as a backup to one of the switch's ports acting as a designated port. If the switch's designated port fails, the switch will use the backup port to immediately take over as the designated port.

balanced hybrid   A term that, over the years, has been used to refer to the logic behind the EIGRP routing protocol. More commonly today, this logic is referred to as advanced distance vector logic.

bandwidth   The speed at which bits can be sent and received over a link.

bandwidth profile   In Metro Ethernet, a contractual definition of the amount of traffic that the customer can send into the service, and receive out of the service. Includes a concept called the committed information rate (CIR), which defines the minimum amount of bandwidth (bits/second) the SP will deliver with the service.

best path selection   The BGP process of choosing the best route by working through an ordered list of comparisons of different BGP path attributes.

BGP neighbor   Another term for BGP peer. A reference to another router with which a router has formed a BGP neighbor or peer relationship.

BGP peer   Another term for BGP neighbor. A reference to another router with which a router has formed a BGP neighbor or peer relationship.

BGP table   The table in each router, maintained by the BGP process, that holds prefixes and path attributes known to BGP.

BGP update   The BGP message that lists BGP path attributes and prefixes.

BGP update source   When running BGP in a router, the interface IP address used to form the TCP connection for the BGP peer relationship with another router.

blocking state   In 802.1D STP, a port state in which no received frames are processed and the switch forwards no frames out the interface, with the exception of STP messages.

boot field   The low-order 4 bits of the configuration register in a Cisco router. The value in the boot field in part tells the router where to look for a Cisco IOS image to load.

Border Gateway Protocol (BGP)   An exterior routing protocol, used today as the primary routing protocol to exchange routes in the Internet.

BPDU   Bridge protocol data unit. The generic name for Spanning Tree Protocol messages.

BPDU Guard   A Cisco switch feature that listens for incoming STP BPDU messages, disabling the interface if any are received. The goal is to prevent loops when a switch connects to a port expected to only have a host connected to it.

bridge ID (BID)   An 8-byte identifier for bridges and switches used by STP and RSTP. It is composed of a 2-byte priority field followed by a 6-byte System ID field that is usually filled with a MAC address.

bridge protocol data unit   *See* BPDU.

broadcast address   Generally, any address that represents all devices, and can be used to send one message to all devices. In Ethernet, the MAC address of all binary 1s, or FFFF.FFFF.FFFF in hex. For IPv4, *see* subnet broadcast address.

broadcast domain   A set of all devices that receive broadcast frames originating from any device in the set. Devices in the same VLAN are in the same broadcast domain.

broadcast subnet   When subnetting a Class A, B, or C network, the one subnet in each classful network for which all subnet bits have a value of binary 1. The subnet broadcast address in this subnet has the same numeric value as the classful network's networkwide broadcast address.

C

cable Internet   An Internet access technology that uses a cable TV (CATV) cable, normally used for video, to send and receive data.

carrier Ethernet   Per MEF documents, the term for what was formerly called Metro Ethernet, generally referring to any WAN service that uses Ethernet links as the access link between the customer and the service provider.

central office (CO)   A term used by telcos to refer to a building that holds switching equipment, into which the telco's cable plant runs, so that the telco has cabling from each home and business into that building.

centralized control plane   An approach to architecting network protocols and products that places the control plane functions into a centralized function rather than distributing the function across the networking devices.

Channel-group   One term Cisco switches use to reference a bundle of links that are, in some respects, treated like a single link. Other similar terms include EtherChannel and PortChannel.

CHAP   Challenge Handshake Authentication Protocol. A security feature defined by PPP that allows either or both endpoints on a link to authenticate the other device as a particular authorized device.

chassis aggregation   A Cisco technology used to combine two distribution or core switches together to act as one, sharing the data plane functions across both switches (called active/active), and centralizing control plane functions on one switch (called active/standby).

CIDR   Classless interdomain routing. An RFC-standard tool for global IP address range assignment. CIDR reduces the size of Internet routers' IP routing tables, helping deal with the rapid growth of the Internet. The term *classless* refers to the fact that the summarized groups of networks represent a group of addresses that do not confirm to IPv4 classful (Class A, B, and C) grouping rules.

CIDR notation   *See* prefix notation.

circuit switching   The switching system in which a dedicated physical circuit path must exist between the sender and the receiver for the duration of the "call." Used heavily in the telephone company network.

Cisco Access Control Server (ACS)   A Cisco product that acts as a AAA server.

Cisco AnyConnect Secure Mobility Client   Cisco software product used as client software on user devices to create a client VPN. Commonly referred to as the Cisco VPN client.

Cisco Express Forwarding (CEF)   A long-time Cisco IOS internal feature that optimizes the forwarding process by creating a more search-efficient forwarding information base (FIB) that is used instead of the IP routing table, along with an adjacency table that caches the new data link headers used to reach the next-hop addresses.

Cisco Intercloud Fabric   Cisco software that provides a variety of functions to help companies connect to different cloud services and to aid the management of and migration between different public cloud services.

Cisco Open SDN Controller (OSC)   A commercial SDN controller from Cisco that is based on the OpenDaylight controller.

Cisco Prime   Graphical user interface (GUI) software that utilizes SNMP and can be used to manage your Cisco network devices. The term *Cisco Prime* is an "umbrella" term that encompasses many different individual software products.

Cisco VPN client   *See* Cisco AnyConnect Secure Mobility Client.

Class of Service (CoS)   The informal term for the 3-bit field in the 802.1Q header intended for marking and classifying Ethernet frames for the purposes of applying QoS actions. Another term for Priority Code Point (PCP).

Class Selector (CS)   The name of eight DSCP values that all end with binary 000, for the purpose of having eight identifiable DSCP values whose first 3 bits match the eight values used for the older IP Precedence field. Originally used for backward compatibility with IP Precedence, but today the values are often used as just more values to use for packet marking.

classful addressing   A concept in IPv4 addressing that defines a subnetted IP address as having three parts: network, subnet, and host.

classful network   An IPv4 Class A, B, or C network. It is called a classful network because these networks are defined by the class rules for IPv4 addressing.

classful routing protocol   An inherent characteristic of a routing protocol. Specifically, the routing protocol does not send subnet masks in its routing updates. This requires the protocol to make assumptions about classful networks and makes it unable to support VLSM and manual route summarization.

classification   The process of examining various fields in networking messages in an effort to identify which messages fit into certain predetermined groups (classes).

classless addressing   A concept in IPv4 addressing that defines a subnetted IP address as having two parts: a prefix (or subnet) and a host.

classless interdomain routing (CIDR)   *See* CIDR.

classless routing   A variation of the IPv4 forwarding (routing) process that defines the particulars of how the default route is used. The default route is always used for packets whose destination IP address does not match any other routes.

classless routing protocol   An inherent characteristic of a routing protocol. Specifically, the routing protocol sends subnet masks in its routing updates, thereby removing any need to make assumptions about the addresses in a particular subnet or network. This allows the protocol to support VLSM and manual route summarization.

client VPN   A VPN for which one endpoint is a user device, like a phone, tablet, or PC.

clock rate   The speed at which a serial link encodes bits on the transmission medium.

clock source   The device to which the other devices on the link adjust their speed when using synchronous links.

clocking   The process of supplying a signal over a cable, either on a separate pin on a serial cable or as part of the signal transitions in the transmitted signal, so that the receiving device can keep synchronization with the sending device.

cloud services catalog   A listing of the services available in a cloud computing service.

Cloud Services Router (CSR)   A Cisco router software image that runs as a virtual machine rather than on Cisco hardware, intended to be used as a consumer-controlled router in a cloud service or in other virtualized environments.

committed information rate (CIR)   In carrier/Metro Ethernet, the concept of the committed amount of bandwidth (typically measured in bits/second) that the SP commits to deliver over a particular EVC; the SP may deliver more bits/second than the CIR, but it commits to the amount defined by the CIR.

composite metric   A term in EIGRP for the result of the calculation of the EIGRP metric for a route.

confidentiality (privacy)   Preventing anyone in the middle of the Internet (a.k.a. man in the middle) from being able to read the data.

configuration revision number   A number used by VTP that identifies the version of the VLAN configuration database. Each time the configuration database changes, a switch increments the configuration revision number by 1.

congestion window   With TCP, a calculation each TCP receiver does that limits the window it grants to the receiver by shrinking the window in response to the loss of TCP segments.

console port   A physical socket on a router or switch to which a cable can be connected between a computer and the router/switch, for the purpose of allowing the computer to use a terminal emulator and use the CLI to configure, verify, and troubleshoot the router/switch.

contiguous network   In IPv4, an internetwork design in which packets being forwarded between any two subnets of a single classful network only pass through the subnets of that classful network.

control plane   Functions in networking devices and controllers that directly control how devices perform data plane forwarding, but excluding the data plane processes that work to forward each message in the network.

convergence   The time required for routing protocols to react to changes in the network, removing bad routes and adding new, better routes so that the current best routes are in all the routers' routing tables.

core   In computer architecture, an individual processing unit that can execute instructions of a CPU; modern server processors typically have multiple cores, each capable of concurrent execution of instructions.

CSU/DSU   Channel service unit/data service unit. A device that connects a physical circuit installed by the telco to some CPE device, adapting between the voltages, current, framing, and connectors used on the circuit to the physical interface supported by the DTE.

customer edge (CE)   A term used by service providers, both generally and also specifically in MPLS VPN networks, to refer to the customer device that connects to the SP's network, and therefore sits at the edge of the SP's network.

customer premises equipment (CPE)   A telco term that refers to equipment on-site at the telco customer site (the enterprise's site) that connects to the WAN service provided by the telco.

D

data integrity   Verifying that the packet was not changed as the packet transited the Internet.

data link connection identifier (DLCI)   The Frame Relay address that identifies a VC on a particular access link.

data plane   Functions in networking devices that are part of the process of receiving a message, processing the message, and forwarding the message.

data VLAN   A VLAN used by typical data devices connected to an Ethernet, such as PCs and servers. Used in comparison to a Voice VLAN.

Database Description   An OSPF packet type that lists brief descriptions of the LSAs in the OSPF LSDB.

DCE   Data circuit-terminating equipment. Also refers to data communications equipment. From a physical layer perspective, the device providing the clocking on a WAN link, usually a CSU/DSU, is the DCE. From a packet-switching perspective, the service provider's switch, to which a router might connect, is considered the DCE.

Dead Interval   In OSPF, a timer used for each neighbor. A router considers the neighbor to have failed if no Hellos are received from that neighbor in the time defined by the timer.

decrypt/decryption   The ability to receive encrypted data and process it to derive the original unencrypted data.

deencapsulation   On a computer that receives data over a network, the process in which the device interprets the lower-layer headers and, when finished with each header, removes the header, revealing the next-higher-layer PDU.

default gateway/default router   On an IP host, the IP address of some router to which the host sends packets when the packet's destination address is on a subnet other than the local subnet.

delay   In QoS, the amount of time it takes for a message to cross a network. Delay can refer to one-way delay (the time required for the message to be sent from the source host to the destination host) or two-way delay (the delay from the source to the destination host and then back again).

delivery header   GRE term to refer to the outer unencrypted IP header used to encapsulate the data (often an encrypted payload packet).

demilitarized Zone (DMZ)   In an Internet edge design at an enterprise, one or more subnets set aside as a place to locate servers that should allow users in the Internet to initiate connections to those servers. The devices in the DMZ typically sit behind a firewall.

denial of service (DoS)   Any type of attack in which the attack causes harm by denying the normal use of the network to legitimate users.

deny   An action taken with an ACL that implies that the packet is discarded.

designated port   In both STP and RSTP, a port role used to determine which of multiple interfaces on multiple switches, each connected to the same segment or collision domain, should forward frames to the segment. The switch advertising the lowest-cost Hello BPDU onto the segment becomes the DP.

designated router   In OSPF, on a multiaccess network, the router that wins an election and is therefore responsible for managing a streamlined process for exchanging OSPF topology information between all routers attached to that network.

DevNet   Cisco's community and resource site for software developers, open to all, with many great learning resources; https://developer.cisco.com.

DHCP attack   Any attack that takes advantage of DHCP protocol messages.

DHCP Binding Table   A table built by the DHCP snooping feature on a switch when it sees messages about a new DHCP lease, with the table holding information about legitimate successful DHCP leases, including the device's IP address, MAC address, switch port, and VLAN.

DHCP snooping   A switch security feature in which the switch examines incoming DHCP messages, and chooses to filter messages that are abnormal and therefore might be part of a DHCP attack.

dial access   A general term referring to any kind of switched WAN service that uses the telco network in which the device must signal (the equivalent of tapping digits on a phone) to establish a connection before sending data.

dial pool   An IOS configuration concept for some interface-related resources that can be used and then released. For PPPoE, it is used to associate the dialer interface with the physical Ethernet interface.

dialer interface   A virtual interface inside a Cisco router, used for a variety of purposes, including for PPPoE to act as the Layer 3 interface, and to hold the PPP configuration used as a template by IOS to create an associated virtual-access interface.

Differentiated Services (DiffServ)   An approach to QoS, originally defined in RFC 2475, that uses a model of applying QoS per classification, with planning of which applications and other traffic types are assigned to each class, with each class given different QoS per-hop behaviors at each networking device in the path.

Differentiated Services Code Point (DSCP)   A field existing as the first 6 bits of the ToS byte, as defined by RFC 2474, which redefined the original IP RFC's definition for the IP header ToS byte. The field is used to mark a value in the header for the purpose of performing later QoS actions on the packet.

Diffusing Update Algorithm (DUAL)   A convergence algorithm used in EIGRP when a route fails and a router does not have a feasible successor route. DUAL causes the routers to send EIGRP Query and Reply messages to discover alternate loop-free routes.

Digital Subscriber Line (DSL)   A public network technology that delivers high bandwidth over conventional telco local-loop copper wiring at limited distances. Typically used as an Internet access technology, connecting a user to an ISP.

Dijkstra Shortest Path First (SPF) algorithm   The name of the algorithm used by link-state routing protocols to analyze the LSDB and find the least-cost routes from that router to each subnet.

disabled port   In STP, a port role for nonworking interfaces—in other words, interfaces that are not in a connect or up/up interface state.

discard route   A static route with an outgoing interface of null0, which causes a router to discard packets that, when forwarded, happen to match that route.

discarding state   An RSTP interface state in which no received frames are processed and the switch forwards no frames out the interface, with the exception of RSTP messages.

discontiguous network   In IPv4, an internetwork design in which packets being forwarded between two subnets of a single classful network must pass through the subnets of another classful network.

distance vector   The logic behind the behavior of some interior routing protocols, such as RIP and IGRP. Distance vector routing algorithms call for each router to send its entire routing table in each update, but only to its neighbors. Distance vector routing algorithms can be prone to routing loops but are computationally simpler than link-state routing algorithms. Also called Bellman-Ford routing algorithm.

distributed control plane   An approach to architecting network protocols and products that places some control plane functions into each networking device rather than centralizing the control plane functions in one or a few devices. An example is the use of routing protocols on each router which then work together so that each router learns Layer 3 routes.

DNS   Domain Name System. An application layer protocol used throughout the Internet for translating hostnames into their associated IP addresses.

DS0   Digital signal level 0. A 64-Kbps line or channel of a faster line inside a telco whose origins are to support a single voice call using the original voice (PCM) codecs.

DS1   Digital signal level 1. A 1.544-Mbps line from the telco, with 24 DS0 channels of 64 Kbps each, plus an 8-Kbps management and framing channel. Also called a T1.

DS3   Digital signal level 3. A 44.736-Mbps line from the telco, with 28 DS1 channels plus overhead. Also called a T3.

DSL modem   A device that connects to a telephone line and uses DSL standards to transmit and receive data to/from a telco using DSL.

DSL   Digital subscriber line. Public network technology that delivers high bandwidth over conventional telco local-loop copper wiring at limited distances. Usually used as an Internet access technology connecting a user to an ISP.

DTE   Data terminal equipment. From a Layer 1 perspective, the DTE synchronizes its clock based on the clock sent by the DCE. From a packet-switching perspective, the DTE is the device outside the service provider's network, usually a router.

dual homed   One design of the Internet edge in which the enterprise connects to one ISP, but with two or more links to that one ISP.

dual multihomed   One design of the Internet edge in which the enterprise connects to two or more ISPs, and with two or more links to each ISP.

dual stack   In IPv6, a mode of operation in which a host or router runs both IPv4 and IPv6.

DUAL   *See* Diffusing Update Algorithm.

Dynamic Multipoint VPN (DMVPN)   A Cisco router feature that dynamically creates GRE tunnels between routers, using a multipoint GRE tunnel to create a multipoint topology, and using the Next Hop Resolution Protocol (NHRP) to dynamically discover other routers.

E

EAP over LAN (EAPoL)   The protocol details for how to deliver EAP messages over a LAN using Ethernet encapsulation; that is, with the EAP message directly encapsulated inside an Ethernet frame.

eBGP multihop   A configuration feature that enables the router to set the TTL for packets sent by BGP for eBGP connections to some value other than 1 (the normal value), so that the packets are delivered to the peer without being discarded.

EIGRP   Enhanced Interior Gateway Routing Protocol. An advanced version of IGRP developed by Cisco. Provides superior convergence properties and operating efficiency and combines the advantages of link-state protocols with those of distance vector protocols.

EIGRP for IPv4 classic mode   The traditional method to configure EIGRP for IPv4, which enables EIGRP on interfaces indirectly using the **network** command in EIGRP router configuration mode.

EIGRP for IPv4 named mode   The newer method to configure EIGRP for IPv4 as compared to classic mode, which enables EIGRP on interfaces directly with interface subcommands, and uses address families within EIGRP router configuration mode.

EIGRP for IPv6   A version of EIGRP that supports advertising routes for IPv6 prefixes instead of IPv4 subnets.

E-LAN   A specific carrier/Metro Ethernet service defined by MEF (MEF.net) that provides a service much like a LAN, with two or more customer sites connected to one E-LAN service in a full mesh, so that each device in the E-LAN can send Ethernet frames directly to every other device.

E-Line   A specific carrier/metro Ethernet service defined by MEF (MEF.net) that provides a point-to-point topology between two customer devices, much as if the two devices were connected using an Ethernet crossover cable.

enable mode   A part of the Cisco IOS CLI in which the user can use potentially disruptive commands on a router or switch, including the ability to then reach configuration mode and reconfigure the router.

encapsulation   The placement of data from a higher-layer protocol behind the header (and in some cases, between a header and trailer) of the next-lower-layer protocol. For example, an IP packet could be encapsulated in an Ethernet header and trailer before being sent over an Ethernet.

encoding   The conventions for how a device varies the electrical or optical signals sent over a cable to imply a particular binary code. For instance, a modem might encode a binary 1 or 0 by using one frequency to mean 1 and another to mean 0.

encrypt/encryption   The ability to take data and send the data in a form that is not readable by someone who intercepts this data.

encryption key   A secret value used as input to the math formulas used by an encryption process.

End of Row (EoR) switch   In a traditional data center design with servers in multiple racks, and the racks in multiple rows, a switch placed in a rack at the end of the row, intended to be cabled to all the Top of Rack (ToR) switches in the same row, to act as a distribution layer switch for the switches in that row.

EtherChannel   A feature in which up to eight parallel Ethernet segments exist between the same two devices, each using the same speed. May be a Layer 2 EtherChannel, which acts like a single link for forwarding and Spanning Tree Protocol logic, or a Layer 3 EtherChannel, which acts like a single link for the switch's Layer 3 routing logic.

Ethernet access link   A WAN access link (a physical link between a service provider and its customer) that happens to use Ethernet.

Ethernet LAN Service   Another term for E-LAN; *see* E-LAN.

Ethernet Line Service   Another term for E-Line; *see* E-Line.

Ethernet Tree Service   Another term for E-Tree; *see* E-Tree.

Ethernet Virtual Connection (EVC)   A concept in carrier/Metro Ethernet that defines which customer devices can send frames to each other over the Ethernet WAN service; includes E-Line, E-LAN, and E-Tree EVCs.

Ethernet WAN   A general and informal term for any WAN service that uses Ethernet links as the access link between the customer and the service provider.

E-Tree   A specific carrier/metro Ethernet service defined by MEF (MEF.net) that provides a rooted multipoint service, in which the root site can send frames directly to all leaves, but the leaf sites can send only to the root site.

EUI-64   Literally, a standard for an extended unique identifier that is 64 bits long. Specifically for IPv6, a set of rules for forming a 64-bit identifier, used as the interface ID in IPv6 addresses, by starting with a 48-bit MAC address, inserting FFFE (hex) in the middle, and inverting the seventh bit.

Expedited Forwarding (EF)   The name of a particular DSCP value, as well as the term for one per-hop behavior as defined by DiffServ. The value, decimal 46, is marked for packets to which the networking devices should apply certain per-hop behaviors, like priority queuing.

extended access list   A list of IOS **access-list** global configuration commands that can match multiple parts of an IP packet, including the source and destination IP address and TCP/UDP ports, for the purpose of deciding which packets to discard and which to allow through the router.

extended ping   An IOS command in which the **ping** command accepts many other options besides just the destination IP address.

Extensible Authentication Protocol (EAP)   An authentication protocol used by IEEE 802.1x.

External BGP   The use of BGP between two routers in different ASNs, with different rules compared to Internal BGP (iBGP).

External Border Gateway Protocol (eBGP)   *See* External BGP.

exterior gateway protocol (EGP)   1) A class of IP routing protocols intended for use between different autonomous systems. 2) An old (no longer used) specific routing protocol that predated BGP.

F

feasibility condition   In EIGRP, when a router has learned of multiple routes to reach one subnet, if the best route's metric is X, the feasibility condition is another route whose reported distance is < X.

feasible distance   In EIGRP, the metric of the best route to reach a subnet.

feasible successor   In EIGRP, a route that is not the best route (successor route) but that can be used immediately if the best route fails, without causing a loop. Such a route meets the feasibility condition.

fiber Internet   A general term for any Internet access technology that happens to use fiber-optic cabling. It often uses Ethernet protocols on the fiber link.

filter   Generally, a process or a device that screens network traffic for certain characteristics, such as source address, destination address, or protocol. This process determines whether to forward or discard that traffic based on the established criteria.

First Hop Redundancy Protocol (FHRP)   A class of protocols that includes HSRP, VRRP, and GLBP, which allows multiple redundant routers on the same subnet to act as a single default router (first-hop router).

flash memory   A type of read/write permanent memory that retains its contents even with no power applied to the memory and that uses no moving parts, making the memory less likely to fail over time.

FlexStack   A switch stacking technology from Cisco, combining up to four 2960-S or 2960-X model switches so that they act as a single logical switch.

FlexStack-Plus   A switch stacking technology from Cisco, as a later improvement to FlexStack, combining up to eight 2960-X or 2960-XR model switches so that they act as a single logical switch.

forward   To send a frame toward its ultimate destination by way of an internetworking device.

forward delay   An STP timer, defaulting to 15 seconds, used to dictate how long an interface stays in the listening state, and the time spent in learning state. Also called the forward delay timer.

forward route   From one host's perspective, the route over which a packet travels from that host to some other host.

Forwarding plane   A synonym for data plane. *See* data plane.

forwarding state   An STP and RSTP port state in which an interface operates unrestricted by STP.

Frame Relay   An international standard data link protocol that defines the capabilities to create a frame-switched (packet-switched) service, allowing DTE devices (usually routers) to send data to many other devices using a single physical connection to the Frame Relay service.

framing   The conventions for how Layer 2 interprets the bits sent according to OSI Layer 1. For example, after an electrical signal has been received and converted to binary, framing identifies the information fields inside the data.

FTP   File Transfer Protocol. An application protocol, part of the TCP/IP protocol stack, used to transfer files between network nodes. FTP is defined in RFC 959.

full duplex   Generically, any communication in which two communicating devices can concurrently send and receive data. Specifically for Ethernet LANs, the ability of both devices to send and receive at the same time. This is allowed when there are only two stations in a collision domain. Full duplex is enabled by turning off the CSMA/CD collision detection logic.

full mesh   From a topology perspective, any topology that has two or more devices, with each device being able to send frames to every other device.

full state   In OSPF, a neighbor state that implies that the two routers have exchanged the complete (full) contents of their respective LSDBs.

full update   With IP routing protocols, the general concept that a routing protocol update lists all known routes. *See also* partial update.

fully adjacent   In OSPF, a characterization of the state of a neighbor in which the two neighbors have reached the full state.

G

Gateway Load Balancing Protocol (GLBP)   A Cisco-proprietary protocol that allows two (or more) routers to share the duties of being the default router on a subnet, with an active/active model, with all routers actively forwarding off-subnet traffic for some hosts in the subnet.

generic routing encapsulation (GRE)   A protocol, defined in RFC 2784, that defines the headers used when creating a site-to-site VPN tunnel. The protocol defines the use of a normal IP header, called the Delivery Header, and a GRE header that the endpoints use to create and manage traffic over the GRE tunnel.

global routing prefix   An IPv6 prefix, which defines an IPv6 address block made up of global unicast addresses, assigned to one organization, so that that organization has a block of globally unique IPv6 addresses to use in their network.

global unicast address   A type of unicast IPv6 address that has been allocated from a range of public globally unique IP addresses as registered through IANA/ICANN, its member agencies, and other registries or ISPs.

GRE tunnel   A site-to-site VPN idea, in which the endpoints act as if a point-to-point link (the tunnel) exists between the sites, while actually encapsulating packets using GRE standards.

H

HDLC   High-level Data Link Control. A bit-oriented synchronous data link layer protocol developed by the International Organization for Standardization (ISO). Derived from synchronous data link control (SDLC), HDLC specifies a data encapsulation method on synchronous serial links using frame characters and checksums.

Hello   (Multiple definitions) 1) A protocol used by OSPF routers to discover, establish, and maintain neighbor relationships. 2) A protocol used by EIGRP routers to discover, establish, and maintain neighbor relationships. 3) In STP, refers to the name of the periodic message sourced by the root bridge in a spanning tree.

Hello BPDU   The STP and RSTP message used for the majority of STP communications, listing the root's bridge ID, the sending device's bridge ID, and the sending device's cost with which to reach the root.

Hello Interval   With OSPF and EIGRP, an interface timer that dictates how often the router should send Hello messages.

Hello timer   In STP, the time interval at which the root switch should send Hello BPDUs.

host   In a virtualized server environment, the term used to refer to one physical server that is running a hypervisor to create multiple virtual machines.

Hot Standby Router Protocol (HSRP)   A Cisco-proprietary protocol that allows two (or more) routers to share the duties of being the default router on a subnet, with an active/standby model, with one router acting as the default router and the other sitting by waiting to take over that role if the first router fails.

HSRP active   A Hot Standby Router Protocol (HSRP) state in which the router actively supports the forwarding of off-subnet packets for hosts in that subnet.

HSRP standby   A Hot Standby Router Protocol (HSRP) state in which the router does not currently support the forwarding of off-subnet packets for hosts in that subnet, instead waiting for the currently active router to fail before taking over that role.

hub-and-spoke   From a topology perspective, any topology that has a device that can send messages to all other devices (the hub), with one or more spoke devices that can send messages only to the hub. Also called point-to-multipoint.

Hyperthreading   The name of Intel's multithreading technology.

hypervisor   Software that runs on server hardware to create the foundations of a virtualized server environment primarily by allocating server hardware components like CPU core/threads, RAM, disk, and network to the VMs running on the server.

I

ICMP-Echo operation   A specific type of IP SLA probe in which the probe message is a standard ICMP Echo Request (that is, the same message sent by a **ping** command).

ICMP Echo Reply   One type of ICMP message, created specifically to be used as the message received by the **ping** command to test connectivity in a network. The **ping** command expects to receive these messages from other hosts, after the **ping** command first sends an ICMP Echo Request message to the host.

ICMP Echo Request   One type of ICMP message, created specifically to be used as the message sent by the **ping** command to test connectivity in a network. The **ping** command sends these messages to other hosts, expecting the other host to reply with an ICMP Echo Reply message.

ICMPv6   Internet Control Message Protocol for IPv6, used for a variety of purposes, including the Echo Request/Reply messages used by the **ping** command, and also including Neighbor Discovery Protocol (NDP).

IEEE 802.11   The IEEE base standard for wireless LANs.

IEEE 802.1AD   The IEEE standard for the functional equivalent of the Cisco-proprietary EtherChannel.

IEEE 802.1D   The IEEE standard for the original Spanning Tree Protocol.

IEEE 802.1Q   The IEEE-standard VLAN trunking protocol. 802.1Q includes the concept of a native VLAN, for which no VLAN header is added, and a 4-byte VLAN header is inserted after the original frame's type/length field.

IEEE 802.1s   The IEEE standard for Multiple Instances of Spanning Tree (MIST), which allows for load balancing of traffic among different VLANs.

IEEE 802.1w   The IEEE standard for an enhanced version of STP, called Rapid STP, which speeds convergence.

IEEE 802.3   The IEEE base standard for Ethernet-like LANs.

IGRP   Interior Gateway Routing Protocol. An old, no-longer-supported interior gateway protocol (IGP) developed by Cisco.

inferior Hello   When STP compares two or more received Hello BPDUs, a Hello that lists a numerically larger root bridge ID than another Hello or a Hello that lists the same root bridge ID but with a larger cost.

infinity   In the context of IP routing protocols, a finite metric value defined by the routing protocol that is used to represent an unusable route in a routing protocol update.

Infrastructure as a Service (IaaS)   A cloud service in which the service consists of a virtual machine that has defined computing resources (CPUs, RAM, disk, and network), and may or may not be provided with an installed OS.

Integrated Services (IntServ)   An approach to QoS, different from Differentiated Services (DiffServ), in which QoS is applied per flow, with reservations made for the necessary QoS characteristics for that flow.

integrity   In data transfers, means that the network administrator can determine that the information has not been tampered with in transit.

interarea prefix LSA   In OSPFv6, a type of LSA similar to the Type 3 summary LSA in OSPFv2, created by an Area Border Router (ABR), to describe an IPv6 prefix in one area in the database of another area.

intercloud exchange   A WAN service that provides connectivity between public cloud providers and their customers, so that customers can install and keep the WAN connections, even when migrating from one cloud provider to another.

interface bandwidth   In OSPF, the numerator in the calculation of an interface's default OSPF cost metric, calculated as the interface bandwidth divided by the reference bandwidth.

Internal Border Gateway Protocol (iBGP)   The use of BGP between two routers in the same ASN, with different rules compared to External BGP (eBGP).

interior gateway protocol (IGP)   A routing protocol designed to be used to exchange routing information inside a single autonomous system.

Internal router   In OSPF, a router with all interfaces in the same non-backbone area.

Internet access technology   Any technology that an ISP offers that allows its customer to send and receive data to/from the ISP, including serial links, Frame Relay, MPLS, Metro Ethernet, DSL, cable, and fiber Internet.

Internet edge   The part of the topology of the Internet that sits between an ISP and the ISP's customer.

Internet service provider   A company or organization that provides Internet services to customers; the company may have a heritage as a telco, WAN service provider, or cable company.

Internetwork Operating System (IOS)   *See* IOS.

Inter-Switch Link (ISL)   The Cisco-proprietary VLAN trunking protocol that predated 802.1Q by many years. ISL defines a 26-byte header that encapsulates the original Ethernet frame.

IOS   Cisco operating system software that provides the majority of a router's or switch's features, with the hardware providing the remaining features.

IOS feature set   A set of related features that can be enabled on a router to enable certain functionality. For example, the Security feature set would enable the ability to have the router act as a firewall in the network.

IOS image   A file that contains the IOS.

IP Control Protocol (IPCP)   A control protocol defined as part of PPP for the purpose of initializing and controlling the sending of IPv4 packets over a PPP link.

IP Precedence (IPP)   In the original definition of the IP header's Type of Service (ToS) byte, the first 3 bits of the ToS byte, used for marking IP packets for the purpose of applying QoS actions.

IP Service Level Agreement (IP SLA)   The Cisco router feature that defines a variety of measurable probe types, so that a network engineer can configure a probe, have the router generate probe messages and measure the responses, and then let the network engineer use those results for troubleshooting and for reporting.

IP SLA operation   A type of test generated by a Cisco router IP SLA feature. The test can generate many different types of test messages, which causes the IP SLA feature on the router to send a particular type of packet, and wait to receive a response, for the purpose of measuring something about the behavior of the network.

IP SLA responder   With the Cisco IP Service Level Agreement (SLA) feature in routers, a process that runs in a router (after being configured on that router) and waits to receive and respond to certain types of IP SLA probe messages.

IP SLA source   With the Cisco IP Service Level Agreement (SLA) feature in routers, the router that is configured to originate IP SLA probe messages of some kind.

IPsec   The term referring to the IP Security protocols, which is an architecture for providing encryption and authentication services, usually when creating VPN services through an IP network.

IPv6 prefix length   A number written as /x, where x is an integer between 0 and 128 inclusive, that defines the number of initial bits in an IPv6 address, used for IPv6 subnetting and for matching with IPv6 ACLs.

ISDN   Integrated Services Digital Network. A communication protocol offered by telephone companies that permits telephone networks to carry data, voice, and video.

ISL   *See* Inter-Switch Link.

ISP prefix   In IPv6, the prefix that describes an address block that has been assigned to an ISP by some Internet registry.

J

jitter   The variation in delay experienced by successive packets in a single application flow.

JSON (JavaScript Object Notation)   A popular method to represent data for exchange by APIs, in a format readable by both programs and computers, and defined as part of the JavaScript language.

K

keepalive   A feature of many data link protocols in which the router sends messages periodically to let the neighboring router know that the first router is still alive and well.

keyboard, video, mouse (KVM)   Three components of a typical desktop computer that are typically not included in a modern server because the server is installed and managed remotely.

KVM (Red Hat)   Kernel-Based Virtual Machine (KVM), a server virtualization/hypervisor product from the Red Hat company.

L

LACP   Link Aggregation Control Protocol is a messaging protocol defined by the IEEE 802.3ad standard which enables two neighboring devices to realize that they have multiple parallel links connecting to each other, and then to decide which links can be combined into an EtherChannel.

LAN broadcast   An Ethernet frame sent to destination address FFFF.FFFF.FFFF, meaning that the frame should be delivered to all hosts on that LAN.

LAPF   Link Access Procedure Frame Bearer Services. Defines the basic Frame Relay header and trailer. The header includes DLCI, FECN, BECN, and DE bits.

Layer 2 EtherChannel (L2 EtherChannel)   An EtherChannel that acts as a switched port (that is, not a routed port), and as such, is used by a switch's Layer 2 forwarding logic. As a result, the Layer 2 switch lists the Layer 2 EtherChannel in switch MAC address tables, and when forwarding a frame based on one of these MAC table entries, the switch balances traffic across the various ports in the Layer 2 EtherChannel.

Layer 3 EtherChannel (L3 EtherChannel)   An EtherChannel that acts as a routed port (that is, not a switched port), and as such, is used by a switch's Layer 3 forwarding logic. As a result, the Layer 3 switch lists the Layer 3 EtherChannel in various routes in the switch's IP routing table, with the switch balancing traffic across the various ports in the Layer 3 EtherChannel.

Layer 3 switch   A LAN switch that can also perform Layer 3 routing functions. The name comes from the fact that this device makes forwarding decisions based on logic from multiple OSI layers (Layers 2 and 3).

learn   Describes how switches discover MAC addresses by examining the source MAC addresses of frames they receive. They add each new MAC address, along with the port number of the port on which it learned of the MAC address, to an address table.

learning state   In STP, a temporary port state in which the interface does not forward frames, but it can begin to learn MAC addresses from frames received on the interface.

leased line   A transmission line reserved by a communications carrier for a customer's private use. A leased line is a type of dedicated line.

Link Control Protocol   A control protocol defined as part of PPP for the purpose of initializing and maintaining a PPP link.

link state   A classification of the underlying algorithm used in some routing protocols. Link-state protocols build a detailed database that lists links (subnets) and their state (up, down), from which the best routes can then be calculated.

link-local address   A type of unicast IPv6 address that represents an interface on a single data link. Packets sent to a link-local address cross only that particular link and are never forwarded to other subnets by a router. Used for communications that do not need to leave the local link, such as neighbor discovery.

link-state advertisement (LSA)   In OSPF, the name of the data structure that resides inside the LSDB and describes in detail the various components in a network, including routers and links (subnets).

link-state database (LSDB)   In OSPF, the data structure in RAM of a router that holds the various LSAs, with the collective LSAs representing the entire topology of the network.

Link-State Request   An OSPF packet used to ask a neighboring router to send a particular LSA.

Link-State Update   An OSPF packet used to send an LSA to a neighboring router.

listening state   A temporary STP port state that occurs immediately when a blocking interface must be moved to a forwarding state. The switch times out MAC table entries during this state. It also ignores frames received on the interface and doesn't forward any frames out the interface.

local loop   A line from the premises of a telephone subscriber to the telephone company CO.

local SPAN   A SPAN monitor session in which the monitored frames and the SPAN destination port are in the same switch.

local username   A username (with matching password), configured on a router or switch. It is considered local because it exists on the router or switch, and not on a remote server.

logical switch   In a switch stack, the term *logical switch* refers to the behavior of the switch stack as a whole in that the entire stack together acts as one switch.

loss   A reference to packets in a network that are sent but do not reach the destination host.

low latency queue   In Cisco queuing systems, a queue from which the queue scheduling algorithm always takes packets next if the queue holds any packets. This scheduling choice means that packets in this queue spend little time in the queue, achieving low delay (latency) as well as low jitter.

Low Latency Queuing (LLQ)   The name of a queuing system that can be enabled on Cisco routers and switches by which messages sensitive to latency and jitter are placed in a queue that is always serviced first, resulting in low latency and jitter for those messages.

LSA   *See* link-state advertisement.

LTE   Literally, Long Term Evolution, but is used as a word itself to represent the type of wireless 4G technology that allows faster speeds than the original 4G specifications.

M

Management Information Base (MIB)   The data structures defined by SNMP to define a hierarchy (tree) structure with variables at the leaves of the tree, so that SNMP messages can reference the variables.

management plane   Functions in networking devices and controllers that control the devices themselves, but that do not impact the forwarding behavior of the devices like control plane protocols do.

man-in-the-middle attack   Any type of attack in which the attacker gains control of some device or process between a user and some server, for the purpose of then capturing the messages sent between the user and the server.

marking   The process of changing one of a small set of fields in various network protocol headers, including the IP header's DSCP field, for the purpose of later classifying a message based on that marked value.

match/action logic   The basic logic done by a networking element: to receive incoming messages, to match fields in the message, to then use logic based on those matches to take action against the message, and to then forward the message.

MaxAge   In STP, a timer that states how long a switch should wait when it no longer receives Hellos from the root switch before acting to reconverge the STP topology. Also called the MaxAge timer.

maximum paths   In Cisco IOS, a reference to the number of equal cost routes (paths) to reach a single subnet that IOS will add to the IP routing table at the same time.

metric   A numeric measurement used by a routing protocol to determine how good a route is as compared to other alternate routes to reach the same subnet.

Metro Ethernet   The original term used for WAN service that used Ethernet links as the access link between the customer and the service provider.

metropolitan-area network (MAN)   A service provided by a service provider to connect customer sites, with the customer sites existing in the same city; it takes its name from the metropolitan area of cities.

MIB   *See* Management Information Base.

MIB view   A concept in SNMPv3 that identifies a subset of an SNMP agent's MIB for the purpose of limiting access to some parts of the MIB to certain SNMP managers.

modem   Modulator-demodulator. A device that converts between digital and analog signals so that a computer may send data to another computer using analog telephone lines. At the source, a modem converts digital signals to a form suitable for transmission over analog communication facilities. At the destination, the analog signals are returned to their digital form.

MPLS   *See* Multiprotocol Label Switching

MPLS Experimental Bits   A 3-bit field in the MPLS label used for QoS marking.

MPLS VPN   A WAN service that uses MPLS technology, with many customers connecting to the same MPLS network, but with the VPN features keeping each customer's traffic separate from others.

MTU   Maximum transmission unit. The maximum packet size, in bytes, that a particular interface can handle.

multiarea   In OSPFv2 and OSPFv3, a design that uses multiple areas.

Multichassis EtherChannel (MEC)   A Cisco technology that allows switches in a switch stack to be one endpoint of an EtherChannel, with links in the EtherChannel connecting to different switches in the switch stack.

multilayer switch   A LAN switch that can also perform Layer 3 routing functions. The name comes from the fact that this device makes forwarding decisions based on logic from multiple OSI layers (Layers 2 and 3).

multilink interface   A virtual interface created by Multilink PPP as the Layer 3 interface used in MLPPP configurations.

Multilink PPP (MLPPP)   A feature of PPP that manages multiple links between two nodes, load balancing data link frames across those multiple links by fragmenting each frame into pieces (fragments), sending one fragment over each active link. It also presents a single Layer 3 interface to the Layer 3 logic in the endpoint devices.

multipoint   A topology with more than two devices in it (in contrast to a point-to-point topology, which has exactly two devices). Without any further context, the term *multipoint* does not define whether all devices in the topology can send messages directly to each other (full mesh) or not (partial mesh).

multipoint GRE   A type of GRE tunnel in which more than two devices can be part of the same tunnel, sending packets directly to each other over the same tunnel, and using one subnet for all devices connected to the tunnel.

Multiprotocol BGP (MPBGP)   A particular set of BGP extensions that allows BGP to support multiple address families, which when used to create an MPLS VPN service gives the SP the method to advertise the IPv4 routes of many customers while keeping those route advertisements logically separated.

Multiprotocol Label Switching (MPLS)   A WAN technology used to create an IP-based service for customers, with the service provider's internal network performing forwarding based on an MPLS label rather than the destination IP address.

multithreading   In computer architecture, a process of maximizing the use of a processor core by sharing an individual core among multiple programs, taking advantage of the typical idle times for the core while it waits on various other tasks like memory reads and writes.

N

named access list   An ACL that identifies the various statements in the ACL based on a name rather than a number.

National Institute of Standards and Technology (NIST)   A U.S. federal agency that develops national standards, including standards for cloud computing.

NBI   *See* Northbound API.

NBMA   *See* nonbroadcast multiaccess.

neighbor   In routing protocols, another router with which a router decides to exchange routing information.

Neighbor Advertisement (NA)   A message defined by the IPv6 Neighbor Discovery Protocol (NDP) and used to declare to other neighbors a host's MAC address. Sometimes sent in response to a previously received NDP Neighbor Solicitation (NS) message.

Neighbor Discovery Protocol (NDP)   A protocol that is part of the IPv6 protocol suite and is used to discover and exchange information about devices on the same subnet (neighbors). In particular, it replaces IPv4 ARP.

Neighbor Solicitation (NS) A message defined by the IPv6 Neighbor Discovery Protocol (NDP) and used to ask a neighbor to reply back with a Neighbor Advertisement, which lists the neighbor's MAC address.

neighbor table For OSPF and EIGRP, a list of routers that have reached neighbor status.

network analyzer Network management software that captures LAN frames (often frames directed to it by a switch SPAN session) for the purpose of then analyzing the contents of those frames for a network engineer.

Network Based Application Recognition (NBAR) A Cisco router feature that looks at message details beyond the Layer 2, 3, and 4 headers to identify over 1000 different classifications of packets from different applications.

Network Layer Reachability Information (NLRI) The formal BGP term for a prefix and matching prefix length that defines an address block, which is included in the BGP Update message.

Network LSA In OSPF, a type of LSA that a designated router (DR) creates for the network (subnet) for which the DR is helping to distribute LSAs.

Network Management System (NMS) Software that manages the network, often using SNMP and other protocols.

Next Hop Resolution Protocol (NHRP) A protocol defined by the IETF, used by Cisco's DMVPN feature for the purpose of allowing routers connected to the Internet to discover each other's public IP addresses and inform each other of their private IP addresses as used by DMVPN.

Nexus 1000v A Cisco Nexus data center switch that runs as a software-only virtual switch inside one host (one hardware server), to provide switching features to the virtual machines running on that host.

NHRP client When using Next Hop Resolution Protocol, a router that registers its public and private IP addresses by informing the NHRP server of the addresses it uses. The NHRP client also asks the NHRP server to inform the client of the public/private address pairs of other routers.

NHRP server When using Next Hop Resolution Protocol, a router that collects and distributes the public and private IP address pairs registered to it from NHRP clients.

NMS Network Management Station. The device that runs network management software to manage network devices. SNMP is often the network management protocol used between the NMS and the managed device.

nonbroadcast multiaccess (NBMA) A characterization of a type of Layer 2 network in which more than two devices connect to the network, but the network does not allow broadcast frames to be sent to all devices on the network.

Northbound API In the area of SDN, a reference to the APIs that a controller supports that gives outside programs access to the services of the controller; for instance, to supply information about the network or to program flows into the network. Also called a Northbound Interface.

Northbound Interface   Another term for Northbound API. *See* Northbound API.

notification community   An SNMP community (a value that acts as a password), defined on an SNMP manager, which then must be supplied by any SNMP agent that that sends the manager any unsolicited SNMP notifications (like SNMP Trap and Notify requests).

NVRAM   Nonvolatile RAM. A type of random-access memory (RAM) that retains its contents when a unit is powered off.

O

ODL   *See* OpenDaylight.

OID   Object identifier. Used to uniquely describe a MIB variable in the SNMP database. This is a numeric string that identifies the variable uniquely and also describes where the variable exists in the MIB tree structure.

on-demand self-service   One of the five key attributes of a cloud computing service as defined by NIST, referring to the fact that the consumer of the server can request the service, with the service being created without any significant delay and without waiting on human intervention.

one-way delay   The elapsed time from sending the first bit of data at the sending device until the last bit of that data is received on the destination device.

ONF   *See* Open Networking Foundation.

Open Networking Foundation   A consortium of SDN users and vendors who work together to foster the adoption of open SDN in the marketplace.

OpenDaylight   An open source SDN controller, created by an open source effort of the OpenDaylight project under the Linux foundation, built with the intent to have a common SDN controller code base from which vendors could then take the code and add further features and support to create SDN controller products.

OpenFlow   The open standard for Software Defined Networking (SDN) as defined by the Open Networking Foundation (ONF), which defines the OpenFlow protocol as well as the concept of an abstracted OpenFlow virtual switch.

OpFlex   The southbound protocol used by the Cisco ACI controller and the switches it controls.

OSPF   Open Shortest Path First. A popular link-state IGP that uses a link-state database and the Shortest Path First (SPF) algorithm to calculate the best routes to reach each known subnet.

OSPF super backbone   Jargon used to refer to how when an MPLS VPN customer uses OSPF, that the MPLS VPN service acts as if it were part of OSPF backbone area 0, with that part of area 0 being called the super backbone.

OSPF version 2   The version of the OSPF routing protocol that supports IPv4, and not IPv6, and has been commonly used for over 20 years.

OSPF version 3   The version of the OSPF routing protocol that originally supported only IPv6, and not IPv4, but now supports IPv4 through the use of address family configuration.

out-of-band   Traffic that does not share the same network paths with user data traffic. Network management traffic is often sent OOB.

overlapping subnets   An (incorrect) IP subnet design condition in which one subnet's range of addresses includes addresses in the range of another subnet.

P

packet switching   A WAN service in which each DTE device connects to a telco using a single physical line, with the possibility of being able to forward traffic to all other sites connected to the same service. The telco switch makes the forwarding decision based on an address in the packet header.

PAgP   Port Aggregation Protocol (PAgP) is a messaging protocol defined by Cisco which enables two neighboring devices to realize that they have multiple parallel links connecting to each other, and then to decide which links can be combined into an EtherChannel.

PAP   Password Authentication Protocol. A PPP authentication protocol that allows PPP peers to authenticate one another, characterized by the weak authentication it uses by sending the username and password as clear text values.

partial mesh   A network topology in which more than two devices could physically communicate, but by choice, only a subset of the pairs of devices connected to the network is allowed to communicate directly.

partial update   With IP routing protocols, the general concept that a routing protocol update lists a subset of all known routes. *See also* full update.

path attribute   In BGP, one of many types of information that describe a route (path), with the path attributes being used for best path selection and other purposes.

periodic update   With routing protocols, the concept that the routing protocol advertises routes in a routing update on a regular periodic basis. This is typical of distance vector routing protocols.

permanent virtual circuit (PVC)   A preconfigured communications path between two Frame Relay DTEs, identified by a local DLCI on each Frame Relay access link, that provides the functional equivalent of a leased circuit but without a physical leased line for each VC.

permit   An action taken with an ACL that implies that the packet is allowed to proceed through the router and be forwarded.

ping   Packet Internet groper. An Internet Control Message Protocol (ICMP) echo message and its reply; ping often is used in IP networks to test the reachability of a network device.

Platform as a Service (PaaS)   A cloud service intended for software developers as a development platform, with a variety of tools useful to developers already installed, so that the developer can focus on developing software rather than on creating a good development environment.

point of presence (PoP)   A term used for a service provider's (SP) perspective to refer to a service provider's installation that is purposefully located relatively near to customers, with several spread around major cities, so that the distance from each customer site to one of the SP's PoPs is short.

point-to-multipoint   *See* hub-and-spoke.

point-to-point   From a topology perspective, any topology that has two and only two devices that can send messages directly to each other.

point-to-point edge port   With 802.1w RSTP, a port type in which the switch believes the port is connected to a single other device, specifically one that is not another switch.

point-to-point port   With 802.1w RSTP, a port type in which the switch believes the port is connected to a single other device, specifically another switch.

poisoned route   A route advertisement in which the routing protocol assigns the route a maximum metric that represents infinity, as a means to advertise that the route is no longer usable.

policing   A QoS tool that monitors the bit rate of the messages passing some point in the processing of a networking device, so that if the bit rate exceeds the policing rate for a period of time, the policer can discard excess packets to lower the rate.

policing rate   The bit rate at which a policer compares the bit rate of packets passing through a policing function, for the purpose of taking a different action against packets that conform (are under) to the rate versus those that exceed (go over) the rate.

port   (Multiple definitions) 1) In TCP and UDP, a number that is used to uniquely identify the application process that either sent (source port) or should receive (destination port) data. 2) In LAN switching, another term for switch interface.

PortChannel   One term Cisco switches use to reference a bundle of links that are, in some respects, treated like a single link. Other similar terms include EtherChannel and Channel-group.

PortFast   A switch STP feature in which a port is placed in an STP forwarding state as soon as the interface comes up, bypassing the listening and learning states. This feature is meant for ports connected to end-user devices.

PPP over Ethernet (PPPoE)   A specific protocol designed to encapsulate PPP frames inside Ethernet frames, for the purpose of delivering the PPP frames between two devices, effectively creating a point-to-point tunnel between the two devices.

PPP   Point-to-Point Protocol. A data link protocol that provides router-to-router and host-to-network connections over synchronous and asynchronous circuits.

PPPoE session   The logical connection between two PPPoE endpoints, used to track the state of the ability of each endpoint to send PPPoE frames to the other endpoint.

prefix notation   A shorter way to write a subnet mask in which the number of binary 1s in the mask is simply written in decimal. For instance, /24 denotes the subnet mask with 24 binary 1 bits in the subnet mask. The number of bits of value binary 1 in the mask is considered to be the prefix.

Priority Code Point (PCP)   The formal term for the 3-bit field in the 802.1Q header intended for marking and classifying Ethernet frames for the purposes of applying QoS actions. Another term for Class of Service (CoS).

priority queue   In Cisco queuing systems, another term for a low latency queue (LLQ).

private address   Several Class A, B, and C networks that are set aside for use inside private organizations. These addresses, as defined in RFC 1918, are not routable through the Internet.

private cloud   A cloud computing service in which a company provides its own IT services to internal customers inside the same company but by following the practices defined as cloud computing.

private IP network   One of several classful IPv4 network numbers that will never be assigned for use in the Internet, meant for use inside a single enterprise.

private key   A secret value used in public/private key encryption systems. Either encrypts a value that can then be decrypted using the matching public key, or decrypts a value that was previously encrypted with the matching public key.

problem isolation   The part of the troubleshooting process in which the engineer attempts to rule out possible causes of the problem, narrowing the possible causes until the root cause of the problem can be identified.

protocol type   A field in the IP header that identifies the type of header that follows the IP header, usually a Layer 4 header, such as TCP or UDP. ACLs can examine the protocol type to match packets with a particular value in this header field.

provider edge (PE)   A term used by service providers, both generally and also specifically in MPLS VPN networks, to refer to the SP device in a point of presence (PoP) that connects to the customer's network, and therefore sits at the edge of the SP's network.

public cloud   A cloud computing service in which the cloud provider is a different company than the cloud consumer.

public key   A publicly available value used in public/private key encryption systems. Either encrypts a value that can then be decrypted using the matching private key, or decrypts a value that was previously encrypted with the matching private key.

PVC   *See* permanent virtual circuit.

PVST+   An STP option in Cisco switches that creates an STP instance per VLAN while using the STP (802.1D) protocol for those STP instances.

Q

Quality of Experience (QoE)   The users' perception of the quality of their experience in using applications in the network.

Quality of Service (QoS)   The performance of a message, or the messages sent by an application, in regard to the bandwidth, delay, jitter, or loss characteristics experienced by the message(s).

queuing   The process by which networking devices hold packets in memory while waiting on some constrained resource; for example, when waiting for the outgoing interface to become available when too many packets arrive in a short period of time.

R

RADIUS   A security protocol often used for user authentication, including being used as part of the IEEE 802.1x messages between an 802.1x authenticator (typically a LAN switch) and a AAA server.

RAM   Random-access memory. A type of volatile memory that can be read and written by a microprocessor.

rapid elasticity   One of the five key attributes of a cloud computing service as defined by NIST, referring to the fact that the cloud service reacts to requests for new services quickly, and it expands (is elastic) to the point of appearing to be a limitless resource.

Rapid PVST+   An STP option in Cisco switches that creates an STP instance per VLAN while using the RSTP (802.1w) protocol for those STP instances.

Rapid Spanning Tree Protocol (RSTP)   Defined in IEEE 802.1w. Defines an improved version of STP that converges much more quickly and consistently than STP (802.1d).

reachability   In BGP, a reference to the goal of BGP to advertise about a prefix/length so that other routers know that the prefix is reachable through the router that advertised the prefix.

read-only community   An SNMP community (a value that acts as a password), defined on an SNMP agent, which then must be supplied by any SNMP manager that sends the agent any messages asking to learn the value of a variable (like SNMP Get and GetNext requests).

read-write community   An SNMP community (a value that acts as a password), defined on an SNMP agent, which then must be supplied by any SNMP manager that sends the agent any messages asking to set the value of a variable (like SNMP Set requests).

Real-time Transport Protocol (RTP)   The transport layer protocol used by many voice and video applications, including between Cisco IP Telephone and other Cisco Unified Communications products.

reference bandwidth   In OSPF, a configurable value for the OSPF routing process, used by OSPF when calculating an interface's default OSPF cost metric, calculated as the interface's bandwidth divided by the reference bandwidth.

Regional Internet Registry (RIR)   The generic term for one of five current organizations that are responsible for assigning the public, globally unique IPv4 and IPv6 address space.

registry prefix   In IPv6, the prefix that describes a block of public, globally unique IPv6 addresses assigned to a Regional Internet Registry by ICANN.

reported distance   From one EIGRP router's perspective, the metric for a subnet as calculated on a neighboring router and reported in a routing update to the first router.

Representational State Transfer (REST)   A type of API that allows two programs that reside on separate computers to communicate, with the messages used to move requests and data across the network using HTTP messages Get, Post, Put, and Delete.

resource pooling   One of the five key attributes of a cloud computing service as defined by NIST, referring to the fact that the cloud provider treats its resources as a large group (pool) of resources that its cloud management systems then allocate dynamically based on self-service requests by its customers.

REST   *See* Representational State Transfer.

REST API   Any API that uses Representational State Transfer (REST), which means that the two programs, on separate computers, use HTTP messages to request and transfer data.

RESTful API   A turn of phrase that means that the API uses REST.

reverse route   From one host's perspective, for packets sent back to the host from another host, the route over which the packet travels.

RFC   Request For Comments. A document used as the primary means for communicating information about the TCP/IP protocols. Some RFCs are designated by the Internet Architecture Board (IAB) as Internet standards, and others are informational. RFCs are available online from numerous sources, including www.rfc-editor.org.

RIP   Routing Information Protocol. An interior gateway protocol (IGP) that uses distance vector logic and router hop count as the metric. RIP Version 1 (RIPv1) has become unpopular. RIP Version 2 (RIPv2) provides more features, including support for VLSM.

root bridge   *See* root switch.

root cost   The STP cost from a nonroot switch to reach the root switch, as the sum of all STP costs for all ports out which a frame would exit to reach the root.

root port   In STP, the one port on a nonroot switch in which the least-cost Hello is received. Switches put root ports in a forwarding state.

root switch   In STP, the switch that wins the election by virtue of having the lowest bridge ID, and, as a result, sends periodic Hello BPDUs (default, 2 seconds).

round robin   A queue scheduling algorithm in which the scheduling algorithm services one queue, then the next, then the next, and so on, working through the queues in sequence.

round-trip delay   The elapsed time from sending the first bit of data at the sending device until the last bit of that data is received on the destination device, plus the time waiting for the destination device to form a reply, plus the elapsed time for that reply message to arrive back to the original sender.

Round Trip Time (RTT)   The time it takes a message to go from the original sender to the receiver, plus the time for the response to that message to be sent back.

routable protocol   *See* routed protocol.

route redistribution   A method by which two routing protocol processes running in the same device can exchange routing information, thereby causing a route learned by one routing protocol to then be advertised by another.

route summarization   The process of combining multiple routes into a single advertised route, for the purpose of reducing the number of entries in routers' IP routing tables.

routed port   A port on a multilayer Cisco switch, configured with the **no switchport** command, that tells the switch to treat the port as if it were a Layer 3 port, like a router interface.

routed protocol   A Layer 3 protocol that defines a packet that can be routed, such as IPv4 and IPv6.

Router Advertisement (RA)   A message defined by the IPv6 Neighbor Discovery Protocol (NDP) and used by routers to announce their willingness to act as an IPv6 router on a link. These may be sent in response to a previously received NDP Router Solicitation (RS) message.

router ID (RID)   In EIGRP and OSPF, a 32-bit number, written in dotted decimal, that uniquely identifies each router.

router LSA   In OSPF, a type of LSA that a router creates to describe itself and the networks connected to it.

Router on a Stick (ROAS)   Jargon to refer to the Cisco router feature of using VLAN trunking on an Ethernet interface, which then allows the router to route packets that happen to enter the router on that trunk and then exit the router on that same trunk, just on a different VLAN.

Router Solicitation (RS)   A message defined by the IPv6 Neighbor Discovery Protocol (NDP) and used to ask any routers on the link to reply, identifying the router, plus other configuration settings (prefixes and prefix lengths).

routing protocol   A set of messages and processes with which routers can exchange information about routes to reach subnets in a particular network. Examples of routing protocols include Enhanced Interior Gateway Routing Protocol (EIGRP), Open Shortest Path First (OSPF), and Routing Information Protocol (RIP).

RSTP   *See* Rapid Spanning Tree Protocol.

S

SBI   *See* Southbound API.

SDM   *See* Switching Database Manager.

Secure Sockets Layer (SSL)   A security protocol that is integrated into commonly used web browsers that provides encryption and authentication services between the browser and a website.

security level   The level of SNMPv3 security applied by the SNMP agent, specifically either noauth, auth, or priv.

segment   (Multiple definitions) 1) In TCP, a term used to describe a TCP header and its encapsulated data (also called an L4PDU). 2) Also in TCP, the set of bytes formed when TCP breaks a large chunk of data given to it by the application layer into smaller pieces that fit into TCP segments. 3) In Ethernet, either a single Ethernet cable or a single collision domain (no matter how many cables are used).

serial cable   A type of cable with many different styles of connectors used to connect a router to an external CSU/DSU on a leased-line installation.

serial link   Another term for leased line.

Service Level Agreement (SLA)   *See* IP Service Level Agreement (IP SLA).

service provider   A company that provides a service to multiple customers. Used most often to refer to providers of private WAN services and Internet services. *See also* Internet service provider.

session key   With encryption, a secret value that is known to both parties in a communication, used for a period of time, which the endpoints use when encrypting and decrypting data.

shaping   A QoS tool that monitors the bit rate of the messages exiting a networking devices, so that if the bit rate exceeds the shaping rate for a period of time, the shaper can queue the packets, effectively slowing down the sending rate to match the shaping rate.

shaping rate   The bit rate at which a shaper compares the bit rate of packets passing through the shaping function, so that when the rate is exceeded, the shaper enables the queuing of packets, resulting in slowing the bit rate of the collective packets that pass through the shaper, so the rate of bits getting through the shaper does not exceed the shaping rate.

shared key   A reference to a security key whose value is known (shared) by both the sender and receiver.

shared port   With 802.1w RSTP, a port type that is determined by the fact that the port uses half duplex, which could then imply a shared LAN as created by a LAN hub.

shortest path first (SPF) algorithm   The algorithm used by OSPF to find all possible routes, and then choose the route with the lowest metric for each subnet.

Simple Network Management Protocol (SNMP)   An Internet-standard protocol for managing devices on IP networks. It is used mostly in network management systems to monitor network-attached devices for conditions that warrant administrative attention.

single homed   One design of the Internet edge in which the enterprise connects to the ISP with a single link.

single multihomed   One design of the Internet edge in which the enterprise connects to two or more ISPs, but with a single link to each.

single point of failure   In a network, a single device or link which, if it fails, causes an outage for a given population of users.

site prefix   In IPv6, the prefix that describes a public globally unique IPv6 address block that has been assigned to an end-user organization (for example, an enterprise or government agency). The assignment usually is made by an ISP or Internet registry.

site-to-site VPN   The mechanism that allows all devices at two different sites to communicate securely over some unsecure network like the Internet, by having one device at each site perform encryption/decryption and forwarding for all the packets sent between the sites.

SLSM   Static-length subnet mask. The usage of the same subnet mask for all subnets of a single Class A, B, or C network.

SNMP   *See* Simple Network Management Protocol.

SNMP agent   Software that resides on the managed device and processes the SNMP messages sent by the Network Management Station (NMS).

SNMP community   A simple password mechanism in SNMP in which either the SNMP agent or manager defines a community string (password), and the other device must send that same password value in SNMP messages, or the messages are ignored. *See also* read-only community, read-write community, and notification community.

SNMP Get message   Used by SNMP to read from variables in the MIB.

SNMP Inform message   An unsolicited SNMP message like a Trap message, except that the protocol requires that the Inform message needs to be acknowledged by the SNMP manager.

SNMP manager   Typically a Network Management System (NMS), with this term specifically referring to the use of SNMP and the typical role of the manager, which retrieves status information with SNMP Get requests, sets variables with the SNMP Set requests, and receives unsolicited notifications from SNMP agents by listening for SNMP Trap and Notify messages.

SNMP Set message   Used in SNMP to set the value in variables of the MIB. These messages are the key to an administrator configuring the managed device using SNMP.

SNMP Trap message   An unsolicited SNMP message generated by the managed device, and sent to the SNMP manager, to give information to the manager about some event or because a measurement threshold has been passed.

SNMPv2c   A variation of the second version of SNMP. SNMP Version 2 did not originally support communities; the term *SNMPv2c* refers to SNMP version 2 with support added for SNMP communities (which were part of SNMPv1).

SNMPv3   The third version of SNMP, with the notable addition of several security features as compared to SNMPv2c, specifically message integrity, authentication, and encryption.

Software as a Service (SaaS)   A cloud service in which the service consists of access to working software, without the need to be concerned about the details of installing and maintaining the software or the servers on which it runs.

Software Defined Networking (SDN)   A branch of networking that emerged in the marketplace in the 2010s characterized by the use of a centralized software controller that takes over varying amounts of the control plane processing formerly done inside networking devices, with the controller directing the networking elements as to what forwarding table entries to put into their forwarding tables.

Southbound API   In the area of SDN, a reference to the APIs used between a controller and the network elements for the purpose of learning information from the elements and for programming (controlling) the forwarding behavior of the elements. Also called a Southbound Interface.

Southbound Interface   Another term for Southbound API. *See* Southbound API.

SPAN destination port   In a SPAN monitor session, the configuration that tells the switch out which port to forward frames copied based on that same SPAN session's source ports or source VLANs.

SPAN monitor session   A function enabled in a Cisco switch that intercepts a defined subset of frames being sent through the switch (as defined by the SPAN monitor session), directing a copy of those frames out a certain port, so that other tools (like network analyzers and intrusion protection systems) can examine the frames.

SPAN session *See* SPAN monitor session.

SPAN source port In a SPAN monitor session, the configuration that tells a switch to copy frames sent or received on a particular port, and to then send those copied frames to the SPAN destination defined by that same SPAN session.

SPAN source VLAN In a SPAN monitor session, the configuration that tells a switch to copy frames sent in that VLAN, and to then send those copied frames to the SPAN destination defined by that same SPAN session.

Spanning Tree Protocol (STP) A protocol defined by IEEE standard 802.1D. Allows switches and bridges to create a redundant LAN, with the protocol dynamically causing some ports to block traffic, so that the bridge/switch forwarding logic will not cause frames to loop indefinitely around the LAN.

split horizon A distant vector routing technique in which information about routes is prevented from exiting the router interface through which that information was received. Split-horizon updates are useful in preventing routing loops.

spurious DHCP server A DHCP server that is used by an attacker for attacks that take advantage of DHCP protocol messages.

SSL *See* Secure Sockets Layer.

Stack Master The one switch in a FlexStack or FlexStack-Plus switch stack that performs the data plane, control plane, and management plane processing on behalf of all switches in the stack.

stacking cable A special cable used to connect stacking modules in switches that are cabled into the same switch stack.

stacking module In Cisco's switch stacking technologies like FlexStack and FlexStack-Plus, the hardware module that is required on each switch to create a communications link between all switches in the stack so that they can forward user frames and also communicate with each other to manage the stack.

standard access list A list of IOS global configuration commands that can match only a packet's source IP address for the purpose of deciding which packets to discard and which to allow through the router.

stateful DHCP A term used in IPv6 to contrast with stateless DHCP. Stateful DHCP keeps track of which clients have been assigned which IPv6 addresses (state information).

stateless address autoconfiguration (SLAAC) A feature of IPv6 in which a host or router can be assigned an IPv6 unicast address without the need for a stateful DHCP server.

stateless DHCP A term used in IPv6 to contrast with stateful DHCP. Stateless DHCP servers do not lease IPv6 addresses to clients. Instead, they supply other useful information, such as DNS server IP addresses, but with no need to track information about the clients (state information).

static-length subnet mask (SLSM) *See* SLSM.

subinterface One of the virtual interfaces on a single physical interface.

subnet   A subdivision of a Class A, B, or C network, as configured by a network administrator. Subnets allow a single Class A, B, or C network to be used and still allow for a large number of groups of IP addresses, as is required for efficient IP routing.

subnet broadcast address   A special address in each subnet—specifically, the largest numeric address in the subnet—designed so that packets sent to this address should be delivered to all hosts in that subnet.

subnet mask   A 32-bit number that describes the format of an IP address. It represents the combined network and subnet bits in the address with mask bit values of 1 and represents the host bits in the address with mask bit values of 0.

subnet prefix   In IPv6, a term for the prefix that is assigned to each data link, acting like a subnet in IPv4.

successor   In EIGRP, the route to reach a subnet that has the best metric and should be placed in the IP routing table.

summary LSA   In OSPFv2, a type of LSA, created by an Area Border Router (ABR), to describe a subnet in one area in the database of another area.

summary route   A route created via configuration commands to represent routes to one or more subnets with a single route, thereby reducing the size of the routing table.

supplicant   With IEEE 802.1x, the end-user device that uses an 802.1x client to listen for messages asking for its identification and then supplies that identification when asked.

switch   A network device that filters, forwards, and floods frames based on each frame's destination address. The switch operates at the data link layer of the Open System Interconnection (OSI) reference model.

switch abstraction   The fundamental idea of what a switch does, in generalized form, so that standards protocols and APIs can be defined that then program a standard switch abstraction; a key part of the OpenFlow standard.

switch stacking   A switch technology that connects a small set of switches using a specialized stacking module and stacking cable hardware, along with control software used on each switch, so that the switches collectively act as one logical switch rather than separate switches.

switched port   A port on a multilayer Cisco switch or a Layer 2 switch, configured with the normal default interface setting of **switchport**, that tells the switch to treat the port as if it were a Layer 2 port, resulting in the switch performing switch MAC learning, Layer 2 forwarding, and STP on that interface.

Switched Port Analyzer (SPAN)   The Cisco switch feature that allows the network engineer to configure the switch to monitor a subset of frames that the switch forwards, to copy those frames, and to send the copies out a specified destination port.

switched virtual interface (SVI)   Another term for any VLAN interface in a Cisco switch. *See also* VLAN interface.

Switching Database Manager (SDM)   A formal term for a Cisco IOS switch feature that allows the user to reconfigure some settings (with the **sdm prefer** global command) about how the switch's forwarding matches messages and how it allocates TCAM memory to store tables such as Layer 2 MAC address tables and Layer 3 routing tables.

synchronous   The imposition of time ordering on a bit stream. Practically, a device tries to use the same speed as another device on the other end of a serial link. However, by examining transitions between voltage states on the link, the device can notice slight variations in the speed on each end and can adjust its speed accordingly.

syslog   A server that takes system messages from network devices and stores them in a database. The syslog server also provides reporting capabilities on these system messages. Some syslog servers can even respond to select system messages with certain actions such as emailing and paging.

System ID Extension   The term for the formatting applied to the original 16-bit STP priority field to break it into a 4-bit priority field and a 12-bit VLAN ID field.

T

T1   A line from the telco that allows transmission of data at 1.544 Mbps, with the capability to treat the line as 24 different 64-Kbps DS0 channels (plus 8 Kbps of overhead).

T3   A line from the telco that allows transmission of data at 44.736 Mbps, with the capability to treat the line as 28 different 1.544-Mbps DS1 (T1) channels, plus overhead.

TACACS+   A security protocol often used for user authentication as well as authorization and accounting, often used to authenticate users who log in to Cisco routers and switches.

tail drop   Packet drops that occur when a queue fills, another message arrives that needs to be placed into the queue, and the networking device tries to add the new message to the tail of the queue but finds no room in the queue, resulting in a dropped packet.

TCAM   *See* ternary content-addressable memory.

TCP synchronization   An effect that happens across many TCP connections whose segments cross the same congested link. The TCP connections increase their windows, the connections send more and more traffic, the link fills, the output queues fill, tail drops occur, causing TCP windows to quickly shrink, resulting in slower data transfer for the TCP connections and an underutilized link for a short period of time. The process can repeat, with the TCP connections synchronized.

TCP window   The mechanism in a TCP connection used by each host to manage how much data the receiver allows the sender to send to the receiver.

telco   A common abbreviation for telephone company.

ternary content-addressable memory (TCAM)   A type of physical memory, either in a separate integrated circuit or built into an ASIC, that can store tables and then be searched against a key, such that the search time happens quickly and does not increase as the size of the table increases. TCAMs are used extensively in higher-performance networking devices as the means to store and search forwarding tables in Ethernet switches and higher-performance routers.

time interval (shaper)   Part of the internal logic used by a traffic shaping function, which defines a short time period in which the shaper sends packets until a number of bytes are sent, and then the shaper stops sending for the rest of the time interval, with a goal of averaging a defined bit rate of sending data.

Top of Rack (ToR) switch   In a traditional data center design with servers in multiple racks, and the racks in multiple rows, a switch placed in the top of the rack for the purpose of providing physical connectivity to the servers (hosts) in that rack.

topology database   The structured data that describes the network topology to a routing protocol. Link-state and balanced hybrid routing protocols use topology tables, from which they build the entries in the routing table.

traceroute   A program available on many systems that traces the path that a packet takes to a destination. It is used mostly to debug routing problems between hosts.

triggered update   A routing protocol feature in which the routing protocol does not wait for the next periodic update when something changes in the network, instead immediately sending a routing update.

trunk   In campus LANs, an Ethernet segment over which the devices add a VLAN header that identifies the VLAN in which the frame exists.

trunk interface   A switch interface configured so that it operates using VLAN trunking (either 802.1Q or ISL).

trunking   Also called VLAN trunking, a method (using either the Cisco ISL protocol or the IEEE 802.1Q protocol) to support multiple VLANs that have members on more than one switch.

trunking administrative mode   The configured trunking setting on a Cisco switch interface, as configured with the **switchport mode** command.

trunking operational mode   The current behavior of a Cisco switch interface for VLAN trunking.

trust boundary   When thinking about a message as it flows from the source device to the destination device, the trust boundary is the first device the message reaches for which the QoS markings in the message's various headers can be trusted as having an accurate value, allowing the device to apply the correct QoS actions to the message based on the marking.

trusted port   A switch port configured with DHCP snooping that may receive frames from DHCP servers, so that the DHCP snooping feature should trust all incoming DHCP messages.

tunnel interface   A virtual interface in a Cisco router used to configure a variety of features, including generic routing encapsulation (GRE), which encapsulates IP packets into other IP packets for the purpose of creating VPNs.

Type of Service (ToS)   In the original definition of the IP header, a byte reserved for the purpose of QoS functions, including holding the IP Precedence field. The ToS byte was later repurposed to hold the DSCP field.

U

unequal-cost load balancing   A concept in EIGRP by which a router adds multiple unequal cost (unequal metric) routes to the routing table, at the same time, allowing equal-metric routes to be used.

Unified Computing System (UCS)   The Cisco brand name for their server hardware products.

unique local unicast address   A type of IPv6 unicast address meant as a replacement for IPv4 private addresses.

untrusted port   A configuration choice for a switch port configured with DHCP snooping and that should never receive frames from DHCP servers. This setting causes the DHCP snooping feature to discard all incoming messages that only a DHCP server would have sent, along with any other DHCP message matching logic that causes the filtering of other incoming DHCP messages.

update timer   The time interval that regulates how often a routing protocol sends its next periodic routing updates. Distance vector routing protocols send full routing updates every update interval.

user network interface (UNI)   A term used in a variety of WAN standards, including carrier/Metro Ethernet, that defines the standards for how a customer device communicates with an service provider's device over an access link.

V

variable-length subnet mask(ing)   *See* VLSM.

variance   A value used in routing protocol decisions by EIGRP. EIGRP computes its metric in a way such that for different routes, the calculated metric seldom results in the exact same value. The variance value is multiplied with the lower metric when multiple routes to the same subnet exist. If the product is larger than the metrics for other routes, the routes are considered to have "equal" metric, allowing multiple routes to be added to the routing table.

virtual-access interface   A virtual interface inside a Cisco router, created by IOS's PPPoE function to act as the Layer 2 interface, with its Layer 2 PPP parameters being built from the configuration listed on an associated dialer interface.

virtual CPU (vCPU)   In a virtualized server environment, a CPU (processor) core or thread allocated to a virtual machine (VM) by the hypervisor.

virtual IP address   For any FHRP protocol, an IP address that the FHRP shares between multiple routers so that they appear as a single default router to hosts on that subnet.

virtual LAN (VLAN)   A group of devices connected to one or more switches that are grouped into a single broadcast domain through configuration. VLANs allow switch administrators to place the devices connected to the switches in separate VLANs without requiring separate physical switches. This creates design advantages of separating the traffic without the expense of buying additional hardware.

virtual MAC address (vMAC)   For any FHRP protocol, a MAC address that the FHRP uses to receive frames from hosts.

virtual machine   An instance of an operating system, running on server hardware that uses a hypervisor to allocate a subset of the server hardware (CPU, RAM, disk, and network) to that VM.

virtual network function (VNF)   Any function done within a network (for example, router, switch, firewall) that is implemented not as a physical device but as an OS running in a virtualized system (for instance, a VM).

virtual NIC (vNIC)   In a virtualized server environment, a network interface card (NIC) used by a virtual machine, which then connects to some virtual switch (vSwitch) running on that same host, which in turn connects to a physical NIC on the host.

virtual private network (VPN)   A set of security protocols that, when implemented by two devices on either side of an unsecure network such as the Internet, can allow the devices to send data securely. VPNs provide privacy, device authentication, anti-replay services, and data integrity services.

Virtual Router Redundancy Protocol (VRRP)   A TCP/IP RFC protocol that allows two (or more) routers to share the duties of being the default router on a subnet, with an active/standby model, with one router acting as the default router and the other sitting by waiting to take over that role if the first router fails.

virtual switch (vSwitch)   A software-only virtual switch inside one host (one hardware server), to provide switching features to the virtual machines running on that host.

VLAN   *See* virtual LAN.

VLAN configuration database   The name of the collective configuration of VLAN IDs and names on a Cisco switch.

VLAN interface   A configuration concept inside Cisco switches, used as an interface between IOS running on the switch and a VLAN supported inside the switch, so that the switch can assign an IP address and send IP packets into that VLAN.

VLAN Trunking Protocol (VTP)   A Cisco-proprietary messaging protocol used between Cisco switches to communicate configuration information about the existence of VLANs, including the VLAN ID and VLAN name.

vlan.dat   The default file used to store a Cisco switch's VLAN configuration database.

VLSM   Variable-length subnet mask(ing). The ability to specify a different subnet mask for the same Class A, B, or C network number on different subnets. VLSM can help optimize available address space.

voice VLAN   A VLAN defined for use by IP Phones, with the Cisco switch notifying the phone about the voice VLAN ID so that the phone can use 802.1Q frames to support traffic for the phone and the attached PC (which uses a data VLAN).

VoIP   Voice over IP. The transport of voice traffic inside IP packets over an IP network.

VPN   *See* virtual private network.

VPN client   Software that resides on a PC, often a laptop, so that the host can implement the protocols required to be an endpoint of a VPN.

VTP   *See* VLAN Trunking Protocol.

VTP client mode   One of three VTP operational modes for a switch with which switches learn about VLAN numbers and names from other switches, but which does not allow the switch to be directly configured with VLAN information.

VTP pruning   The VTP feature by which switches dynamically choose interfaces on which to prevent the flooding of frames in certain VLANs, when those frames do not need to go to every switch in the network.

VTP server mode   One of three sets of operating characteristics (modes) in VTP. Switches in server mode can configure VLANs, tell other switches about the changes, and learn about VLAN changes from other switches.

VTP synchronization   The process by which switches that use VTP exchange VTP messages and realize that one switch now has an updated VLAN configuration database (one that has a higher revision number), resulting in messages that allow the rest of the switches to learn the contents of that updated configuration database.

VTP transparent mode   One of three operating characteristics (modes) in VTP. Switches in transparent mode can configure VLANs, but they do not tell other switches about the changes, and they do not learn about VLAN changes from other switches; however, they can pass VTP messages between other switches that use VTP server and client modes.

W

WAN edge   The device (typically a router) at enterprise sites that connects to private WAN links, therefore sitting at the edge of the WAN.

WAN link   Another term for leased line.

WAN service provider   A company that provides private WAN services to customers; the company may have a heritage as a telco or cable company.

wildcard mask   The mask used in Cisco IOS ACL commands and OSPF and EIGRP **network** commands.

wireless access point (AP)   A wireless LAN device that provides a means for wireless clients to send data to each other and to the rest of a wired network. The wireless access point connects to both the wireless LAN and the wired Ethernet LAN.

write community   *See* read-write community.

X

XML (eXtensible Markup Language)   A popular language used to represent data in a way that is readable both to software and to computers, as defined by the World Wide Web (W3C) consortium.

Z

zero subnet   For every classful IPv4 network that is subnetted, the one subnet whose subnet number has all binary 0s in the subnet part of the number. In decimal, the 0 subnet can be easily identified because it is the same number as the classful network number.

Index

Symbols

2-way state (neighbor relationships), 186, 628

3G wireless, 393

4G wireless, 393

802.1D STP, 58, 62

802.1Q, 20-21

headers, 500-501

trunking. *See* ROAS

802.1w RSTP

defined, 58

port roles, 60

port states, 62

802.11 headers, 501

A

aaa authentication login default command, 149

aaa new-model command, 149

AAA servers

authentication

configuration, 148-150

login authentication rules, 150

login process, 147

TACACS+/RADIUS protocols, 148

configuring for 802.1x, 145

defining, 149

enabling, 149

username/passwords, verifying, 145

aaS (as a Service), 742

ABR (Area Border Router), 190, 625

interface OSPF areas, verifying, 210-211

OSPFv2 multiarea configuration, 209-210

OSPFv3 multiarea configuration, 625

access

Internet, 389

cable Internet, 391

DSLs (digital subscriber lines), 390-391

fiber, 393

WANs, 389

wireless WANs, 392-393

IPv6 restrictions, 685

public cloud services

Internet, 745-746

private WANs, 746-749

VPNs, 747

securing with IEEE 802.1x, 144-146

AAA servers, configuring, 145

authentication process, 145

EAP, 146

switches as 802.1x authenticators, 145

username/password combinations, verifying, 145

access-class command, 486

access control lists. *See* ACLs

Access Control Server (ACS), 147

access interfaces, 24, 113-114

access layer switches, 156-157

access links

MetroE, 365

MPLS, 378

access-list command, 445, 457, 463-466, 486

building ACLs with, 454

examples and logic explanations, 467

extended numbered ACL configuration commands, 467

keywords

any, 448

deny, 448-449

log, 452

permit, 445, 448-449

tcp keyword, 464

upd keyword, 464

reverse engineering from ACL to address range, 454-456

ACI (Application Centric Infrastructure), 773-774

ACLs (access control lists), 586

ACL Analysis tool, 777-778

classification, 497

comparison of ACL types, 442-443

extended numbered ACLs

configuration, 467-470

matching protocol, source IP, and destination IP, 463-464

matching TCP and UDP port numbers, 464-467

overview, 462

GRE tunnel issues, 409-410

HSRP packets, blocking, 563

implementation considerations, 476-477

IPv4, 666-667

IPv6, 664-666

access-list commands, building, 678-679

access restrictions, 685

blocking, 683

capabilities, 669

extended, 674-678

filtering ICMPv6 NDP messages, 679-683

filtering policies, 668

ICMPv6 message filtering, 668-669

implicit filtering ICMPv6 NDP messages, 683-684

IPv4 ACL, compared, 666-667

limitations, 669-670

logging, 670

management control, 685

prefix lengths, 670

problems, 612

router originated packets, 670

standard, configuring, 671-674

testing, 677

tunneled traffic matching, 670

location and direction, 440-441

matching packets, 441-442

named ACLs

configuration, 472

editing, 473-475

overview, 471-472

numbered ACLs, 475-476

overview, 440

QoS tools, compared, 496

SNMP security, 698

standard numbered ACLs
   access-list command, 454
   command syntax, 445
   configuration examples, 448-452
   list logic, 444-445
   matching any/all addresses, 448
   matching exact IP address, 445-446
   matching subset of address, 446-447
   overview, 443
   reverse engineering from ACL to address range, 454-456
   troubleshooting, 452-453
   verification, 452-453
   wildcard masks, 446-448
troubleshooting, 477
   ACL behavior in network, 477-479
   ACL interactions with router-generated packets, 483-485
   commands, 479-480
   common syntax mistakes, 481
   inbound ACL filters routing protocol packets, 481-482
   reversed source/destination IP address, 480-481
ACL Analysis tool, 777-778
ACS (Access Control Server), 147
active HSRP routers, 558
address blocks. *See* **prefixes**
addresses
  families, 619
  global unicast, 593
  IPv4, 197
  IPv6
    assigning to hosts, 595-597
    connectivity, verifying, 600-603
    multicast, 682
    router configuration, 598-599
    static route configuration, 599
    unicast, 593-595
  link, 311-312
  link-local, 595
  MAC, 49
  public cloud assignment services, 756-757
  source/destination, 406
  unique local unicast, 593
adjacent neighbors, 186, 633
administrative distance, 177-178
administratively shutdown interfaces, 49
ADSL (asymmetric DSL), 391
advertising
  BGP routes, 303-304
  eBPG enterprise public prefixes, 307-308
  subnets to ISPs, 318
AF (Assured Forwarding), 502-503
agents (SNMP), 695
  Get/Set messages, 696
  MIB, 697
  NMS polling, 696
  notifications, 696-697
algorithms
  Dijkstra SPF, 180
  DUAL (Diffusing Update Algorithm), 242-243, 646
  IGP routing protocol algorithm, 175
  SPF (Shortest Path First), 180, 186-188
  STA (spanning-tree algorithm), 48
all IP addresses, matching, 448
alternate ports, 60-61, 91-92
Amazon Web Services (AWS), 742

American Registry for Internet Numbers (ARIN), 174

analyzers (network), 719

answering exam questions, 790-792

anti-replay (Internet VPNs), 394

any keyword, 448

any/all IP addresses, matching, 448

APIs (application programming interfaces), 768-769

APIC (Application Policy Infrastructure Controller), 774

APIC EM (APIC Enterprise Module), 774-776

ACL Analysis tool, 777

controller, 777

labs website, 777

Path Trace ACL Analysis tool, 777-778

Path Trace app, 777

Application Centric Infrastructure (ACI), 773-774

Application Policy Infrastructure Controller (APIC), 774

application signatures, 498

application-specific integrated circuit (ASIC), 765

architectures (SDN), 770

APIC Enterprise Module (APIC-EM), 774-776

controller, 777

labs website, 778

Path Trace ACL Analysis tool, 777-778

Path Trace app, 777

Application Centric Infrastructure (ACI), 773-774

comparisons, 776

Open SDN, 771

Open SDN Controller (OSC), 772

OpenDaylight (ODL), 771-772

OpenFlow, 771

Area Border Router. *See* ABR

area design (OSPF), 189-190

ABR, 190, 210-211

areas, 189-190

backbone areas, 190

multiarea on ABR configuration, 625

super, 381

backbone routers, 190

benefits, 191

interarea routes, 190

internal routers, 190

intra-area routes, 190

mismatches, finding, 290-291

MPLS VPNs, 381-382

network size, 189

problems, 188, 281

single-area, 188

SPF workload, reducing, 190

three-area, 189

ARIN (American Registry for Internet Numbers), 174

AS (autonomous system), 174, 304

as a Service (-aaS), 742

ASAv (virtual ASA firewall), 754

ASIC (application-specific integrated circuit), 765

ASNs (AS numbers), 174

BGP, 304

EIGRP, 248

for IPv6, 649

neighbors, 235, 288

Assured Forwarding (AF), 502-503

asymmetric DSL (ADSL), 391

attacks

DHCP-based, 152

types, 150

auth keyword (snmp-server group command), 707

authentication

802.1x, 145

AAA servers

configuration examples, 148-150

login authentication rules, 150

login process, 147

TACACS+/RADIUS protocols, 148

EIGRP neighbors, 235, 286

Internet VPNs, 393

PPP, 342-343

PPP CHAP, 356

PPP PAP, 356

SNMPv3, 699, 707-708

authentication ppp pap command, 346

authenticators, switches as, 145

auto-cost reference-bandwidth command, 222, 643

autonomous system (AS), 174, 304

auto-summary command, 267

defined, 270

EIGRP, 247

EIGRP for IPv4, 648

autosummarization, 266

classful network boundaries, 266-267

discontiguous classful networks, 267-268

AWS (Amazon Web Services), 742

B

backbone areas (OSPF), 190

multiarea on ABR configuration, 625

super, 381

backbone routers, 190

backup DRs (BDRs), 185, 211-212

backup port role (RSTP), 62-63

backup ports, 60, 91-92

bandwidth

EIGRP

for IPv6 routes, 650-651

metrics, 237-239, 265

routes, tuning, 259

interfaces

defaults, 216

higher, 217

OSPF costs based on, 216-217

least-bandwidth, 237

managing, 491

MetroE, 373-374

reference, 216-217

bandwidth command, 216, 359

defined, 222, 270

EIGRP, 247, 647

for IPv6, 662

metrics, 237, 265

OSPFv3 interface, 643

batch traffic, 493

BDRs (backup DRs), 185, 211-212

Bellman-Ford protocols. *See* DV protocols

best path selection (BGP), 305-306

BGP (Border Gateway Protocol), 174, 300, 303

AS, 304

ASNs, 304

best path selection, 305-306

configuring, 310

external. *See* eBGP

IGPs, compared, 302

internal (iBGP), 304

ISP default routes, learning, 320-321

neighbors, 303

disabling, 314

states, 313

prefixes, 303

reachability, 302

route advertising, 303-304

routing table analysis reports website, 303

table entries, injecting, 314

advertising subnets to ISPs, 318

classful network routes, 315-318

static discard routes, 319-320

update messages, 303-310

bgp commands, 311

BIDs (bridge IDs)

STP, 49

root switch election, 50-52

verification, 77

system ID extensions, 73-74

binary-to-hexadecimal conversion, 808

binary wildcard masks, 447

blocking state

interfaces, 47-49

RSTP ports, 92

Border Gateway Protocol. *See* BGP

BPDUs (bridge protocol data units), 49

BPDU Guard, 66

configuring, 81

enabling/disabling, 83

global settings, displaying, 83

verifying, 82-83

branch offices public cloud example, 749-752

email services traffic flow, 750-751

Internet connections, 751

private WAN connections, 751

bridge IDs. *See* BIDs

bridges. *See* switches

broadcast storms, 45-47

burned-in MAC addresses, 49

C

cable Internet, 391

cabling

DTE cables, 335

leased-line WANs, 332-333

stacking cables, 156

CAC (Call Admission Control) tools, 507

carrier Ethernet, 366

Catalyst switches RSTP modes, 88-90

Catalyst switches STP modes, 88-89

CBWFQ (Class-Based Weighted Fair Queuing), 505

CCENT/CCNA ICND1 100-105 Official Cert Guide, 272

CCNA ICND2 200-105 Official Cert Guide Premium Edition eBook and Practice Test, 792

CCNA ICND2 Config Labs website, 796

CCNA Routing and Switching ICND2 Official Cert Guide website, 777

CCNA R&S practice exam, 790

CE (customer edge), 377

centralized control planes, 766

CFN (Cisco Feature Navigator), 531

challenge messages, 342

channel-group command (EtherChannels), 84, 95, 543

incorrect options, troubleshooting, 106-108

Layer 3, troubleshooting, 541

channel service unit (CSU)/data service unit (DSU), 332-334

CHAP (Challenge-Handshake Authentication Protocol)

authentication, 342, 356

configuring, 344-345

verifying, 345-346

chassis aggregation, 159

benefits, 161

design, improving, 160

distribution/core switches high availability, 159-160

switch stacking, 159-161

CIR (committed information rate), 373, 509

Cisco

Access Control Server (ACS), 147

Application Centric Infrastructure (ACI), 773-774

BPDU Guard, 66

Catalyst switches RSTP modes, 88-90

Catalyst switches STP modes, 88-89

DevNet, 777

Feature Navigator (CFN), 531

Intercloud Fabric, 749

nondisclosure agreement (NDA), 788

Open SDN Controller (OSC), 772

Prime management products website, 695

server hardware, 732-733

Unified Communication Manager (CUCM), 35

virtual ASA firewall (ASAv), 754

Class-Based Weighted Fair Queuing (CBWFQ), 505

Class of Service (CoS) fields (802.1Q header), 500-501

Class Selector (CS), 503

classful networks

autosummarization at boundaries, 266-267

discontiguous, 267-268

routes, injecting, 315-318

classful routing protocols, 177, 266

classic mode (EIGRP configuration), 249

classification (QoS), 495

ACLs, 497

matching, 496-497

NBAR, 498

router queuing, 496

routers, 497

with marking, 497

classless routing protocols, 177

clear ip ospf process command, 204, 223

clear-text passwords, 698

CLI skills, 794-796

client VPNs, 396-397

clock rate commands, 349, 359

clocking, 332

cloud computing

address assignment services, 756-757

cloud services catalogs, 740

Cloud Services Routers (CSRs), 747

DHCP services, 757

Infrastructure as a Service (IaaS), 742

NTP, 757-758

Platform as a Service (PaaS), 743-744

private, 739-741

public, 741

    accessing with Internet, 745-746

    accessing with private VPNs, 747

    accessing with private WANs, 746-749

    branch offices example, 749-752

    DNS services, 754-756

    email services traffic flow, 750-751

    intercloud exchanges, 748-749

    Internet connections, 751

    private WAN connections, 751

    VNFs, 752-754

services, 739

Software as a Service (SaaS), 743

Cloud Services Routers (CSRs), 747

codecs, 493

commands

aaa authentication login default, 149

aaa new-model, 149

access-class, 486

access-list, 445, 457, 463-466, 486

    any keyword, 448

    building ACLs with, 454

    deny keyword, 448-449

    examples and logic explanations, 467

    extended numbered ACL configuration commands, 467

    log keyword, 452

    permit keyword, 445, 448-449

    reverse engineering from ACL to address range, 454-456

    tcp keyword, 464

    upd keyword, 464

authentication ppp pap, 346

auto-cost reference-bandwidth, 222, 643

auto-summary, 267, 270

    EIGRP, 247

    EIGRP for IPv4, 648

bandwidth, 216, 222, 270, 359

    EIGRP, 247, 647

    EIGRP for IPv6, 662

    EIGRP metrics, 237, 265

    OSPFv3 interface, 643

bgp, 311

channel-group (EtherChannels), 84, 95, 543

    incorrect options, troubleshooting, 106-108

    Layer 3, troubleshooting, 541

clear ip ospf process, 204, 223

clock rate, 349, 359

command, 222

configure terminal, 28

debug, 286

debug eigrp fsm, 271

debug eigrp packets, 286, 298

debug ip ospf adj, 298

    mismatched OSPF areas, 290

    OSPF neighbors, troubleshooting, 289

debug ip ospf events, 298

debug ip ospf hello, 298

    Hello/dead timer mismatches, 293

    OSPF neighbors, troubleshooting, 289

debug ip ospf packet, 298

debug ipv6 ospf adj, 632

debug ppp authentication, 356, 360

debug ppp negotiation, 360

debug spanning-tree events, 79, 96

default-information originate, 223,
321, 628

default-information originate always,
214

delay, 247, 270, 472-474

EIGRP, 647

EIGRP for IPv6, 662

EIGRP metrics, 237, 265

extended IPv6 ACLs, 675

IPv6 ACLs, 672

deny icmp any any, 683

description, 359

dialer pool, 417, 432

dns-server, 571

eigrp router-id, 246, 252

EIGRP, 647

EIGRP for IPv6, 662

encapsulation, 359, 525

encapsulation dot1q, 543

encapsulation ppp, 344, 350, 417, 432

erase startup-config, 135

frequency, 728

history buckets-kept 6, 728

history enhanced, 717

history enhanced interval, 728

history filter all, 728

history lives-kept 1, 728

hostname, 345

icmp-echo, 728

ifconfig, 568, 600, 615

interface, 25, 37, 543

interface dialer, 432

interface loopback, 196, 222

interface multilink, 360

interface multilink1, 350

interface port-channel, 543

interface range, 27

interface tunnel, 400, 432

interface vlan, 543

ip -6 neighbor show, 615

ip access-group, 450, 457, 467, 477,
486

ip access-list, 472, 486

ip access-list extended, 473

ip address, 568, 584-585

IP addresses on loopback
interfaces, 196

MLPPP, 350

subinterfaces, 525

ip address negotiated, 418, 432

ip domain-lookup, 572

ip hello-interval eigrp, 247, 270, 297,
648

ip helper-address, 573-574

ip hold-time eigrp, 247, 270, 297

ip mtu, 296, 637

ip name-server, 572

ip ospf, 222

ip ospf cost, 222

ip ospf dead-interval, 297

ip ospf hello-interval, 297

ip route, 323

ip routing, 543

ip sla, 728

ip sla restart, 728

ip sla schedule, 715

ipconfig, 568, 600, 615

ipv6 access-list

building, 678-679

IPv6 ACLs, 687

ipv6 access-list deny, 678

ipv6 access-list permit, 678

ipv6 address, 598, 614

ipv6 dhcp relay destination, 614

ipv6 eigrp, 648, 662

ipv6 hello-interval eigrp, 662

ipv6 hold-time eigrp, 662

ipv6 mtu, 637

ipv6 ospf, 614, 624, 643

ipv6 ospf cost, 643

ipv6 router eigrp, 647, 662

ipv6 router ospf, 614, 624, 643

ipv6 traffic-filter, 673, 687

ipv6 unicast routing, 614

ipv6 unicast-routing, 598

mac-address, 432

maximum-paths, 218

    defined, 222, 270

    EIGRP, 247, 647

    EIGRP for IPv6, 651, 662

    EIGRP load balancing, 263

    OSPFv3, 627, 643

monitor session, 721, 728

mtu, 432

name, 25, 40, 135

ndp -an, 615

neighbor, 322

neighbor shutdown, 314

netsh interface ipv6 show neighbors, 615

network

    BGP, 323

    BGP table entries, injecting, 314-320

    EIGRP, 248, 270

    EIGRP, enabling, 246

    EIGRP for IPv4, 648

    EIGRP for IPv6 compatibility, 647

    OSPF single-area configuration, 198-200

    OSPFv2 interface configuration, 218

    OSPFv2 multiarea configuration, 209

no auto-summary, 268

no ip access-group, 476

no ip address, 539

no ip domain-lookup, 572

no ip sla schedule 1, 715

no neighbor shutdown, 314

no passive-interface, 223, 270

no shutdown, 40, 359

    EIGRP for IPv6, 662

    EIGRP for IPv6 routing, 650

    Layer 1 leased-line WAN problems, 354

    OSPF processes, 294

    ROAS subinterfaces, 527

no spanning-tree portfast bpduguard default, 95

no spanning-tree portfast default, 95

no switchport

    Layer 3 EtherChannels, 539

    Layer 3 switches, 543

    routed ports, 535

passive-interface, 205

    defined, 222, 297

    EIGRP, 270

    EIGRP support, 251

    OSPF interfaces as passive, configuring, 196

    OSPFv3, 624

passive-interface default, 205, 270

permit, 471-474, 487

    extended IPv6 ACLs, 675

    GRE tunnel ACLs, 410

    IPv6 ACLs, 672

permit gre, 432

permit icmp any any router-advertisement, 684

permit icmp any any router-solicitation, 684

permit ipv6, 687

ping, 483, 571-574, 615

    IPv6 host connectivity, testing, 600

    IPv6 routes, testing, 602, 614

    leased-line WANs, 353

    self-ping, 483-485

ping6, 615

    IPv6 ACLs, 674

    IPv6 connectivity, testing, 601

ppp authentication, 349, 359

ppp authentication chap, 345

ppp chap hostname, 432

ppp chap password, 432

ppp multilink, 350, 360

ppp multilink group, 360

ppp multilink group 1, 350

ppp pap sent-username, 346, 359

pppoe-client dial-pool-number, 417, 432

pppoe enable, 417, 432

remark, 472, 487

router bgp, 311

router eigrp, 246, 270, 647

router-id, 222, 614, 624

    OSPFv3, 643

    RIDs, defining, 196

router ospf, 196, 222

router ospf 1, 198

sdm prefer, 532

sdm prefer lanbase-routing, 543

show

    IPv6 ACLs, 673

    routing protocol-enabled interfaces, verifying, 275

    STP status, 68

show access-list, 473

show access-lists, 450, 457, 479, 487, 687

show arp, 572

show controllers, 352

show controllers serial, 360

show etherchannel, 96, 543

show etherchannel 1 summary, 86

show etherchannel summary, 107, 540

show interfaces, 298, 360, 543, 569

    EIGRP neighbor requirements, verifying, 286

    MLPPP, 352

    OSPF interfaces, troubleshooting, 283

    OSPF neighbors, troubleshooting, 289

    OSPFv3 interface bandwidth, 640

    PPP CHAP status, 345

    PPP PAP, 346

    routed ports, 536

show interfaces description, 298, 576

show interfaces dialer, 421, 433

show interfaces PPP status, 344

show interfaces status

    Layer 3 EtherChannels, 539

    routed ports, 536

show interfaces switchport, 31-34, 37, 41, 114-116, 135

show interfaces trunk, 32-34, 38, 41, 116-117

show interfaces tunnel, 405, 433

show interfaces virtual-access, 433

show interfaces virtual-access configuration, 423

show interfaces vlan, 543

show ip access-list, 457, 474-476

show ip access-lists, 450, 479, 487

show ip bgp, 323

show ip bgp summary, 313, 323

show ip eigrp interfaces, 271, 297

    EIGRP enabled interfaces, 250-251, 275

    EIGRP neighbor requirements, verifying, 286

    multilink interfaces, 352

show ip eigrp interfaces detail, 250, 271

show ip eigrp neighbors, 271, 297

    neighbor status, displaying, 253

    neighbor verification checks, 285

show ip eigrp topology, 259, 271

    metrics, 262

    successor routes, 258

    topology table, 256

show ip eigrp topology all-links, 260

show ip interface, 450, 457, 479

show ip interface brief, 360

    GRE tunnels, 404

    multilink interfaces, 352

    OSPF interfaces, troubleshooting, 283

show ip interfaces, 286

show ip ospf, 223, 298

    duplicate OSPF RIDs, 291

    OSPF neighbors, troubleshooting, 289

show ip ospf database, 179, 201, 223

show ip ospf interface, 223, 298

    DRs/BDRs details, displaying, 211

    Hello/dead timer mismatches, 293

    OSPF areas for ABR interfaces, 210

    OSPF neighbors, troubleshooting, 289

    OSPFv2 interface configuration, 220

    passive interface, 206

show ip ospf interface brief, 205, 223, 298

    OSPF areas for ABR interfaces, 210

    OSPF-enabled interfaces, identifying, 275

    OSPF neighbors, troubleshooting, 289

    OSPF status on interfaces, 281

    OSPFv2 interface configuration, 221

show ip ospf neighbor, 182, 223, 298

    DRs/BDRs details, displaying, 211

    neighbors, listing, 288

    OSPF processes shutdown, 295

show ip ospf neighbor interface brief, 295

show ip protocols, 223, 271, 297

    EIGRP-enabled interfaces, 251-252, 275

    EIGRP neighbor requirements, verifying, 286

    EIGRP neighbor status, displaying, 253

    IPv4 routing protocols, 202

OSPF configuration errors, 282-283

OSPFv2 interface configuration, 219

show ip route, 223, 271, 323, 577-580

administrative distance, 178

dialer interface Layer 3 orientation, 425

EIGRP-learned routes, displaying, 254

IPv4 routes added by OSPF, 201

routing tables, displaying, 543

show ip route eigrp, 254, 271, 297

show ip route ospf, 223, 298, 577-578

show ip route static, 214

show ip sla enhanced-history distribution-statistics, 729

show ip sla history, 717, 729

show ip sla statistics, 729

show ip sla summary, 729

show ipv6 access-list, 677, 687

show ipv6 eigrp interfaces, 654, 662

show ipv6 eigrp interfaces detail, 662

show ipv6 eigrp neighbors, 663

show ipv6 eigrp topology, 663

show ipv6 eigrp topology | section, 663

show ipv6 interface, 614, 687

show ipv6 neighbors, 614

IPv6 ACL ICMPv6 NDP message filtering, 681

IPv6 IPv4 replacement, 603

show ipv6 ospf, 640, 643

show ipv6 ospf database, 636, 643

show ipv6 ospf interface, 630-631, 643

show ipv6 ospf interface brief, 630, 640, 643

show ipv6 ospf neighbor, 635, 643

show ipv6 protocols, 614, 643

EIGRP for IPv6, 662

EIGRP for IPv6 interfaces, 654

OSPFv3 interfaces, 630

show ipv6 route, 614, 643

EIGRP for IPv6, 663

IPv6 router connectivity, 603

show ipv6 route eigrp, 663

show ipv6 route ospf, 638, 643

show ipv6 route | section, 663

show ipv6 routers, 614, 681

show mac address-table, 114

show mac address-table dynamic, 111

show monitor detail, 724, 729

show monitor session, 724, 729

show monitor session all, 723

show ppp all, 346-347, 360

show ppp multilink, 353, 360

show pppoe session, 424, 433

show running-config, 135, 449, 473-475

show snmp, 703, 729

show snmp community, 702, 728

show snmp contact, 728

show snmp group, 709, 729

show snmp host, 702, 729

show snmp location, 728

show snmp user, 708, 729

show spanning-tree, 96

show spanning-tree bridge, 81

show spanning-tree interface, 96

show spanning-tree interface detail, 82

show spanning-tree root, 77, 81

show spanning-tree summary, 83, 96

show spanning-tree vlan, 96

show spanning-tree vlan 10, 75-77

show spanning-tree vlan 10 bridge, 77

show spanning-tree vlan 10 interface gigabitethernet0/2 state, 92

show standby, 556, 560, 565

show standby brief, 555, 565

show tcp brief, 313

show tcp summary, 323

show vlan, 41, 114, 141

show vlan brief, 26-29, 114

show vlan id, 27, 114

show vlan status, 135

show vlans, 527, 543

show vtp password, 134, 141

show vtp status, 29, 41, 131, 134, 141

shutdown, 40, 359

   EIGRP for IPv6, 662

   EIGRP for IPv6 routing, 650

   Layer 1 leased-line WAN problems, 354

   OSPF processes, 294

   ROAS subinterfaces, 527

shutdown vlan, 135, 140

snmp-server, 700

snmp-server community, 727

snmp-server contact, 727

snmp-server enable traps, 727

snmp-server group, 705

snmp-server host, 701, 710, 727

snmp-server location, 727

snmp-server user, 707

spanning-tree, 95

spanning-tree bpduguard disable, 95

spanning-tree bpduguard enable, 75, 81, 95

spanning-tree mode, 88, 95

spanning-tree mode mst, 72

spanning-tree mode pvst, 72

spanning-tree mode rapid-pvst, 72, 90

spanning-tree pathcost method long, 55

spanning-tree portfast, 75, 81, 95

spanning-tree portfast bpduguard, 95

spanning-tree portfast default, 83, 95

spanning-tree portfast disable, 83, 95

spanning-tree vlan, 74

spanning-tree vlan 10 port-priority 112, 103

speed, 576

standby, 554, 564

standby 1 preempt, 558

standby version, 559

standby version 1 | 2, 564

switchport

   Layer 3 switches, 543

   routed ports, 535

switchport access vlan, 25, 28-29, 37-38, 40, 113, 135

switchport mode, 30, 40

switchport mode access, 25, 28, 37-38, 139

switchport mode dynamic auto, 116

switchport mode dynamic desirable, 32

switchport mode trunk, 30, 116, 524

switchport nonegotiate, 34, 40, 116, 139

switchport trunk allowed vlan, 41, 117

switchport trunk encapsulation, 30, 40

switchport trunk native vlan, 40, 118

switchport voice vlan, 36-38, 41, 135

traceroute, 574

   GRE tunnels, 406

   IPv6 host connectivity, testing, 600

IPv6 network router problems,
    troubleshooting, 611
IPv6 router connectivity, testing,
    602, 614
traceroute6, 615
tracert, 615
tunnel destination, 406-408, 432
tunnel mode gre ip, 404, 432
tunnel mode gre multipoint, 404
tunnel source, 406-407, 432
undebug all, 298
username, 345, 359
variance, 270
    EIGRP, 247, 263, 647
    EIGRP for IPv6, 651, 662
verification, 75
vlan, 25, 37, 40, 135
vlan 10, 122
vlan 200, 137
vtp, 134
vtp domain, 134, 140
vtp mode, 40, 134, 140
vtp mode off, 29, 135
vtp mode transparent, 29, 135
vtp password, 134, 140
vtp pruning, 134, 140
vtp version, 140
committed information rate (CIR),
    373, 509
communities (SNMP), 698-699
Community-based SNMP Version 2
    (SNMPv2c), 699
community strings (SNMP), 698
confidentiality (Internet VPNs), 393
Config Checklist app, 796
configure terminal command, 28

configuring
AAA servers, 148-150
AAA servers for 802.1x, 145
ACLs (access control lists)
    extended numbered, 467-470
    named, 472
    numbered, 475-476
    standard numbered, 448-452
BGP, 310
    disabling eBGP neighbors, 314
    eBGP neighbor verification,
        312-313
    eBGP neighbors using link
        addresses, 311-312
    ISP default routes, learning,
        320-321
    table entries, injecting, 314-320
    transporting messages with TCP,
        310
    update messages, 310
BPDU Guard, 81-83
DHCP snooping, 153-154
EIGRP, 246
    ASNs, 248
    checklist, 246
    classful network numbers, 248
    classic versus named mode, 249
    sample internetwork, 247
    verification. See verifying,
        EIGRP configuration
    wildcard masks, 248-249
EIGRP for IPv6, 647
    commands, 647
    example, 648-649
    load balancing, 651-652
    route metrics, 650-651
    timers, 652

EtherChannels, 84
> dynamic, 86-87
> manual, 84-86

GRE tunnels, 402-404

HDLC, 337-340

HSRP, 554, 560-561

ICMP-Echo operations, 714-715

IGPs, 310

interfaces as passive, 205

IPv6
> addressing on routers, 598-599
> extended ACLs, 674-676
> hosts, 595-597
> routing, 598
> standard ACLs, 671-674
> static routes, 599

ISL, 525

ISP routers, 419

Layer 3
> EtherChannels, 537-539
> switch routed ports, 535-537
> switching with SVIs, 529-531

local SPAN, 721-724

MLPPP, 349-350

multiarea OSPFv2, 206-210
> network commands, 209
> single-area configurations, 207-208
> subnets, 206
> verifying, 210-212

OSPFv2 interfaces, 218-221

OSPFv3, 621
> default routes, 627-628
> load balancing, 627
> multiarea example, 622
> multiarea on ABR, 625

route selection metrics, setting, 626
> single-area, 623-624

overlapping VLSM subnets, 584-585

PortFast, 81-83

PPP, 343-344
> CHAP, 344-345
> PAP, 346-347

PPPoE, 415-416
> ISP router configuration example, 419
> Layer 1, 416-417
> Layer 2, 417-418
> summary, 418-419
> verification, 420-425

RIDs (OSPF), 203-204

ROAS, 524
> native VLANs, 525-526
> subinterface numbers, 525
> subinterfaces, creating, 524-525
> troubleshooting, 528-529
> verifying, 526-527

single-area OSPFv2, 197-198
> IPv4 addresses, 197
> matching with network command, 198-200
> multiarea configurations, 207-208
> network command, 198
> organization, 196-197
> passive interfaces, 204-206
> RIDs, 203-204
> verifying, 200-202
> wildcard masks, 199

SNMPv2
> Get/Set messages, 699-701
> Trap/Inform messages, 701-702
> verifying, 702-704

SNMPv3, 704
  authentication, 707-708
  encryption, 707-708
  groups, 705-707
  notifications, 710-711
  requirements, 704
  summary, 711-712
  users, 707
  verifying, 708-709
STP, 71
  modes, 72
  options, 74-75
  per-VLAN port costs, 74
  port costs, 78-79
  PVST+, 72-73
  root election influence, 80-81
  system ID extensions, 73-74
  topology changes, influencing, 55
  verification commands, 75
VLANs (virtual LANs), 24-25
  data and voice VLANs, 36-38
  full VLAN configuration example, 25-28
  shorter VLAN configuration example, 28-29
  trunking, 30-34
VTP
  common rejections, troubleshooting, 137
  default VTP settings, 129
  example, 130-131
  new VTP configuration settings, 130
  planning, 129
  steps, 129
  storing configuration, 134-135
  transparent mode, 135

congestion avoidance, 512
  TCP windowing, 512-513
  tools, 513-514
congestion management, 504
  Low Latency Queuing (LLQ), 505-507
  multiple queues, 504
  output queuing, 504
  prioritization, 505
  round robin scheduling, 505
  strategy, 507
connections (public cloud access)
  branch offices, 751
  Internet, 745-746
  private WANs, 746-749
  VPNs, 747
contiguous networks, 267
control planes
  centralized, 766
  distributed, 766
  networking devices, 763-764
control protocols (CP), 341
controllers, 766
  APIC-EM, 777
  centralized control, 766-767
  Northbound Interfaces (NBIs), 768-770
  OpenDaylight SDN controller, 771
  Southbound Interfaces (SBIs), 767-768
convergence
  EIGRP, 239
    DUAL process, 242-243
    feasible successor routes, 260-261
    successors, 241-242
  routing protocols, 173
  STP, 48, 105-106

converting
  binary to hexadecimal, 808
  decimal to binary, 805-807
  hexadecimal to binary, 808
core switches, 159-160
CoS (Class of Service) fields (802.1Q header), 500-501
costs. *See* metrics
counters, 715-716
CP (control protocols), 341
CPE (customer premises equipment), 332
CS (Class Selector), 503
CS DSCP values, marking, 503
CSRs (Cloud Services Routers), 747
CSU/DSU (channel service unit/data service unit), 332-334
CUCM (Cisco Unified Communication Manager), 35
customer edge (CE), 377

D

data
  application traffic, 492-493
  EIGRP for IPv6 topology, 657-658
  integrity, 393
  usage (MetroE), 373
    bandwidth used, charging for, 373-374
    overages, controlling, 374-375
data centers (virtual)
  networking, 735
  physical networks, 736
  vendors, 735
  workflow, 737-738
data circuit-terminating equipment (DCE), 334

data plane
  EtherChannel impact on MAC tables, 111-112
  networking devices, 762-763
  STP impact on MAC tables, 110
  VLAN of incoming frames, 112-113
data terminal equipment (DTE), 334-335
databases
  LSDB, 179
    area design, 190
    best routes, finding, 180
    contents, displaying, 201
    exchanging between neighbors, 183-186
    LSAs relationship, 179
    OSPFv3, 636
  MIB, 695-697
    OIDs, 697
    variable numbering/names, 697
    variables, monitoring, 696
    views, 705
  topology, 188
  VLAN, 131-133
DCE (data circuit-terminating equipment), 334
Dead Interval timer, 184
dead timers, 293-294
debug command, 286
debug eigrp fsm command, 271
debug eigrp packets command, 286, 298
debug ip ospf adj command, 298
  mismatched OSPF areas, 290
  OSPF neighbors, troubleshooting, 289
debug ip ospf events command, 298

debug ip ospf hello command, 298

Hello/dead timer mismatches, 293

OSPF neighbors, troubleshooting, 289

debug ip ospf packet command, 298

debug ipv6 ospf adj command, 632

debug messages, 261

debug ppp authentication command, 356, 360

debug ppp negotiation command, 360

debug spanning-tree events command, 79, 96

decimal-to-binary conversion, 805-807

decimal wildcard masks, 446-447

default-information originate always command, 214

default-information originate command, 223, 321

OSPF default routes, 214

OSPFv3, 628

default routes, 627-628

default VLANs, 25

delay command, 270

EIGRP, 247, 647

EIGRP for IPv6, 662

EIGRP metrics, 237, 265

delays

EIGRP

IPv6 routes, 650-651

metrics, 237, 265

managing, 491

delivery headers, 400

deny command, 472-474, 487

extended IPv6 ACLs, 675

IPv6 ACLs, 672

deny icmp any any command, 683

deny keyword, 442, 448-449

dependencies (SPAN), 722

description command, 359

design

improving with chassis aggregation, 160

Internet edge, 306

MetroE Layer 3, 370

E-LAN service, 371-372

E-Line service, 370-371

E-Tree service, 372

MetroE physical, 365-366

MPLS Layer 3, 377

MPLS VPNs Layer 3, 379-382

OSPF area, 189

ABR, 190, 210-211

areas, 189-190

backbone areas, 190

backbone routers, 190

benefits, 191

interarea routes, 190

internal routers, 190

intra-area routes, 190

MPLS VPNs, 381-382

network size, 189

problems, 188, 281

single-area, 188

SPF workload, reducing, 190

three-area, 189

OSPFv3 multiarea, 622

designated ports. See DPs

designated routers. See DRs

destination addresses, 406

destination IP, matching, 463-464

destination ports (SPAN), 719

devices, networking, 762

control, centralizing, 766-767

control plane, 763-764

data plane, 762-763

management plane, 764

switch internal processing, 765-766

DevNet, 777

DHCP (Dynamic Host Control Protocol)

Binding Table, 153

DHCP Relay, 573

public cloud services, 757

snooping

configuration settings, 153

DHCP-based attacks, 152

DHCP Binding Table, 153

features, 151

ports as trusted, configuring, 153

rate limiting, 154

rules summary, 153

trusted/untrusted ports, 151-154

stateful, 608-609

troubleshooting, 573-574

DHCP-based attacks, 152

DHCPv6, 596

dialer interfaces

Layer 3 orientation, 425

PPPoE

configuration, 416-417

verifying, 421-422

dialer pool command, 417, 432

Differentiated Services Code Point. *See* **DSCP**

Diffusing Update Algorithm (DUAL), 242-243, 646

Digital Signal level 0 (DS0), 334

Digital Signal level 1 (DS1), 334

Digital Signal level 3 (DS3), 334

digital subscriber lines (DSLs), 390-391

Dijkstra SPF algorithm, 180

direction (ACLs), 440-441

disabling

BGP neighbors, 314

BPDU Guard, 83

DTP, 116

EIGRP for IPv6 routing, 650

PortFast, 83

ports, 60

VLANs, 114-115

VLAN trunking, 139

discard routes, 319

discarding state

interfaces, 47-49

RSTP, 61

discontiguous classful networks, 266-268

discontiguous networks, 267

discovery (EIGRP neighbors), 234

displaying

BPDU Guard global settings, 83

DRs/BDRs details, 211

EIGRP

enabled interfaces, 275

IPv4 routing table, 253-254

neighbor status, 253

topology table, 255-257

LSDB contents, 201

OSPF-enabled interfaces, 275

passive interfaces, 206

PortFast global settings, 83

TCP connections, 313

distance vector protocols. *See* **DV protocols**

distributed control planes, 766

distribution switches, chassis aggregation, 159-160

DMVPN (Dynamic Multipoint VPN), 411

multipoint GRE tunnels, 411

NHRP (Next Hop Resolution Protocol), 412-413

DNS (Domain Name System)

IPv6 network troubleshooting, 607-608

public cloud services, 754-756

troubleshooting, 571-572

dns-server command, 571

down status (interfaces), 354

DP (designated port), LAN segments, 49, 60

choosing, 54, 104-105

problems, troubleshooting, 105

DR (designated router), 185

backup (BDRs), 185

discovering, 211-212

Ethernet links, 185-186

DROthers routers, 186

DS0 (Digital Signal level 0), 334

DS1 (Digital Signal level 1), 334

DS3 (Digital Signal level 3), 334

DSCP (Differentiated Services Code Point), 497

fields (QoS marking), 501

marking values

AF, 502-503

CS, 503

EF, 502

DSL (digital subscriber line), 390-391

DSLAMs (DSL access multiplexers), 390

DTE (data terminal equipment), 334-335

DTP (Dynamic Trunking Protocol), 116

DUAL (Diffusing Update Algorithm), 242-243, 646

dual Internet edge design, 306

dual stack

OSPFv2/OSPFv3, 619

OSPFv3 address families, 620

strategies, 598

DV (distance vector) protocols, 175, 228

distance/vector information learned, 228

EIGRP as, 232-233

route poisoning, 231-232

split horizon, 230-231

update messages, 229-230

dynamic EtherChannels configuration, 86-87

Dynamic Host Control Protocol. *See* **DHCP**

Dynamic Multipoint VPN. *See* **DMVPN**

Dynamic Trunking Protocol (DTP), 116

E

E1, 334

E3, 334

EAP (Extensible Authentication Protocol), 146

EAPoL (EAP over LAN), 146

earplugs (exam), 786

eBGP (External BGP), 304

Internet edge, 306

design, 306

enterprise public prefixes, advertising, 307-308

ISP default routes, learning, 309

neighbors
>   configuring, *312*
>   disabling, *314*
>   using link addresses, configuring, *311*
>   verifying, *312-313*

Eclipse IDE, **744**

edge ports, **63**

EF (Expedited Forwarding), **501**

EF DSCP value marking, **502**

EF RFC (RFC 3246), **502**

EGP (exterior gateway protocol), **173, 302**

EIGRP (Enhanced Interior Gateway Routing Protocol), **175**

EIGRP for IPv4
>   as advanced DV protocol, 232-233
>   authentication, 286
>   autosummarization, 266
>>   classful network boundaries, 266-267
>>   discontiguous classful networks, 267-268
>   benefits, 227
>   configuration, 246
>>   ASNs, 248
>>   checklist, 246
>>   classful network numbers, 248
>>   classic versus named mode, 249
>>   sample internetwork, 247
>>   wildcard masks, 248-249
>   convergence, 239
>>   DUAL process, 242-243
>>   feasible successor routes, 260-261
>>   successors, 241-242
>   disadvantages, 227

EIGRP for IPv6, compared, 644-646, 653

feasible successor routes
>   convergence, 260-261
>   identifying, 258-260

goals, 302

interfaces
>   configuration problems, 278-281
>   identifying, 275
>   OSPF interfaces, compared, 281
>   troubleshooting, 275-281

K-values, 286

metrics, 236
>   bandwidth, 265
>   calculation, 236-237
>   components, 262
>   delay settings, 265
>   EIGRP topology database, 262
>   example, 237-238
>   FD (feasible distance), 240-241
>   RD (reported distance), 240-241
>   route load balancing, 264
>   serial link bandwidth, 238-239

MPLS VPN challenges, 382

neighbors, 234-235
>   discovery, 234
>   requirements, 284-286
>   status, 233, 253
>   topology information, exchanging, 235-236
>   troubleshooting example, 286-288
>   verifying, 235, 285-286

OSPF, compared, 224

query/reply messages, 242

RIDs, configuring, 252

RIP metrics, compared, 176

RIPv2/OSPFv2, compared, 233

routes

    choosing, 234

    load balancing, 263-264

    tuning with bandwidth changes, 259

    variance, 263-264

successor routes, identifying, 257-258

topology

    database metrics, 262

    exchange, 234

    table, displaying, 255-257

variance, 263-264

verification, 249

    EIGRP enabled interfaces, finding, 250-252

    IPv4 routing table, displaying, 253-254

    neighbor status, displaying, 253

EIGRP for IPv6

configuration, 647

    commands, 647

    example, 648-649

    load balancing, 651-652

    route metrics, 650-651

    timers, 652

DUAL, 646

EIGRP for IPv4, compared, 644-646, 653

FS, 646

interfaces, 654-655

neighbors, 656-657

routes

    ASNs, 649

    enabling/disabling, 650

    FS, 646

    successors, 646

    troubleshooting, 660

    verifying, 659-660

topology data, 657-658

eigrp router-id command, 246, 252, 647, 662

E-LAN (Ethernet LAN) service, 368-372

E-Line (Ethernet Line) service, 367-371

email, 750-751

enabling

  AAA servers, 149

  BPDU Guard, 83

  EIGRP, 246

  EIGRP for IPv6 routing, 650

  IPv6 routing, 598

  OSPF configuration mode, 198

  PortFast, 83

  PPPoE, 417

  VLANs, 115

Encapsulated RSPAN (ERSPAN), 721

encapsulation command, 359, 525

encapsulation dot1q command, 543

encapsulation ppp command, 344, 350, 417, 432

encryption

  IPsec, 395-396

  keys, 395

  SNMPv3, 699, 707-708

  tunnel VPNs, 395

End-to-End QoS Network Design, Second Edition (Cisco Press), 494

end-user traffic, measuring, 713

endpoints, 773

enhanced history, 717

Enhanced Interior Gateway Routing Protocol (EIGRP), 175. *See also* EIGRP for IPv4; EIGRP for IPv6

Enterprise QoS Solution Reference Network Design Guide, 494

enterprises, classification matching, 496-497

eq 21 parameters, 465

erase startup-config command, 135

ERSPAN (Encapsulated RSPAN), 721

EtherChannels, 64-65

  configuring, 84

    dynamic, 86-87

    manual, 84-86

  Layer 3

    configuring, 537-539

    troubleshooting, 541

    verifying, 539-540

  MAC tables impact, predicting, 111-112

  troubleshooting, 106

    configuration checks before adding interfaces, 108-109

    incorrect options, 106-108

Ethernet

  802.1Q headers, 500-501

  802.11 headers, 501

  access links, 365

  carrier, 366

  IEEE standards, 366

  links, 185-186

  WANs, 747

Ethernet LANs

  service, 368-372

  troubleshooting, 575-576

  VLANs (virtual LANs)

    configuration, 24-29

    default VLANs, 25

    IDs, 18

    IP telephony, 34-39

    native VLANs, 20

    overview, 16-18

    routing between, 21-24

    tagging, 18-20

    trunking, 18-21, 29-34

Ethernet Line (E-Line) service, 367-371

E-Tree (Ethernet Tree) service, 369, 372

ETSI (European Telco standards body), 754

EUI-64 rules, 597-599

EVC (Ethernet Virtual Connection), 367

exact IP address matching, 445-446

exam

  CLI skills, 794-796

  earplugs, 786

  exam-day suggestions, 787

  knowledge gaps, finding, 792-793

  practice exams

    answering questions, 790-791

    CCNA R&S, 790

    checklist, 790

    ICND2, 790

    other, 792

    taking, 789-790

  pre-exam suggestions, 786-787

  preparing for failure, 788

  question types, 784

  ready to pass assessment, 797

  scores, 796-797

  study tasks, 798

  studying after failing to pass, 797-798

  time budget versus number of questions, 785

  time-check method, 786

  tutorial, 784-785

Expedited Forwarding (EF), 501

extended IPv6 ACLs

   configuring, 674-676

   examples, 676-678

extended numbered IPv4 ACLs, 462

   configuration, 467-470

   matching protocol, source IP, and destination IP, 463-464

   matching TCP and UDP port numbers, 464-467

Extensible Authentication Protocol (EAP), 146

exterior gateway protocol (EGP), 173, 302

external BGP. *See* eBGP

F

Facebook (Wendell Odom), 799

failed interfaces, 49

failing the exam, 788, 797-798

failures

   CHAP authentication, 356

   HSRP, 552

   keepalive, 355

   PAP authentication, 356

FCS (Frame Check Sequence), 336

FD (feasible distance), 240-241, 256

feasibility conditions, 242, 260

feasible successor (FS), 646

feasible successor routes, 241-242

   convergence, 260-261

   identifying, 258-260

FHRP (First Hop Redundancy Protocol), 544

   features, 550

HSRP, 551

   active/passive model, 551

   active/standby routers, choosing, 555

   active/standby rules, 557

   configuring, 554

   failover, 552

   group numbers, 555

   load balancing, 553

   no preemption, 557

   with preemption, 558

   troubleshooting, 560-563

   verifying, 555-556

   versions, 559-560

   need for, 549

   options, 550-551

fiber Internet, 393

FIFO (first-in, first-out), 504

filtering

   ICMPv6 messages, 668-669, 679-683

   IPv6

      ACL policies, 668

      issues, 604

finding

   EIGRP

      enabled interfaces, 250-252

      feasible successor routes, 258-260

      successor routes, 257-258

   mismatched Hello/dead timers, 293

   OSPF area mismatches, 290-291

   routers best routes, 180

   wildcard masks, 448

firewalls, 754

First Hop Redundancy Protocol. *See* FHRP

first-in, first-out (FIFO), 504

FlexStack, 158

FlexStack-Plus, 158

flooding, 179

flow

   networking, 493

   public cloud traffic, 750-751

Forward delay timer (STP), 56

forwarding

   data. *See* routing

   interface state, 47-49

   paths, 777-778

forwarding plane. *See* data plane

Fractional T1, 334

Fractional T3, 334

Frame Check Sequence (FCS), 336

Frame Relay, 362

frames

   broadcast storms, 45-47

   defined, 495

   HDLC, 336

   incoming, 112-113

   looping, preventing, 44

   multiple frame transmissions, 47

   PPP, 341

   switching, 113

frequency command, 728

FS (feasible successor), 646

full drops, 514

full mesh topology (MetroE), 368

full neighbor state, 186, 628

full updates, 229, 235

full VLAN configuration example, 25-28

fully adjacent neighbors, 186, 633

G

generic routing encapsulation (GRE), 398

"Get IEEE 802" program, 59

Get messages

   agent information, 696

   RO/RW communities, 699

   SNMPv2 support, 699-701

GLBP (Gateway Load Balancing Protocol), 544

global unicast addresses, 593

Google App Engine PaaS, 744

GRE (generic routing encapsulation), 398

GRE tunnels, 398

   between routers, 399

   configuring, 402-404

   details, displaying, 404

   functionality, testing, 406

   large scale environments, 411

   multipoint with DMVPN, 411

   point-to-point, 399

   routes, 405

   troubleshooting, 406

      ACLs, 409-410

      interface state, 407

      Layer 3 issues, 409

      source/destination addresses, 406

      tunnel destination, 408

   tunnel interfaces, 398

   unsecured networks, 400-401

   verifying, 404-406

group numbers (HSRP), 555

groups
endpoint, 773
SNMPv3, 705-707
MIB views, 705
security levels, 705
write views, 706

H

HDLC (High-level Data Link Control), 331, 336-340, 398
headers
802.1Q, 500-501
802.11, 501
delivery, 400
IP, 499-501
MPLS Label, 501
Hello BPDU, 49
Hello Interval, 184, 233
Hello messages (OSPF), 181-182
Hello timer
dead timer mismatches, troubleshooting, 293-294
STP, 56
hexadecimal-to-binary conversion, 808
high availability, 159-160
High-level Data Link Control (HDLC), 331, 336-340, 398
High-speed WICs (HWICs), 332
historical success/failure counters (IP SLAs), 716
history
IP SLA data, 717
OSPF, 619
SNMP, 695
history buckets-kept 6 command, 728
history enhanced command, 717

history enhanced interval command, 728
history filter all command, 728
history lives-kept 1 command, 728
Hold Interval, 233
hostname command, 345
hosts
IPv6, 595
connectivity, verifying, 600-601
issues, 604
missing settings, 608-610
name resolution problems, 607-608
pings fail from default router, 606-607
pings only working in some cases, 605-606
stateful DHCPv6, 596
stateless address autoconfiguration (SLAAC), 597
routes, 357
server virtualization, 734
troubleshooting IPv4 settings
default router IP address setting, 572
DNS problems, 571-572
ensuring IPv4 settings match, 568-569
mismatched masks, 569-571
HSRP (Hot Standby Router Protocol), 544, 551
active/passive model, 551
active/standby routers, choosing, 555
active/standby rules, 557
configuring, 554
failover, 552
group numbers, 555

load balancing, 553

no preemption, 557

with preemption, 558

troubleshooting, 560

    ACL blocks HSRP packets, 563

    configuration, 560-561

    group number mismatches, 563

    misconfiguration symptoms, 561

    routers configuring different VIPs, 563

    version mismatches, 562

verifying, 555-556

versions, 559-560

HSRPv2 (HSRP version 2), 559

hub and spoke topology (MetroE), 369

Huston, Geoff website, 303

HWICs (High-speed WICs), 332

hypervisors, 734

I

IaaS (Infrastructure as a Service), 742

IANA (Internet Assigned Numbers Authority), 174

ASNs, assigning, 174

ICMPv6 parameters, 669

IPv6 multicast address space registry website, 682

website, 174

iBGP (Internal BGP), 304

icmp-echo command, 728

ICMP-Echo operations, 714-715

ICMP Echo probe, 713

icmp keyword, 481

ICMPv6

Echo Request messages, 674

messages, filtering, 668-684

packets, matching, 675

ICND2 practice exam. *See* **practice exams**

IEEE (Institute of Electrical and Electronics Engineers)

802.1D Spanning-Tree states, 58

802.1D standard, 58

802.1w amendment, 58

802.1x

    access, securing, 144-145

    authenticators, 145

    LAN access, securing, 145-146

default port costs, 55

Ethernet standards, 366

"Get IEEE 802" program, 59

ifconfig command, 568, 600, 615

IGP (interior gateway protocol), 173, 226

BGPs, compared, 302

classless/classful, 177

configuring, 310

goals, 302

metrics, 175-176

routing protocol algorithm, 175

subnets, 303

IGRP (Interior Gateway Routing Protocol), 175

implicit filtering, 683-684

incoming frames, 112-113

inferior Hello, 50

infinity, 231

Inform messages, 696-697

SNMPv2, 701-702

SNMPv3, 710-711

Infrastructure as a Service (IaaS), 742

injecting BGP table entries, 314

advertising subnets to ISPs, 318

classful network routes, 315-318

static discard routes, 319-320

instantiating VMs, 742

Institute of Electrical and Electronics Engineers. *See* IEEE

Integrated Intermediate System to Intermediate System (IS-IS), 175

interactive data application traffic, 492

interactive voice traffic, 494

interarea routes, 190, 212, 640

intercloud exchanges, 748-749

Intercloud Fabric, 749

interface command, 25, 37, 543

interface dialer command, 432

interface loopback command, 196, 222

interface multilink command, 360

interface multilink 1 command, 350

interface port-channel command, 543

interface range command, 27

interface tunnel command, 400, 432

interface vlan command, 543

interfaces

　ABR OSPF areas, verifying, 210-211

　access, 113-114

　administratively shutdown, 49

　application programming (APIs), 768-769

　bandwidth

　　defaults, 216

　　EIGRP metric calculations, 265

　　EIGRP routes, tuning, 259

　　higher reference, 217

　　OSPF costs based on, 216-217

　blocking state, 47

　delays, 265

　dialer

　　Layer 3 orientation, 425

　　PPPoE, 416-417, 421-422

　down status, 354

　EIGRP

　　configuration problems, 278-281

　　enabled, finding, 250-252, 275

　　OSPF interfaces, compared, 281

　　troubleshooting, 275-281

　EIGRP for IPv6, 654-655

　EtherChannels, adding, 108-109

　failed, 49

　forwarding state, 47

　LAN speeds, 490

　learning state, 58

　listening state, 58

　loopback, 203

　multilink, 349

　Northbound (NBIs), 768-770

　OSPF

　　bandwidth, 216

　　costs, setting, 216-217

　　EIGRP interfaces, compared, 281

　　identifying, 275

　　passive, 196

　　troubleshooting, 281-283

　OSPFv2 configuration, 218

　　example, 218

　　verifying, 219-221

　OSPFv3, 630

　　influence route selections, setting, 626

　　troubleshooting, 631-632

　　verifying, 630-631, 638-640

　passive

　　EIGRP, 251

　　OSPF, 204-206

　　OSFPv3, 624

　per-VLAN STP costs, 74

routed, 535-537

routing protocol-enabled, verifying, 274

Southbound (SBIs), 767-768

states

   changing with STP, 57-58

   forwarding or blocking criteria, 48-49

status codes, 353

subinterfaces, 524-527

switched virtual. *See* SVIs

tunnel

   ACLs, 409-410

   creating, 400

   destinations, 408

   Layer 3 issues, 409

   replacing serial links, 398

   state, 407

virtual-access, 423

VLAN. *See* SVIs

WANs, 490

working, 49

interior gateway protocol. *See* IGP

Interior Gateway Routing Protocol (IGRP), 175

interior IP routing protocols, 233

internal BGP (iBGP), 304

internal processing (switches), 765-766

internal routers, 190, 623-624

Internet

access, 389

   cable Internet, 391

   DSLs (digital subscriber lines), 390-391

   fiber, 393

   WANs, 389

   wireless WANs, 392-393

edge, eBGP and, 306

   design, 306

   enterprise public prefixes, advertising, 307-308

   ISP default routes, learning, 309

public cloud

   accessing, 745-746

   computing branch office connections, 751

VPNs, 389

   benefits, 394

   clients, 396-397

   security, 393

   site-to-site, 395-396

as WAN service, 389

wireless, 393

Internet Assigned Numbers Authority. *See* **IANA**

Internet service providers. *See* **ISPs**

Inter-Switch Link (ISL), 20-21, 525

intra-area routes, 190

ip -6 neighbor show command, 615

ip access-group command, 450, 457, 467, 477, 486

ip access-list command, 472, 486

ip access-list extended command, 473

IP ACLs (access control lists). *See* **ACLs**

ip address command, 568, 584-585

IP addresses on loopback interfaces, 196

MLPPP, 350

subinterfaces, 525

ip address negotiated command, 418, 432

ip_address parameter (network command), 198

IP addressing

conversions

binary-to-hexadecimal, 808

decimal-to-binary, 805-807

hexadecimal-to-binary, 808

public clouds

address assignment services, 756-757

DHCP services, 757

ip domain-lookup command, 572

IP headers, 499-501

ip hello-interval eigrp command, 247, 270, 297, 648

ip helper-address command, 573-574

ip hold-time eigrp command, 247, 270, 297

IP IGP metrics, 175-176

ip mtu command, 296, 637

ip name-server command, 572

ip ospf command, 222

ip ospf cost command, 222

ip ospf dead-interval command, 297

ip ospf hello-interval command, 297

ip route command, 323

ip routing command, 543

ip sla command, 728

ip sla restart command, 728

IP SLAs (IP Service Level Agreements), 712

historical success/failure counters, 716

history data, troubleshooting with, 717

ICMP-Echo, 713-715

operations, 713

responders, 713

sources, 713

troubleshooting with

counters, 715-716

history data, 717

UDP Jitter probes, 713

ip sla schedule command, 715

IP telephony (VLANs), 34

data and voice VLAN concepts, 34-36

data and voice VLAN configuration and verification, 36-38

summary, 38-39

ipconfig command, 568, 600, 615

IPP (IP Precedence) fields (QoS marking), 501-503

IPsec, 395-396

IPv4 routing

ACLs, 666-667

addresses, 197, 619

EIGRP

configuration, 248-249

load balancing, 263-264

verifying, 253-254

EIGRP verification, 249

EIGRP enabled interfaces, finding, 250-252

IPv4 routing table, displaying, 253-254

neighbor status, displaying, 253

Layer 3 EtherChannels

configuring, 537-539

troubleshooting, 541

verifying, 539-540

Layer 3 switch routed ports, 534-537

Layer 3 switching with SVIs

configuring, 529-531

troubleshooting, 532-534

verifying, 531

matching addresses
  any/all addresses, 448
  exact IP address, 445-446
  subset of address, 446-447
OSPF added, 201
QoS marking, 499
routing protocols
  displaying, 202
  troubleshooting, 273-274
subnet masks
  mismatched masks, 569-571
  *VLSM (variable length subnet
    masking), 581*
troubleshooting, 572
  *default router IP address setting,
    572*
  DHCP issues, 573-574
  DNS problems, 571-572
  *incorrect addressing plans,
    581-585*
  IP forwarding issues, 577-580
  LAN issues, 575-576
  *mismatched IPv4 settings,
    568-569*
  mismatched masks, 569-571
  *packet filtering with access lists,
    586*
  router WAN interface status, 585
ipv6 access-list commands
  building, 678-679
  IPv6 ACLs, 687
ipv6 access-list deny command, 678
ipv6 access-list permit command, 678
ipv6 address command, 598, 614
**ipv6 dhcp relay destination command,
  614**
ipv6 eigrp command, 648, 662
ipv6 hello-interval eigrp command, 662

ipv6 hold-time eigrp command, 662
ipv6 mtu command, 637
ipv6 ospf command, 614, 624, 643
ipv6 ospf cost command, 643
ipv6 router eigrp command, 647, 662
**ipv6 router ospf command, 614, 624,
  643**
IPv6 routing
  access restrictions with IPv6 ACLs,
    685
  ACLs, 664-666
    *access-list commands, building,
      678-679*
    access restrictions, 685
    blocking, 683
    capabilities, 669
    extended, 674-678
    *filtering ICMPv6 NDP messages,
      679-683*
    filtering policies, 668
    *ICMPv6 message filtering,
      668-669*
    *implicit filtering ICMPv6 NDP
      messages, 683-684*
    IPv4 ACL, compared, 666-667
    limitations, 669-670
    logging, 670
    management control, 685
    prefix lengths, 670
    problems, 612
    router originated packets, 670
    standard, configuring, 671-674
    testing, 677
    tunneled traffic matching, 670
  addressing on routers configuration,
    598-599
  connectivity, verifying, 600-601
    hosts, 600-601
    routers, 601-603

EIGRP

  ASNs, 649

  configuration, 647-649

  DUAL, 646

  EIGRP for IPv4, compared, 644-646, 653

  FS, 646

  interfaces, 654-655

  load balancing, 651-652

  neighbors, 656-657

  routes, 650-651, 659-660

  successors, 646

  timers, 652

  topology data, 657-658

global unicast addresses, 593

host configuration, 595

  stateful DHCPv6, 596

  stateless address autoconfiguration (SLAAC), 597

link-local addresses, 595

multicast addresses, 682

OSPF, 619-620

OSPFv3

  configuration, 621-622

  default routes, 627-628

  interface cost metrics, 638-640

  interfaces, 630

  IPv6 MTU mismatches, 636-638

  IPv6 routes, troubleshooting, 640-641

  load balancing, 627

  LSAs, 636

  LSDBs, 636

  multiarea on ABR configuration, 625

  neighbors, 632

  OSPFv2, compared, 621, 628-629

  passive interfaces, 624

  RIDs, 624

  route selection metrics, 626

  single-area configuration, 623-624

  troubleshooting interfaces, 631-632

  troubleshooting neighbors, 633-635

  verifying interfaces, 630-631

  verifying neighbors, 632-633

protocols, 619

QoS marking, 500

routers, enabling, 598

routes

  EIGRP for IPv6 metrics, 650-651

  OSPFv3 metrics, 626, 638-640

  troubleshooting, 640-641

subnetting, 593

unique local unicast addresses, 593

static route configuration, 599

subnetting, 593-594

troubleshooting, 604

  ACLs, 612

  filtering issues, 604

  host issues, 604

  host pings fail from default router, 606-607

  host pings only working in some cases, 605-606

  missing IPv6 settings in host, 608-610

  name resolution problems, 607-608

  router issues, 604

  routing, 611-612

unicast addresses, 593-595

ipv6 traffic-filter command, 673, 687

ipv6 unicast routing command, 598, 614

IS-IS (Integrated Intermediate System to Intermediate System), 175

ISL (Inter-Switch Link), 20-21, 525

ISPs (Internet service providers), 389

    default routes, learning, 320-321

    dial connections with PPP, 414

    Internet edge, learning, 309

    router configuration example, 419

    subnets, advertising, 318

J

Jenkins continuous integration and automation tool, 744

jitter, managing, 491

K

keepalive failures, 355

keyboard, video display, or mouse (KVM), 733

keys (encryption), 395

keywords. *See also* commands

    any, 448

    deny, 442, 448-449

    icmp, 481

    log, 452, 670

    permit, 442, 448-449

    tcp, 464

    udp, 464

knowledge gaps, finding, 792-793

K-values (EIGRP), 286

KVM (keyboard, video display, or mouse), 733

L

labs, completing, 795-796

LACP (Link Aggregation Control Protocol), 86

LANs, 523

    defined, 16

    DPs, 54, 104-105

    interfaces, 490

    redundancy

        problems caused without STP, 45-46

        STP, 42

    security

        IEEE 802.1x, 144-146

        STP security exposures, 65-66

    troubleshooting, 575-576

    VLAN support, adding, 122

Layer 1

    leased-line WANs

        CSU/DSUs, 334

        physical components, 332-333

        speeds, 333-334

        troubleshooting, 354

    leased-line WANs with HDLC, 335-336

    PPPoE

        configuration, 416-417

        switches, 21

        troubleshooting, 427-428

Layer 2

    leased-line WANs, 354-356

    leased-lines with HDLC, 336

    MLPPP, 349

    PPPoE

        configuration, 417

        troubleshooting, 428-429

Layer 3

GRE tunnel issues, 409

leased-line WANs, troubleshooting, 357-358

MetroE design, 370

E-LAN service, 371-372

E-Line service, 370-371

E-Tree service, 372

MLPPP, 348-349

MPLS, 377

MPLS VPNs, 379-380

EIGRP challenges, 382

OSPF area design, 381-382

PPPoE

configuration, 417-418

status, verifying, 425

troubleshooting, 429

switches, 21

EtherChannels, 537-541

routed ports, 534-537

with SVIs, 529-534

VLAN (virtual LAN) routing, 23-24

LCP (Link Control Protocol), 341-342

learning state (interfaces), 58

leased-line WANs, 330-331

building, 335-336

CSU/DSU, 334

with HDLC, 336

configuring HDLC, 337-340

de-encapsulating/ re-encapsulating IP packets, 336

framing, 336

physical components, 332-333

with PPP

authentication, 342-343

configuring PPP, 343-344

configuring PPP CHAP, 344-346

configuring PPP PAP, 346-347

control protocols, 341

framing, 341

multilink. See MLPPP

PPP functions, 340

speeds, 333-334

troubleshooting, 353-354

Layer 1 problems, 354

Layer 2 problems, 354-356

Layer 3 problems, 357-358

mismatched subnets, 358

least-bandwidth, 237

limiting SPAN sources, 725

Link Aggregation Control Protocol (LACP), 86

Link Control Protocol (LCP), 341-342

link-local addresses, 595

link-state advertisements. *See* **LSAs**

link-state database. *See* **LSDB**

link-state protocols, 175. *See also* **OSPF**

Link-State Update (LSU) packets, 183

links

access

MetroE, 365

MPLS, 378

addresses, 311-312

Ethernet, 185-186

RSTP types, 63

serial

bandwidth, 238-239

replacing with IP tunnels, 398

routing IP packets over, 398

list logic (IP ACLs), 444-445

listening state (interfaces), 58

LLQ (Low Latency Queuing), 505-507

load balancing
  EIGRP, 263-264, 651-652
  HSRP, 553
  MLPPP, 349
  OSPF, 217
  OSPFv3, 627
local SPAN, configuring, 721-724
location (ACLs), 440-441
log keyword, 452, 670
log messages, unsolicited, 283
logging IPv6 ACLs, 670
logical switches, 157-158
logins (AAA), 147, 150
Long-Term Evolution (LTE), 393
loopback interfaces, 203
looping frames, preventing, 44
loss, managing, 491
Low Latency Queuing (LLQ), 505-507
LSAs (link-state advertisements), 183
  exchanging with OSPF neighbors,
    183-184
    DRs on Ethernet links, 185-186
    maintenance, 184-185
  flooding, 179
  LSDB relationship, 179
  OSPFv3, 636
  router, 636
LSDB (link-state database), 179
  area design, 190
  best routes, finding, 180
  contents, displaying, 201
  exchanging between neighbors
    DRs on Ethernet links, 185-186
    fully exchanging LSAs, 183-184
    maintaining neighbors, 184-185
  LSAs relationship, 179
  OSPFv3, 636

LSU (Link-State Update) packets, 183
LTE (Long-Term Evolution), 393

M

mac-address command, 432
MAC addresses
  burned-in, 49
  forwarding, 111
  learning, 111
  tables
    EtherChannel impact, predicting,
      111-112
    instability, 47
    STP impact, predicting, 110
maintenance
  EIGRP neighbors, 233
  OSPF neighbors, 184-185
Managed Extensibility Framework
  (MEF), 366
Management Information Base. See
  MIB
management plane (networking
  devices), 764
managing
  bandwidth, 491
  delay, 491
  IPv6 ACLs, 685
  jitter, 491
  loss, 491
  SNMP, 695
manual EtherChannels configuration,
  84-86
marking, 497-499
  with classification, 497
  DiffServ DSCP values
    AF, 502-503
    CS, 503
    EF, 502

Ethernet 802.1Q headers, 500-501

Ethernet 802.11 headers, 501

IP headers, 499-501

MPLS Label headers, 501

trust boundaries, 501-502

matching packets, 441-442

matching parameters

extended numbered ACLs

protocol, source IP, and destination IP, 463-464

TCP and UDP port numbers, 464-467

standard numbered ACLs

any/all addresses, 448

command syntax, 445

exact IP address, 445-446

subset of address, 446-447

wildcard masks, 446-448

MaxAge timer (STP), 56

maximum-paths command, 218, 222, 270

EIGRP

for IPv4, 247, 647

for IPv6, 651, 662

load balancing, 263

OSPFv3, 627, 643

maximum transmission unit. *See* **MTU**

measuring

cloud computing services, 739

end-user traffic, 713

MEC (Multichassis EtherChannel), 161

MEF (Managed Extensibility Framework), 366

memory (TCAM), 766

messages

challenge, 342

debug, 261

EIGRP, 242

Get

agent information, 696

RO/RW communities, 699

SNMPv2 support, 699-701

ICMPv6

Echo request, 674

filtering, 668-669

NDP, filtering, 679-684

Inform, 696-697

SNMPv2, 701-702

SNMPv3, 710-711

NA (neighbor advertisement), 683

NS (neighbor solicitation), 683

OSPF Hello, 181-182

partial update, 232

RA (router advertisement), 610, 684

RS (router solicitation), 610, 684

RSTP, 62

Set

RO/RW communities, 699

SNMPv2 support, 699-701

writing variables on agents, 696

SNMP variables, monitoring, 696

STP Hello BPDU, 49

Trap, 696-697

SNMPv2, 701-702

SNMPv3, 710-711

unsolicited log, 283

update

BGP, 303, 310

DV routing protocols, 229-230

EIGRP, 235-236

metrics

BGP best path selection, 305-306

EIGRP, 236

bandwidth, 265

calculation, 236-237

components, 262

delay settings, 265

EIGRP topology database, 262

example, 237-238

FD (feasible distance), 240-241

RD (reported distance), 240-241

route load balancing, 264

serial link bandwidth, 238-239

IGP, 175-176

infinity, 231

IPv6 routes

EIGRP for IPv6, 650-651

OSPFv3 interface costs, 626

OSPF, 215

based on interface bandwidth, 216-217

higher reference bandwidth, 217

setting, 217

OSPFv3, 638-640

per-VLAN STP, 74

port, 78-79

root, 48

STP port, 53

MetroE (Metro Ethernet), 362-364

access links, 365

data usage, 373

bandwidth used, charging for, 373-374

overages, controlling, 374-375

IEEE Ethernet standards, 366

Layer 3 design, 370

E-LAN service, 371-372

E-Line service, 370-371

E-Tree service, 372

MEF, 366

physical design, 365-366

services, 366

E-LAN, 368-372

E-Line, 367-371

E-Tree, 369-372

topologies

full mesh, 368

hub and spoke, 369

partial mesh, 369

Point-to-Point, 367-368

MIB (Management Information Base), 695-697

OIDs, 697

variables

monitoring, 696

numbering/names, 697

views, 705

mind maps, reviewing, 795

mismatched IPv4 settings, troubleshooting, 568-569

mismatched masks, troubleshooting, 569-571

mismatched subnets, 286

MLPPP (multilink PPP), 348

configuring, 349-350

Layer 2 fragmentation balance, 349

Layer 3, 348-349

load balancing, 349

verifying, 351-353

monitor session command, 721, 728

monitoring MIB variables, 696

MPBGP (Multiprotocol BGP), 380

MPLS (Multiprotocol Label Switching), 362, 375-377

access links, 378

Label headers, 501

Layer 3 design, 377

public cloud connections, 747

QoS, 378-379

virtual private networks. *See* MPLS VPNs

MPLS VPNs (MPLS Virtual Private Networks), 376

EIGRP challenges, 382

Layer 3, 379-382

OSPF area design, 381-382

MST (Multiple Spanning Tree), 72

MTU (maximum transmission unit), 236

IPv6 mismatches, 636-638

OSPF mismatched settings, 296

mtu command, 432

multiarea on ABR OSPFv3 configuration, 625

multiarea OSPFv2 configuration, 206-210

network commands, 209

single-area configurations, 207-208

subnets, 206

verifying, 210-212

multiarea OSPFv3 configuration, 622

multicast addresses, 682

Multichassis EtherChannel (MEC), 161

multihomed Internet edge design, 306

multilayer switches. *See* Layer 3, switches

multilink interfaces, 349

multiple frame transmissions, 47

multiple queues (queuing systems), 504

multiple serial links between routers, 347

Multiple Spanning Tree (MST), 72

Multiprotocol BGP (MPBGP), 380

Multiprotocol Label Switching. *See* MPLS

multithreading, 734

N

NA (neighbor advertisement) messages, 683

name command, 25, 40, 135

named ACLs

configuration, 472

editing, 473-475

overview, 471-472

named mode (EIGRP configuration), 249

names (MIB variables), 697

National Institute of Standards and Technology (NIST), 739

native VLANs, 20

mismatched on trunks, 118

router configuration, 525-526

NBAR (Network Based Application Recognition), 498

NBIs (Northbound Interfaces), 768-770

NCP (Network Control Protocols), 341

NDA (nondisclosure agreement), 788

NDP (Neighbor Discovery Protocol), 593

filtering messages through IPv6 ACLs, 679-683

implicit filtering messages through IPv6 ACLs, 683-684

SLAAC, 597

ndp –an command, 615

neighbor commands, 322

neighbor shutdown command, 314

neighbors

advertisement (NA) messages, 683

BGP, 303

disabling, 314

states, 313

eBGP

configuring, 312

disabling, 314

using link addresses,
configuring, 311

verifying, 312-313

EIGRP for IPv4, 234-235

discovery, 234

requirements, 286

status, 253

topology information,
exchanging, 235-236

troubleshooting, 286-290

verifying, 235, 285-286

EIGRP for IPv6, 656-657

requirements, 656

troubleshooting, 656-657

OSPF

area mismatches, finding,
290-291

duplicate RIDs, 291-293

Hello/dead timer mismatches,
293-294

Hello messages, 181-182

LSDB exchange, 183-186

meeting, 181

requirements, 289

RIDs, learning, 181

states, 182-183, 186, 288

troubleshooting, 288-294

OSPFv3, 632

requirements, 633-634

troubleshooting, 633-635

verifying, 632-633

relationships, 284

neighbor requirements, 284

pinging routers, confirming, 285

routing protocol relationships,
troubleshooting, 274

solicitation (NS) messages, 683

states, 628

netsh interface ipv6show neighbors
command, 615

Network Based Application
Recognition (NBAR), 498

network command, 222, 323

BGP table entries, injecting, 314

advertising subnets to ISPs, 318

classful network routes, 315-318

static discard routes, 319-320

EIGRP, 270

enabling, 246

for IPv4, 648

for IPv6 compatibility, 647

wildcard masks, 248

OSPF single-area configuration,
198-200

OSPFv2

interface configuration, 218

multiarea configuration, 209

Network Control Protocols (NCP), 341

network functions virtualization (NFV),
754

network interface cards (NICs), 718,
735

Network Interface Modules (NIMs),
332

Network Layer Reachability
    Information (NLRI), 303

Network Management Station. *See*
    NMS

Network Time Protocol (NTP),
    757-758

networks
    analyzers, 719
    broad access, 739
    classful
        *autosummarization at
            boundaries, 266-267*
        routes, injecting, 315-318
    contiguous, 267
    controllers
        centralized control, 766-767
        defined, 766
        *Northbound Interfaces (NBIs),
            768-770*
        *Southbound Interfaces (SBIs),
            767-768*
    devices, 762
        control, centralizing, 766-767
        control plane, 763-764
        data plane, 762-763
        management plane, 764
        *security. See authentication,
            AAA servers*
        *switch internal processing,
            765-766*
    discontiguous, 267
    discontiguous classful, 266-268
    flow, 493
    physical data center, 736
    programmability, 760
        *APIC Enterprise Module
            (APIC-EM), 774-776*
        *Application Centric
            Infrastructure (ACI), 773-774*
        comparisons, 776

public cloud
    *address assignment services,
        756-757*
    DHCP services, 757
    DNS services, 754-756
    NTP, 757-758
    VNFs, 752-754
redundancy needs, 547-548
traffic
    bandwidth, managing, 491
    characteristics, 491
    delay, 491
    jitter, 491
    loss, 491
    types, 492-494
unsecured, 400-401
virtual, 735-736, 754
VMs, 736

Nexus 1000v vSwitch, 736

NFV (network functions virtualization),
    754

NHRP (Next Hop Resolution Protocol),
    412-413

    dynamic mapping, enabling, 412
    spoke-to-spoke communication, 413

NICs (network interface cards), 718,
    735

NIMs (Network Interface Modules),
    332

NIST (National Institute of Standards
    and Technology), 739

NLRI (Network Layer Reachability
    Information), 303

NMS (Network Management Station),
    695

    notification community strings, 701
    SNMP, 696-697

no auto-summary command, 268

no ip access-group command, 476

no ip address command, 539

no ip domain-lookup command, 572

no ip sla schedule 1 command, 715

no neighbor shutdown command, 314

no passive-interface command, 223, 270

no shutdown command, 40, 359

   EIGRP for IPv6, 650, 662

   Layer 1 leased-line WAN problems, 354

   OSPF processes, 294

   ROAS subinterfaces, 527

no spanning-tree portfast bpduguard default command, 95

no spanning-tree portfast default command, 95

no switchport command

   Layer 3 EtherChannels, 539

   Layer 3 switches, 543

   routed ports, 535

nondisclosure agreement (NDA), 788

noninteractive data application traffic, 493

nonroot switches (RPs), 101-103

   problems, troubleshooting, 103

   tiebreakers, 102-103

normal-time questions, 785

Northbound Interfaces (NBIs), 768-770

notification community strings, 701

notifications

   SNMP, 696-697

   SNMPv3, 710-711

NS (neighbor solicitation) messages, 683

NTP (Network Time Protocol), 757-758

numbered ACLs, configuring, 475-476

numbers

   AS numbers. *See* ASNs

   HSRP group, 555

   MIB variables, 697

   ROAS subinterfaces, 525

   sequence, editing ACLs with, 473-475

numeric reference table conversions

   binary-to-hexadecimal, 808

   decimal-to-binary, 805-807

   hexadecimal-to-binary, 808

O

ODL (OpenDaylight), 771-772

Odom, Wendell Twitter/Facebook information, 799

OIDs (object IDs), 697

on-demand self-service (cloud computing), 739

one-way delay, 491

ONF (Open Networking Foundation), 771

Open SDN, 771

Open SDN Controller (OSC), 772

Open Shortest Path First. *See* OSPF

OpenDaylight (ODL), 771-772

OpenFlow, 768, 771

operations (IP SLAs), 713-715

OpFlex, 768

OSC (Open SDN Controller), 772

OSPF (Open Shortest Path First), 170, 179

   area design, 189

      ABR, 190, 210-211

      areas, 189-190

      backbone areas, 190

      backbone routers, 190

benefits, 191

interarea routes, 190

internal routers, 190

intra-area routes, 190

MPLS VPNs, 381-382

network size, 189

problems, 188, 281

single-area, 188

SPF workload, reducing, 190

three-area, 189

best routes with SPF, calculating, 186-188

configuration

    errors, troubleshooting, 282-283

    mode, enabling, 198

default routes, 213-215

Dijkstra SPF algorithm, 180

EIGRP, compared, 224

goals, 302

Hello/dead timers, 293-294

history, 619

interarea routes, verifying, 212

interfaces

    costs, setting, 216-217

    EIGRP interfaces, compared, 281

    identifying, 275

    passive, 196

    troubleshooting, 281-283

load balancing, 217

LSAs, 179

metrics, 215

    based on interface bandwidth, 216-217

    higher reference bandwidth, 217

    setting, 217

MTU mismatched settings, 296

neighbors, 181

    area mismatches, finding, 290-291

    DRs on Ethernet links, 185-186

    duplicate RIDs, 291-293

    Hello messages, 181-182

    Hello/dead timer mismatches, 293-294

    LSAs, exchanging, 183-184

    maintaining, 184-185

    meeting, 181

    requirements, 284, 289

    RIDs, learning, 181

    states, 182-186, 288

    troubleshooting, 288-294

process-ids, 198

processes, shutting down, 294-296

RIDs

    configuring, 203-204

    duplicate, troubleshooting, 291-293

super backbone, 381

Version 2. *See* OSPFv2

OSPFv2 (OSPF Version 2), 170

default routes, 213-215

dual stack, 619

history, 619

interface configuration

    example, 218

    verifying, 219-221

load balancing, 217

metrics, 215

    based on interface bandwidth, 216-217

    higher reference bandwidth, 217

    setting, 217

multiarea configuration, 206-210
> *network commands, 209*
> *single-area configurations, 207-208*
> *subnets, 206*
> *verifying, 210-212*

OSPFv3, compared, 621, 628-629

RIPv2/EIGRP, compared, 233

single-area configuration, 197-198
> *IPv4 addresses, 197*
> *matching with network command, 198-200*
> *multiarea configurations, 207-208*
> *network command, 198*
> *organization, 196-197*
> *passive interfaces, 204-206*
> *RIDs, 203-204*
> *verifying, 200-202*
> *wildcard masks, 199*

OSPFv3 (OSPF Version 3), 616

address families dual stack, 620

configuration, 621
> *default routes, 627-628*
> *load balancing, 627*
> *multiarea example, 622*
> *multiarea on ABR, 625*
> *route selection metrics, setting, 626*
> *single-area, 623-624*

dual stack, 619

interfaces, 630
> *troubleshooting, 631-632*
> *verifying, 630-631*

IPv6
> *MTU mismatches, 636-638*
> *routes, 638-641*

LSAs, 636

LSDBs, 636

neighbors, 632
> *requirements, 633-634*
> *troubleshooting, 633-635*
> *verifying, 632-633*

OSPFv2, compared, 621, 628-629

passive interfaces, 624

RIDs, 624

output queuing, 504

overages (MetroE data usage), 374-375

overlapping routes, troubleshooting, 577-580

overlapping subnets

with VLSM, 583-585

without VLSM, 581-583

P

PaaS (Platform as a Service), 743-744

packets

classification, 495
> *ACLs, 497*
> *with marking, 497*
> *matching, 496-497*
> *NBAR, 498*
> *router queuing, 496*
> *routers, 497*

congestion avoidance, 512
> *TCP windowing, 512-513*
> *tools, 513-514*

congestion management, 504
> *Low Latency Queuing (LLQ), 505-507*
> *multiple queues, 504*
> *output queuing, 504*

prioritization, 505

queuing strategy, 507

round robin scheduling, 505

de-encapsulating/re-encapsulating with HDLC, 336

defined, 495

filtering. *See* ACLs

ICMPv6, 675

marking, 499

802.1Q headers, 500-501

802.11 headers, 501

with classification, 497

DiffServ DSCP AF values, 502-503

DiffServ DSCP CS values, 503

DiffServ DSCP EF values, 502

IP headers, 499-501

MPLS Label headers, 501

trust boundaries, 501-502

matching, 441-442

policing, 507

discarding excess traffic, 509

edge between networks, 509-510

features, 510

traffic rate versus configured policing rate, 508

router originated, 670

router queuing, 496

routing over serial links, 398

shaping, 507, 510

features, 512

slowing messages, 510

time intervals, 511-512

TCP, 675

UDP, 675

PAgP (Port Aggregation Protocol), 86

PAP (Password Authentication Protocol)

authentication, 343, 356

configuring, 346-347

parameters

ICMPv6, 669

ip_address, 198

wildcard_mask, 198

partial mesh topology (MetroE), 369

partial updates (EIGRP), 232, 235

passive-interface command, 205

defined, 222, 297

EIGRP, 251, 270

OSPF interfaces as passive, configuring, 196

OSPFv3, 624

passive-interface default command, 205, 270

passive interfaces

EIGRP, 251

OSPF, 196, 204-206

OSPFv3, 624

Password Authentication Protocol. *See* **PAP**

passwords, 698

path attributes (BGP), 305-306

Path MTU Discovery (PMTUD), 668

paths

forwarding

APIC-EM Path Trace ACL Analysis tool, 778

APIC-EM Path Trace app, 777

selections, 172

PBX (private branch exchange), 34

PCP (Priority Code Point) field (802.1Q header), 500

PE (provider edge), 377

Pearson Network Simulator (the Sim), 796

peers (BGPs), 303

periodic updates, 229

permit command, 471-474, 487

  extended IPv6 ACLs, 675

  GRE tunnel ACLs, 410

  IPv6 ACLs, 672

permit gre command, 432

permit icmp any any router-advertisement command, 684

permit icmp any any router-solicitation command, 684

permit ipv6 commands, 687

permit keyword, 442, 448-449

Per-VLAN Spanning Tree Plus (PVST+), 72-73

physical data center networks, 736

physical design (MetroE), 365-366

physical server model, 734

ping command, 483, 571-574, 615

  IPv6

    connectivity, testing, 600-602

    routes, testing, 614

  leased-line WANs, 353

  self-ping, 483-485

ping6 command, 615

  IPv6 ACLs, 674

  IPv6 connectivity, testing, 601

pings (IPv6 hosts)

  failure from default router, 606-607

  name resolution problems, 607-608

  working only in some cases, 605-606

planes (networking devices)

  control, 763-764

  data, 762-763

  management, 764

planning

  EIGRP configuration, 246

  VTP configuration, 129

Platform as a Service (PaaS), 743-744

PMTUD (Path MTU Discovery), 668

point-to-point edge ports, 63, 93

point-to-point GRE tunnels, 399

point-to-point lines, 330-331

  building, 335-336

  CSU/DSU, 334

  with HDLC, 336

    configuring HDLC, 337-340

    de-encapsulating/ re-encapsulating IP packets, 336

    framing, 336

  physical components, 332-333

  with PPP

    authentication, 342-343

    configuring PPP, 343-344

    configuring PPP CHAP, 344-346

    configuring PPP PAP, 346-347

    control protocols, 341

    framing, 341

    multilink. See MLPPP

    PPP functions, 340

  speeds, 333-334

  troubleshooting, 353-354

    Layer 1 problems, 354

    Layer 2 problems, 354-356

    Layer 3 problems, 357-358

    mismatched subnets, 358

Point-to-Point over Ethernet. *See* PPPoE

point-to-point ports, 63, 93

Point-to-Point Protocol. *See* PPP

Point-to-Point topology (MetroE), 367-368

points of presence (PoP), 304, 365

policies

ACI, 773

filtering, 668

policing

data overages (MetroE), 374

QoS, 507

discarding excess traffic, 509

edge between networks, 509-510

features, 510

traffic rate versus configured policing rate, 508

rate, 508

pooling resources, 739

PoP (points of presence), 304, 365

Port Aggregation Protocol (PAgP), 86

PortChannels. *See* EtherChannels

PortFast, 65

configuring, 81

enabling/disabling, 83

global settings, displaying, 83

verifying, 82-83

ports

802.1w RSTP roles, 60

alternate, 60-61, 91-92

backup, 60, 91-92

blocking, choosing, 44

channels, 86

costs

IEEE default, 55

STP, 53, 78-79

designated, 49, 54, 60

disabled, 60

Layer 3 switch routed, 534-537

numbers, matching, 464-467

per-VLAN STP costs, 74

root (RPs), 60

nonroot switches, 101-103

switches, choosing, 52-53

RSTP

backup, 62-63

roles, 60, 91-92

states, 92-93

types, 63, 92

SPAN destination/source, 719

stacking ports, 156

states

RSTP, 92

STP versus RSTP, 62

switch root, choosing, 52-53

trusted/untrusted, 151-153

configuring, 153

DHCP snooping, 154

powers of 2 numeric reference table, 810

PPP (Point-to-Point Protocol), 340, 413

authentication, 342-343

CHAP

authentication, 342, 356

configuring, 344-345

verifying, 345-346

configuring, 343-344

control protocols, 341

dial connections to ISPs, 414

framing, 341

leased-line WANs, 340

multilink (MLPPP), 348

configuring, 349-350

Layer 2 fragmentation balance, 349

Layer 3, 348-349

load balancing, 349

verifying, 351-353

PAP

authentication, 343, 356

configuring, 346-347

PPPoE Layer 2 configuration, 417

status, 344

ppp authentication chap command, 345

ppp authentication command, 349, 359

ppp chap hostname command, 432

ppp chap password command, 432

ppp multilink command, 350, 360

ppp multilink group command, 360

ppp multilink group 1 command, 350

ppp pap sent-username command, 346, 359

PPPoE (Point-to-Point over Ethernet), 413-415

configuring, 415-416

ISP router configuration example, 419

Layer 1, 416-417

Layer 2, 417

Layer 3, 417-418

summary, 418-419

enabling, 417

history, 414

troubleshooting, 425-426

customer router configuration, 426

dialer 2 status, 427

Layer 1, 427-428

Layer 2, 428-429

Layer 3, 429

summary, 430

verification, 420-421

dialers, 421-422

Layer 3 status, 425

session status, 424

virtual-access interfaces, 423

pppoe-client dial-pool number command, 417, 432

pppoe enable command, 417, 432

practice exams

answering questions, 790-791

CCNA R&S, 790

checklist, 790

ICND2, 790

knowledge gaps, finding, 792-793

other, 792

scores, 796-797

taking, 789-790

preemption (HSRP active/standby roles), 557-558

pre-exam suggestions, 786-787

prefixes

BGP, 303

IPv6, 594, 670

preparing for the exam

CLI skills, 794-796

exam-day suggestions, 787

knowledge gaps, finding, 792-793

practice exams

answering questions, 790-791

CCNA R&S, 790

checklist, 790

ICND2, 790

other, 792

scores, 796-797

taking, 789-790

pre-exam suggestions, 786-787

preparing for failure, 788

question types, 784

ready to pass assessment, 797

study tasks, 798

studying after failing to pass, 797-798

tutorial, 784-785

prioritization (congestion management), 505

Priority Code Point (PCP) field (802.1Q header), 500

priority queues, 506

priv keyword (snmp-server group command), 707

private branch exchange (PBX), 34

private cloud computing, 739-741

private WANs

MetroE, 364

access links, 365

data usage, 373-375

E-LAN services, 368-372

E-Line services, 367-371

E-Tree services, 369-372

full mesh topology, 368

hub and spoke topology, 369

IEEE Ethernet standards, 366

Layer 3 design, 370-372

MEF, 366

partial mesh topology, 369

physical design, 365-366

Point-to-Point topology, 367-368

services, 366

MPLS, 375-377

access links, 378

Layer 3 design, 377

MPLS VPNs, 379-382

QoS, 378-379

VPNs, 376

public cloud

accessing, 746-749

branch office connections, 751

types, 362

probes, 713-715

process-ids (OSPF), 198

processes

OSPF, shutting down, 294-296

RSTP, 62

programmability (network), 760

APIC Enterprise Module (APIC-EM), 774-776

Application Centric Infrastructure (ACI), 773-774

comparisons, 776

proprietary routing protocols, 175

protocols, 224

BGP, 174, 300, 303

AS, 304

ASNs, 304

best path selection, 305-306

configuring, 310

external. See eBGP

IGPs, compared, 302

internal (iBGP), 304

ISP default routes, learning, 320-321

neighbors, 303, 313-314

prefixes, 303

reachability, 302

route advertising, 303-304

routing table analysis reports website, 303

table entries, injecting, 314-320

update messages, 303-310

BPDUs (bridge protocol data units), 49

CHAP
    authentication, 342, 356
    configuring, 344-345
    verifying, 345-346
control plane, 764
DHCP
    Binding Table, 153
    DHCP Relay, 573
    public cloud services, 757
    snooping, 151-154
Dijkstra SPF algorithm, 180
DTP, 116
DV (distance vector), 175, 228
    distance/vector information learned, 228
    EIGRP as, 232-233
    route poisoning, 231-232
    split horizon, 230-231
    update messages, 229-230
EAP, 146
EAPoL, 146
eBGP, 304
    Internet edge, 306-309
    neighbors, 311-314
EGP, 173, 302
EIGRP, 175
FHRP, 544
    features, 550
    HSRP. See HSRP
    need for, 549
    options, 550-551
GLBP, 544
HDLC, 331, 336-340, 398
HSRP, 544, 551
    active/passive model, 551
    active/standby routers, choosing, 555

active/standby rules, 557
configuring, 554
failover, 552
group numbers, 555
load balancing, 553
no preemption, 557
with preemption, 558
troubleshooting, 560-563
verifying, 555-556
versions, 559-560
iBGP, 304
IGPs, 173, 226
    BGPs, compared, 302
    classless/classful, 177
    configuring, 310
    goals, 302
    metrics, 175-176
    routing protocol algorithm, 175
    subnets, 303
IGRP, 175
IPv4. *See* IPv4 routing
IPv6. *See* IPv6 routing
link-state, 175
management plane, 765
matching, 463-464
MPBGP, 380
NDP, 593
    filtering messages through IPv6 ACLs, 679-683
    implicit filtering messages through IPv6 ACLs, 683-684
    SLAAC, 597
NHRP, 412-413
    dynamic mapping, enabling, 412
    spoke-to-spoke communication, 413
NTP, 757-758

OSPF. *See* OSPF

OSPFv2. *See* OSPFv2

OSPFv3. *See* OSPFv3

PAgP, 86

PAP

    authentication, 343, 356

    configuring, 346-347

PPP. *See* PPP

PPPoE, 413, 415

    configuring, 415-419

    enabling, 417

    history, 414

    ISP router configuration example, 419

    troubleshooting, 425-430

    verification, 420-425

RADIUS, 146-148

RIP, 175-176, 226

RIPv2, 302

    EIGRP/OSPFv2, compared, 233

    goals, 302

routable, 172

routed, 172

routing

    administrative distance, 177-178

    algorithms, 175

    AS, 174

    autosummarization, 266-268

    classless/classful, 177, 266

    convergence, 173

    defined, 172

    DV. See DV protocols

    EGP (exterior gateway protocol), 173

    functions, 172-173

    IGP, 173-177

    interfaces enabled with, verifying, 274

    interior comparison, 233

    IPv4, 202

    link-state, 175

    path selections, 172

    proprietary, 175

    RIPv1, 226

    RIPv2, 226

    route redistribution, 177

    troubleshooting, 273-274

RSTP

    alternate ports, 60-61

    backup port role, 62-63

    Cisco Catalyst STP modes, 88-90

    implementing, 88

    link types, 63

    port roles, 60, 91-92

    port states, 62, 92-93

    port types, 63, 92

    processes, 62

    standards, 58

    STP, compared, 59-60

RTP, 235

SNMP. *See* SNMP

STA (spanning-tree algorithm), 48

STP. *See* STP

TACACS+, 148

TCP

    BGP connections, displaying, 313

    packets, 675

    port numbers, matching, 464-467

    transporting messages between BGP peers, 310

    windowing, 512-513

UDP

    Jitter probes, 713

    packets, IPv6 ACL matching, 675

    port numbers, matching, 464-467

VRRP, 544

VTP, 120

    automated update powers, 120

    configuration, 129-131

    domains, 125-127

    features, 128

    planning configuration, 129

    pruning, 127-128

    requirements, 126-127

    servers, 124

    standard range VLANs, 123

    storing configuration, 134-135

    switches synchronization to VLAN database, verifying, 131-133

    synchronization, 125-126

    transparent mode, 135

    troubleshooting, 135-139

    versions, 127

    VLAN support, adding, 123

provider edge (PE), 377

pruning (VTP), 127-128

public cloud computing, 741

  accessing with

    Internet, 745-746

    private WANs, 746-749

    VPNs, 747

  address assignment services, 756-757

  branch offices example, 749-752

    email services traffic flow, 750-751

    Internet connections, 751

    private WAN connections, 751

    DHCP services, 757

    DNS services, 754-756

    intercloud exchanges, 748-749

    NTP, 757-758

    VNFs, 752-754

PVST+ (Per-VLAN Spanning Tree Plus), 72-73

Q

QoE (Quality of Experience), 492

QoS (Quality of Service), 378, 488

  bandwidth, 491

  classification, 495

    ACLs, 497

    with marking, 497

    matching, 496-497

    NBAR, 498

    router queuing, 496

    routers, 497

  congestion avoidance, 512

    TCP windowing, 512-513

    tools, 513-514

  congestion management, 504

    Low Latency Queuing (LLQ), 505-507

    multiple queues, 504

    output queuing, 504

    prioritization, 505

    queuing strategy, 507

    round robin scheduling, 505

  defined, 488

  delay, 491

  jitter, 491

  loss, 491

marking, 499

    with classification, 497

    DiffServ DSCP AF values, 502-503

    DiffServ DSCP CS values, 503

    DiffServ DSCP EF values, 502

    Ethernet 802.1Q headers, 500-501

    Ethernet 802.11 headers, 501

    IP headers, 499-501

    MPLS Label headers, 501

    trust boundaries, 501-502

MPLS, 378-379

needs based on traffic types

    data applications, 492-493

    video applications, 494

    voice applications, 493-494

policing, 507

    discarding excess traffic, 509

    edge between networks, 509-510

    features, 510

    traffic rate versus configured policing rate, 508

shaping, 507, 510

    features, 512

    slowing messages, 510

    time intervals, 511-512

switches/routers, 495

tools, 496

VoIP, 493-494

query messages (EIGRP), 242

questions (exam)

  answering, 790-791

  budgeting time, 785

  knowledge gaps, finding, 792-793

  types, 784

queuing

  congestion management, 504

    Low Latency Queuing (LLQ), 505-507

    multiple queues, 504

    output queuing, 504

    prioritization, 505

    round robin scheduling, 505

    strategy, 507

  priority queues, 506

  queue starvation, 506

  routers, classification for, 496

R

RA (Router Advertisement), 610, 684

RADIUS protocol, 146-148

rapid elasticity (cloud computing), 739

Rapid PVST+, 72

Rapid Spanning Tree Protocol. *See* **RSTP**

rate limiting (DHCP snooping), 154

RD (reported distance), 240-241, 257

reachability (BGP), 302

read-only (RO) communities (SNMP), 699

read-write (RW) communities (SNMP), 699

ready to pass assessment (exam), 797

Real-time Transport Protocol (RTP), 235

redistribution

  Internet edge ISP routes, learning, 309

  routes (MPLS VPNs), 380

redundancy

  FHRP

    features, 550

    HSRP. See HSRP

need for, 549

options, 550-551

LANs

  problems caused without STP, 45-46

  STP, 42

network needs for, 547-548

single points of failure, 547

reference bandwidth, 216-217

relationships (neighbors), 284

  EIGRP for IPv6, 656-657

  OSPFv3, troubleshooting, 633-635

  pinging routers, confirming, 285

  requirements, 284

  states, 628

relay agents (DHCPv6), 596

Reliable Transport Protocol (RTP), 235

remark command, 472, 487

Remote SPAN (RSPAN), 721

reply messages (EIGRP), 242

reported distance (RD), 240-241, 257

Representational State Transfer (REST), 769

requirements

  cloud computing services, 739

  EIGRP for IPv6 neighbors, 656

  neighbors, 284

    EIGRP, 286

    OSPF, 289

    OSPFv3, 633-634

  SNMPv3 configuration, 704

  VTP, 126-127

resource pooling (cloud computing), 739

responders (IP SLAs), 713

REST (Representation State Transfer), 769

RESTful APIs, 769

reverse engineering from ACL to address range, 454-456

reversed source/destination IP address, troubleshooting, 480-481

RFC 1065, 694

RFC 4301 *Security Architecture for the Internet Protocol*, 395

RIDs (router IDs), 181

  defining, 196

  EIGRP, configuring, 252

  OSPF, 181

    configuring, 203-204

    duplicate, troubleshooting, 291-293

  OSPFv3, 624

RIP (Routing Information Protocol), 175-176, 226

RIPv2 (RIP Version 2), 226

  EIGRP/OSPFv2, compared, 233

  goals, 302

RO (read-only) communities (SNMP), 699

ROAS (router-on-a-stick), 520, 524

  configuration, 524

    example, 524

    native VLANs, 525-526

    subinterface numbers, 525

    subinterfaces, creating, 524-525

  troubleshooting, 528-529

  verifying, 526-527

    connected routes, 526

    show vlans command, 527

    subinterface state, 527

roles

  ports

    alternate, 60-61

    backup, 62-63

root. See *RPs*

RSTP, *60, 91-92*

STP, 57

root bridge IDs, 50

root costs (switches), 48

root ports. *See* RPs

root switches

electing, 50-52

election influence, configuring, 80-81

ruling out switches, 100-101

STP, verification, 77

troubleshooting, 99-101

round robin scheduling (queuing), 505

round-trip delay, 491

Round Trip Time (RTT), 715

routable protocols, 172

routed ports, 534-537

routed protocols, 172

Router Advertisement (RA) messages, 610, 684

router bgp command, 311

router eigrp command, 246, 270, 647

router-id command, 222, 614

OSPFv3, 624, 643

RIDs, defining, 196

router-on-a-stick. *See* ROAS

router ospf command, 196, 222

router ospf 1 command, 198

Router Solicitation (RS), 610

routers. *See also* routes; routing

ABR (Area Border Router), 190

interface OSPF areas, verifying, 210-211

OSPFv2 multiarea configuration, 209-210

advertisement (RA) messages, 610, 684

backbone, 190

best routes, finding, 180

classification, 497

ACLs, 497

NBAR, 498

Cloud Services Routers (CSRs), 747

configuring different VIPs, troubleshooting, 563

data plane processing, 763

designated (DRs), 185

backup (BDRs), 185

discovering, 211-212

Ethernet links, 185-186

DROthers, 186

flooding, 179

GRE tunnels between, 399

HSRP

active/passive model, 551

active/standby routers, choosing, 555

active/standby rules, 557

configuring, 554

failover, 552

group numbers, 555

load balancing, 553

no preemption, 557

with preemption, 558

troubleshooting, 560-563

verifying, 555-556

versions, 559-560

IDs. *See* RIDs

internal, 190, 623-624

IPv6

addressing configuration, 598-599

connectivity, verifying, 601-603

issues, 604

routing, enabling, 598

static route configuration, 599

troubleshooting, 611-612

ISP, 419

LSAs, 636

multiple serial links between, 347

OSPF interface costs, 216-217

public cloud networks, 754

QoS, 495

queuing

    classification for, 496

    congestion management, 504-507

    strategy, 507

redundant, 549. *See also* FHRP

ROAS, 23, 524

    configuration, 524-526

    native VLANs, 525-526

    subinterfaces, creating, 524-525

    troubleshooting, 528-529

    verifying, 526-527

router WAN interface status, 585

routing IP packets over serial links, 398

solicitation (RS) messages, 610, 684

troubleshooting

    DHCP issues, 573-574

    LAN issues, 575-576

VLAN routing, 21-23

routes. *See also* **routers; routing**

BGP

    advertising, 303-304

    best path selection, 305-306

classful networks, injecting, 315-318

default, 627-628

discard, 319

EIGRP

    choosing, 234

    load balancing, 263-264

tuning with bandwidth, 259

variance, 263-264

EIGRP for IPv6, 659-660

feasibility conditions, 242

feasible successor, 241-242

    convergence, 260-261

    identifying, 258-260

host, 357

interarea, 640

IPv6

    EIGRP for IPv6 metrics, 650-651

    OSFPv3 metrics, 626, 638-640

    static, configuring, 599

    troubleshooting, 640-641

ISP

    default, learning, 320-321

    Internet edge, learning, 309

OSPF

    default routes, 213-215

    interarea, verifying, 212

poisoning, 231-232

redistribution, 177, 380

static discard, 319-320

successor, 257-258

routing. *See also* **routers; routes**

EIGRP for IPv6, enabling/disabling, 650

LANs, 523

protocols. *See* routing protocols

troubleshooting

    default router IP address setting, 572

    DHCP issues, 573-574

    DNS problems, 571-572

    incorrect addressing plans, 581-585

    IP forwarding issues, 577-580

LAN issues, 575-576

mismatched IPv4 settings, 568-569

mismatched masks, 569-571

router WAN interface status, 585

VLAN. *See* VLAN routing

Routing Information Protocol (RIP), 175

routing protocols

administrative distance, 177-178

algorithms, 175

AS, 174

autosummarization, 266

classful network boundaries, 266-267

discontiguous classful networks, 267-268

classless/classful, 177, 266

convergence, 173

defined, 172

DV, 175, 228

distance/vector information learned, 228

EIGRP as, 232-233

route poisoning, 231-232

split horizon, 230-231

update messages, 229-230

EGP (exterior gateway protocol), 173

functions, 172-173

IGP, 173

algorithms, 175

classless/classful, 177

metrics, 175-176

interfaces enabled with, verifying, 274

interior comparison, 233

IPv4, 202

link-state, 175

path selections, 172

proprietary, 175

RIPv1, 226

RIPv2, 226

route redistribution, 177

troubleshooting

configuration errors, 274

internetwork, analyzing, 273

neighbor relationships, 274

routing tables, 273

RPs (root ports), 60

nonroot switches, 101-103

problems, troubleshooting, 103

tiebreakers, 102-103

switches, choosing, 52-53

RS (Router Solicitation) messages, 610, 684

RSPAN (Remote SPAN), 721

RSTP (Rapid Spanning Tree Protocol), 58-59

alternate ports, 60-61

backup port role, 62-63

Cisco Catalyst switch RSTP modes, 88-90

implementing, 88

link types, 63

ports

roles, 60, 91-92

states, 62, 92-93

types, 63, 92

processes, 62

standards, 58

STP, compared, 59-60

RTP (Real-time Transport Protocol), 235

RTP (Reliable Transport Protocol), 235

RTT (Round Trip Time), 715

rules

AAA login authentication, 150

HSRP active/standby, 557

implicit IPv6 ACL ICMPv6 message filtering, 683-684

ruling out switches, 100-101

RW (read-write) communities (SNMP), 699

S

SaaS (Software as a Service), 743

SBIs (Southbound Interfaces), 767-768

scoring exams, 796-797

sdm prefer command, 532

sdm prefer lanbase-routing command, 543

SDN (Software Defined Networking), 760

APIC Enterprise Module (APIC-EM), 774-776

Application Centric Infrastructure (ACI), 773-774

architecture, 770

comparisons, 776

controllers

centralized control, 766-767

Northbound Interfaces (NBIs), 768-770

OpenDaylight SDN controller, 771

Southbound Interfaces (SBIs), 767-768

Open SDN, 771

Open SDN Controller (OSC), 772

OpenDaylight (ODL), 771-772

OpenFlow, 771

Secure Shell (SSH), 765

Secure Sockets Layer (SSL), 396-397

security

AAA servers

configuration, 148-150

login authentication rules, 150

login process, 147

TACACS+/RADIUS protocols, 148

access, 145

attacks

DHCP-based, 152

types, 150

authentication

802.1x, 145

AAA servers, 147-150

Internet VPNs, 393

SNMPv3, 699, 707-708

DHCP snooping

configuration settings, 153

DHCP-based attacks, 152

DHCP Binding Table, 153

features, 151

ports as trusted, configuring, 153

rate limiting, 154

rules summary, 153

trusted/untrusted ports, 151-154

encryption, 699, 707-708

IEEE 802.1x, 144-146

AAA servers, configuring, 145

authentication process, 145

EAP, 146

username/password combinations, verifying, 145

Internet VPNs, 393

IPsec encryption, 395-396

SNMP, 698-699

SNMPv3, 705-707

STP, 65-66

self-ping, 483-485

sender's bridge IDs, 50

sender's root cost, 50

sequence numbers, 473-475

serial cables, 332

serial links. *See* leased-line WANs

servers

  AAA

    authentication, 147-150

    configuring for 802.1x, 145

    defining, 149

    enabling, 149

    username/passwords, verifying, 145

  Cisco hardware, 732-733

  defined, 732

  physical server model, 734

  virtualization, 734-735

    hosts, 734

    hypervisors, 734

    multithreading, 734

    networking, 736

    virtual data centers, 735-738

    VMs, 734

  VTP, 124

service-level agreements (SLAs), 712

service providers (SPs), 362

services

  cloud computing

    broad network access, 739

    cloud services catalogs, 740

    Infrastructure as a Service (IaaS), 742

    measured, 739

    on-demand self-service, 739

    Platform as a Service (PaaS), 743-744

    private, 739-741

    public, 741

    rapid elasticity, 739

    requirements, 739

    resource pooling, 739

    Software as a Service (SaaS), 743

  DHCP, 757

  DNS, 754-756

  Internet as WAN, 389

  MetroE, 366

    E-LAN, 368-372

    E-Line, 367-371

    E-Tree, 369-372

  public cloud

    accessing with Internet, 745-746

    accessing with private WANs, 746-749

    accessing with VPNs, 747

    address assignment, 756-757

    branch offices example, 749-752

    intercloud exchanges, 748-749

session keys, 395

session status (PPPoE), 424

sessions (SPAN), 720-721, 725

Set messages

  RO/RW communities, 699

  SNMPv2 support, 699-701

  writing variables on agents, 696

shaping (QoS), 507, 510

  features, 512

  rate, 510

  slowing messages, 510

  time intervals, 511-512

shaping data overages (MetroE), 375

shared edge ports, 93

shared keys, 395

shared ports, 63, 93

shared session keys, 395

shorter VLAN configuration example, 28-29

Shortest Path First algorithm. *See* SPF algorithm

show access-list command, 473

show access-lists command, 450, 457, 479, 487, 687

show arp command, 572

show commands

    IPv6 ACLs, 673

    routing protocol-enabled interfaces, verifying, 275

    STP status, 68

show controllers command, 352

show controllers serial command, 360

show etherchannel 1 summary command, 86

show etherchannel command, 96, 543

show etherchannel summary command, 107, 540

show interfaces command, 298, 360, 543, 569

    EIGRP neighbor requirements, verifying, 286

    MLPPP, 352

    OSPF

        interfaces, 283

        neighbors, 289

    OSPFv3 interface bandwidth, 640

    PPP CHAP status, 345

    PPP PAP, 346

    PPP status, 344

    routed ports, 536

show interfaces description command, 298, 576

show interfaces dialer command, 421, 433

show interfaces status command

    Layer 3 EtherChannels, 539

    routed ports, 536

show interfaces switchport command, 31-34, 37, 41, 114-116, 135

show interfaces trunk command, 32-34, 38, 41, 116-117

show interfaces tunnel command, 405, 433

show interfaces virtual-access command, 433

show interfaces virtual-access configuration command, 423

show interfaces vlan command, 543

show ip access-list command, 457, 474-476

show ip access-lists command, 450, 479, 487

show ip bgp command, 323

show ip bgp summary command, 313, 323

show ip eigrp interfaces command, 271, 297

    EIGRP-enabled interfaces, 250-251, 275

    EIGRP neighbor requirements, verifying, 286

    multilink interfaces, 352

show ip eigrp interfaces detail command, 250, 271

show ip eigrp neighbors command, 271, 297

    neighbor status, displaying, 253

    neighbor verification checks, 285

show ip eigrp topology all-links command, 260

show ip eigrp topology command, 271

    feasible successor routes, 259

    metrics, 262

successor routes, 258

topology table, 256

show ip interface brief command, 360

GRE tunnels, 404

multilink interfaces, 352

OSPF interfaces, troubleshooting, 283

show ip interface command, 286, 450, 457, 479

show ip ospf command, 223, 298

duplicate OSPF RIDs, 291

OSPF neighbors, troubleshooting, 289

show ip ospf database command, 179, 201, 223

show ip ospf interface brief command, 205, 223, 298

OSPF areas for ABR interfaces, 210

OSPF-enabled interfaces, identifying, 275

OSPF neighbors, troubleshooting, 289

OSPF status on interfaces, 281

OSPFv2 interface configuration, 221

show ip ospf interface command, 223, 298

DRs/BDRs details, displaying, 211

Hello/dead timer mismatches, 293

OSPF areas for ABR interfaces, 210

OSPF neighbors, troubleshooting, 289

OSPFv2 interface configuration, 220

passive interface, 206

show ip ospf neighbor command, 182, 223, 298

DRs/BDRs details, displaying, 211

neighbors, listing, 288

OSPF processes shutdown, 295

show ip ospf neighbor interface brief command, 295

show ip protocols command, 223, 271, 297

EIGRP-enabled interfaces, 251-252, 275

EIGRP neighbors, 253, 286

IPv4 routing protocols, 202

OSPF configuration errors, 282-283

OSPFv2 interface configuration, 219

show ip route command, 223, 271, 323, 577-580

administrative distance, 178

dialer interface Layer 3 orientation, 425

EIGRP-learned routes, displaying, 254

IPv4 routes added by OSPF, 201

routing tables, displaying, 543

show ip route eigrp command, 254, 271, 297

show ip route ospf command, 223, 298, 577-578

show ip route static command, 214

show ip sla enhanced-history distribution-statistics command, 729

show ip sla history command, 717, 729

show ip sla statistics command, 729

show ip sla summary command, 729

show ipv6 access-list command, 677, 687

show ipv6 eigrp interfaces command, 654, 662

show ipv6 eigrp interfaces detail command, 662

show ipv6 eigrp neighbors command, 663

show ipv6 eigrp topology command, 663

show ipv6 eigrp topology | section command, 663

show ipv6 interface command, 614, 687

show ipv6 neighbors command, 614

IPv6 ACL ICMPv6 NDP message filtering, 681

IPv6 IPv4 replacement, 603

show ipv6 ospf command, 640, 643

show ipv6 ospf database command, 636, 643

show ipv6 ospf interface brief command, 630, 640, 643

show ipv6 ospf interface command, 630-631, 643

show ipv6 ospf neighbor command, 635, 643

show ipv6 protocols command, 614, 643

EIGRP for IPv6, 662

EIGRP for IPv6 interfaces, 654

OSPFv3 interfaces, 630

show ipv6 route command, 614, 643

EIGRP for IPv6, 663

IPv6 router connectivity, 603

show ipv6 route eigrp command, 663

show ipv6 route ospf command, 638, 643

show ipv6 route | section command, 663

show ipv6 routers command, 614, 681

show mac address-table command, 114

show mac address-table dynamic command, 111

show monitor detail command, 724, 729

show monitor session all command, 723

show monitor session command, 724, 729

show ppp all command, 346-347, 360

show ppp multilink command, 353, 360

show pppoe session command, 424, 433

show running-config command, 135, 449, 473-475

show snmp command, 703, 729

show snmp community command, 702, 728

show snmp contact command, 728

show snmp group command, 709, 729

show snmp host command, 702, 729

show snmp location command, 728

show snmp user command, 708, 729

show spanning-tree bridge command, 81

show spanning-tree command, 96

show spanning-tree interface command, 96

show spanning-tree interface detail command, 82

show spanning-tree root command, 77, 81

show spanning-tree summary command, 83, 96

show spanning-tree vlan 10 bridge command, 77

show spanning-tree vlan 10 command, 75-77

show spanning-tree vlan 10 interface gigabitethernet0/2 state command, 92

show spanning-tree vlan command, 96

show standby brief command, 555-565

show standby command (HSRP), 565

configuration, 560

status, 556

show tcp brief command, 313

show tcp summary command, 323

show vlan brief command, 26-29, 114

show vlan command, 41, 114, 141

show vlan id command, 27, 114

show vlan status command, 135

show vlans command, 527, 543

show vtp password command, 134, 141

show vtp status command, 29, 41, 131, 134, 141

shutdown command, 40, 359

  EIGRP for IPv6, 650, 662

  Layer 1 leased-line WAN problems, 354

  OSPF processes, 294

  ROAS subinterfaces, 527

shutdown vlan command, 135, 140

shutting down OSPF processes, 294-296

signatures, 498

the Sim (Pearson Network Simulator), 796

Simple Network Management Protocol. *See* SNMP

single-area OSPF, 188

single-area OSPFv2 configuration, 197-198

  IPv4 addresses, 197

  matching with network command, 198-200

  multiarea configurations, 207-208

  network command, 198

  organization, 196-197

  passive interfaces, 204-206

  RIDs, 203-204

  verifying, 200-202

    IPv4 routing protocols, 201-202

    LSDB contents, displaying, 201

  wildcard masks, 199

single-area OSPFv3 configuration, 623-624

single homed Internet edge design, 306

single points of failure, 547

site-to-site VPNs, 394-396

SLA (service level agreement), 712

SLAAC (stateless address autoconfiguration)

  EUI-64, 597

  IPv6 settings, 597

  NDP, 597

  troubleshooting, 609-610

SLBaaS (SLB as a service), 753

SNMP (Simple Network Management Protocol), 692

  agents, 695-696

  clear-text passwords, 698

  communities, 698-699

  Get messages

    agent information, 696

    RO/RW communities, 699

    SNMPv2 configuration, 699-701

  history, 695

  Inform messages, 696-697, 701-702

  managers, 695

  MIB, 696-697

  notifications, 696-697

  read-only (RO) communities, 699

  read-write (RW) communities, 699

  security, 698-699

  Set messages

    RO/RW communities, 699

    SNMPv2 configuration, 699-701

    writing variables on agents, 696

  Trap messages, 696-697, 701-702

snmp-server command, 700

snmp-server community command, 727

snmp-server contact command, 727

snmp-server enable traps command, 727

snmp-server group command, 705

snmp-server host command, 701, 710, 727

snmp-server location command, 727

snmp-server user command, 707

SNMPv2

  configuring

    Get/Set messages, 699-701

    Trap/Inform messages, 701-702

    verifying, 702-704

  security, 699

SNMPv2c (Community-based SNMP Version 2), 699

SNMPv3

  configuring, 704

    authentication, 707-708

    encryption, 707-708

    groups, 705-707

    notifications, 710-711

    requirements, 704

    summary, 711-712

    users, 707

    verifying, 708-709

  groups

    MIB views, 705

    security levels, 705

    write views, 706

  Inform messages, 710-711

  MIB views, 705

  security, 699

  Trap messages, 710-711

Software as a Service (SaaS), 743

Software Defined Networking. *See* SDN

solution apps, 777

sources

  addresses, 406

  IPs, matching, 463-464

  IP SLAs, 713

  ports (SPAN), 719

  SPAN, limiting, 725

Southbound Interfaces (SBIs), 767-768

SPAN (Switched Port Analyzer), 718

  dependencies, 722

  destination ports, 719

  Encapsulated RSPAN (ERSPAN), 721

  local, 721-724

  network analyzer needs for, 719

  Remote (RSPAN), 721

  sessions, 720-721

  source ports, 719

  sources, limiting, 725

  traffic direction, 725

  VLANs, monitoring, 721

spanning-tree algorithm (STA), 48

spanning-tree bpduguard disable command, 95

spanning-tree bpduguard enable command, 81, 95

spanning-tree bpguard enable command, 75

spanning-tree commands, 95

spanning-tree mode command, 88, 95

spanning-tree mode mst command, 72

spanning-tree mode pvst command, 72

spanning-tree mode rapid-pvst command, 72, 90

spanning-tree pathcost method long command, 55

spanning-tree portfast bpduguard default command, 95

spanning-tree portfast command, 75, 81, 95

spanning-tree portfast default command, 83, 95

spanning-tree portfast disable command, 83, 95

Spanning Tree Protocol. *See* STP

spanning-tree vlan 10 port priority 112 command, 103

spanning-tree vlan command, 74

speed command, 576

speeds
  LAN/WAN interfaces, 490
  leased-line WANs, 333-334

SPF (Shortest Path First) algorithm, 180
  Dijkstra SPF, 180
  OSPF best routes, calculating, 186-188

spinning up VMs, 742

split horizon (DV routing protocols), 230-231

spoofing, 422

SPs (service providers), 362

SSH (Secure Shell), 765

SSL (Secure Sockets Layer), 396-397

STA (spanning-tree algorithm), 48

stack masters, 157

stacking cables, 156

stacking modules, 156

stacking ports, 156

stacking switches
  access layer switches, 156-157
  benefits, 155
  chassis aggregation, 159-161
  FlexStack/FlexStack-Plus, 158

operating as single logical switch, 157-158

stack masters, 157

standard ACLs, configuring, 671-674

standard numbered IPv4 ACLs, 443
  access-list command, 454
  command syntax, 445
  configuration examples, 448-452
  list logic, 444-445
  matching any/all addresses, 448
  matching exact IP address, 445-446
  matching subset of address, 446-447
  overview, 443
  reverse engineering from ACL to address range, 454-456
  troubleshooting, 452-453
  verification, 452-453
  wildcard masks
    binary wildcard masks, 447-448
    decimal wildcard masks, 446-447

standard range VLANs, 123

standby 1 preempt command, 558

standby command, 554, 564

standby HSRP routers, 557

standby version 1 | 2 command, 564

standby version command, 559

stateful DHCP, troubleshooting, 608-609

stateful DHCPv6, 596

stateless address autoconfiguration. *See* SLAAC

states
  change reactions (STP topology), 55-56
  discarding, 61
  interfaces
    changing with STP, 57-58
    criteria, 48-49

forwarding/blocking, 47

learning, 58

listening, 58

neighbors

   BGP, 313

   OSPF, 182-183, 186, 288

   OSPFv3, 632

   relationships, 628

ports

   RSTP, 92-93

   STP versus RSTP, 62

ROAS subinterfaces, 527

STP, 57

tunnel interfaces, 407

VLAN mismatched trunking operational, 116

static discard routes, 319-320

static routes (IPv6), configuring, 599

status

   BPDU Guard global settings, 83

   EIGRP neighbors, 233, 253

   HSRP, 555

   interface codes, 353

   PortFast global settings, 83

   PPP, 344

   PPP CHAP, 345

   PPP PAP, 346

   PPPoE

      Layer 3, 425

      sessions, verifying, 424

   STP verification, 75-77

steady-state operation (STP), 56

STP (Spanning Tree Protocol), 42

   802.1D standard, 58

   behind the scenes summary, 72

BIDs

   defined, 49

   root switch election, 50-52

   system ID extensions, 73-74

BPDUs (bridge protocol data units), 49

BPDU Guard

   configuring, 81

   enabling/disabling, 83

   global settings, displaying, 83

   verifying, 82-83

Cisco Catalyst switch STP modes, 88-89

configuration, 71

   modes, 72

   options, 74-75

   per-VLAN port costs, 74

   PVST+, 72-73

   system ID extensions, 73-74

convergence, 48, 105-106

EtherChannels, 64-65

   configuring, 84-87

   MAC tables impact, predicting, 111-112

   troubleshooting, 106-109

forwarding or blocking criteria, 48-49

interface states, changing, 57-58

LAN redundancy, 42-46

LAN segment DPs, choosing, 54

looping frames, preventing, 44

MAC tables impact, predicting, 110

PortFast, 65

   configuring, 81

   enabling/disabling, 83

   global settings, displaying, 83

   verifying, 82-83

ports
> blocking, choosing, 44
> costs, 53, 78-79
> states, 62

purpose, 47-49

roles, 57

root election influence, configuring, 80-81

root switch election, 50-52, 100-101

RSTP (Rapid STP), 58-59
> alternate ports, 60-61
> backup port role, 62-63
> Cisco Catalyst switch RSTP modes, 88-90
> implementing, 88
> link types, 63
> port roles, 91-92
> port states, 92-93
> port types, 63, 92
> processes, 62
> standards, 58
> STP, compared, 59-60

security, 65-66

STA (spanning-tree algorithm), 48

states, 56-57

switch reactions to changes, 56-57

switch RPs, choosing, 52-53

tiebreakers, 102-103

timers, 56-57

topology influences, 55-56

troubleshooting
> convergence, 105-106
> DPs on LAN segments, 104-105
> root switch election, 99-101
> RPs on nonroot switches, 101-103

verification, 75-77

studying after failing the exam, 797-798

studying for exam, 798

subinterfaces
defined, 524
ROAS
> creating, 524-525
> numbers, 525
> state, verifying, 527

subnet masks
mismatched masks, troubleshooting, 569-571
VLSM (variable length subnet masking)
> overlapping subnets, 583-585
> recognizing when VLSM is used, 581

subnets
advertising to ISPs, 318
IGPs, 303
IPv6, 593-594
mismatched
> EIGRP neighbors, 286
> leased-line WANs, 358
OSPFv2 multiarea configuration, 206
overlapping subnets
> with VLSM, 583-585
> without VLSM, 581-583

subset of IP address, matching, 446-447

successors
EIGRP
> identifying, 257-258
> for IPv4, 241-242
> for IPv6, 646
feasible
> convergence, 260-261
> identifying, 258-260

super backbone (OSPF), 381

superior Hello, 50

supplicants, 145

SVIs (switched virtual interfaces), 520, 529

  configuring, 529-531

  troubleshooting, 532-534

  verifying, 531

Switched Port Analyzer. *See* SPAN

switches

  as 802.1x authenticators, 145

  access layer, 156-157

  adding, 137-139

  chassis aggregation, 159

    benefits, 161

    design, improving, 160

    distribution/core switches high availability, 159-160

    switch stacking, 159-161

  Cisco Catalyst

    RSTP modes, 88-90

    STP modes, 88-89

  core, 159-160

  distribution

    design, improving, 160

    high availability with chassis aggregation, 159-160

  internal processing, 765-766

  Layer 2, 21

  Layer 3, 21

    with routed ports, 534-537

    VLAN routing, 23-24

  Layer 3 EtherChannels

    configuring, 537-539

    troubleshooting, 541

    verifying, 539-540

  Layer 3 with SVIs

    configuring, 529-531

    troubleshooting, 532-534

    verifying, 531

  links, 63

  logical, 157-158

  nonroot, 101-103

  PortFast, 65

  QoS, 495

  root

    costs, 48

    electing, 50-52

    election influence, configuring, 80-81

    ruling out switches, 100-101

    STP verification, 77

    troubleshooting, 99-101

  RPs (root ports), choosing, 52-53

  SPAN, 718

    dependencies, 722

    destination ports, 719

    Encapsulated RSPAN (ERSPAN), 721

    limiting sources, 725

    local, 721-724

    network analyzer needs, 719

    Remote (RSPAN), 721

    sessions, 720-721

    source ports, 719

    traffic direction, 725

    VLANs, monitoring, 721

  stacking

    access layer switches, 156-157

    benefits, 155

    chassis aggregation, 159-161

    FlexStack/FlexStack-Plus, 158

operating as single logical switch, 157-158

stack masters, 157

synchronization to VLAN database, verifying, 131-133

ToR (Top of Rack), 736

traditional access switching, 155

virtual (vSwitches), 735

voice switches, 34

as VTP servers, 124

switchport access vlan command, 25, 28-29, 37-40, 113, 135

switchport command

Layer 3 switches, 543

routed ports, 535

switchport mode access command, 25, 28, 37-38, 139

switchport mode command, 30, 40

switchport mode dynamic auto command, 116

switchport mode dynamic desirable command, 32

switchport mode trunk command, 30, 116, 524

switchport nonegotiate command, 34, 40, 116, 139

switchport trunk allowed vlan command, 41, 117

switchport trunk encapsulation command, 30, 40

switchport trunk native vlan command, 40, 118

switchport voice vlan command, 36-38, 41, 135

synchronizing

switches, 131-133

VTP, 125-126, 136-137

system ID extensions (BIDs), 73-74

T

T1. See leased-line WANs

T3, 334

TACACS+, 148

tagging (VLAN), 18-20

tail drops, 513

TCAM (ternary content-addressable memory), 766

T-carrier systems, 333

TCP (Transmission Control Protocol)

BGP connections, displaying, 313

packets, 675

port numbers, matching, 464-467

transporting messages between BGP peers, 310

windowing, 512-513

tcp keyword, 464

TCP/IP networks, 694

TDM (time-division multiplexing), 334

telcos (telephone companies), 331, 390

Telnet, 765

ternary content-addressable memory (TCAM), 766

testing IPv6

ACLs, 677

connectivity

hosts, 600-601

routers, 601-603

three-area OSPF, 189

TID fields (QoS marking), 501

tiebreakers (STP), 102-103

time burners, 785

time-division multiplexing (TDM), 334

time (exam)

budget versus number of questions, 785

checking, 786

time intervals (QoS shaping), 511-512

timers

  EIGRP for IPv6, 652

  EIGRP neighbors, 233

  Hello messages, 184

  Hello/dead mismatches, troubleshooting, 293-294

  STP, 56-57

tools

  APIC-EM ACL Analysis, 777

  APIC-EM Path Trace ACL Analysis tool, 777-778

  APIC-EM Path Trace app, 777

  QoS

    ACLs, compared, 496

    classification, 495-498

    congestion avoidance, 512-514

    congestion management, 504-507

    marking, 499-503

    policing, 507-510

    queuing strategy, 507

    shaping, 507-512

Top of Rack (ToR) switches, 736

topologies

  EIGRP

    displaying, 255-257

    feasible successor routes, 258-261

    metrics, 262

    successor routes, identifying, 257-258

  EIGRP for IPv6, 657-658

  MetroE, 366

    full mesh, 368

    hub and spoke, 369

    partial mesh, 369

    Point-to-Point, 367-368

  OSPF area design, 188

  STP, influences, 55-56

ToR (Top of Rack) switches, 736

ToS (Type of Service) field (IPv4), 499

traceroute command, 574

  GRE tunnels, 406

  IPv6

    connectivity, testing, 600-602

    network router problems, troubleshooting, 611

    routes, testing, 614

traceroute6 command, 615

tracert command, 615

traditional access switching, 155

traffic

  bandwidth, managing, 491

  characteristics, 491

  congestion avoidance, 512

    TCP windowing, 512-513

    tools, 513-514

  congestion management, 504

    Low Latency Queuing (LLQ), 505-507

    multiple queues, 504

    output queuing, 504

    prioritization, 505

    round robin scheduling, 505

    strategy, 507

  delay, managing, 491

  end-user, measuring, 713

  IPv6 ACLs, 670

  jitter, 491

  loss, 491

  policing, 507

    discarding excess traffic, 509

    edge between networks, 509-510

features, 510

traffic rate versus configured policing rate, 508

public cloud branch office email services, 750-751

shaping, 507, 510

features, 512

slowing messages, 510

time intervals, 511-512

SPAN sessions, 725

types

data, 492-493

video, 494

voice, 378, 493-494

Traffic Class field (IPv6), 500

Transmission Control Protocol. See TCP

transparent mode (VTP), 135

Trap messages, 696-697

SNMPv2, 701-702

SNMPv3, 710-711

troubleshooting

CHAP authentication failures, 356

DPs on LAN segments, 105

EIGRP for IPv6

interfaces, 655

neighbors, 656-657

routes, 660

EIGRP interfaces, 275

configuration problems, 278-281

working details, 276-278

EIGRP neighbors

authentication failures, 286

example, 286-288

incorrect ASNs, 288

mismatched subnets, 286

verification checks, 285-286

EtherChannels, 106

channel-group command incorrect options, 106-108

configuration checks before adding interfaces, 108-109

GRE tunnels, 406

ACLs, 409-410

interface state, 407

Layer 3 issues, 409

source/destination addresses, 406

tunnel destination, 408

HSRP, 560

ACL blocks HSRP packets, 563

configuration, 560-561

group number mismatches, 563

misconfiguration symptoms, 561

routers configuring different VIPs, 563

version mismatches, 562

with IP SLA

counters, 715-716

history data, 717

IPv4 ACLs, 477

ACL behavior in network, 477-479

ACL interactions with router-generated packets, 483-485

common syntax mistakes, 481

inbound ACL filters routing protocol packets, 481-482

reversed source/destination IP address, 480-481

troubleshooting commands, 479-480

IPv4 routing

default router IP address setting, 572

DHCP issues, 573-574

DNS problems, 571-572

incorrect addressing plans, 581-585

IP forwarding issues, 577-580

LAN issues, 575-576

mismatched IPv4 settings, 568-569

mismatched masks, 569-571

packet filtering with access lists, 586

router WAN interface status, 585

IPv6 routing, 604

ACLs, 612

filtering issues, 604

host issues, 604

host pings fail from default router, 606-607

host pings only working in some cases, 605-606

missing IPv6 settings in host, 608-610

name resolution problems, 607-608

router issues, 604

routes, 640-641

routing, 611-612

Layer 3 EtherChannels, 541

leased-line WANs, 353-354

Layer 1 problems, 354

Layer 2 problems, 354-356

Layer 3 problems, 357-358

mismatched subnets, 358

neighbors, 285

OSPF

MTU mismatched settings, 296

processes, shutting down, 294-296

OSPF interfaces, 281-283

area design, 281

configuration errors, 282-283

details, checking, 283

unsolicited log messages, 283

OSPF neighbors, 288-294

area mismatches, finding, 290-291

duplicate RIDs, 291-293

Hello timer/dead timer mismatches, 293-294

LAN problems, 289

neighbor states, 288

OSPFv3

interfaces, 631-632

neighbors, 633-635

PAP authentication failures, 356

PPPoE, 425-426

customer router configuration, 426

dialer 2 status, 427

Layer 1, 427-428

Layer 2, 428-429

Layer 3, 429

summary, 430

ROAS, 528-529

routing protocols

configuration errors, 274

internetwork, analyzing, 273

neighbor relationships, 274

routing tables, 273

routing with SVIs, 532-534

RP problems, 103

SPAN sessions, 725

standard numbered ACLs, 452-453

STP

    convergence, 105-106

    DPs on LAN segments, 104-105

    root switch election, 99-101

    RPs on nonroot switches, 101-103

    switch data plane forwarding

        EtherChannel impact on MAC tables, 111-112

        STP impact on MAC tables, 110

        VLAN of incoming frames, 112-113

    VLANs

        access interfaces, 113-114

        frame switching problems, 113

        undefined/disabled VLANs, 114-115

    VLAN trunking

        frame switching problems, 113

        mismatched native VLANs, 118

        mismatched operational states, 116

        mismatched supported VLAN lists, 117-118

    VTP, 135

        adding switches, 137-139

        common configuration rejections, 137

        synchronization, 136-137

trunking (VLANs)

    802.1Q, 20-21

    configuration, 30-34

    disabling, 139

    ISL (Inter-Switch Link), 20-21

    overview, 18

    protocol. *See* VTP

    troubleshooting, 113-118

    VLAN tagging, 18-20

trust boundaries (QoS marking), 501-502

trusted ports, 151

    configuring, 153

    DHCP snooping, 154

tunnel destination command, 406-408, 432

tunnel mode gre ip command, 404, 432

tunnel mode gre multipoint command, 404

tunnel source command, 406-407, 432

tunnels

    destinations, 408

    GRE, 398

        between routers, 399

        configuring, 402-404

        details, displaying, 404

        functionality, testing, 406

        large scale environments, 411

        multipoint with DMVPN, 411

        point-to-point, 399

        routes, 405

        troubleshooting, 406-410

        tunnel interfaces, 398

        unsecured networks, 400-401

        verifying, 404-406

    interfaces

        ACLs, 409-410

        creating, 400

        destinations, 408

        Layer 3 issues, 409

        replacing serial links, 398

        state, 407

    VPN, 394-395

tutorial (exam), 784-785

Twitter (Wendell Odom), 799

Type of Service (ToS) field (IPv4), 499

U

UCS (Unified Computing System), 733

UDP (User Datagram Protocol)

 Jitter probes, 713

 packets, IPv6 ACL matching, 675

 port numbers, matching, 464-467

undebug all command, 298

undefined VLANs, troubleshooting, 114-115

unequal-cost load balancing, 263

UNI (user network interface), 365

unicast IPv6 addresses, 593-595

Unified Computing System (UCS), 733

unique local unicast addresses, 593

unsecured networks (GRE tunnels), 400-401

unsolicited log messages, 283

untrusted ports, 151-154

upd keyword, 464

updates

 BGP, 303, 310

 DV protocols, 229-230

 EIGRP, 235-236

 full, 229

 partial, 232

 periodic, 229

User Datagram Protocol. See UDP

user network interface (UNI), 365

username command, 345, 359

U.S. National Institute of Standards and Technology (NIST), 739

V

v1default MIB view, 706

variable length subnet masking. See VLSM

variables (MIB)

 monitoring, 696

 numbering/names, 697

variance (EIGRP), 263-264

variance command, 270

 EIGRP for IPv4, 247, 263, 647

 EIGRP for IPv6, 651, 662

vCPU (virtual CPU), 734

vector (DV protocols), 228

verification command, 75

verifying

 BPDU Guard, 82-83

 data and voice VLANs, 36-38

 eBGP neighbors, 312-313

 EIGRP configuration, 249

  EIGRP enabled interfaces, finding, 250-252

  IPv4 routing table, displaying, 253-254

  neighbor status, displaying, 253

 EIGRP for IPv6

  interfaces, 654

  routes, 659-660

 EIGRP neighbors, 235, 285-286

 EtherChannel configuration before adding interfaces, 108-109

 GRE tunnels, 404-406

 HDLC, 339

 HSRP, 555-556

 interarea OSPF routes, 212

IPv6 connectivity, 600

   hosts, 600-601

   routers, 601-603

Layer 3 EtherChannels, 539-540

MLPPP, 351-353

OSPFv2 configurations

   interfaces, 219-221

   multiarea, 210-212

   single-area, 200-202

OSPFv3

   interfaces, 630-631, 638-640

   neighbors, 632-633

PortFast, 82-83

PPP

   CHAP, 345-346

   PAP, 347

PPPoE, 420-421

   dialers, 421-422

   Layer 3 status, 425

   session status, 424

   virtual-access interfaces, 423

ROAS, 526-527

routing protocol-enabled interfaces, 274

routing with SVIs, 531

SNMPv2 configuration, 702-704

SNMPv3 configuration, 708-709

standard numbered ACLs, 452-453

STP, 75-77

switches synchronization to VLAN database, 131-133

username/passwords on AAA servers, 145

versions

HSRP, 559-560

OSPF, 619

VTP, 127

video traffic

QoS requirements, 494

shaping time intervals, 512

views (MIB), 705

virtual-access interfaces, 423

virtual LANs. *See* **VLANs**

virtual machines. *See* **VMs**

virtual network functions (VNFs), 752-754

Virtual Private LAN Service (VPLS), 367

Virtual Private Networks. *See* **VPNs**

Virtual Private Wire Service (VPWS), 367

Virtual Router Redundancy Protocol (VRRP), 544

virtualization

ASA firewall (ASAv), 754

CPU (vCPU), 734

data centers

   networking, 735

   physical networks, 736

   vendors, 735

   workflow, 737-738

firewalls, 754

machines. *See* VMs

network functions virtualization (NFV), 754

networks, 735-736, 754

NICs (vNICS), 735

routers (public cloud networks), 754

servers, 734-735

   hosts, 734

   hypervisors, 734

   multithreading, 734

   networking, 736

virtual data center vendors, 735

VMs, 734

switches (vSwitches), 735

VLANs (virtual LANs)

configuration

data and voice VLANs, 36-38

database, VTP synchronization, 125-126

full VLAN configuration example, 25-28

overview, 24-25

shorter VLAN configuration example, 28-29

trunking, 30-34

database, switches synchronization, 131-133

default, 25

enabling/disabling, 115

IDs, 18

incoming frames, choosing, 112-113

interfaces. *See* SVIs

IP telephony, 34

data and voice VLAN concepts, 34-36

data and voice VLAN configuration and verification, 36-38

summary, 38-39

LAN support, adding, 122

mismatched native on trunks, 118

mismatched supported trunk lists, 117-118

native, 20, 525-526

overview, 16-18

routing. *See* VLAN routing

SPAN monitoring, 721

standard range, 123

tagging, 18-20

troubleshooting

access interfaces, 113-114

frame switching process problems, 113

undefined/disabled VLANs, 114-115

trunking

802.1Q, 20-21

configuration, 30-34

disabling, 139

ISL (Inter-Switch Link), 20-21

overview, 18

protocol. See VTP

troubleshooting, 113-118

VLAN tagging, 18-20

vlan 10 command, 122

vlan 200 command, 137

vlan command, 25, 37, 40, 135

VLAN routing, 21

Layer 3 EtherChannels

configuring, 537-539

troubleshooting, 541

verifying, 539-540

Layer 3 switch routed ports, 23-24, 534-537

Layer 3 switching with SVIs

configuring, 529-531

troubleshooting, 532-534

verifying, 531

ROAS, 524

configuration, 524-526

troubleshooting, 528-529

verifying, 526-527

routers, 21-23

VLAN Trunking Protocol. *See* VTP

VLSM (variable length subnet masking)
overlapping subnets, 583-585
recognizing when VLSM is used, 581
VMs (virtual machines), 734
ACI, 773
IaaS, 742
networking, 736
PaaS, 743-744
SaaS, 743
spinning up, 742
virtual NICs (vNICs), 735
VNFs (virtual network functions), 752-754
vNICs (virtual NICs), 735
voice switches, 34
voice traffic, 493
QoS requirements, 494
shaping time intervals, 512
VoIP, 378
VoIP (Voice over IP), 378, 493-494
VPLS (Virtual Private LAN Service), 367
VPNs (Virtual Private Networks)
client, 396-397
dynamic multipoint (DMVPN), 411
multipoint GRE tunnels, 411
NHRP (Next Hop Resolution Protocol), 412-413
Internet, 389
benefits, 394
security, 393
MPLS VPNs, 376
EIGRP challenges, 382
Layer 3, 379-382
OSPF area design, 381-382
public cloud, accessing, 747

site-to-site, 394-396
tunnels, 394-395
VPWS (Virtual Private Wire Service), 367
VRRP (Virtual Router Redundancy Protocol), 544
vSwitches (virtual switches), 735
VTP (VLAN Trunking Protocol), 29, 120
automated update powers, 120
configuration
common rejections, troubleshooting, 137
default VTP settings, 129
example, 130-131
new VTP configuration settings, 130
planning, 129
steps, 129
storing, 134-135
domains, 125-127
features, 128
pruning, 127-128
requirements, 126-127
servers, 124
standard range VLANs, 123
switches synchronization to VLAN database, verifying, 131-133
synchronization, 125
transparent mode, 135
troubleshooting, 135
adding switches, 137-139
common configuration rejections, 137
synchronization, 136-137
versions, 127
VLAN support, adding, 123
vtp commands, 134

vtp domain command, 134, 140

vtp mode command, 40, 134, 140

vtp mode off command, 29, 135

vtp mode transparent command, 29, 135

vtp password command, 134, 140

vtp pruning command, 134, 140

vtp version command, 140

W – Z

WANs

  Ethernet, 747

  Frame Relay, 362

  interface speeds, 490

  Internet access, 389

  Internet as WAN service, 389

  leased-line, 330-331

    building, 335-336

    CSU/DSUs, 334

    mismatched subnets, 358

    physical components, 332-333

    speeds, 333-334

    troubleshooting, 353-358

  leased-line with HDLC, 336

    configuring HDLC, 337-340

    de-encapsulating/ re-encapsulating IP packets, 336

    framing, 336

  leased-line with PPP

    authentication, 342-343

    configuring PPP, 343-344

    configuring PPP CHAP, 344-346

    configuring PPP PAP, 346-347

    control protocols, 341

    framing, 341

    multilink. See MLPPP

    PPP functions, 340

  MetroE, 364

    access links, 365

    data usage, 373-375

    E-LAN service, 368-372

    E-Line service, 367-371

    E-Tree service, 369-372

    full mesh topology, 368

    hub and spoke topology, 369

    IEEE Ethernet standards, 366

    Layer 3 design, 370-372

    MEF, 366

    partial mesh topology, 369

    physical design, 365-366

    Point-to-Point topology, 367-368

    services, 366

  MPLS, 375-377

    access links, 378

    Layer 3 design, 377

    MPLS VPNs, 379-382

    QoS, 378-379

    VPNs, 376

  private

    public cloud access, 746-749

    public cloud branch office connections, 751

    types, 362

  public cloud connections

    Internet as, 745-746

    private WANs, 746-749

  service providers (SPs), 362

  wireless, 392-393

WAN interface cards (WICs), 332

WC masks. *See* wildcard masks

websites

APIC-EM Analysis tool released code, 777

APIC-EM labs, 777

ARIN, 174

BGP routing table analysis reports, 303

CCNA (ICND2) Config Labs, 796

CCNA Routing and Switching ICND2 Official Cert Guide, 777

Cisco

ACI, 774

APIC-EM pages, 777

DevNet, 777

Feature Navigator, 531

Prime management products, 695

Eclipse IDE, 744

ETSI, 754

Google App Engine PaaS, 744

IANA, 174

ICMPv6 parameters, 669

IPv6 multicast address space registry, 682

ICMPv6 packets, 669

Jenkins continuous integration and automation tool, 744

MEF, 366

OpenDaylight SDN controller, 771

OpenFlow, 768

Pearson Network Simulator (the Sim), 796

Wendell Odom's SDN Skills, 777

Wireshark network analyzer, 718

weighting, 505

Wendell Odom's SDN Skills blog, 777

WICs (WAN interface cards), 332

wildcard_mask parameter (network command), 198

wildcard masks

binary, 447

decimal, 446-447

EIGRP configuration, 248-249

finding, 448

OSPF single-area configuration, 199

wireless Internet, 393

wireless WANs, 392-393

Wireshark network analyzer, 718

workflow (virtualized data center), 737-738

working interfaces, 49

write views (SNMPv3 groups), 706

REGISTER YOUR PRODUCT at CiscoPress.com/register
Access Additional Benefits and SAVE 35% on Your Next Purchase

- Download available product updates.
- Access bonus material when applicable.
- Receive exclusive offers on new editions and related products.
  (Just check the box to hear from us when setting up your account.)
- Get a coupon for 35% for your next purchase, valid for 30 days.
  Your code will be available in your Cisco Press cart. (You will also find
  it in the Manage Codes section of your account page.)

Registration benefits vary by product. Benefits will be listed on your account page
under Registered Products.

CiscoPress.com – Learning Solutions for Self-Paced Study, Enterprise, and the Classroom
Cisco Press is the Cisco Systems authorized book publisher of Cisco networking technology,
Cisco certification self-study, and Cisco Networking Academy Program materials.

At CiscoPress.com you can
- Shop our books, eBooks, software, and video training.
- Take advantage of our special offers and promotions (ciscopress.com/promotions).
- Sign up for special offers and content newsletters (ciscopress.com/newsletters).
- Read free articles, exam profiles, and blogs by information technology experts.
- Access thousands of free chapters and video lessons.

Connect with Cisco Press – Visit CiscoPress.com/community
Learn about Cisco Press community events and programs.

Cisco Press